Lecture Notes in Computer Science 1313

Edited by G. Goos, J. Hartmanis and J. van Leeuwen

Advisory Board: W. Brauer   D. Gries   J. Stoer

T0180368

Springer

Berlin
Heidelberg
New York
Barcelona
Budapest
Hong Kong
London
Milan
Paris
Santa Clara
Singapore
Tokyo

John Fitzgerald   Cliff B. Jones
Peter Lucas (Eds.)

FME '97:
Industrial Applications
and Strengthened Foundations
of Formal Methods

4th International Symposium
of Formal Methods Europe
Graz, Austria, September 15-19, 1997
Proceedings

 Springer

Series Editors

Gerhard Goos, Karlsruhe University, Germany

Juris Hartmanis, Cornell University, NY, USA

Jan van Leeuwen, Utrecht University, The Netherlands

Volume Editors

John Fitzgerald
University of Newcastle upon Tyne, Centre for Software Reliability
Bedson Building, NE1 7RU Newcastle upon Tyne, United Kingdom
E-mail: john.fitzgerald@ncl.ac.uk

Cliff B. Jones
Director Applications Division, Harlequin Ltd., Queens Court
Wilmslow Road, SK9 7QD Cheshire, United Kingdom
E-mail: cbj@harlequin.co.uk

Peter Lucas
Technical University Graz, Institute for Software Technology
Münzgrabenstr. 11/2, A-8010 Graz, Austria
E-mail: lucas@ist.tu-graz.ac.at

Cataloging-in-Publication data applied for

Die Deutsche Bibliothek - CIP-Einheitsaufnahme

Industrial applications and strengthened foundations of formal methods : proceedings / FME '97, 4th International Symposium of Formal Methods Europe, Graz, Austria, September 15 - 19, 1997. John Fitzgerald ... (ed.). - Berlin ; Heidelberg ; New York ; Barcelona ; Budapest ; Hong Kong ; London ; Milan ; Paris ; Santa Clara ; Singapore ; Tokyo : Springer, 1997
  (Lecture notes in computer science ; Vol. 1313)
  ISBN 3-540-63533-5

CR Subject Classification (1991): D.1-2, D.3.1, F.3.1, J.1, K.6

ISSN 0302-9743
ISBN 3-540-63533-5 Springer-Verlag Berlin Heidelberg New York

© Springer-Verlag Berlin Heidelberg 1997
Printed in Germany

Typesetting: Camera-ready by author
SPIN 10545840   06/3142 – 5 4 3 2 1 0   Printed on acid-free paper

Preface

This volume contains the proceedings of the fourth international symposium of Formal Methods Europe. The conference, which took place at the Technical University of Graz, Austria, in September 1997, was the eighth in a series which began in Brussels in 1987 with the first of four symposia organised by the VDM Europe group. Later, when VDM Europe widened its scope to become Formal Methods Europe (FME), the current symposium series replaced the VDM conferences. Now FME is a group of practitioners and researchers from industrial and academic institutions who share the aim of encouraging the use of sound mathematically based techniques in the engineering development of computing systems. The group is supported by the Commission of the European Union.

The FME Symposium, which traditionally takes place every eighteen months, reports current work in the area of software development methods that combine mathematical rigour with applicability in the commercial context. The majority of the papers describe industrial applications, extensions to existing techniques or case studies. Papers on theory are accepted only where they show clear potential applicability.

Formal methods are increasingly recognised as a viable technology for the development of computing systems. The papers in this volume bear witness to the importance now being attached to the integration of formal methods with existing development practices. Such integration can be achieved through the provision of common frameworks for a variety of notations and techniques, or by linking formal modelling and analysis techniques to widely accepted tools and notations for systematic development. The problem of gaining acceptance for the use of an unfamiliar formalism is addressed through work to provide graphical notations with sound bases.

As technological advances in formal methods continue to be reported, dissemination of results to industry assumes ever greater importance. Managers and engineers must be able to make informed choices from the range of development tools and techniques available. Since the previous symposium in 1996, FME has responded to this need by organising seminars for industry in ten countries, developing databases, bibliographies and frequently-asked question files recording information on formal methods, their applications and tool support. At the time of writing, the databases provide reports on nearly ninety industrial applications and over fifty support tools. Resources for managers have been developed in variety of media including broadcast video and World Wide Web pages. Further details on these activities are given in the section on FME Dissemination Actions below.

This volume presents 35 papers accepted out of 97 submissions from 21 countries. In addition to submitted papers, the symposium was addressed by four invited speakers: Hermann Kopetz of the Technical University of Vienna, Loe Feijs of Philips Research Laboratories in the Netherlands, Robin Bloomfield of Adelard in the UK and, at the conference dinner, Heinz Zemanek who initiated much of the international collaboration on formal methods with the famous 1964 Baden-bei-Wien conference on "Formal Language Definition Languages".

The international nature of FME'97, its combination of academic and industrial participants and its mixture of reports on technological development and concrete application, continue the tradition of the FME and VDM Symposia. It is to be hoped that this symposium will foster future collaboration to the benefit of the computing industry as a whole.

Newcastle upon Tyne, July 1997   J. S. Fitzgerald
C. B. Jones
P. Lucas

Acknowledgements

We are grateful to the many colleagues who have contributed to the organisation and success of FME'97.

Programme Committee

John Fitzgerald (PC co-Chair)	Brendan Mahony
Cliff Jones (PC co-Chair)	Lynn Marshall
Manfred Broy	Dominique Mery
George Cleland	Peter D. Mosses
Peter Froome	José Oliveira
Chris George	Nico Plat
Shinichi Honiden	Andrzej Tarlecki
Daniel Jackson	Martyn Thomas
Carlos José Pereira de Lucena	Rob Witty
Doug McIlroy	Joakim von Wright

Organising Committee

Peter Lucas (OC Chair)	Petra Pichler
Brigitte Froehlich	Andreas Bollin
Christian Schinagl	Andreas Ausserhofer

We also acknowledge the valuable contributions of Alejandro Moya at the Commission of the European Union, for his continued support of Formal Methods Europe, and Alfred Hofmann at Springer-Verlag for continued interest in publishing the proceedings. The Centre for Software Reliability at the University of Newcastle upon Tyne provided considerable infrastructure support for the programme committee. We are especially grateful to Alison Sheavills for her hard work handling submitted papers, reviews and arrangements for the programme committee.

We would specially like to thank the Principal of the Technical University Graz, Univ.Prof. Irolt Kilman for his support in hosting FME'97. In addition we acknowledge the contributions of the following: Mrs. Almut Fehringer, Tourist Office Graz, for her perfect organising of accommodation; Mrs. Elisabeth Pirker, Technical University Graz, for graphical design and layout and finally Type & Print Ltd. for support and assistance in printing.

Symposium Sponsors

The generous support of the following companies and institutions has contributed to the success of the Symposium:

The Technical University Graz, Austria
The Mayor of the City of Graz, Austria
Tourist Office Graz, Austria
The Austrian Computer Society, Vienna
Canon Office Systems, Austria
TCplus Computer Systems, Austria
Casinos Austria AG, Graz
IFAD - The Institute for Applied Computer Science, Denmark
CRI Computer Resources International A/S, Denmark
The Harlequin Group Limited, U.K.

External Referees

All submitted papers were reviewed by members of the Programme Committee and a number of external referees, without whose hard work the symposium would not be possible. To the best of our knowledge the list below is accurate: we apologise for any inaccuracies or omissions.

Paulo Alencar	José Alferes	Jim Armstrong
Roland Backhouse	Leonor Barroca	José Bernardo Barros
Angelo E. Bean	M.A. Bednarczyk	Sonia Bergamaschi
Marcin Białasik	Andrzej Borzyszkowski	Luc Bougé
Richard J. Boulton	S. Brookes	Michael Butler
Gian Luca Cattani	Antonio Cerone	Tim Clement
Ian Cottam	Radhia Cousot	Régis Cridlig
Paul Curzon	Ludwik Czaja	Dang Van Hung
Juergen Dingel	Katherine Eastaughfte	Javier Esparza
J.L. Fiadeiro	Colin Fidge	Marcus Felipe Fontoura
M. Fuchs	Simon Gay	J. Paul Gibson
Eric Goubault	J.-Ch. Grégoire	Pascal Gribomont
Jim Grundy	Michael R. Hansen	John Harrison
Ian Hayes	Görel Hedin	B. Hemeury
Pedro Rangel Henriques	John Herbert	Ursula Hinkel
Christoph Hofmann	Tadashi Iijima	Misbah Islam
Yoshinao Isobe	Janusz Jabłonowski	David Janin
Tomasz Janowski	P. Johnson	Claire Jones
Darrell Kindred	Carlos Delgado Kloos	Beata Konikowska
Ingolf Krueger	Linas Laibinis	Thomas Långbacka
K. Lano	Kim G. Larson	Sławomir Lasota
Rogerio de Lemos	Kurt Lichtner	Peter Lindsay
Witold Lukaszewicz	Leo Pini Magalhaes	Saeko Matsuura

Bruno Mermet	Stephen Merz	Kees Middelburg
Anna Mikhajlova	Marius Minea	Danilo Montesi
Richard Moore	Olaf Mueller	Kenji Nagahashi
George Necula	Luis Nova	Robert O'Callahan
David Von Oheimb	Peter Ørbæk	Maris Ozols
Paweł Pączkowski	Barbara Paech	Prakash Panangaden
Jan Philipps	Michael Pilling	Anders P. Ravn
Ceri Rees	Mauno Rönkkö	Kristoffer Rose
Olivier Roux	Rimvydas Rukšėnas	Mark Ryan
Amer Saeed	Bernhard Schätz	Birgit Schieder
Monika Schmidt	Erik M. Schmidt	Alexander B. Schmidt
Peter Scholz	Aleksy Schubert	Emil Sekerinski
Kaisa Sere	Oscar Slotosch	Stefan Sokołowski
Katharina Spies	Jason Steggles	Magnus Steinby
J. Straunstrup	Su Thomas	Mitsukazu Unchiyama
Mark Utting	José Manuel Valença	Marina Waldén
Qiwen Xu	J. Yantcher	Hiroka zu Yatsu
George Yee	Lu Yuan	Amy Moormann Zaremski
Zhou Chaochen	John Zic	

Tutorials

The tutorials form an important part of the FME Symposium. We are grateful to all those who kindly submitted tutorial proposals. The following tutorials were scheduled for the two days preceding the research symposium:

Semantics and Logic for Provable Fault-Tolerance
   Tomasz Janowski, UNU/IIST
ACL2
   J. Strother Moore, Matt Kaufmann, William D. Young, Computational Logic Inc.
Formal Software Development Using Cogito
   T. P. Kearney, O. Traynor, University of Queensland
Industrial Training and University Education in Formal Methods
   Michael Hinchey, José Oliveira, New Jersey Institute of Technology, University of Minho

Tool Demonstrations

In parallel with all the other activities at FME'97, tools supporting formal methods were demonstrated in an exhibition. At the time of writing, the following tools were due to be demonstrated at FME'97. However, further demonstrations are expected.

AtelierB demonstration: Thierry Servat, Clement Roches, Steria Mediterranée, France.

3D Visual Tool Supporting Derivation of Operational Specification for Parallel Programs: E. Trichina, J. Oinonen, Advanced Computing Research Center, University of South Australia, Australia.

TAS and IsaWin: Generic Interfaces for Transformational Program Development and Theorem Proving: Christoph Lueth, Bremen Institute for Safe Systems, University of Bremen, Germany.

RAISE Tool Demonstration: Jan Storbank Pedersen, Computer Resources International A/S, Denmark.

VDM Technology: Peter Gorm Larsen, Institute for Applied Computer Science (IFAD), Denmark.

XBarnacle: A Semi-automated Proof Tool: Helen Lowe, Dept. of Computing, Napier University, United Kingdom.

VST Hans Martin Hoercher, Vossloh-Systemtechnik GmbH, Germany.

SDT and ITEX: Magnus Herner, Telelogic AB, Sweden.

FME Dissemination Actions

In the two years prior to this symposium, the members of FME have been involved in three dissemination actions aiming to raise awareness of available formal methods technologies in the wider professional community. The target audience has been industrial software developers, especially those who wish to explore the use of formal techniques but who are unaware of the technical choices, available methods, tools and previous experiences of other applications. Results from the projects described here are all accessible from the FME hub web site at http://www.cs.TCD.ie/FME, or from the addresses indicated below. All three actions have been supported under the European Systems and Software Initiative of the CEU.

The **FMEInfRes** project maintains databases of formal methods applications, support tools, bibliographies and frequently-asked questions. Information may be accessed on the FME hub page mentioned above. Entries for the databases are actively sought. Those with information about industrial applications should contact Nico Plat (Email: Nico.Plat@ACM.org). Providers of support tools should contact Tim Denvir (Email: t-denvir@dircon.co.uk).

The **FMEIndSem** project has organised seminars for industry in ten European countries and has established national industrial interest groups. Further information can be found at http://www.ifad.dk/projects/fmeindsem.html.

The **FM-Guides** project provides information for managers in industry on the benefits of applying formal techniques. Material is provided in a variety of media, including web pages (http://www.cybercable.tm.fr/1997/Formal and video. The main contact is Eric Delalonde (Email: edelalon@ecom.cgs.fr).

Table of Contents

Diagrams and Programming Languages for Programmable Controllers

Stuart Anderson and Konstantinos Tourlas

Laboratory for the Foundations of Computer Science
Department of Computer Science
The Kings Buildings
Edinburgh EH9 3JZ, UK
e-mail: {soa, kxt}@dcs.ed.ac.uk

Abstract. In many domain specific languages diagrammatic notation is used because it conforms to notations used by domain specialists before the deployment of programmable components. The aim is to lessen the possibility of error by changing as little as possible. However the switch to programmable components often means a radical change in the details of the implementation. Such changes can mean that the domain experts' interpretation of the notation diverges significantly from the actual implementation.

We explore this problem, taking programmable controllers as a specific example. The IEC 1131-3 international standard has a diagrammatic notation and a textual language for the description of "function blocks" which are the basic components of controller programs. We take an idealised version of the textual language and its diagrammatic counterpart and show that the diagrams capture equivalence of textual programs under a collection of equational laws.

This result establishes that diagrams relieve the programmer of the need to consider non-significant variants of programs and the match between program texts, their corresponding diagrams and their intended interpretation.

The use of domain-specific languages is becoming ever more widespread as programmable components replace "hard-wired" systems. One feature of such languages is their choice of programming notation. Frequently this is diagrammatic and derived from earlier design practice. The use of such notation is appealing because it eases the transition to new implementation technology. However, it can introduce new risks. Any given diagram can be built in a variety of ways and the notation usually has a concrete representation as a term in some language (or as a representation in the programming system). If the interpretation of the diagram is sensitive to this information it could mean that seemingly identical programs have divergent interpretations and that some of these interpretations differ from what the developer expects. This places an obligation on the language designers to establish that all methods of building the same diagram are interpreted identically. As far as we know there are few results of this kind. Milner's result on the correspondence between flowgraphs and CCS terms [5,4] is a notable exception.

Here we present an exploration of the correspondence between diagrams and their textual form for an idealisation of the IEC 1131-3 [3] languages for programmable controllers. In these languages the user of the graphical language is encouraged to think in a "circuit" paradigm [6,7] – but the programs have a textual form and are interpreted by microprocessors. The potential for divergence of the expected behaviour of diagrammatic notations is obvious. For example, failure of the associativity of composition is certainly possible if care is not taken in defining the meaning of the textual form of the program or in implementing this definition.

1 The Language of Function Blocks

The international standard for programmable controller languages is IEC 1131-3 [3]. The standard defines a number of languages but here we consider only the language of function blocks and its corresponding diagrammatic representation. Function blocks are the basic units of PLC programs and encourage the designer to use pre-defined components which are then composed to form control programs. Figure 1 shows an example of the textual representation of a function block program. The block uses delays (i.e. timers) to debounce a binary input. Figure 2 shows the corresponding diagrammatic representation of the function block. The diagrammatic representation is appealing because it looks like typical circuit schematics used by engineers constructing hard-wired controllers.

```
FUNCTION_BLOCK DEBOUNCE
(** External Interface **)
  VAR_INPUT  IN    : BOOL;                                   END_VAR
  VAR_OUTPUT OUT   : INT;    ET_OFF : TIME;                  END_VAR
  VAR        DB_ON : TMR;    DB_OFF : TMR;  DB_FF : SR; END_VAR
(** Body **)
  DB_ON( IN := IN ); DB_OFF( IN := NOT IN );
  DB_FF( S := DB_ON.Q, R := DB_OFF.Q );
  OUT := DB_FF.Q; ET_OFF := DB_OFF.ET;
END_FUNCTION_BLOCK
```

Fig. 1. Function block DEBOUNCE in ST.

In [8] we introduce a rationalised version of the function block language, provide it with a timed operational semantics and argue that the rationalisation is adequate to describe most PLC programs as well as to support formal reasoning about such programs. Here we are mostly concerned with the relationship between diagrams and the textual form of the language. To compress the

3

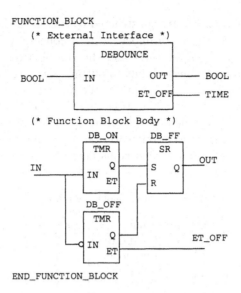

Fig. 2. Example of graphical function block declaration.

presentation we shall omit a detailed account of our language, although a summary of the dynamic semantics will be provided in Sect. 6. For the time being we outline the syntax since it motivates the algebra of diagrams introduced in Sect. 3.

Table 1. Syntactic sets of the language

Set	Description	Metavariable
Time	time constants	t
Con	constants	c
PLab	port labels	$\overline{x}, \overline{y}$
Exp	expressions	e
Fb	function blocks	f

The syntactic sets of the language are summarised in Table 1. Here we are concerned with the category *Fb* of function blocks, defined in terms of the following abstract grammar:

$$S ::= \{\overline{y_1}, \ldots, \overline{y_m}\}$$
$$g ::= \varepsilon \mid \overline{x_1}/\overline{y_1}, \ldots, \overline{x_m}/\overline{y_m}$$
$$f ::= \overline{y} = e \mid \overline{y} = \delta(\overline{x}; (c_1, t_1), \ldots, (c_m, t_m)) \mid$$
$$f \setminus S \mid f[g] \mid f[c; \overline{y} \to \overline{x}] \mid f_1 \circ f_2$$

Composite function blocks are constructed by means of the combinators appearing in Table 2. Every function block f has a collection $\mathcal{I}(f)$ of *input ports* and a collection $\mathcal{O}(f)$ of *output ports* and the combinators use these in their definitions. Composition connects input to output ports, restriction hides some ports, relabelling renames ports according to the function g and looping connects an output port to an input port while specifying the initial value on the loop. In the other two clauses, $\overline{y} = e$ defines the output port $\overline{y}$ to be set to the value of the expression e (which may use input ports) and $\overline{y} = \delta(\overline{x}; (c_1, t_1), \ldots, (c_m, t_m))$ is a delay whose details need not concern us here.

Table 2. Function block combinators

Combinator	Name	Precedence
$f_1 \circ f_2$	Composition	2
$f \setminus S$	Restriction	1
$f[g]$	Relabelling	1
$f[c; \overline{y} \to \overline{x}]$	Loop	1

In the language outlined above, the translation term f_{DB} corresponding to DEBOUNCE will have a single input port labelled $\overline{in}$ and two output ports labelled $\overline{out}$ and $\overline{et\_off}$. The overall decomposition of f_{DB} is

$$f_{DB} \equiv (f_{INV} \circ f_{DB\_ON} \circ f_{DB\_OFF} \circ f_{DB\_FF}) \setminus S \ ,$$

that is a restricted composition where $S = \{\overline{n}, \overline{r}\}$. The f_{INV} component is a simple boolean inverter: $f_{INV} \equiv \overline{n} = not(\overline{in})$. The f_{DB_ON}, f_{DB_OFF} and f_{DB_FF} terms are the instances of TMR and SR with their ports suitably relabelled to specify the desired connections:

$$f_{DB\_ON} \equiv f_{TMR}[\overline{s}/\overline{q}] \setminus \overline{et}$$
$$f_{DB\_OFF} \equiv f_{TMR}[\overline{n}/\overline{in}, \overline{et\_off}/\overline{et}, \overline{r}/\overline{q}]$$
$$f_{DB\_FF} \equiv f_{SR}[\overline{out}/\overline{q}] \ .$$

For instance, the input $\overline{in}$ of f_{TMR} in f_{DB_OFF} has been renamed to $\overline{n}$ so as to be connected to the output port $\overline{n}$ of the inverter f_{INV}. Also, the $\overline{et}$ port of f_{TMR} in f_{DB_ON} has been hidden by the restriction and therefore has been removed from the outputs of f_{DB}. Finally, the restriction $\setminus S$ internalises all those output ports which do not appear among the outputs of f_{DB}.

The SR flip-flop is a simple example of a state-dependent function block, with a possible representation for it being

$$f_{SR} \equiv (\overline{q} = \overline{s} \text{ or } (\overline{r} \text{ and } \overline{q1}))[\textbf{false}; \overline{q} \to \overline{q1}] \ .$$

The current value of output $\overline{q}$ depends not only on the current inputs $\overline{s}$ and $\overline{r}$ but also on the previous value of $\overline{q}$, fed back through the input $\overline{q1}$ via the loop [**false**; $\overline{q} \to \overline{q1}$]. Thus, the role of the loop linking $\overline{q}$ to $\overline{q1}$ in f_{SR} is that of a *local variable* in the terminology of IEC 1131-3 function blocks. In our case, the initial value for that variable is **false**.

Notation Before proceeding to the formal treatment of diagrams, we introduce some frequently used notation. Let h be a function. Then $\operatorname{Dom} h$ and $\operatorname{Ran} h$ are the *domain* and *range* of h, respectively. If $X \subseteq \operatorname{Dom} h$, we write $h{\downarrow}X$ for the *restriction* of h on X and $h(X)$ for the image of X under h. Assuming that g is a function with $\operatorname{Ran} g \subseteq \operatorname{Dom} h$, the *composition* $h \bullet g$ of h with g is then $(h \bullet g)(x) = h(g(x))$. Finally, for X an arbitrary finite set, we let $|X|$ denote the cardinality of X.

2 Diagrams

Informally, a function block diagram consists of a set of nodes, each labelled with a function block term and possessing a set of ports. Each port has an *internal label* and, optionally, an *external label*. All labels are drawn from the set *PLab* of port labels. Furthermore, some input ports may be assigned a constant c from the set *Con*. Finally, ports may be connected by means of *connections*.

We shall assume a harmless restriction on the set of function blocks which may be used to label nodes; namely that such terms have *disjoint input and output sorts*. We shall use Γ to refer to this subset of function blocks obeying the restriction:

$$\Gamma = \{ f \in Fb \mid \mathcal{I}(f) \cap \mathcal{O}(f) = \emptyset \} \ .$$

We are now in position to present the formal definition of diagrams:

Definition 1. A function block diagram $d = (N, F, I, O, C, \lambda, \varepsilon, \iota)$ comprises the following:

1. A *finite* set N of nodes.
2. A map $F{:}N \to \Gamma$ which assigns a function block term $F(n)$ to each node $n \in N$.
3. A set of input ports $I = \bigcup_{n \in N} I(n)$ and a set of output ports $O = \bigcup_{n \in N} O(n)$, where $I(n)$ and $O(n)$ are the sets of *input ports* and *output ports* of node n, respectively. We shall write $P(n)$ for $I(n) \cup O(n)$. Furthermore, for all $n, m \in N$,
   - $I(n) \cap O(n) = \emptyset$
   - $|I(n)| = |\mathcal{I}(F(n))|$, $|O(n)| = |\mathcal{O}(F(n))|$; and
   - $P(n) \cap P(m) = \emptyset$, when $n \neq m$.
4. An *asymmetric* relation $C \subseteq O \times I$, the set of *connections*.
5. A total map $\lambda{:}I \cup O \to PLab$, the *internal label map*, such that $\lambda(I(n)) = \mathcal{I}(F(n))$ and $\lambda(O(n)) = \mathcal{O}(F(n))$ for all $n \in N$.
6. A partial map ε from $I \cup O$ to $PLab$, the *external label map*.
7. A partial map ι from I to Con, the *port initialisation map*. $\qquad\square$

The *input sort* $\mathcal{I}(d)$ of a diagram d is defined to be $\{\varepsilon(p) \mid p \in I \cap \mathrm{Dom}\,\varepsilon\}$, that is the set of all external labels assigned to input ports. Similarly, the *output sort* $\mathcal{O}(d)$ of d is the set of all external labels assigned to output ports: $\{\varepsilon(p) \mid p \in O \cap \mathrm{Dom}\,\varepsilon\}$. The *sort* $\mathcal{S}(d)$ of d is simply $\mathcal{I}(d) \cup \mathcal{O}(d)$. Ports with external labels will be referred to as the *external* ports, whereas those possessing internal labels only will be called the *internal* ports.

Given an arbitrary function block $f \in \Gamma$ with input sort $\{\overline{x_1}, \ldots, \overline{x_m}\}$ and output sort $\{\overline{y_1}, \ldots, \overline{y_{m'}}\}$, it is now possible to define the single-node diagram $\gamma(f)$ of Fig. 3 corresponding to f. Formally, γ is an injective map from Γ into diagrams: Let $\{p_1, \ldots, p_m\}$, $\{p'_1, \ldots, p'_{m'}\}$ be two disjoint sets of ports. Then, $\gamma(f) = (N, F, I, O, C, \lambda, \varepsilon, \iota)$, where

$$N = \{n\} \quad \text{is a singleton}$$
$$F(n) = f$$
$$I = \{p_i \mid i = 1, \ldots, m\}$$
$$O = \{p'_i \mid i = 1, \ldots, m'\}$$
$$C = \emptyset$$
$$\lambda = \{(p_i, \overline{x_i}) \mid i = 1, \ldots, m\} \cup \{(p'_i, \overline{y_i}) \mid i = 1, \ldots, m'\}$$
$$\varepsilon = \lambda$$
$$\iota = \emptyset \ .$$

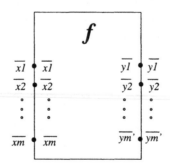

Fig. 3. A single node diagram of function block f.

2.1 Proper Diagrams

Our aim is to define an algebra of diagrams by choosing a suitable set of operations corresponding to the combinators of Table 2. The carrier set of this algebra will then be precisely the set of diagrams generated from $\mathrm{Ran}\,\gamma$ using these operations. We begin by first identifying this set and postpone the introduction of the operations until the next section. Please note that, in a slight abuse of notation, we write $\mathrm{Dom}\,C$ and $\mathrm{Ran}\,C$ to mean those subsets of O and I, respectively, over which the relation C is defined.

Definition 2. A diagram $d = (N, F, I, O, C, \lambda, \varepsilon, \iota)$ is called *proper*, iff

1. C^{-1} is a *function*
2. $\varepsilon{\downarrow}O$ is an injection
3. $\varepsilon(O) \cap \varepsilon(I) = \emptyset$
4. $\mathrm{Dom}\,(\varepsilon{\downarrow}I) = I \setminus \mathrm{Ran}\,C$; and
5. $\mathrm{Dom}\,\iota \subseteq \mathrm{Ran}\,C$. □

Informally, this definition says that an arbitrary diagram d is proper if the following constraints are met:

1. Each input port can be connected to at most one output port.
2. All output ports have *distinct external labels*.
3. No input port is given the same external label as any output port, that is $\mathcal{I}(d) \cap \mathcal{O}(d) = \emptyset$.
4. Only unconnected input ports may have external labels.
5. Only connected input ports may be initialised.

Another easy consequence of the above definition is that, in all proper diagrams d, $\varepsilon(\mathrm{Ran}\,C) = \emptyset$.

3   An Algebra of Diagrams

This section completes the definition of our algebra of diagrams by introducing a set of operations corresponding to those in our programming language. Each element of the algebra describes a particular way of building a diagram and thus the operations are interpreted in terms of the diagrams they construct. The choice of the carrier set made in the previous section is finally justified by demonstrating that all diagrams so constructed are proper.

Definition 3 (Diagram Composition). Let $d_i = (N_i, F_i, I_i, O_i, C_i, \lambda_i, \varepsilon_i, \iota_i)$, $i = 1, 2$, be diagrams with $N_1 \cap N_2 = \emptyset$ and $\mathcal{O}(d_1) \cap \mathcal{O}(d_2) = \emptyset$. Then,

$$d = d_1 \circ d_2 = (N, F, I, O, C, \lambda, \varepsilon, \iota)$$

is given by

$$N = N_1 \cup N_2 \ , F = F_1 \cup F_2 \ , \qquad I = I_1 \cup I_2 \ ,$$
$$O = O_1 \cup O_2 \ , C = C_1 \cup C_2 \cup \widehat{C} \ , \lambda = \lambda_1 \cup \lambda_2 \ ,$$
$$\iota = \iota_1 \cup \iota_2 \ , \varepsilon = \varepsilon_1 \cup (\varepsilon_2 \setminus \{(p, \overline{x}) \mid p \in \mathrm{Ran}\,\widehat{C}\})$$

where $\widehat{C} = \{(p, p') \in O_1 \times I_2 \mid \varepsilon_1(p) = \varepsilon_2(p') \in PLab\}$. □

Definition 4 (Diagram Restriction). If $d = (N, F, I, O, C, \lambda, \varepsilon, \iota)$, then

$$d \setminus \overline{x} = (N, F, I, O, C, \lambda, \varepsilon', \iota) ,$$

where $\varepsilon' = \varepsilon \setminus \{(p, \overline{x}) \mid p \in O\}$. □

Definition 5 (Diagram Relabelling). Let $d = (N, F, I, O, C, \lambda, \varepsilon, \iota)$ and g be a relabelling such that $g \downarrow \mathcal{O}(d)$ is an injection, and $g(\mathcal{I}(d)) \cap g(\mathcal{O}(d)) = \emptyset$. Then

$$d[g] = (N, F, I, O, C, \lambda, g \bullet \varepsilon, \iota) .$$

□

Definition 6 (Diagram Loop). Let $d = (N, F, I, O, A, \lambda, \varepsilon, \iota)$, $c \in Con$ and $\overline{x} \in \mathcal{I}(d)$, $\overline{y} \in \mathcal{O}(d)$. Then

$$d[c; \overline{y} \to \overline{x}] = (N, F, I, O, C \cup \widehat{C}, \lambda, \varepsilon', \iota') ,$$

where $\widehat{C} = \{(p, p') \mid p \in O, p' \in I, \varepsilon(p) = \overline{y}, \ \varepsilon(p') = \overline{x}\}$, $\varepsilon' = \varepsilon \setminus \{(p, \overline{x}) \mid p \in I\}$ and $\iota' = \iota \cup \{(p, c) \mid p \in \operatorname{Ran} \widehat{C}\}$. □

In words, the composition $d_1 \circ d_2$ connects those output ports of d_1 to those input ports of d_2 having matching external labels. The external labels of the inputs thus connected are subsequently removed. The restriction in $d \setminus \overline{y}$ removes all occurrences of the external label $\overline{y}$ in d. Relabelling applies the relabelling function g to recast the external labels of d. Finally, $d[c; \overline{y} \to \overline{x}]$ connects the output port of d having external label $\overline{y}$ to the input port of d having external label $\overline{x}$. The input ports so connected have their external labels subsequently removed and are initialised with the constant c.

Let now D be the least set containing $\operatorname{Ran} \gamma$ and that is closed under the above operations. Our algebra consists of diagram expressions which provide a syntactic means to describe every diagram in D, with each diagram having multiple descriptions in the algebra. As a notational convention, we will use f to stand for $\gamma(f)$ in diagram expressions, and will use w to range over diagram expressions.

Lemma 7. *The diagram operations of Composition, Restriction, Relabelling and Loop preserve properness.*

Proof. Routine from the definitions. □

With the help of this lemma, one may now prove that the proper diagrams are precisely those diagrams generable by the operations:

Proposition 8. *A diagram is in D iff it is proper.*

Proof. To establish the forward implication one needs to show that all diagrams in $\operatorname{Ran} \gamma$ are proper, which holds by definition of γ. Then by Lemma 7, all diagrams in D are proper.

For the converse implication assume $d = (N, F, I, O, C, \lambda, \varepsilon, \iota)$ proper.

1. Add distinct *fresh* labels $\overline{z_1}, \ldots, \overline{z_k}$, i.e. not occuring in $\mathcal{S}(d)$, one for each output port $p_1, \ldots, p_k \in O \setminus \mathrm{Dom}\,\varepsilon$ to form diagram $d' = (N, F, I, O, C, \lambda, \varepsilon', \iota)$ with

$$\varepsilon' = \varepsilon \cup \{(p_i, \overline{z_i}) \mid i \in \{1, \ldots, k\}\} \ .$$

Clearly, d' is proper and

$$d = d' \setminus \overline{z_1} \ldots \setminus \overline{z_k} \ .$$

2. Now, for each initialised input port $p_j \in \mathrm{Dom}\,\iota$, let $p_j' = C^{-1}(p_j)$ be the *unique* output port to which p_j is connected via a connection in C. Such an unique output port always exists since C^{-1} is a function and $\mathrm{Dom}\,\iota \subseteq \mathrm{Dom}\,C^{-1}$. Furthermore, let $\overline{y_j}$ be the *unique* external label assigned to p_j' under ε'. (The existence of $\overline{y_j}$ is guaranteed by the totality of ε' and its uniqueness by the requirement that $\varepsilon \downarrow O$ — and hence $\varepsilon' \downarrow O$ — is an injection.) Add now fresh labels $\overline{x_j} \notin \mathcal{S}(d')$, one for each p_j, and remove all connections in C to the p_j's to form $d'' = (N, F, I, O, C'', \lambda, \varepsilon'', \emptyset)$ with

$$C'' = C \setminus \{(p_j', p_j) \mid p_j \in \mathrm{Dom}\,\iota\} \ ,$$

and

$$\varepsilon'' = \varepsilon' \cup \{(p_j, \overline{x_j}) \mid p_j \in \mathrm{Dom}\,\iota\} \ .$$

Clearly then

$$d' = d''[c_1; \overline{y_1} \to \overline{x_1}] \ldots [c_n; \overline{y_n} \to \overline{x_n}] \ ,$$

where $n = |\mathrm{Dom}\,\iota|$ and $c_j = \iota(p_j)$, $j = 1, \ldots, n$. Furthermore, it is not hard to verify that d'' is also proper.

3. Now consider each node n_i in d'' and let $f_i = F(n_i)$. The map ε'' is defined on every port of d'' except those input ports that are connected, that is those ports $p \in \mathrm{Ran}\,C''$. However, ε'' extends to a *total* map $\eta{:}I \cup O \to PLab$ as follows:

$$\eta = \varepsilon'' \cup \{(p, \varepsilon''(p')) \mid (p', p) \in C''\} \ .$$

Since $\varepsilon'' \downarrow O$ is an injection and $\varepsilon''(I) \cap \varepsilon''(O) = \emptyset$, it follows that $\eta \downarrow O$ is an injection and $\eta(I(n_i)) \cap \eta(O(n_i)) = \emptyset$. Now, for each n_i define a relabelling g_i

$$g_i = \{\eta(p)/\lambda(p) \mid p \in P(n_i)\} \ ,$$

that maps the internal labels of ports in n_i to their corresponding labels under η. By the properties of η and the definition of λ, it follows that each $g_i \downarrow \mathcal{O}(f_i)$ is an injection and that $g_i(\mathcal{I}(f_i)) \cap g_i(\mathcal{O}(f_i)) = \emptyset$. Moreover, it is not hard to see that

$$d'' = f_1[g_1] \circ (f_2[g_2] \circ (\ldots))$$

whence we obtain the diagram expression for d:

$$d = (f_1[g_1] \circ (f_2[g_2] \circ (\ldots)))[c_1; \overline{y_1} \to \overline{x_1}] \ldots [c_n; \overline{y_n} \to \overline{x_n}] \setminus \overline{z_1} \ldots \setminus \overline{z_k}.$$

$\square$

4 Equational Laws

In this section we develop an equational system E for our algebra of diagrams. The system comprises seventeen equational laws which provide the means to link diagrams to the textual form of the language. To establish the result that there is no deviation between diagrammatic and textual programs, one must also establish the validity of these laws in the programming language semantics. This is done in Sect. 6.

Proposition 9 (Equational Laws). *The following identities hold between Γ-diagrams, where we assume that f, f_i are arbitrary diagrams, $\overline{x}, \overline{y}, \overline{z}, \overline{x}_i, \overline{y}_i$ are arbitrary labels, and g, g' are relabellings:*

(E1) $(f_1 \circ f_2) \circ f_3 = f_1 \circ (f_2 \circ f_3)$

(E2) $f_1 \circ f_2 = f_2 \circ f_1$ *if* $\mathcal{O}(f_1) \cap \mathcal{I}(f_2) = \emptyset$ *and* $\mathcal{O}(f_2) \cap \mathcal{I}(f_1) = \emptyset$

(E3) $(f_1[c; \overline{y} \to \overline{x}]) \circ f_2 = (f_1 \circ f_2)[c; \overline{y} \to \overline{x}]$ *if* $\overline{y} \notin \mathcal{O}(f_2)$ *and* $\overline{x} \notin \mathcal{I}(f_2)$

(E4) $f_1 \circ (f_2[c; \overline{y} \to \overline{x}]) = (f_1 \circ f_2)[c; \overline{y} \to \overline{x}]$ *if* $\overline{y} \notin \mathcal{O}(f_1)$ *and* $\overline{x} \notin \mathcal{I}(f_1)$

(E5) $f \setminus \overline{y} = f$ *if* $\overline{y} \notin \mathcal{O}(f)$

(E6) $f \setminus \overline{x} \setminus \overline{y} = f \setminus \overline{y} \setminus \overline{x}$

(E7) $f_1 \setminus \overline{y} \circ f_2 = (f_1 \circ f_2) \setminus \overline{y}$ *if* $\overline{y} \notin \mathcal{O}(f_2) \cup (\mathcal{I}(f_2) \cap \mathcal{O}(f_1))$

(E8) $f_1 \circ f_2 \setminus \overline{y} = (f_1 \circ f_2) \setminus \overline{y}$ *if* $\overline{y} \notin \mathcal{O}(f_1)$

(E9) $f[\,] = f$

(E10) $f[g] = f[g']$ *if* $g \downarrow \mathcal{S}(f) = g' \downarrow \mathcal{S}(f)$

(E11) $f[g][g'] = f[g' \bullet g]$

(E12) $(f \setminus \overline{y})[g] = f[g] \setminus g(\overline{y})$ *if* $\overline{y} \in \mathcal{O}(f)$

(E13) $(f_1 \circ f_2)[g] = f_1[g] \circ f_2[g]$

(E14) $f[c; \overline{y} \to \overline{x}][g] = f[g'][c; g(\overline{y}) \to \overline{z}]$

    where $\overline{z} \notin g(\mathcal{S}(f) \setminus \{\overline{x}\})$ *and* $g'(\overline{w}) = \begin{cases} g(\overline{w}), & \text{if } \overline{w} \neq \overline{x} \\ \overline{z}, & \text{if } \overline{w} = \overline{x} \end{cases}$

(E15) $f \setminus \overline{z}[c; \overline{y} \to \overline{x}] = f[c; \overline{y} \to \overline{x}] \setminus \overline{z}$ *if* $\overline{z} \neq \overline{y}$

(E16) $f[c_1; \overline{y_1} \to \overline{x_1}][c_2; \overline{y_2} \to \overline{x_2}] = f[c_2; \overline{y_2} \to \overline{x_2}][c_1; \overline{y_1} \to \overline{x_1}]$

(E17) $f[c; \overline{y} \to \overline{z}][c; \overline{y} \to \overline{x}] = f[\overline{x}/\overline{z}][c; \overline{y} \to \overline{x}]$

Proof. Routine from the definitions.   □

The following is a useful corollary of Proposition 9.

Corollary 10. *The following identities hold:*

1. $f \setminus \overline{y} = f[\overline{y}/\overline{z}] \setminus \overline{z}$ *if* $\overline{z} \notin \mathcal{S}(f)$
2. $f[c; \overline{y} \to \overline{x}][g] = f[g][c; g(\overline{y}) \to g(\overline{x})]$ *if* $g \downarrow \mathcal{I}(f)$ *is an injection.*   □

5 Completeness

Reverting to the question of which diagram expressions describe the same diagram, we demonstrate that the equational system E of the previous section is *complete* for D. In other words, any two diagram expressions describing the same diagram may be proved equal from laws (E1)–(E17). We shall write $E \vdash w = w'$ to mean "w and w' may be proved equal from E." The proof of the completeness theorem is vastly simplified if one observes that any diagram expression can be converted by the laws into an equivalent *normal form*.

Definition 11 (Normal Form). A diagram expression w is in *normal form* if

$$w \equiv (f_1[g_1] \circ \ldots \circ f_m[g_m])[c_1; \overline{y_1} \to \overline{x_1}] \ldots [c_n; \overline{y_n} \to \overline{x_n}] \setminus \overline{z_1} \ldots \setminus \overline{z_k} ,$$

where

- the $\overline{z_i}$ are *distinct* and all occur in some of the output sorts $\mathcal{O}(f_i[g_i])$, $i = 1, \ldots, m$.
- the $\overline{x_i}$ are *distinct* from the $\overline{z_i}$; and
- the $(\overline{y_i}, c_i)$ are all *distinct* pairs. □

Lemma 12 (Normal Form Lemma). *For every diagram expression w, there is a normal form $w^\star$ such that $E \vdash w = w^\star$.*

Proof. We outline the phases of the transformation of w into $w^\star$, writing w_i for the resulting expression at the end of phase i. First, let

$$X = \{\overline{x} \mid \text{there is a loop } [c; \overline{y} \to \overline{x}] \text{ in } w\} .$$

1. Use (E5) where applicable to remove any unnecessary restrictions; that is restrictions $\setminus \overline{z}$ where $\overline{z}$ is not in the output sort of the subexpression qualified by the restriction.
2. Some of the remaining restrictions may not be distinct from each other or from the labels in $\mathcal{S}(w) \cup X$. In this case, pick up a fresh[1] label $\overline{x}$ for each offending restriction $\setminus \overline{z}$ and use Corollary 10(1) to replace $\setminus \overline{z}$ by $[\overline{x}/\overline{z}] \setminus \overline{x}$.
3. Use (E12), (E13) and (E14) to move all restrictions in w_2 innermost. In particular, (E12) can always be applied as a result of the work done in phase 1. Moreover, any relabellings introduced in phase 2 are, by construction, guaranteed to be injections when restricted to the sorts of the subexpressions they qualify. In using (E14), care must be exercised in choosing $\overline{z} \notin X$ to preserve the work of phase 2. Finally, use (E11) and (E10) to coalesce and simplify innermost relabellings.
4. Move all restrictions $\setminus \overline{z}$ in w_3 outermost, past any occurrences of compositions and loops. The only slightly problematic case is that of composition, which may be analysed as follows:
   - Suppose that $\setminus \overline{z}$ occurs in the context $f' \circ (f'' \setminus \overline{z})$. Now, $\overline{z} \notin \mathcal{O}(f')$ since otherwise $\overline{z} \in \mathcal{O}(w)$ or $\setminus \overline{z}$ occurs further out in w_3, and these possibilities have been eliminated during phase 2.

---

[1] In the context of this proof, a *fresh* label is one not occuring anywhere in the entire expression being manipulated.

- Suppose that $\backslash \overline{z}$ occurs in the context $(f' \backslash \overline{z}) \circ f''$. Again, one has that $\overline{z} \notin \mathcal{O}(f'') \cup (\mathcal{I}(f'') \cap \mathcal{O}(f'))$. Firstly, $\overline{z} \notin \mathcal{O}(f'')$ for reasons similar to those exhibited in the previous case. Secondly, $\overline{z} \notin (\mathcal{I}(f'') \cap \mathcal{O}(f'))$ since otherwise either $\overline{z} \in \mathcal{I}(w) \subseteq \mathcal{S}(w)$, or there is a loop $[c; \overline{y} \to \overline{z}]$ further out which hides $\overline{z}$. Again, phase 2 has precluded these possibilities.

Hence, one may use (E7), (E8) and (E15) freely to move all restrictions $\backslash \overline{z}$ in w_3 outermost.

5. Move all loops $[c; \overline{y} \to \overline{x}]$ in w_4 outside all occurrences of composition. Suppose a loop occurs in the context $(f'[c; \overline{y} \to \overline{x}]) \circ f''$ and $\overline{x} \in \mathcal{I}(f'')$ so that (E3) cannot be applied directly[2]. Then one may use the following sequence of transformations to move the loop out:

$$(f'[c; \overline{y} \to \overline{x}]) \circ f''$$
$$= \quad \langle \text{using (E10)} \rangle$$
$$(f'[c; \overline{y} \to \overline{x}][\ ]) \circ f''$$
$$= \quad \langle \text{using (E14) with } \overline{z} \notin \mathcal{I}(f'') \rangle$$
$$(f'[\overline{z}/\overline{x}][c; \overline{y} \to \overline{z}]) \circ f''$$
$$= \quad \langle \text{using (E3)} \rangle$$
$$(f'[\overline{z}/\overline{x}] \circ f'')[c; \overline{y} \to \overline{z}]$$

In particular, $\overline{z}$ must be distinct from any restriction occuring in w_4 in order to preserve the work of the previous phases. A similar course of action is taken when the loop occurs in the context $f' \circ (f''[c; \overline{y} \to \overline{x}])$.

6. Coalesce relabellings in w_5 using (E11) and simplify them using (E10).

7. w_6 now has the required form, except that some of the $(\overline{y_i}, c_i)$ may not be distinct. In such a case, follow the procedure suggested by the following example, where $w' \equiv f_1[g'_1] \circ \ldots \circ f_m[g'_m]$:

$$w'[c_1; \overline{y_1} \to \overline{x_1}] \ldots [c; \overline{y} \to \overline{x_i}] \ldots [c; \overline{y} \to \overline{x_j}] \ldots [c_n; \overline{y_n} \to \overline{x_n}]$$
$$= \quad \langle \text{repeatedly using (E16)} \rangle$$
$$w'[c; \overline{y} \to \overline{x_i}][c; \overline{y} \to \overline{x_j}][c_1; \overline{y_1} \to \overline{x_1}] \ldots [c_n; \overline{y_n} \to \overline{x_n}]$$
$$= \quad \langle \text{using (E17)} \rangle$$
$$w'[\overline{x_j}/\overline{x_i}][c; \overline{y} \to \overline{x_j}][c_1; \overline{y_1} \to \overline{x_1}] \ldots [c_n; \overline{y_n} \to \overline{x_n}]$$

8. Now move all relabellings generated by the previous phase inwards using (E13). Finally, coalesce and simplify relabellings as in phase 3 and, if some atomic expression f is not qualified by a relabelling, use (E9) to replace it with $f[\ ]$. The resulting expression is $w^\star$, the required normal form. $\qquad \square$

The following auxiliary result concerns the special case in which two diagram expressions constructing the same diagram only involve compositions and relabellings.

---

[2] Obviously, one has that $\overline{y} \notin \mathcal{O}(f'')$ since $\overline{y} \in \mathcal{O}(f')$ by definition and $\mathcal{O}(f') \cap \mathcal{O}(f'') = \emptyset$ by the properness of the diagram being manipulated.

Lemma 13. *For all diagram expressions*

$$w \equiv f_1[g_1] \circ \ldots \circ f_m[g_m]$$

and

$$w' \equiv f_1'[g_1'] \circ \ldots \circ f_{m'}'[g_{m'}']$$

representing the same diagram d, $E \vdash w = w'$.

Proof. Since $d = w = w'$, it follows that the f_k, f_k' and the nodes n_k of d are in bijection, whence $m = m'$. Without loss of generality, assume the bijection between the n_k and f_k to be $n_k \mapsto f_k$. Since composition is not fully commutative, however, there will in general be a permutation $j_1, \ldots, j_{m'}$ of $1, \ldots, m'$ such that the bijection between the n_k and f_k' is $n_k \mapsto f_{j_k}'$. Hence, $f_k = f_{j_k}'$. It follows that one must also have $g_k \downarrow S(f_k) = g_{j_k}' \downarrow S(f_{j_k}')$, otherwise w and w' would not represent the same diagram. Thus, we may further assume $g_k = g_{j_k}'$ via a few applications of (E10).

Also, from the properness of d follows that the $f_k[g_k]$ (and hence the $f_k'[g_k']$) are *distinct*. For supposing the contrary, d would have two external output ports having the same label.

We can now restate our goal as follows: For all diagram expressions

$$w \equiv f_1[g_1] \circ \ldots \circ f_m[g_m]$$

and

$$w' \equiv f_1'[g_1'] \circ \ldots \circ f_m'[g_m']$$

such that $d = w = w'$, $E \vdash w = w'$.

The proof of this is by induction on the length of w and w'. For $m = 1$ one trivially has $E \vdash w = w'$. Now, assume that the induction hypothesis holds for all expressions w, w' of length m describing the same diagram and prove the result for the case of $m + 1$. Then,

$$w \equiv f_1[g_1] \circ \ldots \circ f_{m+1}[g_{m+1}]$$

and

$$w' \equiv f_1'[g_1'] \circ \ldots \circ f_{m+1}'[g_{m+1}'] \ .$$

Take $f_1[g_1]$ and let k be such that $f_1[g_1] = f_k'[g_k']$. Since $f_1[g_1]$ is the first component of w, none of the input ports of the corresponding node n_1 in d will be connected. Consequently, as $f_k'[g_k']$ represents the same node n_1 in w', one has that

$$\mathcal{I}(f_k'[g_k']) \cap \bigcup_{j=1}^{k-1} \mathcal{O}(f_j'[g_j']) = \emptyset \ .$$

Hence, one may use (E2) repeatedly to transform w' as follows:

$$\begin{aligned}
w' &= f_1'[g_1'] \circ \ldots \circ f_k'[g_k'] \circ \ldots \circ f_{m+1}'[g_{m+1}'] \\
&= f_k'[g_k'] \circ (f_1'[g_1'] \circ \ldots \circ f_{k-1}'[g_{k-1}'] \circ f_{k+1}'[g_{k+1}'] \circ \ldots \circ f_{m+1}'[g_{m+1}']) \\
&= f_k'[g_k'] \circ w_1'
\end{aligned}$$

where

$$w_1' \equiv f_1'[g_1'] \circ \ldots \circ f_{k-1}'[g_{k-1}'] \circ f_{k+1}'[g_{k+1}'] \circ \ldots \circ f_{m+1}'[g_{m+1}'] \ .$$

Now, if one lets

$$w_1 \equiv f_2[g_2] \circ \ldots \circ f_{m+1}[g_{m+1}] \ ,$$

then $w = f_1[g_1] \circ w_1$. It is not hard to see that, because $f_1[g_1] = f_k'[g_k']$, both w_1 and w_1' represent the *same* diagram d_1 and that they are both of length m. By applying the induction hypothesis, one now gets that $E \vdash w_1 = w_1'$. Hence, $E \vdash w = w'$ as required.

Proposition 14 (Completeness). $w = w'$ *implies* $E \vdash w = w'$.

Proof. Given Lemma 12 it now suffices to show that, if $d = w = w'$ and w, w' are in normal form, then $E \vdash w = w'$. Suppose then that,

$$w \equiv \overbrace{\underbrace{(f_1[g_1] \circ \ldots \circ f_m[g_m])}_{}[c_1; \overline{y_1} \to \overline{x_1}] \ldots [c_n; \overline{y_n} \to \overline{x_n}]}^{w_1} \backslash \overline{z_1} \ldots \backslash \overline{z_k} \ ,$$

where the w_2 underbrace spans the full bracketed expression.

$$w' \equiv \overbrace{\underbrace{(f_1'[g_1'] \circ \ldots \circ f_{m'}'[g_{m'}'])}_{}[c_1'; \overline{y_1'} \to \overline{x_1'}] \ldots [c_{n'}'; \overline{y_{n'}'} \to \overline{x_{n'}'}]}^{w_1'} \backslash \overline{z_1'} \ldots \backslash \overline{z_{k'}'} \ ,$$

and let d_2, d_2' be the diagrams denoted by w_2, w_2', respectively. Since

$$d = d_2 \backslash \overline{z_1} \ldots \backslash \overline{z_k} = d_2' \backslash \overline{z_1'} \ldots \backslash \overline{z_{k'}'} \ ,$$

those internalised output ports of d are in bijection with $\{\overline{z_1}, \ldots, \overline{z_k}\}$ and with $\{\overline{z_1'}, \ldots, \overline{z_{k'}'}\}$. (Each restriction internalises *exactly* one output port of d.) It follows that $k = k'$ and that

$$d_2 = d_2'[\overline{z_1} \ldots \overline{z_k} / \overline{z_1'} \ldots \overline{z_{k'}'}] \ ,$$

assuming without loss of generality (via (E6)) that the relabelling is $\overline{z_i'} \mapsto \overline{z_i}$. Now, using Corollary 10(2) and the fact that the $\overline{x_i'}$ are distinct from the $\overline{z_i'}$, we have for some $\overline{y_i''}$:

$$
\begin{aligned}
E \vdash \ & w_2'[\overline{z_1} \ldots \overline{z_k} / \overline{z_1'} \ldots \overline{z_{k'}'}] \\
= \ & w_1'[\overline{z_1} \ldots \overline{z_k} / \overline{z_1'} \ldots \overline{z_{k'}'}][c_1'; \overline{y_1''} \to \overline{x_1'}] \ldots [c_{n'}'; \overline{y_{n'}''} \to \overline{x_{n'}'}] \\
= \ & w_1''[c_1'; \overline{y_1''} \to \overline{x_1'}] \ldots [c_{n'}'; \overline{y_{n'}''} \to \overline{x_{n'}'}]
\end{aligned}
$$

where

$$w_1'' \equiv f_1'[g_1''] \circ \ldots \circ f_{m'}'[g_{m'}'']$$

and $g_i'' = (\overline{z_1} \ldots \overline{z_k} / \overline{z_1'} \ldots \overline{z_{k'}'}) \bullet g_i'$. Now, let d_1 and d_1'' be the diagrams denoted by w_1 and w_1'', respectively. Then

$$d_2 = d_1[c_1; \overline{y_1} \to \overline{x_1}] \ldots [c_n; \overline{y_n} \to \overline{x_n}] = d_1''[c_1'; \overline{y_1''} \to \overline{x_1'}] \ldots [c_{n'}'; \overline{y_{n'}''} \to \overline{x_{n'}'}]$$

and consider the set of loop connections in d_2:

$$C_L = \{(p,p') \in C_2 \mid p \in \operatorname{Dom}\varepsilon_2, p' \in \operatorname{Dom}\iota_2\} \ .$$

C_L can now be further partitioned into sets

$$C_{(\overline{l_j},k_j)} = \{(p,p') \in C_L \mid \varepsilon_2(p) = \overline{l_j}, \ \iota_2(p') = k_j\} \ .$$

Informally, each connection in $C_{(\overline{l_j},k_j)}$ emanates from the same output port labelled $\overline{l_j}$ and terminates at some internalised input port initialised with k_j. These sets are clearly disjoint as there can be no output port with more than one external label nor a multiply initialised input port.

Now we know, from assumption that w is in normal form, that the $(\overline{y_j}, c_j)$ are distinct. Similarly, the $(\overline{y_j'}, c_j')$ (and hence the $(\overline{y_j''}, c_j')$) are distinct (the z_i' are distinct and the relabelling $z_i' \mapsto \overline{z_i}$ is one-to-one). Since each loop construction $[c; \overline{y} \to \overline{x}]$ adds a set $C_{(\overline{y},c)}$ of connections, it follows that the $C_{(\overline{l_j},k_j)}$ are in bijection with the $(\overline{y_j}, c_j)$ and with the $(\overline{y_j''}, c_j')$. Furthermore, we may assume via (E16) this bijection to be:

$$(\overline{y_j}, c_j) \mapsto C_{(\overline{l_j},k_j)} \mapsto (\overline{y_j''}, c_j') \ .$$

Then, $\overline{y_i} = \overline{y_i''}$, $c_j = c_j'$ and $n = n'$ and there is a one-to-one relabelling $x_i' \mapsto \overline{x_i}$ such that

$$d_1 = d_1''[\overline{x_1} \ldots \overline{x_n} / \overline{x_1'} \ldots \overline{x_n'}] \ .$$

Hence, one has

$$E \vdash w_1''[\overline{x_1} \ldots \overline{x_n} / \overline{x_1'} \ldots \overline{x_n'}] = f_1'[h_1] \circ \ldots \circ f_{m'}'[h_{m'}] \ ,$$

where $h_i = (\overline{x_1} \ldots \overline{x_n} / \overline{x_1'} \ldots \overline{x_n'}) \bullet g_i''$. Letting

$$w_1''' \equiv f_1'[h_1] \circ \ldots \circ f_{m'}'[h_{m'}] \ ,$$

it is now not hard to see that w_1 and w_1''' represent the same diagram d_1. It follows from Lemma 13 that $E \vdash w_1 = w_1'''$. Finally,

$$
\begin{aligned}
E \vdash w' &= w_1'[c_1; \overline{y_1'} \to \overline{x_1'}] \ldots [c_n; \overline{y_n'} \to \overline{x_n'}] \setminus \overline{z_1'} \ldots \setminus \overline{z_k'} \\
&= w_1'[\overline{z_1} \ldots \overline{z_k} / \overline{z_1'} \ldots \overline{z_k'}][c_1; \overline{y_1} \to \overline{x_1'}] \ldots [c_n; \overline{y_n} \to \overline{x_n'}] \setminus \overline{z_1} \ldots \setminus \overline{z_k} \\
&= w_1'[\overline{z_1} \ldots \overline{z_k} / \overline{z_1'} \ldots \overline{z_k'}][\overline{x_1} \ldots \overline{x_n} / \overline{x_1'} \ldots \overline{x_n'}][c_1; \overline{y_1} \to \overline{x_1}] \ldots [c_n; \overline{y_n} \to \overline{x_n}] \\
&\quad \setminus \overline{z_1} \ldots \setminus \overline{z_k} \\
&= w_1'''[c_1; \overline{y_1} \to \overline{x_1}] \ldots [c_n; \overline{y_n} \to \overline{x_n}] \setminus \overline{z_1} \ldots \setminus \overline{z_k} \\
&= w_1[c_1; \overline{y_1} \to \overline{x_1}] \ldots [c_n; \overline{y_n} \to \overline{x_n}] \setminus \overline{z_1} \ldots \setminus \overline{z_k} \\
&= w \ .
\end{aligned}
$$

$\square$

6 Connecting Diagrams and Programs

To complete the connection we must establish that the equations of Proposition 9 hold for the operational semantics of the programming language.

6.1 Semantics of Function Blocks

The detailed definition of the language is given elsewhere [8]. For simplicity, here we restrict attention to the subset of function blocks excluding delays as the latter play no role in the connection between diagrams and their textual representation.

In general, a function block f is evaluated against a set I of inputs to produce a set O of outputs. As a result of evaluation, f *evolves* into a new term f' which records the new state of f. We use judgements of the form $\langle f, I \rangle \rightarrow \langle f', O \rangle$ to express this fact.

More formally, I and O are both *finite maps* from the set of port labels $PLab$ to constants in Con. Such maps will often be written explicitly as

$$\{\overline{x_1} \mapsto c_1, \ldots, \overline{x_k} \mapsto c_k\} \;,$$

$k \geq 0$. When f, g are finite maps, the map $f + g$, the *modification* of f by g, is the map with domain $\text{Dom}\, f \cup \text{Dom}\, g$ and values

$$(f + g)(x) = \text{if } x \in \text{Dom}\, g \text{ then } g(x) \text{ else } f(x) \;.$$

Also, if f is a finite map and X a finite set, then $f \setminus X$ is $f \downarrow ((\text{Dom}\, f) \setminus X)$. The following definition introduces some notation to deal with the effect of relabellings on input and output maps:

Definition 15. Let $P{:}PLab \rightarrow Con$ and $g{:}PLab \rightarrow PLab$ be a relabelling function. Then,

1. $g \rhd P$, the *relabelling of P by g*, is the map $\{g(\overline{x}) \mapsto P(\overline{x}) \mid \overline{x} \in \text{Dom}\, P\}$, if $g \downarrow \text{Dom}\, P$ is an injection; and
2. $g \lhd P$, the *inverse relabelling of P by g*, is the map

$$\bigcup_{\overline{x} \in \text{Dom}\, P} \{\overline{y} \mapsto P(\overline{x}) \mid \overline{y} \in g^{-1}(\overline{x})\} \;,$$

where $g^{-1}(\overline{x}) = \{\overline{y} \mid g(\overline{y}) = \overline{x}\}$ is the inverse image of $\overline{x}$ under g. □

Function block evaluation depends upon the evaluation of basic expressions. We write $\langle e, I \rangle \rightarrow c$ for the evaluation of expression e to constant c under inputs I. Given this, the rules for function block evaluation have as in Fig. 4.

The evaluation relation $\rightarrow$ can easily be proved *monogenic*, that is $\rightarrow$ is a function.

$$\frac{\langle e, I \rangle \to c}{\langle \overline{y} = e, I \rangle \to \langle \overline{y} = e, \{\overline{y} \mapsto c\}\rangle} \tag{1}$$

$$\frac{\langle f, I \rangle \to \langle f', O \rangle}{\langle f \setminus S, I \rangle \to \langle f' \setminus S, O \setminus S \rangle} \tag{2}$$

$$\frac{\langle f, g \triangleleft I \rangle \to \langle f', O \rangle \quad g {\downarrow} \mathcal{O}(f) \text{ is an injection}}{\langle f[g], I \rangle \to \langle f'[g], g \triangleright O \rangle} \tag{3}$$

$$\frac{\langle f, I + \{\overline{x} \mapsto c\}\rangle \to \langle f', O \rangle}{\langle f[c; \; \overline{y} \to \overline{x}], I \rangle \to \langle f'[O(\overline{y}); \; \overline{y} \to \overline{x}], O \rangle} \tag{4}$$

$$\frac{\langle f_1, I \rangle \to \langle f_1', O_1 \rangle \quad \langle f_2, I + O_1 \rangle \to \langle f_2', O_2 \rangle}{\langle f_1 \circ f_2, I \rangle \to \langle f_1' \circ f_2', O_1 + O_2 \rangle} \tag{5}$$

Fig. 4. Semantic rules: function block evaluation.

Based on the semantics, one can now define a notion of *equality* between function blocks. For our current purposes, the following definition is sufficient[3]:

Definition 16 (Equality). Two function blocks f_1 and f_2 are equal iff, for all I and O,

1. whenever $\langle f_1, I \rangle \to \langle f_1', O \rangle$, then $\langle f_2, I \rangle \to \langle f_2', O \rangle$ and $f_1' = f_2'$; and
2. whenever $\langle f_2, I \rangle \to \langle f_2', O \rangle$, then $\langle f_1, I \rangle \to \langle f_1', O \rangle$ and $f_1' = f_2'$. $\quad\square$

Equality is both an equivalence and a congruence relation. The definition of $=$, together with the fact that evaluation preserves the syntactic structure of function block terms, gives rise to the following proof technique for equality [8]:

Lemma 17. *Let f be some combination $\mathcal{C}(f_1, \ldots, f_n)$ of $f_1, \ldots, f_n$ and let f' be some combination $\mathcal{C}'(f_1', \ldots, f_{n'}')$ of $f_1', \ldots, f_{n'}'$. Define a relation R as follows:*

$$R = \{(\mathcal{C}(f_1, \ldots, f_n), \; \mathcal{C}'(f_1', \ldots, f_{n'}')) \mid f_1, \ldots, f_n, f_1', \ldots, f_{n'}' \in Fb\}$$

Then in order to prove $f = f'$ it suffices to demonstrate that

1. *whenever $\langle f, I \rangle \to \langle h, O \rangle$, then $\langle f', I \rangle \to \langle h', O \rangle$ and $(h, h') \in R$; and*
2. *whenever $\langle f', I \rangle \to \langle h', O \rangle$, then $\langle f, I \rangle \to \langle h, O \rangle$ and $(h, h') \in R$.*

Proof. Equality, $=$, is defined as the greatest fixed point of a function

$$\mathcal{E} : \wp(Fb \times Fb) \to \wp(Fb \times Fb) \; ,$$

the precise definition of which should be obvious from Definition 16. The proof technique amounts to showing that R is a post-fixed point of $\mathcal{E}$; that is $\mathcal{E}(R) \subseteq R$. This, in turn, establishes that $R \subseteq =$. $\quad\square$

---

[3] The full notion of equality must also take the passage of time into account. Having excluded delays, the only time-sensitive elements of the language, full equality reduces to that of Definition 16.

6.2 Verifying the Equational Laws

Checking that each equation in Proposition 9 holds in the semantics is a routine and often tedious task. Here we only prove (E14) to illustrate the use of the general technique described above.

First, assume that $\langle f[c;\ \overline{y} \to \overline{x}][g], I \rangle \to \langle f_1, O \rangle$. Then there is a function block term f' and an output O' such that $f_1 \equiv f'[O'(\overline{y});\ \overline{y} \to \overline{x}][g]$, $O = g \triangleright O'$ and the following is a valid derivation in the semantics:

$$\cfrac{\cfrac{\langle f, (g \triangleleft I) + \{\overline{x} \mapsto c\}\rangle \to \langle f', O'\rangle}{\langle f[c;\ \overline{y} \to \overline{x}], g \triangleleft I\rangle \to \langle f'[O'(\overline{y});\ \overline{y} \to \overline{x}], O'\rangle} \ (4)}{\langle f[c;\ \overline{y} \to \overline{x}][g], I\rangle \to \langle f'[O'(\overline{y});\ \overline{y} \to \overline{x}][g], g \triangleright O'\rangle} \ (3)$$

Now observe that, since $g'(\overline{x}) = \overline{z}$ and $\overline{z} \notin g(\mathcal{S}(f) \setminus \{\overline{x}\})$, $(g \triangleleft I) + \{\overline{x} \mapsto c\} = g' \triangleleft (I + \{\overline{z} \mapsto c\})$. Moreover, $g' \triangleright O' = g \triangleright O'$, since $\overline{x} \notin \mathrm{Dom}\, O'$, and thus $(g' \triangleright O')(g(\overline{y})) = O'(\overline{y})$. By monogenicity of $\to$, $\langle f, g' \triangleleft (I + \{\overline{x} \mapsto c\})\rangle \to \langle f', O'\rangle$. Then we can construct the following derivation:

$$\cfrac{\cfrac{\langle f, g' \triangleleft (I + \{\overline{z} \mapsto c\})\rangle \to \langle f', O'\rangle}{\langle f[g'], I + \{\overline{z} \mapsto c\}\rangle \to \langle f'[g'], g' \triangleright O'\rangle} \ (3)}{\langle f[g'][c;\ g(\overline{y}) \to \overline{z}], I\rangle \to \langle f'[g'][O'(\overline{y});\ g(\overline{y}) \to \overline{z}], g \triangleright O'\rangle} \ (4)$$

Hence,

$$\langle f[g'][c;\ g(\overline{y}) \to \overline{z}], I\rangle \to \langle f'[g'][O'(\overline{y});\ g(\overline{y}) \to \overline{z}], O\rangle$$

and we have shown part 1 of Lemma 17. A completely symmetrical argument establishes the opposite direction, part 2. Thus, the relation

$$R = \{(f[c;\ \overline{y} \to \overline{x}][g], f[g'][c;\ g(\overline{y}) \to \overline{z}]) \mid f \in Fb\}$$

satisfies the criterion of Lemma 17 and, hence,

$$f[c;\ \overline{y} \to \overline{x}][g] = f[g'][c;\ g(\overline{y}) \to \overline{z}]$$

for all $f \in Fb$.

7 Conclusion

Recently, there have been a number of approaches to the formalisation of PLC programming languages, e.g. [1,2]. These have focused on using formal methods to support reasoning about textual representations of these languages. An essential aspect of PLC languages is the ability to program using diagrams. This ability has an impact on the acceptance of the notation and on the designer's ability to reason (formally and informally) about the system.

Here we have established a precise correspondence between diagrams and the semantics of the language. We believe that this has significance both specifically for the programming of PLCs in such notation and more generally it establishes criteria for the use of diagrammatic notations in domain-specific programming languages.

Acknowledgements

We would like to thank the anonymous referees for their helpful comments. The second author in particular wishes to express his gratitude to Professor Rod Burstall for his kind understanding and patience while this article was compiled.

References

1. G. Egger, A. Fett, P. Pepper. *Formal Specification of a Safe PLC Language and Its Compiler.* Proceedings of the SafeComp'94 13th International Conference on Computer Safety, Reliability and Security. ISA, 1994.
2. W. Halang, S. Jung, B. Krämer, J. Scheepstra. *A Safety Licensable Computing Architecture*, World Scientific, 1993
3. IEC *International Standard 1131-3, Programmable Controllers, Part 3, Programming Languages.*, 1993.
4. R. Milner. *Flowgraphs and Flow Algebras.* Journal of the ACM, Vol. 26, No. 4, October 1979, pp. 794-818.
5. R. Milner. *Communication and Concurrency.* Prentice Hall International, 1989.
6. E. Parr. *Programmable Controllers, An Engineer's Guide.* Newnes, 1993
7. F. Swainston. *A Systems Approach to Programmable Controllers.* Newnes, 1991
8. K. Tourlas. *Semantic Analysis and Design of Languages for PLCs.* M.Sc. Project Report, Dept. of Computer Science, The University of Edinburgh, 1996.

Graphical Specification and Reasoning: Case Study Generalised Railroad Crossing*

Henning Dierks and Cheryl Dietz
e-mail: {dierks,dietz}@informatik.uni-oldenburg.de

University of Oldenburg, Germany

Abstract. A benchmark real-time problem, the generalised railroad crossing [9], serves as illustration of a fully graphical approach to the formal development of correct reactive real-time systems. We show how to formally capture requirements with the graphical language Constraint Diagrams [6] and perform graphical refinement steps towards implementable requirements. These requirements correspond directly to PLC-Automata [4], a class of real-time automata suitable to describe the behaviour of Programmable Logic Controllers (PLCs), a hardware widely used in industry in order to control processes. A compilation schema generates runnable PLC-source-code. Optionally, error states can be introduced in the automata to allow checks of correctness of assumptions. While all languages used – except for the PLC-source-code – are visual, their common semantics is formally defined employing Duration Calculus (DC) [20]. Correctness of refinement steps can thus be formally proven. Once established, graphical refinement rules can be used without knowledge of the DC inside. In that way visuality eases application of formal reasoning.

1 Introduction

Application of formal methods for developing reactive real-time systems is a demanding engineering task. A formal foundation enhances clarity of the design process and confidence in the correctness of a resulting system. The price required to pay for these benefits in practice is often considered too high because usually application and software engineers lack experience in interpreting and manipulating logical formulas. Potential industrial users do usually not want to afford a special training for introducing formal methods. This raised the question for simpler representations of formal descriptions for system behaviour and properties. One approach is to use graphical formalisms. A suitably intuitive representation of formulas makes them easier to read and handle. This is the idea we follow here for the development process from top level requirements to the implementation level.

The first step in system development is finding the requirements posed on the intended system. They are normally formulated in natural language. During

---

* This research was partially supported by the German Ministry for Education and Research (BMBF) as part of the project UniForM under grant No. FKZ 01 IS 521 B3.

the phase of requirements capture often misunderstandings between the partners involved occur. These could possibly be avoided if a suitable graphical language for discussion existed. Conciseness of a graphical formalism also supports precise formulations of what is expected. In this work Constraint Diagrams [6] are used for formalising requirements given in natural language. They represent requirements in a style inspired from timing diagrams which are used in hardware design to visualise the timing behaviour of systems considered.

The distance between requirements and implementation is quite big. There are two main streams in formal methods how to bridge this gap. The *model checking* approach (for a survey see [2]) takes an independently written implementation and afterwards checks if it fulfils the desired properties. *Refinement* techniques as e. g. developed in the ProCoS project [8] guarantee correctness of implementations which are stepwise derived from requirements. Here we focus on the refinement approach and show how refinement steps can be done graphically. During refinement suitable assumptions about the environment's behaviour are introduced similar to [15]. Application of refinement rules appears often to be easier in Constraint Diagrams than in formulas; e. g. strengthening of requirements can be done by simply adding suitable parts in the graphics.

At the implementation level we consider Programmable Logic Controllers (PLCs), which are widely used in industry for controlling embedded real-time systems. These devices are machines that frequently poll sensors and compute outputs for actuators. In the UniForM project [12] PLC-Automata have been proposed as description language for the behaviour of PLCs [4]. These automata form a class of real-time automata dedicated to this application. They are used as the interface between the industrial partner Elpro LET GmbH, Berlin, and the universities involved. Here we show how PLC-Automata are derived from the implementable graphical constraints obtained by refinement steps from Constraint Diagrams. It is possible to further refine PLC-Automata, e. g. to enable error detection so that the logic controller becomes more reliable. Finally runnable PLC-source-code is produced through a compilation procedure for PLC-Automata [4].

This development process from informal requirements down to the implementation level is illustrated in Fig. 1.

The underlying formal basis is Duration Calculus [20], an interval temporal logic for real-time. Both Constraint Diagrams and PLC-Automata are equipped with a DC semantics, thus allowing a formal refinement relation in one framework.

Our approach to graphical specification and reasoning is illustrated by a case study. The problem of specifying a generalised railroad crossing and verifying its properties was posed in [9] and suggested as a benchmark problem in comparing the suitability of different formal methods in [10], where many solutions are given. The Duration Calculus approach advocated in [15] inspired us to develop our graphical specifications and refinements for the generalised railroad crossing.

The Constraint Diagram specification shown in Sect. 3.2 corresponds to the informal requirements as found in [10]. Refinement is similar to the steps per-

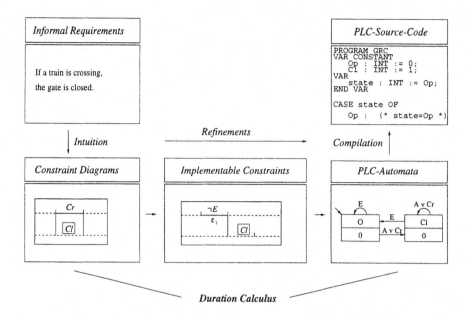

Figure 1. Graphical development of correct real-time systems

formed in [15] without graphics. Section 4 gives an impression of such graphical refinement with Constraint Diagrams. The resulting controller design is the basis for a PLC implementation developed in Sect. 6 after introducing Programmable Logic Controllers and PLC-Automata in Sect. 5. Section 7 demonstrates how additional checks whether assumptions hold can be introduced afterwards in order to enhance the controller. Concluding remarks discuss what is achieved by our work and relate it to other approaches. Duration Calculus and the semantic foundations of Constraint Diagrams and PLC-Automata are described in Apps. A to C.

2 Constraint Diagrams

In hardware design timing diagrams have been used informally to enhance understanding of the timing behaviour of systems developed. Driven by the demand for an easy way to specify formal requirements, attempts to formalise such an approach have been undertaken since the late eighties. The development of Constraint Diagrams [6] was inspired by the work [18] on Symbolic Timing Diagrams.

Requirements concerning the behaviour of reactive systems often consist of a hypothesis and an assertion part. This is known as assumption/commitment style specification. It is exactly this style of formulating requirements which is embodied in Constraint Diagrams. The idea of this graphical language is illustrated using the example of a watchdog in Fig. 2.

Different horizontal lines characterise the behaviour of components of a system considered. E.g. the first line in the watchdog requirement stands for a be-

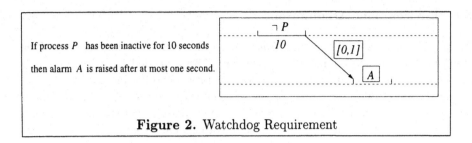

Figure 2. Watchdog Requirement

haviour where process P at the beginning behaves arbitrarily (indicated by the dashed part of the line), then for 10 seconds is inactive and afterwards behaves arbitrary again. The phases on lines are determined by Boolean expressions, so called *phase assertions*, and *length requirements* indicated by time intervals (point intervals like $[10, 10]$ in the example are denoted by their element, i.e. 10); if no particular length is supposed, i.e. a length in $[0, \infty)$ is considered, no annotation is made. Time dependencies between components are introduced by arrows decorated with time intervals between the lines. Assertions are highlighted by boxes. Both hypothesis and assertion of a Constraint Diagram consist of these ingredients. The Duration Calculus semantics of Constraint Diagrams is sketched in App. B.

3 Formalising the Generalised Railroad Crossing

Before coming to the formalisation we cite the description of the case study [9].

> The system to be developed operates a gate at a railroad crossing. The railroad crossing I lies in a region of interest R, i.e. $I \subseteq R$. A set of trains travels through R on multiple tracks in both directions. A sensor system determines when each train enters and exits region R. To describe the system formally, we define a gate function $g(t) \in [0, 90]$, where $g(t) = 0$ means the gate is down and $g(t) = 90$ means the gate is up. We define a set λ_i of *occupancy intervals*, where each occupancy interval is a time interval during which one or more trains are in I. The ith occupancy interval is represented as $\lambda_i = [\tau_i, \nu_i]$, where τ_i is the time of the ith entry of a train into the crossing when no other train is in the crossing and ν_i is the first time since τ_i that no train is in the crossing (i.e., the train that entered at τ_i has exited as have trains that entered the crossing after τ_i).
>
> Given two constants ξ_1 and ξ_2, the problem is to develop a system to operate the crossing gate that satisfies the following two properties:
>
> **Safety Property:** $t \in \cup_i \lambda_i \Rightarrow g(t) = 0$ (The gate is down during all occupancy intervals.)
>
> **Utility Property:** $t \notin [\tau_i - \xi_1, \nu_i + \xi_2] \Rightarrow g(t) = 90$ (The gate is up when no train is in the crossing.)

3.1 Environment Assumptions

To be able to reason about correctness of requirements, certain aspects of the environment's behaviour have to be known. Those needed later in refinement are formalised here. The environment for the gate controller includes tracks and trains. Tracks can be in three states: Either no train is detected, a train is detected after entering R and approaching the crossing, or (at least one) train is crossing the critical region I. The first state is called *empty* (abbr. E), the second one *approaching* (abbr. A) and the third *crossing* (abbr. Cr).

Initialisation and sequencing constraints assumed for the tracks are shown in Fig. 3. The texts give the natural language descriptions which are visualised by the Constraint Diagrams.

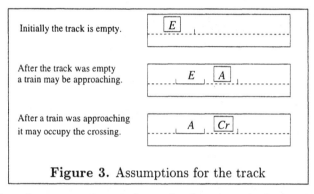

Figure 3. Assumptions for the track

To complete the assumptions, it has to be determined which states can follow a crossing phase. It is realistic to assume that either a new train approaches or the tracks are empty again. This covers all possibles states, so no additional requirement is needed. These requirements together describe the possible phase sequences allowed on the track.

During the refinements in the next section two additional assumptions concerning the speed of trains are needed: The fastest train approaches in ε_1 seconds after the track was empty and the slowest train needs ξ_1 seconds to approach the crossing. They are defined in Fig. 4.

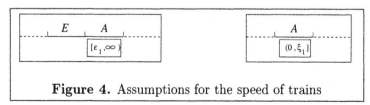

Figure 4. Assumptions for the speed of trains

3.2 Requirements Capture

The gate can be in positions $g(t)$ between 0 to 90 degrees at any time t. The gate is *closed* (abbr. Cl) if the position is 0 degrees and *opened* (abbr. O) if it is 90 degrees. The behaviour of the gate depends on absence or presence of trains in the critical region and shall be controlled accordingly. Two properties are required: *Safety* shown in Fig. 5 and *Utility*.

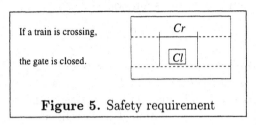

Figure 5. Safety requirement

The utility requirement is that the gate should be open if no train is crossing. To allow a more precise specification, one real constant ξ_2 is assumed to denote the time required for opening the gate after a train passed, while a real constant ξ_1 gives the time needed to close the gate. Assuming a long enough time interval, the utility requirement can then be stated as shown in Fig. 6.

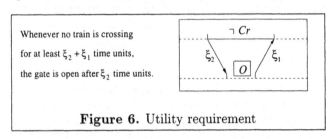

Figure 6. Utility requirement

What is achieved by the development of Constraint Diagrams has been demonstrated here: No temporal logic formulas are needed in requirements capture to gain a requirement specification which can be interpreted formally. The next section shows how a transformational design process can be carried out with Constraint Diagrams.

4 Transformational Design

The requirements Safety and Utility are refined to the design constraints shown in Fig. 7. The first one requires that ε_1 seconds after the track being occupied the gate is closed. The second states that if the track has been empty for ξ_2 seconds, the gate is open.

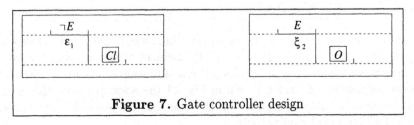

Figure 7. Gate controller design

Before showing the refinement process leading to the requirements for design for both properties, we define the refinement relation and some refinement rules. The refinement relation is defined as follows:

$$D_1 \Leftarrow D_2 \overset{\text{df}}{=} [\![D_1]\!] \Leftarrow [\![D_2]\!] \wedge [\![A]\!] \wedge L(D_1, D_2) \tag{1}$$

where $[\![D]\!]$ denotes the Duration Calculus semantics of design D, $[\![A]\!]$ denotes the DC semantics of the assumptions A and $L(D_1, D_2)$ is a semantic link between D_1 and D_2, for example a simulation relation between different observables used in D_1 and D_2. This refinement notion defines refinement relative to certain assumptions.

Some refinement rules needed in deriving the design in Fig. 7 are given in Figs. 8 and 9.

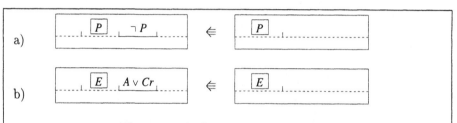

Figure 8. Refinement rule: Initiality
The general refinement rule is given in a) for all state assertions P. An application of this refinement rule in proving Safety is given in b), see Fig. 10.

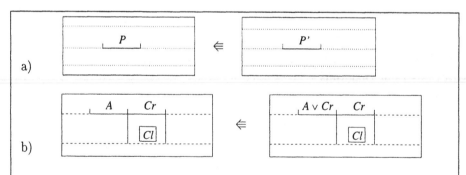

Figure 9. Refinement rule: Monotonicity – weaken phase hypothesis
The general refinement rule is given in a) for all state assertions P, P' if $P' \Leftarrow P$. An application of this refinement rule in proving Safety is given in b) with $P = A$ and $P' = A \vee Cr$.

For Safety it is necessary to find a design which forces the gate to close early enough before a train enters the crossing. Refinement shown in Fig. 10 therefore introduces phases before Cr and utilises the assumption about fast trains.

In the refinement of Utility shown in Fig. 11 the assumption on the slowest train is needed. Assumptions on the track behaviour influence the case analysis in the second step of the refinement.

In [6] Constraint Diagrams have been suggested for requirements capture to simplify comprehensibility of formal requirements for non-formalists. Here we have seen that they can be used even further in a formal development process to perform refinement steps visually.

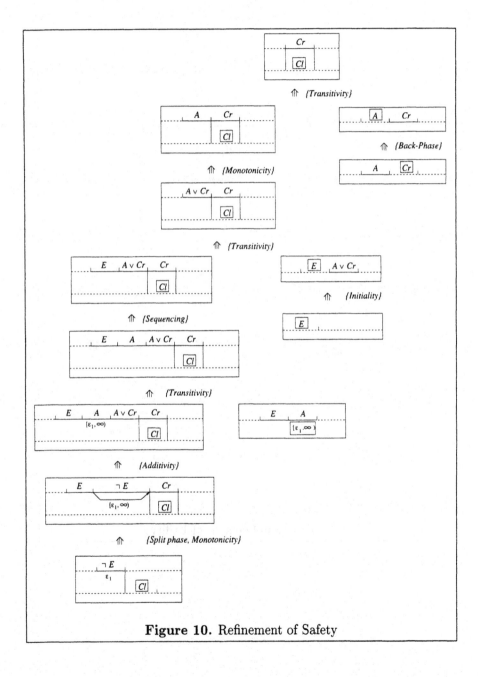

Figure 10. Refinement of Safety

28

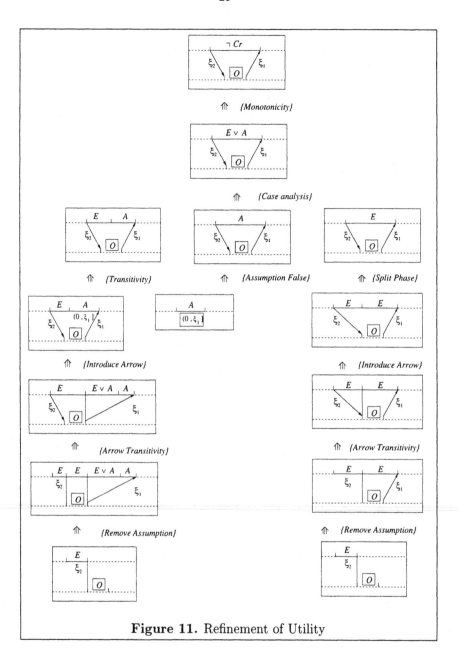

Figure 11. Refinement of Utility

5 Programmable Logic Controllers

Programmable Logic Controllers (PLC) are often used in industry for solving tasks calling for real-time problems like railway crossings, traffic control, or production cells. Due to this special application area PLCs have features for making the design of time- and safety-critical systems easier:

- PLCs have input and output channels where sensors and actuators can be plugged in.
- They behave in a cyclic manner where every cycle consists of the following phases:
  - Poll all inputs and store the read values.
  - Compute the new values for the outputs.
  - Update all outputs.

  The repeated execution of this cycle is managed by the operating system. The only part the programmer has to adapt is the computing phase. Thus, PLCs are implemented polling machines realising the typical method of solving time-critical problems in reality.
- Depending on the program and on the number of inputs and outputs there is an upper time bound for a cycle that can be used to calculate the reaction time.
- Convenient standardised libraries are given to simplify the handling of time.

Although these characteristics are quite useful PLC-programmers have to face the following problem: If an input signal does not hold for at least the maximum amount of time needed for a cycle, one cannot be sure that the PLC will ever read this signal. Note that this is one advantage of using PLCs. It obliges the programmer to check both his sensors and cycle time, which makes the assumptions concerning the hardware explicit.

Furthermore, we want to stress the fact that any computer can be programmed in such a way that it behaves like a PLC. Hence, an implementation on a PLC is equivalent to an implementation on an arbitrary computer system.

Now we present a language which is designed for fitting both the needs of computer scientists and engineers programming PLCs. Engineers, often being electrical engineers, are used to developing PLC-programs in assembler-like languages or languages that are closely related to circuit diagrams.

In the UniForM-project [12] we made the experience that automaton-like pictures can serve as a common basis for computer scientists and engineers because the latter gave them a semantics suitable to PLCs in an intuitive way. This was the motivation for us to formalise a notion of "PLC-Automaton" and to define a formal semantics[1] for it in a suitable temporal logic [4]. On the one hand, this allows formal reasoning; on the other hand, this respects the behaviour of PLCs and the intuitive semantics given by the programmers.

Figure 12 gives an example of a PLC-Automaton. It shows an automaton with three states ($\{q_0, q_1, q_2\}$), that reacts to inputs of the alphabet $\{P, \neg P\}$.

---

[1] The formal semantics can be found in App. C.

30

Every state has two annotations in the graphical representation. The upper one denotes the output of the state, thus in state q_0 the output is ok and in state q_2 the output is A denoting an "Alarm". The lower annotation is either 0 or a pair consisting of a real number d greater than 0 and a nonempty subset A of inputs. The operational behaviour is as follows: If the second annotation of a state q is 0, the PLC-Automaton reacts in every cycle on the inputs that are read and

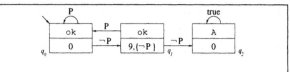

Figure 12. The watchdog as PLC-Automaton

behaves according to the transition relation. If the second annotation of q is a pair (d, A), the PLC-Automaton checks in every cycle the input i according to these parameters. If i is not in A the automaton reacts according to the transition relation. If i is in A and the current state does not hold longer than d, the input will be ignored and the automaton remains in state q. If i is in A and state q held longer than d the PLC-Automaton will react on i according to the transition relation.

The PLC-Automaton in Fig. 12 thus behaves as follows: It starts in state q_0 and holds this state as long as it reads only the input P. The first time it reads $\neg P$ it changes to state q_1 without changing the output. In q_1 the automaton reacts on the input P by changing the state back to q_0 and on the input $\neg P$ by changing the state to q_2. The way back to q_0 is independent from the time state q_1 held. However, the way to q_2 is only possible if q_1 holds longer than 9 seconds. If this transition takes place the automaton enters q_2 and remains there forever. Therefore this PLC-Automaton implements the watchdog as specified in Fig. 2, provided the cycle time of the PLC is fast enough. Note that the delay time of q_1 must be less than 10 because the time consumption of the PLC-cycles has to be reflected.

We formalise this graphic notation using an automaton-like structure extended by some components:

Definition 5.1. A tuple $\mathcal{A} = (Q, \Sigma, \delta, \pi_0, \varepsilon, S_t, S_e, \Omega, \omega)$ is a *PLC-Automaton* if

- Q is a nonempty, finite set of *states*,
- Σ is a nonempty, finite set of *inputs*,
- δ is a function of type $Q \times \Sigma \longrightarrow Q$ (*transition function*),
- $\pi_0 \in Q$ is the *initial state*,
- $\varepsilon > 0$ is the *upper bound* for a cycle.
- S_t is a function of type $Q \longrightarrow \mathbb{R}_{\geq 0}$ assigning to each state π a *delay time* how long the inputs contained in $S_e(\pi)$ should be ignored,
- S_e is a function of type $Q \longrightarrow \mathcal{P}(\Sigma) \setminus \{\emptyset\}$ assigning to each state a set of *delayed inputs* that cause no change of the state during the first time units given by $S_t(\pi)$ the automaton stays in this state,
- Ω is a nonempty, finite set of *outputs*,
- ω is a function of type $Q \longrightarrow \Omega$ (*output function*)

and

$$\forall \pi \in Q, a \in \Sigma : S_t(\pi) > 0 \wedge a \notin S_e(\pi) \Longrightarrow \delta(\pi, a) \neq \pi \qquad (2)$$

holds.

The additional components are needed to model PLC-behaviour and to enrich the language for dealing with real-time aspects. The ε represents the upper bound for a cycle of a PLC and enables us to model this cycle in the semantics. The delay function S_t and S_e represent the annotations of the states. In the case of $S_t(\pi) = 0$ no delay time is given and the value $S_e(\pi)$ is arbitrary. If the delay time $S_t(\pi)$ is greater than 0 the set $S_e(\pi)$ denotes the set of inputs for which the delay time is valid. The restriction (2) is introduced to enable the application of the compilation schema given in [4].

PLC-Automata look similar to Timed Automata [1] but the details are different. Although a transformation of a PLC-Automaton into a Timed Automaton can be given [4], the result is a much more complicated description because we have to switch from a state-based to an event-based formalism. Another reason is that we have to consider that the PLC is not obliged to react to input signals that do not hold longer than ε seconds.

6 Implementation

Now we demonstrate how the graphical requirements gained by the refinement steps in Sect. 4 can be used to develop a PLC-Automaton that fulfils the graphical requirements.

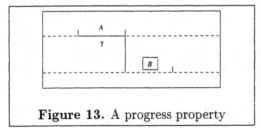

Figure 13. A progress property

Certain forms of graphical requirements can be translated into properties of a PLC-Automaton. The refinement of the graphical requirements in Sect. 4 resulted in such forms, and that makes it possible to translate each requirement into a property for the PLC-Automaton to be developed. The form of graphical requirements we have to consider is given in Fig. 13. This form can be translated into a property for a PLC-Automaton using the rule given in Fig. 14.

The correctness of the rule is proven by a theorem about the behaviour of PLC-Automata given in [4]. This simple rule is sufficient to develop an automaton that refines the final graphical specification of Sect. 4. Both requirements fit to the pattern for the rule in Fig. 14 and thus it is sufficient to give an automaton which has these properties:

- The set of inputs contains $\{E, A, Cr\}$,
- There are two states q_O and q_{Cl} in Q with $\omega(q_O) = O$ and $\omega(q_{Cl}) = Cl$,
- for any state $q \in Q$ holds: $\delta(q, E) = q_O$, $\delta(q, A) = q_{Cl}$ and $\delta(q, Cr) = q_{Cl}$,

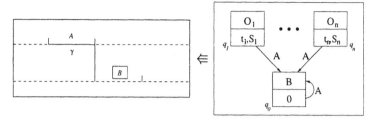

Figure 14. Refining progress requirements by PLC-Automata

A progress requirement of the form as given in Fig. 13 for a set A and an output B is refined by a PLC-Automaton $\mathcal{P} = (Q, \Sigma, \delta, \pi_0, \varepsilon, S_t, S_e, \Omega, \omega)$ with the following properties:

- $Q = \{q_0, \ldots, q_n\}$,
- A is contained in Σ,
- the output in state q_0 is B: $\omega(q_0) = B$,
- $\mathcal{P}$ reacts on A-input by changing the state to q_0: $\forall q_i \in Q : \delta(q, A) = q_0$,
- for the cycle time of $\mathcal{P}$ it holds $2\varepsilon \leq \gamma$, and
- any state $q_i \in Q$ reacts immediately on A-inputs: $t_i = 0 \vee A \cap S_i = \emptyset$.

Note that it is not specified how $\mathcal{P}$ behaves on inputs not contained in A.

- the cycle time is fast enough: $2\varepsilon \leq \min(\varepsilon_1, \xi_2) - \rho_{TS} - \rho_G$ seconds[2] (cf. Fig. 7), and
- in any state $q \in Q$ the automaton reacts immediately on E, A, or Cr-inputs: $S_t(q) = 0 \vee \{E, A, Cr\} \cap S_e(q) = \emptyset$.

The properties are not contradictory which means that we can find an automaton with these properties. The simplest one is given in Fig. 15. It is an automaton that does not use the delay constructs because the requirements given are both progress properties.

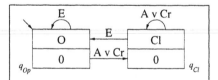

Figure 15. An implementing PLC-Automaton

7 Enhancement

Above we developed an implementation of the generalised railroad crossing that is provably correct. But this correctness is only valid supposing several properties about the environment. Some of these assumptions are given by physical properties like the track behaviour, but other assumptions may produce restrictions to human behaviour. For example the assumption that trains are not too fast can be given, because there is a speed limit for trains although the trains could pass the crossing faster. A dangerous situation can now occur when the

---

[2] We assume that the track sensor reacts within ρ_{TS} and the gate reacts within ρ_G.

engine driver violates the speed limit. Not in all situations these violations can be found by the controller, but sometimes it is possible that the controller gets signals that should not occur and indicate a violation of assumptions. If, for example, the sequence of signals $E - A - Cr$ occurs too fast, the controller could notice the violation of an assumption. The controller in Fig. 15 does not recognise such a violation.

Therefore we present now an enhanced design of a controller that recognises such situations. What one needs in this situation is a way of changing the controller in order to enhance its reactions to unexpected behaviour. In this case we would appreciate a change of the given controller such that it is possible to detect trains that are too fast.

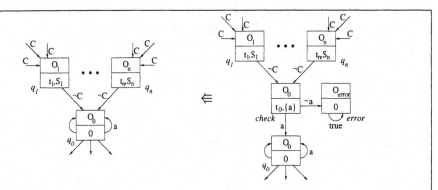

Figure 16. This transformation rule introduces an additional check whether a is stable as assumed

It is a refinement for a set $C \neq \emptyset$ of inputs with $a \notin C$ provided

$\boxed{C}$, $\boxed{C \quad a}$, and $\boxed{\begin{matrix} C & a \\ & [l,\infty) \end{matrix}}$. If

- there is a state q_0 with $\delta(q_0, a) = q_0$ and $S_t(q_0) = 0$,
- all incoming arcs of q_0 are labelled with inputs not contained in C,
- any state q_i with arc to q_0 has only incoming arcs labelled with C, and
- reacts immediately on input a, that means $t_i = 0$ or $a \notin S_i$,

then we can introduce two additional states *check* and *error* as given above with $t_0 \stackrel{\mathrm{df}}{=} t - 4\varepsilon$, supposed that $t_0 > 0$. The output of the "error"-state can be chosen arbitrarily.

In [3] some refinement rules under certain assumptions are given. One of them which fits to our problem is presented in Fig. 16. The application of this rule uses the assumptions of the track behaviour and the assumption that trains are not too fast. Figure 17 shows the result of the application of this rule to the automaton in Fig. 15 with $q_0 = q_{Cl}$, $C = \{E\}$, and $a = A$.

This automaton now consists of four states: *NoTr*: No train is detected; *AppTr*: A new train has entered. This state is held for $\sigma \stackrel{\mathrm{df}}{=} \varepsilon_1 - \rho_{TS} - 4\varepsilon$

seconds[3] if only A-signals are read. After this delay the state *SlowTr* is entered

if A holds on. If the read input
signal is not A during this state,
state *TooFast* is entered; *SlowTr*:
This state holds until the crossing is empty; *TooFast*: If the automaton enters this state, a train
has been too fast. The automaton never leaves this state without
human impact. *NoTr* and *SlowTr*
correspond to q_{Op} resp. q_{Cl} of the
automaton of Fig. 15. *AppTr* is
the *check*-state introduced by the
application of the rule and *TooFast*
represents the *error*-state of the
rule.

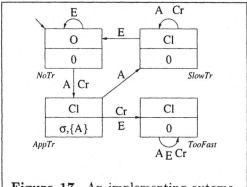

Figure 17. An implementing automaton with additional check for "A"

The implementation of the PLC-Automaton is very easy because in [4] a
compilation schema for PLC-Automata is given. The output of this compilation
is runnable PLC-code using ST ("structured text",[13, 11]), a pascal-like programming language for PLCs. Due to the simplicity of the automaton in Fig. 17
the code is very short:

```
PROGRAM GRC
VAR CONSTANT
    NoTr    :  INT := 0;      AppTr    :  INT := 1;
    SlowTr  :  INT := 2;      TooFast  :  INT := 3;
VAR
    state   :  INT :=NoTr;
    timer   :  TP;
    time_up :  BOOL := FALSE;
END_VAR


CASE state OF
    NoTr :   CASE input OF
                    E : state:= NoTr;
                    A : state:= AppTr;
                    Cr: state:= AppTr;
             END_CASE; (* end of state=NoTr *)
    AppTr :  timer(IN:=TRUE, PT:=σ);
             time_up:=NOT timer.Q;
             CASE input OF
                    E : state:= TooFast;
                        timer(IN:=FALSE, PT:=σ);
                    A : IF time_up THEN
                            state:= SlowTr;
                            timer(IN:=FALSE, PT:=σ);
                        END_IF;
                    Cr: state:= TooFast;
```

---

[3] We know that A should be stable for ε_1 seconds, therefore the output of the track
sensor should be stable for $\varepsilon_1 - \rho_{TS}$ seconds. We assume that $\sigma > 0$, otherwise this
refinement is not allowed.

```
                  timer(IN:=FALSE, PT:=σ);
              END_CASE; (* end of state=AppTr *)
    SlowTr : CASE input OF
                  E : state:= NoTr;
                  A : state:= SlowTr;
                  Cr: state:= SlowTr;
              END_CASE; (* end of state=SlowTr *)
    TooFast :state:= TooFast;
END_CASE
IF state=NoTr THEN output:=Open ELSE output:=Close ENDIF
```

Note that this program is executed once in every cycle of the PLC. So it is the body of an implicit loop-forever statement. The terms "input" and "output" stand for an address of the input ports resp. the output ports of the PLC. "E", "A", and "Cr" correspond to the values delivered by the track sensor. We use the built-in timer constructs of PLCs by the timer-invocations. A timer is set by an invocation when the IN-flag rises from FALSE to TRUE. In this case the timer is set for PT seconds. The flag timer.Q represents the output of the timer, which is true for PT seconds after setting and false otherwise. To get a correct implementation now one has only to check that the PLC-hardware is fast enough to guarantee that every cycle is executed in σ seconds.

8   Concluding Remarks

We have treated the case study completely by transformational design using a common semantical basis. We started by translating the informal requirements into Constraint Diagrams and we want to stress that these diagrams are very useful to convince people that the formal description of a requirement corresponds to the informal one. The reason is that the Constraint Diagrams have a quite intuitive semantics and therefore we believe that it is possible to express requirements without detailed knowledge of the Duration Calculus.

In contrast to [15] the transformation path is also completely on the graphical level, which makes it easier to apply refinement rules. Nevertheless, we ended up with runnable code for a widespread class of machines. Because of these interesting properties of our approach we have the vision of a tool that is equipped with an editor for Constraint Diagrams and PLC-Automata and allows application of transformation rules for them. This tool could be used without reasoning with Duration Calculus semantics.

Though our approach works for this simple case study, there might remain doubts about its scalability. Although it is not clear for which class of problems our method can be successful, we are optimistic that the class of problems we can handle is big enough to be interesting. To prove this statement more complex case studies are needed. But we are sure that problems that could be handled with ProCoS-methods [8] can also be handled by our method and there are many case studies worked out for the ProCoS-method (eg. [17]).

The switch from Constraint Diagrams to PLC-Automata is done at a level where requirements correspond to progress-properties. They belong to the subset of DC called Implementables [16]. The latest result in our research is that our approach can be applied to this subset of DC which was used in the ProCoS-project as a stepping-stone during transformational refinement. In [7] it is shown that this language can be expressed by Constraint Diagrams, and in [5] a synthesis procedure from Implementables to PLC-Automata is presented.

Acknowledgements

We would like to thank E.-R. Olderog, C. Fischer, S. Kleuker, M. Schenke, and other members of the Semantics Group in Oldenburg for detailed comments and various discussions on the subject of this paper. Furthermore, we thank the cafe in the centre of Uppsala — where the ideas of this paper were born — for providing a stimulating atmosphere and a nice coffee.

References

1. R. Alur and D.L. Dill. A theory of timed automata. *Theoret. Comput. Sci.*, 126:183–235, 1994.
2. E. Clarke, O. Grumberg, and D. Long. Verification tools for finite-state concurrent systems. In *A Decade of Concurrency – Reflections and Perspectives*, volume 803 of *Lecture Notes in Computer Science*. Springer-Verlag, 1994.
3. H. Dierks. Rules and Theorems for PLC-Automata. Technical report, University of Oldenburg, November 1996.
4. H. Dierks. PLC-Automata: A New Class of Implementable Real-Time Automata. In M. Bertran and T. Rus, editors, *ARTS'97*, volume 1231 of *Lecture Notes in Computer Science*, pages 111–125. Springer-Verlag, May 1997.
5. H. Dierks. Synthesising Controllers from Real-Time Specifications. In *Proceedings of ISSS'97*. IEEE, 1997. to appear.
6. C. Dietz. Graphical Formalization of Real-Time Requirements. In B. Jonsson and J. Parrow, editors, *Formal Techniques in Real-Time and Fault-Tolerant Systems*, volume 1135 of *Lecture Notes in Computer Science*, pages 366–385, Uppsala, Sweden, September 1996. Springer-Verlag.
7. C. Dietz. Action Diagrams. In *WRTP'97 (to appear)*. Elsevier Science, 1997.
8. Jifeng He, C.A.R. Hoare, M. Fränzle, M. Müller-Olm, E.-R. Olderog, M. Schenke, M.R. Hansen, A.P. Ravn, and H. Rischel. Provably Correct Systems. In H. Langmaack, W.-P. de Roever, and J. Vytopil, editors, *Formal Techniques in Real-Time and Fault-Tolerant Systems*, volume 863 of *Lecture Notes in Computer Science*, pages 288–335. Springer-Verlag, 1994.
9. C. Heitmeyer and N. Lynch. The Generalized Railroad Crossing. In *IEEE Real-Time Systems Symposium*, 1994.
10. C. Heitmeyer and D. Mandrioli, editors. *Formal Methods for Real-Time Computing*, volume 5 of *Trends in Software*. Wiley, 1996.
11. K.-H. John and M. Tiegelkamp. *SPS-Programmierung mit IEC 1131-3*. Springer-Verlag, 1995. in German.
12. B. Krieg-Brückner, J. Peleska, E.-R. Olderog, D. Balzer, and A. Baer. UniForM — Universal Formal Methods Workbench. In U. Grote and G. Wolf, editors, *Statusseminar des BMBF Softwaretechnologie*, pages 357–378. BMBF, Berlin, March 1996.

13. R.W. Lewis. *Programming industrial control systems using IEC 1131-3*. The institution of Electrical Engineers, 1995.
14. B. Moszkowski. A Temporal Logic for Multilevel Reasoning about Hardware. *IEEE Computer*, 18(2):10–19, 1985.
15. E.-R. Olderog, A.P. Ravn, and J.U. Skakkebæk. Refining System Requirements to Program Specifications. In Heitmeyer and Mandrioli [10], pages 107–134.
16. A.P. Ravn. Design of Embedded Real-Time Computing Systems. Technical Report 1995-170, Technical University of Denmark, 1995.
17. M. Schenke and A.P. Ravn. Refinement from a control problem to programs. In J.R. Abrial, E. Börger, and H. Langmaack, editors, *Formal Methods for Industrial Applications: Specifying and Programming the Steam Boiler Control*, volume 1165 of *Lecture Notes in Computer Science*. Springer-Verlag, 1996.
18. R. Schlör and W. Damm. Specification and Verification of System Level Hardware Designs using Timing Diagrams. In *Proc. The European Conference on Design Automation*. Paris, France, 1993.
19. Zhou Chaochen. Duration Calculi: An overview. In D. Bjørner, M. Broy, and I.V. Pottosin, editors, *Formal Methods in Programming and Their Application*, volume 735 of *Lecture Notes in Computer Science*, pages 256–266. Springer-Verlag, 1993.
20. Zhou Chaochen, C.A.R. Hoare, and A.P. Ravn. A Calculus of Durations. *Inform. Proc. Letters*, 40/5:269–276, 1991.

A   Duration Calculus

The Duration Calculus [20, 19] is a real-time interval temporal logic extending earlier work on discrete interval temporal logic of [14]. A formal description of a real-time system using Duration Calculus (DC for short) starts by choosing a number of time-dependent state variables or observables *obs* of a certain type. An interpretation $\mathcal{I}$ assigns to each state variable a function $obs_{\mathcal{I}} : \text{Time} \longrightarrow D$ where Time is the time domain, here the non-negative reals, and D is the type of *obs*.

State assertions P are obtained by applying propositional connectives to elementary assertions of the form $obs = v$ (v for short if *obs* is clear) for a $v \in D$. For a given interpretation $\mathcal{I}$ state assertions denote functions $P_{\mathcal{I}} : \text{Time} \longrightarrow Bool$.

Duration formulae F are evaluated in a given interpretation $\mathcal{I}$ and a given time interval $[b, e] \subseteq \text{Time}$. The basic syntax of duration formulae is as follows:

- **Duration:** $\int P = k$ expresses that the *duration* of the state assertion P in $[b, e]$ is k. Semantically, duration is the measurement $\int_{b}^{e} P_{\mathcal{I}}(t)dt$.
- **Chop:** The composite duration formula $F_1; F_2$ (read as F_1 *chop* F_2) holds in $[b, e]$ if this interval can be divided into an initial subinterval $[b, m]$ where F_1 holds and a final subinterval $[m, e]$ where F_2 holds.
- **Connectives:** Duration formulas are closed under propositional connectives.

Besides this basic syntax various abbreviations are used:

length: $\qquad \ell \stackrel{\mathrm{df}}{=} \int true$

point interval: $\lceil\,\rceil \stackrel{\mathrm{df}}{=} \ell = 0$

everywhere: $\lceil P \rceil \stackrel{\mathrm{df}}{=} \int P = \ell \ \wedge \ \ell > 0$

somewhere: $\Diamond F \stackrel{\mathrm{df}}{=} true; F; true$

always: $\Box F \stackrel{\mathrm{df}}{=} \neg\Diamond\neg F$

$\qquad\qquad F^t \stackrel{\mathrm{df}}{=} (F \wedge \ell = t)$

A duration formula F *holds* in an interpretation $\mathcal{I}$ if F evaluates to true in $\mathcal{I}$ and every interval of the form $[0, t]$ with $t \in \mathsf{Time}$. The following so-called *standard forms* are useful to describe dynamic behaviour:

- *followed-by*: $F \longrightarrow \lceil P \rceil \stackrel{\mathrm{df}}{=} \Box\neg(F; \lceil\neg P\rceil)$
- *timed leads-to*: $F \stackrel{t}{\longrightarrow} \lceil P \rceil \stackrel{\mathrm{df}}{=} (F \wedge \ell = t) \longrightarrow \lceil P \rceil$
- *timed up-to*: $F \stackrel{\leq t}{\Longrightarrow} \lceil P \rceil \stackrel{\mathrm{df}}{=} (F \wedge \ell \leq t) \longrightarrow \lceil P \rceil$

As before we have $t \in \mathsf{Time}$. Intuitively, $F \longrightarrow \lceil P \rceil$ expresses the fact that whenever a pattern given by a formula F is observed, then it will be "followed by" an interval in which P holds. In the "leads-to" form this pattern is required to have a length t, and in the "up-to" form the pattern is bounded by a length "up to" t. Note that the "leads-to" does not simply say that whenever F holds then t time units later $\lceil P \rceil$ holds; rather, a stability of F for t time units is required before we can be certain that $\lceil P \rceil$ holds. The "up-to" form is mainly used to specify certain stability conditions. For example $\lceil\neg\pi\rceil ; \lceil\pi\rceil \stackrel{\leq t}{\Longrightarrow} \lceil\pi\rceil$ is an expression that is true iff π is stable for at least t seconds whenever π becomes true.

B Duration Calculus Semantics of Constraint Diagrams

Semantically, Constraint Diagrams denote an implication between assumptions and commitments of the form

$$\forall\epsilon_1,\ldots,\epsilon_k. \ (\ Assm(\epsilon_1,\ldots,\epsilon_k) \implies \exists\delta_1,\ldots,\delta_l. \ Comm(\epsilon_1,\ldots,\epsilon_k,\delta_1,\ldots,\delta_l))$$

for real variables $\epsilon_i, \delta_j \in Var, i \leq k, j \leq l, k, l \in \mathbb{N}$. Assumptions as well as commitments characterising lines are conjunctions of sequence formulae like

$$(\lceil P_1 \rceil \wedge \ell = \epsilon_1); \ldots; (\lceil P_n \rceil \wedge \ell = \epsilon_n)$$

for state assertions P_i and real variables $\epsilon_i, i \leq n, n \in \mathbb{N}$. Difference formulae characterising arrows have the form

$$\left(\sum_{i=1}^{n} \epsilon_i - \sum_{j=1}^{m} \delta_j \right) \in Int$$

for real variables $\epsilon_i, \delta_j, i \leq n, j \leq m, n, m \in \mathbb{N}$. They are also needed in length requirements between lengths of phases in assumptions and commitments to assure that they concern the same subintervals.

As an example the utility requirement given in Fig. 6 is considered. Let $\epsilon_1^T, \delta_1^T, \ldots, \epsilon_3^G, \delta_3^G$ be real variables. The assumption line for the track behaviour semantically means $\ell = \epsilon_1^T; (\lceil \neg Cr \rceil \wedge \ell = \epsilon_2^T); \ell = \epsilon_3^T$ where lengths of otherwise arbitrary phases are fixed by rigid variables. The commitment line for the gate is $\ell = \delta_1^G; (\lceil O \rceil \wedge \ell = \delta_2^G); \ell = \delta_3^G$. The right arrow is captured by the difference formula relating lengths of phases on the assumed lines $(\epsilon_1^T + \epsilon_2^T) - (\epsilon_1^G + \epsilon_2^G) = t_1$.

Detailed definitions and discussions of the semantics are found in [6].

C   The Duration Calculus Semantics for PLC-Automata

The semantics $[\![A]\!]_{\mathrm{DC}}$ of a PLC-Automaton $A = (Q, \Sigma, \delta, \pi_0, \varepsilon, S_e, S_t, \Omega, \omega)$ is given by the conjunction of the following predicates regarding the observables state : Time $\longrightarrow Q$, input : Time $\longrightarrow \Sigma$ and output : Time $\longrightarrow \Omega$. First of all, the starting of the automaton in the proper initial state is expressed by:

$$\lceil \, \rceil \vee \lceil \pi_0 \rceil ; \mathsf{true} . \tag{3}$$

Note that $\lceil \pi_0 \rceil$ is an abbreviation of $\lceil \mathsf{state} = \pi_0 \rceil$. The transition function, the cyclic behaviour, and the output is modelled by $(\emptyset \neq A \subseteq \Sigma)$:[4]

$$\lceil \neg \pi \rceil ; \lceil \pi \wedge A \rceil \longrightarrow \lceil \pi \vee \delta(\pi, A) \rceil \tag{4}$$

$$\lceil \pi \wedge A \rceil \xrightarrow{\varepsilon} \lceil \pi \vee \delta(\pi, A) \rceil \tag{5}$$

$$\Box(\lceil \pi \rceil \Longrightarrow \lceil \omega(\pi) \rceil) \tag{6}$$

For states without delay requirement $(S_t(\pi) = 0)$ we postulate:

$$\lceil \pi \wedge A \rceil \xrightarrow{2\varepsilon} \lceil \delta(\pi, A) \rceil \tag{7}$$

$$\pi \notin \delta(\pi, A) \Longrightarrow \lceil \neg \pi \rceil ; \lceil \pi \wedge A \rceil^{=\varepsilon} \longrightarrow \lceil \neg \pi \rceil \tag{8}$$

For states with delay requirement $(S_t(\pi) > 0)$ we have:

$$\lceil \pi \rceil ; \lceil \pi \wedge A \rceil^{=2\varepsilon} \xrightarrow{2\varepsilon + S_t(\pi)} \lceil \delta(\pi, A) \rceil \tag{9}$$

$$\lceil \neg \pi \rceil ; \lceil \pi \wedge A \rceil \xrightarrow{\le S_t(\pi)} \lceil \pi \vee \delta(\pi, A \setminus S_e(\pi)) \rceil \tag{10}$$

$$\lceil \neg \pi \rceil ; \lceil \pi \rceil ; \lceil \pi \wedge A \rceil^{=\varepsilon} \xrightarrow{\le S_t(\pi)} \lceil \pi \vee \delta(\pi, A \setminus S_e(\pi)) \rceil \tag{11}$$

$$A \cap S_e(\pi) = \emptyset \Longrightarrow \lceil \pi \wedge A \rceil \xrightarrow{2\varepsilon} \lceil \delta(\pi, A) \rceil \tag{12}$$

$$A \cap S_e(\pi) = \emptyset \Longrightarrow \lceil \neg \pi \rceil ; \lceil \pi \wedge A \rceil^{=\varepsilon} \longrightarrow \lceil \neg \pi \rceil \tag{13}$$

More details can be found in [4].

---

[4] In the formulae we use A as an abbreviation for input $\in A$ resp. $\delta(\pi, A)$ for state $\in \{\delta(\pi, a) | a \in A\}$.

A Graphic Notation for Formal Specifications of Dynamic Systems *

Gianna Reggio – Mauro Larosa

Dipartimento di Informatica e Scienze dell'Informazione
Università di Genova, Italy
Viale Dodecaneso, 35 – Genova 16146, Italy
{ reggio } @ disi.unige.it
http://www.disi.unige.it

Abstract. Given an already fully developed formal specification method for reactive systems, we also develop an alternative graphic notation for its specifications to improve writing and understanding of such specifications and, hopefully, the acceptance of the method by industrial users.

1 Introduction

A good specification formalism, where "good" means technically well founded, expressive, adequate for some phase of the development process, ..., is not enough for having a formal specification method apt to be used for real applications by non-academic people (see e.g. [5] for a discussion on "formalism" and "method"). In our opinion, the formalism must be equipped with:

1. guidelines on how to proceed to use the formalism; for answering the question "How can I produce a specification ?"
2. friendly presentations of the formal specifications; for answering the question "Can I, and the other interested people (clients, implementors, ...) easily read and understand the formal specifications?"
3. supporting software tools.

Our group at the University of Genova in the last years has developed a logic (algebraic) formalism, LTL, for the specification of (concurrent) reactive systems at different levels of abstraction (see e.g. [4, 8]). In this paper by *reactive systems* we denote systems that are able to modify their own state along time interacting with the external (w.r.t. them) world; the concurrent ones are those whose activity is determined by the activity of other (possibly concurrent) reactive systems. Distributed/concurrent/parallel programs, embedded systems, information systems are examples of concurrent reactive systems.

We have also equipped such formalism with several "(also non-software) tools" to help answering the above questions. Among them:

---

* This work has been partially supported by the project 40%: "Progetto di una workstation multimediale ad architettura parallela".

- a textual language, METAL ([12]) for writing the specifications with a sufficiently friendly syntax (e.g. where no esoteric symbols are used, but only catchy keywords);
- techniques for structuring the specifications of complex systems;
- guidelines for producing the specifications;
- a way for writing the formal specifications with associated strictly corresponding informal specifications (just natural language text), see [2];
- a software tool for the rapid prototyping of the specified systems, see [1].

The above "tools" answer to point 1, partly to 3 (no tools to support verification) and to 2 by the associated informal natural language specifications.

The resulting specification method has been successfully applied to several case studies (e.g. [3]), also in projects in cooperation with some industry ([15, 16]). For a detailed comparison with other formal methods, see [4].

However, it is not enough to have a formal specification method to be really used and which can be competitive w.r.t. the commonly used and accepted informal methods (as [6, 7]). A relevant deficiency is the lack of a form of graphic notation. The role of graphic is also shown by the success of some formal methods equipped with them (e.g. Petri nets, SDL [10] and State Charts [9]).

For these reasons, we have tried to give a graphic counterpart to the formal specifications developed following the guidelines of our method and written using the specification language METAL.

Any sensible graphic notation has big advantages: readability, understandability, compactness (the corresponding textual counterpart is usually much longer); but it may have also some disadvantages: drawings larger than one page or resembling a maze are not better than text. To avoid the drawbacks of graphic we need ways to split the drawings in sensible pieces and to give them an appropriate lay-out. In our case, the guidelines for writing textual specifications can be extended to help producing good drawings, and since the specifications are already structured, we have a natural way to split the drawings. For what concerns this point, we have used also some techniques inspired by other graphic methods:

- the drawing associated with a specification consists of several overlapping transparent layers (*views*) determined by the activities required by the original guidelines; and so they are extremely natural and support the application of the guidelines to the development of the specifications. Depending on the complexity we can put in one drawing one or more views. This technique has been inspired by OOA-OOD [6, 7].
- each part of a specification is characterized by an icon, and such icon together the part name (*place holder*) can be used to refer to it inside a drawing, while its full drawing is given apart (as it is done in SDL).
- for the parts that usually are too large, we have developed special ways to split them into page-long pieces, see [17].

Notice that our proposal differs from other approaches having the same aims and present in the literature, which have been designed by putting together an existing informal graphic method with a formal notation (see e.g. [14]); here the graphic part is not given by an existing method but it has been derived from the formal specifications.

In our opinion this attempt seems to be promising. It has worked also for us, strikingly making easier to produce good specifications and reducing their size.

We still have a fundamental task to do: develop software tools for interactively producing the drawings (which cannot be sensibly made by hand), browsing and converting them into the corresponding textual versions (needed e.g. to use the already existing tools) and vice versa.

Our formalism, LTL, allows to write specifications adequate for the different phases of the development process, from the initial requirements till to the detailed design of the developed system. Here, for lack of room we consider only the specifications for what we call *design phases*, i.e. when the structure and the activity of the developed system are fully determined. Notice that "fully determined" must be intended at the abstraction level supported by the formalism, and not at the level of coding in some programming language.

The paper is organized as follows. The formalism LTL is shortly introduced in Sect. 2. Then, we present the guidelines for writing a specification of a system, briefly reporting the textual version and the corresponding graphic one. Reactive systems may be classified as *simple* and *concurrent*, where the latter are those whose activity is determined by the activity of more than one components, which are in turn reactive systems; as the guidelines are different for simple and concurrent systems we consider the first and the latter respectively in Sect. 4 and in Sect. 3. A complete presentation of the method is in [17]. Finally, in Sect. 5 we try to draw some conclusions and point to what should be the next tasks to get a method that may have chances to be really used.

In the paper, we will use, as running toy example, the specification of a very simple pocket calculator, described as follows; for more interesting examples see, e.g., [16, 15].

The calculator consists of a keyboard *for inputting digits and commands, a* display *for showing the pressed keys and the results, an echo that echoes on the* display *the keys pressed on the keyboard and a* computing unit, *which reads the digits and the commands from the keyboard, performs the appropriate calculations and writes the results on the display. A user interacts with the calculator by pressing the keys on the keyboard and by reading the display.*

2 The Formalism: Labelled Transition Logic (LTL)

To model reactive systems LTL uses labelled transition systems (see [11]).

A *labelled transition system* (shortly *lts*) is a triple $(S, L, \rightarrow)$, where S and L are two sets, the *states* and the *labels* of the system, and $\rightarrow \subseteq S \times L \times S$ is the *transition relation*. A triple $(s, l, s') \in \rightarrow$ is said a *transition* and is usually written $s \xrightarrow{l} s'$.

A reactive system R is thus modelled by an lts $LTS = (S, L, \rightarrow)$ and an initial state $s_0 \in S$; the states reachable from s_0 represent the intermediate (interesting) situations of the life of R and the arcs between them the possibilities of R of passing from a state to another one. It is important to note that here an arc (a transition) $s \xrightarrow{l} s'$ has the following meaning: R in the state s has the *capability* of passing into the state s' by performing a transition, where label l represents the interaction with the external (to R) world during such move; thus l contains information on the conditions on the external world for the capability to become effective, and on the transformation of such world induced by the execution of the action; so transitions correspond to *action capabilities*.

Concurrent systems, i.e. having cooperating components that are in turn other reactive systems, can be modelled through particular lts's obtained by composing other lts's describing such components.

An lts can be represented by a first-order structure L on a signature with at least two sorts, *state* and *label*, whose elements correspond to the states and the labels of the system respectively, and a predicate $\rightarrow$: *state label state* representing the transition relation. The triple $(L_{state}, L_{label}, \rightarrow^L)$, whose components are respectively the interpretation of *state*, *label* and of $\rightarrow$, is the corresponding lts.

Obviously we can have lts's whose states are built by states of other lts's (for modelling concurrent systems); in such a case we use first-order structures with different sorts corresponding to states and labels and with different predicates corresponding to transition relations. In a formal model for reactive systems we need to consider data too (e.g. the data used by a process); to handle these cases, we consider structures possibly having also sorts that just correspond to data and neither to states nor labels of lts's.

The first-order structures corresponding to lts's are called *LT-structures* and are formally defined as follows.

- An *LT-signature* $LT\Sigma$ is a pair (Σ, DS), where:
  * $\Sigma = (S, OP, PR)$ is a (first-order) signature,
  * $DS \subseteq S$ (the elements in DS are the *dynamic sorts*, i.e. the sorts corresponding to states of lts's),
  * for all $ds \in DS$ there exist a sort $l\_ds \in S - DS$ (labels of the transitions of the dynamic elements of sort ds) and a predicate $\_ \xrightarrow{\quad} \_: ds\ l\_ds\ ds \in PR$ (transition relation of the dynamic elements of sort ds).
- An *LT-structure* on $LT\Sigma$ (shortly $LT\Sigma$-structure) is a Σ-structure.

In this paper, for some of the operation and predicate symbols, we use a mixfix notation; for instance, $\_ \xrightarrow{\quad} \_: ds\ l\_ds\ ds$ means that we shall write $t \xrightarrow{t'} t''$ instead of $\xrightarrow{\quad} (t, t', t'')$; i.e. terms of appropriate sorts replace underscores.

An *LT-specification* is a pair SP $= (LT\Sigma, AX)$, where $LT\Sigma = (\Sigma, DS)$ is an LT-signature and AX a set of positive conditional formulae on Σ (i.e. of the form $\wedge_{i=1,\ldots,n}\ \alpha_i \supset \alpha_{n+1}$, where for $i = 1, \ldots, n + 1$, α_i is an *atom*, i.e. a formula having form either $t = t'$ or $Pr(t_1, \ldots, t_n)$; $t, t', t_1, \ldots, t_n$ are terms and $Pr \in PR$).

Notice, that since transitions are described by predicate symbols the axioms of an LT-specification allow us also to express properties on the activity of the systems.

SP determines one (up to isomorphism) LT-structure, precisely $I_{SP} = T_{\Sigma}/\equiv_{AX}$, where T_{Σ} is the Σ-structure of the ground terms and $\equiv_{AX}$ is the congruence on T_{Σ} generated by AX, which can be characterized by a Birkhoff-like deductive system.

I_{SP} is called the initial model of SP, since it is initial in $\{L \mid L \models F, F \in AX\}$, i.e. in the class of the models of SP.

It is important to note that in I_{SP}: – each element is the interpretation of a ground term, i.e. it can be represented by a ground term; – two terms are identified iff their equality is consequence of the axioms (can be proved by the deductive system); – a predicate applied to some elements is true iff the truth of the corresponding ground atom is consequence of the axioms (can be proved by the deductive system). As a consequence, since the transitions correspond to the truth of the transition predicates, we have that the transitions in I_{SP} are just those whose corresponding atoms are consequences of the axioms (can be proved by the deductive system).

3 Specifying Simple Systems

In our method specifying a simple system means to abstractly determine an $LT\Sigma$-structure, where $LT\Sigma$ has one dynamic sort (i.e. an lts plus some data structures), by an LT-specification. This means to determine which are the states, the labels, the transitions of the lts, possibly some auxiliary data structures, needed to define such states/labels, and to abstractly specify them. Thus, we decompose the activity of specifying a simple system in four phases, presented in the next subsections; each phase produces a different view of the graphic specification; by overlaying all the views we get the complete graphic presentation.

In this section, as a current example of simple system we consider the computing unit component of the calculator.

The computing unit executes the various commands as follows. When the computing unit is on, it has always stored a partial current result and the command to apply next. The computing unit may read and reset the keyboard anytime a command is pressed; then it proceeds as follows: – by parsing the keyboard content it gets the second operand and the next command to apply; – then it evaluates the old stored command on the partial result and on the new list of digits, obtaining a new partial result; – afterwards it sends such result to the display while simultaneously it also reactivates the echo, returning then to wait for the pressing of a command. If the second operand is the empty list, then the evaluation returns the first operand, i.e. the old partial result; if both the operands are not empty and the command is the equal, then the evaluation returns the second operand, otherwise it applies the command to the two numbers represented by the two lists.

3.1 Basic data structures

In this phase we determine and specify the data structures used by the system. For example, the basic data structures of the computing unit are naturals, lists of digits and lists of keys.

A specification of a data structure is just an LT-specification without dynamic sorts (an algebraic specification of an abstract data type, see [18]); thus sorts, operations and predicates of the signature correspond respectively to the types of values, the operations and the boolean tests of the data structure, and the axioms to their properties. The initial semantics will determine the structure where all values are represented by a ground term and all and only the logical consequences of the axioms hold.

We assume that each data structure has a *main sort*, named as the structure itself.

The icon for a data structure is a rectangle. A graphic specification of a data structure is simply a rectangle including the specification text with below the name of the specification.

Whenever a specification SP uses another specification SP' (thus SP will have also the sorts, the operations, the predicates and the axioms of SP'), a rectangle enclosing the used specification name SP' is included in the icon of SP.

The specification text is split by horizontal lines putting together operations/ predicates with their axioms.

Below we report part of the data structures of the computing unit.

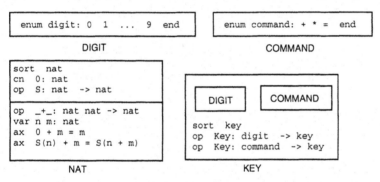

enum srt: Op1 ... Opn end is a METAL shortcut for the specification of a data structure corresponding to an enumeration type, having main sort srt, constant operations Op1, ..., Opn and no identifications on them.

Another view of the basic data structures is the so called *hierarchical schema* representing the mutual relationships among them; it consists of the icons (rectangles) of the various structures and of their names, while the text parts are dropped. Furthermore, this view may be made more compact, by putting the drawing of a structure, used only by another structure, inside the latter. Below we give the whole hierarchical schema for the basic data structures of the computing unit.

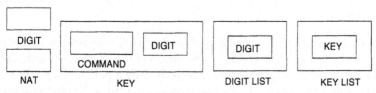

3.2 States

In this phase we determine and specify the (kinds of the) intermediate relevant situations in the life of the system, i.e. the states of the lts modelling it. Each state kind should be conceptually characterized by a natural language sentence corresponding either to an adjective or to a verb in the ing form.

The states are then specified as a data structure, possibly using the basic data structures, with a main sort corresponding to the states themselves, named as the system, and an operation for each state kind. Then the main sort is made dynamic. In this case the specification has no axioms, since we do not want to identify the terms representing the various states.

Each state kind is represented by an oval with below the corresponding operation applied to the sorts of its arguments (we do not need to report the result sort, since it coincides with the system name). The representations of the state kinds are enclosed in the system icon (a rectangle with rounded angles) and the hierarchical view of the basic data structures is reported over the system icon, to have at hand a synthetic view of such structures.

Below we give the specification of the states of the computing unit.

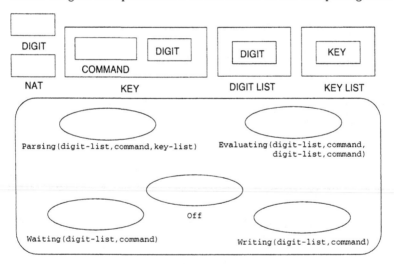

COMPUTING UNIT

For example, the states of kind **Parsing** are characterized by three values of sort respectively **digit-list**, **command** and **key-list** specified by the data structures with the same names.

3.3 Interactions

In this phase we determine and specify the (kinds of the) interactions of the reactive system with the external world, i.e. the labels of the lts modelling it. Each interaction kind should be conceptually characterized by a natural language sentence corresponding to a verb having either active form ("to verb complements")

or passive form ("to be verb-ed complements"). The interactions are then specified as a data structure using the basic data structures, with the sort of labels as
main sort, and having an operation for each interaction kind; these operations
may have several arguments describing the information exchanged between the
system and the external world during each interaction of such kind (informally
described by the complements).

The icon for the interaction kinds is a line attached to the system icon, to
emphasize the idea that interactions are the ways for connecting the system to
the external world. Each line is decorated with the corresponding operation, as
for the states; moreover also in this case we report the hierarchical schema of
the basic data structures.

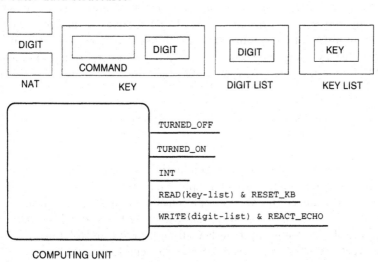

3.4 Activity

In this phase we determine and specify the activity of the system by giving its
action capabilities, i.e. the transitions of the lts modelling it. Formally, they are
represented by the arrow predicate.

The action capabilities/transitions starting from the states of a given kind
are defined by a set of conditional axioms of the form:

(*1) $cond(t_1, \ldots, t_n, t_1'', \ldots, t_k'', t_1', \ldots, t_m') \supset$

$$S\_Kind(t_1, \ldots, t_n) \xrightarrow{I\_Kind(t_1'', \ldots, t_k'')} S\_Kind'(t_1', \ldots, t_m')$$

S_Kind, S_Kind' are state kind operations; I_Kind is an interaction kind operation, t_1, ..., t_n, lab, t_1', ..., t_m' are terms of the appropriate sort; and
$cond(t_1, \ldots, t_n, t_1'', \ldots, t_k'', t_1', \ldots, t_m')$ is a conjunction of atoms in which the sub-
terms and the variables of t_1, ..., t_n, t_1'', ..., t_k'', t_1', ..., t_m' may appear.

We have to give such axioms by recalling that they hold for all possible
instantiations of their variables; thus one axiom determines a possibly infinite
set of transitions, all those obtained by the variable instantiations of the arrow
part for which the condition part holds.

We proceed by first determining the initial states and the transitions starting from such states; then we repeat such procedure for all state kinds reachable from that one, untill all state kinds have been considered.

Each axiom is accompanied by a natural language statement obtained by the natural language explanations of the state and interaction kinds given previously.

It may happen that to determine the action capabilities we have also to consider relevant "static (sequential) aspects" of the system. For example, for the computing unit, we have to define the parsing of key strings and the application of a command to two lists of digits. To accommodate them in the specification, we introduce some "auxiliary" operations/predicates defined by conditional axioms, as those of the data structures, possibly using other auxiliary operations.

The icon for a transition (an action capability) is very naturally an arrow; but decorated by terms with variables, instead of by values as in the various methods based on automata and finite state machines. Furthermore, the states must be represented by using their icon (an oval). Thus, a conditional axiom of the form as (*1), see above, will be represented by

Now, we are ready to represent the whole activity of the system. The chosen icon is a (connected) labelled direct graph. The simplest idea, to get such representation, is to connect the arrows representing the axioms by gluing together states decorated in the same way; unfortunately the result is usually a non-connected graph. So, we group together all nodes referring to states of the same kind, and get what we call a *macro-state*. We represent a macro-state by the same icon of states, the oval, and put the decorations of all particular cases inside such oval.

In Fig. 1 we give the complete graph of the computing unit activity.

To get the full graphic representation of the activity we still need to consider the declaration of the used variables and the auxiliary operations. A variable **v** of sort **str**, where **str** is the main sort of a data structure **STR**, is graphically represented by attaching **v:** to the icon of **STR** in the hierarchical schema of the basic data structures of the system (which is reported also over this view of the system).

The auxiliary operations, if any, are represented as those of the data structures, but in this case we do not need to represent the used data structures, since they can be only the basic data structures. The full representation of the activity of the computing unit is in Appendix A.

4 Specifying Concurrent Systems

Concurrent systems are particular reactive systems having cooperating components (reactive systems) either active or passive. The passive components are

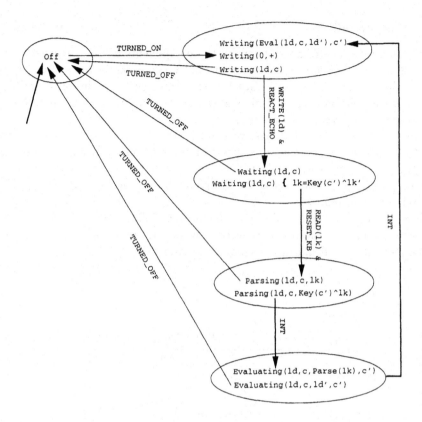

Fig. 1. The graph of the activity of the computing unit

those which can modify their state only because of the activity of some other (active) components. We do not need to describe the interactions and the activity of the passive components, since their states can be changed in any possible way; thus the passive ones are just data structures, while the active components are in turn reactive systems (simple or concurrent).

The calculator is a concurrent system having four components: two active, the computing unit and the echo, and two passive, the keyboard and the display.

The concurrent systems can be classified by considering whether the number of the component is *fixed* or not (all possible states of the system have/have not the same number of components). The guidelines slightly depend on this classification, and here, for lack of room, we consider only the case of systems with fixed number of components; see [17] for the treatment of the other case.

Also the activity of specifying a concurrent system with our method is decomposed in several phases producing the various views; here they are five, instead of the four for the simple systems, because now we also consider the components.

The phases concerning the basic data structures and the interactions are as for the simple systems.

4.1 Components

In this phase we determine and specify the components of the concurrent system. The active ones are reactive systems and we consider them as stand alone systems. The passive components are data structures with a main sort describing the component states. The fact that a system is concurrent and which are its components is graphically as follows.

The icons for active and passive components (reactive systems and data structures) are, as before, the rectangles with rounded angles and the rectangles. We graphically represent the fact that a system is concurrent and which are its components as follows. As usual the hierarchical schema of the basic data structures is reported over.

The structure of the calculator is presented as follows. The computing unit has been specified in the previous section, while the specifications of the other components of the calculator are reported in Appendix A.

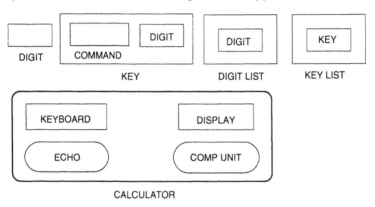

CALCULATOR

4.2 States

Also in this case the states represent the intermediate relevant situations in the life of the system, but now they are just given by putting together the states of the components. For the case of the concurrent systems with fixed components, the states are just sequences of component states. Thus, there is no need of a graphic representation of the states, since they are fully determined by giving the components in the structure representation.

4.3 Activity

The action capabilities of a concurrent system in a state are intuitively described by saying how the components in such state cooperate: precisely, by saying which groups of action capabilities of the active components in such state depending on the states of the passive ones can be performed together, and how the passive ones are consequently modified.

Formally, the system transitions are defined by a set of conditional axioms of the form below, one for each cooperation kind, where we assume without loss of generality that all active components are on the left, and those which act are on the extreme left:

$$(*2) \; a_1 \xrightarrow{lab_1} a_1' \land \ldots \land a_k \xrightarrow{lab_k} a_k' \land cond(l, lab_1, \ldots, lab_k, p_1, \ldots, p_h) \supset$$

$$a_1| \ldots |a_k| \ldots |a_n|p_1| \ldots |p_g| \ldots |p_h| \ldots |p_m| \ldots |p_r \xrightarrow{lab}$$

$$a_1'| \ldots |a_k'| \ldots |a_n|p_1'| \ldots |p_g'| \ldots |p_h| \ldots |p_m'| \ldots |p_r,$$

where lab_1, ..., lab_k, lab are terms; a_1, ..., a_n, a_1', ..., a_k' are variables of sort states of the active components; p_1, ..., p_r, are variables of sort states of the passive components; p_j' are terms of the same sorts.

a_1, ..., a_k, p_1, ..., p_m are the components cooperating as described by this axiom (p_1, ..., p_g are read and modified, p_{g+1}, ..., p_h are only read and p_{h+1}, ..., p_m are only modified); a_{k+1}, ..., a_n, p_{m+1}, ... p_r are the components which do not cooperate.

The above constraints on the form of the axioms ensure that only the interactions of the active component (the labels of the transitions) and the states of the passive ones are relevant for the composition (while the states of the active components cannot be considered), and so that interactions really represent the interfaces of a reactive system.

Also in this case it is possible to use auxiliary operations to specify the static/sequential aspects.

The activity of a concurrent systems cannot be represented by a labelled graph. In the case of the simple system using the macro-states we are able to keep the graph small enough; while if we proceed in this way for a concurrent system we usually get too many nodes. Also for the small example of the calculator the activity graph is too big to be presented in a sensible way. Furthermore, the specification method is conceptually based on the idea of describing how the components cooperate and not on explicitly giving the action capabilities of the whole system. For these reasons we have tried to represent graphically the cooperation, instead of the system action capabilities.

The icon for cooperation is the *hexagon*. The icons for the components have been defined before; those of the passive components are decorated with a variable denoting their generic state.

A line decorated by a term of label sort connecting an active component icon to the hexagon represents that such component cooperates with such interaction. A dashed line from a passive component icon to the hexagon represents that a passive component is involved in the cooperation. Such lines have an arrow from the passive component when the component is read and an arrow towards the hexagon when the component is modified, in such cases the term representing the new component state is put over the line. The interaction with the external world (w.r.t. the concurrent system) is represented by a double line leaving the hexagon decorated with the term representing such interaction.

Thus, a generic axiom describing a cooperation kind of the form (*2), see above, is graphically represented by:

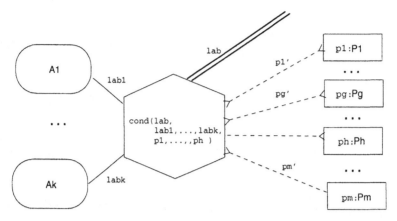

The cooperation of the calculator is represented in Fig. 2, where the double lines labelled by **INT**, corresponding to calculator internal activity, have been dropped.

How to decompose the cooperation diagram Unfortunately, in realistic applications the cooperation drawing may be too large or too complex (too many intersecting lines). We now present a modular way to decompose it.

First we put together the cooperation kinds sharing common features (e.g. those about logically related features, those involving the same components, those having the same interaction with the external world, ...). Each of such parts is called *macro-cooperation kind*.

In the case of the calculator a choice of macro-cooperation kinds may be: those resulting in internal activity, those related to the turning on and off and those related to a user working with the calculator.

The elements of each macro-cooperation kind will be put together in one separate drawing; while in the drawing of the activity of the system they will be replaced by an icon. The icon for macro-cooperation kind is a double hexagon with inside its name. If the cooperation kinds grouped in a macro are C1, ..., Cn, then there is a dashed line [line] connecting the double hexagon with the icons of the passive [active] components taking part in either C1 or ...or Cn [decorated by the set of the interaction kinds appearing in either C1 or ...or Cn], and a double line decorated by the set of the interaction kinds with the external world produced by either C1 or ...or Cn.

The two cooperation kinds about turning on-off of the calculator:

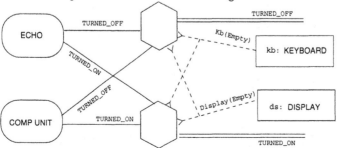

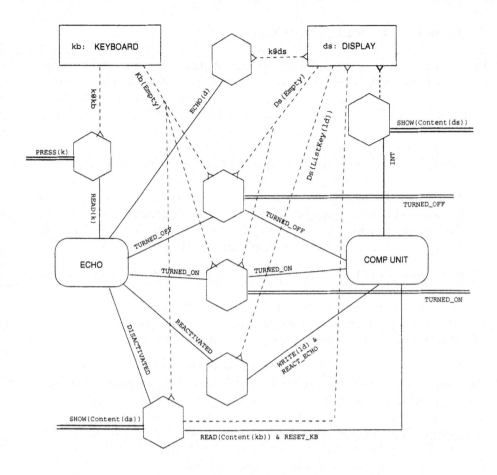

Fig. 2. The activity of the calculator

becomes a macro-cooperation kind graphically represented by

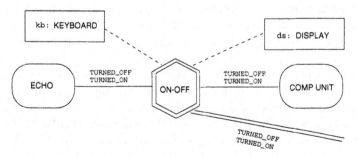

In Appendix A we give the calculator activity in a modular way by using two other macro-cooperation kinds.

5 Conclusions and future work

In this paper we have presented an attempt at making an already developed formal method for the specification of concurrent reactive systems better suited to be used in practice by giving a graphic presentation to its formal specifications.

We have shown how to produce drawings, instead of textual specifications, following our method; thus we have established also a correspondence between graphic and textual specifications, and so we are able to pass from one to another; e.g., see in [17] the corresponding textual specifications for the calculator case.

Some advantages of using the graphic version of the method are as follows.

We have "psychological advantages" when presenting the method; instead of scaring possible users by pages of formulae, we show "appealing" drawings.

The graphic notation supports and makes more explicit the underlying concepts of the method and enforces the application of the guidelines, e.g.:

* we are giving the capabilities of the system of passing from a state to another, when drawing arrows;
* we are giving the interactions of the system with the outside world, when drawing lines (electric wires) attached to the system icon;
* all action capabilities from a state are described together.

We get much more compact presentations of the specifications; instead of three pages of formulae we may have just one page long drawing. That helps also to grasp global aspects of the system with just a glimpse (e.g. whether a state is terminal for a system, whether there is a connection between two components), instead of inspecting a list of formulae.

Clearly, to get these advantages we should give an appropriate lay-out to the drawings, and so the guidelines have to be extended to avoid to convey wrong information by a bad laid-out drawing (see [13]). For example, see in Fig. 3 an alternative wrong lay-out for the activity graph of the computing unit, given before in Fig. 1; now the drawing has a nice symmetry, but now the fact that the computing unit proceeds in a cyclic way is not so easy to grasp.

We have the possibility to discuss/simulate/prototype by hand the behaviour of the specified system just by looking at the drawings and that can be very useful in the validation activity and when discussing the design of the system with clients.

As a short trivial example taken from the calculator, assume that we want to know whether it may be turned off in any moment (but this kind of analysis can be done for interesting point). We look at the calculator activity drawing. There is only one cooperation kind resulting in the interaction TURNED_OFF; it requires that both the computing unit and the echo are turned off and there is no condition on the passive components. The computing unit and the echo can be turned off except when already off. Thus the calculator can be turned off in any case except when already off. If we want that the calculator can be always turned off, we see that it is sufficient to add the turning off action capabilities to the computing unit and to the echo when they are off.

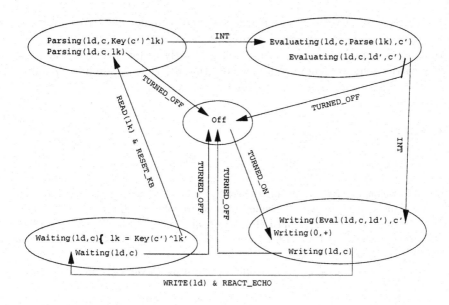

Fig. 3. A bad lay-out for the computing unit graph

In our opinion this attempt seems to be promising; but we still have a fundamental step to do: to develop some software tools for supporting its use. Precisely, we need:

- A graphic editor for producing directly on the screen the drawings.
- A converter from the graphic to the textual presentation and vice versa; to be able, e.g., to use existing tools developed for the textual specifications.
- A browser for examining the specifications able to switch from a view to another and to open the specification of a subpart when clicking its place holder icon inside the representation of some other one.

The above set of tools seem feasible; indeed there are already existing similar tools for other graphic formalisms; we just need some resources.

While the dynamic aspects of the specifications are greatly highlighted by the graphic version, the presented notation offers only a small improvement for the specifications of the data structures: we just make explicit the hierarchical structure and spatially organize the text, grouping related parts. Regarding this point, there are no relevant proposals in the literature; only recently some work on how to graphically represent the terms in the axioms has appeared, but nothing for the resulting data structure. This topic merits to be further studied.

The graphic specifications could be intuitively considered as another concrete syntax for our textual specification language; but here they are not presented as precisely as by means of a BNF grammar. Thus, another future task is to try to use techniques developed in the field of visual languages, to describe the drawings and the correct lay-outs in a more exact way, and to make the correspondence between textual and graphic versions more precise.

Acknowledgments. The present work is strictly connected with other researches carried out in Genova. The authors thank Egidio Astesiano for many fruitful discussions and the referees for helpful comments.

References

1. E. Astesiano, F. Morando, and G. Reggio. The SMoLCS Toolset. In P.D. Mosses, M. Nielsen, and M.I. Schwartzbach, editors, *Proc. of TAPSOFT '95*, number 915 in L.N.C.S., pages 810–811. Springer Verlag, Berlin, 1995.
2. E. Astesiano and G. Reggio. Formally-Driven Friendly Specifications of Concurrent Systems: A Two-Rail Approach. Technical Report DISI–TR–94–20, DISI – Università di Genova, Italy, 1994. Presented at ICSE'17-Workshop on Formal Methods, Seattle April 1995.
3. E. Astesiano and G. Reggio. A Dynamic Specification of the RPC-Memory Problem. In M. Broy, S. Merz, and K. Spies, editors, *Formal System Specification: The RPC-Memory Specification Case Study*, number 1169 in L.N.C.S., pages 67–108. Springer Verlag, Berlin, 1996.
4. E. Astesiano and G. Reggio. Labelled Transition Logic: An Outline. Technical Report DISI–TR–96–20, DISI – Università di Genova, Italy, 1996.
5. E. Astesiano and G. Reggio. Formalism and Method. In M. Bidoit and M. Dauchet, editors, *Proc. TAPSOFT '97*, number 1214 in L.N.C.S., pages 93–114, Berlin, 1997. Springer Verlag.
6. P. Coad and E. Yourdon. *Object-Oriented Analysis*. Prentice-Hall, Englewood Cliffs, N.J., 1991.
7. P. Coad and E. Yourdon. *Object-Oriented Design*. Prentice-Hall, Englewood Cliffs, N.J., 1991.
8. G. Costa and G. Reggio. Specification of Abstract Dynamic Data Types: A Temporal Logic Approach. *T.C.S.*, 173(2):513–554, 1997.
9. D. Harel. Statecharts: A Visual Formalism for Complex Systems. *Science of Computer Programming*, 8:231–274, 1987.
10. ITU. Z.100 ITU Specification and Description Language (SDL). Technical report, ITU, Geneva, 1993.
11. R. Milner. *A Calculus of Communicating Systems*. Number 92 in L.N.C.S. Springer Verlag, Berlin, 1980.
12. F. Parodi and G. Reggio. METAL: a Metalanguage for SMoLCS. Technical Report DISI–TR–94–13, DISI – Università di Genova, Italy, 1994.
13. M. Petre. Why Looking Isn't Always Seeing: Readership Skills and Graphical Programming. *Communications of the ACM*, 38(6), 1995.
14. F. Polak, M. Whiston, and K. Mander. The SAZ Project: Integrating SSADM and Z. In J.C.P. Woodcock and P.G. Larsen, editors, *Proc. FME'93: Industrial-Strength Formal Methods*, number 670 in L.N.C.S. Springer Verlag, Berlin, 1993.
15. G. Reggio. A Graphic Specification of a High-Voltage Substation. Technical Report DISI-TR-96-22, DISI – Università di Genova, Italy, 1996.
16. G. Reggio. A Graphic Specification of a Hydroelectric Power Station. Technical Report DISI–TR–96–21, DISI – Università di Genova, Italy, 1996.

17. G. Reggio and M. Larosa. A Graphic Notation for Formal Specifications of Dynamic Systems. Technical Report DISI–TR–97–3, DISI – Università di Genova, Italy, 1997. Full Version.
18. M. Wirsing. Algebraic Specifications. In J. van Leeuwen, editor, *Handbook of Theoret. Comput. Sci.*, volume B, pages 675–788. Elsevier, 1990.

A   The Complete Graphic Specification of the Calculator

The Structure of the calculator

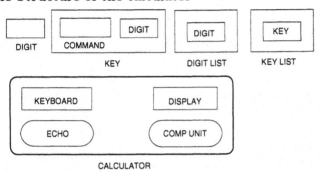

The basic data structures of the calculator

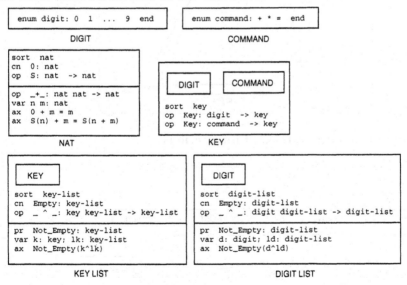

The key-board and the display components

```
┌─────────────┐
│ KEY LIST    │
└─────────────┘

sort  keyboard
op  Kb: key-list -> keyboard

op  _ @ _: key keyboard -> keyboard
var k: key; lk: key-list
ax  k @ Kb(lk) = Kb(k ^ lk)

op  Content: keyboard -> key-list
ax  Content(Kb(lk)) = lk
```
KEYBOARD

```
┌─────────────┐
│ KEY LIST    │
└─────────────┘

sort  display
op  Ds: key-list -> display

op  _ @ _: key display -> display
var k: key; lk: key-list
ax  k @ Ds(lk) = Ds(k ^ lk)

op  Content: display -> key-list
ax  Content(Ds(lk)) = lk
```
DISPLAY

The echo

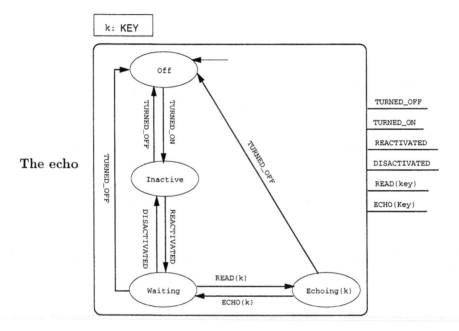

The computing unit states and interactions

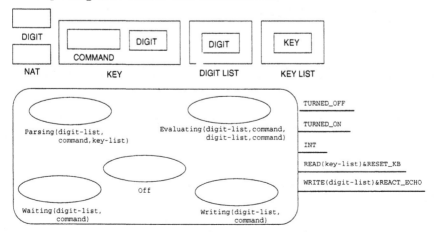

COMPUTING UNIT

The computing unit activity

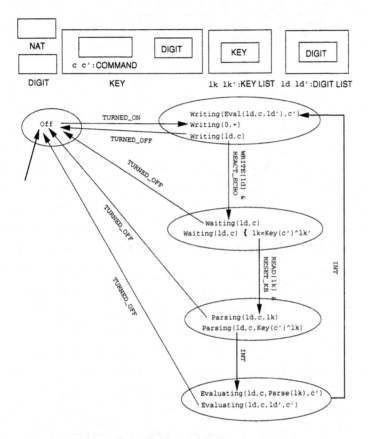

```
**   given a list of keys returns the list of the contained digits
op   Parse: key-list -> digit-list
ax   Parse(Empty) = Empty
ax   Parse(Key(d) ^ lk) = d ^ Parse(lk)
ax   Parse(Key(c) ^ lk) = Parse(lk)
```

```
**   given a number returns its representation as list of digits
op   Cod: nat -> digit-list
op   Cod': nat -> digit-list
ax   Cod'(0,ld) = 0 ^ ld
ax   . . .
ax   Cod'(9,ld) = 9 ^ ld
ax   if k < 10 then Cod'(m*10 + k) = Cod'(m,Cod'(k,ld))
ax   Cod(m) = Cod'(m,Empty)
```

```
op   Decod: digit-list -> nat
ax   Decod(0 ^ ld) = Decod(ld) * 10 + 0
...
ax   Decod(9 ^ ld) = Decod(ld) * 10 + 9

**   given two lists of digits, ld1 and ld2, and a command c returns the
**   list of digits corresponding to the evaluation of c on ld1 and ld2
op   Eval: digit-list command digit-list -> digit-list
ax   Eval(ld,c,Empty) = ld
ax   if Not_Empty(ld2) then Eval(ld1,==,ld2) = ld2
ax   Eval(ld1,+,ld2) = Cod(Decod(ld1) + Decod(ld2))
ax   Eval(ld1,*,ld2) = Cod(Decod(ld1) * Decod(ld2))
ax   Eval(Empty,c,ld) = Eval(0 ^ Empty,c,ld)
```

The interactions of the calculator

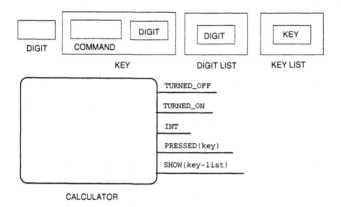

The calculator activity using macro-cooperation kinds

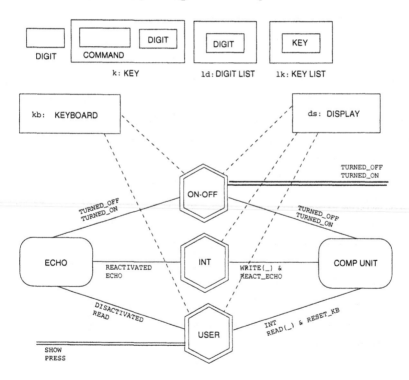

Macro-cooperation kind INT

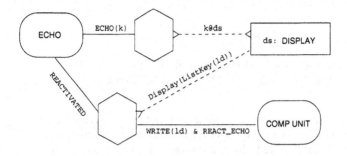

Macro-cooperation kind ON-OFF

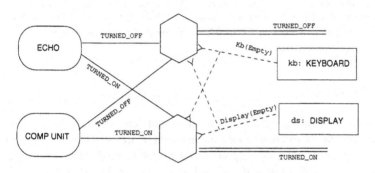

Macro-cooperation kind USER

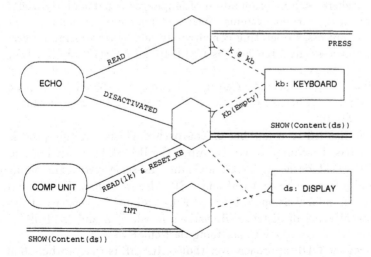

A Semantic Integration of Object-Z and CSP for the Specification of Concurrent Systems

Graeme Smith

Technische Universität Berlin, FB Informatik, FG Softwaretechnik,
Sekr. FR 5-6, Franklinstr. 28/29, D-10587 Berlin

Abstract. This paper presents a method of formally specifying concurrent systems which uses the object-oriented state-based specification language Object-Z together with the process algebra CSP. Object-Z provides a convenient way of modelling complex data structures needed to define the component processes of such systems, and CSP enables the concise specification of process interactions. The basis of the integration is a semantics of Object-Z classes identical to that of CSP processes. This allows classes specified in Object-Z to be used directly within the CSP part of the specification.

1 Introduction

A primary purpose of formal specification is to provide concise and easily comprehensible descriptions of software systems. For particularly large or complex systems, this goal may be more readily achieved by using more than one specification language. While most specification languages can be used to specify entire systems, few, if any, are particularly suited to modelling all aspects of such systems.

An example of where such a combination of languages is particularly useful is the specification of concurrent systems. Such systems comprise a number of distinct component *processes* operating concurrently and synchronising on certain events. While process algebras such as CSP[14] and CCS[18] are ideal for specifying the interactions between these processes, they are not particularly suited to modelling complex data structures which may be needed to describe the processes themselves. This is better specified using a state-based language such as Z[25] or VDM[16].

This realisation has led to a number of approaches which combine process algebras and state-based techniques. For example, the RAISE specification language (RSL)[11] designed for use with complex industrial-scale systems involving concurrency includes features from VDM and CSP. Also, the Open Distributed Processing (ODP) standardisation initiative[15] has adopted a *viewpoint* approach for the specification of distributed systems in which Z and LOTOS[2][1] have been proposed as languages for specifying particular views.

An advantage of the ODP approach over that of RAISE is that, rather than defining a new language, it uses the existing languages without altering their

---

[1] LOTOS includes a process algebra part based on CCS.

syntax or semantics. This makes the approach more accessible to users who are already familiar with the existing languages and also enables the use of tools and methods of verification and refinement developed for these languages. A disadvantage of the ODP approach, however, is that it produces, rather than a single specification, a number of related specifications which must be checked for consistency[6].

In order to produce a single specification while using a combination of existing languages, constructs defined in one of the languages need to be applicable in the other enabling the various parts of the specification to be linked. This is possible if such constructs are given a semantics identical to that of an identifiable construct in the other.

One problem with adopting such an approach, however, is the lack of a construct in most state-based specification languages identifiable with processes in a process algebra. This is not true of object-oriented state-based specification languages such as Object-Z[9]. Central to object orientation is the view of a system as a collection of distinct, interacting objects whose state and operations are encapsulated in *classes*. Hence, there is a strong relationship between classes in object-oriented systems and processes in concurrent systems: interactions between instances of each define the system behaviour. This relationship has been recognised by many researchers in both the theory and practice of object orientation[10, 23, 26, 28].

This paper presents a semantic integration of Object-Z and CSP based on the relationship between classes and processes. Sections 2 and 3 introduce Object-Z and CSP respectively by providing simple examples of their use and an overview of their semantics. Section 4 presents the semantic integration of the languages. Classes in Object-Z are given a *failures-divergences*[4] semantics identical to that of CSP processes. In Sect. 5 the approach to specification using the integrated notations is illustrated through a simple case study. In Sect. 6, verification and refinement are briefly discussed. Although the emphasis in this paper is on the application of the approach to concurrent systems, its applicability extends to other domains. For example, both Z and CSP have been advocated for specifying different aspects of software architectures[21] and a combination of Z and (real-time) CSP has been suggested for the specification of safety-critical systems[13].

2 Object-Z

Object-Z[9] is an extension of Z designed to support an object-oriented specification style. It includes a special class construct to encapsulate a state schema with all the operation schemas which may affect its variables. A class may be used to define one or more components of a system or to specify the interactions between components by referring to instances, i.e. *objects*, of their classes. In the approach adopted in this paper, the interactions between components will be specified using CSP. We restrict our attention, therefore, to classes which do not refer to objects of other classes.

A class in Object-Z is represented syntactically by a named box possibly with generic parameters. In this box there may be local type and constant definitions, at most one state schema and associated initial state schema, and zero or more operation schemas. As an example, consider the following specification of a bounded queue. This specification is generic in that the type T, of the items in the queue, is not specified.

$$
\begin{array}{l}
\hline
Queue[T] \\
\hline
\quad max : \mathbb{N} \\
\hline
\quad items : \text{seq } T \\
\hline
\quad \#items \leqslant max \\
\hline
\quad \underline{INIT} \\
\quad\quad items = \varnothing \\
\hline
\quad \underline{Join} \\
\quad\quad \Delta(items) \\
\quad\quad item? : T \\
\quad\quad\quad \#items < max \\
\quad\quad\quad items' = \langle item? \rangle \frown items \\
\hline
\quad \underline{Leave} \\
\quad\quad \Delta(items) \\
\quad\quad item! : T \\
\quad\quad\quad items \neq \langle \rangle \\
\quad\quad\quad items = items' \frown \langle item! \rangle \\
\hline
\end{array}
$$

The class has a single constant max denoting the maximum length of the queue and a single state variable $items$ denoting the items in the queue. Constants are associated with a fixed value which cannot be changed by any operations of the class. However, the value of constants may differ for different objects of the class.

Initially the queue is empty and the operations *Join* and *Leave* enable items to join and leave the queue, respectively, on a first-in/first-out basis. Each operation schema has a Δ-list of state variables which it may change, a declaration part consisting of input (denoted by names ending in ?) and output (denoted by names ending in !) parameters and a predicate part relating the pre- and post-values (denoted by names ending in ') of the state variables.

A class may also *inherit* the definitions of one or more other classes. Inheritance is a powerful mechanism for incremental specification allowing peripheral concerns to be postponed while specifying the intrinsic behaviour of a class of objects. An inherited class' local types and constants are implicitly available in the inheriting class. Its schemas are also either implicitly available or are implicitly conjoined with common-named schemas declared in the inheriting class. As an example, consider the following definition of a lossy message channel.

Let MSG denote the set of all possible messages.

$$
\begin{array}{|l}
\hline
\quad MsgChannel \\
\hline
Queue[MSG][msgs/items,\ msg?/item?,\ msg!/item!] \\
\\
\quad\begin{array}{|l}
\hline
\quad Lose \\
\hline
\Delta(msgs) \\
\hline
msgs' = tail\ msgs \\
\hline
\end{array} \\
\\
\hline
\end{array}
$$

The class $MsgChannel$ inherits $Queue$ with its generic type T instantiated with MSG and with the state variable $items$ renamed to $msgs$ and the operation parameters $item?$ and $item!$ renamed to $msg?$ and $msg!$ respectively. In general, constants, state variables, operation schemas and operation parameters may be renamed. Objects of $MsgChannel$ behave identically to those of $Queue$ up to renaming, except that they have an additional operation $Lose$ corresponding to the loss of a message.

2.1 Semantics of Object-Z Classes

A class in Object-Z can be modelled as a set of values each corresponding to a potential object of the class at some stage of its evolution. Such a semantics is presented in [23] where, following the work of [8], the value chosen to represent an object is the sequence of states the object has passed through together with the corresponding sequence of operations the object has undergone. This value is referred to as the *history* of the object.

To define the structure and properties of the histories of a class, we first need to define what is meant by its states and the operations it can undergo. The states of a class assign values to the state variables and any constants the state schema may refer to. This includes both constants defined in the class and those defined globally.

Given the set of all possible identifiers, i.e. strings of characters denoting names, Id and the set of all possible values $Value$, the states of a class can be represented by a set[2]

$$S \subseteq (Id \nrightarrow Value)$$

such that the following property holds.

$$s_1 \in S \land s_2 \in S \Rightarrow \text{dom}\ s_1 = \text{dom}\ s_2 \tag{S1}$$

---

[2] $S \nrightarrow T$ denotes the set of finite, partial functions from S to T.

That is, the states of a class refer to a common set of variables.

The operations a class can undergo are instances of the class' operation schemas. They can be represented by the name of an operation schema together with an assignment of values to its parameters.

The operations of a class can be represented by a set

$$O \subseteq Id \times (Id \nrightarrow Value)$$

such that the following property holds.

$$(n, p_1) \in O \land (n, p_2) \in O \Rightarrow \operatorname{dom} p_1 = \operatorname{dom} p_2 \qquad (O1)$$

That is, an operation name is always associated with the same set of parameters.

A history is a non-empty sequence of states together with a sequence of operations. Either both sequences are infinite[3] or the state sequence is one longer than the operation sequence. The histories of a class with states S and operations O can be represented by a set[4]

$$H \subseteq S^\omega \times O^\omega$$

such that the following properties hold.

$$
\begin{aligned}
&(s, o) \in H \Rightarrow s \neq \langle \rangle && (H1)\\
&(s, o) \in H \land s \notin S^* \Rightarrow o \notin O^* && (H2)\\
&(s, o) \in H \land s \in S^* \Rightarrow \#s = \#o + 1 && (H3)\\
&(s_1 \frown s_2, o_1 \frown o_2) \in H \land \#s_1 = \#o_1 + 1 \Rightarrow (s_1, o_1) \in H && (H4)
\end{aligned}
$$

The first three properties capture the requirements on an individual history detailed above. The final property is a condition on the set of histories representing a class. This set must be *prefix-closed*. This is necessary since any prefix of an object's history is the history of that object at some earlier stage of its evolution and hence represents a possible history of the object's class.

3 CSP

CSP has been designed specifically to specify concurrent systems. It models a system as a collection of processes which run concurrently, communicate over unbuffered channels and synchronise on particular events. Processes are specified by guarded, and usually recursive, equations. For example, a simple one-place buffer can be specified as follows.

---

[3] Infinite histories enable liveness properties of classes to be modelled. Such properties have been ignored in the description of Object-Z in this paper.

[4] S^ω and S^* denote the set of sequences and set of finite sequences, respectively, of elements from the set S.

$$\alpha(BUFFER1) = \{in.n \mid n \in \mathbb{N}\} \cup \{out.n \mid n \in \mathbb{N}\}$$
$$BUFFER1 = in?x \rightarrow out!x \rightarrow BUFFER1$$

The first line of the specification defines the *alphabet* of the process $BUFFER1$. The alphabet is the set of all events that the process can possibly engage in. Each event, in this case, is of the form $c.v$ where c is the name of a channel and v is a value communicated along that channel. The second line of the specification defines the temporal order in which the process undergoes those events. The notation $in?x$ corresponds to an event $in.x$ where x is input on channel in. Similarly, $out!x$ corresponds to an event $out.x$ where x is output on channel out.

To compose processes, CSP has a number of operators. One of the most important of these is the concurrency operator $\|$. When two processes are combined using this operator, they run concurrently and synchronise on events with the same name or, in the case of communications events, the same channel name and value. All other events are interleaved in the resulting process. For example, a two-place buffer can be specified in terms of two one-place buffers which are concurrently composed such that the $out.x$ event of the first synchronises and communicates with the $in.x$ of the second. To do this, it is necessary to define the following renaming functions.

$$f(in) = in, \;\; f(out) = transfer$$
$$g(in) = transfer, \;\; g(out) = out$$

The two-place buffer is then specified as follows.

$$BUFFER2 = (f(BUFFER1) \parallel g(BUFFER1)) \setminus \{transfer.n \mid n \in \mathbb{N}\}$$

The events $transfer.n$, where $n \in \mathbb{N}$, are *hidden* in the resulting process so that these events are not available to the environment for further synchronisation.

Although CSP processes are specified without reference to an explicit state, to simplify specifications, they often have parameters which simulate the state information. For example, consider the following equations which specify a queue of arbitrary length.

$$\alpha(Queue) = \{in.n \mid n \in \mathbb{N}\} \cup \{out.n \mid n \in \mathbb{N}\}$$
$$Queue = Queue_{<>}$$
$$Queue_s = in.x \rightarrow Queue_{<x>^\frown s}$$
$$Queue_{s^\frown <x>} = out.x \rightarrow Queue_s$$

The subscript parameters represent the sequence of items in the queue. Parameters can also appear in brackets following the process name.

3.1 Semantics of CSP Processes

The standard semantics of CSP is the failures-divergences semantics developed in [3, 4]. A process is modelled by the triple (A, F, D) where A is its alphabet[5], F is its *failures* and D is its *divergences*. The failures of a process are pairs (s, X) where s is a finite sequence of events that the process may undergo and X is a set of events the process may refuse to perform after undergoing s. That is, if the process after undergoing s is in an environment which only allows it to undergo events in X, it may deadlock. The divergences of a process are the sequences of events after which the process may undergo an infinite sequence of internal events, i.e. livelock. Divergences also result from unguarded recursion.

Failures and divergences are defined in terms of the events in the alphabet of the class. The failures of a process with alphabet A are a set

$$F \subseteq A^* \times \mathbb{P} A$$

such that the following properties hold.

$$(\langle \rangle, \varnothing) \in F \tag{F1}$$
$$(s \frown t, \varnothing) \in F \Rightarrow (s, \varnothing) \in F \tag{F2}$$
$$(s, X) \in F \wedge Y \subseteq X \Rightarrow (s, Y) \in F \tag{F3}$$
$$(s, X) \in F \wedge (\forall x \in Y \bullet (s \frown \langle x \rangle, \varnothing) \notin F) \Rightarrow (s, X \cup Y) \in F \tag{F4}$$
$$(\forall Y \in \mathbb{F} X \bullet (s, Y) \in F) \Rightarrow (s, X) \in F \tag{F5}$$

Properties $F1$ and $F2$ capture the requirement that the sequences of events a process can undergo form a non-empty, prefix-closed set. Property $F3$ states that if a process can refuse all events in a set X then it can refuse all events in any subset of X. Property $F4$ states that a process can refuse any event which cannot occur as the next event. Property $F5$ states that all events in a set can be refused if all events in its finite subsets can be refused.

This final property is not strictly necessary. It was included in [4] in order to enable a particular definition of the semantics of the operators of CSP. However, an alternative definition of the same semantics which doesn't require this property is presented in [19]. This alternative definition also allows some forms of *unbounded nondeterminism* (i.e. where a process makes a choice from an infinite set of options) to be modelled. This is not possible when property $F5$ must hold (see [19] for details). Since unbounded nondeterminism arises naturally in Object-Z, e.g. when declaring a variable to have a value from the set of all natural numbers, we adopt the alternative definition of the semantics, i.e. without property $F5$, in the remainder of this paper.

The divergences of a process with alphabet A and failures F are a set

$$D \subseteq A^*$$

such that the following properties hold.

---

[5] The alphabet is often made implicit by assuming all processes have the same alphabet.

$$D \subseteq \operatorname{dom} F \qquad\qquad (D1)$$
$$s \in D \wedge t \in A^* \Rightarrow s \frown t \in D \qquad\qquad (D2)$$
$$s \in D \wedge X \subseteq A \Rightarrow (s, X) \in F \qquad\qquad (D3)$$

The first property simply states that a divergence is a possible sequence of events of the process. Properties $D2$ and $D3$ capture the idea that it is impossible to determine anything about a divergent process in a finite time. Therefore, the possibility that it might undergo further events cannot be ruled out. In other words, a divergent process behaves *chaotically*.

4 Modelling Classes as Processes

As has been noted, there is a strong relationship between object-oriented and concurrent systems. More precisely, the notion of class corresponds closely to that of process. In this section, we use this correspondence as the basis for a semantic integration of Object-Z and CSP: Object-Z classes are given a failures-divergences semantics identical to that of CSP processes. This allows classes defined in the Object-Z part of the specification to be used directly in the CSP part.

4.1 Operations and Events

In order to relate classes and processes, we need a relationship between operations and events. Since both represent observable, atomic actions[6], we adopt the approach of simply identifying them. This needs to be done in such a way that appropriate input and output parameters of synchronising operations can be identified. We therefore define a meta-function β which returns the basename of a parameter name, i.e. $\beta(x?) = \beta(x!) = x$, and allow it to be applied to the assignment of values to an operation's parameters as follows.

$$\beta(\{(x_1, v_1), \ldots, (x_n, v_n)\}) = \{(\beta(x_1), v_1), \ldots, (\beta(x_n), v_n)\}$$
$$\text{where } \{x_1, \ldots, x_n\} \subseteq Id \text{ and } \{v_1, \ldots, v_n\} \subseteq Value$$

The function relating operations and events is then defined as follows.

$$event((n, p)) = n.\beta(p) \text{ where } n \in Id \text{ and } p \in (Id \nrightarrow Value)$$

The event corresponding to an operation (n, p) is a communication event with the operation name n as the channel and the mapping from the basenames of its parameters to their values $\beta(p)$ as the value 'passed' on that channel. For example, the event corresponding to joining a value x on to a *Queue* object is $Join.\{(item, x)\}$.

This allows operations of different classes to interact as if they were composed using the parallel operator $\|$ of Object-Z (see [9]). That is, in the following three ways.

---

[6] Both operations and events represent instantaneous observations of actions which may themselves take time to occur.

- An output parameter $x!$ can be equated with an input parameter $x?$ in a synchronising operation.

This type of interaction is the most common and models message passing communication between processes. For example, to join two queues so that the values output by one are input by the other, we concurrently compose the following classes which inherit the class *Queue* of Sect. 2.

┌─ *Queue*1[*T*] ────────────
│ *Queue*[*T*][*Transfer*/*Leave*]

┌─ *Queue*2[*T*] ────────────
│ *Queue*[*T*][*Transfer*/*Join*]

The operations *Leave* of *Queue*1 and *Join* of *Queue*2 are renamed to *Transfer* to allow them to synchronise as required. Communication is achieved by the identification of the output *item*! of *Queue*1 with the input *item*? of *Queue*2.

- An input parameter $x?$ can be equated with an input parameter $x?$ in a synchronising operation.

This type of interaction models sharing of an input value. For example, two message channels which concurrently accept broadcast messages can be specified by composing the following classes.

┌── *MsgChannel*1 ─────────────
│ *MsgChannel*[*Leave*1/*Leave*, *Lose*1/*Lose*]
│
└───────────────────────────────

┌── *MsgChannel*2 ─────────────
│ *MsgChannel*[*Leave*2/*Leave*, *Lose*2/*Lose*]
│
└───────────────────────────────

In this case, the *Leave* and *Lose* operations of each class are renamed to prevent them from synchronising. The *Join* operations synchronise and the sharing of inputs is achieved by identifying their *item*? inputs.

- An output parameter $x!$ can be equated with an output parameter $x!$ in a synchronising operation.

This type of interaction models cooperation of two processes to produce an output. It is used when we wish to abstract away from the actual cooperation mechanism which in general would require additional message passing. For example, two exchanges in a mobile phone network may cooperate to output a frequency which neither are currently using for calls. This can be specified as follows.

Let *Freq* be the set of all frequencies.

┌─ *Exchange*1 ───────────────
│
│ *used_freqs* : $\mathbb{P}$ *Freq*
│
│ . . .
│
│ ┌─ *Available* ──────────────
│ │ *freq*! : *Freq* \ *used_freqs*
│ │
│ └──────────────────────────
│
└───────────────────────────────

┌─ *Exchange*2 ───────────────
│
│ *used_freqs* : $\mathbb{P}$ *Freq*
│
│ . . .
│
│ ┌─ *Available* ──────────────
│ │ *freq*! : *Freq* \ *used_freqs*
│ │
│ └──────────────────────────
│
└───────────────────────────────

The exchanges synchronise on the operation *Available* and the necessary output is achieved by identifying their *freq!* outputs.

Note that the interpretation here is simply based on the conventional meaning of the ! decoration and equating two output parameters is semantically identical to equating two input parameters. We have adopted this approach to be consistent with Object-Z. However, as shown in [24], this leads to a restricted form of refinement where, unlike refinement in Z, the constraints on output parameters cannot be strengthened.

In general, our approach is to allow operations with both input and output parameters. Any two operations with the same name and parameters with identical basenames will be modelled by identical events when their parameters have the same values and hence will be able to synchronise. For example, the following operations could synchronise.

$$
\begin{array}{l}
\underline{\textit{Op}} \\
x? : X \\
y! : Y \\
\hline
\ldots
\end{array}
\qquad
\begin{array}{l}
\underline{\textit{Op}} \\
x? : X \\
y? : Y \\
\hline
\ldots
\end{array}
$$

Particular attention must be given, however, to operations which have an input and output parameter with the same basename. When these parameters have the same value, they will be identified in the the set $\beta(p)$, where p is the assignment of values to the operation's parameters, and hence the operation can synchronise with an operation with just one parameter with this basename. When the parameters have different values, any synchronising operation would necessarily have both a corresponding input and output parameter. In this case, however, the inputs of each operation could be equated either to each other or to the outputs of the other operation. Since such specifications could easily lead to misunderstandings, input and output parameters with common basenames should be avoided in operations as a matter of style.

Our use of communications events differs from the conventional usage suggested in [14]. A channel in our approach is a means of bidirectional transfer of multiple messages between processes[7]. Conventionally, however, channels are used for unidirectional transfer of a single message. If desired, conventional usage of channels can be achieved by restricting the individual Object-Z operations to have only inputs or only outputs. In this case, each input, or output, of the operation can be regarded as the field of an input, or output, message to be passed on the channel identified by the operation name.

While identifying operations and events seems an appropriate choice, it should be noted that there are in fact other options. For example, Benjamin[1] suggests identifying operation parameters and events in order to integrate Z and CSP. This leads to a conventional use of channels in communications events, i.e. channels are unidirectional and used to transfer single messages, however it can also

---

[7] Our notion of channel is in fact closer to that of a LOTOS gate[2].

lead to more complex specifications. Ensuring the correct synchronisation when an operation has several parameters can be difficult when each parameter is treated as a separate event.

4.2 Classes and Processes

The essence of the approach presented in this paper is that each Object-Z class can be referred to as a process in the CSP part of the specification. The process representing a class must describe the behaviour of all possible objects of that class. Often, however, it is convenient to refer to the behaviour of particular objects corresponding to particular values of the class' constants. Since constants and state variables are not distinguished in the history semantics of Object-Z, we do not wish to distinguish them here. That is, we do not want to add to the existing semantics of Object-Z. We allow, therefore, any value in a class' initial state to be referred to when the class is used as a process.

A class C is modelled by a parameterised process C_i. The parameter i is an assignment of values to a subset of the state of C satisfying a possible initial state of C. That is, $i \in \{j \mid \exists (s, o) \in H \bullet j \subseteq s(1)\}$[8]. For example, $MsgChannel_{\{(max, 10)\}}$ refers to a message channel of length 10. Classes with generic parameters are referenced with the actual parameters in brackets following the class name. For example, $Queue_\varnothing(\mathbb{N})$ refers to a queue of natural numbers. The $\varnothing$ subscript in this case denotes the fact that there is no restriction on the initial state of the class. That is, the process represents the behaviours of all possible objects of the class. For notational convenience, we introduce the convention that $C = C_\varnothing$ allowing us to write simply $Queue(\mathbb{N})$.

Given a class C with states S, operations O and histories H, the alphabet of process C_i comprises the events corresponding to the operations in O.

$$alphabet(C_i) = \{event(op) \mid op \in O\}$$

To define the failures of a class we use the following function which maps a sequence of operations to a sequence of events.

$$events(\langle \rangle) = \langle \rangle$$
$$events(\langle op \rangle \frown o) = \langle event(op) \rangle \frown events(o)$$

The failures of C_i are derived from the histories in H as follows: (t, X) is a failure of C_i if

- there exists a finite history of C whose initial state is satisfied by i,
- the sequence of operations of the history corresponds to the sequence of events in t and
- for each event in X, there does not exist a history which extends the original history by an operation corresponding to the event.

---

[8] An Object-Z class with no initial states is not given a semantics in this approach. Such degenerate classes are, however, unimplementable and of no practical interest to the specifier.

$$failures(C_i) = \{(t, X) \mid \exists (s, o) \in H \bullet$$
$$s \in S^* \land$$
$$i \subseteq s(1) \land$$
$$t = events(o) \land$$
$$\forall e \in X \bullet \nexists st \in S, op \in O \bullet$$
$$e = event(op) \land (s \frown \langle st \rangle, o \frown \langle op \rangle) \in H \}$$

It is necessary to show that the set of failures of C_i satisfy the properties $F1$ to $F4$ of Sect. 3.

The properties $F1$ and $F2$ follow from the fact that the set of histories are prefix-closed (property $H4$ of Sect. 2).

Proof of $F1$.
Since C_i is only defined for i where $\exists (s, o) \in H \bullet i \subseteq s(1)$ and $\#\langle s(1) \rangle = \#\langle\rangle + 1$, $(\langle s(1) \rangle, \langle\rangle) \in H$ by $H4$. Since $\langle s(1) \rangle \in S^*$ and $events(\langle\rangle) = \langle\rangle$ and $\forall e \in \varnothing \bullet P$ for any predicate P, $(\langle\rangle, \varnothing) \in failures(C_i)$. $\square$

Proof of $F2$.
If $(t_1 \frown t_2, \varnothing) \in failures(C_i)$ then $\exists (s, o) \in H \bullet i \subseteq s(1) \land t_1 \frown t_2 = events(o)$. If $s = s_1 \frown s_2$ and $o = o_1 \frown o_2$ such that $\#o_1 = \#t_1$ and $\#s_1 = \#o_1 + 1$ then $(s_1, o_1) \in H$ by $H4$. Since $s_1(1) = s(1)$, $i \subseteq s_1(1)$ and since $s_1 \in S^*$ and $events(o_1) = t_1$ and $\forall e \in \varnothing \bullet P$ for any predicate P, $(t_1, \varnothing) \in failures(C_i)$. $\square$

The properties $F3$ and $F4$ follow directly from the definition of the function *failures*.

Proof of $F3$.
Since $(\forall e \in X \bullet P) \Rightarrow (\forall e \in Y \bullet P)$ for any predicate P when $Y \subseteq X$, if $(t, X) \in failures(C_i)$ and $Y \subseteq X$ then $(t, Y) \in failures(C_i)$. $\square$

Proof of $F4$.
If $\forall e \in Y \bullet (t \frown \langle e \rangle, \varnothing) \notin failures(C_i)$ then, since $\forall e \in \varnothing \bullet P$ for any predicate P, $\forall e \in Y \bullet \nexists (s, o) \in H \bullet i \subseteq s(1) \land s \in S^* \land t \frown \langle e \rangle = events(o)$. Therefore, given $(s, o) \in H$ such that $i \subseteq s(1)$ and $s \in S^*$ and $t = events(o)$, $\forall e \in Y \bullet \nexists st \in S, op \in O \bullet e = event(op) \land (s \frown \langle st \rangle, o \frown \langle op \rangle) \in H$. Hence, if $(t, X) \in failures(C_i)$ then $(t, X \cup Y) \in failures(C_i)$. $\square$

Since Object-Z does not allow hiding of operations nor recursive definitions of operations[9], divergence is not possible. The set of divergences of C_i are hence defined as follows.

$$divergences(C_i) = \varnothing$$

---

[9] Although recursive definitions of operations have been suggested for Object-Z (e.g. [7]), we have adopted a more conservative view of Object-Z in this paper.

This definition trivially satisfies the properties $D1$ to $D3$ of Sect. 3.

Alternatively, divergences could be used to indicate chaotic behaviour which occurs when an operation is applied outside its precondition as in Z. However, our approach is consistent with Object-Z where operations are "blocked", i.e. can't occur, outside their preconditions (see [23]).

4.3 Unbounded Nondeterminism

As shown in [19], relaxing the failures property $F5$ does not overcome all problems with unbounded nondeterminism when using the failures-divergences semantics. Another problem arises when we specify a process which can undergo any finite sequence of a particular event but not an infinite sequence of the event. For example, consider the following Object-Z class.

```
┌─ A ─────────────────────────────────
│  ┌─────────────────────────────────
│  │  x : ℕ
│  ├─────────────────────────────────
│  │  ┌─ Op ──────────────
│  │  │  Δ(x)
│  │  ├──────────────────
│  │  │  x' = x - 1
│  │  └──────────────────
│  └─────────────────────────────────
└─────────────────────────────────────
```

An object of this class can perform the operation Op v times, where v is the actual value of x. Therefore, the corresponding process can perform any finite sequence of $Op.\varnothing$ events but cannot perform an infinite sequence of $Op.\varnothing$ events. This fact is not captured in the semantics which assumes that the infinite sequences of events can be extrapolated from the finite sequences. Hence, in this case, the semantics assumes that the process can in fact undergo an infinite sequence of $Op.\varnothing$ events. Hence, if $Op.\varnothing$ is subsequently hidden, the process will diverge.

Such a semantics is counter-intuitive and hence the use of hiding in the CSP part of a specification needs to be restricted. This can be achieved by placing a well-definedness condition on the hiding operator as is done in [17]. That is, given a process P with failures F, $P \setminus C$ is well-defined only if

$$\forall s \in \operatorname{dom} F \bullet \neg (\forall n \in \mathbb{N} \bullet \exists t \in C^* \bullet \#t > n \wedge s \frown t \in \operatorname{dom} F)$$

This prevents unbounded sequences of events being hidden.

Another possibility would be to extend the failures-divergences semantics with a component corresponding to the infinite traces of a process as is done in [20]. With the exception of hiding, the definitions of all operators are exactly the same over finite behaviours as in the standard failures-divergences semantics. This approach is adopted for combining CSP and action systems in [5]. However, adopting such a non-standard semantics limits the use of existing methods and tools for standard CSP.

5   Specifying Concurrent Systems

In this section, we describe the approach to specifying concurrent systems using the integrated notations. The approach comprises three phases.

- The first phase involves specifying the component processes using Object-Z. Since all interaction of system components is specified in the CSP part of the specification, a restricted subset of Object-Z is used which does not include instantiation of objects of a class. It also, therefore, does not include polymorphism, class union or object containment which are only used in the context of object instantiation, and the parallel || and enrichment • operators which were introduced in Object-Z to model object interaction (see [9] for details). These restrictions greatly simplify reasoning about the Object-Z part of the specification.
  To maintain a separation of concerns and allow maximum flexibility in describing the component processes, each is described independently of the others and of the environment in which they are to be placed. This also allows classes to be more easily shared between specifications.
- The components specified in the first phase will generally not be in a form that allows them to be composed using CSP operators. The second phase involves modifying the class interfaces so that they will synchronise and communicate as desired. This may be achieved using Object-Z inheritance to rename operations and operation parameters and to add state variables and operation parameters where required. For example, 'dummy' operation parameters may be introduced to allow operations with different parameters to synchronise. Such 'dummy' parameters should not be restricted in the operation's predicate. CSP renaming may also be used on appropriate processes in this phase.
- The final phase involves the specification of the system using CSP operators. Only a subset of the operators defined in [14] is, in fact, required. For example, since we are not specifying processes using the notations for input and output channels, the piping operator $\gg$ intended for use with these notations is not required. Also, since Object-Z classes have no notion of termination, the sequential composition operator ; and its associated notations (see [14] for details) are not required.

To illustrate the approach, we apply it to a simple case study: the game of Life.

5.1   The Game of Life

The game of Life is a simulation of the evolution of an array of cells. The array is set up as shown in Fig. 1 such that each cell has eight neighbours (including its four diagonal neighbours).

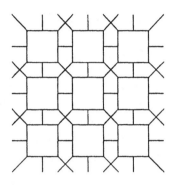

Fig. 1. Array of cells

In each generation of the evolution, each cell is either *alive* or *dead*. The status of a cell in the next generation depends on its present status and the present status of its neighbours as follows:

- a live cell with less than two live neighbours will die (of isolation),
- a live cell with two or three live neighbours will remain alive,
- a live cell with four or more live neighbours will die (of overcrowding), and
- a dead cell with exactly three live neighbours will become alive, otherwise it will remain dead.

In order to discuss concurrency, the cells are regarded as independent processes. Each cell broadcasts its status to its neighbours and when all the cells have broadcasted they synchronise on an event which allows them to change their status.

Specifying the Component Processes. The game of Life has one type of component process, namely a cell. A cell can be specified by a class with three state variables:

status - denoting the cell's status,

num_living - a natural number from 0 to 8 denoting the number of living neighbours that have broadcast their status since the last status change, and

broadcasted - a boolean variable denoting whether or not the cell has broadcasted since the last status change.

```
┌─ Cell ─────────────────────────────────────────────────────────────┐
│ Status == alive | dead                                             │
│ ┌────────────────────────────────────────────────────────────────┐│
│ │ status : Status                                                 ││
│ │ num_living : 0 .. 8                                             ││
│ │ broadcasted : Boolean                                           ││
│ └────────────────────────────────────────────────────────────────┘│
│ ┌─ INIT ─────────────────────────────────────────────────────────┐│
│ │ num_living = 0                                                  ││
│ │ ¬ broadcasted                                                   ││
│ └────────────────────────────────────────────────────────────────┘│
│ ┌─ Broadcast ────────────────────────────────────────────────────┐│
│ │ Δ(broadcasted)                                                  ││
│ │ status! : Status                                                ││
│ │ ───────────────────────────────────────────────────────────────││
│ │ ¬ broadcasted                                                   ││
│ │ status! = status                                                ││
│ │ broadcasted'                                                    ││
│ └────────────────────────────────────────────────────────────────┘│
│ ┌─ Receive ──────────────────────────────────────────────────────┐│
│ │ Δ(num_living)                                                   ││
│ │ status? : Status                                                ││
│ │ ───────────────────────────────────────────────────────────────││
│ │ status? = alive ⇒ num_living' = num_living + 1                  ││
│ │ status? = dead ⇒ num_living' = num_living                       ││
│ └────────────────────────────────────────────────────────────────┘│
│ ┌─ Change ───────────────────────────────────────────────────────┐│
│ │ Δ(status, num_living, broadcasted)                              ││
│ │ ───────────────────────────────────────────────────────────────││
│ │ broadcasted                                                     ││
│ │ (num_living < 2 ∨ num_living > 3) ⇒ status' = dead              ││
│ │ num_living = 2 ⇒ status' = status                               ││
│ │ num_living = 3 ⇒ status' = alive                                ││
│ │ num_living' = 0                                                 ││
│ │ ¬ broadcasted'                                                  ││
│ └────────────────────────────────────────────────────────────────┘│
└────────────────────────────────────────────────────────────────────┘
```

Initially, $num\_living = 0$ and *broadcasted* is false. Therefore, only the operations *Broadcast*, corresponding to a cell broadcasting its status, and *Receive*, corresponding to a cell receiving the status of a neighbouring cell, are enabled. Once a cell has broadcasted, *broadcasted* becomes true and only operations *Receive* and *Change*, corresponding to a cell changing its status, are enabled. Once a cell has changed its status, it returns to a state in which $num\_living = 0$ and *broadcasted* is false.

A cell, therefore, broadcasts its status exactly once before each status change. The number of *Receive* operations occurring before each status change depends on the cell's environment and so is not captured in this class.

Specifying the Component Interfaces. The class *Cell* contains no information about its position in the array or the number of neighbours it has. The class is, therefore, easily reused, e.g. in versions of the game of Life in which the cells are configured in ways other then a standard 2-dimensional array. However, before we can compose the cells in such a way that their operations synchronise and communicate as required, we must add this information. This is done using inheritance.

Let the constants *width* : ℕ and *height* : ℕ denote the width and the height of the cell array respectively. To avoid boundary problems we assume the finite array is a torus. Therefore, the neighbours of a cell with position (x, y) are those, other than the cell itself, whose x value is in the range $(x + width - 1) \bmod width$ .. $(x+1) \bmod width$ and whose y value is in the range $(y + height - 1) \bmod height$ .. $(y+1) \bmod height$.

The following class inherits *Cell* and modifies its interface as required.

```
┌─ CELL ─────────────────────────────────────────────────────────────┐
│ Cell                                                                 │
│  ┌──────────────────────────────────────────────────               │
│  │ x : 0 .. width − 1                                                │
│  │ y : 0 .. height − 1                                               │
│  └──────────────────────────────────────────────────               │
│  ┌─ Broadcast ─────────────────────────────────────────            │
│  │ i! : {x}                                                          │
│  │ j! : {y}                                                          │
│  └──────────────────────────────────────────────────               │
│  ┌─ Receive ───────────────────────────────────────────            │
│  │ i? : (x + width − 1) mod width .. (x + 1) mod width              │
│  │ j? : (y + height − 1) mod height .. (y + 1) mod height           │
│  │ ─────────────────────────────────────────────────               │
│  │ ¬ (i? = x ∧ j? = y)                                              │
│  └──────────────────────────────────────────────────               │
└──────────────────────────────────────────────────────────────────┘
```

The cell's position in the array is captured by the addition of two constants x and y representing the x- and y-coordinates respectively. This position is broadcast with the cell's status by adding to the *Broadcast* operation the output parameters $i! : \{x\}$ and $j! : \{y\}$. This prevents cells with distinct array positions synchronising on their *Broadcast* operations. It also enables only neighbouring cells to receive the broadcast status: cells must only receive a broadcast status when the position broadcast with that status is a neighbouring position. This is captured in the additional declarations and predicates of *Receive*.

For the *Broadcast* event of a cell and the *Receive* events of it neighbours to synchronise, these events must have a common name. Suitable renaming couldn't be done in the class *CELL* as it would have led to a name clash. It can, however, be done in the CSP part of the specification by defining the following renaming function.

$f(Broadcast) = Broadcast$

$f(Receive) = Broadcast$

$f(Change) = Change$

Since we need to refer to the array positions of the cells in the system specification, we apply the renaming function to the process $CELL_{\{(x,i),(y,j)\}}$ where i and j are parameters corresponding to the x- and y-coordinates of the cell's position respectively.

$$CELL_{i,j} = f(CELL_{\{(x,i),(y,j)\}})$$

Specifying the System. The game of Life is now simply specified as the parallel composition of a collection of cell processes: one for each position in the array.

$$LIFE = \left\|\right._{i=0,j=0}^{width-1,height-1} CELL_{i,j}$$

Since all cells will synchronise on the common event $Change.\varnothing$ and the class *Cell* ensures that each cell broadcasts exactly once before each status change, the process *LIFE* will behave as desired. In order to verify properties of the process such as deadlock freedom, a proof system for the integrated notations must be developed. Current work on such a proof system is outlined in the next section.

6   Conclusion and Future Work

This paper has presented an approach to specifying concurrent systems using a combination of Object-Z and CSP. A common semantic basis allows classes specified in the Object-Z part of the specification to be used directly as processes in the CSP part. The explicit modelling of state in Object-Z facilitates the specification of data structures needed to describe the concurrent components of a system. Furthermore, inheritance allows issues concerning a component's interface with the system into which it is to be placed to be separated from the specification of its intrinsic behaviour. This, together with the explicit mechanisms for modelling concurrency and communication in CSP, leads to system specifications which are more concise and, we believe, more easily comprehensible than those specified using just one of the languages.

It is not enough, however, for a specification to be concise and easily comprehensible. A major role of a formal specification is in the formal development of a system through subsequent steps of verification and refinement. Since the system specification in our approach is a CSP specification, a starting point for the development of refinement and verification methods is the existing CSP methods.

A process is a refinement of another in CSP when its failures and divergences are subsets of those of the other process. He[12] and Josephs[17] have developed refinement relations for state transition systems which are both sound and complete with respect to CSP refinement. Woodcock and Morgan[27] have produced similar results using weakest precondition formulae. These approaches could be adopted for refining Object-Z classes in our approach such that any CSP specification in which they were used would also be refined.

Verification in CSP involves showing that a process *satisfies* a predicate over the failures of the process (see [14] for details). Laws exist which allow properties of a process to be proved in terms of properties of its components. Since the components in our approach are Object-Z classes, we need a way of showing that such properties are true for an Object-Z class.

The properties often involve *dynamic* information such as the number of times a particular event has occurred. Although Object-Z has a logic for reasoning about classes[22], it is not particularly suited to reasoning about such dynamic information. However, inheritance can be used to add auxiliary state variables capturing this information. Properties proved for such a class with additional auxiliary variables can then be shown to hold for the original class without the auxiliary variables by proving that the former is refined by the latter. Preliminary work on this approach to verification and the aforementioned approach to refinement can be found in [24].

Acknowledgements

Thanks to Felix Cornelius, Clemens Fischer, Maritta Heisel and Matthias Weber for comments on an earlier draft of this paper. Thanks also to John Derrick and Howard Bowman for interesting discussions about, and related to, this work. The author is supported by a research fellowship granted by the Alexander von Humboldt-Stiftung, Germany.

References

1. M. Benjamin. A message passing system. An example of combining CSP and Z. In J.E. Nicholls, editor, *4th Z Users Workshop*, Workshops in Computing, pages 221–228. Springer-Verlag, 1989.
2. T. Bolognesi and E. Brinksma. Introduction to the ISO specification language LOTOS. *Computer Networks and ISDN Systems*, 14(1):25–59, 1988.
3. S.D. Brookes, C.A.R. Hoare, and A.W. Roscoe. A theory of communicating sequential processes. *Journal of the ACM*, 31(3):560–599, 1984.
4. S.D. Brookes and A.W. Roscoe. An improved failures model for communicating processes. In *Pittsburgh Symposium on Concurrency*, volume 197 of *Lecture Notes in Computer Science*, pages 281–305. Springer-Verlag, 1985.
5. M.J. Butler and C.C. Morgan. Action systems, unbounded nondeterminism, and infinite traces. *Formal Aspects of Computing*, 7(1):37–53, 1995.
6. J. Derrick, H. Bowman, and M. Steen. Viewpoints and objects. In J. Bowen and M. Hinchey, editors, *9th International Conference of Z Users (ZUM'95)*, volume 967 of *Lecture Notes in Computer Science*, pages 449–468. Springer-Verlag, 1995.
7. J. Dong, R. Duke, and G. Rose. An object-oriented approach to the semantics of programming languages. In G. Gupta, editor, *17th Annual Computer Science Conference (ACSC'17)*, pages 767–775, 1994.
8. D. Duke and R. Duke. Towards a semantics for Object-Z. In D. Bjørner, C.A.R. Hoare, and H. Langmaack, editors, *VDM'90:VDM and Z!*, volume 428 of *Lecture Notes in Computer Science*, pages 242–262. Springer-Verlag, 1990.

9. R. Duke, G. Rose, and G. Smith. Object-Z: A specification language advocated for the description of standards. *Computer Standards and Interfaces*, 17:511–533, 1995.

10. H. Ehrich, J. Goguen, and A. Sernadas. A categorical theory of objects as observed processes. In J.W. Bakker, W.P. de Roever, and G. Rozenberg, editors, *Foundations of Object-Oriented Languages*, volume 489 of *Lecture Notes in Computer Science*, pages 203–228. Springer-Verlag, 1991.

11. M. Nielsen et al. The RAISE language, methods and tools. *Formal Aspects of Computing*, 1:85–114, 1989.

12. J. He. Process refinement. In J. McDermid, editor, *The Theory and Practice of Refinement*. Butterworths, 1989.

13. M. Heisel and C. Sühl. Formal specification of safety-critical software with Z and real-time CSP. In E. Schoitsch, editor, *Proceedings 15th International Conference on Computer Safety, Reliability and Security*, pages 31–45. Springer, 1996.

14. C.A.R. Hoare. *Communicating Sequential Processes*. Series in Computer Science. Prentice-Hall International, 1985.

15. ITU Recommendation X.901-904. *Open Distributed Processing - Reference Model - Parts 1-4*, July 1995.

16. C.B. Jones. *Systematic Software Development using VDM*. Series in Computer Science. Prentice-Hall International, 1986.

17. M.B. Josephs. A state-based approach to communicating processes. *Distributed Computing*, 3:9–18, 1988.

18. R. Milner. *Communication and Concurrency*. Series in Computer Science. Prentice-Hall International, 1989.

19. A.W. Roscoe. An alternative order for the failures model. *Journal of Logic and Computation*, 3(2), 1993.

20. A.W. Roscoe. Unbounded nondeterminism in CSP. *Journal of Logic and Computation*, 3(2), 1993.

21. M. Shaw and D. Garlan. Formulations and formalisms in software architecture. In J. van Leeuwen, editor, *Computer Science Today: Recent Trends and Developments*, volume 1000 of *Lecture Notes in Computer Science*, pages 307–323. Springer-Verlag, 1996.

22. G. Smith. Extending $\mathcal{W}$ for Object-Z. In J. Bowen and M. Hinchey, editors, *9th International Conference of Z Users*, volume 967 of *Lecture Notes in Computer Science*, pages 276–295. Springer-Verlag, 1995.

23. G. Smith. A fully abstract semantics of classes for Object-Z. *Formal Aspects of Computing*, 7(3):289–313, 1995.

24. G. Smith and J. Derrick. Refinement and verification of concurrent systems specified in Object-Z and CSP. Submitted for publication, 1997.

25. J.M. Spivey. *The Z Notation: A Reference Manual (2nd Ed.)*. Series in Computer Science. Prentice-Hall International, 1992.

26. F.W. Vaandrager. Process algebra semantics for POOL. Technical Report CS-R8629, Centre for Mathematics and Computer Science, Amsterdam, the Netherlands, 1991.

27. J.C.P. Woodcock and C.C. Morgan. Refinement of state-based concurrent systems. In D. Bjørner, C.A.R. Hoare, and H. Langmaack, editors, *VDM'90: VDM and Z!*, volume 428 of *Lecture Notes in Computer Science*. Springer-Verlag, 1990.

28. A. Yonezawa and M. Tokoro, editors. *Object-Oriented Concurrent Programming*. MIT Press, 1987.

Class Refinement and Interface Refinement in Object-Oriented Programs

Anna Mikhajlova[1] and Emil Sekerinski[2]

[1] Turku Centre for Computer Science, Åbo Akademi University
Lemminkäisenkatu 14A, Turku 20520, Finland
[2] Dept. of Computer Science, Åbo Akademi University
Lemminkäisenkatu 14A, Turku 20520, Finland

Abstract. Constructing new classes from existing ones by inheritance or subclassing is a characteristic feature of object-oriented development. Imposing semantic constraints on subclassing allows us to ensure that the behaviour of superclasses is preserved or refined in their subclasses. This paper defines a class refinement relation which captures these semantic constraints. The class refinement relation is based on algorithmic and data refinement supported by Refinement Calculus. Class refinement is generalized to interface refinement, which takes place when a change in user requirements causes interface changes of classes designed as refinements of other classes. We formalize the interface refinement relation and present rules for refinement of clients of the classes involved in this relation.

1 Introduction

It has been widely recognized that design and development of object-oriented programs is difficult and intricate. The need for formal basis of object-oriented development was identified by many researchers. We demonstrate how formal methods, in particular, Refinement Calculus of Back, Morgan, and Morris [4, 20, 21], can be used for constructing more reliable object-oriented programs.

A characteristic feature of object-oriented program development is a uniform way of structuring all stages of the development by classes. The programming notation of Refinement Calculus is very convenient for describing object-oriented development because it allows us to specify classes at various abstraction levels. The specification language we use is based on monotonic predicate transformers, has class constructs, supports subclassing and subtype polymorphism. Besides usual imperative statements, the language includes specification statements which may appear in method bodies of classes leading to abstract classes. One of the main benefits offered by this language is that all development stages can be described in a uniform way starting with a simple abstract specification and resulting in a concrete program.

We build a logic of object-oriented programs as a conservative extension of (standard) higher-order logic, in the style of [6]. An alternative approach is undertaken by Abadi and Leino in [2]. They develop a logic of object-oriented programs in the style of Hoare, prove its soundness, and discuss completeness issues. Naumann [22] defines the semantics of a simple Oberon-like programming language with similar specification constructs as here, also based on predicate transformers. Sekerinski [24, 25] defines a rich object-oriented programming and specification notation by using a type system with subtyping and type parameters, and also using predicate transformers. In both approaches, subtyping is based on extensions of record types. Here we use sum types instead, as suggested by Back and Butler in [7]. One motivation for moving to sum types is to avoid the complications in the typing and the logic when reasoning about record types: the simple typed lambda calculus as the formal basis is sufficient for our purposes. Another advantage of moving to sum types is that we can directly express whether an object is of exactly a certain type or of one of its subtypes (in the record approach, a type contains all the values of its subtypes). Using summations also allows us to model contravariance and covariance on method parameters in a simple way. Finally, to allow objects of a subclass to have different (private) attributes from those of the superclass, hiding by existential types was used in [24, 25]. It turned out that this leads to complications when reasoning about method calls, which are not present when using the model of sum types. In the latter, objects of a subclass can always have different attributes from those of the superclass.

Constructing new classes from existing classes by inheritance, or subclassing, is one of characteristic features of object-oriented program development. However, when a subclass overrides some methods of its superclass, there are no guarantees that its instances will deliver the same or refined behaviour as the instances of the superclass. We define a class refinement relation and relate the notion of subclassing to this relation. When a class C' is constructed by subclassing from C and class refinement holds between them, then it is guaranteed that any behaviour expected from C will necessarily be delivered by C'.

Class refinement as defined here is based on data refinement [15, 14, 19, 5]. The definition generalizes that of Sekerinski [24] by allowing contravariance and covariance in the method parameters, and by considering constructor methods. Class refinement has also been studied in various extensions of the Z specification languages, e.g. [16, 17], but only between class specifications and not implementations. Other approaches on "behavioural subtyping" of classes [3, 18, 10] also make a distinction between the specification of a class and its implementation. By having specification constructs as part of the (extended) programming language, this distinction becomes unnecessary.

Subclassing requires that parameter types of a method be the same in the subclass and in the superclass or, at most, subject to contravariance and covariance rules, as described in [9, 1]. However, sometimes a change in user requirements causes interface changes of classes designed as refinements of other classes. We formalize the interface refinement relation as a generalization of class refinement, and present rules for refinement of clients of the classes involved in this relation. Interface refinement has also been considered by Broy in [8], but for networks of communicating components rather than for classes.

Paper Outline: In Section 2 we present the required concepts of the Refinement Calculus formalism. In Section 3 we explain our model of objects, classes, subclassing, and subtyping polymorphism. Section 4 defines the class refinement relation. In the following section we generalize class refinement to interface refinement, formalize implicit client refinement, and discuss explicit client refinement. Finally, we conclude with considering applications of our work.

2 Refinement Calculus

A *predicate* over a set of states Σ is a boolean function $p : \Sigma \to Bool$ which assigns a truth value to each state. The set of predicates on Σ is denoted $\mathcal{P}\Sigma$. The *entailment ordering* on predicates is defined by pointwise extension, so that for $p, q : \mathcal{P}\Sigma$,

$$p \subseteq q \;\; \hat{=} \;\; (\forall \sigma : \Sigma \cdot p\,\sigma \Rightarrow q\,\sigma)$$

A *relation* from Σ to Γ is a function $P : \Sigma \to \mathcal{P}\Gamma$ that maps each state σ to a predicate on Γ. We write

$$\Sigma \leftrightarrow \Gamma \;\; \hat{=} \;\; \Sigma \to \mathcal{P}\Gamma$$

to denote a set of all relations from Σ to Γ. This view of relations is isomorphic to viewing them as predicates on the cartesian space $\Sigma \times \Gamma$. The *identity relation* and the *composition* of relations are defined as follows:

$$Id\,x\,y \;\; \hat{=} \;\; x = y$$
$$(P; Q)\,x\,z \;\; \hat{=} \;\; (\exists y \cdot P\,x\,y \land Q\,y\,z)$$

A *predicate transformer* is a function $S : \mathcal{P}\Gamma \to \mathcal{P}\Sigma$ from predicates to predicates. We write

$$\Sigma \mapsto \Gamma \;\; \hat{=} \;\; \mathcal{P}\Gamma \to \mathcal{P}\Sigma$$

to denote a set of all predicate transformers from Σ to Γ. Program statements in Refinement Calculus are identified with weakest-precondition monotonic predicate transformers that map a postcondition $q : \mathcal{P}\Gamma$ to the weakest precondition $p : \mathcal{P}\Sigma$ such that the program is guaranteed to terminate in a final state satisfying q whenever the initial state satisfies p. A program statement S need not have identical initial and final state spaces, though if it does, we write $S : \Xi(\Sigma)$ instead of $S : \Sigma \mapsto \Sigma$.

The *refinement ordering* on predicate transformers is defined by pointwise extension, for $S, T : \Sigma \mapsto \Gamma$:

$$S \sqsubseteq T \;\; \hat{=} \;\; (\forall q : \mathcal{P}\Gamma \cdot S\,q \subseteq T\,q)$$

The refinement ordering on predicate transformers models the notion of total-correctness preserving program refinement. For statements S and T, the relation $S \sqsubseteq T$ holds if and only if T satisfies any specification satisfied by S.

The **abort** statement maps each postcondition to the identically false predicate *false*, and the **magic** statement maps each postcondition to the identically true predicate *true*. The **abort** statement is never guaranteed to terminate, while the **magic** statement is *miraculous* since it is always guaranteed to establish any postcondition.

Sequential composition of program statements is modeled by functional composition of predicate transformers. For $S : \Sigma \mapsto \Gamma$, $T : \Gamma \mapsto \Delta$ and $q : \mathcal{P}\Delta$,

$$(S; T)\ q \ \widehat{=}\ S\ (T\ q)$$

The program statement **skip**$_\Sigma$ is modeled by the identity predicate transformer on $\mathcal{P}\Sigma$.

Given a relation $P : \Sigma \leftrightarrow \Gamma$, the *angelic update statement* $\{P\} : \Sigma \mapsto \Gamma$ and the *demonic update statement* $[P] : \Sigma \mapsto \Gamma$ are defined by

$$\{P\}\ q\ \sigma \ \widehat{=}\ (\exists \gamma : \Gamma \cdot (P\ \sigma\ \gamma) \wedge (q\ \gamma))$$
$$[P]\ q\ \sigma \ \widehat{=}\ (\forall \gamma : \Gamma \cdot (P\ \sigma\ \gamma) \Rightarrow (q\ \gamma))$$

When started in a state σ, $\{P\}$ angelically chooses a new state γ such that $P\ \sigma\ \gamma$ holds, while $[P]$ demonically chooses a new state γ such that $P\ \sigma\ \gamma$ holds. If no such state exists, then $\{P\}$ aborts, whereas $[P]$ behaves as **magic**, i.e. can establish any postcondition.

Ordinary program constructs may be modeled using the basic predicate transformers and operators presented above. For example, in a state space with two components $(x : T, y : S)$, an assignment statement may be modeled by the demonic update:

$$x := e \ \widehat{=}\ [R], \text{ where } R\ (x, y)(x', y') \ =\ (x' = e) \wedge (y' = y)$$

Our specification language includes specification statements. The *demonic specification statement* is written $[x := x' \cdot b]$, and the *angelic specification statement* is written $\{x := x' \cdot b\}$, where b is a boolean expression relating x and x'. The program variable x is assigned a value x' satisfying b. These statements correspond to the demonic and the angelic updates respectively:

$$x := x' \cdot b \ \widehat{=}\ R, \text{ where } R\ (x, y)(x', y') \ =\ b \wedge (y' = y)$$

We also have an *assertion*, written $\{p\}$, where p is a predicate stating a condition on program variables. This assertion behaves as **skip** if p is satisfied and as **abort** otherwise.

Finally, the language supports *local variables*. The construct $\lVert$ **var** $z \bullet S$ $\rVert$ states that the program variable z is local to S:

$$\lVert \textbf{ var } z \bullet S \rVert \ \widehat{=}\ [Enter_z]; S; [Exit_z], \text{ where}$$

$$Enter_z(x, y)(x', y', z') \ \widehat{=}\ (x' = x) \wedge (y' = y) \text{ and}$$
$$Exit_z(x, y, z)(x', y') \ \widehat{=}\ (x' = x) \wedge (y' = y)$$

The semantics of other ordinary program constructs, like multiple assignments, **if**-statements, and **do**-loops, is given, e.g. in [6].

Data refinement is a general technique by which one can change the state space in a refinement. For statements $S : \Xi(\Sigma)$ and $S' : \Xi(\Sigma')$, let $R : \Sigma' \leftrightarrow \Sigma$ be an *abstraction relation* between the state spaces Σ and Σ'. The statement S is said to be data refined by S' via R, denoted $S \sqsubseteq_R S'$, if

$$\{R\};\ S\ \sqsubseteq\ S';\ \{R\}$$

Alternative and equivalent characterizations of data refinement using the inverse relation R^{-1}, are then

$$S;[R^{-1}] \sqsubseteq [R^{-1}];S' \qquad S \sqsubseteq [R^{-1}];S';\{R\} \qquad \{R\};S;[R^{-1}] \sqsubseteq S'$$

These characterizations follow from the fact that $\{R\}$ and $[R^{-1}]$ are each others inverses, in the sense that $\{R\};[R^{-1}] \sqsubseteq \textbf{skip}$ and $\textbf{skip} \sqsubseteq [R^{-1}];\{R\}$.

Refinement Calculus provides laws for transforming more abstract program structures into more concrete ones based on the notion of refinement of predicate transformers presented above. A large collection of algorithmic and data refinement laws is given in [6, 20, 12].

Sum Types and Operators. In our specification language we widely employ sum types for modeling subtyping polymorphism and dynamic binding. The sum or disjoint union of two types Σ and Γ is written $\Sigma + \Gamma$. The types Σ and Γ are called base types of the sum in this case. Associated with the sum types, are the injection relations[1] which map elements of the subsets to elements of the superset summation:

$$\iota_\Sigma : \Sigma \leftrightarrow \Sigma + \Gamma \qquad \iota_\Gamma : \Gamma \leftrightarrow \Sigma + \Gamma$$

and projection relations which relate elements of summation with elements of their subsets:

$$\pi_\Sigma : \Sigma + \Gamma \leftrightarrow \Sigma \qquad \pi_\Gamma : \Sigma + \Gamma \leftrightarrow \Gamma$$

In fact, the projection relation is an inverse of the injection relation for the corresponding subset of the summation.

We define the subtype relation as follows. The type Σ is a subtype of Σ', written $\Sigma <: \Sigma'$, if $\Sigma = \Sigma'$, or $\Sigma <: \Gamma$ or $\Sigma <: \Gamma'$, where $\Gamma + \Gamma' = \Sigma'$. For example, $\Gamma <: \Gamma + \Gamma'$ and, or course, $\Gamma + \Gamma' <: \Gamma + \Gamma'$. If Σ is a subtype of Σ', we can always construct the appropriate injection $\iota_\Sigma : \Sigma \leftrightarrow \Sigma'$ and projection $\pi_\Sigma : \Sigma' \leftrightarrow \Sigma$. The subtype relation is reflexive, transitive and antisymmetric.

A summation operator combines statements by forming the disjoint union of their state spaces. This operator is defined in [7] by extension from the

---

[1] In fact, the injections are functions rather than relations, but for our purposes it is more convenient to treat them as relations.

summation of types. For $S_1 : \Sigma_1 \mapsto \Gamma_1$ and $S_2 : \Sigma_2 \mapsto \Gamma_2$, the summation $S_1 + S_2 : \Sigma_1 + \Sigma_2 \mapsto \Gamma_1 + \Gamma_2$ is a predicate transformer such that the effect of executing it in some initial state σ depends on the base type of σ. If $\sigma : \Sigma_1$ then S_1 is executed, while if it is of type Σ_2, then S_2 is executed.

The summation operator was shown to satisfy a number of useful properties. The one of interest to us is that it preserves refinement, allowing us to refine elements of the summation separately:

$$S_1 \sqsubseteq S_1' \ \wedge \ S_2 \sqsubseteq S_2' \ \Rightarrow \ (S_1 + S_2) \sqsubseteq (S_1' + S_2')$$

Product Types and Operators. The cartesian product of two types Σ and Γ is written $\Sigma \times \Gamma$. The product operator combines predicate transformers by forming the cartesian product of their state spaces. For $S_1 : \Sigma_1 \mapsto \Gamma_1$ and $S_2 : \Sigma_2 \mapsto \Gamma_2$, their product $S_1 \times S_2$ is a predicate transformer of type $\Sigma_1 \times \Sigma_2 \mapsto \Gamma_1 \times \Gamma_2$ whose execution has the same effect as simultaneous execution of S_1 and S_2.

In addition to many other useful properties, the product operator preserves refinement:

$$S_1 \sqsubseteq S_1' \ \wedge \ S_2 \sqsubseteq S_2' \ \Rightarrow \ (S_1 \times S_2) \sqsubseteq (S_1' \times S_2')$$

For $S : \Sigma \mapsto \Sigma$ we define lifting to a product predicate transformer of type $\Sigma \times \Gamma \mapsto \Sigma \times \Gamma$ as $S \times \mathbf{skip}_\Gamma$. When lifting is obvious from the context, we will simply write S instead of $S \times \mathbf{skip}_\Gamma$.

A product $P \times Q$ of two relations $P : \Sigma_1 \leftrightarrow \Gamma_1$ and $Q : \Sigma_2 \leftrightarrow \Gamma_2$ is a relation of type $(\Sigma_1 \times \Sigma_2) \leftrightarrow (\Gamma_1 \times \Gamma_2)$ defined by

$$(P \times Q)\,(\sigma_1, \sigma_2)(\gamma_1, \gamma_2) \ \widehat{=} \ (P \ \sigma_1 \ \gamma_1) \wedge (Q \ \sigma_2 \ \gamma_2)$$

3 Specifying Objects and Classes

Object-oriented systems are characterized by *objects*, which group together data, and operations for manipulating that data. The operations, called *methods*, can be invoked only by sending *messages* to the object. The complete set of messages that the object understands is characterized by the *interface* of the object. The interface represents the signatures of object methods, i.e. the name and the types of input and output parameters. As opposed to the interface, the *object type* is the type of object *attributes*. We consider all attributes as private or hidden, and all methods as public or visible to clients of the object. Accordingly, two objects with the same public part, i.e. the same interface, can differ in their private part, i.e. object types.

We focus on modeling class-based object-oriented languages, which form the mainstream of object-oriented programming. Accordingly, we take a view that objects are instantiated by classes. A class is a pattern used to describe objects with identical behaviour through specifying their interface. Specifically, a class describes what attributes each object will have, the specification for each method, and the way the objects are created. We declare a class as follows:

$$C = \textbf{class}$$
$$attr_1 : \Sigma_1, \ldots, attr_m : \Sigma_m$$

$$C\ (p : \Psi)\ =\ S,$$
$$Meth_1\ (g_1 : \Gamma_1) : \Delta_1\ =\ T_1,$$
$$\ldots$$
$$Meth_n\ (g_n : \Gamma_n) : \Delta_n\ =\ T_n$$
$$\textbf{end}$$

Class attributes $(attr_1, \ldots, attr_m)$ abbreviated further on as $attr$ have the corresponding types Σ_1 through Σ_m. The type of $attr$ is then $\Sigma\ =\ \Sigma_1 \times \ldots \times \Sigma_m{}^2$. A *class constructor* is used to instantiate objects and is distinguished by the same name as the class. Due to the fact that the constructor concerns object creation rather than object functionality, it is associated with the class rather than with the specified interface. We take a view that the constructor signature is not part of the interface specified by the class. The statement $S : \Xi(\Sigma \times \Psi)$ representing a body of the constructor initializes the attributes using input $p : \Psi$.

Methods $Meth_1$ through $Meth_n$ specified by bodies $T_1, \ldots, T_n$ operate on the attributes and realize the object functionality. Every statement T_i is, in general, of type $\Xi(\Sigma \times \Gamma_i \times \Delta_i)$, where Σ is the type of class attributes, Γ_i and Δ_i are the types of input and output parameters respectively. A method may be parameterless with both Γ_i and Δ_i the unit type (), have only input or only output parameters. When a method has an output parameter, a special variable $res : \Delta_i$ represents the result and assignment to this variable models returning a value in the output parameter. The signature of every method is part of the specified interface.

The object type specified by a class can always be extracted from the class and we do not need to declare it explicitly. We use $\tau(C)$ to denote the type of objects generated by the class C. Naturally, $\tau(C)$ is just another name for Σ.

Being declared as such, the class C is modeled by a tuple $(K, M_1, \ldots, M_n)$, where

$$K\ =\ [Enter_{attr}]; S; [Exit_p]$$
$$M_i\ =\ [Enter_{res}]; T_i; [Exit_{g_i}],\ \text{for i} = 1, \ldots, \text{n.}$$

Further on we will refer to K as the constructor and to $M_1, \ldots, M_n$ as the methods, unless stated otherwise.

Instantiating a new variable of object type by class C is modeled by invoking the corresponding class constructor:

$$c.C(e)\ \stackrel{\frown}{=}\ [Enter_p]; p := e; K; c := attr; [Exit_{attr}]$$

Naturally, a variable of object type can be local to a block:

$$|[\ \textbf{var}\ c : C(e)\ \bullet\ S\ ]|\ \stackrel{\frown}{=}\ [Enter_c]; c.C(e); S; [Exit_c]$$

---

^{2} We impose a non-recursiveness restriction on Σ so that none of Σ_i is equal to Σ. This restriction allows us to stay within the simple-typed lambda calculus.

Often a class aggregates objects of another class, i.e. some attributes can be of object types. In this case the class declaration states the object types of these attributes, but only the constructor invocation actually introduces new objects into the state space and initializes them.

Invocation of a method $Meth_i \; (g_i : \Gamma_i) : \Delta_i$ on an object c instantiated by class C is modeled as follows:

$$
\begin{aligned}
d := c.Meth_i \; (g) \quad \widehat{=} \quad & [Enter_{attr}]; [Enter_{g_i}]; \\
& attr := c; g_i := g; M_i; c := attr; d := res; \\
& [Exit_{res}]; [Exit_{attr}]
\end{aligned}
$$

As an example of a class specification consider a class of bank accounts. An account should have an owner, and it should be possible to deposit and withdraw money in the currency of choice and check the current balance. We present the specification of the class *Account* in Fig. 1.

$Account \; = \; \textbf{class}$
  $owner : Name, balance : Currency$

  $Account \; (name : Name, sum : Currency) \; = \; owner := name; balance := sum,$

  $Deposit \; (sum : Currency, from : Name, when : Date) \; =$
    $\{sum > 0\}; balance := balance + sum,$

  $Withdraw \; (sum : Currency, to : Name, when : Date) \; =$
    $\{sum > 0 \; \wedge \; sum \leq balance\}; balance := balance - sum,$

  $Owner \; () : Name \; = \; res := owner,$

  $Balance \; () : Currency \; = \; res := balance$
$\textbf{end}$

Fig. 1. Specification of bank account

Obviously, this specification only demonstrates the most general behaviour of bank accounts. For example, when specifying *Deposit*, we only state that *balance* is increased by *sum* and leave the changes to the other input parameters unspecified. We would like to *subclass* from *Account* more concrete account classes. Let us consider specification of subclasses more closely.

3.1 Subclassing

Subclassing [3] is a mechanism for constructing new classes from existing ones by *inheriting* some or all of their attributes and methods, possibly *overriding* some attributes and methods, and adding extra methods. We limit our consideration

---

[3] We prefer the term *subclassing* to *implementation inheritance* because the latter literally means reuse of existing methods and does not, as such, suggest the possibility of method overriding.

of class construction to inheritance and overriding. Addition of extra methods is a non-trivial issue because of inconsistencies possibly introduced by extra methods which become apparent in presence of subtype aliasing, and is treated in another study.

We describe a subclass of class C as follows:

$$
\begin{aligned}
C' \; = \; & \mathbf{subclass\ of}\ C \\
& attr'_1 : \Sigma'_1, \ldots, attr'_p : \Sigma'_p \\[4pt]
& C'\,(p : \Psi) \; = \; S', \\
& Meth_1\,(g_1 : \Gamma_1) : \Delta_1 \; = \; T'_1, \\
& \quad \ldots \\
& Meth_k\,(g_k : \Gamma_k) : \Delta_k \; = \; T'_k \\
\mathbf{end} &
\end{aligned}
$$

Class attributes $attr'_1, \ldots, attr'_p$ have the corresponding types Σ'_1 through Σ'_p. Some of these attributes are inherited from the superclass C, others override attributes of C, and the other ones are new. The class C' has its own class constructor without inheriting the one associated with the superclass. The bodies $T'_1, \ldots, T'_k$ override the corresponding $Meth_1, \ldots, Meth_k$ body definitions defined in C. The bodies of methods named $Meth_{k+1}, \ldots, Meth_n$ are inherited from the superclass C. The class C' is modeled by a tuple $(K', M'_1, \ldots, M'_n)$, where the statements K' and all M'_i are related to $S', T'_1, \ldots, T'_n$ as described above.

We view subclassing as a syntactic relation on classes, since subclasses are distinguished by an appropriate declaration. Syntactic subclassing implies conformance of interfaces, in the sense that a subclass specifies an interface conforming to the one specified by its superclass. In the simple case the interface specified by a subclass is the same as that of the superclass. In the next section we explain how this requirement can be relaxed.

As an example of subclassing consider extending the class *Account* with a list of transactions, where every transaction has a sender, a receiver, an amount of money being transferred, and a date. We specify a record type representing transactions as follows:

$$
\begin{aligned}
\mathbf{type}\ Transaction \; = \; & \mathbf{record} \\
& from : Name, \; to : Name, \; amount : Currency, \; date : Date \\
\mathbf{end} &
\end{aligned}
$$

Here *Name*, *Currency* and *Date* are simple types. *Date* is a type of six digit arrays for representing a day, a month, and a year, for example as '251296' for December 25, 1996.

Now we can specify in Fig. 2 a class of bank accounts based on sequences of transactions. Notice that we specify only the overriding methods, *Owner* and *Balance* are inherited from the superclass *Account*.

$AccountPlus$ = **subclass of** $Account$
  $owner : Name, balance : Currency, transactions : $ **seq of** $Transaction$

$AccountPlus\ (name : Name, sum : Currency)\ =$
  $owner := name; balance := sum; transactions := \langle \rangle,$

$Deposit\ (sum : Currency, from : Name, when : Date)\ =$
  $\{sum > 0\}; |[$ **var** $t : Transaction \bullet t := (from, owner, sum, when);$
  $transactions := transactions \hat{\ } \langle t \rangle; balance := balance + sum\ ]|,$

$Withdraw\ (sum : Currency, to : Name, when : Date)\ =$
  $\{sum > 0 \wedge sum \leq balance\};$
  $|[$ **var** $t : Transaction \bullet t := (owner, to, sum * (-1), when);$
  $transactions := transactions \hat{\ } \langle t \rangle; balance := balance - sum\ ]|$

end

Fig. 2. Specification of account based on transactions

3.2 Modeling Subtyping Polymorphism

To model subtyping polymorphism, we allow object types to be sum types. The idea is to group together an object type of a certain class and object types of all its subclasses, to form a polymorphic object type. A variable of such a sum type can be instantiated to any base type of the summation, in other words, to any object instantiated by a class whose object type is the base type of the summation. We will call the object types of only one class *ground* and summations of object types *polymorphic*. Since a ground object type uniquely identifies the class of objects, we can always tell whether a certain object is an instance of a certain class.

A sum of object types, denoted by $\tau(C)^+$ is defined to be such that its base types are $\tau(C)$ and all the object types of subclasses of C. For example, if D is the only subclass of C with the object type $\tau(D)$, then $\tau(C)^+ = \tau(C) + \tau(D)$. Naturally, we have that

$$\tau(C) <: \tau(C)^+ \text{ and } \tau(D) <: \tau(C)^+.$$

A variable $c : \tau(C)^+$ can be instantiated by either C or D. The *subsumption* property holds of c, namely, if $c : \tau(C)$ and $\tau(C) <: \tau(C)^+$ then $c : \tau(C)^+$. This property is characteristic of subtype relations, it means that an object of type $\tau(C)$ can be viewed as an object of the supertype $\tau(C)^+$.

Suppose a method $Meth_i$ is specified in both C and D by statements M_i and M_i' respectively. An invocation of $Meth_i$ on an object c of type $\tau(C)^+$ is modeled as follows:

$$c.Meth_i() \; \hat{=} \; \left(\begin{array}{l} [Enter_{attr}]; \\ attr := c; M_i; c := attr; \\ [Exit_{attr}] \end{array} \right) + \left(\begin{array}{l} [Enter_{attr'}]; \\ attr' := c; M_i'; c := attr'; \\ [Exit_{attr'}] \end{array} \right)$$

where $attr : \Sigma$ and $attr' : \Sigma'$ are attributes of C and D respectively. Modeling an invocation of a method having input and output parameters is similar to method invocation on a non-polymorphic object.

Being equipped with subtyping polymorphism, we can allow overriding methods in a subclass to be generalized on the type of input parameters or specialized on the type of output parameters. In the first case this type redefinition is *contravariant* and in the second *covariant*[4]. When one interface is the same as the other, except that it can redefine contravariantly input parameter types and covariantly output parameter types, this interface conforms to the original one.

As an example of using polymorphic object types let us consider a client of the classes *Account* and *AccountPlus*, a bank which maintains a sequence of accounts and can transfer money from one account to another. The specification of the class *Bank* is presented in Fig. 3.

$Bank$ = **class**
    $accounts :$ **seq of** $\tau(Account)$

    $Transfer\ (from : \tau(Account), to : \tau(Account), s : Currency, d : Date)$ =
        $\{sum > 0\};$
        $|[$ **var** $sender, receiver : Name \bullet$
        $sender := from.Owner(); receiver := to.Owner();$
        $from.Withdraw(s, receiver, d); to.Deposit(s, sender, d)\ ]|$
  end

Fig. 3. Specification of bank using accounts

A subclass of *Bank* can redefine the method *Transfer* with input parameters of types $\tau(Account)^+$ to meet the contravariant constraint. The new bank will be able to work with both *Account* and *AccountPlus* instances in this case, provided that the *accounts* attribute is redefined to be of type **seq of** $\tau(Account)^+$.

4 Class Refinement

When a subclass overrides some methods of its superclass, there are no guarantees that its instances will deliver the same or refined behaviour as the instances of the superclass. Unrestricted method overriding in a subclass can lead to an arbitrary behaviour of its instances. When used in a superclass context, such subclass instances may invalidate their clients. For example, the *Deposit* method of *Account* can be overridden so that the money is, in fact, withdrawn from the account instead of being deposited. Then the owner of the account will actually be at a loss.

Therefore, we would like to ensure that whenever C' is subclassed from C, any behaviour expected from C will necessarily be delivered by C'. For this purpose, we introduce the notion of class refinement between C and C'.

---

[4] For a more extensive explanation of covariance and contravariance see, e.g. [1].

Consider two classes $C = (K, M_1, \ldots, M_n)$ and $C' = (K', M'_1, \ldots, M'_n)$ such that $K : \Psi \mapsto \Sigma$ and $K' : \Psi' \mapsto \Sigma'$ are the corresponding class constructors, and all $M_i : \Sigma \times \Gamma_i \mapsto \Sigma \times \Delta_i$ and $M'_i : \Sigma' \times \Gamma'_i \mapsto \Sigma' \times \Delta'_i$ are the corresponding methods. The input parameter types of the constructors and the methods are either the same or contravariant, such that $\Psi <: \Psi'$ and $\Gamma_i <: \Gamma'_i$. The output parameter types of the methods are either the same or covariant, $\Delta'_i <: \Delta_i$.

We define the refinement of class constructors K and K' with respect to a relation R as follows:

$$K \sqsubseteq_R K' \ \widehat{=} \ \{\pi_\Psi\}; K \ \sqsubseteq \ K'; \{R\} \tag{1}$$

where $R : \Sigma' \leftrightarrow \Sigma$ is an abstraction relation coercing attribute types of C' to those of C, and π_Ψ is the projection relation coercing Ψ' to Ψ.

The refinement of all corresponding methods M_i and M'_i with respect to the relation R is defined as

$$M_i \sqsubseteq_R M'_i \ \widehat{=} \ \{R \times \pi_{\Gamma_i}\}; M_i \ \sqsubseteq \ M'_i; \{R \times \iota_{\Delta'_i}\} \tag{2}$$

Here R is as above, $\pi_{\Gamma_i} : \Gamma'_i \leftrightarrow \Gamma_i$ projects the corresponding input parameters, and $\iota_{\Delta'_i} : \Delta'_i \leftrightarrow \Delta_i$ injects the corresponding output parameters. Obviously, when $\Gamma_i = \Gamma'_i$, the projection relation π_{Γ_i} is taken to be the identity relation Id. The same holds when $\Delta_i = \Delta'_i$, namely, $\iota_{\Delta'_i} = Id$.

Now we can define the class refinement relation as follows.

Definition 1 (Class refinement). The class C is refined by the class C', written $C \sqsubseteq C'$, if for some abstraction relation $R : \tau(C') \leftrightarrow \tau(C)$

1. The constructor of C' refines the constructor of C as defined in (1)
2. Every method of C' refines the corresponding method of C as defined in (2).

The class refinement relation shares the properties of statement refinement and is, thus, reflexive and transitive.

Theorem 2. *Let C, C' and C'' be classes. Then the following properties hold:*

1. $C \sqsubseteq C$
2. $C \sqsubseteq C' \land C' \sqsubseteq C'' \ \Rightarrow \ C \sqsubseteq C''$

Declaring one class as a subclass of another raises the proof obligation that the class refinement relation holds between these classes. This is a semantic constraint that we impose on subclassing to ensure that behaviour of subclasses conforms to the behaviour of their superclasses and, respectively, that the subclasses can be used in the superclass context.

As an example of class refinement consider the classes *Account* and *AccountPlus*. Since the latter is declared as a subclass of the former, we get a proof obligation *Account* $\sqsubseteq$ *AccountPlus*. Under the abstraction relation $R\,(o', b', t')(o, b) \ = \ (o' = o) \land (b' = b)$, where o, b correspond to *owner, balance* of *Account* and o', b', t' correspond to *owner, balance, transactions* of *AccountPlus*, this proof obligation can be discharged, but we omit the proof for the lack of space.

5 Interface Refinement

Subclassing requires that parameter types of a method be the same in the subclass and in the superclass or, at most, subject to contravariance and covariance rules. However, sometimes, a change in user requirements causes interface changes of classes designed as refinements of other classes.

When the new interface is similar to the old one, we can identify abstraction relations coercing the new method parameters to the old ones. For every pair of corresponding methods we need to find two such relations, for input and output parameters. The rôle of these parameter abstraction relations is crucial for interface refinement of classes and for refinement of their clients. Let us first define the interface refinement relation between classes with respect to these relations.

Consider two classes $C = (K, M_1, \ldots, M_n)$ and $C' = (K', M_1', \ldots, M_n')$ with attribute types Σ and Σ' respectively, such that $K : \Psi \mapsto \Sigma$ and $K' : \Psi' \mapsto \Sigma'$ are the class constructors, and all $M_i : \Sigma \times \Gamma_i \mapsto \Sigma \times \Delta_i$ and $M_i' : \Sigma' \times \Gamma_i' \mapsto \Sigma' \times \Delta_i'$ are the corresponding methods.

Let $R : \Sigma' \leftrightarrow \Sigma$ be an abstraction relation coercing attribute types of C' to those of C, and $I_0 : \Psi' \leftrightarrow \Psi$ an abstraction relation coercing the corresponding input parameter types. We define the refinement of class constructors K and K' through R and I_0 as follows:

$$K \sqsubseteq_{R,I_0} K' = \{I_0\}; K \sqsubseteq K'; \{R\} \tag{3}$$

Obviously, (3) is a generalization of (1) with $I_0 = \pi_\Psi$ when the input types are contravariant.

Let $R : \Sigma' \leftrightarrow \Sigma$ be as before, and $I_i : \Gamma_i' \leftrightarrow \Gamma_i$ and $O_i : \Delta_i' \leftrightarrow \Delta_i$ be abstraction relations coercing the corresponding input and output parameter types. We define the refinement of corresponding methods M_i and M_i' through R, I_i and O_i as follows:

$$M_i \sqsubseteq_{R,I_i,O_i} M_i' = \{R \times I_i\}; M_i \sqsubseteq M_i'; \{R \times O_i\} \tag{4}$$

Obviously, (4) is a generalization of (2) with $I_i = \pi_{\Gamma_i}$ when the inputs are contravariant, i.e. $\Gamma_i <: \Gamma_i'$, and with $O_i = \iota_{\Delta_i'}$ when the outputs are covariant, i.e. $\Delta_i' <: \Delta_i$.

Definition 3 (Interface refinement). The class C is interface refined by the class C', written $C \sqsubseteq_{I,O} C'$, with respect to parameter abstraction relations $I = (I_0, I_1, \ldots, I_n)$ and $O = (O_1, \ldots, O_n)$ if for some abstraction relation $R : \tau(C') \leftrightarrow \tau(C)$

1. The constructor of C' refines the constructor of C as defined in (3)
2. Every method of C' refines the corresponding method of C as defined in (4).

Being defined as such, interface refinement of classes is a generalization of class refinement. When every I_i and O_i is the identity relation or the projection and injection relations respectively, interface refinement is specialized to class refinement. The interface refinement relation has the basic properties required of a refinement relation, i.e. reflexivity and transitivity.

Theorem 4. *Let C, C' and C'' be classes. Then the following properties hold:*

1. $C \sqsubseteq_{Id,Id} C$
2. $C \sqsubseteq_{I,O} C' \wedge C' \sqsubseteq_{I',O'} C'' \Rightarrow C \sqsubseteq_{I';I,O';O} C''$

where the relational compositions $I'; I$ and $O'; O$ on tuples of relations are taken elementwise.

Proof. The proof of (1) follows directly from reflexivity of statement refinement by taking the abstraction relation R to be Id. To prove (2) we assume that $C \sqsubseteq_{I,O} C'$ and $C' \sqsubseteq_{I',O'} C''$ hold for abstraction relations R and R' respectively. We then show that methods M_i, M_i' and M_i'' of the corresponding classes C, C' and C'' have the property:

$$\{R \times I_i\}; M_i \sqsubseteq M_i'; \{R \times O_i\} \wedge \{R' \times I_i'\}; M_i' \sqsubseteq M_i''; \{R' \times O_i'\} \Rightarrow$$
$$\{(R'; R) \times (I_i'; I_i)\}; M_i \sqsubseteq M_i''; \{(R'; R) \times (O_i'; O_i)\}$$

The proof of the property is as follows:

$$\{(R'; R) \times (I_i'; I_i)\}; M_i \sqsubseteq M_i''; \{(R'; R) \times (O_i'; O_i)\}$$
$$= \quad \text{lemma } (P; P') \times (Q; Q') = (P \times Q); (P' \times Q')$$
$$\{(R' \times I_i'); (R \times I_i)\}; M_i \sqsubseteq M_i''; \{(R' \times O_i'); (R \times O_i)\}$$
$$= \quad \text{homomorphism of angelic update statement } \{P\}; \{Q\} = \{P; Q\}$$
$$\{R' \times I_i'\}; \{R \times I_i\}; M_i \sqsubseteq M_i''; \{R' \times O_i'\}; \{R \times O_i\}$$
$$\Leftarrow \quad \text{assumption } \{R \times I_i\}; M_i \sqsubseteq M_i'; \{R \times O_i\}$$
$$\{R' \times I_i'\}; M_i'; \{R \times O_i\} \sqsubseteq M_i''; \{R' \times O_i'\}; \{R \times O_i\}$$
$$\Leftarrow \quad \text{assumption } \{R' \times I_i'\}; M_i' \sqsubseteq M_i''; \{R' \times O_i'\}$$
$$M_i''; \{R' \times O_i'\}; \{R \times O_i\} \sqsubseteq M_i''; \{R' \times O_i'\}; \{R \times O_i\}$$
$$= \quad \text{reflexivity of statement refinement}$$
$$true$$

The proof of the corresponding property for constructors is similar. $\square$

Theorem 2 follows by specializing I and O appropriately.

As an example of interface refinement consider our previous specification of transactions, accounts and banks. Suppose that facing the start of the new century, we'd like to change the type of dates so that it's possible to specify a four-digit year:

$$\textbf{type } NewDate = \textbf{array } [1..8] \textbf{ of } Digit$$

Accordingly, we define a new transaction record type *NewTran* which is the same as *Transaction* except that the *date* field is now of type *NewDate*. We construct a new class of accounts using *NewTran* transactions as shown in Fig. 4. We omit specifications of *Owner* and *Balance* methods which are straight-forward, and a specification of *Withdraw*, which is similar to that of *Account* with a local variable of type *NewTran* rather than *Transaction*.

$NDAccount$ = **class**

  $owner : Name, balance : Currency, transactions :$ **seq of** $NewTran$

  $NDAccount\ (name : Name, initSum : Currency)\ =$
    $owner := name; balance := initSum; transactions := \langle\rangle,$

  $Deposit\ (sum : Currency, from : Name, when : NewDate)\ =$
    $\{sum > 0\}; |[\ \mathbf{var}\ t : NewTran \bullet t := (from, owner, sum, when);$
    $transactions := transactions\,\widehat{\ }\,\langle t\rangle; balance := balance + sum\ ]|,$

    $\ldots$

end

Fig. 4. Specification of account based on NewTran

It can be shown that $AccountPlus \quad \sqsubseteq_{I,O} \quad NDAccount$, where $I = (Id \times Id, Id \times Id \times D, Id \times Id \times D, Id, Id)$ and $O = (Id, Id, Id, Id)$. The abstraction relation $D : NewDate \leftrightarrow Date$ is defined so that for constants '1' and '9' of type $Digit$ and for any $d : Date$ and $d' : NewDate$:

$$D(d')(d) \quad = \quad (d'[1..4] = d[1..4]) \wedge (d'[5..6] = \text{`1''9'}) \wedge (d'[7..8] = d[5..6])$$

Now let us consider how parameter abstraction relations can be used for refinement of clients of the interface refined classes. Interface changes in class methods certainly affect clients of the class. Examining the ways the clients get affected allows us to discover the situations when the clients can benefit from the interface refinement of their server classes but need not be changed in any way. We can also establish conditions under which the clients can be systematically changed to use the refined server classes. For every *OldClass* and *NewClass*, such that *NewClass* is designed as a refinement of *OldClass* but specifies a different interface, we distinguish two ways clients of *OldClass* can be affected and changed.

5.1 Implicit Client Refinement

This kind of client refinement happens when it is impractical or impossible to redefine clients of *OldClass*, but is, however, desirable that they work with *NewClass* which may offer a more efficient implementation or improved func-tionality to new clients, like in our example. We can implicitly refine clients by employing a so-called *forwarding scheme* illustrated in Fig. 5 using the OMT notation [23]. In this diagram the link with a triangle relates a superclass with

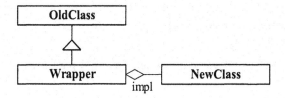

Fig. 5. Illustration of forwarding

a subclass with the superclass above. The link with a diamond shows an aggregation relation, i.e. that *Wrapper* aggregates an instance of *NewClass* in the attribute *impl*.

The idea behind such kind of forwarding is to introduce a subclass of *OldClass*, *Wrapper*, which aggregates an instance of *NewClass* and forwards *OldClass* method calls to *NewClass* through this instance. This has also been identified as a reoccuring design pattern by Gamma et al. in [11]. Clients of *OldClass* can work with *Wrapper*, which is a subclass of *OldClass*, but have all the benefits of working with *NewClass* if

$$OldClass \sqsubseteq Wrapper \text{ and } Wrapper \sqsubseteq_{I,O} NewClass$$

Consider again our example. The client *Bank* wants to use *NDAccount* but cannot do so since the latter specifies the interface different from that specified by *AccountPlus*. We can employ the forwarding scheme by introducing in Fig. 6 a new class *AccountWrapper* which aggregates an instance of *NDAccount* and forwards *AccountPlus* method calls to *NDAccount* via this instance. Specifications of *Withdraw* and *Balance* are straightforward and we omit them for brevity. The function *ToNewDate* (*old* : *Date*) : *NewDate* converts dates from the old format to the new one. In fact, this function can be modeled by the statement $[D^{-1}]$, where $D : NewDate \leftrightarrow Date$ is as before. Provided that the necessary proof obligations are discharged, clients of *AccountPlus*, such as *Bank*, are implicitly refined to work with *NDAccount* via *AccountWrapper*.

$AccountWrapper = $ **subclass of** $AccountPlus$
    $impl : \tau(NDAccount)$

$AccountWrapper (name : Name, initSum : Currency) =$
    $impl.NDAccount(name, initSum),$

$Deposit (sum : Currency, from : Name, when : Date) =$
    $\{sum > 0\}; |[\textbf{ var } d : NewDate \bullet$
    $d := ToNewDate(when); impl.Deposit(sum, from, d)]|,$

$Owner () : Name = res := impl.Owner(),$

    . . .

end

Fig. 6. Specification of wrapper class for implicit interface refinement

---

$Wrapper$ = **subclass of** $OldClass$
  $impl : \tau(NewClass)$

  $Wrapper\ (p : \Psi)$ = $\|[\ \textbf{var}\ e : \Psi' \bullet [e := e' \cdot I_0^{-1}\ p\ e']; impl.NewClass(e)\ ]\|,$
  $Meth_i(g_i : \Gamma_i) : \Delta_i$ =
    $\|[\ \textbf{var}\ c_i : \Gamma_i', d_i : \Delta_i' \bullet [c_i := c_i' \cdot I_i^{-1}\ g_i\ c_i'];$
    $d_i := impl.Meth_i(c_i); \{res := res' \cdot O_i\ d_i\ res'\}\ ]\|,$
  $\ldots$

end

Fig. 7. Schema of wrapper class for implicit interface refinement

Since wrapper classes are of a very specific form, proof obligations can be considerably simplified. Consider a typical wrapper class as given in Fig. 7. The demonic specification statements transform the input parameters of $OldClass$ to the input parameters of $NewClass$ using the corresponding parameter abstraction relations $I_i, i = 0, \ldots, n$. Similarly, the angelic specification statements transform the output parameters of $NewClass$ back to the output parameters of $OldClass$. For the class $Wrapper$ with such a structure, we have the following theorem.

Theorem 5. *For parameter abstraction relations* $I = (I_0, I_1, \ldots, I_n)$ *and* $O = (O_1, \ldots, O_n)$ *the following property holds:*

$$OldClass \sqsubseteq_{I,O} NewClass \quad \Rightarrow \quad OldClass \sqsubseteq Wrapper$$

The form of specification statements gives insight into suitable restrictions when choosing the parameter abstraction relations I_i and O_i. If I_i^{-1} is partial, then the corresponding specification statement can be **magic** and, thus, is not implementable. Hence, I_i has to be surjective, i.e. relate all possible values of the old input parameters to some values of the new input parameters. Likewise, if O_i is non-deterministic (not functional), then the result $res : \Delta_i$ is chosen angelically, and is, therefore, not implementable. Hence O_i must be deterministic (functional), i.e. relate values of the new result parameters $d_i : \Delta_i'$ to at most one value of the old result parameters $res : \Delta_i$.

5.2 Explicit Client Refinement

This kind of client refinement happens quite often in the process of object-oriented development. After $NewClass$ has been developed, using $OldClass$ may become impractical and undesirable, and therefore, a client $OldClient$ of $OldClass$ should be explicitly changed to work with $NewClass$ instead. We can construct $NewClient$ by refinement from $OldClient$. Unfortunately, there are no guarantees that the interface of $NewClient$ will conform to that of $OldClient$. Accordingly, we must consider two cases, when $NewClient$ is a subclass of $OldClient$ and when it is its interface refinement.

When the object type $\tau(OldClass)$ and the types causing the interface change of $OldClass$ to $NewClass$ are not part of $OldClient$ interface, the refinement of $OldClient$, $NewClient$, can be its subclass. In other words, $NewClient$ can specify the interface conforming to that of $OldClient$. Naturally, every class using $OldClient$ can then use $NewClient$ instead and is implicitly refined without respecification.

We feel that there is a strong connection between parameter abstraction relations with respect to which interface refinement is defined and explicit refinement of clients of the refined classes. Investigating how clients can be explicitly refined based on the parameter abstraction relations for the server classes remains the topic of current research.

6 Conclusions

Our approach is suited for documenting, constructing, and verifying different kinds of object-oriented systems because of its uniform way of specifying a program at different abstraction levels and the possibility of stepwise development. We have defined the class refinement relation and the interface refinement relation which allow a developer to construct extensible object-oriented programs from specifications and assure reliability of the final program.

Our model of classes, subclassing, and subtyping polymorphism can be used to reason about the meaning of programs constructed using the separate subclassing and interface inheritance hierarchies, like in Java [13], Sather [26], and some other languages. In that approach interface inheritance is the basis for subtyping polymorphism, whereas subclassing is used only for implementation reuse. By associating a specification class with every interface type, we can reason about the behaviour of objects having this interface. All classes claiming to implement a certain interface must refine its specification class. Subclassing, on the other hand, does not, in general, require establishing class refinement between the superclass and the subclass.

For simplicity we consider only single inheritance, but multiple inheritance does not introduce much complication. With a suitable mechanism for resolving clashes in method names, multiple inheritance has the same semantics as we give for single inheritance. Namely, ensuring that a subclass D preserves behaviour of all its declared superclasses $C_1, \ldots, C_n$ requires proving class refinements $C_1 \sqsubseteq D, \ldots, C_n \sqsubseteq D$ for every corresponding superclass-subclass pair.

Using formal specification and verification is especially important for open systems, such as object-oriented frameworks and component-based systems. Frameworks incorporate a reusable design for a specific class of software and dictate a particular architecture of potential applications. When building an application, the user needs to customize framework classes to specific needs of this application. To do so, he must understand the message flow in the framework and the relationship among the framework classes. The intrinsic feature of open component-based systems is a late integration phase, meaning that components are developed by different manufacturers and then integrated together by their users.

A fine-grained specification can accurately describe the fixed behaviour of classes. In this respect, such a specification is a perfect documentation of a framework or a component, because the user does not have to decipher ambiguous, incomplete, and often outdated verbal descriptions. Neither is it necessary to confront the bulk of source code to gain a complete understanding of the system behaviour. The programming notation we use allows the developer to abstract from implementation details and specify classes with abstract state space and non-deterministic behaviour of methods, expressing only the necessary functionality. Moreover, a certain implementation can be a commercial secret, whereas a concise and complete specification distributed instead of source code enables the user to understand the functionality and protects corporate interests.

Formal verification in the form of establishing a class refinement relation between specifications and their implementations guarantees that any behaviour expected from the specifications will be delivered by the implementations.

It has been acknowledged that frameworks are usually developed using a spiral model that takes feedback from actual use of the framework into account. It can be expected that such development iterations may result in an interface change of some classes. In this case, interface refinement can be used to verify behavioural compatibility of the corresponding classes and the rules for interface refinement of clients can be used to refine the whole framework.

Acknowledgments

We would like to thank Ralph Back for a number of fruitful discussions and Martin Büchi for useful comments.

References

1. M. Abadi and L. Cardelli. *A Theory of Objects*. Springer-Verlag, 1996.
2. M. Abadi and K. R. M. Leino. A logic of object-oriented programs. In *Theory and Practice of Software Development: Proceedings / TAPSOFT '97*, volume LNCS 1214, pages 682–696. Springer, April 1997.
3. P. America. Designing an object-oriented programming language with behavioral subtyping. In J.W. de Bakker, W. P. de Roever, and G. Rozenberg, editors, *Foundations of Object-Oriented Languages, REX School/Workshop*, volume LNCS 489, pages 60–90, New York, N.Y., 1991. Springer-Verlag.
4. R. J. R. Back. *Correctness Preserving Program Refinements: Proof Theory and Applications*, volume 131 of *Mathematical Center Tracts*. Mathematical Centre, Amsterdam, 1980.
5. R. J. R. Back. Changing data representation in the refinement calculus. In *21st Hawaii International Conference on System Sciences*. IEEE, January 1989.
6. R. J. R. Back and J. von Wright. Refinement calculus I: Sequential nondeterministic programs. In W. P. deRoever J. W. deBakker and G. Rozenberg, editors, *Stepwise Refinement of Distributed Systems*, pages 42–66. Springer-Verlag, 1990.

7. R.J.R. Back and M.J. Butler. Exploring summation and product operators in the refinement calculus. In B. Möller, editor, *Mathematics of Program Construction, 1995*, volume LNCS 947. Springer-Verlag, 1995.

8. M. Broy. (Inter-)Action Refinement: The Easy Way. In M. Broy, editor, *Program Design Calculi*, pages 121–158, Berlin Heidelberg, 1993. Springer-Verlag.

9. L. Cardelli and P. Wegner. On understanding types, data abstraction, and polymorphism. *ACM Computing Surveys*, 17(4):471–522, 1985.

10. K. K. Dhara and G. T. Leavens. Forcing behavioral subtyping through specification inheritance. In *Proceedings of the 18th International Conference on Software Engineering*, pages 258–267, Berlin, Germany, 1996.

11. E. Gamma, R. Helm, R. Johnson, and J. Vlissides. *Design Patterns: Elements of Reusable Object-Oriented Software*. Professional Computing Series. Addison-Wesley, 1995.

12. P.H. Gardiner and C.C. Morgan. Data refinement of predicate transformers. *Theoretical Computer Science*, 87(1):143–162, 1991.

13. J. Gosling, B. Joy, and G. Steele. *The Java Language Specification*. Sun Microsystems, Mountain View, 1996.

14. J. He, C. A. R. Hoare, and J. W. Sanders. Data refinement refined. In B. Robinet and R. Wilhelm, editors, *European Symposium on Programming*, volume LNCS 213. Springer-Verlag, 1986.

15. C. A. R. Hoare. Proofs of correctness of data representation. *Acta Informatica*, 1(4):271–281, 1972.

16. K. Lano and H. Haughton. Reasoning and refinement in object-oriented specification languages. In O. Lehrmann Madsen, editor, *European Conference on Object-Oriented Programming '92*, volume LNCS 615. Springer-Verlag, 1992.

17. K. Lano and H. Haughton. *Object-Oriented Specification Case Studies*. Prentice-Hall, New York, 1994.

18. B. Liskov and J. M. Wing. A behavioral notion of subtyping. *ACM Transactions on Programming Languages and Systems*, 16(6):1811–1841, 1994.

19. C. C. Morgan. Data refinement by miracles. *Information Processing Letters*, 26:243–246, 1988.

20. C. C. Morgan. *Programming from Specifications*. Prentice-Hall, 1990.

21. J. M. Morris. A theoretical basis for stepwise refinement and the programming calculus. *Science of Computer Programming*, 9:287–306, 1987.

22. D. A. Naumann. Predicate transformer semantics of an Oberon-like language. In Ernst-R. Olderog, editor, *Programming Concepts, Methods and Calculi*, pages 460–480. International Federation for Information Processing, 1994.

23. J. Rumbaugh, M. Blaha, W. Premerlani, F. Eddy, and W. Lorensen. *Object-Oriented Modelling and Design*. Prentice Hall, Englewood Cliffs, 1991.

24. E. Sekerinski. *Verfeinerung in der Objektorientierten Programmkonstruktion*. Dissertation, Universität Karlsruhe, 1994.

25. E. Sekerinski. A type-theoretic basis for an object-oriented refinement calculus. In S.J. Goldsack and S.J.H. Kent, editors, *Formal Methods and Object Technology*. Springer-Verlag, 1996.

26. C. A. Szyperski, S. Omohundro, and S. Murer. Engineering a programming language – the type and class system of Sather. In *Proceedings, First Intl Conference on Programming Languages and System Architectures*, volume LNCS 782, Zurich, Switzerland, 1994. Springer.

Formalizing Requirements for Distributed Systems with Trace Diagrams[*]

Stephan Kleuker

University of Oldenburg - FB Informatik
P.O. Box 2503, 26111 Oldenburg, Germany
email: kleuker@informatik.uni-oldenburg.de

Abstract. Graphical formalisms can be useful to bridge the gap between informal requirements written by application experts and formal requirements used by formal methods experts. *Trace diagrams* are a new graphical formalism that was developed during several case studies in the telecommunications area to express relations between allowed and disallowed sequences of communications. This paper introduces the graphical and textual syntax as well as its formal semantics. It is shown that trace diagrams can easily be extended at the informal and formal level to serve other applications.

1 Introduction

The research project *Provably Correct Communication Networks* — abbreviated as Co-CoN — was carried out from 1993 to 1996 in close cooperation between Philips Research Laboratories Aachen and the Department of Computer Science at the University of Oldenburg. The overall goal of this project was to improve the software quality of future communication systems by the application of formal methods. More precisely, the aim of the project CoCoN was to support a stepwise and verified development of communication systems from the requirement phase over the specification phase to an implementation. Our method is based on results of the ESPRIT Basic Research Action ProCoS [4, 16, 27, 28] (Provably Correct Systems). ProCoS was a wide-spectrum verification project where embedded communicating systems are studied at various levels of abstraction ranging from requirements' capture over specification language and programming language down to the machine language. It emphasizes a constructive approach to correctness, using stepwise transformations between specifications, designs, programs, compilers, and hardware.

The ideas of ProCoS are extended in CoCoN with a method for the development of *extensible* systems [19, 22]. Extensibility means that *new functionality* can be added step by step to an existing system. In each step it is important to fix a new set of requirements that have to be fulfilled by the final result of the step. The task of finding requirements, so called *requirements engineering* is the most difficult part in the application of formal methods because the gap between the informal and the formal world has to be closed at this point. The case studies of CoCoN come from different telecommunication areas (Intelligent Network, Private Alternating Branch Exchange, multiuser multimedia systems), with the general property that the set of usable communications

---

[*] This research was supported by the Leibniz Programme of the Deutsche Forschungsgemeinschaft (DFG) under grant No. Ol 98/1-1

between the components is fixed and that an informal description of the protocols exists. Therefore requirements have to be formalized which describe relations between sequences of communications (so called *traces*). We choose trace logic [32] as our requirement language (see section 4) because the logic deals directly with communications and sequences thereof. Nevertheless it is a problem to come to an agreement with engineers without detailed knowledge of logic that requirements formalized in trace logic are indeed a formalization of informal requirements. A solution is to find a language in-between that fits both the needs of engineers and experts in formal methods. Such a graphical language is presented with *trace diagrams* (abbreviated as *TrDs*) in this paper.

Graphical visualisation of requirements is also applied in several other areas, e.g. timing diagrams are nowadays successfully applied in the development of hardware. The formalization and application of such diagrams is described e.g. in [2, 5]. Some of these diagrams can be formalized in terms of temporal logic formulas. Temporal logics allow also the reasoning about properties of protocols and have several useful graphical representations. The supported logics range from CTL (e.g. [30]) to interval logics (e.g. [10, 29]) and the Duration Calculus [9].

The graphical support for the formalization of requirements for already existing protocols is not studied in such detail so far. Although the approaches mentioned before can be applied, sometimes a tricky and not self-explaining encoding of communications as properties is needed. Standardisation Committees use *Message Sequence Charts* [15, 26] and *Time Sequence Diagrams* [14] to describe allowed sequences of standardized protocols. An extension of these languages is under development, but nowadays they can only describe examples of allowed traces. The approach presented in this paper allows formal reasoning about the desired relation between arbitrary traces.

The case studies in CoCoN have shown that requirements usually have the form *"if something happens then something else should/ should not have happened or has to /has not to happen"*. Therefore logical implication is the most important constructor in the presented approach. It turns out that *safety* (a possible trace fulfils certain conditions) and *future* (a trace can/must follow after an executed trace) requirements are particularly important in practice. *TrDs* are well suited to support these features. Although this approach focuses on distributed systems with synchronous communication (sender and receiver must execute a common communication together) it is discussed in section 6 that also requirements for asynchronous systems can be supported. Moreover it is shown that *TrDs* can be structured such that complex *TrDs* are a composition of several auxiliary diagrams which can also be reused in other *TrDs*.

One important property that all visual formalisms should fulfil is *intuitive power*. Intuitive power means that it should be possible for non-experts after a short introduction to understand most requirements without further information. Intuitive power is reached with *TrDs* by the approach that the number of used symbols is kept as small as possible without loosing too much expressive power.

The next section presents some examples for *TrDs*. Section 3 introduces a textual representation of *TrDs* which is used in the following two sections to define a formal semantics. Possible simplifications and extensions enhancing the practicality are discussed in section 6. A case study from an application area other then telecommunications systems is sketched in section 7. Section 8 adds some short remarks w.r.t. a relation to other logics than trace logic. We conclude with some further remarks at the end of this paper.

2 Graphical representation of typical requirements

The first part of this section presents the general structure of *TrDs* and the second part explains the details with some examples.

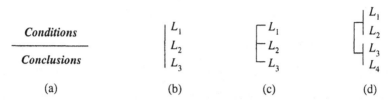

Fig. 1. Different elements of *TrDs*

Figure 1(a) shows the general structure of *TrDs*. A long horizontal line separates the *conditions* above the line and the *conclusions* below the line. A requirement which is represented as a *TrD* is fulfilled by a system if it always holds for the system that the conditions imply the conclusions. Conditions and conclusions are described as several *lines* which are composed by symbols for conjunction and disjunction. A vertical line (see figure 1(b)) is used to express conjunction (i.e. $L_1 \wedge L_2 \wedge L_3$) and a square bracket (in general a "comb", see figure 1(c)) is used to express disjunction (i.e. $L_1 \vee L_2 \vee L_3$). Therefore, figure 1(d) represents $(L_1 \wedge L_2) \vee (L_3 \wedge L_4)$. The possible structures of the lines are now explained with some examples.

The following informal requirements and their graphical representation are motivated by a case study in which among other things a protocol for a multiuser multimedia system [20, 21] was formalized. Several parts of the protocol are simplified in this text to avoid the presentation of unnecessary details of the formalized protocol. It is assumed that several sites are connected with a network such that arbitrary subsets of sites can be connected in a conference. Only sites that have joined the conference can send and receive data.

Four types of messages are used in general to exchange informations. Let us assume that an information shall be transmitted from a site A to a site B. Site A initiates the transmission with a request message to the network (the suffix _rq is used to identify requests), the message is transmitted as an indication (_id) to B. The receiver B answers with a response message (_rp) to the network which is transmitted as a final confirm message (_cf) to A.

A first typical informal requirement is: If a sender T_i sends a value msg to a site T_j and gets the confirm message that the transmission is successful then it is guaranteed that in-between these two communications T_j has received the value msg and has answered with a positive response communication.

It follows with a more detailed analysis of the informal text and the application that this requirement contains the additional assumption that the confirm message belongs to the last transmitted value and that no other request to the same site was sent between the mentioned request and confirm.

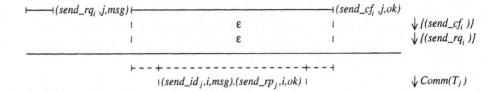

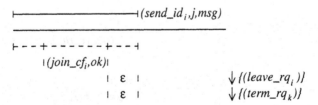

Fig. 2. Graphical representation of a requirement with a trace diagram

The graphical representation of this informal requirement is given in figure 2. The first line of the *TrD* denotes that at first an arbitrary sequence of communications happens which is presented as a simple horizontal line (⊢———⊣). This sequence is followed by a $(send\_rq_i, j, msg)$ communication.[1] Then, a second arbitrary sequence of communications is followed by a confirmation communication $send\_cf_i$.

The second line denotes that the second arbitrary sequence is a member of the language $\{\varepsilon\}$ (ε denotes the empty sequence) when the second arbitrary sequence is projected (by the projection operator $\downarrow$) onto the set $\{send\_cf_i\}$. Similarly, the third line denotes that there is no communication $send\_rq_i$ in the arbitrary sequence. In general, any formal language over the alphabet of all possible communications of the system can replace ε in other *TrDs*. The right margin is used to describe restrictions w.r.t. the observed alphabet.

It can be summarized that the first three lines describe that a request is followed by a confirm and that there was no confirm and no request in-between these communications. The line below the long horizontal line denotes that there exists a splitting of the second arbitrary trace into three parts. Dashed horizontal lines (⊢ - - ⊣) are used in general for existential quantification. The last line formalizes that the middle part is the sequence $send\_id_j.send\_rp_j$ w.r.t. all communications that belong to T_j (denoted by the set $Comm(T_j)$). There are no restrictions w.r.t. the other parts of the trace. All lines above the long horizontal line and all lines below are combined by conjunctions which is the default combination of lines.

The second informal requirement is that if a site T_i gets a message from a conference member then T_i has joined the conference before. The graphical representation of this requirement is given with a *TrD* in figure 3.

$$\text{⊢————————⊣}(send\_id_i, j, msg)$$

$$\text{⊢ - - + - - - - - - + - - ⊣}$$
$$|(join\_cf_i, ok)|$$
$$| \quad \varepsilon \quad | \qquad\qquad \downarrow \{(leave\_rq_i)\}$$
$$| \quad \varepsilon \quad | \qquad\qquad \downarrow \{(term\_rq_k)\}$$

Fig. 3. An information can only be received by members of a conference

The first line denotes that T_i receives a message after an arbitrary sequence of com-

---

[1] Each communication has the form *(name, list of parameters)*, i.e. here a $send\_rq_i$ is sent by the site T_i with parameters j and msg. If a communication has no parameters then the surrounding brackets can be omitted.

munications. The second part under the long horizontal line ensures that the sequence can be divided in three parts such that T_i has joined the conference ($join\_cf_i$) in the second part, that T_i has not left the conference ($leave\_rq_i$) in the third part, and that the conference is not terminated ($term\_rq_k$) by the known fixed initiator T_k of this conference in the third part. There is no restriction w.r.t. the set of relevant communications in the line with $join\_cf_i$ on the right margin because all communications are relevant for this line.

Note that some simplifications for the graphical representation and some remarks w.r.t. the handling of indices and parameters are added in section 6.

The requirements presented so far are safety requirements. The following two examples show that it is also possible to present requirements for possible communications in the future with *TrDs*. The next informal requirement is that if a site T_i asks to join a conference then the next communications w.r.t. T_i has to be either a message that it is allowed to join or that it is denied or that the conference is terminated.

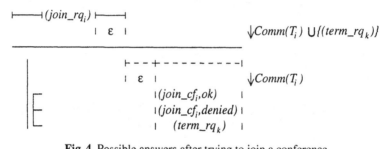

Fig. 4. Possible answers after trying to join a conference

The first two lines denote that T_i asks to join the conference and that T_i waits, i.e. does not participate in any other communication (other processes can continue). The other lines denote that then there exists an extension of the trace that w.r.t. T_i the next communication is either ($join\_cf_i$, ok) or ($join\_cf_i$, $denied$) or ($term\_rq_k$).

The last informal requirement is that whenever a site is a member of a conference then the site can decide at any time to leave the conference or the conference is terminated by the initiator.

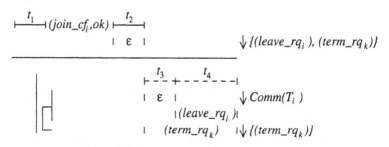

Fig. 5. A conference can be left at any time

The first two lines of the *TrD* in figure 5 denote that T_i has joined the conference and not left the conference afterwards and that the conference is not terminated. The four lines below the long horizontal line denote that for such a sequence there exists a possible extension such that T_i can transmit a *leave_rq$_i$* without participating in any further communication. The last line denotes the alternative that the conference is terminated by the initiator.

Each sequence is annotated in figure 5 with a unique name, a so called *trace variable*. These annotations are used in the following section to come to a textual representation of *TrDs*. A *TrD* without annotations (as in figures 2, 3, 4) is called a *simple TrD*, the *TrD* in figure 5 is called an *annotated TrD*. Annotations are usually not necessary in the process of formalizing informal requirements, but they are needed in the formalization of the graphical representation.

3 Textual syntax of trace diagrams

A textual representation of a graphical entity can be useful in several ways, e.g. it is easier to store, transmit and manipulate simple ASCII files in computers, and a formal semantics can be based on the textual syntax.

The textual representation of trace diagrams uses the following idea. Each line of the annotated *TrD* is translated into one text line. We refer to each initial and final point of a sequence by so called *selectors*, i.e. the selector $\mathbf{b}(t_i)$ denotes the initial point and $\mathbf{e}(t_i)$ the final point for a trace t_i . The order of the lines is recorded using strictly increasing line numbers for each line. To describe the logical combination of the lines we add two "link" lines at the end of the textual representation.

Therefore each *TrD* can be described by the following BNF-rules (the non-terminal $<LINK>$ is decorated with two different subscripts in the clause (1) such that the occurrences can be distinguished afterwards):

(1) $<TrD>$ ::= $<INIT>$ $<COND>^*$ **then** $<CONCL>$ $<LINK_1>$ $<LINK_2>$
(2) $<INIT>$::= $< LN >$**: trvars:** $<LIST\_TVARS>$ **seq:** $<TRACESEQ>$
(3) $<LN>$::= $<line\_number>$
(4) $<LIST\_TVARS>$::= $<TRACEVAR>$**,** $<LIST\_TVARS>$ | $<TRACEVAR>$
(5) $<TRACEVAR>$::= t_i
(6) $<TRACESEQ>$::= $<TRACEVAR>$ | $<COMM>$
        | $<TRACEVAR>$**.**$<TRACESEQ>$ | $<COMM>$**.**$<TRACESEQ>$
(7) $<COMM>$::= c_j
(8) $<COND>$::= $<LN>$**:** $<QUANTIFIER>$ $<SEL1>$**.**$<SEL2>$**=**$<LIST\_TVARS>$
        | $<LN>$**:** $<SEL1>$**.**$<SEL2>$ **in** $<language>$ **proj:** $<alphabet>$
(9) $<QUANTIFIER>$::= **forall** | **exists**
(10) $<SEL1>$::= $\mathbf{b}($$<TRACEVAR>$$)$
(11) $<SEL2>$::= $\mathbf{e}($$<TRACEVAR>$$)$
(12) $<CONCL>$ ::= $<LN>$**:** $<QUANTIFIER>$ **new:** $<LIST\_TVARS>$ $<COND>^+$
        | $<COND>^+$
(13) $<LINK>$::= $<LN>$ **or** $<LINK>$ | $<LN>$ **and** $<LINK>$ | $($$<LINK>$$)$ | $<LN>$

Figure 6 shows the relation between the graphical representation and the non-terminals mentioned in clause (1) above. The *TrD* in figure 5 has the following textual representation.

Fig. 6. Relation between graphical and textual representation

```
1: trvars: t_1,t_2 seq: t_1.(join_cf_i,ok).t_2
2: b(t_2).e(t_2) in {eps} proj:{(leave_rq_i), (term_rq_k)}
then
3: exists new:t_3,t_4
4: b(t_3).e(t_3) in {eps} proj:Comm(T_i)
5: b(t_4).e(t_4) in {(leave_rq_i)} proj:all
6: b(t_3).e(t_4) in {(term_rq_k)} proj:{(term_rq_k)}
1 and 2
3 and ((4 and 5) or 6)
```

There are several non-contextfree conditions that have to be fulfilled by a *TrD*, the most important ones are mentioned in the following informal explanations. Clause (1) of the BNF-grammar presents the general structure of a *TrD*. A special initial line is followed by an arbitrary number of additional conditions. The keyword **then** denotes the long horizontal line which is followed by the conclusions that have to hold. The last two parts denote the combination of the lines before and after the **then**. Clause (2) describes the typical structure of a first line of a *TrD*. Several trace variables are declared and it is possible that in-between these trace variables several communications (see clauses (6) and (7)) can occur (after the keyword **seq**). Note that each other line than the last two lines and the **then**-line begins with a *line number* which is a natural number. The line numbers are unique and increasing in the *TrD*.

A condition can have the following form. Either it denotes that a sequence of trace variables is split into another one. Then, the first selector denotes the initial point for the split sequence and the second selector denotes the final point. It is assumed that trace variables mentioned in the selectors in the clauses (10) and (11) must be introduced before they are used in another line of the *TrD*. The sequence of the new trace variables follows after the assignment symbol. Or a condition claims that a sequence of trace variables (fixed by **b(t_i).e(t_i)**) which is projected onto a certain alphabet (**proj:**) shall be an element of a certain language.

The conclusion in clause (12) can have another form to describe future requirements. The keyword **new** is used to declare that the subsequent list of trace variables follows after the sequence described in clause (2). Only one future extension is allowed in this version. A more general version with more future properties is omitted here because otherwise several technical details have to be formalized in the following semantics.

Clause (13) is used to describe the combination of the numbered lines. It is required that each line number is used exactly once in one of the two *<LINK>* lines. Line numbers which appear before the **then** are used in the first $<LINK_1>$ part of clause (1), the others are used in the second $<LINK_2>$ part.

A grammar representing the languages mentioned in clause (8) is omitted here because any desired presentation can be chosen. One solution is a restriction to regular languages represented by regular expressions.

We can summarize that *four* different kinds of lines are possible in the textual representation. The lines 1, 2 and 3 show examples for three different cases. The missing case is the possibility to split a sequence of traces into another sequence of traces. Such a splitting appears e.g. in the textual representation of the *TrD* in figure 3 and has the following form:

$$2: \textbf{exists } \mathtt{b(t\_1).e(t\_1)} = \mathtt{t\_2,t\_3,t\_4}$$

An important question is whether it is also possible to translate the textual representation back into its graphical form. The answer is yes although two problems occur. The first problem is that there are several textual representations for one *TrD*. One example is the part of a *TrD* in figure 7(a). The last line of the diagram can either be presented as **forall** $\mathtt{b(t\_1).e(t\_1)=t\_4,t\_5,t\_6}$ or as **forall** $\mathtt{b(t\_2).e(t\_3)=t\_4,t\_5,t\_6}$. Nevertheless this is no problem because it can be derived from the context that e.g. $\mathtt{e(t\_1)}$ and $\mathtt{e(t\_3)}$ denote the same point.

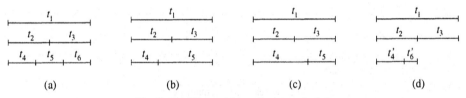

Fig. 7. Possible problems for a translation

A more serious problem which is also related to the informal understanding of *TrDs* is that the *TrDs* in figure 7(b) and (c) are equivalent although (b) suggests that the point between t_4 and t_5 is before the point between t_2 and t_3 and (c) suggests the other order of the points. The problem is that *TrDs* do not define any relation between intermediate points for different lines. If it is desired that the point between t_4 and t_5 is before the point between t_2 and t_3 as suggested in (b) then it is possible to add an auxiliary trace variable as shown in (d) and to substitute t_5 in (b) with $t_6'.t_3$ in the other parts. A strict "before" can be expressed with the additional condition $t_6' \neq \varepsilon$.

The next question that has to be answered is: Which kinds of properties *cannot* be expressed with *TrDs*? As mentioned before, *TrDs* focus on requirements of the form "if something then something". Therefore requirements of other forms have to be translated into this form. Another problem is that it is not allowed to express properties between trace variables that are declared in a *TrD* before. Formulas like $t_1 = t_2 \lor t_1 = t_3$ or $t_1 \leq t_2$ (t_1 is a prefix of t_2) are disallowed so far, because they were not needed in our case studies. An extension of the formalism to allow such formulas is possible but several additional notations must be declared such that some of the intuitive power gets lost. Another restriction is that only finite traces are taken into account. Therefore arbitrary liveness requirements in the sense of [1] like "a *c*-communication eventually happens" cannot be expressed (see also the short discussion in section 8). Nevertheless our case studies have shown that this form of liveness requirements is usually not needed or can be weakened such that they can be expressed in trace logic.

4   A short introduction to trace logic

The informal semantics presented so far can be formalized in several logics. Particularly appropriate is trace logic [32] because it deals directly with sequences of communications and their relations. This section is a short introduction into trace logic and shows how trace logic can be used as a requirement language for distributed systems.

The *semantics* of a system can be formalized by a logical predicate with suitable free variables describing its observable behaviour [11, 12]. If concrete values are substituted for the variables then the logical predicate can be evaluated to *true* or *false*. Only if the result is *true* these values describe a desired (allowed) behaviour. We are interested in all possible traces of a system. Therefore, its semantics is formalized by a predicate with one free variable tr ranging over traces. The resulting situation is sketched in figure 8.

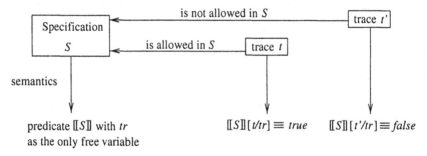

Fig. 8. predicative semantics

For a system S let $[\![S]\!]$ denote its semantics which is a trace logic predicate. For example, if S can do a communication a we can observe the empty trace ε and a trace where a has been performed. As a predicate:

$$[\![S]\!] \equiv (tr = \varepsilon \ \vee \ tr = a)$$

The formal proof that the communication a can happen is:

$$[\![S]\!][a/tr] \equiv (tr = \epsilon \ \vee \ tr = a)[a/tr]$$
$$\equiv a = \varepsilon \vee a = a \ \equiv \ false \vee true \ \equiv \ true$$

(Here $[a/tr]$ denotes the substitution of a for tr in the predicate, letters $tr, t, t_1, \ldots$ always denote trace variables, and $\equiv$ denotes logical equivalence).

It is also possible to formalize requirements for systems in trace logic. Then we additionally employ a second-order free variable X ranging over simple trace predicates with tr as the only free variable. X stands for the unknown system for which we are to specify the requirements for its traces.

Requirements are of the form "if some communications $c_1, \ldots, c_n$ happen in a special order (possibly interrupted by sequences $t_1, \ldots, t_{n+1}$ of other communications) then these sequences fulfil certain conditions". It is formalized as: if a trace of the form $t_1.c_1.t_2.c_2.\ldots.c_n.t_{n+1}$ is possible in a system and the *side_conditions* are fulfilled then the *desired_behaviour* is guaranteed. The trace variables $t_{n+2}, \ldots t_{n+l}$ which are used in the following formalization are introduced to describe possible splittings of the other trace variables. It has been shown in several case studies in CoCoN that many requirements for telecommunication systems can be expressed in this way [20].

Definition (syntax of basic trace logic predicates): Let Δ be a finite set of communications and $c_1, \ldots, c_n \in \Delta \cup \{\varepsilon\}$. A formal *basic requirement in trace logic* has the following form ($n \geq 0$):

$$\forall t_1, \ldots, t_{n+1} \ \forall t_{n+2}, \ldots, t_{n+k} \ \exists t_{n+k+1}, \ldots, t_{n+\ell} \bullet$$
$$((X[t_1.c_1.t_2.c_2.\ldots.c_n.t_{n+1}/tr] \wedge side\_conditions(t_1, \ldots, t_{n+\ell}))$$
$$\rightarrow \ desired\_behaviour(t_1, \ldots, t_{n+\ell}))$$

The predicates *side_conditions* and *desired_behaviour* are of the form P described by the following BNF-grammar:

$$< P > ::= < P_1 > \wedge < P_2 > \ | \ \neg < P_1 > \ | \ (< P_1 >) \ | \ true$$
$$| \ t_{p_1}.\ldots.t_{p_q} = t_{i_1}.\ldots.t_{i_m} \ | \ t_i \in < L > \quad (1 \leq i \leq n + \ell)$$

where $k \geq 1$, $\ell \geq k$, $< L >$ can be any subset of Δ^*, $free(P) \subseteq \{t_1, t_2, \ldots, t_{n+\ell}\}$ (*free* denotes the set of free variables of a predicate) and for the set of equations $t_{p_1}.\ldots.t_{p_q} = t_{i_1}.\ldots.t_{i_m}$ it holds that each index j with $1 \leq j \leq n + 1$ never appears on the right-hand side and each index j with $n + 2 \leq j \leq n + l$ appears at least once on the right-hand side, i.e. $t_1 = t_2.t_3 \wedge t_2 = t_3$ is disallowed. $\square$

Remarks: Disjunction can be expressed in terms of negation and conjunction. Other operators that can be used and are equivalent to formulae which can be described by the above BNF-grammar are: the projection operator $\cdot \downarrow \cdot$ ($t \downarrow A \in L \equiv t \in L_1$, with $A \subseteq \Delta^*$ and $L_1 = \{w \in \Delta^* | w \downarrow A \in L\}$), the equality of a trace and a word ($t = w \equiv t \in \{w\}$, with $w \in \Delta^*$), the relation of the length of a trace ($| \cdot |$ denotes this length) and a constant $n \in I\!N$ ($|t| \diamond n \equiv t \in \{w \in \Delta^* | \ |w| \diamond n\}$, with $\diamond \in \{<, \leq, =, \geq, >\}$). $\square$

An example for a requirement is:

$$Req \equiv \forall t_1, t_2 \bullet X[t_1.a.t_2/tr] \rightarrow t_1 = \varepsilon$$

It formalizes that if a communication a is possible in the system then it is the first communication.

A requirement Req is fulfilled by a specification S iff S is substituted for X in the requirement ($Req[S/X]$) and the resulting trace predicate is a tautology. E.g.:

$$Req[S/X] \equiv \forall t_1, t_2 \bullet ((tr = \varepsilon \vee tr = a)[t_1.a.t_2/tr] \rightarrow t_1 = \varepsilon)$$
$$\equiv \forall t_1, t_2 \bullet ((t_1.a.t_2 = \varepsilon \vee t_1.a.t_2 = a) \rightarrow t_1 = \varepsilon)$$
$$\equiv \forall t_1, t_2 \bullet (t_1.a.t_2 = a \rightarrow t_1 = \varepsilon)$$
$$\equiv t_1 = \varepsilon \wedge t_2 = \varepsilon \wedge t_1.a.t_2 = a \rightarrow t_1 = \varepsilon$$
$$\equiv true \qquad \square$$

This is a very detailed version of a proof. For an experienced specifier it is possible to shorten such a proof by summarizing steps.

The term *basic* is used in the previous definition because it is not possible to express future requirements with the formulas introduced so far. Nevertheless, the *desired_behaviour* can be extended in such a way that here the free variable X occurs again. Then, it is possible to describe requirements of the form "if a communication c

happens then is guaranteed that a communication u can happen later". The formal trace requirement is:

$$\forall t_1, t_2 \bullet \; X[t_1.c.t_2/tr] \to (\exists t_3 \bullet X[t_1.c.t_2.t_3/tr] \wedge t_3 \downarrow \{u\} \neq \varepsilon)$$

5   Semantics of trace diagrams

The semantics of a *TrD* is defined for its textual representation as a translation into a trace logic formula. Each *TrD* is translated line by line by the following algorithm. Let $\mathcal{M}$ denote the mapping from textual *TrDs* to trace logic formulas. First, the general structure of the formula can be given by the following function as a translation of clause (1) (non-terminals are now place-holders for the concrete derived parts of the formula, **and** is replaced by $\wedge$, **or** is replaced by $\vee$):

$$\mathcal{M}[\![< TrD >]\!] = \mathcal{Q} \bullet \; (< LINK_1 > \to (\mathcal{R} \bullet (< LINK_2 >)))$$

The symbols $\mathcal{Q}$ and $\mathcal{R}$ are special place-holders for the quantification of the variables which are replaced by the following translations of the lines. Each line number in the concrete *LINK*-expressions is translated now always using the line with the smallest not translated line number so far. It is shown for each of the possible kinds of lines described in the BNF-grammar in which way the line number is substituted with a formula and what changes happen to $\mathcal{Q}$ and $\mathcal{R}$, i.e. several context sensitive rules are presented now. The first part of the rule states the syntax of the examined line, the other parts denote the substitutions for the place-holders $\mathcal{Q}$ and $\mathcal{R}$ and for the line number in the formula.

[1] *<LN>*: **trvars**: *<LIST_TVARS>* **seq**: *<TRACESEQ>*
leads to the following substitutions:

$\qquad \mathcal{Q} \rightsquigarrow \forall <LIST\_TVARS> \mathcal{Q}$ $\qquad\qquad$ ($\rightsquigarrow$ denotes "is exchanged with")
$\qquad <LN> \rightsquigarrow X[<TRACESEQ>/tr]$
$\qquad \mathcal{R} \rightsquigarrow \mathcal{R}$

An auxiliary variable *seq* gets the value *<TRACESEQ>*. The variable is used to store the initial trace sequence for possible extensions of the sequence in the **then**-part.

[2] *<LN>*: *<QUANTIFIER>* *<SEL1>* . *<SEL2>* = *<LIST_TVARS>*
with $<LN> \in lines(< LINK_1 >)$ ($lines(l)$ denote the set of line numbers appearing in l)

leads to the following substitutions:

$\qquad \mathcal{Q} \rightsquigarrow \exists <LIST\_TVARS> \mathcal{Q}$ $\qquad$ if $<QUANTIFIER>=$**forall**[2]
$\qquad \mathcal{Q} \rightsquigarrow \forall <LIST\_TVARS> \mathcal{Q}$ $\qquad$ if $<QUANTIFIER>=$**exists**
$\qquad <LN> \rightsquigarrow sequence(<SEL1.SEL2>) = \rho(<LIST\_TVARS>)$
$\qquad \mathcal{R} \rightsquigarrow \mathcal{R}$

The function $sequence(\cdot)$ calculates the sequence of trace variables mentioned in the

---

[2] Note that $\forall x \bullet ((\exists y \bullet P(x,y)) \to (\forall z \bullet Q(x,z))) \equiv \forall x, y \bullet (P(x,y) \to (\forall z \bullet Q(x,z))$ if y is not free in Q.

$<SEL1>$ and $<SEL2>$ part. The calculation uses the previous lines of the *TrD* as additional input. The function $\rho(\cdot)$ exchanges commas with dots, e.g. $\rho(\texttt{t\_1}, \texttt{t\_2}, \texttt{t\_3}) = t_1.t_2.t_3$.

[3] $<LN>$: $<QUANTIFIER>$ $<SEL1>$. $<SEL2>$ = $<LIST\_TVARS>$
with $<LN> \in lines(< LINK_2>)$
leads to the following substitutions:

$\quad Q \rightsquigarrow Q$
$\quad \mathcal{R} \rightsquigarrow \forall <LIST\_TVARS> \mathcal{R}$ if $<QUANTIFIER>$=**forall**
$\quad \mathcal{R} \rightsquigarrow \exists <LIST\_TVARS> \mathcal{R}$ if $<QUANTIFIER>$=**exists**
$\quad <LN> \rightsquigarrow sequence(<SEL1.SEL2>) = \rho(<LIST\_TVARS>)$

[4] $<LN>$: $<SEL1>$. $<SEL2>$ **in** $<language>$ **proj** : $<alphabet>$
leads to the following substitutions:

$\quad Q \rightsquigarrow Q$
$\quad <LN> \rightsquigarrow sequence(<SEL1> . <SEL2>) \downarrow alphabet \in \mathcal{L}[\![language]\!]$
$\quad \mathcal{R} \rightsquigarrow \mathcal{R}$

[5] $<LN>$: $<QUANTIFIER>$ **new** : $<LIST\_TVARS>$
leads to the following substitutions:

$\quad Q \rightsquigarrow Q$
$\quad <LN> \rightsquigarrow X[seq.\rho(<LIST\_TVARS>)/tr]$
$\quad \mathcal{R} \rightsquigarrow \forall <LIST\_TVARS> \mathcal{R}$ if $<QUANTIFIER>$=**forall**
$\quad \mathcal{R} \rightsquigarrow \exists <LIST\_TVARS> \mathcal{R}$ if $<QUANTIFIER>$=**exists**

If each line is translated then Q and $\mathcal{R}$ are removed.

The semantics of the *TrD* in figure 5 can now be calculated in the following way (some steps are omitted, the rules are applied in the sequence [1],[4],[5],[4],[4],[4]). Some small simplifications are made w.r.t. the used languages.

$$
\begin{aligned}
\mathcal{M}[\![< TrD >]\!] &= Q \bullet (< LINK_1> \rightarrow (\mathcal{R} \bullet (< LINK_2>))) \\
&= Q \bullet (1 \wedge 2 \rightarrow (\mathcal{R} \bullet (3 \wedge ((4 \wedge 5) \vee 6)))) \\
&= \forall t_1, t_2 \; Q \bullet (X[t_1.(join\_cf_i, ok).t_2/tr] \wedge 2 \\
&\qquad \rightarrow (\mathcal{R} \bullet (3 \wedge ((4 \wedge 5) \vee 6)))) \\
&= \forall t_1, t_2 \bullet (X[t_1.(join\_cf_i, ok).t_2/tr] \wedge t_2 \downarrow \{leave\_rq_i, term\_rq_k\} = \varepsilon \\
&\qquad \rightarrow (\exists t_3, t_4 \bullet (X[t_1.(join\_cf_i, ok).t_2.t_3.t_4/tr] \\
&\qquad\qquad \wedge ((t_3 \downarrow Comm(T_i) = \varepsilon \wedge t_4 = leave\_rq_i) \\
&\qquad\qquad \vee t_3.t_4 \downarrow \{term\_rq_k\} \neq \varepsilon))))
\end{aligned}
$$

Such trace logic formulas are often difficult to read because one has to guess the right pair of matching brackets. Therefore long formulas should be presented in Lamport's notation [24], e.g.

$$
\begin{aligned}
\forall t_1, t_2 \bullet \;& \wedge \; X[t_1.(join\_cf_i, ok).t_2/tr] \\
& \wedge \; t_2 \downarrow \{leave\_rq_i, term\_rq_k\} \in \{\varepsilon\} \\
& \rightarrow \exists t_3, t_4 \bullet \; \wedge \; X[t_1.(join\_cf_i, ok).t_2.t_3.t_4/tr] \\
&\qquad\qquad \wedge \; \vee \; t_3 \downarrow Comm(T_i) = \varepsilon \; \wedge \; t_4 = leave\_rq_i \\
&\qquad\qquad\qquad \vee \; t_3.t_4 \downarrow \{term\_rq_k\} \neq \varepsilon
\end{aligned}
$$

The semantics in this section is defined as a translation algorithm which can be implemented straightforwardly in a tool. Alternative approaches using a denotational semantics or rewriting rules and expressing the same semantics can be written to allow formal reasoning inside the semantics.

6 Enhancing the applicability

Simplifications. The syntax and semantics of *TrDs* can be easily extended because the only things that have to be done are to add a line in the grammar of the textual representation and to formalize a transformation into a formula in the transformation algorithm. Nevertheless it is important to keep the number of used symbols small such that an intuitive understanding of the graphics is possible.

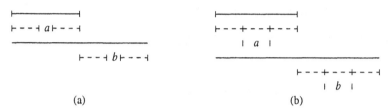

(a)   (b)

Fig. 9. Mixture of trace variables and communications

Some extensions can be formalized as a translation into the already known syntax. A typical example is that until now we need two lines to express the introduction of new trace variables together with communications. Figure 9(a) presents an abbreviation for this requirement and its translation into the known (and formalized) form in figure 9(b).

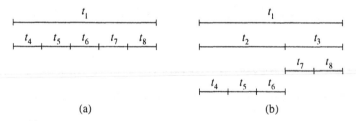

(a)   (b)

Fig. 10. Reducing the number of trace variables

The simplification presented in figure 10 is also useful to reduce the time in verifying that a requirement is fulfilled because the number of trace variables is reduced. Another possible reduction of the number of trace variables is presented in figure 10. Here, figure (b) shows the initial requirement and figure (a) the simplified one. The trace variable t_2 has to be substituted with $t_4.t_5.t_6$ in other parts of the simplified version.

Equivalence. A more tricky part is that it is sometimes necessary to express equivalence (if and only if) instead of implication (if). An example is that we want to express "if and only if a trace belongs to a language L then it should be possible in the desired system". One way to express that is to add a new symbol as proposed in figure 11(a). The disadvantage is that a new symbol is introduced which is not often needed. Another solution is to split the equivalence into the conjunction of two implications as presented in the figures 11(b) and 11(c). Note that in this case it is necessary to guarantee that the

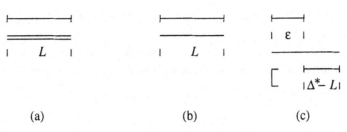

Fig. 11. Expressing equivalence

trace ε is possible in the final system because otherwise a system that is not allowed to perform any trace would fulfil this requirement, too. Figure (b) guarantees that each possible trace belongs to L and figure (c) guarantees that (after the empty trace) for all traces holds that they are either possible in the system or do not belong to L (Δ denotes the set of all possible communications), i.e. all traces which belong to L are possible.

Logical combinators. Further extensions of *TrDs* are possible. Another approach can be to allow other main combinators than implication. If such an expressiveness is needed then it should be allowed to combine any set of lines with any kind of combinators. This approach is chosen for the Graphical Interval Logic [10, 29].

Negation. Note that no special symbol for negation appears in the *TrDs*. The reason is that it is possible to transform each requirement with a negation into a requirement in which negations are placed before formal languages. This denotes the complement of the formal language in the set of all possible sequences of communications, i.e. the trace logic formula $\neg(t_1 \in L_1 \wedge t_2 \in L_2)$ is equivalent to $t_1 \in (\Delta^* - L_1) \vee t_2 \in (\Delta^* - L_2)$.

Quantification of free variables. If we look carefully at the last trace logic formula in the previous section then we can observe that the index i is a free variable in the formula. Of course, the requirement should hold for an arbitrary i but this information is not included in the *TrD*. Case studies have shown that it is often the case that quantifiers for indices and parameters can be derived from quantifiers of the surrounding trace variables, i.e. the universal quantification can be derived from t_1 in the example. If this "default quantification" leads to wrong results it is possible to express the quantification on the left margin of the *TrD* with a solid box around the variable for a universal quantification and a dashed box around the variable for an existential quantification.

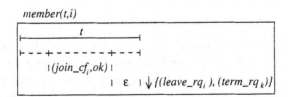

Fig. 12. An auxiliary predicate as a diagram

Structuring. Another problem of the application of *TrDs* in praxis is that some requirements are quite complicated and several lines are needed to express them. But, with an increasing number of lines, the intuitive power of graphical representations decreases drastically. A related problem is that it is often necessary to express a certain property again and again, e.g. "if a certain communication happens and *the system is in* *a certain mode* do ...". Therefore a modular or hierarchical approach is needed to solve this problem.

The solution for *TrDs* is that some properties can be summarized as an auxiliary predicate in a graphical way and that the name of the auxiliary predicate can be used in the *TrDs*. If necessary, it is also possible to replace the predicate with its graphical representation to come to a complete *TrD* without abbreviations.

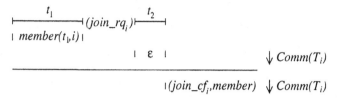

Fig. 13. A trace diagram with an auxiliary predicate

A typical auxiliary predicate is presented in figure 12. The predicate $member(t, i)$ formalizes that T_i is a member of the conference after the trace t. This predicate can now be used in other *TrDs*. An example for such a requirement is that if a site that is a member of a conference asks again to become a member then the information that this site is already a member is transmitted next. The *TrD* for this requirement is presented in figure 13. Note that it is easy to substitute figure 12 with a simple renaming of t with t_1 into figure 13. The introduction of auxiliary predicates in the textual representation is straightforward and omitted here.

Non-determinism. Another possible extension of *TrDs* can deal with a special form of non-determinism. If the set of next possible communications (also called *ready-sets* [13]) needs not be fixed for a system after an executed trace then this should be expressible in *TrDs*. The ready-sets can be used as labels at the end of the graphical representation of a trace. The introduced trace logic has to be extended with other observables, i.e. ready-sets or an information about the state which is reached after an executed trace.

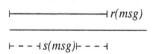

Fig. 14. Formalizing asynchronous communication

Asynchronous Communication. It is mentioned in the introduction that *TrDs* are used to formalize requirements for synchronously communicating systems. A communication which appears once in a *TrD* is meant to be executed by the sender and the receiver together. If support for asynchronous communication is desired, i.e. communications are put by the sender into an input buffer of the receiver and the sender can continue without synchronization, then the send and receive actions have to be distinguished in the *TrDs*. A solution is to add an s and an r before the communication to indicate whether the communication is sent of received. Figure 14 presents the property that each communication must be sent before it can be received (it is assumed that each communication is unique).

7 Sketch of a railway case study

This section sketches another example for the application of *TrDs* using some of the enhancements of the previous section. The example is taken from a railway case study that is currently studied in the project UniForM [23] (Unified Formal Methods Workbench) together with an industrial partner, the ELPRO Let GmbH in Berlin. The task is to develop a control system for a single track railway, i.e. for a part of track which can be used by trains in both directions. Figure 15(a) describes the scenario. A train can enter from the left and pass the entrance sensor $ES1$, pass the sensor $CS1$ indicating that the critical section is entered and finally pass the sensor $LS1$ which indicates that the train has left the critical part. A train entering from the right-hand side passes the sequence $ES2.CS2.LS2$ of sensors.

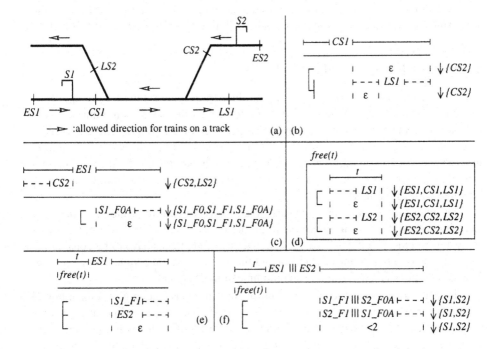

Fig. 15. Requirements for a single track railway control

There are two signals $S1$ and $S2$ for each direction. The following values can be transmitted to the signals: $F0$ for a red light (trains have to stop), $F1$ for a green light (trains can pass) and $F0A$ for a red flashing light which shows an incoming train that the signalling system has recognized the train but that the train has to stop. Signal names and values are combined into one communication name, i.e. a communication $S1\_F0$ denotes that the red light should go on for the signal $S1$ (this is the default situation).

The requirement in figure 15(b) ensures that if a train has entered the critical section from the left ($CS1$) then either no train enters from the right or the train from the left has left the critical section and no train from the right has entered before (for simplicity it is assumed that $ES1$ can only happen after $LS1$, i.e there is only one train for each direction in the critical section). The requirement in (c) ensures that if a train approaches from the left and a train from the right is already in the critical section then the next communication w.r.t. signal $S1$ starts the flashing red light. The last line denotes the allowed situation that no communication has followed after $ES1$ so far.

Figure (d) shows an auxiliary predicate for the case that the track is free, $LS1$ and $LS2$ were the last passed sensors or nothing has happened so far. This predicate is used in the requirement in the figure (e). If a train approaches from the left and the track is free then the next communication guarantees either a green signal or a train approaches immediately from the other side. The indices 1 and 2 can be exchanged in the requirements presented in (b), (c) and (e). Requirement (f) ensures that if trains are approaching in both directions at nearly the same time ($|||$ denotes the interleaving operator of CSP, e.g. $a|||b \equiv a.b + b.a$ and < 2 denotes arbitrary traces with length smaller than two) then one train gets a green light and the other a red flashing light.

The approach presented in [19] was used to develop a specification that fulfils these requirements. Information about a distributed solution are omitted here due to lack of space.

8 Trace-Diagrams and other logics

The last sections have shown that *TrDs* and their trace logic semantics are appropriate to reason about communicating systems for which the set of communications is well known. Another advantage is that the semantics of the programming specification language SL [27, 28] that we have in mind as a target language is also based on an extended trace logic and that this semantics is already encoded [3] in an interactive theorem prover. SL can roughly be described as language based on finite automata extended by local variables.

The main limitation of the *TrDs* and trace logic is that only finite sequences are taken into account. This was no problem for the several case studies so far but if someone wants to reason about arbitrary liveness then infinite traces have to be considered. An example for a requirement which cannot be expressed in trace logic is, if a communication c happens then eventually a communication d happens.

There are several ways to solve this problem. If it is possible to give a fixed bound for the "eventually", e.g. d will be under the next 1000 communications, then this requirement can be formalized in the introduced trace logic. If this is not possible then infinite sequences have to be studied. *TrDs* can be extended to handle infinite traces which could also lead to a promising graphical representation of requirements in that area, e.g. for the stream based approach in FOCUS [6] which uses trace logic over infinite sequences as a requirement language.

On the other hand it is also possible to express most requirements in a temporal logic (see [8, 25, 31] for overviews). The disadvantage is that these logics deal with properties rather than communications. Therefore an automaton has to be translated into a so called *Kripke-Structure*, a transition system with states which are labelled by properties that hold in this state. One possibility is to guess the properties from the informal description of the protocols. The other possibility is to encode the communications. Two examples for such an encoding are shown in the figure 16. The automata in (a) and (c) are translated into the structures in (b) and (d). Each communication c has to be encoded with two properties, $rd(c)$ denotes that the system is *ready* to execute c and $ex(c)$ that

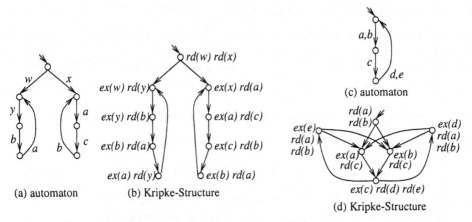

(a) automaton   (b) Kripke-Structure

(c) automaton

(d) Kripke-Structure

Fig. 16. Relation between Automata and Kripke-Structures

the system *has executed* c as the last communication. This encoding guarantees that an executed communication can be identified with the formula $rd(c) \wedge X\ ex(c)$ where X denotes the temporal next operator. If different transitions lead to the same state then the states must be doubled in the structure to allow to identify which communication is executed.

Note that not all requirements presented so far can be described for example in linear temporal logic (LTL) because informations about sequences of arbitrary length between two communications have to be stored to be analyzed several times which is directly not possible in LTL (which can sometimes be solved with tricky encodings). It is also not possible to express the future operator of the introduced trace logic because this corresponds to a branching operator.

The final alternative are logics in which it is possible to argue directly over communications. It is e.g. possible to rewrite the transformation algorithm of section 5 (without the future operation) for Monadic Second Order Logic on strings. This logic also offers two model checkers [17, 18] which were applied in some non-trivial case studies. Finally it also possible to encode trace logic formulas in the μ-calculus as it is used in [7] for several efficient decision procedures.

The above mentioned logics and their applications are the motivation for further research in trace logic. In the appendix of [20] it is e.g. shown that if we restrict ourselves to regular languages in clause (8) of the definition of *TrDs* then it is possible to write a model checking algorithm for trace logic. Therefore it is possible to check with an algorithm for a set of requirements given as *TrDs* and a specification formalized as a finite automaton whether the specification fulfils the requirements or not. In the negative case it is possible to produce counter examples.

Timing Diagrams which can be formalized in temporal logics are sometimes used in hardware development to synthesize hardware from the diagrams [30]. It can be shown that *synthesis* is also possible for a subset of *TrDs*. If the only allowed quantification is a universal quantification in the first part of the requirement and if we focus again on regular languages then a finite automaton can be derived which accepts the unique largest language that fulfils the requirement.

9 Conclusions and further remarks

Trace Diagrams are introduced as a suitable graphical approach to formalizing requirements for distributed systems that goes beyond the possibilities of message sequence charts which can only describe allowed sequences of communications. Following the typical form of requirements, the graphical formalism is developed with an intuitive informal semantics which is formalized in trace logic. Case studies with telecommunication protocols [20, 21] and a single track railway control point out that this formalism can be applied for real applications.

It also is shown in this paper that the formalism can easily be extended on the informal and formal level such that further areas of distributed systems can be served.

Of course, tool support for the development of complex systems (not only at the requirements level) is needed. Therefore such tools are considered which may lead to small changes in the presented syntax. Case studies in other areas will be done to observe which extensions of the trace diagrams are needed to serve their special interests.

Acknowledgements. The author thanks H. Tjabben of Philips Research Laboratories Aachen and E.-R. Olderog and the other members of the "semantics" group in Oldenburg for helpful discussions.

References

1. B. Alpern und F.B. Schneider, Defining Liveness, Information Processing Letters, 21(4), 181–185, 1985

2. C. Antoine, B. Le Goff, Timing Diagrams for Writing and Checking Logical and Behavioural Properties of Integrated Systems, in P. Prinetti, P. Camurati (eds.), Correct Hardware Design Methodologies, Elsevier Science Publishers, 1992

3. J. Bohn, S. Rössig. On automatic and interactive design of communicating systems, in E. Brinksma, W. R. Cleaveland, K. G. Larsen, T. Margaria, and B. Steffen (eds.), Proceedings of TACAS'95, LNCS 1019 (Springer), 1995

4. D. Bjørner, H. Langmaack, C.A.R. Hoare, ProCoS I Final Deliverable, ProCoS Technical Report ID/DTH db 13/1, January 1993

5. G. Boriello, Formalized Timing Diagrams, in Proc. European Conference on Design Automation, Belgium, 1992

6. M. Broy, F. Dederichs, C. Dendorfer, M. Fuchs, T.F. Gritzner, R. Weber, The Design of Distributed Systems – An Introduction to FOCUS -Revised Version, technical report TUM-I9202-2, Technical University of Munich, 1993

7. J.R. Burch et al., Symbolic Model Checking: 10^{20} States and Beyond, in Proc. of the Fifth Annual Logic in Computer Science, 1990

8. E.M. Clarke et al., Automatic Verification of Finite State Concurrent Systems Using Temporal Logic Specifications, ACM TOPLAS 8, 1986

9. C. Dietz, Graphical Formalization of Real-Time Requirements, in B. Jonsson, J. Parrow (eds.), Formal Techniques in Real-Time and Fault-Tolerant Systems '96, LNCS 1135 (Springer), 1996

10. L.K. Dillon, G. Kutty, L.E. Moser, P.M. Melliar-Smith, Y.S. Ramakrishna, A Graphical Interval Logic for Specifying Concurrent Systems, ACM Transactions on Software Engineering and Methodology, vol. 3, no. 2, April 1994

11. E.C.R. Hehner, Predicative Programming, Comm. ACM 27 (2), 1984

12. C.A.R. Hoare, Programs are Predicates, in C.A.R. Hoare, J.C. Shepherdson (Eds.), Mathematical Logic and Programming Languages, Prentice-Hall, London, 1985

13. C.A.R. Hoare, Communicating Sequential Processes, Prentice-Hall, London, 1985

14. ISO, revised text of CD 10731, information technology - Open Systems Interconnection - conventions for the definition of OSI services, technical report, ISO/OEC JTC 1/SC 21 N 6341, ISO, 1991

15. ITU-TS, ITU-TS Recommendation Z.120: Message Sequence Chart (MCS), ITU-TS, Geneva, 1994

16. Jifeng He, C.A.R. Hoare, M. Fränzle, M. Müller-Olm, E.-R. Olderog, M. Schenke, M.R. Hansen, A.P. Ravn, H. Rischel, Provably Correct Systems, in H. Langmaack, W.P. de Roever, Y. Vytopil (eds.), Formal Techniques in Real-Time and Fault-Tolerant Systems '94, LNCS 863 (Springer), 1994

17. J.G. Henriksen et al., MONA: Monadic Second-Order Logic in Practice, in E. Brinksma, W. R. Cleaveland, K. G. Larsen, T. Margaria, and B. Steffen (eds.), Proceedings of TACAS'95, LNCS 1019 (Springer), 1995

18. P. Kelb, T. Margaria, M. Mendler, C. Gsottberger, Mosel: A Flexible Toolset for Monadic Second-Order Logic, in E. Brinksma (ed.), Proc. of TACAS'97, LNCS 1217 (Springer), 1997

19. S. Kleuker, H. Tjabben, The Incremental Development of Correct Specifications for Distributed Systems, in M.-C. Gaudel, J. Woodcock (eds.), Formal Methods Europe '96, LNCS 1051 (Springer), 1996

20. S. Kleuker, H. Tjabben, A Formal Approach to the Development of Reliable Multi-User Multimedia Applications, Philips Research Laboratories Aachen, Technical Report, 1168/96, ftp://ftp.informatik.uni-oldenburg.de/pub/procos/cocon/mumu.ps.gz

21. S. Kleuker. Using Formal Methods in the Development of Protocols for Multi-User Multimedia Systems, in R. Gotzhein, J. Bredereke (eds.), Formal Description Techniques IX, Chapman & Hall, London, 1996.

22. S. Kleuker, Incremental Development of Deadlock-Free Communicating Systems, in E. Brinksma (ed.), Proc. of TACAS'97, LNCS 1217 (Springer), 1997

23. B. Krieg-Brückner, J. Peleska, E.-R. Olderog, D. Balzer, A. Baer, UniForM: Universal Formal Methods Workbench, in Statusseminar des BMBF, Softwaretechnologie, Berlin, March 1996

24. L. Lamport, How to Write a Long Formula, technical research report, Digital Equipment Corporation, in http://www.research.digital.com/SRC/proofs/proofs.html, 1994

25. Z. Manna, A. Pnueli, Temporal Verification of Reactive Systems – Safety, Springer, 1995

26. S. Mauw, M.A. Reniers, An algebraic semantics of Basic Message Sequence Charts, The computer journal, 37(4), 1994

27. E.-R. Olderog, Towards a Design Calculus for Communicating Programs, LNCS 527 (Springer), p. 61-77, 1991

28. E.-R. Olderog, S. Rössig, J. Sander, M. Schenke, ProCoS at Oldenburg: The Interface between Specification Language and OCCAM-like Programming Language. Technical Report Bericht 3/92, Univ. Oldenburg, Fachbereich Informatik, 1992.

29. Y.S. Ramakrishna, P.M. Melliar-Smith, L.E. Moser, L.K. Dillon, G. Kutty, Really Visual Temporal Reasoning, in Proc. 14th RTSS, Raliegh-Durham, IEEE Press, 1993

30. R. Schlör, W. Damm, Specification and Verification of System Level Hardware Designs using Timing Diagrams, in Proc. The European Conference on Design Automation, Paris, France, 1993

31. M.Y. Vardi, An Automata-Theoretic Approach to Linear Temporal Logic, in F. Moller, G. Birteistle (eds.), Logics for concurrency, , LNCS 1043 (Springer), 1996

32. J. Zwiers, Compositionality, Concurrency and Partial Correctness - Proof Theories for Networks of Processes and their Relationship, LNCS 321 (Springer), 1989

Consistent Graphical Specification of Distributed Systems[*]

Franz Huber, Bernhard Schätz, Geralf Einert

Fakultät für Informatik,
Technische Universität München,
Arcisstraße 21,
80333 München
Email: huberf@informatik.tu-muenchen.de,
schaetz@informatik.tu-muenchen.de,
einert@informatik.tu-muenchen.de

Abstract: The widely accepted possible benefits of formal methods on the one hand and their minor use compared to informal or graphical description techniques on the other hand have repeatedly lead to the claim that formal methods should be put to a more indirect or transparent use. We show how such an indirect approach can be incorporated in a CASE tool prototype by basing it upon formally defined hierarchical description techniques. We demonstrate the immediate benefits by introducing consistency notions gained from the formalization. Additionally, we show how the formalization can be used to apply automated property validation. Finally, we discuss some further techniques that could be based on the underlying formalization.

1 Distributed Systems Development

Development of distributed systems has become a main objective of software engineering today. Intelligent networks providing multimedia-related services, distributed information systems like for instance car rental booking systems, or embedded controller systems used, for example, in avionics systems or industrial production lines: all of these are examples of distributed systems.

The increasing complexity of those applications, in particular the complex interactions between the components of such systems, make their development complicated and error prone. Intuitive graphical formalisms to specify and develop such systems, provided by a number of development tools, are already in widespread use in industry. Many of these notations and tools, however, lack a precise interpretation in the sense of a formal semantics. Thus, in a number of cases the interpretation of certain properties of a modeled system is unclear or even ambiguous. Such ambiguously specified system properties easily lead to insecure systems where, for example, behavior under certain conditions may be unpredictable or dependent on factors not accounted for by the developers. Situations like these are intolerable especially in the development of safety-critical systems like those, upon which human lives are dependent, or mission-critical applications for companies. In such applications, the correctness of a system in relation to the system specification is crucial. Nonetheless,

---

[*] This work was carried out within the sub-project A6 of the "Sonderforschungsbereich 342 (Werkzeuge und Methoden für die Nutzung paralleler Rechnerarchitekturen)" and the SysLab project, sponsored by the German Research Community (DFG) under the Leibniz program and by Siemens-Nixdorf.

many systems that are in use today bear inconsistencies that are undetected until particular situations arise, where the effects often are disastrous [9].

1.1 Applicable Formal Methods

Despite the benefits that can be gained by using formal techniques, their use in large-scale industrial systems development is still quite uncommon. As has repeatedly been stated, the reasons for this fact are mainly due to the complexity and clumsiness of the mathematical formalisms used there. Development strictly adhering to such formalisms is too time-consuming for industrial systems development and requires too much time for developers to get acquainted with.

As a consequence, it has often been proposed to combine the advantages of both approaches, intuitive graphical notations on the one hand, and mathematically precise formalisms on the other hand, in development tools encapsulating as much as possible of the mathematical formalisms under the hood of pragmatical graphical notations. AUTOFOCUS, the tool presented in this paper, tries to reach this goal in selected areas: AUTOFOCUS uses a formal method for the development of distributed systems called FOCUS [2] as the underlying basis. FOCUS describes distributed systems as collections of components that are spatially or conceptually/logically distributed. The components communicate, that is, exchange messages, over communication channels. Components may be hierarchically refined by networks of subcomponents in the development process. The behavior of these components is specified using mathematical concepts like stream processing functions or traces. AUTOFOCUS uses a set of practice-oriented, mainly graphical notations, embedded into FOCUS, to specify different aspects of these concepts.

The following section briefly introduces the AUTOFOCUS tool giving a short description of general aspects. Afterwards, we outline the AUTOFOCUS description techniques, characterizing some aspects of their relationships to the underlying semantical concepts of FOCUS. Subsequently, the notion of syntactical consistency of development documents is introduced. In this section, a classification of consistency conditions according to their use and implementation is given, followed by a description of how consistency is controlled during the process of systems development and how inconsistencies, which are inevitable under certain circumstances, are treated. After that we show how the mathematical basis of AUTOFOCUS, provided by the FOCUS method, is used to verify system properties exceeding syntactical consistency. The paper is concluded by an outlook to the future development of the AUTOFOCUS tool.

2 The AUTOFOCUS Tool

This section briefly describes important aspects of the current implementation of the AUTOFOCUS tool. For a further description of its architecture and implementation, we refer the reader to [6].

2.1 Distributed Client/Server Architecture

Because of their complexity distributed systems are generally developed in teams by several developers at the same time, often using different computer platforms. Therefore, AUTOFOCUS is implemented as a client/server system with a central repository where all development documents are stored. An arbitrary number of clients can access these documents over a network connection. Thus system developers can use the specification documents simultaneously. By implementing the clients in Java, AUTOFOCUS can be used on most of the usual operating system platforms.

2.2 Version Management

Specifications are repeatedly revised, especially in the early phases of development. Therefore, the possibility to use version control of single documents as well as of whole projects is absolutely necessary. Tool support should allow to rule out inconsistencies (other than the ones mentioned above) caused by team members working on the same specification documents. Therefore, the AUTOFOCUS repository offers version control of both documents and projects as well as locking mechanisms for documents based on the usual pattern of one write access and multiple read accesses.

2.3 Graphical User Interface

On the client side, the complete functionality of AUTOFOCUS is accessible in a graphical user interface, parts of which are shown in figure 1. A project browser provides access to the development projects in the repository as well as to the associated document hierarchies grouped by document classes. For each of the graphical description techniques that will be introduced in the following section AUTOFOCUS provides a graphical editor. These editors, which support the hierarchy concepts of FOCUS, are shown in figure 1 as well.

All editors use an identical user interface concept with mouse-based user interactions to facilitate editing development documents. To use AUTOFOCUS diagrams in common word processors for documentation purposes the diagrams can be exported into encapsulated PostScript graphics files.

3 AUTOFOCUS - The Description Techniques

3.1 View-based Systems Development

AUTOFOCUS, like many tools and methods that are in practical use, does not aim at capturing a complete system description within a single formalism. Instead, different views of a system are each specified using an appropriate notation called *description technique*.

A distributed system can be characterized from several points of view, as

- the structure of a system including its components and the communication paths between them providing both a component interface specification and topological information,
- the behavioral description of the system as a whole or of one of its components,
- the data processed by the system and transmitted across the communication paths, and
- the interaction of the components and the system environment via message exchange.

Only a description including all these views forms a complete picture of the system. Therefore, AUTOFOCUS offers five different description techniques: system structure diagrams (SSDs), state transition diagrams (STDs), data type definitions (DTDs) as well as component data declarations (CDDs), and extended event traces (EETs), covering all the above aspects. Conforming with the hierarchical concepts of FOCUS, each of the graphical description techniques allows to model on different levels of granularity, supporting a top-down approach where, for example, components or behavioral modules can be either atomic or consist of sub-components or sub-modules themselves.

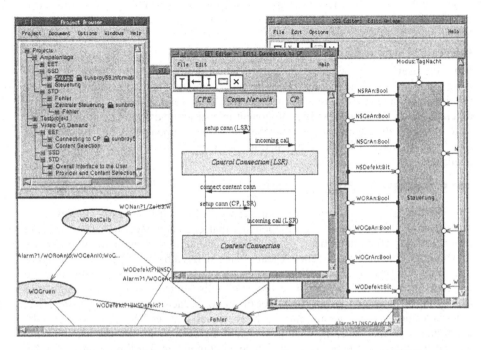

Figure 1: The AUTOFOCUS Client Application – Project Browser and Editors

3.2 Document Oriented Description

In AUTOFOCUS, a project, representing a system under development, consists of a number of documents that are representations of views using the description techniques introduced above. Thus each description technique is mapped to a corresponding class of documents (also called diagrams). Combined, these documents provide a complete characterization of a system in its current development status. Access and version control is done on the document level of granularity in the repository, which keeps track of the complete version history of every document. For a changed document, the user may choose whether it should be stored by default, simply incrementing the version number, or if it should be saved under a version number explicitly given by the user. In order to reuse documents, a document may be referenced by more than one project. Projects are subject to version control as well: in our approach, versions of a project are collections of specific versions of development documents.

Hierarchical Documents

As already mentioned, all graphical AUTOFOCUS description techniques share the concept of hierarchy. Both system structure diagrams and state transition diagrams -

which are essentially graphs - as well as extended event traces allow hierarchical refinement. In a system structure diagram, a system component may be viewed as a conceptual unit made up of a network of sub-components specified in another structure diagram document. In the same way, a state in a state transition diagram can be characterized by another state transition diagram document refining this state on a more detailed level. In extended event trace diagrams, so-called "boxes" are introduced as an abbreviating notation for parts of system runs specified in different event trace diagrams.

Integrated Documents

From the user's point of view, the documents of a development project are tightly integrated, both vertically along the refinement hierarchies and horizontally along the relationships between documents of different kinds: for instance, a state transition diagram can be associated with a component in a structure diagram denoting that this state transition diagram specifies the behavior of the component. Along relationships like these, quick and intuitive navigation mechanisms between the documents are available.

3.3 System Structure Diagrams (SSDs)

System structure diagrams describe static aspects of a distributed system, viewing it as a network of interconnected components that exchange messages over directed channels. Each component has a unique identifier and a set of input and output ports to which the channels are attached. Channels are defined by identifiers and data types describing the sets of messages that may be sent across them. Thus system structure diagrams provide both the topological view of a distributed system and the signature (the syntactic interface, given by the set of ports) of each individual component. As remarked above, components may be hierarchically refined by networks of sub-components. In that case, the document specifying such a sub-network has the same set of communication ports as the higher-level component that this refined view belongs to. Graphically, as shown in figure 1, system structure diagrams are represented as graphs, where rectangular vertices symbolize components and arrow-shaped edges stand for channels. Both of them are annotated with their identifiers and, in the case of channels, also with their data types. Component ports are visualized as small hollow or filled circles, depending on whether they are input or output ports.

This graphical notation similar to data flow networks is a direct representation of the semantical concepts of a distributed system used in FOCUS. A textual representation to define such component networks, omitting the graphical context of SSDs, is given by the *Agent Network Description Language* defined in [14]. ANDL can easily be transformed into notations suitable for verification of system properties like, for example, the HOLCF package for the *Isabelle* theorem prover (see also section 5.3).

3.4 State Transition Diagrams (STDs)

State transition diagrams are extended finite automata similar to the concepts introduced in [4]. They are used to describe the dynamic aspects, that is, the behavior, of a distributed system or of its components. Each system component can be associated with an STD consisting of states and transitions between them. Each transition has a set of annotations: a pre- and a post-condition, encoded as predicates over the data state of the component satisfied before and after the transition, and a set of input and output patterns describing the messages that are read from or written to the input and output ports of the component. The notation used to specify the input and output patterns is similar to CSP. For hierarchical refinement of states in STDs, we use a concept similar to the one used in the SSDs. Graphically, automata are represented as graphs with labeled ovals as states and arrows as transitions. Figure 1 shows an example of an AUTOFOCUS state transition diagram.

Semantically, STDs are flat, thus hierarchy in this case is only a mechanism of visual representation. They represent system or component behaviors given by stream processing functions or traces. A mapping to stream processing functions can be accomplished based on the concepts from [3].

3.5 Datatype Definitions (DTDs)

The types of the data processed by a distributed system are defined in a textual notation. We use basic types and data type constructors similar to those found in the functional programming language Gofer [8] for this purpose. The data types defined here may be referenced from within other development documents, for example, as channel data types in SSDs.

In order to use such data type definitions for verification of system properties they can be transformed into HOLCF using the HOLCF domain construct introduced in [15]. Subsets of Gofer data type definitions can be efficiently transformed into model checker input format.

3.6 Component Data Declaration (CDDs)

Additionally to receiving and sending messages, components generally store information locally to process those messages. For this purpose, local variables may be defined for each component by associating a component data declaration to it. A CDD simply consists of a set of variable identifiers and their associated types as defined in the DTD of the system, plus a possible initial value.

Those variables locally defined for a component may be addressed in the definition of the STD of this component in the input and output patterns as well as in the pre- and post-conditions.

3.7 Extended Event Traces (EETs)

Extended event traces are used to describe exemplary system runs from a component-based view. As shown in figure 1, we use a notation similar to the ITU-standardized message sequence charts (MSCs) with some core concepts taken from MSC'96 (ITU Z.120, [7]). As well as the other graphical AUTOFOCUS notations, EETs support hierarchy. Using so-called boxes a number of sub-EETs can be nested to specify variants of behavior in parts of an EET. Additionally, indicators can be used to define optional or repeatable parts of an EET. A complete description of EETs can be found in [13].

EETs carry somewhat redundant information in relationship to the other AUTOFOCUS notations. From the methodological point of view, they are intended to be used in the very early stages of systems development to specify elementary functionality of a system on an exemplary basis. Additionally, EETs can be used to specify system behavior in error situations as well. Later in the development process, the system specifications given by SSDs, STDs, and DTDs can be checked against the EETs, whether they fulfill the properties specified in them.

Further applications of EETs consist in the visualization of model checking and simulation results. For instance, witnesses obtained by model checking state transition diagrams can be visualized using EETs.

4 Consistency of Descriptions

If a specification exceeds the toy world size, the contained information in general is spread across several documents, like in different modules or libraries of a large programming package. A large number of errors arises out of the fact that those information pieces are created separately and thus do not automatically fit together. Here, simple checks based on the abstract syntax of the description techniques can already be an enormous help. Since AUTOFOCUS uses different classes of documents as well as hierarchically organized document structures, it becomes even more important to make sure that the information spread out over those documents is consistent.

Therefore, consistency checks are offered to ensure that the produced documents fit together. Consistency includes several different classes of syntactical correctness criteria like

- **Grammatical Correctness:** The corresponding document obeys the syntactical rules for textual documents or the graph-grammatical rules for graphical documents.
- **Document Interface Correctness:** If a document is embedded into another document according to the hierarchical concepts introduced before, those documents must have compatible interfaces to each other (components in SSDs, states in STDs, or boxes in EETs).
- **Definedness:** If a document makes use of objects not defined in the document itself, those objects must be defined in a corresponding document (channel types in SSDs or STDs, for example).
- **Type Correctness:** The type of an object assigned and the type of the object it is assigned to must coincide (channels and ports in SSDs, or channel values and channel types in STDs, for example).
- **Completeness:** All necessary documents of a project have to be present.

Those syntactical conditions can be split in two classes according to their definition and treatment:

- **Intra-document Conditions:** Conditions that can be checked using only information found in the document itself.
- **Inter-document Conditions:** Conditions that can only be checked by using two or more documents at the same time.

In the following two sections we give some examples for each class using SSD documents.

4.1 Intra-document Consistency

Intra-document consistency basically corresponds to the syntactical and semantical analysis performed during the parsing of program code. In general, the grammatical correctness and the type correctness are checked here. We give some simple consistency conditions for an SSD:

- Each component has a non-empty name.

- Each port has a non-empty name, a non-empty type and a direction (input or output).
- Each channel has a non-empty name and a non-empty type.
- Each port is bound to a channel.
- Each channel is bound to one port per direction with the same type.

Note that no notion of a document is used here. These conditions can easily be formalized using typed first order predicate logic with equality if we introduce appropriate individuals for the elementary objects like identifiers, components, channels, ports, or directions, and appropriate functions like *name_of*, *type_of*, or *direction_of*.

Thus, the last two conditions may be formalized as

$\forall con : Connector.(\exists chan : Channel.channel\_of(con) = chan)$

$\forall chan : Channel.\exists icon, ocon : Connector.(inconnector\_of(chan) = icon \wedge$
$outconnector\_of(chan) = ocon \wedge type\_of(icon) = type\_of(chan) \wedge$
$type\_of(ocon) = type\_of(chan))$

4.2 Inter-document Consistency

For inter-document consistency, we use checks that are performed in a similar way during the linking process of a program code. Primary checks for this case are the document interface correctness, the definedness and the completeness. Like in the case of the above intra-document conditions we define conditions for SSDs that need more than one document to be checked:

- Each sub-document has a defined corresponding component in a different super-document
- For each port of a sub-document bound to the environment there exists a single port bound to the corresponding component of the super-document having the same name, same type and opposite direction.
- If a component has a defined sub-document, then for each port of the component there exists a single port in this sub-document, having the same name, type and the opposite direction.

Again, these conditions can be formalized as above. Note that now, however, we have to add documents as individuals and corresponding functions to the language.

$\forall comp:Component, doc:Document.(subdocument\_of(comp) = doc \Rightarrow$

$(\forall father:Port.(component\_of(father) = comp \Rightarrow$

$(\exists son:Port.(document\_of(son) = doc \wedge name\_of(father) = name\_of(son) \wedge$

$type\_of(father) = type\_of(son) \wedge direction\_of(father) \neq direction\_of(son) \wedge$

$\forall port:Port.((name\_of(port) = name\_of(son) \wedge$

$document\_of(port) = doc) \Rightarrow port = son))))))$

4.3 Consistency and Development

During the development process of a system, its specification documents are in fact inconsistent most of the time. In view-based systems development, these views, although describing different aspects of a system, are not independent of each other. For instance, a structural description in an SSD uses the data types defined in DTDs to identify the data transmitted on channels. Transitions in STDs use port names from related SSDs to identify the data read (written) when the transition is performed.

Quite naturally, in a typical development scenario, these descriptions are incomplete for most of the time in a development process: SSDs are drawn before all necessary data type definitions are finished; behavior is specified for components for which the interface definition has not yet been completed; the revision of the refined structure (network of sub-components) of a system component requires a change in the interface of the component, thus rendering the component's interface temporarily inconsistent with that of its refined structure, and many more situations like these. Having many developers working on one system specification independently usually even worsens these circumstances producing more inconsistencies.

Consequently, in our view, inconsistency in the development is a natural and inevitable phenomenon that should be treated accordingly by the tool used.

User Controlled Inconsistencies

From the observations stated above, we conclude that a tool should give its users, that is, the developers working with it, control over when to check the system descriptions for consistency. The tool should not try to enforce consistency of descriptions automatically. Instead, developers should be able to decide when to have the tool perform appropriate checks for consistency. This approach, in our view, conforms much more to the way in which human developers work.

Many CASE tools that are commercially available are not being used just for this reason: developers feel too restricted when working with them, as they have to change their habits of working only to fulfill consistencies enforced by the tool. Similar experiences were made with syntax-driven editors for programming languages like Pascal, or C++. These editors, although intended to serve as an aid for programmers, have quickly proven to be more of an impediment than a help as they are usually too restrictive in their use.

Definition of Consistency Conditions

In AUTOFOCUS, the actual conditions upon which consistency checks are based, are defined using a declarative textual notation, similar to first order predicate logic with a simple type system. This approach, in contrast to hard-coding the consistency conditions in the AUTOFOCUS implementation language Java, which would be more efficient, provides a clear and simple way for developers to extend the set of consistency conditions if needed. In particular, no program code of the tool has to be modified or added. Thus it is unnecessary to know the internal program structure of AUTOFOCUS in order to write new consistency checks or to modify existing ones. The textual documents containing the consistency conditions stored in the repository of AUTOFOCUS also hold further information, like an informal explanation about the consistency condition, and whether it is an intra- or an inter-document condition.

The basic language elements of the textual notation used for the consistency conditions are

- quantors (universal quantor and existential quantor),
- selectors to access properties of documents, and
- operators on logical expressions and the equational operator.

A number of examples for the concrete syntactical representation of such consistency conditions in AUTOFOCUS is given subsequently:

Example 1: Intra-document condition

```
forall c: Component . Name(c) != ""
```

This very simple intra-document consistency condition states that no component in the SSD document being checked may have an empty name. It only uses selectors referring to items within that document and is thus classified as intra-document condition.

Note that the universe of components that the quantor is bound to in this case is implicitly restricted to those belonging to the SSD document being checked.

Example 2: Inter-document condition

```
forall ea: Axis .
    exists sc: Component .
      name(ea) == name(sc)
```

This condition for component axes in EET documents refers to elements from external documents, namely SSD documents, and is thus an inter-document condition. It checks whether for each component axis in a given EET, a corresponding component (in an SSD) is existing.

Example 3: Inter-document condition

```
forall c: Component .
    (exists ssd: SSDDocument . refinement(c, ssd)) or
    (exists std: STDDocument . behavior(c, std))
```

This consistency condition relating components with SSD documents and STD documents asserts that each component must either be refined by an SSD document specifying its sub-structure or be related to an STD that specifies its behavior. This consistency condition is an example for a simple completeness property of a system specification.

Integration of Inconsistency Treatment

In AUTOFOCUS, developers can invoke consistency checks from within different environments: editors and the hierarchical project browser.

In editors, where just a single document is being edited, all intra-document consistency checks for the respective kind of document can be started. This provides a quick and handy way for developers to ensure a minimum level of consistency within one single document. Checks of that kind are started simply by selecting a menu command in the editor of the document.

In the project browser, developers have several options to perform consistency checks. By selecting a whole project, a global consistency check for all development documents of that particular project, using all available consistency conditions, is started. This includes all intra-document checks, which are each performed for every appropriate document. Partial consistency can be checked by selecting a special class of documents, for example, by selecting the SSD category, which means that all SSD documents will be checked applying all appropriate intra-document checks and all inter-document checks suitable for SSD documents. Figure 2 shows this case, where the command to perform the consistency checks was invoked with the SSD document category selected. All consistency checks currently defined for this document category are then lined up in a dialog, grouped by the categories they belong to. These checklists are generated at runtime, based on the selection in the project browser and on the available consistency checks. Usually, all checks in these lists are to be executed, but in case only a selection of them should be carried out, individual ones can be deselected, thus performing only an arbitrary subset of all possible checks.

The tool then performs the selected checks on the appropriate documents. As a result, it displays a list of all the consistency conditions that have been found violated by at least one of the documents checked. By selecting one of these conditions, users may bring up a list of all documents violating it, and, from there, directly navigate to the individual documents, that is, open the documents using the corresponding editors with the items violating consistency already highlighted. For consistency checks invoked from within editors, this is obviously not necessary, as the editor is already open; here the components violating consistency are directly highlighted.

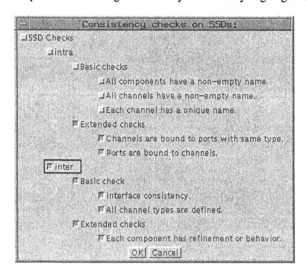

Figure 2: Sample List of Available Consistency Checks for SSDs

5 Verification of Specifications

After having introduced the description techniques and having defined several syntactical consistency conditions on them we now define their exact meaning. After giving an intuitive description we will introduce their semantics using μ calculus logic [10]. Since those descriptions can be automatically verified in a restricted range we will show how those checks can be performed using a μ calculus model checker like μ-cke [1].

The verification based on the relational μ calculus described in this section is ongoing work currently being implemented, the verification based on interactive theorem proving at the end of the section only exists in fragments. For easier understanding, we describe the formalization in a non-optimized version which makes the basic concepts more obvious.

5.1 Informal Semantics

While the meaning of DTDs, CDDs, and SSDs is quite obvious and needs no further explanation, the exact meaning of the behavioral description techniques STDs and EETs was left open so far. In the following two sections we will give an informal description of the meaning of those techniques. These informal descriptions will be formalized accordingly using μ calculus logic.

Meaning of STDs

An STD characterizes the behavior of a system or a system component reacting on input received from its environment and producing output sent to the environment. Those reactions depend on the actual state of the component and influence the future behavior of the component by setting a new state. Since an STD describes an extended finite state machine by using variables local to the characterized component, the state of a component is defined both by the control state (that is, the state of the finite state machine) and the values of the local variables of the component. A new state of the component as a result of the reaction to input is a new control state and new values of the local variables.

As mentioned in section 3.4, input and output patterns are used to describe the messages read from the input ports and written to the output ports. Each pattern consists of one or more port patterns. An input port pattern is built from an input port identifier and a message type construct of a type matching the port type. A message type construct can be built using constants and data type constructors from the DTD of the system, variables defined in the CDD of the component or free variables. An input port pattern matches an actual message at this port, if the constants and the values of the defined variables match the corresponding values of the read message. The free variables are bound to the actual values as found in the message.[1] Thus, while the CDD defined variables are only read in an input pattern, the free variables get set during the matching process. Output port patterns are constructed correspondingly, the message written to the port is generated by simply assigning the current value of both defined and free variables to their identifiers.

In pre-conditions only defined variables may be used to define predicates over the current data state. In post-conditions, defined and free variables can be used to the define the predicates. Like in output port patterns, defined and free variables are bound to their current values. Additionally, for each defined variable x a primed variable x' can be used to address the value of the variable *after* the execution of the transition.

It is important to note that in our approach the input is read simultaneously from all input ports. Input patterns used in an STD are complete in the sense that unspecified combinations of input patterns are interpreted to result in an empty valued output and leave both control state and local variables unchanged. If no input pattern is defined for a certain port, the input pattern will only match if no message is received on this port. Analogously, output messages are produced simultaneously for all output ports. If no output pattern is defined for an output port, the value of the message written to this port is empty. As a consequence, the meaning of STDs is closer to

---

[1] More formally, a match is considered successful if a data element equal to the actual message can be constructed according to the pattern using its type constructors, the constants, the CDD defined variables with their current assignment and the free variabales with an arbitrary assignment.

hardware oriented description mechanisms like Statecharts than abstract description languages like SDL. Since, furthermore, no implicit message buffering is done by the components, buffering must be explicitly introduced into the specifications if desired.

Meaning of EETs

For sake of brevity we will only discuss simple EETs without indicators or boxes. Those extensions, however, can be easily integrated in the formalization given later. Informally, the interpretation of an EET is given by the following statements:

- The system behavior is interpreted as the concurrent runs of its components, each run described by the incoming and outgoing messages of the respective component shown at the corresponding axis. By identifying which incoming message of the receiving component corresponds to which outgoing message of the sending component those single descriptions are merged into a complete system description. Note that this is a more general version than used in [13] since only a partial ordering of events is assumed here.

- The transmission of a message between components is interpreted to happen instantaneously, no delay is introduced during transmission.

- Only the sending and receiving of a message can be observed as an event using EETs.

- Two consequent events observed at a component take place either at the same time or with an unknown finite delay in between. During this delay no other events can be observed at this component.

5.2 Exploration and Model Checking

The above described model of computation for STDs was chosen for two reasons:

- A lot of embedded systems as mentioned above are described on hardware oriented levels. In such a setting, synchronized and unbuffered communication is the natural paradigm. Therefore, this paradigm is generally adopted in tools used in this area [5].

- If unbuffered communication is used, the space needed to describe the current system space is fixed during execution.[2] For such systems, in general, model checking techniques offer a reasonable possibility to automatically verify behavioral properties.

In the remainder of this section we describe how the informal semantics given above can be formalized to be used with a relational μ calculus model checker.

Transformation of STDs

Basically, STDs are formalized by describing all possible sequences of states of the corresponding machine starting in a initial state of the STD. The sequences include the messages consumed and produced. To characterize those sequences, we simply describe the transition relation generating the sequences. To formalize STDs and combinations of STDs via SSDs we have to give a μ calculus representation of channels, ports, the control state space, the variable state space, and the transitions.

Channels are formalized as variables shared between the two adjacent components of these channels addressed via ports. A channel will therefore only hold one value of the corresponding channel type at a time. Thus, messages are not buffered. If

---

[2] Given fixed size data types.

an incoming message is not explicitly stored in a local variable by the receiving process, it will be lost after transmission. Since the lifetime of a value is restricted to a single step of the state machine, we need a special value to describe the absence of a message on a channel. Therefore each data type contains the special value *nil* representing such an absence.

The variable state space of an STD, that is, the collection of the local variables of the corresponding component as defined in its CDD, is formalized as the product of all variables.

The control state space of an STD is formalized by introducing an additional state variable containing the actual control state of the corresponding machine.

Additionally, a predicate *Init*(s, x) on the control and variable state space is defined, characterizing initial configurations of the system as given by the initial state of the STD and the initial variable assignment in the CDD.

Transitions may be of the form

$$S_1 \xrightarrow{P(x);I(x,v)/O(x,v);C(x,x',v)} S_2$$

where

- x is the set of local variables defined for the component described by the STD; the definition of these variables can be found in the CDD of the component.
- $v = \{v_1, \ldots, v_k\}$ is a set of variables $v_1, \ldots, v_k$ local to the definition of the transition; these are variables used in the transition definition without being defined as variables local to the STD.
- $P(x)$ is a predicate over the set of variables of the state transition diagram x. and the set of variables of the transition definition v. At the moment, only propositional logic plus equality on the individuals and individual variables are allowed to form those predicates.
- $I(x, v) = I_1(x, v); \ldots; I_m(x, v)$ is a list of input port patterns over the set of variables x where the pattern for port i_i $I_i(x, v)$ may either be empty or $i_i ? c_i(x, v)$ with $c_i(x, v)$ being a data type constructor using the variables from x. and v.
- $O(x, v) = O_1(x, v); \ldots; O_n(x, v)$ is a list of output port patterns corresponding to the input patterns which may either be empty or $o_i ? d_j(x, v)$ with $d_j(x, v)$ being a data type constructor using the variables x and v.
- $C(x, x', v)$ is a predicate over the variables of the state transition diagram and the transition definition similar to the pre-condition; additionally to the variables x, corresponding primed variables x' may be used to describe the values of the variables before and after the transition is executed.

For each transition of the above form a clause

$$\exists v_1, \ldots, v_k . s = S_1 \wedge P(x) \wedge i_1 = c_1(x, v) \wedge \ldots \wedge i_m = c_m(x, v) \wedge$$

$$t = S_2 \wedge o_1 = d_1(x, v) \wedge \ldots \wedge o_n = d_n(x, v) \wedge C(x, x', v)$$

is introduced. If an empty port pattern was used for port i_i or o_j, $i_i = nil$ and $o_j = nil$, respectively, are used in the above clause.

The complete transition relation is defined as the disjunction of all the clauses introduced for the defined transitions plus clauses for all unspecified behaviors. Note that in case of conflicting transitions, that is, transitions with the same start state, precondition and input pattern but differing output pattern, post-condition or end state, these conflicts are interpreted - as usual - to be solved nondeterministically: All computations picking one of those conflicting transitions are included in the semantics.

Combination of SSDs/STDs

If a system is described as a collection of several communicating components, the behavior of the system must be generated from the description of the behavior of the single components and the static aspects of intercommunication via the channels. As in the case of EETs, we assume communication to take place instantaneously without introducing delay. Therefore, this formalization is basically done by simply combining the description of the components and identifying the shared communication channels. More formally,

- the new control state space is the product of all the control state spaces of the components,
- the new variable state space is the product of all the variable state spaces of the components and the internal channels as the defined by the SSD,
- the new input and output channels are the external channels as defined by the SSD, and
- the set of initial states is the product of all the sets of initial states of the components.

Furthermore, the transition relation R for the hierarchical system is defined to be the product of the single transition relations of each component.

SSD/STD-Refinement

One possible application of the above formalization and the model checking mechanism is the verification of refinement relations of SSDs together with the corresponding STDs. This becomes necessary if a component of an SSD has an associated sub-document, and for both the component itself and the components of the sub-document STDs are given to describe their behavior. Here, we have to show that the behavior of the complete hierarchical system described by the corresponding STD of the component is a more abstract version of the complete behavior of its components. The behavior of the complete system can be described as the combination of the behaviors of the individual components, abstracting from internal channels.

In FOCUS, on the requirements level we use trace equivalence as behavioral equivalence notion, and inclusion on trace sets as behavioral refinement notion. Since these notions are used in the *Isabelle* HOLCF-implementation of Focus, a corresponding notion of equivalence and refinement has to be defined for STDs using the relational μ calculus. Otherwise, the semantics given by the theorem prover *Isabelle* and by the model checker μ-cke would differ, yielding two different semantics for the same description techniques.

In general, bisimulation is the equivalence notion used on state-based description techniques and, in particular, in many model-checking based approaches. It cannot, however, be used in our case, since bisimulation and trace equivalence do not coincide here. Since we use STDs without a notion of fairness like, for example, fairness sets used in Buechi automata, we can apply the standard approach to show language inclusion of two given automata without any major complexity difference. Thus, to show that the set of traces $L(S_1)$ of STD S_1 is a subset of the corresponding set $L(S_2)$ of S_2, that is,

$$L(S_1) \subseteq L(S_2)$$

we show that

$$L(S_1) \cap \overline{L}(S_2) = \emptyset$$

where $\overline{L}(S_2)$ denotes the complement of S_2 regarding the set of all traces. The complement automaton $\overline{S_2}$ of S_2 can be effectively constructed by adding a new state f to the set of states of S_2 and defining the transition relation $\overline{R}$ to be

$$\overline{R} = R \cup \{(s,i,o,f) \mid \forall t. \ (s,i,o,t) \notin R\} \cup \{(f,i,o,f) \mid i \in I \wedge o \in O\}$$

Additionally, we define a relation $Final_i$ characterising final states in both automata. As mentioned above, we do not use fairness conditions in our approach. Thus it suffices to compare finite prefixes of execution traces of S_1 and $\overline{S_2}$ instead of their infinite traces, and to show that no common finite prefixes of infinite execution traces of S_1 and S_2 exist. Therefore, every state of S_1 is a final state. For $\overline{S_2}$, only f is a final state since only traces not possible in S_2 are considered.

Finally, the emptiness of the intersection of the trace sets is simply checked by making sure that no computation of the product automaton of S_1 and S_2 will lead to a final state of the automaton, or - conversely - that by computing backwards no initial state can be reached from a final state. Therefore we define a relation $LeadsToFinal$ to characterise states leading to a final state of the product automaton of S_1 and $\overline{S_2}$:

$$\mu \ LeadsToFinal(s_1, s_2) =$$

$$(Final_1(s_1) \wedge Final_2(s_2)) \vee$$

$$\exists i,o,t_1,t_2. \ R_1(s_1,i,o,t_1) \wedge \overline{R_2}(s_2,i,o,t_2) \wedge LeadsToFinal(t_1,t_2)$$

Here, μ characterises the operator for the smallest fixed point. Now, the check itself simply consists of

$$\forall s_1, s_2. Init_1(s_1) \wedge Init_2(s_2) \rightarrow \neg LeadsToFinal(s_1, s_2)$$

If this condition does not hold, that is, a trace of S_1 is found not contained in $L(S_2)$, a counter example can be produced to demonstrate the mismatch.

Transformation of EETs

While STDs were basically formalized by giving a transition relation, we will formalize EETs as conditions on these transition relations. In order to demonstrate the core concept of this formalization we will first define the formalization only for EETs consisting of only one axis. After that, we will sketch how such single axis EETs can be combined to form general EETs.

Using the relational μ calculus, for each step within the corresponding EET we can define a relational μ calculus formula characterizing the described behavior. In case of the EET shown in Figure 3 we have to define the steps 1 through n+1 according to the following scheme:

$$\nu EET_{n+1}(s) = \exists i,o.(C(i,o) \wedge \exists t.(R(s,i,o,t) \wedge EET_{n+1}(t))$$

$$\mu EET_n(s) = \exists i,o.(P_n(i,o) \wedge \exists t.(R(s,i,o,t) \wedge EET_{n+1}(t))) \vee$$
$$(C(i,o) \wedge \exists t.(R(s,i,o,t) \wedge EET_n(t))$$

$$\vdots$$

$$\mu EET_i(s) = \exists i, o.(P_i(i,o) \wedge \exists t.(R(s,i,o,t) \wedge EET_{i+1}(t)))$$
$$\vee\, (C(i,o) \wedge \exists t.(R(s,i,o,t) \wedge EET_i(t))$$
$$\vdots$$
$$EET(s) = Init(s) \wedge EET_1(s)$$

Here, $\vee$ and μ characterize the greatest and least fixed points of the corresponding equation. The variables s and t contain the complete state space of the system, that is, both the variable and control state space. C describes a step of the component where no messages are sent or received between two observed events:

$$i_1\, ?\, nil \wedge \ldots \wedge i_m\, ?\, nil \wedge o_1\, !\, nil \wedge \ldots o_n\, !\, nil$$

Finally, P_i describes the fact that the corresponding messages were sent or received while no events occurred at the other channels of the component:

$$i_1\, ?\, v_1 \wedge \ldots \wedge i_m\, ?\, v_m \wedge o_1\, !\, w_1 \wedge \ldots o_n\, !\, w_n$$

with v_i and w_j being the values received or sent, or nil otherwise.

By using a similar construction as in the case of the hierarchical SSDs described for the combination of SSDs and STDs, the combination of single component EETs to complete system EETs can be defined. The system state space is the product of the component state spaces, and the in-between states (defined by the EET_i predicates) are the products of those states.

STDs and EETs

Note that EETs are defined as requirements for the transition relation of a system. This is due to the fact that the μ calculus definition of EET as given above makes use of the transition relation R as defined by the corresponding STD. They are not descriptions of a system in themselves. So we need not use some kind of language inclusion relation to verify the relationship between STDs and EETs as we have done in case of SSD/STD refinement.

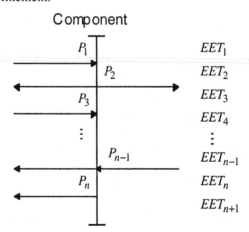

Figure 3: One Component EET

Instead, to check that an EET formalized as $EET(s)$ using a transition relation R describes a possible run of the system with transition relation R we just have to prove

$$\exists s.EET(s)$$

Thus, EETs can be seen as "use cases" describing a possible expected behavior of the transition relation of the system. Similarly, to prove that an EET describes a run not possible for the system, we have to prove

$$\forall s.\neg EET(s)$$

This, in turn, applies EETs as "negative use cases" describing behavior patterns not allowed for the transition relation of the system.

Further Properties

Besides from checking the behavioral consistency of hierarchical systems or STDs and EETs, the full expressiveness of the relational μ calculus can be used to verify additional properties. By formalizing properties like liveness of a component, deadlock freedom or similar properties as a relational μ calculus expression without using the graphical notations these properties may be verified automatically using the translation of the graphical specification. Since formalizing these properties using the relational μ calculus however requires quite some mathematical knowledge, easier specification front-ends to the μ calculus like CTL might be more appropriate in this framework.

Witnesses

A major advantage of model checking is the possibility of witness generation. If we try to prove the incorrect assumption that a component can be implemented by a subsystem of components, we get a counterexample describing a system run leading to a contradiction instead. This counterexample can be visualized using the EET description technique, thus showing why the refinement relation does not hold. Similarly, if we check whether an EET describes a legal system run, we can mark the point of failure where an event prescribed by the EET cannot be produced by the system.

5.3 Theorem Proving

In general, model checking of the described systems may not be feasible under all circumstances due to the state space being too large, even using sophisticated mechanisms to reduce the size of the internal representation like variable interleaving. In this case it may be necessary to apply interactive theorem proving to verify certain system properties. Therefore, in addition to the relational μ semantics a semantics suitable for interactive theorem proving must be given. We use the semantical model of stream processing functions defined in the Focus methodology [2]. By defining a corresponding semantics [12] on basis of the HOLCF [11] logics, we can use the *Isabelle* theorem prover as interactive verification tool. Of course, this semantics has to be consistent with the semantics introduced using the relational μ calculus. Basically, the semantics described in [3] can be used.

6 Future Work

AUTOFOCUS in its current state is the result of a number of student projects. It was started in a practical project course in software engineering in the 1996 summer term and has since then been enhanced to its current state.

Based on this status, a number of further extensions are currently planned or implemented. The present implementation of AUTOFOCUS is intended to be the core of a complete tool-set for developing distributed systems. Extensions currently in work or under investigation are listed subsequently.

6.1 Code Generation

Code Generation is an important core functionality for various other functions, like prototyping, simulation, and more. Since transformation done by hand is not only laborious but also error-prone, it is an important feature in a formally-based approach. As we use an implementation-oriented description technique to describe system behavior, code generation becomes a simple process. In addition to the specialized generation mechanisms used in the simulation framework as mentioned in section 6.2, it is planned to implement a generic code generator that can be customized according to specific needs.

6.2 Simulation

Simulation, particularly in combination with sophisticated visualization tools, is a very important means for developers to gain a deeper understanding of how a developed system works. The area of simulation covers a wide range of applications, reaching from elementary animation of single diagrams, like STDs, visualizing the state transitions according to the inputs received, to concurrent simulation of several or all system components processing input and producing output simultaneously. In this context, the ability to generate protocols of simulation runs is desirable: we are planning to use EETs, showing the recorded communication history of selected components for this purpose.

6.3 Graphical Development Steps

Graphical development steps for the same description techniques as used here, guaranteeing consistent refining transformations of the specifications were already discussed in [13], using a slightly different semantics. Since the semantics introduced here is basically compatible with the original version, the same graphical transformation steps can safely be applied. Thus, enhancing the AUTOFOCUS tool with these mechanisms is a straight-forward step.

6.4 Reuse and Libraries

We intend to integrate library mechanisms into AUTOFOCUS, enabling developers to easily reuse documents that have been developed earlier, a functionality that is essential for industrial systems development. Thus, developers can develop libraries of reusable system components, structures, and behaviors that can be incorporated into new development projects.

7 Bibliography

[1] A. Biere. *Eine Methode zur μ-Kalkül-Modellprüfung*. Slides for the AKFM from 23.05.96, GI/ITG-Fachgespräch „Formale Beschreibungstechniken für verteilte Systeme" (in German), 1996.

[2] M. Broy, C. Dendorfer, F. Dederichs, M. Fuchs, T. Gritzner, and R. Weber. *The Design of Distributed Systems - An Introduction to FOCUS*. Technical Report TUM-I9225, Technische Universität München, 1992.

[3] M. Fuchs and M. Mendler. *Functional Semantics for Delta-Delay VHDL based on Focus.* In: C. Delgado Kloos and P. Breuer (eds.). Formal Semantics for VHDL, Kluwer Academic Publishers, 1994, Chapter I, pp. 9 - 38.

[4] R. Grosu, C. Klein, B. Rumpe, and M. Broy. *State Transition Diagrams.* Technical Report TUM-I9630, Technische Universität München, 1996.

[5] D. Harel and A. Naamad. *The Statemate Semantics of Statecharts.* IEEE Transactions of Software Engineering Methods, 1996.

[6] F. Huber, B. Schätz, A. Schmidt, and K. Spies. *AutoFocus - A Tool for Distributed System Specification.* In: B. Jonsson and J. Parrow (eds.). Proceedings FTRTFT´96. Lecture Notes in Computer Science 1135, Springer, 1996, pp. 476-470.

[7] International Telecommunication Union. *Message Sequence Charts, 1996.* ITU-T Recommendation Z.129. Geneva, 1996.

[8] M. P. Jones. *Introduction to Gofer 2.20.* Technical Report, Yale University, 1991.

[9] J.-L. Lions et al. *Ariane 5 Flight 501 Failure.* ESA Press Release 33-96, Paris, 1996.

[10] D. Park. *Finitness is μ-ineffible.* Theoretical Computer Science 3(2), 1976, pp. 173-181.

[11] F. Regensburger. *HOLCF: Higher Order Logic of Computable Functions.* In: T. Schubert, P. Windley, and J. Alves-Foss (eds.). Higher Order Logic Theorem Proving and Its Application (HOL95), 1995, pp. 293-307.

[12] R. Sandner and Olaf Müller. *Theorem Prover Support for the Refinement of Stream Processing Functions.* Proc. 3rd Int. Workshop on Tools and Algorithms for the Construction and Analysis of Systems (TACAS´97). Lecture Notes in Computer Sience Vol. 1217. Springer, 1997, pp. 351-365.

[13] B. Schätz, H. Hußmann, and M. Broy. *Graphical Development of Consistent System Specifications.* In: J. Woodcock, M.-C. Gaudel (eds.). FME' 96. Lecture Notes in Computer Science Vol. 1051, Springer, 1996, pp. 248-267.

[14] B. Schätz and K. Spies. *Formale Syntax zur logischen Kernsprache der Focus-Entwicklungsmethodik.* Technial Report TUM-I9529, Technische Universität München, 1995.

[15] D. von Oheimb. *Datentypspezifikationen in HOLCF.* Master´s Thesis, Technische Universität München, 1996.

Design of Reactive Control Systems
for Event-Driven Operations

K. Lano
Dept. of Computing, Imperial College, 180 Queens Gate, London SW7 2BZ
A. Sanchez
Centre for Process Systems Engineering, Imperial College, London SW7 2BY.
Current address: Departmento de Ingenieria Electrica. CINVESTAV-Gdl.
Apdo. Postal 31-438. Guadalajara 45090, Jalisco, Mexico

Abstract. This paper explores the combination of formal methods with techniques taken from control engineering for specifying, designing and verifying reactive systems.

In particular, it is shown how to use techniques for specification and verification in VDM^{++} in combination with the synthesis of *procedural controllers*, a mathematical abstraction of the logic controlling an event-driven sequential operation. The procedural controller is used as a provably correct specification of an event-driven operation to be implemented using VDM^{++}. The resulting method enables a systematic approach for creating formalized designs of controllers for this type of operations, and proof obligations for the correctness of the designs against specifications to be generated. The approach is illustrated using an example.

1   Introduction

This paper shows how to use a theoretical framework taken from control engineering, termed Procedural Control Theory (PCT) [11, 13], to obtain the specification of a reactive system which is then developed in VDM^{++}. PCT provides tools for synthesizing a class of model-based *controllers* (a device that schedules commands to a given system according to a predetermined *control law*), named *procedural controllers* for event-driven sequential operations satisfying safety and operability properties. Such controllers are state-transition structures that describe the constrained (in control engineering jargon, closed-loop) system behaviour that is theoretically guaranteed to achieve desired goal states in a safe manner and never reach forbidden situations. The *procedural controller* is then used as a provably correct specification of the constrained behaviour for which proof obligations are posed in VDM^{++} to guarantee a correct implementation. The modularity mechanisms of VDM^{++} support a decomposition of verification into a number of steps, showing that the controller operations at the lowest level of implementation (i.e. opening and closing valves, etc.) maintain the safety invariants (that undesired states are avoided), provided they are called within their preconditions, and that the controller at a higher level of abstraction invokes these low-level operations within their preconditions.

As an illustration of the methodology, the paper presents the synthesis and implementation of a controller for a simplified burner system. A similar example has been used to demonstrate verification techniques in chemical engineering [8]. Applications of PCT to larger systems are presented elsewhere [10, 11].

The paper starts by briefly introducing VDM^{++} specification language. Afterwards, Section 3 describes the proposed method to obtain an implementable design of the control system. The method comprises requirement, specification, refinement and implementation steps. PCT is used in the specification step to obtain the provably correct specification of the control system to be implemented. The notion of *procedural controller* and how to synthesize it are sketched in Section 4. References are given where a complete treatment of this topic can be found. Finally, Section 5 illustrates the method using the burner example. Due to space restrictions many details are omitted. A complete report is available from the authors upon request.

2 VDM^{++}

VDM^{++} is an extension of the VDM-SL notation to cover object-oriented structuring, concurrency and real-time specification elements. It is oriented to the description of reactive systems, but has advantages over languages such as statecharts or SDL in providing a fully formal specification language for abstractly describing complex data types and state transitions in a model-based style, together with a precise definition of refinement. A VDM^{++} specification consists of a set of *class* definitions, where these have the general form:

```
class C
types ...
values ...
functions ...
time variables ...
instance variables
    vC : TC ;
inv objectstate == InvC ;
init objectstate == InitC
methods
    m(x : Xm,C) value y : Ym,C
      pre Prem,C(x, vC)   ==   Defnm,C ;
    ...
sync ...
thread ...
aux reasoning ...
end C
```

The **types**, **values** and **functions** components define types, constants and functions as in conventional VDM. Although class reference sets @D for class names **D** can be used as types in these items – such classes **D** are termed *suppliers* to **C**, as are instances of these classes. **C** is then a *client* of **D**. The **instance variables** component defines the attributes of the class, and the **inv** defines an invariant over a list of these variables (including time variables): `objectstate` is used to include all the attributes. The `init` component defines, via a statement, a set of initial states in which an object of the class may be at object creation. Object creation is achieved via an invocation of the operation **C!new**, which returns a reference to a new object of type **C** as its result. The initialisation is executed on object creation.

Time variables can be used to express timing constraints or assumptions about the continuous/hybrid behaviour of physical systems.

The methods of **C** are listed in the `methods` clause. Methods can be defined in an abstract declarative way, using *specification statements*, or by using a hybrid of specification statements, method calls and procedural code. Input parameters are indicated within the brackets of the method header, and results after a `value` keyword. Preconditions of a method are given in the `pre` clause. Other clauses of a class definition control how **C** inherits from other classes: an optional `is subclass of` clause in the class header lists classes which are being extended by the present class – that is, all their methods become exportable facilities of **C**. An `inherits` clause in **C** lists classes which are being included via *controlled inheritance*: whereby some inherited methods are made internal to **C**. Dynamic behaviour of objects of **C** is specified in the `sync` and `thread` clauses.

A set of internal consistency requirements are associated with a class, which assert that i) its state space is non-empty; ii) the definition of each method maintains the invariant of the class; iii) the initialisation establishes the invariant. Refinement obligations, based on theory extension, can also be given [7].

2.1 Refinement Concepts

The semantics of a VDM^{++} class **C** can be given as a real-time action logic (RAL) [7] theory $\Gamma_{\mathbf{C}}$ which expresses the typing of its attributes and methods, the effect of its methods, and its dynamic behaviour and constraints.

Refinement of classes is then based on theory interpretations between the Γ theories. Theory interpretations in RAL are similar to those for the object calculus [4]. A morphism $\sigma : \mathbf{Th1} \rightarrow \mathbf{Th2}$ maps each type symbol **T** of **Th1** to a type symbol $\sigma(\mathbf{T})$ of **Th2**, each function symbol of **Th1** to a function symbol of **Th2**, and each attribute of **Th1** to an attribute of **Th2**. Actions of **Th1** are mapped to actions of **Th2**. We can construct a category of theories with theory morphisms as categorical arrows as usual.

The concepts of subtyping and refinement in VDM^{++} correspond to a particular form of theory morphism. Class **C** is a supertype of class **D** if there is a *retrieve function* $\mathbf{R} : \mathbf{T_D} \rightarrow \mathbf{T_C}$ between the respective states, and a renaming ϕ of methods of **C** to those of **D**, such that for every $\varphi \in \mathcal{L_C}$, $\Gamma_{\mathbf{C}} \vdash \varphi$ implies that $\Gamma_{\mathbf{D}} \vdash \phi(\varphi[\mathbf{R}(v)/u])$ where **v** is the tuple of attributes of **D**, **u** of **C**. ϕ must map internal methods of **C** to internal methods of **D**, and external methods to external methods. The notation $\mathbf{C} \sqsubseteq_{\phi,\mathbf{R}} \mathbf{D}$ is used to denote this relation. **D** is a refinement of **C** if it is a subtype of **C** and the retrieve function **R** satisfies the condition of *adequacy*:

$$\forall \mathbf{u} \in \mathbf{T_C} \cdot \mathbf{Inv_C}(\mathbf{u}) \Rightarrow \exists \mathbf{v} \in \mathbf{T_D} \cdot \mathbf{Inv_D}(\mathbf{v}) \wedge \mathbf{R}(\mathbf{v}) = \mathbf{u}$$

That is, **R** is onto. No new external methods can be introduced in **D**.

As usual, refinement proofs can be decomposed into modular proofs of stronger but more local obligations.

3 Constructing a Reactive System

The proposed development method for reactive systems in VDM^{++} involves the following steps:

1. **System modelling**. The goal of this first stage is twofold. First, to gain understanding of the process behaviour which will ease a correct capture of the requirements and behaviour specifications. Second, to guarantee model consistency through all the development process by using the model as a basis for the generation of a low level description of the system in VDM^{++} and for the synthesis of the procedural controller. Three stages are distinguished:

   (a) **Generation of system architecture**. Given the system components, a system architecture is built using standard techniques. In this case a data and control flow diagram is used for this purpose.

   (b) **Capture of elementary components behaviour**. A description of the system behaviour using continuous or hybrid descriptions must be obtained which are then encapsulated in classes. In this case, Finite State Machines (FSMs) capture the behaviour of each hardware component.

   (c) **Construction of unconstrained system VDM^{++} specification**. The unconstrained system VDM^{++} specification comprises all possible behaviour declared in the elementary component FSMs. It is captured as a subclass of the elementary component classes.

2. **Capture of system abstract specification**. Obtaining the abstract specification of the system's behaviour is carried out using PCT. The input information required is a) state-transition models for each hardware component defined in step 1.a; b) forbidden states that the system must avoid and; c) dynamic behaviour that must be achieved in normal and abnormal operation. The last two are captured using logical formalisms. The result is a *procedural controller*, an FSM where states represent system states and the language accepted by the FSM models the system behaviour. The *procedural controller*, if it exists, is mathematically guaranteed to minimally satisfy the dynamic specifications while avoiding forbidden states. Thus the *procedural controller* is used as a high level description that the system must achieve. A sketch description of techniques used to carry out this task is given in the following section.

3. **Generation of VDM^{++} specification**. This comprises the following steps:

   (a) **Generation of constrained system specification**. The existence of a *procedural controller* guarantees a minimal satisfaction of forbidden states and dynamic behaviour specifications. Thus, the constrained systems is formed by the inclusions in the invariant section of such statements. New operations are also defined, if needed, satisfying such invariants.

(b) **Specification of the abstract controller**. It usual that the cardinality of the FSM modelling the *procedural controller* reaches the order of magnitude of hundreds of states and transitions. Thus, it has been found convenient to reduce the size of the machine by grouping states by mode of operation (e.g. in the burner example meta states are defined as **idle**, **try_ignite**, etc.) in which transitions among the states correspond to inputs in the data and control flow diagram. A class named **AbstractController** captures this as a VDM^{++} specification.

(c) **Refinement of abstract controller**. The next step is the transformation of the abstract requirements (expressed, for example, in **whenever** statements [3]) into method definitions which carry out the required changes, in response to polling or interrupts. The result is the **HL_Controller** class. Separation of polling mechanisms from the controller into special-purpose objects are also carried out. This leads to a 'pure' reactive system specification that describes the reaction to each of the events sent to the controller.

4. **Definition of the hardware wrapper**. The **HL_Controller**, together with the polling mechanisms are captured in the hardware wrapper allowing an easy implementation.

4   Procedural Control

Procedural Control Theory is a formal framework for the specification, analysis and synthesis of feedback model-based control mechanisms, termed *procedural controllers*, targeted to discrete-event sequential systems [11, 13]. Two key components of PCT are the notions of *procedural controller* and *controllability*.

A *procedural controller* is a mathematical representation of the logic controlling an event-driven operation. It is represented by a finite state machine (FSM) describing possible system behaviour in which each state either has: (i) a unique transition leaving it, representing an output from the controller to the controlled system, i.e. a control command; or (ii) transitions modelling process responses that can be issued in the current system state. Type i) transitions are said to be controllable because the controller is capable of issuing these commands, whilst type ii) transitions are termed incontrollable since the controller does not have any authority upon them. In this paper, states where type (ii) transitions occur will be called *wait* states. PCT gives sufficient conditions of existence for a procedural controller fulfilling safety properties. That is, if a procedural controller exists for a given specification, it can be guaranteed that the process behaviour will be kept by the controller within desired boundaries, avoiding any hazardous or unsafe operation by issuing control commands. Thus, it is said that a process is *controllable* if in each state of its state-transition representation, all corresponding process responses are declared as possible candidates of occurrence or there exists at least one control command to be executed. Thus, a procedural controller exists which forces desired states to be reached and undesired states to be avoided, by the use of control commands.

The synthesis of a procedural controller comprises the following stages [9]:

1. **Input-output modelling of processing system components.** Elementary process components (e.g. valves, switches, timers) are modelled as state-transition structures in which transitions are classified as described above as: i) control commands (controllable transitions from the controller point of view), and ii) process responses (uncontrollable transitions from the controller point of view). The former will correspond to events generated by the controller whilst the latter will usually form the list of events to which the controller must respond. Important states to be reached during operation such as the initial state, a state of desired activity, etc., are identified in each model. They are termed *marked* states.

   A model of the unconstrained (open-loop) behaviour of the whole system is built by combining the elementary component models using FSM operators [11]. Extra behaviour not captured for each elementary component is usually added (e.g. if an exit valve in a storage tank is closed, the level should not decrease). This model will serve as a basis for the synthesis of the procedural controller realising such behaviour.

2. **Prescription of forbidden states.** States that must be avoided during operation must be declared as forbidden. Logical invariants are used to model the avoidance of these states [11].

3. **Prescription of dynamic specifications.** Desired dynamic behaviour to be imposed upon the process by the procedural controller must be declared. These include normal, abnormal and emergency operation. They can be captured as temporal logic (RAL [7] or LTL [11]) formulas.

4. **Procedural controller superstructure synthesis.** This superstructure represents the maximal feasible (i.e. closed-loop controllable) behaviour that avoids all forbidden states [13]. Its construction is a preliminary step in the synthesis of the procedural controller. The superstructure usually contains states in which several control actions can be executed. It is the task of the procedural controller synthesis to resolve this underspecification.

5. **Procedural controller synthesis.** Given the dynamic specifications and the controller superstructure, the constrained (closed-loop) behaviour is found which satisfies the dynamic specifications and is controllable [13]. In other words, an FSM is found that i) accepts minimally the behaviour described by the dynamic specifications and ii) is guaranteed to describe the behaviour produced by the system and controller synchronised by the execution of transitions. This FSM is termed a procedural controller [13].

Note that it is possible that no procedural controller exists satisfying the stated specifications. This becomes a design problem in which either the system equipment or the specification must be modified. A *procedural controller* synthesized in this manner is mathematically guaranteed to be correct with respect to its specification.

5 Gas Burner Case Study

We will begin the development of this system from an initial design stage, at which the physical components to be used and the data and control flow diagram have already been determined, and discrete finite state models of components defined. Real-time components such as the **Timer** have also been modelled as finite state machines in order to enable procedural control synthesis.

The process to be controlled in the case study is the simplified burner system shown in Figure 1. It consists of the following process items: an on/off valve to feed air (av); an on/off valve to feed fuel (gv); a flame igniter (fv); a flame detector (fd); an on/off switch to start/stop the operation of the burner (bu); an alarm indicator to indicate abnormal/emergency conditions in the burner (al); a timer to time the start-up operation (ti). The data and control flow diagram of the system is given in Figure 2.

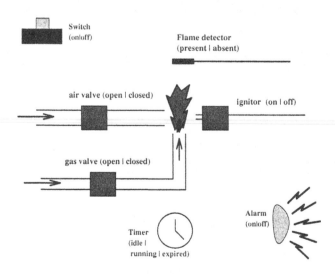

Fig. 1. Gas Burner Components

The objective of the exercise is to generate a reactive control system to operate the burner, namely i) to start it up, maintain it with an ignited flame and to shut it down when requested, in the safest possible way and ii) to deal with abnormal and emergency conditions that may arise during operation. The

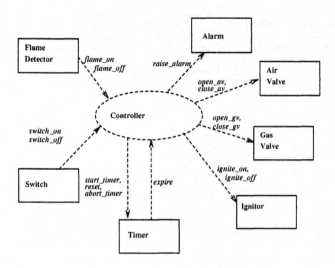

Fig. 2. Data and Control Flow Diagram of Burner System

safest start up is achieved by minimising the time in which the air/fuel mixture is present in the chamber without the occurrence of flame. In order to maximise the life of the igniter, it must be used only when the system must ignite.The initial state of the system is when all valves are closed, and the rest of the components are off. The desired operation of the burner is divided into normal, alarm activation and emergency modes. These are captured using natural language resulting in 16 statements. Some examples are given in appendix 1.

5.1 System Modelling

Models are constructed to represent the input-output behaviour of each system element. In this case, each item is modelled as an FSM as shown in Table 1. Each FSM gives a description of the component behaviour in terms of operational states and transitions representing the inputs and outputs of the given system.

5.2 Generation of the VDM++ Unconstrained System Specification

The VDM++ models of components can be immediately generated from the FSMs, together with some choices over the naming of states and transitions being supplied by the developer. For example, the **Timer** is formalised by:

```
class Timer
  is subclass of GBTypes
instance variables
  tstate: TState;
init objectstate ==
  tstate := <idle>
inv objectstate ==
  whenever tstate = <running>
```

| elementary | state–variable | | state | | transition | | |
component	description	value	label	label	description	from st	to st
air	valve	av_closed	1	11	open_av	1	2
valve	position	av_open	2	12	close_av	2	1
gas	valve	gv_ closed	1	21	open_gv	1	2
valve	position	gv_open	2	22	close_gv	2	1
igniter	igniter	off	1	31	ignite_on	1	2
valve	status	on	2	32	ignite_off	2	1
flame	detector	present	1	41*	flame_on	1	2
detector	status	absent	2	42*	flame_off	2	1
emergency	alarm	alarm_off	1	51	activate_alarm	1	2
alarm	status	alarm_on	2	52	deactivate_alarm	2	1
switch	switch	off	1	61*	switch_on	1	2
	status	on	2	62*	switch_off	2	1
timer	timer	idle	1	71	start_timer	1	2
	status	running	2	72	abort_timer	2	1
		expired	3	73*	expire	2	3
				74	reset	3	1

Table 1. Elementary models of the burner system (* = uncontrollable transition).

```
  also from p ==>
    tstate = <idle>  or  tstate = <expired>
methods
  start_timer()
    pre tstate = <idle>  ==  tstate := <running>;

  abort_timer()
    pre tstate = <running>  ==  tstate := <idle>;

  expire()
    pre tstate = <running>  ==  tstate := <expired>;

  reset()
    pre tstate = <expired>  ==  tstate := <idle>
end Timer
```

The **whenever** statement asserts that "Whenever the timer enters the state
< **running** >, within **p** time units it must enter the state < **idle** > or the state
< **expired** >." The timer will become part of the environment (the 'hardware
wrapper') and must be implemented in a way that satisfies this invariant.

GBTypes encapsulates shared type definitions such as **TState** = < **idle** > |
< **running** > | < **expired** >. The preconditions of the **Timer** actions express
physical constraints: it is not possible for a **expire** event to occur unless the
timer is < **running** >, for example.

The VDM^{++} specification of the unconstrained system is formed by inheriting each of the classes corresponding to individual components into a new class:

```
class UnconstrainedSystem
   is subclass of AirValve, GasValve, FlameDetector, Switch, Timer, Ignitor,
             Alarm
end UnconstrainedSystem
```

5.3 Capture of system abstract specification

Given the system to be controlled, and the desired behaviour to achieve in the form of the statements of appendix 1, the abstract specification for the controller is obtained following the steps outlined in section 4. Due to space limitations, each stage procedure is sketched and references are given as needed.

Input-output modelling of processing system components. The FSMs given in Table 1 are used as the elementary models for each processing component. The overall open-loop model is given by the asynchronous product of the seven elementary system components [11]. The resultant FSM contains 192 states. Relevant states for the operation are defined in Table 2 as *marked*. These are the initial state of the system and safe goal states that may be reached during normal or abnormal operation.

state	*state–variables*						
	air valve	gas valve	igniter	flame detector	alarm	switch	timer
initial	av_closed	gv_closed	off	absent	alarm_off	off	idle
normal	av_open	gv_open	off	present	alarm_off	on	idle
safe alarm	av_closed	gv_closed	off	any value	alarm_on	any value	any value

Table 2. List of marked states

Prescription of Forbidden States (Invariants). The forbidden states are obtained from the initial description of the case study in Section 5. In order to minimise the time in which the air/fuel mixture is present without flame present, if the gas valve is open then so must the air valve, irrespective of the state of any of the other process components. This is described by the invariant (1):
gvstate = < gv_open > $\Rightarrow$ avstate = < av_open >.

Likewise, in order to maximise the life of the igniter, it must be used only when the system must ignite. Therefore, the ignitor is on only if the air valve is open (2): istate = < on > $\Rightarrow$ avstate = < av_open >.

Prescription of Dynamic Specifications. The description of the desired behaviour must be formalised as well. This is achieved by capturing the specifications using RAL, a temporal logic formalism [7]. As an example, two of some of the specifications listed in appendix 1 are translated into RAL.

Normal Operation. If the system is in the initial state and the switch changes to on then start up the system: (i) Launch timer; (ii) Open air valve; (iii) Switch on igniter; (iv) Open gas valve.

In RAL the constraint could be written as (**TA**1):

$$(\text{avstate} = < \text{av\_closed} > \wedge \text{gvstate} = < \text{gv\_closed} > \wedge$$
$$\text{istate} = < \text{off} > \wedge \text{fdstate} = < \text{absent} > \wedge$$
$$\text{astate} = < \text{alarm\_off} > \wedge \text{sstate} = < \text{switch\_off} > \wedge$$
$$\text{tstate} = < \text{idle} > \wedge \text{switch\_on}) \Rightarrow$$
$$\bigcirc \text{start\_timer} \wedge \bigcirc \bigcirc \text{open\_av} \wedge$$
$$\bigcirc \bigcirc \bigcirc \text{ignite\_on} \wedge \bigcirc \bigcirc \bigcirc \bigcirc \text{open\_gv}$$

$\bigcirc$**act** asserts that the next method to execute in the history of the object is **act**.

Similarly, if the system is starting up and flame is detected, it must: (i) Switch off ignitor; (ii) Abort timer. In temporal logic:

$$(\text{avstate} = < \text{av\_open} > \wedge \text{gvstate} = < \text{gv\_open} > \wedge$$
$$\text{istate} = < \text{on} > \wedge \text{fdstate} = < \text{absent} > \wedge$$
$$\text{astate} = < \text{alarm\_off} > \wedge \text{sstate} = < \text{switch\_on} > \wedge$$
$$\text{tstate} = < \text{running} > \wedge \text{flame\_on}) \Rightarrow$$
$$\bigcirc \text{ignite\_off} \wedge \bigcirc \bigcirc \text{abort\_timer}$$

Synthesis of Procedural Controller Superstructure. Applying the method for synthesising the maximal controller superstructure [13], the FSM satisfying the forbidden states (1) and (2) declared above and rendering a controllable behaviour, diminishes the size of the original open-loop model from 192 states to 120 states.

Synthesis of Procedural Controller. Using the controller superstructure and the 16 dynamic specifications, a procedural controller for this system is generated using the techniques of [9, 13]. It has 39 states, and is shown in Figure 3. Wait states are shown as ovals. For simplicity, numeric labels are used according to the key given in Table 1 with the following order:

(air valve, gas valve, igniter, flame detector, alarm, switch, timer)

Dashed line arrows represent uncontrollable transitions (i.e. system responses), whilst continuous line arrows are control commands. The initial state is shown at the top of the FSM. The behaviour generated by this procedural controller can be visually checked to be controllable.

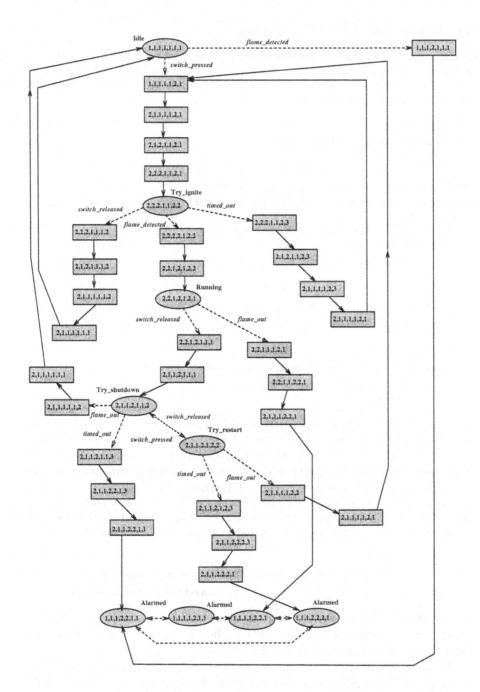

Fig. 3. FSM representing the Procedural Controller

5.4 Generation of VDM^{++} specification

Generation of VDM^{++} constrained system specification. With the certainty that forbidden states can be safely avoided by the correct sequencing of control actions given by the procedural controller, these are expressed in the **inv** clause of a **ConstrainedSystem** class:

```
class ConstrainedSystem
  is subclass of UnconstrainedSystem
inv objectstate ==
  (gvstate = <gv_open>  =>  avstate = <av_open>) and
  (istate = <on>  =>  avstate = <av_open>)
methods /* restrict some transitions of unconstrained system: */
  close_av()
    pre istate = <off> and gvstate = <gv_closed> and
        avstate = <av_open>  ==
      self!AirValve'close_av();

  open_gv()
    pre avstate = <av_open> and gvstate = <gv_closed>  ==
          self!GasValve'open_gv();

  ignite_on()
    pre avstate = <av_open> and istate = <off>  ==
          self!Ignitor'ignite_on()
end ConstrainedSystem
```

The operations **close_av**, etc are redefined in this class to ensure that they preserve the new invariant, if they are called in states which satisfy their preconditions. The statement **self!AirValve'close_av()** is a way of invoking the **AirValve** definition of this action. Other operations, **flame_on**, **open_av**, etc, retain the definitions they were given in **UnconstrainedSystem**.

These preconditions can be calculated from the invariants **Inv** and definitions **Def** of the atomic transitions. They are: **Pre** $\equiv$ (**Inv** $\Rightarrow$ [**Def**]**Inv**) where [ ] is the weakest precondition operator [1]. For example, for the action **close_av**:

$$\text{Pre}_{\text{close\_av}} \equiv$$
$$[avstate := <av\_closed>](gvstate = <gv\_open> \Rightarrow$$
$$avstate = <av\_open>)$$

is (**gvstate** $= <$ **gv_open** $> \Rightarrow <$ **av_closed** $> = <$ **av_open** $>$), ie.: **gvstate** $= <$ **gv_closed** $>$. Notice that [ ] distributes over $\wedge$, so that the conjuncts of the invariant can be treated separately.

These specifications are introduced as additional properties of **Constrained System** enforcing active behaviour on any implementation of the system, in addition to requiring that the actions of the actuators are invoked by the controller in particular orders. The specifications are expressed as formulae in the theory of the **ConstrainedSystem** class – this class is fully mutex (methods cannot overlap in their executions) and so has a history consisting of intervals in which either no action executes, or in which exactly one of the atomic actions from one of the gas burner components is executing. The procedure specifications are of the form **current_state = val** $\land$ α $\Rightarrow$ $\bigcirc \theta$ where α is an uncontrolled action, and θ contains only controlled actions. Other forms of dynamic constraint include liveness requirements of the form $\mathbf{P} \Rightarrow \Diamond \mathbf{Q}$ or $\mathbf{P} \Rightarrow (\mathbf{A}\,\mathcal{U}\,\mathbf{B})$ [5].

Timing constraints could also be included. For instance, that the gas valve should never open for a continuous period of more than 30 seconds with the flame being absent (**RT**1):

$$\forall\, t_1, t_2 : \mathbf{TIME}\ \cdot\ t_1 < t_2\ \Rightarrow$$
$$(\text{gvstate} = <\text{gv\_open}> \land \text{fdstate} = <\text{absent}>)\odot[t_1, t_2]\ \Rightarrow$$
$$t_2 - t_1\ \leq\ 30$$

where $\varphi\odot\mathbf{I}$ means that φ holds throughout the interval $\mathbf{I}$. **TIME** is usually taken to be the non-negative real numbers in VDM^{++}.

Specification of the abstract controller. The abstract controller for the system is built in an *ad-hoc* manner using a copy of the data of the unconstrained system. Meta states are defined with some operational meaning (e.g. try_ignite, alarmed) with transitions for the events given in the data and control flow diagram. The resulting FSM is shown in fig. 4.

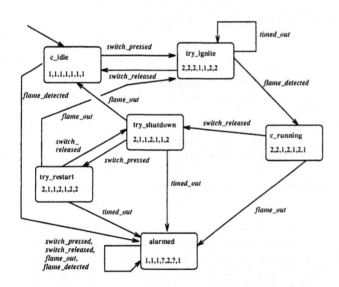

Fig. 4. Abstract Controller FSM

A class capturing the above is given as follows. Its methods correspond to the events which are inputs to the controller on the data and control flow diagram:

```
class AbstractControl
    is subclass of AirValve, GasValve, FlameDetector, Switch,
                   Timer, Ignitor, Alarm
```

```
inherit /* No methods of the superclasses appear in the interface of
           AbstractControl */
types
  CState = <c_idle> | <try_ignite> | <c_running> | <try_shutdown> |
           <try_restart> | <alarmed>
instance variables
  cstate: CState;
inv objectstate ==
  (cstate = <c_idle>  <=>
           (avstate = <av_closed> and gvstate = <gv_closed> and
            istate = <off> and fdstate = <absent> and
            astate = <alarm_off> and sstate = <switch_off> and
            tstate = <idle>) ) and
  (cstate = <try_ignite>  <=>
           (avstate = <av_open> and gvstate = <gv_open> and
            istate = <on> and fdstate = <absent> and
            astate = <alarm_off> and sstate = <switch_on> and
            tstate = <running>) ) and ...


  /* Similar equivalences for other controller states. */
init objectstate ==   cstate := <c_idle>
methods
  switch_pressed() ==   /* Reaction to switch_on event */
    [ext wr avstate, gvstate, istate, sstate, tstate,
            cstate
     post
       (cstate~ = <c_idle>  =>
                                (cstate = <try_ignite> and ...
                                 tstate = <running>))        and

       (cstate~ = <try_shutdown>  =>
                                (cstate = <try_restart> and ...
                                 tstate = tstate~)) ];


  ..... /* Other event handlers */

end AbstractControl
```

This specification describes *what* the controller actions should achieve, not *how* they are implemented in terms of the atomic actions of the system. The notation **var**~ denotes the value of **var** at commencement of the operation in which it occurs. **var** without decoration in the postcondition refers to the new value of **var**.

Refinement of abstract controller. The initial refinement step is to "implement" the complete system model represented by **ConstrainedSystem** by interacting components: components representing the environment of the system, and components representing the software controller which will actually be developed. The VDM^{++} class of the abstract controller refinement is:

```
class HL_Controller
-- refines AbstractControl
types
  CState = <c_idle> | <try_ignite> | <c_running> | <try_shutdown> |
           <try_restart> | <alarmed>
instance variables
  cstate: CState;
  burner: @LL_Controller;
  timer: @Timer;
init objectstate ==  cstate := <c_idle>
methods
  switch_pressed()  ==
    if cstate = <c_idle>
    then
      (timer!start_timer();
       burner!open_av();
       burner!ignite_on();
       burner!open_gv();
       cstate := <try_ignite>)
    else
      if cstate = <try_shutdown>
      then
        cstate := <try_restart>;

  .... /* Other event handlers */

end HL_Controller
```

This design is derived from the data and control flow diagram: the components which are purely receivers of commands from the controller have been gathered together into the **LL_Controller** class, together with the invariants from the static specifications[1]. An object of this class is then made a client of the controller. Since there is a two-way flow of signals between the controller and the timer, these components need to be clients of each other. The controller is also a client of the flame detector and switch.

The workspace class creates and links the objects of the controller, sensor and actuator classes:

```
class Workspace
instance variables
  burner: @LL_Controller;
  controller: @HL_Controller;
  detector: @FlameDetector;
  switch: @Switch;
  timer: @Timer;
init objectstate ==
    (burner := LL_Controller!new;
```

---

[1] This can always be achieved, since the static specifications involve only *controllable* state variables.

```
controller := HL_Controller!new;
detector := FlameDetector!new;
switch := Switch!new;
timer := Timer!new;
topology
  [post controller.timer = timer and
        controller.burner = burner and
        detector.controller = controller and
        switch.controller = controller and
        timer.controller = controller])
end Workspace
```

The theory interpretation of **ConstrainedSystem** into this refined system is given in Table 3. We can reason that this interpretation preserves the axioms of

Symbol of ConstrainedSystem	Symbol of Workspace
avstate	burner.avstate
astate	burner.astate
gvstate	burner.gvstate
istate	burner.istate
fdstate	detector.fdstate
sstate	switch.sstate
tstate	timer.tstate
ignite_on	burner!ignite_on
ignite_off	burner!ignite_off
open_av	burner!open_av
close_av	burner!close_av
open_gv	burner!open_gv
close_gv	burner!close_gv
start_timer	timer!start_timer
reset	timer!reset
abort_timer	timer!abort_timer
switch_on	switch!switch_on
switch_off	switch!switch_off

Table 3. Interpretation of **ConstrainedSystem** in **Workspace**

ConstrainedSystem as follows. Certainly the typing of all the symbols concerned is preserved in the refinement, and the invariants for constraints (1) and (2) of Section 5.3 are ensured in their interpreted forms as the constraints are duplicated in **LL_Controller**. It is also direct to show that the effects of the methods of **ConstrainedSystem** are achieved, under the above interpretation, by the corresponding operations in **Workspace**. The proof obligations concern the satisfaction of the temporal constraints. These follow from the procedural definitions of the operations of **HL_Controller**.

5.5 Definition of hardware wrapper

The design structure of the resulting system is shown in Figure 5. This design

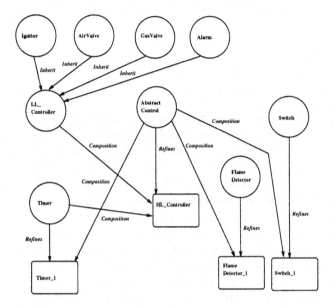

Fig. 5. Design Architecture

could be further refined by implementation using a polling or interrupt-driven architecture.

The refinement reasoning depends upon:

1. The controller states being up-to-date with respect to the monitored components before input events occur (so that if all the components are idle/off then the controller is in the $<$ c_idle $>$ state);

2. The order in which the controller reacts to events is the same in which the events occurred (so that if **switch_on** occurs, the next controller method to initiate must be **switch_pressed**);

3. The controller reacts to events quickly enough, compared with the minimum inter-arrival time of events, that it is never executing a method at a time point where an input event occurs (otherwise, the controller could be reacting to a **switch_off** event, for example, when **switch_on** occurs, so that it need not invoke **burner!start_timer** as the next action, contradicting (**TA1**)). The use of **whenever** statements in place of temporal sequencing formulae would provide a time tolerance for the reactions.

A polling approach could lead to the second condition failing, since the occurrence of an event would be detected by comparing the states of a component at successive polls. Since several components could change state between these polls, there would be no general way of determining the order in which these state changes occurred. If enough information was present in the model, it would however be possible to deduce the actual order of events in particular cases, by ruling out orders incompatible with the model.

6 Conclusions

6.1 Comparison with Other Approaches

We have also specified and developed the gas burner controller using the B Abstract Machine Notation [6]. Whilst B provides greater tool support for animation, proof, refinement and code generation than VDM^{++}, it is more restrictive in the forms of design that can be expressed. In particular, the reflexive relationship between the timer and controller in the VDM^{++} design cannot be directly achieved in the B version. Instead, a separate polling task must be defined which periodically samples the timer, flame detector and switch state, and informs the controller of any change in these states in order to trigger controller responses. However the controller specification itself can use an almost identical structure to the VDM^{++} version. The complexity of the polling design resulted in 100 proof obligations for the polling task, far in excess of the other components of the system. Two-thirds of these obligations could not be automatically discharged.

B does not provide a means of specifying of temporal logic requirements or of continuous system descriptions, which VDM^{++} does. Both B and VDM^{++} are more restrictive as languages than formalisms such as the duration calculus [12] or Metric Temporal Logic [2], but provide a more familiar language for software and control engineers.

References

1. J. Abrial. *The B Book: Deriving Programs from Meaning*, Cambridge University Press, 1996.
2. M. Celiktin. *Interval-based techniques for the specification and analysis of real-time requirements.* Technical report, Universite Catholique de Louvain, 1994.
3. E. Durr, S. Goldsack, and J. van Katjwick. *Specification of a cruise controller in VDM^{++}*. In Proceedings of Real Time OO Workshop, ECOOP 96, 1996.
4. J. Fiadeiro and T. Maibaum *Describing, Structuring and Implementing Objects*, in de Bakker *et al.*, Foundations of Object Oriented languages, LNCS 489, Springer-Verlag, 1991.
5. K. Lano. *Specification of a Chemical Process Controller in VDM^{++} and B*, ROOS Project Document GR/K68783-11, September 1996. Department of Computing. Imperial College, UK.
6. K. Lano, J. Bicarregui and A. Sanchez. *Using B to Design and Verify Controllers for Chemical Processing*, B Conference, IRIN, Nantes, France, 1996.
7. K. Lano, G. Goldsack, J. Bicarregui and S. Kent. *Integrating VDM^{++} and Real-Time System Design*, Z User Meeting, 1997.

8. I. Moon, G. Powers, J. R. Burch and E. M. Clarke. *Automatic Verification of Sequential Control Systems using Temporal Logic*, American Institute of Chemical Engineers (AIChE) Journal, 38(1):67–75, January 1992.
9. A. Sanchez and S. Macchietto. *Design of Procedural Controllers for Chemical Processes*, Computers and Chemical Engineering, 19, S381-S386, 1995.
10. N. Alsop, L. Camillocci, A. Sanchez and S. Macchietto. *Synthesis of Procedural Controllers – Application to a batch plant*, Computers and Chemical Engineering, 20, S1481-S1486, 1996
11. A. Sanchez. *Formal Specification and Synthesis of Procedural Controllers for Process Systems.* Springer-Verlag. Lecture Notes in Control and Information Sciences, vol. 212. 1996.
12. M. Schenke and A. Ravn. *Refinement from a Control Problem to Programs*, in J. Abrial, E Börger and H. Langmaack (Eds.), *Formal Methods for Industrial Applications*, Lecture Notes in Computer Science Vol. 1165, Springer-Verlag, 1997.
13. G. E. Rotstein, A. Sanchez and S. Macchietto. *Procedural Control of Discrete Event Systems*, Submitted to J. Discrete Event Systems, 1997.

Appendix 1. Exemplars of Dynamic Specification Statements.

– Normal Operation
1. If the system is in the initial state and the button changes to on then the start-up initiates with the following sequence: Launch timer; Open air valve; Switch on igniter; Open gas valve.
2. If the system is starting up and flame is detected, the system must be driven to the normal operation state, that is: Switch igniter off; Abort timer.
3. If the system is starting up waiting for the occurrence of flame (that is air and gas valves are open, igniter is on, timer is running and flame has not been detected) and timer expires, then initiate recovery procedure, namely: Close gas valve; Switch igniter off; Restart timer; Close air valve.

– Alarm activation
1. During normal operation, if flame extinguishes, activate alarm.
2. During shut down, regardless of the switch position, if timer expires, then activate alarm
3. If gas valve is closed and flame occurs, activate alarm.

– Emergency Operation
If the alarm is activated, the controller must drive the system to a safe state. That is, to a state in which gas and air valves are closed, igniter is off and timer is idle. It must be guaranteed that the safest sequence of actions will be executed. Thus, once the alarm has been activated and the gas valve is open, it must be closed immediately. Then, timer and igniter must be guaranteed to be off. Finally, the air valve must be closed. The above is captured in the following statements:
1. If the alarm has been activated and the gas valve is open, it must be closed immediately.
2. Afterwards, if the igniter is on, it must be switched off.
3. Same for timer, if it is running.
4. Same for timer, if it is aborting.
5. Finally, if the air valve is on, it must be closed.

An M-Net Semantics for a Real-Time Extension of µSDL

Hans Fleischhack and Josef Tapken
Fachbereich Informatik
Carl-von-Ossietzky-Universität Oldenburg
D-26111 Oldenburg
{fleischhack, tapken}@informatik.uni-oldenburg.de

Abstract

In this paper an extension of SDL by real-time assertions is suggested. A denotational compositional semantics in terms of timed high level Petri nets is given. This semantics allows to reason about timed SDL-specifications by simulation of the underlying high level nets as well as by unfolding these into timed low level nets and then applying analysis methods for timed Petri nets or temporal model checking. The approach is embedded in the MOBY-tool.

1 Introduction

In the MOBY-project (Modelling of distributed systems; [1]), a design environment for SDL-specifications (Specification and Description Language; [8]) has been developed. Based on a high level Petri net semantics and a temporal logic for SDL, the MOBY-tool allows to reason about functional and qualitative temporal properties of such specifications. Reasoning is done by simulation or by checking SDL-specifications against properties expressed by temporal logic formulae, using the model checker of the the PEP project (Programming Environment Based on Petri Nets; cf. [4, 11]).

In general, the behaviour of a distributed system does depend on its real-time as on its functional and qualitative temporal properties. Therefore, a formal description method should offer features to express real-time requirements. In standard SDL, this is done by the timer concept. But, since – with the exception of the timer part – there are no assumptions about the timed behaviour of (the other parts of) an SDL-specification, the timer concept leads to certain anomalies. E.g., as Leue [13] points out, in some cases no finite bound of the delay between the point of time when a timer expires, and the moment at which the SDL-specification reacts to the expiry can be found.

As a solution in this paper an extension of SDL-specifications by real-time assertions is suggested. The assertions are given by time intervals and allow the specification of lower and upper time bounds for all events which may be observed in an SDL-system.

In accordance with the time model for timers in standard SDL (cf. Annex F3 of Z.100 [8]), our notion of time is discrete. We have chosen time intervals rather than time points, to be able to describe minimal as well as maximal reaction times of (parts of) SDL systems.

A compositional denotational semantics for the extended language SDL/R by means of high level Petri nets is developed. For this purpose the algebra of M-nets [6] is augmented by additional inscriptions which, for each transition, denote the earliest and latest possible firing time, yielding the algebra of TM-nets. A semantic function is then defined which specifies a TM-net for each (fragment of an) SDL/R-program.

There have been other proposals for real time extensions of SDL: In [2], information about the (average) amount of time the system will remain in a certain state and/or probabilities of transitions to other states, may be added to SDL specifications. This approach enables probabilistic validation and performance evaluation of SDL-specifications based on stochastic processes. Hence, the domain of properties to be analysed using this approach is rather different from the one presented here.

In [13], quantitative aspects of SDL-systems are modelled by additional specifications in terms of real-time extended temporal logic (MTL-) formulae. The allowed behaviour of an SDL system is given via a global state transition system, and is constrained by the MTL-formulae. In this approach, SDL-system and MTL-formula are viewed as complementary parts of the specification, while in ours the SDL-system rather establishes an abstract implementation which is checked against a temporal logic specification.

The paper is organized as follows: The real-time extension SDL/R of μSDL (cf. [1]) is presented in section 2. Section 3 contains the definition of the TM-net algebra. The core of the paper consists of the TM-net semantics of SDL/R in section 4. In the concluding section 5 we discuss verification of real-time properties of SDL/R-specifications and the embedding in the MOBY-tool.

2 SDL/R-Specifications

Over many years SDL has emerged as a standard language for the specification of distributed systems, especially in the area of telecommunication. An SDL-specification describes a *system* consisting of *processes*. Processes are extended communicating finite state machines. For processes timing constraints may be modelled by *timers*. Processes may be *created* and *terminated dynamically* and may also contain *procedures*. There is a notion of *hierarchy* which supports structured development of specifications. For the purpose of communication and for local variables *objects* are definable in SDL. Among others the fact that SDL-specifications may also be *represented graphically* has contributed to the wide acceptance of SDL.

The prototype implemented in the MOBY-project concentrates on that subset of SDL that deals with concurrency and communication [1]. In this setting a system appears as a set of non-deterministic sequential finite automata with

τ-transitions, extended by local variables and communicating asynchronously with one another. In this paper, we extend the language under consideration by timers. To avoid the anomalies mentioned in the introduction section, we also augment input queues, channels and atomic actions with time expressions, denoting the minimal and maximal delay time for an input queue or a channel or, respectively, the minimal and maximal execution time for an action. Our notion of time is *discrete*; hence we use natural numbers to denote time points. Still, we do not consider procedures, dynamic handling of processes, hierarchy, and abstract data types/objects.

$$
\begin{array}{lll}
< timerdef > & ::= \texttt{timer}\ t\ ; & (1) \\
< set > & ::= \texttt{set}\ (t, \texttt{now} + < expr >) & (2) \\
< reset > & ::= \texttt{reset}\ (t) & (3) \\
< timeint > & ::= [< expr >, < expr >\ ] & (4)
\end{array}
$$

Table 1. Extension of the SDL-syntax pertaining to timers.

The syntax pertaining to timers is shown in Table 2. Timers are used to handle time supervision and have to be declared inside a process like local variables (1). It is assumed that a global time is available through the global variable now. A timer is set with an expiry time, which usually depends on the variable now (2). When the expiry time is reached, a signal with the name of the timer is inserted in the input queue of the process. A timer is cancelled by a reset statement (3). Setting a timer, which is already set, implies overwriting the original expiry time. Setting a timer to an earlier expiry time than the actual time now, causes an immediate insertion of the timer signal in the input queue. Resetting a timer that is not set has no effect. When the timer is set and neither consumed from the input queue nor reset, it is called *active*. Timer parameters are not considered in this paper. They may be treated like signal parameters, which are handled by our semantics.

Like in [1], as parameter types of signals and as types of local variables we allow the set of Boolean values and the set of integers (both with the usual operations). The resulting part of the language is called *SDL/R*.

The formal syntax of SDL/R is based on the *textual representation* of SDL and is given in appendix A. To increase readability, all examples in this text will be given using the *graphical representation*.

In the remaining part of this section, an example of an SDL/R-specification is given which describes a simple communication protocol, the ARQ (automatic repeat request) protocol with alternating acknowledgement.

The top level of the specification consists of a system ARQ (cf. Figure 1) comprising two processes, a process *sender* and a process *receiver*.

Via the channel d the *sender* sends data packages which are labelled alternately by 0 and 1 to the *receiver*. The data packages are modelled by a signal type *data* with parameter type $\{0, 1\}$. The channel d causes a delay of at least 5 time units and at most 10 time units.

The *receiver* either receives a data package correctly and answers, via the a channel, the label of the next data package. Otherwise, an error occurs. There are two types of error. First, the *receiver* may receive a faulty package. In this case it answers by repeating the label of the last package. Second, a package may get lost. In this case, the *receiver* does nothing. The possibility of erroneous transmission of data is modelled in the *receiver* process by the non-deterministic choice between the answers 0, 1, and no answer, respectively. For the answers there is a signal type *ack*, also with parameter type $\{0,1\}$. Also channel a delays signals for at least 5 and at most 10 time units.

Before sending a data package, the *sender* sets a timer t, which will be reset, if the *receiver*'s acknowledge arrives in time and which otherwise forces the sender to send the last data package again.

The processes *sender* and *receiver* are modelled separately (cf. Figure 2). We assume that internal actions of a process consume 1 time unit and that access to a channel needs 2 time units. Timing constraints are given in additional square brackets; intervals of the form $[eft, eft]$ are abbreviated by (eft).

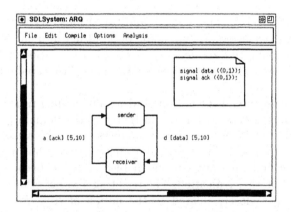

Fig. 1. The ARQ-System with time constraints

3 An Algebra of Timed Multi Labelled Petri Nets

M-nets (multi labelled nets) form an algebra of high level Petri nets. They were introduced in [6] as an abstract and flexible semantic model for concurrent programs and used in [7] for the definition of a high level net semantics of the experimental programming language $B(PN)^2$.

The most distinguishing feature of the algebra of M-nets is given by the rich set of composition operators they provide. These allow the compositional construction of complex nets from simple ones, thereby satisfying various algebraic properties.

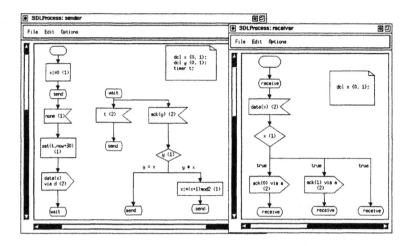

Fig. 2. The *sender* and *receiver* Process

Annotations of places (sets of allowed tokens), arcs (multisets of variables or values or tuples of variables and values), and transitions (occurrence conditions – called value terms) support the unfolding of an M-net into an elementary net. Communication capabilities are denoted by labels of transitions (action terms), while labels of places (called status) denote their interface capabilities. A status can be 'entry', 'exit' or 'internal'.

In this section we extend the notion of M-nets by adding time restrictions to transitions. *Discrete time* is assumed and therefore the domain for time points is restricted to the set $\mathbf{N}$ of the natural numbers. To each transition t, a time interval $[eft, lft]$ is attached. The informal meaning is that t has to occur at least *eft* and at most *lft* time units after being enabled, unless it becomes disabled by the occurrence of another transition. The resulting TM-net (time multi labelled Petri net) algebra is closely related to the notion of *time Petri net* (cf. e.g. [3, 14, 15]). We restrict the class of nets under consideration to *safe* nets. A (T)M-net N is called safe, if each marking m reachable in N from the standard initial marking m_0 (cf. section 3.2) is a set[1].

3.1 Definition of TM-Nets

The building blocks (places, transitions, arcs) of a TM-net N are equipped with inscriptions which are important for the behaviour as well as for the compositional structure of N.

There are three kinds of *places* in TM-nets: *entry* places (without incoming arcs; labelled by e), *exit* places (without outgoing arcs; labelled by x), and *internal* places (labelled by i). Moreover, each place s has a *type* which comprises the set of possible values for any tokens on that place. A type is a nonempty finite subset of the set VAL^*, where $VAL = \mathbf{N} \cup \mathbf{B} \cup \{\bullet\}$, with the set of Boolean

---

[1] I.e., $(m(s))(v) \in \{0,1\}$ for all $s \in S$ and $v \in \alpha_s$.

values **B** and the usual token in Petri nets •. Hence the inscription ι_s of a place s consists of a pair (λ_s, α_s), where λ_s and α_s denote the label and the type of s, respectively. All entry places as well as all exit places have type $\{\bullet\}$.

We also assume a set VAR of typed variables called *value variables* and ranging over the types.

Each *transition* t has a triple $\iota_t = (\lambda_t, \alpha_t, \chi_t)$ of inscriptions. The first component λ_t expresses the synchronisation capabilities of t and consists of a finite multiset of *simple action terms*. A simple action term is an expression of the form $A(a_1, ..., a_n)$ where A is an *action symbol* with arity $S_1 \times ... \times S_n$ and a_i is either a value variable of type S_i or an element of S_i, $1 \leq i \leq n$.

On the set ACT of action symbols we assume a *conjugation function* $con: ACT \rightarrow ACT$ such that, for all $A \in ACT, con(A) \neq A, con(con(A)) = A$, and $arity(A) = arity(con(A))$. We use $\overline{A}$ as abbreviation for $con(A)$.

The second inscription α_t of a transition t consists of a set of value expressions.[2] *Value expressions*[2] are built up by elements of VAL, value variables, and the usual relational, arithmetic, and boolean operators. Value expressions denote elements of VAL.

The third inscription χ_t of a transition restricts the set of time points, at which t may occur. It consists of a pair (eft, lft) of value terms which may be evaluated to a natural number. The intended meaning is that eft (lft, resp.) denotes the minimal (maximal, resp.) number of time units, which may pass between enabling of t and occurrence of t. The earliest firing time eft may be 0, the latest firing time lft may be ∞. Usually, χ_t is denoted by $[eft(t), lft(t)]$.

Finally, each *arc* (s, t) $((t, s)$, resp.) of an TM-net is inscribed by a finite multiset $\iota_{s,t}$ ($\iota_{t,s}$, resp.) of value variables of type α_s.[3]

Hence, altogether, an TM-net is a triple $N = (S, T, \iota)$ such that

1. S is a set (of places).
2. T is a set (of transitions) satisfying $S \cap T = \emptyset$.
3. ι is a mapping with domain $S \cup T \cup (S \times T) \cup (T \times S)$ as described above,

satisfying the additional requirements that N has at least one entry place and one exit place and that each transition t has at least one incoming and one outgoing arc.

In part (i), Figure 3 shows a simple TM-net N_1.

3.2   The Transition Rule

First, the transition rule for M-nets is described. Let N be an TM-net and M its underlying M-net, which is given by forgetting about N's time restrictions.

A *marking* m of an M-net M maps each place s to a finite multiset over α_s. Under the *standard initial marking* there is exactly one token on each entry place and no token on any other place.

---

[2] In examples, this set is given as the conjunction of its elements; in particular, the empty set of value expressions is represented by the value expression **true**.

[3] Since we only consider safe nets, arc inscriptions are in fact sets.

An *assignment* is a mapping $\beta : VAR \rightarrow VAL$ which associates a value $v \in \tau$ to each variable $a \in VAR$ of type τ. A transition t is called *enabled* under the marking m w.r.t. the assignment β iff $\beta(\alpha_t)$ evaluates to **true** and $\beta(\iota_{s,t}) \leq m(s)$ for each arc (s,t) entering t.

A pair (t, β), is called *firing event* of M. Firing events (t, β) and (t', β') are called *in conflict* $((t, \beta) \bowtie (t', \beta'))$ iff $\beta(\iota(s, t)) \cap \beta'(\iota(s, t')) \neq \emptyset$ for some place s. The set of all firing events which are enabled under the marking m, is denoted by $act(m)$.

If the *firing event* (t, β) is enabled in a marking m, then (t, β) may occur, yielding a new marking m' such that $m'(s) = m(s) - \beta(\iota_{s,t}) + \beta(\iota_{t,s})$ for all places s.

Now the transition rule for TM-nets is introduced. A *configuration* of N is a pair (m, n), consisting of a marking m and a mapping n which maps each firing event (t, β) of N to an element of $(\mathbf{N} \cup \{\$\})$. For each firing event (t, β), $n(t, \beta)$ may be seen as a clock showing the number of time units that passed since the enabling of (t, β), $\$$ indicating that the event is not enabled. The *initial configuration* (m_0, n_0) for N is given by the standard initial marking m_0 and by n_0, mapping each firing event which is enabled under m_0 to 0 and any other firing event to $\$$. Now we consider two types of steps, namely steps where time passes (which we call *time-steps*) and steps where a nonempty set of firing events occurs (which we call *occur-steps*):

1. *Time-steps*: A time-step may occur in a configuration (m, n), if no firing event is forced to occur, i.e. if, for any firing event (t, β), $n(t, \beta) < \beta(lft(t))$, whenever $n(t, \beta) \neq \$$. In this case, the successor configuration (m', n') is given by $m' = m$ and

$$n'(t, \beta) = \begin{cases} n(t, \beta) + 1 & \text{if } n(t, \beta) \neq \$ \\ \$ & \text{otherwise} \end{cases}$$

2. *Occur-steps*: An occur-step is possible in a configuration (m, n), if some firing event may occur, i.e. if there is a firing event (t, β) such that $n(t, \beta) \in \mathbf{N}$ and $\beta(eft(t)) \leq n(t, \beta) \leq \beta(lft(t))$. In this case, the successor configuration (m', n') w.r.t. (m, n) and (t, β) is given by $m'(s) = m(s) - \beta(\iota_{s,t}) + \beta(\iota_{t,s})$ for all places s and

$$n'(t', \beta') = \begin{cases} \$ & \text{if } (t', \beta') \notin act(m') \\ 0 & \text{if } (t', \beta') \in act(m') \\ & \text{and } ((t', \beta') \bowtie (t, \beta) \text{ or } (t', \beta') \notin act(m)) \\ n(t', \beta') & \text{otherwise} \end{cases}$$

E.g., in the TM-net N_1 of part (i) of Figure 3, transition t is enabled under the current marking w.r.t. the assignments β_1 given by $\beta_1(a) = 1$ and $\beta_1(b) = 2$ and β_2 given by $\beta_2(a) = 2$ and $\beta_2(b) = 1$, respectively. Event (t, β_1) may occur at time 1, event (t, β_2) may occur at time 1 or time 2. The possible behaviour of N_1 is described by its occurrence graph which is displayed in Figure 4. Here, the configurations are represented as tuples, whose components denote, respectively, $m(s)$, $m(s')$, $n(t, \beta_1)$, and $n(t, \beta_2)$.

Remark A TM-net N may be unfolded to a low level time Petri net.

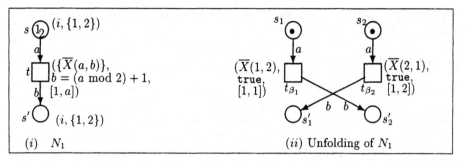

Fig. 3. A simple TM-net N_1 and its unfolding

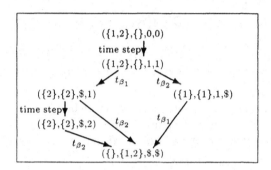

Fig. 4. Occurrence graph of N_1

3.3 Operations on TM-Nets

In this section we define composition operations on TM-nets corresponding to the operators of the PBC [5]. These create a new TM-net out of one, two, or three given TM-nets.

We consider the following *basic nets*:

1. $M(\iota) = \begin{pmatrix} e & \{c\} & \iota & \{c\} & x \\ \bigcirc & \longrightarrow & \square & \longrightarrow & \bigcirc \end{pmatrix}$ with $\iota = (\lambda, \alpha, \chi)$, in particular
2. $M_{silent} = M(\emptyset, \text{true}, [0,0])$
3. $M_{stop} = \begin{pmatrix} e & x \\ \bigcirc & \bigcirc \end{pmatrix}$

TM-nets may be combined *vertically* by means of

- *parallel composition* $N_2 \| N_3$: The nets are executed independently (cf. Figure 5, (iii)).
- *sequential composition* $N_2; N_3$: The nets are executed one after the other (cf. Figure 5, (iv)).
- *choice composition* $N_2 \,\square\, N_3$: One of the nets is nondeterministically chosen for execution (cf. Figure 5, (v)).
- *iteration* $[M_1 * M_2 * M_3]$: An (initial) net M_1 is executed once, followed by zero or more executions of the (iterated) net M_2, followed by one execution

of the (final) net M_3. The repetition of the iterated part is enabled by $M_4 = M_{silent}$ (cf. Figure 5, (vi)).

and also *horizontally* by means of

- *synchronisation*: The synchronisation N **sy** A of an M-net N with respect to an action symbol A is constructed by exhaustively applying basic synchronisation w.r.t. A. A transition t'' arises through a *basic synchronisation* w.r.t. A of two transitions t and t' iff

  1. $A(\tau_1, ..., \tau_n) \in \lambda_t$ and $\overline{A}(\tau_1', ..., \tau_n') \in \lambda_{t'}$.
  2. There exists a common most general unifier β of the pairs (τ_i, τ_i'), $1 \leq i \leq n$, such that
     (a) $\lambda_{t''} = \beta(\lambda_t) + \beta(\lambda_{t'}) \setminus \beta(\{A(\tau_1, ..., \tau_n), \overline{A}(\tau_1', ..., \tau_n')\})$,
     (b) $\alpha_{t''} = \beta(\alpha_t) \wedge \beta(\alpha_{t'})$,
     (c) $\chi_{t''} \doteq [min(\beta(eft(t)), \beta(eft(t'))), max(\beta(lft(t)), \beta(lft(t')))]^4$,
     (d) $\iota(s, t'') = \beta(\iota(s, t)) + \beta(\iota(s, t'))$ and $\iota(t'', s) = \beta(\iota(t, s)) + \beta(\iota(t', s))$ for all $s \in S$.

  An example of a basic synchronisation step (which in this case already covers the **sy** -operator) is shown in Figure 5, (vii)).
- *restriction*: The restriction N **rs** A of an M-net N with respect to an action symbol A is N with all transitions t removed such that A or $\overline{A}$ occurred in λ_t (cf. Figure 5, $(viii)$).
- *scoping*: Scoping is synchronisation followed by restriction:
  $[A : N] = N$ **sy** A **rs** A.

Note that synchronisation and restriction – and, hence, scoping – are associative and commutative. Therefore, for an TM-net N, and for $ACT' \subseteq ACT$, N **sy** ACT', N **rs** ACT', and $[ACT' : N]$ are all well defined.

4 Translation of SDL/R-specifications into TM-Nets

An SDL/R-specification describes a system consisting of a set of sequential processes which may communicate asynchronously with each other. In this section, we define a semantic function which associates to each such system S a

TM-net $M(S)$, the *high level semantics* of S. $M(S)$ may then be unfolded to a (safe) time Petri net $U(M(S))$, the *low level semantics* of S.

The standard semantic model of SDL-specifications contains two types of infinite objects, namely channels and input queues of processes, which both are unbounded. This fact causes no problem as far as simulation is concerned, but, for the purpose of verification of properties of SDL-systems, one has to assume a bound for the capacity of channels and input queues. Often, an upper bound for these queues is explicit part of the problem specification. Otherwise, if such a bound exists at all, it may be determined using a model checker by checking

---

[4] For intervals $[eft(t), lft(t)]$ and $[eft(t'), lft(t')]$ with constant bounds this term denotes intersection.

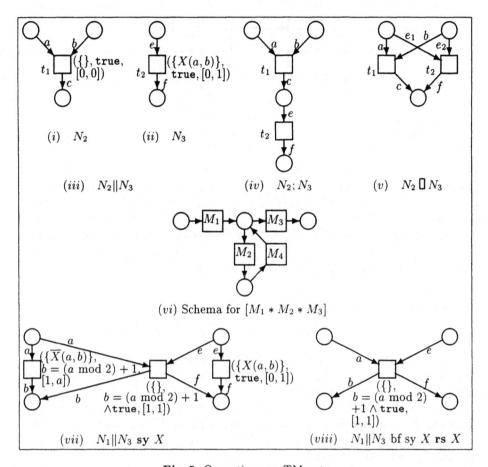

Fig. 5. Operations on TM-nets

with an increasing upper bound until the queue cannot be filled completely. In this paper, we assume a finite bound $k \in \mathbf{N}$ for channels and input queues. Unbounded versions of channels and input queues may be constructed similarly.

In the following, we illustrate the semantic function using the ARQ example. The formal definition is given in appendix A.

The high level semantics of a system S is given by the parallel composition of TM-nets $M_1, ..., M_n$ for the different processes and channels. To model the communication between processes, according to the semantic model of SDL (cf. [8]), each process has an implicit input queue. Like channel variables in $B(PN)^2$, these input queues are represented by TM-nets $I_1, ..., I_k$ (cf. [7]). The TM-net representing the whole system is then given by the parallel composition of $M_1, ..., M_n$ and $I_1, ..., I_k$, respectively, followed by synchronising and restricting the resulting net according to the action symbols occurring in the input queues and the channels.

The relevant parts of the semantic model of the ARQ system (cf. Figure 6)

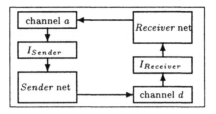

Fig. 6. Structure of the standard semantics of the ARQ-system

consist of the process *sender* together with its input queue I_{sender}, the process *receiver* together with its input queue $I_{receiver}$, and the channels a and d. These parts have to be synchronised and restricted w.r.t. the corresponding read and write actions of the channels $(A^!, A^?, D^!, D^?)$ and of the input queues of the processes $(I^!_{sender}, I^?_{sender}, I^!_{receiver}, I^?_{receiver})$. Hence, the semantics for the whole ARQ system is described by the following equation:

$$M(ARQ) = [\{I^!_{sender}, I^?_{sender}, I^!_{receiver}, I^?_{receiver}, A^!, A^?, D^!, D^?\} :$$
$$M(sender)\|M(receiver)\|M(a)\|M(d)]$$

The semantics of a channel is given by the net $M_{channel}(c, k, Set, [eft, lft])$ (also called *channel box*; cf. section 4.2), where c, k, Set, $[eft, lft]$ denote the name, the capacity, the type, and the time interval of the channel. This net is connected to the target process of the channel by a transition which in turn is embedded in an infinite loop, thus synchronising each read operation of the channel with a corresponding write operation to the input queue of the target process. E.g., for channel d this yields:

$$M(d) = M_{channel}(d, Capacity(d), \{\text{data.0}, \text{data.1}\}, [5, 10])\|$$
$$[M(\{D^?(s_1), I^!_{receiver}(s_2)\}, \{s_1 = s_2\})$$
$$*M(\{D^?(s_1), I^!_{receiver}(s_2)\}, \{s_1 = s_2\})$$
$$*M_{stop}]$$

The TM-net of a single process P consists of

1. a part for the input queue of the process. This is given by the net $M_{input}(P)$, cf. section 4.3.
2. a part for each declaration dcl $v : Set$; of a local variable, given by a special TM-net $M_{data}(v, Set)$, called *data box*, cf. section 4.1.
3. a part for the set *States* of states of the process. These are treated as a local variable q and are represented by the data box $M_{data}(q, States \cup \{\bullet\})$.
4. a part for each declaration of a timer t, which is given by a *timer box* $M_{timer}(P, t)$, cf. section 4.4.
5. a part for the control flow of the process, cf. section 4.5.

These parts are put in parallel and then synchronised and restricted according to the (action symbols for the) local variables, the timers, and the states of the process. Hence e.g. for the *sender* process we get the following:

$$M(sender) = [\{X, Y, Q, T_{set}, T_{reset}, I_{sender}^{rem}\} \quad :$$
$$M_{input}(sender, Capacity(I_{sender}), \{\mathsf{data.0}, \mathsf{data.1}\}) \parallel M_{data}(q, \{\mathsf{send}, \mathsf{wait}, \bullet\})$$
$$\parallel M_{data}(x, \{0, 1\})$$
$$\parallel M_{data}(y, \{0, 1\})$$
$$\parallel M_{timer}(sender, t)$$
$$\parallel M(body(sender))]$$

The semantics for the control part consists of the choice composition of the action sequences for each pair (q, in) of state (q) and input symbol (in) such that an SDL- transition is defined for (q, in). This is embedded in an infinite loop, e.g. for the body of the *sender* process, which consists of a start transition *start* and two transitions $transition_1$ and $transition_2$ we have:

$$M(body(sender)) = [M(start)$$
$$*(M(transition_1) \,\square\, M(transition_2))$$
$$*M_{stop}]$$

4.1 Semantics of Data Declarations

The semantics of the declaration of a local variable v with value set *Set* inside a process P is given by the *data box* $M_{data}(v, Set)$ as shown in Figure 7. The first access to v is done by firing of transition T_1, which has to synchronise with an appropriate transition within the control part of process P, as is indicated by the action label of T_1. All further access to v is handled by transition T_2 in the same manner. The actual value of the variable is held in the central place S_2. Place S_3 is only needed for compositions of the data box.

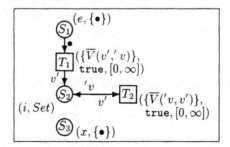

Fig. 7. TM-net $M_{data}(v, Set)$ for the declaration of variable v with value set *Set*

4.2 Semantics of Channel Declarations

In SDL/R, a channel c is used as a unidirectional connection from a process P to a process Q. Signals of a certain type *Set*, which are written to c by P, are delivered after a time delay which ranges from the minimum *eft* to the maximum *lft*, to the input queue of Q. Thereby, the arrival order of the signals is retained. The TM-net semantics of a channel c of capacity k is depicted in Figure 8[5].

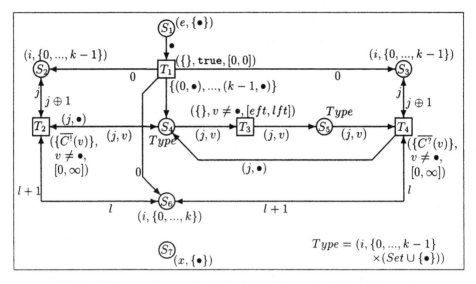

Fig. 8. TM-net $M_{channel}(c, k, Set, [eft, lft])$ for the delayed channel

By firing of transition T_2, a signal v may be written to place S_4 – which contains the undelayed signals – if the current write position j (contents of place S_2) is empty (i.e., the pair $(j, \bullet)$ is on S_4) and the channel contains at most $(k-1)$ entries (i.e., the contents l of place S_6 satisfies $l < k$.

Upon firing of T_2, the current write position (S_2) and the current number of entries (S_6) are updated. T_2 has to synchronise with an appropriate transition of the control flow as is indicated by its action label. The time behaviour of T_2 is not restricted, but T_2 will 'inherit' some time constraints through synchronisation.

For each entry (j, v) of the channel transition T_3 nondeterministically chooses a delay time from the interval $[eft, lft]$ and puts the delayed entry on place S_5[6].

Signals may be read from the channel by firing of transition T_4 which is enabled if at the current read position j (contents of place S_3) there is an entry $v \neq \bullet$. As is indicated by its action label, also T_4 has to synchronise with an appropriate transition of the control part. Upon firing, T_4 removes the entry

---

[5] To enhance readability, here and in the following pictures, as abbreviation expressions are allowed as arc inscriptions. Also, arcs pointing in both directions are used. Inscriptions of these are placed next to the source node of that direction of the arc to which they refer.

[6] The inscription of transition T_3 is somewhat simplified. In fact the action part should contain the action terms for all variables occurring in *eft* and *lft*, respectively. Using the denotations of appendix A, the inscription would read $\iota_{T_3} = (AS, v \neq \bullet, [E', E''])$, where $AS = AS' \cup AS''$, $\zeta(eft) = (AS'/E')$, and $\zeta(lft) = (AS''/E'')$, respectively.

(j, v) from P_5, adds $(j, \bullet)$ to S_4, and also updates the read index S_5 and the current number of entries S_6.

Transition T_1 initialises write position (S_2), read position (S_3), and current number of entries (S_6) with 0. Place S_7 is only needed for compositions of the channel box.

4.3 Semantics of Input Queues

As pointed out above, the standard semantic model of SDL assigns an implicit input queue to each process P, which takes up all signals sent to P. The semantics of an input queue is given by the TM-net $M_{input}(P, k, Set)$, as shown in figure 9, where Set denotes the union of all types of signals which may be sent to P by any other process. The net for the input queue is very similar to the net for a channel. It may be generated by first collapsing S_4, T_3, and S_5 of the channel, yielding the place S_8 and then adding a new transition, T_5. The purpose of T_5 is to remove timer signals, that have been invalidated, from the input queue. To do so, it has to synchronise with an appropriate transition in a timer box.

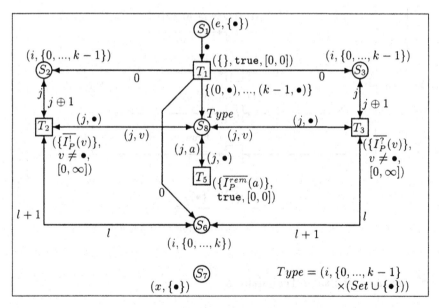

Fig. 9. TM-net $M_{input}(P, k, Set)$ for the input queue of process P

4.4 Semantics of Timers

The semantics for the declaration of timer t within process P is given by the TM-net $M_{timer}(P, t)$. It contains two central places: S_2 to hold the expiry time for t when a **set**-command was executed and S_3 to remember whether a timer signal for t was inserted in the input queue of the process P. Depending on the contents of S_3, there are two transitions for set (T_3, T_4) and for reset (T_5, T_6), respectively. If t is set with expiry time a, a is put on place S_2, thereby enabling transition T_2, which - after a time units, inserts a t-signal in the input queue of P, unless it looses concession in the meantime. If there was already a t-signal in the input queue (i.e., S_3 was marked with a 1), it has to be removed first. This is done through the additional action label $I_P^{rem}(t)$ which causes a synchronisation with transition T_5 of the input box. If t is reset, the expiry time is removed from S_2 (if there is any). In addition, a timer signal is removed from the input queue (if there is any).

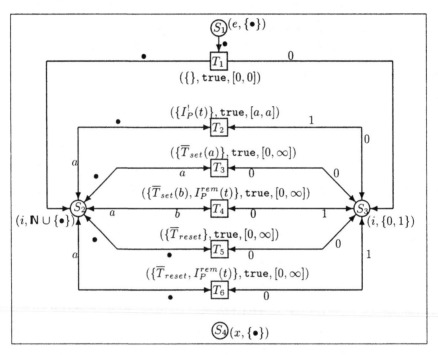

Fig. 10. TM-net $M_{timer}(P, t)$ for declaration of timer t in process P

4.5 Semantics of State Transitions

We will not describe the compositional derivation of the semantics of a state transition here, but merely show the semantics of one transition of the *sender* process as an example in Figure 11. The state transition consists of four parts which are composed sequentially: Consuming of input none in state *send* (which consumes 1 time unit), setting timer t to react after 30 time units (which also consumes 1 time unit), output of $data(x)$ via channel d (which consumes 2 time units), and entering of state *wait* (without consuming time). These parts are represented in the semantic model by four transitions which are also connected sequentially. The first makes the current state be undefined (represented by

$q' = \bullet$) and has to synchronise with the data box for the states. The second transition, which has to synchronise with a "**set** -transition" of the timer box for t causes delivery of the delay time on place S_2 of the timer box. By synchronising with the data box for the local variable x and with the write transition of the channel box for channel d, the third transition inserts the pair $m = (data, x)$ into the channel d. Finally, the last transition, which has to synchronise with the data box for the states, changes the state to *wait*. All timing requirements of the SDL-actions are just passed to the according transitions.

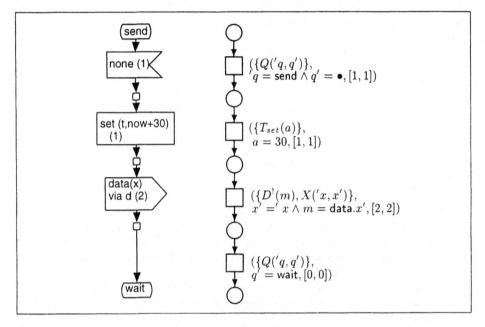

Fig. 11. Semantics of an SDL-transition

5 Conclusion

In this paper, we have extended SDL by real-time requirements to be able to deal also with quantitative temporal aspects of distributed systems. A compositional denotational semantics for the resulting language SDL/R has been defined, which allows to analyse SDL/R-specifications using methods from time Petri nets.

Currently, the real-time extension is being implemented in the MOBY-tool. The next step will consist in expanding the approach to the verification of qualitative and quantitative temporal properties.

For the verification of qualitative temporal properties of SDL/R-systems, a translation of the low level semantics into equivalent (untimed) Petri boxes will be implemented. This will enable us to use the model checker for μSDL-specifications of the MOBY-tool also for SDL/R-specifications.

To deal with quantitative temporal properties, first a real-time extension of the temporal logic for SDL has to be developed. We will then extend Esparza's partial order model checking algorithm to cope also with this extension. As an alternative, we will apply other verification methods. E.g., we will translate the low level semantics for SDL/R-systems as well as formulae of the (extended) temporal logic for SDL to formulae of Monadic Second Order Logic (M2L) and then use a proof-tool for M2L like the MONA-tool (cf. [12]).

We also plan to extend our approach to complete SDL. E.g., we have defined an M-net semantics for procedures and dynamic process creation and termination in SDL [10].

Acknowledgement

The authors would like to thank the members of the Oldenburg semantics group for helpful comments on the paper.

References

1. P. Amthor, H. Fleischhack, and J. Tapken: *MOBY – more than a Tool for the Verification of SDL-Specifications*, Research Paper, Universität Oldenburg, 1996.
2. F. Bause and P. Buchholz, Protocol Analysis Using a Timed Version of SDL, in J. Quemada, J. Mañas, and E. Vazquez (Eds.), *Formal Description Techniques, III*, pp. 269-285, North-Holland, 1991.
3. B. Berthomieu and M. Diaz, Modelling and Verification of Time Dependent Systems Using Time Petri Nets, *IEEE Transactions on Software Engineering*, Volume 17/3, pages 259 – 273 (1991).
4. E. Best, *Partial Order Verification with PEP*, Report HIB 26/96, Universität Hildesheim, 1996.
5. E. Best, R. Devillers, and J. G. Hall. The box calculus: a New Causal Algebra With Multi-Label Communication. In G. Rozenberg, (Ed.), *Advances in Petri Nets 92*, Volume 609 of *Lecture Notes in Computer Science*, pages 21 – 69. Springer, 1992.
6. E. Best, H. Fleischhack, W. Fraczak, R. P. Hopkins, H. Klaudel, and E. Pelz. A Class of Composable High Level Petri Nets. In G. De Michelis and M. Diaz, (Eds.), *Application and Theory of Petri Nets 1995*, Volume 935 of *Lecture Notes in Computer Science*, pages 103-118. Springer, 1995.
7. E. Best, H. Fleischhack, W. Fraczak, R. P. , H. Klaudel, and E. Pelz. An M-net Semantics of B(PN)^2. In J. Desel, (Ed.), *Structures in Concurrency Theory*, Workshops in Computing, Springer, 1995.
8. CCITT. *Specification and Description Language*, CCITT Z.100, International Consultative Committee on Telegraphy and Telephony, Geneva, 1992.
9. J. Esparza. *Model Checking Using Net Unfoldings*, Science of Computer Programming, Volume 23, pages 151-195, Elsevier, 1994.
10. H. Fleischhack, and B. Grahlmann, *Towards Compositional Verification of SDL Systems*, Research Paper, 1997. (submitted)

11. B. Grahlmann and E. Best: PEP – More Than a Petri Net Tool. In T. Margaria and B. Steffen, (Eds.), *Tools and Algorithms for the Construction and Analysis of Systems*, Volume 1055 of *Lecture Notes in Computer Science*, pages 397–401, Springer, 1996.

12. J. Henriksen e.a., MONA: Monadic Second-Order Logic in Practice, in Brinksma, Cleaveland, Larsen, Margaria, and Steffen, (Eds.) *TACAS '95, Tools and Algorithms for The Construction and Analysis of Systems*, Volume 1019 of *Lecture Notes in Computer Science*, pages 89-110, Springer, 1995.

13. S. Leue, *Specifying Real-Time Requirements for SDL Specifications – a Temporal Logic-Based Approach*, Research Paper, University of Waterloo, Canada, 1996.

14. P. Merlin and D. Farber, Recoverability of Communication Protocols – Implication of a Theoretical Study, *IEEE Transactions on Software Communications* Vol. 24, 1036 – 1043 (1976).

15. L. Popova: On Time Petri Nets. *Journal of Information Processing and Cybernetics*, Volume 1055 of *Lecture Notes in Computer Science*, Springer, 1991.

A   Appendix

Syntax of SDL/R:

$< systemdef >$	::=	**system** $syst$; $< signaldef >^*$ $< channeldef >^*$ $< processdef >^+$ **endsystem;**
$< signaldef >$	::=	**signal** $sign$ [($< sortlist >$)] ;
$< sortlist >$	::=	$< sort >$, $< sortlist >$ | $< sort >$
$< sort >$	::=	Set
$< channeldef >$	::=	**channel** $< timeint >$ $chan$ **from** $proc1$ **to** $proc2$ **with** $< signallist >$;
$< signallist >$	::=	$sign$, $< signallist >$ | $sign$
$< processdef >$	::=	**process** $proc$; $< vardef >^*$ $< timerdef >^*$ $< processbody >$ **endprocess;**
$< vardef >$	::=	**dcl** w $< sort >$;
$< timerdef >$	::=	**timer** t ;
$< processbody >$	::=	**start** ; $< transition >$ $< state >^+$
$< state >$	::=	**state** st ; $< input >^+$
$< input >$	::=	**input** { $sign$ [($< varlist >$)] $< timeint >$ | **none** } ; $< transition >$
$< varlist >$	::=	w , $< varlist >$ | w
$< transition >$	::=	$< transaction >$ $< timeint >$; $< transition >$ | $< decision >$ | **nextstate** st ;
$< transaction >$	::=	**task** $v :=$ $< expr >$ | $< set >$ | $< reset >$ | **output** $sign$ [($< exprlist >$)] **via** $chan$
$< set >$	::=	**set** $(t, \mathbf{now} + < expr >)$
$< reset >$	::=	**reset** (t)
$< exprlist >$	::=	$< expr >$, $< exprlist >$ | $< expr >$
$< expr >$	::=	w | $const$ | $< expr >$ op $< expr >$ | op $< expr >$
$< decision >$	::=	**decision** w $< timeint >$; $< answer >^+$ **enddecision;**
$< answer >$	::=	($< expr >$) : $< transition >$
$< timeint >$	::=	$[< expr >, < expr >]$

Auxiliary Semantic Functions:

$Proc$	: set of all process names in the system.
$Chan$	: set of all channel names in the system.
$InputChan(p)$	: set of all names of channels with receiver p.
$State(p)$	: set of all state names in p, without 'input none'.
$StateNone(p)$	: set of all state names in p, with 'input none'.
$InputSignal(p, s)$	: set of all input signals (without parameter), which p may consume in state s.
$Signal(c)$	: set of all (parametrised) signals of channel c.
$Capacity(B)$	: capacity for the buffer B (channel or input queue).

Semantic Rules:

$\mathcal{M}(\textbf{system } syst; < signaldef >^* < channeldef >^* < processsdef >^+ \textbf{ endsystem};) =$

$$[\bigcup_{p \in Proc} \{I^!_p, I^?_p\} \cup \bigcup_{c \in Chan} \{C^!, C^?\} : \mathcal{M}(< channeldef >^* < processsdef >^+)] \qquad (1)$$

$\mathcal{M}(< channeldef >^+ < processsdef >^+) = \mathcal{M}(< channeldef >^+) \parallel \mathcal{M}(< processsdef >^+) \qquad (2)$

$\mathcal{M}(< channeldef_1 >< channeldef >^+) = \mathcal{M}(< channeldef_1 >) \parallel \mathcal{M}(< channeldef >^+) \qquad (3)$

$\mathcal{M}(< processsdef_1 >< processsdef >^+) = \mathcal{M}(< processsdef_1 >) \parallel \mathcal{M}(< processsdef >^+) \qquad (4)$

$\mathcal{M}(\textbf{channel } < timeint > c \textbf{ from } p1 \textbf{ to } p2 \textbf{ with } < signallist >) =$

$\qquad M_{channel}(c, Capacity(c), Signal(c), < timeint >)$

$\qquad \parallel [M(\{C^?(s1), I^!_{p2}(s2)\}, \{s1 = s2\}) * M(\{C^?(s1), I^!_{p2}(s2)\}, \{s1 = s2\}) * M_{stop}] \qquad (5)$

$\mathcal{M}(\textbf{process } p ; < vardef >^+ < timerdef >^* < processsbody > \textbf{endprocess};) =$

$\qquad [\delta(< vardef >^+) : \mathcal{M}(< vardef >^+)$

$\qquad \parallel \mathcal{M}(\textbf{process } p ; < timerdef >^* < processsbody > \textbf{endprocess};)] \qquad (6)$

$\qquad \text{with } \delta(< vardef_1 >< vardef >^+) = \delta(< vardef_1 >) \cup \delta(< vardef >^+)$

$\qquad \text{and } \delta(\textbf{dcl } w \ Set;) = \{W\}$

$\mathcal{M}(\textbf{process } p ; < timerdef >^+ < processsbody > \textbf{endprocess};) =$

$\qquad [\delta(< timerdef >^+) : \mathcal{M}^P(< timerdef >^+)$

$\qquad \parallel \mathcal{M}(\textbf{process } p ; < processsbody > \textbf{endprocess};)] \qquad (7)$

$\qquad \text{with } \delta(< timerdef_1 >< timerdef >^+) = \delta(< timerdef_1 >) \cup \delta(< timerdef >^+)$

$\qquad \text{and } \delta(\textbf{timer } t;) = \{T_{set}, T_{reset}\}$

$\mathcal{M}(< vardef_1 >< vardef >^+) = \mathcal{M}(< vardef_1 >) \parallel \mathcal{M}(< vardef >^+) \qquad (8)$

$\mathcal{M}(\textbf{dcl } w \ Set;) = M_{data}(w, Set) \qquad (9)$

$\mathcal{M}^P(< timerdef_1 >< timerdef >^+) = \mathcal{M}^P(< timerdef_1 >) \parallel \mathcal{M}^P(< timerdef >^+) \qquad (10)$

$\mathcal{M}^P(\textbf{timer } t;) = M_{timer}(p, t) \qquad (11)$

$\mathcal{M}(\textbf{process } p ; < processsbody > \textbf{endprocess};) =$

$$[\{Q, I^{rem}_p\} : M_{input}(I_p, Capacity(I_p), \bigcup_{c \in InputChan(p)} Signal(c))$$

$\qquad \parallel \mathcal{M}^P(< processsbody >) \parallel M_{data}(q, State(p) \cup \{\bullet\})] \qquad (12)$

$\mathcal{M}^P(\textbf{start}; < transition >< state >^+) = [\mathcal{M}^P(< transition >)*$

$$\mathcal{M}^P(< state >^+) \ \Box \ M(\{Q('q, q'), I^?_p(m)\}, \{'q = q' \wedge \bigwedge_{s \in StateNone(p)} ('q \neq s)$$

$$\wedge \bigwedge_{s \in State(p)} ('q = s \Rightarrow \bigwedge_{i \in InputSignal(p,s)} m[0] \neq i)\}, [0, 0]) * M_{stop}] \qquad (13)$$

$$\mathcal{M}^P(< state_1 >< state >^+) = \mathcal{M}^P(< state_1 >) \,\Box\, \mathcal{M}^P(< state >^+) \tag{14}$$

$$\mathcal{M}^P(\textbf{state } st; < input_1 >< input >^+) = \mathcal{M}^P(\textbf{state } st; < input_1 > \textbf{state } st; < input >^+) \tag{15}$$

$$\mathcal{M}^P(\textbf{state } st; \textbf{input none; } [< expr_1 >, < expr_2 >]; < transition >) =$$
$$M(\{Q('q,q')\} \cup AS_1 \cup AS_2, \{'q = st \wedge q' = \bullet\}, [E_1, E_2]); \mathcal{M}^P(< transition >) \tag{16}$$

$$\mathcal{M}^P(\textbf{state } st; \textbf{input } s(v_1, \ldots, v_n) \; [< expr_1 >, < expr_2 >]; < transition >) =$$
$$M(\{Q('q,q'), I_p^?(m), V_1('v_1, v_1'), \ldots, V_n('v_n, v_n')\} \cup AS_1 \cup AS_2,$$

$$\{'q = st \wedge q' = \bullet \wedge m[0] = s \wedge len(m) = n \wedge \bigwedge_{i=1}^{n} m[i] = v_i'\}, [E_1, E_2]);$$

$$\mathcal{M}^P(< transition >) \quad\quad , \text{ for } n \geq 0 \tag{17}$$

and $\zeta(< expr_j >) = (AS_j/E_j), j = 1, 2$ with

$$\zeta(w) = (\{W('w, w')\}/'w)$$
$$\zeta(const) = (\emptyset/const)$$
$$\zeta(< expr_1 > op < expr_2 >) = (AS_1 \cup AS_2/E_1 \, op \, E_2)$$
$$\quad\quad\quad\quad\quad\quad\quad\quad\quad\quad \text{if } \zeta(< expr_i >) = (AS_i/E_i) \,, \, i=1,2$$
$$\zeta(op < expr >) = (AS/op \, E) \quad\quad \text{if } \zeta(< expr >) = (AS/E)$$

$$\mathcal{M}^P(< transaction > ; < transition >) = \mathcal{M}^P(< transaction >); \mathcal{M}^P(< transition >) \tag{18}$$

$$\mathcal{M}^P(\textbf{task } v :=< expr_1 > [< expr_2 >, < expr_3 >]) = M(AS \cup \{V('v, v')\},$$
$$\{v' = E_1\} \cup \{'w = w' \mid w \neq v \text{ and } w \text{ in } < expr_i > i = 1, 2 \text{ or } 3\}, [E_2, E_3]) \tag{19}$$

if $\zeta(< expr_j >) = (AS_j/E_j), 1 \leq j \leq 3,$ and $AS = \bigcup_{j=1}^{3} AS_j$

$$\mathcal{M}^P(\textbf{output } s(< expr_1 >, \ldots, < expr_n >) \textbf{ via } c \, [< expr_{n+1} >, < expr_{n+2} >]) =$$

$$M(\{C'(m)\} \cup \bigcup_{i=1}^{n+2} AS_i, \{m[0] = s \wedge len(m) = n \wedge \bigwedge_{i=1}^{n} m[i] = E_i\}, [E_{n+1}, E_{n+2}]) \tag{20}$$

with $n \geq 0$ and $\zeta(< expr_i >) = (AS_i/E_i)$ for all $i = 1, \ldots, n+2$.

$$\mathcal{M}^P(\textbf{set } (t, \text{now} + < expr_1 >), [< expr_2 >, < expr_3 >]) =$$
$$M(\{T_{set}(b)\} \cup AS, \{b = E_1\}, [E_2, E_3]) \tag{21}$$

if $\zeta(< expr_i >) = (AS_i/E_i), 1 \leq i \leq 3,$ and $AS = \bigcup_{i=1}^{3} AS_i.$

$$\mathcal{M}^P(\textbf{reset } (t), [< expr_1 >, < expr_2 >]) = M(\{T_{reset}\} \cup AS, \{\}, [E_1, E_2]) \tag{22}$$

if $\zeta(< expr_i >) = (AS_i/E_i), 1 \leq i \leq 2,$ and $AS = AS_1 \cup AS_2.$

$$\mathcal{M}^P(\textbf{decision } w < timeint > ; < answer >^+ \textbf{ enddecision;}) =$$
$$\mathcal{M}^P_{<timeint>}(< answer >^+) \tag{23}$$

$$\mathcal{M}^P_{<timeint>}(< answer_1 >< answer >^+) =$$
$$\mathcal{M}^P_{<timeint>}(< answer_1 >) \,\Box\, \mathcal{M}^P_{<timeint>}(< answer >^+) \tag{24}$$

$$\mathcal{M}^P_{<timeint>}((< expr >) :< transition >) =$$
$$\mathcal{M}^P(< expr >< timeint >); \mathcal{M}^P(< transition >) \tag{25}$$

$$\mathcal{M}^P(< expr_1 > [< expr_2 >, < expr_3 >]) =$$
$$M(AS, E_1 \cup \{'w = w' \mid w \text{ in } < expr_i > i = 1, 2 \text{ or } 3\}, [E_2, E_3]) \tag{26}$$

if $\zeta(< expr_j >) = (AS_j/E_j), 1 \leq j \leq 3,$ and $AS = \bigcup_{j=1}^{3} AS_j$

$$\mathcal{M}^P(\textbf{nextstate } st;) = M(\{Q('q, q')\}, \{q' = st\}, [0, 0]) \tag{27}$$

Reconciling Real-Time
with Asynchronous Message Passing

M. Broy, R. Grosu, C. Klein*

Institut für Informatik, TU München, D-80290 München
email: {broy,grosu,klein}@informatik.tu-muenchen.de

Abstract. At first sight, real-time and asynchronous message passing like in SDL and ROOM seem to be incompatible. Indeed these languages fail to model real-time constraints accurately. In this paper, we show how to reconcile real-time with asynchronous message passing, by using an assumption which is supported by every mailing system throughout the world, namely that messages are time-stamped with their sending and arrival time. This assumption allows us to develop a formalism which is adequate to model and to specify real-time constraints. The proposed formalism is shown at work on a small real-time example.

1   Introduction

Asynchronous message passing has gained a lot of popularity in the industrial community. Two of the most prominent specification and description languages for real-time systems use it as their basic communication and synchronization scheme between processes: the ITU-T specification and description language SDL [OFMP+94, IT93] and the ObjecTime specification and description language ROOM [SGW94].

Basically, the behavior of a system in SDL or ROOM is given as a set of asynchronously communicating extended finite state machines (EFSM). A signal instance, i.e., a message, is created when an EFSM executes an output and ceases to exist when the receiving EFSM consumes the signal in an input. Communication channels convey the signal instance from the sender to the receiver. When the signal arrives, it is kept in the input port of the receiver, which is an unbounded FIFO queue, until the receiver consumes it. The virtue of this communication scheme is the loose coupling between system parts: a sender is never blocked because a receiver is not ready to communicate.

In order to express real-time constraints, both SDL and ROOM allow to access the global, *actual time* and to set and reset *timers*. A timer is a stopwatch which is set with an expiration time. The expiration of the timer is then signaled to

---

* This work is partly sponsored by the Deutsche Forschungs Gemeinschaft (DFG) project SYSLAB

the process as an ordinary input signal. When a timer is no longer needed, it can be reset before its expiration, to avoid spurious expirations.

Unfortunately, these timing facilities are not precisely defined in the SDL and ROOM semantics [Hin96, Leu95, BB91, SGW94] and therefore implementation dependent. Practical experience has shown that the SDL timing facilities behave well only if the tolerance intervals are at least 100 times the average instruction time of the CPU used for the implementation [OFMP+94]. Moreover, these timing facilities are not always expressive enough. In order to understand why this is the case, let us examine a small fragment of a telephone protocol.

" After the caller has lifted the phone receiver, he must receive a dial tone within 0.1s."

Assuming that no delay occurs on the communication lines, this protocol can be expressed very intuitively by using a timed variant of message sequence charts, as shown in Figure 1, left, where offH is the abbreviation for off-hook, dtB is the abbreviation for dial-tone-begin and a,b are points in time (see [IT96] for the MSC standard).

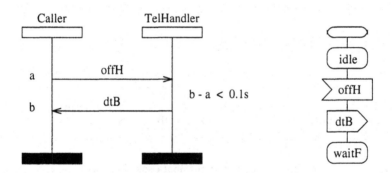

Fig. 1. MSC and EFSM for the protocol fragment

This requirement is neither expressible in SDL nor in ROOM. The best one can do is to write the EFSM given in SDL-notation in Figure 1, right. It consists of a start symbol, the control states idle and waitF, and a transition labeled by the input offH and the output dtB. This EFSM neither guarantees that the transition is taken synchronously with the generation of the offH message nor that the transition takes less than 0.1s. The transition can be delayed, even if the dtB message was already queued in the input port. Moreover, it is unknown how long does it take to produce the output dtB. Note that timers are not helpful in this case, since they can only be used to enforce a reaction if a signal does not *arrive* within a given time interval.

One of the most successful formal models for specifying and verifying real-time systems are timed automata [AD94, HNSY92]. The formalism of timed automata generalizes finite state machines over infinite strings to generate (or accept) infinite sequences of states which are additionally constrained by timing requirements.

A timed automaton operates with finite control – a finite set of locations, a finite set of propositions and a finite set of real-valued clocks. All clocks proceed at the same rate and measure the amount of time that has elapsed since they were reset. Each edge of the automaton may reset some of the clocks and assign new values to a set of propositional variables. Each edge and each location may put certain constraints on the values of the clocks and propositions corresponding to that location.

Using a syntax similar to the one given in [HNSY92], the caller and the telephone handler automata can be expressed as shown in Figure 2. Suppose the channels i and o and the timer x are modeled with shared variables, and that composition is done by interleaving. If initially i ≠ offH, then only the caller automaton can proceed by "sending" offH along i simultaneously with reseting the timer x. The telephone handler is then able to make its first transition. The second transition of the telephone handler can than be taken at any moment such that x < 0.1s with the effect of "sending" dtB.

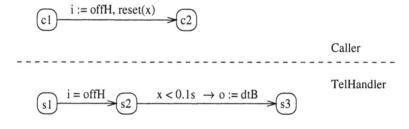

Fig. 2. The timed automata solution

The above timed-automata solution uses shared variables both for communication and for time synchronization. Although shared variables are appropriate for single-processor systems, they are unnatural in the context of distributed systems. Moreover, the timed automata approach is not modular, since timed automata may constrain their environment, as we will show in the next section.

Note that the sharing of the timer variable x between the caller and the telephone handler implies that the receiver knows when the offH message has been sent. In the following, we use essentially the same idea, but in a modular way, and within a message-passing communication paradigm. In the solution we propose, each message is time-stamped both with the sending and the arrival time, as this is a common practice of any mailing system. To simplify the semantics (but without loss of generality because the communication medium can be modeled again as a component) we assume instantaneous delivery, i.e., the sending and the arrival time are considered to be the same.

As in SDL and ROOM, we describe the behavior of processes with extended finite-state machines which we call *timed state transition diagrams* (TSTDs). We also assume asynchronous communication and the presence of a timer variable now containing at each moment the actual time. However, in contrast to SDL and ROOM we allow to access the arrival time of a message by using time-stamped input patterns. For example, the pattern i?offH@t matches the first offH message in the input port i, and updates the variable t with the arrival time of this message. This variable can be used in conjunction with now to guard a transition, as in now - t < 0.1s. When the transition is taken, it takes place instantaneously.

Using our approach, the timing requirement of the telephone protocol fragment can be expressed with only one TSTD – the telephone handler – as shown in Figure 3.

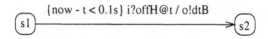

Fig. 3. Our solution

The input and the output patterns are separated by a slash, and written in a syntax inspired by CSP [Hoa85]. The guard (or precondition) is written within curly brackets before the input/output patterns. Assignments to the state variables can be written between curly brackets after the input/output patterns (the postcondition).

Intuitively, a component specified by this TSTD behaves as follows. If the component is in the control state s1, the first message on the port i is offH, and the arrival time t of this message is such that now-t<0.1s, then the component has the choices either to perform the transition immediately, or to perform it at any later moment now' which also satisfies the condition now'-t<0.1s.

To express timeouts and priorities between transitions, we also allow to test for the absence of any message in a given port. For example, the input pattern i?⊖ is satisfied if no message is in the input port i at time moment now. The input pattern i?a, j?⊖ is satisfied if at time point now the "prioritized" port j is empty whereas the first message in the port i is a. Hence, if a transition is labeled with i?a, j?⊖ and another with j?b, and both have the same source control node, then the second transition has a higher priority.

If a transition has no pattern for an input port, then no message is discarded from that port in this transition. Similarly, if a transition has no pattern for an output port, then no message is sent on this output port.

If no transition can be taken in a given state, then the behavior of the component is completely unspecified ("chaotic"). This implies that we have to handle undesired input explicitly. This is in contrast to SDL, where input messages without a matching transition are implicitly ignored. Although at first sight the SDL approach might seem more convenient, this implicit assumption often leads to subtle errors in SDL specifications.

Note that time stamping the input can be avoided, if the input transition of the receiver is synchronous with the output transition of the sender. This assumption however, would change the communication paradigm. In contrast, our time-stamped model is fully asynchronous and contains the SDL and the ROOM models as a particular case, in which all timing constraints equal true. This allows for a modular specification formalism along the lines of [BDD+93, BS97, GS96], and for a stepwise development process, where timing constraints are omitted in the first step [GKRB96] and introduced gradually in the next steps. The above would not hold, however, if we would change our model such that transitions are taken as soon as they become enabled. Moreover, in this case one would also have to introduce prophecies in order to express an arbitrary delay within a given interval.

Our paper is organized as follows. In Section 2, we intuitively introduce timed state transition diagrams by specifying a simplified telephone handler. In Section 3 we introduce the abstract syntax of timed state transition diagrams. Section 4 defines the semantics of TSTDs in terms of timed input-/output relations. Section 5 is concerned with the syntax and the semantics of input- and output patterns. In section 6 we discuss the composition of TSTDs. Finally, in section 7 we draw some conclusions.

2 Dialing a Telephone Number

In order to get more intuition about our model and to show how we deal with timeouts, let us formalize the behavior of a telephone handler, which controls the dialing of a four-digit telephone number. The telephone handler has to satisfy the following requirements:

1. *After the caller has lifted the phone receiver, he must receive a dial tone within 0.1s*

2. *If the caller does not respect the following timing requirements, then the telephone handler should return a timeout tone and disconnect the line:*

   (a) *After receiving the dial tone, the caller must dial the first digit within 30s.*

   (b) *After a digit has been dialed, the next digit must be dialed within 20s.*

   (c) *After the caller has lifted the phone receiver, he must dial a complete number within 60s*

The specification of the telephone handler is given in Figure 4.

```
tstd TelHandler = {

    input      i : TelI
    output     o : TelO
    attributes n, c, dt, nt : Nat
    transitions
```

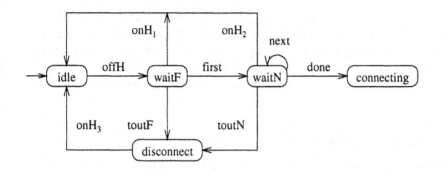

transition	precondition	input	output	postcondition
offH	now $-$ t $<$ 0.1s	i?offH @ t	o!dtB	dt' = nt' = now
first	t $-$ dt $<$ 30s	i?d(a) @ t	o!dtE	n' = a $\land$ c' = 1 $\land$ dt' = now
next	t $-$ dt $<$ 20s $\land$ t $-$ nt $<$ 60s $\land$ c $<$ 3	i?d(a) @ t		n' = n * 10 + a $\land$ c' = c + 1 $\land$ dt' = now
done	t $-$ dt $<$ 20s $\land$ t $-$ nt $<$ 60s $\land$ c = 3	i?d(a) @ t		n' = n * 10 + a
onH$_1$	now $-$ t $<$ 0.1s	i?onH @ t	o!dtE	
onH$_2$	t $-$ dt $<$ 20s $\land$ t $-$ nt $<$ 60s	i?onH @ t		
onH$_3$		i?onH	o!dcE	
toutF	now $-$ dt = 30s	i?$\ominus$	o!dcB	
toutN	now $-$ dt $=$ 20s $\lor$ now $-$ nt $=$ 60s	i?$\ominus$	o!dcB	

Fig. 4. The telephone handler

The specification consists of an interface declaration part, an attribute declaration part and a state transition diagram. The interface declaration lists the names of the input and the output ports together with their types. The attributes are defined by their name, type, and (optionally) an initial value. The telephone handler has an input port i : TelI and an output port o : TelO, where the message sets TelI and TelO are defined as follows:

> **data** TelI = offH | onH | d(Digit)
> **data** TelO = dtB | dtE | dcB | dcE

The above types define the set of messages allowed to flow between the caller and the telephone handler. Each message consists of a message name and optional data. For example, offH contains no data while d(8) contains both the message name d(igit) and the data value $8 \in$ Digit, where Digit is assumed to range between 0 to 9. The bar notation is used to separate alternatives. It is similar to data-type declarations as they are used in functional languages like ML (see [Pau91]).

The abbreviations onH, dtE, dcB and dcE are used for on-hook, dial-tone-end, disconnect-begin and disconnect-end respectively.

The attribute n is used to store the telephone number, the attribute c is used to count the number of digits already received, the attribute nt is used to save the arrival time of the first digit and the attribute dt is used to save the arrival time of the previous digit.

To enhance the readability of the state transition diagrams we allow to define the transitions separately in tabular form and to refer them by their name. A good practice is to use for the transition's name the name (or a common attribute) of the transition's input message(s). For example, the transition offH is defined as follows: if the component is in the control state idle and the first message in its input port i is offH, then it sends the message dtB along its output port o provided that offH was received at a time t such that now − t < 0.1s. Additionally, the current time is saved in dt and nt. This is needed to raise a timeout if the first digit is not dialed within 30s or if the number is not dialed within 60s. The other transitions are defined analogously.

Note that if no message has arrived on the port i, then a timeout transition takes place exactly at the moment when the time limit has expired. Contrast this with SDL and ROOM, where a timeout message is queued as an ordinary message after the timeout has expired. As a consequence, it can be only guaranteed that timeout processing does not happen before the time limit has expired. Contrast this also with timed automata, where the input is not inspected in the timeout transitions. This is not necessary in that approach, because the correct traces of the environment *and* the automaton are generated together.

Since we use transition diagrams primarily for specification purpose, the preconditions and the postconditions are allowed to be arbitrary predicates. However, often one might be interested in a specification technique which can be used for validation purposes or for direct code generation. In such cases, one is free to use some restricted form of predicates, such as equations or executable statements of some programming language. Let us now give the formal definition of the state transition diagrams introduced so far.

3 Timed State Transition Diagrams

A real-time component described by a timed state transition diagram communicates with its environment along typed input and output ports. They define the interface of the component and are given formally by a *port signature*.

Definition 1. (Port signature) Let I and O be disjoint sets of *input* and respectively *output port names*. Let D be a mapping assigning to each port $c \in I \cup O$ a type D_c. A *port signature* is a tuple $\Sigma = (I, O, D)$.

Let φ denote the time-stamped sequence of message which is expected to arrive along the input interface before a transition is taken. Since the input ports are named and typed, φ is a record (or named tuple), and for each $i \in I$, $\varphi.i$ represents the sequence of messages which is expected to arrive along the port i. Formally[2], φ is an element of the named product $\Pi_{i \in I}(D_i \times \mathbb{N})^*$, where $\mathbb{N}$ denotes the domain of time stamps. In the following, we denote this set of *input actions* by Act_{Σ}^I. Similary, let ψ denote the sequence of messages which are sent along the output interface when a transition is taken. Since the output ports are named and typed and the output sequences are sent on all ports in the same time unit, ψ is an element of the set of *output actions* $Act_{\Sigma}^O = \Pi_{o \in O} D_o^*$. This powerful concept of input and output actions often allows us, in contrast to SDL, to eliminate trivial intermediate states and transitions.

Definition 2. (State Transition Diagram) A state transition diagram is a tuple $\mathcal{D} = (\Sigma, S, G, \nu, \eta)$ where:

$\Sigma = (I, O, D)$ is a port signature.

$S = \Pi_{a \in A} D_a$ defines the data state space of $\mathcal{D}$. Each $a \in A$ is an *attribute a* with associated type D_a. One special, read only attribute now $\in \mathbb{N}$ contains at each moment the current time.

$G = (N, E \subseteq N \times N, n_0)$ is the *control graph* of $\mathcal{D}$. Each node $n \in N$ defines a *control state* and each edge $(n_1, n_2) \in E$ defines a *control transition*. $n_0 \in N$ is the *initial control node*.

$\nu \in N \to (S \to \mathbb{B})$ is the *node labeling* of $\mathcal{D}$. It marks each control state $n \in N$ with a predicate ν_n giving the associated data states.

---

[2] Given an arbitrary set M, we denote by M^* the set of finite sequences over M. Given a set of names I and a mapping D assigning to each name $i \in I$ a type D_i, we denote by $\Pi_{i \in I} D_i$ the set of named tuples $\{f : I \to \bigcup_{i \in I} D_i | f.i \in D_i\}$

$\eta \in E \to \wp((S \times Act_\Sigma^I \to \mathbb{B}) \times (S \times Act_\Sigma^I \times Act_\Sigma^O \times S \to \mathbb{B}))$ is the *edges label-ing* of $\mathcal{D}$. It marks each edge $e \in E$ with a set of precondition/postcondition pairs $(pre, post)$. The *precondition* acts as a guard on the transition's source state and input. The transition is taken only if the guard is true. In that case the *postcondition* defines the next state and the output, possibly by referring to the current state and the input.

Although state predicates ν_n were not used in our telephone protocol, they are convenient to impose for example an upper bound timing constraint for a given control node n. If all transitions leaving node n have only lower bounds, then the upper bound constraint for n enforces that one of the transitions is taken before the upper bound is reached.

From a methodological point of view, it might be appropriate to require cer-tain well-formedness conditions for the predicates involved. For example, the enabledness of a transition should depend only on the precondition, i.e., the postcondition should not constrain the current state and the input. Formally, for all data states $s \in S$, inputs $i \in Act_\Sigma^I$, edges $e \in E$ and precondition/postcondition pairs $(pre, post) \in \eta_e$:

$$pre(s, i) \quad \Rightarrow \quad \exists s', o.\ post(s, i, o, s')$$

A state transition diagram satisfying this property is called *precondition con-trolled*. Similarily, the destination data state s' should be a valid state of the destination control node. We call such a node *postcondition complete*. Formally, for all states $s, s' \in S$, inputs $i \in Act_\Sigma^I$, outputs $o \in Act_\Sigma^O$, edges $(n, n') \in E$ and precondition/postcondition pairs $(pre, post) \in \eta_{(n,n')}$:

$$pre(s, i) \land post(s, i, o, s') \quad \Rightarrow \quad \nu_{n'}(s')$$

However, we do not enforce these conditions in the semantics. They should be treated on the methodological level, either by restricting the language or by automatically generating proof obligations.

4 The Semantics of TSTDs

The semantics of a timed state transition diagram is given as a relation between the communication histories along its input and its output ports. For simplicity, the communication histories are defined over a discrete time domain which is taken to be the set of natural numbers $\mathbb{N}$. However, this semantics could easily be extended to a dense time domain [MS96].

As usual in weakly monotonic discrete time semantics [AH92], each complete communication history is an infinite sequence of finite sequences of messages. Each finite sequence contains the messages occuring within the same time unit. Given a set of messages D, the set $(D^*)^*$ is the set of *partial* communication histories over D and the set $(D^*)^\infty$ is the set of *complete* communication histories over D. In the following we abbreviate $(D^*)^\infty$ by $D^\mathbb{N}$.

The ports of a component in our semantic model are named and typed. As a consequence the communication histories over its input and respectively output ports are named products of communication histories. We call them *named communication histories*. Formally, if the port signature of the timed state transition diagram is $\Sigma = (I, O, D)$, then the set of complete named communication histories over the input and the output ports are given by $\prod_{i \in I} D_i^{\aleph}$ and $\prod_{o \in O} D_o^{\aleph}$, respectively. The set of partial named communication histories is given by $\prod_{i \in I} (D_i^*)^*$ and $\prod_{o \in O} (D_o^*)^*$. The named communication sequences within a time unit are denoted by $\prod_{i \in I} D_i^*$ and $\prod_{o \in O} D_o^*$. In the following we also refer to named communication histories as communication histories when no confusion arises.

Given $\alpha \in D^{\aleph}$ and $i \in \mathbb{N}$, then $\alpha \downarrow_i \in (D^*)^*$ denotes the partial communication history consisting of the first i finite sequences in the complete communication history α. This operation is overloaded to named communication histories and to sets of named communication histories in a point-wise and an element-wise style, respectively.

The input/output relation corresponding to a TSTD is a *set valued function*

$$F : \prod_{i \in I} D_i^{\aleph} \to \wp(\prod_{o \in O} D_o^{\aleph})$$

mapping complete input histories to sets of complete output histories. However, not every relation with this functionality is adequate to give the semantics of a TSTD: *In reality, TSTDs can not predict the future.* The output produced by a TSTD until some point in time must not depend on input the TSTD will receive in the future. This condition is formally captured by the following definition:

Definition 3. (Timed relations) We call an input/output relation $F \in \prod_{i \in I} D_i^{\aleph} \to \wp(\prod_{o \in O} D_o^{\aleph})$ *weakly time guarded*, if for all $\alpha, \beta : \prod_{i \in I} D_i^{\aleph}$ and $i \in \mathbb{N}$

$$\alpha \downarrow_i = \beta \downarrow_i \quad \Rightarrow \quad F(\alpha) \downarrow_i = F(\beta) \downarrow_i$$

We call an input/output relation *strongly time guarded*, if the following stronger condition holds

$$\alpha \downarrow_i = \beta \downarrow_i \quad \Rightarrow \quad F(\alpha) \downarrow_{i+1} = F(\beta) \downarrow_{i+1}$$

Before we give the formal definition of the input output relation generated by a TSTD, let us introduce some operators on sequences which are used in this definition.

For any finite sequences s, s_1, s_2 and element a, $a :: s$ is the sequence s with a appended in front of s, $s_1 \frown s_2$ is the concatenation of s_1 and s_2 and $\#s$ is the length of s. $[]$ is the empty sequence and $[a_1, \ldots, a_n]$ is the sequence $a_1 :: (a_2 :: \ldots (a_n :: []))$. If $a_1 = a_2 = \ldots = a_n$ we also write $[a^n]$. The operations $::$ and $\frown$ are overloaded for the case in which the second argument is an infinite sequence.

On sequences of sequences, an operation related to $\frown$ is the paste operation $.\smile. : (D^*)^* \times D^{\aleph} \to D^{\aleph}$. It only differs from the conventional concatenation $\frown$

in that the last sequence of s_1 is pasted with the first sequence of s_2.

$$\forall a, b \in D^*, s_1 \in (D^*)^*, s_2 \in D^\aleph. \ (s_1 \frown [a]) \smile ([b] \frown s_2) = s_1 \frown [a \frown b] \frown s_2$$

This operation allows us to take a prefix of a communication history, by cutting the history in the middle of a sequence of messages occurring in the same time unit. Formally, we say that φ is a prefix of α, written as $\varphi \sqsubseteq \alpha$ if the following holds:

$$\varphi \sqsubseteq \alpha \quad \Leftrightarrow \quad \exists \beta. \ \varphi \smile \beta = \alpha$$

Given a partial communication history $\varphi \in (D^*)^*$ and a time value $t \in \mathbb{N}$, we denote by $\varphi@t \in (D \times \mathbb{N})^*$ the time-stamped communication history, i.e., the communication history with time information made explicit and adjusted to the time point t. Formally, for every $a \in D, u \in D^*$ and $\varphi \in (D^*)^*$ the time-stamped sequence $((a :: u) :: \varphi)@t$ is defined as below. Remember that a and all the messages in u occurr in the same time unit.

$$((a :: u) :: \varphi)@t = \langle a, t \rangle :: ((u :: \varphi)@t)$$

$$([] :: \varphi)@t \quad = \varphi@(t+1)$$

$$[]@t \quad = [\langle \ominus, t \rangle]$$

If no confusion can arise, a tuple $\langle a, t \rangle$ from a time stamped sequence is also written as $a@t$. In this definition and in the following, we tacitly assume that the symbol $\ominus$ is also an element of D. The last element $\langle \ominus, t \rangle$ of a time stamped sequence is needed to distinguish between timed sequences ending with a different number of trailing empty sequences. As we shall see in Section 5, this allows us to give a different semantics to empty- and to negative patterns, respectively. Empty patterns like i?[] are satisfied when no message in the input port is consumed, whereas negative patterns like i?$\ominus$ are satisfied only if no message has arrived on the input port until now.

All operators introduced in this section are overloaded to named communication histories and to sets of communication histories in a point-wise and an element-wise style, respectively[3]. If $\gamma, \delta \in \prod_{i \in I} \mathbb{N}$ and $k \in \mathbb{N}$ then we write $\gamma + \delta$ and $\gamma + k$ for the named product which is obtained by summing γ and δ componentwise and by adding k to each component of γ respectively. Moreover, for a state s of the TSTD we write $s + k$ for the state in which now is incremented by k.

The operational intuition is as follows: The state space of the component consists of a control part (node), a data part (attributes), a time part (now variable), and a tuple $f \in \Pi_{i \in I} \mathbb{N}$. The value $f.i$ indicates the arrival time of the first message in the input port i which has not yet been processed by the component. The component starts in an initial data state s_0 satisfying the predicate ν_{n_0} of the start node, and $f.i = (s_0).\text{now}$ for all $i \in I$. In each state, the component can wait for some amount of time until a transition is taken. However, waiting is

---

[3] Note that $\prod_{i \in I} D_i^\aleph \cong (\prod_{i \in I} D_i^*)^\infty$. For $\varphi \in \prod_{i \in I} D_i^*$ and $\alpha \in \prod_{i \in I} D_i^\aleph$ we therefore consider $\varphi :: \alpha$ to be also an element of $\prod_{i \in I} D_i^\aleph$.

only allowed either if no transition was already enabled or if waiting does not lead to a chaotic behavior. The transition consumes part of the input, updates f accordingly, and sends some output in the current time interval. If the component performs a transition, then the transition is instantaneous, i.e., the value of the timer now is the same in the next state. In the definition below, we will assume that now cannot be modified, i.e., it does not occur primed in the postcondition of the TSTD.

Definition 4. (History Semantics of TSTDs) Given a state transition diagram $\mathcal{D} = (\Sigma, S, G, \nu, \eta)$. Then the semantics of $\mathcal{D}$ is the input/output relation $\mathcal{F}$ which is defined as follows:

$$\mathcal{F} \in \prod_{i \in I} D_i^{\aleph} \to \wp(\prod_{o \in O} D_o^{\aleph})$$

$$\mathcal{F}(\alpha) = \bigcup_{s \in \nu(n_0)} F(s, n_0, \lambda i \in I.(s.\text{now}))(\alpha)$$

F is the greatest weakly time guarded input/output relation parametric with respect to the current data state, current control state and arrival time of the first messages in the named input communication history that satisfies the following equation:

$$F \in S \times N \times \prod_{i \in I} \mathbb{N} \to \prod_{i \in I} D_i^{\aleph} \to \wp(\prod_{o \in O} D_o^{\aleph})$$

$$F(s, n, f)(\alpha) = \{ \beta \in \prod_{o \in O} D_o^{\aleph} \quad |$$

$\forall k \in \mathbb{N}.$	$--$	the delay measured in ticks
$\forall m \in N.$	$--$	the next control node
$\forall \varphi \in \prod_{i \in I} (D_i^*)^*.$	$--$	the timed input of the TSTD
$\forall \psi \in \prod_{o \in O} D_o^*.$	$--$	the output of the TSTD
$\forall s' \in S.$	$--$	the next state of the TSTD
$\forall pre \in S \times Act_{\Sigma}^I \to \mathbb{B}.$	$--$	the transition's precondition
$\forall post \in S \times Act_{\Sigma}^I \times Act_{\Sigma}^O \times S \to \mathbb{B}.$	$--$	the transitions's postcondition
$(\varphi \sqsubseteq \alpha \wedge$	$--$	φ is a prefix of α
$(pre, post) \in \eta_{(n,m)} \wedge$	$--$	$(pre,post)$ is in the TSTD
$\nu_n(s) \wedge \nu_m(s') \wedge$	$--$	src/dest predicates are satisfied
$pre(s+k, \varphi@f) \wedge post(s+k, \varphi@f, \psi, s')$	$--$	pre/post predicates are satisfied
$\Rightarrow$	$--$	chaos completion
$\exists \alpha' \in \prod_{i \in I} D_i^{\aleph}, \beta' \in \prod_{o \in O} D_o^{\aleph}.$	$--$	the suffixes of α and β
$\alpha = \varphi^{\smallfrown} \alpha' \wedge$	$--$	α' is indeed a suffix of α
$\beta = [[]^{k-1}, \psi]^{\smallfrown} \beta' \wedge$	$--$	β' is indeed a suffix of β
$\beta' \in F(s', m, f+\#\varphi)(\alpha')$	$--$	β' is in the continuation of F
$)$		
$\wedge$	$--$	no chaos for time:

$(\forall k' \leq k.$ $--$ an enabled transition

$\nu_n(s) \wedge \nu_m(s') \wedge$ $--$ has to be taken

$pre(s+k', \varphi @ f) \wedge post(s+k', \varphi @ f, \psi, s')$ $--$ before

$\Rightarrow$ $--$ it becomes disabled

$\nu_n(s) \wedge \nu_m(s') \wedge$ $--$ because of

$pre(s+k, \varphi @ f) \wedge post(s+k, \varphi @ f, \psi, s')$ $--$ time progression

$)$

$\}$

As usual we define that $F_1 \subseteq F_2$ holds if $\forall \alpha. F_1(\alpha) \subseteq F_2(\alpha)$. Since the F occurs only positively on the right-hand side of the equation, the corresponding functional is monotone w.r.t. this ordering, which implies the existence of a greatest solution. By the greatest weakly time guarded input-/output relation we mean the relation which is obtained by removing all behaviors which are not weakly time guarded in this solution.

5 Pattern Syntax of Transitions

The concrete syntax for state transition diagrams, and for the underlying predicate logic may depend on the concrete objectives for which timed state transition diagrams are used, and on the available tool support. One possible syntax has been given in the telephone protocol example.

However, we found it convenient to use transition rules of the following form:

$\{ Pre \}$ ip $/$ op $\{ Post \}$

where Pre and $Post$ are $predicate$ $expressions$ and ip and op are $input$ and $output$ $patterns$ (see the next two sections). The precondition Pre may contain as free variable the current state $s \in \Pi_{a \in A} D_a$ and the variables occuring free in the input pattern. The postcondition $Post$ may contain as free variables s and the next state s', as well as the variables occuring free in the input and output patterns. Since attributes not mentioned explicitly primed in the postcondition $Post$ are assumed to remain unchanged, we denote by $\overline{Post}$ the conjunction of $Post$ with equations $s'.a = s.a$ for all these attributes.

Suppose that ρ and η are environments for the free variables contained in the input and respectively the output patterns, that φ denote the current input action, and that ψ denotes the current output action. Then the predicates pre and $post$ with respect to Pre, $Post$, ip and op are defined as follows:

$pre(s, \varphi) \quad = \exists \rho : \; [\![Pre]\!]_{s,\rho} \wedge [\![ip]\!]_{s,\rho,\varphi}$

$post(s, \varphi, \psi, s') = \exists \rho, \eta : \; [\![ip]\!]_{s,\rho,\varphi} \wedge [\![\overline{Post}]\!]_{s,s',\rho,\eta} \wedge [\![op]\!]_{s,s',\rho,\eta,\psi}$

Here, $[\![PredExp]\!]_{env}$ denotes the interpretation (i.e. a truth value) of the predicate expression $PredExp$ with respect to some environment env. We assume the interpretation function to be given as usual for predicate expressions. The definition of the input and the output patterns together with their interpretations is the subject of the next two sections.

5.1 The Input Patterns

The input patterns are used to simplify the definition of the precondition/postcondition. An *input pattern* has the following form:

$$ip ::= i_1?p_1, \ldots, i_n?p_n$$
$$p ::= [m_1[@t_1], \ldots, m_k[@t_k]] \mid \ominus$$

where the port names i_k are all distinct. It associates each input port name i_k, $1 \leq k \leq n$, with an *input port pattern* p_k. The port pattern $[m_1[@t_1], \ldots, m_k[@t_k]]$ tests for the presence of the message sequence $[m_1, \ldots, m_k]$ on the associated port. Each message m_k may be optionally *time stamped* with the time of the message arrival. The empty pattern $[]$ indicates that input is ignored on the associated port. To simplify the diagrams, input port patterns with empty patterns are not explicitly written, and one-element patterns like $i?[m]$ are written as $i?m$. The port pattern $\ominus$ tests for the absence of any message on the associated port. It allows us to specify priorities and to model timeouts and interrupts. Note again the subtle difference between the empty pattern $[]$ and the negative pattern $\ominus$. $[]$ expresses that input is not required for the transition, while $\ominus$ expresses that there is no input.

Given the current state s, an environment ρ for the free variables in ip and an input sequence φ we define the interpretation of an input pattern

$$i_1?p_1, \ldots, i_m?p_m$$

as below. Without loss of generality, we assume that $I = \{i_1, \ldots, i_m, \ldots\}$.

$$[\![i_1?p_1, \ldots, i_m?p_m]\!]_{s,\rho,\varphi} \stackrel{\text{def}}{=} \forall_{k \leq m} : [\![i_k?p_k]\!]_{s,\rho,\varphi} \wedge \forall_{k > m} : [\![i_k?[]]\!]_{s,\rho,\varphi}$$

$$[\![i?[m_1[@t_1], \ldots, m_k[@t_k]]]\!]_{s,\rho,\varphi} \stackrel{\text{def}}{=} [[\![m_1@t_1]\!]_{s,\rho}, \ldots, [\![m_k@t_k]\!]_{s,\rho}, [\![\ominus@t]\!]_{s,\rho}] = \varphi.i$$

$$[\![i?\ominus]\!]_{s,\rho,\varphi} \stackrel{\text{def}}{=} [\![\ominus@s.\text{now}]\!] = \varphi.i$$

For messages not explicitly time stamped in the input patterns as well as for the negative pattern $\ominus$, we assume the existence of fresh, anonymous time variables in the environment ρ.

For simplicity, all patterns in the example in Section 2 have used only one-element lists. However, it is often convenient to use the more general form of patterns introduced in this section. For instance, the requirement that the time between the dialing of two consecutive digits is limited to 20s can be expressed as follows:

$$\{\forall i.1 \leq i \leq 3.t_{i+1} - t_i < 20s\} \quad i?[d(a_1)@t_1, \ d(a_2)@t_2, \ d(a_3)@t_3, \ d(a_4)@t_4]$$

5.2 The Output Patterns

The output patterns are used to simplify the definition of the postcondition. An *output pattern* has the following form:

$$op ::= o_1!p_1, \ldots, o_n!p_n$$
$$p \ ::= [m_1, \ldots, m_k]$$

where the port names o_k are all distinct. It associates each output port name o_k, $1 \leq k \leq n$, with an *output port pattern* p_k. The port pattern $[m_1, \ldots, m_k]$ defines the message sequence on the associated output port.

Given two states s and s', environments ρ, η for the free variables, and an output sequence ψ, we define the interpretation of an output pattern

$$o_1!p_1, \ldots, o_m!p_m$$

as below. Without loss of generality, we assume that $O = \{o_1, \ldots, o_m, \ldots\}$.

$$[\![o_1!p_1, \ldots, o_m!p_m]\!]_{s,s',\rho,\eta,\psi} \overset{\text{def}}{=} \forall_{k \leq m} : [\![o_k!p_k]\!]_{s,s',\rho,\eta,\psi} \ \wedge \ \forall_{k > m} : \psi.o_k = [\,]$$

$$[\![o![m_1, \ldots, m_k]]\!]_{s,s',\rho,\eta,\psi} \overset{\text{def}}{=} [[\![m_1]\!]_{s,s',\rho,\eta}, \ldots, [\![m_k]\!]_{s,s',\rho,\eta}] = \psi.o$$

6 Composition

Given two timed state transition diagrams $tstd_1$ and $tstd_2$ with port signatures $\Sigma_1 = (I_1, O_1, D_1)$ and $\Sigma_2 = (I_2, O_2, D_2)$, respectively. If $O_1 \cap O_2 = \emptyset$ and for all $i \in (I_1 \cap O_2) \cup (I_2 \cap O_1)$ it holds that $(D_1)_i = (D_2)_i$, then we call the two port signatures *compatible*. For compatible signatures Σ_1 and Σ_2, the composition $\Sigma_1 \otimes \Sigma_2$ is defined as follows: each output port of Σ_1 is connected with an input port of the same name of Σ_2, and similarily, each output port of Σ_2 is connected to an input port of Σ_1. The *feedback channels* introduced this way are hidden in $\Sigma_1 \otimes \Sigma_2$. Formally, $\Sigma_1 \otimes \Sigma_2 = (I, O, D)$, where[4]

$$I = (I_1 \setminus O_2) \cup (I_2 \setminus O_1) \quad O = (O_1 \setminus I_2) \cup (O_2 \setminus I_1) \quad D = D_1 + D_2$$

The resulting network is graphically depicted in Figure 5.

---

[4] Given two type mappings $(D_i)_{i \in I}$ and $(D'_j)_{j \in J}$, their *sum* is defined such that $(D + D').i = D.i$ if $i \in I$, and $(D + D').i = D'.i$ if $i \in J$. Given two named tuples $\varphi \in \Pi_{i \in I} D_i$ and $\psi \in \Pi_{j \in J} D'_j$, and $K \subseteq I$, their *sum* $\varphi + \psi$ is defined such that $(\varphi + \psi).i = \varphi.i$ if $i \in I$, and $(\varphi + \psi).i = \psi.i$ if $i \in J$. The projection $\varphi|_K$ is defined such that $(\varphi|_K).i = \varphi.i$ for all $i \in K$.

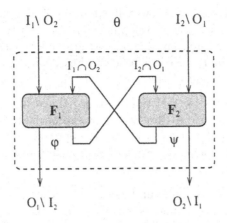

Fig. 5. Composition

Let the semantics of $tstd_1$ and $tstd_2$ with compatible port signatures be given by

$$[\![tstd_1]\!] : \prod_{i \in I_1} (D_1)_i^{\aleph} \to \wp(\prod_{i \in O_1} (D_1)_i^{\aleph}),$$
$$[\![tstd_2]\!] : \prod_{i \in I_2} (D_2)_i^{\aleph} \to \wp(\prod_{i \in O_2} (D_2)_i^{\aleph}).$$

The semantics $[\![tstd_1 \otimes tstd_2]\!]$ of their composition is equal to the *parallel composition with feedback* $[\![tstd_1]\!] \otimes [\![tstd_2]\!]$ of their input-/output-relations. The operator $\otimes$ is defined for relations as follows:

$$[\![tstd_1]\!] \otimes [\![tstd_2]\!] : \prod_{i \in I} D_i^{\aleph} \to \wp(\prod_{i \in O} D_i^{\aleph})$$

$$([\![tstd_1]\!] \otimes [\![tstd_2]\!])(\alpha) =$$

$$\{\beta|_O \in \prod_{i \in O} D_i^{\aleph}| \ \beta|_{O_1} \in [\![tstd_1]\!](\alpha|_{I_1} + \beta|_{I_1}) \wedge \beta|_{O_2} \in [\![tstd_2]\!](\alpha|_{I_2} + \beta|_{I_2})\}$$

For the above equation a unique solution exists if both input-/output relations are time guarded on the feedback channels [GKR96, BS97].

7 Conclusion

We have presented timed state transition diagrams, a new formalism for the specification of real-time aspects of reactive systems. The formalism is based on a semantic model where components communicate asynchronously via unbounded FIFO-channels. We have shown that existing approaches using this communication paradigm, like SDL and ROOM, fail to model real-time aspects accurately. The basic idea of our formalism is to time-stamp messages with their arrival time and to allow the specifier to label transitions with timing constraints. By using negative patterns, we can also easily deal with priorities. Therefore, timed state diagrams can be seen as a powerful extension of SDL and ROOM. In particular, it allows for a stepwise development process, where timing constraints are omitted in the first step and introduced gradually in the next steps. Our approach is fully modular, since it is based on FOCUS, a formal approach for the specification and refinement of reactive systems [BDD+93, BS97, GS96].

Among other formalisms for real time systems, timed input/output automata [LV96, LSVW95] seem to be closest to our approach. However, whereas the main goal of timed input/output automata is to provide a semantical model for real time systems, our main concern was to provide a pragmatic and tractable specification formalism for real time systems.

Timed state transition diagrams can be extended in several ways. A first extension would be to use a dense time model. We believe that such an extension can easily be accomplished along the lines of [MS96]. Dense time models are gaining more and more attention in theory and practice for the modeling of real-time systems. Of great importance is also the development of a tractable refinement calculus, as it has been presented for a similar, time-independent notation in [RK96]. Future extensions will also include an extension to hierarchical state transition diagrams à la statecharts [Har87]. The semantic foundations needed for hierarchical AND-states have already been presented in this paper. In constrast to the various approaches under way to define a semantics for statecharts [Von94], we start from a semantic model and define an appropriate notation for specifying components.

Acknowledgments

We thank Jan Philipps, Ursula Hinkel and Christian Prehofer for reading a draft version of the paper.

References

[AD94]   Rajeev Alur and David L. Dill. A theory of timed automata. *Theoretical Computer Science*, 2(126):183–235, April 1994.

[AH92]   R. Alur and T.A. Henzinger. Logics and models of real time: a survey. In J.W. de Bakker, K. Huizing, W.-P. de Roever, and G. Rozenberg, editors, *Real Time: Theory in Practice*, Lecture Notes in Computer Science 600, pages 74–106. Springer-Verlag, 1992.

[BB91]   F. Bause and P. Buchholz. Protocol analysis using a timed version of SDL. In J. Quemada, J. Mañas, and E. Vazquez, editors, *Formal Description Techniques*. North Holland, 1991.

[BDD+93] M. Broy, F. Dederichs, C. Dendorfer, M. Fuchs, T.F. Gritzner, and R. Weber. The Design of Distributed Systems - An Introduction to

FOCUS. Technical Report SFB 342/2/92 A, Technische Universität München, Institut für Informatik, 1993.

[BS97]   M. Broy and K. Stølen. *Interactive System Design.* To appear, 1997.

[GKR96]   Radu Grosu, Cornel Klein, and Bernhard Rumpe. Enhancing the SYSLAB system model with state. TUM-I 9631, Technische Universität München, 1996.

[GKRB96]   Radu Grosu, Cornel Klein, Bernhard Rumpe, and Manfred Broy. State transition diagrams. TUM-I 9630, Technische Universität München, 1996.

[GS96]   Radu Grosu and Ketil Stoelen. A Model for Mobile Point-to-Point Dataflow Networks without Channel Sharing . In Martin Wirsing and Maurice Nivat, editors, *Proceedings of the 5th International Conference on Algebraic Methodology and Software Technology, AMAST'96, Munich, Germany*, pages 505–519. Lecture Notes in Computer Science 1101, 1996.

[Har87]   D. Harel. Statecharts: A visual formalism for complex systems. *Science of Computer Programming*, 8, 1987.

[Hin96]   Ursula Hinkel. SDL and Time – A Mysterious Relationship. 1996. submitted to SDL Forum 97.

[HNSY92]   T.A. Henzinger, X. Nicollin, J. Sifakis, and S. Yovine. Symbolic model checking for real-time systems. In *Proceedings of the Seventh Annual Symposium on Logic in Computer Science*, pages 394–406. IEEE Computer Society Press, 1992.

[Hoa85]   C.A.R. Hoare. *Communicating sequential processes.* Prentice-Hall International series in computer science. Prentice Hall, Inc., Englewood Cliffs, New Jersey, 1985.

[IT93]   ITU-T. *Recommendation Z.100, Specification and Description Language (SDL).* ITU-T, Geneva, 1993.

[IT96]   ITU-T. *Z.120 – Message Sequence Chart (MSC).* ITU-T, Geneva, 1996.

[Leu95]   S. Leue. Specifying Real-Time Requirements for SDL Specifications - A Temporal Logic-Based Approach. In *Proceedings of the Fifteenth International Symposium on Protocol Specification, Testing, and Verification PSTV'95.* Chapmann & Hall, 1995.

[LSVW95]   N. Lynch, R. Segala, F. Vaandrager, and H.B. Weinberg. Hybrid I/O automata. Technical Report CS-R9578, CWI, Computer Science Department, Amsterdam, 1995. Also appeared in: Hybrid Systems III, Lecture Notes in Computer Science. Available under http://www.cs.kun.nl/~fvaan/.

[LV96]   N.A. Lynch and F. Vaandrager. Forward and backward simulations – part II: Timed systems. *Information and Computation*, 128(1):1–25, 1996.

[MS96]   Olaf Müller and Peter Scholz. Specification of real-time and hybrid systems in FOCUS. TUM-I 9627, Technische Universität München, 1996.

[OFMP⁺94] A. Olsen, O. Færgemand, B. Møller-Pedersen, R. Reed, and J. R. W. Smith. *Systems Engineering Using SDL-92*. Elsevier Science, North-Holland, 1994.

[Pau91]   L.C. Paulson. *ML for the Working Programmer*. Cambridge University Press, 1991.

[RK96]   B. Rumpe and C. Klein. Automata describing object behavior. In H. Kilov and W. Harvey, editors, *Specification of Behavioral Semantics in Object-Oriented Information Modeling*, pages 265–286, Norwell, Massachusetts, 1996. Kluwer Academic Publishers.

[SGW94]   B. Selic, G. Gullekson, and P. T. Ward. *Real-Time Object-Oriented Modeling*. John Wiley and Sons, Inc., 1994.

[Von94]   M. Von der Beeck. A Comparison of Statecharts Variants. *Lecture Notes in Computer Science*, 863:128–148, September 1994.

Specifying the Remote Controlling of Valves in an Explosion Test Environment

Martin Schönhoff* and Mojgan Kowsari**

Technical University of Braunschweig, Computer Science, Databases,
Postfach 3329, D–38023 Braunschweig, Germany,
email: M.Kowsari@tu-bs.de

Abstract. We present parts of the specification of a program to remote control and monitor different devices, especially valves, in an explosion test environment. The program was developed within an industrial national project called CATC carried out in PTB, the German federal institute of weights and measures. The CATC information system supports various activities of different user groups that are responsible for testing and certifying explosion proof electrical equipment in PTB. Our approach is based on the formal object-oriented specification language TROLL. We describe the advantages of the use of the formal method in our project.

1 Introduction

In the past few years, there has been considerable activity in the area of modelling large information systems. Many industrial methods have been developed for every platform and for different users, local or in networks. But they do not reach the level of formality achieved by formal specification languages. One main problem remains when designing a real world aspect: "Do we get what we need?" There is a small but growing community of people who propose and promote formal methods in software engineering [BH94]. The acceptance of formal methods in industry is still low. This is mainly due to the fact that formal methods are thought to be complex, hard to handle, and not suitable for real world applications [FBGL94, BH95].

In this paper, we present our experiences with the formal specification language TROLL, gained while using TROLL to design a large information system in an industrial environment [KHDE96, KKH+96, Kow96]. TROLL helps to discover and eliminate ambiguities and vaguenesses in the modelling phases. When we started our project in 1994, no formal method was applied. Soon some problems arose [HS94], and mid 1995, we became aware that the project was already

---

* Now at University of Zurich, Department of Computer Science, Database Technology Research Group, Winterthurerstr. 190, CH–8057 Zurich, Switzerland, email: mschoen@ifi.unizh.ch

** Work reported in this paper is supported by the Physical Technical Federal Board, lab 3.51, project Computer Aided Testing and Certifying

likely to fail. One of the problems of informal methods we encountered was that they require the designer to think about implementation aspects. However, our application domain and its data are too complex to mix design and implementation without loosing the global view of the system. Hence, we decided to use a formal approach. Using formalism allows us to concentrate more on the data and data structure and to determine what the system has to do under exceptional circumstances. Due to safety-critical aspects of our problem domain, emphasis on this point was especially important and useful in the process of requirement acquisition of the remote controlling of the valves.

The TROLL approach incorporates many ideas which have been developed over the past eight years. TROLL supports the declarative specification of conceptual models. TROLL defines an abstract model called the *Universe of Discourse* to cover all aspects which are relevant with respect to organisational activities in complex information systems. It includes the functional requirements of the later system and excludes non-functional requirements (like technology bindings of later implementations).

The remainder of this paper is structured as follows. Section 2 provides a summary of the concepts of TROLL. In Sect. 3, we give a short introduction to the problem domain of testing electrical apparatus in flameproof enclosures. Some of the requirements for VENTIL are presented in Sect. 4, while Sect. 5 shows the resulting TROLL specification. Our experiences are discussed in Sect. 6. Finally, Sect. 7 concludes the paper.

2 TROLL

In this section, we give a short introduction to the specification language TROLL.

TROLL ("Textual Representations of an Object Logical Language") is a formal language for the specification of object systems on a high level of abstraction. The basic ideas and concepts of TROLL can be summarised as follows:

- The basic building blocks of information systems are objects.
- Objects are classified into classes and described by a set of attributes and actions.
- Every object describes a set of *sequential life cycles*, i.e. sequences of *local actions* on the object.
- An object system is composed of a number of concurrent objects. These objects are the *nodes* of the system. Nodes usually have other objects as components. To establish global communication in an object system, nodes can be connected through global interactions.

The following are the basic features of the language:

- A *system specification* consists of a set of *data type* definitions, a set of *object class* specifications (prototypical object descriptions), and a number of *object declarations*.

- *Parameterised data types* allow for the construction of new data types based on a fixed universe of predefined data types.
- An object class specification is a set of *attributes*, *actions*, and *constraints*.
- Object classes may be constructed over other object classes (*aggregation*) to describe complex objects, i.e. objects which contain component objects.
- An object class may be the *specialisation* of another object class. The specialised class (*subclass*) may have properties in addition to those inherited from its *superclass*.
- Concurrent objects are declared over object classes. These declarations describe the potential objects in the system. Interactions (through *action calls*) between different objects describe the global synchronisation relations. All actions which are called within one *event* are understood to take place concurrently. Action parameters are exchanged through unification.

The case study which will be introduced in Sect. 4 illustrates some of the language features. For more details, see [Har97, DH97].

Semantics are assigned to TROLL specifications using different techniques: The static structure of an object system is semantically described with algebraic methods, statements over object states are expressed with a logic calculus, and the dynamic structure of the system, i.e. its evolution, is reflected via a temporal logic which is interpreted in terms of event structures. For an exhaustive description of the underlying theory, semantics, and logics see [Ehr96, ES95, EH96], for the refinement of object specifications refer to [Den96, Den95].

3   Problem Domain

In this section, we provide a short introduction to the application domain. We offer basic information about electrical apparatus in flameproof enclosures and the explosion test environment needed to certify them.

The Physical Technical Federal Board (PTB) [RBH87] is a federal institute for science and technology and the highest technical authority for metrology and physical safety in Germany. Its tasks are research in physics and technology, realisation and dissemination of SI units[3], cooperation in national and international technical committees, physical safety engineering serving against explosions, etc.

The PTB's group 3.5 "explosion protected electrical equipment" is concerned with the testing and certifying of explosion proof electrical equipment. Such equipment may only be used in hazardous areas after it has been approved and certified following the harmonised European standards EN 50014–50028. The assessment procedure consists of testing the formal and informal documents, checking the design papers (technical drawings) and experimental tests (such as explosion, flame propagation, and thermal-electrical tests). Currently, all steps which are necessary during the testing procedure and the issuing of about 1000 certificates each year are carried out manually and individually by the approximately 100 employees who make up the three labs of group 3.5. Because of

---

[3] international system of units

the huge amount of data, a standardised archive and catalogue of all existing certificates of explosion proof equipment is planned. It will be integrated into a software package called CATC (Computer Aided Testing and Certifying). Since 1994, the design and modelling of CATC is the long-term aim of the cooperation between the PTB and the database group of the Technical University of Braunschweig.

CATC has to support three different problem domains: *administration management, design approval,* and *experimental tests,* which are performed in a test lab. CATC is not a standalone information system, but it has to be embedded into an existing environment. Besides, we have to deal with existing application programs which have to be re-specified because they are erroneous. These re-specified parts have to be embedded into the new information system structure. In addition, there is a link to the frequently accessed PTB-wide database. To summarise, we have a safety-critical application area that comprises both technical and database aspects in a complex heterogeneous environment as well as existing and re-developed applications.

4 Requirements for VENTIL

This section focuses on some requirements for VENTIL[4], a program to remote control and monitor explosion test stands in the test lab of group 3.51. It is a part of the experimental test software of CATC. PTB's group 3.51 deals with the certification of *electrical apparatus in flameproof enclosures* according to the standards EN 50014 and EN 50018 [EN 87a, EN 87b] (motors, pumps, and switches, for instance). For *flameproof enclosure,* all parts which can ignite an explosive atmosphere are placed in an enclosure. In the case of an explosion inside, the enclosure withstands the pressure developed and prevents the transition of the explosion to the surrounding explosive atmosphere. The critical places for explosion transition are the *joints,* the places where corresponding surfaces of two parts of an enclosure come together and therefore a *gap* arises. For a flameproof enclosure, each gap must be narrow enough so that only *flameproof joints* are formed [ORW83].

Consequently, *flameproof joint tests* are among the experiments undertaken in the test lab to certify flameproof enclosures [EN 87b]. In a flameproof joint test (Fig. 1), a prototype (2) is placed inside the test chamber (1, called an *autoclave*) of an *explosion test stand* and is filled with an explosive atmosphere (eA). Then, a spark (S) ignites the atmosphere inside the enclosure. A prototype passes the test if the enclosure withstands the developing pressure and temperature (°C) and the explosion does not continue into the autoclave.

The main equipment of an explosion test stand are a gas source, the autoclave, analysis tools, pumps, and valves. All of these devices are connected in a

---

[4] This is German for "valve". The name originates from the previously used program which only let the user open and close valves. The name VENTIL was kept for the newly developed application because of habit.

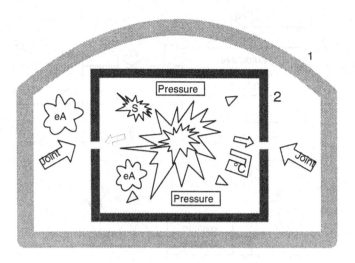

Fig. 1. Flameproof joint test.

net of tubes and pipes. Figure 2 shows a schematic view of the smallest explosion test stand in the test lab, the so called *Ex–Eva*[5]. VENTIL is used to control and monitor most of the devices of the Ex–Eva in order to create explosive atmospheres in the autoclave. The actual measuring of explosion pressure during an experiment is done separately [Hoh96, Sch96a].

Besides the obvious tasks to let users (i.e. the *testers*) mix gases, open, close, and monitor valves, turn on and off pumps, etc., VENTIL provides two more advanced features: the automatic *observance of dependencies* between devices and the *calculation of the gasflow*.

4.1 Observance of Dependencies

VENTIL prevents testers from accidently violating *dependencies* between devices. Dependencies are rules which have to be observed to protect the equipment and the environment (including the testers themselves) of the explosion test stand. The dependencies can be formulated as a kind of "master-slave" functions — one device depends on the state or state change of one or more other device(s).

These example dependencies (to which we will refer throughout Subsect. 5.2) are needed to protect the fragile oxygen analyser of the Ex–Eva (cf. Fig. 2) from extreme pressure and soot developed in the autoclave during an explosion:

1. Valve 31 may be open if and only if valve 26 is open.
2. (a) Before valve 31 is opened, valve 34 is opened automatically.
   (b) Before valve 34 is opened, valve 35 is opened automatically.
   (c) One second after valve 31 has been closed, valve 34 is closed automatically.
   (d) After valve 34 has been closed, valve 35 is closed automatically.

---

[5] **Explosions–Versuchs Anlage** (German for "explosion test stand")

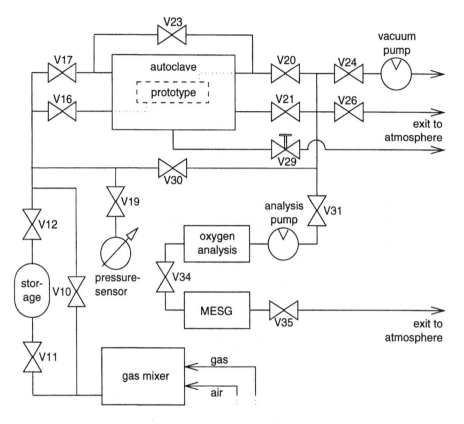

Fig. 2. Schematic view of the Ex–Eva. Vxx denotes a valve.

4.2 Calculation of the Gasflow

In a schematic display similar to the one of the Ex–Eva in Fig. 2, VENTIL offers to the testers a calculated view of the gasflow in the test stand. Unfortunately, this calculation is not at all trivial, but depends on parameters like the expected (yet not measured) gas pressure and the pumping direction of pumps. We will not go into the details of the parameters, but we use significantly simplified requirements for the visualisation of the gasflow here:

- A gasflow may begin or end at any gas entry or exit point of the test stand (e.g., the exit to the atmosphere) as well as at the gas mixer, reservoir, autoclave, or pressure sensor (altogether referred to as *endpoints*).
- There has to be an "open way" from one endpoint to another, i.e. all valves need to be open and the pumps turned on in a gasflow. All the other devices, the oxygen analyser, for instance, do not influence the gasflow and are treated here simply like a pipe.

Nevertheless, these reduced requirements will still be sufficient to present the implications of the gasflow calculation as far as this paper is concerned. An unabridged description is given in [Sch96b].

5   Specification of VENTIL using TROLL

The main components of the TROLL specification of VENTIL are presented in this section. First, a general overview of the object hierarchy of the information system node is given. Afterwards, the two most interesting parts of the specification are treated in detail: the observance of dependencies and the calculation of the gasflow. The diagrams illustrating this section use a notation similar to OMT [RBP+91] which was adapted to TROLL [JWH+94, WJH+93].

5.1   Overview

The specification of the VENTIL system is made up of three *nodes* (cf. Sect. 2), namely the user, hardware, and information system nodes. The user node describes the possible behaviour of the different user groups (testers, technicians, etc.) and their interfaces to the main system. For instance, in the `Tester`[6] object class (which is a part of the user node) it is specified that valves can be opened and closed or what data must be provided for the gas mixer. These specifications solely focus on functionality and data and are therefore abstractions of possible implementations (like dialog boxes or other user interface elements). Digital outputs (e.g., "open valve"), digital and analogue sensors ("valve is open", voltage representing measured pressure), etc. are modelled in the hardware node.

One merit of specifying VENTIL in TROLL is the possibility to examine the information system node isolated from the nodes describing user interaction [Sch96b] and hardware behaviour [Hoh96]. In this paper, the latter nodes and global interactions are not treated any further. We only discuss the specification of the information system node, beginning with the introduction of its object classes in the remainder of this subsection. The Community Diagram in Fig. 3 gives an overview of the component and inheritance hierarchies used.

The Object Class Knot   The calculation of the gasflow requires the most complex algorithm in VENTIL. Hence, the structure of the specification has been designed to suit this algorithm best. From Fig. 2 and the description in Subsect. 4.2 it is rather obvious that a gasflow can be formalised as a path in a *directed graph* representing the explosion test stand. The *nodes* of the graph stand for the devices[7] of the test stand, and the *vertices* for its pipes[8]. Although pipes are generally undirected, the graph's vertices need to be directed here, because at one time gas can only flow one way, determined by the pumping directions of the pumps and the gas mixer.

All basic properties of a node in the graph are modelled in the abstract (i.e. not instantiable) object class **Knot**. It is a superclass of any object class

---

[6] Throughout this paper, we print all terms referring to the TROLL specification in typewriter font and TROLL keywords in *italics*.

[7] Subsequently, devices also subsume the joins between two or more pipes, and the entry and exit points of the test stand (e.g., the external gas supply).

[8] To simplify reading, we will no longer distinguish tubes from pipes.

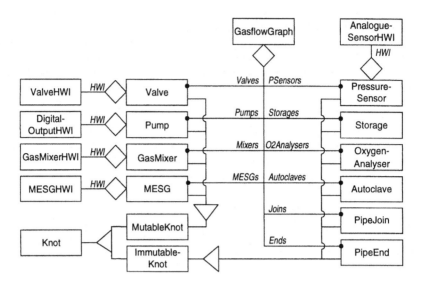

Fig. 3. Community Diagram of the information system node of VENTIL. The triangles symbolise inheritance, the diamonds component relationships. The dots are read as "zero or more" components.

representing a concrete device[9]. Hence, the devices become nodes of the graph, but do not need to take care of their connections to other nodes or their behaviour during the gasflow calculations themselves. This is an excellent example for the use of inheritance in TROLL: Each device class inherits the basic properties of a Knot. Evolution within these properties does not have any effect on object classes apart from Knot, thus facilitating the maintenance of the specification a great deal. All devices (including those which may be added to the test stand in future) reuse the specification of Knot and are therefore modelled more quickly and understandably. Furthermore, a Knot does not need to know which kinds of devices it is connected to, because it does not need any specialised properties of its neighbouring Knots.

Here is a part of the TROLL specification of Knot:

data type **vertex** = *record*(knot: |Knot|, flow: *bool*)
data type **names** = *string*(3)
data type **switch** = *enum*(activate, deactivate)
object class **Knot**

attributes Vertices: *set*(vertex) *isConstant*;
        Type: *enum*(endpoint, through) *isConstant*;
        Status: *enum*(closed, opening, open, closing);
        Name: names;

---

[9] While we are discussing the specification of VENTIL, we will use the name of a real-world object synonymous to its representing TROLL object; e.g., by "valve 31", we generally mean "the object representing valve 31 in the specification". The few exceptions are made clear through phrases like "the hardware of valve 31".

actions FindFlow(visited:*set*(|Knot|), flow:*set*(|Knot|),
 ! newFlow:*set*(|Knot|), *!* success:*bool*);
  FindFlowNo(no:*nat*, vertices:*list*(vertex), visited:*set*(|Knot|),
    flow:*set*(|Knot|), *!* newFlow:*set*(|Knot|), *!* success:*bool*);
  Switch(action:switch, ...) -- for the second parameter, see Subsect. 5.2
constraints cnt(Vertices) > 0,
    cnt(Vertices) = cnt(*toSet*(*select* v.knot *from* v *in* Vertices)),
    all vert *in* Vertices (vert.knot # *self*);
end;

We do not use a vertex object class in the specification of VENTIL. It is
sufficient to keep a set of references to neighbouring **Knots** (together with a
flag denoting whether this **vertex** is in the gasflow or not) to store outgoing
vertices[10]. The three constraints on **Vertices** make sure for each **Knot** (i) that it
is connected to at least another one, (ii) that there are no two vertices to the same
Knot, and (iii) that there is no vertex to itself ((i) to (iii) are always fulfilled for
an explosion test stand). Subclasses of **Knot** add constraints according to their
specialised needs: A pump, for example, must always have one incoming and
one outgoing vertex to denote the pumping direction. Note how simple allowed
states of an object can be defined in TROLL. Constraint (ii) also serves as one of
many examples in VENTIL where the power of the descriptive *select* statement
is exploited to yield a compact specification.

The constant attribute **Type** specifies whether a **Knot** is an **endpoint** of a
gasflow or the flow just runs **through** the **Knot**. The **Status** attribute stands for
the states different devices may take. For a valve, **open** means it is open, **opening**
that it is no longer closed, but not yet open (due to the mechanical switching
delay) and so on. Figure 4a shows the Object Behaviour Diagram of **Valve**;
due to mechanical malfunction, any state transition is possible. The **Status** of
a pump can only be either **open** (turned on) or **closed** (turned off) (Fig. 4b)
— enforced by a constraint. The **Type** and **Status** attributes and the actions
FindFlowNo and **FindFlow** are needed in the gasflow calculation and are treated
in detail in Subsect. 5.3.

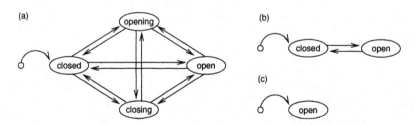

Fig. 4. Object Behaviour Diagrams: (a) **Valve**, (b) **Pump**, (c) **ImmutableKnot**.

---

[10] Specifying vertices is more complicated with the complete gas flow algorithm (using gas pressure, cf. Subsect. 4.2), because the graph needs to be traversed along
incoming vertices as well. A direction part is added to the **vertex** data type and an
additional constraint is needed to control the resulting redundancy [Sch96b].

The enumeration **switch** generalises the notions of "opening a valve", "turning on a pump", etc. to **activate** and the respective counterparts to **deactivate**. It is used as the first parameter to the action **Switch** which is overloaded in any subclass of **Knot** to perform the required task for the individual subclass.

Finally, the **Name** is a user-defined identification of a **Knot**. It is simply a three character string like 'V11' for valve 11. For every operation a user likes to perform on a specific device, he inputs the **Name** to denote the device.

The Object Classes MutableKnot and ImmutableKnot Devices like the oxygen analyser or pressure sensors cannot be manipulated through VENTIL. With regard to their **Status** in the gasflow, those devices are always **open**. They are modelled as subclasses of the abstract object class **ImmutableKnot** which is a subclass of **Knot** (see Fig. 3). **ImmutableKnot** constrains the **Status** to **open** (Fig. 4c) and disables the inherited switching operation.

Devices that can be controlled by testers (e.g., valves, pumps) also have a common abstract superclass, **MutableKnot**. Obviously, only **MutableKnots** may need to observe dependencies, since only if the state of a device is mutable, it may depend on the state of another device. Hence, the observance of dependencies is handled in **MutableKnot**. See Subsect. 5.2.

The Device Object Classes The different device classes of the test stand are modelled as separate object classes in VENTIL. Each of these object classes is a subclass of either **MutableKnot** or **ImmutableKnot** and hence indirectly a subclass of **Knot**.

Several device object classes have components specifying hardware interfaces. By convention, the names of hardware interface classes all end on **HWI**. For instance, **ValveHWI** models the interface to an object class within the hardware node of VENTIL. **ValveHWI** provides actions to open and close a valve, to check the current status of the hardware, etc. A detailed introduction to the device and hardware interface object classes of VENTIL is beyond the scope of this paper. Refer to Fig. 3 for an overview and to [Sch96b] for details. However, it should be mentioned that TROLL served well in the description of **HWI**-classes which not only form the interface to the real hardware, but also to the work of another member of the CATC team [Hoh96].

The Object Class GasflowGraph The management of our graph and the initiation of the gasflow calculation is modelled in the object class **GasflowGraph**. Here follows the part of its specification relevant for this paper:

object class **GasflowGraph**
components Valves: *map* (names) *to* (|Valve|);
          Pumps: *map* (names) *to* (|Pump|);
          . . .
attributes Knots: *map* (names) *to* (|Knot|) *derived*
          Knots(name):= *select* knot *from* knot *in* dom(Valve)+dom(Pump)+...
                    where knot.Name = name;

actions Gasflow();
      GasflowNo(no:*nat*, knots:*list*(|Knot|), flow:*set*(|Knot|),
          ! newFlow:*set*(|Knot|));
constraints all name *in* names (
         cnt(*select* knot *from* knot *in* *dom*(Valves)+*dom*(Pumps)+...
         where knot.Name = name) <= 1);
end;

In the *components* section, parametrised components are declared for each of the device subclasses of **Knot**. The parameter domains are always the range of possible **names** for Knots. In TROLL, it is necessary to specify the exact class of a component and not just one of its superclasses. It is therefore not possible to have one parametrised component containing instances of any of the subclasses of **Knot**. But since all **names** within a test stand are supposed to be unique even for different device classes, a well-defined map from **names** to **Knots** is required. It is achieved through the constraint given above which states that each **name** may appear at most once in the union of all domains (i.e. the actually existing instances) of the parameterised components. Convenient access to the map from **names** to **Knots** is provided through the derived attribute **Knots**. The two actions **Gasflow** and **GasflowNo** initiate the search for gasflow in the graph. They are treated in detail in Subsect. 5.3.

5.2   Observance of Dependencies

Classification of Dependencies The formalisation of dependencies (like those of the examples in Subsect. 4.1) leads to the distinction of three types: static, dynamic, and delayed dependencies[11].

Static dependencies involve at most *one state change* in one device. This state change depends on the state of another device which is only watched, but not changed. Example 1 is a static dependency: Valve 31 may only be open if and only if valve 26 is open.

Dynamic dependencies always involve the possibility of *two state changes* in two devices, *as fast as possible*. From the point of view of one of the involved devices, there are three possible executions of the own state change: *before* or *after* the other device or both in *parallel*. Specifying the parallel and after cases is straightforward. For the before case, we take a look at Example 2b, where valve 35 must be opened *before* valve 34. The two following TROLL events must take place if valve 34 is commanded to open itself:

1. If valve 35 is already open, valve 34 opens and nothings else needs to be done. Otherwise, valve 34 commands valve 35 to open.
2. As soon as the hardware of valve 35 is opened, its corresponding object is notified and commands valve 34 to open.

---

[11] Following the vocabulary of the engineers in lab 3.51, there is also a fourth type of "dependencies" in the original requirements analysis. But its formal definition revealed that it must be treated differently from the other three [Sch96b].

Delayed dependencies are a special case of dynamic dependencies. They also involve the possibility of *two state changes* in two devices, but introduce a *delay time* between the switching operations. Obviously, *parallel* delayed dependencies do not make sense, thus leaving the *before* and *after* cases.

Delayed dependencies are treated similarly to the other dynamic dependencies, but another event is added. In Example 2c, valve 34 has to be closed one second after valve 31 is closed. Listing the required TROLL events for the closing command on valve 31, we get:

1. Valve 31 closes.
2. As soon as the hardware of valve 31 is closed, its corresponding object is notified. If valve 34 is already closed, nothing else needs to be done. Otherwise, the delay time begins.
3. As soon as the delay time has expired, valve 31 commands valve 34 to close.

Modelling Dependencies with Duties The observance of any type of dependency is modelled in a system of *duties*. One dependency can result in a number of duties imposed on several devices (e.g., see below how Example 1 is treated). Duties are specified as *record*-types in VENTIL. They are stored as attributes in the *duty list*[12] of the MutableKnots they are imposed on. The duty list is checked before any switching operation is applied to the device. A duty *object class* would not be helpful, because all actions which process duties only modify attributes of Knot, but never the values of a duty (except for creation and deletion, of course).

Duty types are modelled as follows in TROLL:

```
data type execution = enum(now, before, parallel, after)
data type duty = record(trigger : switch,    exec : execution,
                        delay : time,         target : |Knot|,
                        action : switch,      once : bool)
data type delayedDuty = record(time : time,
                        duty : duty)
```

The enumeration execution is used to distinguish static (now) from dynamic dutys. In the latter case, the time of execution of the second state change is given as either before, after, or in parallel with the first state change, as explained above.

The first component of the duty *record* holds the information on which switch the duty must be fulfilled; e.g., a duty with the trigger value activate imposed on a valve must be fulfilled each time the valve is opened. The exec component determines the type of the duty. For before and after duties, delay holds the time between the first and second switching operation; a delayed dependency has a value greater then 0. To fulfill the duty, action has to be passed to the Switch operation of the target. The flag once is set for dutys that have to be removed from the duty list as soon as they are fulfilled. A delayedDuty is an ordinary duty which has to be fulfilled at a certain system time.

---

[12] The name "duty *list*" emerged during development although no sequencing is needed; see the declarations for MutableKnot below.

Fulfilling Duties The declarations of **MutableKnot**, as far as the observance of dependencies is concerned, look like this:

object class **MutableKnot**
aspect of Knot *on* ...   -- Knot is the superclass of MutableKnot
attributes DutyList : *set*(duty);
       DelayedDutyList : *set*(delayedDuty);
     ...

actions AreDutiesFulfilled(trigger:switch, *!* now:*bool*, *!* before:*bool*)
       FulfillDuty(duty:duty)
       FulfillAllDuties(trigger:action, exec:execution)
       FulfillDelayedDuties()
       Switch(action:switch, duties:*set*(duty))
     ...

end;

AreDutiesFulfilled returns (denoted by a '*!*') for a given action whether all now and before dutys in the DutyList are fulfilled. The return values are used by the switching operation of specialised ImmutableKnots to determine whether the desired action is allowed now or later or must be rejected. FulfillAllDuties calls FulfillDuty to fulfill all dutys in the DutyList for the given trigger and exec parameters, e.g., to fulfill all dutys before the MutableKnot is activated. Similar to FulfillAllDuties, FulfillDelayedDuties is used to process the delayedDutys in the DelayedDutyList as soon as their delay time has expired.

The action Switch is inherited from the superclass Knot (see Subsect. 5.1). Here, we introduce the second parameter, the set duties. All members of duties are added to the DutyList. Usually, duties is empty, but to fulfill a before duty, one new duty is passed; see below.

Lead by the examples introduced earlier, we will now take a look at how these actions work together if a static, dynamic, or delayed dependency must be fulfilled.

Fulfilling a static dependency is as simple as expected. Example 1 requires two dutys:

(activate, now, 0, *Valve 26*, activate, *false*)

imposed on **Valve** 31 and

(deactivate, now, 0, *Valve 31*, deactivate, *false*)

imposed on **Valve** 26.

While opening, the first duty must be fulfilled for **Valve** 31. The Switch action of **Valve** 31 checks the Status of the dutys target, *Valve 26*[13]. If **Valve** 26 is activated (i.e. the Status of **Valve** 26 is not closed), the hardware of valve 31 can be activated, too. Otherwise, the switching command is rejected. Similarly, **Valve** 26 must check the status of **Valve** 31 before closing (according to the second duty given above).

The dynamic dependency of Example 2b results in the duty

---

[13] This is meant to be the identity of the object representing valve 26.

(activate, before, 0, *Valve 35*, deactivate, *false*)

imposed on **Valve** 26.

What happens if the dynamic dependency of Example 2b must be fulfilled is shown in the Object Communication Diagram in Fig. 5. In the first TROLL event (shown as continuous arrows), the **Switch** action is called to open **Valve** 34. **Switch** uses **AreDutiesFulfilled** to find out that there is at least one unfulfilled **before duty** and calls **FulfillAllDuties** with the parameters **activate** and **before**. **FulfillAllDuties** calls **FulfillDuty** to fulfill all necessary **dutys**, including the one of our example above. To fulfill the **duty**, **Switch** is called for **Valve** 35. The arguments passed are **activate** to open the valve (what is done by a call to the hardware interface object) and a *set(**duty**)* containing

(activate, after, 0, *Valve 34*, activate, *true*).

This new **duty** is added to the **DutyList** of **Valve** 35.

As soon as the hardware of **Valve** 35 is opened, the second TROLL event is initiated (dashed arrows). Because the event takes place **after Valve** 35 has been **activated**, the new **duty** must be fulfilled and then deleted from the **DutyList** (the last component of the **duty** is *true*). Fulfilling the **duty** results in the opening of **Valve** 34, thus we have **Valve** 34 opened after **Valve** 35 — as required by the dependency.

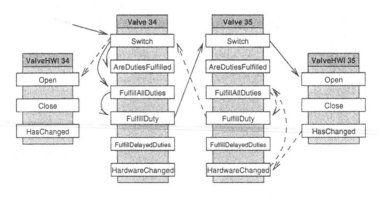

Fig. 5. Object Communication Diagram for Example 2b (dynamic dependency).

Finally, we take a glance at Example 2c and the respective Object Communication Diagram (Fig. 6). The **duty** which is imposed on **Valve** 31 is

(deactivate, after, 1, *Valve 34*, deactivate, *false*).

If the **duty** must be fulfilled (event one, continuous arrows), the hardware of **Valve** 31 can be **Close**d immediately, because we talk about an **after duty**. After **Valve** 31 is closed, it tries to **FulfillAllDuties** (event two, dashed arrows). It therefore delays our example **duty** by adding

(current time + 1 sec, (deactivate, after, 1, *Valve 34*, deactivate, *false*))

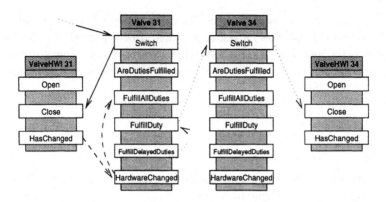

Fig. 6. Object Communication Diagram for Example 2c (delayed dependency).

to the `DelayedDutyList` of `Valve` 31. As soon as the specified time is reached the third event takes place (dotted arrows): `FulfillDelayedDuties` calls once again `FulfillDuty`, and `Valve` 34 is `Closed`, too.

5.3 Calculation of the Gasflow

Searching the Gasflow Based on the requirements mentioned in Subsect. 4.2, we derived the algorithm to calculate the gasflow in an explosion test stand. In short, an action `Gasflow` searches all `Knots` in the `GasflowGraph` and determines whether they are endpoints or not. If a `Knot` is an endpoint, `Gasflow` finds all directed, acyclic paths (called *gasflows*) to a different endpoint, leading only through `Knots` with a `Status` different from `closed` (all `ImmutableKnots`, for instance).

This search is done by calling the recursive action `FindFlow` in the endpoint. In the case of a successful search, `FindFlow` returns the set of `Knots` which are contained in any of the gasflows beginning in this endpoint. The union of all those sets for all endpoints obviously contains all `Knots` through which gas flows. This union is called *the* gasflow, because the following can be shown: The vertices between any of the `Knots` in the gasflow represent exactly those pipes of the test stand which contain gas. This means, to show the gasflow in the test stand to the users, it is sufficient to mark the vertices between each two `Knots` in the gasflow.

Recursive Search for Endpoints We stated above that `Gasflow` must find each endpoint of the graph, call `FindFlow` for them, and calculate the union of the resulting gasflow sets. To start with, it is necessary to explain the signature of `FindFlow`:

```
FindFlow(visited: set(|Knot|), flow: set(|Knot|),
         ! newFlow: set(|Knot|), ! success: bool);
```

The set `visited` contains all `Knots` of the graph which are already part of the current recursion. This parameter is used to avoid cycles in the search. The other input parameter, **flow**, holds the set of **Knots** which have already been discovered to be in the gasflow currently searched. Corresponding to **flow** is the output parameter **newFlow**. In this set, all the members of **flow** are returned plus the identity of the current **Knot**, if it is in the gasflow, too. In this case, **success** is set to *true*.

For the specification of **Gasflow** it is therefore necessary to call

```
inGasflow : set(|Knot|);
ignore : bool;
FindFlow({}, {}, inGasflow, ignore);
```

to each endpoint of the graph and unite the resulting **inGasflow** sets. The **success** parameter can be ignored here.

The calls to **FindFlow** and the collection of their results is easily specified if we can use command sequences. But with TROLL, we encounter the challenge that the whole calculation has to be done in *one shot*. There is no *while* statement. There is no way to make an arbitrary number of action calls and keep the results for "later" processing. The only possibility we have is to use the unification of action calls to imitate a sequence of calls. In such a "sequence", the **newFlow** result of a call has to be inserted as the **flow** parameter of the next call.

We use the additional recursive action

```
GasflowNo(no:nat,knots:list(|Knot|),flow:set(|Knot|),!newFlow:set(|Knot|))
```

for this task. The first two parameters control the recursion: **knots** contains a *list* of all **Knots** in the graph (in arbitrary, but fixed order), **no** the current index in the list. The recursion is initiated with the parameter **no** set to the number of **Knots**. The index is decremented in each recursion step until 1 is reached. The parameters **flow** and **newFlow** are used like their counterparts in **FindFlow**.

Here is the complete specification of **GasflowNo** and **Gasflow**. The *first* **Knot** for which **FindFlow** may be called is **knots[1]**. For the calculation of **newFlow**, note that the results **flowNo** and **flowOut** are undefined if the respective action calls do not take place.

```
GasflowNo(no:nat,knots:list(|Knot|),flow:set(|Knot|),!newFlow:set(|Knot|))
    variables flowNo, flowOut : set(|Knot|);
            ignore : bool;
    do onlyIf(no > 1): GasflowNo(no-1, knots, flow, flowNo);
        onlyIf(knot[no].Type = endpoint):            -- start recursing Knots here
            knot[no].FindFlow({}, no > 1 ? flowNo : flow, flowOut, ignore);
        newFlow := (knot[no].Type = endpoint) ? flowOut
                                        : (no > 1 : flowNo : flow);
    od
Gasflow()
    variables knots : list(|Knot|) derived knots := toList(dom(Knots));
            flow : set(|Knot|);
    do GasflowNo(length(knots), knots, {}, flow);            -- initiate recursion
        ShowGasflow(knots);                        -- visualise gasflow to users
    od
```

Recursive Search in the Graph and in the Knots We just discussed how the actions `Gasflow` and `GasflowNo` are used, so we do not need to cover any details of the `FindFlow` and `FindFlowNo` actions; they are used to recursively search the arbitrary number of **Vertices** within *a single* **Knot** analogous to the **Knots** of the graph. Additionally, `FindFlowNo` calls `FindFlow` in *a neighbouring* **Knot** to traverse the graph recursively.

Thus we have three nested recursions to calculate the gasflow — all of them carried out concurrently, only "sequentialised" through TROLL's unification mechanism. Figure 7 visualises the three recursions on instance level. Note that each **Knot** can be a part of several calling "sequences".

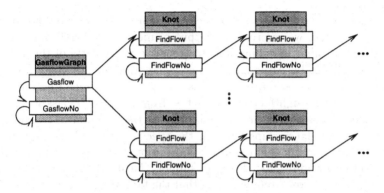

Fig. 7. Object Communication Diagram for the three nested recursions of the gasflow calculation.

6 Experiences

We have developed a specification of VENTIL that successfully exploits the features TROLL provides.

The object-orientation of TROLL helped us to find a modular structure and well-defined module interfaces. Inheritance became an important factor in the specification of the graph, since we were able to separate general properties of a node (e.g., during the gasflow calculation) from those of specialised device nodes. The general design and specification of a **Knot** is reused in every (future) device object class, and no change to some device class will influence other **Knots**.

Constraints, often in conjunction with the powerful descriptive *select* statement, proved to be very helpful, too. They allow for compact and yet simple restrictions of the possible behaviour of objects.

Because of the similarities to the transaction concept of databases, the virtues of parallelism are obvious if a "usual" information system is designed. But even in VENTIL, concurrent execution has advantages, e.g., whenever one device is the target of several duties. During the implementation, we were troubled by serialisation, because two duties that are fulfilled simultaneously in one TROLL event can have two different effects if they are fulfilled one after the other.

On the other hand, sequential execution would have been useful during the gasflow calculation. The implementation which we successfully derived from our specification has been simplified. It requires only one level of recursion instead of three in TROLL and is therefore probably easier to understand. We nevertheless specified the complete algorithm to allow for the *animation* of the whole VEN-TIL model[14]. Discovering that TROLL has deficiencies in the domain of VENTIL was not surprising though. Recall from Sect. 1 and 2 that TROLL is primarily designed for the development of information systems. As a rather technical application, VENTIL is situated at least on the edge of TROLL's target domain, if not even outside.

Finally, some more notes on the implementation are appropriate. From about 2500 lines of TROLL, we received an output of more than 20000 lines of C++ code. We derived rules describing how to translate many parts of the specification into C++ [Sch96b]. Although no tools where available, the transition from the compact TROLL notation to C++ was, except for the difficulties mentioned above, surprisingly straightforward. In fact — from the overall class structure to algorithmic details in the gasflow calculations — there are on any design level almost one-to-one relationships between the specification and the implementation. On the code level though, the direct translation of the specification required to implement many additional classes to support TROLL data types (like sets of Knots, etc.). Overall, we strongly believe that the formal specification of VENTIL has payed off.

7   Conclusions and Future Work

In this paper, we presented the specification of VENTIL, a program to monitor and control the devices in an explosion test environment. VENTIL is a part of the ongoing development of a large information system in the PTB. We also presented our experiences with the use of the formal specification language TROLL in our project. So far, they were positive. One advantage of using TROLL was to achieve first a rather global view before considering details. Changes to the finer grained specification documents did not affect the global view. Furthermore, the formality and clearly defined semantics of TROLL specifications carried over to the implementation. The work for one laboratory is finished and we are currently implementing systems for the other two laboratories [HDK+97].

In the next step of the development of TROLL, we will establish tool support [Gra97]. Most important are tools that allow for a fast modification of the specification documents while ensuring consistency throughout the project. The reification from specification to implementation is another objective we want to reach in the near future.

---

[14] At least theoretically, since there is no animation tool available for the current version of TROLL.

Acknowledgements

We thank the employees of the PTB's group 3.51 for their support, especially Achim Kühne for his patience in discussing the technical details of VENTIL. We also thank Peter Hartel and Grit Denker for answering specific questions on TROLL. Finally, we thank the anonymous reviewers for their useful hints on preparing the final version of this paper.

References

[BH94]   J. P. Bowen and M. G. Hinchey. Seven more myths of fomal methods: Dispelling industrial prejudices. In M. Naftalin, T. Denvir, and M. Bertrani, editors, *FME'94: Industrial Benefit of Formal Methods*, number 873 in LNCS, pages 105–117. Springer-Verlag, Berlin, 1994.

[BH95]   J. P. Bowen and M. G. Hinchey. Seven more myths of formal methods. *IEEE Software*, 12(3):34–41, 1995.

[Den95]   G. Denker. Transactions in object-oriented specifications. In E. Astesiano, G. Reggio, and A. Tarlecki, editors, *Recent Trends in Data Type Specification, 10th Workshop on Specification of Abstract Data Types, Joint with the 5th COMPASS Workshop; S. Margherita, Italy*, number 906 in LNCS, pages 203–218. Springer-Verlag, Berlin, May 1995.

[Den96]   G. Denker. Semantic refinement of concurrent object systems based on serializability. In B. Freitag, C. B. Jones, C. Lengauer, and H.-J. Schek, editors, *Object Orientation with Parallelism and Persistence*, pages 105–126. Kluwer Academic Publ., 1996. ISBN 0-7923-9770-3.

[DH97]   G. Denker and P. Hartel. TROLL – an object-oriented formal method for distributed information systems design: Syntax and pragmatics. Informatik-Bericht 97-03, Technical University of Braunschweig, 1997.

[EH96]   H.-D. Ehrich and P. Hartel. Temporal specification of information systems. In A. Pnueli and H. Lin, editors, *Logic and Software Engineering*. World Scientific, 1996.

[Ehr96]   H.-D. Ehrich. Object Specification. Informatik-Bericht 96-07, Technical University of Braunschweig, 1996.

[EN 87a] CELENEC: Europäische Norm EN 50014. Elektrische Betriebsmittel für explosionsgeschützte Bereiche, Allgemeine Bestimmungen. VDE–Verlag, Berlin, Offenbach, 1987.

[EN 87b] CELENEC: Europäische Norm EN 50018. Elektrische Betriebsmittel für explosionsgeschützte Bereiche, Druckfeste Kapselung "d". VDE–Verlag, Berlin, Offenbach, 1987.

[ES95]   H.-D. Ehrich and A. Sernadas. Local specification of distributed families of sequential objects. In E. Astesiano, G. Reggio, and A. Tarlecki, editors, *Recent Trends in Data Type Specification, 10th Workshop on Specification of Abstract Data Types, Joint with the 5th COMPASS Workshop; S. Margherita, Italy*, number 906 in LNCS, pages 219–235. Springer-Verlag, Berlin, May 1995.

[FBGL94] J.S Fitzgerald, T.M Brookes, M.A Green, and P.G Larsen. First results in a comparative study. In M. Naftalin, T. Denvir, and M. Bertrani, editors, *FME'94: Industrial Benefit of Formal Methods*, number 873 in LNCS. Springer-Verlag, Berlin, 1994.

[Gra97]   A. Grau. An Animation System for Validating Object-Oriented Conceptual Models. In J.P. Tolvanen and A. Winter, editors, *4th Doctoral Consorcium on Advanced Information Systems Engineering (CAiSE'97), Barcelona*. Fachberichte Informatik 14/97, University Koblenz-Landau, June 1997.

[Har97]   P. Hartel. *Konzeptionelle Modellierung von Informationssystemen als verteilte Objektsysteme*. Reihe DISDBIS. infix-Verlag, Sankt Augustin, 1997.

[HDK⁺97]   P. Hartel, G. Denker, M. Kowsari, M. Krone, and H.-D. Ehrich. Information systems modelling with TROLL formal methods at work. *Information Systems*, 22(2-3):79–99, 1997.

[Hoh96]   T. Hohnsbein. Objektorientierte Realisierung eines Meßdatenerfassungssystems für druckfeste Kapselung. Diploma thesis, Technical University of Braunschweig, 1996.

[HS94]   T. Hohnsbein and H. Schafiee. Reengineering des Programms DRUCKMESS in der PTB. Project work, Technical University of Braunschweig, 1994.

[JWH⁺94]   R. Jungclaus, R.J. Wieringa, P. Hartel, G. Saake, and T. Hartmann. Combining TROLL with the Object Modeling Technique. In B. Wolfinger, editor, *Innovationen bei Rechen- und Kommunikationssystemen. GI-Fachgespräch FG 1: Integration von semi-formalen und formalen Methoden für die Spezifikation von Software*, Informatik aktuell, pages 35–42. Springer-Verlag, Berlin, 1994.

[KHDE96]   M. Kowsari, P. Hartel, G. Denker, and H.-D. Ehrich. A case study in information system design, the CATC system. FME'96: Industrial Benefit and Advances in Formal Methods, Oxford, UK, poster session, March 1996. Available on http://www.cs.tu-bs.de/idb/publications/pub_96.html.

[KKH⁺96]   M. Krone, M. Kowsari, P. Hartel, G. Denker, and H.-D. Ehrich. Developing an information system using TROLL – an application field study. In *Conference on Advanced Information Systems Engineering (CAiSE'96), Crete, Greece*, number 1080 in LNCS. Springer-Verlag, Berlin, 1996.

[Kow96]   M. Kowsari. Formal object oriented specification language TROLL in information system design. In H.-M. Haav and B. Thalheim, editors, *Doctoral Consortium of 2nd International Baltic Workshop on Databases and Information Systems, Tallinn, Estonia*, 1996.

[ORW83]   H. Olenik, H. Rentzsch, and W. Wettstein. *Explosion Protection Manual*. W. Girardet, Essen, 2nd revised edition, 1983.

[RBH87]   H. Rechenberg, J. Bortfeld, and W. Hanser. *100 Jahre Physikalisch–Technische Bundesanstalt 1887–1987*. VCH Verlagsgesellschaft, Munich, 1987.

[RBP⁺91]   J. Rumbaugh, M. Blaha, W. Premerlani, F. Eddy, and W. Lorenson. *Object–Oriented Modeling and Design*. Prentice Hall, Englewood Cliffs, New Jersey, 1991.

[Sch96a]   H. Schafiee. Objektorientierte Realisierung der Benutzerschnittstellen eines Meßdatenbearbeitungssystems für druckfeste Kapselung. Diploma thesis, Technical University of Braunschweig, 1996.

[Sch96b]   M. Schönhoff. Objektorientierte Realisierung eines Steuerungs- und Überwachungssystems für Explosionsprüfstände. Diploma thesis, Technical University of Braunschweig, 1996. Available on http://www.ifi.unizh.ch/~mschoen.

[WJH⁺93]   R. Wieringa, R. Jungclaus, P. Hartel, T. Hartmann, and G. Saake. OMTROLL – Object modeling in TROLL. In U.W. Lipeck and G. Koschorreck, editors, *International Workshop on Information Systems – Correctness and Reusability (IS-CORE'93), Technical Report No. 01/93, University of Hanover*, pages 267–283, 1993.

PICGAL: Practical Use of Formal Specification to Develop a Complex Critical System

Lionel Devauchelle[1], Peter Gorm Larsen[2] and Henrik Voss[2]

[1] AEROSPATIALE espace et defense, department SY/YI -BP 3 002, F 78 133 Les Mureaux CEDEX, FRANCE
[2] IFAD (The Institute of Applied Computer Science), Forskerparken 10, DK-5230 Odense M, Denmark

Abstract. This paper reports on the experiment PICGAL which aims to assess the benefits of using VDM to develop high reliability related software in the space industry in a practical way. The application used in this project is a code generator from a next generation environment to be used in the development of ground application software for boosters such as ARIANE V. The experiment is constructed as a parallel development of the code generator; using the conventional approach and using formal specification. This allows detailed measurements of the effects resulting from the introduction of VDM. This work is adding to the existing body of evidence of the effect of using a moderate amount of formal methods in an industrial context in a new critical domain. This paper provides an overview of the domain, the application and it shows how the formal specification has been structured. Finally, results and key lessons are presented.

1 Introduction

AEROSPATIALE Espace & Defense is prime contractor or industrial architect of space launchers and vehicles, and the critical role of software in this sector is increasing continuously. In the experiment described in this paper, we focus on the highly reliable ground application software development environment used to develop the required control command functionality. In order to decrease the cost of such developments as well as the associated time, a future generation environment entitled SCALA is being studied by AEROSPATIALE.

The SCALA environment will include a code generator from the control specification language SCALA to the ANSI C programming language. The dependability of the ground application software will rely on the reliability of the code generator. This component is a high dependability related piece of software, which therefore should be carefully checked and validated. In the PICGAL[3]

---

[3] PICGAL is an acronym for "Process Improvement experiment of a Code Generator to the Ariane Launcher" and the project is supported by the European Commission (ESSI project – PIE no 21 716).

project this code generator is developed twice. One development uses the conventional development approach at AEROSPATIALE with natural text in the early phases of the life-cycle, and another development uses VDM with the IFAD VDM-SL Toolbox and the associated VDM-SL$_{to}$C++ Code Generator. During the project a number of metrics are being collected to measure the effect of using the VDM technology.

The Vienna Development Method (VDM) [5] is one of the most mature formal methods, primarily intended for formal specification and subsequent development of functional aspects of software systems. Its specification language VDM-SL [1] is used during the specification and design phases of a software development project, and it supports the production of correct high quality software. VDM-SL is standardised under the auspices of the International Standard Organization (ISO) [8].

A modular extension to ISO VDM-SL is supported by the IFAD VDM-SL Toolbox [2, 7, 9]. The Toolbox supports extensive type checking, LaTeX pretty-printing facilities, test coverage, code generation, interpretation and many debugging facilities. A large subset of IFAD VDM-SL can be execute by the existing interpreter of the Toolbox. As part of the modular extension the IFAD VDM-SL Toolbox supports Dynamic Linked modules (DL modules) [4]. DL modules are used to describe the interface between modules which are fully specified in VDM-SL and parts of the overall system which are only available as C++ code. This facility enables users to employ existing C++ libraries while a specification is being interpreted/debugged.

Related work has been carried out using an earlier version of the same technology by British Aerospace for communications software [3, 10, 6]. The results of this work were very promising and showed that the use of formal specification for critical components was slightly less expensive than the conventional way, and in addition an exceptional situation was discovered already at the system design phase which was never discovered with the conventional development process. At the time of this experiment no code generator for VDM-SL was available so the final code was produced manually. In the PICGAL experiment we use the VDM-SL$_{to}$C++ Code Generator.

In line with the experiment at British Aerospace we have focused, on purpose, on using VDM-SL as a high-level language to describe a model of the system. Thus, we have not stressed formal proof or refinement at any stage in this project. The motivation for this more pragmatic approach is that we feel that it is better first to learn to think in terms of VDM concepts and be able to validate such a model using well-known techniques such as testing. However, we consider this to be a first step towards a more rigorous development of industrial software systems. When the engineers are confident with this technology it may be feasible to introduce more components from the VDM methodology and introduce formal verification. We believe that making too large a step in one go would be too difficult for industrial engineers in most cases.

This paper is organised as follows: in the next section a short introduction to the application domain and the purpose of the SCALA environment is given. In Section 3 it is explained how the experiment is organised in a parallel development of the SCALA to C code generator. This section also includes material about the background for the use of VDM and the comparisons and tests to be performed during the experiment in order to assess the benefits of using VDM in this application. The following three sections present an overview of the specification and the way it is being validated. Section 7 presents some results from the project and this is followed by a section illustrating how we envisage this kind of technology to be used in the space domain in the future. Finally, a few concluding remarks are given.

2 The Application Domain

In this section an introduction to the control command systems domain and the SCALA environment is given.

2.1 Control Command Systems

The control command systems are ground systems used to check-out the different parts of a booster during its assembly process and to perform the lift-off. Their main functions are:

- to bring the booster or a part of it into operation;
- to test the availability of the booster equipment;
- to synchronise the operation of the booster with external events during lift-off; and
- to monitor the equipment in order to keep the booster safe and to avoid damage to the environment.

An overview of a control command stand is shown in Fig. 1. Many of these components are not of relevance to this project, but it provides an idea about the environment in which the work presented here is carried out. For this paper the most important part is the software architecture which is divided into three layers:

Level 1 includes the operating system and the hardware handlers;
Level 2 provides basic services for the application software such as sequencing, and basic check-out functions; and
Level 3 is the application software layer. It is to this kind of software that the SCALA code generator described in this paper is to be applied.

2.2 The Purpose of the SCALA Environment

In the development of Level 3 software components of a control command application there is currently a relatively long turn-around time when requirements changes are introduced. To increase the productivity and decrease the

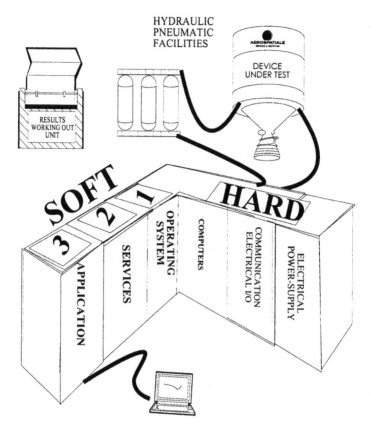

Fig. 1. Control Command Stand Overview

turn-around time of the application software, AEROSPATIALE is planning to produce a new development environment named SCALA. This environment will include the following tools:

- a specification editor,
- a specification validation tool, and
- an automatic code generator.

The most critical part of this environment is the code generator. The reliability of the developed application will depend on it. This automatic code generator will automatically translate SCALA specifications into the ANSI C programming language.

SCALA will be used by booster equipment engineers or system engineers to specify easily readable, comprehensive and unambiguous control command requirements as shown in Fig. 2.

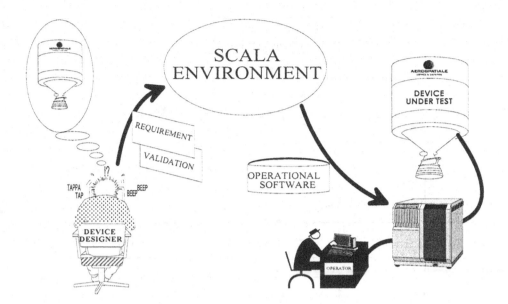

Fig. 2. SCALA Development Environment Use

3 Description of the Experiment

3.1 Parallel Development

Fig. 3 provides an overview of the different phases of the two parallel and separate developments of the code generator. The initial requirements phase determined the purpose of the generator but do not indicate its structure, the algorithms to be used or the output code. The general design phase is common to both developments: the baseline and the PICGAL line. With the structure of the generated code, this phase provides the functions of the generator as well as some required algorithms (e.g. the naming of data).

The conventional development consists of the following steps:

- software design to refine the general design in accordance with the implementation constraints;
- coding and unit testing; and
- integration.

The VDM development consists of the following steps:

- architecture design to refine the general design in accordance with the VDM modelling principles;
- VDM modelling;
- specification test;
- code generating through the VDM tool and complementary coding in C++.

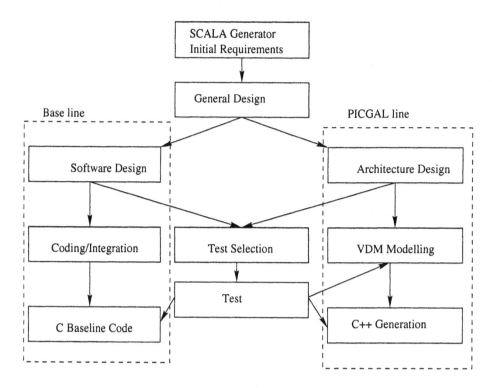

Fig. 3. PICGAL Project Phases

In addition, a test environment testing both systems with the same test cases is developed. In order to prevent the results from being biased by the skills of the developing engineers, one key engineer is used on both developments. In order to illustrate the benefits of the VDM approach this engineer always work on the baseline development before dealing with the corresponding VDM work.

3.2 Background for the use of VDM

The AEROSPATIALE team had no prior experience with formal methods. VDM was chosen because of the availability of strong tool support in form of the IFAD VDM-SL Toolbox. The team was trained by IFAD in VDM modelling and use of the different features of the VDM-SL Toolbox during two one week courses.

During the project, IFAD has been acting as a VDM consultant. Periodically IFAD has reviewed the VDM model developed by the AEROSPATIALE team. However, both in the consultancy and in the reviews IFAD has only pointed out problems and suggestions for the kind of constructs which could be used to improve a given specification. No part of the specification has been written by IFAD so that a fair comparison in the experiment can be provided.

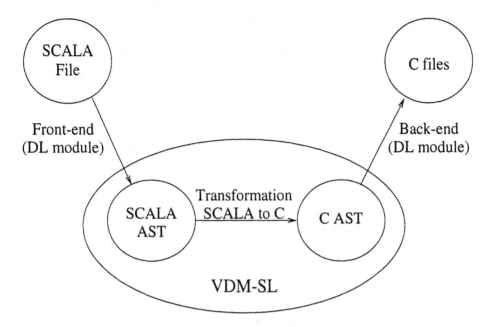

Fig. 4. The general structure of the SCALA to C code generator.

4 Structure of the VDM Model

In this section we will present the architectural structure of the SCALA to C code generator. The general structure of the specification is presented and subsequently broken down into a modular structure showing the dependencies between these modules.

4.1 General Structure of the Specification

The purpose of the final code generator is to translate a SCALA ASCII file into C ASCII files (.cc and .h files). VDM-SL does not provide I/O facilities so this notation cannot be used for the entire translation. Thus, the code generator has been divided into three components as shown in Fig. 4. The first phase is the front-end. The purpose of the front-end is to parse the SCALA ASCII file and produce an intermediate VDM-SL representation in terms of a SCALA abstract syntax tree. In the second phase the VDM-SL specification transforms the abstract syntax of SCALA into the abstract syntax of C. The third part is the back-end, and it converts the C AST into files containing the concrete ASCII representation of the generated C program.

The front-end and the back-end are written directly in C++. In order to include these parts in the VDM-SL specification dynamically linked modules have been used. This enables the VDM-SL part to be interpreted in combination with the front-end and the back-end.

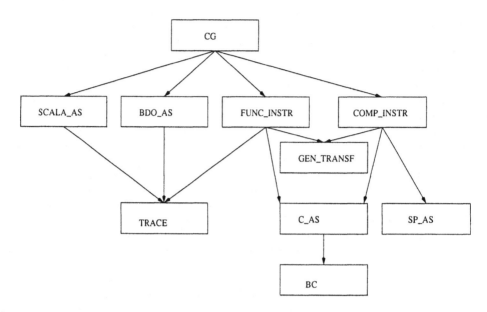

Fig. 5. Specification Module Overview

4.2 Modular Structure of the Specification

The modular structure of the specification and the dependencies between the different modules can be seen in Fig. 5. An arrow between two modules indicates that the first module is using constructs from the second one.

The main module is the CG module which is responsible for the overall code generation of a SCALA specification into a number of C files. It needs information about the abstract syntax of the SCALA notation, SCALA_AS, and the operational database information, BDO_AS providing information of the data used. The transformation of different kinds of instructions takes place in respectively the FUNC_INST, COMP_INST and GEN_TRANSF modules. The abstract syntax and the functions to build C abstract syntax are placed in C_AS and BC. The SP_AS module provides an interface to the subprograms used as level 2 services. Finally, the TRACE module is used to manage trace and error messages.

5   Transformation of a selected SCALA Instruction

The SCALA language contains approximately 30 different statements dealing with actions of setting, acquiring, checking and computing as well as with the associated data management.

In this section we will show how the transformation from SCALA to C of a single SCALA instruction is specified using VDM-SL. The transformation of each instruction is documented using:

1. Examples of the SCALA instruction and its corresponding C code in different cases.
2. Textual description of the steps in the transformation.
3. A formal VDM-SL definition of the transformation.

In order to illustrate the approach we show below how the SCALA instruction **AFFECTER** (meaning "change" in French) is transformed into C. In addition to the items above, we have included the definition of the abstract syntax for the **AFFECTER** instruction and the abstract syntax definition of C needed to understand the VDM-SL definition of the transformation.

The SCALA instruction **AFFECTER** and its corresponding C code can be divided into the following five cases:

SCALA instruction	Corresponding C code
AFFECTER var1 ind1 var2 ind2	var1[ind1-1] = var2[ind2-1]
AFFECTER var1 ind1 var2	var1[ind1-1] = var2
AFFECTER var1 var2 ind2	var1 = var2[ind2-1]
AFFECTER var1 var2 (in case of numeric copy)	var1 = var2
AFFECTER var1 var2 (in case of string copy)	strcpy(var1,var2)

The abstract syntax of the **AFFECTER** instruction is defined below. The **AFFECTER** instruction will always have a variable, var1, on the left-hand side of the assignment and a variable or a value, var2, on the right-hand side of the assignment. Furthermore, var1 and var2 can have optional indices, ind1 and ind2, which can be values or variables.

```
Affecter :: var1 : Variable
            ind1 : [Variable | Valeur]
            var2 : Variable | Valeur
            ind2 : [Variable | Valeur];
```

As shown in the table above, the **AFFECTER** instruction is transformed into an assign statement or a function call to strcpy. The C abstract syntax of a function call is defined as:

```
FctCall:: fct : Id
          arg : seq of Expr
```

In order to build C abstract syntax trees a number of auxiliary functions are defined. The function GenFctCall is one of those and it is used to build a C function call. A general principle in the specification has been to build C AST's only using such auxiliary functions. That is, nodes like FctCall will never be built using a record constructor expression anywhere else than in the auxiliary functions for this purpose.

```
GenFctCall: Id * seq of Expr -> FctCall
GenFctCall(fct,args) ==
  mk_FctCall(fct,args)
```

The function **TransformAffecter** formalises the transformation from **Affecter** to C **Stmt**. The function makes use of some definitions which are not included in this paper. These can be divided into two main categories: 1) General auxiliary functions like **DataType**, which is used to look up the type of the variable on the left-hand side of the assignment, and 2) functions to build C AST's (**GenId**, **GenIntegerLit**, **GenFctCall**, **GenArrayApply** and **GenAsgnStmt**).

```
TransformAffecter: Affecter -> Stmt
TransformAffecter(mk_Affecter(var1,ind1,var2,ind2)) ==
  let id1 = GenId(var1),
      id2 = GenId(var2),
      one = GenIntegerLit(1)
  in
    if DataType(var1) = <car>
    then GenFctCall(StrCpyId,[id1,id2])
    else let e1 = if ind1 = nil
                  then id1
                  else GenArrayApply(id1,GenMin(id1,one)),
             e2 = if ind2 = nil
                  then id2
                  else GenArrayApply(id2,GenMin(id2,one))
         in
           GenAsgnStmt(e1,e2)
  pre DataType(var1) = <car> => ind1 = nil and ind2 = nil
```

Notice that the structure of the **TransformAffecter** function is structured into five different cases corresponding to the different cases of the **AFFECTER** instruction. The first let expression simply provides a name for the two identifiers, id1 and id2 and the integer one. In case the left-hand side variable is defined to be a string the standard string-copy function must be called. Otherwise an assignment statement is made with or without indexing in an array depending on the value of the index parts of the **AFFECTER** instruction.

The precondition of **TransformAffecter** documents that if variable **var1** is a string then the instruction must have the form **AFFECTER var1 var2**. This strategy has been used to document assumptions about the SCALA specification used as input to the code generator. In addition to preconditions it has appeared to be very valuable to use invariants e.g. on the SCALA abstract syntax to document assumptions about SCALA files and instructions.

6 Testing the VDM Specification

The specification of the SCALA to C code generator is tested at two levels:

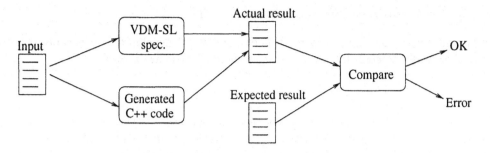

Fig. 6. Specification Test Overview

- at specification level using the Toolbox's interpreter and
- at implementation level using the automatically generated C++ code produced by the VDM-SL$_{to}$C++ Code Generator.

At both levels test coverage information is collected during the tests and metrics are used for comparison with the conventionally developed SCALA to C code generator.

In order to facilitate the test procedures a test environment has been developed. This test environment is common to both levels of testing, and it is illustrated in Fig. 6. It consists of:

- a graphical user interface;
- test drivers (UNIX scripts) for both levels of testing;
- test cases and expected results;
- editors and browsers to view results of tests, test coverage, create new test cases and update existing test cases;
- report (log) generation facilities;
- history information about earlier tests; and
- configuration management interface to the specification and implementation of the code generator.

This testing environment enables easy measurement of code metrics for the different versions of the developments.

7   Measured Results

7.1   Work Amount

The total amount of work turned out to be the same for both developments if the two weeks of direct training in VDM-SL and the C++ code generator are omitted. However, the additional time to get acquainted with the technology is included in this figure. Since this was the first project where the Aerospatiale team used VDM we estimate that in a new project, this team would be able to develop another system with less effort using the VDM technology.

7.2 Test Coverage, Size and Speed of code

For the final source files from the baseline and VDM development a number of metrics was collected. In the table below some of these are shown:

	C baseline	VDM model	C++ generated from VDM	Total VDM C++
Total lines	3938	4252	11708	14565
Actual lines	2471	2215	11400	14000
Functions	79	175	175	200
Test coverage	82 %	89 %	67 %	67 %
CPU speed	100 %			60 %

The difference between most of these figures can be explained by the difference in the overall architecture of the two developments. The general approach of the C code produced in the baseline project is to directly translating from the sequence of characters in the various input files to the corresponding output files. As shown in Fig. 4 the VDM development is structured into three parts (input processing, transformation between abstract syntax trees, and output processing). Naturally this more structured approach requires more types and functions to be defined than the direct approach. We believe that this is the main reason why the size of the C baseline code and the VDM model is approximately equal (the type definitions of the SCALA abstract syntax and the C abstract syntax alone is 20 % of the VDM model). The VDM approach has also structured the model into significantly more functions than the C baseline development (175 versus 79). Concerning the test coverage it is slightly higher in the VDM model using the same set of test cases. The test coverage of the generated C++ code is rather low but this can be explained by the defensive programming style used by the C++ code generator. The main surprising result in this experiment was that the speed of the generated code actually was significantly faster than the hand coded C code from the baseline development. This is not because the C++ code generator is producing outstanding fast code, so it can only be explained by a better design encouraged by the use of VDM.

7.3 Lessons Learnt

The pragmatic approach focusing on validation of the VDM model using conventional testing techniques has shown to be appropriate for an application such as the code generator from SCALA to C. In comparison to a conventional baseline process, the VDM-SL notation has shown to be an adequate software specification language to be used after the engineering design phase to check requirements and to reduce functional complexity. The formalism is unambiguous allowing direct code generation for a large subset of VDM-SL. The VDM modelling allowed a better structured, more flexible and general development than the conventional way. This resulted in a better quality code generation from SCALA to C.

The VDM-SL notation proved to be adequate to model this application by providing the necessary constructs, keeping the data in a logic form in the functional description and by being capable of checking the generation algorithm.

Considering the extensive use of the interpreter and of the C++ code generator made in this experiment, most of the benefits accounted for come from the tool support provided by the IFAD VDM-SL Toolbox. In particular the ability to obtain fast feedback from a model using the interpreter and the powerful type-checking capabilities turned out to be valuable.

The following points have been learnt from the experiment :

Introduction of the VDM technology: Initial training (2 weeks) and the assistance of IFAD's consultants were sufficient to enable a correct use of the technology. Naturally, better skilled people would have benefited more from the particular notation existing in the VDM language. Trying to introduce the model to engineers who had not been trained turned out to be difficult. A general introduction to the basic concepts of formal methods is missing in order to spread the understanding of formal languages among the data processing engineers.

Scope of use: Formal methods are applied to the specification field of a critical software component and not of a whole software system. The VDM technology deals with functional requirements without offering easy modelling of hardware or real-time constraints. However, the VDM language covers a large field of data processing and can be used beyond small automatic logical security systems.

The reliability domain: The reliability of the software comes from careful test coverage measurements available from the VDM-SL Toolbox. The VDM language allows the tracking of invariants, pre- and post conditions which are important points in order to prevent large development teams from misunderstandings and software units from discrepancies.

Work efficiency: After requirements capturing, specification using formal methods can be applied to functional requirements in order to be modelled and checked. The work efficiency comes from the use of a high level language associated with an interpreter (which makes partial test during the modelling) and a code generator. However, the use of the VDM notation as a programming language turned out to be as productive as the C language (same programming time for the same size program). The interpreter allows tests at the modelling level in order to clearly identify the behaviour of the VDM concepts right after formulating them.

8   A Possible Future Use

According to the lessons learnt in the experiment, the VDM technology is a highly efficient modelling tool and allows functional test coverage measurement

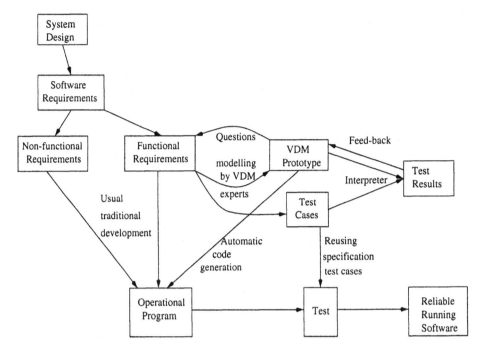

Fig. 7. Future Development Process Using the VDM Technology

at specification level. So, the VDM technology could be used by designers to check the accuracy, the completeness and the coherence of the functional requirements of critical software components.

Even with the use of VDM we feel that the natural language has to be maintained to write such requirements because it is commonly used in space projects and it belongs to the European industrial background. However, this does not prevent developers from using the VDM technology to analyse the requirements. In Fig. 7 it is illustrated how we envisage that the development process could be adjusted to incorporate the VDM technology in a practical way in space applications. In case the natural language explanation and the formal definition are in conflict with each other there must be a clear definition of which one takes precedence. We propose that the formal definition shall be the correct one if such situations should occur, but it is not certain that such an approach would be politically acceptable.

For natural language requirement specifications it is of primary importance to remove all discrepancies, misunderstandings and flaws that would prevent a reliable achievement. In a first step, formal method experts could use the VDM technology to model the functional requirements coming from the system design in order to detect any discrepancy or inaccuracy. This model could be interpreted in order to check the requirements and to study test cases to get an optimal functional test coverage. In a second step, the operational software could be developed as usual, taking into account all the requirements (operational and functional) and could benefit from the code automatically generated from the VDM model. The test cases used at specification level are selected to a high level of test coverage using the test coverage facility from the VDM-SL Toolbox. All these test cases are then reused for the validation of the final program.

9 Concluding Remarks

In this experiment we have not used the methodology part of the formal method VDM. We have taken a pragmatic approach and mainly used the VDM-SL notation for a high level description of the system under development. In comparison to a conventional process, the VDM-SL notation has showed to be an adequate software specification language after the engineering design phase. The formalism is unambiguous and allow direct correct code generation for a large subset of VDM-SL.

The VDM-SL notation proved to be adequate to model a code generator by providing the necessary constructs, keeping the data in a logic form in the functional description and in giving the capability of checking the generation algorithm. We have to point out that such a critical application does not include any synchronisation or real-time needs. If this had been the case we do not expect that we would be able to use the VDM-SL$_{to}$C++ Code Generator, and VDM-SL might not be the best notation to use for such an application. We believe the main benefits of this particular notation is the powerful tool support which is provided by the IFAD VDM-SL Toolbox.

The VDM-SL notation was found easy to use after the first one-week training. A second week of training was used to upgrade the engineers from C to C++ and showing how to interface to the generated code from the VDM-SL$_{to}$C++ Code Generator. However, it turned out that engineers who had not been trained had difficulty in understanding the VDM model being produced.

The specification has been written using an executable subset of VDM-SL on purpose. Dynamic link modules have been used to interface the specified parts with input and output to and from files. This enabled the specifiers to use the interpreter/debugger functionality from the Toolbox on the test arguments used for the final code as well. In addition, this also meant that we did not have to write a lot of C++ code manually.

Acknowledgements

We would like to thank the deputy manager Daniel Claude for setting up this project and the Commission of the European Union for financially supporting the project. Special thanks also go to the members of the development teams in particular to Michelle Lesage, Dennis Couturier and Robert Pastor. Finally, we would like to thank Sten Agerholm, Paul Mukherjee, Anne Berit Nielsen and Ole Storm for their valuable comments to an earlier version of this paper.

References

1. John Dawes. *The VDM-SL Reference Guide*. Pitman, 1991. ISBN 0-273-03151-1.
2. René Elmstrøm, Peter Gorm Larsen, and Poul Bøgh Lassen. The IFAD VDM-SL Toolbox: A Practical Approach to Formal Specifications. *ACM Sigplan Notices*, 29(9):77–80, September 1994.
3. John Fitzgerald, Peter Gorm Larsen, Tom Brookes, and Mike Green. *Applications of Formal Methods*, chapter 14. Developing a Security-critical System using Formal and Convential Methods, pages 333–356. Prentice-Hall International Series in Computer Science, 1995.
4. Brigitte Fröhlich and Peter Gorm Larsen. Combining VDM-SL Specifications with C++ Code. In Marie-Claude Gaudel and Jim Woodcock, editors, *FME'96: Industrial Benefit and Advances in Formal Methods*, pages 179–194. Springer-Verlag, March 1996.
5. Cliff B. Jones. *Systematic Software Development Using VDM*. Prentice-Hall International, Englewood Cliffs, New Jersey, second edition, 1990. ISBN 0-13-880733-7.
6. Peter Gorm Larsen, John Fitzgerald, and Tom Brookes. Applying Formal Specification in Industry. *IEEE Software*, 13(3):48–56, May 1996.
7. Paul Mukherjee. Computer-aided Validation of Formal Specifications. *Software Engineering Journal*, pages 133–140, July 1995.
8. P. G. Larsen and B. S. Hansen and H. Brunn N. Plat and H. Toetenel and D. J. Andrews and J. Dawes and G. Parkin and others. Information technology — Programming languages, their environments and system software interfaces — Vienna Development Method — Specification Language — Part 1: Base language, December 1996.
9. The VDM Tool Group. The IFAD VDM-SL Language. Technical report, IFAD, May 1996. IFAD-VDM-1.
10. T.M. Brookes and J.S. Fitzgerald and P.G. Larsen. Formal and Informal Specifications of a secure System Component: Final Results in a Comparative Study. In Marie-Claude Gaudel and Jim Woodcock, editors, *FME'96: Industrial Benefit and Advances in Formal Methods*, pages 214–227. Springer-Verlag, March 1996.

Mathematical Modeling and Analysis
of an External Memory Manager

William D. Young and William R. Bevier

Computational Logic, Inc.,
1717 West 6th Street, Suite 290
Austin, TX 78704, USA

Abstract. We have modeled and formally analyzed a simple external
memory manager (EMM) system loosely based on the memory management strategies of Mach. The modeling was carried out via a series
of refinements from a very abstract model to a simple concrete model.
Each successive model is an implementation of the next more abstract
level. We have stated theorems that describe formally the relationships
among these models; these theorems have been proven for a subset of the
functionality of the system. The result is a "stack" of progressively more
realistic and complex systems (partially) proven to satisfy an *implements*
relation with a simple high-level design.

1 Introduction

An external memory manager (EMM) is a system module outside the kernel
that mediates access to a collection of memory objects.[1] These objects are made
accessible to client processes through interactions among the client, EMM, and
kernel. Figure 1 illustrates very abstractly this type of system. The objects managed by the EMM initially become available to a client task by mapping them
into the client's virtual address space. A client's reference to a virtual address
may trigger a request by the kernel to the EMM to supply a value or modify
the object. Typically the object is cached in resident memory (RAM) managed
by the kernel. This strategy obviates frequent calls to the EMM. However, since
the kernel memory is limited, it requires that the kernel/EMM interface allow
for paging-out resident objects to allow for paging-in non-resident objects on
demand.

We have implemented a simple external memory manager system via a series of refinements from a very abstract implementation model. The refinement
process produced a "stack" of progressively more realistic and complex systems
each proven[2] to satisfy an *implements* relation with our most abstract design.

---

[1] An excellent description of EMMs in Mach and the complete design of an EMM is
given in [2].

[2] Because of limited time, we attacked a vertical "slice" of the specification. We have
proved the correctness of two of five operations, *Alloc* and *Read*, at each level. We
believe that these are representative operations and will have shown any major shortcomings in our appoach. However, there may be errors in the other operations, the
correctness of which is stated axiomatically at each level.

There are currently five levels in our stack. Below, we describe each of these in turn.

Due to the limited duration of our study, we have deliberately chosen to focus on modeling and analysis of *selected* aspects of the EMM system problem and to ignore others. In particular, we concentrate on the issues involved in: modeling finite resources and the necessary interactions between client, EMM, and kernel. We have ignored other important aspects of external memory management as implemented in a system such as Mach[2].

- We have abstracted away the detailed structure of memory objects, treating pages as if they were simple variables.
- We have eliminated consideration of multiple client tasks. We believe that our work could be easily generalized to handle this complication.
- We have not considered the question of how a client process becomes aware that a memory object is available for mapping.
- We have ignored several obvious optimizations such as recording when a cached memory object is "dirty," allowing a more efficient flushing of the cache.
- We have assumed that a client always supplies a virtual address for mapping. In real systems such as Mach, the virtual address is often selected automatically by the system on behalf of the client.
- We have modeled synchronous interfaces among client, kernel, and EMM. More realistic systems allow asynchronous interactions.

These are important issues for consideration and modeling; we simply did not have the leisure to consider them. We believe that our work could be extended readily to consider some of these aspects.

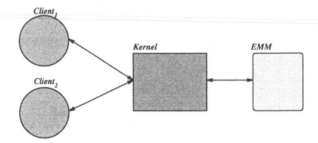

Fig. 1. External Memory Management

In the following section we describe our overall modeling strategy. Sections 3 through 7 describe the five levels of models we have produced and the relationships among them. Finally, Section 8 gives some conclusions of the study.

All of our modeling and analysis has been carried out using the ACL2 logic and theorem prover of Kaufmann and Moore[3, 6]. All definitions presented have been accepted by the ACL2 prover and all of the theorems demonstrated in this paper have been mechanically checked *for some representative cases*, as explained below. Correctness of the other cases was assumed axiomatically. The ACL2 prover is the successor to the Boyer-Moore Nqthm system[4] and is freely available from CLI. ACL2 is a logic of Common Lisp and, like Nqthm, is an untyped logic. Therefore, the various types and signatures used in our presentation are not enforced by typing mechanisms built into the specification language, but rather by explicit "type" hypotheses on our theorems.

2 Our Modeling Strategy

Our strategy has been to take an extremely abstract view of memory management and to model this view as our highest level specification of the system. In this most abstract view, clients have *direct* access to a collection of objects stored on the system disk. That is, unlike the view of Figure 1 in which there is a visible system structure incorporating separate kernel and EMM, the system visible to clients is more like that of Figure 2, in which the maintenance of memory objects is merely a service provided by the system without any of the implementation details being present. In particular, there is no visible division of kernel from memory manager.

A direct implementation of this abstraction is inefficient, because it supposes that client processes read and write directly to backing store without the advantages provided by caching to RAM. However, this abstract model approximates the illusion provided to client processes by the memory management system. Ideally, at all levels the client process is blissfully unaware of any of the details of the complex dance—deferred allocation, copy-on-write, demand paging, etc.— between kernel and EMM that supplies seamless access to memory objects. The client process is presented with the illusion that reading and writing of objects is immediate and direct.

To maintain this illusion in the implementation, we have derived an implementation of our abstract model by refining it through a series of steps that introduce these more complex but more efficient mechanisms. In each step we maintain the abstraction provided by our highest level model and establish the correctness of our implementations by *proving* that each step maintains this abstract interface.

At the lowest level, we have a system in which accessed objects are cached (as needed) into a bounded RAM. Attempted access to non-resident objects results in an interaction between kernel and EMM to page-in the requested object, with the possibility that some other object must be paged-out. At this level, the EMM is a separate module maintaining its private storage of objects separate from the kernel state.

We distinguish two types of objects: temporary and permanent. Permanent objects are those managed by the EMM; temporary objects are created and destroyed at the behest of the client and are managed by the kernel. The client requests that the system:

- *map* permanent memory objects into its virtual address space;

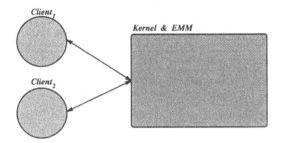

Fig. 2. Client's Model of Memory Management

- *allocate* and *deallocate* temporary memory objects; and,
- *read* and *write* objects, whether temporary or permanent.

Between top and bottom are three intermediate levels representing refinement steps toward this implementation. Our five levels may be summarized as follows.

Level$_0$ Clients have *direct and immediate access* to memory objects on disk that have been mapped into their virtual address space.

Level$_1$ The kernel assumes unbounded physical memory; *objects are copied* into RAM from disk when first *mapped* and remain resident thereafter.

Level$_2$ The kernel assumes unbounded physical memory; *objects are paged in on demand* (i.e., when first read or written), but remain resident thereafter.

Level$_3$ The kernel's *physical memory is bounded*; paging in an object may require freeing space by paging out some other object.

Level$_4$ The state is divided into *kernel and EMM components*. The EMM is a separate module called synchronously by the kernel.

Each successive level is shown to implement the level above and to preserve the abstraction provided by Level$_0$.

In the following sections we describe these five system models and their relationship in some detail. At each level of abstraction, we model the execution of the system in an "operational" style. That is, we define a structure representing the "state" of the system; functions operating on this state model the five available system calls. We also identify an invariant on the state and prove that it is preserved by each of the operations. This invariant places reasonable "well-formedness" conditions on the state. At each level below Level$_0$ we state a correctness theorem that establishes that this level implements the abstraction provided by Level$_0$.

3 Level$_0$: The Abstract Model

3.1 The Level$_0$ State

Our computing model at this and subsequent levels is defined in terms of a number of sets including: the set $\mathcal{B}$ of Booleans; a set $\mathcal{V}$ of virtual addresses; a set $\mathcal{P}$ of physical addresses; a set $\mathcal{M}$ of object names; and a set $\mathcal{D}$ of values.

The Level$_0$ system state is a four-tuple $\langle as,\ tb,\ ds,\ rg \rangle$ where:

- $as : \mathcal{V} \to \mathcal{M}$;
- $tb : \mathcal{M} \to \mathcal{B}$;
- $ds : \mathcal{M} \to \mathcal{D}$;
- $rg : \mathcal{D}$.

Here as is the client address space—a mapping from virtual addresses to memory object names. Table tb records attributes of all memory objects. At this level the only attribute of a memory object is whether or not it is *temporary*. Temporary objects are transient objects conceptually managed by the kernel; permanent objects are persistent entities conceptually managed by the EMM. Mapping ds (disk space) is the model of external storage; it maps object names to values. Notice that we are not concerned here with the internal structure of objects and deal with them as if they were simple variables. Finally, rg is a register private to the client and used in read and write operations.

At Level$_0$, when a client requests access to a memory object known to that client by virtual address va, the kernel uses the corresponding object name $as[va]$ as a pointer to the disk storage of the object. There is only one copy of an object (i.e., in disk space), so no issue of consistency arises at this level.

3.2   The Level$_0$ Invariant

The invariant at this level is particularly important because Level$_0$ is our most abstract system specification. If we place unrealistic or unrealizable assumptions on Level$_0$ they will be carried throughout our entire development. We make the following assumptions about our Level$_0$ state s:[3]

1. $dom\,(s.tb) = dom\,(s.ds)$;
2. $ran\,(s.as) \subset dom\,(s.tb)$;
3. $\forall x, y \in \mathcal{V}; m \in \mathcal{M} : (s.as[x] = s.as[y] = m \land s.tb[m]) \to x = y$.

These say that our table tb contains information regarding all objects on disk, that all objects mapped into our virtual address space as actually exist in the system, and that temporary objects are only mapped to a single virtual address. These seem like fairly innocuous restrictions, but we have no doubt that others would have served as well. In particular, the requirement that there be no extraneous objects on the disk could have been eliminated with very minor changes in our model.

3.3   The Level$_0$ Operations

Each operation is defined as a function on states returning a *labeled state*—a pair consisting of a state and label. A label of *success* indicates that the operation

---

[3] We will always use the notation *structure.component* to reference a particular component of a structured entity such as the system state.

succeeded; any other label indicates an error. Five operations are defined at Level0: $Alloc_0$, Map_0, $Dealloc_0$, $Read_0$, and $Write_0$. We now consider each of them in turn. Note that because of space limitations, at subsequent levels we will only describe *Alloc* and *Read* in detail. These are the two operations which were formally verified. Full descriptions of the other operations at all levels and the full formal ACL2 specification is included in a longer version of this report[7].

Definition 1. The function $Alloc_0 : \mathcal{V} \times \mathcal{S}_0 \to \langle \mathcal{L}, \mathcal{S}_0 \rangle$ is defined as follows:[4]
$Alloc_0 (va, s) = \langle flg, s' \rangle$ where

$$
\begin{cases}
flg = \texttt{already-allocated} \ \wedge \ s = s' & \text{if } va \in dom(s.as), \\[2mm]
\begin{aligned}
flg &= \texttt{success} \\
\wedge \ s'.as &= s.as[va \leftarrow m] \\
\wedge \ s'.tb &= s.tb[m \leftarrow true] \\
\wedge \ s'.ds &= s.ds[m \leftarrow 0]
\end{aligned} & \text{otherwise,}
\end{cases}
$$

and where m is a "new" memory object name.

A call to $Alloc_0 (va, s)$ returns a pair $\langle flg, state \rangle$ where flg is either *success* or some error value. In this case, the only possible error[5] arises if we attempt to overwrite an already allocated virtual address. Otherwise, we return an updated state in which we bind our input virtual address va to a new memory object name m in the virtual address space, indicate in our table that m denotes a temporary object, and bind m to value 0 on the disk. Since m is a new name, this involves creating new locations in tb and ds.

Definition 2. The function $Map_0 : \mathcal{V} \times \mathcal{M} \times \mathcal{S}_0 \to \langle \mathcal{L}, \mathcal{S}_0 \rangle$ is defined as follows:

$Map_0 (va, m, s) = \langle flg, s' \rangle$ where

$$
\begin{cases}
flg = \texttt{already-allocated} \ \wedge \ s = s' & \text{if } va \in dom(s.as), \\[2mm]
flg = \texttt{temporary-memory} \ \wedge \ s = s' & \text{if } s.tb[m], \\[2mm]
\begin{aligned}
flg &= \texttt{success} \\
\wedge \ s'.as &= s.as[va \leftarrow m]
\end{aligned} & \text{otherwise.}
\end{cases}
$$

Given an existing *permanent* memory object, we "map" it to an unused address va in our virtual address space. Such mapping is necessary before we can read or write the object. Notice that we map only permanent objects; we use $Alloc_0$ to create and map temporary objects into our address space.

---

[4] We use the notation $z[x \leftarrow y]$ for $(z/\{x, z(x)\}) \cup \{(x, y)\}$ (i.e., bind y to x in mapping z) and $z[x \leftarrow \phi]$ for $z/\{x, z(x)\}$ (i.e., remove the binding for x from mapping z).

[5] Actually errors can also arise if our actual parameters do not match their intended "types"; but we ignore that possibility here and in subsequent definitions.

Definition 3. The function $Dealloc_0 : \mathcal{V} \times \mathcal{S}_0 \rightarrow \langle \mathcal{L}, \mathcal{S}_0 \rangle$ is defined as follows:

$Dealloc_0 (va, s) = \langle flg, s' \rangle$ where

$$
\begin{cases}
flg = \texttt{unallocated-va} \wedge s = s' & \text{if } va \notin dom(s.as), \\[2ex]
\begin{aligned}
&flg = \texttt{success} \\
&\wedge\, s'.as = s.as[va \leftarrow \phi] \\
&\wedge\, s'.tb = s.tb[m \leftarrow \phi] \\
&\wedge\, s'.ds = s.ds[m \leftarrow \phi]
\end{aligned} & \text{if } s.tb[m], \\[2ex]
\begin{aligned}
&flg = \texttt{success} \\
&\wedge\, s'.as = s.as[va \leftarrow \phi]
\end{aligned} & \text{otherwise,}
\end{cases}
$$

and where $m = s.as[va]$.

This definition requires a bit more explanation than the previous two. We first see that the supplied virtual address is bound in the address space. We then check whether the designated object is temporary. If so, we are free to discard the object. Temporaries are mapped at most once (by $Alloc_0$); consequently, they are not shared and may be freely discarded. We remove the temporary from our address space, table, and disk space. On the other hand, if the object is permanent we merely discard the reference to it in our virtual address space, retaining the object in our table and on disk. There is no need to "flush" its value to disk because, at this level, there is no storage other than disk.

The $Read_0$ operation uses the rg register component of the state as the destination of data read from memory.

Definition 4. The function $Read_0 : \mathcal{V} \times \mathcal{S}_0 \rightarrow \langle \mathcal{L}, \mathcal{S}_0 \rangle$ is defined as follows:

$Read_0 (va, s) = \langle flg, s' \rangle$ where

$$
\begin{cases}
flg = \texttt{unallocated-va} \wedge s = s' & \text{if } va \notin dom(s.as), \\[2ex]
\begin{aligned}
&flg = \texttt{success} \\
&\wedge\, s'.rg = s.ds[m]
\end{aligned} & \text{otherwise.}
\end{cases}
$$

Notice that it is in $Read_0$ (and $Write_0$) where our assumption that data objects act as simple variables comes into play. That is, reading and writing occurs at the granularity of an entire *object*. Removing this limitation is an obvious potential later refinement of our specification.

Finally, $Write_0$ uses rg as the source of data copied into memory.

Definition 5. The function $Write_0 : \mathcal{V} \times \mathcal{S}_0 \rightarrow \langle \mathcal{L}, \mathcal{S}_0 \rangle$ is defined as follows:

$Write_0 (va, s) = \langle flg, s' \rangle$ where

$$
\begin{cases}
flg = \texttt{unallocated-va} \wedge s = s' & \text{if } va \notin dom(s.as), \\[2ex]
\begin{aligned}
&flg = \texttt{success} \\
&\wedge\, s'.ds = s.ds[m \leftarrow s.rg]
\end{aligned} & \text{otherwise,}
\end{cases}
$$

and where m is $s.as[va]$.

3.4 Defining the Level$_0$ Interpreter

In order to establish the correspondence between levels in our hierarchy, it is desirable that we be able to refer to the execution of a *sequence* of commands. Therefore, we define a concrete syntax for invoking operations at each level and an interpreter for the resulting simple command language. This is extremely straightforward. In fact, since the interpreter is defined almost identically at each level in our stack, we will only describe it at Level$_0$.

We specify a simple concrete syntax for virtual address, memory object names and instructions. For example, we represent an invocation of $Alloc_0(v, s)$ with concrete syntax `Alloc0 (v)`, where the state is an implicit argument assumed to be the current state at the time of the invocation. Assume that $\mathcal{I}_i$ is the instruction set at Level$_i$ in our hierarchy.[6] We then define a "single-stepper" $Step_0$ for the language.

Definition 6. The function $Step_0 : \mathcal{I}_0 \times \mathcal{S}_0 \to \langle \mathcal{L}, \mathcal{S}_0 \rangle$ is defined as follows:

$Step_0 \ (ins, \ s) =$

$$
\begin{cases}
Alloc_0(v, s) & \text{if } ins = \texttt{Alloc(v)}, \\
Map_0(v, m, s) & \text{if } ins = \texttt{Map(v,m)}, \\
Dealloc_0(v, s) & \text{if } ins = \texttt{Dealloc(v)}, \\
Read_0(v, s) & \text{if } ins = \texttt{Read(v)}, \\
Write_0(v, s) & \text{if } ins = \texttt{Write(v)}, \\
\langle \texttt{failure}, s \rangle & \text{otherwise},
\end{cases}
$$

and where v and m are the virtual address and memory object name designated by the syntactic entities `v` and `m`, respectively.

Finally, we define the language interpreter recursively, calling the single stepper on individual instructions in the obvious way.

Definition 7. The function $Int_0 : \mathcal{I}_0^* \times \langle \mathcal{L}, \mathcal{S}_0 \rangle \to \langle \mathcal{L}, \mathcal{S}_0 \rangle$ is defined as follows:

$Int_0 \ (prog, \ \langle l, \ s \rangle) =$

$$
\begin{cases}
\langle l, s \rangle & \text{if } l \neq \text{success} \vee prog = \langle \rangle, \\
Int_0(prog', Step_0(i, s)) & \text{if } prog = i \circ prog'.
\end{cases}
$$

3.5 Establishing the Level$_0$ Invariant

An initial "sanity check" on the model is to show that each of the five operations preserves the invariant defined at this level. That is, if Inv_0 is the Level$_0$ invariant described in Section 3.2, for each of the five operations we can prove a theorem such as the following for $Alloc_0$.

Theorem 8 $Alloc_0$ Preserves Inv_0.
For all $v \in \mathcal{V}, s \in \mathcal{S}_0 : Inv_0(s) \to Inv_0(Alloc_0(v, s).state)$.

---

[6] Since the instructions will be identical at all levels, we usually drop the subscript.

Here *.state* extracts the state component from the $\langle label, state\rangle$ labeled state pair returned by each of the operations. More generally, we prove:

Theorem 9 Int_0 Preserves Inv_0.
For all $prog \in \mathcal{I}^*, \langle l, s\rangle \in \langle \mathcal{L}, \mathcal{S}_0\rangle$:

$$Inv_0(s) \rightarrow Inv_0(Int_0(prog, \langle l, s\rangle).state).$$

This concludes our overview of $Level_0$. Since there is no more abstract system specification than $Level_0$, at this point we should have convinced ourselves that this level provides a reasonable abstraction of memory access and one worth implementing. We now proceed to describe the subsequent levels (in somewhat less detail) and show how they implement the $Level_0$ abstraction.

4 $Level_1$: Resident Memory

At $Level_1$ we add to our model the key feature of memory management systems, namely the notion that the kernel maintains a store (RAM) in which memory object values are cached for improved access. At this level the cache is of un-bounded size. Objects are copied into this primary store when mapped by the client. Consequently, they are always resident when accessed; no page-faults occur. Flushing an object to disk [7] need only occur when a permanent object is deallocated and is no longer mapped in any client's address space.

4.1 The $Level_1$ State

The $Level_1$ system state is a five-tuple $\langle as, tb, pm, ds, rg\rangle$ where:

- $as : \mathcal{V} \rightarrow \mathcal{M}$;
- $tb : \mathcal{M} \rightarrow \langle \mathcal{B}, \mathcal{P}\rangle$;
- $pm : \mathcal{P} \rightarrow \mathcal{D}$;
- $ds : \mathcal{M} \rightarrow \mathcal{D}$;
- $rg : \mathcal{D}$.

Our state at this level contains an additional component not present at $Level_0$, the primary (or physical) memory or RAM, pm, maintained by the kernel. It is represented by a mapping from addresses to values. The system table, tb, again contains the attributes of memory objects, but at this level we have both the status of the object (temporary or permanent), and the physical address of the object (or the special value NR indicating an object that is non-resident). For object name x, we will refer to the corresponding status and address as $tb[x].temp?$ and $tb[x].addr$, respectively. The other state components are identical to those of $Level_0$.

---

[7] "Flushing an object" means updating the disk copy of an object from the cached value (which may have been altered).

At $Level_1$, when a client requests access to a memory object mapped into his virtual address space and known to that client by virtual address va, the kernel first looks up the corresponding object name $as[va]$. This in turn is used to fetch from tb the physical address of the resident copy in pm. This resident copy is the one accessed. Following this chain of pointers should always succeed at this level since objects become resident (are copied into pm) when mapped by the client. However, writing to an object may cause the disk copy and resident copy to become inconsistent.

4.2 The $Level_1$ Invariant

We make the following assumptions about our $Level_1$ state s:

1. $dom\,(s.tb) = dom\,(s.ds)$;
2. $ran\,(s.as) \subset dom\,(s.tb)$;
3. $\forall\, x, y \in \mathcal{V}, m \in \mathcal{M}, s.as[x] = s.as[y] = m \land s.tb[m].temp? \rightarrow x = y$;
4. $\forall\, x \in dom\,(s.tb) : s.tb[x].addr = \text{NR} \lor s.tb[x].addr \in dom\,(s.pm)$;
5. $\forall\, x \in dom\,(s.tb) : s.tb[x].addr \neq \text{NR} \rightarrow x \in ran\,(s.as)$.

To the three invariant properties of $Level_0$, we add two new requirements. Any address stored in tb must be a legal address into pm. This is merely an integrity constraint on our state that prevents dangling pointers. The second is more subtle: if an object is marked as resident (has an associated address in tb) it must be mapped by some client. This precludes having any resident objects that are not mapped into the client's virtual address space. This is a rather dubious requirement and it is needed only because of the implementation theorem we prove. We'll say more on this shortly; but we believe that this restriction could be eliminated with the some minor changes to our model.

4.3 The $Level_1$ Operations

Five operations are defined at this level: $Alloc_1$, Map_1, $Dealloc_1$, $Read_1$, and $Write_1$. We only describe $Alloc$ and $Read$ in detail here, an approach followed in all subsequent levels. The other operations were defined at each level and the state invariant properties proved, but the implementation proofs only carried out for these two operations.

Definition 10. The function $Alloc_1 : \mathcal{V} \times \mathcal{S}_1 \rightarrow \langle \mathcal{L}, \mathcal{S}_1 \rangle$ is defined as follows:

$Alloc_1\,(va,\,s) = \langle flg, s' \rangle$ where

$$
\begin{cases}
flg = \text{already-allocated} \land s = s' & \text{if } va \in dom(s.as), \\[2ex]
\begin{aligned}
& flg = \text{success} \\
& \land s.as' = s.as[va \leftarrow m] \\
& \land s.tb' = s.tb[m \leftarrow \langle true, pa \rangle] \\
& \land s.pm' = s.pm[pa \leftarrow 0] \\
& \land s.ds' = s.ds[m \leftarrow 0]
\end{aligned} & \text{otherwise,}
\end{cases}
$$

and where m is a "new" memory object name and pa an unused physical address.

$Alloc_1$ is quite similar to $Alloc_0$ except that the newly allocated memory object is stored both in RAM and on the disk, with its RAM address stored in tb. Notice that we can always find an unused address at this level because RAM is unbounded.

Definition 11. The function $Read_1 : \mathcal{V} \times \mathcal{S}_1 \rightarrow \langle \mathcal{L}, \mathcal{S}_1 \rangle$ is defined as follows:

$Read_1 (va, s) = \langle flg, s' \rangle$ where

$$
\begin{cases}
flg = \texttt{unallocated-va} \wedge s = s' & \text{if } va \notin dom(s.as), \\[1em]
\begin{aligned} flg &= \texttt{success} \\ \wedge\ s.rg' &= s.ds[m] \end{aligned} & \text{if } pa = \text{NR}, \\[1em]
\begin{aligned} flg &= \texttt{success} \\ \wedge\ s.rg' &= s.pm[pa] \end{aligned} & \text{otherwise},
\end{cases}
$$

and where m is $s.as[va]$, and $pa = s.tb[m].addr$.

$Read_1$ is supposed to read a value from memory into its register rg. It gets this value from the resident copy of the source memory object. *But suppose the object isn't resident?* We know this shouldn't occur because, at this level, objects are made resident when mapped. Consequently, a client shouldn't have a virtual address for an object that is not resident. But our invariant doesn't guarantee that property. It could, but that would cause a problem in lower levels where it won't be true. Therefore, we simply add a clause to our definition of $Read_1$ to assure that we do the "right" thing if this situation ever arises (even though we know it won't). The right thing in this case is to read directly from disk, as at $Level_0$. Notice that this is the precise analogue of what we do at lower levels; when there is a page fault we page the object value from disk into memory and read that value. So this level is the natural bridge between our $Level_0$ abstraction and our lower level implementation.

4.4 Level₁ Implements Level₀

We note in passing that the interpreter for $Level_1$ is built exactly equivalently to that for $Level_0$ as described in Section 3.4. We also prove the same types of theorems to establish that our $Level_1$ invariant is preserved by each of the five operations operations available at this level, as described in Section 3.5. But we have an additional obligation at $Level_1$, namely, showing that $Level_1$ is a *correct implementation* of $Level_0$.

The relationship between these two levels is evident from the following observation. At $Level_0$ the client effectively accesses the disk ds directly. At $Level_1$, we have object values cached in pm and it is these that we access. The cached values may not be consistent with the values stored on disk. But, at any time, we should be able to "flush" the cache and create a $Level_1$ disk state equivalent to our $Level_0$ disk state. This is possible because we are careful to avoid having multiple (and possibly inconsistent) resident copies of any memory object. The idea of using "flushing" in the specification to reach a state which can be compared to the abstract non-caching version is one which has recently been used in the specification of pipelined hardware architectures.[5] We were not aware of that work until after this modeling project had been completed.

Flushing the cache and throwing away pm and the addresses in tb converts a $Level_1$ state into a $Level_0$ state. We can define this mapping formally.

Definition 12. The function $State_{1 \to 0} : S_1 \to S_0$ is defined as follows:

$State_{1 \to 0}(s) = \langle s.as,\ tb',\ ds',\ s.rg \rangle$ where

$$\left\{ \begin{array}{l} dom\,(tb') = dom\,(s.tb) \\ \wedge\ \forall\, x \in dom\,(s.tb) : tb'[x] = s.tb[x].temp? \\ \wedge\ dom\,(ds') = dom\,(s.ds) \\ \wedge\ \forall\, x \in dom\,(s.ds) : s.tb[x] \neq \mathrm{NR} \to ds'[x] = s.pm[x] \\ \wedge\ \forall\, x \in dom\,(s.ds) : s.tb[x] = \mathrm{NR} \to ds'[x] = s.ds[x]. \end{array} \right.$$

Since the interpreter returns a labeled state, and since we use the same labels at the different levels, we can trivially write a function to map $Level_1$ labeled states to $Level_0$ labeled states as well.

Definition 13. The function $LS_{1 \to 0} : \langle \mathcal{L}, S_1 \rangle \to \langle \mathcal{L}, S_0 \rangle$ is defined as follows:

$$LS_{1 \to 0}(\langle l, s \rangle) = \langle l,\ State_{1 \to 0}(s) \rangle.$$

We can prove easily that: $s \in S_1 \to State_{1 \to 0}(s) \in S_0$. However we additionally want to prove the theorem expressed graphically in Figure 3. We show that extracting a $Level_0$ state from the result after executing a sequence of instructions at $Level_1$, is identical to the result of first mapping up to $Level_0$ and then executing the same instruction sequence at that level, i.e., the diagram in Figure 3 commutes.

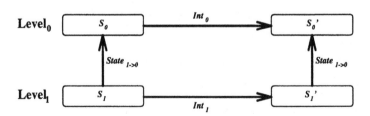

Fig. 3. $Level_1$ Implements $Level_0$

Theorem 14 $Level_1$ Implements $Level_0$.
For all $ins \in \mathcal{I}^*$, $\langle l, s \rangle \in \langle \mathcal{L}, S_1 \rangle$:

$$inv_1(s) \to LS_{1 \to 0}(Int_1(ins, \langle l, s \rangle)) = Int_0(ins, LS_{1 \to 0}(\langle l, s \rangle)).$$

Notice that it suffices to map the state but not the instruction list, since we are using the same instructions and same concrete syntax at both levels.

The subcases of this theorem have been completely mechanically checked for *Alloc* and *Read*. Modulo the proofs of the other three operations, we take this theorem as establishing our claim that $Level_1$ "implements" $Level_0$.[8]

5 $Level_2$: Demand Paging

At $Level_2$ we add the notion of *demand paging* to our model. In $Level_1$, objects mapped into the virtual address space of the client are immediately copied into main memory. This is potentially inefficient if the object is not subsequently accessed. At the current level, objects are copied into memory only when first accessed via a *Read* or *Write* operation. Thus, there is never a need to create a copy of the object on RAM until (and if) it is actually accessed. At $Level_2$ we still assume unbounded memory, so there is no need ever to page-out an object to make room for another.

5.1 The $Level_2$ State and Invariant

The $Level_2$ system state and system invariant are identical to those at $Level_1$. Only the operations differ. At $Level_2$, when a client requests access to a memory object mapped into its virtual address space and known to that client by virtual address *va*, the kernel first looks up the corresponding object name $as[va]$. This in turn is used to fetch from *tb* the physical address of the resident copy in *pm*, if the object is resident. The object will not be resident if it has not previously be read or written. If not resident, a *page fault* occurs and the object is paged into memory and then accessed.

5.2 The $Level_2$ Operations

As at higher levels, five operations are defined at this level: $Alloc_2$, Map_2, $Dealloc_2$, $Read_2$, and $Write_2$. Again, we only describe $Alloc_2$ and $Read_2$ in detail.

Definition 15. The function $Alloc_2 : \mathcal{V} \times \mathcal{S}_2 \rightarrow \langle \mathcal{L}, \mathcal{S}_2 \rangle$ is defined as follows:

$Alloc_2 (va, s) = \langle flg, s' \rangle$ where

$$
\begin{cases}
flg = \texttt{already-allocated} \ \wedge \ s = s' & \text{if } va \in dom(s.as), \\
\\
\begin{aligned}
flg &= \texttt{success} \\
\wedge \ s.as' &= s.as[va \leftarrow m] \\
\wedge \ s.tb' &= s.tb[m \leftarrow \langle true, \texttt{NR} \rangle] \\
\wedge \ s.pm' &= s.pm \\
\wedge \ s.ds' &= s.ds[m \leftarrow 0]
\end{aligned} & \text{otherwise,}
\end{cases}
$$

and where m is a "new" memory object name.

---

[8] See [1] for a fuller discussion and justification of this approach to proving implementations.

We allocate the temporary object, associate it with a virtual address, and record its properties in our object table. But notice that we do not create a copy of the object in physical memory, and consequently, do not generate a new physical address for the object in this operation.

Read and *Write* are more complicated at Level$_2$ than at higher levels. Here, we cannot rely on the accessed object being resident. The first access to an object causes a page-fault and prompts the kernel to page in the object.

Definition 16. The function $Read_2 : \mathcal{V} \times \mathcal{S}_2 \rightarrow \langle \mathcal{L}, \mathcal{S}_2 \rangle$ is defined as follows:

$Read_2\,(va,\ s) = \langle flg,\ s' \rangle$ where

$$
\begin{cases}
flg = \texttt{unallocated-va} \wedge s = s' & \text{if } va \notin dom(s.as), \\[2ex]
\begin{aligned}
& flg = \texttt{success} \\
& \wedge\ s.tb'.addr = s.tb[m \leftarrow new\text{-}pa].addr \\
& \wedge\ s.pm' = s.pm[new\text{-}pa \leftarrow val] \\
& \wedge\ s.rg' = val
\end{aligned} & \text{if } s.tb[m].addr = \texttt{NR}, \\[2ex]
\begin{aligned}
& flg = \texttt{success} \\
& \wedge\ s.rg' = s.pm[s.tb[m].addr]
\end{aligned} & \text{otherwise,}
\end{cases}
$$

and where $m = s.as[va]$, *new-pa* is a new physical address, and $val = s.ds[m]$.

5.3 Level$_2$ Implements Level$_1$

We would like to prove the exact analogue of Theorem 14 to establish the relationship between Level$_2$ and Level$_1$. That is, we would like to prove the assertion:

$$\forall\ ins \in \mathcal{I}^*,\ \langle l,\ s \rangle \in \langle \mathcal{L},\ \mathcal{S}_2 \rangle,$$

$$inv_2(s) \rightarrow LS_{2 \rightarrow 1}\,(Int_2(ins, \langle l,\ s \rangle)) = Int_1\,(ins, LS_{2 \rightarrow 1}\,(\langle l,\ s \rangle)).$$

However, because objects are copied into physical memory at different times in the two levels, it may happen that the physical addresses associated with specific objects differ in the two resulting states. Therefore, the above "obvious" correctness assertion will not be a theorem of our system.

We solve this dilemma by noting that the result we really care about is that our implementation preserves the abstraction provided by Level$_0$. We note that the resulting states should be identical if we "flush the cache" after both executions. This is captured formally in the following theorem.

Theorem 17 Level$_2$ Implements Level$_1$.
For all $ins \in \mathcal{I}^*,\ \langle l,\ s \rangle \in \langle \mathcal{L},\ \mathcal{S}_2 \rangle$:
$$inv_2\,(s)$$
$$\rightarrow LS_{1 \rightarrow 0}\,(LS_{2 \rightarrow 1}\,(Int_2(ins, \langle l,\ s \rangle))) = LS_{1 \rightarrow 0}\,(Int_1\,(ins, LS_{2 \rightarrow 1}\,(\langle l,\ s \rangle))).$$

The theorem is represented schematically in Figure 4, minus the dotted portions. Since the mapping from Level$_2$ to Level$_1$ is the identity mapping, this theorem and Theorem 14 allow us to prove:

Theorem 18 Level$_2$ Implements Level$_0$.
For all $ins \in \mathcal{I}^*$, $\langle l, s \rangle \in \langle \mathcal{L}, \mathcal{S}_2 \rangle$:
$$inv_2(s) \rightarrow LS_{2\rightarrow 0}\left(Int_2(ins, \langle l, s \rangle)\right) = Int_0\left(ins, LS_{2\rightarrow 0}\left(\langle l, s \rangle\right)\right),$$
where $LS_{2\rightarrow 0}$ is simply the composition of $LS_{2\rightarrow 1}$ and $LS_{1\rightarrow 0}$.

This contributes the dotted portions to Figure 4. We take this theorem as establishing that Level$_2$ maintains the abstraction provided by Level$_0$.

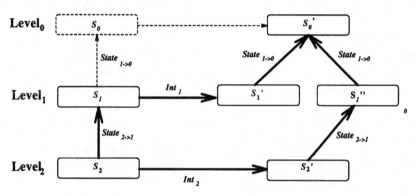

Fig. 4. Level$_1$ Implements Level$_0$

6 Level$_3$: Bounded Physical Memory

At Level$_3$ we introduce a bound on the size of RAM. This implies that there may be more objects accessed than locations in the cache. Consequently, we must be able to page-out some objects to make room for others. Page-out occurs in reading and writing when a page-fault occurs and there are no currently unused physical addresses.

6.1 The Level$_3$ State and Invariant

The Level$_3$ system state is again identical to the system state at Level$_1$ except that all physical addresses appearing in tb and pm are required to be less than or equal to some fixed but unspecified upper bound. The system invariant is also unchanged.

6.2 The Level$_3$ Operations

As at all previous levels, five operations are defined: $Alloc_3$, Map_3, $Dealloc_3$, $Read_3$, and $Write_3$. Again, we describe only $Alloc_3$ and $Read_3$.

$Alloc_3$ is identical to its $Level_2$ counterpart. As at $Level_2$, we have the possibility that *Read* will cause a page-fault. New at this level is the additional possibility that there will be no free RAM locations. We must choose some resident object to page-out.

Definition 19. The function $Read_3 : \mathcal{V} \times \mathcal{S}_3 \rightarrow \langle \mathcal{L}, \mathcal{S}_3 \rangle$ is defined as follows:

$Read_3 \, (va, \, s) = \langle \mathit{flg}, \, s' \rangle$ where

$$
\left\{
\begin{array}{ll}
\mathit{flg} = \texttt{unallocated-va} \, \wedge \, s = s' & \text{if } va \notin dom(s.as), \\
\\
\mathit{flg} = \texttt{success} & \\
\wedge \, s.rg' = s.pm[s.tb[m].addr] & \text{if } s.tb[m].addr \neq \text{NR}, \\
\\
\mathit{flg} = \texttt{success} & \\
\wedge \, s.tb' = s.tb[m \leftarrow \textit{new-pa}] & \text{if } s.tb[m].addr = \text{NR} \, \wedge \\
\wedge \, s.pm' = s.pm[\textit{new-pa} \leftarrow val] & \textit{new-pa} \text{ is unused}, \\
\wedge \, s.rg' = s.ds[m] & \\
\\
\mathit{flg} = \texttt{success} & \\
\wedge \, s.tb'[m] = \langle s.tb[m].temp?, \, pa \rangle & \\
\wedge \, s.tb'[tm] = \langle s.tb[tm].temp?, \, \text{NR} \rangle & \text{if } s.tb[m].addr \neq \text{NR} \, \wedge \\
\wedge \, s.pm' = s.pm[pa \leftarrow s.ds[m]] & \text{no addr is unused.} \\
\wedge \, s.ds' = s.ds[tm \leftarrow s.pm[pa]] & \\
\wedge \, s.rg' = s.ds[m] & \\
\end{array}
\right.
$$

and where $m = s.as[va]$ and pa is some physical address such that $s.tb[tm].addr = pa$.

If the requested object is resident, we read from RAM. If the object is non-resident but there is a free slot, we page it in and return the value. If we have the need to page in an object but RAM is full (i.e., there are no unused physical addresses), we select some address currently in use. The object at that location is flushed to disk and the address reused. The choice of an object to page out is axiomatized to return some unspecified element in the domain of *pm*. This permits implementations that use any of the standard strategies, such as "least recently used," to select the target for replacement.

6.3 $Level_3$ Implements $Level_2$

Again, because we are reusing physical addresses from a limited pool rather than generating them as needed, the physical addresses recorded in *tb* and *pm* may differ from $Level_2$ to $Level_3$. Therefore, we cannot prove a simple version of the correctness theorem such as that illustrated in Figure 3. Instead we prove the equivalence of the final states obtained by flushing the cache.

Theorem 20 $Level_3$ Implements $Level_2$.
For all $ins \in \mathcal{I}^*$, $\langle l, s \rangle \in \langle \mathcal{L}, \mathcal{S}_3 \rangle$:

$$inv_3(s) \rightarrow LS_{1 \rightarrow 0} \, (Int_3(ins, \langle l, s \rangle)) = LS_{1 \rightarrow 0} \, (Int_2 \, (ins, \, \langle l, s \rangle)).$$

There would seem to be several type errors here since, for example, we are applying the function $LS_{1 \to 0}$ to Level$_2$ states. However, we have simply eliminated calls to $LS_{3 \to 2}$ and $LS_{2 \to 1}$, which are both the identity function. From this theorem, it is an easy step to:

Theorem 21 Level$_3$ Implements Level$_0$.
For all $ins \in \mathcal{I}^*$, $\langle l, s \rangle \in \langle \mathcal{L}, \mathcal{S}_3 \rangle$:

$$inv_3(s) \to LS_{3 \to 0}\left(Int_3(ins, \langle l, s \rangle)\right) = Int_0\left(ins, LS_{3 \to 0}\left(\langle l, s \rangle\right)\right).$$

where $LS_{3 \to 0}$ is simply the composition of $LS_{3 \to 2}$, $LS_{2 \to 1}$, and $LS_{1 \to 0}$.

This lemma establishes that we have carried our Level$_0$ abstraction down to Level$_3$.

7 Level$_4$: Separating the Kernel and EMM

To this point, we have not clearly distinguished the separate roles of kernel and external memory manager (EMM) in providing memory access. At Level$_4$ we make the division of the state into two parts, showing the separate responsibilities of these two modules. The EMM will be responsible for managing the disk ds, with the kernel managing the other components of the state. At this, the lowest implementation level we will consider, the EMM is still subservient to the kernel in the sense that it is called as a subroutine (synchronously) by the kernel. A next logical step in this development would be to introduce a Level$_5$ implementation at which communication between kernel and EMM was implemented via an asynchronous message-passing interface as in Mach. We have not done so, however.

7.1 The Level$_4$ State and Invariant

The Level$_1$ system state is a $\langle ks, es \rangle$ pair comprising the kernel state and EMM state. The EMM state is identical to the ds component of higher levels. The kernel state is a four-tuple $\langle as, tb, pm, rg \rangle$ with components structurally identical to the as, tb, pm, and rg of Level$_3$. The invariant is identical to the Level$_3$ invariant, modulo the changes needed to access the components of the state.

7.2 The Level$_4$ Operations

The EMM. The EMM is a module, separate from the kernel, that accepts requests for services and either updates its internal state or returns a value. Level$_4$ is the first level at which the separate existence of the EMM becomes apparent. It is coded as a command interpreter that returns a triple consisting of an error flag, value, and an updated state. We use $.vl$, and $.st$ to access the value and state components of this triple. The value is usually not relevant. The only commands acceptable to our current version of the EMM are alloc, dealloc, store, and fetch. We assume a concrete syntax $\mathcal{E}$ of EMM commands.

Definition 22. The function $EMM_4 : \mathcal{E} \times (\mathcal{M} \to \mathcal{D}) \to \langle \mathcal{L}, \mathcal{D}, (\mathcal{M} \to \mathcal{D}) \rangle$ is defined as follows:

$EMM_4\,(i,\ ds) =$

$$
\begin{cases}
\langle \texttt{success},\ 0,\ ds[m \leftarrow 0] \rangle & \text{if } i = \texttt{alloc(m)}, \\
\langle \texttt{success},\ 0,\ ds[m \leftarrow \phi] \rangle & \text{if } i = \texttt{dealloc(m)}, \\
\langle \texttt{success},\ 0,\ ds[m \leftarrow v] \rangle & \text{if } i = \texttt{store(m, v)}, \\
\langle \texttt{success},\ ds[m],\ ds \rangle & \text{if } i = \texttt{fetch(m)}, \\
\langle \texttt{unrecognized-request},\ 0,\ ds \rangle & \text{otherwise.}
\end{cases}
$$

The kernel requests service from the EMM by generating an appropriate request string and calling the EMM with that string. The kernel is not allowed to access the EMM state directly. As at all previous levels, five kernel operations are defined: $Alloc_4$, Map_4, $Dealloc_4$, $Read_4$, and $Write_4$. Some of these call the EMM to update the disk or to return the current value of an object. As usual, we show only $Alloc_4$ and $Read_4$.

Definition 23. The function $Alloc_4 : \mathcal{V} \times \mathcal{S}_4 \to \langle \mathcal{L}, \mathcal{S}_4 \rangle$ is defined as follows:

$Alloc_4\,(va,\ \langle ks,\ es \rangle) = \langle flg,\ \langle ks',\ es' \rangle \rangle$ where

$$
\begin{cases}
flg = \texttt{already-allocated} & \text{if } va \in dom(ks.as), \\
\wedge\ ks = ks'\ \wedge\ es = es' & \\[1.2em]
flg = \texttt{success} & \\
\wedge\ ks.as' = ks.as[va \leftarrow m] & \\
\wedge\ ks.tb' = ks.tb[m \leftarrow \langle true,\ \text{NR} \rangle] & \text{otherwise,} \\
\wedge\ ks.pm' = ks.pm & \\
\wedge\ es' = EMM(\texttt{alloc}\ (m),\ es).st,
\end{cases}
$$

and where m is a "new" memory object name.

We should additionally allow for the case in which the call to EMM returns an error. However, by examining the definition of EMM we see that it will not do so in any of the cases we consider in Level$_4$.

Definition 24. The function $Read_4 : \mathcal{V} \times \mathcal{S}_4 \to \langle \mathcal{L}, \mathcal{S}_4 \rangle$ is defined as follows:

$Read_4\,(va,\ \langle ks,\ es \rangle) = \langle flg,\ \langle ks',\ es' \rangle \rangle$ where

$$\left\{\begin{array}{ll}
\begin{aligned}
& flg = \texttt{unallocated-va} \\
& \wedge\; ks = ks' \;\wedge\; es = es'
\end{aligned} & \text{if } va \notin dom(ks.as), \\[2em]

\begin{aligned}
& flg = \texttt{success} \\
& \wedge\; ks.rg' = ks.pm[ks.tb[m].addr]
\end{aligned} & \text{if } ks.tb[m].addr \neq \text{NR}, \\[2em]

\begin{aligned}
& flg = \texttt{success} \\
& \wedge\; ks.tb' = ks.tb[m \leftarrow new\text{-}pa] \\
& \wedge\; ks.pm' = ks.pm[new\text{-}pa \leftarrow val] \\
& \wedge\; ks.rg' = val
\end{aligned} & \begin{aligned} & \text{if } ks.tb[m].addr = \text{NR} \wedge \\ & new\text{-}pa \text{ is unused,} \end{aligned} \\[3em]

\begin{aligned}
& flg = \texttt{success} \\
& \wedge\; ks.tb'[m] = \langle tmp1,\ pa \rangle \\
& \wedge\; ks.tb'[tm] = \langle tmp2,\ \text{NR} \rangle \\
& \wedge\; ks.pm' = ks.pm[pa \leftarrow val] \\
& \wedge\; es' = EMM(\texttt{store}\ (tm,\ v),\ es).st \\
& \wedge\; ks.rg' = val
\end{aligned} & \begin{aligned} & \text{if } ks.tb[m].addr \neq \text{NR} \wedge \\ & \text{no addr is unused.} \end{aligned}
\end{array}\right.$$

and where $m = ks.as[va]$, pa is some physical address such that $ks.tb[tm].addr = pa$, $tmp1 = ks.tb[m].temp?$, $tmp2 = ks.tb[tm].temp?$, $val = EMM(\texttt{fetch}\ (m), es).val$, and $v = ks.pm[pa]$.

7.3 Level$_4$ Implements Level$_3$

We can see that there is a very direct mapping from Level$_4$ up to Level$_3$ and no real change in functionality in the operations. We have merely reorganized the state and partitioned the functionality between the kernel and EMM. Consequently, the correctness theorem at this level does assert the equality of the final states without having to flush the cache.

Theorem 25 Level$_4$ Implements Level$_3$.
For all $ins \in \mathcal{I}^*$, $\langle l,\ s \rangle \in \langle \mathcal{L},\ \mathcal{S}_4 \rangle$:

$$inv_4(s) \rightarrow LS_{4 \rightarrow 3}\left(Int_4(ins, \langle l,\ s \rangle)\right) = Int_3\left(ins,\ LS_{4 \rightarrow 3}\left(\langle l,\ s \rangle\right)\right).$$

From this and Theorem 21, we easily see that:

Theorem 26 Level$_4$ Implements Level$_0$.
For all $ins \in \mathcal{I}^*$, $\langle l,\ s \rangle \in \langle \mathcal{L},\ \mathcal{S}_4 \rangle$:

$$inv_4(s) \rightarrow LS_{4 \rightarrow 0}\left(Int_4(ins, \langle l,\ s \rangle)\right) = Int_0\left(ins,\ LS_{4 \rightarrow 0}\left(\langle l,\ s \rangle\right)\right).$$

where $LS_{4 \rightarrow 0}$ is simply the composition of $LS_{4 \rightarrow 3}$ with $LS_{3 \rightarrow 0}$.

Theorem 26 establishes that our lowest level model is a faithful implementation of our abstract model.

8 Conclusions

We have modeled and formally analyzed a simple external memory manager system loosely based on the memory management strategies of Mach [2]. The modeling was carried out via a series of refinements from a very abstract model to a substantially more complex concrete model. The abstract model conveys an idealized view of memory management in which all functions are provided by a monolithic kernel/EMM and direct access by a user process to (disk) memory is implemented. At our most concrete level, this abstraction has been implemented via a demand paging system in which bounded RAM is utilized as a cache, objects are paged in as needed, and paged-out to free RAM locations when required. Between the highest and lowest level abstractions are several intermediate layers providing incremental steps from abstract to concrete.

We have stated theorems that describe formally the relationships among these models and have proven these theorems for a representative "slice" of the functionality of the system. The result is a (partially) verified stack of progressively more realistic and complex systems satisfying an *implements* relation with a simple high-level design.

We believe that this strategy of incremental refinement and proof is a powerful one. It provides a means of controlling complexity while preserving rigor during the implementation process. That is, following a systematic stepwise refinement process in developing our implementation, we were able to concentrate on particular implementation issues in isolation. A single leap from abstract to concrete would have been much less manageable, both intellectually and as a verification target.

Because of the small size of our study, we focused on modeling and analysis of *selected* aspects of the EMM system problem and ignored others. Several potential extensions to this work were described Section 1. We believe that it would be valuable to carry out these extensions, but do not think that any of our omissions detract from the value of this work. However, one of our goals was to investigate approaches toward modeling and analysis of client/server systems, as exemplified by a client/kernel/EMM system. This portion of the study was only partially successful because we did not have time to study the asynchronous level that really exposes many of the behaviors characteristic of realistic client/server systems.

However, we believe that our approach of top-down refinement from a monolithic system into a collection of co-operating components is a promising one. Moreover, we strongly endorse the notion that the particular decomposition of the functionality of a system among modules is an implementation strategy that should be largely invisible to the user.

References

1. W.R. Bevier, W.A. Hunt, Jr., J S. Moore, and W.D. Young. An approach to systems verification. *Journal of Automated Reasoning*, 5(4):411–428, December 1989.
2. J. Boykin, D. Kirschen, A. Langerman, and S. LoVerso. *Programming under Mach*. Addison Wesley Unix and Open Series System, Reading, Mass., 1993.
3. B. Brock, M. Kaufmann and J Strother Moore. ACL2 theorems about commercial microprocessors, in M. Srivas and A. Camilleri, eds., *Proceedings of Formal Methods in Computer-Aided Design (FMCAD '96)*, Springer-Verlag, pp. 275-293, 1996.
4. R.S. Boyer and J S. Moore. *A Computational Logic Handbook*. Academic Press, Boston, 1988.
5. J. R. Burch and D. L. Dill. Automatic verification of pipelined microprocessor control, in D. Dill, ed., *Computer Aided Verification*, Lecture Notes in Computer Science 818, Springer Verlag, 1994, page 68-80.
6. M. Kaufmann and J Moore. An industrial strength theorem prover for a logic based on Common Lisp, to appear in *IEEE Transactions on Software Engineering*, 1997. This is a revised version of "ACL2: An industrial strength version of Nqthm," which appeared in *Proceedings of the Eleventh Annual Conference on Computer Assurance*, IEEE Computer Society Press, June, 1996, pp 23-34.
7. W.D. Young and W.R. Bevier. Mathematical modeling and analysis of an external memory manager. CLI Technical Report 105, Computational Logic, Inc., September, 1995.

Automatic Translation of VDM-SL Specifications into Gofer

Paul Mukherjee

School of Computer Studies, University of Leeds, Leeds LS2 9JT, UK.

Abstract. Interest in the use of functional languages for prototyping and animating formal specifications has decreased recently, as some of the limitations of traditional approaches have become apparent, in comparison to direct execution of the specification. In this paper we attempt to inject new life into this debate by describing how programs in a modern functional language may be automatically generated from formal specifications. We demonstrate how drawbacks of previous approaches are solved, and illustrate the success of the approach by describing errors found in published specifications.

1   Introduction

Formal methods of system specification and development are state of the art techniques that allow the construction of reliable computer systems. However recent interest has focused on the problem of errors in the initial specification that are not identified until an implementation is obtained and executed. As the initial specification will be based on informal user requirements, it is clear that we can not *prove* its correctness, therefore a number of techniques have been proposed which allow us to increase our confidence in the correctness of a specification. These are known as techniques for *validation* of the specification.

A number of validation techniques exist [15] such as syntax and type checking of specifications, and proof of validation conjectures [3]. A popular approach is to obtain an executable specification by transforming the original specification, since in general specifications are not executable [9, 8]. Initially this approach was based on mapping the specification into a functional or logic programming language [5, 6], but more recently dedicated tools for the execution of specifications have become available [7, 17], and have proved more effective than the previous approach.

This is because the previous approach suffered from a number of severe limitations such as weak support for abstract datatypes provided by the specification language, limited coverage of the specification language, and manual, heuristic-based generation of programs from specifications.

In this paper we describe automatic generation of programs in the functional language Gofer [11] from formal specifications written in VDM-SL [19]. The tool which performs this translation supports most of the VDM-SL language (including notions of looseness) and provides full support for most of the data types available in VDM-SL. We describe the strategy for translation of VDM-SL into Gofer, highlighting drawbacks and any differences in semantics as we proceed. We illustrate the success of this approach by giving examples of errors found by the tool in publically-available specifications, previously subjected to other forms of validation analysis. Our approach is based on naive translation, that is, it is syntax directed. The basis of the tool is the VDM-SL parser produced by the Technical University of Braunschweig[1]. Our objective is to discover the limitations, both theoretical and practical, of the naive translation approach, based on a modern functional programming language.

Thus this paper is organized as follows: in the next section we briefly describe the Gofer language; we then describe the strategy we employ for translation of VDM-SL specifications into Gofer programs, starting by looking at VDM-SL's type system, then functions and expressions, and finally operations and statements. We describe results to date, emphasising cases where errors were found in specifications. Following this we discuss problems that arise, and (as this is ongoing work) future work. Finally we draw some conclusions. Throughout the paper we assume familiarity with VDM-SL, but assume no knowledge of Gofer. Wherever possible examples are drawn from the specification of the Single Transferable Vote algorithm [16] to ensure continuity, though knowledge of this algorithm is not necessary to understand the current work.

2   The Gofer programming language

Gofer is a pure functional programming language. That is, it contains no state variables, has no concept of assignment, and is side-effect free. Therefore it exhibits referential transparency: the ability to replace any expression with its value without changing the value of the overall expression. This is a highly desirable property as it greatly eases reasoning and understanding of programs. In this section we give a description of the language which is sufficient to understand the following sections.

2.1   Expressions and Types

Gofer employs lazy (non-strict) evaluation for its expressions; that is, expressions are only evaluated when no other reduction is possible, and therefore undefinedness does not necessarily propagate through expressions. Expressions in gofer are strongly typed, and all types can be statically inferred. Expressions and functions may be polymorphic for instance

```
id :: a -> a
id x = x
```

(Here x is the argument pattern and a is a type variable.) Primitive types available are Int, Float, Bool and Char. Types are syntactically distinguished from other objects by having capitalized names.

Gofer allows lambda expressions, which we make extensive use of. So for instance the expression \x -> x+1 represents the expression $\lambda x \cdot x + 1$.

---

[1] Obtainable from ftp://ftp.ips.cs.tu-bs.de/ftp/pub/local/sw/

2.2 Overloading

Symbols and functions may be overloaded in Gofer, though it must be possible to resolve applications of overloaded operators statically. We can also define overloaded functions and values ourselves using Gofer's *class* system. A class is a collection of types which share an overloaded function. Elements of a class are called *instances*. For example, suppose we wish to define an overloaded infix operator `divide` such that x `divide` y yields the `Float` quotient of x and y whether x and y are `Int`s or `Float`s etc. (We can use a function f as an infix operator by writing it 'f'.)

```
class Divclass a b where
    divide :: a -> b -> Float
```

This says that each instance of `Divclass` is a pair of types (a,b), and we are defining an overloaded function `divide` over this class. We then declare instances of this class, of which in this case there are four (a or b may be `Int` or `Float`). For example

```
instance Divclass Int Float where
    x 'divide' y = (fromInteger x) / y
```

where `fromInteger` maps an `Int` to its corresponding `Float`.

Classes are crucial to our translation strategy as VDM-SL employs overloading extensively, ranging from equality testing to apply expressions (function, map and sequence application share the same syntax).

2.3 Lists

A feature of Gofer is its support for list processing; the type of lists containing elements of type T is written [T]. Another notable aspect of lists in Gofer is the support for list comprehensions. That is, expressions of the form

$$[f(x_1, \ldots, x_n) \mid x_1 \leftarrow l_1, \ldots, x_n \leftarrow l_n, p(x_1, \ldots, x_n)]$$

where $x_1, \ldots, x_n$ are patterns, $l_1, \ldots, l_n$ are list expressions and p is a predicate. For instance, the list comprehension [x * x | x <- [1..10], even x] represents the list [4, 16, 36, 64, 100]. List comprehensions are convenient as they allow direct translation of similar expressions in VDM-SL.

2.4 Type Constructors and Unions

As well as providing a range of built-in types, Gofer provides a mechanism for user-defined types. Suppose we want to define a type `Candidate_names` with 2 elements (known as *constructors*) `Adam` and `Bill`. We have

```
data Candidate_names = Adam | Bill
```

We can associate values with constructors for instance

```
data Numtype = I of Int | R of Float
```

which represents values such as I 1, R 1.0 etc. We can even make polymorphic types e.g.

```
data UnionT a b = In1 of a | In2 of b
```

2.5 Monads

In pure functional languages such as Gofer, there is no such thing as reference or state variables. Therefore, recent interest has centred on ways of simulating state-like variables in pure functional languages, to allow state-oriented applications (e.g. GUIs) to be implemented, whilst retaining referential transparency. The most popular and successful of these approaches is that of monads [21]. In this section we describe this approach with a view to using monads to represent VDM-SL state variables.

The approach we use, initially described in [13] is an extension of the original monad idea (which itself was aimed directly at functional treatment of I/O) called *state transformers*. Our description here is based on that source. The key notion is that a value of type ST s a is a computation which transforms a state indexed by type s and delivers a value of type a. (Here the type ST stands for state transformer.) That is, ST is a polymorphic type with two parameters: the first refers to the state thread that we will transform, and the second refers to the type of value delivered by the transformation.

State transformers may have inputs in addition to the initial state, giving rise to state transformers with functional types. For instance, the trivial state transformer that delivers its argument without changing the state is:

```
returnST :: a -> ST s a
```

We can sequentially compose two state transformers using the function thenST:

```
thenST:: ST s a -> (a -> ST s b) -> ST s b
```

So the expression s1 'thenST' s2 performs s1 then uses its output state and delivered value as input to s2. (A specialized version of this function is thenST_ where a is the type () i.e. the unit type.) As a simple example, the state trans-former while shown below, repeatedly applies a state transformation s as long as a boolean-delivering state transformer yields the value True.

```
while :: ST s Bool -> ST s () -> ST s ()
while e s = e 'thenST' (\b -> if b
                               then (s 'thenST_' (while e s))
                               else returnST())
```

For our purposes, a state is just a finite mapping from references to values. We may think of a reference as the name of an updatable location in the state that can store a value. In a state indexed by type s, we represent a reference holding values of type a by the primitive type MutVar s a. Then we have a number of primitive transformers on this type: newVar takes an initial value and delivers a reference to it newVar :: a -> ST s (MutVar s a); readVar takes a reference and delivers the value currently stored in it readVar :: MutVar s a -> ST s a;

`writeVar` takes a reference and a new value, and transforms the state so that the given reference stores the new value `writeVar :: MutVar s a -> a -> ST s ()`.

As we shall see later, monads provide a convenient and powerful way of representing VDM-SL state variables, giving rise to a concise encoding of VDM-SL operations as Gofer functions over monadic state variables. Note that there is an important distinction between the state transformers defined above, and those defined in VDM-SL: the ones defined above *all* preserve referential transparency whereas those in VDM-SL need not. This is a key aspect of the rationale behind the design of monads.

2.6 Summary

As we have seen, Gofer contains a number of sophisticated features, which make it suitable for prototyping and animating VDM-SL Specifications. In particular, the presence of classes and user-defined overloading allows the problems of previous approaches to be overcome. Gofer's monads allow a clean representation of VDM-SL's state, and its type system shares other similarities with that of VDM-SL. The use of lazy evaluation allows more subtle techniques such as infinite precision arithmetic; this is discussed further in section 7.

3 Implementation of the VDM-SL type system

In this and the following two sections, we describe our strategy for translating VDM-SL into Gofer. In particular, we concentrate on aspects of VDM-SL that have proved difficult to translate in the past, and also aspects affected by the desire to perform the translation automatically.

Gofer is a strongly-typed functional language, and therefore provides a rich type system in which we may embed the type system of VDM-SL. However while the type system of VDM-SL is intended to describe arbitrary systems, the type system of Gofer is designed to perform computation. Therefore there are limitations to the extent to which we may map VDM-SL's type system into that of Gofer. In this section we describe this mapping, its limitations, and consider some of the consequences of these limitations. We begin by considering the basic types of VDM-SL.

3.1 Basic Types

Gofer's basic types correspond closely to the basic types of VDM-SL. Thus VDM-SL's bool type maps to Gofer's `Bool` type and VDM-SL's char type maps to Gofer's `Char` type. VDM-SL's quote type maps to Gofer's data type of constructors. VDM-SL's numeric types present more of a challenge as in Gofer we have only `Int` and `Float`. Clearly we will map nat, nat1 and int to `Int`, and real and rat to `Float`. The problem of course, is that in VDM-SL all the numeric types are essentially considered as sub-types of real, so we can use values from the various types within a given expression and still have a well-defined type for the expression. In Gofer (in line with most languages), `Int` and `Float` are considered to be distinct types, and there is no automatic type coercion. In practice this means that we need to be careful about representing constants (for instance, writing 0.0 rather than 0 in a specification if we are performing a real calculation rather than an integer one).

Token types in VDM-SL present an entirely different problem, as a token type declaration says that we are defining a type on which the only operation we will perform is equality. However, for a basic type in Gofer, we need to be able to enumerate the members of a type in order to be able to *define* equality. Thus we cannot directly translate token types, but require them to be endowed with more structure in the specification.

3.2 Compound Types

We use Gofer's lists to implement VDM-SL's sets, sequences and maps. For instance, the map $\{2 \mapsto' b', 3 \mapsto' c'\}$ would be represented in Gofer as `Map [(2 ,'b'),(3 ,'c')]`.

Record types in VDM-SL have no direct counterpart in Gofer, so we simulate their effect using data type constructors and tuples. Therefore we need to define the corresponding selector functions, as well as mk- functions and is- functions. Consider the following definition of a record type:

$$Score :: name : Candidate\text{-}names$$
$$count : \mathbb{R}$$

In Gofer, this would be translated to

```
data Score = Score (Candidate_names,Float )
```

and we would need to define two corresponding selector functions:

```
sel_name (Score (x,_)) = x
sel_count (Score (_,x)) = x
```

A drawback of this approach is that any other record types we define must have different field names to this one. This is because otherwise the field selector functions would be overloaded, which the Gofer compiler would not be able to resolve. A possible solution to this would be to use a Gofer class definition to resolve the overloading, but this would not be possible without performing more sophisticated type analysis in the translator (which is beyond the remit of our naive translator). Similarly we can not prefix selector functions with the type name (e.g. `sel_Score_name`) as then to translate an expression $x.name$, we would need to compute the unique name of the type of x.

Our approach to union types is also limited. There is no direct counterpart to a VDM-SL type definition of the form $numtype = \mathbb{Z} \mid \mathbb{R}$. In general, we could define a type `data Numtype = I of Int | R of Float` and translate values of $numtype$ accordingly e.g. a function return $n : numtype$ would be translated to a function returning `I n` or `R n` depending on the type of `n`. However this would mean that the translator be able to compute the type of a given VDM-SL expression, which in general is not computable, and in any case is certainly beyond the capabilities of a naive translator such as this.

However we are able to translate unions of quote types. For instance, the type

$$Candidate\text{-}names = \text{ADAM} \mid \text{BILL} \mid \text{CHARLIE}$$

would be translated to

```
data Candidate_names = Adam  | Bill  | Charlie
```

Nonetheless, our inability to translate arbitrary unions means that, for instance, we cannot translate BNF-style grammars which make heavy use of union types. Note that other approachs [18, 5] face similar difficulties or ignore the issue, but the IFAD VDM-SL Toolbox has no such problems.

One of the major flaws of the approach in [18] is that compound values whose components are non-basic can not be tested for equality. That is a test such as $\{\{1,2,3\},\{1,2\}\} = \{\{1,2,3,4\}\}$ could not be made in the SML code generated by the translator. This is because equality testing in SML may not be extended to user-defined types. However in Gofer, we may extend equality testing using Gofer's class-based system of overloading. Thus, for instance, to define equality on sets, we assert that the type of sets is an instance of the class of equality types, and define our equality operation:

```
instance Eq a => Eq (Set a) where
Set xs == Set ys  =  xs 'subset' ys  &&  ys 'subset' xs
                     where xs 'subset' ys =
                                   all  ('elem' ys) xs
```

This is an example of a conditional class (the => in the instance): we can only define equality over sets of type a if equality is defined over type a itself.

4 Functions and Expressions

As functions and expressions do not involve state, their interpretation in Gofer is relatively straightforward.

4.1 Functions

In general, functions are interpreted as Gofer functions. However special functions such as polymorphic functions need more care. Also, of course arbitrary functions specified by pre- and post-condition can not be directly interpreted (though in some cases we can translate the pre- and post-conditions into Gofer predicates).

Normal explicit functions are directly translated into Gofer functions. For instance the function

$$calc\text{-}non\text{-}transf\text{-}value : \mathbb{R} \times Value \rightarrow Value$$

$$calc\text{-}non\text{-}transf\text{-}value\,(surplus, total\text{-}value) \triangleq$$
$$\quad \text{if } surplus > total\text{-}value \text{ then } surplus - total\text{-}value \text{ else } 0.0$$

would be translated to:

```
calc_non_transf_value ::(Float , Value) -> Value
calc_non_transf_value (surplus,total_value) =
if surplus > total_value then surplus - total_value
else 0.0
```

An implicit function would have its pre- and post-conditions translated into Gofer predicates (provided the bodies of the conditions may be translated). Thus

$$sqrt\,(x:\mathbb{R})\ s:Realp$$
$$\text{pre}\ \ x \geq 0.0$$
$$\text{post}\ s \geq 0.0 \wedge s \uparrow 2 = x$$

would be translated as

```
pre_sqrt::(Float ) -> Bool
pre_sqrt(x) = (x  >= 0.0 )
post_sqrt::(Float ,Realp) -> Bool
post_sqrt(x,s) = ((s  >= 0.0 ) && ((s  ^ 2 ) == x ))
```

4.2 Automatically generated functions

A number of functions are automatically generated by a specification, that is, is-functions and type constructor functions. The precise nature of these functions is specification dependent, and therefore some care needs to be taken in their interpretation in Gofer.

We can divide is- functions into those which are applied to VDM-SL's basic types, and those which are defined for user-defined record types. Considering the former category first, a function is-$T(x)$ where T is a basic type, is defined for all expressions x in the VDM type universe. Thus is-T is an overloaded function with type $t \to \mathbb{B}$, where t is any type in the VDM type universe. This is interpreted in Gofer by defining a class **VDMtypes**, representing all of the basic types in VDM-SL, all user-defined types, and all compound types built using these types. Then we define is-T as an overloaded function of this class. For instance, we have

```
class VDMtypes a where
is_Bool   :: a -> Bool
is_Bool   x = False
. . .
instance VDMtypes Bool where
is_Bool   x = True

instance VDMtypes a => VDMtypes (Set a)

    . . .
```

Thus we define **is_Bool** for every type in the class **VDMtypes** and by default it returns false for every argument. However for the particular instance of the type **Bool**, **is_Bool** returns the value true. User-defined types are then instantiated as VDMtypes, and therefore is_Bool will be well-defined (and false) for all such types.

For a user-defined record type R, the interpretation of is-R is similar. We define a class C_R for the type, and define an overloaded function over this class is_R in the above manner. Then instances of this class are given for all types in the class VDMtypes. Note that as we need to know all of the record types defined in the specification to list all of these instances, this interpretation cannot be performed inline, but must be performed after a full pass through the specification.

Type constructor functions (mk-) functions may be interpreted easily: for each record type defined in the specification, we define a mk- function. So for instance, given the type definition

$$Score :: name : Candidate\text{-}names$$
$$count : \mathbb{R}$$

as well as the corresponding Gofer type definition, we would have the following function definition:

```
mk_Score (x0,x1) = Score (x0,x1)
```

4.3 Expressions

Most expressions in VDM-SL may be translated into corresponding Gofer expressions in the expected manner. However a few expressions have non-trivial translations, and are therefore worthy of further study.

In line with the executable subset of VDM-SL [12] used in the IFAD VDM-SL Toolbox [7], expressions based around searching types, such as quantification over types, and let ...be st expressions over types may not be translated. However there is no problem if we are able to use finite sets instead of types in such cases.

Expressions such as set comprehensions may be implemented directly in Gofer using list comprehensions. (In [16] such expressions were formulated using the list functionals map, filter and concat, which though functionally equivalent, gave a less clear correspondence than the use of list comprehensions.) For instance the VDM-SL expression

$$\{cand.cname \mid cand \in s.elected \cup s.excluded \cup s.continuing\}$$

would be interpreted as

```
Set [ sel_cname(cand ) |
cand <- set_to_list (sel_elected(s )) 'union'
                     (sel_excluded(s ))'union'
                     (sel_continuing(s )) ]
```

VDM-SL's let expressions may be directly implemented using Gofer's let expression. However there is no direct counterpart in Gofer to VDM-SL's let be expression. Therefore we implement them using lambda expressions. The expression let $x \in s$ be st $p(x)$ in $E(x)$ would be translated to the Gofer expression

```
(\x -> E x)(choose s (\x -> p x))
```

where **choose** is an auxiliary function which takes a set and a predicate, and returns an arbitrary member of the set satisfying the predicate.

Apply expressions cause more difficulty due to overloading: function application, map application and sequence indexing all share the same syntax $e(x)$. In a naive translation, it is not normally possible to compute which kind of application is involved. We resolve this by defining a class of types over which apply expressions may be used, then defining an overloaded function to perform applications. We call this class **Apply_type**, and define an overloaded function **apply** over this class.

```
class Apply_type a b c where
apply :: a -> b -> c
```

Then we define instances of **Apply_type** for functions, maps and sequences. For instance

```
fun_apply :: (a->b) -> a -> b
fun_apply f x = f x

instance Apply_type (a->b) a b where
apply = fun_apply
```

The last kind of expression that we consider are record modifiers (μ-expressions). It suffices to explain how modification of one field in a record is dealt with, as multiple modifications are interpreted as a sequence of single modifications by the translator.

As one would expect, we use a function to represent μ expressions. If we wish to interpret an expression $\mu\,(r, f \mapsto f')$ in Gofer, we do not know *a priori* how to update r, since in our Gofer interpretation field tags have no semantic value. Therefore we allocate a number to each field, then use this field number to locate (during translation) which component in the tuple representing r is to be replaced.

Clearly this means that our function representing μ will be overloaded, as the types of the field to be updated may vary. Therefore we define a class for all record types, and define the overloaded function **mu** over this class.

```
class Record_types a b where
mu :: (a,Int,b) -> a
```

Thus in **mu(r,i,f)**, the component i represents the position number of field **f** in the record **r**. As we define each record type, we declare it to be an instance of this class, and define mu for each field in the record type. For instance, with the record type *Score* defined in section 3.2 we would have the following declaration:

```
instance Record_types Score Float  where
mu (Score (x0,x1), 2, x') = Score (x0,x')
instance Record_types Score Candidate_names where
mu (Score (x0,x1), 1, x') = Score (x',x1)
```

Finally, we note that most of the patterns available in VDM-SL are also available in Gofer. However loose patterns (i.e. set union patterns and sequence concatenation patterns) have no counterpart in Gofer, and in our naive translation system, there is no obvious equivalent Gofer formulation. Therefore we are unable to interpret such patterns. This contrasts with the IFAD VDM-SL Toolbox where loose patterns may be executed.

5 Implementation of operations and statements

A typical VDM-SL specification consists of a collection of function and value definitions, together with a state and the operations that may be performed on this state. Previous attempts at animating VDM-SL specifications in functional (style) languages have focused on Standard ML (SML) [14], as the presence of reference variables in that language provides a natural way of representing the state. (However the presence of such variables makes SML an impure language from a functional point of view, as referential transparency is lost.)

In this section we describe how we may use monads in Gofer to represent VDM-SL state variables, and how VDM-SL operations and statements may be automatically translated into Gofer to utilize this representation.

5.1 Monadic Representation of State

We represent VDM-SL state variables using Gofer references, using the initialization predicate from the state definition to supply the initial values for the references, or by using dummy values if no initialization predicate is given. (Note it is not always possible to do this automatically.) For instance, given the following state definition:

```
state St of
    stages : Stage*
    continuing : Candidate-set
    excluded : Candidate-set
    elected : Candidate-set
end
```

We would start a state-based computation with the following initialization:

```
newVar (List []) 'thenST' \stages ->
newVar (Set [])  'thenST' \continuing ->
newVar (Set [])  'thenST' \excluded ->
newVar (Set [])  'thenST' \elected -> ...
```

So the expression evaluated at ... will have the references **elected**, **excluded**, **continuing** etc in scope.

5.2 Statements

Having constructed a monadic model of the state, we interpret VDM-SL statements as Gofer state transformers. The correspondence is the obvious one and proceeds in a straightforward manner, but it is useful to see a few examples to demonstrate the idea. The general strategy is that for each statement, we dereference any state variables and local variables referred to in that statement, then transform the state. Dereferencing is performed using Gofer's primitive function **readVar**.

The most simple statement in VDM-SL is the assignment statement. The function **assign** used below, writes the value represented by its second argument to the reference represented by its first argument. So the simple assignment

$$elected := elected \cup continuing$$

would be translated to the Gofer expression

```
readVar continuing 'thenST' \continuing_val ->
readVar elected 'thenST' \elected_val ->
assign elected (elected_val 'union' continuing_val )
```

Note here that despite our naive translation, only state variables referred to on the right-hand side of the assignment are dereferenced.

The sequential composition of two statements is interpreted as the two state transformers composed using **thenST_**. Therefore we require that the first component returns no value. This is different from the semantics of VDM-SL, where in a composition, if the first component returns a value, then that terminates the composition and the result of the composition is this value. Thus the simple composition

$$(excluded := excluded \setminus continuing;$$
$$elected := elected \cup continuing)$$

is translated to

```
(readVar continuing 'thenST' \continuing_val ->
readVar excluded 'thenST' \excluded_val ->
assign excluded (excluded_val 'diff' continuing_val ))
  'thenST_'
(readVar continuing 'thenST' \continuing_val ->
readVar elected 'thenST' \elected_val ->
assign elected (elected_val 'union' continuing_val ))
```

Note that we dereference the state for each component; this is because state variables dereferenced in the first component will not be in scope in the second component; even if they were, the action of the first component might render those values obsolete.

Loops are implemented in the usual way using recursive state transformers. For instance, for *while* loops we use the state transformer described in section 2.5. (In fact, the function is slightly more complex than this due to our treatment of exceptions described below.) So for instance, in the context of the state definition given earlier, the simple loop

$$\text{while } i \neq \text{len } sub\text{-}parcels$$
$$\text{do } i := i + 1$$

would be translated to

```
while (returnST(i  /= (len sub_parcels ))) (assign i (i +1 ))
```

5.3   Operations

Since Gofer is a pure functional language, VDM-SL operations are implemented using functions over monadic state variables. The state components, as defined by the VDM-SL state definition, are encoded as a tuple which is then passed as the first argument to the function. Any operation arguments are passed as later arguments to the function. So the operation

$$PROCESS\text{-}SUB\text{-}PARCELS : Candidate \times Sub\text{-}parcel^* \xrightarrow{o} ()$$

$$PROCESS\text{-}SUB\text{-}PARCELS \, (ex\text{-}cand, sub\text{-}parcels) \triangleq$$

$$\ldots$$

would be implemented as a function of type

```
pROCESS_SUB_PARCELS ::
(MutVar s (List Stage), MutVar s (Set Candidate),
MutVar s (Set Candidate), MutVar s (Set Candidate)),
Candidate, (List Sub_parcel)) -> ST s (OpResult e  ())
```

(Note here that capitalized identifiers are reserved for type names in Gofer, hence the lower-case **p**. The type **OpResult e ()** is described below.) Then, a call to this operation

$$PROCESS\text{-}SUB\text{-}PARCELS(excluded\text{-}candidate, sorted\text{-}sub\text{-}parcels)$$

is implemented as a monadic function call:

```
pROCESS_SUB_PARCELS((stages, continuing,excluded,
        elected), excluded_candidate, sorted_sub_parcels))
```

5.4   Exceptions

In order to accommodate exceptions and exception handlers, it is necessary to modify some of our earlier ideas. In particular, we require that functions which represent VDM-SL statements return values of type **OpResult**, where

```
data OpResult a b = Error a | Ok b
```

Ok x represents successful termination returning the value **x**, and **Error y** represents exceptional termination with data packet **y**.

Sequential composition of two statements is then performed by the function **opcompr** (and its companion **opcomp**, used when the first statement does not return a value). If the first statement terminates successfully, the second is executed normally. Otherwise the second statement is ignored and the exception packet returned by the first statement is the result of the composite statement.

```
opcompr :: ST s (OpResult a b) -> (b -> ST s (OpResult a c))
    -> ST s (OpResult a c)
s1 'opcompr' s2 = s1 'thenST' \s1_res -> case s1_res of
                                Error e ->  returnST (Error e)
                                Ok v -> s2(v)
```

To raise an exception, we return a value **Error x**. Thus the statement exit 3 would be implemented as **returnST (Error 3)**. More complex exception handling mechanisms are captured in a similar manner.

5.5 Example

In order to see how all of the components in the translation of operations fit together, we now describe the translation of a complete operation. In fact, translation of this operation led to the discovery of an error in the original specification, purely due to Gofer's strong type system.

The operation *CHOOSE-SURPLUS-TO-TRANSFER* takes no arguments and returns a value of type *Candidate-names*. It demonstrates the use of local state variables, conditional statements, translation of patterns, and operation calls.

$CHOOSE\text{-}SURPLUS\text{-}TO\text{-}TRANSFER : () \xrightarrow{o} Candidate\text{-}names$

$CHOOSE\text{-}SURPLUS\text{-}TO\text{-}TRANSFER () \triangleq$
  (dcl *leaders* : *Candidate-names*-set :=
                  {*score.name* | *score* ∈ elems hd *stages* ·
                        score.count = hd hd *stages.count*};
    if card *leaders* = 1 then let {*n*} = *leaders* in return *n*
    else if ∃ *n* ∈ *leaders* · *greatest-value-at-earliest-stage*(*n*, *stages*)
        then return ι *name* ∈ *leaders* ·
                        greatest-value-at-earliest-stage(*name*, *stages*)
        else *RANDOM-ELEMENT*(*leaders*))
  pre *stages* ≠ []

The translated function takes the tuple of monadic state variables, and transforms them in the manner described by the specification, delivering a value of type **Candidate_names**. A local state variable is created using the primitive **newVar** for *leaders*. State variables are dereferenced whenever their values are referred to in the following expression or statement. The complete translation is given in figure 1. Note that in the call to the function **rANDOM_ELEMENT**, state variables are passed by reference, whereas operation arguments are passed by value. This is because in VDM-SL, state is global and persists throughout all operations, and parameter passing is by value. Another relevant observation is that the pre-condition of the operation is a predicate over values, rather than state variables, as there is no concept of state in the pre-condition. From the translation we can see that although the Gofer code is less readable than the VDM-SL, the correspondence between the two is clear.

```
cHOOSE_SURPLUS_TO_TRANSFER ::
  (MutVar s (List Stage), MutVar s (Set Candidate),
   MutVar s (Set Candidate), MutVar s (Set Candidate)) ->
   ST s (OpResult e Candidate_names)
cHOOSE_SURPLUS_TO_TRANSFER((stages,continuing,excluded,elected)) =
  (readVar stages 'thenST' \stages_val ->
   newVar (Set [ sel_name score |
                 score <- set_to_list (elems (hd stages_val)),
                 ((sel_count score) ==
                             (sel_count(hd (hd stages_val))))])
  'thenST' \leaders ->
  (readVar leaders 'thenST' \leaders_val ->
  if (card leaders_val) == 1
  then readVar leaders 'thenST' \leaders_val ->
       let { Set [n] = leaders_val }
       in  returnST(Ok n)
  else readVar stages 'thenST' \stages_val ->
       readVar leaders 'thenST' \leaders_val ->
       (if exists (\n -> (apply (greatest_value_at_earliest_stage)
                                (n, stages_val))) leaders_val
        then readVar stages 'thenST' \stages_val ->
             readVar leaders 'thenST' \leaders_val ->
             returnST(Ok(iota(\name ->
                           (apply
                            (greatest_value_at_earliest_stage)
                            (name,stages_val ))) leaders_val))
        else rANDOM_ELEMENT((stages,continuing,excluded,elected),
                            leaders_val))))

pre_cHOOSE_SURPLUS_TO_TRANSFER ::
  (List Stage, Set Candidate, Set Candidate, Set Candidate) ->
  Bool
pre_cHOOSE_SURPLUS_TO_TRANSFER(stages_val,continuing_val,
                          excluded_val,elected_val) =
  stages_val  /= List []
```

Fig. 1. Gofer interpretation of *CHOOSE-SURPLUS-TO-TRANSFER*

5.6   Semantic differences

The semantics of the functional portion of VDM-SL coincide fairly closely with
their interpretation in VDM-SL, as one would expect. However, the interpretation of operations within the constraints of a strongly-typed pure functional
language mean that the semantics of some VDM-SL statements differ from their
interpretation in Gofer.

There are two major semantics differences between VDM-SL statements and
their Gofer interpretations. The first concerns conditional statements. In VDM-
SL, the various branches of a conditional statement need not return values of
the same type. So for instance if *expr* then return 3 else return [4] would be a

valid statement in VDM-SL. However in Gofer, as statements are interpreted as functions over a monadic state, the values returned by each branch must be of the same type to ensure that the type of the function is well-defined and statically computable. In particular, this means that if one branch in a conditional statement delivers a value, then we are not allowed to have another branch in which the identity statement is performed. This restriction also applies to the values returned as exception data packets. So the statement if *expr* then exit 3 else exit "error" would generate an error in the Gofer interpreter when translated.

The second difference relates to sequential composition. In VDM-SL, a composite statement $S_1; S_2$ behaves such that if S_1 terminates successfully and delivers a result, then that result is the returned by the composite; if it delivers no result, then S_2 is executed and the result of the composite is the result of S_2. However in Gofer, the composition s1 'opcomp' s2 requires that s1 returns no value (technically, s1 returns the value Ok ()), and the result of the composition is the result of s2. Again, the reason for this is that Gofer's type system needs to compute the unique type of the composite statement. Related to this difference, there is a difference in the semantics of loops; in VDM-SL loop iteration may be terminated prematurely by the body of the loop delivering a value. However for the reason described above, this is not possible in Gofer. Therefore loop bodies in Gofer are not allowed to return values.

Other than these, there are no major differences between the semantics of VDM-SL statements and the semantics of their Gofer interpretation. Of course there are general issues concerning looseness and non-determinism, but we discuss these in section 7.

6 Results To Date

The automatic translation tool described in the previous sections has been tested on a number of specifications drawn from the VDM-SL examples repository[2]. Most of these specifications have previously been subjected to other forms of mechanical analysis, and therefore are unlikely to contain many errors. Also, not all of these specifications could be translated as several contained constructs and expressions outside the subset of VDM-SL that can be automatically translated. Finally, in general the absence of test data means that validation of the specifications was limited to translation into Gofer followed by type checking and dependency analysis by the Gofer interpreter.

Despite these provisos, a number of errors were discovered; some minor, some less so. For instance, consider the extract of the specification of the Message Authentication Algorithm (MAA), used in banking [20], shown in figure 2. Here, on line 5 M''' has type *Number* | *Key*, where *Number* is a sub-type of the naturals, and *Key* consists of sequences of *Numbers*. However on line 8 the function *Z-of-SEG* expects its first argument to have type *Number**, so the argument given need not coincide with the type of the argument expected, giving a type error. This type error was rapidly pinpointed by the Gofer compiler, but

---

[2] http://www.ifad.dk/examples/examples.html

1.0 $MAC : Message\text{-}in\text{-}bits \times Key \rightarrow Number$

.1 $MAC\,(M,K) \stackrel{\triangle}{=}$
.2   let $M' = Pad\text{-}out\text{-}Message(M)$ in
.3   let $M'' = Form\text{-}Message\text{-}into\text{-}blocks(M')$ in
.4   if len $M'' \leq Maximum\text{-}No\text{-}of\text{-}blocks\text{-}for\text{-}MAC$ then $Z(M'',K)$
.5   else let $M''' = [Z(Get\text{-}head\text{-}in\text{-}blocks(M'',$
.6 $Maximum\text{-}No\text{-}of\text{-}blocks\text{-}for\text{-}MAC),K),K] \frown$
.7 $Get\text{-}tail\text{-}in\text{-}blocks(M'', Maximum\text{-}No\text{-}of\text{-}blocks\text{-}for\text{-}MAC)$
.8   in $Z\text{-}of\text{-}SEG(M''', K, Maximum\text{-}No\text{-}of\text{-}blocks\text{-}for\text{-}MAC\text{-}plus\text{-}1)$

Fig. 2. Extract of MAA Specification

eluded detection in the IFAD VDM-SL Toolbox (under **pos** type checking; see below).

More interesting errors were to be found in the specification of an animation tool designed for use in the validation of complex real-time reactive systems using the Timed Reactive Object Model formalism [2]. As well as uncovering a small number of type errors, translation into Gofer revealed that a significant number of operations were translated into non-monadic (i.e. normal) Gofer functions; that is, these operations did not alter the state. Since these operations did not use any looseness, they could safely be converted to VDM-SL functions, thus simplifying the specification without altering its meaning.

As demonstrated above, by translating VDM-SL specifications into Gofer, we are able to highlight a number of errors in the specification that eluded the IFAD VDM-SL Toolbox. This is not a reflection on the Toolbox, but merely indicative of the richness of VDM-SL, and the consequent difficulty in static analysis of the language.

The IFAD VDM-SL Toolbox offers two levels of type checking, corresponding to the two levels of well-formedness defined in the static semantics of VDM-SL [19]:

possible well-formedness – the specification cannot be judged to be ill-formed statically;
definite well-formedness – we can statically confirm that the specification is well-formed.

The errors listed above would undoubtedly have been identified by checking for definite well-formedness (**def** type checking), but probably eluded the test for possible well-formedness (**pos** type checking). In practice most well-formed specifications satisfy (i.e. generate no error messages) **pos** type checking, but fail to satisfy **def** type checking. This is because most specifications exploit constructs which have limitations on their domain of application (such as taking the head of a sequence). Consequently **def** type checking normally results in a stream of error messages relating to well-formedness criteria which can not be deduced statically, but which are trivial to prove. Often some real type errors may be interleaved with these messages, and will therefore be missed or ignored. However this problem is currently being addressed [1].

In this context it is clear that the kind of automated analysis described here does have a role to play, not withstanding the availability of tools such as the IFAD VDM-SL Toolbox. Moreover evidence so far suggests that this role is complementary to that of the other tools.

Finally, as a postscript we observe that using this tool an error was found in the specification of the Single Transferable Vote algorithm [16], a specification which had already been subject to two separate validation exercises [15]. The moral of this is that *no* amount of validation *guarantees* the absence of errors in a specification.

7   Problems and Future work

As the work described here is on-going, it is appropriate to consider some of the drawbacks to this approach, and indicate the direction of future work.

In comparison to the IFAD VDM-SL Toolbox, the approach described here has a number of shortcomings. Principal amongst these is the limited subset of VDM-SL which may be translated into Gofer and executed. Although the IFAD VDM-SL Toolbox also only allows execution of a subset of the language, this subset is a strict superset of that which can be automatically translated into Gofer. There are two reasons for this:

- Limitations of the Gofer language itself: Gofer does not support all VDM-SL expressions, and some that it does not support can not be simulated (e.g. set union patterns), or may only be simulated in a limited fashion (e.g. record types).
- The approach taken is naive: that is, our approach is syntax directed; although we have identified a subset of VDM-SL which can be captured in Gofer with similar semantics, little attempt is made to analyse the semantics of a particular specification (such as building the type universe) before translation into Gofer. This is the reason for our restricted approach to union types.

The first of these reasons might be negated if we chose a different language. However, as we shall see below, our options are limited by our wish to use a lazy functional language. Nonetheless in the future we will consider the use of Haskell [10], a more extensive lazy functional language.

The second reason is a deliberate choice we have made in this work; we could have opted for a more sophisticated approach whereby we perform careful analysis of specifications, and explicitly construct the type universe. However to do this would be to repeat what has already been successfully achieved in the IFAD VDM-SL Toolbox. Our current objective is to discover the limitations of our ability to automatically translate, and then execute, VDM-SL specifications into Gofer.

Our approach also suffers from a number of drawbacks shared by the IFAD VDM-SL Toolbox, such as deterministic (but underdetermined) execution (i.e. non-determinism is resolved algorithmically but in a manner unknown to the user), and limited precision. This latter point is of interest, as our choice of a lazy functional language was motivated by the possibility of performing infinite precision arithmetic [15, 4]. To this end, we have written a package of Gofer functions which perform infinite precision arithmetic, and in the future we plan to incorporate these functions into our translation tool. This will allow more accurate execution of specifications, as well as aiding the generation of test data in numerical applications.

Another future area of work is code generation: it is possible to automatically generate C code from Gofer programs, and therefore we can generate C code from VDM-SL specifications. It will be interesting to compare this to the C++ code generation facility available in the IFAD VDM-SL Toolbox.

8 Conclusions

In this paper we have discussed a method of validating specifications based on automatic generation of programs in the functional language Gofer. Previous experience [15, 16] has highlighted the need for validation, and this conviction has been reaffirmed here, due to the errors found in specifications that had previously been analysed. This would suggest that a variety of validation techniques should be employed in order to minimize the number of errors in a specification.

The original aim of the work described here was to ascertain the extent to which it is possible to automatically translate VDM-SL specifications into Gofer programs using a naive, syntax-directed approach. In this sense the work has been successful, as we have been able to identify a large subset of the executable subset of VDM-SL described in [12] which is amenable to translation. Additionally, we have been able to explain why the complement of these two sets (the area shaded in figure 3) can not be translated (due to the naive approach or inherent limitations of Gofer). The benefit we gain from restricting ourselves to this

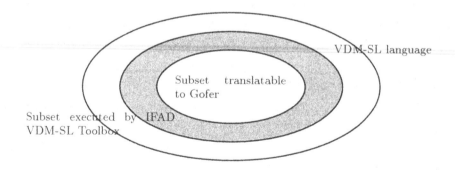

Fig. 3. Subsets of VDM-SL

smaller subset is the strong type-checking provided by Gofer, which led to the discovery of errors in existing specifications described in section 6. As described there, we hope to take this approach further by incorporating infinite precision arithmetic into the translation process. This will provide a greater contrast with the IFAD VDM-SL Toolbox, and other VDM-SL tools, thus leading to a greater variety of tools available for use, in line with our observation above.

References

1. B. K. Aichernig and P. G. Larsen. A Proof Obligation Generator for VDM-SL. Submitted to FME '97, 1997.
2. V.S. Alagar, D. Muthiayen, and R. Achuthan. Animating Real-Time Reactive Systems. In A. Stoyenko, editor, *ICECCS '96*. IEEE Computer Society, 1995.
3. J.C. Bicarregui, J.S. Fitzgerald, P.A. Lindsay, R. Moore, and B. Ritchie. *Proof in VDM: A Practitioner's Guide.* Springer-Verlag, 1994.
4. H. Boehm and R. Cartwright. Exact Real Arithmetic. In D. Turner, editor, *Research Topics in Functional Programming.* Addison-Wesley, 1990.
5. P. Borba and S. Meira. From VDM Specifications to Functional Prototypes. *Journal of Systems and Software*, 21:267–278, 1993.
6. A. J. J. Dick, P. J. Krause, and J. Cozens. Computer Aided Transformation of Z into Prolog. In J. Nicholls, editor, *Z User Workshop.* Springer-Verlag, 1989.
7. R. Elmstrøm, P.G. Larsen, and P.B. Lassen. The IFAD VDM-SL Toolbox: A Practical Approach to Formal Specifications. *ACM Sigplan Notices*, 29(9), 1994.
8. N.E. Fuchs. Specifications are (preferably) executable. *Software Engineering Journal*, September 1992.
9. I.J. Hayes and C.B. Jones. Specifications are not (necessarily) executable. *Software Engineering Journal*, 4(6), 1989.
10. P. Hudak, S.L. Peyton-Jones, and P. L. Wadler. Report on the Functional Programming Language Haskell: A Non-strict Purely Functional Language. *ACM SIGPLAN Notices*, 27(5), March 1992.
11. M. P. Jones. The implementation of the Gofer functional programming system. Technical Report YALE U/DCS/RR-1030, Yale University, 1994.
12. P.G. Larsen and P.B. Lassen. An Executable Subset of Meta-IV with Loose Specification. In Prehn and Toetenel [22].
13. J. Launchbury and S. Peyton-Jones. Lazy Functional State Threads. In *ACM Programming Languages Design and Implementation.* ACM Press, 1993.
14. D. MacQueen, R. Harper, and Milner R. Standard ML. Technical Report ECS-LFCS-86-2, Department of Computer Science, University of Edinburgh, 1986.
15. P. Mukherjee. Computer-aided Validation of Formal Specifications. *Software Engineering Journal*, 10(4):133–140, July 1995.
16. P. Mukherjee and B.A. Wichmann. Formal Specification of the STV Algorithm. In M.G. Hinchey and J. P. Bowen, editors, *Applications of Formal Methods.* Prentice Hall, 1995.
17. D. S. Neilson and I. H. Sørenson. The B-Technologies: a system for computer-aided programming. In *6th Nordic Workshop on Programming Theory*, 1994.
18. G. O' Neill. Automatic Translation of VDM specifications into Standard ML programs. *The Computer Journal*, 35(6), 1992.
19. P. G. Larsen and B. S. Hansen and H. Brunn N. Plat and H. Toetenel and D. J. Andrews and J. Dawes and G. Parkin and others. Information technology — Programming languages, their environments and system software interfaces — Vienna Development Method — Specification Language — Part 1: Base language, December 1996.
20. G. I. Parkin and G. O'Neill. Specification of the MAA standard in VDM. In Prehn and Toetenel [22].
21. S. Peyton-Jones and P. Wadler. Imperative Functional Programming. In *20th ACM Symposium on Principles of Programming Languages.* ACM Press, 1993.
22. S. Prehn and W. J. Toetenel, editors. *VDM'91: Formal Software Development Methods*, number 551 in Lecture Notes in Computer Science. Springer-Verlag, 1991.

Towards an Integrated CASE and Theorem Proving Tool for VDM-SL

Sten Agerholm[1] and Jacob Frost[2]

[1] The Institute of Applied Computer Science (IFAD), Forskerparken 10,
DK-5230 Odense M, Denmark
[2] Department of Information Technology, Technical University of Denmark,
DK-2800 Lyngby, Denmark

Abstract. While CASE tools for formal methods have been relatively successful in industry, the up-take of the theorem proving technology has been quite slow. This suggests that more focus should be put on specification notations and pragmatic features of existing CASE tools in building proof support tools. This paper presents a prototype integrated CASE/TP tool which combines the benefits of a general-purpose theorem prover called Isabelle with those of a commercial CASE tool for the VDM-SL formal specification language—the IFAD VDM-SL Toolbox. The integrated tool supports pragmatic test and rigorous proof at the same time. Moreover, the tool supports proofs in the notation of the CASE tool by handling "difficult" constructs such as patterns and cases expressions in an untraditional way using reversible transformations.

1 Introduction

CASE tools for formal software development support the validation of specifications through static checks and animation. Proofs can add rigor to the software development process and, if supported by proper tools, provide an efficient, supplementary approach to debugging and validating specifications. Traditionally, CASE tools for formal methods and theorem provers have been separate systems, e.g. supporting different notations. While CASE tools support industrially widely-used notations such as Z and VDM-SL, theorem provers have their own notations. This has been a major obstacle to the up-take of theorem proving technology in industry, because a major effort is required to incorporate the technology in already existing work practices with CASE tools. There seems to be an obvious need for integrated CASE and theorem proving systems that allow the user to stay within the notation of the CASE tool while conducting proofs.

Some will argue that industry is not interested in proofs, and claim that there are not many convincing examples of industrial use, thus indicating that an attempt to build an integrated CASE/TP tool is not worthwhile. Today the technology may not be mature to build fully verified (Pentium) chips or (Ariane) rocket software, but industry may wish to use the technology for a small subset of critical components in economic and safety high risk applications, and when mandated by customers or one of the existing (or emerging) standards for safety critical systems.

A large part of industry's reluctance towards theorem proving is also caused by the "take it or leave it" approach that has been taken when presenting the technology to industry. The focus has traditionally been on fully verified systems, and the theorem prover has been the starting point of discussion. We suggest instead taking a more pragmatic and more realistic starting point, such as a CASE tool, and step by step "upgrading" this tool with support for proofs. More light-weight use of theorem provers is to "debug" specifications by proving various consistency conditions, such as type checking conditions in PVS [17] and type checker generated proof obligations in the IFAD VDM-SL Toolbox [4]. More heavy-weight use is, for example, to prove refinements of specifications.

This paper presents the first steps towards building an industrially applicable proof support tool for VDM-SL using this CASE tool oriented approach. Our starting point is the IFAD VDM-SL Toolbox [14, 8, 10], which is a widely used commercial tool environment that supports a range of development activities, including source level execution/debugging and code generation to C++. We try to combine the benefits of this toolset with the benefits of the generic theorem prover Isabelle[3] [15] in a single system. Constructing a theorem prover for VDM-SL from scratch is a far too time consuming task, and systems like Isabelle are designed to allow fast construction of theorem provers for new logics. Our intended use of the combined tool is mainly for proving type consistency proof obligations. Experiments have already shown this to be a powerful approach to debugging specifications [2], and for proving safety properties for operations in state-based systems. However, it will also be possible to prove general correctness requirements of specifications.

The main contribution of the work reported here is the integration of Isabelle with the IFAD Toolbox in a way that gives the user a consistent view on the specification and the proof process. The combined tool provides a way to deal with difficult constructs like patterns and cases expressions that we have not seen in theorem provers before, based on reversible transformations and special-purpose derived proof rules that mimic the original expressions. Moreover, there is little theorem-proving support currently available for VDM-SL, so the present work represents a useful contribution to the literature. The first attempt to build proof support for VDM-SL was in the Mural project [12, 6], but unfortunately, to our knowledge, the Mural tool was based on a platfrom which is no longer supported. The results of the Mural project has been an important starting point for this work, in particular [6]. However, our combined tool extends the subset of VDM-SL supported in Mural with (at least) let expressions, cases expressions, patterns, enumerated expressions, quote types and the character type.

The paper is organized as follows. First we give an overview of our approach in Section 2 and of the Isabelle instantiation in Section 3. Section 4 presents transformations from VDM-SL to the subset formalized in Isabelle. Section 5 describes the generation of axioms for user specifications by considering a small but interesting example. The conclusions are provided in Section 6.

---

[3] A generic theorem prover provides a logical framework in which new logics can be formulated. A new logic is called an instantiation, or an object-logic.

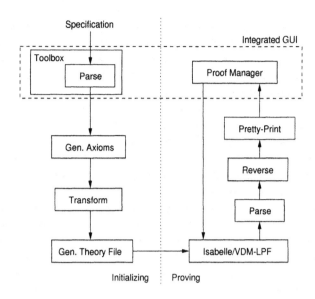

Fig. 1. Overview of system architecture.

2 Overview of Approach

The overall idea is that a user writes a VDM-SL specification using the IFAD VDM-SL Toolbox to syntax check, type check and possibly validate the specification. When the user wants to prove a property or a proof obligation generated by the type checker[4], he can start the Proof Support Tool (PST), generate axioms from a specification and load these into a VDM-SL instantiation of Isabelle. The PST will then provide a Graphical User Interface (GUI) to Isabelle through which proofs can be conducted and managed in a flexible way. This system architecture is illustrated in Fig. 1. We call this a two-layered architecture in the sense that the theorem prover is the bottom layer and the proof support tool and its graphical user interface is the top layer. In between the layers, transformation, parsing and pretty-printing occur.

2.1 Reading of Fig. 1

The left part of Fig. 1 concerns initializing the proof support tool for a specification. The specification is written and then syntax and type checked using the Toolbox. It must be type checked because axioms are generated on basis of this assumption (see Section 5). The resulting abstract syntax tree representation of the specification is communicated to the proof support tool (via a file link). From the syntax tree, axioms are generated as proof rules whose hypotheses are stated

---

[4] Work is currently in progress to extend the Toolbox type checker to generate proof obligations [4].

using abstract syntax for VDM-SL and type judgments. The expression parts of axioms are then transformed to a subset of VDM-SL. This subset does not contain for instance patterns and cases expressions. Finally, the transformed axioms are printed together with signature information for new constants to an Isabelle theory file. This is read into an instantiation of Isabelle, called Isabelle/VDM-LPF, which contains a proof theory for the VDM-SL subset.

The right part of the figure concerns making proofs. Proofs of theorems and proof obligations are conducted by sending commands to Isabelle via the PST graphical user interface. Such commands could tell Isabelle to start a new proof or to apply some tactic in an on-going backwards proof. Proof states in backwards proofs are represented as proof rules in Isabelle and the Toolbox parser has been extended to read Isabelle's notation for these. After parsing proof states to abstract syntax, a transformation function is applied, which reintroduces for instance patterns and cases expressions. Finally, a VDM-SL ASCII pretty-printer produces concrete syntax which can be displayed to the user.

2.2 Status of the Current Prototype

The current prototype does not completely integrate the Toolbox and the theorem prover Isabelle, since the proof manager and the graphical user interface have not been implemented. The design of this is still in progress. Important sources of inspiration are the Mural book [12] and a paper by Ross and Lindsay [18] presented at FME'93.

However, the current prototype does provide the bits and pieces to support the integration. One shell script generates and transforms axioms, another parses, reverse transforms and pretty-prints Isabelle proof states. Both the generation of axioms, the transformation and the pretty-printing are specified in VDM-SL itself. The underlying "programs" work by executing specifications using the Toolbox. Proofs are presently conducted by interacting with Isabelle directly, which is feasible since the Isabelle instantiation supports a subset of the ISO standard for VDM-SL ASCII notation.

By exploiting transformations, we are able to treat essentially the full functional subset of VDM-SL. We have not considered, for instance, constructs like let-be-such-that expressions and union patterns, whose underdetermined semantics destroys reflexivity of equality [13]. As in Mural, we can treat state definitions and implicit operations. However, we have not yet considered explicit operations and statements, which form an imperative subset of VDM-SL, but already existing work on formalizing Hoare logic in the HOL theorem prover may be useful [1]. Features of VDM-SL like exception handling have not been considered either. In short, we treat the subset supported in Mural, plus let expressions, cases expressions, patterns, enumerated expression, quote types and the character type.

3 Isabelle and VDM-LPF

The theorem proving component of the proof support tool consists of an instantiation of the generic theorem prover Isabelle [15] with the "Logic of Partial Functions" (LPF) [5, 7]. This instantiation supports a subset of the ISO standard for the VDM-SL ASCII notation by exploiting distinguishing features of Isabelle for defining new logics.

This section gives an overview of the Isabelle based proof component and motivates some of the major decisions behind the current design. The instantiation of Isabelle is presented in more detail in [3]. We first give short introductions to the Isabelle system and LPF.

3.1 Isabelle

Isabelle can be instantiated to support reasoning in a new so-called *object-logic* by extending its *meta-logic* [15]. The language of the meta-logic is typed lambda-calculus. The syntax of an object-logic is implemented by extending this language with new types and constants. The inference rules of an object-logic are implemented by extending the meta-logic with corresponding meta-axioms. Object-level natural deduction proofs can be carried out as meta-level proofs using different forms of resolution to apply rules.

The Isabelle system contains a range of useful features. For example, it provides unknowns, which are essentially free variables that can be instantiated gradually during a proof by higher-order unification. It also provides syntax annotations, syntax declarations and several translation mechanisms that are useful for handling concrete syntax. In addition, it has a tactic language and generic packages to write powerful proof procedures for object logics with little effort.

3.2 LPF

The "Logic of Partial Functions" (LPF) is a well-established basis for reasoning about VDM-SL specifications [11, 12, 6]. Consequently we have chosen to base the theorem prover component of our system on LPF.

LPF is designed specifically to cope with "undefined values" resulting from partiality of functions. Logics such as first-order classical logic are two-valued in the sense that formulas are either true or false. In contrast, LPF is three-valued, allowing formulas to be undefined as well. Because many of the connectives are non-strict, a formula can be defined even though its subformulas are undefined. For example, the formula e1 or e2 is true whenever one of its subformulas e1 or e2 is true. To be false both subformulas must be false. In the remaining situations the disjunction is undefined.

The definition of LPF means that it has many nice properties. For example, both disjunction and conjunction behave symmetrically. In fact, all inference rules valid in LPF are also valid in classical logic. However, the opposite is not true. Most noticeably, the law of the excluded middle e or not e does not hold, due to the third value representing undefinedness.

3.3 VDM-SL Syntax in Isabelle

In order to ensure quick implementation and smooth representation of the VDM-SL syntax in Isabelle, the *higher-order abstract syntax* approach of [16] has been employed to build the instantiation. For instance, this means that object-level variables are identified with meta-level variables, meta-level abstraction is used to represent object-level variable binding, and renaming of and substitution for bound variables is handled by α- and β-conversion in the meta-logic. Meta-level abstraction is only supported for variables, not for patterns like in VDM-SL, and therefore patterns are treated outside the instantiation. Moreover, the transformation of patterns needs information in the abstract syntax tree representation of the Toolbox, and could therefore not be performed in Isabelle.

The point of abstract versus concrete syntax is that the abstract syntax is used internally and constructed with the aim of making reasoning as simple as possible, while the concrete syntax is constructed more with presentation in mind. For instance, the concrete syntax supports universal quantifications and let expressions of the form:

```
forall x:nat, y:nat & x = y
let x=true, y=false in [x,y]
```

Internally, a more unreadable prefix format is used.

The concrete syntax is implemented using Isabelle's syntax declaration and annotation mechanisms which can express an arbitrary context-free priority grammar [15]. In cases where the correspondence is not trivial, the concrete syntax is related to the abstract syntax by using Isabelle's powerful translation mechanisms. For more details see [3].

3.4 Proof Theory

In the work reported here we focus on the ability to do realistic proofs about VDM-SL specifications, not on the theoretical aspects of semantics and proof theory. We have therefore chosen to build on already existing work in this area. In particular, the Mural project invested a lot of effort in the proof theory for VDM-SL. We have exploited this work by copying the large listing of proof rules in the book [6]. This collection contains proof rules for both propositional and predicate LPF as well as a large number of proof rules for theories about products, natural numbers, sequences, sets, maps, booleans, etc. As in many other textbooks on VDM-SL, these rules are formulated as natural deduction rules. This fits well with our choice of Isabelle since Isabelle supports natural deduction particularly well. Implementing the rules as meta-level axioms was straightforward, consisting mostly of changing the syntax.

The proof rules of VDM-SL are stated in a standard way in Isabelle. For example, the proof rule for conjunction introduction, traditionally stated as

P; Q

P and Q

is stated in Isabelle as follows:

```
"[| P; Q |] ==> P and Q"
```

Here, meta-implication ==> is used to represent hypotheses of rules. The notation

```
[| a1; a2; ... ; an |] ==> c
```

abbreviates

```
a1 ==> (a2 ==> ... ==> (an ==> c)...)
```

A proof rule like exists introduction is stated by

```
"[| a:A; P(a) |] ==> exists x:A & P(x)"
```

where β-reduction in the meta-logic is used to substitute the witness a for the bound variable x.

3.5 Proofs and Proof Procedures

Using the VDM-SL instantiation of Isabelle described above we are already able to prove properties of VDM-SL specifications fairly conveniently. The basic resolution tactics of Isabelle allow the rules to be applied in a backwards manner. Moreover, rules can be applied repeatedly, and several rules can be applied at the same time for simple proof search. However, to make the system genuinely useful in practice it is necessary to be able to carry out proofs at a higher level of abstraction.

An Isabelle proof tool which we believe is of great importance for this is a general purpose reasoner for VDM-SL. The main purpose of this is to automatically prove the most basic theorems, allowing the user to concentrate on the hard and interesting parts of proofs. Unfortunately it is not possible to use Isabelle's generic classical reasoner directly for this purpose. The problem is that it requires the logic to be classical, which LPF is not. Instead we have constructed a suitable variant, based on ideas of [7], which is able to automatically prove most of the 120 derived propositional and predicate logic rules listed in [6] (see [3]).

It is also important to be able to reason effectively and conveniently about equality. We are therefore also working on building a simplifier for LPF, based on ideas from Isabelle's powerful generic simplifier.

4 Transformations

VDM-SL was designed for writing large specifications in industry, and this is reflected in both its syntax and data types. On the syntax side, it has constructs such as pattern matching and cases expressions, which are difficult to represent in a theorem prover (see Section 3.3). On the data type side, it has non-disjoint unions and arbitrary-length tuples, which are not nested pairs. Moreover, it has finite maps (and sets and sequences) and record types with a postfix field selection notation. It has universal and existential quantifiers with lists of type and set bindings, which may contain patterns, and it has set, map and sequence comprehensions. Again patterns are supported such that specifications can be written in a compact way.

In other words, VDM-SL is a real specification language with constructs that are designed for actually writing specifications and not for embedding in a theorem prover. This section describes how we treat some of the complex constructs by transforming expressions down to expanded expressions in a subset of the language that can be formalized in Isabelle.

Throughout this section we use a record type R of the following form:

```
R :: a:T1
     b:T2
     c:T3
```

Thus, the record type R has three fields, called a, b and c respectively, which have types T1, T2 and T3. We construct elements of this type by writing mk_R(x,y,z). Note that the order in which the fields appear is important since mk_R(x,y,z).a equals x, while mk_R(x,y,z).c equals z.

4.1 Pattern Matching

We represent pattern matching by transforming patterns to combinations of if and let expressions where a boolean condition for matching is expressed using an existential quantification. The user of the system does not see these expanded forms since the expansion is reversed before showing output from Isabelle to the user (after this has been parsed by the Toolbox parser).

In this section we illustrate how to treat patterns in let, quantified and comprehension expressions. In the presentation, we just use expression templates, but the transformation does work for real specifications, see Section 5.

Let Expressions The VDM-LPF instantiation of Isabelle supports only simple let expressions of the form

```
let x = e1, y = e2[x], z = e3[x,y] in expr
```

where x, y and z are variables. Note that the first variable of the let expression may be used in the second expression, etc.

However, a VDM-SL let expression may contain general patterns in addition to variables. Assuming R is a record with fields a:T1, b:T2 and c:T3, then a let expression may have the form

```
let mk_R(x,-,z) = e1,
    mk_((e),y) = e2
in body
```

Here, x, z and y are pattern variables, - is the don't care pattern and (e) is a value pattern, i.e. the expression e is evaluated. The expression e1 must be a record of type R for the first pattern to match, and for the second pattern to match, e2 must be a tuple with two components where the first component is equal to the value of e. If one of the patterns does not match, then the expression is undefined.

The above expression is transformed to an equivalent expanded expression containing if expressions, existential quantifiers and simple let expressions:

```
let new = e1 in
if (exists x:T1, z:T3, dc:T2 & mk_R(x,dc,z) = new) then
  let x = new.a, z = new.c in
  let new2 = e2 in
  if (exists y:Ty & mk_(e,y) = new2) then
    let y = new2.#2 in body
  else undefined
else undefined
```

This expression lies within Isabelle's subset. The variables new, new2 and dc must be new identifiers generated by the transformation (see Section 5). The & ends a binding list and corresponds to "such that". The selector #2 takes the second component of a tuple. The type information on e.g. y in the second exists is available in the Toolbox abstract syntax tree after type checking. Note that we illustrate the transformation on concrete syntax due to readability, but it is really performed on the abstract syntax tree.

Quantified Expressions Patterns in quantified expressions are represented using an existential quantifier and an implication =>. Consider for example

```
forall mk_(mk_R(x,-,z),(e)) in set s & expr[x,z]
```

which could be generalized to a list of bindings. This is transformed to:

```
forall new in set s &
  (exists x:T1, z:T3, dc:T2 & mk_(mk_R(x,dc,z),e) = new) =>
  let x = new.#1.a, z = new.#1.c in expr[x,z]
```

For existential quantification we must replace implication by conjunction.

Comprehensions Set, map, and sequence comprehensions can all be treated in the same way. For example the set comprehension

```
{expr[x,z] | mk_(mk_R(x,-,z),(e)) in set s & p[x,z]}
```

is transformed to:

```
{let x = new.#1.a, z = new.#1.c in expr[x,z] | new in set s &
  exists
    x:T1, z:T3, dc:T2 & mk_(mk_R(x,dc,z),e) = new and p[x,z]}
```

This is also illustrated in the example in Section 5.

4.2 Cases Expressions

Cases expressions are not supported at all in the instantiation of Isabelle. VDM-SL cases expressions are transformed to certain combinations of if and simple let expressions, in a fairly similar way as let expressions with patterns. However, to the user these combinations appear to be cases expressions since the transformation to expanded expressions is reversed before expressions are displayed. Moreover, there are proof rules which make the if-let combinations appear to be cases expressions.

Consider the following example which uses the same patterns that were also used above:

```
cases expr:
  mk_R(x,-,z) -> e1,
  mk_((e),y) -> e2,
  others -> e3
end
```

This is transformed to the following expanded expression:

```
let new = expr in
if (exists x:T1, z:T3, dc:T2 & mk_R(x,dc,z) = new) then
  let x = new.a, z = new.c in e1
elseif (exists y:Ty & mk_(e,y) = new) then
  let y = new.#2 in e2
else e3
```

A difference between the expanded forms of let and cases expressions is the use of elseifs in expanded cases expressions.

A number of proof rules has been derived to make the expanded forms mimic cases expressions, i.e. these rules can be applied on let-if combinations in such a way that it appears to the user that these are real cases expression (due to reverse transformation):

```
cases_match
  "[| P(e); e:A; e1(e):B |] ==>
   (let x = e in if P(x) then e1(x) else e2(x)) = e1(e)"
cases_not_match
  "[| not P(e); e:A; e2(e):B |] ==>
   (let x = e in if P(x) then e1(x) else e2(x)) =
   (let x = e in e2(x))"
cases_form_sqt
  "[| def P(e); e:A;
      [| P(e) |] ==>  e1(e):B;
      [| not P(e) |] ==> let x = e in e2(x):B |] ==>
   (let x = e in if P(x) then e1(x) else e2(x)) : B"
```

Let us explain why these proof rules mimic cases expressions from the viewpoint of a user. For simplicity we consider a slightly different example than above.

Suppose we are doing a proof where we would like to reduce a cases expression of the form:

```
cases ex:
  mk_(n,m,m) -> n+m,
  mk_(n,-,n) -> n,
  others      -> 0
end
```

Further, suppose that we expect the first pattern to not match. We would then use the proof rule `cases_not_match` to reduce the cases expression. In conducting a proof this rule would be instantiated to:

```
"[| not exists n:nat, m:nat & mk_(n,m,m) = ex; ex:A;
    if (exists n:nat, dc:nat & mk_(n,dc,n) = ex) then n
    else 0:B |] ==>
 (let new = ex in
  if (exists n:nat, m:nat & mk_(n,m,m) = new) then
    let n = new.#1,
        m = new.#2 in n+m
  elseif (exists n:nat, dc:nat & mk_(n,dc,n) = new) then
    let n = new.#1 in n
  else 0) =
 (let new = ex in
  if (exists n:nat, dc:nat & mk_(n,dc,n) = new) then n else 0)"
```

Isabelle would typically do this instantiation and the necessary β-reductions automatically, a user just tells it to apply the rule (by providing the name of the rule). It is important to realize that the left-hand side of the equality is the expanded form of the original cases expression and that the right-hand side of the equality is still a cases expression, namely:

```
cases ex:
  mk_(n,-,n) -> n,
  others      -> 0
end
```

Hence, the first cases expression above reduces to a cases expression where the first pattern has been thrown away, if this pattern does not match. Note that the if-then-else structure of the derived cases rules works because

```
if b1 then e1
elseif b2 then e2
else e3
```

is just syntactic sugar for

```
if b1 then e1
else if b2 then e2
     else e3
```

5 Generating Axioms: An Example

In order to support reasoning about specifications, we automatically generate axioms stated as proof rules which formalize the meaning of the definitions in a specification. These axioms are stated in Toolbox abstract syntax extended with a construction for proof rules, type judgments and subtypes. Once the axioms have been transformed to the Isabelle subset, they can be read into Isabelle and then used in proofs. The specification of the axiom generator, which was done in VDM-SL and developed using the Toolbox itself, is straightforward and based on [6]. Therefore we shall not go into the details here. Note that in addition to axioms for specifications, Isabelle needs the signatures of new constants. These are also straightforward to generate, again the specification of this was done in VDM-SL using the Toolbox.

In this section we illustrate the working of the axiom (and signature) generator on a small example, which is adapted from an example of a forthcoming book on VDM-SL [9] and inspired by a real industrial system. The example concerns an alarm paging system for a chemical plant. A safety requirement of the system is that for any period of time and any possible alarm code (and location) there must be experts with the required qualifications to deal with the alarm on duty according to a certain plan.

The specification below is stated in the expression (or functional) subset of VDM-SL, but we could as well have used a state to model the plant and defined some of the functions as implicit operations on the state (using preconditions and postconditions). The approach to state definitions and implicit operations is borrowed from the Mural project. A state definition is treated in essentially the same way as a record and implicit operations are treated as functions on the state (taking the state as an extra argument and result).

5.1 Type Definitions

We shall model the chemical plant as a record type whose invariant specifies the safety requirement:

```
Plant :: plan   : Plan
         alarms : set of Alarm
inv mk_Plant(plan,alarms) ==
    forall per in set dom plan, alarm in set alarms &
       QualificationsOK(alarm,plan(per));
```

The record has two fields, containing a plan and a set of alarms respectively. The function QualificationsOK defines the safety requirement and will be specified later.

A plan is simply a map from periods to sets of experts:

```
Plan = map Period to set of Expert
inv plan == forall exs in set rng plan & exs <> {};

Period = token;
```

The invariant says that there should always be at least one expert associated with any period. The data type of periods is left unspecified (using the `token` type which just denotes an infinite set with equality).

An expert has an ID and a set of qualifications:

```
Expert :: expertid : ExpertId
          quali    : set of Qualification
inv mk_Expert(-,q) == q <> {};

ExpertId = token;

Qualification = <Elec> | <Mech> | <Chem> | <Chief>;
```

Qualifications are modeled as an enumeration type. An expert must have at least one qualification.

The datatype of alarms is modeled as a record type with two fields, one for the alarm codes and one for the location of the alarms:

```
Alarm :: code : AlarmCode
         loc  : Location;

AlarmCode = <A> | <B> | <C>;

Location = <P1> | <P2> | <P3> | <P4> | <P5> | <P6> | <P7>
```

A function is clearly needed to specify which qualifications are required for the different alarms, this is done below.

We shall now consider the signature of new constants and axioms generated for these type definitions. We cannot include all axioms in this paper, due to lack of space. Axioms are generated by executing the shell script `genax` with the file name of our specification `alarm.vdm` as an argument. The result is a file `alarm.thy` which contains the Isabelle theory file for the specification. This is ready to be loaded into the Isabelle/VDM-LPF instantiation, which is started by executing the binary `vdmlpf` in a shell.

The theory file starts with the signature of new constants. For a record type, like `Plant` used for illustration in the following, a record constructor function is introduced:

```
mk_Plant :: [ex,ex] => ex
```

This means that `mk_Plant` is a function in the Isabelle meta-logic, which takes two expressions as arguments, corresponding to the two fields, and yields an expression as a result, corresponding to a record with these two field values. The field selectors of the record type are defined in both an abstract and a concrete syntax version which allows the concrete syntax to support VDM-SL field selection using a postfix notation:

```
plan'   :: ex => ex   ("_.plan" [500] 500)
alarms' :: ex => ex   ("_.alarms" [500] 500)
```

The primes are used on constants of the abstract syntax by convention. The parenthesis on the right specifies a priority grammar for the postfix notation, we shall not go into details here. For a record type with an invariant, the signature of the invariant function must also be included:

```
inv_Plant :: ex
```

In contrast to the constructor and selector functions this is represented as an object-logic function. A special object-logic application operator is defined in VDM-LPF and written using an @. The invariant function could be represented as a meta-logic function but there are technical reasons for not doing this. VDM-SL map application and sequence indexing must be done in the object-logic and application of invariant, and many other functions is not distinguished from these first forms of applications in the abstract syntax tree of the IFAD Toolbox.

After the signature declarations the generated axioms are stated as proof rules. The definition axiom for the invariant function is stated as follows:

```
inv_Plant_defn
  "inv_Plant@(mk_Plant(plan, alarms)) ==
    forall per in set dom plan, alarm in set alarms &
      QualificationsOK@(alarm, plan@(per))"
```

This is stated as a simple meta-equality rewrite rule. A number of formation and definition axioms are introduced for record types. For the record constructor function, the following two axioms are needed:

```
mk_Plant_form
  "[| gax41 : Plan; gax42 : set of Alarm;
      inv_Plant@(mk_Plant(gax41, gax42)) |] ==>
  mk_Plant(gax41, gax42) : Plant"
```

```
mk_Plant_defn
  "gax5 : Plant ==> mk_Plant(gax5.plan, gax5.alarms) = gax5"
```

The **gax** variables may look strange, they are automatically indexed by the axiom generator. Each field selector of a record type yields two similar axioms:

```
plan_Plant_form
  "gax5 : Plant ==> gax5.plan : Plan"
```

```
plan_Plant_defn
  "[| gax41 : Plan; gax42 : set of Alarm |] ==>
  mk_Plant(gax41, gax42).plan = gax41"
```

In order to ensure definedness of object equality =, typing hypotheses appear everywhere [6].

Basic type definitions like the definition of **Plan** and **AlarmCode** yield fewer axioms. Hence, for **Plan** just two definition axioms are generated:

```
inv_Plan_defn
  "inv_Plan@(plan) == forall exs in set rng plan & exs <> {}"
```

```
Plan_defn
  "Plan ==
  << gax1 : map Period to set of Expert & inv_Plan@(gax1) >>"
```

The latter defines Plan as a subtype of a map type, restricted using the invariant
of Plan. The AlarmCode definition just yields one axiom

```
AlarmCode_defn
  "AlarmCode == <A> | <B> | <C>"
```

but as a side effect axioms are also generated for each of the quote types, for
example:

```
A_axiom
  "<A> : <A>"
```

```
A_singleton
  "gax47 : <A> ==> gax47 = <A>"
```

```
A_B_disjoint
  "<A> <> <B>"
```

Disjointness axioms are needed for all pairs of quotes. In VDM-SL, the notation
<A> is used for both a quote type and its one element. This can be supported
in Isabelle since the corresponding constants of the meta-logic have different
meta-types. Ambiguities are resolved by the Isabelle type checker.

5.2 Function Definitions

We shall now continue the example from above by specifying a few functions.
As already noted we need a function to map alarm codes and locations to qualifications required of experts. We also need a function to specify the safety requirement, and a function to page a set of experts to handle a specific alarm.

However, consider first a simpler function that tests whether a given expert
is on duty in a certain period:

```
OnDuty: Expert * Period * Plant -> bool
OnDuty(ex,per,plant) ==
  ex in set plant.plan(per)
pre per in set dom plant.plan;
```

This function has as precondition that the period is valid, i.e. it is covered by
the plan. This ensures that the map application in the body of the function is
defined.

All functions of specifications are represented as object-logic functions, just
like invariants. Hence, the signature of OnDuty is simply:

```
OnDuty :: ex
```

The signature of the precondition function `pre_OnDuty` is the same.

A function definition like this, with a precondition and in the explicit style, results in two axioms, one defining the precondition and one defining the function:

```
pre_OnDuty_defn
   "pre_OnDuty@(ex, per, plant) == per in set dom plant.plan"

OnDuty_defn
   "[| ex : Expert; per : Period; plant : Plant;
       pre_OnDuty@(ex, per, plant) |] ==>
   OnDuty@(ex, per, plant) = ex in set plant.plan@(per)"
```

Strictly speaking the latter should include a type judgment in the hypotheses saying that the body of the function is well-typed, in order to ensure that the LPF equality is defined. However, as mentioned in Section 2, we assume that the specifications have been checked using the Toolbox type checker (extended with proof obligations), and for convenience we shall therefore omit this condition. Note that we could include the condition as a hypothesis, prove the hypothesis once and for all, and then derive the above axiom. This integration could be taken further in a very tightly integrated system where the Toolbox type checker could be integrated even more with the proof process to "prove" type judgments arising in proofs.

The following function interprets alarms:

```
AlarmQualifications: Alarm -> set of Qualification
AlarmQualifications(alarm) ==
   cases alarm:
     mk_Alarm(<A>,-)   -> {<Mech>},
     mk_Alarm(<B>,loc) ->
         if loc in set {<P1>,<P3>,<P7>}
         then {<Chief>,<Elec>,<Chem>}
         else {<Elec>},
     others -> {<Chief>}
   end;
```

Alarms with code <A> require a mechanic, regardless of the location (specified using a "don't care" pattern). Alarms with code <B> at the locations <P1>, <P3> and <P7> are more serious, they require three qualifications, including a chief. <B> alarms at other locations require an electrician. The pattern variable `loc` is bound to the value of the location field of <B> alarms. Finally, all other alarms require a chief (e.g. for inspecting the situation).

The axiomatization of this definition is straightforward of course, it just yields one axiom. However, the interesting aspect of the definition is the cases expression in the function body, which is translated to nested let and if expressions:

```
AlarmQualifications_defn
  "alarm : Alarm ==>
  AlarmQualifications@(alarm) =
  (let tf21 = alarm in
   if exists dc22 : Location & mk_Alarm(<A>,dc22) = tf21 then
     {<Mech>}
   elseif exists loc : Location & mk_Alarm(<B>,loc) = tf23 then
     let loc = tf23.loc in
     if loc in set {<P1>, <P3>, <P7>} then
       {<Chief>, <Elec>, <Chem>}
     else {<Elec>}
   else {<Chief>})"
```

The variables **tf** are generated automatically during the transformation. Again, as discussed above, a type judgment for the function body should strictly speaking be included in the hypotheses.

We can now define the safety requirement, which was stated in the invariant of **Plant**, using the function:

```
QualificationsOK: Alarm * set of Expert -> bool
QualificationsOK(alarm,exs) ==
  let reqquali = AlarmQualifications(alarm) in
    forall quali in set reqquali &
      exists ex in set .exs & quali in set ex.quali
```

The axiomatization is obvious:

```
QualificationsOK_defn
  "[| alarm : Alarm; exs : set of Expert |] ==>
  QualificationsOK@(alarm, exs) =
  (let reqquali = AlarmQualifications@(alarm) in
    forall quali in set reqquali &
      exists ex in set exs & quali in set ex.quali)"
```

Again, this is in principle a derived axiom.

The function definitions above are all stated in the explicit style, which means that an algorithm is given for calculating the results. VDM-SL also supports an implicit style, where the result is just specified by a postcondition. The following function definition is in the implicit style:

```
Page(a:Alarm,per:Period,plant:Plant) r:set of Expert
pre per in set dom plant.plan and
    a in set plant.alarms
post r subset plant.plan(per) and
     AlarmQualifications(a) subset
        dunion {quali | mk_Expert(-,quali) in set r};
```

This function uses the plan of a plant to page a set of experts for a given alarm and period. A valid implementation of this function could just calculate all experts on duty for a certain period, regardless of the alarm, but a better implementation would probably try to minimize the set in some way.

Implicit function definitions yield four axioms, two defining the preconditions and postcondition respectively, and one definition and one formation axiom for the new function:

```
pre_Page_defn
  "pre_Page@(a, per, plant) ==
  per in set dom plant.plan and a in set plant.alarms"

post_Page_defn
  "post_Page@(a, per, plant, r) ==
  r subset plant.plan@(per) and
  AlarmQualifications@(a) subset
  dunion {let quali = tf31.quali in quali | tf31 in set r &
    exists quali : set of Qualification, dc32 : ExpertId &
      mk_Expert(dc32, quali) = tf31 and true}"

Page_defn
  "[| a : Alarm; per : Period; plant : Plant;
      pre_Page@(a, per, plant) |] ==>
  post_Page@(a, per, plant, Page@(a, per, plant))"

Page_form
  "[| a : Alarm; per : Period; plant : Plant;
      pre_Page@(a, per, plant) |] ==>
  Page@(a, per, plant) : set of Expert"
```

Note that the body of the postcondition is expanded slightly in order to treat the pattern in the set comprehension expression. The Toolbox parser inserts true when there is no restriction predicate in a comprehension expression. The Toolbox type checker ensures that the third axiom makes sense by generating a satisfiability proof obligation. Hence, also axioms for implicit functions are generated on the assumption that specifications are type correct.

6 Conclusion

It is a major challenge to build proof support for VDM-SL. The language was designed for writing large specifications in industry, and this is reflected in both its syntax and its data types. On the syntax side, it supports pattern matching in for example let and quantifier expressions, and it has constructs such as cases expressions, again with patterns, which are difficult to represent in a theorem prover. On the data type side, it has non-disjoint unions, record types with post-fix field selection, and arbitrary-length tuples that are not equivalent to nested pairs. Moreover, the underlying logic of VDM-SL is the non-classical three-valued

Logic of Partial Functions, which makes traditional classical approaches to, for example, proof search infeasible.

We are able to handle traditionally difficult constructs of VDM-SL by transforming these to expanded expressions in a subset of the ISO standard for the VDM-SL ASCII notation formalized in Isabelle (see [3]). However, the user never realizes the transformations while writing proofs, unless he wants to, since we can reverse transformations and provide a collection of derived proof rules which mimic the original expressions, though these actually work on expanded expressions. The transformations are dependent on the abstract syntax tree representation of expressions in the Toolbox, and would not be possible in Isabelle.

As a further consequence of the fact that the Isabelle instantiation supports the VDM-SL standard, we can use the Toolbox parser to read output from Isabelle. It has only been slightly modified to read proof rules, type judgments and subtypes, which are not part of the VDM-SL standard. Similarly, an ASCII pretty-printer for VDM-SL can be used to print abstract syntax both after it has been transformed to a subset understood by Isabelle and after Isabelle output has been parsed and reverse transformed to the original abstract syntax. Hence, no major changes or additions were needed to the IFAD Toolbox, in order to build the present prototype of an integrated system. Finally, as another consequence, the Isabelle instantiation can be used directly to reason in a subset of VDM-SL.

A main feature of the CASE/TP tool is that pragmatic test and rigorous proof for specification validation can be employed at the same time. All facilities of the IFAD VDM-SL Toolbox are available while conducting proofs. Moreover, the user always works in the notation provided by the Toolbox and is not limited by restrictions on syntax imposed by the proof component. Furthermore, industrial requirements like proof management, automation and version control, which typically are not well-addressed in theorem provers, could be supported by the proof support tool outside the theorem prover. Isabelle does provide some features for automating proofs, but these appear not to be directly usable with VDM-SL (cf. the discussion in [3]). Work will continue on improving the current prototype, e.g. by refining the proof theory formalized in Isabelle and by developing a graphical user interface with proof management and integrated transformations.

Acknowledgments

We would like to thank Peter Gorm Larsen for useful discussions concerning this work. Bernhard Aichernig and Peter Gorm Larsen commented on drafts of this paper. The work was financially supported by the Danish Research Councils.

References

1. S. Agerholm. Mechanizing program verification in HOL. In *Proceedings of the 1991 International Workshop on the HOL Theorem Proving System and Its Applications.*

IEEE Computer Society Press, 1992. A full version is in Technical Report IR-111, University of Aarhus, Department of Computer Science, Denmark.

2. S. Agerholm. Translating specifications in VDM-SL to PVS. In J. von Wright, J. Grundy, and J. Harrison, editors, *Proceedings of the 9th International Conference on Theorem Proving in Higher Order Logics (TPHOLs'96)*, volume 1125 of *Lecture Notes in Computer Science*. Springer-Verlag, 1996.

3. S. Agerholm and J. Frost. An Isabelle-based theorem prover for VDM-SL. In *Proceedings of the 10th International Conference on Theorem Proving in Higher Order Logics (TPHOLs'97)*, LNCS. Springer-Verlag, August 1997.

4. B. Aichernig and P. G. Larsen. A proof obligation generator for VDM-SL. In *FME'97*, LNCS. Springer-Verlag, September 1997.

5. H. Barringer, J. H. Cheng, and C. B. Jones. A logic covering undefinedness in program proofs. *Acta Informatica*, 21:251–269, 1984.

6. J. C. Bicarregui, J. S. Fitzgerald, P. A. Lindsay, R. Moore, and B. Ritchie. *Proof in VDM: A Practitioner's Guide*. FACIT. Springer-Verlag, 1994.

7. J. H. Cheng. A logic for partial functions. Ph.D. Thesis UMCS-86-7-1, Department of Computer Science, University of Manchester, Manchester M13 9PL, England, 1986.

8. R. Elmstrøm, P. G. Larsen, and P. B. Lassen. The IFAD VDM-SL Toolbox: A practical approach to formal specifications. *ACM Sigplan Notices*, 29(9):77–80, September 1994.

9. John Fitzgerald and Peter Gorm Larsen. *Software System Design: formal methods into practice*. Camdridge University Press, The Edinburgh Building, Cambridge CB2 2RU, UK, 1997. To appear.

10. IFAD World Wide Web page. http://www.ifad.dk.

11. C. B. Jones. *Systematic Software Development using VDM*. Prentice-Hall International Series in Computer Science. Prentice-Hall, 1986.

12. C. B. Jones, K. D. Jones, P. A. Lindsay, and R. Moore. *mural: A Formal Development Support System*. Springer-Verlag, 1991.

13. P. G. Larsen and B. S. Hansen. Semantics for underdetermined expressions. *Formal Aspects of Computing*, 8(1):47–66, January 1996.

14. P. Mukherjee. Computer-aided validation of formal specifications. *Software Engineering Journal*, pages 133–140, July 1995.

15. L. C. Paulson. *Isabelle: A Generic Theorem Prover*. Number 828 in Lecture Notes in Computer Science. Springer-Verlag, Berlin, 1994.

16. F. Pfenning and C. Elliott. Higher-order abstract syntax. In *Proceedings of the SIGPLAN'88 Conference on Programming Language Design and Implementation*, pages 199 – 208, Atlanta, Georgia, June 1998.

17. PVS World Wide Web page. http://www.csl.sri.com/pvs/overview.html.

18. K. J. Ross and P. A. Lindsay. Maintaining consistency under changes to formal specifications. In J.C.P. Woodcock and P.G. Larsen, editors, *FME'93: Industrial-Strength Formal Methods*, pages 558–577. Formal Methods Europe, Springer-Verlag, April 1993. Lecture Notes in Computer Science 670.

Specification of Required Non-determinism

K Lano, J Bicarregui
Dept. of Computing, Imperial College, 180 Queens Gate, London SW7 2BZ
J Fiadeiro, A Lopes
Dept. of Informatics, University of Lisbon, Campo Grande, 1700 Lisbon.

Abstract. We present an approach to the specification of *required external non-determinism*: the willingness of a component to respond to a number of external action requests, using a language, COMMUNITY, which provides both permission and willingness guards on actions.

This enables a program-like declaration of required non-determinism, in contrast to the use of a branching-time temporal logic. We give a definition of parallel composition for this language, and show that refinement is compositional with respect to parallel composition. We use the concepts developed for COMMUNITY to identify extensions to the B and VDM^{++} model-based specification languages to incorporate specification of required non-determinism. In particular, we show that preconditions may be considered as a form of willingness guard, separating concerns of acceptance and termination, once module contracts are re-interpreted in a way suitable for a concurrent environment.

1 Introduction

Non-determinism is usually regarded as an aspect of abstract specification which is to be eliminated during the refinement process. Indeed this view equates non-determinism in specifications with *under-specification*: the incomplete description of a value or operation which leaves open the choice of several deterministic implementations[1]. For example, in B [1] we could write:

CONSTANTS **ff**
PROPERTIES
  ff $\in$ N $\rightarrow$ N $\land$
  $\forall$ **xx**.(**xx** $\in$ N $\Rightarrow$ **ff**(**xx** + 1) > **ff**(**xx**))

This is an underspecified description of **ff** – we know that **ff** must be strictly increasing, but no other constraint is provided. An implementation of this function **ff** must be deterministic – one possible choice would be the successor function on N.

  Thus if we had defined an operation using **ff**:

yy $\longleftarrow$ **op(xx)** =
  PRE **xx** $\in$ N
  THEN

---

[1] Both B and VDM-SL take the interpretation that loosely-specified values are actually deterministic, just unknown, whilst operations may be internally non-deterministic.

$$\mathbf{yy} \ := \ \mathbf{ff}(\mathbf{xx})$$
$$\text{END}$$

we would expect the same result from calling **op** with a particular argument value **xx** each time this call is made.

In contrast an operation specified as

$$\mathbf{yy} \ \longleftarrow \ \mathbf{random} \ =$$
$$\text{ANY } \mathbf{vv}$$
$$\text{WHERE } \mathbf{vv} \ \in \ \mathbb{N}$$
$$\text{THEN } \mathbf{yy} \ := \ \mathbf{vv}$$
$$\text{END}$$

could, in principle, be implemented in a non-deterministic manner: successive calls of **random** could yield different elements of $\mathbb{N}$ as their results.

An example where such genuinely non-deterministic operation implementations are useful is a random number generator [9]. Applications in the field of security – where it is important that some clients of an operation cannot use its result to deduce certain secure information – also arise. However, the B language, or similar model-based languages such as VDM or Z cannot be used for such specification: the operation **random** above can validly be implemented by an operation which always returns the answer 5, for instance.

The property that all possible non-determinism in the effects of an operation is actually observable will be termed *required internal non-determinism* in this paper. Our main focus will be on a related form, termed *required external non-determinism*. This refers to the willingness of a component to answer a range of operation requests at a given time. This is particularly important in a concurrent execution context, where we need some guarantees that a parallel composition of two components, where one requests services from another, will not deadlock.

The use of *permission* guards for operations has become a common mechanism for concurrent object-based and object-oriented languages [5, 8]. A permission guard **G** for an operation **op** of a server object **obj** expresses that **obj** will refuse to provide the service **op** to external callers unless **G** holds. The caller will be "blocked", ie, suspended in its thread of execution, if it attempts to call **op** at a time when **G** does not hold, and will only be freed to complete the call if **obj** changes state (as a result of other calls from other clients) so that **G** becomes true.

Such guards allow a passive shared server object to protect its internal state. For example, a buffer with several clients would need to block clients that wish to execute a **get** method until there are some elements in the buffer. In VDM[++] notation [10] this could be specified as:

```
class Buffer
instance variables
  contents :  seq of N;
init objectstate == contents  := []
methods
  put(x :  N)  ==
      contents  :=  contents  ⌢  [x];
```

```
get() value y :  N  ==
      (y  :=  hd(contents);
        contents  :=  tl(contents);
        return y)
sync
  per get   ⇒   len(contents)  >  0
end Buffer
```

The permission guard len(contents) > 0 for get in the synchronisation clause asserts that get can only initiate execution if this condition holds.

Permission guards are used rather than preconditions because the presence of concurrency requires a change in the usual interpretation of module contracts [5, Chapter 11]: instead of producing an arbitrary result or behaviour if it is called outside the stated assumptions of its contract, a supplier operation such as get must suspend the client until the operation assumptions hold.

In terms of the semantics of classes [10], a permission guard G for op must be true at each time $\uparrow(\mathbf{op}, \mathbf{i})$ which is the initiation of the i-th invocation of op:

$$\forall \mathbf{i} : N_1 \cdot G \odot \uparrow(\mathbf{op}, \mathbf{i})$$

$\varphi \odot \mathbf{t}$ asserts that φ holds at time $\mathbf{t}$.

Hence, permission guards can be *strengthened* as development or specialisation proceeds. This ensures internal consistency, at the risk of system deadlock. In terms of theory extension, this is valid, as subtypes or refinements will then have stronger theories (the $\odot$ operator is monotonic in the RAL formalism [10] used as a semantics for VDM^{++}). This is not totally satisfactory however, as it allows a class to be "implemented" by a class with false permission guards for each of its methods, ie, whose objects refuse to execute any methods. The alternative, to leave these guards essentially unchanged through refinement [3], is not adequately flexible if we wish to combine subtyping and synchronisation [12].

We propose therefore a means of specifying an upper bound on the strength of permission guards, at specification time, via the use of "willingness" guards which provide a guarantee that implementations of a class will answer requests for services under certain conditions. The willingness guards imply the permission guards (if an object is willing to execute a method, then certainly it must permit itself to do so) and may be *weakened* during refinement. We have the situation shown in Figure 1: the grey area, where the permission guard is true but the willingness guard is not, may be eliminated during refinement or specialisation. It represents a form of under-specification whereby it is not known whether an object of the class will accept or refuse a request for the particular service under these conditions.

Such predicates can also be of use in B. A frequent style of abstract specification in B is to leave unspecified how a choice between error and normal behaviour is to be made:

add_data(dd) =

not(Willing),
not(Permitted)

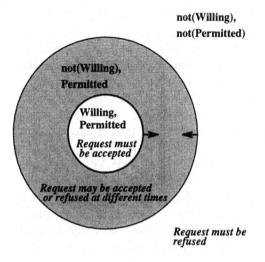

Fig. 1. Permission and Willingness Conditions

```
PRE dd ∈ Data
THEN
    CHOICE
        memory := memory ⌢ [dd]
    OR
        SKIP
    END
END
```

In this case the SKIP statement is meant only to be executed if the data cannot be stored because memory is exhausted – however according to the semantics of B a developer could implement the entire operation by a SKIP. Using permission and willingness guards we could express precisely under what conditions the addition of data is *guaranteed* to be carried out by an implementation (perhaps if memory usage is below 70% of capacity), under what conditions it *cannot* be performed (eg., if memory capacity has been reached), and (the remaining states) when we are uncertain as to the behaviour of the eventual implementation (the request may be refused or accepted). Similar examples concern the withdrawal of money from a bank account, etc.

In Sections 2 and 3 we describe the COMMUNITY language, its semantics and relation to branching temporal logic. We give the definitions of refinement and parallel composition in this language, and show that refinement is compositional with respect to parallel composition. Section 4 identifies suitable extensions of the B language to cover concurrent specification with required non-determinism. Section 5 considers the extension of VDM^{++} with specification of required non-determinism.

2 COMMUNITY

COMMUNITY [7] is based on the UNITY language of [4] but uses shared actions and private attributes. In this paper we extend COMMUNITY with the specification of *willingness* guards in addition to the usual permission guards. A COMMUNITY program is a pair (Θ, Δ) where Θ is a *program signature*: a pair $(\mathbf{V}, \Gamma)$ of sets of attribute symbols $\mathbf{V}$ and action symbols Γ. Each action symbol $\mathbf{g} \in \Gamma$ has a *write frame* (the set of attribute symbols that it may change) $\mathbf{D}(\mathbf{g}) \subseteq \mathbf{V}$.

The second component Δ of a program is a tuple $(\mathbf{I}, \mathbf{F}, \mathbf{P}, \mathbf{W})$ where $\mathbf{I}$ is an initialisation for the program (module): a predicate over the attributes $\mathbf{V}$. $\mathbf{F}$ gives for each action $\mathbf{g}$ and attribute $\mathbf{a}$ an effect statement $\mathbf{F}(\mathbf{g}, \mathbf{a})$ which describes how $\mathbf{a}$ is changed by $\mathbf{g}$. $\mathbf{P}$ gives for each action a permission guard $\mathbf{P}(\mathbf{g})$: when $\mathbf{P}(\mathbf{g})$ is false, $\mathbf{g}$ cannot be executed. $\mathbf{W}$ gives a willingness guard $\mathbf{W}(\mathbf{g})$ for each action: when $\mathbf{W}(\mathbf{g})$ holds the program is willing to execute $\mathbf{g}$ if the environment requests it.

We can also attach an invariant predicate to a program. The program will be *internally consistent* if the initialisation implies the invariant and the invariant is preserved by the execution of each possible combination of actions.

As a simple example, consider the task of maintaining a bank account. This has an invariant that the account **balance** is always above the overdraft **limit**, and actions to deposit and withdraw money:

var
   balance : $\mathbb{Z}$;
   limit : $\mathbb{Z}$
initialisation
   balance $= 0$ $\wedge$ **balance** $\geq$ **limit**
invariant
   balance $\geq$ **limit** $\wedge$ $0 \geq$ **limit**
do
   deposit(amt : $\mathbb{N}$) : [**true, true** $\rightarrow$ **balance** := **balance** + **amt**] []
   withdraw(amt : $\mathbb{N}$) : [**balance** $-$ **amt** $\geq$ **limit**,
                 balance $-$ **amt** ≥ 0 $\rightarrow$
                    balance := **balance** $-$ **amt**]

An action specification has the form $\mathbf{g}(\mathbf{p}) : [\mathbf{P}(\mathbf{g}), \mathbf{W}(\mathbf{g}) \rightarrow \mathbf{F}(\mathbf{g})]$: the permission guard $\mathbf{P}(\mathbf{g})$ is written before the willingness guard $\mathbf{W}(\mathbf{g})$. $\mathbf{F}(\mathbf{g})$ is the effect statement of the action, using the abstract generalised substitution notation of B.

The above specification asserts that **deposit** is always available for clients. However the **withdraw** action will definitely not be accepted for execution if **balance** $-$ **amt** $<$ **limit**: the permission guard for **withdraw** is false. It is guaranteed to be accepted if **balance** $-$ **amt** ≥ 0: the willingness guard for **withdraw** is true. In other cases the bank may use its discretion in accepting or rejecting the request.

In general, a COMMUNITY program may execute several actions in the same time interval (but the effects of such actions must not conflict – so **deposit**(x) cannot occur with **withdraw(x)** unless **x** = 0). Over a time interval, a given attribute **att** may only change its value if there is some action **g** executing in that interval with **att** in the write frame of **g**.

We can define a semantics $\models$ for programs using transition systems termed Θ-*interpretation structures* (see Appendix A).

Definition A program $\mathbf{P} = (\Theta, \Delta)$ is *realisable* iff (i) **I** is satisfiable, and (ii) every Θ-interpretation structure **S** that satisfies conditions 1 – 4 of the definition of model has that $\mathbf{S} \models \mathbf{W(g)} \Rightarrow \mathbf{P(g)}$ for every $\mathbf{g} \in \Gamma$.

A realisable program that has a model of the permission and functionality constraints also has a model of its willingness constraints:

Proposition If **P** is realisable, then every Θ-interpretation structure $\mathbf{S}_1$ that satisfies conditions 1 – 4 has an extension (ie, with more states and transitions) $\mathbf{S}_2$ which is a Θ-interpretation structure that is a model of **P**.

Usually we will write programs with $\mathbf{W(g)}$ implying $\mathbf{P(g)}$ in any case. Henceforth in this paper we will omit the part of $\mathbf{W(g)}$ which simply repeats $\mathbf{P(g)}$ and only explicitly write the additional conditions.

2.1 Parallel Composition

Program signatures and morphisms define a category $\mathcal{SIG}$:

Definition Given program signatures $\Theta_1 = (\mathbf{V}_1, \Gamma_1)$ and $\Theta_2 = (\mathbf{V}_2, \Gamma_2)$, a *signature morphism* σ from Θ_1 to Θ_2 consists of a pair $(\sigma_\alpha : \mathbf{V}_1 \to \mathbf{V}_2, \sigma_\gamma : \Gamma_1 \to \Gamma_2)$ of functions such that for every $\mathbf{a} \in \mathbf{V}_1$:

$$\{\mathbf{g} \in \Gamma_2 \mid \sigma(\mathbf{a}) \in \mathbf{D}_2(\mathbf{g})\} = \sigma(\!\{\mathbf{g} \in \Gamma_1 \mid \mathbf{a} \in \mathbf{D}_1(\mathbf{g})\}\!)$$

Given a signature morphism σ we can translate a predicate φ in the language of Θ_1 into a predicate $\sigma(\varphi)$ in the language of Θ_2 by applying σ to all the attribute and action symbols of φ.

Definition A *superposition* (component-of) morphism $\sigma : (\Theta_1, \Delta_1) \to (\Theta_2, \Delta_2)$ is a signature morphism $\sigma : \Theta_1 \to \Theta_2$ such that:

1. for all $\mathbf{g}_1 \in \Gamma_1$, $\mathbf{a}_1 \in \mathbf{D}_1(\mathbf{g}_1)$,

   $$\models_2 \mathbf{P}_2(\sigma(\mathbf{g}_1)) \Rightarrow \mathbf{F}_2(\sigma(\mathbf{g}_1), \sigma(\mathbf{a}_1)) = \sigma(\mathbf{F}_1(\mathbf{g}_1, \mathbf{a}_1))$$

   in the case the effects are assignments $\mathbf{a}_i := \mathbf{F}_i(\mathbf{g}_i, \mathbf{a}_i)$; other cases are similar.

2. $\models_2 \mathbf{I}_2 \Rightarrow \sigma(\mathbf{I}_1)$

3. for every $\mathbf{g}_1 \in \Gamma_1$, $\models_2 \mathbf{P}_2(\sigma(\mathbf{g}_1)) \Rightarrow \sigma(\mathbf{P}_1(\mathbf{g}_1))$

4. for every $\mathbf{g}_1 \in \Gamma_1$, $\models_2 \mathbf{W}_2(\sigma(\mathbf{g}_1)) \Rightarrow \sigma(\mathbf{W}_1(\mathbf{g}_1))$.

Programs and superposition morphisms constitute a finitely co-complete category c-$\mathcal{PROG}$ [11].

We can define interconnections between COMMUNITY programs using these morphisms and *channels*, which are programs with a single action **c** : [**true, true** → **skip**] which allow synchronisation of actions of other programs (see Figure 2). The co-limit of such a diagram of programs {**P**$_i$: i ∈ **Ind**} is a program || {**P**$_i$: i ∈ **Ind**} defined as follows:

1. Its actions are all those actions from any **P**$_i$ which are not synchronised by any channel between programs, together with all the composite actions induced by these synchronisations

2. Its initialisation is the conjunction of the initialisations of the **P**$_i$

3. The write frame of a composite action is the union of the write frame of its parts

4. The effect of a composite action is the || combination (in the sense of B) of the individual effects

5. The permission guard of a composite action is the conjunction of the individual permission guards (compare with the definition of || for actions in [3])

6. The willingness guard of a composite action is the conjunction of the individual willingness guards.

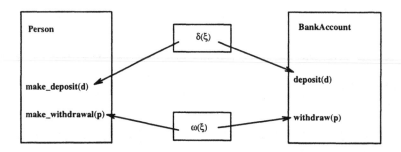

Fig. 2. Concurrent Composition via Synchronisation

This composition is similar to the synchronised interleaving of traces in VDM^{++} [10], or the || operator of CSP. A parallel composition should only be willing to perform a composite action **g** if every component involved in the execution of **g** is willing to accept it for execution: hence the use of ∧ in the final clause of the above definition.

Channels with attributes can be used to represent the form of || composition of actions with input and output parameters defined in [3].

In the example of Figure 2, if **Person** has the form:

var
    cash : $\mathbb{N}$
do
    make_deposit(amt : $\mathbb{N}$) : [amt $>$ 0 $\wedge$ amt $\leq$ cash, true $\rightarrow$
                                            cash := cash $-$ amt] []
    make_withdrawal(amt : $\mathbb{N}$) : [amt $>$ 0, true $\rightarrow$
                                            cash := cash $+$ amt]

(that is, the willingness guards for the two actions are equivalent to the permission guards), then the concurrent composition of the two modules has two parameterised actions **dep**(x : $\mathbb{N}$) which is the composite

$$\textbf{make\_deposit}(x) \parallel \delta(x) \parallel \textbf{deposit}(x)$$

and **with**(x : nat) which is the composite

$$\textbf{make\_withdrawal}(x) \parallel \omega(x) \parallel \textbf{withdraw}(x)$$

The first has the derived definition

    dep(amt : $\mathbb{N}$) : [amt $>$ 0 $\wedge$ amt $\leq$ cash, true $\rightarrow$
                        cash := cash $-$ amt $\parallel$ balance := balance $+$ amt]

and the second the definition

    with(amt : $\mathbb{N}$) : [amt $>$ 0 $\wedge$ balance $-$ amt $\geq$ limit,
                        balance $-$ amt $\geq$ 0 $\rightarrow$
                        cash := cash $+$ amt $\parallel$ balance := balance $-$ amt]

2.2 Subtyping and Refinement

We will define subtyping of COMMUNITY programs in terms of morphisms which allow permission guards to be *strengthened* and willingness guards to be *weakened* (see Figure 1). This means that the degree of uncertainty about the behaviour of a subtype object will be lower than for a supertype object – it may both definitely refuse more requests and definitely accept more requests.

Definition A *subtyping morphism* $\sigma : (\Theta_1, \Delta_1) \rightarrow (\Theta_2, \Delta_2)$ is a signature morphism $\sigma : \Theta_1 \rightarrow \Theta_2$ such that:

1. for all $g_1 \in \Gamma_1$, $a_1 \in D_1(g_1)$,

$$\models_2 P_2(\sigma(g_1)) \Rightarrow F_2(\sigma(g_1), \sigma(a_1)) = \sigma(F_1(g_1, a_1))$$

2. $\models_2 I_2 \Rightarrow \sigma(I_1)$

3. for every $g_1 \in \Gamma_1$, $\models_2 P_2(\sigma(g_1)) \Rightarrow \sigma(P_1(g_1))$

4. for every $g_1 \in \Gamma_1$, $\models_2 \sigma(W_1(g_1)) \Rightarrow W_2(\sigma(g_1))$.

Programs and subtyping morphisms constitute a category s-$\mathcal{PROG}$. σ is a *refinement* morphism if σ_γ is surjective: ie., no new external actions are introduced.

   A central result is that refinement is compositional with respect to parallel composition:

Proposition If there are subtyping morphisms $\eta_1 : \mathbf{P}_1 \to \mathbf{P}'_1$ and $\eta_2 : \mathbf{P}_2 \to \mathbf{P}'_2$ then there is a unique subtyping morphism $\eta : \mathbf{P}_1 \parallel \mathbf{P}_2 \to \mathbf{P}'_1 \parallel \mathbf{P}'_2$ for any parallel composition of $\mathbf{P}_1$ and $\mathbf{P}_2$ (and corresponding composition of their subtypes or refinements).

The same applies with regard to refinement morphisms.

Informally this is clear because parallel composition is a monotonic operator in terms of the logical and functional elements of its components. The full proof is given in [11].

3 Temporal Logic Specification of Required Non-Determinism

We can more abstractly and generally specify the required availability of actions by using a *branching time* temporal logic [13]. Specifically we will use the CTL* language which contains a branch quantifier $\mathbb{E}\varphi$ "on some path φ holds" and the derived $\mathbb{A}\varphi$ quantifier "on all paths φ holds".

Definition The computational tree logic CTL* is defined as follows:

- Its category of signatures is $\mathcal{SET} \times \mathcal{SET}$

- The grammar functor defines, for every signature $\Theta = (\mathbf{V}, \Gamma)$, the set of *state formulas* $\mathbf{CTL}^*(\Theta)$:

$$\phi_{\mathbf{S}} ::= \mathbf{a} \mid \neg \phi_{\mathbf{S}} \mid \phi_{\mathbf{S}} \Rightarrow \psi_{\mathbf{S}} \mid \mathbf{beg} \mid \mathbb{E}\phi_{\mathbf{P}}$$

and the set $\mathbf{CTL}^*_{\mathbf{P}}(\Theta)$ of *path formulas*:

$$\phi_{\mathbf{P}} ::= \mathbf{g} \mid \phi_{\mathbf{S}} \mid \neg \phi_{\mathbf{P}} \mid \phi_{\mathbf{P}} \Rightarrow \psi_{\mathbf{P}}$$
$$\mid \bigcirc \phi_{\mathbf{P}} \mid \phi_{\mathbf{P}} \mathcal{U} \psi_{\mathbf{P}}$$

The specification of the bank account given in Section 2 can be alternatively presented as a $\mathbf{CTL}^*$ theory with data and initialisation axioms:

> **balance** $\in \mathbb{Z}$
> **limit** $\in \mathbb{Z}$
> **beg** $\Rightarrow$ **balance** $= 0 \wedge$ **balance** $\geq$ **limit**
> **balance** $\geq$ **limit**

locality axioms:

> $\bigcirc$**limit** $=$ **limit**
> $\bigcirc$**balance** $=$ **balance** $\vee \exists$ **amt** $: \mathbb{N} \cdot$ **deposit(amt)** $\vee$
> $\qquad \exists$ **amt** $: \mathbb{N} \cdot$ **withdraw(amt)**

permission/effect axioms:

$$\forall \, amt : N \cdot deposit(amt) \Rightarrow$$
$$\bigcirc balance \, = \, balance + amt$$
$$\forall \, amt : N \cdot withdraw(amt) \Rightarrow$$
$$balance - amt \geq limit \, \wedge \, \bigcirc balance = balance - amt$$

and willingness axioms:

$$\forall \, amt_1 : N \cdot \mathbb{E}(\forall \, amt_2 : N \cdot \neg \, deposit(amt_1) \wedge \neg \, withdraw(amt_2))$$
$$balance \geq 0 \, \Rightarrow \, \mathbb{E}(deposit(0) \wedge withdraw(0))$$
$$\forall \, amt_2 : N \cdot balance - amt_2 \geq 0 \, \Rightarrow$$
$$\mathbb{E}(\forall \, amt_1 : N \cdot withdraw(amt_2) \wedge \neg \, deposit(amt_1))$$
$$\forall \, amt_1 : N \cdot \mathbb{E}(\forall \, amt_2 : N \cdot deposit(amt_2) \wedge \neg \, withdraw(amt_1))$$

There are concepts of morphism and refinement for such theories, and a mapping from programs to theories: the above theory is an example of application of this mapping.

4 Extending B with Required Non-Determinism

A model of action-based concurrency for B has been developed in [3]. In this approach the operations of B machines are viewed as actions similar to those of COMMUNITY programs, and operations of different machines may be synchronised under certain conditions. This language already possesses a form of *permission* guard, since the SELECT **G** statement of B may be interpreted as asserting that "there are no possible executions unless **G** holds". However it has no separate willingness guard – effectively this is taken to be equivalent to the permission guard since the permission guard cannot be essentially strengthened during refinement.

The wp semantics [**S**]**P** of a statement **S** gives a predicate **Q** for which every execution of **S** started from a state satisfying **Q**, will result in a post-state satisfying **P**. In the case of SELECT we have

$$[\text{SELECT } \mathbf{G} \text{ THEN } \mathbf{S} \text{ END}]\mathbf{P} \quad = \quad \mathbf{G} \Rightarrow [\mathbf{S}]\mathbf{P}$$

In the case that **G** does not hold initially, this says that every execution of the SELECT will achieve **P**, even if **P** is **false**. This can only be true if "every" is a null quantifier, ie, there are no executions of the statement if **G** fails.

However in B there is no explicit willingness guard, so that it is always possible to refine a system by strengthening permission guards to **false**, since

$$(\mathbf{G}_1 \Rightarrow \mathbf{G}_2) \Rightarrow$$
$$\text{SELECT } \mathbf{G}_2 \text{ THEN } \mathbf{S} \text{ END} \quad \sqsubseteq \quad \text{SELECT } \mathbf{G}_1 \text{ THEN } \mathbf{S} \text{ END}$$

where $\sqsubseteq$ is the refinement relation between substitutions.

We can however interpret *preconditions* as a form of willingness guard. Consider the usual "design by contract" meaning of a precondition **P** of an operation **op**. This asserts that if **P** holds when an attempt is made to execute **op**, then:

1. execution of **op** will be accepted

2. execution of **op** will terminate in a valid state, as specified by the postcondition.

In a sequential environment the first property is assumed to always hold, so the focus is on the guarantee of termination. Nevertheless, since

$$\text{PRE } \mathbf{G} \text{ THEN } \mathbf{S} \text{ END } \sqsubseteq \text{ SELECT } \mathbf{G} \text{ THEN } \mathbf{S} \text{ END}$$

one possible implementation of the preconditioned substitution is the corresponding guarded command, and therefore one possible behaviour of the operation outside its precondition is a refusal to execute.

We can reinterpret the design by contract use of the precondition to represent just the first kind of guarantee to the environment – that execution of the operation will be accepted. Proof of termination will be performed separately.

Given this interpretation, we can write the bank account example of Section 1 as:

```
MACHINE Account
CONSTANTS limit
PROPERTIES limit ∈ Z ∧ limit ≤ 0
VARIABLES balance
INVARIANT
    balance ∈ Z ∧ balance ≥ limit
INITIALISATION balance := 0
OPERATIONS
  deposit(amt) =
      PRE amt ∈ N
      THEN
          balance := balance + amt
      END;

  withdraw(amt) =
      SELECT amt ∈ N ∧ balance − amt ≥ limit
      PRE balance − amt ≥ 0
      THEN
          balance := balance − amt
      END

END
```

A "double guard" statement SELECT $\mathbf{P(op)}$ PRE $\mathbf{W(g)}$ THEN $\mathbf{S}$ END is used in the definition of **withdraw**. This extends the suggestion of [2] that guards are made "first-class citizens". We can see the two guards as successive filters – if the first guard fails then execution of the operation is not *permitted*, so the second guard need not be tested. If the first guard is passed successfully then the second guard is tested to see if acceptance of this execution is *obliged*.

A similar approach works for the memory management example. We can relate this modified B to COMMUNITY as follows.

4.1 Relationship of B to COMMUNITY

Taking the above interpretation of guards and preconditions, B can be interpreted/implemented in COMMUNITY, provided a facility for hiding data and actions was added to COMMUNITY. The results of Section 3 show that a definition of parallel composition can be given for this extended language which is monotonic with respect to refinement.

A specification-level B machine can be viewed as a COMMUNITY module:

1. Machine parameters can be defined as variables in a module which is then made a component (via a superposition morphism) of the machine module;

2. Machine constants and variables can be defined as attributes of the machine module, with their properties and invariant expressed as an invariant;

3. The machine initialisation $\mathbf{T}$ can be re-expressed as a predicate $(\neg [\mathbf{T}](\mathbf{x} \neq \mathbf{x}'))[\mathbf{x}/\mathbf{x}']$ in the initialisation of the machine module;

4. Operations $\mathbf{y} \longleftarrow \mathbf{op}(\mathbf{x}) = $ SELECT $\mathbf{P}$ PRE $\mathbf{W}$ THEN $\mathbf{S}$ END can be expressed as actions

$$\mathbf{op}(\mathbf{x}) : [\mathbf{P}, \mathbf{W} \rightarrow \mathbf{S}]$$

where the output parameters $\mathbf{y}$ have been converted into new attributes (unique to $\mathbf{op}$).

The locality axiom is true for modules derived from B machines, because B allows variables to be modified only via operations of the machine in which this data is declared. Additionally, at most one of the operations declared in a particular machine can execute at any time – this must be expressed by a specific axiom in the translated module.

Machine inclusion mechanisms can be expressed in terms of colimits wrt suitable superposition morphisms:

1. If machine $\mathbf{B}$ SEES machine $\mathbf{A}$, then we can express the meaning of $\mathbf{B}$ as the colimit of a diagram (Figure 3) where $\mathbf{B}'$ is $\mathbf{B}$ with the seen data $\mathbf{x}$ renamed to $\mathbf{y}'$, and $\mathbf{C}$ just contains the seen data (therefore, this data must be constant). σ' is the identity morphism;

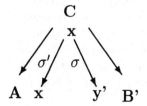

Fig. 3. Diagram of Modules for SEES

2. If machine **B** USES machine **A**, the same construction can be used, however now **B** may refer to the shared data in its invariant;

3. If machine **B** INCLUDES machine **A**, then **C** will have an action symbol α for every pair of operations **op** of **B** and $\mathbf{op}_1$ of **A** which is called by **op**. For example, if **op** was defined in **B** as

$$
\begin{array}{llll}
\mathbf{op} & = & \text{PRE} & \mathbf{P} \\
& & \text{THEN} & \\
& & & \mathbf{S} \parallel \mathbf{op}_1 \\
& & \text{END} &
\end{array}
$$

then the two superposition morphisms would map α to **op** and α to $\mathbf{op}_1$. In **B'** **op** is defined without any subordinate calls.

More complex cases of calling, involving conditional behaviour, can also be expressed via such unifying theories.

C must also contain a copy of all the data of **A**, and use this copy to identify the data of **A** with the included version of this data in **B'**.

The operations included from **A** must be hidden in the co-limit, except for PROMOTEd operations.

Internal consistency conditions for a machine now include additionally that the explicit willingness guards given in the PRE clause, together with the permission guards given in the SELECT clause, ensure the termination of the body of the operation.

5 Extending VDM^{++}

VDM^{++} is an extension of the VDM-SL notation to cover object-oriented structuring, concurrency and real-time specification elements.

We noted in Section 1 that the absence of willingness guards in VDM^{++} leads to the danger of introducing deadlock during refinement, because permission guards may be arbitrarily strengthened in implementations. The same applies to subtyping.

We propose the use of a predicate **enabled(m)** which asserts that **m** is available for execution, ie, that a request for **m** will be accepted (in terms of the RAL semantics of VDM^{++} this only means that **m** may be the next executed action of an object of the class, with no intermediate interruption by other actions). Implementations of specifications containing such assertions therefore cannot strengthen the permission guards of **m** further than these asserted willingness conditions: the willingness conditions give an upper bound on how far the permissions can be strengthened.

In fact, we will interpret a permission guard

$$\text{per } \mathbf{m} \quad \Rightarrow \quad \mathbf{G}$$

by the formula **enabled(m)** $\Rightarrow$ **G** in the semantics of VDM^{++} in the RAL formalism [10].

A willingness guard could be simply written as

```
enabled m ⇐ W
```

in the **sync** clause of a class, and is interpreted by the formula **W** $\Rightarrow$ **enabled(m)**.

Interpreting refinement by theory extension, it is clear that willingness guards can be weakened (**m** can be asserted to be accepted under more conditions) and permission guards can be strengthened, provided we do not assert non-permission in cases where willingness has been asserted.

A natural example making use of these extra conditions would be a general buffer specification. This would express only a very loose form of synchronisation, whereby update methods such as **put** and **get** would be asserted to be self and mutually exclusive, and to exclude enquiry methods such as **full**, but the latter could co-execute. The permission guards would therefore have the form:

```
sync
   per get ⇒
          #active(get) + #active(put) + #active(full) = 0;
   per put ⇒
          #active(get) + #active(put) + #active(full) = 0;
   per full ⇒
          #active(get) + #active(put) = 0
```

where **#active(M)** counts the number of active instances of the method **M**, ie, the number of invocations of this method that have been initiated but not yet terminated. However, we do want to assert also that every subtype must guarantee acceptance of methods whenever possible. Since we may strengthen the synchronisation policy to one which is fully mutex, and in which **get** can only be executed if there are elements to get, ie, if **len(contents)** > 0, we can only make the following guarantees:

```
enabled put   ⇐   #active(get) + #active(put) + #active(full) = 0
enabled full  ⇐   #active(get) + #active(put) + #active(full) = 0
enabled get   ⇐   #active(get) + #active(put) + #active(full) = 0 ∧
                              len(contents) > 0
```

Subtypes of this buffer can strengthen the permissions to define fully mutex behaviour and to prevent **get** executing on an empty buffer – in this case the permissions and willingness conditions would be equivalent and could not be further changed.

Alternatively, we could implement an internally concurrent buffer that obeyed the readers/writers protocol with **get** guarded by the empty buffer condition. In this case the willingness for **full** could be weakened to assert its availability if neither **put** or **get** are executing:

```
enabled full   ⇐   #active(get) + #active(put) = 0
```

In this case again the permission and willingness guards would coincide.

6 Required Internal Non-Determinism

A similar treatment can be given to internal non-determinism. We could specify upper and lower bounds on the possible refinements of an operation effect by a pair POSS S_l REQD S_u END where the S_i are B-like substitutions with a wp semantics, such that $S_l \sqsubseteq S_u$. This pair is refined by POSS H_l REQD H_u END iff $S_l \sqsubseteq H_l$ and $H_u \sqsubseteq S_u$ in the usual sense.

The intuitive meaning of such a pair is that all its "executions" obey the specification S_l, and that every execution that obeys S_u is an execution of the pair. There is underspecification if S_u is not equivalent to S_l, in that it is not known which executions of specifications "between" S_l and S_u are included in its implementation. This underspecification can be resolved in different ways in distinct subtypes or alternative refinements.

Thus we could specify a random number generator which must at least provide a non-deterministic choice between the numbers $0, \ldots, 10$ by:

POSS $x :\in N$ REQD $x :\in 0 .. 10$ END

This can be refined by POSS $x :\in 0..20$ REQD $x :\in 0..20$ END or by POSS $x :\in 0..10$ REQD $x :\in 0..10$ END for example, but not by POSS $x := 0$ REQD $x := 0$ END which is equivalent to the single statement $x := 0$.

If S is non-deterministic[2] then POSS S REQD S END cannot be simplified to S – because then subsequent refinement could remove the non-determinism – but must be implemented by a program element which genuinely exhibits the required non-determinism.

In terms of semantics, we can represent the "executions" of a statement by actions in the logics of Section 3. Requiring a certain level of internal non-determinism can then be expressed as asserting that a certain collection of these actions are possible next steps, ie, $\mathbb{E}\gamma$ holds for each such execution action γ.

Specifically, let $\alpha_{x,n}$ be the action with effect $x := n$ where x is a list of attributes, and n a list of corresponding values. Then to assert that the full non-determinism expected from a statement S such as POSS $x :\in 0 .. 10$ REQD $x :\in 0 .. 10$ END occurs, we write:

$$\mathbb{E}\alpha_{x,0} \wedge \mathbb{E}\alpha_{x,1} \wedge \ldots \wedge \mathbb{E}\alpha_{x,10}$$

In other words, there *are* executions of the statement S for each of the specified behaviours. In terms of Kripke models, there are paths starting from the current state which begin with some $\alpha_{x,i}$ for each choice of $i \in 0 .. 10$. Notice that the logic does not distinguish between choices that are made externally from those that are made internally – $\mathbb{E}\alpha$ simply asserts that *some* behaviour starting with an execution of α will occur.

For an action definition

$\alpha \;=\;$ POSS L REQD U END

---

[2] That is, $\exists x' \cdot [S](x = x')$ fails where x is the write frame of S.

we have the axioms

$$\alpha \Rightarrow [\![\mathbf{L}]\!]$$

where $[\![\mathbf{L}]\!]$ is the temporal logic semantics of $\mathbf{L}$ as given in Appendix B, and

$$\alpha \Rightarrow \bigwedge_{\alpha_{x.n}} \mathbb{E}\alpha_{x,n}$$

where the $\alpha_{x,n}$ are all those assignment actions which have $\mathbf{U} \sqsubseteq \alpha_{x,n}$.

7 Discussion

We have proposed adding one extra guard to a B, VDM^{++} or UNITY specification, and subsuming the usual precondition under a willingness guard. There may be justification in retaining three separate guards: a precondition **Pre**, a permission guard **G** and a willingness guard **W**. The meaning of these guards for an action α with postcondition **Post** would be expressed by the axioms:

1. $\alpha \wedge \mathbf{Pre} \Rightarrow \bigcirc\mathbf{Post}$ "If α executes when **Pre** holds, then it terminates, and **Post** is achieved at termination".

2. $\alpha \Rightarrow \mathbf{G}$ "α can only execute if **G** holds".

3. $\mathbf{W} \Rightarrow \mathbb{E}\alpha$ "If **W** holds, α must be accepted if called".

If **G** contains only attributes, and no temporal operators or action symbols, then $\mathbb{E}\mathbf{G} \Rightarrow \mathbf{G}$ and hence $\mathbf{W} \Rightarrow \mathbf{G}$. There are thus 6 possible behaviours for various combinations of the guards being true or false (Table 1). The final case

Pre	G	W	
✓	×	×	No execution
✓	✓	×	Execution is permitted. Executions that occur will be valid
✓	✓	✓	Acceptance of execution guaranteed. Executions will be valid
×	×	×	No execution
×	✓	×	Execution permitted, but non-termination or arbitrary behaviour may occur
×	✓	✓	Execution guaranteed, but non-termination or arbitrary behaviour may occur

Table 1. Behaviour Depending on Guards

would be eliminated if we required that $\mathbf{W} \Rightarrow \mathbf{Pre}$, which would be the case if we adopted the suggestion of Section 4 that $\mathbf{W}$ ensures termination of the operation statement.

Internal actions are used in [3, 2] in order to decompose an operation into a sequence of subordinate operations. The same approach could be taken in our version of B/COMMUNITY if internal actions and action hiding were included in the language.

Required non-determinism can be expressed in the traces/failures semantics of CSP. If s is a trace and a an action, then

$$(s \frown \langle a \rangle, X) \in F \ \wedge \ (s, \{a\}) \in F$$

for a failures set **F** indicates that **a** is permitted but not required to be available in 'state' **s**. This corresponds to **s** being in the 'grey area' in Figure 1.

$$(s \frown \langle a \rangle, X) \in F \ \wedge \ (s, \{a\}) \notin F$$

indicates that **a** is permitted and required, whilst

$$(s, \{a\}) \in F \ \wedge \ (s \frown \langle a \rangle, X) \notin F$$

indicates that **a** is not permitted.

Refinement in CSP terms then means that the first kind of non-determinism may be eliminated.

8 Conclusion

We have introduced a means of specifying required external non-determinism in model-based languages: providing the environment with a guarantee of acceptance of one of a choice of possible actions, by means of *willingness guards*. We have defined languages for specifying and implementing systems with required external non-determinism, and shown how these languages can be related to specification languages such as B and VDM^{++}. Similar extensions could be made to the Syntropy [5] or $\pi o \beta \lambda$ [8] languages. We have also described how required internal non-determinism can be treated in this context.

References

1. J-R Abrial. *The B Book: Assigning Programs to Meanings.* Cambridge University Press, 1996.
2. J-R Abrial. *Extending B Without Changing it (for Developing Distributed Systems),* B Conference, IRIN, Nantes, November 1996.
3. M Butler. *Stepwise Refinement of Communicating Systems,* Southampton University, 1997.
4. K M Chandy and J Misra. *Parallel Program Design – A Foundation.* Addison-Wesley, 1988.
5. S Cook and J Daniels. *Designing Object Systems: Object-Oriented Modelling with Syntropy.* Prentice Hall, Sept 1994.
6. J Fiadeiro and T Maibaum. *Temporal Theories as Modularisation Units for Concurrent System Specification,* Formal Aspects of Computing 4(3), pp. 239–272, 1992.

7. J Fiadeiro and T Maibaum. *Categorical Semantics of Parallel Program Design*, Science of Computer Programming, 28 (1997), pp. 111–138, 1997.
8. C B Jones. *Accommodating Interference in the formal design of concurrent object-based programs*. Formal Methods in System Design, 8(2): 105–122, March 1996.
9. R Kuiper. *Enforcing Nondeterminism via Linear Time Temporal Logic Specification using Hiding*, in B Banieqbal, H Barringer and A Pnueli (eds) *Temporal Logic in Specification*, LNCS 398, Springer-Verlag 1989, 295–303.
10. K Lano, S Goldsack, J Bicarregui and S Kent. *Integrating VDM^{++} and Real-Time System Design*, Z User Meeting, 1997.
11. A Lopes. *COMMUNITY and Required Non-determinism*, Department of Informatics, University of Lisbon, 1996.
12. C McHale. *Synchronisation in Concurrent, Object-oriented Languages: Expressive Power, Genericity and Inheritance*. PhD Thesis, University of Dublin, 1995.
13. C Stirling. Comparing linear and branching time temporal logics. In B Banieqbal, H Barringer and A Pnueli (eds) *Temporal Logic in Specification*, LNCS 398, Springer-Verlag 1989.

A   Semantics of COMMUNITY

The semantics of a program is expressed by a form of transition system.

Definition A Θ-*interpretation structure* for a signature $\Theta = (\mathbf{V}, \Gamma)$ is a pair $(\mathcal{T}, \mathcal{A})$ where

- $\mathcal{T}$ is a transition system $(\mathcal{W}, \mathbf{w}_0, 2^{\Gamma}, \rightarrow)$
- $\mathcal{A}$ is a map $\mathcal{A} : \mathbf{V} \rightarrow (\mathcal{W} \rightarrow \{\mathbf{t}, \mathbf{f}\})$

Definition Given a signature $\Theta = (\mathbf{V}, \Gamma)$ and Θ-interpretation structure $\mathbf{S} = (\mathcal{T}, \mathcal{A})$, the truth $(\mathbf{S}, \mathbf{w}) \models \varphi$ of a formula φ at a world $\mathbf{w} \in \mathcal{W}$ of $\mathbf{S}$ is recursively defined by:

$$(\mathbf{S}, \mathbf{w}) \models \mathbf{a} \quad \text{iff} \quad \mathcal{A}(\mathbf{a})(\mathbf{w})$$
$$(\mathbf{S}, \mathbf{w}) \models (\phi_1 \Rightarrow \phi_2) \quad \text{iff} \quad (\mathbf{S}, \mathbf{w}) \models \phi_1 \text{ implies } (\mathbf{S}, \mathbf{w}) \models \phi_2$$
$$(\mathbf{S}, \mathbf{w}) \models \phi_1 \vee \phi_2 \quad \text{iff} \quad (\mathbf{S}, \mathbf{w}) \models \phi_1 \text{ or } (\mathbf{S}, \mathbf{w}) \models \phi_2$$
$$(\mathbf{S}, \mathbf{w}) \models \neg \phi \quad \text{iff} \quad \neg ((\mathbf{S}, \mathbf{w}) \models \phi)$$

Definition A formula ϕ is *true* in a Θ interpretation structure $\mathbf{S}$, written $\mathbf{S} \models \phi$, iff $(\mathbf{S}, \mathbf{w}) \models \phi$ at every state $\mathbf{w}$ of $\mathbf{S}$.

Definition Given a program $\mathbf{P} = (\Theta, \Delta)$ where $\Theta = (\mathbf{V}, \Gamma)$ and $\Delta = (\mathbf{I}, \mathbf{F}, \mathbf{P}, \mathbf{W})$, a *model of P* is a Θ-interpretation structure $\mathbf{S} = (\mathcal{T}, \mathcal{A})$ such that:

1. $(\mathbf{S}, \mathbf{w}_0) \models \mathbf{I}$.   The initialisation is true in the first state;
2. for every set $\mathbf{e} \subseteq \Gamma$ of actions, action $\mathbf{g} \in \mathbf{e}$ and attribute $\mathbf{a} \in \mathbf{D}(\mathbf{g})$, if $\mathbf{w}, \mathbf{w}' \in \mathcal{W}$ have $\mathbf{w} \rightarrow^{\mathbf{e}} \mathbf{w}'$ then $\mathcal{A}(\mathbf{a})(\mathbf{w}')$ iff $(\mathbf{S}, \mathbf{w}) \models \mathbf{F}(\mathbf{g}, \mathbf{a})$.   The effect of $\mathbf{F}(\mathbf{g})$ is achieved on $\mathbf{a}$;
3. for every attribute $\mathbf{a}$, $\mathbf{w}, \mathbf{w}' \in \mathcal{W}$, and $\mathbf{e} \subseteq \Gamma$, if $\mathbf{w} \rightarrow^{\mathbf{e}} \mathbf{w}'$ and no $\mathbf{g} \in \mathbf{e}$ has $\mathbf{a} \in \mathbf{D}(\mathbf{g})$, then $\mathcal{A}(\mathbf{a})(\mathbf{w})$ iff $\mathcal{A}(\mathbf{a})(\mathbf{w}')$.   Attributes outside the frame of every action currently executing are unchanged;
4. for every action $\mathbf{g} \in \Gamma$, $\mathbf{w} \in \mathcal{W}$ and $\mathbf{e} \subseteq \Gamma$ with $\mathbf{g} \in \mathbf{e}$, if there exists some $\mathbf{w}' \in \mathcal{W}$ with $\mathbf{w} \rightarrow^{\mathbf{e}} \mathbf{w}'$, then $(\mathbf{S}, \mathbf{w}) \models \mathbf{P}(\mathbf{g})$.   Any action that occurs from $\mathbf{w}$ must be permitted in this state;

5. for every $e \subseteq \Gamma$ and $\mathbf{w} \in \mathcal{W}$, if $(\mathbf{S}, \mathbf{w}) \models \mathbf{W}(\mathbf{g})$ for every $\mathbf{g} \in e$ and $(\mathbf{S}, \mathbf{w}) \models \mathbf{F}(\mathbf{g}, \mathbf{a})$ iff $(\mathbf{S}, \mathbf{w}) \models \mathbf{F}(\mathbf{g}', \mathbf{a})$ for each $\mathbf{g}, \mathbf{g}' \in e$ and $\mathbf{a} \in \mathbf{D}(\mathbf{g}) \cap \mathbf{D}(\mathbf{g}')$, then there exists some $\mathbf{w}'$ such that $\mathbf{w} \to^e \mathbf{w}'$. A program must be capable of executing a set of actions all of whose willingness conditions are true, and whose effects are consistent.

Implicitly, only the actions of a program can possibly change the attributes of that program – all concurrency in COMMUNITY is achieved by the sharing of actions rather than sharing of data.

B Temporal Logic Specifications

A Θ model of a CTL* theory is a tuple $(\mathcal{W}, \mathcal{R}, \mathcal{V}, \mathcal{E}, \mathbf{w}_0)$ where $\mathcal{R} \subseteq \mathcal{W} \times \mathcal{W}$ is a transition relation over the set $\mathcal{W}$, $\mathcal{V} : \mathbf{V} \to \mathbb{P}(\mathcal{W})$ and $\mathcal{E} : \Gamma \to \mathbb{P}(\mathcal{W} \times \mathcal{W})$ give the interpretation of attributes and actions. $\mathbf{w}_0$ is the initial state.

Each Θ-model $\mathbf{M}$ generates a set of *paths* through $\mathcal{R}$, **path(M)**, defined by

$$\{\pi \in \mathbb{N} \to \mathcal{W} : \forall i : \mathbb{N} \cdot \mathcal{R}(\pi(i), \pi(i+1))\}$$

The satisfaction relation $\models$ is defined by: $(\mathbf{M}, \mathbf{w}) \models \phi$ for state formulae ϕ iff

- for all $\mathbf{a} \in \mathbf{V}$, $(\mathbf{M}, \mathbf{w}) \models \mathbf{a}$ iff $\mathbf{w} \in \mathcal{V}(\mathbf{a})$
- $(\mathbf{M}, \mathbf{w}) \models \neg \phi$ iff $\neg ((\mathbf{M}, \mathbf{w}) \models \phi)$
- $(\mathbf{M}, \mathbf{w}) \models \phi \Rightarrow \psi$ iff $(\mathbf{M}, \mathbf{w}) \models \phi$ implies $(\mathbf{M}, \mathbf{w}) \models \psi$
- $(\mathbf{M}, \mathbf{w}) \models \mathbf{beg}$ iff $\mathbf{w} = \mathbf{w}_0$
- $(\mathbf{M}, \mathbf{w}) \models \mathbb{E}\phi$ iff there exists a path $\pi \in \mathbf{path(M)}$ such that $\pi(0) = \mathbf{w}$ and $(\mathbf{M}, \pi) \models \phi$

For path formulae $\models$ is defined by:

- for all $\mathbf{g} \in \Gamma$, $(\mathbf{M}, \pi) \models \mathbf{g}$ iff $(\pi(0), \pi(1)) \in \mathcal{E}(\mathbf{g})$
- for all state formulae ϕ, $(\mathbf{M}, \pi) \models \phi$ iff $(\mathbf{M}, \pi(0)) \models \phi$
- $(\mathbf{M}, \pi) \models \neg \phi$ iff $\neg ((\mathbf{M}, \pi) \models \phi)$
- $(\mathbf{M}, \pi) \models \phi \Rightarrow \psi$ iff $(\mathbf{M}, \pi) \models \phi$ implies $(\mathbf{M}, \pi) \models \psi$
- $(\mathbf{M}, \pi) \models \bigcirc\phi$ iff $(\mathbf{M}, \pi^1) \models \phi$ where $\pi^j(i)$ is $\pi(j+i)$
- $(\mathbf{M}, \pi) \models \phi \mathcal{U} \psi$ iff there exists $\mathbf{j} > 0$ such that $(\mathbf{M}, \pi^j) \models \psi$, and such that for all $\mathbf{k}$ with $0 < \mathbf{k} \le \mathbf{j}$, $(\mathbf{M}, \pi^k) \models \phi$.

We can relate programs in COMMUNITY to specifications in **CTL*** by defining a mapping from a program to a specification which gives an axiomatic expression of its semantics.

Definition Given a program $\mathbf{P} = (\Theta, \Delta)$ where $\Delta = (\mathbf{I}, \mathbf{F}, \mathbf{P}, \mathbf{W})$ we define:

1. **Safe(P)** is the following set of formulae in **LTL(Θ)**:
   - $\mathbf{beg} \Rightarrow \mathbf{I}$
   - For every action $\mathbf{g} \in \Gamma$, the proposition $\mathbf{g} \Rightarrow \mathbf{P}(\mathbf{g}) \wedge \bigwedge_{\mathbf{a} \in \mathbf{D}(\mathbf{g})} \bigcirc \mathbf{a} = \mathbf{F}(\mathbf{g}, \mathbf{a})$
   - For every $\mathbf{a} \in \mathbf{V}$, the proposition $(\bigvee_{\mathbf{a} \in \mathbf{D}(\mathbf{g})} \mathbf{g}) \vee \bigcirc \mathbf{a} = \mathbf{a}$.
2. **ND(P)** is the following set of formulae in **CTL$^*(\Theta)$**:
   - for every set $\gamma \subseteq \Gamma$ of actions: $\mathbb{A}(\mathbf{W}(\gamma) \wedge \mathbf{sync}(\gamma) \Rightarrow \mathbb{E}\gamma)$ where

$$\mathbf{W}(\gamma) \equiv \bigwedge_{\mathbf{g} \in \gamma} \mathbf{W}(\mathbf{g})$$
$$\gamma \equiv \bigwedge_{\mathbf{g} \in \gamma} \mathbf{g} \wedge \bigwedge_{\mathbf{g} \notin \gamma} \neg \mathbf{g}$$
$$\mathbf{sync}(\gamma) \equiv \bigwedge \{\mathbf{F}(\mathbf{g}, \mathbf{a}) = \mathbf{F}(\mathbf{g}', \mathbf{a}) : \mathbf{g}, \mathbf{g}' \in \gamma \wedge \mathbf{a} \in \mathbf{D}(\mathbf{g}) \cap \mathbf{D}(\mathbf{g}')\}$$

Safe(P) gives the axioms for the effects and permissions of the actions, together with typing axioms (for COMMUNITY with general variables). **ND(P)** gives the axioms for willingness.

We can generalise the semantics to deal with B substitutions other than $\mathbf{a} := \mathbf{F}(\mathbf{g}, \mathbf{a})$ by defining a temporal logic semantics $[\![\,\mathbf{S}\,]\!]$ for substitutions $\mathbf{S}$:

$$
\begin{aligned}
[\![\,\mathbf{x} := \mathbf{e}\,]\!] &= \bigcirc \mathbf{x} = \mathbf{e} \\
[\![\,\mathbf{x} :\in \mathbf{s}\,]\!] &= \bigcirc \mathbf{x} \in \mathbf{s} \\
[\![\,\mathbf{S_1} \parallel \mathbf{S_2}\,]\!] &= [\![\,\mathbf{S_1}\,]\!] \wedge [\![\,\mathbf{S_2}\,]\!] \\
[\![\,\text{IF } \mathbf{E} \text{ THEN } \mathbf{S_1} \text{ ELSE } \mathbf{S_2} \text{ END}\,]\!] &= (\mathbf{E} \Rightarrow [\![\,\mathbf{S_1}\,]\!]) \wedge (\neg\, \mathbf{E} \Rightarrow [\![\,\mathbf{S_2}\,]\!]) \\
[\![\,\mathbf{op(x)}\,]\!] &= \mathbf{op(x)}
\end{aligned}
$$

with similar clauses for PRE, ANY and SELECT.

A Corrected Failure-Divergence Model for CSP in Isabelle/HOL [1]

H. Tej, B. Wolff

Universität Bremen, FB3
Postfach 330440
D-28334 Bremen
{bu,ht}@informatik.uni-bremen.de

Abstract. We present a failure-divergence model for CSP following the concepts of [BR 85]. Its formal representation within higher order logic in the theorem prover Isabelle/HOL [Pau 94] revealed an error in the basic definition of CSP concerning the treatment of the termination symbol tick.
A corrected model has been formally proven consistent with Isabelle/-HOL. Moreover, the changed version maintains the essential algebraic properties of CSP. As a result, there is a proven correct implementation of a "CSP workbench" within Isabelle.

1 Introduction

In his invited lecture at FME'96, C.A.R. Hoare presented his view on the status quo of formal methods in industry. With respect to formal proof methods, he ruled that they "are now sufficiently advanced that a [...] formal methodologist could occasionally detect [...] obscure latent errors before they occur in practice" and asked for their publication as a possible "milestone in the acceptance of formal methods" in industry.

In this paper, we report of a larger verification effort as part of the UniForM project [Kri+95]. It revealed an obscure latent error that was not detected within a decade. It can not be said that the object of interest is a "large software system" whose failure may "cost millions", but it is a well-known subject in the center of academic interest considered foundational for several formal methods *tools*: the theory of the failure-divergence model of CSP ([Hoa 85], [BR 85]). And indeed we hope that this work may further encourage the use of formal proof methods at least in the academic community working on formal methods.

Implementations of proof support for a formal method can roughly be divided into two categories. In *direct tools* like FDR [For 95], the logical rules of a method (possibly integrated into complex proof techniques) are hard-wired into the code of their implementation. Such tools tend to be difficult to modify and to formally reason about, but can possess enviable automatic proof power in specific problem domains and comfortable user interfaces.

---

[1] This work has been supported by the German Ministry for Education and Research (BMBF) as part of the project **UniForM** under grant No. FKZ 01 IS 521 B2.

The other category can be labelled as *logical embeddings*. Formal methods such as CSP or Z can be logically embedded into an LCF-style tactical theorem prover such as *HOL* [GM 93] or *Isabelle*[Pau94]. Coming with an open system design going back to Milner, these provers allow for user-programmed extensions in a logically sound way. Their strength is flexibility, generality and expressiveness that makes them to *symbolic programming environments*.

In this paper we present a tool of the latter category (as a step towards a future combination with the former). After a brief introduction into the failure divergence semantics in the traditional CSP-literature, we will discuss the revealed problems and present a correction. Although the error is not "mathematically deep", it stings since its correction affects many definitions. It is shown that the corrected CSP still fulfils the desired algebraic laws. The addition of fixpoint-theory and specialised tactics extends the embedding in Isabelle/HOL to a formally proven consistent proof environment for CSP. Its use is demonstrated in a final example.

2 The Failure Divergence Semantics

In this section, we follow closely the presentation of [Cam 91], whose contribution is a formal, machine-assisted version of a subset of CSP based on [BR 85] and [Ros 88] *without* the sequential operator, the parallel interleave operator and a proof-theory based on fixpoint induction. With [Cam 91], we share some major design decisions, in particular the choice of the alternative process ordering in [Ros 88] (see below).

In its trace semantics model it is not possible to describe certain concepts that commonly arise when reasoning about concurrent programs. In particular, it is not possible to express non-determinism, or to distinguish deadlock from infinite internal activity. The failure-divergence model incorporates the information available in the trace-semantics, and in addition introduces the notions of *refusal* and *divergence* to model such concepts.

Example 2.1: Non-Determinism

Let a and b be any two events in some set of events Σ. The two processes

$$(a \rightarrow Stop) \; \Box \; (b \rightarrow Stop) \tag{1}$$

and

$$(a \rightarrow Stop) \; \sqcap \; (b \rightarrow Stop) \tag{2}$$

cannot be distinguished under the trace semantics, in which both processes are capable of performing the same sequences of events, i.e. both have the same set of traces $\{\langle\rangle,\langle a\rangle,\langle b\rangle\}$. This is because both processes can either engage in a and then *Stop*, or engage in b and then *Stop*. We would, however, like to distinguish between a deterministic choice of a or b (1) and a non-deterministic choice of a or b (2).

This can be done by considering the events that a process can refuse to engage in when these events are offered by the environment; it cannot refuse either, so we say its *maximal refusal* set is the set containing all elements of Σ other than a and b, written $\Sigma\backslash\{a,b\}$, i.e. it can refuse all elements in Σ other than a or b. In the case of the non-deterministic process (2), however, we wish to express that if the environment offers the event a say, the process non-deterministically chooses either to engage in a,

/ to refuse it and engage in *b* (likewise for b). We say therefore, that process (2) has two maximal refusal sets, $\Sigma\backslash\{a\}$ and $\Sigma\backslash\{b\}$, because it can refuse to engage in either *a* or *b*, but not both. The notion of refusal sets is in this way used to distinguish non-determinism from determinism.

Example 2.2: Infinite Chatter

Consider the infinite process

$$\mu X. a \to X$$

which performs an infinite stream of *a*'s. If one now conceals the event *a* in this process by writing

$$(\mu X. a \to X) \backslash a \tag{3}$$

it no longer becomes possible to distinguish the behaviour of this process from that of the deadlock process *Stop*. We would like to be able to make such a distinction, since the former process has clearly not stopped but is engaging in an unbounded sequence of internal actions invisible to the environment. We say the process has diverged, and introduce the notion of a *divergence set* to denote all sequences events that can cause a process to diverge. Hence, the process *Stop* is assigned the divergence set {}, since it can not diverge, whereas the process (3) above diverges on any sequence of events since the process begins to diverge immediately, i.e. its divergence set is Σ^*, where Σ^* denotes the set of all sequences with elements in Σ. Divergence is undesirable and so it is essential to be able to express it to ensure that it is avoided.

2.3 The Original Version of CSP-Semantics

The Semantic Domain. In the model of CSP presented in [BR 85] a process communicates with its environment by engaging in events drawn from some *alphabet* Σ. In the failure-divergence semantics a process is characterised by:

- its *failures* — these are sets of pairs (s,X), where s is a possible sequence of events a process can engage in (a *trace*), and X is the set of events that process can refuse to engage in (the *refusals*) after having engaged in *s*,
- its *divergences* — these are the traces after which a process may diverge.

Processes are therefore represented by pairs *(F,D)*, where *F* is a failure set and *D* is a divergence set.

The failures and divergences of a process must satisfy six well-definedness conditions (following [Ros 88]): (i) the initial trace of a process must be empty, (ii) the prefixes of all traces of a process are themselves traces of that process, i.e. traces are *prefix-closed*, (iii) a process can refuse all subsets of a refusal set, (iv) all events which are impossible to perform in the next step can be included in a refusal set, (v) a divergence set is *suffix closed*, and (vi) once a process has diverged, it can engage in, or refuse, any sequence of events.

More formally, given a (possibly infinite) set of events Σ and sets *F* and *D* such that:

$$F \subseteq \Sigma^* \times P(\Sigma)$$
$$D \subseteq \Sigma^*$$

then using a set theory and predicate calculus notation similar to that adopted in [Ros 88], the above six well-definedness conditions for processes are stated as:

is_well_defined(F,D) $\overset{\text{def}}{\Leftrightarrow}$

$\quad\quad (\langle\rangle,\{\}) \in F$ (i)

$\wedge \quad \forall s,t.\ (s \wedge t, \{\}) \in F \Rightarrow (s, \{\}) \in F$ (ii)

$\wedge \quad \forall s,X,Y.\ (s, X) \in F \wedge Y \subseteq X \Rightarrow (s, Y) \in F$ (iii)

$\wedge \quad \forall s,X,Y.\ (s, X) \in F \wedge (\forall c \in Y.\ ((s \wedge \langle c\rangle, \{\}) \notin F)) \Rightarrow$

                                        $(s, X \cup Y) \in F$ (iv)

$\wedge \quad \forall s,t.\ s \in D \Rightarrow s \wedge t \in D$ (v)

$\wedge \quad \forall s,t.\ s \in D \Rightarrow (s \wedge t, X) \in F$ (vi)

where $\langle\rangle$ denote the empty trace, and the notation $s \wedge t$ is used to represent the concatenation of two traces s and t.

In the model originally presented in [BR 85], the converse of (iii) is also a well-definedness condition. This condition, which is shown formally below, states that a set is refusable if all its finite subsets are refusable:

$$(\forall Y \in F(X).\ (s,Y) \in F) \Rightarrow (s,X) \in F \quad\quad\quad\quad (4)$$

In [Ros 88], Roscoe explains that this condition can in fact be omitted from the definition of process, but if this is done, a coarser, more complex ordering on processes must be defined since the ordering used in [BR 85] is no longer a *complete* partial order otherwise. This ordering will be called *process ordering*.

We prefer to use the process ordering of [Ros 88] (extended in [RB 89]), since we plan to investigate combinations of Z and CSP. In such a combination, Z is used to specify system-transitions via pre-and postconditions. Therefore we need a model that can cope with unbounded nondeterminism. In such a setting, a separation of the process-ordering from the refinement ordering seems unavoidable (see the detailed discussion of the counter examples in [Ros 88]). We will show in chapter 5 how one can live with two orderings from a proof theory point of view.

The semantics of the operators. We will consider the set of well-formed processes over alphabet Σ as a type *process* Σ. Then the language of CSP can now be given by the following signature (using infix notation):

Stop, Skip : process Σ

$\_\rightarrow\_$: $\Sigma \times$ process $\Sigma \rightarrow$ process Σ (* prefix of single event *)

$\square\_:\_\rightarrow\_$: P $\Sigma \times (\Sigma\rightarrow$process $\Sigma) \rightarrow$ process Σ (* multi-prefix of events*)

$\_\backslash\_$: process $\Sigma \times$ P $\Sigma \rightarrow$ process Σ (* hide *)

$\_\square\_, \_\sqcap\_,$ (* det. & non-det. choice *)

$\_;\_$: process $\Sigma \times$ process $\Sigma \rightarrow$ process Σ (* seq. composition*)

$\mu \_$: (process $\Sigma \rightarrow$ process Σ)$\rightarrow$process Σ (* recursion *)

$\cdots$

The signature above is the precise equivalent of the "grammar" in [BR 85] in higher-order abstract syntax. We will write $\square x : A \rightarrow P\ x$ for $(\square\_:\_\rightarrow\_)\ A\ (\lambda x.P\ x)$.

In the traditional CSP-literature, a distinguishable particular element $\sqrt{}$ ("tick") within Σ is required. It is used to indicate the termination of a process. It is crucial that it has not been distinguished on the level of the definition of the semantic domains.

Let $\mathcal{D}$ be the projection into the divergences and $\mathcal{F}$ be the projection into the failures of a process. The semantics for the CSP-operators can now be given following the lines of the example below:

$$\mathcal{D}(P;Q) \quad = \quad \mathcal{D}P \cup \{\, s \wedge t \mid \text{tick-free}(s) \wedge s\wedge\langle\sqrt{}\rangle \in \text{traces}(\mathcal{F}P) \wedge t \in \mathcal{D}Q\}$$

$$\mathcal{F}(P;Q) \quad = \quad \{(s, X) \mid \text{tick-free}(s) \wedge (s, X \cup\{\sqrt{}\}) \in \mathcal{F}P\}$$

$$\cup \quad \{(s \wedge t, X) \mid (s\wedge\langle\sqrt{}\rangle,\{\}) \in \mathcal{F}P \wedge \text{tick-free}(s) \wedge (t,X) \in \mathcal{F}Q\}$$

$$\cup \quad \{(s, X) \mid s \in \mathcal{D}P)\}$$

where *traces* denotes the projection into the traces and the predicate *tick-free* discriminates traces not containing tick.

Of course, for any operator it has to be shown that the results of $\mathcal{D}$ and $\mathcal{F}$, when composed to a pair, form in fact an object of type *process*, i.e. it remains to be shown that failures and divergences produced by an operator according to definitions above respect the well-formedness condition of the semantical domain, i.e. *is_well_defined($\mathcal{F}P$, $\mathcal{D}P$)*. (Theorem 1 in [BR 85]).

In fact, this is not possible for the sequential operator.

2.4 The Problem

The problem is that from the definition one can not prove the following part of *is_well_defined*:

$$(s \wedge t,\{\}) \in \mathcal{F}(P;Q) \Rightarrow (s,\{\}) \in \mathcal{F}(P;Q)$$

Consider the following case:

- $(s \wedge t, \{\}) \in \mathcal{F}(P;Q)$ and
- $s \wedge t \in \mathcal{D}P$ and
- $s \notin \mathcal{D}P$ and
- s is not tick-free, i.e there exist s' and s'' such that $s = s' \wedge \langle\sqrt{}\rangle \wedge s''$

From the definition for ; and the *is_well_defined* we can only prove that:

$$(s',\{\}) \in \mathcal{F}(P;Q)$$

but we can say nothing about *(s,{})*.

The problem is independent from axiom (4).

Conceptually, this is a consequence of an incoherent treatment of tick-freeness in divergence sets and failure sets. Although this is extremely ugly, our intuition that ticks "can appear only at the end of a trace" ([Hoa 85], pp.57, paragraph 1.9.7) has to be formally represented in the notion of well-formedness (which was, to our knowledge, never done in the CSP-Literature).

This means that the sequential operator of CSP in the sense of the definition does not form a process. This problem has meanwhile been recognised by other researchers of the CSP community ([Ros 96]), together with the fact that the problem ranges over "traditional CSP literature". Roscoe independently found this error recently and proposes a solution similar to ours.

3 Isabelle/HOL

3.1 Higher Order Logic (HOL)

In this section, we will give a short overview of the concepts and the syntax. Our logical language HOL goes back to [Chu 40]; a more recent presentation is [And 86]. In the formal methods community, it has achieved some acceptance, especially in hardware-verification. HOL is a classical logic with equality formed over the usual logical connectives $\neg$, $\wedge$, $\vee$, $\Rightarrow$ and $=$ for negation, conjunction, disjunction, implication and equality. It is based on total functions denoted by λ-abstractions like "$\lambda x.x$". Function application is denoted by $f\,a$. Every term in the logic must be typed, in order to avoid Russels paradox. Isabelle's type discipline incorporates polymorphism with type-classes (as in Haskell). HOL extends predicate calculus in that universal and existential quantification $\forall x.\ P\ x$ rsp. $\exists x.\ P\ x$ can range over functions.

3.2   Conservative Extensions in HOL

The introduction of new axioms while building a new theory may easily lead to inconsistency. Here, a *theory* is a pair of a signature Σ and a set of formulas Ax (the axioms). A theory extension can be characterised by a relation on theories:

$$(\Sigma, Ax) \rightsquigarrow (\Sigma \cup \Delta\Sigma, Ax \cup \Delta Ax)$$

Fortunately there are a number of syntactic schemes for theory extensions that maintain the consistency of the extended one — such schemes are called *conservative extensions schemes*. (For a more formal account the reader is referred to [GM 93]; one may also find a proof of soundness there). Some syntactic schemes for theory-increments $\Delta\Sigma$ and ΔAx are:

- the *constant definition* $c \equiv t$ of a fresh constant symbol c and a closed expression t not containing c and not containing a free type variable that does not occur in the type of c,
- the *type definition* (a set of axioms stating an isomorphism between a non-empty subset $S = \{x :: R \mid P\ x\}$ of a base-type R and the type T to be defined),

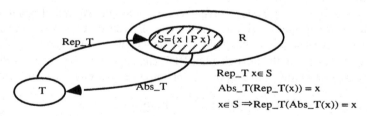

$$Rep\_T\ x \in S$$
$$Abs\_T(Rep\_T(x)) = x$$
$$x \in S \Rightarrow Rep\_T(Abs\_T(x)) = x$$

- a set of equations forming a *primitive recursive scheme* over a fresh constant symbol f.

The basic idea of these extension schemes is to avoid logical paradoxes by avoiding general recursive axioms provoking them. Desired properties have to be derived from conservative extensions. We will build up all theories by the above extension schemes, which constitutes a consistency proof w.r.t. HOL.

3.3 Isabelle

Isabelle is a *generic* theorem prover that supports a number of logics, among them first-order logic (FOL), Zermelo-Fränkel set theory (ZF), constructive type theory (CTT), the Logic of Computable Functions (LCF), and others. We only use its set-up for higher order logic (HOL). Isabelle supports natural deduction style. Its principal inference techniques are resolution (based on higher-order unification) and term-rewriting. Isabelle provides syntax for hierarchical theories (containing signatures and axioms).

In the sequel, all Isabelle input and output will be denoted in this FONT throughout this paper — enriched by the usual mathematical notation for $\forall$, $\exists$,... instead of ASCII-transcriptions.[2]

Isabelle belongs to the family of LCF-style theorem provers. This means it is a set of data types and function definitions in the ML-environment (or: "data-base"). The crucial one is the abstract data type "thm" (protected by the ML type discipline) that contains the formulas accepted by Isabelle as theorems. thm-objects can only be constructed via operations of the logical kernel of Isabelle. This architecture allows to provide user-programmed extensions of Isabelle without corrupting the logical kernel.

Technically, the proofs were done by ML-scripts performing sequences of kernel operations. These scripts were attached to the theory documents that constitute a larger system of theories, "the CSP-theory" in our case. While Isabelle is loading the theory documents and checking the proof-scripts, Isabelle can produce an HTML-document allowing to browse the CSP-theory.

4 Formalising CSP Semantics in HOL

Our formalisation of CSP profits from the powerful logical language HOL in several aspects:

- Higher order abstract syntax leads to a more compact notation avoiding auxiliary instruments like environments, updates, substitutions and process-and alphabet-variables. These issues were handled uniformly and precisely by the type-discipline.
- The data type invariant is_process (corresponding to is_well_defined in 2.3.1) can be encapsulated within a HOL-type. This leads to explicit treatment of notational assumptions and makes them amenable to static type checking.
- As we will see in the next chapter, HOL can cope with the issue of *admissibility* (as a prerequisite for fixpoint induction) in an extremely elegant way.

4.1 A Corrected Version for CSP Semantics

Whenever we changed a definition or a theorem, we will mark this by * in the sequel. The modified process invariant reads as follows[3]:

---

[2] We do not distinguish quantifications and implications at the different logical levels throughout this paper; see [Pau 94].

[3] In his "Notes on CSP" [Ros 96], Roscoe proposes two additional conditions. We have also proved formally that the CSP-theory is consistent on this basis.

is_process(F, D) $\overset{\text{def}}{\Leftrightarrow}$

$\wedge$ $(\langle\rangle,\{\}) \in F$ (i)

$\wedge$ $\forall$s,X. (s,X) $\in$ F $\Rightarrow$ front-tick-free(s)   (*)

$\wedge$ $\forall$s,t. (s $^\wedge$ t, {}) $\in$ F$\Rightarrow$ (s, {}) $\in$ F   (ii)

$\wedge$ $\forall$s,X,Y. (s, X) $\in$ F$\wedge$ Y$\subseteq$X $\Rightarrow$ (s, Y) $\in$ F   (iii)

$\wedge$ $\forall$s,X,Y. (s, X) $\in$ F$\wedge$ ($\forall$c$\in$ Y. ((s $^\wedge$ $\langle$c$\rangle$,{}) $\notin$ F)) $\Rightarrow$ (s, X $\cup$ Y) $\in$ F (iv)

$\wedge$ $\forall$s,t. s $\in$ D $\wedge$ tick-free(s) $\wedge$ front-tick-free(t) $\Rightarrow$ s $^\wedge$ t $\in$ D   (v*)

$\wedge$ $\forall$s,t. s $\in$ D $\Rightarrow$ (s, X) $\in$ F   (vi)

The condition * requires all traces to be front-tick-free (i.e. $\sqrt{}$ can occur at most at the end of a trace). Note that from (v *) and (vi) follows also front-tick-freeness for all divergences.

4.2 The Type Process

The encapsulation of the data type invariants *is_process* of the previous section within a type is accomplished by a type definition (see section 3.2). Note that Isabelle's notation for type constructor instances differs from the one used throughout this paper.

We introduce a type abbreviation trace Σ as synonym for $(\Sigma \oplus \{\sqrt{}\})^*$ where $\oplus$ denotes the disjoint sum on sets. Further, a type abbreviation p Σ will be used for the product of failures and divergences:

$$p\ \Sigma \overset{\text{def}}{=} P(\text{trace } \Sigma \times P\ (\Sigma \oplus \{\sqrt{}\})) \times P\ (\text{trace } \Sigma)$$

The set of all these tuples of p Σ represents the base type R of the type definition scheme. According to this extension scheme, fresh constant symbols are introduced:

Abs_process : p Σ $\to$ process Σ
Rep_process : process Σ $\to$ p Σ

together with the new axioms:

Rep_process X : {p. is_process p}   (Rep_process)
Abs_process(Rep_process(X)) = X   (Abs_inverse)
is_process X $\Rightarrow$ Rep_process(Abs_process(X)) = X   (Rep_inverse)

In Isabelle, this whole instance of the conservative extension scheme is abbreviated with the following statement in the theory ProcessType:

subtype (process) process Σ= "{p. is_process p}"

A first important theorem of this extension is[4]:

is_process (Rep_process P)   (is_process_Rep)

---

[4] In fact, the methodology entails a proof obligation that the type is non empty, i.e. that there is a witness for which is_process holds. This trivial proof is omitted here.

We proceed with the definitions of the projections for failures and divergences:

$\mathcal{D}$ P ≡ snd (Rep_process P)
$\mathcal{F}$ P ≡ fst (Rep_process P)

where fst and snd are the usual projections into cartesian products.

The encapsulation of well-formedness within a type has the price that the constant definitions of the semantic operators are slightly unconventional. The definition of the prefix-operator in Isabelle theory notation, for instance, proceeds as follows:

```
Prefix = ProcessType +
consts   "→"  :: Σ → process Σ → process Σ            (infix  75)
defs
      Prefix_def    " a → P ≡
              Abs_process({(s,X) I s = ⟨⟩ ∧ ev a ∉ X} ∪
                              {(s, X) I s ≠ ⟨⟩ ∧ hd s = ev a ∧ (tl s,X)∈ 𝓕 P},
                              {d I d ≠ ⟨⟩ ∧ hd d = ev a ∧ tl s ∈ 𝒟 P} )"

   end
```

The first line indicates that the theory Prefix is a hierarchical extension of the theory ProcessType. The pragma (infix 75) sets up Isabelle's powerful parsing machinery to parse the prefix operator the way it is used throughout this paper. The next axiom is declared to be a constant definition (Isabelle checks the syntactic side conditions) containing the abstracted tuple of failures and divergences, where hd and tl are the usual projection in lists and ev is just the injection of an element into Σ ⊕ {√}.

From this definition, the traditional equations for $\mathcal{F}$ and $\mathcal{D}$ are *derived* as theorems:

$\mathcal{D}$(a → P)   = {(⟨ev a⟩^s, X) I s ∈ $\mathcal{D}$ P}
$\mathcal{F}$(a → P)   = {(⟨⟩,X) I ev a ∉ X}} ∪ {(⟨ev a⟩^s,X) I (s,X) ∈ $\mathcal{F}$ P}

The proof requires Rep_inverse and hence a proof of is_process for the prefix operator. We follow this technique to develop conservatively $\mathcal{F}$ and $\mathcal{D}$ for all operators.

4.3 The Semantics of the CSP-Operators

In the sequel, we will omit the technical definitions like Prefix_def and start with a listing of the derived theorems for the process projections, bearing in mind that they already subsume the proof of process well-formedness.

$\mathcal{D}(\text{Bot})$ = {d | front-tick-free d}   (*)

$\mathcal{F}(\text{Bot})$ = {(s,X) | front-tick-free s}   (*)

$\mathcal{D}(\text{Skip})$ = {}

$\mathcal{F}(\text{Skip})$ = {($\langle\rangle$,X) | $\sqrt{} \notin$ X} $\cup$ {($\langle\sqrt{}\rangle$,X)}

$\mathcal{D}(\text{Stop})$ = {}

$\mathcal{F}(\text{Stop})$ = {($\langle\rangle$,X)}

$\mathcal{D}(\Box x{:}A{\rightarrow}P\ x)$ = {($\langle$ev a$\rangle{}^{\wedge}$s, X) | a $\in$ A $\wedge$ s $\in$ $\mathcal{D}$ P}

$\mathcal{F}(\Box x{:}A{\rightarrow}P\ x)$ = {($\langle\rangle$,X) | X $\cap$ ev A = {}}
           $\cup$ {($\langle$ev a$\rangle{}^{\wedge}$s,X) | a $\in$ A $\wedge$ (s,X) $\in$ $\mathcal{F}$P}

$\mathcal{D}(P\ ;\ Q)$ = $\mathcal{D}$P $\cup$ {s $^{\wedge}$ t | s$^{\wedge}\langle\sqrt{}\rangle \in$ traces($\mathcal{F}$P) $\wedge$ t $\in$ $\mathcal{D}$ Q}   (*)

$\mathcal{F}(P\ ;\ Q)$ = {(s,X) | tick-free(s) $\wedge$ (s, X $\cup${$\sqrt{}$}) $\in$ $\mathcal{F}$P}
           $\cup$ {(s$^{\wedge}$t,X) | (s$^{\wedge}\langle\sqrt{}\rangle$,{}) $\in$ $\mathcal{F}$P $\wedge$ (t,X) $\in$ $\mathcal{F}$Q}
           $\cup$ {(s,X) | s $\in$ $\mathcal{D}$(P;Q)}   (*)

$\mathcal{D}(P \sqcap Q)$ = $\mathcal{D}$P $\cup$ $\mathcal{D}$Q

$\mathcal{F}(P \sqcap Q)$ = $\mathcal{F}$P $\cup$ $\mathcal{F}$Q

$\mathcal{D}(P \Box Q)$ = $\mathcal{D}$P $\cup$ $\mathcal{D}$Q

$\mathcal{F}(P \Box Q)$ = {($\langle\rangle$,X) | ($\langle\rangle$,X) $\in$ $\mathcal{F}$P $\cap$ $\mathcal{F}$Q}
           $\cup$ {(s,X) | s $\neq \langle\rangle$ $\wedge$ (s,X) $\in$ $\mathcal{F}$P $\cup$ $\mathcal{F}$Q}
           $\cup$ {($\langle\rangle$,X) | $\langle\rangle$ $\in$ $\mathcal{D}$P $\cup$ $\mathcal{D}$Q}

$\mathcal{D}(P \setminus A)$ = {s | $\exists$ t u.front-tick-free u $\wedge$ s=(hide t(ev A))$^{\wedge}$u $\wedge$
           (t $\in$ $\mathcal{D}$ P $\wedge$ (u = $\langle\rangle$ $\vee$ tick-free t) $\vee$
           ($\exists$ M. M $\notin$ F {x.True} $\wedge$ t $\in$ M $\wedge$
           ($\forall$ w$\in$M,w'$\in$M.t$\leq$w $\wedge$ (w$\leq$w' $\vee$ w'$\leq$w)) $\wedge$
           ($\forall$ w $\in$ M. hide w (ev A) = hide t (ev A) $\wedge$
                  w $\in$ traces($\mathcal{F}$ P))))}   (*)

$\mathcal{F}(P \setminus A)$ = {(s, X) | $\exists$ t. s = hide t (ev A) $\wedge$
           (t, X $\cup$ ev A) $\in$ $\mathcal{F}$ P}
      $\cup$ {(s, X) | s $\in$ $\mathcal{D}$(P\A) }   (*)

$\mathcal{D}(P\ [|A\ |]\ Q)$ = {s | $\exists$ t u r w. front-tick-free w $\wedge$
           (tick-free r $\vee$ w=$\langle\rangle$) $\wedge$ s = r$^{\wedge}$w $\wedge$
           r inter((t,u),(ev A) $\cup$ {$\sqrt{}$}) $\wedge$
           (t $\in$ $\mathcal{D}$P $\wedge$ u $\in$ traces($\mathcal{F}$Q) $\vee$
           t $\in$ $\mathcal{D}$Q $\wedge$ u $\in$ traces($\mathcal{F}$P))}   (*)

$\mathcal{F}(P\ [|A\ |]\ Q)$ = {(s,R) | $\exists$ t u X Y. (t,X) $\in$ $\mathcal{F}$P $\wedge$ (u,Y) $\in$ $\mathcal{F}$Q $\wedge$
           s inter ((t,u), (ev A) $\cup$ {$\sqrt{}$}) $\wedge$
           R=((X$\cup$Y) $\cap$ ((ev A) $\cup$ {$\sqrt{}$})) $\cup$ X $\cap$ Y}
      $\cup$ {(s,R) | s $\in$ $\mathcal{D}$(P [|A |] Q)}   (*)

hide t A yields the trace obtained from t when concealing all events contained in A. The expression r inter ((t,u),A) means that r is obtained from t and u by synchronising their events which are contained in A and interleaving those which are not.

We adopt the more recent concept of the parallel interleave operator P[lA l]Q from the CSP-literature and define the parallel operator and the interleave operator as special cases:

$$P \text{ ||| } Q \equiv P[l \{\} l] Q \qquad\qquad P \text{ || } Q \equiv P [l\{x \mid True\}l] Q$$

4.4 The Generic Theory of Fixpoints

The keystone of any denotational semantics is its fixpoint theory that gives semantics to systems of (mutual) recursive equations. Meanwhile, many embeddings of denotational constructions in HOL-Systems have been described in the literature; in the Isabelle/HOL world alone, there is HOLCF [Reg 94]. However, HOLCF is a logic of *continuous functions*, while the fixpoint-theory is only a very small part of it. In contrast to HOLCF, we aim at a more lightweight approach that is parameterized (generic) with the underlying domain-theory (here: processes). Beyond the advantage of a separation of concerns, this paves the way for the reuse of this theory in other problem domains and for a future combination of CSP with pure functional programming. It is also possible with little effort to exchange the fixpoint-theory by another, for example, based on metric spaces via Banach-fixpoints.

Our formalisation of fixpoint theory in HOL will use a particular concept of Isabelle/HOL, namely polymorphism with (axiomatic) *type classes*. This is a constraint on a type variable (similar to the functional programming language Haskell) restricting it to the class of types fulfilling certain syntactic and semantic requirements.

For example, the type class $\alpha :: po$ (partial ordering) can restrict the class of all types α to those for which there is a symbol $\leq : \alpha \times \alpha \rightarrow bool$ that enjoy the property $x \leq x$ (refl_ord), $x \leq y \wedge y \leq x \Rightarrow x = y$ (antisym_ord) and $x \leq y \wedge y \leq z \Rightarrow x \leq z$ (trans_ord). Showing that a particular type (say nat with its standard ordering $\leq$) is an *instance* of this type-class, i.e. nat::po is a legal type assertion, requires the proof of the above properties follow from the definition of $\leq : nat \times nat \rightarrow bool$. Once this proof has been done while establishing the instance judgement, Isabelle can use this semantic information during static type checking.

We apply this construction to the class cpo that is an extension of po. It requires the symbol $\bot : \alpha::cpo$ and the semantic properties $\bot \leq x$ (least) and directed $X \Rightarrow X \neq \{\} \wedge \exists b. X \ll b$ (complete). Here, directed : (a::po) set $\rightarrow$ bool and "is least upper bound" $\_\ll\_:(a::po)set \rightarrow a \rightarrow bool$ are defined in the usual way for the class of partial orderings, together with lub : (a::po)set $\rightarrow \alpha$ defined as lub S $\equiv$ $\varepsilon x. S \ll x$. For the class of cpo's, the crucial notions for continuity cont : ($\alpha::cpo$ $\rightarrow \beta::cpo) \rightarrow bool$ and the fixpoint operator fix : ($\alpha::cpo \rightarrow \alpha) \rightarrow \alpha$ are defined in the usual way.

From the definition of continuity it is easy to show several proof-rules like cont($\lambda x.x$) (cont_id) and cont($\lambda x.c$) (cont_const_fun), stating the identity or any constant function to be continuous.

The first key result of the fixpoint theory is the proof of the fixpoint theorem:

$$cont\ f \Rightarrow fix\ f = f(fix\ f)$$

from the definition of fix $f \equiv \text{lub}(_{i \in \mathbb{N}} f^i \bot)$. The second key result is the fixpoint induction theorem, that can be used as general proof principle (see chapter 5).

A third result consists in the fact that the definitions $x \leq y \equiv \text{fst } x \leq \text{fst } y \wedge \text{snd } x \leq \text{snd } y$ and $\bot \equiv (\bot, \bot)$ extend cpo's to product cpo's. From these definition the instance judgement for the type constructor "×" itself can be proved:

instance "×" : (cpo,cpo)cpo

On this basis Isabelle's parser can parse mutual recursive definitions of the scheme:

$$\text{letrec} \quad x_1 = E_1(x_1,...,x_n)$$
$$...$$
$$x_n = E_n(x_1,...,x_n)$$
$$\text{in} \quad F(x_1,...,x_n)$$

as $\text{let}(x_1,...,x_n) = \text{fix } \lambda(x_1,...,x_n).(E_1(x_1,...,x_n),...,E_n(x_1,...,x_n))$ in $F(x_1,...,x_n)$. Note that the necessary inference that $(x_1,...,x_n)$ forms a cpo is done by Isabelles type inference and not by tactical theorem proving.

Similarly, the usual extension of cpo's to function spaces can be constructed. This adds arbitrary abstractions to an instance of the fixpoint theory with a concrete language; for CSP, this means an optional extension to "Higher Order CSP" allowing the expression of process schemes within this language (similar algorithmic schemes like *map* and *fold* in functional programming languages).

4.5 The Process Instance of the Fixpoint Theory

The crucial point of the instantiation is the definition of the process ordering. As already mentioned, instead of the usual refinement ordering (which is a partial ordering):

$$P \sqsubseteq Q \equiv \mathcal{F}P \supseteq \mathcal{F}Q \wedge \mathcal{D}P \supseteq \mathcal{D}Q$$

we use the more complex process ordering of [Ros 88] since otherwise the operators will not be continuous in presence of unbounded nondeterminism. A prerequisite is the definition "refusals after" $\mathcal{R}$: process $\Sigma \to$ trace $\Sigma \to P(P \; (\Sigma \oplus \{\sqrt{}\}))$:

$$\mathcal{R}P \, s \equiv \{ X \mid (s,X) \in \mathcal{F}P \}$$

Then the process ordering is introduced as:

$$P \leq Q \equiv \mathcal{D}P \supseteq \mathcal{D}Q$$
$$\wedge \; s \notin \mathcal{D}P \Rightarrow \mathcal{R}P \, s = \mathcal{R}Q \, s$$
$$\wedge \; \mu(\mathcal{D}P) \subseteq \textit{traces} \; \mathcal{F}Q$$

where $\mu \, T$ denotes the set of minimal elements of a set T of finite traces. The difference between these orderings is that $\leq$ orders just approximation, but not non-determinism, i.e.:

$$\text{Bot} \; \leq \; a {\to} \text{Bot} \; \leq \; a {\to} a {\to} \text{Bot} \; ...$$

but:

$$a {\to} \text{Bot} \; \not\leq \; a {\to} \text{Bot} \sqcap b {\to} \text{Bot} \; \not\leq \; a {\to} \text{Bot} \sqcap b {\to} \text{Bot} \sqcap c {\to} \text{Bot} \; \not\leq \; ...$$

Note that the chain outlined above is ordered w.r.t. $\sqsubseteq$, however.

The well-known theorem:

$$P \leq Q \Rightarrow P \sqsubseteq Q \hspace{3cm} \text{(ord\_imp\_ref)}$$

expresses that the process ordering is just a coarser ordering than the refinement ordering.

The definition of $\leq$ proves to be an instance of po. With Bot identified with $\perp$, the type α process is proven to form an instance of the type class cpo. As a consequence we inherit all definitions and theorems from the generic fixpoint theory. The CSP-operator μ is just identified with fix:(process $\Sigma \to$ process Σ) $\to$ process Σ.

A quite important consequence of ord_imp_ref is that the fixpoints (which are known to uniquely exist in the generic fixpoint theory) have a very particular form in the process-instance:

$$\text{fix } f = \text{Abs\_process } (\bigcap_{i \in N} \mathcal{F}(f^i \text{ Bot}), \bigcap_{i \in N} \mathcal{D}(f^i \text{ Bot})) \hspace{1cm} \text{(fix\_eq\_lim\_proc)}$$

i.e. if a fixpoint exists w.r.t. $\leq$, than it coincides with the fixpoint w.r.t. $\sqsubseteq$.

The most complex part of the entire theory is the proof of continuity for the CSP-operators. The required properties have the following form:

$$\text{cont } F \Rightarrow \text{cont } (\lambda x. a \to F x) \hspace{2cm} \text{(cont\_prefix)}$$
$$\text{cont } F \wedge \text{cont } G \Rightarrow \text{cont } (\lambda x. F x \,\square\, G x) \hspace{1cm} \text{(cont\_ndet)}$$
$$\text{cont } F \wedge \text{cont } G \Rightarrow \text{cont } (\lambda x. F x \,\sqcap\, G x) \hspace{1cm} \text{(cont\_det)}$$
$$\text{cont } F \wedge \text{cont } G \Rightarrow \text{cont } (\lambda x. F x \,;\, G x) \hspace{1cm} \text{(cont\_seq)}$$
$$\text{cont } F \wedge \text{cont } G \Rightarrow \text{cont } (\lambda x. F x \,[|A\,|]\, G x) \hspace{1cm} \text{(cont\_parint)}$$
$$\text{cont } F \wedge \text{finite } A \Rightarrow \text{cont } (\lambda x. F x \setminus A) \hspace{1.5cm} \text{(cont\_hide)}$$

. . .

Especially the last two theorems can pass as "highly non-trivial" even by mathematically rigorous standards; as formal proofs, they must be considered as hard. Phrases like "By Königs lemma follows the existence of finitely many traces of the form ... " required weeks of intensive work.

The collection of the above theorems (together with cont_id and cont_const_fun) is used to instantiate Isabelle's simp_tac procedure (see [Pau 94]), that applies them in a backward-chaining technique similarly to PROLOG-interpreters. This yields a tactical program that decides the continuity of arbitrary CSP-expressions with finite hide-sets as required for the application of the Knaster-Tarski theorem or for the fixpoint induction.

4.6 Laws

From the definitions of the CSP-operators the usual CSP-laws can be derived as formally proven theorems. Among them there is also the list drawn from [BR 85]:

$P \square P = P$ $P \square Q = Q \square P$

$P \square (Q \square R) = (P \square Q) \square R$ $P \square (Q \sqcap R) = (P \square Q) \sqcap (P \square R)$

$P \sqcap (Q \square R) = (P \sqcap Q) \square (P \sqcap R)$ $P \square \, Stop = P$

$a \to (P \sqcap Q) = a \to P \sqcap a \to Q$ $a \to P \square a \to Q = a \to P \sqcap a \to Q$

$P \sqcap P = P$ $P \sqcap Q = Q \sqcap P$

$P \sqcap (Q \sqcap R) = (P \sqcap Q) \sqcap R$

$P \parallel Q = Q \parallel P$ $P \parallel (Q \parallel R) = (P \parallel Q) \parallel R$

$P \parallel (Q \sqcap R) = P \parallel Q \sqcap P \parallel R$

$a \to P \parallel b \to Q = Stop \quad$ if $a \neq b$ $a \to P \parallel b \to Q = a \to (P \parallel Q)$ if $a = b$

$P \parallel Stop = Stop$

$P \parallel\parallel Q = Q \parallel\parallel P$ $P \parallel\parallel (Q \parallel\parallel R) = (P \parallel\parallel Q) \parallel\parallel R$

$P \parallel\parallel (Q \sqcap R) = P \parallel\parallel Q \sqcap P \parallel\parallel R$

$a \to P \parallel\parallel b \to Q = a \to (P \parallel\parallel b \to Q) \square b \to (a \to P \parallel\parallel Q)$

$Skip \, ; P = P$ $Stop \, ; P = Stop$

$(a \to P); Q = a \to (P \, ; Q)$ $P \, ; (Q \, ; R) = (P \, ; Q) \, ; R$

$P \, ; (Q \sqcap R) = (P \, ; Q) \sqcap (P \, ; R)$ $(Q \sqcap R) \, ; P = (Q \, ; P) \sqcap (R \, ; P)$

$P \setminus \{a\} \setminus \{a\} = P \setminus \{a\}$ $P \setminus \{a\} \setminus \{b\} = P \setminus \{b\} \setminus \{a\}$

$(a \to P) \setminus \{b\} = a \to P \setminus \{b\} \quad$ if $a \neq b$ $(a \to P) \setminus \{a\} = (P \setminus \{a\})$

$(Q \sqcap R) \setminus A = Q \setminus A \sqcap R \setminus A$

Note that the law $P \parallel\parallel Stop = P$ (as in [BR 85]) does not hold as a consequence of its definition based on the parallel interleave operator. Instead, we have:

$$P \parallel\parallel Stop = P; Stop.$$

5 Proof Support for CSP

Fixpoint theory comes with a general induction principle called fixpoint induction. We will see that it can be expressed particularly elegant in HOL. Moreover, it will be shown that fixpoint induction can be used as proof principle for refinement proofs.

5.1 Fixpoint Induction

The idea of this proof principle is to induce a property P over ascending chains in directed sets. If P is *admissible*, i.e. if validity of P for all elements of a directed set Y always implies validity of P for the least upper bound of Y, then the task of proving a property P for a fixpoint fix f reduces to prove P for all its approximations.

Admissibility is a second order concept and can not be represented inside a first-order logic. In the days of the late Edinburgh LCF-prover, the task was resolved by built-in syntactical checks over predicates, the principles of which had been worked out by meta-theoretic reasoning. These checks were a constant source of errors and annoyance since they inherently conflicted with the overall design goal to keep the core of a theorem-prover small and simple.

In HOL admissibility adm: $(\alpha::cpo \to bool) \to bool$ is just an ordinary predicate (to our knowledge, the idea of an object-logical representation of admissibility is due to [Reg 94]) defined by:

$$adm\ P \equiv \forall Y.\ directed\ Y \Rightarrow (\forall x : Y.\ P\ x) \Rightarrow P(lub\ Y) \qquad (adm\_def)$$

which leads naturally to a list of theorems that implement the reminiscent syntactic checks in ordinary derived proof-rules *inside* the logic:

$adm\ (\lambda x.c)$	(adm_const_fun)
$adm\ P \wedge adm\ Q \Rightarrow adm\ (\lambda x.\ P\ x \wedge Q\ x)$	(adm_conj)
$adm\ P \wedge adm\ Q \Rightarrow adm\ (\lambda x.\ P\ x \vee Q\ x)$	(adm_disj)
$cont\ f \wedge cont\ g \Rightarrow adm\ (\lambda x.\ f\ x \leq g\ x)$	(adm_ord)
etc.	

Admissibility is used in the fixpoint induction principle in the following way:

$$\lfloor\ cont\ f \wedge adm\ P \wedge (\forall\ x.\ P\ x \Rightarrow P(f\ x))\ \rfloor \Rightarrow P\ (fix\ f) \qquad (fix\_ind)$$

The crucial question arises, if the refinement ordering is also admissible. This is vital for the applicability of fixpoint induction for the highly desirable refinement proofs. To our knowledge, this question has not been risen so far in the literature.

Of course, such a property cannot be proven in the generic fixpoint theory (as all theorems above) but only in the process instance.

Proposition: The refinement ordering is admissible, i.e.

$$cont\ f \wedge cont\ g \Rightarrow adm\ (\lambda x.\ f\ x \sqsubseteq g\ x) \qquad (adm\_ref\_ord)$$

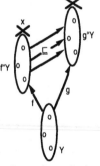

Proof-Sketch: Let f and g be continuous, Y be directed and let $(\forall x:Y.\ f\ x \sqsubseteq g\ x)$ hold. Let f"Y and g"Y denote the image sets of Y w.r.t. f and g. Then the figure aside gives an overview over the situation.

Here x and xa denote the lub's w.r.t. $\leq$. As a consequence of ord_imp_ref and of transitivity of $\sqsubseteq$, both x and xa must be upper bounds w.r.t. $\sqsubseteq$ for f"Y. The question arises if they are also related via $\sqsubseteq$. The answer is positive as a consequence of fix_eq_lim_proc and the definition of $\sqsubseteq$, i.e. x is also *least* upper bound w.r.t. $\sqsubseteq$.

This fact gives us that living with two orders in CSP (as a price for unbounded nondeterminism) is perhaps inelegant and uncomfortable, but perfectly possible.

5.2 Take Lemmas

Fixpoint induction proofs are usually quite ingenious proofs. In this section we will discuss a more specialised proof-scheme that is more amenable to automated reasoning. This principle will also shed some light on the potential of model-checking techniques (seen from the perspective of symbolic reasoning).

The principle of take lemmas is enclosed in the take operator $\_\downarrow\_ : process\ \Sigma \to nat \to process\ \Sigma$, that cuts a behaviour of a process up to a depth n, for example:

$$fix\ (\lambda x.\ a \to x) \downarrow 1 = a \to Bot.$$

The definition of this operator along the usual lines yields the characterising theorems:

$\mathcal{H}(P \downarrow n) = \mathcal{F}P \cup \{ (s, X) \mid s \in \mathcal{D}(P \downarrow n) \}$

$\mathcal{D}(P \downarrow n) = \mathcal{D}P \cup \{ s \wedge t \mid |s|=n \wedge \text{tick-free } s \wedge \text{front-tick-free}(t) \wedge s \in \text{traces } P \}$

From there the following *cutting-rules* are derived:

$P \downarrow 0 = \text{Bot}$ $\qquad\qquad (a \to P) \downarrow n = a \to (P \downarrow n\text{-}1)$

$(Q \sqcap R) \downarrow n = (Q \downarrow n \sqcap R \downarrow n)$

...

The principal characteristic of this operator is that it is monotone w.r.t. $\leq$:

$n \leq m \Rightarrow P{\downarrow}n \leq P{\downarrow}m$

This fact allows us to specialise the fixpoint-induction to the $\leq$-take-lemma:

$\forall m \, ((\forall n. \, n < m \wedge P{\downarrow}n \sqsubseteq Q{\downarrow}n) \Rightarrow P{\downarrow}m \sqsubseteq Q{\downarrow}m) \Rightarrow P \sqsubseteq Q$

Note the strong similarity of this rule to Noetherian induction. Using this take-lemma, we can perform the following backward-proof example:

$\qquad$ $\text{fix}(\lambda x. \, a \to x) \sqsubseteq \text{fix}(\lambda x. \, a \to x \sqcap \lambda x. \, b \to x)$

$\Leftarrow \quad \{ \text{by} \leq\text{-take-lemma}, \forall\text{-intro}, \Rightarrow\text{-intro} \}$

$\qquad$ $|[\forall n. \, n < m \wedge \text{fix}(\lambda x. \, a \to x){\downarrow}n \sqsubseteq \text{fix}(\lambda x. \, a \to x \sqcap \lambda x. \, b \to x){\downarrow}n]| \Rightarrow$
$\qquad\qquad$ $\text{fix}(\lambda x. \, a \to x){\downarrow}m \sqsubseteq \text{fix}(\lambda x. \, a \to x \sqcap \lambda x. \, b \to x){\downarrow}m$

$\Leftarrow \quad \{ \text{by knaster-tarski} \}$

$\qquad$ $|[...]| \Rightarrow (a \to \text{fix}(...)){\downarrow}m \sqsubseteq (a \to \text{fix}(...) \sqcap b \to \text{fix}(...)){\downarrow}m$

$\Leftarrow \quad \{ \text{by cutting rules} \}$

$\qquad$ $|[...]| \Rightarrow a \to(\text{fix}(...){\downarrow}m\text{-}1) \sqsubseteq a \to(\text{fix}(...){\downarrow}m\text{-}1) \sqcap b \to(\text{fix}(...){\downarrow}m\text{-}1)$

$\Leftarrow \quad \{ \text{by refinement projection left} \}$

$\qquad$ $|[...]| \Rightarrow a \to(\text{fix}(...){\downarrow}m\text{-}1) \sqsubseteq a \to(\text{fix}(...){\downarrow}m\text{-}1)$

$\Leftarrow \quad \{ \text{by refinement monotonicity} \}$

$\qquad$ $|[\forall n. \, n < m \wedge \text{fix}(...){\downarrow}n \sqsubseteq \text{fix}(...){\downarrow}n]| \Rightarrow \text{fix}(...){\downarrow}m\text{-}1 \sqsubseteq \text{fix}(...){\downarrow}m\text{-}1$

$\Leftarrow \quad \{ \text{by arithmetic and assumption} \}$

$\qquad$ True

Even without knowing anything about tactical programming in Isabelle, it is not hard to see how this proof-technique can be mechanised. The essential difficulties are to unfold fix-terms only in a controlled way, to "drive inside" the take-operator occurrences while decreasing their offsets and to control the necessary backtracking for refinement projection left rsp. refinement projection right.

The technique resembles very much the usual graph-exploration techniques in labelled transition diagrams (as implemented in FDR). The nodes in the graph correspond to equivalence-classes on take-terms, the edges applications of the refinement monotonicity. If problematic pathological cases were avoided (so-called *non-contracting* bodies of fix like $\text{fix}(\lambda x.x)$), and if graph-regularity can be assured, this tactical program will be a (proven correct) decision procedure.

6 Example

The following example is drawn from [For 95], pp. 5. It specifies a process *COPY* that behaves like a one place buffer. Then an implementation using a separate sender *SEND* and receiver processes *REC*, communicating via a channel *mid* and an acknowledgement *ack*. Instead of using model-checking for a known, finite alphabet of events, we will prove via fixpoint induction for arbitrary alphabets that the implementation refines the specification. Note, however, that the alphabets must still be finite because of the hiding operator in *SYSTEM*, which is known to be noncontinuous for infinite alphabets (see [BR 86]).

On the top-level of our CSP theory in Isabelle, new syntax for channels has been introduced. Hence *writing* c!a→P is represented by (c,a)→P and *receiving* c?x→P x is mapped to an appropriate representation with multi-prefixes.

Our can be represented in an Isabelle theory by introducing a data type for all involved channels. This can be done in an ML-like definition:

datatype channel = left | right | mid | ack

The process COPY : process (channel × Σ) is defined as follows:

COPY ≡ (letrec COPY = left?x → right!x → COPY in COPY   (COPY_def)

The definition of the implementation reads as follows:

SYSTEM ≡ (letrec   SEND = left?x → mid!x → ack?y → SEND;
                       REC = mid?x → right!x → ack!x → REC
              in   SEND [I SYN I] REC) \ SYN)   (SYSTEM_def)

where SYN ≡ {x I fst x = mid ∨ fst x = ack}.

Now we can state the desired proof-goal COPY ⊑ SYSTEM (under premise P : finite SYN) with COPY acting as specification of the behaviour of SYSTEM.

In the following presentation of the backward-proof, we suppress the required proofs of continuity (which were eliminated by an appropriate tactic). For convenience, we introduce G as abbreviation for the often re-occurring term:

(λu. (left?x→mid!x→ack?y→fst u, mid?x→right!x→ack!x→snd u))

Then, the main steps of the refinement proof are:

COPY ⊑ SYSTEM
⇐   {by COPY_def, SYSTEM_def, fix_ind, adm_ref_ord }
1)   Fixpoint induction base:
        Bot ⊑ SYSTEM
     ⇐   {by Bot ⊑ X }
        True
2)   Fixpoint induction step:
        I[x ⊑   (fst (fix G) [I SYN I] snd (fix G)) \ SYN]I ⇒
              left?xa → right!xa → x
           ⊑
              (fst (fix G) [I SYN I] snd (fix G)) \ SYN
     ⇐   {by knaster_tarski over both fix-terms, fst-snd-simplification}
        I[...]I ⇒
              left ? xa → right ! xa → x
           ⊑
              (left?x → mid!x → ack?y → fst (fix G)
              [I SYN I]
              mid?x → right!x → ack!x → snd (fix G)) \ SYN

$\Leftarrow$ {by distributive laws of the hiding operator, the
parallel interleave operator and the Mprefix operator}

|[...]| $\Rightarrow$

    left?xa $\to$ right!xa $\to$ x

$\sqsubseteq$

    left?x $\to$ right!x$\to$((fst(fix G)|]SYN[|snd(fix G)\SYN)

$\Leftarrow$ {by monotonicity of multiprefix operator w.r.t refinement
order $\sqsubseteq$ and by assumption}

True

The premise P was only used in the proof of admissibility, when applying adm_ref_ord. A careful analysis of its proof reveals that it can be strengthened to cont f $\wedge$ mono g $\Rightarrow$ adm (λx. f x $\sqsubseteq$ g x), while on the other hand a proof of monotonicity for the hide operator with arbitrary sets seems feasible. This seems to suggest that at least the class of typical refinements fix f $\sqsubseteq$ (fix g)\A (provided that f and g continuous) with one outermost hiding operator hiding away an arbitrary internal communication channel introduced by the refinement step can be handled also in the infinite case.

7 Conclusion

We have presented a corrected, shallow embedding of CSP into higher-order logic that nevertheless preserves the algebraic properties of CSP for which we have formal, machine-checked proofs. This embedding forms an implementation of a "CSP Workbench" that allows interactive theorem proving in CSP-specifications with infinite alphabet (complementary to the FDR-tool that allows automatic proofs on specialised, finite CSP-specifications). The collection of theories has been converted directly by Isabelle into a "textbook on CSP theory" available under "http://www. informatik.uni-bremen.de/~bu/isa_doc/CSP/doc/html/index.html".

Some remarks should be given on the amount of verification work. The theory presented so far required one man year (excluding a first attempt of five man months invested in a model much closer to [Hoa 85] that turned out to be infeasible). This effort could probably have been reduced by better expert advice, since our major problems came from wrong theoretic foundations, gaps in proofs etc. and not from the technicalities of "embedding" or proving. Although the effort still may be qualified as considerable, we see a need for more machine assisted verification work, since there is a tendency to dilute the formal core of a research programme, especially a successful one. In the meantime there are so many different variants of CSP, that they are very likely to be incompatible. Due to the high publication pressure, authors tend to modify the definitions according to their needs and cite the proofs from elsewhere ("proof is done analogously to [XY ??]"). In such a situation, research peers can shift more research effort to *canonical* theory representations that were verified by machine assistance.

We are not denying that formal proof activity without mathematical intuition is blind, but we would like to emphasise that intuition tends to delude more often in foundational theories of computer science that in other mathematical research areas, perhaps due to their discrete nature and resulting combinatorial complexity. The treatment of tick is an example for a unintuitive, combinatorically complex part of a complex theory. Obviously, the situation gets even worse if combinations of formal methods — as envisaged by the UniForM project [Kri+95] — are undertaken. Nevertheless, such combination-methods are particularly desirable since "there is no single theory for all stages of the development of software [...]. Ideas, concepts, methods and calculations will have to be drawn from a wide range of theories, and they are going to have to work together consistently [...]" (again from Hoare's invited lecture at FME'96).

7.1 Future Work

We will investigate to prove the denotational semantics as described in this paper consistent with the operational semantics of FDR [For 95], i.e. we prove consistency with the formal specification of this tool (we are not planning to "prove FDR" w.r.t. this specification). As a result, one can embed the FDR-tool as a proof-oracle (external decision procedure) within Isabelle in order to build up a logically consistent, combined environment for the reasoning over CSP. This is particularly attractive, since both tools deliver complementary deduction support: Isabelle/CSP provides interactive proof support for infinite CSP, while FDR excels at automatic refinement proofs for specialised, finite CSP specifications. In such an environment, general requirements-engineering is possible, followed by a sequence of "massage steps" that make a specification amenable for FDR, concluded by combined proof-efforts of FDR and Isabelle/CSP.

We are interested in designing a transformational methodology in CSP. This means that a collection of "transformation rules" in the sense of [KSW 96a] should be designed that allow the construction of a CSP-process by identifying and refining *design-patterns*.

We work at a safe and semantically clean integration of CSP with other industry-standard specification languages like Z (whose representation in Isabelle/HOL has been worked out in [KSW 96b]). First conceptual studies for such an integration are [Fis 97].

Finally we admit that an encapsulation of the Isabelle/CSP embedding in an integrated *tool* is of crucial importance for further acceptance in industry. Following the lines of [KSW 96a], a generic user interface has been developed that can be instantiated with LCF-style theorem-prover in order to encapsulate them as a specialised tool (see [KLMW 96]). An instance of this technology with Isabelle/CSP has been envisaged. Moreover, an even wider goal of UniForM is to provide a workbench to integrate these tools and to provide them with inter-tool communication, version-management and development-management. We believe that this technology should ease the construction of powerful formal methods tools and simplify the technical side of interchanging information between them.

Acknowledgement. We would like to thank A.W.Roscoe for several hints helping us to bridge big steps in rigorous mathematical proofs. Prof. Bernd Krieg-Brückner, Thomas Santen, Sabine Dick, Christoph Lüth and Clemens Fischer read earlier versions of this paper.

References

[And 86]   P.B. Andrews: *An Introduction to Mathematical Logic and Type Theory: To Truth Through Proof*, Academic Press, 1986.

[BH 95]   J. P. Bowen, M. J. Hinchey: Seven more Myths of Formal Methods: Dispelling Industrial Prejudices, in *FME'94: Industrial Benefit of Formal Methods*, proc. 2nd Int. Symposium of Formal Methods Europe, LNCS 873, Springer Verlag 1994, pp. 105-117.

[BR 85]   S.D. Brookes, A.W. Roscoe: An improved failures model for communicating processes. In: S.D.Brookes (ed.): Seminar on Semantics of Concurrency. LNCS 197, Springer Verlag, pp. 281-305. 1985.

[Cam 91]   A.J. Camillieri: A Higher Order Logic Mechanization of the CSP Failure-Divergence Semantics. G. Birtwistle (ed): *IVth Higher Order Workshop*, Banff 1990. Workshops in Computing, Springer Verlag, 1991.

[Chu 40]   A. Church: A formulation of the simple theory of types. *Journal of Symbolic Logic*, 5, 1940, pp. 56-68.

[Fis 97]   C. Fischer: Combining CSP and Z. Submitted for publication.

[For 95]   Formal Systems (Europe) Ltd: Failures-Divergence Refinement: FDR2, Dec.1995. Preliminary Manual.

[GM 93]   M.J.C. Gordon, T.M. Melham: *Introduction to HOL: a Theorem Proving Environment for Higher order Logics*, Cambridge Univ. Press, 1993.

[Hoa 85]   C.A.R.Hoare: Communication Sequential Processes.Prentice-Hall, 1985

[KLMW96]   Kolyang, C. Lüth, T. Meier, B. Wolff: Generic Interfaces for Formal Development Support Tools. In: Workshop for Verification and Validation Tools, Bremen. to appear in LNCS.

[Kri+95]   B. Krieg-Brückner, J. Peleska, E.-R. Olderog, D. Balzer, A. Baer, : Uniform Workbench — Universelle Entwicklungsumgebung für formale Methoden. Technischer Bericht 8/95, Universität Bremen, 1995. See also the project home-page: http://www.informatik.uni-bremen.de/~uniform.

[KSW 96a]   Kolyang, T. Santen, B. Wolff: Correct and User-Friendly Implementations of Transformation Systems. Proc. Formal Methods Europe, Oxford. LNCS 1051, Springer Verlag, 1996.

[KSW 96b]   Kolyang, T. Santen, B. Wolff: A structure preserving encoding of Z in Isabelle/HOL. In J. von Wright, J. Grundy and J. Harrison (eds): Theorem Proving in Higher/Order Logics — 9th International Conference, LNCS 1125, pp. 283-298, 1996.

[Pau 94]   L. C. Paulson: *Isabelle - A Generic Theorem Prover*. LNCS 828, 1994.

[RB 89]   A.W. Roscoe, G. Barett: Unbounded Nondeterminism in CSP. In: M. Main, A.Melton,M.Mislove,D.Schmidt (eds): 9th International Conference in Mathematical Foundations of Programming Semantics. LNCS 442,pp. 160-193, 1989.

[Reg 94]   F. Regensburger: HOLCF: Eine konservative Einbettung von LCF in HOL. Phd thesis, Technische Universität München. 1994.

[Ros 88]   A.W. Roscoe: An alternative Order for the Failures Model. In: Two Papers on CSP. Technical Monograph PRG-67, Oxford university Computer Laboratory, Programming Research Group, July 1988.

[Ros 96]   A.W. Roscoe, e-mail communication with the authors.

A Proof Obligation Generator for VDM-SL

Bernhard K. Aichernig[1] and Peter Gorm Larsen[2]

[1] Graz University of Technology, Institute of Software Technology (IST),
Münzgrabenstr. 11/II, 8010 Graz, Austria
[2] Institute of Applied Computer Science (IFAD), Forskerparken 10, 5230 Odense M,
Denmark

Abstract. In this paper an extension of the IFAD VDM-SL Toolbox
with a proof obligation generator is described. Static type checking in
VDM is undecidable in general and therefore the type checker must be
incomplete. Hence, for the "difficult" parts introducing undecidability,
it is up to the user to verify the consistency of a specification. Instead
of providing error messages and warnings, the approach of generating
proof obligations for the consistency of VDM-SL specifications is taken.
The overall goal of this work is to automate the generation of proof
obligations for VDM-SL. Proof obligation generation has already been
carried out for a number of related notations, but VDM-SL contains a
number of challenging constructs (e.g. patterns, non-disjoint union types,
and operations) for which new research is presented in this paper.

1   Introduction

During the last few years the interest in formal software development has been
growing rapidly. One of the main reasons for this is the availability of tools to support the developer in using these formal methods. This paper describes an extension of the IFAD VDM-SL Toolbox [13, 24], a commercial CASE tool supporting
the Vienna Development Method (VDM). Amongst other features the Toolbox
provides parsing and type checking of specifications written in VDM-SL, the
specification language of VDM, which has been standardised under ISO [23, 26].

VDM is one of the most widely used formal methods, and it can be applied
to the construction of a large variety of software systems. It is a *model-oriented*
method, i.e. its formal descriptions (VDM specifications) consist of an explicit
model of the system being constructed. A system design is generated through a
series of specifications, where each specification is more concrete and closer to
the implementation than the previous one [21]. Each of these development steps
introduces a formal refinement statement which, when appropriately verified,
ensures the (relative) correctness of the implemented system.

The existing type checker of the IFAD VDM-SL Toolbox supports extensive consistency checks according to the static semantics of the ISO standard.
However, the problem of static type checking VDM-SL specifications is that
it is undecidable in general, which means that the consistency checks must be
incomplete. Thus, it is up to the user to check the "difficult parts" in a specification, which causes the undecidability. The existing type checker generates

error messages and warnings to identify places with possible inconsistencies. In VDM-SL the undecidability is introduced by partial operators, functions with pre-conditions, union types and subtypes. Division is one of the most well-known examples of partial operators. Considering the expression a/b, the requirement for the expression to be consistent is that b is not equal to zero. In general, this cannot be guaranteed by static type checking, which means the expression may or may not be consistent.

Instead of generating error messages, this work improves the existing type checker by generating proof obligations for those parts of a specification which cause the undecidability and cannot be checked automatically. These proof obligations (PO) are unproved theorems stating that a certain condition must hold in order to ensure that a specification is consistent in itself. For a/b the condition for consistency is $b \neq 0$. If all POs generated for a specification can be proved, then the specification is consistent. Therefore, the POs are designed to be loaded into the proof tool of the Toolbox, which is currently under development at IFAD [3, 2]. However, many of the generated proof obligations are trivial or simple, and can be informally justified by simply inspecting the PO.

The notion of POs for VDM has been based on previous work [21, 20, 6]. The main contribution of this work is the automation of the generation of POs. In addition, Sections 5 and 6 present new work in the areas of patterns and explicit operations where no existing research for POs was present.

The proof obligation generator (POG) is an extension of the existing specification of the static semantics and has been formally specified using an executable subset of VDM-SL. To distinguish between the meta and the object level in this paper, the specification parts of the POG are pretty printed using the mathematical concrete syntax of VDM-SL, and the used examples with their generated POs are printed in the ASCII VDM-SL notation.

After this introduction an overview of the existing type checker is provided. This is followed by a series of sections presenting the proof obligation generator. In this technical part of the paper the approach dealing with the unique features of VDM-SL are explained and a little familiarity with VDM-SL is assumed. In Section 7 the relation to existing work is given and finally Section 8 contains some concluding remarks and identification of possible directions for future work.

2 The Existing Type Checker

This section is an overview of the existing type checker focusing on the parts which are essential for the POG. The specification document of the existing type checker contains more than 250 pages organised in 12 different modules. In addition there is a test environment with a large number of test cases used for regression testing. Due to the fact that the IFAD VDM-SL Toolbox is a commercial product, the specification document is confidential. Thus, we are only able to show very small extracts from this specification here.

2.1 Rejection and Acceptance

Type checking for VDM-SL is somewhat different from what is usually found in programming languages [7, 10]. According to the standard of VDM-SL [23] a dual strategy of type checking is applied: (1) Impossibly consistent specifications are rejected. For example, the type checker will raise an error message if a specification contains the expression $1 + true$. This kind of rejection approach is usually used for traditional programming languages. (2) Definitely consistent specifications are accepted. For example, $1 + 2$ is definitely consistent.

However, for many VDM-SL constructs it cannot be decided if they are definitely consistent, although they are possibly consistent. These are the "difficult parts" introducing the undecidability. For example, the expression a/b is possible consistent if a and b are of a numeric type, but it cannot be statically checked that b is unequal to zero. In fact, only some very simple specifications are accepted by the existing type checker to be definitely consistent.

According to the dual strategy in the static semantics the type checker can be used in two different modes: (1) in possible mode (POS) error messages indicate not possibly consistent parts; and (2) in definite mode the absence of error messages indicates the acceptance of a specification. In the IFAD VDM-SL Toolbox the two modes of type checking are selected by setting an option [16].

As mentioned in the introduction not only partial operators cause undecidability, but also the rich type system of VDM-SL. This is mainly due to the fact that the union type is an ordinary set-theoretic union without injection and projection functions. In addition subtypes are described by type invariants restricting the "legal" values of a type in a set-theoretic manner without any requirement for explicitly "casting" the values to be members of the subtype. In general such invariants can be arbitrarily complex and thus it is impossible to statically determine whether an expression belongs to a required subtype.

The following algorithm for checking the compatibility of two types reflects the dual strategy of type checking in VDM-SL.

2.2 Type Compatibility

The central task of the type checker is to check if two types, an expected and an actual, are compatible. Due to the rich type system of VDM-SL a simple comparison is not possible in general. Furthermore, the task is statically undecidable in general, because of non-disjoint unions and subtypes [10].

The operation[3] performing the compatibility check *IsCompatible* takes three arguments. The first argument specifies the kind of type checking that should be performed (POS or DEF). The next two arguments (*TpR1*, *TpR2*) are the types that must be checked. They are of type *TypeRep*, the internal type representation in the type checker.

---

[3] An operation is used, because the auxiliary operations *IsOverlapping* and *IsSubType* refer to the environment state containing type names and their type binding.

$IsCompatible : (\text{POS} \mid \text{DEF}) \times TypeRep \times TypeRep \xrightarrow{o} \mathbb{B}$

$IsCompatible\ (i,\ TpR1,\ TpR2) \triangleq$
  if $TpR1 = TpR2$
  then return true
  else cases i:
       POS $\rightarrow IsOverlapping(TpR1,\ TpR2)$,
       DEF $\rightarrow IsSubType(TpR1,\ TpR2)$
    end;

In the trivial case that the two types are the same, true is returned. Otherwise, depending on the kind of type-checking (possible or definite), the function checks whether the types are overlapping or whether one is a subtype of the other.

Two types are possibly compatible if they are overlapping, which means that the sets of values they denote are non-disjoint. In VDM-SL two different basic types are overlapping if both of them are numeric types. If two types are not overlapping, they cannot possibly be consistent (rejection).

In definite mode all values denoted by an actual type must be compatible to an expected type. Therefore, the algorithm has to check that the set of values denoted by the actual type is a subset of the set of values denoted by the expected type. In short, the actual type must be a subtype of the expected type. For example, every numeric type is a subtype of the type **real** denoting the real numbers.

2.3 Well-formedness of Expressions

According to the strategy of rejection and acceptance, the static semantics defines two kinds of predicates in order to check whether an expression is well-formed. These predicates denote the possible and definite well-formedness of an expression [10, 23].

If the existing type checker of the IFAD VDM-SL Toolbox performs possible type checking (POS mode) an expression is rejected if it is not possibly well-formed. In definite mode (DEF) the type checker only accepts expressions if they are definitely well-formed, which means that an error message is raised if the definite well-formedness cannot be statically checked. As an example the specification of the well-formedness predicate for a division expression is given below:

$wf\text{-}NUMDIV : (\text{POS} \mid \text{DEF}) \times BinaryExpr \xrightarrow{o} \mathbb{B} \times TypeRep$

$wf\text{-}NUMDIV\ (i, \text{mk-}BinaryExpr\ (lhs, \text{-}, rhs)) \triangleq$
  let mk- $(wf\text{-}lhs, lhstype) = wf\text{-}Expr\ (i, lhs)$,
    mk- $(wf\text{-}rhs, rhstype) = wf\text{-}Expr\ (i, rhs)$,
    $ExpectedLhsAndRhsType = \text{mk-}BasicTypeRep\ (\text{REAL})$ in
  let $lhscomp = IsCompatible\ (i, lhstype, ExpectedLhsAndRhsType)$,

$rhscomp = IsCompatible\,(i, rhstype, ExpectedLhsAndRhsType)$ in
(if $\neg\ lhscomp$
then $GenErr("Lhs\ of\ '/'\ is\ not\ a\ numeric\ type")$;
if $\neg\ rhscomp$
then $GenErr("Rhs\ of\ '/'\ is\ not\ a\ numeric\ type")$
elseif $i = \text{DEF} \wedge rhstype \neq \text{mk-}BasicTypeRep\,(\text{NATONE})$
then $(GenErr("Rhs\ of\ '/'\ must\ be\ non\ zero")$;
    return mk-$(\text{false}, ExpectedLhsAndRhsType)$);
return mk-$(wf\text{-}lhs \wedge wf\text{-}rhs \wedge lhscomp \wedge rhscomp,$
    $ExpectedLhsAndRhsType)$)

The choice of possible and definite well-formedness is conveyed to the well-formedness operation via the first parameter i. The second parameter is the expression to be checked, which in this case is a binary expression with the binary operator '$/$'. The signature shows that in addition to the well-formedness of subexpressions, the type of the expression is returned. Analysing the body, four parts can be distinguished: (1) The well-formedness and the types of the left- and right-hand side (lhs and rhs) are determined. (2) The check whether the left- and right-hand side are compatible to the expected type. (3) Error Messages are raised. Note the additional error message in definite mode: To be accepted, rhs must be of type N_1, which denotes the natural numbers excluding zero. This type is needed for static acceptance, because no other basic numeric type in VDM-SL excludes zero. (4) The well-formedness and type of the division expression are returned. It is the goal of this work to generate proof obligations instead of error messages in definite mode. In the following section this modification of the type checker is explained.

3 The Proof Obligation Generator

The existing type checker specification document was extended with one extra module and the total size became approximately 300 pages [4]. The test cases and the test environment were naturally also adapted to take these changes into account.

The central idea underlying the approach presented here (proposed in [10, 11]) is to extend type checking by generating proof obligations for the "difficult" parts which cause the undecidability. In this section we will describe how the existing type checker has been extended and modified to perform this task. The proof obligations (PO) should replace the error messages, raised by the definite type checker.

Fig. 1 provides an overview of the data flow to and from the type checker. A VDM-SL specification is syntax checked by the parser which produces an abstract syntax tree of the specification. The abstract syntax tree is the input for the type checker (static semantics). If type checking in possible mode fails, a list of error messages is generated. In definite mode the type checker becomes the proof obligation generator. These proof obligations can be inspected through the graphical user interface (GUI) and/or they can be loaded into the proof tool.

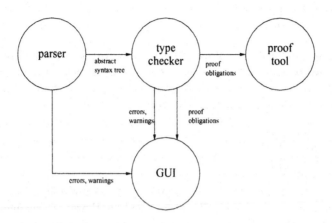

Fig. 1. Interaction of the new type checker.

The main advantage of this approach is the combination of a type checker and a proof tool. In the cases where the type checker is not able to check the consistency, the proof theory in the proof tool can be applied to prove the consistency. The link between the two components are the generated proof obligations. Minor simplifications and proofs of trivial proof obligations could be made directly by the POG. However, in the present approach the decision has been made to forward these tasks to the proof tool, which is designed for these purposes.

3.1 Proof Obligations

A proof obligation for type consistency is a statement that must be proved in order to ensure type consistency. Therefore, the POG is a conditional type checker which returns true under the assumption that the POs generated during the type check can be proved. This process is called conditional type checking. In order to be able to prove POs, they contain context information. The general form of a proof obligation is that of a proof rule, where the assumptions are generated out of the context and the conclusion is the property that must hold. Thus, the general form of a PO is

$$\frac{\text{context information}}{\text{predicate}}$$

In the examples below, the proof obligations will be given in an ASCII representation which is:

```
PO: context information ==> predicate
```

A proof obligation is modelled as a proof (inference) rule consisting of a list of hypotheses and a conclusion. The rule states that the conclusion holds whenever the hypotheses hold [6, 20]. The abstract syntax for a proof rule is:

PrfRule :: *hyp* : *Sequent**
         con : *AllExpr*;

To be compatible with the proof theory a hypothesis is defined as a sequent $P \vdash R$. Its meaning is that the local conclusion R is derivable from the local assumptions P in a subproof. Formally, a sequent is composed of local variables, a sequence of local assumptions, and a local conclusion:

Sequent :: *vars* : *Name**
        lhyp : *AllExpr**
        lcon : *AllExpr*;

However, it turned out that for formulating the proof obligations the use of local assumptions is not needed. Therefore, the hypotheses are sequents without local assumptions ($\vdash R$). In the following, we skip the turnstile in the hypotheses, when we present a proof obligation.

AllExpr is a syntactic extension of VDM-SL expressions with type judgements (e.g., $3 : \mathbb{N}$). This extension is necessary in order to reason over types.

AllExpr = *Expr* | *TypeJudgement*;

TypeJudgement :: *expr* : *Expr*
               type : *TypeRep*

3.2 Context Generation

Context information forms the hypothesis of a proof obligation. Therefore, the existing specification of the type checker has been extended in order to generate the context. The context of a certain location in a specification is the summation of logical conditions that must hold in order to reach this location during evaluation. The following example illustrates the notion of context:

```
if is-nat(x) then x + 1 else 1
```

To reach `x + 1` during the evaluation, the condition `is-nat(x)` must be true. Therefore, the context of `x + 1` is `is-nat(x)`. Obviously, the context of 1 in the else branch is `not is-nat(x)`.

For generating proof obligations we distinguish between two kinds of context:

Type judgements of the form *identifier* : *Type* are used to record membership of a type. This may be read as "*identifier* is of type *Type*". They are provided as context information to infer over types in the typed logic of partial functions and to provide the proof tool with the needed type information. The type information is stored in the environment of the type checker.

Boolean expressions like `is-nat(x)` in our example above are stored in a context stack, while performing the consistency check. When checking the then-branch of an if-expression the test expression (above: `is-nat(x)`) is pushed onto the stack. Checking the else branch, we first remove the test expression from the stack (pop), then the negated test expression (above: `not is-nat(x)`) is pushed onto the stack.

4 Proof Obligations for Expressions and Functions

When type checking VDM-SL expressions, two categories of consistency checks can be distinguished: (1) Type compatibility and (2) domain checking, which checks whether functions and operators are applied to their defined domains. Both may be undecidable. The first because of union and subtypes, the second because of partial operators and functions with pre-conditions. In addition to these two categories the new POG also generates satisfiability obligations for implicitly defined functions and operations [21].

4.1 Type Compatibility

A compatibility check fails if the actual type and an expected type are overlapping, but the first is not a subtype of the second. This undecidable case occurs if the actual type is a union type or if the expected type is a subtype of the actual type.

Consider the function f, which increases its argument if it is a natural number, otherwise 1 is returned.

```
f: bool | nat -> N1
f(x) == if is-nat(x) then x + 1 else 1
```

The returned value is restricted by an invariant to the natural numbers unequal to zero: `N1 = nat inv n == n <> 0`. The function is consistent, which means it will not cause a run-time error. However, the existing type checker fails to accept it, because: (1) the plus operator in `x + 1` expects numeric types and therefore x must be compatible to (here: a subtype of) `real`. However, the actual type of x is the union type `bool | nat` which only overlaps the type `real`, but is not a subtype of it. (2) To check the consistency of the return value the type checker would have to statically determine, whether the invariant function is true or false, which is is not possible.

Therefore the extended type checker raises two proof obligations stating the needed properties that in cases: (1) x is of type `real` and (2) the invariant holds:

```
PO1: is-nat(x)  ==>  x:real
PO2: x:bool | nat  ==> inv-N1( if is-nat(x) then x + 1 else 1 )
```

PO1 trivially states that if x is a natural number then it is a real number. Note that this theorem is only valid for VDM-SL, with non-disjoint types. This PO can be proved automatically by the proof tool. PO2 states that for the function body the implicitly defined invariant function for N1 holds.

4.2 Domain Checking

For domain checking, proof obligations are generated for partial operators and for function applications if the function has a pre-condition. These POs ensure that the operands/parameters are in the defined domain. Examples of partial operators are division, head and tail. A pre-condition in a function restricts the domain by an additional predicate. The use of such a function generates a proof obligation stating that the pre-condition function holds. Below the general POs for a / b and g(a), where g is defined with a pre-condition, are given:

```
PO1: context ==> b <> 0
PO2: context ==> pre-g(a)
```

Below we illustrate how such domain checking is carried out for partial operators. Again, the well-formedness operation of a division expression serves as the demonstrating part of the specification to illustrate the changes made for the POG. To see the modifications compare the following with the specification in Section 2.3:

$wf\text{-}NUMDIV\text{-}POG : (\text{POS} \mid \text{DEF}) \times BinaryExpr \xrightarrow{o} \mathbb{B} \times TypeRep$

$wf\text{-}NUMDIV\text{-}POG\,(i, \text{mk-}BinaryExpr\,(lhs, \text{-}, rhs)) \triangleq$
    let mk-$(wf\text{-}lhs, lhstype) = wf\text{-}Expr\,(i, lhs),$
       mk-$(wf\text{-}rhs, rhstype) = wf\text{-}Expr\,(i, rhs),$
       $ExpectedLhsAndRhsType = \text{mk-}BasicTypeRep\,(\text{REAL})$ in
    let $lhscomp = IsCompatible\,(i, lhstype, ExpectedLhsAndRhsType),$
       $rhscomp = IsCompatible\,(i, rhstype, ExpectedLhsAndRhsType)$ in
   (if $\neg\, lhscomp$
   then if $i = \text{DEF}$
      then $GenPO(\text{mk-}TypeJudgement\,(lhs, ExpectedLhsAndRhsType))$
      else $GenErr(\text{"Lhs of '/' is not a numeric type"})$;
   if $\neg\, rhscomp$
   then if $i = \text{DEF}$
      then $GenPO(\text{mk-}TypeJudgement\,(rhs, ExpectedLhsAndRhsType))$
      else $GenErr(\text{"Rhs of '/' is not a numeric type"})$;
   if $i = \text{DEF} \wedge rhstp \neq \text{mk-}REP\text{'}BasicTypeRep\,(\text{NATONE})$
   then $GenPO(\text{mk-}BinaryExpr\,(rhs, \text{NE}, \text{mk-}RealLit\,(0), \text{nil}\,))$;
   if $i = \text{DEF}$
   then return mk-$(wf\text{-}lhs \wedge wf\text{-}rhs, ExpectedLhsAndRhsType)$
   else return mk-$(wf\text{-}lhs \wedge wf\text{-}rhs \wedge lhscomp \wedge rhscomp,$
            $ExpectedLhsAndRhsType)\,)$

The main difference compared to the previous specification is the generation of proof obligations in DEF mode, instead of error messages: If the compatibility check is not successful a PO is generated ($GenPO$) stating that the expression (rhs or lhs) is of the expected type. This is done using a type judgement. For domain checking a PO stating that the right-hand side is not equal (NE) to zero is generated. In definite mode only the well-formedness of the left- and right-hand side is returned, because the compatibility and the domain constraint are assumed to be true. This assumption is verified later using the proof tool by proving the generated proof obligations. The operation *GenPO* takes the conclusion of the PO as an argument. During type checking the context is collected from the abstract syntax tree and is stored separately and updated in a context stack. This context together with the conclusion argument is used by *GenPO* to synthesise a proof obligation.

4.3 Satisfiability

Satisfiability obligations state that it must be possible to find a model for implicitly defined constructs such that for all valid input a valid output must exist. The satisfiability of an implicit function is thus another VDM-SL concept that is covered by the POG. Implicit functions are defined by means of pre- and post-conditions. A post-condition is a truth valued expression which specifies what must hold after the function is evaluated. A post-condition can refer to the result identifier and the parameter values. Consider an implicit specification of the division:

```
Div( a:real, b:real) r:real
pre b <> 0
post a = r * b
```

The pre-condition restricts the domain of div. The post-condition states a relation between the operands a, b and the result r. For an implicit function definition to be consistent, there must exist a return value satisfying the post-condition when the pre-condition is satisfied. This property is called the satisfiability of implicit functions. Below the satisfiability PO for Div is given:

```
PO: b <> 0 ==> exists r:real &  a = r * b
```

As in explicit functions the pre-condition is taken as the context. A similar strategy is used for implicitly defined operations.

5 Pattern Matching

Pattern matching is one of the advanced features of VDM-SL. All constructs containing patterns are powerful tools in specifying. However, patterns raise some difficulties in type checking that are worth investigating. The use of patterns depends on the expressions containing them. In this section let and cases expressions will serve as the demonstrating example constructs.

A pattern is a template for a value of a particular class of type. It is always used in a context where it is matched to a value of a certain type. Consider the set enumeration pattern {a, 2}. This pattern matches only set values with two elements, where one of the elements is 2. The identifier a is called a pattern identifier and matches any value, of any type. The match value 2 can only be matched against the value itself. Possible values matching the set enumeration pattern are {1, 2} or {true, 2}. A full description of all different kinds of patterns can be found in [12, 31].

In general, type checking patterns can be seen as checking if the patterns can match associated values. If they cannot, the specification has to be rejected. A pattern identifier, for example, is compatible to all types, but a set enumeration pattern expects a set type. This corresponds to type checking for possible consistency (POS mode). However, definite consistency demands more advanced checks, which depend on the usage of patterns. In the following it will be demonstrated that these definite checks are often statically undecidable and how the extended type checker overcomes this problem by generating proof obligations.

5.1 Let expressions

In let expressions patterns are used to improve the readability of complicated expressions or to decompose complex structures. The general form of a simple let expression is let *pattern* = *value* in *expr*. We consider the following example in order to investigate the behaviour of the type checker:

```
let {a,b} = if true then {1,2} else 0 in a + b
```

In practice the example would be useless and of poor quality, because the else branch is in fact "dead code". However, the expression is consistent and serves to look into the edges of type checking pattern expressions. The expression evaluates to 3. The if expression is of the union type `set of nat | nat`. As explained, the set enumeration pattern matches only with set values. In possible mode the type checker checks if the pattern possibly matches the value, i.e. if the set of values the pattern denotes overlaps the values denoted by the expression. In the example above this is the case. To be definite consistent the type checker has to guarantee the match. This is not possible, without evaluating the expression. A check of this kind is undecidable in general and therefore a proof obligation stating that the pattern matches the expression/value is needed. Using an existential quantification we are able to formulate a predicate "*pattern* matches *value*". The match proof obligation for the example above looks like:

```
PO: exists a, b:nat & {a,b} = if true then {1,2} else 0
```

Verifying this PO ensures formally that the pattern matches the value. During the process of generating a proof obligation, the pattern {a,b} is turned into an expression. Note that for patterns containing a match value in any case a proof obligation has to be generated to ensure the definite consistency. The following example makes this obvious:

```
let {a,2} = {1,2} in a
```

The let expression above evaluates to 1. The match value 2 restricts the matching property: The pattern matches only sets of two elements where 2 is one of the elements. This is not decidable in general. Therefore the PO

```
PO: exists a:nat & {a,2} = {1,2}
```

is generated.

5.2 Cases Expressions

The use of patterns in cases expressions is very different from what was presented above. Cases expressions allow the choice of one from a number of expressions on the basis of the value of a particular expression. Consider the following cases expression:

```
let a in set {1, 2, {1,0}, {2,0}} in
cases a:
    1,
    {1,b}           ->  DoThis(1),
    2,
    {2} union b  ->  DoThat(2),
    others          ->  0
end
```

The possible values of a are defined by a let be-such-that expression. Here patterns are used to define the branches of a cases expression. The expression which is going to be evaluated is selected by pattern matching, where several patterns can be used to define one branch.

Cases expressions need special treatment in definite type checking. The existing type checker had to be improved, because errors were returned in almost all cases. Type checking the example above produced several error messages "Pattern cannot match". However, the expression is in fact type consistent. The reason for the overly strict behaviour of the type checker was, like for let expressions above, that every pattern was checked for its well-formedness in definite mode.

However, the semantics of pattern matching used this way is different from that in let-expressions. Type checking a pattern in definite mode assures that it will match definitely. This approach is not feasible in a cases expression, where pattern matching serves to select, not to define a value. The patterns in the cases expression above have to be able to match to a, which means that the sets of values they denote must overlap the value domain of the expression a. Therefore, patterns in cases expressions only need to be possibly well-formed (consistent). If the possible well-formedness check fails for a pattern, this pattern can never match and the corresponding expression will become "dead code" (holds for a single pattern). Figure 2 shows the type relations for cases expressions. The grey areas indicate the set of values to which the patterns in the cases expression match. The white area (*expr.a*) is the set of values denoted by the type of a. The different possibilities for the pattern types are: (1) The pattern is overlapping *expr. a* (*p1* to *p3*). (2) The pattern does not overlap *expr.a* (*p4*) and therefore cannot match. (3) The pattern is a subtype of *expr.a* (*p5*). (4) The type of *expr.a* is a subtype of the pattern. (5) A pattern identifier, which matches with every value, occurs. It covers the whole type universe of VDM-SL. (6) The others alternative is present. It covers the white area of the domain of *expr.a*, which is not covered (overlapped) by the alternative patterns.

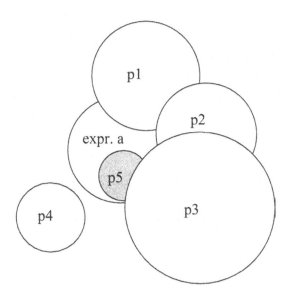

Fig. 2. The sets of values which match the patterns in a cases expression.

In VDM-SL the **others** alternative is not mandatory, if the expression to which the alternative patterns are matched (*expr.a*) is fully covered (overlapped) by these patterns. Thus, the **others** construct can be skipped, if one of the alternatives will match the expression definitely. In the example above the others construct can be omitted, because the other alternatives fully cover the possible values. To ensure the coverage of the expression by the patterns in a cases expression without an others branch or a pattern identifier a proof obligation has to be generated. The coverage PO for the above cases expression without an others construct would be:

```
PO:   a in set {1, 2, {1,0}, {2,0}}
      ==> exists b: nat | set of nat &
            a in set {1,2}   or
            {1,b} = a        or
            {2} union b = a
```

The proof obligation states that for all **a** in the set, a match must be possible. The match values are summarised in a value set. The provability of this proof obligation shows the definite consistency of the example even without the **others** branch.

6   Operations

In VDM-SL functionality can be defined both by functions and operations. What separates operations from functions is the use of states (variables in traditional programming languages). Operations can manipulate local and global states and are therefore imperative. As functions they can be defined both implicitly and explicitly. An explicit operation contains a sequence of statements which is very similar to statements found in ordinary programming languages.

The main problem concerning our work is that no proof theory covering the full imperative part of VDM-SL exists. Also the proof tool does not yet deal with operations and statements. The main reason for this lack is the totally different way of proving in the imperative world: Due to side effects [30], the whole history of state changes has to be considered.

Traditional proof systems for statements use a pre-post strategy where a pre-predicate describes what is supposed to hold before execution of a specific statement and a post-predicate describes what will hold after executing the statement [19, 5]. A few proof rules for VDM-SL statements, which are adapted for exception handling, can be found in [22].

Implicit operations can be treated as implicit functions, which means a satisfiability proof obligation is generated to ensure consistency. However, explicit operations need another approach.

6.1 Generating Assertions

The central idea in the POG to ensure the definite consistency of VDM-SL operations is to generate assertions and include them into the specification. An assertion is a pre-predicate stating the property that must hold before a statement. Thus, in type checking operations the generated proof obligations are not proof rules but assertions. The abstract syntax for an assertion is:

$Assertion :: loc : Location$
$\qquad\qquad prd : Sequent;$

The assertion is composed of a sequent and a location. As in a PO above, a sequent states the needed property. The need for a sequent will be explained later. The location is needed due to the fact that an assertion is always related to a certain location in the specification.

$Location :: oper : Name$
$\qquad\qquad stmt : \mathbb{N}_1$

The *Location* is defined by the operation name and the nth statement for which the assertion represents a pre-predicate. Nested statements are counted in the order of their appearance in the specification. Consider the following specification to calculate the average of a set of numbers:

```
SmallNat = nat
inv s == s < 256

Average: set of SmallNat ==> real
Average (s) ==
```

```
( dcl sum : SmallNat := 0;
  for all e in set s do
    ( if sum > 255 - e then exit <ToLarge>;
      sum := sum + e );
  return sum / card s )
```

As in traditional programming languages the numbers are restricted to a certain size (SmallNat). The operation takes the set of numbers as an argument and uses the local state sum and a loop to compute the result. In the loop an exception <ToLarge> is raised if the sum is going to exceed its maximum.

The loop statement is a good example of a construct for which it is impossible to generate a context as in the sections above. Therefore the POG generates and inserts the following assertions to ensure definite consistency:

```
Average: set of SmallNat ==> real
Average (s) ==
  ( --PO1: inv-SmallNat(0)
    dcl sum : SmallNat := 0;
    for all e in set s do
      ( if sum > 255 - e then exit <ToLarge>;
        --PO2: inv-SmallNat(sum + e)
        sum := sum + e );
    --PO3: card s <> 0
    return sum / card s )
```

PO1 must hold before the first declaration statement to ensure that the initialisation of sum will not violate the invariant. PO2 will be inserted before the assignment statement. It must be proved in order to ensure that the assignment will not exceed the maximum of sum. Finally, PO3 has to be included before the return statement. It can be seen as the obligatory pre-condition of the division expression. The return statement is definitely not consistent, because PO3 is not provable.

In the following we will change the specification to be consistent and will explain how we treat expressions in statements.

6.2 Expressions in Statements

Like the return statement above, statements may include expressions. Therefore undecidability could occur in an expression. Consider the consistent version of the specification:

```
Average2: set of SmallNat ==> real
Average2 (s) ==
  ( dcl sum : SmallNat := 0;
    for all e in set s do
      ( if sum > 255 - e then exit <ToLarge>;
        sum := sum + e );
```

```
return if s <> {}
        then sum / card s
        else 0 )
```

Average2 returns zero if the set of numbers is the empty set by using an if expression. To be able to use the context in the expression the POG collects the context in expressions as in functions. The difference from functions is that the POG type checking an operation generates a sequent assertion. The sequent notation is used to express the context of an expression as local context. The generated assertions for **Average2** demonstrate this approach:

```
Average2: set of SmallNat ==> real
Average2 (s) ==
  ( --PO1: inv-SmallNat(0)
    dcl sum : SmallNat := 0;
    for all e in set s do
      ( if sum > 255 - e then exit <ToLarge>;
        --PO2: inv-SmallNat(sum)
        sum := sum + e );
    --PO3: s <> {} ==> card s <> 0
    return if s <> {}
            then sum / 0
            else 0 )
```

Now **PO3** states that under the assumption that s is unequal to the empty set, the cardinality of s is unequal to zero. Which is by definition of cardinality true (==> is the turnstile ⊢).

7   Relation to Previous Work

Some similar work has been done before, but the specified proof obligation generator is the first one for VDM-SL covering the advanced topics of pattern matching and the non-functional part (operations and states). The central idea influencing this work comes from Flemming M. Damm, Hans Bruun, and Bo Stig Hansen [10, 11]. But also some other tools (methods) already generating proof obligations motivated this extension of the IFAD VDM-SL Toolbox with a proof obligation generator.

RAISE: In the RAISE Specification Language [15, 27] an expressive notion of types is also used for type checking. As a separate facility, not part of type checking, proof obligations called "confidence conditions" may be generated. These rule out, e.g., dynamic type errors.

PVS: PVS (Prototype Verification System) [25] is an environment for specification and verification consisting of a specification language, a parser, a type checker, and an interactive theorem prover. The type checker in PVS generates proof obligations called TCCs (Type Correctness Condition). However,

PVS only supports (tagged) disjoint union types, which do not cause undecidability like the non-disjoint unions in VDM-SL. The TCCs relate to subtypes, partial operators and the termination of recursive functions.

B-Method: The B-Toolkit [17] has a proof obligation generator, that can be invoked from the "Main Environment". The POs are generated according to the correctness criteria which are required to hold within the B-Method [1]. Thus, for example the criteria requires that an Abstract Machine initialisation must establish the invariant, and that each operation re-establishes the invariant.

Z/EVES: The Z/EVES system [28, 29], a Z front-end to the theorem prover EVES [9] provides domain checking for Z specifications, which is the generation of proof obligations to ensure that all functions and operators are applied with parameters inside their domain. The same is done in our work, but Z does not have a type system as rich as VDM [18]. Our work covers a wider area, e.g. union types and patterns. Thus, domain checking is a subset of our consistency checks.

SPARK: SPARK is an annotated subset of Ada, designed to eliminate ambiguities and insecurities of the full Ada language [8]. The SPARK Examiner, a tool which checks conformance of a program to the rules of SPARK, also generate POs called "verification conditions". Mandatory annotations in a program are used to generate these POs. However, SPARK does not allow exceptions and overloading and has simplified scope and visibility rules. Unlike in our approach to operations, where annotations (assertions) are generated as proof obligations, in SPARK the annotations are added by the programmer in order to be able to generate POs [14].

8   Concluding Remarks

In this paper we have presented an approach for automatic generation of proof obligations for VDM-SL. We have shown the general strategy and presented more details about the kinds of constructs for which this kind of proof obligation generation has not been done before. The approach presented has also been formalised in terms of a VDM-SL specification for which a few extracts have been shown. From a tool point of view this work is an improvement of the existing VDM-SL Toolbox. For a more detailed presentation of this work we refer the reader to [4].

At present no work has been done on generating proof obligations for termination of recursive functions. This work could also be extended by a closer integration with the proof tool being developed. In particular we envisage a possibility for the proof tool to automate the proof of type judgements by sending it to the POG.

The proof obligation generation approach presented here has several advantages: (1) A larger subset of specifications can be formally checked according to their internal consistency. (2) By using a proof tool many simple proof obligations can be proved automatically. Thus, the link of automatic type checking and theorem proving extends the set of specifications that can be checked automatically. (3) Proof obligations provide more information than an error message. The user who is familiar with the basics of logic reasoning, will often detect the missing parts in a specification. (4) By feeding the type errors as proof obligations into a theorem prover, it leaves less for human examination, which reduces the possibility of errors being disregarded by the user.

We feel that the combination of a proof obligation generator as presented here and a proof support tool currently being developed will be a powerful combination. However, more work is needed to make a tighter integration between such tools.

Acknowledgement

The authors would like to thank their friends and colleagues for a careful reading of this article: Sten Agerholm, Brigitte Fröhlich, Jeppe Nyløkke Jørgensen, Paul Mukherjee and Anne Berit Nielsen. Particularly Sten Agerholm has provided considerable input on the directions of the work reported in this paper. We are grateful to the support of the Austrian Federal Ministry of Science, Research and the Arts (Kurt Gödel Scholarship) for Bernhard K. Aichernig's stay at IFAD. Finally, we want to thank Bernhard's professor, Peter Lucas, who made his stay possible.

References

1. J.-R. Abrial. *The B Book – Assigning Programs to Meanings.* Cambridge University Press, August 1996.
2. S. Agerholm and J. Frost. An Isabelle-based theorem prover for VDM-SL. In *Proceedings of the 10th International Conference on Theorem Proving in Higher Order Logics (TPHOLs'97)*, LNCS. Springer-Verlag, August 1997.
3. S. Agerholm and J. Frost. Towards an integrated CASE and theorem proving tool for VDM-SL. FME'97, September 1997.
4. Bernhard K. Aichernig. A Proof Obligation Generator for the IFAD VDM-SL Toolbox. Master's thesis, Technical University Graz, Austria, March 1997.
5. K. Apt. Ten Years of Hoare's Logic: A survey - Part I. *ACM-TOPLAS*, 3(4):431–483, Oct 1981.
6. Juan Bicarregui, John Fitzgerald, Peter Lindsay, Richard Moore, and Brian Ritchie. *Proof in VDM: A Practitioner's Guide.* FACIT. Springer-Verlag, 1994. ISBN 3-540-19813-X.
7. Hans Bruun, Flemming Damm, and Bo Stig Hansen. An Approach to the Static Semantics of VDM-SL. In *VDM '91: Formal Software Development Methods*, pages 220–253. VDM Europe, Springer-Verlag, October 1991.
8. Bernard Carre, William Marsh, and Jon Garnsworthy. SPARK: A Safety-Related Ada Subset. In *Ada UK Conference*, pages 1–19, August 22 1992.
9. Dan Craigen, Sentot Kromodimoeljo, Irwin Meisels, Bill Pase, and Mark Saaltink. Eves: An overview. In S. Prehn and W.J. Toetenel, editors, *VDM'91 – Formal Software Development Methods*, pages 389–405. Springer-Verlag, October 1991.

10. Flemming Damm, Hans Bruun, and Bo Stig Hansen. On Type Checking in VDM and Related Consistency Issues. In *VDM '91: Formal Software Development Methods*, pages 45–62. VDM Europe, Springer-Verlag, October 1991.

11. Flemming M. Damm and Bo Stig Hansen. Generation of Proof Obligations for Type Consistency. Technical Report 1993-123, Department of Computer Science, Technical University of Denmark, December 1993.

12. John Dawes. *The VDM-SL Reference Guide*. Pitman, 1991. ISBN 0-273-03151-1.

13. René Elmstrøm, Peter Gorm Larsen, and Poul Bøgh Lassen. The IFAD VDM-SL Toolbox: A Practical Approach to Formal Specifications. *ACM Sigplan Notices*, 29(9):77–80, September 1994.

14. Jon Garnsworthy, Ian O'Neill, and Bernhard Carré. Automatic Proof of Absence of Run-time Errors. In *Ada UK Conference*. London Docklands, October 1993.

15. The RAISE Language Group. *The RAISE Specification Language*. The BCS Practitioners Series. Prentice-Hall, 1992.

16. The VDM Tool Group. User Manual for the IFAD VDM-SL Toolbox. Technical report, IFAD, May 1996. IFAD-VDM-4.

17. Howard Haughton. *Specification in B: An Introduction Using the B Toolkit*. World Scientific Publishing, 1996.

18. I.J. Hayes, C.B. Jones, and J.E. Nicholls. Understanding the Differences Between VDM and Z. *FACS Europe*, pages 7–30, Autumn 1993.

19. C.A.R. Hoare. An Axiomatic Basis for Computer Programming. *Communications of teh ACM*, 12(10):576–581, October 1969.

20. Cliff Jones, Kevin Jones, Peter Linsay, and Richard Moore, editors. *mural: A Formal Development Support System*. Springer-Verlag, 1991. ISBN 3-540-19651-X.

21. Cliff B. Jones. *Systematic Software Development Using VDM*. Prentice-Hall International, Englewood Cliffs, New Jersey, second edition, 1990. ISBN 0-13-880733-7.

22. Peter Gorm Larsen. *Towards Proof Rules for VDM-SL*. PhD thesis, Technical University of Denmark, Department of Computer Science, March 1995. ID-TR:1995-160.

23. P.G. Larsen, B. S. Hansen, H. Brunn, N. Plat, H. Toetenel, D. J. Andrews, J. Dawes, G. Parkin, and et. al. Information Technology – Programming languages, their environments and system software interfaces – Vienna Development Method – Specification Language – Part 1: Base language, ISO/IEC 13817-1, December 1996.

24. Paul Mukherjee. Computer-aided Validation of Formal Specifications. *Software Engineering Journal*, pages 133–140, July 1995.

25. Sam Owre, John Rushby, Natarajan Shankar, and Friedrich von Henke. Formal Verification for Fault-Tolerant Architectures: Some Lessons Learned. In J.C.P. Woodcock and P.G. Larsen, editors, *FME'93: Industrial-Strength Formal Methods*, pages 482–501. Formal Methods Europe, Springer-Verlag, April 1993. Lecture Notes in Computer Science 670.

26. Nico Plat and Peter Gorm Larsen. An Overview of the ISO/VDM-SL Standard. *Sigplan Notices*, 27(8):76–82, August 1992.

27. The RAISE Method Group. *The RAISE Development Method*. The BCS Practitioners Series. Prentice-Hall International, 1995.

28. Mark Saaltink. Z and EVES. In J.E. Nicholls, editor, *Z User Workshop, York 1991*, pages 223–242. Springer-Verlag, 1992. Workshops in Computing.

29. Mark Saaltink. The Z/EVES system. Technical report, ORA Canada, September 1995.

30. R.D. Tennent. *Principles of Programming Languages*. Prentice-Hall International, Englewood Cliffs, New Jersey 07632, 1981.
31. The VDM Tool Group. The IFAD VDM-SL Language. Technical report, IFAD, May 1996. IFAD-VDM-1.

Verification of Cryptographic Protocols: An Experiment

Marc Mehdi Ayadi[1*] and Dominique Bolignano[2]

[1] Cap Gemini/Division Finance,
76, avenue Kléber 75784, Paris France
mayadi@capgemini.fr
[2] Dyade
B.P.105 78153 Le Chesnay Cedex France
Dominique.Bolignano@dyade.fr

Abstract. The objective of this paper is to present the verification of some confidentiality features of the SESAME protocol, an extension of Kerberos. We do that by using the formal approach presented in [7]. This approach is based on the use of state-based general purpose formal methods. It makes a clear separation between modeling of reliable agents and that of intruders. After we have extended this approach to take into account the use of signatures, we use it to formalize SESAME which includes many functionalities among them access control, delegation and multi-level security facilities. The approach is then transposed together with the protocol description quite directly into the Coq prover's formalism. For the sake of conciseness we only describe here formal proofs of confidentiality properties. We prove more precisely the privacy of the session keys in addition to that of the secret keys the principals share with servers. The main advantage of the approach is to provide within a completely formal framework, a systematic verification of a protocol based on its exact and precise specification and not an approximation or simplification of it. The approach is thus complementary with modal logic based methods which allow for a concise, elegant, but superficial verification of protocols: in such logics confidentiality properties, which we prove here to be preserved provided they are true initially, are considered to be hypotheses that are not verified or justified by any formal means.
Keywords: formal methods, cryptographic protocols, security, Coq.

1 Introduction

Verification of cryptographic protocols is a topic of growing importance. Cryptographic protocols employ cryptography to achieve two fundamental security aspects : *integrity* and *confidentiality*. Integrity denotes protecting of information against unsuspected modifications. Confidentiality is concerned with the non-disclosure of information. Cryptographic protocols are generally based on the use of cryptographic functions, ie. encryption and decryption functions. These functions are used either to achieve confidentiality requirements of a message m by encrypting it or to achieve integrity ones

---

* This work was done while the author was at LAMSADE-Université Paris IX Dauphine

by signing it. Signing a message means attaching it a mark (called a *signature*) which cannot be forged nor denied and which is closely tied to the message in such a way that the message cannot be altered without destroying this mark.

Hence a cryptographic protocol is just a communication algorithm that combines encryption, decryption, signing and verification of signature to protect information communicating against unsuspected modifications. The sender and the receiver of messages are called *principals*. We distinguish between two types of principals the client to whom secrets are distributed (who is often designed as a principal) and the server who is a trusted principal to (from) whom principals may send (or receive) secrets.
Authentication protocols, that is, protocols that provide to principals the ability to mutually identify themselves, and not be misled by malicious principals, are particular cryptographic protocols.
Encryption and signature are based on the use of keys which may be *symmetric* if the same key is used both to encrypt and decrypt a message or *asymmetric* if two different keys have to be used for this purpose. A key is said to be *private* if it is only known by principals that are supposed to use it. A *symmetric* key is always private. In the case of *asymmetric* keys one key is *public* and its inverse is usually private.

But the use of encryption and decryption functions does not prevent protocols from having flaws (i.e. [8][18][7],...). In fact designing an authentication protocol is a particularly error-prone process and many popular and largely used protocols been shown to have flaws. This motivates the need to use formal methods that are strong-enough to model and verify such protocols in a systematic and formal way.

The formal verification of authentication protocols may be done in basically three ways. The first one is to use a modal logic for authentication, that is a logic which has some modalities for expressing adequately authentication properties. One such logic is the BAN logic which was proposed by Burrows, Abadi and Needham [8] to transform a correctness requirement into a proof obligation in a formal logic. It is a logic of beliefs which aims at showing how the trust of the participants in a protocol evolves during a protocol run. A protocol fulfills the expected security requirements if it can be shown that at the end of the run, the participants have the beliefs that are intended by the protocol. This has motivated the emergency of many other logics for protocols analysis among them [12] and [1]. The BAN logic and its successors have been used successfully for the verification of many protocols. But these logics also have limitations which have been the subject of many research activities. A survey of these limitations can be found in [17] and [2]. A second possibility is to use model checking to detect the cryptographic protocols flaws, an example of that can be found in [26] and [18]. But model checking techniques apply on finite models, and thus require the simplification of the problem : for example only looking for flaws or problems that only involve a predefined number of untrustable principals, with limited resources (typically, due to state explosion problems, one untrustable principal, with only one additional private key, and only one additional nonce, etc). The third possibility is to use general purpose formal methods. Such methods have been designed and used for various kinds of software applications: safety-critical embedded systems for trains, nuclear power; etc. The use of general purpose formal methods has the advantage of relying on well-defined and largely used techniques. Formal verification can for example be done using theorem provers or simplifiers for standard logics which may take advantage of all research in the area of automatic or assisted proving. The main approaches in this area can be found in [14],

[10] [5] and [19, 20, 21, 22]. With the exception of Meadows' approach, most of these approaches either do not allow for the verification of authentication protocols or do not allow for the definition of a large class of protocols. A survey of the application of formal methods in the area of cryptographic protocols can be found in [27]. More recently a new approach has been proposed in [7]. Although based on general purpose formal methods, this approach achieves at the same time greater precision in modeling and greater concision in proofs than most comparable approaches. The approach is based on a clear separation between the modeling of reliable principals and that of unreliable ones. A specific modeling for the knowledge of unreliable principals that allows for easy and precise proofs, in the style of modal logic proofs, is proposed. The formalization of the approach using Coq has been presented in [6]. The main objective of this paper is to show that this approach can be used to formally verify large protocols. We use the Coq prover [11] for this purpose, and a significant extension of the well known *Kerberos* authentication service [13],[15]. Kerberos provides a means for verifying the identities of each principal (e.g. a workstation user or a network server) on an open network. It makes the assumption that messages traveling along the network can be manipulated at will and performs authentication as a trusted third party authentication service. Kerberos can operate across organizational boundaries. A principal in one organization can be authenticated to a server in another one. Each organization wishing to run a Kerberos server establishes its own *realm*. The name of the realm in which a principal is registrated is part of his name. Realms are organized hierarchically and each realm shares a key with its parents and a different key with each child.

Despite all this, Kerberos is subject to many practical limitations that have been pointed in [4].

SESAME ([23] and [24, 25]) has been proposed to overcome some of these limitations. It aims at reducing the management overheads encountered when Kerberos is employed in securing communications between different realms, some of which may have loosely coordinated security policies. SESAME provides Kerberos with some useful extensions, among them:

- an access control: by defining a scheme for securely propagating principal's privileges. Thanks to that it can decide of applications that can be accessed or act as delegated.
- a symbolic inter-realm key distribution to make scalable secure inter-working practical between inter-realms.

Many Authentication protocols with some having properties similar to that of Kerberos have already been formally verified and presented. But none having the size nor the functionalities of SESAME. This makes such a verification (to our knowledge) the only one on a protocol of this importance and including properties such as delegation, access control, mixing of many encrypting techniques or inter-realm authentication.

According to the way SESAME is used, the authentication properties we want to verify and the protocol itself may change depending on whether communication is performed within a realm or between two realms, if it is accompagned with delegation or not. Due to the lack of space and in the sake of clarity we will content ourselves here of the confidentiality property verification. The rest of the properties (delegation, resistance to replay attacks, access control and inter-realm authentication) will be presented later.

The rest of this paper is organized as follows. In the next section we give an overview of SESAME protocol. In section 3 we describe our formalization of the protocol in Coq.

In section 4 we present the security properties we want the protocol to satisfy. We then show how to express these properties as invariants the verification of which ensure that the protocol fulfills its requirements (the proofs will be detailed in appendices[3]). Finally in section 5 we discuss our conclusions.

2   SESAME: An Overview

The protocol SESAME includes Kerberos features and components as well as new ones. It supports communication confidentiality, integrity and access control in which access to services may be restricted according to specific levels of security. The authentication service extension provides support for authentication based on public keys (principals may authenticate using their private key).

A session in SESAME can be separated into two steps: a first step when an initiator attempts to obtain access rights allowing him to interact with a target. A second one when the target is reached making communication possible.

1. A successful authentication by numerous (3 in fact) authentication authorities from whom an initiator requests successively credentials allowing to check his or her identity, and to check and deliver to him or her access rights in the form of a *Privilege Attribute Certificate* (*PAC*),
2. At the time when he knows the application to be accessed (a target), the initiator attempts to obtain keying information for communicating with him or her. Keying information include keys for securing communicating of the *PAC* and keys for guaranteeing integrity or confidentiality of user data passed between him and the target.

According to the cryptographic algorithms adopted by the target (symmetric or asymmetric key), the keying information is either fully constructed by the initiator or with the involvement of a particular server: the *Key Distribution Service* (*KDS*).

Keying information and a *PAC* are presented by the initiator to a target application each time access to protected resources is requested. Depending on the initiator's security attributes and access control information attached to the resources, access is allowed or not to the initiator. *PACs* may be delegated or used with more than one target. The structure of *PACs* will be presented in the next section.

2.1   Authorities in SESAME

To satisfy its requirements SESAME distinguish between the different classes of servers or *authorities* that manage keys and the principals which, under their control, are acting as initiators or as targets. More specifically, two classes of security authorities are defined: *off-line* authorities and *on-line* ones.

Off-line authorities: are called *Certification Authorities (CA)*. A *CA* is responsible of the generating of *Directory Certificates* containing public keys in such a manner that anybody who trusts the *CA* can check a signature produced by an entity whose public key is known by the *CA*. *CAs* are used when public key technology is adopted. Since

---

[3] for the sake of conciseness, proofs are not presented here and can be obtained from http://www.dyade.fr/actions/VIP/SESAME-proofs1.ps.

knowledge of all principal's public keys is impossible in a large distributed system, a trusted CA is used to guarantee the public key of principals.

On-line authorities : have to manage keys and distribute $PACs$ and *tickets*.

□ $PACs$ are needed because since SESAME's access control policies are based on roles, a principal playing a particular role is likely to need particular privileges and controls which allow access to particular applications and services. Roles are associated to principals by the administrator. He also defines a set of Privileges Attributes, which is associated with a role, and controls which are to apply to the use of these privileges. All this is precisely by the mean of $PACs$.

□ Because several authorities (servers) are involved in the protocol, a *ticket* is delivered by each authority to the initiator. This ticket is to be presented to the next authority the initiator is going to talk to. Tickets are encrypted messages with symmetric key technology. A symmetric key -which is typically shared by two principals- is used and only authorities sharing it are able to read the ticket's content. Typically the ticket creator passes it to a principal who is unable to understand its contents but who uses it as a proof for other authorities that he was really talking to its creator. Tickets are also used for conveying secrets which have to be distributed to some groups of principals.

If we assume that a message m encrypted with a key k is denoted by $\{m\}_k$, then a ticket looks like this:

...$\{$ **secret information included in this ticket** $\}$A_SECRET_KEY....

There are four trusted on-line authorities:

1. **The Authentication Server (AS)**: authenticates principals acting as initiators. It maintains a database of principals with their authentication information. After the AS has successfully authenticated the principal, he returns a ticket which includes the authenticated identity of the principal and a key for communicating with the remaining authorities. The initiator identity will be used further by the next authority (the PAS) as an entry point to the database to get the access privileges of the principal.

2. **The Privilege Attribute System (PAS)**: is responsible for granting $PACs$ to principals. Of course before that, he must be sure of the principal identity. He also generates a specific identifier associated to the initiator which is added to the ticket generated before by the AS to create a new one. The PAS also passes in the new ticket the cryptographic key that will be used by the initiator to protect his (or her) subsequent communications with the next authority (the Key Distribution Service).

3. **The Key Distribution Server (KDS)**: provides principals, either as initiator or target, with keys used (during the authentication process) to protect communicating of the session key (which will be used to protect used data communicating). More specifically its responsibilities are:

   • to deliver cryptographic keys to be used with the authority (the PVF which is presented hereafter) who manages access control to the target application.

   • to manage long term secret keys shared with the PVF of the target application.

4. **The Local Registration authority (LRA)**: from which entities may request the generation of asymmetric keys pairs.

and one on-line untrusted service:

5. **The Certification Authority Agent (CAA)** : who receives and responds to the requests for the generation of asymmetric key pairs.

Some other authorities are defined for $PACs$ verification purposes and are only solicited when a principal acts as a target. One such major authority is:

6. **The PAC Validation Facility (PVF):** is a trusted per-host daemon that verifies tickets and $PACs$. Each target application is associated with the single PVF in that end-system. Hence, more than one application may be associated with him.

   A PVF is used in order to handle establishment of basic keys, to validate $PACs$, to extract and return the information in the PAC that is applicable to the target, to obtain the dialogue keys under which its communication with the initiator can be protected and to provide the means for performing delegation operations by using the PAC. If the validation operation succeeds the PVF returns to the target an *Integrity Dialogue Key* and a *Confidentiality Dialogue Key*. These can be used to protect communication between the initiator and the target application.

The security model of SESAME is based upon an interaction between the AS, PAS, KDS and the *initiator* in one side and between the *initiator*, the PAC Validation Facility (PVF) and the *target* in the other side.

Now, each target application is given a name and is associated with a PVF she trusts. This association is recorded in the PVF and in the KDS. In addition, the KDS knows the different applications supported by every PVF with whom he shares a secret key. For every principal, an access is granted only if both the PAC and the keying information are acceptable to the PVF.

<u>NOTATION</u> : In the sequel we denote respectively the AS by A, the PAS by P, the KDS by G, the PVF by V, the initiator by X and the target by Y.

2.2 SESAME for Intra-realm communication

The part of SESAME we are concerned with here, is related to the description of a complete walk-through of basic security context establishment within a realm. The intra-realm protocol is essentially the same as defined in [16] with the addition of support for privilege acquisition, and authentication to the PVF rather than an individual target application. In the sequel we adopt the following notations:

o Principals when they appear as identifiers, always appear in capital letters. But every time we describe an object attached to a principal we represent this principal by a small letter.

o Sending of a message m from X to Y is denoted by: $X \rightarrow Y : m$.

o The symbol comma will be used to denote the concatenation operator.

o $\{m\}_k$ will be the representation of a message m encrypted with a key k.

o Signed messages are represented using square brackets subscribed by a key: $[m]_k$.

o A key shared between two principals X and Y is denoted by BK_{xy} if it is a temporary (only for one session) key, KI_{xyd} and KC_{xyd} if it is an integrity or confidentiality key. LK_{xy} denotes a long term key (valid for several sessions).

o The private key of X is denoted by KPR_x, the public one by KPU_x.

o A timestamp created by X for communicating with Y is denoted by T_{xyi} where i denotes the creation number of the timestamps.

o In the same manner, a key lifetime is denoted by L_{xsy} where S is the server who generates the key for X and Y. A request for an *object* (a timestamp, a validity period etc..) is represented by $Robject$.

o The result of applying of a function f to an argument x is denoted by $f(x)$.

o Finally, a list distributed by a server S and which represents objects accessible from a principal X is denoted by $(X)_s$.

Initial Assumptions : the protocol starts with the following initial assumptions:

- **in the initiator side :**
  - LK_{xa}: the principal X possesses a long term key LK_{xa} which corresponds for human principals to a derivative of their password. He shares this key with A.
  - LK_g: At the local security server, A shares a long term key LK_g with G and P.
  - LK_{vg}: G knows the key LK_{vg} he shares with V.
- **in the target side :**
  - V knows LK_{vg}. Thanks to that, he can decrypt tickets on behalf of Y.
  - KPU_p: V also knows KPU_p the public key of P and uses it to verify the PAC generated by P.
  - V also knows $(Y)_g$ the list of target applications servers for which the ticket obtained for Y from G by the initiator is valid (the identities of the local applications V supports).

The SESAME version for intra-realm exchanges is presented in figure 1.

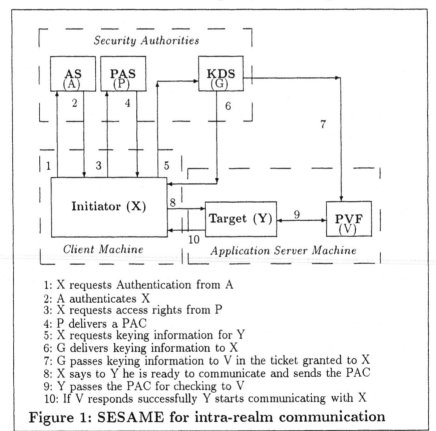

1: X requests Authentication from A
2: A authenticates X
3: X requests access rights from P
4: P delivers a PAC
5: X requests keying information for Y
6: G delivers keying information to X
7: G passes keying information to V in the ticket granted to X
8: X says to Y he is ready to communicate and sends the PAC
9: Y passes the PAC for checking to V
10: If V responds successfully Y starts communicating with X

Figure 1: SESAME for intra-realm communication

$$1.X \rightarrow A : X, G, I(T_{xan}), RL_{xag}$$

Purpose: The objective of this message is **to request** from A the generating of a key which will allow X to securely communicate with P and G.

Description: The protocol starts with X sending a message containing his own identity, the KDS identity G and includes a number $I(T_{xan})$ derived from a timestamp T_{xan} created by him for A. Timestamps are used in authentication protocols to indicate when a message is constructed so as to prove its freshness. This prevents an intruder from replaying it in other sessions. Use of timestamps requires synchronized clocks and this is not unrealistic since technology advances make loosely and closely synchronized clocks available system-wide and nationwide. This message is completed by a request RL_{xag} to A to associate a validity period to the ticket he will respond with.

$$2.A \rightarrow X : \{BK_{xg}, I(T_{xan}), G, L_{xag}, T_{axn}\}_{LK_{xa}}, \{T_{axn}, L_{xag}, BK_{xg}, X\}_{LK_g}$$

Purpose: The first purpose of this message is to **provide** X with a key BK_{xg} to communicate with P and G. The second one is to **distribute** this key to P and G. But rather than passing it directly to P (which may be source of attacks by message replay or false identities) A creates a ticket that includes this key. Thanks to that P will be able to verify that the key included in the ticket is that used by X to protect his messages.

Description: Consecutively to the receipt of message 1, A generates a ticket:

$$\{T_{axn}, L_{xag}, BK_{xg}, X\}_{LK_g}$$

This ticket is denoted by TGT_{xg} for *(Ticket Granting Ticket) for X to join G*. Principal X cannot decrypt TGT_{xg} since he does not possess LK_g. Hence he views it just as a single message that makes him recognizable by P. Every sealed or encrypted component of this message incorporates a new timestamp T_{axn}, L_{xag} the requested validity period of TGT_{xg} and the new session key BK_{xg} (called basic key) for X and G. We have to mention here that SESAME adopts a two level key scheme in which there are *basic keys* and *dialogue keys*. Basic keys are essentially temporary keys established between an initiator and a KDS, a PVF or the target itself.

The ticket lifetime L_{xag} ensures that the ticket will not be used more than allowed. All these information are encrypted either with the long term key LK_g or with LK_{xa}. Use of these symmetric keys makes the two sub-messages unreadable for every principal but P, G and A (resp. X and A).

$$3.X \rightarrow P : \{T_{axn}, L_{xag}, BK_{xg}, X\}_{LK_g}, \{X, T_{xpi}\}_{BK_{xg}}$$
$$[T_{xpi}, R_{xi}]_{BK_{xg}}, [I(T_{xpi}), G, RL_{xpg}]_{BK_{xg}}$$

Purpose: This message **requests** a PAC from P. A PAC is created only for X and includes the identity of X. This is why X must prove his identity by the mean of a ticket and the use of BK_{xg}. Signatures here allow P to check that the key BK_{xg} he has is really the good key.

Description: Once the X-A initialization (i.e. login) has taken place, X requests a PAC from P by sending a message which includes the ticket TGT_{xg}, a component containing a new timestamp T_{xpi} and encrypted using BK_{xg} and two separate components both signed with BK_{xg}. The first one, R_{xi} requesting a PAC, and the second one RL_{xpg} requesting a validity period for the ticket P is expected to generate.

$$4.P \rightarrow X : \{BK_{xg}, I(T_{xpi}), G, L_{xpg}, T_{axn}\}_{BK_{xg}}, [T_{xpi}, [PA_{xi}, PPID_x]_{KPR_p}]_{BK_{xg}},$$
$$\{T_{axn}, L_{xpg}, BK_{xg}, X, PPID_x\}_{LK_g}$$

Purpose: If the request of message 3 is successful P delivers a PAC and a ticket for G. This PAC contains the set PA_{xi} of PAC attributes and controls granted by P to X, concatened to a unique identifier $PPID_x$ associated by P to X. To protect the PAC from modification it is signed with P's private (asymmetric) key KPR_p. This is a first use of the public key technology in SESAME. This ensures that only P can create the PAC (since only P knows his private key).

Description: After he has concatened the PAC $[PA_{xi}, PPID_x]_{KPR_p}$ to T_{xpi}, P signs (and hence integrity protects) it a second time with BK_{xg}. This avoids situations in which a PAC is substituted by an old one. P also creates a ticket which is identical TGT_{xg} except that it includes $PPID_x$. This ticket is called $PTGT_{xg}$ and will be used by X for G. It is the part $\{T_{axn}, L_{xpg}, BK_{xg}, X, PPID_x\}_{LK_g}$ where LK_g is the KDS G masterkey. We may notice here that each time X sends a message either to a server or to the target, he attaches a timestamp (T_{xgn} in this case) to it.

$$5.\mathbf{X \rightarrow G} : \{\mathbf{T_{axn}, L_{xpg}, BK_{xg}, X, PPID_x}\}_{\mathbf{LK_g}},$$
$$\{\mathbf{X, T_{xgn}}\}_{\mathbf{BK_{xg}}}, [\mathbf{I(T_{xgn}), Y}]_{\mathbf{BK_{xg}}}$$

Purpose: This message asks G to create a key for X and Y and to generate a ticket allowing V to identify X. In addition to the ticket, G has also to create a key for X and V (to communicate directly once X is correctly authenticated by V).

Description: X requests a ticket for Y from G. For this, he sends a message which includes $PTGT_{xg}$, an encrypted component that contains a timestamp T_{xgn} and a signed one specifying Y's identity. X is thus forced to prove his identity to G by the use of BK_{xg} to encrypt and sign some parts of the message.

$$6.\mathbf{G \rightarrow X} : \{\mathbf{BK_{xv}, I(T_{xgn}), Y, L_{xgy}, T_{axn}}\}_{\mathbf{BK_{xg}}}, [\mathbf{T_{xgn}, (Y)_g}]_{\mathbf{BK_{xg}}},$$
$$\{\mathbf{T_{axn}, L_{xgv}, BK_{xv}, X, PPID_x}\}_{\mathbf{LK_{vg}}}$$

This step is characterized by the generation by G of: BK_{xv} the basic key X and V will use to communicate, a ticket that allows X to be recognizable by V (for that G uses the symmetric key LK_{vg} he shares with V) and $(Y)_g$ the list of applications supported by V and accessible to X.

The list $(Y)_g$ instead of being crypted is just signed. This prevents its modification. No principal but X and G should be given the possibility to add or to erase an application from this list.

The key BK_{xv} is assumed to be securely passed to V by G. This is why this step is not considered as a part of the protocol.

$$7.\mathbf{X \rightarrow Y} : [\{\mathbf{T_{axn}, L_{xgv}, BK_{xv}, X, PPID_x}\}_{\mathbf{LK_{vg}}}, \mathbf{Y}, [\mathbf{PA_{xi}, PPID_x}]_{\mathbf{KPR_p}},$$
$$DKP_{xyd}]_{BK_{xv}}, [\mathbf{C, M, X, T_{xyi}, C_{xyi}}]_{\mathbf{KI_{xyd}}}$$

Purpose: Now, X is able to contact directly Y. For that, he uses the ticket $PTGT_{xg}$ he has received from G and transmits it to Y with the keys he has generated for the purpose of communicating with him.

Description: when X receives the ticket from G he constructs a message which contains the ticket for Y, the PAC and a dialogue key package DKP including integrity and confidentiality dialogue key seeds ($DKP = [..KI_{xyd}, KC_{xyd}..]_{BK_{xv}}$). A dialogue key is a temporary key established between the initiator and target, to be used for protecting the user level operations that takes place subsequent to the transmission of the PAC. Separate dialogue keys can be established for integrity protection and for confidentiality protection. The distinction between dialogue and basic keys enables V to control whether dialogues between the initiators and targets can take place. The dialogue keys that the initiator is expecting to use are released to the target only if the PAC is successfully validated by V. X also signs with his integrity dialogue key a message for Y which contains a message type M, a timestamp T_{xyi} and a sequence number C_{xyi}. Sequence numbers are used to order the messages and to prevent their duplication.

$$8. \mathbf{Y} \rightarrow \mathbf{X} : \{\mathbf{M}, \mathbf{T_{xyi}}, \mathbf{C_{yxi}}\}_{KI_{xyd}}$$

Purpose: This message indicates to X that Y is ready to communicate with him.

Description: When Y receives the context establishment message from X, Y submits it to V for verification (communication between Y and V is not represented here, but it will be the case in our modelization). If it succeeds, V passes the integrity and confidentiality keys present in the ticket to Y.
Y responds to X and signs a message with KI_{xyd} which includes a timestamp and a sequence number.

$$9. \mathbf{X} \rightarrow \mathbf{Y} : \{\mathbf{M}, \mathbf{C_{xyi}}, \{\mathbf{D_{xy}}\}_{KC_{xyd}}\}_{KI_{xyd}}$$

Now that a security context has been successfully constituted, subsequent user data D_{xy} can be securely communicated between X and Y. The data is sequence protected and integrity protected and may, according to policy, be confidentiality protected. To every message is attached a sequence number but no timestamp.

$$10. \mathbf{Y} \rightarrow \mathbf{X} : \{\mathbf{M}, \mathbf{C_{yxi}}, \{\mathbf{D_{yx}}\}_{KC_{xyd}}\}_{KI_{xyd}},$$
$$11. \mathbf{X} \rightarrow \mathbf{Y} : \{\mathbf{M}, \mathbf{T_{xy(j+m)}}, \mathbf{C_{xy(j+m)}}\}_{KI_{xyd}}$$

After the application has completed and when context termination is requested, X sends an unconfirmed termination request to Y. No data is included here.

3   The Protocol Modelization

The protocol modeling follows the strategy presented in [7]. We start by identifying the principals involved in the protocol. Among them we distinguish between some that we may consider as trustable and some not.

First the different principals involved in the protocol have to be identified. Communication media can be considered as principals that receive messages on one end and emit other messages at another end. Some principals will be considered to be trustables (or reliables) and some won't. Communication media are usually considered to be non-trustable as messages can usually be spied upon, replayed, removed or created by intruders. We will consider that this is the case in the following, although this is not central to our approach in any way . The same protocol can be studied under many different hypotheses. In the case of the protocol at hand we will take X, Y, A, P, G and V to be the only trustable principals.

All trustable principals will always be assumed to play their role as stated by the protocol. For non-trustable principals the situation is different as we do not know how many they are, how they work, how they cooperate and we have to imagine the worst case. So instead of modeling each non-trustable principal separately, and instead of

1. $X \to A : X, G, I(T_{xan})$
2. $A \to X : \{BK_{xg}, I(T_{xan}), G, L_{xag}, T_{axn}\}_{LK_{xa}}, \{T_{axn}, L_{xag}, BK_{xg}, X\}_{LK_g}$
3. $X \to P : \{T_{axn}, L_{xag}, BK_{xg}, X\}_{LK_g}, \{X, T_{xpi}\}_{BK_{xg}}, [T_{xpi}]_{BK_{xg}}, [I(T_{xpi}), G]_{BK_{xg}}$
4. $P \to X : \{BK_{xg}, I(T_{xpi}), G, L_{xpg}, T_{axn}\}_{BK_{xg}}, [T_{xpi}, [PA_{xi}, PPID_x]_{KPR_p}]_{BK_{xg}},$
   $\{T_{axn}, L_{xpg}, BK_{xg}, X, PPID_x\}_{LK_g}$
5. $X \to G : \{T_{axn}, L_{xpg}, BK_{xg}, X, PPID_x\}_{LK_g}, \{X, T_{xgn}\}_{BK_{xg}}, [I(T_{xgn}), Y]_{BK_{xg}}$
6. $G \to X : \{BK_{xv}, I(T_{xgn}), Y, L_{xgy}, T_{axn}\}_{BK_{xg}}, [T_{xgn}, (Y)_g]_{BK_{xg}},$
   $\{T_{axn}, L_{xgv}, BK_{xv}, X, PPID_x\}_{LK_{xv}}$
7. $X \to Y : [\{T_{axn}, L_{xgv}, BK_{xv}, X, PPID_x\}_{LK_{vg}}, Y, [PA_{xi}, PPID_x]_{KPR_p}$
   $, DKP_{xyd}]_{BK_{xv}}, [C, M, X, T_{xyi}, C_{xyi}]_{KI_{xyd}}$
8. $Y \to V : [\{T_{axn}, L_{xgv}, BK_{xv}, X, PPID_x\}_{LK_{vg}}, Y, [PA_{xi}, PPID_x]_{KPR_p},$
   $DKP_{xyd}]_{BK_{xv}}$
9. $V \to Y : \{KI_{xyd}, KC_{xyd}\}_{LK_{yv}}$
10. $Y \to X : \{M, C_{yxi}, \{D_{yx}\}_{KC_{xyd}}\}_{KI_{xyd}}$

Table 1. Security Context establishment- intra realm

describing how they work, we will model the set of all such principals and call it "the external world" or more concisely the *hostile environment*.

The intruder is modeled as a principal who may know some data initially and who will store and decrypt all data components passed to the malicious principals and thus all information circulating on the communication media. The intruder will also be able to encrypt data components to create new messages he or she will send to mislead trustable principals. But he or she will only be able to decrypt and encrypt data components with keys he or she knows. This modeling will in particular allow us to tell, at any time, which data component is potentially known by the intruder under the chosen "trustability" hypothesis.

3.1 Principals and Data modelisation

Now let us detail the way we model SESAME. First, we consider two trusted principals which act as an initiator and a target, namely X and Y. Then th servers A, P, G and the PAC validation facility PVF of Y which does not appear in the above description, but which we include to make more precise the communicating process. Conversely, we focus our attention only on the steps closely tied to authentication, consequently communicating of user data is entirely ignored. The protocol we effectively model is represented in table 1.

Data communicated by principals can be modeled using recursive (abstract data) type *composed*. At the bottom level, we distinguish between *basic* data types representing *cleartext* messages such as principal names, stamps or nonces, and *keys*. Elements of *cleartext* cannot be used as cryptographic keys. Now at a high level, we have a composed message obtained by composition either by using the pair operator which takes two data c_1 and c_2 of type *composed* and returns the pair (c_1, c_2), or by encryption of a data c using key k (the corresponding encrypted data will be noted $\{c\}_k$).

Keys may either be symmetric or asymmetric since, as we have seen, SESAME makes use of the two encryption schemes. The pair operation is used to represent reversible constructors. The taking into account of other reversible constructors such as the sequence, set or aggregate constructors as well as that of operations that are irreversible because of some loss of information (e.g. the modulo operation) are done in a straight-forward manner and is omitted here for the sake of conciseness.

Messages circulating over the system (and hence, intruders knowledge) will be modeled by the set of data components the principal who represents the environment will have collected or deduced previously. He exploits available data to deduce new ones by using these six basic operations: pairing of two known data, decomposition of a pair, encryption, verification, signature and decryption of a known data using a known key. Coq data types definitions are presented in appendices. The data type *composed* is for example defined as:

```
Variables Word : Set.
Inductive Key   : Set :=  inv  : Key -> Key | KeyXY : Word->Word->Key|
                          KeyS : Word-> Key.
Variables Cleartext : Set.
Inductive Basic : Set   :=  Key2Basic        : Key -> Basic |
                            Cleartext2Basic : Cleartext -> Basic.
Inductive Composed : Set := encrypt : Composed -> Key -> Composed |
                            pair    : Composed -> Composed -> Composed |
                            Basic2Composed : Basic -> Composed.
Inductive Collector : Set:= empty : Collector |
                            cons  : Composed -> Collector -> Collector.
```

3.2   Messages manipulation

Exploitation of collected knowledge, which in our case is a set of messages, to deduce new data is possible by application of one or more of the above operations any number of times and in any order. Hence, starting from a set of data s, we say that another set s' is deducible if there exists a sequence of application of the six basic operations that leads to s'. This relation is formalized using the predicate *known_in*: s' *known_in* s. In [7] an axiomatization of the predicate is presented and proved. The axiomatization is presented in Table 2. It makes use of another predicate *comp_of* to allow for more conciseness in proofs. Intuitively *comp_of* specializes *known_in* by considering just decryption and decomposition operations. The proposed axiomatization allows in particular to deduce negative facts (i.e. the impossibility of deducing some set of data components). An example of such rule is : (c, c') comp_of $s \Rightarrow c$ comp_of $s \wedge c'$ comp_of s and: $\neg(c$ comp_of $s \cup c')$ $c \neq \{c'\}_k \Rightarrow \neg(c$ comp_of $s \cup \{c'\}_k)$.
The transposition of such rules in Coq gives:

> Axiom C2:$(c1, c2 : \text{Composed})(k : \text{Key})(s : \text{Collector})$
> $\neg(\text{comp\_of } c1 \text{ } (\text{cons } c2 \text{ } s)) \rightarrow \neg(\text{equiv } c1 \text{ } (\text{encrypt } c2 \text{ } k)) \rightarrow$
> $\neg(\text{comp\_of } c1 \text{ } (\text{cons } (\text{encrypt } c2 \text{ } k) \text{ } s)).$

3.3   The protocol decomposition

In order to model the protocol we use a basic but yet powerful paradigm sometimes referred to as the chemical abstract machine paradigm: a system is described as a set of atomic actions which may be applied repeatedly and in any order and whenever pre-condition holds. If $\mathcal{GS}$ stands for the domain of possible states, every action can be described as a relation on $\mathcal{GS} \times \mathcal{GS}$ binding the state before application to the state after application. Instead of using a formalism based on this paradigm, such as Unity [9], or

A1. c known_in s $\land$ c' known_in s $\Rightarrow$ (c, c') known_in s

A2. (c, c') known_in s $\Rightarrow$ c known_in s $\land$ c' known_in s

A3. c known_in s $\land$ k known_in s $\Rightarrow$ $\{c\}_k$ known_in s

A4. $\{c\}_k$ known_in s $\land$ k known_in s $\Rightarrow$ c known_in s

A5. s' known_in s $\land$ s'' known_in s $\Rightarrow$ (s' $\cup$ s'') known_in s

A6. (s' $\cup$ s'') known_in s $\Rightarrow$ s' known_in s $\land$ s'' known_in s

A7. s known_in s

A8. $\emptyset$ known_in s

B1. (c, c') comp_of s $\Rightarrow$ c comp_of s $\land$ c' comp_of s

B2. $\{c\}_k$ comp_of s $\land$ k comp_of s $\Rightarrow$ c comp_of s

B3. s' comp_of s $\land$ s'' comp_of s $\Rightarrow$ (s' $\cup$ s'') comp_of s

B4. (s' $\cup$ s'') comp_of s $\Rightarrow$ s' comp_of s $\land$ s'' comp_of s

B5. s comp_of s

B6. $\emptyset$ comp_of s

C1. $\neg$(c comp_of s) $\land$ $\neg$(k comp_of s) $\land$ c $\neq \{c'\}_k$ $\Rightarrow$ $\neg$(c comp_of s $\cup \{c'\}_k$)

C2. $\neg$(c comp_of s $\cup$ c') $\land$ c $\neq \{c'\}_k$ $\Rightarrow$ $\neg$(c comp_of s $\cup \{c'\}_k$)

C3. $\neg$(c comp_of s) $\land$ c $\neq$ d $\Rightarrow$ $\neg$(c comp_of s $\cup$ d)

C4. $\neg$(c comp_of s $\cup$ c$_1$ $\cup$ c$_2$) $\land$ c $\neq$ (c$_1$, c$_2$) $\Rightarrow$ $\neg$(c comp_of s $\cup$ (c$_1$, c$_2$))

C5. $\neg$(c comp_of $\emptyset$)

C6. $\neg$(s' comp_of s) $\lor$ $\neg$(s'' comp_of s) $\Rightarrow$ $\neg$((s' $\cup$ s'') comp_of s)

C7. c $\notin$ s $\land$ setofkeys(s) $\Rightarrow$ $\neg$(c comp_of s)

C8. setofkeys(s) $\Rightarrow$ setofkeys(s $\cup$ k)

C9. setofkeys($\emptyset$)

D1. $\neg$(s' known_in s) $\Rightarrow$ $\neg$(s' comp_of s)

D2. $\neg$(b comp_of s) $\Rightarrow$ $\neg$(b known_in s)

D3. $\neg$($\{c\}_k$ comp_of s) $\land$ $\neg$(k comp_of s) $\Rightarrow$ $\neg$($\{c\}_k$ known_in s)

D4. $\neg$($\{c\}_k$ comp_of s) $\land$ $\neg$(c known_in s) $\Rightarrow$ $\neg$($\{c\}_k$ known_in s)

D5. $\neg$((c, c') comp_of s) $\land$ ($\neg$(c known_in s) $\lor$ $\neg$(c' known_in s)) $\Rightarrow$ $\neg$((c, c') known_in s)

D6. $\neg$(s known_in s'') $\lor$ $\neg$(s' known_in s'') $\Rightarrow$ $\neg$(s $\cup$ s' known_in s'')

E1. (s known_in s') $\Rightarrow$ (s known_in s' $\cup$ s'')

Table 2. Knowledge acquisition rules

Gamma [3], which would require presenting its syntax and semantics, for presentation reasons we just use here a simple and basic mathematical notation. But the formalism used in the verification -namely Coq- is presented in appendices.

Sending and reception of a message are not synchronous. Consequently the transmission of a message cannot be considered as an atomic action but as the combination of two events or actions, one for sending and one for receiving. Our modeling of the SESAME protocol will thus distinguish 20 different kinds of atomic actions, two for each message type. Instead of using one relation of $\mathcal{GS} \times \mathcal{GS}$ for each action we will use a single subset $\mathcal{GS} \times \mathcal{A} \times \mathcal{GS}$, where $\mathcal{A} = \{1_s, 1_r, 2_s, 2_r, .., 10_s, 10_r\}$, for describing the whole system. Each label n_s stands for the sending and n_r for the reception of message n. the set $\mathcal{GS}$ is defined as a subset of $\mathcal{LS}_X \times \mathcal{LS}_A \times \mathcal{LS}_P \times \mathcal{LS}_G \times \mathcal{LS}_Y \times \mathcal{LS}_V \times \mathcal{LS}_I$ where each component describes the domain of local states of principals X, A, P, G, Y, V. Intuitively $\mathcal{LS}_I$ the local state of the intruder, is the domain of sets of data that have been collected from the communication channel and that malicious principals may know or may have known or built since the beginning of the protocol. The local state of a principal is defined as an aggregate of sensitive information he knows and uses. Such information comprise nonces, keys, identities as well as PACs, tickets or sequence numbers. The local state of principal X is represented by the following:

$$\mathcal{LS}_X = \text{target:Principal, } BK_{xg}, BK_{xv}, LK_{xa} : \text{Key } L_{xag}, L_{xpg}, L_{xgy}: \text{Integer,}$$
$$TGT_{xg}, PTGT_{xg}, PAC, Ticket, DKP_{xyd}, T_{xan}, T_{xpi}, T_{xgn}, List_{(Y)},$$
$$T_{xyi} : \text{Cleartext,nseq : Sequence Number, pc : Program Address}$$

The field *target* is used to store the identity of the target application. Conversely, the field *initiator* is used to store the identity of the supposed requester. We assume that keys are never changed. Fields BK_{xg} and BK_{xv}, contain the current values of keys shared by X with respectively G and V. LK_{xa} contains the value of a long term key shared between A and X. Hence, these fields contains keys that are either used before the protocol starts or received according to the protocol description.

Fields T_{xan}, T_{xpn},T_{xgn} and T_{xyn} contains the current values of nonces produced during the protocol execution. Encrypted messages which X has just to convey, or use without knowing their contents, are represented by fields which contain cleartext messages, such fields are TGT_{xg}, $PTGT_{xg}$ and the ticket for Y. The local state related to the KDS G contains the following:

$$\mathcal{LS}_G = \text{initiator, target : Principal, Key}X : \text{Principal} \rightarrow \text{Key, Key}_{XY}: \text{Principal} \rightarrow$$
$$\text{Principal} \rightarrow \text{Key } Lxpg, Lxgv, Lxgy, List_{(Y)}, Txgn, Taxn, PPID_x : \text{Cleartext,}$$
$$\text{pc : Program Address}$$

two functions $keyX$ and $keyXY$ permit respectively, to retrieve the key G shares with one given principals and to retrieve the session key two principals share.

In all cases, fields pc hold the value of the abstract program counter for the algorithm used by the corresponding principal.

Other local states related respectively to A,P, V and Y are all formalized in the same manner. To every sensitive information appearing in messages, or which are used to decrypt or integrity verify them, is associated a specific field which is supposed to hold their value. A program counter pc is also present in every local state. Hence, their formalization is straightforward and is detailed in appendices.

As mentioned previously, the set $\mathcal{A}$ of actions contains twenty actions, partitioned between sending actions and reception ones. To model local states we use state variables. Since states may change consecutively to application of an operation, we use primed variables to represent the new values of the state variables. We adopt here the convention that every state variable which is not explicitly changed is supposed to remain unchanged. Here a the description for the first operation.

$$action(\mathbf{S_X}.pc, 1s, \mathbf{S_X}'.pc) \wedge \mathbf{S_I}' = \mathbf{S_I} \cup (X, \mathbf{S_X}'.KDS, I(\mathbf{S_X}'.T_{xan})) \tag{1}$$
$$action(\mathbf{S_A}.pc, 1r, \mathbf{S_A}'.pc) \wedge (\mathbf{S_A}'.initiator, \mathbf{S_A}'.KDS, I(\mathbf{S_A}'.T_{xan})) \, known\_in \, \mathbf{S_I} \tag{2}$$

after the first operation only $\mathbf{S_X}.pc$ and $\mathbf{S_I}$ has changed, thus we assume that $\mathbf{S_X}.KDS = \mathbf{S_X}'.KDS,..$ $\mathbf{S_Y} = \mathbf{S_Y}'$ and so on. Later, these equalities will be explicited in the Coq formalization. The protocol contains 20 actions where each one models an interaction between one trusted principal and the intruder. We use the predicate *action* to describe every action. This predicate, specifies the management of the field program counter pc which represents the current position in the protocol execution.

Because we are reasoning in terms of global states instead of local ones, each action is a relation which relates the global state before activation of the action to the global state after. We have also to define initial hypothesis related to the intruder. Other initial conditions (e.g. secrecy or not of specific messages) are made explicit when required. Every principal performs actions in a specific way, for example X necessarily performs action $1.s$, $2.r$, $3.s$, $4.r$, $5.s$, $6.r$, $7.s$ and a certain number of communicating actions that we may represent by $e.s$ and $e.r$ followed by a disconnect action $d.s$ or $d.r$. Because they are not related to authentication nor confidentiality aspects, data communicating and disconnect actions are not modeled here. Hence, we may consider that X only repeats a loop $(1.s, 2.r, 3.s, 4.r, 5.s, 6.r, 7.s)$ when assuming the initiator role. In the same manner, G is assumed to repeat a loop $(5.r, 6.s)$ where he responds by a ticket in $6.s$ to a request received in $5.r$. The same applies to the rest of principals.

4 Security Properties

We have now to describe the confidentiality requirements we want SESAME to respond to. The first aspect of confidentiality we have to express is that of keys confidentiality: the principal X wants to be sure, on completion of actions $2.r$, $4.r$ and $6.r$, that BK_{xg} the key he just received is still private. He also must be sure of the same, after action $6.r$, for BK_{xg}. The confidentiality and integrity keys KC_{xyd} and KI_{xyd} must also remain private on completion of action $19.r$. For this, G (resp. P) must be sure of the privacy of BK_{xg} after completion of the action $5.r$ (resp. $3.r$).

The second property consists in being sure that the distributed keys are really those assumed (and created) by servers A and G and not replays of old ones.

Authentication of principals is another aspect of verification we are doing. Because of the interaction of many principals during the protocol unfolding, each principal must be sure that he is talking to the principal he wants to talk to and not to an usurper. For this, we suppose an external observer which has a complete view of the system. Whoever be the trustable principals he selects, the observer wants to be sure that none of these principals believes that he has performed a correct authentication session with the other while he is communicating with an intruder.

If we except the first four interactions ($1.s$, $1.r$, $2.s$ and $2.r$) where A cannot be sure that he has really been talking to X, in the rest of the protocol authentication of principals can be ensured. For example, the server G can be sure of whether he has been talking to A and P or not.

Because of its features, comparatively to "traditional protocols" SESAME integrates some new functionalities, among them: the delegation. Hence, the property SESAME must satisfy here is just that the protocol will not grant an intruder some access rights he has not legitimately gained. More specifically the protocol must ensure that:

1. the signed PAC, X is granted, cannot be used by another principal to access the servers he is not legitimated to access to.
2. the list of the target applications servers for which the ticket -for Y, from G is valid- cannot be changed.

In the following, we will just present the formal proof of the keys confidentiality. The rest will be treated later. This invariant will be called $Privacy\_of\_new\_keys$ in the sequel. It just expresses the following:

$$\neg(S_{\mathbf{X}}.BKxg\ known\_in\ s) \wedge \neg(S_{\mathbf{X}}.BKxv\ known\_in\ s) \wedge \neg(S_{\mathbf{X}}.KIxyd\ known\_in\ s)$$

we have deliberately omitted the key of $KCxyd$ because their treatment is identical to that of $KIxyd$.

5 Intra-realm sessions verification

After we have described each action of the protocol sparately, we express the protocol description in the language of the prover Coq. It is given by the predicate execution:

Definition execution := [st1 : GlobalState][st2 : GlobalState]
  (action1s st1 st2) ∨ *(action1r st1 st2)* ∨ *(action2s st1 st2)* ∨ *(action2r st1 st2)* ∨
  (action3s st1 st2) ∨ *(action3r st1 st2)* ∨ *(action4s st1 st2)* ∨ *(action4r st1 st2)* ∨
  (action5s st1 st2) ∨ *(action5r st1 st2)* ∨ *(action6s st1 st2)* ∨ *(action6r st1 st2)* ∨
  (action7s st1 st2) ∨ *(action7r st1 st2)* ∨ *(action8s st1 st2)* ∨ *(action8r st1 st2)* ∨
  (action9s st1 st2) ∨ *(action9r st1 st2)* ∨ *(action10s st1 st2)* ∨ *(action10r st1 st2)*.

where each sending or receipt action i (not including the program counter management) is described by a function *(action$_i$ st1 st2)* and $st1$ and $st2$ are the global state before and after firing of the action.

In order to formally prove using Coq that *Privacy_of_new_keys* is an invariant property, we first prove some intermediate properties which can also be expressed as invariants. The proof of *Privacy_of_new_keys* faces the following problem: many messages contain in their bodies, some encrypted parts that the receptor cannot decrypt. Since these components contain complex data, we have to prove that their sending does not violate the invariant by providing some sensitive information to the intruder. This means that we must express, when proving *Privacy_of_new_keys* that the intruder already knows them. This is the subject of the first intermediate property we have to prove.

Another property that needs to be guaranteed in order for the protocol to work properly is confidentiality of secret keys (i.e. long terms keys). In SESAME, we have identified five such keys namely: LK_{xa}, LK_g, LK_{gv}, LK_{yv} and P's private key K_{PRp}. We express that as an invariant that we call *Privacy_of_secret_keys* and we try to prove that it is preserved by all protocol actions.

5.1 Distribution of tickets

The first invariant concerns both the target and initiator principals, since only them receive sub-messages they cannot decrypted. We have identified three such messages concerning X and two others related to Y. The principal X receives the foloowing tickets for P, G and then V:

TGTxg   : $\{T_{axn}, L_{xag}, BK_{xg}, X\}_{LK_g}$
PTGTxg   : $\{T_{axn}, L_{xpg}, BK_{xg}, X, PPID_X\}_{LK_g}$
a ticket for V : $\{T_{axn}, L_{xgv}, BK_{xv}, X, PPID_X\}_{LK_{gv}}$

which he cannot decrypt. But, nothing proves to him that BK_{xg}, BK_{xv}, KC_{xyd} and KI_{xyd} are not disclosed in these tickets. This means that we must be sure when proving the privacy of BK_{xg}, BK_{xv}, KC_{xyd} and KI_{xyd} that, even if an intruder knows $TGTxg$, $PTGTxg$ and the *ticket* for V, by no mean he can exploit them to deduce the new session keys. This invariant will be called $Disclosed2IforX$ and expresses the following property:

$S_{\mathbf{X}}.TGTxg\ known\_in\ s\ \wedge\ S_{\mathbf{X}}.PTGTxg\ known\_in\ s\ \wedge\ S_{\mathbf{X}}.ticket\ known\_in\ s$

Its formalization in Coq is straightforward:

$Definition$ **Disclosed2IforX** $:= [st : GlobalState]\ <Prop>\ Match\ st\ with$
$[stx : XState][sta : AState][stp : PState][stg : GState]\ [sty : YState]$
$[stv : VState][s : Collector]$
$<Prop>\ Match\ stx\ with$
$[y : Cleartext][bkxg, bkxv : Key][lxag, lxpg, lxgy, tgtxg, ptgtxg : Cleartext]$
$[pac : Composed][ticket : Cleartext][dkpxyd : Composed]$
$[txan, txpi, txgn : Cleartext][listeY : Composed][txyi, taxn, nseq : Cleartext]$
$\quad (known\_in\ (Basic2Composed\ (Cleartext2Basic\ tgtxg))s)\ \wedge$
$\quad (known\_in\ (Basic2Composed\ (Cleartext2Basic\ ptgtxg))s)\ \wedge$
$\quad (known\_in\ (Basic2Composed\ (Cleartext2Basic\ ticket))s)\ end\ end.$

The preservation of the invariant leads to the following Coq proof obligation:

$Lemma$ **Disclosed2I** $: (st1 : GlobalState)(st2 : GlobalState)$
$\qquad (Disclosed2IforX\ st1)\ \rightarrow\ (execution\ st1\ st2)\ \rightarrow$
$\qquad (Disclosed2IforX\ st2).$

5.2 Secret keys privacy

The invariant $Privacy\_of\_secret\_keys$ introduced earlier can now be formalized as:

$\neg(\mathbf{S_G}.LK_g\ known\_in\ s\ )\wedge\ \ \neg(\mathbf{S_G}.LK_{vg}\ known\_in\ s)\ \wedge$
$\neg(\mathbf{S_G}.LK_{yv}\ known\_in\ s)\ \wedge\ \neg(\mathbf{S_P}.K_{PRp}\ known\_in\ s\ )\wedge\ \ \neg(\mathbf{S_X}.LK_{xa}\ known\_in\ s\ )$

its transposition into Coq is straightforward:

$Definition$ **SecretKeysPrivacy** $:= [st : GlobalState]\ <Prop>\ Match\ st\ with$
$[stx : XState][stA : AState][stp : PState][stg : GState]\ [sty : YState]$
$[stv : VState][s : Collector]$
$\qquad \neg(known\_in\ (Basic2Composed\ (Key2Basic\ LKga))\ s)\ \wedge$
$\qquad \neg(known\_in\ (Basic2Composed\ (Key2Basic\ LKvg))\ s)\ \wedge$
$\qquad \neg(known\_in\ (Basic2Composed\ (Key2Basic\ LKyv))\ s)\ \wedge$
$\qquad \neg(known\_in\ (Basic2Composed\ (Key2Basic\ Kprp))\ s)\ \wedge$
$\qquad \neg(known\_in\ (Basic2Composed\ (Key2Basic\ LKxa))\ s)\ end.$

The preservation of the invariant is written:

$Lemma$ **Privacy_of_secret_keys** $: (st1 : GlobalState)(st2 : GlobalState)$
$\qquad (disclosed2IforX\ st1)\ \rightarrow\ (secretKeysPrivacy\ st1)\ \rightarrow$
$\qquad (execution\ st1\ st2)\ \rightarrow\ (secretKeysPrivacy\ st2).$

5.3 Confidentiality of the session key

The generation of every new key imposes from the server the respect of some basic constraints:

$\forall X, Y, Z\ \in\ \mathbf{Principals}\ \bullet$
$\quad (X\ \neq\ Y)\ \Rightarrow\ KeyX(X)\ \neq\ KeyX(Y) \wedge\ (KeyX(Z)\ \neq\ KeyXY(X,Y))$

where $KeyX$ is a function used by the server to associate to each principal X the corresponding private key he shares with this server. In the same manner, $KeyXY$ is a function used by the server to return the session key genered for X and Y.

Now, we can express our final invariant. It states that the keys BK_{xg}, BK_{xv} and KI_{xyd} remain secret to all principals but those who have legitimately obtained them[4].

$$\neg(S_{\mathbf{X}}.BK_{xg} \; known\_in \; s') \wedge \; \neg(S_{\mathbf{X}}.BK_{xv} \; known\_in \; s') \wedge \; \neg(S_{\mathbf{X}}.KI_{xyd} \; known\_in \; s')$$

Its Coq formalization is:

$Definition$ **SessionKeysPrivacy** $:= [st : GlobalState] < Prop > Match \; st \; with$
$[stx : XState][stA : AState][stp : PState][stg : GState] \; [sty : YState]$
$[stv : VState][s : Collector]$
$\qquad \neg(known\_in \; (Basic2Composed \; (Key2Basic \; BK_{xg})) \; s) \wedge$
$\qquad \neg(known\_in \; (Basic2Composed \; (Key2Basic \; BK_{xv})) \; s) \wedge$
$\qquad \neg(known\_in \; (Basic2Composed \; (Key2Basic \; KI_{xyd})) \; s) \; end.$

the preservation of this invariant starts with the assumptions that long term keys are not accidentally disclosed and that the different tickets appearing in the protocol are known and may be exploited (if possible) by intruders.

$Lemma$ **Privacy_of_new_keys** $: \qquad (st1 : GlobalState)(st2 : GlobalState)$
$\qquad (Disclosed2IforX \; st1) \rightarrow (secretKeysPrivacy \; st1) \rightarrow$
$\qquad (sessionKeysPrivacy \; st1) \rightarrow (execution \; st1 \; st2) \rightarrow$
$\qquad (sessionKeysPrivacy \; st2).$

The proof can then be done in a quite systematic way using the Coq prover. We should notice here that proofs may often be reused. For example, the proof of the confidentiality of the long term $\mathsf{LK_{xa}}$ key and that of $\mathsf{LK_g}$ are very similar and one can be used as a starting point for the other. The proof process in Coq although quite tedious at hand, can however be reduced thanks to a set of tools. Up to now, we have only developped a tool for generating directly the protocols specifications in Coq. This reduces considerably the verifier effort who can focus on discharging the proof obligations. In many situation however the user will have to manually modify the generated specifications. Depending on the adequacy of the automatically generated invariants with his or her intuitive view of the property, an adjustement effort may be required. The proof process in any case is not completly automated and will typically require some manual interaction.

The formal proof in Coq of a basic property is about a one week effort for trained Coq users. Adjusting the generated specification is a matter of hours. Furthermore, the complexity of the proof can almost be entirely hidden to non-Coq users using a Coq tool which translates the formal proofs into an unformal description of the proof. This is currently being experimented for the production of documents in the context of ITSEC criteria based evaluation, for which the presented approach is used.

6 Conclusion

This paper has explored how to formally verify authentication protocols using the approach proposed in [7]. The verification is made on the protocol SESAME which is

---

[4] We may notice here that the confidentiality key KC_{xyd} has not been included in $Privacy\_of\_secret\_keys$. This is in the sake of conciseness since the proofs are similar to those of BK_{xg}, BK_{xv} and KI_{xyd}.

an extension of the Kerberos protocol which integrates several advanced functionalities such as access control, delegation and inter-realm authentication. Due to the important size of the protocol we have restricted ourselves to presentation of confidentiality properties.

The approach and the formalization of the protocol were obtained quite directly using the Coq formalism. The formal proofs although more tedious than informal one may be obtained in a quite systematic way. The confidentiality property we have proved concerns the privacy of the secret keys shared at the beginning of the session and that of session keys (keys which are created during the session for the purpose of communicating data later). In the framework of most modal properties Such properties have to be assumed and cannot be verified. More generally the main advantage of the approach followed here as compared to modal logic based approaches is the finer level of precision that can be achieved in modeling and proofs. The approach is thus an alternative to modal logic-based approaches when a detailed analysis of a protocol is required. It differs from other approaches based on formal methods such as Meadows' approach, in that it focuses on proof simplification whereas the second focuses on proof automation. More account on this can be found in [7]. Another significant advantage that was exploited here is the ability to use general purpose proof environments, such as the Coq environment. As we show in appendices some proofs may be reused. This considerably reduces the proving effort.

In future works, we intend prove properties relevant to the authenticity of privileges and of delegation (in addition to confidentiality) for the inter-realm. Although the complete formal verification can already be done at a reasonable costs (i.e. a few weeks for each property following if reusing the formalization presented here), it is expected that this situation can still be significantly improved as invariants are very similar from one protocol to the other and can be associated to particular features of the protocol (distribution of certificate, use of tickets, etc). This will be the subject of future research.

References

1. M. Abadi and Marc.R. Tuttle. A Semantics for a Logic of Authentication. In *Proceedings of the 10th Annual ACM Symposium On Principles of Distributed Computing*, pages 201–216, August 1991.
2. M. Ayadi. Logics for Cryptographic Protocols: a Survey. Technical report, University of Paris IX- Dauphine, 1997.
3. J.P. Banâtre and D. LeMétayer. Programming by Multiset Transformation. Technical Report 117, IRISA Rennes, March 1990.
4. S.M. Bellovin and M. Merritt. Limitations of the Kerberos Authentication System. In *Computer Communications Review 20(5)*, pages 119–132. , October 1990.
5. P. Bieber and N. Boulahia-Cuppens. Formal Development of Authentication Protocols. In *BCS-FACS sixth Refinement Workshop*, 1994.
6. D. Bolignano. Vérification Formelle de Protocoles Cryptographiques à l'aide de Coq. In *Actes des journées GDR*, 1995.
7. D. Bolignano. Formal Verification of Cryptographic Protocols. In *Proceedings of the third ACM Conference on Computer and Communication Security*, 1996.
8. M. Burrows, M. Abadi, and R. Needham. A Logic of Authentication. In *Proceedings of the Royal Society of London A Vol.426*, pages 233–271, 1989.
9. K.M. Chandy and J. Misra. Parallel Program Design. Addison-Wesley, 1990.

10. P.C. Chen and V.D. Gligor. On the Formal Specification and Verification of a Multiparty Session Protocol. In *Proceedings of the IEEE Symposium on Research in Security and Privacy*, 1990.

11. G.Huet. The Gilbreath Trick : A Case Study in Axiomatization and Proof Development in the Coq Proof Assistant. In *INRIA Research Report 1511*, September 1991.

12. L. Gong, R. Needham, and R. Yahalom. Reasoning about Belief in Cryptographic Protocols. In *Proceedings of the IEEE Symposium on Research in Security and Privacy*, pages 234–248. IEEE, 1990.

13. B.C. Neuman J.G. Steiner and J.I. Schiller. Kerberos: An Authentication Service for Open Network Systems. *Usenix Conference Proceedings, Dallas, Texas*, pages 191–202, Feb 1988.

14. R.A. Kemmerer. Analyzing Encryption Protocols Using Formal Verification Techniques. *IEEE Journal on Selected Area in Communications, volume 7(4)*, 1989.

15. J.T Kohl. The Evolution of the Kerberos Authentication Service. *European Conference Proceedings, Troms, Norway*, pages 295–313, May 1991.

16. J.T Kohl and B.C. Neuman. The Kerberos Network Authentication Service (V5). *Internet RFC 1510*, Sep 1993.

17. Armin Liebl. Authentification in Distributed Systems: A Bibliography. *ACM Operating Systems Review, 27(4)*, pages 31–41, October 1993.

18. Gavin Lowe. An Attack on the Needham-Schroeder Public-Key Authentication Protocol. *Information Processing Letters*, 1995.

19. C. Meadows. Using Narrowing in the Analysis of Key Management. In *Proceedings of the IEEE Symposium on Research in Security and Privacy.* , June 1989.

20. C. Meadows. Representing Partial Knowledge in an Algebraic Security Model. In *Proceedings of the IEEE Computer Security Foundations Workshop VII, Franconia, New-Hampshire.* , June 1990.

21. C. Meadows. A System for the Analysis of a Key Management Protocol. In *Proceedings of the IEEE Symposium on Research in Security and Privacy.* , June 1991.

22. C. Meadows. Applying Formal Methods to the Analysis of a Key Management Protocol. In *Journal of Computer Security.* , June 1992.

23. T.A. Parker. A Secure European System for Applications in a Multi-vendor Environment (The SESAME project). In *Proceedings of the 14th American National Security Conference.* , 1991.

24. D. Pinkas and T.A. Parker. SESAME Technology Version Two- an Overview. , Sep 1994.

25. D. Pinkas and T.A. Parker. SESAME Technology Version Three- Overview. , Sep 1995.

26. A. W. Roscoe. Developing and Verifying Protocols in CSP. In *Proceedings of Mierlo workshop on protocols.* TU Eindhoven, 1993.

27. A.D. Rubin and P. Honeyman. Formal Methods for the Analysis of Authentication Protocols. Technical report, Center for Information Technology Integration, 1993. University of Michigan. Internal Draft.

TLA + PROMELA: Conjecture, Check, Proof
Engineering New Protocols Using Methods and Formal Notations

J-Ch. Grégoire
INRS-Télécommunications

Abstract. Refinement is the best established method to verify complex models using proof-theoretic techniques. One of the challenge of applying this method, besides the tediousness of the proofs, is the slow feedback in assessing the adequacy of the models. In this paper, we show how the tool SPIN has been used to help with formal proofs of a hierarchy of models specified in TLA$^+$. Without being a substitute for a formal proof, using SPIN in this context can reduce the workload by providing a means to quickly assess models, invariants and refinement mappings.
keywords TLA$^+$, TLA, SPIN, PROMELA, refinement, implementation.

1 Introduction

Proving the correctness of a new protocol is hardly ever a straightforward task. Analysis based on reachability analysis [1] is the traditional technique of choice for verification. This is not exactly formal proof, but can be suitable for most purposes, in a "best effort" form of validation.

In this paper, we study the following questions:

- Is it possible to reduce the amount of effort involved in the formal verification of a new protocol (or more precisely, of a new retransmission mechanism)?
- Is it possible for a proof-based technique to share a common framework with a reachability analysis technique?

We propose an extension to a formal method based on a refinement method, which combines formal proofs and reachability analysis. Refinement allows us to minimize the work required to validate a new protocol by relating it to an already existing one. Integrating model checking in the process allows us to have quick, albeit not quite formal, feedback on the quality of the specification.

We start with a description of the method and its extension. We follow with the introduction of the formal tools we have used, namely the *Temporal Logic of Actions* (TLA) [9] and SPIN [6]. We discuss the issues of generating a model for SPIN from a TLA specification. We then proceed to illustrate the method with an example of the derivation of a generic sliding windows mechanism and

---

[1] We use the term reachability analysis in the sense of Holzmann [7].

a non-trivial extension. We end with a discussion on our accomplishments, and comparison with related work.

Note that the context of this work is communication protocols. This is our primary application domain, and there are plenty of challenging examples for state of the art verification techniques. We do not discuss other possible applications of this work here, although some transposition should be obvious.

caveat Because of the space constraint, a few TLA$^+$ modules and PROMELA models were not included.

2 A method

Refinement methods are quite straightforward. In our example domain, protocols, or rather, the *critical mechanisms* of a protocol (such as sliding windows) are modeled in a formal language. This formal language must support the analysis of a form of refinement, or abstract *implementation*, that is, to show that different variations of the mechanisms still essentially behave like a more abstract, general version. This notion of implementation is recursive, as an "implementation" can be viewed as a less abstract "specification".

Our methodological extension, as we shall expose it, is to use reachability analysis tools as a separate step to "check" *the quality of the specifications as well as the soundness of the implementation relation.* This is done independently of the proof step itself, although the proof can use reachability analysis to "test" possible invariants.

Why is reachability analysis not sufficient? For real-life protocols, reachability analysis is typically done with dramatically scaled down parameters, and even then one may have to resort to a form of randomized search because the number of states to explore remains too high for the memory available. Reachability analysis does not support symbolic parameters, except in some special cases.

Why is reachability analysis interesting? In spite of these limitations, reachability analysis is typically quite sufficient to give us a general feeling of soundness of our work. Furthermore, reachability analysis can be done in fairly little time, whereas a formal proof, even with the aid of tools, can take quite long. Published data show that reachability analysis is done in matters of days or weeks, whereas proof checking takes months (see for example [4] for a survey).

Furthermore, reachability analysis tools can act as *design animation* tools, which let us explore specific aspects of a design and test for specific properties. Such tools help to provide quick turnaround in design sessions, thereby reducing overall design time.

Why is time critical? Most protocols are not of a critical nature, but rather developed as a quite minor part of large products. Our own experience has shown that industry is not interested in spending too much effort on verification when a product has to be delivered. At least, that effort should not unduly slow down implementation.

Why bother with a proof then? One may want to do a proof off-line anyway, or (better?) ask an academic to do the proof in parallel with development. Only a proof brings certainty in this method. Nevertheless, we feel that it is critical that a form of rapid check be available to minimize the risks of late discovery of trouble.

Where is the leverage? We tend to look at implementation as a single step, but it doesn't have to be the case. With formal notations, implementation can be seen as a *recursive* concept, where an implementation remains an abstract, yet more refined specification which can itself be implemented. In that sense, an implementation can still be non-deterministic, and partial.

A hierarchy of implementations present methodological advantages, in two different fronts. First, it is easier to prove the correctness of a little implementation step rather than a large one, where most abstractions have been dramatically changed. Second, when intermediate steps correspond to concrete problems, they can be used independently of the rest of the derivation of implementations. Sliding windows are a good case in point: the abstract sliding windows mechanism can be implemented with different forms of acknowledgments, but can also be refined in another abstract model with more complex feedback, or different retransmission mechanisms, as we shall illustrate later. Proving that the refined protocol implements sliding windows, which itself implements a buffer with FIFO discipline will be easier than doing a single implementation proof. Furthermore, we may want to establish that intermediate specifications satisfy other properties.

Proceeding this way is also easier than the more traditional technique a single specification is used, and the "desirable properties" are captured by an invariant. There is then a single proof step of the form

$$Specification \Rightarrow Invariant$$

Such invariants tend to be fairly complex.

2.1 The example hierarchy

Because of space limitations, we use only three specifications in this paper, and thus have non-trivial implementation steps. The first specification is a perfect channel, that is, a buffer with FIFO discipline. The second is an abstract sliding windows model with modulo-N numbering. The third one is a sliding windows protocol with a rather intricate retransmission mechanism aimed at minimizing duplicate transmissions.

3 The tools

We have chosen for this work the Temporal Logic of Actions for the proof work and SPIN for reachability analysis. TLA is a logic which supports the concept of implementation, and has a long history of practical use. SPIN is without contest one of the, if not the, best tool currently available to analyze protocols through reachability analysis.

3.1 The Temporal Logic of Actions

TLA is essentially first order logic combined with temporal operators. The reader interested in a description of TLA should look at the excellent introduction of Abadi and Merz [1], Ladkin's example-tutorial [8] or Lamport's original paper [9] for a more in-depth presentation. In this paper, we give a simple illustration of TLA and its features through an example, our first specification *AbstractChannel*.

In TLA, a specification is simply a formula, typically written in a canonical form as we shall illustrate later. The semantic model of TLA is the sequence of states, or *behavior*. Each state defines a valuation for the variables of the specification. Behaviors represent the execution or "run" of a system. Of course, for reactive systems, such executions can be infinite.

A specification implicitly characterizes all behaviors which satisfy it. We say that a system whose behaviors all satisfy a specification *implements* the specification.

Let us look at the following example. A specification is written in a *module*, which is simply a convenient way to encapsulate declarations. The language used to write the specification is TLA$^+$ [10]. TLA$^+$ extends TLA with the module structure, Zermelo-Frænkel's set theory with the axiom of choice, and significant syntactic sugar to help large, structured specifications.

The following example is the specification of a buffer with FIFO behavior, similar to Ladkin's [8]. Messages are tagged with an index and *Put*'d into a set. They are *Get*'d from that set in FIFO order using another index variable. Both indexes are unbounded. The module *MiscDefinitions* is presented in the appendix; it contains the declaration of the constants (*BufferLength* and *Messages*) as well as a few auxiliary definitions.

────────────── **module** *AbstractChannel* ──────────────

EXTENDS *MiscDefinitions*   We use definitions from module MiscDefinitions
EXTENDS *Sequences*   and Sequences.

VARIABLE *channel*   Flexible variable (quantified over behaviors) used in the formulæ

$ACvars \triangleq \langle channel \rangle$
$Init \triangleq channel = \langle \rangle$ Init defines the initial values of the variables.

$Put(a) \triangleq \land a \in Messages$
$\qquad\qquad \land Len(channel) < BufferLength$
$\qquad\qquad \land channel' = channel \circ \langle a \rangle$
$Get \triangleq \land channel \neq \langle \rangle$
$\qquad\qquad \land channel' = Tail(channel)$

Put and *Get* are the *actions* of the specification. They describe pairs of states, with the primes denoting the values of the variables in the new state, which belong to behaviors. Such pairs are called *steps*.

$SomeAction \triangleq \quad \lor \exists a : Put(a)$
$\qquad\qquad\qquad \lor Get$

A step is either a Put or a Get step.

$Spec \triangleq \quad \land Init$
$\qquad\qquad \land \Box[SomeAction]_{ACvars}$
$\qquad\qquad \land WF_{ACvars}(Get)$

The specification is the conjunction of the initial state, steps and fairness constraints on some steps.

THEOREM
$Spec \Rightarrow \Box \land Len(channel) \geq 0$
$\qquad\qquad\quad \land Len(channel) \leq BufferLength$

This theorem is a consequence of the specification.

TLA specifications allow the repetition of *stuttering steps*, where the state of the "environment" changes, but not the state of the model (i.e. all variables of the specification, represented by the tuple *Cvars* keep the same value, while variables not used in the specification may change). Stuttering steps are necessary for implementation. Yet, they allow behaviors where variables never change. To avoid such situations, it is necessary to add *fairness conditions* (WF in the channel example) to the specification.

In TLA, we say that a specification Φ implements a specification Π if and only if every behavior that satisfies Φ also satisfies Π. This is written in classical fashion as $\Phi \Rightarrow \Pi$ and implementation is implication.

The TLA specification method typically proceeds from a very abstract specification such as the one we have described which almost trivially establish the core properties that we want our more refined specifications to display. By showing that the more refined specification, in our case the sliding windows, implements the simple channel, we'll have established FIFO behavior. We proceed similarly to demonstrate that refined models still behave like a sliding windows mechanism.

3.2 PROMELA/SPIN

SPIN is a reachability analysis tool whose roots go back to the late seventies [3]. This tool is dedicated to the analysis of (software based) communication systems and as such is a natural choice for our purposes.

These biases are strongly reflected in its modeling language, PROMELA. This is essentially a process-based imperative language, without functional abstractions and with very limited data abstractions. It integrates Dijkstra's guarded command notation for iteration and selection with the combination of non-determinism, which is, of course, quite fundamental for modeling. Communications between processes can be done either through shared variables, or through communication channels.

PROMELA is a rather unusual modeling language in the formal methods community, but the choice of its features is largely a pragmatic one. By the admission of his creator, a language that remains close to automata and "classical" programming languages has better chances of being accepted by practitioners at large than purer forms of automata or algebraic forms.

SPIN supports quite a large range of verifications and checks on PROMELA models, including deadlock and livelock detection, model checking of linear temporal logic formulæ and unreached code.

The following example shows how a similar FIFO buffer could be coded in PROMELA. PROMELA doesn't have set abstractions nor unbounded models. We use an array to model the set, and allow only fixed size operations.

```
#define BufferLength 3
#define ModelSize 10

int indexR, indexS;
int buffer[ 11 ]; /* ModelSize + 1 */

#define InBounds(x) x < ModelSize
#define AtBounds(x) x == ModelSize

proctype Channel() {
  do
  ::
    assert( indexR <= indexS );
    assert( indexS - indexR <= BufferLength );
    if
    :: indexS - indexR < BufferLength && InBounds(indexS) ->
      buffer[ indexS ] = 1; indexS = indexS + 1;
    :: InBounds(indexR) && buffer[ indexR ] != 0 ->
      indexR = indexR + 1;
    :: AtBounds(indexR) && AtBounds(indexS) -> break;
    fi;
  od;
}

init {
  indexR = 0; indexS = 0;
  run Channel();
}
```

We see that finiteness forces us to add constraints to the model. This matter will be analyzed further below.

3.3 Why not ...

Are there alternatives to these tools? Certainly, but, as we have said, both are well established, mature and have examples of practical industry-level applications. The critical feature for our method is the ability to relate hierarchies of specifications through implementation; TLA does it well, but there are others, such as TLR [11], or B [2].

Our interest is *engineering* and our prime focus is to concentrate on how to *improve the quality* of the job done, rather than comparing formal notations. From what we can judge, no other notation or tool has any critical advantage over our selection. TLA has behind it a history of 20 years of formal specification and refinement of concurrent algorithms. SPIN's ancestry has similar maturity.

3.4 Caveat emptor

Purists would probably at this stage, quite rightly, reflect that they have never seen a formal definition (i.e. syntax and semantics) of PROMELA or TLA$^+$. This is quite correct. There have been efforts to define the semantics of PROMELA, but they are not complete. The best effort to date is reported in [12]. TLA$^+$ was defined informally in a report written by Lamport [10]. More recently, a new formal syntax has been formally defined. At the time of this writing, the semantics are under (formal) definition.

We use the new TLA$^+$ syntax in this work. For PROMELA, we have (incidentally) used only parts of the language which are in the formal definition.

4 Sliding windows

Simple "send and wait for an acknowledgment" protocols are the most straightforward communication mechanisms and are quite easy to implement. In communication systems with high latency, however, they result in very poor utilization of the communication bandwidth, especially when short frames are transmitted over channels with high propagation delays. To improve on such simple protocols, several techniques have been introduced over the years, including the *anticipation of acknowledgments*, *clustering of acknowledgments*, *embedding of acknowledgments* and full duplex communications. These techniques allow one to send multiple frames before requesting an acknowledgment, thus effectively increasing the size of the frames, to similarly group acknowledgments but also to piggyback the acknowledgments on other messages rather than waiting for an explicit polling request.

Sliding windows mechanisms combine the benefits of these techniques, using also modulo-N numbering, to avoid obvious problems of fixing a-priori the size of frame identifiers. Frames must be kept by the sender until their acknowledgment is received. The more frames that are kept, the larger the buffer memory required to store them. There is a limit on the number of outstanding acknowledgments, which is commonly called the *sender's window*. We have the usual relation, for all indices f_i of frames in the sender's window:

$$lb \leq f_i < lb + WindowSize$$

with *lb* being the lower bound of the window, that is the number of the first unacknowledged frame. Note that this relation must be appropriately defined when modulo-N arithmetic is taken into account.

We know also that the range of numbers must be greater than the size of the window. How much bigger depends on the flavor of the protocol. In some protocols, the receiver will not do any buffering, and simply send a negative acknowledgment whenever something is received out of sequence. This is sometime called a *go-back-n* scheme. This is still not very efficient and it is possible to improve this scheme by *selectively rejecting* a specific frame which was in error, without thereby rejecting the subsequent ones. In this case, we also need a window on the receiver side, which defines the range of frame identifiers acceptable by the receiver. Selective reject still gives us several refinement alternatives. If we keep the bottom of the sender's window synchronized (through acknowledgments) with the bottom of the sender's window, the receiver's window should be equal in size to the sender's window.

Across various flavors of sliding windows mechanisms, we then find the following property (in absolute numbers):

$$bottom_{senderWindow} \leq bottom_{receiverWindow}$$

Under such conditions, it is easy to demonstrate that the numbering range need only be twice as large as the window size. Indeed, since sender and receiver are not synchronized, the receiver never knows where the bottom of the sender window is with regard to its current value. Imagine that the bottom of the receiver window has jumped by the whole length of the window. As long as the value as not been updated on the sender side, it will send up to *windowSize* frames with identifiers lower than $bottom_{receiverWindow}$. After the bottom of the window has been updated, it will send frames with identifiers equal or greater than $bottom_{receiverWindow}$, up to $bottom_{receiverWindow} + windowSize - 1$, or *windowSize* distinct identifiers. It is easy to show that this is a worst case scenario.

From these observations, we can derive a few more general properties:

- there can only be at most $2 \times windowSize$ distinct frames in the system composed of the sender, the receiver and the communication channels.
- it is not possible to introduce more than *windowSize* messages in this system unless they are removed on the receiver side,
- the set of identifiers of frames held in the receiver's window is a subset of the sender's window.

Variants of sliding windows mechanisms will essentially differ in the resend strategy: once the whole window has been sent, is the oldest or the newest frame resent first. Such choices usually depend on the expected behavior of the channels.

4.1 A formal model

The following module specifies sliding windows behavior, with modulo-N arithmetic. The module defining the modulo-N arithmetic operators can be found in the appendix.

In this specification, *Put* and *Get* keep the same function as for the earlier abstract buffer. On the sender side, *SendMsg* transfers a frame (message-index pair) to the receiver side and *ReadAck* reads the acknowledgment. The actions *ReadMsg* and *SendAck* specify the dual operations on the receiver side. Communications are modeled with a one-position buffer (one for each direction). Loss is modeled by overwriting the previous content of the buffer.

---

module *Sliding Windows*

EXTENDS *MiscDefinitions*
EXTENDS *ModularArithmetic*

ASSUMPTION
$IndexRange = 2 \times BufferLength$
All arithmetic is done modulo IndexRange

VARIABLES $sSet, rSet, index_r, index_s, fBuffer, bBuffer$

$SLvars \triangleq \langle sSet, rSet, modIndex_r, modIndex_s, fBuffer, bBuffer \rangle$

$Init \triangleq \ \land modIndex_r = 0$
$\quad\quad\quad \land modIndex_s = 0$
$\quad\quad\quad \land sSet = \emptyset$
$\quad\quad\quad \land rSet = \emptyset$
$\quad\quad\quad \land fBuffer = \langle 0, \perp_{Messages} \rangle$
$\quad\quad\quad \land bBuffer = 0$

$Put(a) \triangleq \ \land a \in Messages$
$\quad\quad\quad\quad \land (sSet = \emptyset) \lor (modIndex_s \ominus ModSetMin(sSet) < BufferLength)$
$\quad\quad\quad\quad \land sSet' = sSet \cup \{\langle modIndex_s, a \rangle\}$
$\quad\quad\quad\quad \land modIndex_s' = modIndex_s \oplus 1$
$\quad\quad\quad\quad \land$ UNCHANGED $rSet, modIndex_r, fBuffer, bBuffer$

$Get \triangleq \ \land \exists a : \land \langle modIndex_r, a \rangle \in rSet$
$\quad\quad\quad\quad\quad\quad\quad \land rSet' = rSet \setminus \{\langle modIndex_r, a \rangle\}$
$\quad\quad\quad \land modIndex_r' = modIndex_r \oplus 1$
$\quad\quad\quad \land$ UNCHANGED $sSet, modIndex_s, fBuffer, bBuffer$

$SendMsg \triangleq \ \land \exists f : \land f \in sSet$
$\quad\quad\quad\quad\quad\quad\quad \land fBuffer' = f$
$\quad\quad\quad\quad \land$ UNCHANGED $modIndex_s, modIndex_r, sSet, rSet, bBuffer$

$ReadMsg \triangleq \ \land fBuffer \neq \langle 0, \perp_{Messages} \rangle$
$\quad\quad\quad\quad \land InRange(fBuffer[1], modIndex_r, modIndex_r \oplus BufferLength)$
$\quad\quad\quad\quad \land rSet' = rSet \cup \{fBuffer\}$
$\quad\quad\quad\quad \land fBuffer' = \langle 0, \perp_{Messages} \rangle$
$\quad\quad\quad\quad \land$ UNCHANGED $modIndex_s, modIndex_r, sSet, bBuffer$

$SendAck \triangleq \ \land bBuffer' = modIndex_r$
$\quad\quad\quad\quad \land$ UNCHANGED $modIndex_s, modIndex_r, sSet, rSet, fBuffer$

$ReadAck \triangleq \ \land sSet' = sSet \setminus \{\langle i, m \rangle \mid \neg InRange(i, bBuffer, modIndex_s) \land \langle i, m \rangle \in sSet\}$
$\quad\quad\quad\quad \land$ UNCHANGED $modIndex_s, modIndex_r, rSet, fBuffer, bBuffer$

$$
\begin{aligned}
SomeAction \;\triangleq\; & \lor\; \exists\, a : Put(a)\\
& \lor\; Get\\
& \lor\; SendMsg\\
& \lor\; ReadMsg\\
& \lor\; SendAck\\
& \lor\; ReadAck\\
Spec \;\triangleq\; & \land\; Init\\
& \land\; \Box[SomeAction]_{SLvars}\\
& \land\; WF_{SLvars}(ReadMsg)\\
& \land\; WF_{SLvars}(ReadAck)\\
& \land\; WF_{SLvars}(SendAck)\\
& \land\; WF_{SLvars}(Get)
\end{aligned}
$$

4.2 The Implementation

Another module, *SWimplementsFIFO* not included here, defines the implementation theorem between sliding windows and the FIFO buffer. This implementation is however not straightforward and requires special auxiliary variables to keep track of the real number of messages which have been transmitted (which is lost in the modulo-N numbering). Such variables are called *history variables*.

The main theorem of this module states that the sliding windows with modulo-N arithmetic implement a channel. The proof of such theorems requires a *refinement mapping*, that is, an abstraction function which gives a value to the bound variables of the right hand side (i.e. *tSet*) in terms of the other variables. An invariant is also required, which helps to establish step simulation, that is, that for any step of the abstract specification, there exists a sequence of steps of the implementation which achieve the same behavior. This is vintage TLA, and beyond the scope of this work.

5 A Translation Process

A translation from a TLA$^+$ model into a PROMELA model isn't obvious, nor straightforward. The abstractions used in either models are of a very different nature. TLA$^+$ uses *set abstractions* extensively. PROMELA, on the other hand, has no provision for abstract data types and the only homogeneous container is the array. The other critical issue is the finiteness of the PROMELA model. We must give bounds to the size of the structures and to the range of variables.

5.1 Overall structure

The canonical form of a TLA specification is the conjunction of the initial conditions, the disjunction of all possible actions (and stuttering steps), and fairness conditions. This structure can be mapped onto a single PROMELA process quite easily.

Initial conditions are mapped directly. We use a single do loop for all the actions, with a little twist. The do loop has a single entry, which allows to check an invariant first before executing an action chosen through an if statement. Fairness conditions can be handled by flagging so-called *progress* cycles, or fair cycles in SPIN.

5.2 Nondeterminism

There are two forms of nondeterminism relevant here: "don't care" and "don't know". The first case can be seen as a random selection process: we pick anyone satisfying some conditions, and different turns will result in different picks, all other conditions being identical. The don't know nondeterminism simply reflects that we do not know how an item is picked, yet the same one will always be picked. The first one is modeled with an existential quantifier. The second, with the CHOOSE construct.

SPIN's nondeterminism is restricted to transitions. Because of its interleaving semantics, when several transitions are enabled simultaneously, all possible orders of execution will be considered (up to "partial-order" reductions, which eliminate some equivalent interleavings). This is a form of "don't care" nondeterminism and it is the only mechanism we can use.

Whenever we must make a nondeterministic choice, we must map that choice to a set of transitions which give the alternatives.

5.3 Finiteness

One major advantage of the logical form is of course to have quantification of critical values, viz. to show that implementation works for all buffer sizes. This is not possible with reachability analysis, where the model must be finite and we must give values to all domains.

Typically, values are chosen in an ad-hocish manner, to limit the explosion of the models. Choices must however be consistent, to guarantee that the range of different variables will be compatible. In our case, for example, $modIndex_r$ and $modIndex_s$ must have the same range.

5.4 Coding Sets

In TLA, as in other set-theoretic languages, sets are the abstraction of choice for data structures. Sets, however, because of their nature, do not carry much structural information. Although TLA$^+$ does give us some syntactic sugar for sequences and tuples, we are still far from the computational structures of PROMELA. Therefore, a generic mapping for sets is not realistic. We can however define different mappings from which we can choose depending on our needs.

We consider three possibilities :

- use an array, a value is stored at an index matching the element;
- use an array, store an element at the first free position, fill the whole when it is removed;

— use *bitsets*, that is, code the presence of an element in a set as a bit in a word.

In all cases, the array or the word will have to be large enough w.r.t the cardinality of the set. We may also need a mapping from set elements to naturals. In the first two cases, we also need a value which does not belong to the domain of the elements to mark emptiness.

In the PROMELA models, we also introduce simplifications when we need to compute the minimum of a set as well as a test for emptiness.

5.5 Domains

All domains must be finite. When we use modulo-N numbering, this isn't a problem. Otherwise, we must define a finite range, and guard variables to guarantee that the range won't be exceeded, but only in specific cases, namely in supplementary constraints in guards.

As we said before, we also need out of domain values to initialize arrays to empty sets. We simply take a number out of all ranges.

5.6 Sliding Windows in Promela

The following PROMELA model matches the TLA$^+$ specification of the sliding windows with history variables. Because we do not have functions in PROMELA, an extra variable is used to keep track of the bottom of the sender's buffer. This variable is equal to *modIndex$_s$* when the set is empty.

```
byte indexR, modIndexR, modIndexS, indexS;

#define MAXb 7
#define BLength 3
#define Modular 6
#define OofR   10

byte sSet[Modular];
byte rSet[Modular];

byte sSetMin;
byte fBuffer, bBuffer;
byte loopVar, data;

#define InRange(a,b,c) ( (b<=a && a<c)||(c<b && b<=a)||(a<c && c<b) )
#define modInc(a) ( (a + 1) % Modular)
#define modSub(a,b) ( (a>b -> a-b : (a + Modular - b)))
#define modAdd(a,b) ( ((a+b) % Modular) )

#define Inbounds() (indexR < MAXb && indexS < MABb && data < MAXb)
#define Atbounds() (indexR == MAXb && indexS == MABb && data == MAXb)
/*
```

```
   d_steps are not strictly necessary in such synchronous models, but they
   reduce the number of states.
*/
proctype unique() {
  do
   :: (1) ->
     /* check invariant */
     d_step{
       assert (indexS >= indexR);
       assert (indexS-indexR <= BLength );
       assert (rSet[modIndexR] == 0 || rSet[ modIndexR ] == indexR + 1 );
     };
     /* end of invariant */
/* Put */
     if
     :: ((sSetMin == modIndexS) || modSub(modIndexS, sSetMin) < BLength )
     && (data < MAXb) ->
       sSet[modIndexS] = data;
       data = data + 1;
       modIndexS = modInc(modIndexS);
       indexS = indexS + 1;
/* get */
     :: indexR < MAXb && rSet[ modIndexR ] != 0  ->
       rSet[ modIndexR ] = 0;
       indexR = indexR + 1;
       modIndexR = modInc(modIndexR);
/* SendMsg */
:: InRange(0, sSetMin, modIndexS) && sSet[0]!=0 -> progress0: fBuffer=0;
:: InRange(1, sSetMin, modIndexS) && sSet[1]!=0 -> progress1: fBuffer=1;
:: InRange(2, sSetMin, modIndexS) && sSet[2]!=0 -> progress2: fBuffer=2;
:: InRange(3, sSetMin, modIndexS) && sSet[3]!=0 -> progress3: fBuffer=3;
:: InRange(4, sSetMin, modIndexS) && sSet[4]!=0 -> progress4: fBuffer=4;
:: InRange(5, sSetMin, modIndexS) && sSet[5]!=0 -> progress5: fBuffer=5;
/* ReadMsg */
     :: fBuffer != OofR
     && InRange(fBuffer, modIndexR, modAdd(modIndexR,BLength)) ->
        rSet[ fBuffer ] = sSet[ fBuffer ]; fBuffer =OofR;
/* SendAck */
     :: (1) -> progressSA: bBuffer = modIndexR;
/* ReadAck */
     :: sSetMin != bBuffer ->
        d_step {
          do
          :: sSetMin != bBuffer ->
             sSet[ sSetMin ] = 0; sSetMin = modInc(sSetMin);
          :: sSetMin == bBuffer -> break
          od;
        }
/* exit */
     :: (indexR == MAXb) && (indexS == MAXb) -> break;
```

```
/* end of simulation */
    fi
  od;
}

init{
  /* 0 is a null value for data; OofR is a null value for indices */
  indexR = 0; indexS = 0; modIndexR = 0; modIndexS = 0;
  fBuffer = OofR; bBuffer = 0; sSetMin = 0; data = 1;
  run unique();
}
```

Results

```
(Spin Version 2.9.4 -- 4 November 1996)
        + Partial Order Reduction
Full statespace search for:
        never-claim             - (not selected)
        assertion violations    +
        cycle checks            - (disabled by -DSAFETY)
        invalid endstates       +
State-vector 40 byte, depth reached 279, errors: 0
   12437 states, stored
    4780 states, matched
   17217 transitions (= stored+matched)
       0 atomic steps
hash conflicts: 1107 (resolved)
(max size 2^19 states)

2.89838e+06    memory usage (bytes)

unreached in proctype unique
        line 80, state 59, "-end-"
        (1 of 59 states)
unreached in proctype :init:
        (0 of 10 states)
```

5.7 Checking the implementation

The PROMELA model can also be used to check if the implementation relation is correct. This is done simply by merging the two specifications into a single model, computing them in lockstep, and making sure that the refinement mapping is always valid. By "lockstep" we mean that we still validate the implementation, but make sure that any action of the implementation are compatible with a matching action (if any) of the specification. In this case, there is a one to one mapping between *Put* actions in both models as well as between *Get* actions. Both pairs of actions can be combined in a common branch of the if, but using different variables for the indices. After executing any branch of the if, we check if the indices still match, and is the computed *tSet* still equals the value given by the refinement mapping.

6 More complex windows

This more sophisticated model implements sliding windows while minimizing the number of retransmissions. An auxiliary queue is used to keep track of the order of transmission and acknowledgments contain a bitmap of the receiver's entire window. This information allows us to decide what has been lost for certain, as long as we receive a feedback: anything that has been sent before an acknowledged message, but hasn't been acknowledged, can be resent. Note that this hypothesis is valid only if the communication channels do not reorder or duplicate messages.

When we no longer have feedback, and the whole sender's window has been sent, a deadlock can occur. In this case, we resend the last item in the queue, until we do receive an acknowledgment. This preserves the transmission order, while relaxing the uniqueness of reception rule. The multiple copies will be deleted by the receiver.

In this model, we distinguish between $SetMin(sSet)$ and $bottom$, which is simply an image of $modIndex_r$ on the receiver side. Items below $bottom$ will be purged from the queue in due time when they reach the head of the queue.

— module *NoRetransmit* —

EXTENDS *MiscDefinitions*
EXTENDS *ModularArithmetic*
EXTENDS *Sequences*
VARIABLES $sSet$, $rSet$, $aSet$, $sQueue$, $bottom$, $modIndex_r$, $modIndex_s$, $fBuffer$, $bBuffer$

ASSUMPTION
$IntervalRange = 2 \times BufferLength$

$NRvars \triangleq \langle sSet, rSet, aSet, sQueue, bottom, modIndex_r, modIindex_s, fBuffer, bBuffer \rangle$
$Init \triangleq \;\land modIndex_r = 0$
$\qquad\quad \land modIndex_s = 0$
$\qquad\quad \land bottom = 0$
$\qquad\quad \land aSet = \emptyset$
$\qquad\quad \land rSet = \emptyset$
$\qquad\quad \land sSet = \emptyset$
$\qquad\quad \land fBuffer = \langle 0, \perp_{Messages} \rangle$
$\qquad\quad \land bBuffer = \langle \emptyset, 0 \rangle$
$\qquad\quad \land sQueue = \langle \rangle$

$Put(a) \triangleq \;\land a \in Messages$
$\qquad\qquad \land sSet \neq \emptyset \land modIndex_s \ominus ModSetMin(sSet) < BufferLength$
$\qquad\qquad \land sSet' = sSet \cup \{\langle modIndex_s, a \rangle\}$
$\qquad\qquad \land modIndex'_s = modIndex_s \ominus 1$
$\qquad\qquad \land$ UNCHANGED $aSet, rSet, sQueue, bottom, modIndex_r, fBuffer, bBuffer$

$Get \;\triangleq\; \wedge\, \exists\, a \,:\, \wedge\, \langle modIndex_r, a\rangle \in rSet$
$\qquad\qquad\qquad \wedge\, rSet' = rSet \setminus \{\langle modIndex_r, a\rangle\}$
$\qquad\quad\;\, \wedge\, modIndex_r' = modIndex_r \oplus 1$
$\qquad\quad\;\, \wedge\, \text{UNCHANGED } aSet, sSet, sQueue, modIndex_s, bottom, fBuffer, bBuffer$

$SendNewMsg \;\triangleq\; \wedge\, f \notin \{j \,:\, \langle i,j\rangle \in sQueue\}$
$\qquad\qquad\qquad\;\; \wedge\, |sQueue| < BufferLength$
$\qquad\qquad\qquad\;\; \wedge\, fBuffer' = f$
$\qquad\qquad\qquad\;\; \wedge\, sQueue' = sQueue \circ \langle f\rangle$
$\qquad\qquad\qquad\;\; \wedge\, \text{UNCHANGED } bottom, modIndex_s, modIndex_r, aSet, sSet, rSet, bBuffer$

$ResendMsg \;\triangleq\; \wedge\, Head(sQueue)[1] \notin aSet$
$\qquad\qquad\qquad\;\; \wedge\, InRange(Head(sQueue)[1], bottom, modIndex_s)$
$\qquad\qquad\qquad\;\; \wedge\, \vee\, aSet \neq \emptyset$
$\qquad\qquad\qquad\qquad\;\; \vee\, \exists f \,:\, \wedge\, f \in sQueue$
$\qquad\qquad\qquad\qquad\qquad\qquad\;\, \wedge\, \neg InRange(f[1], bottom, modIndex_s)$
$\qquad\qquad\qquad\;\; \wedge\, fBuffer' = Head(sQueue)$
$\qquad\qquad\qquad\;\; \wedge\, sQueue' = Tail(sQueue) \circ \langle Head(sQueue)\rangle$
$\qquad\qquad\qquad\;\; \wedge\, \text{UNCHANGED } bottom, modIndex_s, modIndex_r, aSet, sSet, rSet, bBuffer$

$PurgeMsg \;\triangleq\; \wedge\, Head(sQueue)[1] \in aSet$
$\qquad\qquad\qquad \wedge\, aSet' = aSet \setminus Head(sQueue)[1]$
$\qquad\qquad\qquad \wedge\, sSet' = sSet \setminus Head(sQueue)[1]$
$\qquad\qquad\qquad \wedge\, sQueue' = Tail(sQueue)$
$\qquad\qquad\qquad \wedge\, \text{UNCHANGED } bottom, modIndex_s, modIndex_r, rSet, fBuffer, bBuffer$

$PurgeBottom \;\triangleq\; \wedge\, \neg InRange(Head(sQueue)[1], bottom, modIndex_s)$
$\qquad\qquad\qquad\quad \wedge\, sSet' = sSet \setminus Head(sQueue)$
$\qquad\qquad\qquad\quad \wedge\, sQueue' = Tail(sQueue)$
$\qquad\qquad\qquad\quad \wedge\, \text{UNCHANGED } bottom, modIndex_s, modIndex_r, rSet, aSet, fBuffer, bBuffer$

$UnblockQueue \;\triangleq\; \wedge\, InRange(Head(sQueue)[1], bottom, modIndex_s)$
$\qquad\qquad\qquad\quad\;\; \wedge\, aSet = \emptyset$
$\qquad\qquad\qquad\quad\;\; \wedge\, \nexists f \,:\, \wedge\, f \in sQueue$
$\qquad\qquad\qquad\qquad\qquad\;\; \wedge\, \neg InRange(f[1], bottom, modIndex_s)$
$\qquad\qquad\qquad\quad\;\; \wedge\, fBuffer' = Last(sQueue)$
$\qquad\qquad\qquad\quad\;\; \wedge\, \text{UNCHANGED } bottom, modIndex_s, modIndex_r, rSet, aSet, sSet, bBuffer$

$ReadMsg \;\triangleq\; \wedge\, fBuffer \neq \langle 0, \bot_{Messages}\rangle$
$\qquad\qquad\qquad \wedge\, InRange(fBuffer[1], modIndex_r, modIndex_r + BufferLength)$
$\qquad\qquad\qquad \wedge\, rSet' = rSet \cup fBuffer$
$\qquad\qquad\qquad \wedge\, fBuffer' = \langle 0, \bot_{Messages}\rangle$
$\qquad\qquad\qquad \wedge\, \text{UNCHANGED } bottom, sQueue, modIndex_s, modIndex_r, aSet, sSet, rSet, bBuffer$

$SendAck \;\triangleq\; \wedge\, bBuffer' = \langle\{i \,:\, \exists m \,:\, \langle i,m\rangle \in rSet\}, modIndex_r\rangle$
$\qquad\qquad\qquad \wedge\, \text{UNCHANGED } bottom, sQueue, modIndex_s, modIndex_r, aSet, rSet, sSet, fBuffer$

$ReadAck \;\triangleq\; \wedge\, bBuffer \neq \langle\emptyset, 0\rangle$
$\qquad\qquad\qquad \wedge\, bBuffer' = \langle\emptyset, 0\rangle$
$\qquad\qquad\qquad \wedge\, aSet' = bBuffer[1]$
$\qquad\qquad\qquad \wedge\, bottom' = bBuffer[2]$
$\qquad\qquad\qquad \wedge\, \text{UNCHANGED } modIndex_s, sQueue, modIndex_r, sSet, rSet, fBuffer$

$$
\begin{aligned}
SomeAction \;\triangleq\; &\;\vee\; \exists\, a\,:\, Put(a) \\
&\;\vee\; Get \\
&\;\vee\; SendNewMsg \\
&\;\vee\; ResendMsg \\
&\;\vee\; PurgeMsg \\
&\;\vee\; UnblockQueue \\
&\;\vee\; ReadMsg \\
&\;\vee\; SendAck \\
&\;\vee\; ReadAck \\
&\;\vee\; PurgeBottom
\end{aligned}
$$

$$
\begin{aligned}
Spec \;\triangleq\; &\;\wedge\; Init \\
&\;\wedge\; \Box[SomeAction]_{NRvars} \\
&\;\wedge\; WF_{NRvars}(ReadMsg, ReadAck, PurgeBottom, PurgeMsg, Get)
\end{aligned}
$$

$$\text{---------------------- module } NRimplementsSLW \text{ ----------------------}$$

EXTENDS NR

EXTENDS $MiscDefinitions$

EXTENDS $ModularArithmetic$

VARIABLES $SLWsSet, SLWrSet, SLWfBuffer, SLWbBuffer$

$$
\begin{aligned}
HLS \;\triangleq\; \text{INSTANCE } SLW \text{ with } &sSet \leftarrow SLWsSet,\; rSet \leftarrow SLWrSet, \\
&SLWfBuffer \leftarrow fBuffer,\; SLWbBuffer \leftarrow bBuffer
\end{aligned}
$$

THEOREM

$\exists\, sSet, rSet, aSet, sQueue, bottom, fBuffer, bBuffer : Spec$

$\Rightarrow \exists\, SLWsSet, SLWrSet, SLWfBuffer, SLWbBuffer : HLS.Spec$

The validation of the translated PROMELA model yielded the following results.

```
Spin Version 2.9.4 -- 4 November 1996)
        + Partial Order Reduction
Full statespace search for:
        never-claim            - (none specified)
        assertion violations   +
        cycle checks           - (disabled by -DSAFETY)
        invalid endstates      +
State-vector 48 byte, depth reached 623, errors: 0
1.6451e+06 states, stored
  421859 states, matched
2.06696e+06 transitions (= stored+matched)
        0 atomic steps
hash conflicts: 2.98002e+06 (resolved)
(max size 2^18 states)

8.76979e+07      memory usage (bytes)

unreached in proctype NR
        line 135, state 141, "-end-"
        (1 of 141 states)
unreached in proctype :init:
        (0 of 25 states)
```

7   Discussion

The three step specification we have illustrated here is actually a simplification from the real specifications we have been working on. In practice, we have used more intermediate steps, e.g. for the introduction of modulo-N numbering and for the bitmap acknowledgments. Space hasn't allowed us to explore these specifications in more detail. The principle of our method appears more clearly on non-trivial examples.

With this method, we simply check some properties on a finite version of the abstract model, without making any claim to the generalization of the results. The intuition is that, if there is something wrong with the parameterized model, the problem will most likely appear in the finite model. But the lack of problem with the finite model doesn't lead to any conclusion with the parameterized model, only that our feeling of correctness is reinforced.

How general is this method? Obviously, the difficulty lies in the ability to generate computable models from an abstract specification. Whenever we substitute a computation to a declarative style, we change the specification, and increase the risk of introducing an error. High level specifications tend to be very abstract and may thus be difficult to model.

Can this method be automated? The translation of data abstractions is ad-hocish. With TLA$^+$ as it is defined, it is difficult to do better, and we do not want to change this language. Through the use of macros and macro generators, however, the process can be greatly simplified.

Should there be a formal link between the two notations? Ideally, yes. But in practice, even an informal translation can be quite helpful, as we have observed experimentally. Several errors in the TLA$^+$ models were exposed through the PROMELA models, in very little time.

Is this a combination of theorem-proving and model-checking? Yes, but not in the sense that it is normally interpreted. Although reachability analysis tools tend to be assimilated under the term "model checker", we are not interested in the satisfiability of temporal logic formulæ. Nor do we have a formal relation between the TLA$^+$ and the PROMELA models. We further discuss this matter below.

7.1   Comparison with other work

Herrmann & Krumm Herrmann and Krumm's work [5] is also based on TLA and aims at being able to perform verification both in a theorem proving and reachability analysis context. The focus of their work is quite narrow, as they concentrate on building a framework to define and validate transfer protocols. They do not use TLA$^+$ but a closely related, but more specific formalism based on processes and joint actions. They do not exploit refinement but rather composition of specification and implementation components by conjunction. They have developed for this framework an extensive set of tools, which include an automatic checker for refinement mappings through reachability analysis. Although the application domain is similar, our focus differs, and the principle of checking we have presented here is more general.

Havelund & Shankar Havelund & Shankar in [4] report on a number of experiments in using theorem provers to verify protocols, as well as their own experience in combining a theorem prover and model checkers. Their framework, as most other's, is a classical invariant proof and they do not consider refinement, nor liveness properties. Furthermore, although they did experiment with a reachability analysis tool, their major focus was to try to derive a "property-preserving finite state abstraction" which could be verified automatically. In their proposed methodology, they do recommend the construction of a scaled-down version of the protocol for debugging. The models and proofs are done directly in the PVS [13] tool rather than being coded in a specification logic such as Unity or TLA, which gives us a solid foundation for refinement.

The authors reach similar conclusions on the interest of "exploring" the specification with a reachability analysis tool.

INRS-Télécommunications In a related activity, another group at INRS is building tools to help with the TLA proof process. The persons involved have studied the RLP1 protocol, although they haven't exploited refinement to the same extent. Nevertheless, our activities are complementary.

8 Conclusions

We have presented a part of a larger effort to validate a large protocol with RLP. In this paper, we have focused on the checking of (some of) the models with PROMELA. The benefits of complementing formal proofs with checking are quite clear. In fact, for this type of protocols and with the current state of the art, it is unlikely that a complete proof would be done in practice, considering the amount of work required, for marginal incremental payback w.r.t. checking. The major weakness of this process is certainly the manual translation (and interpretation) of the TLA$^+$ model into PROMELA. In this experience, however, we have accomplished the translation and the validation in a few hours each time, and some problems of the TLA$^+$ model were indeed identified. The proof of the pudding ...

Acknowledgments The NR protocol is actually an approximation of the RLP1 TDMA protocol. Early specifications of (quite) abstract versions of RLP1 where written by B. Johnston. A (hierarchical) proof that an unbounded sliding windows (*SlidingWindows* without modulo-N numbering) implements an abstract buffer is being constructed by T. Gerdsmeier, D. Henkel and P. Ladkin at the University of Bielefeld. The specification presented here are related to a hierarchy of specifications developed jointly with Prof. Ladkin and his students, borrowing also some concepts from M. Ferguson and B. Johnston. A few safety proofs of the hierarchy have been completed at this stage.

References

1. Martín Abadi and Stephan Merz. On TLA as a logic. In Manfred Broy, editor, *Deductive Program Design*, pages 235–271. NATO ASI Series, Springer-Verlag, 1995.
2. J.-R. Abrial. *The B Book: Assigning Programs to Meanings*. Cambridge University Press, 1996.
3. J. Hajek. Automatically verified data transfer protocols. In *4th ICCC*, pages 749–756, 1978.
4. Klaus Havelund and N. Shankar. Experiments in theorem proving and model checking for protocol verification. In *Formal Methods Europe FME '96*, number 1051 in Lecture Notes in Computer Science, pages 662–681, Oxford, UK, March 1996. Springer-Verlag.
5. P. Herrmann and H. Krumm. Re-usable verification elements for high-speed transfer protocol configu ration. In *Protocol Specification, Testing and Verification XV*, pages 171–186. Chapman & Hall, 1995.
6. Gerard J. Holzmann. *Design and Validation of Computer Protocols*. Prentice Hall, 1991.
7. Gerard J. Holzmann and Doron Peled. An improvement in formal verification. In Dieter Hogrefe and Stefan Leue, editors, *7th Int. Conf. on Formal Description Techniques*. Chapman and Hall, 1994.
8. Peter Ladkin. Formal but lively buffers in TLA$^+$. Technical report, Universität von Bielefeld, 1996. from http://www.rvs.uni-bielefeld.de/.
9. Leslie Lamport. The temporal logic of actions. *ACM TOPLAS*, 16(3):872–923, 1994.
10. Leslie Lamport. TLA$^+$. Technical report, DEC-SRC, 1995. from http://www.research.digital.com/SRC/personal/Leslie_Lamport/tla/papers.html.
11. Zoar Manna and Amir Pnueli. A Temporal Proof Methodology for Reactive Systems. In *Program Design Calculi, NATO ASI Series, Series F*. Springer Verlag, 1993.
12. Natarajan and G.J. Holzmann. Towards a formal semantics of PROMELA. In *Proceedings of the 2nd SPIN Workshop*, 1996.
13. S. Owre, J. Rushby, N. Shankar, and F. von Henke. Formal verification of fault-tolerant architectures: Prolegmena to the design of PVS. *IEEE Transactions on Software Engineering*, 21(2):107–125, 1995.

A TLA Solution to the Specification and Verification of the RLP1 Retransmission Protocol

Abdelillah Mokkedem, Michael J. Ferguson, and Robert deB Johnston

INRS-Telecommunications
16, Place du Commerce, Nun's Island
Québec H3E 1H6, Canada
Email: mokkedem@inrs-telecom.uquebec.ca

Abstract. This paper presents a series of TLA$^+$ specification/implementations that lead to an implementation of the retransmission policy of RLP1, the Radio Link Protocol proposed for TDMA (Time Division Multiple Access) digital cellular radio. Both safety and liveness properties are proved for SWPInitial, a very abstract, but formal, specification of a sliding window protocol. The rest of the work consists of a series of refinements which finally result in a model of RLP1. Each refinement step is formally proved. In all cases the most difficult part of the proof is for liveness. We prove, formally and rigorously, and parametrised by the window size N, that the model of RLP1 obtained from the last refinement step is an implementation of the initial specification SWPInitial, and thus inherits safety and liveness properties proved for all the higher-level specifications. The specifications are written in TLA$^+$, a formal language based on TLA, and proofs are given in Lamport's hierarchical proof-style. Most proof steps are checked mechanically in Eves.

1 Introduction

In this paper, we investigate the use of TLA (Temporal Logic of Actions) due to Lamport [1,8,9], for the specification and verification of a series of sliding window protocols, the last of which captures the actual retransmission algorithm of an early version of the real protocol RLP1 (Radio Link Protocol) [13]. RLP1 is the data link protocol for TDMA (Time Division Multiple Access) digital cellular radio and has recently been standardized by TIA (Telecommunications Industry Association). RLP1 is the first protocol that has been standardised where there was a formal language, namely SDL [2], that was the definitive specification of the standard rather than informal text [4,5]. In addition, the entire protocol, including connection processing and retransmission algorithm was modeled and validated [5] during the actual standardisation using a combination of SDL and Promela/SPIN [6].

TLA is a (linear) temporal logic with an associated *specification/implementation* methodology [9] for refining abstract specification to a *concrete* implementation. This methodology was used to create a sequence of models for that started with simple finite, but unbounded sets as data structures, unbounded naturals for message identifiers, and a conventional retransmission algorithm, and then incrementally added detail for creating finite and bounded data structures and identifiers, finally adding the retransmission details of RLP1. Each new specification was proven to be an *implementation* of the previous *specification*, and various invariants and liveness theorems that were relevant to the new specification were proved. The TLA *specification/implementation* methodology ensures that the *implementation* inherits all the invariants and theorems that were true of the previous *specification*. The complete proofs, which may be found in [11], have been done with sufficient low-level detail that it has been possible to check the low level action steps with the theorem prover Eves [3,12] (developed by ORA Canada). Due to space limitations, most proofs have been omitted from the paper. However, because of the difficulty of proving non-trivial liveness properties, an example of such a proof is given in Section 4.

The paper is organised as follows: Section 2 gives a brief description of TLA and Section 3 gives a brief description of the retransmission algorithm of RLP1. Sections 4 to 7 give the series of specifications that add the detail necessary to create the final RLP1 specification. These are

Section 4: SWP with unbounded naturals as message identifiers, complete receiver state feedback, fixed window of size N, and message retransmission if unacknowledged. Sender State consists of the (unbounded) sets of Acknowledged messages (A) and Sent messages (S), and the Receiver state by the (unbounded) set of Received messages (R).

Section 5: The unbounded Receiver and Sender states are represented by finite bounded structures consisting of lower window edges, message maps, and the actions to manipulate them.

Section 6: The naturals used for message ids are replaced by ids modulo M.

Section 7: The Basic and Pre-emptive retransmission modes for RLP1 are added.

Section 8 discusses a simple unification and improvement of the algorithm for declaring a message *known lost* while Section 9 concludes.

2 A Short Introduction to TLA and TLA$^+$

TLA is a (linear) temporal logic. Temporal logic formulas contain *flexible variables* that may change with a change in state while *rigid variables* do not. The meaning $[\![S]\!]$ of a TLA formula S is a boolean function on behaviors, where a behavior is an infinite sequence of states and a state is an assignment of values to all flexible variables. A behavior σ *satisfies* a formula S iff $[\![S]\!](\sigma)$ equals TRUE. A formula is *valid* iff it is satisfied by all behaviors. A full description of TLA may be found in [9]. TLA$^+$ is a formal language based on TLA and Zermelo-Fraenkel set theory [10]. Figure 1 gives the complete set of inference rules for TLA and Figure 2 the meaning of TLA$^+$ keywords and symbols.

Temporal Logic Rules

$STL1.$ $\dfrac{F \text{ a tautology}}{\square F}$ $\qquad$ $STL4.$ $\dfrac{F \Rightarrow G}{\square F \Rightarrow \square G}$

$STL2. \vdash \square F \Rightarrow F$ $\qquad$ $STL5. \vdash \square(F \wedge G) \equiv (\square F) \wedge (\square G)$

$STL3. \vdash \square\square F \equiv \square F$ $\qquad$ $STL6. \vdash (\Diamond\square F) \wedge (\Diamond\square G) \equiv \Diamond\square(F \wedge G)$

$LATTICE.$ $\quad$ $\succ$ a well–founded partial order on a set S

$\qquad\qquad$ c not free in F or G

$$\dfrac{F \wedge (c \in S) \Rightarrow (H_c \rightsquigarrow (G \vee \exists d \in S : (c \succ d) \wedge H_d))}{F \Rightarrow ((\exists c \in S : H_c) \rightsquigarrow G)}$$

Basic TLA Rules

$TLA1.$ $\dfrac{P \wedge (f' = f) \Rightarrow P'}{\square P \equiv P \wedge \square[P \Rightarrow P]_f}$ $\qquad$ $TLA2.$ $\dfrac{P \wedge [\mathcal{A}]_f \Rightarrow Q \wedge [\mathcal{B}]_g}{\square P \wedge \square[\mathcal{A}]_f \Rightarrow \square Q \wedge \square[\mathcal{B}]_g}$

Invariance and Fairness Rules

$INV1.$ $\dfrac{I \wedge [\mathcal{N}]_f \Rightarrow I'}{I \wedge \square[\mathcal{N}]_f \Rightarrow \square I}$ $\qquad\qquad$ $INV2. \vdash \square I \Rightarrow (\square[\mathcal{N}]_f \equiv \square[\mathcal{N} \wedge I \wedge I']_f)$

$WF1.$

$$\dfrac{\begin{array}{l} P \wedge [\mathcal{N}]_f \Rightarrow (P' \vee Q') \\ P \wedge \langle \mathcal{N} \wedge \mathcal{A} \rangle_f \Rightarrow Q' \\ P \Rightarrow \text{ENABLED} \langle \mathcal{A} \rangle_f \end{array}}{\square[\mathcal{N}]_f \wedge \text{WF}_f(\mathcal{A}) \Rightarrow (P \rightsquigarrow Q)}$$

$WF2.$

$$\dfrac{\begin{array}{l} \langle \mathcal{N} \wedge \mathcal{B} \rangle_f \Rightarrow \langle \overline{\mathcal{M}} \rangle_{\overline{g}} \\ P \wedge P' \wedge \langle \mathcal{N} \wedge \mathcal{A} \rangle_f \wedge \overline{\text{ENABLED} \langle \mathcal{M} \rangle_g} \Rightarrow \mathcal{B} \\ P \wedge \overline{\text{ENABLED} \langle \mathcal{M} \rangle_g} \Rightarrow \text{ENABLED} \langle \mathcal{A} \rangle_f \\ \square[\mathcal{N} \wedge \neg \mathcal{B}]_f \wedge \text{WF}_f(\mathcal{A}) \wedge \square F \\ \qquad \wedge \Diamond\square\overline{\text{ENABLED} \langle \mathcal{M} \rangle_g} \Rightarrow \Diamond\square P \end{array}}{\square[\mathcal{N}]_f \wedge \text{WF}_f(\mathcal{A}) \wedge \square F \Rightarrow \overline{\text{WF}_g(\mathcal{M})}}$$

$SF1.$

$$\dfrac{\begin{array}{l} P \wedge [\mathcal{N}]_f \Rightarrow (P' \vee Q') \\ P \wedge \langle \mathcal{N} \wedge \mathcal{A} \rangle_f \Rightarrow Q' \\ \square P \wedge \square[\mathcal{N}]_f \wedge \square F \Rightarrow \Diamond\text{ENABLED} \langle A \rangle_f \end{array}}{\square[\mathcal{N}]_f \wedge \text{SF}_f(\mathcal{A}) \wedge \square F \Rightarrow (P \rightsquigarrow Q)}$$

$SF2.$

$$\dfrac{\begin{array}{l} \langle \mathcal{N} \wedge \mathcal{B} \rangle_f \Rightarrow \langle \overline{\mathcal{M}} \rangle_{\overline{g}} \\ P \wedge P' \wedge \langle \mathcal{N} \wedge \mathcal{A} \rangle_f \Rightarrow \mathcal{B} \\ P \wedge \overline{\text{ENABLED} \langle M \rangle_g} \Rightarrow \text{ENABLED} \langle A \rangle_f \\ \square[\mathcal{N} \wedge \neg \mathcal{B}]_f \wedge \text{SF}_f(\mathcal{A}) \wedge \square F \\ \qquad \wedge \square\Diamond\overline{\text{ENABLED} \langle M \rangle_g} \Rightarrow \Diamond\square P \end{array}}{\square[\mathcal{N}]_f \wedge \text{SF}_f(\mathcal{A}) \wedge \square F \Rightarrow \overline{\text{SF}_g(\mathcal{M})}}$$

where $\quad$ F, G, H_c are TLA formulas $\qquad$ P, Q, I are predicates

$\qquad\qquad$ $\mathcal{A}, \mathcal{B}, \mathcal{N}, \mathcal{M}$ are actions $\qquad$ f, g are state functions

Fig. 1. Axioms and proof rules used of TLA.

ASSUME Asserts named assumptions about constant parameters.

BOOLEAN Specifies that a parameter is a boolean-valued constant.

CONSTANT   Specifies that a parameter is a nonboolean constant.

EXTEND M Adds parameters, assumptions, definitions, and theorems from module M.

instance M as N Adds definitions from module M with parameters instantiated and "N." appended to defined names. If N has the form $P(x_1, \ldots, x_n)$, then the x_i become additional formal parameters of each included definition.

module Begins a module.

theorem Asserts that named theorems are deducible from the module's assumptions.

VARIABLE   Specifies that a parameter is a flexible variable.

$\stackrel{\Delta}{=}$ Defines an operator.

$f[x : S] \stackrel{\Delta}{=} \ldots$ Defines f to be a function with domain S.

├──────┤ Decoration that ends the scope of an **assumption** or **theorem** section.

└──────┘ Marks the end of a module.

Fig. 2. Syntactic keywords and symbols of TLA$^+$.

A concrete specification C is said to *implement* a specification S iff every behavior satisfying C satisfies S, which is true iff the formula $C \Rightarrow S$ is valid. In general to prove that a *concrete* specification implements another *abstract* specification one has to prove the following general formula:

$$\exists\, y \,:\, CInit \wedge \Box[CNext]_v \wedge CL \Rightarrow \exists\, x \,:\, Init \wedge \Box[Next]_w \wedge L$$

The standard higher-level TLA proof of such a formula is presented according the Theorem 1 given below (more details are given by Ladkin in [7]), where $CInv$ is a suitable predicate called the invariant, $\overline{x}$ is a refinement mapping, and $\overline{G} \stackrel{\Delta}{=} G$ with $x \leftarrow \overline{x}$.

Theorem 1. $\exists\, y \,:\, CInit \wedge \Box[CNext]_v \wedge CL \Rightarrow \exists\, x \,:\, Init \wedge \Box[Next]_w \wedge L$
if there is a formula $CInv$ and a refinement mapping $\overline{x}$ such that the following steps are provable using predicate logic, except the fifth step which may involve temporal logic:

$\langle 1 \rangle 1.\ \ CInit \Rightarrow CInv$

$\langle 1 \rangle 2.\ \ CInv \wedge [CNext]_v \Rightarrow CInv'$

$\langle 1 \rangle 3.\ \ CInit \Rightarrow \overline{Init}$

$\langle 1 \rangle 4.\ \ [CInv \wedge CInv' \wedge CNext]_v \Rightarrow \overline{[Next]}_{\overline{w}}$

$\langle 1 \rangle 5.\ \ \Box CInv \wedge \Box[CNext]_v \wedge CL \Rightarrow \overline{L}$

This theorem will be used to prove the validity of *implementations*.

3 An Informal Description of RLP1 and Sliding Window Protocols

A Sliding Window Protocol (SWP) is used at the data link layer to provide reliable data communication. In the basic mechanism the sender breaks a stream of bytes or bits received from the network layer into messages, also known as "frames", numbers them sequentially, and sends the numbered messages to the receiver. The receiver *acknowledges* messages that it receives. The sender is only allowed to send messages that are inside its "transmit" window. The "transmit" window is of size N and starts at the "lower-window-edge" which is the oldest-unacknowledged message from the receiver. In order to allow the window to slide up, the sender will retransmit the unacknowledged messages. When the lower-window-edge is acknowledged, the window slides up so that the new oldest-unacknowledged message becomes the lower-window-edge. If all the sent messages have been acknowledged, the lower-window-edge becomes identical to the next new message id. Current sliding window protocols differ in the details of their retransmission algorithm. RLP1 [13] brings a number of new variations to its retransmission which aim to reduce unnecessary message retransmission. In RLP1, the receiver sends back a complete map of all received messages, consisting of its lower-window-edge (the first *missing* message) and a bit map of all received messages above that. Thus the sender knows, with some delay, the complete state of the receiver. In addition, messages are retransmitted by the sender in either a *Basic Mode* or in a *Pre-emptive mode*. A message is retransmitted in the *Basic mode* only if it is *known lost*. It is *known lost* only if it is unacknowledged, if there is only one copy in the system (a new message or one retransmitted in the *Basic* mode) and if there has been a message with only one copy in the system that was acknowledged, and sent after it. Messages can be unacknowledged but not yet *known lost*. The protocol switches to the *Pre-emptive mode*, which may retransmit a message before it is *known lost*, when either there are no new messages to transmit or the window is full, and no messages are permitted for basic-mode retransmission.

4 Sliding Window Protocols with unbounded structures

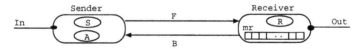

Fig. 3. The structure of SWP.

Figure 3 gives a block diagram, and the variables that are used in the initial model *SWPInitial*. *In* is an (unbounded) sequence of arbitrary messages from the upper layer, each carrying some arbitrary, undefined data. *Out*, which is empty initially, is the sequence of messages at the exit of the receiver. The interlayer specification of the protocol consists in transferring messages from *In* to *Out* without loss and duplication.

SWPInitial (Figure 4), declares internal parameters and specifies the actions, safety and liveness properties which defines an abstract model of a sliding window protocol. It imports *SwpParameters*, Figure 5, which contains some free

```
┌──────────────────────── module SWPInitial ────────────────────────┐
│ EXTEND SwpParameters                                               │
│  ┌───────────────────────── module Inner ─────────────────────┐   │
│  │ VARIABLE  S, A, R, mr, F, B                                 │   │
│  ├─────────────────────────────────────────────────────────────┤   │
```

$hi(X) \triangleq$ if $X = \{\}$ then 0
      else $maxSet(X) + 1$

$lo(X) \triangleq minSet(S \setminus X)$

$Init \triangleq \land In \in [i \in Nat^+ \mapsto Messg] \land Out = \langle\rangle$
    $\land mr = [i \in Nat \mapsto \bot_m]$
    $\land (S = \{\}) \land (A = \{\}) \land (R = \{\}) \land (F = \langle\rangle) \land (B = \{\})$

Comment: In $\langle hi(S), In[hi(S) + 1])\rangle$, the message ids start at 0 but the sequence position identifiers start at 1.

$NewMsg \triangleq \land hi(S) < lo(A) + N$
     $\land S' = S \cup \{hi(S)\}$
     $\land F' = F \circ \langle\langle hi(S), In[hi(S) + 1])\rangle\rangle$
     $\land$ UNCHANGED In, Out, A, B, R, mr

$RtxMsg(i) \triangleq \land i \in (S \setminus A)$
      $\land F' = F \circ \langle\langle i, In[i + 1])\rangle\rangle$
      $\land$ UNCHANGED In, Out, S, A, B, R, mr

$LosMsg \triangleq \land F \neq \langle\rangle$
     $\land F' = Tail(F)$
     $\land$ UNCHANGED In, Out, S, A, B, R, mr

$RcvMsg \triangleq \land F \neq \langle\rangle$
     $\land F' = Tail(F)$
     $\land R' = R \cup \{Head(F).num\}$
     $\land \lor \land Head(F).num = lo(R)$
       $\land mr' = [mr$ EXCEPT $![Head(F).num] = Head(F).val]$
       $\land Out' = Out \circ [i \in (1(lo(R') - lo(R))) \mapsto$ if $(i = lo(R))$ then $Head(F).val$
                    else $\quad mr'[i + lo(R) - 1]]$
      $\lor \land Head(F).num > lo(R)$
       $\land mr' = [mr$ EXCEPT $![Head(F).num] = Head(F).val]$
       $\land$ UNCHANGED Out
      $\lor \land Head(F).num < lo(R)$
       $\land$ UNCHANGED Out, mr
     $\land$ UNCHANGED In, S, A, B

$SndAck \triangleq \land B' = R$
     $\land$ UNCHANGED In, Out, S, A, F, R, mr

$LosAck \triangleq \land B' = \{\}$
     $\land$ UNCHANGED In, Out, S, A, F, R, mr

$RcvAck \triangleq \land B \neq \{\}$
     $\land A' = A \cup B$
     $\land$ UNCHANGED In, Out, S, B, F, R, mr

$Next \triangleq \lor NewMsg \lor (\exists i : RtxMsg(i)) \lor LosMsg$
     $\lor RcvMsg \lor SndAck \lor LosAck \lor RcvAck$

$vars \triangleq \langle In, Out, S, A, R, mr, F, B\rangle$

$spec \triangleq \land Init \land \Box[Next]_{vars}$
     $\land$ WF$_{vars}(NewMsg) \land$ WF$_{vars}(RtxMsg(lo(A)) \land (hi(S) = lo(A) + N))$
     $\land$ WF$_{vars}(SndAck) \land$ WF$_{vars}(RcvMsg)$
     $\land$ SF$_{vars}(RcvAck \land lo(A) \in B)$
     $\land$ SF$_{vars}(RcvMsg \land Head(F).num = lo(A))$

$Spec \triangleq \exists S, A, R, mr, F, B : Inner.spec$

Fig. 4. Module SWPInitial.

---

module *SwpParameters* ────────────────────────

EXTEND *Naturals, Sequences*

VARIABLE *In, Out*

CONSTANT *Messg, N*

───

ASSUME *Assump* $\stackrel{\Delta}{=}$ $N > 0 \wedge Messg \neq \{\}$

───

$\perp_m$ $\stackrel{\Delta}{=}$ CHOOSE $i : i \notin Messg$

Nat^+ $\stackrel{\Delta}{=}$ $Nat \setminus \{0\}$

$minSet(E)$ $\stackrel{\Delta}{=}$ CHOOSE $z : (z \in E \wedge \forall y : y \in E \Rightarrow z \leq y)$

$maxSet(E)$ $\stackrel{\Delta}{=}$ CHOOSE $z : (z \in E \wedge \forall y : y \in E \Rightarrow z \geq y)$

Fig. 5. Module *SwpParameters*

parameters and definitions. The state is made up of four parts, the sender, the forward channel (sender-receiver), the receiver, and the ack channel (receiver-sender) in Figure 3. S and A represent the set of sent messages and the set of acknowleged messages, respectively. The variable R represents the set of received messages and mr represents the buffer for storing the message content before delivering to Out. The channel is described by two variables F and B: F for carrying messages transiting from the sender to the receiver and B for carrying acknowledgements transiting from the receiver to the sender. F is a FIFO queue of arbitrary length while B is queue of length one.

$lo(A)$ and $hi(S)$ represents the lower-window-edge and the next new message number respectively at the sender. Messages are represented by the pair $\langle i, v \rangle$, where i represents the message id and v represents its content.

If the window is not full, the action *NewMsg* sends a new message from the input sequence In by placing it in the message channel F. *RtxMsg* resends a unacknowledged message. *LosMsg* models message loss on the message channel. *RcvMsg* gets the message at the head of the message channel F, puts its number into the set R and its content into the buffer, and, when the lower-window-edge moves, the receiver delivers all the received messages between the old value and the new value of the lower-window-edge to Out. *SndAck* puts a copy of the set of received messages R into the ack channel B and *LosAck* resets the value of B to empty. *RcvAck* receives the set of messages acknowledged from the ack channel B. For a pair $c = \langle i, v \rangle$ representing an entire message, $c.num$ denotes the number i and $c.val$ denotes the content v.

Verification of SWPInitial

The verification of the specification *SWPInitial* is achieved by proving the validity of the module *SWPInitialVerification* (Figure 6). The theorems *InvThm* (invariance property) and *LiveThm* (liveness property) follow from the assumption ASSUME $N > 0 \wedge Messg \neq \{\}$. *LiveThm* asserts that the lower-window-edge $lo(A)$ increases forever, which implies that the specified system is deadlock free and livelock free. $lo(A)$ can increase only after the message corresponding to $lo(A)$ is first received by the receiver, hence $(lo(A) \in R')$, and then this new state R' is sent back to sender in B and is received to update A. As an illustra-

---

————————— module *SWPInitialVerification* —————————

EXTEND *SWPInitial*

$SwpInv \triangleq \ \wedge\ hi(S) \in Nat\ \wedge\ S = 0..<hi(S)$
$\wedge\ \forall i,j\ :\ 1 \leq i < j \leq Len(F) \Rightarrow F[i].num < (F[j].num + N)$
$\wedge\ \forall i \in 1\,Len(F)\ :\ \wedge\ (hi(R) - N) \leq F[i].num < hi(S)$
$\wedge\ F[i].val = In[F[i].num + 1]$
$\wedge\ R \subseteq S\ \wedge\ B \subseteq R\ \wedge\ (A \subseteq B \vee B = \{\})$
$\wedge\ (A \subseteq R)\ \wedge\ (0 \leq hi(S) - lo(A) \leq N)\ \wedge\ (\forall i \in R\ :\ mr[i] = In[i+1])$
$\wedge\ ([i \in (1\,lo(R)) \mapsto mr[i-1]] \preceq In)\ \wedge\ (Out \preceq In)$

theorems
$InvThm \triangleq Inner.spec \Rightarrow \Box SwpInv$
$LiveThm \triangleq Inner.spec \Rightarrow (lo(A) = i) \rightsquigarrow (lo(A) > i)$

Fig. 6. Module SWPInitialVerification.

tion, a summary of the liveness proof is given below, while complete proofs are in [11].

Sketch of the Liveness Proof This proof makes use of the TLA inference rules: Strong Fairness (SF1), Lattice Rule, Weak Fairness (WF1), and a Simple Temporal Logic (STL2) rule which are given in Figure 1.

LET:
$WFair \triangleq \ \wedge\ WF_{vars}(NewMsg) \wedge WF_{vars}(RtxMsg(lo(A))) \wedge hi(S) = lo(A) + N$
$\wedge\ WF_{vars}(SndAck) \wedge WF_{vars}(RcvMsg)$
ASSUME $N > 0 \wedge Messg \neq \{\}$

PROVE: $Inner.spec \Rightarrow (lo(A) = i) \rightsquigarrow (lo(A) > i)$

The proof is done in two steps. The first proves that the message identified by $lo(A)$ will be eventually received. The second proves that every received message will be eventually acknowledged. The main property follows from the transitivity of $\rightsquigarrow$.

The structure of the first proof step is: the high level is an application of SF1; the next lower level consists of its three premises. The third of these is the tricky one, justified by a conclusion of Lattice Rule plus some temporal logic. The conclusion of the Lattice Rule is justified by the premise. The premise is justified by an application of WF1. The three premises of WF1 are shown directly.

$\langle 1 \rangle 1.$ $\Box[Next]_{vars} \wedge SF_{vars}(RcvMsg \wedge Head(F).num = lo(A)) \wedge WFair$
$\Rightarrow (lo(A) \notin R) \rightsquigarrow (lo(A) \in R)$
PROOF: The next three steps form the premises of the TLA Rule SF1.

$\langle 2 \rangle 1.$ $(lo(A) \notin R) \wedge [Next]_{vars} \Rightarrow$
$(lo(A') \notin R') \vee (lo(A') \in R')$

PROOF: Immediate by propositional logic.

$\langle 2 \rangle 2.$ $(lo(A) \notin R) \wedge \langle Next \wedge (RcvMsg \wedge Head(F).num = lo(A)) \rangle_{vars} \Rightarrow$
$(lo(A') \in R')$
PROOF:

$\langle 2 \rangle 3.$ $\square(lo(A) \notin R) \wedge \square[Next]_{vars} \wedge WFair \Rightarrow$
$\Diamond$ENABLED $\langle RcvMsg \wedge Head(F).num = lo(A) \rangle_{vars}$
PROOF: This step is proved as a *leadsto* property. The rule proved in the next step allows to transform it into a *leadsto* form.

LET: X, Y, Z : PROPOSITIONAL VARIABLES
$\langle 3 \rangle 1.$ $\dfrac{Z \Rightarrow X \rightsquigarrow Y}{(\square X \wedge Z) \Rightarrow \Diamond Y}$

$\quad \langle 4 \rangle 1.$ $\dfrac{X \rightsquigarrow Y}{\square X \Rightarrow \Diamond Y}$

$\quad\quad$ PROOF: $X \rightsquigarrow Y \triangleq \square(X \Rightarrow \Diamond Y)$
$\quad\quad \vdash \{STL2\}$
$\quad\quad X \Rightarrow \Diamond Y$
$\quad\quad \vdash \{STL4\}$
$\quad\quad \square X \Rightarrow \square \Diamond Y$
$\quad\quad \vdash \{STL2 \text{ and propositional logic}\}$
$\quad\quad \square X \Rightarrow \Diamond Y$

$\quad \langle 4 \rangle 2.$ Q.E.D.
$\quad\quad$ Follows form $\langle 4 \rangle 1$ and propositional logic.

$\langle 3 \rangle 2.$ $\square[Next]_{vars} \wedge WFair$
$\quad \Rightarrow lo(A) \notin R \rightsquigarrow (F \neq \langle \rangle \wedge Head(F).num = lo(A)) \wedge (lo(A) \notin R)$
PROOF: This step is proved in two steps: the first guarantees that whenever $lo(A)$ is over the message channel, it will eventually advance to head of the channel. The second step guarantees that $lo(A)$ will eventually be put in the channel.

$\langle 3 \rangle 3.$ $lo(A) \notin R \wedge (F \neq \langle \rangle \wedge Head(F).num = lo(A)) \Rightarrow$ ENABLED $\langle RcvMsg \wedge Head(F).num = lo(A) \rangle_{vars}$
PROOF: Follows by quantifier rules of predicate logic from the definition of RcvMsg and ENABLED and the typing invariant : $\square(lo(A) \in Nat \wedge R \subseteq Nat)$ whose proof is straightforward using especially *SwpInv*. Notice that the substitution axiom INV2 is used to strengthen the hypothesis of assertions with invariants in order to complete their proofs.

$\langle 3 \rangle 4.$ Q.E.D.
$\quad$ PROOF: Follows by rule $\dfrac{X \rightsquigarrow Y, \quad Y \Rightarrow Z}{X \rightsquigarrow Z}$ (which can be proved in simple temporal logic), and rule proved in $\langle 3 \rangle 1$ with hypotheses $\langle 3 \rangle 2$, $\langle 3 \rangle 3$ and the substitution
$\quad X \triangleq lo(A) \notin R \quad\quad\quad Z \triangleq \square[Next]_{vars} \wedge WFair$
$\quad Y \triangleq$ ENABLED $\langle RcvMsg \wedge Head(F).num = lo(A) \rangle_{vars}$
$\langle 2 \rangle 4.$ Q.E.D.

PROOF: Immediate from the TLA theorem $WFair \equiv \Box WFair$ and the TLA Rule SF1 with hypotheses $\langle 2 \rangle 1$, $\langle 2 \rangle 2$, $\langle 2 \rangle 3$, under the substitution

$$P \triangleq (lo(A) \notin R) \qquad\qquad Q \triangleq (lo(A) \in R)$$
$$A \triangleq (RcvMsg \wedge Head(F).num = lo(A)) \quad \mathcal{N} \triangleq Next$$
$$f \triangleq vars \qquad\qquad\qquad\qquad F \triangleq WFair.$$

This completes the proof of the first step of the liveness property. The proof of the second step has almost the same structure of the first step: the high level is an application of SF1; the next low-level consists of its three premises. The third of these is in turn justified by a conclusion of the rule WF1 plus some temporal logic.

$\langle 1 \rangle 2.$ $[Next]_{vars} \wedge SF_{vars}(RcvAck \wedge lo(A) \in B) \wedge WFair$
$\Rightarrow (lo(A) = i \wedge i \in R) \rightsquigarrow (lo(A) > i)$
PROOF:

This step is justified by the next substep and manipulation of arithmetic, set-theory, and simple temporal logic using the definition of $lo(A)$. We prove that $(lo(A) = i \wedge i \in R) \rightsquigarrow i \in A$ follows from the specification. By definition of $lo(A)$, it is not difficult to derive $(lo(A) = i \wedge i \in R) \rightsquigarrow (lo(A) > i)$. The next step is proved using the rule SF1. The subsequent three substeps are the premises of this rule.

$\langle 2 \rangle 1.$ $[Next]_{vars} \wedge SF_{vars}(RcvAck \wedge lo(A) \in B) \wedge WFair \Rightarrow (lo(A) = i \wedge i \in R) \rightsquigarrow i \in A$
PROOF:

$\langle 3 \rangle 1.$ $(lo(A) = i \wedge i \in R) \wedge [Next]_{vars} \Rightarrow (lo(A') = i \wedge lo(A') \in R') \vee (i \in A')$
PROOF: The only actions that change A or R (and therefore require closer inspection) are $RcvMsg$ and $RcvAck$. The case of $RcvMsg$ is simple, because $RcvMsg \Rightarrow R' \subseteq R$. For the case of $RcvAck$:

$\langle 4 \rangle 1.$ $(lo(A) = i \wedge i \in R) \wedge RcvAck \Rightarrow (lo(A') = i \wedge lo(A') \in R') \vee (i \in A')$
For the case $i \in B$, the second disjunct $i \in A'$ holds. For the case $i \notin B$, the first disjunct $(lo(A') = i \wedge lo(A') \in R')$ holds because $R' = R$ (by definition of $RcvAck$) and $lo(A') = lo(A)$ (by definition of $lo(A)$ and the invariant $SwpInv$; more precisely the invariant $A \subseteq B \vee B = \{\}$).
$\langle 3 \rangle 2.$ $(lo(A) = i \wedge i \in R) \wedge \langle Next \wedge (RcvAck \wedge lo(A) \in B) \rangle_{vars} \Rightarrow (i \in A')$
PROOF:

$\langle 3 \rangle 3.$ $\Box(lo(A) = i \wedge i \in R) \wedge \Box[Next]_{vars} \wedge WFair \Rightarrow \Diamond \text{ENABLED} \langle RcvAck \wedge lo(A) \in B \rangle_{vars}$
PROOF:

⟨4⟩1. □[*Next*]$_{vars}$ ∧ *WFair* ⇒ (*lo*(*A*) = *i* ∧ *i* ∈ *R*) ↝ ENABLED ⟨*RcvAck* ∧ *lo*(*A*) ∈ *B*⟩$_{vars}$

PROOF:

⟨5⟩1. *lo*(*A*) ∈ *B* ⇒ ENABLED ⟨*RcvAck* ∧ *lo*(*A*) ∈ *B*⟩$_{vars}$
PROOF: Follows by quantifier rules of predicate logic from the definition of *lo*(*A*) and *RcvAck*.

⟨5⟩2. □[*Next*]$_{vars}$ ∧ *WFair* ⇒ (*lo*(*A*) = *i* ∧ *i* ∈ *R*) ↝ *lo*(*A*) ∈ *B*
PROOF: The proof uses the TLA Rule WF1 under substitution

$P \triangleq lo(A) = i \land i \in R \land lo(A) \notin B \qquad Q \triangleq lo(A) \in B$

$\mathcal{N} \triangleq Next$

$A \triangleq SndAck \qquad f \triangleq vars$

(see [11]).

⟨5⟩3. Q.E.D.
PROOF: Follows from ⟨5⟩1 and ⟨5⟩2 by the rule $\frac{X \rightsquigarrow Y, \; Y \Rightarrow Z}{X \rightsquigarrow Z}$ which can be proved in simple temporal logic.

⟨4⟩2. Q.E.D.
PROOF: Follows from ⟨4⟩1, by the rule $\frac{Z \Rightarrow X \rightsquigarrow Y}{(\Box X \land Z) \Rightarrow \Diamond Y}$ proved in a substep of ⟨1⟩1.

⟨3⟩4. Q.E.D.
PROOF: Immediate from TLA Rule SF1 with hypotheses ⟨3⟩1, ⟨3⟩2, ⟨3⟩3, under substitution

$P \triangleq (lo(A) = i \land i \in R) \qquad Q \triangleq i \in A \qquad F \triangleq WFair$

$\mathcal{N} \triangleq Next \qquad A \triangleq RcvAck \land lo(A) \in B \qquad f \triangleq vars$

⟨2⟩2. Q.E.D.
PROOF: Follows by arithmetic, standard axioms of set-theory ans simple temporal logic from the definition of *lo*(*A*) and ⟨2⟩1.

⟨1⟩3. Q.E.D.
PROOF: Immediate from ⟨1⟩1, ⟨1⟩2, by Transitivity of ↝ and the definition of *Inner.spec*.

5 SWP with finite structures

In the abstract specification *SWPInitial*, the message sets *S*, *R*, *A* and the message identifiers are finite but unbounded. In the protocol standard, modulo-numbering *M* (where *M* ≥ 2 × *N*) is used and thus sets represented by *S*, *R* and *A* are finite and bounded. In *SWPFiniteStruct*[11], the variables *S*, *R* and *A* are implemented with finite data structures. The second refinement step, *SWPModulo*, introduces the modulo-numbering. The key to implementing finite structures is the observation that *A* of the sender state can be completely described by a variable *loA* (which takes a natural value) and a finite set *upA* (see Figure 7) which contains all the sent-messages greater than *loA*, and similarly for the receiver state *R*.

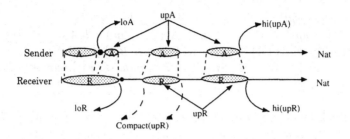

Fig. 7. Finite structures.

The specification *SWPFiniteStruct* implements *SWPInitial* by representing *S* with a variable *hiS* which takes a natural value, *A* with the two variables *loA* and *upA*, and *R* with two variables *loR* and *upR*.

————— **module** *SWPFiniteStructImplementsSWPInitial* —————

EXTEND *SwpParameters*

$SwpI \triangleq$ **instance** *SWP*
$SwpFS \triangleq$ **instance** *SWPFiniteStruct*

theorem $SwpFS.Spec \Rightarrow SwpI.Spec$

Fig. 8. Module *SWPFiniteStructImplementsSWPInitial*

Proof of SWPFiniteStructImplementsSWPInitial (Figure 8) The picture given in figure 7 gives a simple way to get a refinement mapping for the proof of *SWPFiniteStructImplementsSWPInitial*. The refinement mapping is defined as follows:

$$\overline{S} \triangleq 0.._{<hiS} \qquad\qquad \overline{A} \triangleq 0.._{<loA\cup upA}$$

$$\overline{B} \triangleq \text{ if } B = \bot \text{ then } \{\} \qquad\qquad \overline{R} \triangleq 0.._{<loR\cup upR}$$
$$\qquad\qquad \text{else} \quad 0.._{<B[1]\cup B[2]}$$

$$\overline{F} \triangleq F \qquad\qquad\qquad\qquad \overline{mr} \triangleq mr$$

The invariant[1] used for the refinement proof is :

---

[1] There is no systematic method to invent a suitable invariant for the refinement proof. It relies on the experience gained from a deep study of the problem in question.

$$Inv \triangleq \land (loA \in Nat) \land (loA \leq loR \leq hiS \leq (loA + N))$$
$$\land (\forall i \in upR : loR < i < hiS) \land (\forall i \in upA : loA < i < hiS)$$
$$\land (loR \leq hi_r(upR) \leq hiS) \land (B = \bot \lor B[1] \leq loR)$$
$$\land \forall i,j : 1 \leq i < j \leq Len(F) \Rightarrow F[i].num < (F[j].num + N)$$
$$\land \forall i \in 1Len(F) : (hi_r(upR) - N) \leq F[i].num < hiS$$

This invariant implies that *Finite-Structure*; $\sharp(upR) \leq N \land \sharp(upA) \leq N$ follows straightforwardly from *Inv*, where $\sharp X$ denotes the cardinality of the set X. hi_r is defined in *SWPFiniteStruct* [11] as follows:

$$hi_r(X) \triangleq \textbf{if } X = \{\} \textbf{ then } loR$$
$$\textbf{else } maxSet(X) + 1$$

The proof follows Theorem 1 with details given in [11].

6 SWP with modulo-numbering

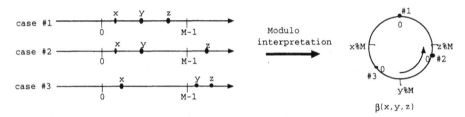

Fig. 9. Modulo-numbering and the new order relation.

Although the sets in *SWPFiniteStruct* are finite, the values of their elements are unbounded. *SWPModulo* (Figures 12 and 13) is an implementation of *SWPFiniteStruct* in which message identifiers take numbers modulo a fixed number M. The validity of *SWPFiniteStructImplementsSWPInitial* proved in Section 5 allows *SWPFiniteStruct* to inherit the invariants and liveness proved for the specification *SWPInitial*. The key to the refinement mapping for this implementation is a relation that allows the unique decoding of a modulo number relative to natural number. The restrictions imposed by the window N in the cycle modulo M with $2N \leq M$ imply that for any three messages that may occur in the channel, there are only three possible cases to place their numbers over the extremities of a segment of length equal to M as illustrated in Figure 9. The module *ModuloNumbering* (figure 10) uses this relationship to define numbering modulo a constant M. The relation $\beta(x, y, z)$ states that the (modulo) number y is between x and z according to the direction of the (modulo) circle as explained in Figure 9 while $dec(\underline{k}, x)$ uniquely relates the modulo values $\underline{k}$ relative to the natural x (see Figure 11).

By convention, underlined names (like $\underline{a}, \underline{n}, \ldots$) will be used to denote modulo numbers. The parameters N, M in the module *SWPModulo* and assump-

─── module *ModuloNumbering* ───

EXTEND *Naturals*

CONSTANT N, M

ASSUME $N > 0 \wedge M \geq 2 \times N$

$u..{<}v \; \triangleq \; \{i \in Nat : (u \leq i) \wedge (i < v)\}$

$u\%M \; \triangleq \; u - ((u/M) \times M)$:The modulo operator.

$\underline{u} \oplus_M \underline{v} \; \triangleq \; (\underline{u} + \underline{v})\%M$

$\underline{u} \ominus_M \underline{v} \; \triangleq \;$ if $\underline{u} \geq \underline{v}$ then $(\underline{u} - \underline{v})\%M$
$\qquad\qquad$ else $(\underline{v} - \underline{u})\%M$

$\beta(\underline{a}, \underline{b}, \underline{c}) \; \triangleq \; (0 \leq \underline{a} \leq \underline{b} < \underline{c} < M) \vee (0 \leq \underline{c} \leq \underline{a} \leq \underline{b} < M) \vee (0 \leq \underline{b} < \underline{c} \leq \underline{a} < M)$

$dec(\underline{k}, x) \; \triangleq \;$ if $\underline{k} = x\%M$
$\qquad\qquad$ then x
$\qquad\qquad$ else if $\beta(x\%M, \underline{k}, (x+N)\%M)$
$\qquad\qquad\qquad$ then if $\beta((x+1)\%M, 0, (\underline{k}+1)\%M)$ then $(x/M+1) \times M + \underline{k}$
$\qquad\qquad\qquad\qquad$ else $(x/M) \times M + \underline{k}$
$\qquad\qquad\qquad$ else if $\beta((x-N)\%M, \underline{k}, x\%M)$
$\qquad\qquad\qquad\qquad$ then if $\beta((x+1)\%M, 0, (\underline{k}+1)\%M)$ then $(x/M) \times M + \underline{k}$
$\qquad\qquad\qquad\qquad\qquad$ else $(x/M-1) \times M + \underline{k}$

theorems

$Thm1 \; \triangleq \; \forall \underline{a}, \underline{b}, \underline{c} \in 0..{<}M : \vee \; \beta(\underline{a}, \underline{b}, \underline{c})$
$\qquad\qquad\qquad\qquad\qquad\quad \vee \; \beta(\underline{c}, \underline{b}, \underline{a})$

$Thm2 \; \triangleq \; \wedge \; \beta(\underline{a}, i, \underline{b}) \wedge \beta(\underline{a}, \underline{b}, \underline{c}) \Rightarrow \beta(\underline{a}, i, \underline{c}) \;\wedge\; \beta(i, \underline{b}, \underline{c})$
$\qquad\qquad \wedge \; \beta(\underline{a}, \underline{b}, \underline{c}) \wedge \beta(\underline{b}, i, \underline{c}) \Rightarrow \beta(\underline{a}, i, \underline{c}) \;\wedge\; \beta(\underline{a}, \underline{b}, i)$
$\qquad\qquad \wedge \; \forall k \in Nat : \beta(\underline{a}, \underline{b}, \underline{c}) \Rightarrow \beta(\underline{a} \oplus_M k, \underline{b} \oplus_M k, \underline{c} \oplus_M k)$
$\qquad\qquad \wedge \; \forall a, b, c : a \leq b < c \leq a + M \Rightarrow \beta(a\%M, b\%M, c\%M)$

$Thm3 \; \triangleq \; (x - N \leq dec(\underline{k}, x) < x + N) \wedge dec(\underline{k}, x)\%M = \underline{k}$

$Thm4 \; \triangleq \; \forall x \in Nat, \underline{k} \in 0..{<}M : (\underline{k} < (M - N) + x) \wedge \beta(x \ominus_M N, \underline{k}, x \oplus_M N)$
$\qquad\qquad\qquad \Rightarrow \exists! b \in Nat : (x - N \leq b < x + N) \wedge (b = dec(\underline{k}, x))$

$Thm5 \; \triangleq \; \forall x, y \in Nat, \underline{k} \in 0..{<}M : \wedge \; (\underline{k} < (M - N) + x) \;\wedge\; (x \leq y \leq x + N)$
$\qquad\qquad\qquad\qquad\qquad\qquad\quad \wedge \; \beta(x \ominus_M N, \underline{k}, x \oplus_M N)$
$\qquad\qquad\qquad\qquad\qquad \Rightarrow dec(\underline{k}, x) = dec(\underline{k}, y)$

Fig. 10. The module ModuloNumbering.

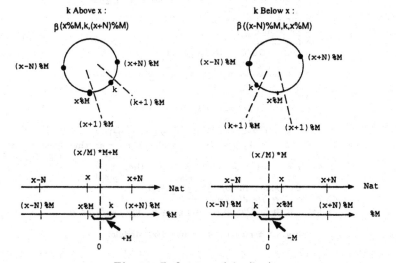

Fig. 11. Definition of dec(k,x).

—————————— module *SWPModulo* ——————————

EXTEND *SwpParameters*, *ModuloNumbering*

—————————— module *Inner* ——————————

VARIABLE *loA*, *loR*, $\underline{ns}$, $\underline{na}$, $\underline{nr}$, *upA*, *upR*, $\underline{mr}$, $\underline{F}$, $\underline{B}$

——

$\perp \;\triangleq\;$ CHOOSE $i : i \notin Nat$

$minSet_r(E) \;\triangleq\;$ CHOOSE $i : (i \in E \wedge \forall j \in E : \beta(\underline{nr}, i, j) \vee j = i)$

$maxSet_r(E) \;\triangleq\;$ CHOOSE $i : (i \in E \wedge \forall j \in E : \beta(\underline{nr}, j, i) \vee j = i)$

$hi_r(X) \;\triangleq\;$ **if** $X = \{\}$ **then** $\underline{nr}$
$\qquad\qquad\qquad$ **else** $\;\; maxSet_r(X) \oplus_M 1$

$Compact(X) \;\triangleq\;$ **if** $X = \{\}$ **then** $\{\}$
$\qquad\qquad\qquad$ **else** $\qquad$ UNION $\{ Y : \wedge\; Y \subseteq X \qquad\qquad\qquad\qquad\qquad \}$
$\qquad\qquad\qquad\qquad\qquad\qquad\qquad\qquad \wedge\; minSet_r(X) \in Y$
$\qquad\qquad\qquad\qquad\qquad\qquad\qquad\qquad \wedge\; \forall i \in Y : (i \oplus_M 1) \in Y \vee i = maxSet_r(Y)$

——

$Init \;\triangleq\; \wedge\; In \in [i \in Nat^+ \mapsto Messg] \;\wedge\; (Out = \langle\rangle) \;\wedge\; (\underline{mr} = [i \in 0.._{<M} : i \mapsto \perp_m])$
$\qquad\qquad \wedge\; (loA = 0) \;\wedge\; (loR = 0) \;\wedge\; (\underline{upA} = \{\}) \;\wedge\; (\underline{upR} = \{\})$
$\qquad\qquad \wedge\; (\underline{ns} = 0) \;\wedge\; (\underline{nr} = 0) \;\wedge\; (\underline{na} = 0) \;\wedge\; (\underline{F} = \langle\rangle) \;\wedge\; (\underline{B} = \perp)$

$NewMsg \;\triangleq\; \wedge\; \beta(\underline{na}, \underline{ns}, \underline{na} \oplus_M N)$
$\qquad\qquad\quad \wedge\; \underline{ns}' = \underline{ns} \oplus_M 1$
$\qquad\qquad\quad \wedge\; \underline{F}' = \underline{F} \circ \langle\langle \underline{ns}, In[dec(\underline{ns}, loA) + 1]\rangle\rangle$
$\qquad\qquad\quad \wedge\;$ UNCHANGED $In, Out, loA, loR, \underline{na}, \underline{nr}, upA, upR, \underline{mr}, \underline{B}$

$RtxMsg(i) \;\triangleq\; \wedge\; \beta(\underline{na}, i, \underline{ns})$
$\qquad\qquad\qquad \wedge\; i \notin upA$
$\qquad\qquad\qquad \wedge\; \underline{F}' = \underline{F} \circ \langle\langle i, In[dec(i, loA) + 1]\rangle\rangle$
$\qquad\qquad\qquad \wedge\;$ UNCHANGED $In, Out, loA, loR, \underline{ns}, \underline{na}, \underline{nr}, upA, upR, \underline{mr}, \underline{B}$

$LosMsg \;\triangleq\; \wedge\; \underline{F} \neq \langle\rangle$
$\qquad\qquad\quad \wedge\; \underline{F}' = Tail(\underline{F})$
$\qquad\qquad\quad \wedge\;$ UNCHANGED $In, Out, loA, loR, \underline{ns}, \underline{na}, \underline{nr}, upA, upR, \underline{mr}\,\underline{B}$

$RcvMsg \;\triangleq\; \wedge\; \underline{F} \neq \langle\rangle$
$\qquad\qquad\quad \wedge\; \underline{F}' = Tail(\underline{F})$
$\qquad\qquad\quad \wedge\; \vee\; \wedge\; \beta(\underline{nr}, Head(\underline{F}).num, \underline{nr} \oplus_M N)$
$\qquad\qquad\qquad\qquad \wedge\; \vee\; \wedge\; \underline{nr} \neq Head(\underline{F}).num$
$\qquad\qquad\qquad\qquad\qquad\quad \wedge\; \underline{upR}' = upR \cup \{Head(\underline{F}).num\}$
$\qquad\qquad\qquad\qquad\qquad\quad \wedge\; \overline{mr}' = [\underline{mr}$ EXCEPT $![Head(\underline{F}).num] = Head(\underline{F}).val]$
$\qquad\qquad\qquad\qquad\qquad\quad \wedge\;$ UNCHANGED $In, Out, loA, loR, \underline{ns}, \underline{na}, \underline{nr}, upA, \underline{B}$
$\qquad\qquad\qquad\qquad \vee\; \wedge\; \underline{nr} = Head(\underline{F}).num$
$\qquad\qquad\qquad\qquad\qquad\quad \wedge\; (\underline{nr} \oplus_M 1) \notin upR$
$\qquad\qquad\qquad\qquad\qquad\quad \wedge\; \underline{nr}' = \underline{nr} \oplus_M 1$
$\qquad\qquad\qquad\qquad\qquad\quad \wedge\; loR' = loR + 1$
$\qquad\qquad\qquad\qquad\qquad\quad \wedge\; Out' = Out \circ \langle= Head(\underline{F}).val\rangle$
$\qquad\qquad\qquad\qquad\qquad\quad \wedge\; \underline{mr}' = [\underline{mr}$ EXCEPT $![\underline{nr}] = \perp_m]$
$\qquad\qquad\qquad\qquad\qquad\quad \wedge\;$ UNCHANGED $In, loA, \underline{ns}, \underline{na}, upA, upR, \underline{B}$
$\qquad\qquad\qquad\qquad \vee\; \wedge\; \underline{nr} = Head(\underline{F}).num$
$\qquad\qquad\qquad\qquad\qquad\quad \wedge\; (\underline{nr} \oplus_M 1) \in \underline{upR}$
$\qquad\qquad\qquad\qquad\qquad\quad \wedge\; \underline{nr}' = hi_r(Compact(upR))$
$\qquad\qquad\qquad\qquad\qquad\quad \wedge\; upR' = upR \setminus Compact(upR)$
$\qquad\qquad\qquad\qquad\qquad\quad \wedge\; \overline{loR}' = loR + (hi_r(Compact(upR)) \ominus_M \underline{nr})$
$\qquad\qquad\qquad\qquad\qquad\quad \wedge\; Out' = Out \circ [i \in 1(\underline{nr}' \ominus_M \underline{nr}) \mapsto$ **if** $(\; i = \underline{nr})$ **then** $Head(\underline{F}).val$
$\qquad\qquad\qquad\qquad\qquad\qquad\qquad\qquad\qquad\qquad\qquad\qquad\qquad$ **else** $\qquad mr[i \oplus_M \underline{nr} \oplus_M 1]]$
$\qquad\qquad\qquad\qquad\qquad\quad \wedge\; \underline{mr}' = [i \in 1.._{<M} \mapsto$ **if** $\beta\;(\underline{nr}, i, \underline{nr}')$ **then** $\perp_m\;]$
$\qquad\qquad\qquad\qquad\qquad\qquad\qquad\qquad\qquad\qquad\qquad\quad$ **else** $\qquad mr[i]$
$\qquad\qquad\qquad\qquad\qquad\quad \wedge\;$ UNCHANGED $In, loA, \underline{ns}, \underline{na}, upA, \underline{B}$
$\qquad\qquad\quad \vee\; \wedge\; \beta(\underline{nr} \oplus_M N, Head(\underline{F}).num, \underline{nr})$
$\qquad\qquad\qquad\quad \wedge\;$ UNCHANGED $In, Out, loA, loR, \underline{ns}, \underline{na}, \underline{nr}, upA, upR, \underline{mr}, \underline{B}$

Fig. 12. First part of module SWP.Modulo.

$$SndAck \triangleq \land \underline{B}' = \langle \underline{nr}, \underline{upR} \rangle$$
$$\land \text{UNCHANGED } In, Out, loA, loR, \underline{ns}, \underline{na}, \underline{nr}, \underline{upA}, \underline{upR}, \underline{mr}, \underline{F}$$

$$LosAck \triangleq \land \underline{B}' = \bot$$
$$\land \text{UNCHANGED } In, Out, loA, loR, \underline{ns}, \underline{na}, \underline{nr}, \underline{upA}, \underline{upR}, \underline{mr}, \underline{F}$$

$$RcvAck \triangleq \land \underline{B} \neq \bot$$
$$\land \underline{na}' = \underline{B}[1]$$
$$\land loA' = dec(\underline{na}', loA)$$
$$\land \underline{upA}' = \underline{B}[2]$$
$$\land \text{UNCHANGED } In, Out, loR, \underline{ns}, \underline{nr}, \underline{upR}, \underline{mr}\underline{F}, \underline{B}$$

$$Next \triangleq \lor NewMsg \lor (\exists i : RtxMsg(i)) \lor LosMsg$$
$$\lor RcvMsg \lor SndAck \lor LosAck \lor RcvAck$$

$$vars \triangleq \langle In, Out, loA, loR, \underline{ns}, \underline{na}, \underline{nr}, \underline{upA}, \underline{upR}, \underline{mr}, \underline{F}, \underline{B} \rangle$$

$$spec \triangleq \land Init \land \Box[Next]_{vars}$$
$$\land \text{WF}_{vars}(NewMsg) \land \text{WF}_{vars}(RtxMsg(\underline{na}) \land (\underline{ns} = \underline{na} \oplus_M N))$$
$$\land \text{WF}_{vars}(SndAck) \land \text{WF}_{vars}(RcvMsg)$$
$$\land \text{SF}_{vars}(RcvAck \land \underline{na} = \underline{B}[1]) \land \text{SF}_{vars}(RcvMsg \land Head(\underline{F}).num = \underline{na})$$

$$Spec \triangleq \exists loA, loR, \underline{ns}, \underline{na}, \underline{nr}, \underline{upA}, \underline{upR}, \underline{mr}, \underline{F}, \underline{B} : Inner.spec$$

Fig. 13. Second part of module SWPModulo.

tions on these constants are imported from the module *ModuloNumbering*. Theorems *Thm4* and *Thm5* of the module *ModuloNumbering* (when $\underline{k}$ takes the values *loA* or *loR*) guarantee the existence of a refinement mapping between *SWPFiniteStruct* and *SWPModulo*. They assert that the natural references *loA* and *loR* at the sender and the receiver, always decode a modulo number in the system into the same natural number and thus the sender and the receiver are continuously synchronized, since $loA \leq loR \leq loA + N$ is an invariant of the implementation. The complete proof of this refinement step may be found in [11].

7 RLP1 with Modulo-Numbering

The last refinement step introduces new actions specific to RLP1 described in Section 3. The refinement especially affects the action *RtxMsg*. The action *NewMsg* is slightly strengthened in order to update the internal variables introduced by the refinement. The other actions remain unchanged. Three internal variables are introduced : (i) *Ssn* is a function which assigns the upper send sequence number (a stamp!) for each message, (ii) *Nssn* : the next send sequence number, (iii) *PM* the set of messages sent in pre-emptive mode and which still may occur in the channel (i.e not known lost). The module *RLP1* (figure 15) is a possible model of RLP1, we will prove it implements *SWPModulo* (Figure 14).

The proof of theorem *LostPolicy* requires the following stronger invariant :

```
┌──────────────── module RLP1ImplementsSWPModulo ─────────────────┐
│ EXTEND SwpParameters, ModuloNumbering                            │
├──────────────────────────────────────────────────────────────────┤
│ SwpMod  ≜  instance SWPModulo                                    │
│ Rlp  ≜  instance RLP1                                            │
│ theorem                                                          │
│    LostPolicy  ≜  Rlp.Spec ⇒ □ ∧ β(ns, v, na) ⇒ v ∉ PM          │
│                              ∧ Lost(i) ⇒ (¬InSeq(i, F) ∧ i ∉ upR)│
│    Impl  ≜  Rlp.Spec ⇒ SwpMod.Spec                              │
└──────────────────────────────────────────────────────────────────┘
```

Fig. 14. Module RLP1ImplementsSWPModulo.

$$Inv \; \triangleq \; \land \; \beta(ns, v, na) \Rightarrow v \notin PM$$
$$\land \; Lost(i) \Rightarrow (\neg InSeq(i, F) \land i \notin upR)$$
$$\land \; \forall i,j : (0 < i < j \leq Len(F) \land F[i] \notin PM) \Rightarrow Ssn[F[i]] < Ssn[F[j]]$$
$$\land \; \forall i,j : (0 < i < j \leq Len(F) \land F[i] = F[j]) \Rightarrow F[j] \in PM$$
$$\land \; (j \in (upA \setminus PM) \land Ssn[j] > Ssn[i]) \Rightarrow \neg InSeq(i, F)$$
$$\land \; (j \in (upA \setminus PM) \land (i \notin upA) \land (Ssn[j] > Ssn[i])) \Rightarrow i \notin upR$$

LET : $vars_1 \; \triangleq \; loA, loR, Nssn, ns, na, nr, upA, upR, mr, F, B, Ssn, PM$

$vars_2 \; \triangleq \; loA, loR, ns, na, nr, upA, upR, mr, F, B$

The proof of *LostPolicy* requires the proof of $Rlp.Init \Rightarrow Inv$ and $[SwpRlp.Next]_{vars_1} \land Inv \Rightarrow Inv'$ which are done by considering a proof-step for each action of *SwpRlp.Next*.

The proof of the theorem *Impl* requires the proof of $Rlp.Init \Rightarrow \overline{SwpMod.Init}$ and $[Rlp.Next \land Inv \land Inv']_{vars_1} \Rightarrow [\overline{SwpMod.Next}]_{\overline{vars_2}}$, neither of which require any temporal reasoning. The proof of the first condition is straightforward. Since the mapping doesn't introduce stuttering steps, the proof of the second condition is simpler. Indeed, each step of *Rlp* is a step of *SWPMod*, which is shown by proving $[Rlp.Act \land Inv \land Inv']_{vars_1} \Rightarrow [\overline{SwpMod.Act}]_{\overline{vars_2}}$ for each individual action *Act* in *Next*.

The interesting part of the proof of *Impl* involves the temporal formula $\Box Inv \land \Box[SwpMod.Next]_{vars_1} \land L_1 \Rightarrow \overline{L_2}$. Each action of *RLP1*, except for *RtxMsg*, simulates the corresponding action of *SWPModulo* and fairness of the abstract actions follows from fairness of the concrete actions. In [11] we show how fairness of $\overline{SwpMod.RtxMsg}$ follows from fairness of both concrete actions. The details of these proofs can be found in [11].

8 A Modest Improvement on the Determination of *Known Lost* Messages

The proof and modeling of the conditions that a message is *lost* and *known lost* is the key to the retransmission algorithm of RLP1. The necessity to formalise these conditions resulted in an extension and unification of the Basic and Preemptive modes of the RLP1 retransmission algorithm. The key observation was

─────────────────────── module *RLP1* ───────────────────────

EXTEND *SwpParameters*, *ModuloNumbering*

─────────────────────── module *Inner* ───────────────────────

VARIABLE *loA*, *loR*, *Nssn*, $\underline{ns}$, $\underline{na}$, $\underline{nr}$, *upA*, *upR*, $\underline{mr}$, $\underline{F}$, $\underline{B}$, $\underline{Ssn}$, *PM*

$SwpMod \triangleq$ **instance** *SWPModulo*

$Lost(i) \triangleq \;\land\; \beta(\underline{na}, i, \underline{ns})$
$\qquad\qquad \land\; i \notin upA$
$\qquad\qquad \land\; \exists j \in \overline{(upA \setminus PM)} : (\underline{Ssn}[i] < \underline{Ssn}[j])$

$LostSet \triangleq \{i \in 0.._{< M} : Lost(i)\}$

$Init \triangleq \;\land\; SwpMod.Init$
$\qquad\quad \land\; PM = \{\}$
$\qquad\quad \land\; \underline{Ssn} = [i \in 0.._{< M} \mapsto 0]$
$\qquad\quad \land\; Nssn = 1$

$NewMsg \triangleq \;\land\; SwpMod.NewMsg$
$\qquad\qquad\quad \land\; \underline{Ssn}' = [\underline{Ssn} \text{ EXCEPT }![\underline{ns}] = Nssn]$
$\qquad\qquad\quad \land\; Nssn' = Nssn + 1$
$\qquad\qquad\quad \land\; \text{UNCHANGED } PM$

$RtxMsg(i) \triangleq \;\lor\; \land\; Lost(i)$
$\qquad\qquad\qquad\quad \land\; SwpMod.RtxMsg(i)$
$\qquad\qquad\qquad\quad \land\; \underline{Ssn}' = [\underline{Ssn} \text{ EXCEPT }![i] = Nssn]$
$\qquad\qquad\qquad\quad \land\; PM' = PM \setminus \{i\}$
$\qquad\qquad\qquad\quad \land\; Nssn' = Nssn + 1$
$\qquad\qquad\quad \lor\; \land\; LostSet = \{\}$
$\qquad\qquad\qquad\quad \land\; \underline{ns} = \underline{na} \oplus_M N$
$\qquad\qquad\qquad\quad \land\; SwpMod.RtxMsg(i)$
$\qquad\qquad\qquad\quad \land\; \underline{Ssn}' = [\underline{Ssn} \text{ EXCEPT }![i] = Nssn]$
$\qquad\qquad\qquad\quad \land\; PM' = PM \cup \{i\}$
$\qquad\qquad\qquad\quad \land\; Nssn' = Nssn + 1$

$LosMsg \triangleq \;\land\; SwpMod.LosMsg$
$\qquad\qquad\quad \land\; \text{UNCHANGED } Nssn, \underline{Ssn}, PM$

$RcvMsg \triangleq \;\land\; SwpMod.RcvMsg$
$\qquad\qquad\quad \land\; \text{UNCHANGED } Nssn, \underline{Ssn}, PM$

$SndAck \triangleq \;\land\; SwpMod.SndAck$
$\qquad\qquad\quad \land\; \text{UNCHANGED } Nssn, \underline{Ssn}, PM$

$RcvAck \triangleq \;\land\; SwpMod.RcvAck$
$\qquad\qquad\quad \land\; \lor\; \land\; \underline{na}' \neq \underline{na}$
$\qquad\qquad\qquad\qquad \land\; PM' = PM \setminus \{v : \beta(\underline{na}, v, \underline{na}')\}$
$\qquad\qquad\qquad \lor\; \land\; \underline{na}' = \underline{na}$
$\qquad\qquad\qquad\qquad \land\; \text{UNCHANGED } PM$
$\qquad\qquad\quad \land\; \text{UNCHANGED } Nssn, \underline{Ssn}$

$Next \triangleq \;\lor\; NewMsg \lor (\exists i : RtxMsg(i)) \lor LosMsg$
$\qquad\qquad \lor\; RcvMsg \lor SndAck \lor LosAck \lor RcvAck$

$vars \triangleq \langle In, Out, loA, loR, Nssn, \underline{ns}, \underline{na}, \underline{nr}, upA, upR, \underline{mr}, \underline{F}, \underline{B}, \underline{Ssn}, PM \rangle$

$spec \triangleq \;\land\; Init \land \Box[Next]_{vars}$
$\qquad\quad \land\; \text{WF}_{vars}(NewMsg) \land \text{WF}_{vars}(RtxMsg(\underline{na})) \land \text{WF}_{vars}(SndAck) \land \text{WF}_{vars}(RcvMsg)$
$\qquad\quad \land\; \text{SF}_{vars}(RcvAck \land \underline{na} = \underline{B}[1]) \land \text{SF}_{vars}(RcvMsg \land Head(\underline{F}).num = \underline{na})$

$Spec \triangleq \exists loA, loR, Nssn, \underline{ns}, \underline{na}, \underline{nr}, upA, upR, \underline{mr}, \underline{F}, \underline{B}, \underline{Ssn}, PM : Inner.spec$

Fig. 15. Module RLP1.

that a particular message a may be declared *known lost* through the acknowledgment of a second message b if *all* the outstanding copies of a were sent before all the outstanding copies of b. If $Ssl(x)$ is defined as the Ssn of the first outstanding copy of message x and $Ssu(x)$ the Ssn of the most recently transmitted copy then an acknowledgment of b will declare a, *known lost* if and only if, $[Ssl(a), Ssu(a)] \bigcap [Ssl(b), Ssu(b)] = \{\}$ where $[i, j]$ represents the closed interval of integers between i and j. A message x has only one copy outstanding if and only if, $Ssl(x) = Ssu(x)$. It is clear that this extension will declare more messages *known lost* than the original protocol. It is also clear that it will complicate all the invariant and liveness proofs that have already been obtained for the module *RLP1*.

9 Conclusion and future work

This work is an example of the use of TLA$^+$ and theorem proving techniques applied to prove and discover properties of a real protocol, and to prove that all these properties are valid for any window size N. The detail required to approach the actual data structures and algorithms used in RLP1 was considerable, and required much work. Even at that, the final model in Section 7 captures only the early version of the protocol. One result of the validation [5] during the standardisation was the replacement of the unbounded Ssn by a bounded queue where the unacknowledged messages were maintained in transmit order. It appears to be relatively straightforward to add this refinement to our model, but not without increasing the already high level of detail.

However, because the refinement methodology forced us to concentrate on the essence of the retransmission algorithm, as noted in Section 8, it was discovered that the retransmission policy of RLP1 may be strengthened by storing both the upper and the lower Ssn (Send sequence number) of messages instead of the upper Ssn only. More lost messages may be detected and the protocol performance is improved.

The work involved in proving the properties of this fragment of the complete RLP1 protocol was considerable. Although the discovery of an improved method of retransmission was gratifying, and the fact that all of the properties are true for any window size N, it appears that it is probably easier to prove the complete correctness of a concrete protocol such as RLP1 using model-checking techniques as was reported in [5].

References

1. ABADI, M., AND LAMPORT, L. The existence of refinement mappings. *Theoretical Computer Science 82*, 2 (may 1991), 253–283.
2. CCITT. CCITT specification and description language (SDL). ITU-T Standard Recommendation Z.100, ITU, 1988.
3. CRAIGEN, D. EVES, an overview. In *Proceedings VDM'91* (1991), Springer-Verlag.
4. FERGUSON, M. J. On the syntactic, semantic, and functional analysis of the RLP1 (layer2) protocol standard. Contribution TR45.3.2.5/94.06.10.01, Data Services Task Group of ANSI Accredited TIA TR45-3, jun 1994.

5. FERGUSON, M. J. Formalization and validation of the Radio Link Protocol (RLP1). *Computer Networks and ISDN Systems 29*, 3 (feb 1997), 357–372.

6. HOLZMANN, G. *Design and Validation of Computer Protocols.* Prentice Hall, Englewood Cliffs, NJ, 1991.

7. LADKIN, P. Formal but lively buffers in tla$^+$. WWW page, http://www.techfak.uni-bielefeld.de/techfak/persons/ladkin, 1995.

8. LAMPORT, L. A temporal logic of actions. Tech. Rep. 57, Digital, SRC, apr 1990.

9. LAMPORT, L. The temporal logic of actions. *ACM Transactions on Programming Languages and Systems 16*, 3 (may 1994), 872–923.

10. LAMPORT, L. TLA WWW page. WWW page, http://www.research.digital.com/SRC/tla/tla.html, 1996.

11. MOKKEDEM, A., FERGUSON, M., AND DEB. JOHNSTON, R. A TLA solution to the specification and verification of the RLP1 retransmission protocol. WWW page, http://www.inrs-telecom.uquebec.ca/users/telesoft/Ferguson/FME97fullpaper.ps.gz, 1997.

12. ORA, CANADA. EVES — http://www.ora.on.ca/eves.html. WWW page, ORA, 1996.

13. SACUTA, A. D. PN-3306: Radio link protocol 1 (ballot resolution draft). TIA Draft Standard TR45.3.2/95.02.28.03, Data Services Task Group of ANSI Accredited TIA TR45-3, feb 1995.

An Efficient Technique for Deadlock Analysis of Large Scale Process Networks

J.M.R.Martin[1] and S.A.Jassim[2]

[1] Oxford University Computing Services,
13 Banbury Road,
Oxford OX2 6NN, UK
[2] Department of Mathematics,
Statistics, and Computer Science,
University of Buckingham,
MK18 1EG, UK

Abstract. Nowadays we are becoming increasingly dependent on parallel or distributed computer systems for many safety critical applications. Therefore, in order to avoid software precipitated catastrophes, we must look for ways to enable software engineers to design systems that are free from pathological problems such as deadlock. Traditionally deadlock has been one of the most feared problems in parallel computing. Existing tools which perform deadlock analysis can usually cope only with rather small networks due to the problem of exponential state explosion. Here we describe the implementation of a new, highly efficient, graph-theoretical approach to automatically proving deadlock-freedom which can be used to analyse CSP networks of arbitrary size. Our methods exploit previous work by S. D. Brookes, A. W. Roscoe and N. Dathi.

1 Introduction

Deadlock is a phenomenon pertaining to networks of communicating processes which occurs when no two processes can agree to communicate with each other and so the whole system becomes permanently frozen. This is potentially catastrophic in safety-critical computing applications. A network which can never exhibit deadlock is said to be *deadlock-free*. It is essential that a safety-critical network should be so.

The deadlock problem was first identified by Dijkstra [5] in the early days of multi-user operating systems. Early work focused on the scenario of *user-resource* networks, where a collection of user processes compete for allocation of a set of shared resources, without any direct communication between the user processes (see, for example, [1]).

Three approaches to the problem arose. The first was *deadlock-detection and recovery* which is still widely used in multi-user distributed database technology[10]. The second was *deadlock-avoidance* which involves adding extra processes to a system which stop it from entering any of its known deadlock states.

The third approach was *deadlock-prevention* which means building systems provably free of deadlock. Deadlock-prevention is the most general technique of the three and is the theme of this paper.

It is not usually possible to prove a network deadlock-free by experimental testing (there might be deadlocks that require many years of running time to appear). Proving a network deadlock-free by hand is often found to be infeasibly difficult and time consuming. To combat these problems, some simple design rules emerged for building networks guaranteed to be deadlock-free. For instance the *resource-allocation* protocol (described in [18]), the *master-slave* (or *client-server*) protocol[1], and the *cyclic* protocol [6].

With the onset of formal methods, rigorous proof techniques for deadlock-freedom were developed, notably by Brookes, Dathi and Roscoe[2,18,4], influenced by Chandy and Misra[3]. Many networks have been analysed using these methods but they are still difficult to apply in general.

Recent years have seen the arrival of *model checkers* (for instance [19] and [15]). These are programs that work by checking every possible state of a system to verify some specified property such as deadlock-freedom. A major limitation of model checking is the problem of *exponential state explosion*. The number of states of a network tends to increase exponentially in relation to the number of constituent processes. State compression techniques have been used successfully in certain restricted cases to enable the analysis of significantly larger networks[15,20], but this has made only a small inroad into the state explosion problem.

The current state of the art as regards building deadlock-free systems seems to be that, at best, designers of large-scale systems use informally specified design rules (such as [21]) which are open to human error and misinterpretation. Model Checkers are used only to verify small networks. How might this gap be bridged?

In this paper we present an $O(nlogn)$ efficient checking algorithm which overcomes the problem of exponential state explosion by restricting its analysis to pairs of neighbouring processes within a network. The price of this is incompleteness – there exist deadlock-free networks which cannot be proven so using our technique. Nonetheless our method is found to be widely applicable. In particular it is applicable to networks built using the specific design rules mentioned above and various combinations of these.

The rest of this paper is organised as follows. Section 2 describes a terminology and framework for deadlock analysis of CSP networks, based on that of Brookes, Dathi and Roscoe[2,4,18], but updated to embrace the concept of *normal form transition systems* [19]. In section 3 we present the main innovation of the paper – the *state dependence digraph*, a novel tool for deadlock analysis of large networks. We illustrate its application to certain well-known systems. In section 4 we show how to add information to the state dependence digraph to analyse certain more stubborn networks. Finally in section 5 we compare our technique with competing methods and discuss directions for further work. For the reader who is unfamiliar with the CSP language of C.A.R.Hoare, reading the first three chapters of [9] will be a necessary requirement in order to follow this paper.

2 Terminology and a Fundamental Result

In order to perform meaningful deadlock analysis we shall need a precise mathematical characterisation of concurrent systems. We use the CSP language for this purpose [9], with which we shall assume that the reader is familiar. Here processes are defined according to the following grammar

$$P = STOP \mid SKIP \mid a \to P \mid P \square P' \mid P \sqcap P' \mid P; P' \mid$$
$$P \setminus A \mid c?x \to P \mid c!x \to P \mid P \parallel P' \mid P \mathbin{|||} P' \mid$$
$$\text{if } b \text{ then } P \text{ else } P' \mid name$$

where a is an event, A is a set of events, b is an expression, c is a channel name, $name$ is a process identifier, and x is a datum. Events are drawn from a *universal event set* Σ.

We shall now introduce a couple of simple processes to help illustrate the subsequent terminology. First consider a process to represent a typical vending machine.

$$VM = coin \to tea \to VM \sqcap coin \to VM$$

The vending machine is supposed to accept a coin, then dispense a cup of tea. However sometimes it swallows up the coin without dispensing anything, quite unpredictably. Now consider a process to describe the behaviour of a consumer of hot drinks.

$$TD = coin \to tea \to TD \square coffee \to TD$$

The tea drinker is happy either to pay for cups of tea, or to drink coffee free of charge.

The standard semantic model of CSP is that of *failures* and *divergences*. A failure (s, X) of a process P consists of a possible *trace* of events s that P may perform, after which it may refuse to perform any event from a *refusal* set X. For example

$$(\langle coin, tea, coin \rangle, \{tea\}) \in failures(VM)$$
$$(\langle coffee, coin, tea, coin \rangle, \{coin\}) \in failures(TD)$$

A divergence s is a trace after which P may perform an unbounded sequence of concealed actions. (We shall not be interested in processes which may diverge in this paper.) Each CSP process is uniquely defined by its failures and divergences.

We say that an individual process P is *deadlock-free* if there is no trace after which it may refuse to perform every event in the universe Σ, *i.e.*

$$\not\exists s : \Sigma^*.(s, \Sigma) \in \mathit{failures}(P)$$

Clearly both *VM* and *TD* are deadlock-free processes.

The reader will observe that the failures sets for most interesting processes will be infinite, certainly for any deadlock-free process. For our analysis we shall need to find a compact finite representation. This will be given by the *normal form transition system* devised by A.W.Roscoe for use in the refinement checking program FDR[19]. Here any process P, with a finite number of recognisable states, is represented by $NF(P)$. This is a finite transition system (S, T, σ_0, l), where S is a set of states, T is a set of labelled transitions from the set $S \times \Sigma \times S$, σ_0 is the initial state, and l is a *labelling* of states, $l : S \to (\mathbb{P}\,\mathbb{P}\,\Sigma) \cup \{\bot\}^1$. Each state in S corresponds to a set of traces of P after which the subsequent behaviour is identical. We define an equivalence relation $\sim$ on $\mathit{traces}(P)$ given by

$$s_1 \sim s_2 \iff P \text{ after } s_1 = P \text{ after } s_2$$

(For example, in the case of process *VM* we can see that $\langle \mathit{coin,tea} \rangle \sim \langle \rangle$ because the behaviour of the process after it has dispensed a cup of tea is identical to its initial behaviour.) The set S is formally defined as the set of equivalence classes $\mathit{traces}(P)/ \sim$. If there exist any divergent traces of P, *i.e.* $\mathit{divergences}(P) \neq \emptyset$, then they belong to a single equivalence class which corresponds to a state labelled with a flag $\bot$. States which correspond to non-divergent classes of traces are labelled with a set of *minimal acceptance sets* $\{A_1, .., A_m\}$. Minimal acceptance sets are the complement in Σ of maximal refusal sets. They will clearly be the same for any particular class of equivalent traces. Minimal acceptances are used instead of refusals because they usually require less storage space. The set of labelled transitions T of $NF(P)$ is given by

$$(\forall s : S_1. s \,^\frown \langle x \rangle \in S_2) \iff (S_1, x, S_2) \in T$$

The initial state σ_0 of $NF(P)$ is that state which is the class of traces equivalent to the empty trace $\langle \rangle$.

An elegant algorithm for compiling to a normal form transition system from a CSP expression has been developed by Roscoe. First the expression is compiled into an ordinary transition system, using operational rules for CSP. Then two transformations are applied. The first, called *pre-normalisation*, involves removing all non-determinism from the structure of the transition system, and replacing it with state labelling of the form described above. The second, called *compaction*, folds together classes of states from which the future behaviour is identical, by constructing the fixed point of a particular sequence of equivalence

---

[1] $\mathbb{P}$ is the *power set* operator, i.e. $\mathbb{P}\,\Sigma$ is the set of all subsets of Σ and $\mathbb{P}\,\mathbb{P}\,\Sigma$ is the set of all subsets of the power set of Σ.

relations on states. Assuming that the process is finite-state, the procedure will terminate and deliver the normal-form transition system for the process. A full description is given in [19].

Let us consider the normal form transition systems for our processes VM and TD, which have been calculated as follows

$$NF(VM) =
\begin{pmatrix}
S = \{0, 1\}, \\
T = \{(0, coin, 1), (1, coin, 1), (1, tea, 0)\}, \\
\sigma_0 = 0, \\
l = \{(0, \{\{coin\}\}), (1, \{\{coin\}, \{tea\}\})\}
\end{pmatrix}$$

$$NF(TD) =
\begin{pmatrix}
S = \{0, 1\}, \\
T = \{(0, coin, 1), (0, coffee, 0), (1, tea, 0)\}, \\
\sigma_0 = 0, \\
l = \{(0, \{\{coin, coffee\}\}), (1, \{\{tea\}\})\}
\end{pmatrix}$$

Here, for convenience, we use integer annotations for the two normal form states of each process, instead of the classes of equivalent traces that they represent. These transition systems are illustrated in figure 1. Observe that the action of the nondeterministic choice operator $\sqcap$ is absorbed into state 1 of $NF(VM)$. The nondeterminism is represented by the presence of two distinct minimal acceptance sets.

Fig. 1. Normal Form Transition Systems

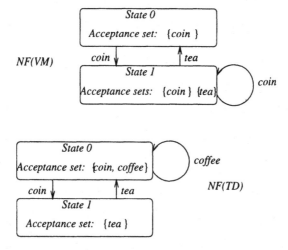

The failures of *VM* are exactly those pairs (s, X) such that there is a *walk* in $NF(VM)$, starting from state 0, with transitions labelled as s, ending at a state σ labelled with an acceptance set A where $X \subseteq \Sigma - A$.

In general, if P is a divergence-free process for which $NF(P)$ is defined then, for every maximal failure (s, X) of P^2 there is a corresponding walk in $NF(P)$ starting from state σ_0, with transitions labelled as s, to some state σ labelled with an acceptance set $\Sigma - X$.

We define a *network* of CSP processes as a list of processes $\langle P_1, .., P_n \rangle$ where with each process P_i is associated an *alphabet* αP_i of events that it may perform. The parallel composition of all the processes in the network is written as $PAR(V)$ which is defined recursively as follows:

$$PAR(\langle P_1, .., P_{k-1}, P_k \rangle) = PAR(\langle P_1, .., P_{k-1} \rangle) \parallel P_k$$
$$PAR(\langle P_1 \rangle) = P_1$$

There are two desirable properties of networks that we shall insist upon for our deadlock analysis technique. Firstly the network must be *busy*: each component process P_i must be free from deadlock and divergence, *i.e.*

$$\nexists s : \Sigma^*.(s, \Sigma) \in failures(P_i)$$

[3] Secondly the network must be *triple-disjoint*: no event shall belong to the vocabulary of more than two processes, *i.e.*

$$i, j, k \text{ distinct} \Longrightarrow \alpha P_i \cap \alpha P_j \cap \alpha P_k = \emptyset$$

These properties are required in order to enable us to determine deadlock-freedom by pairwise process analysis (although note that the property of being busy may be slightly relaxed[4]).

Let us consider the traces of $PAR(V)$. Events that belong to the alphabet of more than one process must be performed jointly by these processes. Formally, this is written as follows

$$s \in traces(PAR(V)) \Longleftrightarrow \wedge_{i=1}^n s \upharpoonright \alpha P_i \in traces(P_i)$$

[4] So each trace s of network V corresponds to a particular trace $s \upharpoonright \alpha P_i$ of each process P_i. This trace, in turn, belongs to a particular state of each normal form transition system $NF(P_i)$, which we shall write as $\sigma_i(s)$. We shall define a *network state* to be a sequence $\langle \sigma_1, .., \sigma_n \rangle$ consisting of one normal form state from each $NF(P_i)$, such that there is some trace s of $PAR(V)$ satisfying $\sigma_i = \sigma_i(s)$ for each i. (This is usually a *strict* subset of the cartesian product of the normal form state spaces of each process P_i.)

---

[2] A *maximal failure* of a process P is a pair (s, X) such that $(s, X) \in failuresP$ and $\nexists(s, X') : failuresP. \quad X' \supset X$.

[3] From the point of view of normal form transition systems, a network is busy if no process has a reachable state either labelled as $\perp$ or with $\emptyset$ as a minimal acceptance.

[4] For a trace s and event set X, $s \upharpoonright X$ means trace s restricted to events contained within X, i.e. with all other events removed.

Let us consider the network $\langle VM, TD \rangle$, where $\alpha VM = \{tea, \ coin\}$ and $\alpha TD = \{tea, \ coin, \ coffee\}^5$. We can see that it has a network state $\langle 1, 1 \rangle$ corresponding, for example, to trace $\langle coffee, \ coin, \ tea, \ coin \rangle$.

In order to decide whether deadlock is possible in a particular network state we need to look at the acceptance set labelling of each state. A *stable configuration* of a network state $\langle \sigma_1, .., \sigma_n \rangle$ is a sequence of acceptance sets $\langle A_1, .., A_n \rangle$ such that, for each i, $A_i \in l_i(\sigma_i)$. It represents a situation where every process P_i has stabilised, that is to say it can perform no internal events, and is ready to perform *exactly* those events in A_i. A *deadlock configuration* is a stable configuration from which no further progress is possible, which can only happen if every event is refused by at least one process, *i.e.*

$$\bigcup_{i=1}^n (\alpha P_i - A_i) = \bigcup_{i=1}^n \alpha P_i$$

It can easily be shown that the process $PAR(V)$ is deadlock-free if, and only if, V has no network state with a deadlock configuration.

Notice that state $\langle 1, 1 \rangle$ of network $\langle VM, TD \rangle$ has a deadlock configuration $\langle \{coin\}, \{tea\} \rangle$, representing a situation where the vending machine has swallowed up the tea drinker's coin without being prepared to dispense any tea. No further progress is possible.

In a particular stable configuration $\delta = \langle A_1, .., A_n \rangle$ we say that P_i has an *ungranted request* to P_j *with respect to* an event set C, if P_i is ready to communicate with P_j, but P_j is not willing to perform any event that P_i offers, and neither P_i nor P_j is ready to perform any event outside C, *i. e.*

$$A_i \cup A_j \subseteq C \wedge \emptyset \neq A_i \cap \alpha P_j \subseteq \alpha P_j - A_j$$

This is written, using the notation of [18], as

$$P_i \overset{\delta, C}{\rightarrow} \bullet P_j$$

A *cycle of ungranted requests* with respect to a set C is a sequence of ungranted requests

$$P_{i_1} \overset{\delta, C}{\rightarrow} \bullet P_{i_2} \overset{\delta, C}{\rightarrow} \bullet .. \overset{\delta, C}{\rightarrow} \bullet P_{i_k} \overset{\delta, C}{\rightarrow} \bullet P_{i_1}$$

The set of shared events in the network is referred to as its *vocabulary*, and is written

$$\Lambda(V) = \bigcup_{i \neq j} (\alpha P_i \cap \alpha P_j)$$

Usually we are interested in ungranted requests with respect to the network's vocabulary, as in the following well-known and fundamental theorem.

Theorem 1. *In any deadlock configuration $\delta = \langle A_1, .., A_n \rangle$ of a busy, triple-disjoint network $V = \langle P_1, .., P_n \rangle$ there is a cycle of ungranted requests with respect to the network vocabulary Λ.*

---
[5] In the rest of this paper we shall only explicitly define alphabets when they are not obvious from the context

Proof. Suppose the network is deadlocked in configuration δ and consider some process P_{i_1}. P_{i_1} is ready to perform the events of A_{i_1}, which is non-empty as the network is busy. Clearly this set must be contained within the vocabulary of V, as the network is deadlocked, so we have

$$\emptyset \neq A_{i_1} \subseteq \Lambda$$

Therefore P_{i_1} must be able to communicate events shared with some other process P_{i_2}, *i.e.*

$$\exists\, i_2 \neq i_1 . A_{i_1} \cap \alpha P_{i_2} \neq \emptyset$$

As the network is triple-disjoint, if there were any event that both P_{i_1} and P_{i_2} could perform then it could go ahead and the network would not actually be deadlocked. So, in network configuration δ, P_{i_2} refuses every event that P_{i_1} wishes to communicate with it, *i.e.*

$$A_{i_1} \cap \alpha P_{i_2} \subseteq \alpha P_{i_2} - A_{i_2}$$

Like P_{i_1}, P_{i_2} is unable to communicate outside the vocabulary in configuration δ, *i.e.*

$$A_{i_2} \subseteq \Lambda$$

So we have now established that

$$P_{i_1} \xrightarrow{\delta,\Lambda} \bullet P_{i_2}$$

We may continue this argument to build an arbitrarily long chain of ungranted requests

$$P_{i_1} \xrightarrow{\delta,\Lambda} \bullet P_{i_2} \xrightarrow{\delta,\Lambda} \bullet P_{i_3} \xrightarrow{\delta,\Lambda} \bullet .. \xrightarrow{\delta,\Lambda} \bullet P_{i_h}$$

As the network is finite, this sequence must eventually cross itself, giving us a cycle of ungranted requests

$$P_{i_k} \xrightarrow{\delta,C} \bullet P_{i_{k+1}} \xrightarrow{\delta,C} \bullet .. \xrightarrow{\delta,C} \bullet P_{i_{k+m}} \xrightarrow{\delta,C} \bullet P_{i_k}$$

This completes the proof$\square$

Note that the network properties of being busy and triple-disjoint are both required to complete this proof.

3 The State Dependence Digraph

We are now ready to present the main innovation of this paper. The conventional method for checking deadlock-freedom of a network, as practised by the FDR tool[19,8] for example, is to expand the entire network into a transition system of global states, and then to check that progress is possible from every state. The problem with this approach is that the number of global states of a system tends to grow exponentially with the number of constituent processes. Now we shall describe a method that avoids any consideration of global states, working only with pairs of adjacent processes to build a global *state dependence digraph*, which, if free from circuits, guarantees deadlock-freedom. This method is found to be highly efficient.

We define the state dependence digraph (SDD) of a busy, triple-disjoint network V as follows. The digraph contains vertices of the form (P_i, σ_j, A_k): one for each minimal acceptance set of each state of each process. The arcs in the digraph represent all the various *local* ungranted requests of the system. To be more precise, the digraph contains arc $((P_i, \sigma_j, A_k), (P_{i'}, \sigma_{j'}, A_{k'}))$ if, and only if the following two conditions apply

- $\langle \sigma_j, \sigma_{j'} \rangle$ is a network state of the subnetwork $\langle P_i, P_{i'} \rangle$
- In stable configuration $\langle A_k, A_{k'} \rangle$ of $\langle \sigma_j, \sigma_{j'} \rangle$ P_i has an ungranted request to $P_{i'}$ with respect to the vocabulary of the network as a whole: $\Lambda(V)$.

The usefulness of this digraph is shown by the following result.

Theorem 2. *A busy, triple-disjoint network, which has a circuit-free state dependence digraph, is deadlock-free.*

Proof. Consider a deadlock configuration $\delta = \langle A_1, .., A_m \rangle$ of a state $\langle \sigma_1, .., \sigma_n \rangle$ of a busy, triple-disjoint network $V = \langle P_1, .., P_n \rangle$. By theorem 1 there is a cycle of ungranted requests

$$P_{i_1} \overset{\delta, \Lambda}{\to} \bullet P_{i_2} \overset{\delta, \Lambda}{\to} \bullet .. \overset{\delta, \Lambda}{\to} \bullet P_{i_h} \overset{\delta, \Lambda}{\to} \bullet P_{i_1}$$

Clearly each ungranted request $P_{i_q} \overset{\delta, \Lambda}{\to} \bullet P_{i_{q+1}}$ corresponds to an arc

$$((P_{i_q}, \sigma_{j_q}, A_{k_q}), (P_{i_{q+1}}, \sigma_{j_{q+1}}, A_{k_{q+1}}))$$

in the state dependence digraph. Together these arcs form a circuit in the SDD□

Because the information carried by the state dependence digraph may be calculated by purely local analysis of process pairs, it may be constructed in an efficient manner, as we shall now show.

Algorithm to Construct and Analyse the SDD

We are presented with a network of normal form transition systems $\langle N_1, .., N_n \rangle$. The analysis proceeds as follows

1. Set up a digraph, SDD. Its vertices consist of elements of the form (N, σ, A) – one for each minimal acceptance set A of each state σ of each normal form process N in the network, and initially it has no arcs.
2. Check network prerequisites. First we check for triple-disjointedness as follows.

a. Assume that the events in the network are numbered from 1 to m. Set up two arrays *first* and *second*, with dimension m, which are initially "undefined".

b. Scan the alphabet of each process N_i in turn. For each event $e \in \alpha N_i$, if *first*(e) is undefined then set

$$first(e) := i$$

otherwise if *second*(e) is undefined then set

$$second(e) := i$$

otherwise halt, because event e lies in the alphabet of at least three processes, so the network is not triple-disjoint

Then we check that the network is busy. We examine every state of every process to make sure that it is not labelled as divergent and also does not have the empty set as a minimal acceptance.

3. Calculate the network vocabulary Λ and the list L of pairs (N, N') of processes which communicate with each other. This is done as follows.

a. Start with the two arrays, *first* and *second*, that were calculated above. Scan the arrays to construct a list L of process pairs of the form

$$(first(e), second(e))$$

such that both elements of the pair have been defined. The set of values of e which contribute to this list is the vocabulary of the network. This is stored as a boolean array of size m.

b. Purge duplicate pairs from L. (This may be performed using a standard merge sort.)

$$L := setof(L)$$

4. For each pair (N, N') in L calculate the set of all states $\langle \sigma, \sigma' \rangle$ of subnetwork $\langle N, N' \rangle$. Call this set $S(N, N')$. Do this as follows (this state-expansion technique is well-known)

a. Define a set *pending* of states $\langle \sigma, \sigma' \rangle$. Initially set

$$pending := \{\langle \sigma_0(N), \sigma_0(N') \rangle\}$$
$$S(N, N') := \{\}$$

b. Take a state s from *pending* to be processed.

$$s := \langle \sigma, \sigma' \rangle \in pending$$
$$pending := pending - \{s\}$$
$$S(N, N') := S(N, N') \cup \{s\}$$

c. construct the list *new* of 'successor' states from s, given by

$$
\begin{aligned}
new \ :=& \\
& \{\langle \psi, \sigma' \rangle \mid \exists x : \alpha N - \alpha N'. \sigma \xrightarrow{x} \psi\} \quad \cup \\
& \{\langle \sigma, \psi' \rangle \mid \exists x : \alpha N' - \alpha N. \wedge \sigma' \xrightarrow{x} \psi'\} \quad \cup \\
& \left\{\begin{array}{l} \langle \psi, \psi' \rangle \mid \\ \exists x : \alpha N \cap \alpha N'. \wedge \sigma \xrightarrow{x} \psi \wedge \sigma' \xrightarrow{x} \psi' \end{array}\right\}
\end{aligned}
$$

d. Now we eliminate states from *new* that have already been discovered and merge the remainder into *pending*.

$$pending := pending \cup (new - S(N, N'))$$

e. If *pending* $\neq \emptyset$ then return to step b, otherwise the construction of set $S(N, N')$ is complete.

5. For each stable configuration $\langle A, A' \rangle$ of each state $\langle \sigma, \sigma' \rangle$ from each set $S(N, N')$, if there is an ungranted request from N to N' with respect to Λ then add arc $((N, \sigma, A), (N', \sigma', A'))$ to SDD. If there is a an ungranted request from N' to N with respect to Λ then add arc $((N', \sigma', A'), (N, \sigma, A))$.

6. (The SDD has now been constructed). Check digraph SDD to see whether it contains any circuit. This is done by performing a *depth-first search*. [7]. If none is found report the network as deadlock-free, otherwise report that the network has a possible cycle of ungranted requests.

Let the number of processes in the network be n. Our calculation for the complexity of the SDD algorithm will be based on the following design criterion – the network building-blocks should be kept simple. Hence we shall assume that the following upper bounds apply to all well designed networks: k_1 for the number of states of each process, k_2 for the number of minimal acceptances of any state, and k_3 for the alphabet size of each process.

Given these upper bounds, we calculate the time complexity of the algorithm as follows. The number of vertices in the SDD is bounded by $k_1 k_2 n$ so step 1 has complexity $O(n)$. The number of events in the network is bounded by $k_3 n$ so step 2 also has complexity $O(n)$ (assuming a constant time array lookup facility). The calculation of list L in step 3 involves a merge-sort of a list bounded by $k_3 n$. For this the complexity is known to be $O(nlogn)$. The number of steps in the state-space expansion for any process pair of the network is clearly bounded by some constant K derived from k_1, k_2 and k_3. The number of process pairs to be analysed is bounded by $k_3 n$. Hence step 4 has complexity $O(n)$ and the same argument applies to step 5. The number of arcs in the SDD is bounded by $k_1 k_2 k_3 n$ and so the depth first search analysis may be performed in $O(n)$ steps too[7].

This gives an overall complexity for the algorithm of $O(nlogn)$ which compares most favourably with the exponential complexity of the technique of exhaustive state analysis, as used by FDR[19,8].

Example: Dining Philosophers

As an example, let us consider the famous problem of the Dining Philosophers. A number of philosophers sit around a table, and a fork is positioned on the table between each pair of neighbours. There lies in the middle of the table an everlasting bowl of tangled spaghetti. A philosopher spends most of his time engrossed in deep thought, but whenever he becomes hungry he picks up his left hand fork then his right hand fork in order to dine. Once he has finished eating he places both the forks back on the table. Deadlock would occur if every philosopher picked up his left hand fork at the same time. This is, of course, a simple case of a *user-resource* network.

For the purpose of illustration we shall consider the case of there being only two philosophers. The network is coded in CSP as follows.

$$PHIL(i) = takes.i.i \to takes.i.((i-1) \bmod 2) \to eats.i \to$$
$$drops.i.((i-1) \bmod 2) \to drops.i.i \to PHIL(i)$$
$$FORK(i) = takes.i.i \to drops.i.i \to FORK(i) \ \Box$$
$$takes.((i+1) \bmod 2).i \to drops.((i+1) \bmod 2).i \to FORK(i)$$
$$PHILS2 = \langle PHIL(0), PHIL(1), FORK(0), FORK(1) \rangle$$

The SDD algorithm has been implemented as part of our program *Deadlock Checker*[11,13]. This is a prototype tool for deadlock analysis written in the java language. It uses the FDR software as a base to perform compilation from *machine-readable CSP* to normal form transition systems. Here is the SDD analysis of the above dining philosophers network.

```
Welcome to Deadlock Checker
Command:load phils2
Command:sdd
Network phils2 is triple-disjoint
Network phils2 is busy
State Dependence Digraph:
(PHIL(1), state 0, acct 1)-->*(FORK(1), state 1, acct 1)
(FORK(1), state 2, acct 1)-->*(PHIL(1), state 1, acct 1)
(FORK(1), state 2, acct 1)-->*(PHIL(1), state 3, acct 1)
(FORK(0), state 0, acct 1)-->*(PHIL(1), state 0, acct 1)
(PHIL(1), state 1, acct 1)-->*(FORK(0), state 1, acct 1)
(FORK(0), state 0, acct 1)-->*(PHIL(1), state 4, acct 1)
(FORK(1), state 0, acct 1)-->*(PHIL(0), state 0, acct 1)
(PHIL(0), state 1, acct 1)-->*(FORK(1), state 2, acct 1)
(FORK(1), state 0, acct 1)-->*(PHIL(0), state 4, acct 1)
(PHIL(0), state 0, acct 1)-->*(FORK(0), state 2, acct 1)
(FORK(0), state 1, acct 1)-->*(PHIL(0), state 1, acct 1)
(FORK(0), state 1, acct 1)-->*(PHIL(0), state 3, acct 1)
```

430

Fig. 2. Two Dining Philosophers

Normal Form Transition Systems

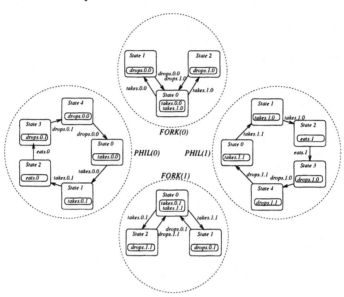

State Dependence Digraph

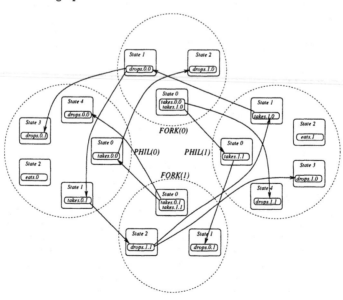

```
Found possible cycle of ungranted requests:
FORK(1) ready to do drops.1.1 blocked by PHIL(1)
PHIL(1) ready to do takes.1.0 blocked by FORK(0)
FORK(0) ready to do drops.0.0 blocked by PHIL(0)
PHIL(0) ready to do takes.0.1 blocked by FORK(1)
```

The state dependence digraph is illustrated in figure 2. It contains a single circuit corresponding to the potential deadlock of both philosophers having picked up their left hand fork.

A standard way to remove the deadlock in the dining philosophers network is to make one of the philosophers 'left-handed', *i.e.* he picks up his right hand fork first. The new definitions are as follows

$$LPHIL(i) = takes.i.((i-1) \bmod 2) \to takes.i.i \to eats.i \to$$
$$drops.i.i \to drops.i.((i-1) \bmod 2) \to LPHIL(i)$$
$$OKPHILS2 = \left\langle \begin{array}{l} LPHIL(0),\ PHIL(1), \\ FORK(0),\ FORK(1) \end{array} \right\rangle$$

Now the state dependence digraph is found to be circuit-free so Deadlock Checker reports that the network is deadlock-free.

```
Command:load okphils2
Command:sdd
Network okphils2 is triple-disjoint
Network okphils2 is busy
Network okphils2 is deadlock-free
```

Deadlock Checker is able to prove deadlock-freedom for a network of 100 philosophers and 100 forks in under ten seconds on a Sun Sparcstation 10. For this network the state dependence digraph has 800 vertices. To check this network by exhaustive state analysis would require looking at $10^{\sim 50}$ states of the *global* state graph – clearly infeasible.

Example: The Mad Postman Routing Protocol

Freedom from deadlock is a significant consideration in the design and implementation of message routing protocols. The SDD algorithm has been found to be useful for verifying many such applications. Here we shall consider an implementation of J. Yantchev's 'Mad Postman' routing protocol[22]. Suppose that we have a rectangular grid of processors and we might wish to send a message from any one of these nodes to any other, at any time. There is clear potential for deadlock here, but we can prevent it as follows. We set up two connected processes at each node: one whose function is to input messages and to route them downwards and right, if required; the other to route messages upwards and left and output them at their destination. The overall process configuration forms a systolic array of buffers, which ensures that traffic is always able to flow through the system. It is, in fact, a simple example of a *client-server* network[1,21].

For a 3×2 processor grid the CSP code may be written as follows (closely following an example given in [17]).

$$I(i,j) = in.i.j?x?y?mess \to I'(i,j,x,y,mess)$$
$$\Box \ \text{if } j > 0 \text{ then}$$
$$I\_down.i.(j-1)?x?y?mess \to I'(i,j,x,y,mess)$$
$$\text{else } STOP$$
$$\Box \ \text{if } i > 0 \text{ then}$$
$$I\_right.(i-1).j?x?y?mess \to I'(i,j,x,y,mess)$$
$$\text{else } STOP$$

$$I'(i,j,x,y,mess) = \text{if } i < x \text{ then } I\_right.i.j!x!y!mess \to I(i,j)$$
$$\text{else if } j < y \text{ then } I\_down.i.j!x!y!mess \to I(i,j)$$
$$\text{else } over.i.j!x!y!mess \to I(i,j)$$

$$O(i,j) = over.i.j?x?y?mess \to O'(i,j,x,y,mess)$$
$$\Box \ \text{if } j < 1 \text{ then}$$
$$O\_down.i.j?x?y?mess \to O'(i,j,x,y,mess)$$
$$\text{else } STOP$$
$$\Box \ \text{if } i < 2 \text{ then}$$
$$O\_right.i.j?x?y?mess \to O'(i,j,x,y,mess)$$
$$\text{else } STOP$$

$$O'(i,j,x,y,mess) = \text{if } x < i \text{ then } O\_right.(i-1).j!x!y!mess \to O(i,j)$$
$$\text{else if } y < j \text{ then } O\_down.i.(j-1)!x!y!mess \to O(i,j)$$
$$\text{else } out.i.j!x!y!mess \to O(i,j)$$

$$POSTMAN = \left\langle \begin{array}{l} O(0,0),\ I(0,0),\ O(0,1),\ I(0,1), \\ O(1,0),\ I(1,0),\ O(1,1),\ I(1,1), \\ O(2,0),\ I(2,0),\ O(2,1),\ I(2,1) \end{array} \right\rangle$$

where i and x range over $\{0,1,2\}$, j and y range over $\{0,1\}$, and *mess* ranges over some arbitrary set of messages, for which we use $\{datum1, datum2\}$.

It is no problem for Deadlock Checker to prove this network deadlock-free using the SDD algorithm. Note that more detail is provided in this specification than is required for proving deadlock-freedom. We could have completely hidden all details of message destination and content and still proved deadlock-freedom for the abstract system.

4   Augmenting the State Dependence Digraph

In the previous section we defined and illustrated an efficient algorithm for solving a problem which is essentially exponentially complex. Inevitably there is a price to pay for this level of efficiency. Although the SDD algorithm has been used to prove deadlock-freedom for many useful networks, there are certain deadlock-free networks for its power is insufficient. We shall now consider two examples of these and show how to add extra information to the SDD in order to make it rise to the occasion.

Example: Roscoe's ring

Roscoe has developed a sophisticated deadlock-free message passing ring protocol [16]. Each process on the ring has a buffer capacity of two. It may receive messages from either its anti-clockwise neighbour or via a local user channel, but it is only prepared to accept a message from its local user channel when both its buffers are empty. These messages are then either passed on to the next process in the ring or output locally. An abstract CSP representation of this protocol for a ring with four processes is as follows.

$$NODE(i) = in.i \rightarrow NODE1(i)$$
$$\square \quad pass.((i-1) \bmod 4) \rightarrow NODE1(i)$$
$$NODE1(i) = pass.((i-1) \bmod 4) \rightarrow NODE2(i)$$
$$\square \quad \begin{pmatrix} pass.i \rightarrow NODE(i) \\ \sqcap \quad out.i \rightarrow NODE(i) \end{pmatrix}$$
$$NODE2(i) = pass.i \rightarrow NODE1(i)$$
$$\sqcap \quad out.i \rightarrow NODE1(i)$$
$$RING4 = \left\langle \begin{matrix} NODE(0),\ NODE(1), \\ NODE(2),\ NODE(3) \end{matrix} \right\rangle$$

Unfortunately the SDD technique fails to prove deadlock-freedom for the ring network, despite the fact that this property has been shown to hold by analytic methods.

```
Found possible cycle of ungranted requests:
NODE(3) ready to do pass.3 blocked by NODE(0)
NODE(0) ready to do pass.0 blocked by NODE(1)
NODE(1) ready to do pass.1 blocked by NODE(2)
NODE(2) ready to do pass.2 blocked by NODE(3)
```

We get around this problem by storing extra information in the SDD as follows. Arcs are now set to either be *flashing* or *non-flashing*. An arc

$$((P_i, \sigma_j, A_k), (P_{i'}, \sigma_{j'}, A_{k'}))$$

Fig. 3. Roscoe's Ring

Normal Form Transition Systems

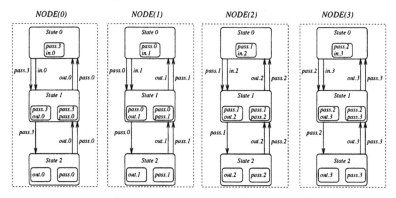

State Dependence Digraph

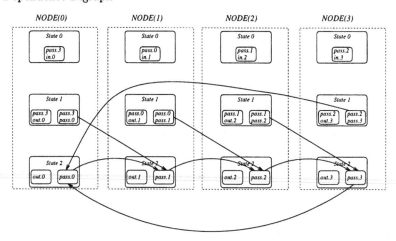

is set to be flashing only if it is known that the state $\langle \sigma_j, \sigma_{j'} \rangle$ of the subnetwork $\langle P_i, P_{i'} \rangle$ can arise only when $P_{i'}$ has communicated with P_i at least once, and more recently than with any other process. Now consider a circuit of flashing arcs in the SDD. $\left\langle \begin{array}{l} (P_{i_1}, \sigma_{j_1}, A_{k_1}), (P_{i_2}, \sigma_{j_2}, A_{k_2}), .. \\ (P_{i_m}, \sigma_{j_m}, A_{k_m}), (P_{i_1}, \sigma_{j_1}, A_{k_1}) \end{array} \right\rangle$. The ungranted requests that these represent cannot all occur simultaneously for, if they did, we would know that each process in the cycle had communicated with its predecessor more recently than with its successor, and following this argument around the circuit would lead to a contradiction. This is, of course, the argument that Roscoe used to prove deadlock-freedom for his ring protocol. We summarise this result with the following statement.

Theorem 3. *A busy, triple-disjoint network is deadlock-free if its FSDD contains no non-flashing arc which lies on a circuit*□

In order to calculate the flashing state dependence digraph (FSDD) the above algorithm needs to be slightly modified. While searching for states $\langle \sigma, \sigma' \rangle$ of each subnetwork $\langle N, N' \rangle$ we must keep track of pairs of processes that N and N' have most recently communicated with. So once the flashing digraph has been constructed we need to check to see whether there is any non-flashing arc which lies on a circuit. This is done by partitioning the vertices of the FSDD into *strongly connected components.* Then an arc (u, v) lies on a circuit if, and only if, u and v belong to the same component. This check can be done in $O(n)$ time complexity using a variant of the depth-first search algorithm[7].

When the algorithm is applied to the ring network it is actually found that every arc of the FSDD is flashing, and so the network is reported as being deadlock-free.

```
Command:fsdd
Network ring4 is triple-disjoint
Network ring4 is busy
Command (h for help, q to quit):fsdd
Flashing State Dependence Digraph:
FLASHING:(NODE(2), state 2, acct 2)-->*(NODE(3), state 2, acct 2)
FLASHING:(NODE(2), state 1, acct 2)-->*(NODE(3), state 2, acct 2)
FLASHING:(NODE(1), state 2, acct 2)-->*(NODE(2), state 2, acct 2)
FLASHING:(NODE(1), state 1, acct 2)-->*(NODE(2), state 2, acct 2)
FLASHING:(NODE(3), state 2, acct 2)-->*(NODE(0), state 2, acct 2)
FLASHING:(NODE(3), state 1, acct 2)-->*(NODE(0), state 2, acct 2)
FLASHING:(NODE(0), state 2, acct 2)-->*(NODE(1), state 2, acct 2)
FLASHING:(NODE(0), state 1, acct 2)-->*(NODE(1), state 2, acct 2)
Network ring4 is deadlock-free
```

Example: Toroidal Cellular Array

Processes with cyclically repeating communication patterns are an important ingredient of many parallel systems[6,12,21]. Now we consider a deadlock-free communication protocol for a toroidal cellular array, originally presented in [12]. Each process communicates cyclically, exchanging messages with its neighbours in clockwise order. So as to avoid deadlock, processes alternate as to whether to start by communicating to the left or to the right, according to a chess board pattern. Here is the CSP code for a 4×4 mesh.

$$CELL(i,j) = \text{if } ((i + j) \bmod 2 = 0) \text{ then } LEFT(i,j) \text{ else } RIGHT(i,j)$$

$$LEFT(i,j) = e.i.j.left \rightarrow e.((i - 1) \bmod 4).j.right \rightarrow UP(i,j)$$
$$\square \; e.((i - 1) \bmod 4).j.right \rightarrow e.i.j.left \rightarrow UP(i,j)$$

$$UP(i,j) = e.i.j.up \rightarrow e.i.((j - 1) \bmod 4).down \rightarrow RIGHT(i,j)$$
$$\square \; e.i.((j - 1) \bmod 4).down \rightarrow e.i.j.up \rightarrow RIGHT(i,j)$$

$$RIGHT(i,j) = e.i.j.right \rightarrow e.((i + 1) \bmod 4).j.left \rightarrow DOWN(i,j)$$
$$\square \; e.((i + 1) \bmod 4).j.left \rightarrow e.i.j.right \rightarrow DOWN(i,j)$$

$$DOWN(i,j) = e.i.j.down \rightarrow e.i.((j + 1) \bmod 4).up \rightarrow LEFT(i,j)$$
$$\square \; e.i.((j + 1) \bmod 4).up \rightarrow e.i.j.down \rightarrow LEFT(i,j)$$

$$TORUS = \left\langle \begin{array}{l} CELL(0,0),\ CELL(1,0),\ CELL(2,0),\ CELL(3,0), \\ CELL(0,1),\ CELL(1,1),\ CELL(2,1),\ CELL(3,1), \\ CELL(0,2),\ CELL(1,2),\ CELL(2,2),\ CELL(3,2), \\ CELL(0,3),\ CELL(1,3),\ CELL(2,3),\ CELL(3,3) \end{array} \right\rangle$$

The raw SDD algorithm fails to establish deadlock-freedom for this network.

```
Found possible cycle of ungranted requests:
CELL(2,3) ready to do e.3.3.left e.2.3.right blocked by CELL(3,3)
CELL(3,3) ready to do e.3.2.down e.3.3.up blocked by CELL(3,2)
CELL(3,2) ready to do e.0.2.left e.3.2.right blocked by CELL(0,2)
CELL(0,2) ready to do e.0.1.down e.0.2.up blocked by CELL(0,1)
CELL(0,1) ready to do e.0.1.left e.0.1.right blocked by CELL(1,1)
CELL(1,1) ready to do e.1.0.down e.1.1.up blocked by CELL(1,0)
CELL(1,0) ready to do e.2.0.left e.1.0.right blocked by CELL(2,0)
CELL(2,0) ready to do e.2.3.down e.2.0.up blocked by CELL(2,3)
```

The cycle of ungranted requests reported cannot actually happen. This is because some of these ungranted requests can only occur when the first process has completed one more communication cycle than the second, otherwise both processes have completed the same number of communication cycles. Following this line of argument all the way around the loop takes us back to the initial process on a previous communication cycle. Clearly no process can perform two communication cycles simultaneously so the potential cycle reported by Deadlock Checker actually represents a harmless spiral of ungranted requests backwards in time.

We solve this problem by colouring the arcs of the SDD as follows. We define the number of times a process P has *crossed* its initial state after trace s to be equal to the number of times that the equivalent walk in $NF(P)$ passes through the initial state. An arc $((P_i, \sigma_j, A_k), (P_{i'}, \sigma_{j'}, A_{k'}))$ is coloured *red*, if it can be shown that the state $\langle \sigma_j, \sigma_{j'} \rangle$ of the subnetwork $\langle P_i, P_{i'} \rangle$ can only arise when P_i and $P_{i'}$ have both crossed their initial state the same number of times. It is coloured *green* if this configuration can only occur when P_i has crossed its initial state more times than $P_{i'}$. Otherwise the arc is coloured *blue* to represent uncertainty. Any circuit in the coloured state dependence digraph (CSDD) which contains a blue arc remains a potential cause of deadlock, as does one consisting entirely of red arcs. But a circuit containing only red and green arcs, at least one of which is green, does not represent a cycle of ungranted requests as the requests cannot all occur simultaneously.

Theorem 4. *A busy, triple-disjoint network is deadlock-free if its coloured SDD contains neither a blue arc which lies on a circuit nor a circuit composed entirely from red arcs*□

As with the flashing state dependence digraph, our algorithm needs to be slightly modified in order to calculate the coloured state dependence digraph (CSDD). While searching for states $\langle \sigma, \sigma' \rangle$ of each subnetwork $\langle N, N' \rangle$ we keep track of the number of times more (or less) that process N has crossed its initial state than process N'. If any inconsistency is found in this quantity, *i.e.* a state $\langle \sigma, \sigma' \rangle$ is found where the number of times that N has crossed its initial state more than N' is variable, then we colour *all* the arcs between states of N and N' blue. Otherwise we colour the arcs red, green or blue according to the above scheme.

So once the coloured digraph has been constructed we need to check whether there is any blue arc which lies on a circuit. This is done by the same technique of strongly connected components as is used to analyse the FSDD. If there is no blue arc which lies on a circuit we need to check whether there is a circuit consisting entirely of red arcs. We do this by deleting all the green and blue arcs, and then checking the remaining red subgraph for circuit-freedom.

When the CSDD is calculated for the torus network it is found to have 576 arcs: 288 red and 288 green. There are no exclusively red circuits, so the network is deadlock-free.

```
Command:csdd
Network torus is triple-disjoint
Network torus is busy
Coloured State Dependence Digraph:
GREEN: (CELL(3,3), state 0, acct 1) -->*
  (CELL(2,3), state 6, acct 1)
...
RED:   (CELL(2,3), state 6, acct 1) -->*
  (CELL(1,3), state 0, acct 1)
...
Network torus is deadlock-free
```

Interestingly, deadlock-freedom for the torus network depends on both its dimensions being even. If either dimension is odd the network deadlocks[12].

5 Discussion

Conclusions

In this paper we have presented an efficient technique for deadlock analysis of large scale networks. Using the SDD, FSDD, and CSDD algorithms we have been able to prove deadlock freedom for many useful networks.

We tested the performance of Deadlock Checker on differently sized versions of the torus network of section 4. Deadlock-freedom for the 4×4 network takes $\sim$ 20s to compute on a Sun Sparcstation 10 (1.25 seconds per process). For the 8×8 network it takes 93 seconds (1.45 seconds per process). For the 12×12 network it takes 230 seconds (1.60 seconds per process). These and other results are in line with the near linear scalability of our algorithm predicted by complexity analysis[6]. The 12×12 toroidal array is far beyond the power of exhaustive state checking programs, such as FDR and ARC[15].

Unfortunately, unlike FDR and ARC, our method is not complete. Although there is certainly room for further improvement, it seems unlikely that a proof technique for the global property of deadlock freedom based mainly on local analysis will ever be complete. So relying on our program Deadlock Checker for proving deadlock freedom on a trial and error basis might sometimes be unsatisfactory. Past experience shows that it usually best to build concurrent systems according to known design rules that guarantee deadlock-freedom[21]. The CSDD technique has been shown in [11] to be sufficiently powerful to verify deadlock-freedom for *client-server* networks [1,21] (such as the Mad Postman routing protocol), *resource allocation* networks [18] (such as the Dining Philosophers), and *cyclic* networks (such as the toroidal cellular array) [6,12,18,21], plus various hybrid forms of these. These design rules are suitable for the development of a rich variety of deadlock-free concurrent systems[14], for which Deadlock Checker then provides a very powerful debugging aid. Within this framework, it succeeds in bridging the gap between the requirement of programmers to build large-scale process networks that are deadlock-free and the ability of conventional model checkers to analyse only small-scale networks.

One significant application that was developed with the help of Deadlock Checker was a genetic algorithm based breeding colony for neural networks based on a toroidal array of transputers, written using the occam language[7]. Much multiplexing and demultiplexing of channels over physical links was required to implement the conceptual design, and the programmers were having significant problems to prevent deadlock. We were able to modify their network to conform to the design rules and then verify it deadlock-free using Deadlock Checker.

The prototype version of Deadlock Checker has been used to prove deadlock-freedom for networks with several hundred processes, but the efficiency of the

---

[6] Unfortunately we are unable to test significantly larger networks at present due to system limits within the FDR software that we use to compile from CSP code to transition systems.

[7] This program was developed by Ian East and Jon Rowe, University of Buckingham

algorithm is such that it will soon be possible to perform automatic deadlock analysis of networks with many millions of processes.

Our use of normal-form transition systems probably needs some justification. It would be simple to rephrase our work in terms of operational semantics for CSP based on non-deterministic transition systems, hence avoiding the potentially costly step of normalisation. However, as long the individual processes in the network do not have large numbers of states (as required by our network construction rule), this cost should be small.

The main reason that we need to use normal form transition systems concerns the CSDD algorithm, which places special importance on the initial state of each process and relies on the fact that the normal form for a process is unique. It would not be guaranteed to work so well were we to use simple transition systems, as the initial state of the normal form could map onto two or more distinct states of a simple transition system. Consider, for example, the cyclic processes

$$P = a \to b \to a \to b \to P$$
$$Q = a \to b \to Q$$

P has a simple transition system with 4 states, whereas the transition system for Q has only 2. However the normal-form transition systems for the equivalent processes P and Q have two states and are identical.

The second point in favour of normalisation is that it usually reduces significantly the overall number of states of non-deterministic systems.

Thirdly normal-form transition systems have a very close relationship with the *failures* model, as described in section 2, which means they are more suitable for certain other forms of network analysis that might be required in conjunction with deadlock analysis. For instance a new method for checking failures specifications such as

$$tr \downarrow choc - tr \downarrow coin > 0 \implies coin \notin ref$$

which uses networks of normal-form transition systems is described in [11]. This technique is used for checking exact adherence to design rules such as the *client-server* protocol.

Further Work

We shall briefly discuss several areas for improvement that we have explored. First of all it is worth making the point that a cycle of ungranted requests does not necessarily imply deadlock. The cycle might subsequently be broken by the intervention of a process from outside. In fact, it is sometimes rather useful to allow networks to have cycles of ungranted requests of length two. We have extended the power of the SDD algorithm by treating cycles of length two as a special case, using a theorem of Brookes and Roscoe [2]. This extension is useful for proving deadlock-freedom for particular types of communication protocols, and is explained in full in [11,13].

Secondly we have discovered cases where the Deadlock Checker reports a cycle of ungranted requests which involves two different states of the same process. This is clearly impossible but we have not found any *efficient* way of 'filtering out' circuits of this nature. We seem to have uncovered an interesting problem in algorithmic graph theory which may be described abstractly as follows. Given a digraph where each vertex is coloured, decide whether there is a circuit such that every vertex has a different colour. (We are now using colours to identify states of particular processes).

Deadlock Checker also has the ability to prove *livelock-freedom* for certain networks, which is often as important as deadlock-freedom, using a simple technique from [4]. Full details are given in [11,13].

References

1. P. Brinch Hansen: Operating System Principles, Prentice-Hall 1973.
2. S. D. Brookes and A. W. Roscoe: Deadlock Analysis in Networks of Communicating Processes, Distributed Computing (1991)4, Springer Verlag.
3. K. M. Chandy and J. Misra: Deadlock Absence Proofs for Networks of Communicating Processes, Information Processing Letters. Volume 9 number 4 1979.
4. N. Dathi: Deadlock and Deadlock-Freedom, Oxford University D. Phil Thesis 1990.
5. E. W. Dijkstra: Cooperating Sequential Processes, Technological University Eindhoven, The Netherlands 1965. (Reprinted in Programming Languages, F. Genuys, ed., Academic Press, New York 1968.)
6. E. W. Dijkstra: A Class of Simple Communication Patterns, Selected Writings on Computing: A Personal Perspective, Springer-Verlag 1982.
7. S. Even: Graph Algorithms, Computer Science Press, Inc. 1979.
8. FDR User Manual and Tutorial: Formal Systems (Europe) Ltd. 3 Alfred Street, Oxford OX1 4EH. Available at
   ftp://ftp.comlab.ox.ac.uk/pub/Packages/FDR
9. C. A. R. Hoare: Communicating Sequential Processes, Prentice Hall 1985
10. E. Knapp: Deadlock Detection in Distributed Databases, ACM Computing Surveys, Vol 19, No 4, December 1987.
11. J. M. R. Martin: The Design and Construction of Deadlock-Free Concurrent Systems, D. Phil. Thesis, University of Buckingham (Department of Mathematics, Statistics and Computer Science) 1996. Available at
   http://www.hensa.ac.uk/parallel/theory/formal/csp
12. J. M. R. Martin, I. East, and S. Jassim: Design Rules for Deadlock-Freedom, Transputer Communications, September 1994
13. J. M. R. Martin and S. A. Jassim: A Tool for Proving Deadlock Freedom, in Parallel Programming and Java, Proceedings of the 20th World Occam and Transputer User Group Technical Meeting, IOS Press 1997
14. J. M. R. Martin and S. A. Jassim: How to Design Deadlock-Free Networks Using CSP and Verification Tools – A Tutorial Introduction, in Parallel Programming and Java, Proceedings of the 20th World Occam and Transputer User Group Technical Meeting, IOS Press 1997
15. A. N. Parashkevov and J. Yantchev: ARC – A Tool for Efficient Refinement and Equivalence Checking for CSP, IEEE International Conference on Algorithms and Architectures for Parallel Programming (ICA3PP) '96, Singapore 1996.

16. A. W. Roscoe: Routing Messages Through Networks: An Exercise in Deadlock Avoidance, Proceedings of the 7th occam User Group Technical Meeting, IOS Press 1988.
17. A. W. Roscoe: Notes on CSP, Oxford University Lecture Notes 1995
18. A. W. Roscoe and Naiem Dathi: The Pursuit of Deadlock-Freedom, Oxford University Computing Laboratory (Technical Monograph PRG-57) 1986.
19. A. W. Roscoe: Model Checking CSP, A Classical Mind, Prentice Hall 1994.
20. A. W. Roscoe, P. H. B. Gardiner, M. H. Goldsmith, J. R. Hulance, D. M. Jackson and J. B. Scattergood: Hierarchical compression for model-checking CSP or how to check 10^{20} dining philosophers for deadlock, in TACAS'95 Workshop, pages 133-152, LNCS 1019, Springer-Verlag 1995.
21. P. H. Welch, G. R. R. Justo, and C. J. Willcock: High Level Paradigms for Deadlock-Free High-Performance Systems, Transputer Applications and Systems '93, IOS Press 1993.
22. J. Yantchev and C. R. Jesshope: Adaptive, low latency, deadlock-free packet routing for networks of processors, IEE Proceeding, Vol 136, Pt. E, No 3, May 1989

Implementing a Model Checker for LEGO

Shenwei Yu and Zhaohui Luo**

Department of Computer Science, University of Durham,
South Road, Durham, DH1 3LE, UK

Abstract. Interactive theorem proving provides a general approach to modelling and verification of both hardware and software systems but requires significant human efforts to deal with many tedious proofs. To be effectively used in practice, we need some automatic tools such as model checkers to deal with those tedious proofs. In this paper, we formalise a verification system of both CCS and an imperative language in the proof development system LEGO which can be used to verify both finite and infinite problems. Then a model checker, LegoMC, is implemented to generate LEGO proof terms for finite-state problems automatically. Therefore people can use LEGO to verify a general problem with some of its finite sub-problems verified by LegoMC. On the other hand, this integration extends the power of model checking to verify more complicated and infinite models as well.

1 Introduction

Interactive theorem proving gives a general approach to modelling and verification of both hardware and software systems but requires significant human efforts to deal with many tedious proofs. Even a simple model like the 2-processes mutual exclusion problem is fairly complicated to verify. On the other hand, model checking is automatic but limited to certain problems - i.e., simple finite state processes, although this limitation can be partially overcome to deal with more complicated problems by improving the efficiency through BDD techniques [4]. Since theorem proving and model checking are complementary techniques, both schools have been trying to combine the strength of these two approaches by using theorem provers to reduce or divide the problems to ones which can be checked by model checkers.

Wolper and Lovinfosse [26] and Kurshan and McMillan [14] extended model checking for inductive proofs by using an invariant to capture the induction hypothesis in the inductive step. Joyce and Seger [11] used HOL theorem prover to verify formulas which contain uninterpreted constants as lemmas which are verified by Voss's model checker. Kurshan and Lamport [12] proved a multiplier where the 8-bit multiplier can be verified by COSPAN model checker [13] and the n-bit multiplier composed from 8-bit multipliers can be verified by TLP theorem prover [10]. In principle, these approaches are to divide the whole problem to

---

* Email address:{Shenwei.Yu, Zhaohui.Luo}@durham.ac.uk

separated sub-problems and then use different tools to solve individual problems. Their works based on paper and pencils are the early attempts of combining theorem proving and model checking.

However, the integration of these two approaches is still not tight enough. Müller and Nipkow [20] used HOL theorem prover to reduce the alternating bit protocol expressed in I/O automata to a finite state one to be verified by their own model checker. PVS proof checker [21] even includes a model checker as a decision procedure which presented the possibility of combining theorem proving and model checking in a smooth and tight way [24]. However, the correctness of model checkers is still a big concern since they themselves are computer softwares which could contain bugs. The output of most model checkers including the model checker of PVS for a correct system is only a "TRUE." People can only choose to believe that "TRUE" as a pure act of faith, or not at all.

On the other hand, the proofs of type theory based theorem provers, such as LEGO [16], ALF [1, 17], Coq [8] and Nuprl [6], are proof terms(λ terms) which in principle can be justified by different proof checkers so that people can have more confidence on formal proofs. Moreover, proof terms provide a common interface for different tools so that we can easily integrate various tools to complete more complicated proofs. Our work is to implement a model checker for LEGO by producing proof terms. One of the major contributions of our model checker is the automatic generation of proof terms so that we can enhance the efficiency of verification in a general theorem prover, LEGO.

We use the Calculus of Communicating Systems (CCS) [19], a message-passing concurrent language, to model the systems and propositional μ-calculus to express the system properties. Both CCS and propositional μ-calculus are formalised in LEGO for both finite and infinite state systems. Our model checker (LegoMC) is an independent program which takes the syntax of CCS and propositional μ-calculus in LEGO and then returns a string which is a proof term in the syntax of LEGO. We can therefore integrate this proof term with other proof terms to complete a larger proof. This system can also deal with other temporal logics by giving their abbreviations in μ-calculus. Furthermore, the domain model can be changed to imperative languages as well. The system structure is shown in Fig. 1.

Using this system, we have successfully verified some finite state processes automatically such as the ticking clock, the vending machine, 2-process mutual exclusion . . .. For infinite state problems, we have verified a n-process mutual exclusion problem by reducing the model to a finite state abstract model. LEGO is used to prove that the abstract model preserves the property of the original model, and LegoMC is used to verify the abstract model. We have also verified some finite examples in an imperative language such as Peterson's algorithm and the dining philosophers problem.

In the following section, a brief introduction to CCS and propositional μ-calculus is given. Their formalisation in LEGO is presented in section 3. The implementation of the model checker is discussed in section 4. Section 5 presents an example of a n-process token ring network. In section 6, we discuss the exten-

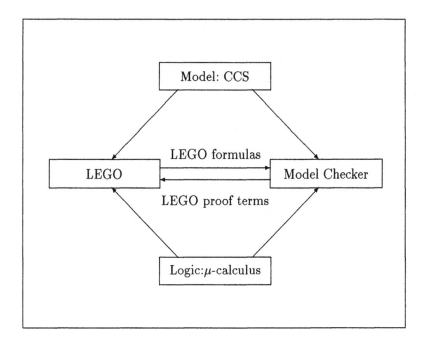

Fig. 1. The system structure of LegoMC

sion to an imperative programming language. Conclusions are given in section 7.

2 Model and Logic

2.1 CCS: Calculus of Communicating Systems

We recall only the essential information about *pure* CCS, which does not involve value passing, and refer to [19] for more details.

Let *Act* be a set of *actions* consisting of *internal* action τ, *base* actions a and *complement* actions $\bar{a}$ with the property $\bar{\bar{a}} = a$. The *process* expressions are defined by the following grammar.

$$P ::= Nil \mid X \mid \alpha.P \mid P_1 + P_2 \mid P_1|P_2 \mid P\backslash L \mid P[f] \mid rec\ X.P$$

where α ranges over actions, P, P_1, P_2 range over processes, L is a subset of base actions or complement actions, f is a relabelling function from *Act* to *Act* with $f(\bar{a}) = \overline{f(a)}$ and $f(\tau) = \tau$. The operational semantics is given via a *labelled transition system* with processes as states and actions as labels. The transition relations are given by the following transition rules in terms of the structure of process expressions.

$$\alpha.P \xrightarrow{\alpha} P \qquad \frac{P_1 \xrightarrow{\alpha} P}{P_1 + P_2 \xrightarrow{\alpha} P} \qquad \frac{P_2 \xrightarrow{\alpha} P}{P_1 + P_2 \xrightarrow{\alpha} P}$$

$$\frac{P_1 \stackrel{\alpha}{\rightarrow} P}{P_1|P_2 \stackrel{\alpha}{\rightarrow} P|P_2} \qquad \frac{P_2 \stackrel{\alpha}{\rightarrow} P}{P_1|P_2 \stackrel{\alpha}{\rightarrow} P_1|P} \qquad \frac{P_1 \stackrel{a}{\rightarrow} P_1 \quad P_2 \stackrel{\bar{a}}{\rightarrow} P_2}{P_1|P_2 \stackrel{\tau}{\rightarrow} P_1|P_2}$$

$$\frac{P \stackrel{a}{\rightarrow} P'}{P\backslash L \stackrel{a}{\rightarrow} P'\backslash L}(a, \bar{a} \notin L) \qquad \frac{P \stackrel{\alpha}{\rightarrow} P'}{P[f] \stackrel{f(\alpha)}{\rightarrow} P'[f]} \qquad \frac{P[(rec\ X.P)/X] \stackrel{\alpha}{\rightarrow} P'}{rec\ X.P \stackrel{\alpha}{\rightarrow} P'}$$

Whenever $P \stackrel{\alpha}{\rightarrow} P'$, we call the pair (α, P') an *immediate derivative* of P, α an *action* of P, and P' an α-*derivative* of P.

2.2 μ-calculus

Kozen's (propositional) modal μ-calculus(μK) has expressive power subsuming many modal and temporal logics such as LTL and CTL [4, 5, 9]. We take a negation-free version of the modal μ-calculus and use Winskel's construction of *tagging* fixed points with sets of states [25]. The assertions are constructed from the following grammar:

$$\Phi ::= X \mid \Phi \vee \Psi \mid \Phi \wedge \Psi \mid \langle K \rangle \Phi \mid [K]\Phi \mid \mu Z.U\Phi \mid \nu Z.U\Phi$$

where U is called a *tag* which is a subset of states, X ranges over a set of assertion variables, and K ranges over subsets of labels. We will use $-K$ to abbreviate the universal set of labels except K. The tag-free fixed points $\mu Z.\Phi$ and $\nu Z.\Phi$ are special cases with empty tags.

Let S be the set of states in a labelled transition system. The semantics of assertions $[\![\Phi]\!]_\rho \subseteq S$ is given by induction on the structure of Φ as follows.

$$
\begin{aligned}
[\![X]\!]_\rho &= \rho(X) \\
[\![\Phi \vee \Psi]\!]_\rho &= [\![\Phi]\!]_\rho \cup [\![\Psi]\!]_\rho \\
[\![\Phi \wedge \Psi]\!]_\rho &= [\![\Phi]\!]_\rho \cap [\![\Psi]\!]_\rho \\
[\![\langle K \rangle \Phi]\!]_\rho &= \{s \in S | \exists \alpha \in K.\exists s' \in S.s \stackrel{\alpha}{\rightarrow} s' \text{ and } s' \in [\![\Phi]\!]_\rho\} \\
[\![[K]\Phi]\!]_\rho &= \{s \in S | \forall \alpha \in K.\forall s' \in S.s \stackrel{\alpha}{\rightarrow} s' \text{ implies } s' \in [\![\Phi]\!]_\rho\} \\
[\![\nu Z.U\Phi]\!]_\rho &= \{s \in S | \exists P \subseteq S.P \subseteq [\![\Phi]\!]_{\rho[P/Z]} \cup U \text{ and } s \in P\} \\
[\![\mu Z.U\Phi]\!]_\rho &= \{s \in S | \forall P \subseteq S. [\![\Phi]\!]_{\rho[P/Z]}/U \subseteq P \text{ implies } s \in P\}
\end{aligned}
$$

where the map ρ is an evaluation function which assigns to each assertion variable X a subset of S, and $\rho[\Phi/Z]$ is the evaluation ρ' which agrees with ρ everywhere except on Z when $\rho'(Z) = [\![\Phi]\!]_\rho$. Satisfaction between a state s and an assertion Φ is now defined by: $s \models \Phi$ iff $s \in [\![\Phi]\!]_\rho$ for all ρ.

The inference rules for ν and μ operators can be expressed as follows, where $\vdash_s \Phi$ means that state s satisfies the property Φ.

nu_base

$$\frac{}{\vdash_s \nu Z.U\Phi}(s \in U)$$

nu_unfold

$$\frac{\vdash_s \Phi[\nu Z.U \cup \{s\}\Phi/Z]}{\vdash_s \nu Z.U\Phi}(s \notin U)$$

mu_base

$$\frac{}{\not\vdash_s \mu Z.U\Phi}(s \in U)$$

mu_unfold

$$\frac{\vdash_s \Phi[\mu Z.U \cup \{s\}\Phi/Z]}{\vdash_s \mu Z.U\Phi}(s \notin U)$$

To simplify the proof terms, we define two functions *Succ* and *Filter* for [ ] and ⟨ ⟩ operators. (*Succ s*) generates a list of successor (label-state) pairs of a state *s*. (*Filter K slist*) filters the states satisfying the Modality *K* from *slist* which is the output of *Succ*. Thus we can prove lemma_dia and lemma_box as follows.

lemma_dia

$$\frac{\vdash_{s'} \Phi}{\vdash_s \langle K \rangle \Phi}(s' \in \text{Filter } K \ (\text{Succ } s))$$

lemma_box

$$\frac{\vdash_{s_1} \Phi, \ldots, \vdash_{s_n} \Phi}{\vdash_s [K]\Phi}(\{s_1, \ldots, s_n\} = \text{Filter } K \ (\text{Succ } s))$$

3 The Formalisation in LEGO

The syntax and semantics of both CCS and μ-calculus can be formalised by means of inductive data types of LEGO. Before describing the formalisation, we will give a brief introduction to LEGO. Further details of LEGO are referred to [16].

3.1 LEGO

LEGO is an interactive proof development system designed and implemented by Randy Pollack in Edinburgh [16]. It implements the type theory UTT [15]. LEGO is a powerful tool for interactive proof development in the natural deduction style and supports refinement proof as a basic operation and a definitional mechanism to introduce definitional abbreviations. LEGO also allows users to specify new inductive data type (computational theories), which supports the computational use of the type theory. General applications of LEGO at the moment are to formalise a system and reason about its properties, such as the verification of proof checkers [23].

There is an **Inductive** command in LEGO [22] to simplify the declaration of inductive types and relations by automatically constructing the basic LEGO syntax from a 'high level' presentation. The syntax is as follows.

```
Inductive [T1:M1] ... [Tm:Mm]
Constructors [CONS1:L1] ... [CONSn:Ln]
<Options>
```

This command declares the mutually recursive datatype T1 ... Tm with the constructors CONS1 ... CONSn which have corresponding types L1 ... Ln.

3.2 CCS

We use lists to represent sets and natural numbers to introduce the base names of actions and variables of processes: Base = nat and Var = nat. Then we define the types of actions and processes as follows.

```
Inductive [ActB : SET] ElimOver Type
Constructors [base : Base->ActB][comp : Base->ActB];

Inductive [Act : SET] ElimOver Type
Constructors [tau:Act][act : ActB->Act];

Inductive [Process : SET] ElimOver Type
Constructors
[Nil : Process]
[dot : Act->Process->Process]
[cho : Process->Process->Process]
[par : Process->Process->Process]
[hide: Process->(list ActB)->Process]
[ren : Process->(Base->Base)->Process]
[var : Var->Process]
[rec : Process->Process];
```

In the above, the natural way to express **rec** constructor should be [rec:(Process->Process)->Process]. However, LEGO does not allow this sort of expressions since in general they could introduce paradoxes [15]. Instead, we use de Bruijn's indexes [7] to deal with variable binding.

The transition relation can be defined as an inductive relation with each of the constructors in the definition corresponding to one or two rules. For instance, the constructor of rule $Dot : \alpha.P \xrightarrow{\alpha} P$ is

```
[Dot   : {a:Act}{p:Process}
(*----------------------------------------------------*)
TRANS a (dot a p) p
]
```

which means $\forall a \in Act \; \forall p \in Process$ (p is an a-derivative of $a.p$). The constructor of rule $ChoL : \dfrac{P_1 \xrightarrow{\alpha} P}{P_1+P_2 \xrightarrow{\alpha} P}$ is

```
[ChoL : {a:Act}{p1,p2,p:Process}
(TRANS a p1 p)->
(*----------------------------------------------------*)
(TRANS a (cho p1 p2) p)
]
```

which means $\forall a \in Act \; \forall p, p1, p2 \in Process$ (if p is an a-derivative of $p1$, then p is an a-derivative of $p1 + p2$).

The complete definition of the transition relation in LEGO syntax is given in Appendix 1.

3.3 μ-calculus

First of all, we formalise the label sets of [ ] and ⟨ ⟩ operators as an inductive data type *Modality*. The modality type has two constructors, *Modal* and *Negmodal*, which correspond to the positive operator [K] and negative operator [-K], respectively. The precise LEGO definition is as follows, where we use de Bruijn's indexes to deal with the binding of ν and μ operators.

```
Inductive [Modality:SET] ElimOver Type
Constructors [Modal:(list Label)->Modality]
            [Negmodal:(list Label)->Modality];

[Tag= list State];

Inductive [Form:SET] ElimOver Type
Constructors
[VarF:Var->Form]
[OrF:Form->Form->Form]
[AndF:Form->Form->Form]
[Dia:Modality->Form->Form]
[Box:Modality->Form->Form]
[Tnu:Tag->Form->Form]
[Tmu:Tag->Form->Form] ;
```

3.4 The Semantics and Inference Rules

The semantics is defined as a function which takes a μ-calculus formula and an evaluation mapping as arguments and returns a predicate over states. A function in LEGO can be defined by constructing a proof of the function type. Because LEGO proof scripts are not easy to read, we present the construction of the μ-calculus semantics in Appendix 2 in equational form to make it more understandable.

Using the above formalisation of syntax and semantics, we are able to prove the rules and the lemmas, nu_base, nu_unfold, mu_unfold, lemma_box and lemma_dia, in LEGO. We note that our embedding is *deep embedding*, not *shallow embedding*.

4 The Model Checker, LegoMC

We can verify finite and infinite problems using the above formalisation already. However, there are so many tedious and trivial proof steps; we expect to use model checking to develop parts of the proofs automatically. In the following subsection, we describe the structure of our LegoMC. We then discuss the implementation in subsection 4.2.

4.1 The Structure of LegoMC

Given a file which contains the definition of a finite model and a specification (formula), LegoMC will produce the proof term of LEGO which could be put into LEGO proof processes if the model satisfies the specification. If the model does not satisfy the specification, LegoMC simply produces an error message. The rules are as follows, where $p : (\vdash_s P)$ means p is a proof term of $\vdash_s P$.

OR

$$\frac{p : (\vdash_s P)}{\text{inl } p \; q : (\vdash_s P \vee Q)} \qquad \frac{q : (\vdash_s Q)}{\text{inr } p \; q : (\vdash_s P \vee Q)}$$

AND

$$\frac{p : (\vdash_s P) \quad q : (\vdash_s Q)}{\text{pair } p \; q : (\vdash_s P \wedge Q)}$$

BOX

$$\frac{p_1 : (\vdash_{s_1} \Phi), \ldots, p_n : (\vdash_{s_n} \Phi)}{\text{lemma\_box prove\_state\_list} : (\vdash_s [a]\Phi)} (\{s_1, \ldots, s_n\} = \text{Filter M (Succ s)})$$

where prove_state_list=$[s':\text{State}]$mem_ind $p_1 \ldots$ mem_ind p_n(not_mem_nil s')

DIA

$$\frac{p' : (\vdash_{s'} P)}{\text{lemma\_dia (ExIntro } s' \; p') : (\vdash_s \langle K \rangle P)} (s' \in \text{Filter M (Succ s)})$$

NU

$$\frac{}{\text{nu\_base} : (\vdash_s \nu Z.U\Phi)} (s \in U) \qquad \frac{p : (\vdash_s \Phi[\nu Z.U \cup \{s\}\Phi/Z])}{\text{nu\_unfold } p : (\vdash_s \nu Z.U\Phi)} (s \notin U)$$

MU

$$\frac{p : (\vdash_s \Phi[\mu Z.U \cup \{s\}\Phi/Z])}{\text{mu\_unfold } p : (\vdash_s \mu Z.U\Phi)} (s \notin U)$$

In the above rules, *inr* and *inl* are the or-introduction proof operators, *pair* is that for and-introduction, *ExIntro* for exists-introduction, *mem_ind* for the membership induction rule and *not_member_nil* for the rule that no element is the member of an empty set.

4.2 The Implementation

We have implemented LegoMC as a separate program in ML given in Appendix 3. In the following, we explain the implementation of And, Dia and Mu operators, and the others are omitted.

AND

Assume we want to find a proof term p of $\vdash_s P_1 \wedge P_2$. We should find the proof term p_1 of $\vdash_s P_1$ and the proof term p_2 of $\vdash_s P_2$. If we can find both p_1 and p_2, then p is 'pair p_1 p_2'.

DIA

Assume we want to find a proof term p of $\vdash_s \langle K \rangle P$. By lemma_dia, that is $\exists s' \in$ Filter K (Succ s). $\vdash_{s'} P$. Therefore we try to find the proof term p' of $\vdash_{s'} P$ for all the states in *Filter K (Succ s)*. If p' exists, then p is 'lemma_dia (ExIntro s' p')'.

MU

Assume we want to find a proof term p of $(\vdash_s \mu Z.U\Phi)$, we check whether $s \in U$ first. If $s \notin U$, we try to find the proof term p' of $\vdash_s \Phi[\mu Z.U \cup \{s\}\Phi/Z]$. If we can find p', then p is 'mu_unfold p''.

5 An Example

One of the applications is to find an abstract finite-state model which is *bisimular* to the original model. Since *bisimulation equivalence* preserves the properties of a model[19], we can then use abstract model instead of the original one. Here bisimilarity is proved in LEGO, and LegoMC is used to prove the abstract finite-state model. We take a simple token ring network from [3] as an example to explain the above approach.

Assume that there are n workstations in a ring network as shown in Fig. 2. Every workstation which wants to enter its critical section should hold a token which passes around the ring. The workstation which holds the token can also merely do nothing and pass on the token. If the workstation enters its critical section, it can only exit the critical section but still keep the token. The whole model can be expressed in CCS as follows:

$$I = \tau.I + pass.IT$$

$$IT = enter.exit.IT + \tau.IT + \overline{pass}.I$$

$$Ring(n) = (IT|I|\ldots|I)\backslash\{pass\} \text{ with } n + 1 \ Is(n \geq 0)$$

where I is the idle workstation and IT is the workstation which holds the token.

We can find that the abstract model

$$Ring_{abst} = \tau.Ring_{abst} + enter.exit.Ring_{abst}$$

is a bisimular of $Ring(n)$. The Bisimulation is $\{(Ring_{abst}, Ring(n)), (exit.Ring_{abst}, (exit.IT|I|\ldots|I)\backslash\{pass\})\}$. As a result, we can use LegoMC to prove $Ring_{abst}$ against various properties such as mutual exclusion and deadlock freedom.

First, we prove in LEGO the bisimularity,

$$\vdash \text{Bisimular } Ring(n) \ Ring_{abst},$$

and we have the lemma

$$\vdash \text{Bisimular } A \ B \text{ and } \vdash_A \Phi \longrightarrow \vdash_B \Phi.$$

Therefore the proof term of $\vdash_{Ring_{abst}} \Phi$, which is generated by LegoMC, can be integrated into LEGO to complete the whole proof.

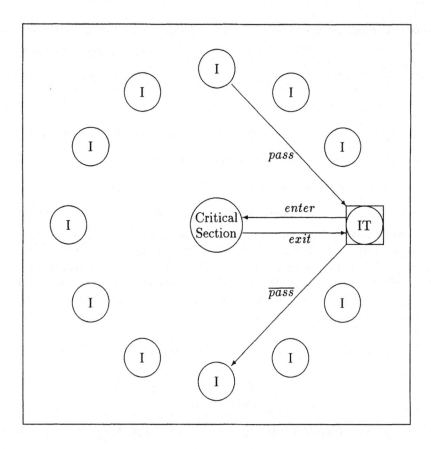

Fig. 2. A token ring network with 12 workstations

6 A Simple Imperative and Concurrent Language

Our system has been extended to a simple imperative and concurrent language and used to verify some finite state examples. In the following subsection, we describe the syntax and semantics of the imperative language. An example is given in subsection 6.2.

6.1 The Syntax and Semantics

We consider a concurrent program as several sequential processes in progress at the same time by interleaved execution sequences of atomic statements. There is an underlying set of global variables that are shared among the processes for inter-process communication and synchronisation. We define labels as primitive statements and boolean expressions, the sequential processes as lists of statements and the programs as lists of processes. The syntax of our language can be described as follows, where BE ranges over boolean expressions, NE ranges over natural number expressions, and *wait* and *signal* are semaphore statements.

1. primitive statements

Primitive ::= $x := NE$ | skip | wait_until BE | wait s | signal s

2. processes

Statement ::= Primitive | if BE Process Process | while BE Process

Process = Statement list

Program = Process list

3. labels

Label ::= Primitive | BE

We define a state as a pair (P, M), consisting of a program P and a memory M. The memory is a table containing the current values of variables represented as a list of (Variable, Value) pair. We shall use $M(e)$ to denote the value of e under evaluation in memory M and M_e^x to denote changing the value of x to $M(e)$ in memory M. Therefore, the operational semantics of our language can be defined via a labelled transition system as follows.

$$([x := e, p], M) \xrightarrow{x := e} ([p], M_e^x)$$

$$([skip, p], M) \xrightarrow{skip} ([p], M)$$

$$\frac{M(b) = true}{([wait\_until(b), p], M) \xrightarrow{wait\_until(b)} ([p], M)}$$

$$\frac{M(s) > 0}{([wait(s), p], M) \xrightarrow{wait(s)} ([p], M_{s-1}^s)}$$

$$([signal(s), p], M) \xrightarrow{signal(s)} ([p], M_{s+1}^s)$$

$$\frac{M(b) = true}{([\text{if } b \text{ then } p_1 \text{ else } p_2, p], M) \xrightarrow{b} ([p_1, p], M)}$$

$$\frac{M(b) = false}{([\text{if } b \text{ then } p_1 \text{ else } p_2, p], M) \xrightarrow{\neg b} ([p_2, p], M)}$$

$$\frac{M(b) = true}{([\text{while } b \text{ do } p, p'], M) \xrightarrow{b} ([p, \text{while } b \text{ do } p, p'], M)}$$

$$\frac{M(b) = false}{([\text{while } b \text{ do } p, p'], M) \xrightarrow{\neg b} ([p'], M)}$$

$$\frac{(p_1, M) \xrightarrow{l} (p, M')}{(p_1 \| p_2, M) \xrightarrow{l} (p \| p_2, M')}$$

$$\frac{(p_2, M) \xrightarrow{l} (p, M')}{(p_1 \| p_2, M) \xrightarrow{l} (p_1 \| p, M')}$$

6.2   An Example

As an example, we consider a semaphore solution of the mutual exclusion problem for two processes. The individual sequential process is as follows.

$$Critical = skip$$

$$P = [\text{while True } [\text{wait } S, \text{ Critical, signal } S]]$$

The program is $Pro = [P, P]$. The initial value of semaphore S is 1, $init = [(S, 1)]$. The mutual exclusion property defined in μ-calculus is "For all the states after the initial state, if the program can perform $wait\ S$ to enter the critical section, the program cannot perform $wait\ S$ again unless it performs $signal\ S$ first." The μ-calculus formula is as follow.

$$\text{ME} = \Box([\text{wait } S]\nu Z.(\text{inable } [\text{wait } S]) \wedge [\text{-(signal } S)]Z)$$

where $\Box \Phi = \nu Z.[-]Z \wedge \Phi$ and inable $X = [X]\mu Z.Z$.
We can prove the following two theorems by LegoMC.

$$\vdash_{(init,Pro)} ME$$

$$\vdash_{(init,Pro)} deadlockfree$$

where deadlockfree $= \Box(\langle - \rangle \nu Z.Z)$.
The second author of this paper used the direct LEGO formalisation to prove these properties, it is much harder.

7   Conclusions and Future Work

Theorem proving based on type theory produces not only a 'TRUE' or 'FALSE' answer to a problem but also an explicit proof term. We can therefore integrate various *proof generators*, interactive or automatic ones, if they can produce proof terms. No matter how complicated those proof generators are, the correctness of proofs is assured by the simple proof checking algorithm. In this paper, we have showed how to verify concurrent programs in LEGO by combining interactive theorem proving with model checking. This approach can be generalised to other temporal logic model checker such as SMV [18].

Beside the proof terms, another difference of LegoMC with model checkers in HOL and PVS is the domain languages. Rather than automata, we use CCS and the imperative language which are more natural to express a software system. Another difference is that we use deep embedding instead of shallow embedding so that we can prove the correctness of our model checking rules.

In this paper, the proof of infinite part is mostly based on the semantics. Although we can use LegoMC to simplify the proof work significantly, part of the proof which cannot use LegoMC to solve can still be difficult. Bradfield and Stirling developed a sound and complete tableau proof system of local model checking for infinite state spaces [2]. It is expected that we can formalise their proof system in LEGO to help the verification of infinite problems.

Since LegoMC generates the proof terms of LEGO syntax, it depends on the formalisation of concurrent languages (CCS) in LEGO. Once the formalisation is changed, the model checker has to be changed as well. However, we design the interface to μ-calculus as a *succ* function which takes a state and returns a list of successor states so that we do not have to change the μ-calculus part if we change the concurrent languages. In this way, we have implemented a simple imperative language using the same formalisation of μ-calculus. In the future, it is expected that the model checker can accept the inductive definition of LEGO directly so that the model checker can become generic.

At the moment, the size of generated proof terms is quite big so that LegoMC is not very efficient and also needs a lot of memory. To enhance the efficiency, we need to further develop some pre-proved lemmas and use abbreviations; this will be done in the near future.

References

1. L. Augustsson, Th. Coquand, and B. Nordström. A short description of another logical framework. In G. Huet and G. Plotkin, editors, *Preliminary Proc. of Logical Frameworks*, 1990.
2. Julian Bradfield and Colin Stirling. Local model checking for inifinite state spaces. *Theoretical Computer Science*, 96:157–174, 1992.
3. Glenn Bruns. Algebraic Abstraction with Process Preorders. in preparation, 1995.
4. J.R. Burch, E.M. Clarke, K.L. McMillan, D.L. Dill, and L.J. Hwang. Symbolic model checking: 10^{20} states and beyond. *Information and Computation*, 98(2):142–170, June 1992.
5. E.M. Clarke, O. Grumberg, and K. Hamaguchi. Another look at LTL model checking. In D.L. Dill, editor, *Proc. 6th Conference on Computer Aided Verification*, volume 818 of *Lecture Notes in Computer Science*, pages 415–427, Stanford, CA, June 1994. Springer Verlag.
6. R. L. Constable et al. *Implementing Mathematics with the NuPRL Proof Development System*. Pretice-Hall, 1986.
7. Nicolaas G. de Bruijn. Lamda calculus notation with nameless dummies, a tool for automatic formula manipulation, with application to the Church-Rosser theorem. *Indag. Math.*, 34:381–392, 1972.
8. G. Dowek et al. *The Coq Proof Assistent: User's Guide (version 5.6)*. INRIA-Rocquencourt and CNRS-ENS Lyon, 1991.
9. E.A. Emerson and C.L. Lei. Efficient model checking in fragments of the propositional mu-calculus. In *Proceedings of the 10th Symposium on Principles of Programming Languages*, pages 84–96, New Orleans, LA, January 1985. Association for Computing Machinery.
10. Urban Engberg, Peter Gronning, and Leslie Lamport. Mechanical verification of concurrent systems with TLA. In G.V. Bochmann and D.K. Probst, editors, *Computer-Aided Verification 92*, volume 663 of *Lecture Notes in Computer Science*, pages 44–55. Springer-Verlag, 1992.
11. Jeffrey J. Joyce and Carl-Johan H. Seger. Linking Bdd-based symbolic evaluation to interactive theorem proving. In *Proceedings of the 30th Design Automation Conference*. Association for Computing Machinery, 1993.

12. R. Kurshan and L. Lamport. Verification of a multiplier: 64 bits and beyond. In Costas Courcoubetis, editor, *Computer-Aided Verification 93*, volume 697 of *Lecture Notes in Computer Science*, pages 166–179, Elounda, Greece, June/July 1993. Springer Verlag.

13. Robert P. Kurshan. *Computer-Aided Verification of Coordinating Processes: The Automata-Theoretic Approach*. Princeton University Press, Princeton, New Jersey, 1994.

14. R.P. Kurshan and K. McMillan. A structural induction theorem for processes. In *8th ACM Symposium on Principles of Distributed Computing*, pages 239–248, Edmonton, Albera, Canada, August 1989.

15. Z. Luo. *Computation and Reasoning: A Type Theory for Computer Science*. International Series of Monographs on Computer Science. Oxford University Press, 1994.

16. Z. Luo and R. Pollack. LEGO Proof Development System: User's Manual. LFCS Report ECS-LFCS-92-211, Department of Computer Science, University of Edinburgh, 1992.

17. L. Magnusson. The new implementation of ALF. In *Informal Proceedings of Workshop on Logical Frameworks*, Bastad, 1992.

18. Kenneth L. McMillan. *Symbolic Model Checking*. Kluwer Academic Publishers, Boston, MA, 1993.

19. R. Milner. *Communication and Concurrency*. Prentice Hall, 1989.

20. Olaf Müller and Tobias Nipkow. Combining Model Checking and Deduction for I/O-Automata. In *Tools and Algorithms for the Construction and Analysis of Systems*, volume 1019 of *Lecture Notes in Computer Science*, pages 1–16. Springer-Verlag, 1995.

21. S. Owre, J.M. Rushby, and N. Shankar. PVS: A prototype verification system. In Deepak Kapur, editor, *11th International Conference on Automted Deduction(CADE)*, volume 607 of *Lecture Notes in Artificial Intelligence*, pages 748–752, Saratoga, NY, June 1992. Springer-Verlag.

22. Randy Pollack. *Incremental Changes in LEGO: 1994*, May 1994. Available by ftp with LEGO distribution.

23. Robert Pollack. A Verified Typechecker. In M. Dezani-Ciancaglini and G. Plotkin, editors, *Proceedings of the Second International Conference on Typed Lambda Calculi and Applications*, volume 902 of *Lecture Notes in Computer Science*, Edinburgh, 1995. Springer-Verlag.

24. S. Rajan, N. Shankar, and M. K. Srivas. An Integration of Model Checking with Automated Proof checking. In *Computer Aided Verification, Proc. 7th Int. Conference*, volume 939 of *Lecture Notes in Computer Science*, pages 84–97, Liège, Belgium, July 1995. Springer-Verlag.

25. Glynn Winskel. A note on model checking the modal ν-calculus. In G. Ausiello, M. Dezani-Ciancaglini, and S. Ronchi Della Rocca, editors, *Proceedings of ICALP*, volume 372 of *Lecture Notes in Computer Science*, pages 761–772. Springer-Verlag, 1989.

26. P. Wolper and V. Lovinfosse. Verifying properties of large sets of processes with network invariants. In J. Sifakis, editor, *International Workshop on Automatic Verification Methods for Finite State Systems*, volume 407 of *Lecture Notes in Computer Science*, pages 68–80, Grenoble, France, June 1989. Springer-Verlag.

Appendix 1: The Transition Relation of μ-calculus

```
Inductive [TRANS : Act->Process->Process->Prop] Relation
Constructors
[Dot   : {a:Act}{p:Process}
(*------------------------------------------------------*)
TRANS a (dot a p) p
]
[ChoL : {a:Act}{p1,p2,p:Process}
(TRANS a p1 p)->
(*------------------------------------------------------*)
(TRANS a (cho p1 p2) p)
]
[ChoR : {a:Act}{p1,p2,p:Process}
(TRANS a p2 p)->
(*------------------------------------------------------*)
(TRANS a (cho p1 p2) p)
]
[ParL : {a:Act}{p1,p2,p:Process}
(TRANS a p1 p)->
(*------------------------------------------------------*)
(TRANS a (par p1 p2) (par p p2))
]
[ParR : {a:Act}{p1,p2,p:Process}
(TRANS a p2 p)->
(*------------------------------------------------------*)
(TRANS a (par p1 p2) (par p1 p))
]
[Tau1 : {n:Base}{p1,p2,q1,q2:Process}
(TRANS n.base.act p1 q1)->(TRANS n.comp.act p2 q2)->
(*------------------------------------------------------*)
(TRANS tau (par p1 p2) (par q1 q2))
]
[Tau2 : {n:Base}{p1,p2,q1,q2:Process}
(TRANS n.comp.act p1 q1)->(TRANS n.base.act p2 q2)->
(*------------------------------------------------------*)
(TRANS tau (par p1 p2) (par q1 q2))
]
[Hide : {a:ActB}{p,q:Process}{R:list ActB}
(TRANS a.act p q)->
(is_false (orelse(member_act a R)(member_act a.comple R)))->
(*------------------------------------------------------*)
(TRANS a.act (hide p R) (hide q R))
]
[Ren  : {a:Act}{p,q:Process}{f:Base->Base}
(TRANS a p q)->
```

```
(*------------------------------------------------------*)
(TRANS (rename f a) (ren p f) (ren q f))
]
[TauH : {p,q:Process}{R:list ActB}
(TRANS tau p q)->
(*------------------------------------------------------*)
(TRANS tau (hide p R) (hide q R))
]
[Rec  : {a:Act}{p,p':Process}
(TRANS a (subst p one p.rec) p')->
(*------------------------------------------------------*)
(TRANS a p.rec p')];
```

Appendix 2: The Semantics of μ-calculus

```
Sem : Form -> map_Form -> State.Pred

Sem (VarF X) V = V X
Sem (OrF P Q) V = Or (Sem P V) (Sem Q V)
Sem (AndF P Q) V = And (Sem P V) (Sem Q V)
Sem (Dia (Modal K) P) V = [s:State]Ex[l:Label]Ex[s':State]
and3 (Member l K)(Trans l s s')(Sem P V s')
Sem (Dia (Negmodal K) P) V = [s:State]Ex[l:Label]Ex[s':State]
and3 (not(Member l K))(Trans l s s')(Sem P V s')
Sem (Box (Modal K) P) V = [s:State]All[l:Label]All[s':State]
((Member l K).and (Trans l s s'))->(Sem P V s')
Sem (Box (Negmodal K) P) V = [s:State]All[l:Label]All[s':State]
((not(Member l K)).and (Trans l s s'))->(Sem P V s')
Sem (Tnu T P) V = [s:State]Ex[Q:State.Pred]
(Q.Subset ((Sem P (change V Q one)).Union T).and (Q s)
Sem (Tmu T P) V = [s:State]All[Q:State.Pred]
(((Sem P (change V Q one)).Minus T).Subset Q)->(Q s)
```

458

Appendix 3: The Model Checking Algorithm

```
fun check s Φ =
   case Φ of
   Var V      ⟶ error
   Φ₁ ∨ Φ₂    ⟶ return "inl "+(check s Φ₁) or "inr "+(check s Φ₂)
   Φ₁ ∧ Φ₂    ⟶ return "pair "+(check s Φ₁)+(check s Φ₂)
   ⟨K⟩Φ′      ⟶ if exists a state s'∈ xs=Filter K (succ s) such that check s' Φ'
                   is provable
                   then return "lemma_dia (ExIntro "+state2str(s')+")
                   ([s':State] and (Member s' (Filter "+(modality2str K)
                   +"(Succ "+state2str(s)+")))(sem_Form "+(form2str Φ')
                   +" V s'))(pair "+(prove_member s' xs)+(check s' Φ')
                   else error
   [K]Φ′      ⟶ return "lemma_box|"+(modality2str K)+"|?|"+(state2str s)
                   +" ([s':State]"+(checklist (Filter K (Succ s)) Φ')+"))"
   νX.UΦ′     ⟶ if s ∈ U then return "nu_base "+(prove_member s U)
                   else return "nu_unfold|?|"+(form2str Φ')
                   +(check s Φ'[νX.(U ∪ s)Φ'/X])
   μX.UΦ′     ⟶ if s ∈ U then error
                   else return "mu_unfold|?|"+(form2str Φ')
                   +(check s Φ'[μX.(U ∪ s)Φ'/X])
fun checklist xs P =
   case xs of
   [ ]        ⟶ return "([h: Member s' (nil State)] Not_Member_nil h
                   (sem_Form "+(form2str P)+" V s'))"
   y::ys      ⟶ return "([h:Member s' (cons ("+(state2str y)+") ("
                   +(liststate2str ys)+")]Mem_ind1 h "+(checklist ys P))
                   +"([h:Eq "+(state2str y)+" s'] Eq_subst h ([z:State]sem_Form"
                   +(form2str P)+" V z) "+(check y P)+"))"
fun prove_member s U =
   case U of
   [ ]        ⟶ error
   x::xs      ⟶ if s=x then "member_head|?|?|?" else "member_tail "
                   +prove_member s xs
```

where *Succ* is a function with type *state → list (label*state)* which takes a state
and returns a list of successor states with the corresponding labels, *Filter* is a
function which takes a list of *(label*state)* pairs and returns the list of states with
corresponding labels which satisfy the modality K. Several ***2str** functions are
used to convert a type value to a corresponding string in LEGO's syntax.

Formal Verification of Transformations for Peephole Optimization*

A. Dold, F.W. von Henke, H. Pfeifer, H. Rueß

Fakultät für Informatik
Universität Ulm
D-89069 Ulm, Germany
{dold,vhenke,pfeifer,ruess}@informatik.uni-ulm.de

Abstract. In this paper we describe a formal verification of transformations for peephole optimization using the PVS system [12]. Our basic approach is to develop a generic scheme to mechanize these kinds of verifications for a large class of machine architectures. This generic scheme is instantiated with a formalization of a non-trivial stack machine [14] and a PDP-11 like two-address machine [2], and we prove the correctness of more than 100 published peephole optimization rules for these machines. In the course of verifying these transformations we found several errors in published peephole transformation steps [14]. From the information of failed proof attempts, however, we were able to discover strengthened preconditions for correcting the erroneous transformations.

Keywords: formal verification, transformations, higher-order logic, reusability of specifications.

1 Introduction

Peephole optimization is generally understood as the replacement of a sequence of instructions by a semantically equivalent but more efficient one. Typically, a peephole optimizer works by moving a "window" consisting of two or three consecutive instructions through the object code, and, whenever a peephole pattern is detected replacing it by the "better" sequence. Hence, a peephole optimizer usually works locally and does not incorporate global data-flow knowledge of the machine program. Experience has shown that optimizers of this kind can tremendously improve the object code [2, 7–10, 14], especially when this object code has been automatically generated by a code generator.

On the other hand it is crucial to ensure that the process of peephole optimization indeed replaces sequences of instructions with semantically equivalent ones; one important step in increasing the trustworthiness of peephole optimizers is to verify the correctness of the underlying transformations. Although verification of local optimizations seems to be a relatively easy task, we demonstrate the importance of a rigorous formal treatment, having detected some errors in

---

* This research has been funded in part by the German Research Council (DFG) under project "Verifix"

published transformations for peephole optimization. Moreover, corrected applicability conditions were discovered through formal proof.

In this paper we present a generic scheme for formally verifying peephole optimizations in PVS [13] and use this scheme to formally prove correct sets of peephole optimizations for different machines. The purpose of the scheme is to provide a tool for simplifying the verification and administration burden. Our scheme is generic in the sense that we abstract from a specific machine architecture. It consists of an abstract machine description, a correctness criterion, and a number of definitions based on this description useful for the verification of local transformations, such as conditional transformations.

We applied the scheme to different machine architectures, including a stack machine (for intermediate code) consisting of more than 50 instructions and a PDP-11 like two-address machine with several addressing modes. For these machines, we tried to verify the sets of peephole optimization rules published by Tanenbaum [14], and by Davidson and Fraser [2], respectively. Nearly all of these transformations could be proven mechanically using a simple proof tactic. More interestingly, we found that 5 transformations for the stack machine were erroneous in the general form stated by Tanenbaum [14]. In each of the cases in which we encountered unprovable transformations, however, unsolved subgoals of failed proof attempts pointed us to strengthened admissibility conditions of optimization rules for which the given transformations indeed become equality-preserving.

The paper is organized as follows: in the following we give an overview of related work. Then a brief description of the PVS system is provided. Section 3 presents the generic peephole optimization scheme, and Section 4 describes an instantiation of this scheme for a non-trivial stack machine together with proofs of peephole optimizations for this machine. Finally, Section 5 contains some concluding remarks.

Related Work

There are, of course, quite a number of researchers who have constructed powerful peephole optimizers, for example [2–4, 8–10, 14].

One of the first machine-independent peephole optimizer has been developed by Davidson and Fraser [2]. Their idea is to simulate pairs of consecutive instructions and replace them, where possible, with an equivalent single instruction. The machine is described by register and memory transfers. Their optimizer is enhanced further using a simple data-flow analysis about which resources are accessed or modified by an instruction pair [3], and by automatically generating rules from a test set [4].

Tanenbaum's peephole optimizer [14] operates on a stack-machine-based intermediate code suitable for imperative languages and several machine architectures. A large set of optimizations is given in advance in a table including more than 100 rules (pattern/replacement pairs).

In all these approaches, however, neither a formal machine semantics is provided nor are the transformations formally verified.

McNerney [11] validates transformations on basic blocks by automatically enumerating a set of test programs p, then evaluating both p and its transformation using abstract interpretation. The transformation is meaning-preserving if both p and its transformation are mapped to the same graph in the abstract domain. He implemented an equivalence prover to check this property and used it to validate the register allocation phase of his compiler. It is not clear how his prover can be reused to verify transformations for other target languages.

Windley [15, 16] also uses *generic schemes* but in the realm of hardware verification. He models microprocessors on different levels of abstraction using a generic state transition system (interpreter) to represent each level. The machine specification described in Section 3 is quite similar to Windley's specification of the assembly language level (macro level).

2 A Brief Description of PVS

This section provides a brief overview of PVS. For more details consult [1, 12].

The PVS system combines an expressive specification language with an interactive proof checker. The PVS specification language builds on classical typed higher-order logic with the usual base types, `bool`, `nat`, `rational`, `real`, among others, and the function type constructor `[A -> B]`. The type system of PVS is augmented with *dependent types* and *abstract data types*. A distinctive feature of the PVS specification language are *predicate subtypes*: the subtype `{x:A | P(x)}` consists of exactly those elements of type `A` satisfying predicate `P`. Predicate subtypes are used, for instance, for explicitly constraining the domains and ranges of operations in a specification and to define partial functions. Predicates in PVS are elements of type `bool`, and `pred[A]` is a notational variant for the function type `[A -> bool]`. Sets are identified with their characteristic predicates, and thus the expressions `pred[A]` and `set[A]` are interchangeable. For a predicate `P` of type `pred[A]`, the notation `(P)` is just an abbreviation for the predicate subtype `{x:A | P(x)}`. In general, type-checking with predicate subtypes is undecidable; the type-checker generates proof obligations, so-called *type correctness conditions* (TCCs) in cases where type conflicts cannot immediately be resolved. A large number of TCCs are discharged by specialized proof strategies, and a PVS expression is not considered to be fully type-checked unless all generated TCCs have been proved. A built-in *prelude* and loadable *libraries* provide standard specifications and proved facts for a large number of theories.

Proofs in PVS are presented in a sequent calculus. The capabilities of the PVS prover component include induction, quantifier instantiation, automatic conditional rewriting, simplification using arithmetic and equality decision procedures and type information, and propositional simplification using binary decision diagrams. Finally, PVS has an LCF-like strategy language for combining inference steps into more powerful proof strategies.

3 The Generic Specification

In this section we describe a generic scheme for formalizing peephole optimizations for abstract state machines; the main idea is to identify the minimal requirements that still permit expressing local transformations and correctness thereof.

More precisely, we identified the following set of parameters suitable for verifying peephole optimizations for a large class of abstract state machines:

1. `instr`: the set of (assembly) instructions of an abstract machine is simply given as an uninterpreted type. An instantiation of this uninterpreted instruction type then normally consists of a (non-recursive) abstract data type where each instruction is given by a constructor.

2. `state`: in order to represent the (operational) semantics one has to define the machine state. Again, a concrete interpretation of this state is not needed for developing the generic scheme. Usually, machine states are given as a tuple or record type consisting of the register set, the memory, status registers, and flags.

3. `admissible?`: for each instruction a precondition constrains the set of states in which the instruction is applicable. For example, in order to apply a store instruction of a stack machine which stores the top element of the stack into memory the stack obviously has to be non-empty. In PVS one represents the `admissible?`-predicate as a higher-order boolean function which takes an instruction and yields a state predicate.

4. `effect`: for the purpose of local optimizations it suffices to give the semantics of the state machine in terms of a one-step interpreter which specifies the effect of each instruction. The concept of predicate subtypes is used to formalize the condition that the one-step interpreter is only defined for states which are admissible for a specific instruction.

Altogether, this parameter list leads to the parameterized PVS theory in $\boxed{1}$ for the generic peephole optimization scheme; note also that there are no further semantic constraints on these parameters.

```
pho_scheme                                                        1
  [instr       : TYPE,
   state       : TYPE,
   admissible? : [instr -> pred[state]],
   effect      : [i:instr ->  [(admissible?(i)) -> state]]] : THEORY

BEGIN
  [... theory body (see below) ...]
END pho_scheme
```

Given a specific machine, one has to instantiate these formal parameters with machine-specific types and functions. The following definitions, based on this abstract machine description, constitute the body of theory pho_scheme.

The application of local transformations is restricted to linear code sequences. We assume that the code sequences considered here do not contain jumps, i.e. conditional and unconditional jumps or returns from a subroutine. Consequently, we disregard the program counter component of the machine state.

An interpreter for a linear code sequence can easily be defined as a repeated execution of the semantics of the single instructions **effect**. Since **effect** can be applied only in states which are admissible for a specific instruction, the interpreter has to be defined as a partial function. We use relations to model partial functions. In PVS, a relation $R \subseteq A \times B$ can be specified as a function mapping elements of type A to a set of elements of type B. Partial functions are then described by restricting the range to sets with at most one element. The recursive function[2] **interprete** $\boxed{2}$ takes an instruction sequence **c**, a state **s** and yields a singleton state set which is the result of consecutively executing the instructions if all the instructions of the sequence can be executed, otherwise the empty set denoting undefinedness is returned.

```
% Code : TYPE = list[instr]                                    2

interprete(c:Code)(s:state) : RECURSIVE set[state] =
  CASES c OF
      null     : singleton(s),
      cons(i,r) : IF admissible?(i)(s)
                     THEN interprete(r)(effect(i)(s))
                     ELSE emptyset
                     ENDIF
  ENDCASES
   MEASURE length(c)
```

Obviously, given a sequence **c1 ++ c2** where **++** denotes concatenation, the interpretation of **c1 ++ c2** can be split: the results of interpreting **c1** and **c2** can be relationally composed $\boxed{3}$. Note that the operator **++** is overloaded here; the second occurrence in $\boxed{3}$ denotes relational composition.

```
interprete_split : LEMMA                                        3
  interprete(c1 ++ c2) = interprete(c1) ++ interprete(c2)
```

Using this interpreter, two linear code sequences, say **c1** and **c2**, are said to be (semantically) equal if the interpretations of **c1** and **c2**, starting from a state **s**, lead to the same result.

```
==(c1:Code,c2:Code) : [state -> bool] =                         4
  LAMBDA (s:state): interprete(c1)(s) = interprete(c2)(s)
```

---

[2] In PVS only total functions are allowed. For recursive functions a well-founded measure has to be provided for which one has to show that it decreases for each recursive call. Here, one simply uses the length of the instruction sequence.

Now we have collected all the ingredients to represent peephole optimization rules on linear code sequences and a corresponding correctness criterion. Since transformations consist of an applicability condition, a pattern sequence, and the replacement sequence, they can be encoded as triples of a type **rule** as in $\boxed{5}$.

```
rule : TYPE = [# pattern     : Code,                                    5
                replacement : Code,
                condition    : pred[state] #]
```

A transformation is said to be correct (formalized by **correct?** in $\boxed{6}$) if the pattern and the replacement are semantically equal under the given precondition.[3] Furthermore, the type **correct_rule** comprises all correct transformation rules.

```
correct?(r:rule) : bool =                                               6
 condition(r) IMPLIES pattern(r) == replacement(r)

correct_rule: TYPE = (correct?)
```

The following theorem expresses the fact that applying an applicable *correct* transformation within a code sequence results in a semantically equivalent sequence.[4]

```
% r: VAR correct_rule, fp,lp: VAR Code                                  7

applicable?(r, fp) : bool =
 FORALL (start:state): interprete(fp)(start) IMPLIES condition(r)

% --- rule application is correct

applicable_equal : THEOREM
 applicable?(r, fp)
   IMPLIES fp ++ pattern(r) ++ lp == fp ++ replacement(r) ++ lp
```

Here, **fp** and **lp** respectively represent the instructions before and after the sequence of instructions to be replaced, and **applicable?(r, fp)** holds if the interpretation of sequence **fp** yields a state satisfying the applicability condition of the transformation rule **r**. The proof of this theorem is by unfolding definitions and using the splitting lemma $\boxed{3}$ above.

Using this theorem, a simple peephole optimizer can be specified and proved correct. A function **apply_rule(r, c)** for applying a correct transformation rule **r** within a sequence **c** can be specified using a predicate subtype: the result of applying **apply_rule** is a code sequence **cc** in which an instance of the pattern

---

[3] Note that the boolean operator **IMPLIES** is overloaded here:

IMPLIES(p1,p2:pred[state]):bool = FORALL s: p1(s) IMPLIES p2(s)

[4] The conversion mechanism of the PVS type-checker is used here to include implicit coercions from type pred[state] to bool.

of **r** has been replaced by the replacement sequence of **r** if there is a match and this rule is applicable; otherwise function `apply_rule` returns **c**. We have carried out a simple implementation of this specification using list functions, but not included it in this presentation.

```
apply_rule(r:correct_rule, c:Code) :                           8
  { cc:Code | (EXISTS (fp,lp:Code):
                 c = fp ++ pattern(r) ++ lp &
                 applicable?(r, fp) &
                 cc = fp ++ replacement(r) ++ lp)
                OR (cc = c) }
```

An obvious consequence of the theorem above $\boxed{7}$ is the corollary

```
rule_application_correct : COROLLARY c == apply_rule(r, c)      9
```

Our simple peephole optimizer **pho** takes a list of *correct* rules, and a code sequence **c**, and tries to consecutively apply the rules in **rs** to **c**:

```
pho(rs:list[correct_rule], c:Code) : RECURSIVE Code =          10
 CASES rs OF
  null         : c,
  cons(r,rest) : pho(rest, apply_rule(r, c))
 ENDCASES
  MEASURE length(rs)
```

An easy proof by structural induction shows that our simple peephole optimizer does not change the semantics of a code sequence **c**.

```
pho_correct : THEOREM c == pho(rs, c)                          11
```

In the rest of this paper we concentrate on the correctness of local transformation rules. In order to establish this correctness, we have developed a proof strategy $\boxed{12}$.

```
(defstep pho (&optional theories rewrites exclude)             12
  (THEN*
   (GRIND :defs ! theories rewrites exclude)
   (REWRITE "singleton_lem")
   (REPEAT (APPLY-EXTENSIONALITY :HIDE? T))
   (REDUCE))
    "(pho &OPTIONAL THEORIES REWRITES EXCLUDE) :
     Sets up auto-rewrites from definitions in the statement,
     from THEORIES and REWRITES,
     and stops rewriting on EXCLUDE.
     Then tries to prove the correctness of an optimizing pattern."
   "~%Applying peephole-optimization strategy")
```

The strategy can be called with additional parameters for installing and excluding definitions and theorems for automatic rewriting. THEN* is a strategy which applies the first command that follows to the current goal; the rest of the commands are then applied to each subgoal generated by the first command application. GRIND is the most powerful built-in strategy. It combines rewriting with propositional simplification using BDD's and decision procedures. Most of the optimization steps presented in the next section can be proved simply with GRIND. However, some additional effort is required for a few of them. Unfolding the definition of the interpreter, two singleton state sets have to be compared in the final proof state. This can be reduced to proving the equality of the states using the corollary singleton_lem 13 .

```
singleton_lem : COROLLARY                                                    13
  s1 = s2 IMPLIES singleton(s1) = singleton(s2)
```

Repeatedly applying the extensionality axiom and then applying REDUCE may finish the proof. All but a few optimizations given in the next section can be proved automatically using this strategy.

4 Verification of Stack Machine Optimizations

In this section we formally represent a non-trivial stack machine with more than 50 instructions as an instance of the generic scheme developed in Section 3. Then, we describe the proof efforts for proving the correctness of the optimization patterns as listed by Tanenbaum [14] for this architecture.

The machine consists of a stack on which all arithmetic instructions are executed, i.e. the operands are fetched from top of the stack and the result is put back onto the stack. The machine does not have general registers. Besides arithmetic instructions it provides instructions for loading operands onto the stack and popping them off into memory using several addressing modes (offset, indirect, parameter, direct, etc). Furthermore, instructions for conditional and unconditional jumps, for shifting operands, and special purpose instructions for incrementing, memory clearing, comparisons and block moves are provided. Our formalization includes all instructions except those dealing with transfer of control (i.e. jumps, procedure calls, returns etc.)

It is convenient, though not necessary, to represent the instruction set as an abstract data type (sm_inst in 14). The instruction blm(n), for example, moves a memory block, lop(n) indirectly loads the contents of a memory cell n onto the stack, and sti(k) stores (k div 2) elements from the stack into memory where the base memory address is taken from the top of the stack.[5]

---

[5] Since memory addresses have to be even we model ramadr as the type of even natural numbers {n:nat | even(n)}. Type value denotes integers.

```
sm_inst : DATATYPE                                              14
BEGIN

  ...
  blm(blm_n:ramadr)      : blm?
  lop(lop_adr: ramadr)   : lov?
  sti(sti_n:ramadr)      : sti?
  ...

END sm_inst
```

The machine state consists of the stack and the memory. Since we do not model jumps the program counter is not included in the state. In 15, memory is modeled as a function from memory locations (**ramadr**) to values and the state as a record with selector fields **mem, stk**; the theory of parameterized stacks is defined as abstract datatypes in the obvious way.

```
memory  : TYPE  = [ramadr -> value]                             15
state   : TYPE+ = [# mem : memory, stk : Stack #]
```

In addition, for each instruction one has to constrain the states in which it is applicable. For example, the **sti(k)** instruction for storing **(k div 2)** elements from the stack into memory requires the stack consisting of at least **(k div 2) + 1** elements (predicate **n_tops?**). Also, it must be ensured that the top element of the stack denotes a valid memory address, i.e. it has to be an even natural number. The higher-order function **sm_admissible** is given by a case analysis on the instruction type:[6]

```
sm_admissible(i:sm_inst) : pred[state] =                        16
LAMBDA (s:state):
  CASES i OF
  ...
  add    : twotops?(stk(s)),
  sti(k) : nonempty?(stk(s)) &
           n_tops?(pop(stk(s)), div2(k)) &
           top(stk(s)) >= 0 &
           even(top(stk(s)))),
  ...
ENDCASES
```

The semantics of the stack machine is given by a one-step interpreter which defines the effects of each instruction separately. Instructions with similar behavior can be grouped together into instruction classes and their effect can then be defined by means of higher-order functions. For example, all binary machine operations (**add, sub, mul, xor,** ...) have a similar behavior: they fetch two operands from the stack, apply the binary operation, and push the result back onto the stack 17 . [7]

---

[6] Predicate **twotops?** is true if a stack contains at least two elements.

[7] In PVS the **WITH** expression is used to denote updating a record at a specific field.

```
% bop : VAR [value,value -> value]                                      17

binop_sem(bop)(s:{s1:state | twotops?(stk(s1))}) : state =
  LET t1 = top(stk(s)), t2 = top(pop(stk(s))) IN
    s WITH [(stk) := push(bop(t2,t1), pop(pop(stk(s))))]
```

The effect of unary operations can be defined similarly. Compare instructions pop the top operand from the stack, compare it with 0 using the associated relation **rel**, and push 1 or 0 onto the stack if the comparison yields true or false, respectively $\boxed{18}$.

```
% rel : VAR [value,value -> bool]                                       18

comp_sem(rel)(s:{s1:state | nonempty?(stk(s1))}) : state =
  LET t = top(stk(s)),
      newstk = (IF rel(t, 0) THEN push(1, pop(stk(s)))
                ELSE push(0, pop(stk(s)))
                ENDIF)
  IN s WITH [(stk) := newstk]
```

The one-step interpreter **sm_ip** $\boxed{19}$ is then defined using these functions.

```
sm_ip(i:sm_inst)(s:{s1:state | (sm_admissible(i))(s1)}) : state =    19
  CASES i OF
    ...
    add    : binop_sem(LAMBDA v1,v2: v1 + v2)(s),
    teq    : comp_sem(LAMBDA v1,v2: v1 = v2)(s),
    sti(k) : sti_aux(s WITH [(stk) := pop(stk(s))], top(stk(s)), div2(k)),
    ...
  ENDCASES
```

The meaning of **sti(k)** is given by means of an auxiliary recursive function **sti_aux** which stores (**k div 2**) words starting at base address **top(stk(s))**.

To utilize the generic specification from Section 3 for this stack machine, the following actual parameters are used for the formal parameters stated in $\boxed{1}$:

- **sm_inst**, the (abstract data type) of instructions,
- **state**, the record, consisting of the memory, and the stack,
- **sm_admissible**, the admissible functional, and
- **sm_ip**, the effect function.

4.1 Correctness-Preserving Optimizations for the Stack Machine

In [14] more than 100 transformations are given in a pattern/replacement table. We have examined nearly all transformations, formalized and proved them correct or falsified them. We have omitted only transformations containing jump instructions and instructions concerning procedures.

```
tan1    : LEMMA correct?((# pattern      := (: loc(a), loc(b), add :),
                              replacement := (: loc(a + b) :),
                              condition   := true #))

tan17   : LEMMA correct?((# pattern      := (: neg,add :),
                              replacement := (: sub :),
                              condition   := true #))

tan23   : LEMMA correct?((# pattern      := (: loc(2), mul :),
                              replacement := (: loc(1), shl :),
                              condition   := true #))

tan32   : LEMMA correct?((# pattern      := (: loc(0), add :),
                              replacement := null,
                              condition   := nonempty? #))

tan65   : LEMMA correct?((# pattern      := (: lav(n), blm(4) :),
                              replacement := (: loi(4), sdv(n) :),
                              condition   := LAMBDA s: nonempty?(stk(s)) &
                                             top(stk(s)) /= n + 2 #))

tan123  : LEMMA correct?((# pattern      := (: div, neg :),
                              replacement := (: neg, div :),
                              condition   := true #))
```

Fig. 1. Some Peephole Optimizations for Stack Machine

An excerpt of the list of peephole optimizations can be found in Fig. 1. Consider, for example, rule **tan1** in Fig. 1.[8] This rule is always applicable, and permits replacing the *pattern* part with the *replacement* part, since loading constants a and b onto the stack followed by an application of **add** is equivalent to simply loading the constant **a + b**. The pattern in **tan32** is a redundant code sequence since adding 0 to a value is redundant. However, this rule is only applicable if the stack is non-empty. We found that the simple strategy **pho** described in the preceding section suffices to prove the vast majority of peephole optimizations fully automatically.

In some cases, proof attempts failed and, altogether, we have discovered 5 erroneous transformation rules in Tanenbaum's [14] list of peephole optimizations. Consider, for example, the rule **tan62** in [20].

---

[8] The conversion mechanism of the PVS type-checker is used here to include implicit coercions from type **bool** to **pred[state]** and from type **pred[Stack]** to **pred[state]**

```
tan62 : LEMMA correct?(                                              20
    (# pattern      := (: stv(n), lov(m), stv(n + 2) :),
       replacement  := (: lov(m), sdv(n) :),
       condition    := LAMBDA s: n /= m #))
```

This transformation tries to combine consecutive push and pop operations into
a single one. stv(n) stores the top element at location m, lov(n) pushes the
content of location n onto the stack, and stv(n) stores the two top elements
at locations n + 2 and n, respectively. Tanenbaum lists this rule without the
precondition n /= m. Trying to prove this erroneous transformation with our
specialized proof strategy, the prover stops in a subgoal which can only be solved
if the locations given by m and n are distinct, since omitting this precondition
results in a memory writing conflict:

```
{-1} n!1 = m!1
{-2} ...
  |-------
{1}  mem(s!1) WITH [(n!1)      := top(stk(s!1))]
             WITH [(2 + n!1) := top(stk(s!1))]

     =

     mem(s!1) WITH [(2 + n!1) := mem(s!1)(m!1),
                    (n!1)      := top(stk(s!1))]
{2} ...
```

A similar inspection leads to strengthened preconditions for some of the
other incorrect transformations. In addition, some transformations have been
corrected by changing one or more instructions in the pattern or the replacement.
Note, however, that the discovery of strengthened preconditions from failed proof
attempts is not automated and requires a close analysis of the unsolved subgoals.
    Summarizing the results, we have formalized and proved correct 108 trans-
formations (out of 123 in [14]), 101 of them are proved automatically by our
specialized proof strategy, 7 require some additional interaction. However, only
4 of these 7 transformations require a non-trivial interaction. These 4 all deal
with indirect loading and storing for which some additional properties have to
be established. We have discovered 5 erroneous transformations in Tanenbaum's
list of peephole optimization steps. In all these cases, however, we were able to
identify strengthened admissibility conditions for which the optimization step is
correct.

5   Concluding Remarks

We have outlined how to represent a general scheme for verifying local optimizations, how to instantiate it for a specific machine architecture, and how to
encode and prove correct a set of peephole optimization rules using a specialized
proof strategy. By detecting errors in published peephole optimization rules, we
have demonstrated once again the importance of a rigorous formal treatment.

In order to demonstrate the wide applicability of the approach and the specialized proof strategy, we also instantiated this scheme with a formalization of a PDP-11 like two-address machine with different addressing modes [2], and proved all the optimization steps for this machine as stated in [2] to be correct [5]. In addition, we instantiated the generic scheme with the Tamarack [17] micro-processor and verified peephole optimization rules for this processor. In [5], however, we used an older version of PVS which did not provide powerful built-in proof strategies such as GRIND. There, the degree of automation was much lower, only 83 of 108 transformations from [14] could be proved automatically using a specific strategy.

Besides the correctness proofs of peephole optimization steps, the generic developments described in this paper can also used for establishing the correctness of other local optimization tasks like transformations to improve scheduling on RISC architectures, since these transformations can also be formalized as transformations on linear code sequences.

The generic interpreter has also been used within the Verifix project to verify local code generation rules from an intermediate language into DEC Alpha code. In addition, it has been utilized to specify and verify the compilation of standard imperative language constructs into code of an arbitrary machine [6]. To implement conditionals and while loops, jump instructions have been added to the linear code, and an interpreter for this code has been provided. Our linear interpreter presented in this paper has been embedded into this machine code interpreter. Future work will consider the verification of optimizations on code including jumps using this interpreter.

Acknowledgment

We thank all members of the Verifix team for helpful discussions on optimization techniques. The constructive criticisms and suggestions provided by the anonymous referees have greatly improved the paper.

References

1. J. Crow, S. Owre, J. Rushby, N. Shankar, and M. Srivas. A Tutorial Introduction to PVS. Technical report, Computer Science Laboratory, SRI International, Menlo Park CA 94025, USA, March 1995. To presented at WIFT'95: Workshop on Industrial-Strength Formal Specification Techniques, Boca Raton, Florida.
2. Jack W. Davidson and Christoper W. Fraser. The Design and Application of a Retargetable Peephole Optimizer. *ACM Transactions on Programming Languages and Systems*, 2(2):191–202, April 1980.
3. Jack W. Davidson and Christoper W. Fraser. Register Allocation and Exhaustive Peephole Optimization. *Software – Practice and Experience*, 14(9):857–865, September 1984.
4. Jack W. Davidson and Christoper W. Fraser. Automatic Inference and fast Interpretation of Peephole Optimization Rules. *Software – Practice and Experience*, 17(11):801–812, November 1987.

5. A. Dold, F.W. von Henke, H. Pfeifer, and H. Rueß. A Generic Specification for Verifying Peephole Optimizations. Technical Report UIB-95-14, Universität Ulm, Fakultät für Informatik, 89069-Ulm, Germany, December 1995.

6. A. Dold, F.W. von Henke, H. Pfeifer, and H. Rueß. Generic Compilation Schemes for Simple Programming Constructs. Technical Report UIB-96-12, Universität Ulm, Fakultät für Informatik, 89069-Ulm, Germany, December 1996.

7. Andrew Gill. A Novel Approach Towards Peephole Optimisations. In *Proceedings of the 4th Annual Glasgow Workshop on Functional Programming*, Workshops in Computer Science. Springer-Verlag, August 1991.

8. Peter B. Kessler. Discovering Machine Specific Code Improvements. *Sigplan Notices*, 21(7):249–254, 1986.

9. Robert R. Kessler. Peep - an Architectural Description Driven Peephole Optimizer. *Sigplan Notices*, 19(6):106–110, June 1984.

10. David Alex Lamb. Construction of a Peephole Optimizer. *Software – Practice and Experience*, 11(6):639–647, June 1981.

11. Timothy S. McNerney. Verifying the Correctness of Compiler Transformations on Basic Blocks using Abstract Interpretation. *Sigplan Notices*, 26(9):106–115, 1991.

12. S. Owre, J. Rushby, N. Shankar, and F. von Henke. Formal Verification for Fault-Tolerant Architectures: Prolegomena to the Design of PVS. *IEEE Transactions on Software Engineering*, 21(2):107–125, February 1995.

13. S. Owre, J. M. Rushby, and N. Shankar. PVS: A Prototype Verification System. In Deepak Kapur, editor, *11th International Conference on Automated Deduction (CADE)*, volume 607 of *Lecture Notes in Artificial Intelligence*, pages 748–752, Saratoga, NY, 1992. Springer-Verlag.

14. Andrew S. Tanenbaum, Hans van Staveren, and Johan W. Stevenson. Using Peephole Optimization on Intermediate Code. *ACM Transactions on Programming Languages and Systems*, 4(1):21–36, January 1982.

15. P.J. Windley. A Theory of Generic Interpreters. In George J. Milne and Laurence Pierre, editors, *Correct Hardware Design and Verification Methods*, volume 683 of *Lecture Notes in Computer Science*, pages 122–134. Springer-Verlag, May 1993.

16. P.J. Windley. Specifying Instruction-Set Architectures in HOL: A Primer. In Thomas F. Melham and Juanito Camilleri, editors, *Proceedings of the 7th International Workshop on the Higher-Order Logic Theorem Proving and Its Applications*, volume 859 of *Lecture Notes in Computer Science*, pages 440–455. Springer-Verlag, September 1994.

17. P.J. Windley and M. Coe. Microprocessor Verification: A Tutorial. Technical Report LAL-92-10, University of Idaho, Department of Computer Science, Laboratory for Applied Logic, 1992.

A Meta-Method for
Formal Method Integration

Richard F. Paige

*Department of Computer Science, University of Toronto,
Toronto, Ontario, M5S 3G4, Canada.* `paige@cs.toronto.edu`*

Abstract. We describe a meta-method for formal method integration [Pai97]. The approach is applied to combining formal methods with other formal and semiformal methods. We discuss the theory behind formal method integration, present two example combinations, and use an integrated method in solving a small problem.

1 Introduction

Method integration involves defining relationships between different methods so that they may be productively used together to solve problems. In a software engineering context, method integration has seen recent research on combining specific methods [LKP91, SFD92], and on the formulation of systematic techniques [Kro93, Pai97]. In this paper, we follow the latter theme and describe a meta-method for formal method integration based on heterogeneous notations [Pai97].

We commence with a brief overview of method integration and the general means we take to accomplishing it. Our approach is based on heterogeneous notations, combinations of existing formal and semiformal notations. After providing the background for heterogeneous notations, and discussing their role in method integration, we describe a meta-method for method integrations involving at least one formal method, and then briefly apply the technique to examples.

Due to space restrictions, this paper only provides high-level details concerning our approach to formal method integration and heterogeneous notations. The interested reader may find further results in [Pai97].

1.1 Method integration

When integrating methods, incompatibilities between techniques are resolved so that the approaches can be safely and effectively used together [Kro93]. Method integration in a software engineering context is a problem of growing research interest. A significant reason for this is that it is unlikely that one method will suffice for use in the development of increasingly complex systems [Jac95,

---

* *Current address:* Department of Computer Science, York University, North York, Ontario, Canada, M3J 1P3. `paige@cs.yorku.ca`

DeM82]; method integration provides systematic techniques for dealing with this complexity. Furthermore, method integration has been used and has proved to be useful in practice in various forms, e.g., at Rolls-Royce [Hil91], BT [SFD92], Westinghouse [Ham94], Praxis [Hal96], and elsewhere.

1.2 Heterogeneous notations and specifications

A notation is an important part of any method; it is used to describe the concrete products of the technique. Notations play a key role in how we integrate methods. In particular, we combine notations as a first step towards combining formal methods. A *heterogeneous notation* is a combination of notations. A heterogeneous notation is used to write heterogeneous specifications.

Definition 1. A specification is *heterogeneous* if it is a composition of partial specifications written in two or more notations.

We do not constrain what is to be allowed as a composition. Useful compositions will depend on the context and the notations to be used. Compositions may occur through use of specification combinators, by use of shared state or shared names, or in other ways. We supply some examples later.

Heterogeneous notations are useful for a number of reasons: for producing simpler specification languages [ZaJ93]; for writing simpler specifications than might be produced using a single language [ZaM93]; for ease of expression [BoH94]; and because they have been proven to be successful in practice [ZaJ95, SFD92, Hal96].

The formal meaning of a heterogeneous specification is given by defining the semantics of all the notation compositions. Formal meaning is provided by a heterogeneous basis.

Definition 2. A *heterogeneous basis* is a set of notations, translations between formalisms, and formalizations, that provides a formal semantics to compositions of specifications written in two or more notations.

The heterogeneous basis that is used in this paper is partially presented in [Pai97]. It is created by translation. We discuss it in the next subsection, and in Section 2 outline the process of its construction.

1.3 A heterogeneous basis

A heterogeneous basis supplies a formal semantics to a heterogeneous specification [Pai97]. It is used to provide the foundation on which integrated formal methods are defined. The basis in this paper consists of a set of languages with translations defined between them. It is depicted in Fig. 1.

The predicate notation is from [Heh93]; Z is from [Spi89]; specification statements (i.e., $w : [pre, post]$) are from [Mor94]; CSP is from [Hoa85]; and the two Larch languages are from [GuH93]. The remaining semiformal notations are from SA/SD [DeM79, YoC79], SADT [MaM88], and Coad-Yourdon object oriented

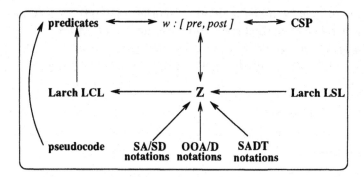

Fig. 1. A heterogeneous basis

analysis and design [CoY90]. More notations are considered in [Pai97]. Notations were chosen to be placed in the basis for a variety of reasons: because they are well-known, or because they have proven to be useful in practice, or because there are existing method integrations involving such notations that can be used for comparison.

In Fig. 1, the arrows represent translations between notations. Many of the translations in Fig. 1 are described in detail in [Pai97]. We will give a few examples in Section 2, considering both formal and semiformal notations, and will demonstrate the general technique that can be used for constructing (or extending) a heterogeneous basis that consists of formal and semiformal notations.

A specification written using the notations from Fig. 1 is given a semantics in terms of a formal specification written using only one of the formal notations of the basis. The user of the basis chooses the formal notation to use for their particular application and context, and defines the meaning of a heterogeneous specification in this formal notation. Specific context-level problems must be dealt with by the specifier and user of the heterogeneous basis, e.g., how to resolve parsing problems, and how to deal with differences in expressive capabilities (we address some of these issues in Section 2).

The existence of the heterogeneous basis means that we can give a formal semantics to compositions of partial specifications written in the notations of the basis. It does not provide us with any results regarding the feasibility (or even the possibility) of using specific notations in composition. Such compatibility issues must be examined in a case-by-case setting.

1.4 Integrating methods with heterogeneous notations

Heterogeneous specifications are written using two or more notations. Formal method integration is carried out by first precisely combining the notations used by the methods. This first step occurs by constructing or extending a heterogeneous basis consisting of the notations of interest, and by resolving syntactic differences among the notations. Once this is done, the method integration process continues by *generalizing* method steps to use heterogeneous notations (i.e., by adding notations from one method to another method), and by interleaving (perhaps generalized) method steps from the methods that are to be combined.

Heterogeneous notations will not solve all the problems of method integration; issues with respect to method compatibility and models of procedure remain to be dealt with. We claim that heterogeneous notations provide a systematic and lightweight basis for formal method integration, and we provide evidence to support this claim herein.

1.5 Overview

We commence the paper by describing a general process for constructing the heterogeneous basis of Fig. 1. We suggest a meta-method for formal method integration and use it to combine methods: we integrate two refinement-based methods in one example, and combine a refinement-based and structured method in a second example. We then use the first integration in solving a small problem (detailed examples using combined formal and semiformal methods are given in [Pai97]).

2 A Heterogeneous Basis

A heterogeneous basis is shown in Fig. 1. The basis is created by translation: a set of mappings are given that transform a specification in one notation into a specification in a second notation. In this section, we summarize the process of constructing the heterogeneous basis of Fig. 1. In particular, we consider the addition of formal notations (by translation), and the process of adding semiformal notations to an existing basis (by formalization).

2.1 Formal translations

A formal notation may be added to a heterogeneous basis by providing a translation from the formal notation into a second formal notation already in the heterogeneous basis. In doing so, the extender of the basis must analyze the expressive capabilities of the new notation, viz., what can and cannot be translated into and from the new notation. The expressive capabilities of the notations will affect the use of the translations, and will also affect how a semantics is given to a heterogeneous specification that uses the new notation.

We present several example translations here, building on those that have been previously given in the literature [Kin90, HeM88, Mor94]. We also identify several examples of untranslatable specifications. In a meta-method, differences in notation expressiveness should be handled in a way that is most appropriate to the users of the meta-method and heterogeneous basis; this might be carried out by restricting translation domains, or by extending languages. In this paper, we restrict translation domains, and therefore take an 'intersection' approach to semantics (i.e., only mutually expressible concepts in combinations of languages are used). Alternative approaches—e.g., 'union' approaches to semantics—are considered or discussed in [ZaJ93, Pai97]. As we shall see, the meta-method for formal method integration does not require that an intersection (or union) approach to semantics be used. However, the examples in this paper only make use of an intersection approach.

To simplify the process of integration, we assume that all languages use the primed/unprimed notation of Z to distinguish poststate from prestate. We also assume that types and type constructors can be freely translated. We retain the convention of [Pai97] and describe each translation as a function from language to language.

A predicate specification **frame** $w \bullet P$ that does not refer to the time variables t, t' [Heh93] can be translated to a specification statement [Mor94] using the mapping $PredToSS$.

$$PredToSS(\textbf{frame } w \bullet P) \,\hat{=}\, w : [\,true, P\,]$$

(Translations are given in [Pai97] for handling time variables.)

A specification statement can be translated to a predicate as follows.

$$SSToPred(w : [\,pre, post\,]) \,\hat{=}\, \textbf{frame } w \bullet (pre \Rightarrow post)$$

[Pai97] describes how to translate a specification statement to a predicate that includes references to the time variables t and t'. The predicative notation cannot represent angelic specifications [BaV89] and terminating but otherwise arbitrary behaviour (i.e., **havoc** [Mor94]), and so $SSToPred$ cannot translate these specifications and maintain their interpretation.

The Z schema $Op \,\hat{=}\, [\,\Delta S;\ i? : I;\ o! : O \mid pred\,]$ can be mapped into a specification statement using the function $ZToSS$. This result is due to [Kin90].

$$ZToSS(Op) \,\hat{=}\, w : [\,(\exists w' : T \mid inv \bullet pred), pred\,]$$

(The Δ-schema denotes those state elements Op can change. The inputs to the operation are denoted by $i?$, and the outputs by $o!$. inv is a state invariant obtained from the Δ-schema in the declaration of Op, and w consists of variables in S together with the operation outputs.)

The specification statement $w : [\,pre, post\,]$ can be translated into Z using function $SSToZ$.

$$SSToZ(w : [\,pre, post\,]) \,\hat{=}\, [\,\Xi\rho;\ \Delta w \mid pre \wedge post\,]$$

ρ is all state variables not in the frame w. The user of $SSToZ$ may identify input components (using a ?), or output (using a !) in the schema, instead of placing all state components in Δ or Ξ components. Miraculous specifications (i.e., terminating and establishing *false*) cannot be translated under maintenance of interpretation using this function.

We can add CSP [Hoa85] to the heterogeneous basis by translating from CSP to *action systems* [Bac90] following the work of [WoM91]. An action system consists of a state, an initialization, and a number of labelled guarded commands on the state (a labelled guarded command is called an *action*). An example is shown below.

$$\textbf{var } n \bullet \textbf{initially } n := 0$$
$$count : n < 100 \rightarrow n := n + 1$$
$$reset : true \rightarrow n := 0$$

The initialization is executed, and then repeatedly one of the labelled commands with a true guard is chosen and executed. The system deadlocks if no guard is true, and diverges whenever a command aborts.

A communicating sequential process consists of an alphabet of events, and a set of behaviours described in one of the models of CSP: traces, failures, or failures-divergences.

In [WoM91] it is shown how to construct the traces, failures, and divergences of an action system, thus mapping from action systems into CSP. First, define for any sequences of actions s and t, the *sequential composition* P_s, as follows:

$$P_{\langle\rangle} \mathrel{\widehat{=}} \textbf{skip}, \quad P_{\langle a \rangle} \mathrel{\widehat{=}} P_a, \quad P_{s^\frown t} \mathrel{\widehat{=}} P_s; \ P_t$$

We can now construct the traces, failures and divergences. Consider an action system P with initialization P_i and a set of actions A. Three laws from [WoM91] are used for calculating traces, failures, and divergences of an action system.

Law 2.1 *A sequence tr is a **trace** of P providing that* $\neg wp(P_{\langle i \rangle^\frown tr}, false)$.

Law 2.2 *For a sequence of actions tr and a set of actions ref, the pair (tr, ref) is a **failure** of P if tr is a trace of P and:*

$$\neg wp(P_{\langle i \rangle^\frown tr}, \exists x : ref \bullet gd \ P_x)$$

where gd P_x is the guard of the action P_x.

Law 2.3 *A sequence tr is a **divergence** if* $\neg wp(P_{\langle i \rangle^\frown tr}, true)$.

Justifications for the laws are given in [WoM91].

The transformation from a CSP specification (given in terms of traces, failures, and divergences) into an action system is also possible. Suppose we have a set of traces T, a set of failures F, and a set of divergences D. First we construct a set of actions L (these are simply names for actions). An action system P for this specification is as follows. The declaration and initialization of P is

$$\textbf{var } tr : L^*; \ \mathcal{R} : \mathbb{P}L \bullet$$
$$\textbf{initially } tr := \langle\rangle; \ \mathcal{R} : [\, tr \notin D, (tr, \mathcal{R}) \in F \,]$$

and for every $l \in L$ we form the guarded command

$$l : (l \notin \mathcal{R} \wedge (tr \frown \langle l \rangle) \in T) \to tr := tr \frown \langle l \rangle;\ \mathcal{R} : [\ tr \notin D, (tr, \mathcal{R}) \in F\ ]$$

Further details can be found in [WoM91].

The issue of whether specific combinations of formal notations in the heterogeneous basis are usable together is not directly considered here. Feasibility (or compatibility) of use depends on the context in which the notations are to be used, and on how compositions between notations are to be defined. We do provide some evidence that particular notations are compatible, and can be used productively together (see the examples, and the further case studies in [Pai97]). More work remains to be done on examining the soundness of using all combinations of the notations of the heterogeneous basis.

2.2   Semiformal translations

The heterogeneous basis contains semiformal notations, including those from SADT [MaM88], Coad-Yourdon OOA/D [CoY90], and SA/SD [DeM79, YoC79]. To include a semiformal notation in the basis, we must fix an interpretation for it and then express specifications in this notation in one of the formalisms in the basis [Pai97]. If this interpretation or formalization is not appropriate for a development setting, then it should be changed. Once a formalization of a semiformal specification has been constructed, the formalization can be used to check for ambiguity or inconsistency.

We demonstrate how to add semiformalisms to the heterogeneous basis by using examples of SADT notations. Other semiformal notations, e.g., data flow diagrams and object notations, are dealt with in [Pai97].

There are many interpretations that might be taken for a semiformalism. In particular, an interpretation and formalization will probably be useful only for a specific problem context, or particular development context. Therefore, it is important that the approach to heterogeneous basis construction be extendible to new notations, interpretations, and formalizations. Our examples have convinced us that the basis is partwise extendible and changeable; that is, we can change formalizations without altering the rest of the heterogeneous basis.

An SADT actigram box is shown in Fig. 2. An actigram is made up of interconnected boxes and arrows, with boxes representing functions and arrows representing data flow. Actigram boxes may be annotated with processing details, just as data flow diagrams may be annotated with process specifications (PSPECs).

The interpretation placed on an actigram is that it represents an operation on a state; this maps conveniently into a Z style of specification. If this interpretation is inappropriate for the task at hand, it can be changed according to the users' needs. For example, with this interpretation (and formalization) it will not be straightforward to model nondeterminism or triggering conditions. If we need to

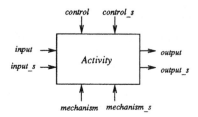

Fig. 2. An SADT actigram

model such concepts, we should use a more appropriate formalization (e.g., akin to [LKP91, ZaJ95]). We represent the actigram of Fig. 2 in Z as follows. First, we define appropriate types for the inputs, outputs, mechanisms, and controls. We create a state schema, *ActivityState*, for the actigram. This represents the part of the outputs of the actigram that are used elsewhere, and is equivalent to declaring an implicit data store.

$$
\begin{array}{|l}
\hline
\_ActivityState _____ \\
\; output\_s : O_s \\
\hline
\end{array}
$$

We next construct a Z specification of the box. In Fig. 2, flow labelled with a _s suffix comes from or goes to another box. Non-suffixed labels indicate data flow from or to the environment. In the Z schema we annotate external interactions with the Z syntax for input and output, and do not annotate the internal interactions.

A Z schema for *Activity* is as follows.

$$
\begin{array}{|l}
\hline
\_Activity_____ \\
\; control? : C_e \\
\; input? : I_e \\
\; output! : O_e \\
\; mechanism? : M_e \\
\; \Xi\, input\_s \\
\; \Xi\, mechanism\_s \\
\; \Xi\, control\_s \\
\; \Delta\, ActivityState \\
\hline
\end{array}
$$

Each of *input_s*, *mechanism_s*, and *control_s* are names of state schemas declared elsewhere. They can be annotated with Δ instead of Ξ if necessary. An invariant may be added to *Activity*, by formalizing any associated processing details, if such information is important for proofs.

An SADT datagram box is shown in Fig. 3.

Boxes represent data, and arrows represent activities on data. The interpretation we place on a datagram box is that it is an entity (a set), and arrows between datagrams (or between the environment and a box) represent relations between entities. This can be modelled in Z as follows.

481

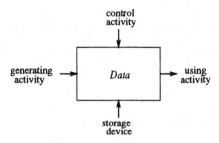

Fig. 3. An SADT datagram

1. Create a type $[ENVTYPE]$, the type of the environment. Model the environment as a state schema with component env.

    ___Environment_____
    | $env : ENVTYPE$

    All external interactions will be with the entity *Environment*.
2. For each datagram box *Data*, declare a type $[DATA]$. Represent the box in Z as a state schema.

    ___Data_____
    | $data : DATA$

3. Each arrow labelled r between the environment and a datagram box D is modelled as a one-to-one function from the environment to the box.

    | $r : Environment \rightarrowtail D$

    If there is more than one instance of D in the system that is represented by the box, then the relation should instead be one-to-many.
4. Each arrow r from a datagram D to the environment is described as a one-to-one function from the box to the environment.

    | $r : D \rightarrowtail Environment$

    If there is more than one instance of D in the system that is represented by the box, the relation should instead be many-to-one.
5. Each arrow from a datagram D_1 to a datagram D_2 is modelled as a pair of appropriately-named relations. For example, consider the arrow in Fig. 4. It is described in Z as follows.

    | $gen : D_1 \leftrightarrow D_2$
    | $use : D_2 \leftrightarrow D_1$

    Constraints on the domain and range of the relation can be added as invariants, e.g., to make relations one-to-one.

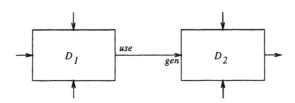

Fig. 4. A use-generate relationship

The addition of other semiformalisms (e.g., data flow diagrams, structure charts, object notations, pseudocode) is considered in [Pai97]. Therein, examples of how to extract semiformal specifications from formal specifications are also considered.

3 A Meta-Method for Formal Method Integration

Heterogeneous notations can be used in the production of a meta-method for formal method integration. We present such a technique here. The meta-method describes an abstract strategy for constructing relationships between procedural steps.

The meta-method itself does not place constraints or restrictions on how the methods are to be used when integrated. This is the task of the method engineer, i.e., the user of the meta-method. The meta-method is designed to support the method engineer in placing constraints on using methods in combination. Whether particular methods are to be considered *complementary* is dependent on the context in which they are to be used.

1. *Fix a base method.* Fixing a base method is step aimed at assisting method engineers in determining roles that individual methods can play in the integrated method. A base method can suggest a set of steps (i.e., a partial meta-model [Met94]) that is to be supported and complemented by other (invasive) methods. A base method may support more of the software development cycle than other methods; it may also provide those steps that a developer may want to use the most during development.

2. *Choose the invasive method(s).* Invasive methods augment, are embedded, or are interleaved with the base method. In this step, possible relationships between the base and invasive methods are decided. The selection of invasive methods might be done in terms of: notational convenience, e.g., for adding operational details to flow diagrams, or for adding formality to semiformal specifications; methodological convenience, e.g., for adding new sets of procedures to a base method, such as procedural refinement to a non-refinement based technique; or, internal constraints dictated by requirements, management or company policy, or regulatory bodies.

3. *Construct or extend a heterogeneous basis.* This is accomplished by constructing or adding notations from the base and invasive methods to a heterogeneous basis. A single formal notation from the heterogeneous basis (that

is to be used to provide a formal semantics to system specifications that arise in the use of the integrated method) can be chosen and fixed at this point.

4. *Generalization and relation of method steps.* The method steps for the base and invasive methods are manipulated in order to define how they will work together in combination. Either one or both of the generalization and relation manipulations can be applied. In more detail, the manipulations are as follows.

   - *Generalization.* The steps of the base or invasive methods are generalized to use heterogeneous notations; effectively, notations are added to a method, and the method steps are generalized to using the new notations. An example of a generalization integration is demonstrated in [WiZ92], where SA is combined with Larch.
   - *Relation.* Relation of method steps can follow generalization. Relationships between the (generalized) base steps and (generalized) invasive steps are defined. Examples of relationships include the following.

     • Linking of method steps, by defining a translation between notations of different methods, e.g., as in the SAZ Project [PWM93].

     • Replacement of entire steps in a base method by (generalized) steps of an invasive method. The invariant in such a replacement is that the steps being added must do at least the tasks of the steps they are replacing.

     • Supplementation of method steps. Specific steps of one method are identified and are supplemented by steps from a second method. Supplementation does not change the ordering of steps, i.e., the ordering in the integrated method is identical to that in the method being supplemented. Invariance of ordering can be obtained by ensuring that the steps being added do not overlap with steps of the supplemented method outside of those method steps being supplemented.

     • Parallel use of steps, by describing relationships that interleave the use of two or more separate sets of method steps. An example of this kind of relation is suggested in [LKP91].

5. *Guidance to the user.* Hints, examples, and suggestions on how the integrated method can be used is provided.

The meta-method does not provide a formal (meta-) model of each method (e.g., as is done in meta-modelling techniques like [Met94]); for this reason, we consider the meta-method to be a "lightweight" approach to method integration. The meta-method also requires that all notations have (or can be given) a formal semantics, and that the method engineer eliminate syntactic ambiguity among the notations of the methods.

In the next two sections, we use the meta-method to integrate formal and semiformal techniques, and use these examples to discuss some of the properties of the meta-method.

4 Integrating Formal Methods

Of the formalisms considered in the heterogeneous basis, two include methods based on procedural refinement; the remaining techniques are specification styles (possibly with rules for data transformation), associated with informal rules for writing the specification, and for checking for its consistency.

We integrate several formal methods (a Z 'house method', Morgan's refinement calculus, predicative programming) using the meta-method of the previous section. We choose the Z house method as the base method, in order to make use of its specification style. The refinement calculus and predicative programming are selected as the invasive methods. A heterogeneous basis containing these notations (and translations between them) was constructed in Section 2. For each combination of used notations, the use of notations is restricted to those mutually expressible specifications (i.e., when combining Z and predicates, no miracles or **havoc** specifications are used).

In applying Step 4 of the meta-method, we first generalize the Z house method specification procedures (that require informal documentation of specification parts) to include the predicative notation and the refinement calculus notation. Then, we supplement the Z house method steps with proof rules (for procedural refinement and data transformation) from predicative programming and the refinement calculus. The supplementation step requires us to show how procedural refinement (and other proof techniques, e.g., for data transformation) apply to heterogeneous specifications. We summarize how procedural refinement applies to heterogeneous specifications here; other proof techniques are discussed in [Pai97].

The procedural refinement rules are based on the refinement relations from [Heh93] and [Mor94]. Their definitions are summarized here for completeness.

Definition 3 [Mor94]. A specification statement S is refined by a specification statement T (written $S \sqsubseteq T$) if $\forall R' \bullet wp(S, R') \Rightarrow wp(T, R')$, where R' is a relation on pre- and poststate.

Definition 4 [Heh93]. A predicative specification P is refined by a specification Q if $\forall \sigma, \sigma' \bullet (P \Leftarrow Q)$, where σ and σ' denote the prestate and poststate, respectively.

We now outline a small collection of rules for refinement over formal heterogeneous specifications. Further rules—and results on proof of satisfiability and data transformation—can be found in [Pai97].

4.1 Application of refinement

We briefly summarize several rules that demonstrate how to apply the refinement relations $\Leftarrow$ and $\sqsubseteq$ to operands of types other than predicate and specification statement. In the following, σ is the state.

Rule 4.1 *Let P and Q be predicates. If $\forall \sigma, \sigma' \bullet (P \Leftarrow Q)$ then $P \sqsubseteq Q$.*

Proof:

$$P \sqsubseteq Q = \forall \sigma, R' \bullet (wp(P, R') \Rightarrow wp(Q, R'))$$

$$\{\text{translation } PredToWp \text{ from [Pai97]}\}$$

$$= \forall \sigma, R' \bullet ((\forall \sigma' \bullet P \Rightarrow R') \Rightarrow (\forall \sigma' \bullet Q \Rightarrow R'))$$

$$\{\text{monotonicity}\}$$

$$\Leftarrow \forall \sigma, R' \bullet \forall \sigma' \bullet ((P \Rightarrow R') \Rightarrow (Q \Rightarrow R'))$$

$$\{\text{antimonotonicity}\}$$

$$\Leftarrow \forall \sigma, \sigma' \bullet (P \Leftarrow Q)$$

Rule 4.2 *For Z schemas S_p, S_q with invariants P and Q,*

$$S_p \sqsubseteq S_q = (\exists \sigma' \bullet P \Rightarrow \exists \sigma' \bullet Q) \wedge (\exists \sigma' \bullet P \Rightarrow \forall \sigma' \bullet (P \Leftarrow Q)).$$

Proof: By translation *ZToSS*, Definition 3, and manipulation.

We can also apply the refinement relation of the predicative notation to non-predicate operands. We show how it applies to Z schemas and Larch interface language operations.

Rule 4.3 *For Z schemas S_p, S_q with invariants P and Q,*

$$(S_p \Leftarrow S_q) = \forall \sigma, \sigma' \bullet ((\exists \sigma' \bullet Q) \Rightarrow Q) \Rightarrow ((\exists \sigma' \bullet P) \Rightarrow P)$$

Proof: By translations *ZToSS*, *SSToPred*, and manipulation.

Rule 4.4 *Let L and M be LCL functions with identical function interfaces, where both have* **modifies** *clause w, and where L and M have* **requires** *clauses P and U respectively, and* **ensures** *clauses Q and V respectively. Then*

$$L \Leftarrow M = \forall w, w' \bullet ((P \Rightarrow Q) \Leftarrow (U \Rightarrow V)).$$

A further result tells us that a specification statement is always refined by its predicate translation.

Rule 4.5 *If $S \mathrel{\widehat{=}} w : [\ pre, post\ ]$ is a specification statement and $preds$ is its predicate translation, then $S \sqsubseteq preds$.*

Proof:

$$S \sqsubseteq preds = \forall R' \bullet wp(S, R') \Rightarrow wp(preds, R')$$

$$\{\text{definition, distributivity, } PredToWp \}$$

$$\Leftarrow \forall w', R' \bullet (pre \wedge (post \Rightarrow R')) \Rightarrow ((pre \Rightarrow post) \Rightarrow R'),$$

and the last line is a theorem.

We can generalize the result of Rule 4.5: two further rules allow us to introduce predicates or specification statements in the process of a development.

Rule 4.6 *Let P and Q be predicates, and $spec_P$ and $spec_Q$ their translations into specification statements (using translation $PredToSS_1$ or $PredToSS_2$). If $P \Leftarrow Q$ then $P \sqsubseteq spec_Q$.*

Rule 4.7 *Let S and T be specification statements, and $pred_S$ and $pred_T$ their translations into predicates. If $S \sqsubseteq T$ then $S \sqsubseteq pred_T$.*

Proof of 4.7 By Rule 4.5, $T \sqsubseteq pred_T$. If $S \sqsubseteq T$, then by monotonicity of $\sqsubseteq$, $S \sqsubseteq pred_T$.

Finally, we discover that refinement is actually preserved over translation from specification statements to predicates.

Rule 4.8 *For specification statements S and T, and their predicate translations $pred_S$ and $pred_T$, $(S \sqsubseteq T) \Rightarrow (pred_S \Leftarrow pred_T)$.*

Proof: By translation $PredToSS$, and since $[a \Rightarrow (c \wedge (b \Leftarrow d))] \Rightarrow [(a \Rightarrow b) \Leftarrow (c \Rightarrow d)]$ is a tautology for all a, b, c, and d.

Other results and rules are possible; they can be obtained by generalizing or specializing the results presented, and by using the basic translations.

4.2   Refinement over conjunction and disjunction

We describe refinement rules for application over conjunction and disjunction. More rules are described in [Pai97]; see [War93] for an alternative approach to combining specification statements with Z combinators. In the following, let S, S' and T be specification statements, and P and Q be predicates.

Rule 4.9 *If $S \sqsubseteq T$ then $P \wedge S \sqsubseteq P \wedge T$.*

Proof:

$$
\begin{aligned}
P \wedge S \sqsubseteq P \wedge T &= \forall R' \bullet (wp(P \wedge S, R') \Rightarrow wp(P \wedge T, R')) \\
&\qquad \{PredToWp,\ \text{splitting law}\} \\
&= \forall R', \sigma' \bullet ((P \wedge S \Rightarrow R') \Rightarrow (P \wedge T \Rightarrow R')) \\
&\qquad \{\text{antimonotonicity}\} \\
&\Leftarrow \forall \sigma' \bullet (P \wedge T \Rightarrow P \wedge S) \\
&\qquad \{\text{monotonicity, Rule 4.7}\} \\
&\Leftarrow S \sqsubseteq T
\end{aligned}
$$

Rule 4.10 *Let $pred_S$ and $pred_T$ be the predicate specification equivalents of S and T (assuming S and T are not angelic). If $\forall \sigma, \sigma' \bullet (pred_S \Leftarrow pred_T)$ then $P \vee S \sqsubseteq P \vee T$.*

Combining Rule 4.10 with Rule 4.8, we determine that:

Corollary 1 *If $S \sqsubseteq T$ then $P \vee S \sqsubseteq P \vee T$.*

Specification statements that are conjoined or disjoined together can also be refined by parts.

Rule 4.11 *Providing that S, S', and T are all expressible in predicates,*

$$(S \wedge T \sqsubseteq S' \wedge T) \Leftarrow S \sqsubseteq S',$$
$$(S \vee T \sqsubseteq S' \vee T) \Leftarrow S \sqsubseteq S'.$$

Rule 4.11 gives us a form of monotonicity over predicate combinators. The proof is similar to that for Rule 4.9.

As is shown in [War93], refinement over schema conjunction and disjunction is not monotonic. However, we can combine schemas (and other specifications) via predicate operators $\vee$ and $\wedge$ and refine them. Let S_x, S_y, and S_z be schemas. Then:

Rule 4.12

$$(S_x \wedge S_y \sqsubseteq S_z \wedge S_y) \Leftarrow S_x \sqsubseteq S_z,$$
$$(S_x \vee S_y \sqsubseteq S_z \vee S_y) \Leftarrow (S_x \Leftarrow S_z).$$

Rules for refinement over sequential composition are given in [Pai97], as are rules for heterogeneous development, i.e., rules for changing notation during a development via a refinement step. We give an example of how to use some of these rules in Section 6.

5 Combining Formal and Semiformal Methods

Structured Analysis and Design Technique (SADT) [MaM88] was invented by Ross in the early 1970s. It claims to allow easy representation of system characteristics like control, feedback and mechanism. It contains explicit procedures for group work, and is based on the specification and elucidation of diagrams. There is a rigorous set of rules for the construction of the diagrams. We consider a basic version of the SADT method here solely in the context of software specification and design.

We apply the meta-method from Section 3 in integrating SADT with predicative programming. The base method is SADT; predicative programming is the invasive method. SADT procedures will be generalized to using predicative notations. Specifically, the procedures for authoring and data modelling will be generalized to use predicative notations. After generalization, the procedures will be supplemented by predicative programming refinement rules. In particular, the SADT steps for refinement, data modelling, authoring, and implementation will be supplemented by predicative refinement rules. We depict the integrated method in Fig. 5.

In Fig. 5, ellipses represent procedure steps (and thick arrows between ellipses represent ordering of steps), and boxes describe heterogeneous products. Arrows from ellipses to boxes denote usage or creation of the product by the procedure step.

In more detail, the integrated method procedure is as follows.

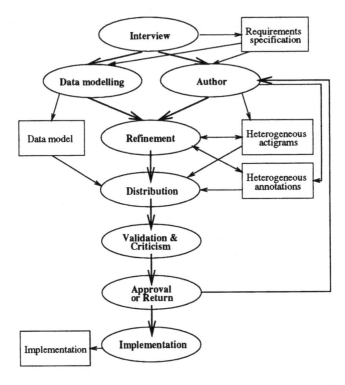

Fig. 5. SADT/predicative programming integrated method

1. *Interview.* The clients, customers, and users are interviewed so as to gather requirements. A requirements specification is written in a notation appropriate for the task.

> **ASIDE.** Steps 2, 3, and 4 can occur in parallel. We write them sequentially here for ease of presentation. **END OF ASIDE.**

2. *Authoring of heterogeneous specifications.* A heterogeneous system specification is constructed. Actigrams, datagrams, and annotations are produced using compositions of SADT notations and predicate notations. Typically, the predicate notation will be confined to the expression of annotations, but visual depictions of predicates could be used, too.
3. *Data modelling and data dictionary construction.* Data is designed and modelled, and a heterogeneous data dictionary (written using pseudocode, regular expressions, and predicate notations) is constructed.
4. *Refinement of heterogeneous specifications.* The actigrams and datagrams are refined hierarchically. SADT rules are used to syntactically check the steps. Predicate partial specifications are refined using Definition 4, and proof rules from [Heh93].
5. *Distribution.* The refined heterogeneous specification is distributed to a review committee. The committee should be familiar with the SADT notations and conventions, and at least one member should be familiar with the

predicative notation, for reading processing details. The specification writers should be prepared to informally explain or document the formal parts of the heterogeneous specification, and to explain the heterogeneous basis.

6. *Validation and Criticism.* The specification is reviewed and criticized. Syntax is validated according to SADT rules. The syntax and satisfiability of predicate specifications is checked. The connections between the SADT boxes and the predicate specifications are validated given the precise meaning of the composition. The SADT and predicate interfaces should be syntactically verified using the syntactic rules of SADT; predicate parts will be informally treated as SADT annotations for the purposes of review.

7. *Approval or Repair.* The specification is approved, or sent back to Step 2 (or Step 4) for repair.

8. *Implementation.* The specification is implemented in a hierarchical fashion by standard SADT practice and by predicate refinement, data transformation, transliteration, and component integration. Testing of the product should also occur.

At several steps of the method, SADT produces documentation (e.g., glossaries, diagrams, supplements, narratives; see [MaM88]). We do not discuss the effects of method integration on these products here in the interests of conserving space. One can take the view that the predicative notation is just another form of documentation for the SADT method, though it is documentation that can be formally manipulated.

Some of the properties we obtain with this integrated method are as follows.

- *Restrictability:* the predicate notation need be used only when required for describing actigram annotations. Restrictability is convenient to obtain with this integration, due to the structured style of specification offered by the use of SADT actigram and datagram notations.
- *Gradual introduction:* predicative programming can be gradually introduced into the SADT method by restricting the use of predicates to the specification and development of those system parts where the notation seems necessary, and by applying restrictability over time.
- *Semantic gaps:* the semantic gaps introduced by using a formal method in a development are reduced due to the heterogeneous basis and restrictability.
- *Method transformation:* transformations between the heterogeneous specifications of the SADT/predicate method and pure predicate or pure SADT are possible, as are partial transformations, by the translations from Section 2 and by producing informal extraction procedures.

6   A Small Formal Example

We have only the space to present a very small example of using integrated formal methods. For this reason, we choose to demonstrate the use of a combination of formal methods. The example combines predicative programming [Heh93] and the refinement calculus [Mor94]. The intent is only to give the flavour of using multiple methods together. Further examples are presented in [Pai97]; these examples in particular include integrations of formal and semiformal methods, and further examples of integrating and using multiple formal methods.

The problem is as follows. We are presented with two equal-length lists of lower-case letters (representing, typically, English words). We are to determine if the two lists are anagrams (i.e., permutations) of each other. If they are, we are to compute the number of *position differences* over the two lists (a position difference for a character c that is in both L and M is the absolute difference in indices for c in L and M. A strategy must be developed for handling multiple occurrences of characters in lists.)

We specify the problem in two parts. The two lists are L and M. We declare a constant list $ALPH = [`a; `b; ..; `z]$. The global variables are b, which is set to true iff L and M are anagrams; and np, the number of position differences between L and M. The initial specification is as follows.

$$anagram \ .$$

$$\textbf{if } b \rightarrow numpos$$
$$[]\neg b \rightarrow \textbf{skip}$$
$$\textbf{fi}$$

(The predicate . operator is dependent composition, i.e., sequencing.) *anagram* is a predicate. It is defined as follows, using the notation of [Heh93].

$$anagram \mathrel{\hat{=}} b' = \forall j : 0, ..26 \bullet ((\mathord{\mathsf{\phi}}\,\S i : 0, ..\#L \bullet Li = ALPH(j)) =$$
$$(\mathord{\mathsf{\phi}}\,\S i : 0, ..\#L \bullet Mi = ALPH(j)))$$

(§ is the bunch quantifier [Heh93], and $\mathord{\mathsf{\phi}}$ is the bunch cardinality operator.) *numpos* is a specification statement that counts the number of position differences between L and M.

$$numpos \mathrel{\hat{=}} \ np : [\ np' = \sum i : 0, ..26 \bullet \sum j : 0, ..\#N \bullet$$
$$abs([k : 0; ..\#L \mid L(k) = ALPH(i)]j -$$
$$[k : 0; ..\#L \mid M(k) = ALPH(i)]j)$$
$$]$$

where $N \mathrel{\hat{=}} \S k : 0, ..\#L \bullet L(k) = ALPH(i)$. Note that for multiple occurrences of c, we always take the difference of the smallest *unmatched* indices.

The refinement relation $\Leftarrow$ is monotonic over dependent composition. Therefore, we can refine *anagram* without affecting *numpos* or the guarded selection. The approach to refining the *anagram* specification will be to iterate through the alphabet, and for each letter of the alphabet count the number of occurrences of the letter in each of lists L and M. L and M are permutations iff they have the same number of occurrences of each letter. A refinement goes as follows. First, define P like so.

$$P \mathrel{\hat{=}} ((\mathord{\mathsf{\phi}}\,\S i : 0, ..\#L \bullet Li = ALPH(j)) = (\mathord{\mathsf{\phi}}\,\S i : 0, ..\#L \bullet Mi = ALPH(j))$$

Then:

$$anagram \Leftarrow b := \mathsf{T}.\ k := 0.\ b' = b \wedge \forall j : k, ..26 \bullet P \qquad (1)$$

The predicate at the end of the dependent composition (1) is refined as a selection.

$$\Leftarrow \textbf{if } k = 26 \textbf{ then skip}$$
$$\textbf{else } k \neq 26 \Rightarrow b' = b \wedge \forall j : k, ..26 \bullet P$$

The predicate in the **else**-branch can be implemented by defining three new variables, s, sM, and sL, that will be used to iterate through the lists L and M and to keep track of the number of occurrences of the letter $ALPH(k)$.

$$\Leftarrow \textbf{var } s, sL, sM : nat \bullet$$
$$s, sL, sM := 0, 0, 0 .$$
$$k \neq 26 \Rightarrow b' = b \wedge \forall j : k, ..26 \bullet Q .\quad \lhd$$
$$k := k + 1 .\ b' = b \wedge \forall j : k, ..26 \bullet P$$

where

$$Q \mathrel{\widehat{=}} (sL + \natural \S i : s, ..\#L \bullet Li = ALPH(j)) =$$
$$(sM + \natural \S i : s, ..\#L \bullet Mi = ALPH(j))$$

Finally, the predicate marked with a $\lhd$ can be refined by a simple selection that updates the counters.

$$\Leftarrow \textbf{if } s = \#L \textbf{ then } b := b \wedge (sL = sM) \textbf{ else } ($$
$$sL, sM, s := sL + (\textbf{if } Ls = ALPH(k) \textbf{ then } 1 \textbf{ else } 0),$$
$$sM + (\textbf{if } Ms = ALPH(k) \textbf{ then } 1 \textbf{ else } 0),$$
$$s + 1 .$$
$$k \neq 26 \Rightarrow b' = b \wedge \forall j : k, ..26 \bullet Q)$$

The development is now complete. Notice that we have used a recursive refinement [Heh93] in the last step above, instead of developing a loop structure.

The next step is to refine *numpos*. We can do this using $\sqsubseteq$ due to Rule 4.8. The refinement requires two loops. The outer loop will iterate over the alphabet, while the inner loop will iterate over the lists and will calculate the lists of indices where specific letters of the alphabet appear. The refinement proceeds as follows (omitting details due to space constraints), based on the standard development steps outlined in [Mor94] for loops (this includes using *leading* and *following* assignment laws).

$$numpos \sqsubseteq i, np := 0, 0;$$
$$\textbf{do } i \neq 26 \rightarrow$$
$$np : [\, (0 \leq i < 26) \wedge I, I' \,];\quad \lhd$$
$$i := i + 1$$
$$\textbf{od}$$

An invariant is $I \mathrel{\hat{=}} np = \sum r : 0, ..i \bullet R$, where R is:

$$R \mathrel{\hat{=}} \sum j : 0, ..\#N \bullet$$
$$abs([k : 0; ..\#L \mid L(k) = ALPH(r)]j - [k : 0; ..\#L \mid M(k) = ALPH(r)]j)$$

A bound function is $26 - i$. The new specification statement marked with a $\lhd$ can be refined by adding three fresh variables and a loop over the list; these variables are used in determining the indices for a specific letter of the alphabet. The results of the list determination are subtracted, and this new result added to np to preserve the loop invariant. We again apply the laws leading and following assignment, and introduce the loop using the checklist from [Mor94].

$$\sqsubseteq \;\| [\;\mathbf{var}\; j : \mathbb{N}; \; A, B : \mathrm{seq}_{\#L} \,\mathbb{N} \cdot$$
$$j, A, B := 0, \langle \rangle, \langle \rangle;$$
$$\mathbf{do}\; j \neq \#L \rightarrow$$
$$A, B : [\; (0 \leq j < \#L) \wedge J, J'; \;]; \qquad \lhd$$
$$j := j + 1$$
$$\mathbf{od};$$
$$np := np + \sum k : 0, ..\#A \bullet abs(A(k) - B(k))$$
$$] |$$

The invariant J in the above loop is

$$J \mathrel{\hat{=}} A = [k : 0; ..j \mid M(k) = ALPH(i)] \wedge B = [k : 0; ..j \mid L(k) = ALPH(i)]$$

The bound function is $\#L - j$. The final refinement of the specification marked with $\lhd$ is straightforward: a selection is added that concatenates the current value of j to the lists A and B if the conditions in the invariants are met.

$$\sqsubseteq \mathbf{if}\; M(j) = ALPH(i) \rightarrow A := A \frown [j] \;\mathbf{fi};$$
$$\mathbf{if}\; L(j) = ALPH(i) \rightarrow B := B \frown [j] \;\mathbf{fi}$$

(where $\frown$ is list concatenation). If $\sum$ is not an implemented combinator in the programming language, then we need to refine the last sum (and addition to np) in the last line of the refinement tree. This can be done by introducing a simple loop or recursive refinement (which we omit here due to space constraints). Note that such a refinement can be done using either predicative refinement *or* weakest precondition refinement; the preferences of the developer can be taken into account.

By Rule 4.8 and the monotonicity of $\Leftarrow$ and $\sqsubseteq$ over dependent composition, the composition of the refinements is a refinement of the original specification, and we have implemented a solution.

7 Conclusions

We have briefly described a meta-method for integrating formal methods with other methods. We have provided two examples of using the meta-method: an integration of several formal methods; and an integration of a program design calculus with a structured method. The approach to integration is based on combining notations; formal method integration is based on combining notations, and manipulating procedures of methods to accommodate and use the new notations. Future work will encompass more and larger case studies, and will see us consider a wider spectrum of methods in integration. We will also look at constructing formal models of methods, in order to be able to speak precisely about the relationships we are defining between them. Finally, we will consider other approaches to giving semantics to heterogeneous specifications—particularly, union approaches, where the semantics of all specifications can be expressed in compositions.

Acknowledgements

Thanks to Ric Hehner, Pamela Zave, and the three anonymous referees for their excellent suggestions and advice.

References

[Bac90]   R.J.R. Back. Refinement calculus II: parallel and reactive programs. In *Stepwise Refinement of Distributed Systems*, LNCS 430, Springer-Verlag, 1990.

[BaV89]   R.J.R. Back and J. von Wright. A Lattice-Theoretical Basis for a Specification Language. In *Mathematics of Program Construction*, LNCS 375, Springer-Verlag, 1989.

[BoH94]   J. Bowen and M. Hinchey. Ten Commandments of Formal Methods. Oxford University Computing Laboratory Technical Monograph, 1994.

[CoY90]   P. Coad and E. Yourdon. *Object-oriented Analysis*, Prentice-Hall, 1990.

[DeM79]   T. DeMarco. *Structured Analysis and System Specification*, Yourdon Press, 1979.

[DeM82]   T. DeMarco. *Controlling Software Projects: Management, Measurement, and Estimation.* Yourdon Press, 1982.

[GuH93]   J.V. Guttag and J.J. Horning. *Larch: Languages and Tools for Formal Specification*, Springer-Verlag, 1993.

[Hal96]   A. Hall. Using Formal Methods to Develop an ATC Information System. *IEEE Software*, March 1996.

[Ham94]   J. Hammond. Producing Z Specifications from Object-Oriented Analysis. In *Proc. Eighth Z User Meeting*, Cambridge, Springer-Verlag, 1994.

[HeM88]   E.C.R. Hehner and A.J. Malton. Termination Conventions and Comparative Semantics, *Acta Informatica*, 25 (1988).

[Heh93]   E.C.R. Hehner. *A Practical Theory of Programming*, Springer-Verlag, 1993.

[Hil91]   J.V. Hill. Software development methods in practice. In *Proc. Sixth Annual Conference on Computer Assurance*, 1991.

[Hoa85]   C.A.R. Hoare. *Communicating Sequential Processes*, Prentice-Hall, 1985.

494

[Jac95]   M.A. Jackson. *Software Requirements and Specifications*, Addison-Wesley, 1995.

[Kin90]   S. King. Z and the refinement calculus. In *VDM '90: VDM and Z - Formal Methods in Software Development*, Third international symposium of VDM Europe, LNCS 428, Springer-Verlag, 1990.

[Kro93]   K. Kronlöf, ed. *Method Integration: Concepts and Case Studies*, Wiley, 1993.

[LKP91]   P. Larsen, J. van Katwijk, N. Plat, K. Pronk, and H. Toetenel. Towards an integrated combination of SA and VDM. In *Proc. Methods Integration Workshop*, Springer-Verlag, 1991.

[MaM88]   D.A. Marca and C.L. McGowan. *SADT - Structured Analysis and Design Technique*, McGraw-Hill, 1988.

[Met94]   Project MetaPHOR Group, MetaPHOR: Metamodeling, Principles, Hypertext, Objects and Repositories. Technical Report TR-7, University of Jyvaskyla, 1994.

[Mor94]   C.C. Morgan. *Programming from Specifications*, Prentice-Hall, Second Edition, 1994.

[Pai97]   R.F. Paige. *Formal Method Integration via Heterogeneous Notations*, PhD Dissertation, July 1997.

[PWM93]   F. Polack, M. Whiston, and K.C. Mander. The SAZ Project: Integrating SSADM and Z. In *Proc. FME '93: Industrial-strength Formal Methods*, LNCS 670, Springer-Verlag, 1993.

[ScR77]   K. Schoman and D. Ross. Structured Analysis for requirements definition, *IEEE Trans. on Software Engineering*, 3(1), 1977.

[SFD92]   L.T. Semmens, R.B. France, and T.W. Docker. Integrated Structured Analysis and Formal Specification Techniques, *The Computer Journal* 35(6), June 1992.

[Spi89]   J.M. Spivey. *The Z Notation: A Reference Manual*, Prentice-Hall, 1989.

[War93]   N. Ward. Adding specification constructors to the refinement calculus. In *Proc. FME '93: Industrial-strength Formal Methods*, LNCS 670, Springer-Verlag, 1993.

[WiZ92]   J.M. Wing and A.M. Zaremski. Unintrusive ways to integrate formal specifications in practice. In *VDM '91: Formal Software Development Methods*, Fourth International Symposium of VDM Europe, LNCS 551, Springer-Verlag, 1992.

[WoM91]   J.C.P. Woodcock and C.C. Morgan. Refinement of state-based concurrent systems. In *VDM '90: VDM and Z - Formal Methods in Software Development*, Third International Symposium of VDM Europe, LNCS 428, Springer-Verlag, 1990.

[YoC79]   E. Yourdon and L. Constantine. *Structured Design*, Prentice-Hall, 1979.

[ZaJ93]   P. Zave and M. Jackson. Conjunction as Composition, *ACM Trans. on Software Engineering and Methodology*, 2(4), October 1993.

[ZaJ95]   P. Zave and M. Jackson. Where do operations come from? An approach to multiparadigm specification, *IEEE Trans. on Software Engineering*, 12(7), July 1996.

[ZaM93]   P. Zave and P. Mataga. A formal specification of some important 5ESS features, Part I: Overview. AT&T Bell Laboratories Technical Memorandum, October 1993.

Reuse of Verified Design Templates
Through Extended Pattern Matching

David Hemer and Peter A. Lindsay

Software Verification Research Centre
School of Information Technology,
The University of Queensland, Brisbane 4072, Australia
{hemer,pal}@it.uq.edu.au

Abstract. CARE provides a framework for construction and verification of programs, based around the recording of reusable design knowledge in parameterized templates. This paper shows how pattern-matching can be used to aid in the selection and application of design templates from a reusable library. A general framework is presented which is independent of the particular matching algorithm used at the level of mathematical expressions. A prototype has been built which supports a large subset of the Z mathematical language.

Keywords: formal methods, program development, refinement, software verification, pattern matching

1 Introduction

1.1 Outline of CARE

Development of formally verified software is often seen as a difficult, time consuming task, requiring somewhat esoteric mathematical skills. The CARE approach [4, 9] attempts to address this problem by providing a library of reusable, pre-proven design templates, which the software engineer can use to develop formally verified programs.

CARE stands for **Computer Assisted Refinement Engineering**. CARE provides a framework within which specification, programming and verification knowledge can be recorded and reused with minimal need for re-proof. The CARE project has been exploring the use of a library of design templates for which most of the difficult parts of modelling and proof have been done once, off-line, by suitably skilled experts. CARE tools then help the user build applications by selecting and instantiating pre-proven refinements to fit the problem at hand, and generating and discharging correctness-of-fit proof obligations. Other CARE tools synthesize compilable source code programs which can be integrated with other system components and tested using common integration testing techniques.

The CARE method is generic and can be tailored for use with different specification languages, programming languages and theorem provers. In particular, it can be used to construct verified software for programming languages which themselves do not have a full formal semantics, by restricting use of target-language code to formally specified library routines which have been verified off-line using techniques appropriate to the target language.

CARE was developed through a collaboration between Telectronics Pacing Systems and the Software Verification Research Centre. Telectronics develops and manufactures software-driven medical devices such as implantable defibrillators. The company has long been motivated to investigate the use of formal methods for the economical and timely development of provably correct software. Specifically, Telectronics had used formal specifications in the development of some of its products, but wanted a method and tools to help verify code and to enable tracing of requirements from specifications through to code and construction of product variants [2]. A grant from the Australian Government enabled more extensive development of the ideas and the construction of a prototype tool-set to support the method.

The prototype tool-set has been populated with a large library of design templates and primitive components for numbers, sets, lists, arrays and records. We have used the CARE method on a number of medium-sized applications including verification of the design of an event logger such as might be used in an embedded device [8]. The tools themselves have been formally specified [3].

1.2 CARE programs

A CARE program consists of types, fragments and theorems. CARE types correspond to data structures; fragments correspond roughly to functions and procedures in a procedural programming language; and theorems correspond to definitions, lemmas and CARE proof obligations (explained below).

Each CARE program component has its own formal specification, which may include constraints on how the component can be used. Program components are classified as *primitive* or *higher-level*. In essence, primitive components are those whose proof of correctness is outside the scope of CARE, while higher-level components have associated proof obligations. More specifically:

Primitive components are supplied as part of the CARE library, and are not written by the ordinary user. Primitive types and fragments are implemented directly in the target programming language and provide access to target language data structures and basic functionality. (B uses a similar approach [7].) The specification of such a component describes the component in terms of a mathematical model of the semantics of the target language and its compiler: a primitive type's specification describes the set of mathematical values corresponding to the associated data structure; a primitive fragment's specification describes the associated target code's functionality. Primitive theorems are axioms; their statement is their "specification".

Higher-level components are constructed from other components. Higher-level types and fragments express data refinements and algorithm designs respectively, and are implemented in a special-purpose language with a formally-defined mathematical semantics; using this semantics, CARE tools generate proof obligations which show that the component's implementation is correct with respect to its specification (see §3.2 below). Higher-level theorems (lemmas) are "implemented" by proofs.

CARE differs from most other formal software development methods by supporting incremental working – top-down, bottom-up or in a mixture of styles. During development a CARE program may contain components which have specifications but which do not yet have implementations. A complete CARE program is one in which all components are implemented.

1.3 This paper

This paper explains the CARE approach and illustrates some of the main concepts. §2 below introduces the CARE integrated specification and implementation language. §3 outlines how verified programs are developed using CARE. §4 discusses matching at the level of mathematical expressions, §5 extends it to CARE program components, and §6 extends it to whole design templates. §7 illustrates how matching can be used to develop verified programs from a library of pre-verified design templates. §8 discusses ways of improving the effectiveness of library searches by modifying the matching function to take advantage of the semantics of CARE constructs. The examples all use Z-like naming conventions.

2 The CARE language

This section describes the CARE language in more detail. In the rest of this paper, CARE values and types are written in `typewriter` font and mathematical expressions are written in *italics*.

2.1 Mathematical definitions

The mathematical theory part of a CARE program consists of: signatures and axiomatic definitions of constants, functions and predicates; declarations of "generic" (not-further-defined) sorts and definitions of other sorts; and lemmas, with or without their proofs. For example, Fig. 1 shows the definition of a function *append* which appends a value onto the head of a list, and a lemma for calculating the range of an appended list.

2.2 Types

A CARE type declaration consists of a name, a specification and an implementation. The specification is an expression denoting the sort of mathematical values that objects of the type can take. For example, Fig. 4 contains specifications of CARE types for natural numbers, elements and sequences of elements.

Primitive types are implemented by some target language data structure. A higher-level type (the *refined type*) is implemented in terms of one or more other

---

Theory definition of function *append*.

$append : Elem \times \text{seq } Elem \to \text{seq } Elem;$

$\forall h : Elem; \ t : \text{seq } Elem \bullet append(h,t) = \langle h \rangle \frown t,$

$\forall s : \text{seq } Elem \bullet \#s \neq 0 \Rightarrow append(head(s), tail(s)) = s.$

Lemma ran_of_append.

$\forall e : X; \ s : \text{seq } X \bullet \text{ran}(append(e,s)) = (\text{ran } s) \cup \{e\}$

Fig. 1. Example theory components.

---

types (the corresponding *concrete types*) by data refinement; the specification describes the relationship between values of the refined type and their concrete representations (the *refinement relation*), an optional condition restricting the values that the refined type may take (the *constraint*), and an optional condition restricting the values the concrete types may take (the *invariant*). An example refined type is given in Fig. 5.

2.3 Fragment specifications

There are two kinds of fragments: *simple* and *branching*. Simple fragments correspond roughly to functions in a procedural programming language; they take inputs and return outputs.[1] Branching fragments differ from simple fragments by also allowing branching of control during execution. A non-standard feature of the CARE language is that branching fragments can return different numbers and kinds of outputs on different branches.

The number and type of inputs taken by a fragment is fixed. The specification of a simple fragment consists of a name, an optional *precondition*, a list of outputs and their types, and the required input/output relationship (or *postcondition*). For example, Fig. 3 gives specifications of the simple fragments nil, car and cdr for manipulating lists, using LISP-like naming conventions.

The specification of a branching fragment consists of its name, an optional precondition and a sequence of guarded branches. Each branch contains a *test*, a description of the outputs and their types, an optional postcondition, and a *report*, which identifies the branch. (The test in the last branch is true by default.) Fig. 4 gives examples of specifications of branching fragments search and decompose. Note that the number and type of outputs on each branch is fixed but may differ from branch to branch. For example, the search(s,e) fragment has two cases: when e occurs in s, it reports found and returns an index i at which e can be found; otherwise it simply reports notfound with no outputs. The *guard* of a branch is its test conjoined with the negations of the tests of the preceding branches. For example the guard of the nonempty branch of decompose(s) is $\neg (\#s = 0)$.

---

[1] CARE has been extended to handle state-changing operations (not treated here).

Note that fragment specifications may be under-determined, in the sense that more than one output may satisfy the postcondition for any given input: e.g. i in `search(s,e)`. In practice however, the postcondition is often an equation defining the output variables directly as a function of the input variables.

2.4 Fragment implementations

Primitive fragments are implemented by giving code segments in the target language. Higher-level fragments are implemented in terms of calls to other fragments. The CARE implementation language supports the following simple design constructs: assignment of values to local variables, fragment calls, sequencing, branching of control, and data refinement transformations. An *abort* statement is also provided, for use in branches which will never be executed.

Recursive calls and mutual recursion are allowed, provided the recursion eventually terminates. To establish termination, the CARE user supplies a well-founded variant function (or *variant* for short) whose value decreases on recursive calls and is bounded below. Fig. 4 contains example implementations, for branching fragments `search` and `searchAux`.

3 Construction of verified software with CARE

3.1 CARE programs

A CARE program consists of a collection of theories, types and fragments. Components may be specified but not yet implemented. A program is said to be *complete* if all components in the program have been implemented (and in particular, all proof obligations and lemmas have been proven); otherwise it is said to be *partial*.

3.2 Proof obligations

For each higher-level fragment in the program, a CARE tool generates proof obligations that check that the fragment's implementation satisfies its specification. The proof obligations for fragments fall into four categories:

Partial correctness: The result returned at each (non-aborting) leaf of an implementation tree satisfies the appropriate postcondition.
Termination: For recursively-defined fragments, the variant is strictly decreasing on recursive calls.
Well-formedness: For each fragment call, the fragment's precondition (if any) is satisfied.
Non-execution: Execution cannot reach an 'abort' leaf (at least, not for input values which satisfy the fragment's precondition).

For refined types, there are proof obligations to check that the refinement relation defines a function whose domain is given by the invariant and whose range is given by the constraint.

3.3 Templates

A CARE *design template* (or template, for short) is a reusable, parameterised collection of CARE types, fragments and theories, which together encapsulate a piece of design knowledge.[2] Templates can make use of formal parameters as well as textual parameters, ranging over component names. The prototype CARE library contains templates in each of the following categories:

theories: e.g. the theory for ordered sequences - see Fig. 2;

primitives: e.g. a template containing operations for manipulating linked lists, using LISP-like naming conventions - see Fig. 3;

families of algorithms: e.g. a search algorithm for lists - see Fig. 4;

data refinements: e.g. sets implemented as non-repeating lists - see Fig. 5.

Template Ordered Sequences is

Formal parameters: $X, \_ < \_ : X \times X$.

Applicability conditions:
$\forall a, b, c : X \bullet a < b \wedge b < c \Rightarrow a < c,$
$\forall a, b : X \bullet a < b \vee a = b \vee b < a.$

Theory definition of predicate *isOrderedSeq*.
$isOrderedSeq : \text{seq } X;$
$\forall s : \text{seq } X \bullet isOrderedSeq(s) \Leftrightarrow \forall i : 1 .. \#s - 1 \bullet s(i) < s(i+1).$

Lemma **singleton_isOrderedSeq**.
$\forall e : X \bullet isOrderedSeq(\langle e \rangle)$

Lemma **append_isOrderedSeq**.
$\forall h : X; \ t : \text{seq } X \bullet isOrderedSeq(append(h, t)) \Leftrightarrow$
$t = \langle \rangle \vee (h < head\ t \wedge isOrderedSeq(t))$

end template.

Fig. 2. A template containing theory for ordered sequences

Some or all of the types and fragments may have specifications but not implementations: in such cases, the template user is obliged to supply implementations later in the development. Similarly, some or all of the lemmas in the theory part may be assumptions (called *applicability conditions*); the template user is obliged to show that these follow as logical consequences from the definitions already

---

[2] CARE also provides a mechanism for modularisation of templates; space does not permit details to be presented here.

in the CARE program; for example, the template **Ordered Sequences** given in Fig. 2 has two applicability conditions, stating that the ordering relation must be transitive and it must obey the trichotomy law.

Note that in practice, the user may require only part of a template. The CARE template instantiation tool allows the user to indicate what components of the template are of interest; it then determines the complete set of components on which the nominated components depend (including all applicability conditions) and extracts them from the template, appropriately instantiated.

4 Matching on mathematical constructs

In what follows (a dialect of) Z is used to model an abstract syntax for the CARE language and matching functions over the language.[3] To start with, a mathematical expression can be either a sort, a formula or a term:

$$MathExpr == Sort \cup Fmla \cup Term$$

Note that mathematical expressions may contain formal parameters.

4.1 Instantiation

A *formal parameter instantiation* indicates the sorts, predicates and functions by which parameters are to be instantiated:

$$FPInst == FParam \twoheadrightarrow \text{seq } Var \times MathExpr$$

We shall write, e.g. $f(x, y) \rightsquigarrow body$ for $f \mapsto (\langle x, y \rangle, body)$. In practice, signatures are also supplied for predicate and function parameters as part of the instantiation, but they will not be modelled here.

The function *instantiate* takes a mathematical expression (the *pattern*) and an instantiation and forms a new mathematical expression (the *target*) by replacing occurences of formal parameters in the pattern in accordance with the instantiation map. The form of instantiation used in CARE is logically sound: the result of instantiating all expressions in a proof is again a proof. The function's signature only is given here; details are straightforward.

$$instantiate : MathExpr \times FPInst \twoheadrightarrow MathExpr$$

When formal parameters remain in the *target*, the instantiation is referred to as a *partial* instantiation.

---

[3] As presented here, some of the definitions are not type-correct with respect to standard Z, but the explanation should be clear enough to satisfy most readers. $\twoheadrightarrow$ represents finite functions, $\twoheadrightarrow$ partial functions, $\mathbb{F}$ finite power sets, and $\mathbb{P}$ arbitrary power sets.

Template **Linked Lists** is

    Formal parameters: X.

    Type **Elem** has specification: X.

    Type **LList** has specification: seq X
    implementation: *appropriate code for linked list type declarations*

    Fragment **nil()** has specification:
        output **s:LList** such that $s = \langle \rangle$
    implementation: *code for the empty list*

    Fragment **car(s:LList)** has specification:
        precondition $\#s \neq 0$
        output **h:Elem** such that $h = head(s)$
    implementation: *code for finding the head of the list*

    Fragment **cdr(s:LList)** has specification:
        precondition $\#s \neq 0$
        output **t:LList** such that $t = tail(s)$
    implementation: *code for finding the tail of the list*

    Fragment **cons(e:Elem,s:LList)** has specification:
        output **r:LList** such that $r = append(e, s)$
    implementation: *code for appending an element onto the front of a linked list*

    Branching fragment **null(s:LList)** has specification:
        result defined by cases:
            if $\#s = 0$ then report **yes** else report no
    implementation: *code for checking for the null list*

    Branching fragment **decompose(s:LList)** has specification:
        result defined by cases:
            if $\#s = 0$ then report **empty**
            else report **nonempty** with outputs **h:Elem,t:LList**
                such that $s = append(h, t)$
    implementation:
        case **null(s)** of
          yes: report **empty**.
          no: report **nonempty** and return **car(s),cdr(s)**.
end template.

Fig. 3. Part of a template for linked lists primitives.

Example: The result of instantiating the expression

$$\forall\, a, b : S \bullet P(f(a, b)) \Rightarrow P(f(b, a))$$

with instantiation $S \leadsto \mathbb{FN}, P(x) \leadsto \#x = 0, f(x, y) = x \cap y$ is

$$\forall\, a, b : \mathbb{FN} \bullet \#(a \cap b) = 0 \Rightarrow \#(b \cap a) = 0.$$

4.2 Matching

The function *match* can be specified in terms of the *instantiate* function:

$$
\begin{array}{|l}
\hline
match : MathExpr \times MathExpr \rightarrow \mathbb{P}\, FPInst \\
\hline
\forall\, i : match(m_1, m_2) \bullet instantiate(m_1, i) =_\alpha m_2 \\
\end{array}
$$

where $=_\alpha$ is α-equivalence: i.e., equality up to renaming of bound variables.

Note that this is an underspecification of matching, in-as-much-as it requires that only matches be returned, but does not strictly require that all possible matches are returned. (A fuller specification might require, for example, that at least one match from each possible equivalence class of matches be returned [5]). The above specification is sufficient for the purposes of this paper however.

Example: Suppose P is a formal parameter ranging over 1-ary predicates, and a ranges over 0-ary functions (constants); then $P(a)$ matches the formula $0 = 0$ in each of the following ways:

$P(x) \leadsto$	$x = x$	$x = 0$	$0 = x$	$0 = 0$
$a \leadsto$	0	0	0	?

Space does not permit a full description of the matching algorithm used by CARE. Basically, it works on structural induction on the pattern, and returns a finite set of instantiations at each step. For example when the pattern is of the form $f(p_1, \ldots, p_m)$, and f is a constant (i.e. a non-parametric function), then the pattern matches only targets of the form $f(a_1, \ldots, a_m)$ such that each p_i matches a_i. Turning this around, the set of matches against $f(p_1, \ldots, p_m)$ can be found by merging (if possible) the sets formed by matching each p_i against a_i, using the following function:

$$
\begin{array}{|l}
\hline
mergeInstSets : \mathbb{F}(\mathbb{F}\, FPInst) \rightarrow \mathbb{F}\, FPInst \\
\hline
mergeInstSets\; \varnothing = \varnothing,\; mergeInstSets\; \{is\} = is \\
rest \neq \varnothing \Rightarrow \mathbf{let}\; is_2 = mergeInstSets(rest)\, \mathbf{in} \\
\qquad mergeInstSets(\{is_1\} \cup rest) = \{i_1 : is_1;\; i_2 : is_2 \bullet mergeInsts(i_1, i_2)\} \\
\end{array}
$$

Two instantiations are mergeable if they agree on their common part:

$$
\begin{array}{|l}
\hline
mergeInsts : FPInst \times FPInst \rightarrow FPInst \\
\hline
mergeInsts(i_1, i_2) = \mathbf{if}\; (\mathrm{dom}\, i_2) \lhd i_1 =_\alpha (\mathrm{dom}\, i_1) \lhd i_2 \\
\qquad\qquad \mathbf{then}\; i_1 \oplus i_2\; \mathbf{else}\; \varnothing \\
\end{array}
$$

where $=_\alpha$ stands for element-wise α-equivalence.

These ideas can be extended to give a complete matching algorithm for mathematical expressions. (Complete in the sense that all possible matches are returned, up to α-equivalence and subsetting: see [6] for details for a very similar syntax).

5 Extending matching to CARE program components

5.1 Modelling CARE program components

To extend matching to CARE program components, we need first to model their abstract syntax. For the purposes of this paper, CARE type specifications can be modelled as follows:

```
┌─ TypeSpec ──────────────────────────────
  name : TypeName
  spec : Sort
```

Fragment specifications can be modelled as follows:

```
┌─ FragSpec ──────────────────────────────
  name : FragName
  inputvars : VarDeclars
  precond : Fmla
  gsparts : seq₁ GSPart
```

Each guarded specification part is modelled as a 4-tuple, consisting of a guard, report, output variables and a post-condition:

$$GSPart == Fmla \times Report \times VarDeclars \times Fmla$$

The input and output variables (together with any local variables in fragment bodies) are modelled as an ordered sequence of variable/type pairs.

$$VarDeclars == \mathrm{seq}(Var \times TypeName)$$

A theorem specification can be modelled as follows:

```
┌─ TheoremSpec ───────────────────────────
  name : TheoremName
  statement : Fmla
```

Space does not permit treatment of component implementation here, but the details are straightforward.

5.2 Textual parameters, renaming and instantiation

At the CARE component level, as well as being able to instantiate formal parameters, we also need to be able to rename textual parameters. Using *Renaming* to stand for such renamings, we can define appropriate functions for performing renamings: e.g. *rename : TypeName × Renaming ↦ TypeName*. (To preserve meaning, the renaming function will sometimes need to rename bound variables within constructs, to avoid capture of free variables). In what follows, we overload *rename* and extend it to other CARE constructs.

A (CARE-level) *instantiation* thus consists of an instantiation of formal parameters together with a renaming of textual parameters:

$$Inst == FPInst \times Renaming$$

We can now extend the definition of *instantiate* appropriately:

> *instantiate : TypeSpec × Inst ↦ TypeSpec*
> ───
> *instantiate*$(T, (i, r))$*.name* = *rename*$(T.name, r)$
> *instantiate*$(T, (i, r))$*.spec* = *instantiate*$(T.spec, i)$

5.3 Component-wise matching

This section considers *exact* matching of CARE components; i.e. the situation where, after renaming textual parameters and instantiating formal parameters in the pattern, the result is α-equivalent to the target. (Here α-equivalence means equality up to renaming of variables bound anywhere in the component, including input and output variables.) It turns out that this form of matching is too strict to be much use in practice; in Section 8 we explore useful ways of relaxing the requirements to take advantage of the semantics of CARE constructs components and how they are used.

To start with however, we simply extend the specification of pattern-matching to CARE components in the obvious way: e.g.

> *match : TypeSpec × TypeSpec → ℙ Inst*
> ───
> $\forall i : match(T_1, T_2) \bullet instantiate(T_1, i) =_\alpha T_2$

It is now a straightforward matter to extend the matching algorithm for mathematical expressions to CARE constructs. For example to match type specification T_1 against T_2, where $T_1.name$ is a textual parameter, suppose i is a match for sorts $(T_1.spec, T_2.spec)$ and r is the renaming $\{T_1.name \leadsto T_2.name\}$; then (i, r) is a match for (T_1, T_2).

Similarly, the algorithm for matching a fragment specification pattern A with a target B proceeds as follows:

1. try to match the input variables and types of A and B;
2. try to match the output variables and types for each branch of A with the output variables in the corresponding branch of B (this only succeeds when there are equal numbers of branches);

3. try to match the guard and postconditions for each branch of A with the guard and postconditions in the corresponding branch of B;

4. finally, try to match the preconditions of A and B.

At each stage of the algorithm, zero or more instantiations are found. The results of these are merged with the instantiations found in the previous stage using a merge function similar to the one given in §4.2, but extended to include renaming of textual parameters. If any stage fails, then the algorithm terminates and returns the empty set of instantiations.

6 Matching and templates

6.1 Instantiation

Templates and programs can be modelled simply as sets of CARE components. To extend the definition of instantiation to templates, we must also include the set of (names of) components in which the user is interested:

$$TempInst == FPInst \times Renaming \times \mathbb{F} \, CompName$$

where

$$CompName == FragName \cup TypeName \cup TheoremName$$

Space does not permit a full definition of the template instantiation function here, but its signature is given by:

$$\mid \quad instantiate : Template \times TempInst \rightarrow ComponentSet$$

The results returned by the template instantiation tool are then processed by the *worksheet manager* which checks that no conflicts will arise. For example, if A is a fully implemented component whose specification agrees with that of a specified-only component B on the worksheet, then A can be added to the worksheet to provide an implementation of B.

6.2 Matching

To search the library for appropriate templates, we supply a *search query*, consisting of a set of component specifications. The search tool then looks for templates which contain components which match any or all of the components in the query. The tool uses the following function:

$$\begin{array}{|l} match : Template \times Query \rightarrow \mathbb{P} \, TempInst \\ \hline \forall \, \tau : match(t,q) \bullet instantiate(t,\tau) =_s q \end{array}$$

where the relation $=_s$ between two component sets holds if for each component specification in one set there is an α-equivalent component specification in the other set.

An algorithm for finding the matches between a template with components $\{t_1, .., t_m\}$ and search query with components $\{q_1, .., q_n\}$ is as follows:

1. Form the set F of all partial surjective mappings from $\{1, .., m\}$ to $\{1, .., n\}$ (since m and n are finite, then F is also finite).
2. For each $f \in F$:
   (a) form the instantiation sets $match(t_j, q_{f(j)})$ for each $j \in \text{dom} f$;
   (b) merge the sets to form a single set of instantiations i_f;
   (c) from i_f, form the set of template instantiations τ_f, by replacing each 2-tuple of the form (i, r), with the 3-tuple

   $$(i, r, \{t_j.name \mid j \in \text{dom} f\})$$

3. Return the union of all τ_f's: i.e. $\bigcup\{f \in F \bullet \tau_f\}$.

7   Example uses of matching

We illustrate how matching can be applied to a library of design templates to develop CARE programs.

7.1   Development of an algorithm

To illustrate the use of templates and matching, suppose we are given the following specifications for a search problem:

Branching fragment find(s:WordList,e:Word) has specification:
  result defined by cases:
    if $e \in \text{ran} \, s$ then report found
    with output i:Index such that $s(i) = e$
    else report notfound.

Type Index has specification: $\mathbb{N}$.

Type Word has specification: *Word*.

Type WordList has specification: seq *Word*.

An implementation could be developed using the following steps:

Step 1: We begin by giving a library search query containing the above specifications. A match can be found with the template Linear Search given in Fig. 4, with renaming {List ⤳ WordList, Element ⤳ Word, Index ⤳ Index} and formal parameter instantiation {$E \rightsquigarrow Word$}.

Step 2: Next we might look for an implementation of WordList by supplying a search query containing the specifications of the types WordList, Word and the fragment decompose. A match with the template Linked List in Fig. 3 can be found, with renaming {LList ⤳ WordList, Element ⤳ Word, decomposeList ⤳ decompose} and instantiation {$Elem \rightsquigarrow Word$}.

Step 3: We could then use the specifications of **zero**, **increment** and the type **Index** as a search query to find a template containing primitives for natural numbers.

Step 4: Finally, implementations of **Word** and **equal** (for checking equality of list elements) need to be chosen. The choice for **Word** obviously depends on the intended application. As a general rule, templates which introduce a new type would usually define a branching fragment for determining equality; thus, we could expect to find an appropriate implementation included in the same template as chosen for **Word**.

Note that the user has not had to discharge any proof obligations in the above development.

7.2 A data refinement

Fig. 5 gives a template for representing sets as non-repeating lists. To illustrate use of the template, suppose we were given the following specification of an operation for adding a new element to a set:

> Fragment **insert(e:Elem,u:Set)** has
> specification:
> > precondition $e \notin u$
> > output **v:Set** such that $v = u \cup \{e\}$.

Upon applying the data refinement, matching **insert** with **abstractOperation** and renaming **concreteOperation** to **insertList**, we are left with the problem of implementing the following fragment:

> Fragment **insertList(e:Elem,s:List)** has specification:
> > precondition $isNonRep(s) \land e \notin \text{ran } s$
> > output **r:List** such that $isNonRep(r) \land \text{ran } r = (\text{ran } s) \cup \{e\}$.

But this fragment can be implemented by simply appending **e** onto list **s**:

> Fragment **insertList(e:Elem,s:List)** has
> implementation: **cons(e,s)**.

From the specification of **cons**, the output r of **insertList(e,s)** satisfies $r = append(e, s)$, and correctness of the implementation follows easily from the lemmas **range_of_append** and **append_isNonRep** in Fig. 1 and Fig. 6 respectively.

8 Improvements

This section considers relaxations of the definition of component matching to make library searches more effective.

Template **Linear Search** is
  formal parameters: E.
  Type **Index** has specification: $\mathbb{N}$.
  Type **Element** has specification: E.
  Type **List** has specification: seq E.

Branching fragment **search(s:List,e:Element)** has specification:
  result defined by cases:
    if $e \in$ ran s then report **found** with output i:**Index** such that $s(i) = e$
    else report **notfound**
implementation: **searchAux(s,e,zero)**.

Branching fragment **searchAux(s:List,e:Element,i:Index)** has
specification:
  result defined by cases:
    if $e \in$ ran s then report **found** with output j:**Index**
        such that $s(j - i) = e$
    else report **notfound**
implementation:
  case **decompose(s)** of
    empty: report **notfound**.
    nonempty: assign outputs to h:**Element**,t:**List**;
               case **equal(e,h)** of
                   yes:report **found** and return **increment(i)**.
                   no: **searchAux(t,e,increment(i))**.
  variant: $\#s$.

Branching fragment **decompose(s:List)** has specification:
  result defined by cases:
    if $\#s = 0$ then report **empty**
    else report **nonempty** with outputs h:**Element**,t:**List**
        such that $s = append(h, t)$.

Branching fragment **equal(a,b:Element)** has specification:
  result defined by cases: if $a = b$ then report **yes** else report **no**.

Fragment **zero()** has specification:
output n:**Index** such that $n = 0$.

Fragment **increment(m:Index)** has specification:
output n:**Index** such that $n = m + 1$.
end template.

Fig. 4. Template for implementation of a list searching algorithm.

Template Sets As Non-repeating Lists is

include Non-repeating Sequences with $X \rightsquigarrow X$.

Formal parameters: X, $P : X \times \mathbb{F}X$, $Q : X \times \mathbb{F}X \times \mathbb{F}X$.

Type Element has specification: X.

Type List has specification: seq X.

Type Set has specification: $\mathbb{F}X$
implementation:
    value u:Set is refined by s:List with invariant $isNonRep(s)$
    with refinement relation $u = \operatorname{ran} s$.

Fragment abstractOperation(e:Element,u:Set) has
specification:
    precondition $P(e, u)$
    output v:Set such that $Q(e, u, v)$
implementation:
    decompose u into s:List;
    compose concreteOperation(e,s) to v:Set;
    return v.

Fragment concreteOperation(e:Element,s:List) has
specification:
    precondition $isNonRep(s) \wedge P(e, \operatorname{ran} s)$
    output r:List such that $isNonRep(r) \wedge Q(e, \operatorname{ran} s, \operatorname{ran} r)$.

end template.

Fig. 5. Template for data refinement of sets into non-repeating lists, with corresponding refinement of a simple operation on sets.

8.1 Reordering fragment arguments

Note that the order in which input and output variables appear in a fragment's specification is not of great importance: e.g. whether one defines cons(e:Elem, s:List) or cons(s:List,e:Elem) is largely a matter of taste. Thus one particularly effective improvement is to make the matching function insensitive to the order of inputs and outputs in query fragments and to extend the definition of instantiation to allow reordering of variables. The instantiation function can then make the corresponding changes to arguments throughout the fragments being instantiated. To achieve this, we modified the syntax of variable declarations in template fragments to remove ordering of arguments:

$VarDeclars_1 == Var \twoheadrightarrow TypeName$

The information about desired variable ordering can be added to instantia-

Template **Non-repeating Sequences** is

    Formal parameters: X.

    Theory definition of predicate *isNonRep*.
       isNonRep : seq X;
       $\forall s : \text{seq } X \bullet isNonRep(s) \Leftrightarrow (\forall i, j : 1 .. \#s \bullet i \neq j \Rightarrow s(i) \neq s(j))$.

    Lemma **singleton_isNonRep**.
       $\forall e : X \bullet isNonRep(\langle e \rangle)$.

    Lemma **append_isNonRep**.
       $\forall e : X; \ s : \text{seq } X \bullet isNonRep(append(e,s)) \Leftrightarrow isNonRep(s) \wedge e \notin \text{ran } s$.

end template.

Fig. 6. A template containing theory for non-repeating sequences

---

tions by including data of the following type:

    $VarOrdering ==$ seq Var
    $Inst_1 == FPInst \times Renaming \times VarOrdering$

The definition of the instantiation function for variable declarations becomes:

$$instantiate_1 : VarDeclars_1 \times Inst_1 \rightarrow VarDeclars$$
$$instantiate_1(vs, (i, r, p)) = \{j : 1 .. \#p \bullet j \mapsto (p(j), rename(vs(p(j)), r))\}$$

The specification of the match function for variable declarations is analogous.

Example: Given input variable declaration set $vs = \{\mathbf{x} : \mathbf{X}, \mathbf{y} : \mathbf{Y}, \mathbf{z} : \mathbf{Z}\}$ renaming $r = \mathbf{X} \rightsquigarrow \mathbf{List}, \mathbf{Y} \rightsquigarrow \mathbf{Element}, \mathbf{Z} \rightsquigarrow \mathbf{List}$ and permutation $p = \langle \mathbf{z}, \mathbf{x}, \mathbf{y} \rangle$, then

$$instantiate_1(vs, (i, r, p)) = \langle \mathbf{c} : \mathbf{List}, \mathbf{a} : \mathbf{List}, \mathbf{b} : \mathbf{Element} \rangle$$

Remark: A slightly more sophisticated generalisation of this approach would be to allow template fragments to have optional arguments; the above solution can be further adapted to cover this case.

8.2 Matching up to other forms of equivalence

Note that, in many cases, the requirement for α-equivalence can be relaxed to "weaker" forms of equivalence: e.g. for formulae, logical equivalence will usually suffice, where it is used in matching preconditions, etc:

$$match_2 : Fmla \times Fmla \rightarrow \mathbb{P}\,FPInst$$

$$\forall\,i : match_2(\phi_1, \phi_2) \bullet instantiate(\phi_1, i) \Leftrightarrow \phi_2$$

The CARE semantics can be used to justify the soundness of implementing one component by another component with an equivalent specification.

8.3 Substitution matching on components

When looking for a fragment which implements a given fragment specification, it is often useful to further relax the requirement for equivalence and look for a fragment which might have a weaker precondition and/or a stronger postcondition than the query fragment. Such a fragment is substitutable for the original in the CARE program without further change, since the resulting proof obligations are weaker than for the original. This leads to the following definition, for example:

$$match_3 : SimpleFragSpec \times SimpleFragSpec \rightarrow \mathbb{P}\,Inst$$

$$\forall\,\tau : match_3(F_1, F_2) \bullet \text{let } F = instantiate(F_1, \tau)\,\text{in}$$
$$F.name = F_2.name$$
$$F_2.precondition \Rightarrow F.precondition$$
$$F_2.precondition \wedge F.postcondition \Rightarrow F_2.postcondition$$

For example, this form of matching would yield **cons** as a possible instantiation of **insertList** in the example in §7.2; the fragment could be implemented by direct instantiation, thereby absolving the user from establishing correctness.

If automated reasoning support is available, the matching algorithm in §6.2 can be adapted to meet the above specification. Note that full logical deduction is not an absolute necessity: even quite weak deductive abilities promise to increase the effectiveness of library template searching. (Generating proof obligations is another possibility). We plan to prototype such an adaptation in the near future by modifying the abstract syntax of formulae.

9 Comparison to other work

The paper by Zaremski and Wing [15] describes how specification matching can be used to compare two components; the application they consider include retrieval for reuse and determination of subtyping relationships. The paper investigates a number of different ways of relaxing the requirement for exact matching, and compares the effectiveness of the resulting search mechanisms. (Note however that our "substitution matching" is not one of those considered.) The framework is extended to matching of modules, which is similar in its goals to our template matching. Their system requires interactive theorem proving support to determine whether or not components match. By contrast our motivation has primarily been to improve browsing of template libraries and "retrieval for reuse", so we have been mainly interested in the case where matching is fully automatable. However, the framework will also support other paradigms which might be content to use of interactive matching (e.g. correctness by construction).

A number of systems are available that perform specification matching at the component level. The Inscape system [10] uses the Inquire predicate-based search mechanism to aid the user in the search for reusable components. The Inquire search mechanism can look for predicates that are equivalent to the query predicate, as well as predicates that are weaker or stronger. The VCR system [1] uses implicit VDM specifications as queries for retrieval of software components. The search mechanism used searches for components with weaker preconditions and stronger postconditions. Rollins and Wing [12] describe a system, implemented in λProlog similar to our "substitution matching", which is used to match Larch specifications. The search mechanism looks for specifications with weaker preconditions and stronger postconditions.

A restricted form of specification matching is signature matching [11, 13], where properties of the type system can be used to define various forms of matches. This however is not as powerful, or as successful in retrieving desired components, as the above methods using specification matching.

Finally, the reader's attention is drawn to the AMPHION system [14], which makes use of a library of formally-specified FORTRAN routines. AMPHION converts space scientists' graphical specifications into mathematical theorems and uses automated deduction to try to construct and verify a program that satisfies the specification. The success of AMPHION in its particular problem domain is further evidence that reuse of library routines can be made effective with appropriate tool support.

10 Conclusions

This paper has outlined the CARE approach to constructing and formally verifying software, and explored the use of pattern-matching as an aid in the selection and application of design templates from a reusable library. By minimizing the user's need for mathematical inventiveness, both in modelling and proof, CARE is better suited to industrial development of verified software than many methods.

The method is general and can be used in conjunction with a variety of other development methods, both formal and informal. It can be used with a wide variety of specification languages, theorem provers and target languages. It can even be used with programming languages which do not have a full formal semantics. A prototype tool-set has been built [4] which supports a large subset of the Z mathematical language and can synthesize source-code programs in C; the prototype includes a purpose-built automatic theorem prover together with a generic interactive theorem prover extended with CARE-specific tactics and theories.

Acknowledgements: The authors would like to thank their colleagues on the CARE project, and in particular Keith Harwood who proposed the original ap-

514

proach from which CARE has evolved. Thanks also for the constructive comments made by many of our colleagues at Telectronics and the SVRC.

SVRC technical reports are available by anonymous ftp from ftp.cs.uq.edu.au in the directory /pub/SVRC/techreports.

References

1. B. Fischer, F. Kievernagel, and W. Struckman. VCR: A VDM-based software component retrieval tool. Technical report, Technical University of Braunschwieg, Germany, November 1994.
2. K. Harwood. Towards tools for formal correctness. In *The Fifth Australian Software Engineering Conference*, pages 153–158. IREE Australia, May 1990.
3. D. Hemer and P.A. Lindsay. Formal specification of proof obligation generation in CARE. Technical Report 95-13, Software Verification Research Centre, The University of Queensland, 1995.
4. D. Hemer and P.A. Lindsay. The CARE toolset for developing verified programs from formal specifications. In O. Frieder and J. Wigglesworth, editors, *Proceeding of the Fourth International Symposium on Assessment of Software Tools*, pages 24–35. IEEE Computer Society Press, May 1996.
5. G.P. Huet. A unification algorithm for typed λ-calculus. *Theoretical Computer Science*, 1:27–57, 1975.
6. C. B. Jones, K. D. Jones, P. A. Lindsay, and R. Moore. *mural: A Formal Development Support System*. Springer-Verlag, 1991.
7. K. Lano. *The B Language and Method: A Guide to Practical Formal Development*. FACIT Series. Springer-Verlag, 1996.
8. P.A. Lindsay. The data logger case study in CARE. In *Proc 5th Australasian Refinement Workshop (ARW'96)*, 1996. http://www.it.uq.edu.au/conferences/arw96/.
9. P.A. Lindsay and D. Hemer. An industrial-strength method for the construction of formally verified software. In *Proceedings of the 1996 Australian Software Engineering Conference*, pages 27–36. IEEE Computer Society Press, July 1996.
10. D.E. Perry and S.S. Popovich. Inquire: Predicate-based use and reuse. In *Proceedings of the 8th Knowledge-Based Software Engineering Conference*, pages 144–151, September 1993.
11. M. Rittri. Using types as search keys in function libraries. In *Proceedings of the Fourth International Conference on Functional Programming and Computer Architecture*, pages 174–183. ACM Press, 1989.
12. E.J. Rollins and J.M. Wing. Specifications as search keys for software libraries. In *Eighth International Conference on Logic Programming*, pages 173–187. 1991.
13. C. Runciman and I. Toyn. Retrieving re-usable software components by polymorphic type. In *Proceedings of the Fourth International Conference on Functional Programming and Computer Architecture*, pages 166–173. ACM Press, 1989.
14. M. Stickel, R. Waldinger, M. Lowry, T. Pressburger, and I. Underwood. Deductive composition of astronomical software from subroutine libraries. In *Proceedings 12th International Conference on Automated Deduction*, pages 341–355, June 1994.
15. A. Moormann Zaremski and J.M. Wing. Specification matching of software components. In *Third ACM SIGSOFT Symposium on the Foundations of Software Engineering*, 1996.

A Compositional Proof System
for Shared Variable Concurrency

F.S de Boer [*,1], U. Hannemann[2] and W.-P. de Roever[2]

[1] Utrecht University, Department of Computer Science, P.O. Box 80.089, 3508 TB
Utrecht, The Netherlands, Email: frankb@cs.ruu.nl.
[2] Christian-Albrechts-Universität zu Kiel, Institut für Informatik und Praktische
Mathematik II, Preusserstrasse 1-9, 24105 Kiel, Germany, Email:
{uha,wpr}@informatik.uni-kiel.de.

Abstract. This paper presents a compositional proof system for shared
variable concurrency. The proof system is based on an assertion language
which describes a computation, i.e. a sequence of state-changes, in terms
of a qualitive notion of time represented by a discrete total well-founded
ordering.

1 Introduction

In 1965 E.W. Dijkstra introduced the **parbegin** statement for describing parallel
composition between processes which communicate via shared variables. But it
is only recently that the compositional and fully abstract semantics of shared
variable concurrency has been studied in [3, 4]. On the other hand the first
complete logic for proving partial correctness properties of concurrent programs
appeared already in 1976 and was developed by S. Owicki and D. Gries in [21].

The central concept of the logic of S. Owicki and D. Gries is that of *proof-
outlines* which are free from *interference*. A proof-outline consist of an annotation
of the control points of a (sequential) line of code by predicates which respect
the local flow of control. The test for interference freedom additionally ensures
that the truth of the predicates of a (local) proof-outline is not affected by the
actions of the other parallel components. These concepts have been generalized
to the model of concurrency as described by CSP by K.R. Apt, N. Francez and
W.-P. de Roever in [1].

However, due to the presence of the above described test for interference
freedom the proof method of S. Owicki and D. Gries is not *compositional* in the
sense that it does not allow a derivation of a correctness specification of a parallel program in terms of local specifications of its components *without* reference
to their internal structure. Consequently this proof method cannot be used to
support *top-down* program-design. Moreover, the relevance of a compositional
reasoning pattern with respect to the complexity of (mechanically supported)
correctness proofs of concurrent systems lies in the fact that the verification (in

---

* The research of F. S. de Boer has been partially supported by Human Capital and
Mobility network EXPRESS.

a compositional proof system) of the local components of a system can in most practical cases be mechanized fully (or at least to a very large extent). What remains is a proof that some logical combination of the specifications of the components implies the desired specification of the entire system. This latter proof in general involves purely mathematical reasoning about the underlying data-structures and as such does not involve any reasoning about specific control structures (see also [14] where the use of 'mathematics' for specification and verification of concurrent programs is strongly advocated). This abstraction from the flow of control allows for a greater control of the complexity of correctness proofs.

For the model of concurrency described by CSP, which is based on a synchronous communication mechanism, after lots of intensive research in, e.g., [5, 9, 12, 15, 16, 18, 19, 24], several (relatively) complete compositional proof methods have been introduced by J. Zwiers in [25], notably a pre/post based characterization. The so-called assumption/commitment (A/C) method [15] introduced by Misra and Chandy in 1981 is similarly compositional and especially suited to describe *open* systems, for it states that an A/C specification of a process is valid when provided that the environment of a process fulfills assumption A then the process itself fulfills commitment C. A/C style proofs can easily be mapped to pre/post style proofs. These proof methods formalize reasoning about synchronous communication in terms of a *trace* logic, a trace being a sequence of communications. For the parallel composition of processes it is important to notice that their specification must only refer to projections of the trace onto those communications that involve the process at hand.

The first compositional characterization of shared variable concurrency was called the Rely/Guarantee (R/G) method and was conceived by Jones [11]; for complete versions of this proof system consult [17, 22]. Again validity of a R/G specification of a process states that provided the environment satisfies the rely condition R that process fulfills the guarantee condition G. The difference with the A/C system being that validity of an A/C specification of a process S stipulates that C holds after each communication of S provided A holds after all communications before that particular one, whereas for any given so-called *reactive sequence* of a process, as described in [3, 4], the assumption R in the R/G method refers to *all* its environmental moves and the commitment G to *all* its process transitions. The A/C and R/G methods have in common that soundness of the network rules in both system can be proved by an inductive argument on the length of their computation sequence (respectively, traces or reactive sequences). The R/G method can be regarded as a compositional reformulation of the Owicki/Gries method as argued in [23] on the basis of a comparison of their respective completeness proofs, since both are based on the introduction of a special kind of *auxiliary* variables, namely the so-called *history* variables which record the sequence of state-changes, and both proofs use the same style of *strongest postcondition* assertions.

The compositional proof method presented in this paper formalizes reasoning about shared variable concurrency *directly* in terms of histories, i.e. they needn't be introduced through the addition of extra auxiliary variables. In other words, histories form an integral part of our programming logic, similarly as in the compositional proof method of [25] for CSP. In order to be able to describe parallel composition logically as *conjunction* we represent histories by *time-diagrams*: Given a discrete total well-founded ordering which represents *time* abstractly, a program variable then is naturally viewed as a function from this abstract notion of time to the domain of values, a so-called time-diagram. Interpreting time-instances as possible *interleaving points* and introducing boolean variables (so-called *action* variables) which indicate for each time-instance whether the given process is active or not (these action variables are also used for the same purpose in[2]), we can describe logically the compositional semantics of [3, 4] in terms of time-diagrams. Thus we show in this paper that a compositional pre/post style reasoning about shared variable concurrency, apart from the given underlying data structures, involves reasoning about a discrete total well-founded ordering, the first-order logic of which is decidable. We demonstrate that R/G style proofs can be embedded in our proof method. On the other hand, there is still a not understood difference between R/G and our time diagram based method in that until now nobody succeeded in extending the R/G method to *real time*, whereas for our approach this extension is only natural.

To describe and reason about time-diagrams we introduce a multi-sorted assertion language with first-order quantification over variables which range over points in time. The advantage of such an explicit first-order quantification over time instead of using *temporal logic* is, for example, that it allows for a straightforward axiomatizion of sequential composition, whereas in temporal logic compositional reasoning about the sequential composition operator requires the introduction of the *chop* operator which complicates the underlying logic considerably ([2]). Moreover explicit first-order quantification over time also allows for a simple logical formulation of abstraction from *finite stuttering* and *granularity of interleaving* as described in [3, 4]. These abstractions are formulated in terms of the rules of the proof system. Consequently the specifications derived by the proof system describe a fully abstract semantics, and thus can be used as a basis for a *refinement calculus*.

In [13], in order to define a theory of *refinement*, a temporal logic is designed the (temporal) *operators* (notably the next-time operator) of which are insensitive to finite stuttering. In our framework however both the abstraction from stuttering and granularity of interleaving relate to the behavior of the *action* variables, which are introduced in order to describe parallel composition as conjunction (as such the action variables play a similar role as the projection operator on traces in the logic of CSP as described in [25]): Abstraction from stuttering is obtained by the addition of stuttering steps caused by the process (and consequently marked as such by an action variable) and abstraction from the granularity of interleaving is obtained in our framework by the introduction of *instantaneous* state-changes.

However the assertion language of time-diagrams itself does not coincide yet with the fully abstract semantics: For example, there exist assertions which do distinguish between the statements $x := x + 1$ and $skip; x := x + 1$ (statements which are identified in a fully abstract semantics). Clearly the advantage of such a fully abstract assertion language is that one does not need to describe abstraction of finite stuttering and from the granularity of interleaving *explicitly* anymore as we have to do within our proof system: It is built-in in the assertion language, so to speak.

Thus, despite more than 3 decades of research on shared variable concurrency, the quest remains to define an assertion language for specification and compositional verification of shared variable concurrency which is insensitive to finite stuttering and abstraction from the granularity.

The plan of the paper is as follows: In the next section we describe a programming language for shared variable concurrency. In section 3 we introduce the assertion language and partial correctness specifications and describe their semantics. The proof system is presented in section 4. An example of a correctness proof of a mutual exclusion algorithm is presented in section 5. Section 6 discusses an embedding of the Rely/Guarantee formalism. The last section discusses a a modification of the proof system which generates fylly abstract specifications.

2 Programming language

In this section we present a programming language for shared variable concurrency.

Let *Pvar* be the set of program variables, with typical elements $x, y, \ldots$. For ease of presentation we restrict to the domain of values consisting of the integers and booleans only.

Definition 1. In the grammar of the programming language below, boolean expressions are denoted by b, whereas e denotes either an arithmetic or a boolean expression (we abstract from the syntactical structure of arithmetic and boolean expressions).

$$S ::= b.x := e \mid S_1; S_2 \mid [\!]_{i=1}^n b_i \to S_i \mid *[\!]_{i=1}^n b_i \to S_i \mid S_1 \parallel S_2$$

The execution of the guarded assignment $b.x := e$ corresponds with the execution of an await-statement of the form

$$\textbf{await } b \to x := e$$

Namely, the execution $b.x := e$ is suspended in case b evaluates to false. In case b evaluates to true control proceeeds immediately with the execution of the assignment $x := e$ which is executed atomically. Thus the evaluation of the guard and the execution of the assignment cannot be interleaved. Sequential composition is denoted as usual by the semicolon. Execution of the choice construct $[\!]_{i=1}^n b_i \to S_i$ consists of the execution of S_i for which the corresponding guard b_i evaluates to true. The control point between the evaluation of b_i and the subsequent execution of S_i constitutes an interleaving point. The evaluation of a boolean guard itself is atomic. In case none of the boolean guards evaluate to true the execution of the choice construct suspends. The execution of the iterative construct $*[\![_{i=1}^n b_i \to S_i$ consists of the repeated execution of $[\![_{i=1}^n b_i \to S_i$ until all the boolean guards are false. Parallel composition of the statements S_1 and S_2 is denoted by $S_1 \parallel S_2$. Its execution consists of an interleaving of the atomic actions, that is, the guarded assignments and the boolean guards, of S_1 and S_2.

3 The mathematics of shared-variable concurrency

In this section we discuss the mathematical structures and corresponding logics needed to describe and reason about shared-variable concurrency in a compositional manner.

In [3, 4] a compositional semantics for shared variable concurrency is introduced based on so-called *reactive sequences*. A reactive sequence is a sequence of pairs of states: $\langle \sigma_1, \sigma_1' \rangle, \langle \sigma_2, \sigma_2' \rangle, \ldots$. A pair of states $\langle \sigma, \sigma' \rangle$ represents a computation step of the process which transforms the input state σ into σ'. A 'gap' $\langle \sigma_1', \sigma_2 \rangle$ between two consecutive computation steps $\langle \sigma_1, \sigma_1' \rangle$ and $\langle \sigma_2, \sigma_2' \rangle$ represents the state-changes introduced by the environment. Parallel composition in this model is then described by *interleaving* of reactive sequences.

In order to be able to describe parallel composition logically as *conjunction* we therefore introduce a representation of reactive sequences as *time-diagrams*: Given a discrete total well-founded ordering which represents *time*, a program variable then is naturally viewed as a function from time to the domain of values, a so-called time-diagram. Interpreting time-instances as possible *interleaving points* and introducing boolean variables which change in time to indicate whether the given process is active or not, we can describe logically the compositional semantics of [3, 4] in terms of time-diagrams.

Thus compositional reasoning about shared variable concurrency, apart from the underlying data structures, involves reasoning about a discrete total well-founded ordering. In the context of mechanically supported program verification it is of interest here to note that the first-order logic of discrete total well-founded orderings is decidable. Moreover it should be observed here that we have only a qualitive notion of time which is introduced in order to model interleaving of parallel processes and as such it should be distinguished from the notion of *real time* as studied in [10].

Formally we define the (typed) assertion language for describing and reasoning about time-diagrams as follows. We assume given the standard types of the integers, denoted by **int**, and the type of booleans, denoted by **bool**. Furthermore we assume given the type of points in time, denoted by **time**. As introduced in the previous section, the set of program variables is given by *Pvar*. For each $x \in Pvar$ we have that x is either an integer or a boolean variable. We distinguish a set *Avar* $\subseteq$ *Pvar* of boolean variables. Variables of *Avar*, with typical element $a, \ldots$, will also be called action variables, since they will be used to indicate whether a given process is active or not. We assume that *action* variables do not occur in statements. The set of logical variables is denoted by *Lvar* (which is supposed to be disjoint from *Pvar*). A logical variable can be of any of the above given types **int, bool** or **time**. In the sequel we will use the symbols $t, \ldots$ both for denoting time variables and time-instances (i.e. the elements of a given time-domain T).

Definition 2. We present the following main cases of a logical expression l.

$$
\begin{aligned}
l ::= \; & time \\
| \; & z & z \in Lvar \\
| \; & x(l) & x \in Pvar \\
| \; & l_1 \preceq l_2
\end{aligned}
$$

In the above definition *time* is a constant of type **time** which is intended to denote the *current time* instant. The intended meaning of a logical expression $x(l)$, where it is implicitly assumed that l is of type **time**, is the value of the program variable x at the time-instant denoted by l. The precedence relation in time is denoted by $\preceq$. More complex logical expressions can be constructed using the standard vocabulary of the integers and booleans.

Definition 3. Next we define the syntax of an assertion p.

$$
\begin{aligned}
p ::= \; & l \\
| \; & \neg p \\
| \; & p \wedge q \\
| \; & \exists z. \, p \;\; z \in Lvar \\
| \; & \exists a. \, p \;\; a \in Avar
\end{aligned}
$$

Assertions are constructed from boolean logical expressions by means of the logical operations of negation, conjunction and (existantial) quantification over logical variables and action variables. Note that we thus do not allow quantification of variables of $Pvar \setminus Avar$, that is, the variables which may occur in statements.

In order to describe formally the semantics of the assertion language we need the following definitions.

Definition 4. Let *Val* denote the set of all possible values. The set of states Σ, with typical element σ, is given by $Pvar \to Val$ (assuming that a state maps integer variables to integers and boolean variables to booleans).

A state thus assigns values to the program variables.

Definition 5. Given a discrete well-founded total ordering $(T, \sqsubseteq)$, a time-domain T for short, a (time-) diagram d is an element of $D = T \to_{fd} \Sigma$, where $T \to_{fd} \Sigma$ denotes the set of partial functions from T to Σ the domain of which is finite (and non-empty) and downward-closed, i.e. if $d(t)$ is defined and $t' \sqsubseteq t$ then also $d(t')$ is defined.

A time-diagram thus describes the state-changes in time. The domain of a diagram d we denote by $dom(d)$. The last time instant of a diagram d, that is the maximal time instant t such that $d(t)$ is defined, we denote by $max(d)$.

Semantically assertions are evaluated with respect to a (time) diagram $d \in D = T \rightarrow_{fd} \Sigma$ and a logical environment $e \in Lvar \rightarrow Val$. Formally we have the following truth-definition.

Definition 6. Let $\sigma =_v \sigma'$, where $v \subseteq Pvar$, if for all $x \in v$ we have that $\sigma(x) = \sigma'(x)$. This notion we lift to diagrams as follows: $d =_v d'$ if $dom(d) = dom(d')$ and, in case both $d(t)$ and $d'(t)$ are defined, $d(t) =_v d'(t)$, for every t.

The value of a logical expression l in a logical environment e and a diagram d, denoted by $[\![l]\!](e)(d)$, is defined by a straightforward induction on l, for example,

$$[\![time]\!](e)(d) = max(d)$$

and

$$[\![x(l)]\!](e)(d) = d([\![l]\!](e)(d))(x).$$

The truth-value of an assertion p in a logical environment e and a diagram d, denoted by $[\![p]\!](e)(d)$ (or sometimes also by $e, d \models p$), is defined by induction on p. We give the following cases:

- For $z \in Lvar$ of type **int** or **bool**, we define $[\![\exists z p]\!](e)(d)$ if there exists a value v of a corresponding type such that $[\![p]\!](e\{v/z\})(d)$.
- For $z \in Lvar$ of type **time**, we define $[\![\exists z.\, p]\!](e)(d)$ if there exists a $t \in dom(d)$ such that $[\![p]\!](e\{t/z\})(d)$.
- For $a \in Avar$, we define $[\![\exists a.\, p]\!](e)(d)$ if there exists a d' such that $d =_v d'$, for $v = Pvar \setminus \{a\}$, and $[\![p]\!](e)(d')$.

Note that thus quantification over time is restricted to the domain of the given diagram.

Definition 7. A logical environment e and a time-diagram d are defined to be consistent if e maps every time variable to an element of the domain of d. An assertion p is valid if for any discrete well-founded total ordering $(T, \sqsubseteq)$, we have that $[\![p]\!](e)(d)$, for any consistent e and d.

For notational convenience we introduce the next-time operator $\bigcirc l$, where l is an expression of type **time**, and the strict precedence relation $\prec$. Note that the next-time operator (like all the other standard temporal operators) and the strict precedence relation can be expressed.

In order to describe logically progress in time we introduce the following substitution operation.

Definition 8. Given an assertion p and a time variable t, the assertion $p[t/time]$ denotes the result of (the usual) replacement of (occurrences of) $time$ in p by t and, additionally, the replacement of every subformula $\exists t'.\, q$ ($\forall t'.\, q$) by the bounded quantification $\exists t'(t' \preceq t \wedge q)$ ($\forall t'(t' \preceq t \rightarrow q)$). (Formulas of the form $\exists t'(t' \preceq t \wedge q)$ and $\forall t'(t' \preceq t \rightarrow q)$ we will also denote by $\exists t' \preceq t.\, q$ and $\forall t' \preceq t.\, q$, respectively.)

For example, given an assertion p the passing of one time-unit we can describe by $\exists t(p[t/time] \wedge time = \bigcirc t)$. Observe that due to the introduction of bounded quantification the assertion $p[t/time]$ thus refers to the time interval determined by t which by the substitution operation is initialized to the 'old' value of $time$. This is formalized by the following substitution lemma.

Lemma 9. *Let d_t, with t a time-instance, denote the time-diagram d restricted to the set of time-instances preceding (and including) t. For any consistent logical environment e and time-diagram d, and assertion p we have*

$$e, d \models p[t/time] \text{ iff } e, d_{e(t)} \models p$$

Definition 10. Partial correctness specifications are of the form $\{p\}S\{q\}$.

Intuitively we have the following semantics of a correctness specification $\{p\}S\{q\}$:

> The postcondition q is guaranteed to hold in any extension consisting of a terminating execution of S of a time-diagram which satisfies initially p.

In the full paper a compositional interleaving semantics of statements is presented which, given a time-domain $(T, \sqsubseteq)$, assigns to every statement S a meaning function

$$M[\![S]\!] \in (T \rightarrow_{fd} \Sigma) \rightarrow \mathcal{P}(T \rightarrow_{fd} \Sigma)$$

(the semantics M is a straightforward reformulation of the semantics introduced in [3]). The intuition is that $d' \in M[\![S]\!](d)$ if d' is an extension of d which consists of an interleaved terminating execution of S. The semantics M uses a fixed action variable a to indicate the state-changes induced by the process itself.

We then can define the truth of a partial correctness specification, denoted by $\models \{p\}S\{q\}$, formally in terms of the semantics M:

> $\models \{p\}S\{q\}$ if we have that whenever $[\![p]\!](e)(d)$ evaluates to true and $d' \in M[\![S]\!](d)$ then $[\![q]\!](e)(d')$ evaluates to true as well.

4   The proof system

In this section we present a proof system for deriving partial correctness specifications as introduced in the previous section.

We will describe the semantics of a statement S axiomatically in terms of a generic action variable a which will indicate when S is active. For notational convenience we introduce $idle_b(t, t')$ as an abbreviation of the assertion

$$\forall t''(t \preceq t'' \prec t' \rightarrow \neg a(t'')) \wedge a(t') \wedge b(t') \wedge time = \bigcirc t'$$

This assertion expresses that the process during the interval determined by the values of t and t' is non-active, and at time t' the boolean test b evaluates to true while at the same time the process resumes activity. Furthermore the assertion expresses that time has progressed till the next time-instant of t'.

A guarded assignment $b.x := e$ is characterized by the following axiom.

Assignment axiom: Let $\bar{y}$ be a sequence of variables different from x.

$$\{p\}b.x := e\{\exists t, t'(p[t/time] \wedge idle_b(t, t') \wedge x(time) = e(t') \wedge \bar{y}(time) = \bar{y}(t'))\}$$

Here $\bar{y}(time) = \bar{y}(t'))$ denotes the conjunction $\bigwedge_i y_i(time) = y_i(t')$ $(\bar{y} = y_1, \ldots y_n)$. Due to the subsitution of $time$ by t in p, the (quantified) time variable t in the postcondition refers to the value of $time$ before the execution of $b.x := e$. The idling period which represents possible interleavings of parallel processes is given by the values of t and t'. Execution of $b.x := e$ takes place at time t' and it takes one time-unit.

It worthwhile to remark that the above assignment axiom is modeled after the following well-known characterization of the *strongest postcondition* of a standard assignment statement $x := e$ in sequential programming:

$$\{p\}x := e\{\exists y(p[y/x] \wedge x = e[y/x])\}$$

The 'fresh' variable y in the postcondition represents the 'old' value of x.

The use of the substitution operation $p[t/time]$ in the assigment axiom (and in the rules below) is best explained by a small example: Let p be the precondition $\forall t'.\ x(t') = 0$ and consider the assignment $x := 1$. The precondition p thus expresses that before the assignment $x := 1$ the value of x has always been 0. The formula $\forall t' \preceq t.\ x(t') = 0$ then expresses that x equals 0 for some bounded period of time (the upperbound of which is given by t). Without the introduction of this bounded quantification the formula $p[t/time]$ in the postcondition still would express that the value of x is equal to 0 at all times, which now also includes the moment just after the assignment $x := 1$, which is clearly incorrect. Summarizing, the introduction of the bounded quantification is needed for a correct treatment of the changing scope of the quantified time variables.

The rule for sequential composition is as usual.

Sequential rule:

$$\{p\}S_1\{r\}, \{r\}S_2\{q\}$$

$$\overline{\qquad\qquad\qquad\qquad}$$

$$\{p\}S_1; S_2\{q\}$$

In order to axiomatize the choice and iteration construct we introduce a guarded skip-statement $b.skip$. The assignment axiom for a skip-statement $b.skip$ reduces to the following skip axiom.

Skip axiom: Let $\bar{y}$ be a sequence of variables.

$$\{p\}b.skip\{\exists t, t'(p[t/time] \wedge idle_b(t, t') \wedge \bar{y}(time) = \bar{y}(t'))\}$$

For the choice construct we then have the following simple rule.

Choice rule:

$$\{p\}b_i.skip; S_i\{q\} \quad \text{for } i = 1, \ldots, n$$

$$\overline{\qquad\qquad\qquad\qquad}$$

$$\{p\}[\!]_{i=1}^n b_i \to S_i\{q\}$$

Iteration is described similarly as follows.

Iteration rule:

$$\frac{\{p\}[\![_{i=1}^{n} b_i \rightarrow S_i\{p\} \quad \{p\} \bigwedge_i \neg b_i.skip\{q\}}{\{p\} * [\![_{i=1}^{n} b_i \rightarrow S_i\{q\}}$$

Parallel composition is described axiomatically by the following rule.

Parallel rule:

$$\frac{\{p_1\}S_1\{q_1\} \quad \{p_2\}S_2\{q_2\}}{\{p_1 \wedge p_2 \wedge time = t_0\}S_1 \parallel S_2\{\exists a_1, a_2, t_1, t_2(q_1' \wedge q_2' \wedge par)\}}$$

where q_i' denotes the formula $q_i[a_i, t_i/a, time]$, for $i = 1, 2$, par denotes the conjunction of the formulas: $time = max(t_1, t_2)$, $\forall t. \, t_i \preceq t \preceq time. \, \neg a_i(t)$, for $i = 1, 2$, and the formula $\forall t. \, t_0 \preceq t \preceq time. \, \neg(a_1(t) \wedge a_2(t)) \wedge a(t) \leftrightarrow (a_1(t) \vee a_2(t))$.

The quantified action variables a_1 and a_2 in the postcondition of the conclusion of the above rule are introduced to distinguish the computation steps of S_1 and S_2, respectively. The execution times of S_1 and S_2 are given by the time variables t_1 and t_2, respectively. The initial time of the execution of the parallel composition of S_1 and S_2 is given by the time variable t_0, which is initialized to the value of $time$ in the precondition. Given the execution times t_1 and t_2 of S_1 and S_2 the execution time of $S_1 \parallel S_2$ is given by the maximum of t_1 and t_2. In order to obtain a complete description we have to add the information that S_1 and S_2 are non-active when they have terminated. This is expressed by the assertion

$$\forall t. \, t_1 \preceq t \preceq time. \, \neg a_1(t) \wedge \forall t. \, t_2 \preceq t \preceq time. \, \neg a_2(t)$$

Finally the assertion

$$\forall t. \, t_0 \preceq t \preceq time. \, \neg(a_1(t) \wedge a_2(t)) \wedge a(t) \leftrightarrow (a_1(t) \vee a_2(t))$$

expresses that the execution of $S_1 \parallel S_2$ consists of an interleaving of S_1 and S_2.

Moreover we have the (standard) elimination rule, the conjunction rule and the consequence rule.

Reasoning about a statement under the assumption that it cannot be interleaved, a so-called *closed* system, can be axiomatized simply by the following rule.

Non-Interleaving rule:

$$\frac{\{p\}S\{q\}}{\{p\}S\{q \wedge \forall t.a(t)\}}$$

The additional information in the postcondition of the conclusion of the above rule expresses that S is active at all times.

In the full paper we prove soundness, i.e. every derivable correctness specification is valid, and completeness, i.e. every valid correctness specification is derivable, of the proof system wrt the compositional semantics M. The completeness proof follows the lines of the general pattern introduced by Cook in

[6]. It is based on the expressibility in the assertion language of the *strongest postcondition*.

Definition 11. For a given statement S and precondition p the strongest post-condition, denoted by $SP(p, S)$, is defined by

$$\{d \mid \text{there exists } d' \text{ s.t. } d' \models p \text{ and } d \in M(S)(d')\}$$

(we assume that p does not contain free logical variables, therefore reference to a logical environment is ommited).

It is worthwhile to remark here that we can express the strongest postcondition in the assertion language *directly*, that is, we do not need the usual coding techniques (see [20]). This is due to the presence of quantification over action-variables which introduces a second-order feature of the logic (namely quantification over sequences of time-instances).

Since the compositional semantics M is correct wrt observing only the initial/final values of the program variables we also have the following completeness result: Let ϕ and ψ be ('untimed') first-order assertions specifying the values of the program variables only. Then, if $\{\phi\}S\{\psi\}$ is a valid specification of the initial/final values of the program variables of S then there exists a (temporal) assertion p such that $\{\phi(time)\}S\{p\}$ is derivable and p implies $\psi(time)$ (the formulas $\phi(time)$ and $\psi(time)$ are obtained from ϕ and ψ by replacing every occurrence of a program variable x by $x(time)$).

5 Example: Proving a mutual exclusion property

In order to illustrate our proof system we consider the following program $P_0\|Q_0$ due to Dijkstra [8], with P_0 and Q_0 given by:

$$P_0 :: in_1 := true$$
$$*[in_2 \rightarrow in_1 := false; in_1 := true\,];$$
$$critical\ section1;$$
$$in_1 := false;$$
$$noncritical\ section1$$

$$Q_0 :: in_2 := true$$
$$*[in_1 \rightarrow in_2 := false; in_2 := true\,];$$
$$critical\ section2;$$
$$in_2 := false;$$
$$noncritical\ section1$$

The claim is that $P_0\|Q_0$ guarantees the mutual exclusion of the ciritical sections "*critical section*1" and "*critical section*2". Consequently $P_0\|Q_0$ is called a *mutual exclusion* algorithm.

Note that program $P_0\|Q_0$ does not necessarily terminate. There exists an interleaving of the atomic actions of P_0 and Q_0, called the so-called *"after-you-after-you blocking"*, which leads to an infinite computation sequence, namely:

$$in_1 := true; in_2 := true; (in_1 := false; in_1 := true; in_2 := false; in_2 := true;)^\infty.$$

The mutual exclusion inside $P_0\|Q_0$ is caused by the nontermination of $P\|Q$ - part, given by:

$$P :: in_1 := true$$
$$*[in_2 \to in_1 := false; in_1 := true]$$

$$Q :: in_2 := true$$
$$*[in_1 \to in_2 := false; in_2 := true]$$

This guarantees that when, e.g., P terminates Q does not terminate and, therefore, execution of *critical section*1 inside P_0 cannot overlap with that of *critical section*2 inside Q_0, because no assignment to in_1 occurs inside *critical section*1. Only when, after finishing *critical section*1, $in_1 := false$ has been executed, Q is allowed to terminate. Then *critical section*2 is executed, thus mutual exclusion is guaranteed if this program $P\|Q$ does not terminate, which can be expressed in our partial correctness framework by $\{true\}\ P\|Q\ \{false\}$, and will be proved below.

We freeze the starting time of process P using a logical variable t_0 and get for the first assignment by the assignment axiom and a simple application of the consequence rule:

$$\{time = t_0\}in_1 := true\{\exists t_1.idle(t_0, t_1) \wedge in_1(time)\}.$$

(Note that we use *idle* to denote $idle_{true}$.) This postcondition clearly implies our loop invariant, denoted by I_1:

$$I_1 \overset{\text{def}}{=} \forall t.t_0 \preceq t \prec time \to ((\neg a(t) \to in_1(t) = in_1(\bigcirc t)) \to in_1(time))$$

The assertion I_1 states that if the environment does not change the value of in_1, at the time-instant denoted by *time* the value of in_1 will be true. In order to prove that I_1 is a loop invariant of $*[in_2 \to in_1 := false; in_1 := true]$ it suffices to observe that (by the assignment axiom and a simple application of the consequence rule) we have

$$\{true\}in_1 := true\{in_1(time)\}$$

and thus (by the consequence rule)

$$\{true\}in_1 := true\{I_1\}$$

Moreover we have that

$$\exists t_1, t_2.I_1[t_1/time] \wedge idle_{\neg in_2}(t_1, t_2) \wedge in_1(time) = in_1(t_2) \wedge in_2(time) = in_2(t_2)$$

implies

$$I_1 \wedge \neg in_2(time)$$

It follows by the skip axiom and the consequence rule that

$$\{I_1\}\neg in_2.skip\{I_1 \wedge \neg in_2(time)\}$$

Putting the above together we thus obtain a local proof for

$$\{time = t_0\}\ P\ \{I_1 \wedge \neg in_2(time)\}.$$

We next have, since in_2 is a read-only variable of P, that

$$\{time = t_0\}\ P\ \{\forall t_0 \preceq t \prec time.a(t) \rightarrow in_2(t) = in_2(\bigcirc t)\}$$

The proof of which is straightforward and therefore ommitted. Using conjunction and consequence rule, we derive the following postcondition for P:

$$\forall t. t_0 \preceq t \prec time.(a(t) \rightarrow in_2(t) = in_2(\bigcirc t)\ \wedge$$
$$\forall t. t_0 \preceq t \prec time.((\neg a(t) \rightarrow in_1(t) = in_1(\bigcirc t)) \rightarrow in_1(time))\ \wedge$$
$$\neg in_2(time)$$

This postcondition reflects a rely/guarantee intuition behind the specification: process P relies on the fact that no other process changes in_1 to establish $in_1(time)$, guarantees that it does not change in_2 and has as local assertion on its termination $\neg in_2(time)$.

We have a similar correctness specification for Q. Now the Parallel rule is applied, resulting in

$$\{t_0 = time\}$$
$$P\|Q$$

$\{\ \ \exists t_1, t_2, a_1, a_2.\forall t. t_0 \preceq t \prec t_1.(a_1(t) \rightarrow in_2(t) = in_2(\bigcirc t))\ \ \wedge$
$\quad \forall t. t_0 \preceq t \prec t_1.((\neg a_1(t) \rightarrow in_1(t) = in_1(\bigcirc t)) \rightarrow in_1(t_1))\ \ \wedge$
$\quad \neg in_2(t_1)\qquad\qquad\qquad\qquad\qquad\qquad\qquad\qquad\qquad\qquad\qquad\wedge$
$\quad \forall t. t_0 \preceq t \prec t_2.(a_2(t) \rightarrow in_1(t) = in_1(\bigcirc t))\qquad\qquad\quad\wedge$
$\quad \forall t. t_0 \preceq t \prec t_2.((\neg a_2(t) \rightarrow in_2(t) = in_2(\bigcirc t)) \rightarrow in_2(t_2))\ \wedge$
$\quad \neg in_1(t_2)\qquad\qquad\qquad\qquad\qquad\qquad\qquad\qquad\qquad\qquad\qquad\wedge$
$\quad par$
$\}$

We proceed next as follows. We consider the case that $t_1 \sqsubseteq t_2$: We apply the Non-interleaving rule, so we know that at all times t the assertion $a(t)$ holds, and par, namely $a(t) = a_1(t) \vee a_2(t)$, for all times t, to infer from the invariance of in_1 in Q that $in_1(t_1)$. Another application of the Non-interleaving rule and par gives us $in_1(t_2)$, which contradicts $\neg in_1(t_2)$. Elimination of the logical variable t_0 in the precondition finally results in the correctness specification

$$\{true\}\ P\|Q\ \{false\}$$

that was to be proved.

6 Embedding the rely and guarantee formalism

In the Rely/Guarantee formalism [11, 17, 22] a specification is split up into four parts. There exist two assumptions on the environment: a *precondition pre* characterizing the initial state and a *rely* condition on state *pairs* that characterizes a relation any transition from the environment is supposed to satisfy. These assumptions describe conditions under which the program is used. The expected behavior of the program when used under these conditions consists of a *postcondition post* on the final state of the program in case it terminates, and a *guarantee* predicate *guar* which characterizes a relation any transition performed by the program itself should satisfy.

We consider the following partial correctness interpretation: A program P satisfies such a specification, denoted by P *sat* (*pre, rely, guar, post*) if for all terminating computations τ of P, whenever τ starts in a state which satisfies *pre*, and any environment transition in τ satisfies *rely*, then any component transition in τ satisfies *guar* and upon termination its final state satisfies *post*.

Now we can embed the R/G formalism into our (generalized) system in the following way. First note that the pre- and postcondition of the R/G formalism correspond to a restricted kind of pre- and postcondition in our system, namely, we have only to 'time' them: *pre(time)* and *post(time)* denote the formulas obtained from *pre* and *post* by replacing every occurrence of a program variable x by $x(time)$. Using the action variable a to indicate the environmental steps by requiring $\neg a$ and the steps of the process itself by a , the *rely* part is described by

$$\forall t.t_0 \preceq t.(\neg a(t) \rightarrow rely(\overline{x}(t), \overline{x}(\bigcirc t)))$$

and the *guar* part by

$$\forall t.t_0 \preceq t.(a(t) \rightarrow guar(\overline{x}(t), \overline{x}(\bigcirc t)))$$

Hence we can express a R/G formula within our system as follows:

$$P \; sat \; (pre, \; rely, \; guar, \; post)$$
$$\overset{def}{\Leftrightarrow}$$
$$\{pre(time) \wedge time = t_0\}P\{rely \rightarrow (quar \wedge post(time)\}$$

where *rely* and *quar* in the postcondition denote the assertions given above.

In order to embed the full R/G formalism (which also specifies non-terminating computations) we generalize our formalism by the inclusion in a correctness specification of a global invariant which is interpreted over non-terminating computations. Given this (straightforward) generalization of our formalism we can embed the full R/G formalism in a similar manner as described above. The details are given in the full paper.

7   Full abstraction and refinement

The proof system presented in the previous section can also be viewed as providing a compositional translation of the programming language into the assertion language: Let $\bar{x}$ be the program variables of S and $\bar{z}$ be a set of corresponding logical variables. Using the rules of the proof system we can construct inductively an assertion which describes the strongest postcondition of S wrt precondition $\bar{x}(time) = \bar{z}$, that is, the set $SP(\bar{x}(time) = \bar{z}, S)$ defined in the previous section, and derive the so-called *gorelick* specification

$$\{\bar{x}(time) = \bar{z}\}S\{SP(\bar{x}(time) = \bar{z}, S)\}$$

However this gorelick specification describes a semantics which is not fully abstract wrt to observing the initial and final values of the program variables. Therefore the proof system presented cannot be used yet as a refinement calculus since it introduces unobservable distinctions. For example, in a fully abstract semantics (see [3, 4]) the following two statements S and S' should be identified:

$$S \equiv x := x + 1$$
$$S' \equiv x := x; x := x + 1$$

However, the gorelick specification of S is not satisfied by S', and vice versa.

To identify the two statements above one needs to abstract from *finite stuttering*. Semantically this abstraction is described in terms of reactive sequences in [3, 4] by *adding randomly* stuttering steps, that is, computation steps of the form $\langle \sigma, \sigma \rangle$. Proof theoretically this abstraction can be specified in terms of time-diagrams by the following modification of the assertion $idle_b(t, t')$ used in the proof system to describe an idling period. We assume given a finite set of program variables v. Let $idle_b^v(t, t')$ now stand for:

$$\forall t''(t \preceq t'' \prec t' \wedge a(t'') \rightarrow \bigwedge_{x \in v} x(\bigcirc t'') = x(t'')) \wedge a(t') \wedge b(t') \wedge time = \bigcirc t'$$

Thus during the idling period determined by the values of t and t' the process now either idles or it gives rise to stuttering steps, that is, steps which leave the values of the program variables unchanged.

However, as described in [4] we also need to abstract from the *granularity of interleaving* as given by the atomic actions. For example, consider the following two statements

$$S \equiv [true \rightarrow x := x + 1; x := x + 1]$$
$$S' \equiv [true \rightarrow x := x + 1; x := x + 1 \square true \rightarrow x := x + 2]$$

The added possible computation of S' stems from hiding the interleaving point of the computation $x := x + 1; x := x + 1$. In a fully abstract semantics the above two statements should be identified.

In order to specify proof theoretically the needed abstraction we first introduce the following substitution operation:

Definition 12. Let z be a logical variable then $p[z/x]$ denotes the result of replacing every occurrence of an expression $x(l)$ in p by the conditional expression

if $l = time$ **then** z **else** $x(l)$ **fi.**

Thus intuitively z in $p[z/x]$ denotes the value of x at the current time-instant (which is given by the value of $time$). This is formalized by the following substitution lemma.

Lemma 13. *Let time-diagram d' be obtained from d by assigning to the variable x in $d(max(d))$ the value of z in the logical environment e. Then*

$$e, d \models p[z/x] \text{ iff } e, d' \models p$$

As above we assume given a finite set $\bar{y}$ of program variables. Abstraction from the granularity of interleaving can be obtained by allowing assignments to take place *instantaneously* as described in [4]. Given a precondition p such an instantaneous execution of an assignment $b.x := e$ can be described by the formula

$$\exists \bar{z}(p[\bar{z}/\bar{y}] \wedge a(\ominus time) \wedge b(\bar{z}) \wedge x(time) = e[\bar{z}/\bar{y}])$$

The assertion $a(\ominus time)$ (the *past-time* operator $\ominus$ yields the *previous* time-instant) states that the process is already active. The quantified logical variables $\bar{z}$ specify the internal (hidden) intermediate state, that is, the values of the variables $\bar{y}$ at the time-instant denoted by $time$ just before the execution of the assignment $b.x := e$.

Summerizing we obtain the following assigment axiom The following assignment axiom additionally specifies abstraction from the granularity of interleaving.

$$\{p\}b.x := e\{q_1 \vee q_2\}$$

where q_1 denotes the above assertion which describes the instantaneous execution of the assignment. The other disjunct q_2 describes the assignment as before.

In the full paper we introduce a fully abstract semantics M_α based on time-diagrams and we show that we can derive in the proof system, which results from introducing the above described modification of the notion of idling and the assignment axiom, for each statement S a correctness specification

$$\{\bar{x}(time) = \bar{z}\}S\{SP_\alpha(\bar{x}(time) = \bar{z}, S)\}$$

which describes the fully abstract semantics of S (as before, $\bar{x}$ denotes the program variables of S and $\bar{z}$ are corresponding logical variables). The assertion $SP_\alpha(\bar{x}(time) = \bar{z}, S)$ in fact expresses the strongest postcondition of S defined wrt the fully abstract semantics of S.

531

References

1. K.R. Apt, N. Francez and W. P. de Roever. *A proof system for Communicating Sequential Processes.* In ACM Transactions on Programming Languages and Systems, 2:359-385, 1980.
2. H. Barringer, R. Kuiper, and A. Pnueli. *Now you may compose temporal logic specifications.* In 16th ACM symposium on Theory of Computation, pages 51–63, 1984.
3. F.S. de Boer, J.N. Kok, C. Palamidessi, and J.J.M.M. Rutten. *The failure of failures: Towards a paradigm for asynchronous communication.* In Proceedings of Concur '91, Lecture Notes in Computer Science, Vol. 527, pages 111–126, 1991.
4. S. Brookes. *A fully abstract semantics of a shared variable parallel language.* In Proceedings 8th Annual IEEE Symposium on Logic in Computer Science, IEEE Computer Society Press, pages 98–109, 1993.
5. S.D. Brookes, C.A.R. Hoare and A.W. Roscoe. *A Theory of Communicating Sequential Processes.* JACM 31(7), pp. 560 – 599, 1984.
6. S.A. Cook. *Soundness and completeness of an axiom system for program verification.* In SIAM J. on Computing 7, pp. 70-90, 1978.
7. E.W. Dijkstra. *Solution of a problem in concurrent programming control.* In Comm. ACM 8, 1965.
8. E.W. Dijkstra. *Co-operating sequential processes.* In Academic Press, New York, 1968.
9. E.C.R. Hehner, C.A.R. Hoare. *A more complete model of Communicating Processes.* TCS 26, pp. 134 – 120 , 1983.
10. J. Hooman. *Specification and compositional verification of real-time systems.* Lecture Notes in Computer Science, Vol. 558, 1992.
11. C.B. Jones. *Development methods for computer programs including a notion of interference.* PhD thesis, Oxford University Computing Laboratory, 1981.
12. M. Joseph, P. Pandya. *Specification and Verification of Total Correctness of Distributed Programs.* Research report RR 96, University of Warwick, 1987.
13. Y. Kesten, Z.Manna and A. Pnueli, *Temporal verification of simulation and refinement* In A Decade of Concurrency (eds. J.W de Bakker, W.-P. de Roever and G. Rozenberg), Lecture Notes in Computer Science, Vol. 803, 1993.
14. L. Lamport. *Verification and specification of concurrent programs.* In A Decade of Concurrency (eds. J.W de Bakker, W.-P. de Roever and G. Rozenberg), Lecture Notes in Computer Science, Vol. 803, 1993.
15. J. Misra and K.M. Chandy. *Proofs of networks of processes.* IEEE Transactions on Software Engeneering, 7(7):417–426, 1981.
16. E.-R. Olderog and C.A.R. Hoare. *Specification oriented Programming in TCSP.* Proc. of the 10th ICALP, LNCS 154, 1983.
17. K. Stølen. *Development of Parallel Programs on Shared Data-structures.* PhD thesis, Computer Science Department, Manchester University, 1990.
18. N. Sounderarajan. *Axiomatic semantics of communicating sequential processes.* TOPLAS, 6:647–662, 1984.
19. J. Widom, D. Gries and F.B. Schneider. *Completeness and Incompleteness of Trace-based Network Proof Systems.* Proc. of the 14th ACM SIGACT-SIGPLAN Symposium on Principles of Programming Languages, pp. 27 – 38, 1987.
20. J.V. Tucker and J.I. Zucker. *Program correctness over abstract data types, with error-state semantics.* In CWI Monograph Series, vol. 6, Centre for Mathematics and Computer Science/North-Holland, 1988.

21. S. Owicki and D. Gries. *An axiomatic proof technique for parallel programs.* In Acta Informatika, 6:319-340, 1976.

22. Q. Xu. *A theory of state -based parallel programming.* PhD thesis, Oxford University Computing Laboratory, 1992.

23. Q. Xu, W.-P. de Roever and J. He. *Rely- guarantee method for verifying shared variable concurrent programs.* Formal Aspects of Computing 1997 (To appear).

24. C.C. Zhou and C.A.R. Hoare. *Partial Correctness of CSP.* Proc. IEEE Int. Conf. on Distributed Computer Systems, pp. 1– 12, 1981.

25. J. Zwiers. *Compositionality, Concurrency, and Partial Correctness.* Lecture Notes in Computer Science, Vol.321, Springer-Verlag, 1989.

A Framework for Modular Formal Specification and Verification

Pierre Michel and Virginie Wiels
{michel,wiels}@cert.fr

ONERA-CERT, 2 av. E. Belin, BP 4025, 31055 Toulouse cedex, France

Abstract. This paper presents a specification formalism that combines temporal logic with actions and algebraic modules. This formalism allows to write modular specifications of complex systems and is supported by a tool. We show that we can also exploit the structure of the specification in order to realize modular verifications. It is applied to a telecommunication example.

1 Introduction

In this paper, we present an approach that combines algebraic modules and temporal logic. Several authors (one of the first was Kroger in 1987 [10], and more recently Fiadeiro and Maibaum [5]) have noticed that a combination of temporal logic and algebraic structure based on categories was interesting because temporal logic is very expressive and well-suited to the specification of reactive systems while categories allows to structure the logical descriptions and provides composition laws. In [17], we had besides proposed a categorical and logical approach and applied it to compositionally specify and verify a fault-tolerance mechanism. But this solution is not sufficient in many cases: it lacks notions of interface and there is only one kind of interaction between components.

This paper presents the continuation of that work (and completes [13]): we improve the previous formalism by adding a structuration level: a component of a system is no more described by a specification but by a module composed of several specifications, This allows to specify the component more precisely and to increase the possible kinds of interactions between components.

We have adapted the calculus of modules proposed in [3]: Ehrig and Mahr define powerful means of describing modules and a lot of classical modularity concepts such as encapsulation or genericity. Their calculus of modules is based on categorical concepts and is well-adapted to top-down but also to bottom-up approaches. Ehrig and Mahr use the abstract data types as description formalism inside the modules. We have decided to extend their modules with the logical concepts developed in [17].

The proposed approach is expressive and modular. Expressiveness, given by the use of logic, is necessary to specify complex systems. The description of a system is structured in modules and each module is also structured in a way that allows a very precise description. There are three levels of description:

- system level: a system is described by modules that are interconnected by morphisms and on which composition operations can be performed;
- module level: a module is composed of four specifications linked by specification morphisms;
- specification level: each specification is a logical theory (a signature that gives the vocabulary (attributes and methods) and a set of formulae to describe the behavior).

One of the four specifications constituting a module is the hidden part of the module (its implementation part); three specifications constitute the interface of the module: a parameter specification contains the parameters in case of a generic module, an export specification gives the elements of the module that are accessible from the environment and an import specification contains the elements used by the module but defined elsewhere. This structure gives important properties to the modules: encapsulation, information hiding, abstraction and reusability. Our approach has the same goal as Fiadeiro and Maibaum one ([6]), but the way we structure the description of a component is different: they chose to describe a component by a kernel specification and to have an interface for each interconnection with another component while we describe a component by a module with fixed interfaces and interconnections with other modules are simply described by a morphism. Moreover, we adapt an existing calculus and consequently inherit from the work on operations between modules for example.

Our approach is based on well-defined formal concepts and allows a verification process (we adapt the verification methodology proposed in [17]). Finally, this approach is supported by a tool that implements all the categorical concepts and operations needed for the definition of modules. The tool can perform all the composition operations defined on modules and thus automatically build the specification of systems from the specifications of their components.

This paper is organised as follows. Section 2 presents the application that will be taken as example in the whole paper. This is a telecommunication application that was developed during a collaboration with the CNET[1]. Section 3 presents the specification modules and a methodology of specification. Section 4 deals with their semantics. Section 5 describes the interconnections between modules and the construction of a module representing the whole system. Section 6 describes the tool associated to the approach. In section 7, the verification aspects are explained. Section 8 presents our future work.

2 Application

We will take as examples applications that we have developed as part of a project supported by CNET [1]. We first present a "Notification Selection and Dispatching Function" (NSDF). Then we present two applications that used the NSDF: an alarm mechanism and an appointment dispatching function.

---

[1] Centre National d'Etudes des Telecommunications - France Telecom

2.1 Notification Selection and Dispatching Function

General presentation This application is presented in [1] as an example of a system described following the RM-ODP (Reference Model for Open Distributed Processing) [9] and more precisely following the G.851-01 recommendation [8].

A client provides an information to dispatch and a list of destinations. The provider of the service checks that the information is correct with respect to an internal criterion and that the set of destinations is included in its potential destination domain and then delivers the information. If one of the conditions is not respected, it sends an error message back to the client.

In [1], the function is described more precisely following three of the five viewpoints of the RM-ODP: enterprise, information and computational. We will not enter in great details about the ODP methodology but it is interesting to notice that our formalism was well-suited to the specification process described in this methodology, as showed in [12].

Specification of the NSDF The provider is decomposed in three components called *Configuration*, *Manager* and *Transmitter*.

Configuration contains all the data used by the provider that is to say the destination sets (a potential destination domain, a default destination set and an actual destination set) and the selection criterion for the information.

Manager is the part of the provider which is in charge of the update of the data in *Configuration*.

Transmitter is the part of the provider that actually executes the delivery of the information. If the client asks for a delivery of information, *Transmitter* checks that the provided information is correct with respect to the criterion and that the provided set of destinations (if there is one) is included in the default destination set. If no destination set is provided, the information is delivered to the provider destination set.

2.2 Applications of the NSDF

The NSDF is a general service which is used to define more specialized applications.

Alarms. This application describes an alarm that, when a given sensor goes beyond a limit value, delivers an alarm message to all the concerned persons.

Appointment dispatching. This application specializes the NSDF by taking a particular kind of information to be delivered: an appointment information, that is to say a start time, an end time and an activity.

3 Specification modules

We first give the structure of a specification module, then we define the notion of specification.

3.1 Definitions

A specification module MOD consists of four specifications PAR, IMP, EXP, BOD and of four specification morphisms e, i, s, v between these specifications (as shown on the following figure) such that $v \circ e = s \circ i$ (the notions of specification and specification morphism are defined in the next section):

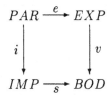

The intuitive meaning of the four parts of a module is the following:

- the **parameter** part contains the parameters in case of a generic module; it is a common part to IMP and EXP. In fact, it declares those of the resources (among all the resources of the system) that are used by the module.
- the **import** part identifies the elements which must be imported by the module, i.e. which are used in the current module, but defined into an other one. The import part may contain equations that give information about the use of the imported elements. This is very interesting, particularly in a top-down approach.
- the **export** part identifies the elements that are visible outside the module and can be accessed by other components. It must not contain attributes in order to respect the encapsulation principle. This export part allows to hide some elements in the body.
- the **body** part contains the whole description of the component, that is to say the construction of the exported elements from the imported ones. This part of the module can not be accessed by the environment.

Remark: it is particularly interesting to have equations in the interface parts because it allows to express constraints on the environment or to give information about the elements exported by the module.

The four parts of a module are linked by specification morphisms that allow identification of resources and name abstraction inside the module.

Morphisms. A module morphism $MOD_X \longrightarrow MOD_Y$ is a quadruplet $f = (f_P, f_E, f_I, f_B)$ of specification morphisms :

$$f_P : PAR_X \longrightarrow PAR_Y \qquad \text{such that:} \qquad f_E \circ e_X = e_Y \circ f_P$$

$$f_E : EXP_X \longrightarrow EXP_Y \qquad\qquad f_I \circ i_X = i_Y \circ f_P$$
$$f_I : IMP_X \longrightarrow IMP_Y \qquad\qquad f_B \circ v_X = v_Y \circ f_E$$
$$f_B : BOD_X \longrightarrow BOD_Y \qquad\qquad f_B \circ s_X = s_Y \circ f_I$$

The modules and module morphisms constitute a category.

3.2 Specifications

A specification SPEC is composed of four parts:
  an algebraic signature $\Sigma = (S, \Omega)$,
  a family of attributes ATT,
  a family of events EV,
  a set of axioms AX.
Σ, ATT and EV are disjoint and finite. They give the vocabulary of the specification, while AX gives its behaviour by means of logical formulae.

* Σ is a classical algebraic signature where S is a set of sorts and Ω a family of operators (indexed by $S^* \times S$) on these sorts. This part of the specification describes all the data structures that are needed by the component. These data structures will be used to give the type of the attributes and of the parameters of the actions.

* ATT is a family of attribute symbols indexed by $S^* \times S$. These attributes are necessary to describe the component. The values of these attributes will characterize the current state of the component.

From the sets of symbol names Ω and ATT, we can define the set of terms. The set of well-formed and well-typed terms of sort s TR_s is inductively defined as follows:

every variable x of sort s is in TR_s
if $c \in \Omega_s$, then $c \in TR_s$
if $v \in ATT_s$, then $v \in TR_s$
if $f \in \Omega_{<s1,..,sn>,s}$ and t_i are terms of TR_{si}, then $f(t_1, ..., t_n) \in TR_s$
if $f \in ATT_{<s1,..,sn>,s}$ and t_i are terms of TR_{si}, then $f(t_1, ..., t_n) \in TR_s$

* EV is a family of symbols indexed by S^*. Events represent "types" of actions the component can execute. More precisely, the set ACT of all the actions of the component is defined from EV as follows:

if $a \in EV_{<s1,...,sn>}$ and t_i are terms of sort s_i, then $a(t_1, ..., t_n) \in ACT$.

Moreover, we add to ACT an action τ to represent all the actions that are non significant for the object (actions executed by other components of the system).

* AX is a set of axioms that describe the behavior of the component. We chose to write these axioms with a temporal logic with actions that we defined in [17]. This logic has proved to be adapted to the specification and verification of systems: the linear temporal logic is well suited for expressing properties of concurrent and reactive systems; and the behavior of systems is easily described thanks to the explicit use of actions. But these advantages can be found in other logics near to this one (such as TLA) as well.

The set of well-formed formulae is inductively defined as follows:

* every equality between terms is a wff.
* if A and B are wff over C and if $\alpha \in ACT \cup \{\tau\}$ then $\neg A$, $A \to B$, $A \wedge B$, $A \vee B$, $A \leftrightarrow B$, t, f, $[\alpha]A$, $\langle\alpha\rangle A$, $\Diamond A$, $\Box A$, $(\forall x : s)A$ are wff over C.

$\neg$, $\to$, $\wedge$, $\vee$, $\leftrightarrow$ are the connectives of classical logic, $[\alpha]$, $\langle\alpha\rangle$ those of dynamic logic and $\Diamond$, $\Box$ those of temporal logic.

$[\alpha]A$ means that after every execution of α, the formula A is true.
$\langle\alpha\rangle A$ means that α can be executed and after this execution of α, A is true.
$\Box A$ means that the formula A is always true.
$\Diamond A$ means that there exists a time where A will be true.

Locality We add an important property to each component description: the locality property. This property says that the attributes of a component C can only be modified by the actions of C. This property can be expressed by an axiom that is added to each component description.

Morphisms A specification morphism $m : SPEC1 \to SPEC2$ is a classical (see for example [2]) signature morphism $\Sigma1 \to \Sigma2$ that moreover associates:
   * to each at1 in ATT1 an attribute at2 in ATT2
   * to each ev1 in EV1 an event ev2 in EV2
such that

   – if $at1 \in ATT1_{<s1,...,sn>,s}$, then $m(at1) \in ATT2_{<m(s1),...,m(sn)>,m(s)}$
   – if $ev1 \in EV1_{<s1,...,sn>}$, then $m(ev1) \in EV2_{<m(s1),...,m(sn)>}$
   – the image by m of each formula of $AX1$ is a theorem of $SPEC2$ [2]

Specifications and specification morphisms constitute a cocomplete category as proved in [5] and in the implementation of our tool (cf section 6).

3.3 Methodology and specification of the example

We give here some methodology rules to write a specification module on the example of the description of the *Configuration* and *Transmitter* components (*Manager* is not described here because it is a very simple module).

---

[2] this is in particular true for the locality axiom.

Configuration. Let us first consider the body of the module. *Configuration* contains four attributes: *dest_set*, *dest_dom*, *default_set* of type *DS* (destination set) and *criterion* of type *Filter*. There are also eight actions standing for the reading and writing of each attribute. Each action has a parameter of type *DS* or *Filter* that represents the value of the attribute. Moreover, the body contains some formulae that describe the behavior of *Configuration*. We determined five classes of formulae in order to guide the specifier:

- **initial formulae**: formulae describing the initial state,
- **necessary preconditions** to perform an action; there is no such formula in *Configuration* but this would be of the following kind:
  $\Box(\langle action\rangle t \rightarrow cond)$ (the action is possible only if the condition is true).
- **reactivity or fairness formulae** to guarantee the triggering of enable actions. For example, we have:
  $\Box(cond \rightarrow \Diamond\langle action\rangle t)$ to ensure the action will be done if the preconditions are satisfied.
- **weakest post-conditions** to describe the effects of the actions. For example, after the execution of *put_dest(x)*, the attribute *dest_set* has the value x:
  $\Box([put\_dest(x)](dest\_set = x))$
- **invariants**: constraints that must always be verified; for example, one of the invariant specified in the NSDF is that the default destination set must always be included in the potential destination domain:
  $\Box(Included(default\_set, dest\_dom) = True)$

The specification of the body of *Configuration* can be summarized as follows:

$Sorts$: $DS, Filter, Bool$

$Operators$: $True, False :\rightarrow Bool$
$Included : DS, DS \rightarrow Bool$
$Empty\_set :\rightarrow DS$

$Attributes$: $dest\_set, dest\_dom, default\_set : DS, criterion : Filter$

$Actions$: $get\_dest(DS), get\_dom(DS), get\_default(DS), get\_criterion(Filter)$
$put\_dest(DS), put\_dom(DS), put\_default(DS), put\_criterion(Filter)$

$Axioms$: $x : DS, y : Filter$
$\Box(Included(default\_set, dest\_dom) = True)$
$\Box(Included(dest\_set, default\_set) = True)$
$\Box([put\_dest(x)](dest\_set = x))$
$\Box([put\_dom(x)](dest\_dom = x))$
$\Box([put\_default(x)](default\_set = x))$
$\Box([put\_criterion(y)](criterion = y))$

Then we have to define the interface parts. The elements that are used by the body part but not defined in this module are the sorts *DS*, *Filter*, *Bool* and the operators *True*, *False*, *Included* and *Empty_set*. These elements constitute the import part.

The elements of the body that will be accessible for the environment are the eight actions (and consequently the sorts *DS* and *Filter* and all the operators).

The parameters of the module are thus its sorts and operators (PAR = IMP).

The last things to define are the morphisms that link the four parts of the module. Here the morphisms are straightforward.

Transmitter. It is the part of the provider that will offer the service to the client. It must have in export two actions: *info_dispatch_req(DS,I)* that represents the request of the client to have some information (of type I) delivered to a set of destinations and *error(E)* that tells the client that an error has occurred because of a problem described by the parameter of type E (it can be either *Incorrect_info* or *Wrong_dest_set* which are both constant operators of type E). The export part of *Transmitter* thus contains the two actions, the useful sorts (DS, I, E) and the two constant operators of type E.

In order to implement the service, *Transmitter* needs to have the criterion, the destination set and the default destination set. It consequently imports three functions that give these values: *get_criterion*, *get_dest* and *get_default*[3]. Moreover, *Transmitter* needs a sort describing the information, we suppose that *Transmitter* is generic with respect to I and thus I is in its parameter and import parts. It also needs an operator $Correct : I, Filter \rightarrow Bool$ that says if an information is correct with respect to a given criterion of type *Filter*. The import part thus contains I, *Correct*, the three actions and the sorts needed for them.

The body part contains the implementation of the service, it is described as follows:

$Sorts :$ $DS, Filter, Bool, I$
$Operators :$ $imported\ ones, exported\ ones$
$Attributes :$ $request : Bool, cl\_dest : DS, cl\_info : I,$
           $dest : DS, default : DS, criterion : Filter$
$Actions :$ $imported\ ones, exported\ ones, info\_dispatch(I, DS)$
$Axioms :$ $x : DS, z : I$
(1) $(request = False)$
(2) $\Box(\langle erreur(Incorrect\_info)\rangle t \rightarrow$
           $(Correct(cl\_info, criterion) = False) \wedge (request = True))$
(3) $\Box(\langle info\_dispatch(cl\_info, cl\_dest)\rangle t \rightarrow$
           $(Correct(cl\_info, criterion) = True) \wedge (request = True)$
           $\wedge not(cl\_dest = Empty\_set) \wedge (Included(cl\_dest, default) = True))$
(4) $\Box([info\_dispatch\_req(z, x)]((cl\_info = z) \wedge (cl\_dest = x) \wedge (request = True)$
           $\wedge \langle get\_criterion(criterion)\rangle t \wedge \langle get\_default(default)\rangle t))$

...

---

[3] we give them the same name as in *Configuration* but we could have called them differently. Anyway, we will see in section 5 that the morphisms make the necessary associations.

request is a boolean that is true when a client has made a request, *cl_dest* stores the destination set provided by the client, *cl_info* stores the information provided by the client, *dest* stores the value of the provider destination set, *default* stores the value of the provider default destination set and *criterion* stores the value of the provider criterion. The actions in the body are the imported ones, the exported ones and one action more: *info_dispatch* which represents the dispatching of information. Then we have examples of formulae that describe the behavior of the *Transmitter*. (1) gives the initial value of *request*. (2) and (3) express necessary preconditions. (2) means that an error message "incorrect information" is sent to the client if the information provided by this client is not correct with respect to the provider criterion. (3) means that the information is dispatched to a set of destinations if the information is correct with respect to the criterion and there was a request and the destination set is not empty and is included in the default destination set. (4) is a weakest post-condition: when a request happens, the attributes *info* and *dest* take the values provided by the client, *request* becomes true and we fetch the values of the criterion and default destination set by means of the "get" functions.

4 Semantics

In this section, we give the semantics of specifications and of modules.

4.1 Semantics of specifications

Structures The formulas defined above are interpreted on the following structures:

$$M = (W, w_0, ACT_M, R_g, g \in ACT_M, U, I_s, I_\Omega, I_{ATT}, I_{EV})$$

* W is a set of states

* $w_0 \in W$ is the initial state

* ACT_M is the set of action names that allow to interpret actions.

* $R_g, g \in ACT_M$ is a family of elementary transitions between states such that each family of transition R_g is a partial function of profile $W \to W$ and such that $\cup R_g$ is an application (denoted Π) .

* U is a Σ-algebra (S_U, F_U)

* I_s is the interpretation function for the sorts: $I_s : S \to S_U$.

* I_Ω is the interpretation function for the operators: $I_\Omega : \Omega \to F_U$ such that $\forall f \in \Omega_{<s1,...,sn>,s}, I_\Omega(f) \in F_{U<Is(s1),...,Is(sn)>,Is(s)}$.

* I_{ATT} is the interpretation function for the attributes: $I_{ATT} : ATT \rightarrow (S_U^* \times W \rightarrow S_U)$ such that $\forall at \in ATT_{<s1,..,sn>,s}, I_{ATT}(at) : Is(s1) \times ... \times Is(sn) \times W \rightarrow Is(s)$.

* I_{EV} is the interpretation function for the actions: $\forall ac \in EV_{<s1,..,sn>}, I_{EV}(ac) : Is(s1) \times ... \times Is(sn) \rightarrow ACT_M$.

Interpretation of terms Let $f(t_1, .., t_n)$ be a term of TR_s. The interpretation $[f(t_1, ..., t_n)](w)$ of this term in a state w is defined in the following way:

if x is a variable of sort s, $[x](w) = V(x)$, where V is an assignment
if $f \in \Omega_{<s1,...,sn>,s}$, $[f(t_1, ..., t_n)](w) = I_\Omega(f)([t_1](w), ..., [t_n](w))$
if $f \in ATT_{<s1,...,sn>,s}$, $[f(t_1, ..., t_n)](w) = I_{ATT}(f)(([t_1](w), ..., [t_n](w)), w)$

We can notice that the operators have an interpretation that is independent from the state while the interpretation of attributes depends on the state.

Interpretation of formulas The satisfaction of a formula in a structure M and a state w is defined as follows:

$M, w \models (t_1 =_s t_2)$ iff $[t_1](w) = [t_2](w)$
$M, w \models \neg A$ iff $not(M, w \models A)$
$M, w \models A \wedge B$ iff $M, w \models A$ and $M, w \models B$
$M, w \models \Diamond A$ iff $\exists i$ such that A is satisfied by M in $\Pi^i(w)$
$M, w \models \Box A$ iff $\forall i \geq 0$, A is satisfied by M in $\Pi^i(w)$
$M, w \models < a > A$ iff $\exists w'$ such that $(w, w') \in R_{(I_{EV}(a))}$ and $M, w' \models A$
$M, w \models [a]A$ iff $\forall w'$, if $(w, w') \in R_{(I_{EV}(a))}$, then $M, w' \models A$

Models A model for a specification $sp = ((S, \Omega), ATT, EV, AX)$ is a structure M such that $M, w_0 \models ax, \forall ax \in (AX \cup \{locality\,axiom\})$.

4.2 Semantics of modules

In Ehrig and Mahr calculus, the semantics of a module is defined by a functor SEM, composition of a free functor (between Cat(IMP) and Cat(BOD)) and of the forgetful functor associated to v.

But we adopt another solution for the semantics, rather following Fiadeiro and Maibaum. In [6], they defined a design structure to specify a component of a system. This structure is composed of a kernel, an extension and several interfaces. These parts are specifications and there is no particular semantics added except a methodology of use. Here, we also consider that a component is described by four specifications linked by morphisms that impose constraints. There is a methodology of use described at the beginning of section 3, and the specifications have a well-defined semantics that we have found sufficient in practise in order to specify and verify (cf section 7) systems.

5 Interconnection of components and description of the system

Now that we are able to describe a module in a system, the next step is to interconnect these descriptions and to obtain a specification of the whole system. We have defined several patterns of interconnection.

The principle is the same in all cases:

- first we express the relationships between the modules by means of morphisms: we get a diagram where modules are linked by morphisms;
- then we used a categorical operation to build the module resulting from the interconnection. It is very interesting to build this module because it can be reused later as a component in another system.

The specification morphisms are flexible but precise means to express the interconnection between two modules. They allows renaming and identification of resources and they guarantee that the matching of the corresponding components of the two modules being interconnected is consistent with the declaration in these components. In other words, the morphisms that interconnect two modules can be defined if the constraints of the two modules are compatible.

We are going to describe three kinds of interconnection: use (client/server), sharing and actualization.

5.1 Use (client/server) relationships

Interconnecting components. This kind of interconnection between two modules M1 and M2 is expressed by a morphism between IMP1 (import part of M1) and EXP2 (export part of M2). In a general way, this morphism means that some elements imported by M1 are associated to some elements exported by M2. But, depending on the content of the specifications and the definition of morphisms, this link may express several kinds of interconnections. We are going to illustrate that on the NSDF example.

First such a link may express the synchronisation of two modules on some elements (attributes or actions). For example, *Manager* is the part of the provider that is responsible for the updating of the data stored in *Configuration*. It is a simple module that will use the write functions of *Configuration*. We want thus to connect *Manager* and *Configuration* and express that the action *update_dest(x)* of *Manager* is exactly the action *put_dest(x)* of *Configuration*. it is in fact client-server relationships where only one client is allowed (*Manager* uses the service *put_dest* offered by *Configuration* in order to implement its action *update_dest* (in this case, it is very simple: *update = put*)). This kind of interconnection is expressed in the following way:

544

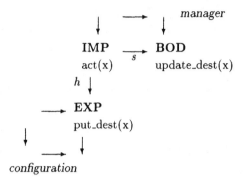

configuration

$s : act(x) \rightarrow update\_dest(x)$
$h : act(x) \rightarrow put\_dest(x)$

Remark: this kind of interconnection does not always imply an identification of actions: *Manager* could also have used the action *put_dest* to implement its updating function or there could have been more than one client using *put_dest* (in this case, there is no more an equivalence between *update_dest* and *put_dest* but only an implication).

Construction operation. Once the modules corresponding to all the components of the system are interconnected, the module corresponding to the description of the whole system has to be built. Several construction operations are possible for the type of interconnection described above.

1. A first possible operation is **composition**. The corresponding scheme is the following (where M stand for *Manager* and C for *Configuration*):

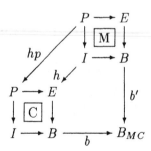

In this case, the resulting module is (P_M, I_C, E_M, B_{MC}) where B_{MC} is the push-out of B_M and of B_C over I_M. The behavior of the resulting module is described in its BODY part and corresponds in fact to the parallel composition of the behaviors described in the two initial BODY parts with the synchronisation due to the links expressed by h.

Remark: in addition to the morphism h whose role has been explained in the previous section, a morphism hp is needed between the two PARAMETER parts and the following property must be respected : $h \circ i_M = e_C \circ hp$. This morphism indicates a compatibility between the parameters of the two modules and is indispensable to link the PARAMETER and IMPORT parts of the resulting module.

In the NSDF example, we obtain in this way a module that represents the composition of *Manager* and *Configuration* with respect to the links described just before.

2. In the composition operation, the resulting module exports only the elements exported by M. The **product** operation is a version of the composition operation where the resulting EXPORT part is the push-out of the two initial EXPORT parts. Thus the resulting module exports also the elements exported by C.

3. A module often imports elements coming from several different modules. In this case, the useful operation is the **partial composition** which is a generalisation of the composition operation. In this operation, the import is decomposed in several parts (each part containing elements defined in one module of the environment) and the morphism h associates the elements of one of these parts to the exported elements of the corresponding module.

For example, in the NSDF example, partial composition is needed between *Transmitter* and *Configuration*. Indeed, *Transmitter* imports elements that are defined in *Configuration* (*get_dest*, *get_default* and *get_criterion*) but it also imports I that is not defined in *Configuration*. The scheme is the following:

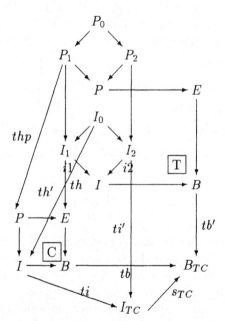

I_1 contains all the elements that *Transmitter* imports and that are defined in *Configuration* (*DS, Filter, Bool, Included, True, False, Empty_set, get_dest, get_default* and *get_criterion*) while I_2 contains the other imported elements: *I, Filter, Bool, Correct* (*Filter* and *Bool* are necessary to express the profile of *Correct*). I_0 is the intersection of I_1 and I_2, it is necessary to identify the two versions of *Filter* and *Bool* (to express that *Filter* and *Bool* are the same in I_1 and I_2).

The resulting module is $(P_T, I_{TC}, E_T, B_{TC})$, its construction is done in the same way as for the composition, except that a new import must be computed (to take into account I_2): I_{TC} is the push-out of I_C and I_2 on I_0.

We thus obtain a module that represents the composition of *Transmitter* and *Configuration*.

5.2 Share

Interconnecting components. Now we want to express that two modules share some elements (attributes or actions). In the NSDF example, we need this to build the module specifying the whole system. Indeed we have to make the union of MC and TC but taking into account the fact that these two modules share some elements.

In order to do that, we have to define a new module that contains all the elements that are common to the two modules and two module morphisms that make the necessary associations.

Let us explain this more precisely on the example of MC and TC. We create a module S, the body of S contains an action $a1(DS)$, this action will be matched by means of morphisms on one hand to the action *update_dest(DS)* of MC and on the other hand to the action *put_dest(DS)* of TC. (This must be repeted for each shared action). The corresponding scheme is the following:

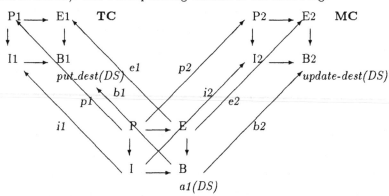

The morphisms $b1$ and $b2$ that associates $a1(DS)$ to both *put_dest(DS)* and *update_dest(DS)* expresses that the two actions are synchronised.

Remark: we have only represented the relations between the body parts but there are also associations between the other parts (for example, there must be a sort DS in P and the two morphisms p1 and p2 must associate DS to the respective DS in P1 and P2).

Construction operation. The operation used here to build the module corresponding to the two modules MC and TC sharing the elements of S is called

union (it is the adaptation to the extended module of the union operation of Ehrig and Mahr). In fact, it is a pushout in the category of modules.

Each part of the resulting module (P', E', F', B') represents the union of the two corresponding parts of MC and TC with synchronization on the elements of the corresponding part of S.

5.3 Actualization

This interconnection is a particular case: it is the operation that allows to instantiate a generic module to get a specific one.

Interconnecting components. For this operation, we take as example the instantiation of the generic specification of the NSDF obtained above by a specific kind of information: appointment information. We have the generic module Syst = (PAR,IMP,EXP,BOD) and a reduced module R describing the actual parameter as follows:

$$\text{PAR'} \longrightarrow \text{ACT}$$

The ACT part contains the description of the actual parameter that will replace the generic parameter of Syst, and this actual parameter can itself be parameterized by a generic parameter that is in this case declared in the PAR' part.

In the example, the sort that instantiates I is a record of three elements: a start time, an end time and an activity. We will call this sort App (for appointment). The ACT part will be described as follows:

$$
\begin{aligned}
Sorts : \quad & App, Time, Activity \\
Operators : \quad & Beg : App \rightarrow Time \\
& End : App \rightarrow Time \\
& Act : App \rightarrow Activity
\end{aligned}
$$

The PAR' part will thus contains the sorts *Time* and *Activity* that will be the new parameters of the module.

The interconnection between Syst and R is made by a morphism h between PAR and ACT that associates to the generic parameter of Syst the actual parameter in ACT.

Construction operation. The new module (PAR',IMP',EXP',BOD') is then built as shown on the following scheme:

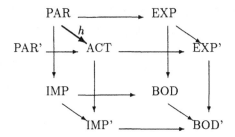

IMP', EXP' and BOD' are obtained by push-out (of IMP and ACT, EXP and ACT, BOD and EXP' respectively). The new module is the instantiation of Syst with the actual parameter in ACT.

5.4 Remarks on the application

If we briefly recalls the structure of the application, we have three main modules: *Transmitter*, *Manager* and *Configuration*. *Manager* and *Transmitter* use some elements exported by *Configuration*.

A possible way to build the module describing the whole system is the one described above: we build MC by composition of *Manager* and *Configuration*, we build TC by partial composition of *Transmitter* and *Configuration* and we finally build *Syst* by union of MC and TC (for this operation, we need an additional module that precises the shared elements between MC and TC).

Another possibility would have been to first make the union of *Manager* and *Transmitter* (with an additional module describing the intersection, but this module would have contained only the sorts DS, Filter, Bool and the operators Included, True and False) to obtain a module MT. Then we would have (partially) composed this module MT with *Configuration* to obtain *Syst*. In this case, the morphisms describing the interaction between MT and *Configuration* can be automatically computed from the morphims linking *Manager* and *Configuration* and the ones linking *Transmitter* and *Configuration*.

In the two cases, we obtain the same module (for equivalences of different constructions see [14]) ; this module specifies the whole NSDF, and we can reuse it in others applications like the alarm or the appointment delivery.

6 Tool

We have developed a tool to support our formalism. The kernel of this tool is based on the ideas of Rydeheard and Burstall [15] and defines all the useful notions of category theory. Above this kernel, the calculus of modules is implemented. And a third level provides user-friendly services like a parser and a graphical interface.

6.1 The categorical kernel

The tool defines a categorical kernel based on the ideas of Rydeheard and Burstall [15]. This kernel, written in SML, first defines the types that represent the basic notions in category theory. For example, the type of a category is defined as follows:

```
datatype ('o,'a)Cat = cat of ('a -> 'o) * ('a -> 'o) * ('o -> 'a) *
('a * 'a -> 'a)
```

It means that in order to define a category with objects of type o and arrows of type a, we need a *source* function ('a -> 'o) that gives the source object of an arrow, a *target* function ('a -> 'o) that gives the target object of an arrow, an *identity* function ('o -> 'a) that gives the identity arrow of an object and a *composition* function ('a * 'a -> 'a) that gives the arrow corresponding to the composition of two arrows.

All the objects in the tool are defined in the same way: the type of the object includes the elements that prove that the definition of this object is correct.

From the basic types, the tool defines several notions:

- graphs and diagrams (useful for the definition of functions that compute colimits);
- colimits and cocomplete categories (in order to define a cocomplete category, we have to give the initial object and means to compute the coproduct and coequalizer) ;
- functors, adjoints, natural transformations;
- the categories of sets and infinite sets;
- comma categories.

6.2 The calculus of modules

Above the categorical kernel, the category of algebraic signatures and the category of modules (Ehrig and Mahr ones) have been defined as particular cocomplete comma-categories. The categorical kernel and the two previous categories were defined in 1992 [16]. More recently, we have added the definition of the extended modules (with attributes, actions and axioms) and the horizontal operations on these modules: actualization, union, composition, product, and partial composition.

Remark: we defined all useful categories as cocomplete categories, this is a way to verify the proofs evoked in section 3.

6.3 Interface

Finally, we have defined a language for the modules and an associated parser, because the structures used by the tool are quite complex and not easy to handle; and a graphical interface written in Python [18] which gives an easy access to all the functionalities of the module calculus.

We can fetch files describing a module in the file system and enter these descriptions in the environment (parsing, verification of syntax). Then we can execute operations on the modules of the environment. This allows to automatically build a specification of a system from the specifications of its components.[4]

The NSDF, alarm and appointment dispatching applications have been modelised with the tool.

7 Verification

We have explained how to specify a system in a modular way. What is very interesting then is to be able to exploit the structure of the specification in order to make some modular verifications. We first recall that our formalism allows to control the interconnections and then consider the verification of a logical property : we explain how the proof of a global property can be modularized.

7.1 Control of the interconnections

We must insist on the fact that a first verification is done when the modules are interconnected (thanks to the import and export parts and to the morphisms). Indeed, the operations are possible only if the interconnected modules are compatible. More precisely, interconnections are expressed by specification morphisms between parts of module and two kinds of constraints must be respected (see definition of specification morphisms, section 3.2):

- type constraints: the profiles of the associated elements must be compatible. If they are not, it is detected by the tool and the operation is not executed.
- constraints concerning the axioms: the image of the axioms of the source specification must be theorems in the target one. The tool generates proof obligations that must be discharged for the operation to be executed.

It is thus an efficient way to control that the interconnections are coherent and this is interesting, particularly when the system is large.

7.2 Verification strategy

The definition of specification morphism is constraining but ensures the following property: for a morphism $m : Spec1 \rightarrow Spec2$, if a property $P1$ is true in $Spec1$, then $m(P1)$ is true in $Spec2$ (see [5]). We use this property in order to make modular verifications. The strategy is the following:

- For a property that we want to prove on a given specification, we first scan the operator, attribute and action names occuring in the formula. We intend to select the smallest specification which may enable the proof. The order between specifications is induced by the specification morphisms used to interconnect specifications: we say $S2$ is greater than $S1$ if the specifications

---

[4] A documentation about this tool can be found at http://www.cert.fr/francais/deri/wiels/Francais/wiels.html

are connected in the whole system by a morphism f: $S1 \to S2$. When we have achieved the proof in the small specification, we can translate back the theorem in the wished theory by means of the morphisms.

– When the least specification results from operation computation, we try to decompose the property in elementary lemmas provable in more basic specifications (and these lemmas are translated along the morphisms to the global description).

Following these basic principles, we develop several specific strategies, depending on the structure of the global specification and on the property to prove. For exemple, if we want to prove a global property on the system body and if we have a scheme like the following (the body parts are always linked in a hierarchical way, see the operation schemes in section 5):

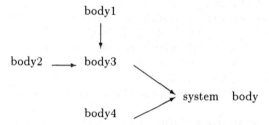

In this scheme, a property of the system may in fact be expressed and proved in body 3, and this property is then translated to the system body. Another property of the system body may result from the conjonction of two lemmas, each lemma being provable in smallest specifications (body 3 and 4).

The decomposition of global properties into local lemmas is made by hand, but it is relatively easy once a good knowledge about the application is acquired: the structure of the system is of great help in the process of decomposing properties. In [17], we had already applied a similar methodology to verify some properties of a fault-tolerance mechanism in a modular way.

8 Future work

As future work, we want to combine our tool for specification with existing verification and proof tools. But for the moment, we use an ad-hoc logic that we have defined and for which no tool exists. We thus have to define modules where behaviors are defined with another logic. We have began to work on TLA [11] in order to use tools associated to TLA (such as TLP [4]). We are also studying TRIO [7]: it is a temporal logic with a notion of duration and there exist tools for the proof of logical properties and for model and test case generation. We are involved in a project where our aim is to work on the modularization of the specification and validation of an aeronautics application in TRIO.

For long-dated work, we plan to study the vertical aspects of Ehrig and Mahr calculus (they have defined refinement operations). We also plan to combine the modules with several different formalisms and to study the possibilities to have heterogeneous modules in the same system specification. The final goal of modules is to bring modularity in several specification and verification formalisms.

References

1. CNET - Note technique NT/PAA/TSA/4727. *Specification de la fonction de selection et de diffusion de notifications*, 1996.
2. H. Ehrig and B. Mahr. *Fundamentals of Algebraic Specification 1*, volume 6 of *EATCS Monographs on Theoretical Computer Science*. Springer-Verlag, 1985. Equations and initial semantics.
3. H. Ehrig and B. Mahr. *Fundamentals of Algebraic Specification 2*, volume 21 of *EATCS Monographs on Theoretical Computer Science*. Springer-Verlag, 1990. Modules specifications and constraints.
4. U. Engberg. *Reasoning in the Temporal Logic of Actions*. PhD thesis, Department of Computer Science, University of Aarhus, September 1995.
5. J. Fiadeiro and T. Maibaum. Temporal theories as modularisation units for concurrent system specification. *Formal Aspects of Computing*, 4(3):239–272, 1992.
6. J. Fiadeiro and T. Maibaum. Design structures for object-based systems. In S. Goldsack and S.Kent, editors, *Formal Methods and Object Technology*. Springer-Verlag, 1996.
7. C. Ghezzi, D. Madrioli, and A. Morzenti. TRIO: A logic language for executable specifications of real-time systems. *jss*, 12(2), 1990.
8. ITU Draft Rec. G.851-01. *Management of the transport network - Application of the RM-ODP framework*, 1996. Study Group 15 Contribution.
9. ITU Rec. X.901, ISO DIS 10746-1. *Reference Model of Open Distributed Processing-Part1: Overview and Guide to Use*, 1994.
10. F. Kroger. Abstract modules: Combining algebraic and temporal logic specification means. *Technique et Science Informatiques*, 6(6), 1987.
11. L. Lamport. The Temporal Logic of Actions. Technical Report 79, SRC, 1992.
12. P. Michel and V.Wiels. Assistance au développement et à la maintenace de logiciels basée sur la composition. In *Les logiciels de télécommunications*, Actes des séminaires action scientifique France Telecom, mars 1997.
13. P. Michel and V. Wiels. Modular specification and validation of systems. In *ECOOP Workshop on Proof Theory of Concurrent Object-Oriented Programming*, July 1996.
14. P. Michel and V. Wiels. Un calcul de modules pour combiner les développements ascendants et descendants. In *Journee Formalisation des Activites Concurrentes LAAS-CNRS*, 1996.
15. D.E. Rydeheard and R.M. Burstall. *Computational Category Theory*. International Series in Computer Science. Prentice Hall, 1988.
16. J. Sauloy. A calculus of modules built on a kernel for categorical computations. unpublished.
17. C. Seguin and V. Wiels. Using a Logical and Categorical Approach for the Validation of Fault-tolerant Systems. In *Proceedings of FME'96*, volume 1051 of *Lecture Notes in Computer Science*. Springer-Verlag, 1996.
18. G. van Rossum. Python tutorial. http://www.python.org/, 1996.

A Timed Semantics for the STATEMATE Implementation of Statecharts

Carsta Petersohn* and Luis Urbina**

Institut für Informatik und Praktische Mathematik,
Christian–Albrechts–Universität Kiel, Preußerstr. 1–9, D–24105 Kiel, Germany***

Abstract. The two central simulation algorithms of the STATEMATE tool for Statecharts are formalized following the most recent description by Harel and Naamad [7]. Our semantics is given in terms of fair and clocked transition systems [15, 12]. The main benefit from providing such formal semantics is that analysis tools developed for these transition systems can now be applied to STATEMATE specifications. We also discuss typical properties of synchronous languages for our semantics.

1 Introduction

Statecharts [4] is a widely used specification language for complex reactive systems. From the beginning, it was intended to be used by actual engineers in specifying real systems. Typical application fields are automobile industry, aerospace and telecommunications. Statecharts has the advantage to be good readable since it is graphical and its concepts of parallel and hierarchically ordered states allow a very compact specification. The executable semantics of Statecharts implemented in the commercial tool STATEMATE [6] has been described in [7]. The toolset is dominated by Statecharts. Activitycharts, another specification language of STATEMATE, is used to structure a system representation by functional aspects, but the semantics of the system representation is established mainly by its statecharts. STATEMATE supports, for instance, simulators and code generators.

Many variants of formal semantics [11, 19] for Statecharts have been proposed, but the simulation algorithms implemented in STATEMATE have not been given a formal semantics. The main difference between the semantics [7] and these formal semantics is that by [7] changes that occur in a system step take effect in the next system step and not within the current one as, for instance, in [9, 17]. In [13] and [14] real–time semantics for Statecharts have been

---

* Supported by the German Research Council (DFG) within the project AMFORES (Applicable Formal Methodologies for Reactive and Real–Time Systems) under grant Ro. 1122/1-2.

** Supported by the German Research Council (DFG) within the special program KONDISK (Analysis and Synthesis of Technical Systems with Continuous-discrete Dynamics) under the grants Ro 1122/2 and En 152/19.

*** E–mail: { cp, lu }@informatik.uni–kiel.de

proposed, however, both contain real–time features which differ from those given in [7]. In [14], time durations are associated with transitions and in [13] transitions can be delayed.

The most recent description of the Statecharts semantics implemented in STATEMATE is given in [7] in natural language. In this paper we provide a formal semantics for an essential part of Statecharts. Time–dependent properties typical for synchronous languages can be verified. We formalize the concepts of complex state structure, full compound transitions, simple data processing, and timeout events. We do not consider history operators and complex data processing, but believe that their addition requires only an extension of our formalism. Our approach follows [7] as closely as possible so that only little argumentation is needed to show that both the formal model and the natural language description are 'equivalent'. Moreover, we give theorems allowing to abstract from some implementation details. Our basic formalization is influenced by [9, 18, 10], but to reach our goal we had to extend and change definitions contained in these papers. Our formalization consists of the following four parts:

1. We capture the syntax of graphical Statecharts by an abstract textual syntax. We formalize basic semantic concepts. Based on this, we also formalize conclusions stated in [7] and prove them to be correct (Appendix). For passages in [7] with more than one interpretation we introduce several definitions and investigate their equivalence (Sect. 2).

2. We formalize different stages of the basic step algorithm as different kinds of steps. They are the basis of the formalization of the simulation algorithms (Sects. 3.1, 3.2). The central step is a system step in which a maximal set of non–conflicting transitions is taken simultaneously in zero time [7]. The general principles underlying system steps are: (i) calculations in one step are based on the situation at the beginning of the step, (ii) changes that occur in a step can be sensed only after the completion of the step, and (iii) events "live" for the duration of one step only and are not "remembered" in subsequent system steps.

3. The untimed parts of STATEMATE's simulation algorithms Go-Step and Go-Repeat are formalized in terms of fair transition systems (Sect. 3.3). These parts deal with the scheduling of steps. Go-Step models that after every system step new input is considered, and Go-Repeat that a system reaction due to an input is completed until a stable state is reached before new input from the environment is considered.

4. The timed parts of the algorithms dealing also with an internal clock and timeout events are formalized in terms of clocked transition systems over **N** (Sect. 4). Go-Step underlies a synchronous time model. It increments the internal clock after every system step. Go-Repeat underlies an asynchronous time model. The internal clock is incremented by Go-Repeat only after reaching a stable state.

Section 5 discusses in which way concurrency and concepts of synchronous languages are modeled by our formalization. We conclude with Sect. 6. Proofs are given in the appendix.

555

2 Preliminaries

The subset of Statecharts we consider in this paper consists of the basic components *states* and *labeled transitions* which we informally introduce by Fig. 1. In Sects. 2.1, 2.2 and 2.3 we will give mathematical descriptions for these concepts.

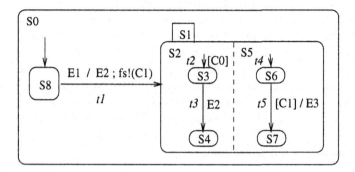

Fig. 1. Example of a Statecharts Specification

There are three types of states: *AND*, *OR*, and *BASIC* states. In Fig. 1, for instance, $S1$ is an AND state, $S0$, $S2$, $S5$ are OR states, and $S3$, $S4$, and $S8$ are BASIC states. States obey a hierarchical order. For instance, $S2$ and $S5$ are substates of state $S1$. Substates of an AND state are called *parallel states*. A *configuration* is a maximal set of states a system can simultaneously reside in. If an AND (OR) state is contained in a configuration, then all substates (only one of its substates) are (is) also contained in it. Figure 1 contains *events* E_1, E_2, E_3 and *condition variables* C_0 and C_1. For the specification of real–time aspects *timeout events* are used. A timeout event '$tm(e, d)$' is generated iff the last occurrence of event e has happened $d \in \mathbf{N}$ time units ago.

In the context of Statecharts *transitions* are arrows connecting non–empty source sets with target state sets. *Default transitions* have no source state and as target state a substate of an OR state, e.g, transition $t_2 = (\emptyset, \{S3\})$. The labels $t_1, \ldots, t_5$ are not part of the graphical Statecharts, but added to provide the transitions with names. Transitions can be marked by *labels* '$e[c]/a$', where 'e', 'c', and 'a' are an *event*, a guard *condition* and an *action expression*, respectively. All these parts are optional. Intuitively, event e will trigger the transition if the guard c is true, and taking the transition will cause the execution of action a. Event and condition expressions are boolean combinations of (simple) events and conditions, respectively. An action expression contains assignments, e.g., '$fs!(C1)$' means that the variable $C1$ gets the value *false*. Moreover, events can be emitted, e.g., event $E2$ is generated by the action '$E2$'. Action expressions can be composed by ';', e.g., '$E2; fs!(C1)$'.

The semantics given in [7] is based on *full compound transitions*. These are a combination of a transition with a not–empty source and several default transitions. More precisely, for every entered OR state one default transition is added and the label of a full compound transition is the combination of the labels of the component transitions. For instance, in the figure above the combination of transitions t_1, t_2 and t_4 with label $E1[C0]/E2; fs!(C1)$ constitutes a full compound transition, which we denote by t_6. When transition $t_1 = (\{S8\}, \{S1\})$ is taken, state $S8$ is left and state $S1$ entered. Then, entering $S3$ and $S6$ is determined by transitions t_2 and $t_4 = (\emptyset, \{S6\})$. After the execution of a full compound transition a new configuration is reached.

Following the STATEMATE implementation a graphical statechart is internally extended by two extra states r and $init$, where r is the new *root state*, the substates of which are state $init$ and the old root state of the graphical statechart. The state $init$ captures the situation that no state of the graphical statechart is active before the simulation starts. The statechart is extended by a default transition the target state of which is $init$ and by a transition from $init$ to the old root state. In this paper, we consider all transitions the source of which is a non–empty set of states to be extended to full compound transitions and eliminate all default transitions.

2.1 States

Formal Syntax: We formalize the hierarchical structure of the states by a finite directed marked tree:

A *state hierarchy* is a tuple $\mathcal{H} = (\mathcal{S}, down, type)$, where

- $\mathcal{S}$ is a finite set of *states*,
- $down : \mathcal{S} \to 2^{\mathcal{S}}$ defines for every state its substates, such that:
  1. There exists a unique state $r \in \mathcal{S}$, such that $\forall s \in \mathcal{S} : r \notin down(s)$. Moreover, $|down(r)| = 2$ and there is a state $init \in \mathcal{S}$ with $init \in down(r) \wedge down(init) = \emptyset$.
  2. For each $s \in \mathcal{S} \setminus \{r\}$ there exists exactly one *path* $r = s_1, s_2, \ldots, s_n = s$, $n \in \mathbf{N}, n \geq 1$ along states $s_i \in \mathcal{S}$, with $s_{i+1} \in down(s_i)$ for $1 \leq i \leq n-1$.
- $type : \mathcal{S} \to \{AND, OR, BASIC\}$ defines for every state its type, such that:
  1. $type(r) = OR$,
  2. $\forall s \in \mathcal{S} : down(s) \neq \emptyset \Leftrightarrow type(s) \in \{AND, OR\}$,
  3. $\forall s_1 \in \mathcal{S} : (type(s_1) = AND \Rightarrow \forall s_2 \in down(s_1) : type(s_2) = OR)$.

For a given state hierarchy we introduce the terminology related to descendants and ancestors of states. The function $down^* : \mathcal{S} \to 2^{\mathcal{S}}$, which computes for a state $s \in \mathcal{S}$ its *descendants*, is the function satisfying the following requirements: 1.) $s \in down^*(s)$, 2.) $s_2 \in down^*(s_1) \Rightarrow down(s_2) \subseteq down^*(s_1)$, 3.) for all sets $X \subseteq \mathcal{S}$ satisfying the previous two conditions $down^*(s) \subseteq X$. The function $up : (\mathcal{S} \setminus \{r\}) \to \mathcal{S}$ defines for a state $s \in \mathcal{S} \setminus \{r\}$ its *direct ancestor*, i.e. $up(s) = u \Leftrightarrow s \in down(u)$. The function $up^* : \mathcal{S} \to 2^{\mathcal{S}}$, which computes for a state $s \in \mathcal{S}$ its *ancestors*, is the function satisfying the following requirements: 1.) $s \in up^*(s)$, 2.) $\forall s_1 \in (\mathcal{S} \setminus \{r\}) : (s_1 \in up^*(s_2) \Rightarrow up(s_1) \in up^*(s_2))$, and 3.) for all sets $X \subseteq \mathcal{S}$ satisfying the previous two conditions $up^*(s) \subseteq X$. The generalization of the definitions $down^*$ and up^* for sets of states $X \subseteq \mathcal{S}$

is as usual: $down^*(X) = \bigcup_{s \in X} down^*(s)$, and $up^*(X) = \bigcup_{s \in X} up^*(s)$. We introduce the partial order $\leq$ on states by: $s_1 \leq s_2$ iff $s_1 \in down^*(s_2)$. The transitive, irreflexive and antisymmetric relation $<$ on states is defined as follows: $s_1 < s_2$ iff $s_1 \leq s_2$ and $s_1 \neq s_2$. The *lowest common ancestor* of a non–empty set of states $X \subseteq S$, denoted by $LCA(X)$, is defined as follows: $\forall s \in X : s \leq LCA(X)$ and $\forall s' \in S : (\forall s \in X : s \leq s') \Rightarrow (LCA(X) \leq s')$.

Configurations: 'A configuration is a maximal set of states that the system can be in simultaneously' (cf. [7], Sect. 3). The function $C_{all} : S \to 2^{2^S}$ mapping a state s_r to the set of configurations C relative to s_r is the function satisfying the following requirements: 1.) $s_r \in C$, 2.) $s \in C \wedge type(s) = AND \Rightarrow down(s) \subseteq C$, 3.) $s \in C \wedge type(s) = OR \Rightarrow |down(s) \cap C| = 1$, and 4.) $\forall s \in (C \setminus \{s_r\}) : up(s) \in C$, i.e., for all $s \in C$ there exists a path from s_r to s where all states of the path are also contained in C. We abbreviate $C_{all}(r)$ by C_{all}.

'To uniquely determine a configuration it is sufficient to know its basic states' (cf. [7], Sect. 3). Let $C \in C_{all}(s_r)$, $B = \{s \in C \mid down(s) = \emptyset\}$, then $up^*(B) \cap down^*(s_r) = C$ (cf. Lemma 1). The set B is called a *basic configuration* (relative to r).

2.2 Transitions

Now, we give an abstract syntax for Statecharts transitions. In order to do so, we introduce legal transitions, full compound transitions, sets of exited and entered states, and conflict and priority between two transitions.

Formal Syntax: A *transition* is a triple $t = (X, l, Y)$, where l is a label and $X, Y \subseteq S$ are the sets of source and target states, respectively. As we eliminated default transitions of the considered graphical statechart it follows that $X, Y \neq \emptyset$ and either $X, Y \subseteq (S \setminus \{r, init\})$ or $X = \{init\}$ and $Y \subseteq (S \setminus \{r, init\})$. Transitions satisfying the latter condition are called *initial transitions*. By T we denote the set of all transitions.

'For a transition to be legal every two states in the source and every two states in the target must be mutually orthogonal' (cf. [7], Sect. 6). The definition of orthogonality given below is sufficient to ensure that source and target states of a transition are contained in configurations. Two states $s_1, s_2 \in S$ are said to be *orthogonal*, denoted by $s_1 \perp s_2$, iff $type(LCA(\{s_1, s_2\})) = AND \wedge \neg(s_1 \leq s_2 \vee s_2 \leq s_1)$. A transition $t = (X, l, Y)$ is *legal* iff $(\forall s_1, s_2 \in X : s_1 \neq s_2 \Rightarrow s_1 \perp s_2) \wedge (\forall s_1, s_2 \in Y : s_1 \neq s_2 \Rightarrow s_1 \perp s_2)$. The set of legal transitions is denoted by T_l.

States Entered and Exited by a Transition : To define the set of entered and exited states of a transition the scope of a transition is introduced. 'The scope of a transition is the lowest OR state in the hierarchy of states that is a proper common ancestor of all the sources and targets of the transitions' (cf. [7], Sect. 6). The function $scope : T \to S$ mapping a transition t to its scope is a function which satisfies the following requirements: 1.) $\forall s \in (X \cup Y) : s < scope(t) \wedge$

$type(scope(t)) = OR$, and 2.) $\forall s' \in \mathcal{S} : ((\forall s \in (X \cup Y) : s < s') \wedge type(s') = OR) \Rightarrow scope(t) \le s'$.

'When a transition t is taken, all proper descendants of its scope in which the system resided at the beginning of the step are exited and all proper descendants of that scope in which the system will reside as a result of executing t are entered' (cf. [7], Sect. 6). For a given transition the set of entered and exited states are defined by functions $Exit$ and $Enter$ as follows. The function $ExitMax : \mathcal{T}_l \to \mathcal{S}$ determines for a taken transition $t = (X, l, Y)$ the *uppermost exited state* $ExitMax(t) \in \mathcal{S}$, i.e., $ExitMax(t) \in down(scope(t))$ and $LCA(X) \le ExitMax(t)$. The function $Exit : \mathcal{T}_l \times \mathcal{C}_{all} \to \mathcal{S}$ determines for a taken transition t and a configuration $\mathcal{C}$ the set of exited states by $down^*(ExitMax(t)) \cap \mathcal{C}$. $EnterMax : \mathcal{T}_l \to \mathcal{S}$ determines for a taken transition $t = (X, l, Y)$ the *uppermost entered state* $EnterMax(t) \in \mathcal{S}$ defined by $EnterMax(t) \in down(scope(t))$ and $LCA(Y) \le EnterMax(t)$.

We characterize full compound transitions by a condition on the target set. This condition determines which substate of an OR state will be entered when that OR state is entered. We call a transition $t = (X, l, Y) \in \mathcal{T}$ *full compound* iff for all substates s of $EnterMax(t)$ of type OR either an entered substate is determined by Y, i.e. $Y \cap down^*(down(s)) \ne \emptyset$, or the state s itself is not entered, i.e. $\exists s' \in up^*(s), s'' \in up^*(Y) : s' \ne s'' \wedge up(s') = up(s'') \wedge type(up(s')) = OR$. By $\mathcal{T}_w$ we denote the set of all legal full compound transitions. The function $Enter : \mathcal{T}_w \to 2^{\mathcal{S}}$ maps a taken transition $t = (X, l, Y)$ to the set of entered states $up^*(Y) \cap down^*(EnterMax(t))$. The condition on the target set of a full compound transition can be replaced by the following simpler one. A set of states is an allowed target set of a legal full compound transition $t \in \mathcal{T}_w$ and $En = EnterMax(t)$ iff it is a basic configuration relative to a state $En \in States$ (Theorem 2). When a transition $t = (X, l, Y)$ is taken in a configuration $\mathcal{C}$, a new configuration $\mathcal{C}' \in \mathcal{C}_{all}$ is reached. That is, if $X \subseteq \mathcal{C}$, then $((\mathcal{C} \setminus Exit(t, \mathcal{C})) \cup Enter(t)) \in \mathcal{C}_{all}$ (Theorem 3). Consider $t_6 = (\{S8\}, l_6, \{S3, S6\})$ in Fig.1. Then, $scope(t_6) = S0$, $ExitMax(t_6) = S8$ and $EnterMax(t_6) = S1$. Given $\mathcal{C} = \{r, S0, S8\}$, then $Exit(t_6, \mathcal{C}) = \{S8\}$, $Enter(t_6) = \{S1, S2, S3, S5, S6\}$.

Conflict between two Transitions and Priority: The notions of 'conflict' and 'priority' between two transitions are introduced to compute a set of transitions which can be taken simultaneously. 'Two transitions are in conflict if there is some common state that would be exited if any one of them were to be taken' (cf. [7], Sect. 7). This can be interpreted in two ways. Two transitions $t_i = (X_i, l_i, Y_i) \in \mathcal{T}$, $i = 1, 2$, are *in conflict* with respect to a configuration $\mathcal{C} \in \mathcal{C}_{all}$ if 1. $(Exit(t_1, \mathcal{C}) \cap X_2) \ne \emptyset \vee (Exit(t_2, \mathcal{C}) \cap X_1) \ne \emptyset$, or 2. $Exit(t_1, \mathcal{C}) \cap Exit(t_2, \mathcal{C}) \ne \emptyset$ holds. Other definitions of conflict found in the literature are independent of a configuration. These are 3. $ExitMax(t_1) \le ExitMax(t_2) \vee ExitMax(t_2) \le ExitMax(t_2)$, 4. $type(LCA(\{scope(t_1), scope(t_2)\})) = OR$, and 5. $\neg(scope(t_1) \bot scope(t_2))$. If $X_1, X_2 \subseteq \mathcal{C}$, then conditions $1 - 5$ are all equivalent (Theorem 4).

If two transitions $t_1, t_2 \in \mathcal{T}_l$ are in conflict and one of them has a higher priority, then this one is taken (cf. [7], Sect. 7). In STATEMATE a transition t_1 has a higher *priority* than transition t_2, which we denote by $t_1 > t_2$, iff $scope(t_1) > scope(t_2)$. The definition of priority is changed, for instance, in the semantics of Statecharts supporting object–oriented methodologies [5]. However, priority of transitions is only used in Sect. 3.1, where only $<$ is used. There is only needed that $<$ is a relation between transitions. In fact, all proofs of the theorems given in the appendix do not depend on the definitions of priority.

Let $\mathcal{C} = \{r, S0, S1, S2, S3, S5, S6\}$ be a configuration in Fig. 1. Then, $t_3 = (\{S3\}, l_3, \{S4\})$ and $t_5 = (\{S6\}, l_5, \{S7\})$ are not in conflict. According to definitions 1 and 2 of conflict, transitions t_6 and t_3 are in conflict, and according to definitions 3–5 of conflict, they are not. This does not contradict our theorem because there does not exist any configuration such that $\{S8, S3\}$ is contained in it. If t_6 had the opposite direction, they would be in conflict according to all definitions. Transition t_6 has a higher priority than transition t_3.

2.3 Labels of Transitions

Let *Events* denote the set of event and *Conds* the set of condition variables occurring in a statechart. A label of a transition 'e[c]/a' consists of an event, a condition and an action expression. An event expression is defined by the grammar $S_e ::= \varepsilon \mid E$, $E ::= e \mid \neg E \mid E \vee E \mid E \wedge E$, where $e \in Events$. A condition expression is similar to an event expression where condition variables occur instead of events. Let $T_{cond} = \{fs!(C), tr!(C) \mid C \in Conds\}$ be the set of all assignments to condition variables, then action expressions are generated by the grammar $S_a ::= \varepsilon \mid A$, $A ::= e \mid ca \mid A; A$, where $e \in Events$ and $ca \in T_{cond}$. Let $\mathcal{L}_e, \mathcal{L}_c$ and $\mathcal{L}_a$ denote the sets of event, condition and action expressions, respectively.

A transition is said to be *enabled* iff the event expression evaluates to true for the set of available events and the condition expression evaluates to true for the set of true condition variables. For instance, $E1[C0]$ evaluates to true iff event $E1$ is available and condition variable $C0$ is true. For the evaluation of event and condition expressions we introduce the relations $EvalEv \subseteq \mathcal{L}_e \times 2^{Events}$ and $EvalCo \subseteq \mathcal{L}_c \times 2^{Conds}$, the definitions of which are straightforward.

Assignments to condition variables can be regarded in STATEMATE as the set of internally generated tuples (C, val), where val is a new value for C. Let $Val = Conds \times \{tt, ff\}$. By Val^* we denote lists over Val. For the evaluation of action expressions we introduce the functions $EvalAc$ and $EvalCl$ defined as follows. Function $EvalAc : \mathcal{L}_a \times 2^{Conds} \rightarrow 2^{(2^{Events} \times Val^*)}$ yields for an action expression and values of the condition variables a set where each element consists of a set of generated events and a list of new values for condition variables. The most interesting evaluation is that of an action expression $a_1; a_2$, which leads to a non–deterministic execution of a_1 and a_2:

$$EvalAc(a_1; a_2) = \{ (E_1 \cup E_2, Cl_i * Cl_j) \mid i, j, \in \{1, 2\}, i \neq j,$$
$$(E_1, Cl_1) \in EvalAc(a_1), (E_2, Cl_2) \in EvalAc(a_2)\} \ .$$

The function $EvalCl : Val^* \times 2^{Conds} \rightarrow 2^{Conds}$ yields for the previous set of true conditions and a list of new values for condition variables a set of true conditions.

3 Semantics – Qualitative Time Abstraction

Statecharts is used to model reactive systems by specifying the system as a statechart and the only thing known about the environment is that it provides inputs. Here, we consider a qualitative time abstraction, that is, we can only observe that an event precedes another one, but not how much time has passed. We formalize parts of the basic step algorithm in Sects. 3.1 and 3.2 and then the simulation algorithms Go-Step and Go-Repeat in Sect. 3.3.

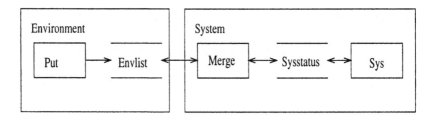

Fig. 2. Functional Overview

Figure 2 shows the interactions between the system and the environment. The system part consists of a system processing step Sys, a system status $SysSt$, and a step $Merge$. The environment part consists of an environment status $Envlist$, and a step Put. The step Put is an extension of the basic step algorithm. The interactions between the system and the environment take place over $Envlist$, where step Put provides inputs to the system, and step $Merge$ adds inputs from the environment to the system status. $SysSt$ contains the last system status on which the system processing step Sys depends. The result of step Sys is a new system status.

3.1 The Basic Step System Part

The abstract syntax of a statechart is described by a tuple $(\mathcal{H}, \mathcal{T}, Events, Conds)$, where $\mathcal{H}$ is the state hierarchy, $\mathcal{T}$ is the set of full compound transitions containing at least one initial transition, $Events$ is the set of events and $Conds$ is the set of condition variables occurring in the labels of the transitions.

Definition 1 System Status, Initial System Status. *A system status is a tuple $(S, E, C) \in \mathcal{C}_{all} \times 2^{Events} \times 2^{Conds}$ consisting of a configuration of the state hierarchy $S \in \mathcal{C}_{all}$, a set of events $E \in 2^{Events}$ and a set of true condition variables $C \in 2^{Conds}$. By $SysSt_{all}$ we denote the set of statuses. A system status $(S, E, C) \in SysSt_{all}$ with $S = \{r, init\}$, $E = \emptyset$ and $C = \emptyset$ is called* initial system status. *The set of initial statuses is denoted by Θ_{Sys}.*

The system processing step consists of the execution of enabled transitions. A transition is said to be *enabled* in a system status (S, E, C) iff its source states are included in the actual configuration S and both the event e and condition expressions c evaluate to true (cf. [7], Sect. 6).

Definition 2 Enable. *By* Enable $\subseteq \mathcal{T} \times SysSt_{all}$ *we denote the set of tuples* $(t, (S, E, C))$, *such that the transition* t *is enabled in the system status* (S, E, C). *That is,* $(t, (S, E, C)) \in$ Enable *iff* $t = (X, e[c]/a, Y)$, $X \subseteq S$ *and both* $EvalEv(e, E)$ *and* $EvalCo(c, C)$ *evaluate to true.*

Intuitively, an internal system step, as an essential part of the basic step algorithm, consists of the execution of a set of transitions that can be executed simultaneously. Such a set of transitions $Tr \subseteq \mathcal{T}$ depends on the actual system state $SysSt \in SysSt_{all}$. Let Max $\subseteq SysSt_{all} \times 2^{\mathcal{T}}$ and $(SysSt, Tr) \in$ Max. Then the set of transitions Tr is computed as follows ([7], Sect. 8):

- Compute for $SysSt$ the maximal set of enabled transitions:
  Enable$_{SysSt} = \{t \in \mathcal{T} \mid$ Enable$(t, SysSt)\}$.
- Remove from Enable$_{SysSt}$ those transitions which are in conflict with other enabled transitions of higher priority: Enable$^-_{SysSt}$ = Enable$_{SysSt} \setminus$ $\{t_c \in$ Enable$_{SysSt}$ $\mid \exists t \in$ Enable$_{SysSt} : t_c < t \wedge conflict(t, t_c)\}$.
- Compute Tr as a maximal subset of Enable$^-_{SysSt}$ containing no conflicting transitions. That is, Tr must satisfy the following two conditions:
  - $\forall t_1, t_2 \in Tr : t_1 = t_2 \vee \neg conflict(t_1, t_2)$, and
  - $\forall t_c \in$ Enable$^-_{SysSt} : t_c \in Tr \vee (\exists t \in Tr : (t_c \neq t \wedge conflict(t_c, t)))$.

The general principles of [7], Sect. 2, underlying a system step of simultaneously executed transitions are the following 'calculations in one step are based on the situation at the beginning of the step, changes that occur in a step can be sensed only after completion of the step, and events "live" for the duration of a step, and are not "remembered" in subsequent steps.' This is modeled by the step Sys defined next.

Definition 3 Sys Step. *The system step* Sys *is defined as the relation* $Sys \subseteq$ $(SysSt_{all} \times 2^{\mathcal{T}} \times SysSt_{all})$, *such that* $((S_0, E_0, C_0), Tr, (S', E', C')) \in Sys$ *iff* $((S_0, E_0, C_0), Tr) \in$ Max *and exactly one of the following conditions is satisfied:*

- *If no transition is enabled, that is* $|Tr| = 0$, *the step is empty and* $(S', E', C') = (S_0, \emptyset, C_0)$.
- *Otherwise, let* $\{t_1, \ldots, t_{|Tr|}\} = Tr$, *and* $t_i = (X_i, e_i[c_i]/a_i, Y_i)$ *for* $i \in \{1, \ldots, |Tr|\}$. *Then, for all* $i \in \{1, \ldots, |Tr|\}$ *there exist tuples* $(S_i, E_i, Cl_i) \in \mathcal{C}_{all} \times 2^{Events} \times T^*_{cond}$, *such that* $(E_i, Cl_i) \in EvalAc(a_i, C_0) \wedge$ $S_i = (S_{i-1} \setminus Exit(t_i, S_0)) \cup Enter(t_i)$ *and* $S' = (S_{|Tr|}, E' = \bigcup_{i \in \{1, \ldots, |Tr|\}} E_i, C' = EvalCl(C_0, Cl_1 * \ldots * Cl_{|Tr|}))$.

This formalizes an essential part of the basic step algorithm. For $((S_0, E_0, C_0), Tr, (S', E', C')) \in Sys$ we write briefly $((S_0, E_0, C_0), (S', E', C'))$. The final configuration does not depend on the order of the execution of the transitions (Theorem 6), that is $S' = (S_0 \setminus \bigcup_{i \in \{1, \ldots, n\}} Exit(t_i, S_0)) \cup \bigcup_{i \in \{1, \ldots, n\}} Enter(t_i)$.

3.2 The Basic Step Interface Part

The interface between the system and the environment is modeled in the basic step algorithm by a list which contains the changes generated by the environment since the last internal system step [7].

Definition 4 Interface Status, Initial Interface Status. *A status of the interface list is a pair* $(E, C) \in 2^{Events} \times T^*_{cond}$, *where* E *is a set of events and* C *is a list of actions over condition variables. The set containing all statuses of the interface list is denoted by* $Envlist_{all}$. *A status of the interface list satisfying the predicate* $\Theta_{Env}(E_{env}, C_{env}) \equiv E_{env} = \emptyset \land C_{env} = \varepsilon$ *is called* initial status.

The basic step algorithm adds the external events to the list of internal generated events and executes all actions implied by the external changes (cf. [7], Sect. 8). This is modeled by the *Merge* step defined next.

Definition 5 Merge Step. *The* Merge *step is a relation* $Take \subseteq (SysSt_{all} \times Envlist_{all} \times SysSt_{all} \times Envlist_{all})$, *such that* $((S, E, C), (E_{Env}, Cl_{Env}), (S', E', C'), (E'_{Env}, Cl'_{Env})) \in Take$ *iff the new system status* $(S', E', C') = (S, (E \cup E_{Env}), EvalCl(C, Cl_{Env}))$ *and the new interface status* $(E'_{Env}, Cl'_{Env}) = (\emptyset, \varepsilon)$. *Thus, the* Merge *step adds to the actual system the interface status.*

How the environment is influenced by the system is not described in [7]. To model the situation in which the environment provides inputs to the system the *Put* step is introduced. Notice that this is not part of the simulation algorithms. To be general we consider the general case that the step leads to arbitrary changes of the interface list.

Definition 6 Put Step. *The relation* $Put \subseteq Envlist_{all} \times Envlist_{all}$ *models the changes of the environment status.*

3.3 The Untimed Part of Go-Step and Go-Repeat

Now, the untimed parts of the algorithms Go-Step and Go-Repeat are formalized in terms of fair transition systems denoted by FTS_S and FTS_R, respectively. Both FTS_S and FTS_R are based on our formalization of system status and environment status and contain the sets of variables $V_{sys} = \{S, E, C\}$ and $V_{env} = \{E_{env}, C_{env}\}$. We introduce mappings σ_{Sys} and σ_{Env} which capture the actual system status by $(\sigma_{Sys}(S), \sigma_{Sys}(E), \sigma_{Sys}(C))$ and the actual environment status by $(\sigma_{Env}(E_{env}), \sigma_{Env}(C_{env}))$.

The part of algorithm Go-Step (cf. [7], Sect. 9) considered here is: 1.) execute all external changes reported since the completion of the previous step, 2.) execute one step. Point one is formalized by the *Take* step and point two by the *Sys* step. Moreover, we introduce step *Put* to model that the environment has provided input to the system. We extend the algorithm to the transition system shown in Fig. 3.

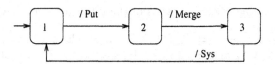

Fig. 3. Transition System FTS_S

The corresponding FTS_S consists of the following components:

1. The set of variables $V = V_{sys} \cup V_{env} \cup V_{loc}$, where $V_{loc} = \{\pi\}$ and $\sigma_{loc}\{\pi\} \rightarrow \{1, 2, 3\}$. Let Σ be the set of mappings with domain V consistent with $\sigma_{Sys}, \sigma_{Env}$ and σ_{loc}.
2. The set of initial states $\Theta \subseteq \Sigma$ is identified by the predicate $\Theta(V)$, such that $\Theta(V) \equiv \Theta_{Sys}(V_{Sys}) \wedge \Theta_{Env}(V_{Env}) \wedge \pi = 1$.
3. The set of transitions $\mathcal{T}$ containing $\tau_{12}, \tau_{23}, \tau_{31} \subseteq \Sigma \times \Sigma$. These relations are identified by their characteristic predicates, i.e., assertions as follows:
$\rho_{12}(V, V') : \pi = 1 \wedge Put(V_{Env}, V'_{Env}) \wedge V'_{sys} = V_{sys} \wedge \pi' = 2$
$\rho_{23}(V, V') : \pi = 2 \wedge Merge(V_{sys}, V_{Env}, V'_{sys}, V'_{Env}) \wedge \pi' = 3$
$\rho_{31}(V, V') : \pi = 3 \wedge Sys(V_{sys}, V'_{sys}) \wedge V'_{Env} = V_{Env} \wedge \pi' = 1$
The set of transitions is well–defined, since for every state $s \in \Sigma$ there exists a transition $\tau \in \mathcal{T}$ which is enabled.

The part of algorithm Go-Repeat (cf. [7], Sect. 9) considered here is : 1.) execute all external changes reported since the completion of the previous step, 2.) repeatedly execute one step till the system is in a stable state, i.e., there are no generated events and no enabled compound transition left. To formalize this we introduce the set $stable \subseteq SysSt_{all}$ containing all system statuses $(S, E, C) \in SysSt_{all}$ in which the system is in a stable state, i.e., for which $E = \emptyset \wedge \neg\exists t \in \mathcal{T} : Enab(t, (S, E, C))$ holds.

To ensure that a system reaction as modeled by Go-Repeat terminates, we give two solutions: a.) The first solution is to restrict to a subclass of statecharts specifications which terminate for all input. This makes only sense if this set of statecharts is recursive. This is the case, since we consider only statecharts which are finite. b.) The second solution is to introduce a constant $c \in \mathbf{N}$ which restricts the allowed number of repetitions of Sys step. Such a constant is not part of the described algorithm in [7], but used within STATEMATE. We model the simulation algorithm by $c = \infty$. The transition system for algorithm Go-Repeat is depicted in Fig. 4.

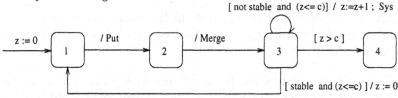

Fig. 4. Transition System FTS_R

The corresponding FTS_R consists of the following components:

1. The set of variables $V = V_{sys} \cup V_{env} \cup V_{loc}$, where $V_{loc} = \{\pi, z\}$ with σ_{loc} : $\{\pi\} \to \{1, 2, 3, 4\}$ and $\sigma_{loc}\{z\} \to \mathbf{N}$. Let Σ be the set of mappings with domain V consistent with $\sigma_{Sys}, \sigma_{Env}$ and σ_{loc}.
2. The set $\Theta \subseteq \Sigma$ is identified by $\Theta(V) \equiv \Theta_{Sys}(V_{Sys}) \wedge \Theta_{Env}(V_{Env}) \wedge \pi = 1 \wedge z = 0$.
3. The set of transitions $\mathcal{T}$ containing $\tau_{12}, \tau_{23}, \tau_{33}, \tau_{31}, \tau_{34}, \tau_{44} \subseteq \Sigma \times \Sigma$, where ρ_{12}, and ρ_{23} are similarly defined as in FTS_S, and

$$\rho_{33}(V, V') \; : \; \pi = 3 \; \wedge \; z \leq c \wedge \neg stable(V_{sys}) \; \wedge \; Sys(V_{sys}, V'_{sys}) \wedge$$
$$V'_{Env} = V_{Env} \; \wedge z' = z + 1 \; \wedge \; \pi' = 3$$

$$\rho_{31}(V, V') \; : \; \pi = 3 \; \wedge \; z \leq c \wedge stable(V_{sys}) \; \wedge \; (V'_{sys}, V'_{Env}) = (V_{sys}, V_{Env}) \; \wedge$$
$$z' = 0 \; \wedge \; \pi' = 1$$

$$\rho_{34}(V, V') \; : \; \pi = 3 \; \wedge \; z > c \; \wedge \; (V'_{sys}, V'_{Env}) = (V_{sys}, V_{Env}) \; \wedge$$
$$z' = z \; \wedge \; \pi' = 4$$

$$\rho_{44}(V, V') \quad \pi = 4 \; \wedge \; V' = V \; \wedge \; \pi' = 4$$

The set of transitions is well–defined, since for every state $s \in \Sigma$ there exists a transition $\tau \in \mathcal{T}$ which is enabled.

4 Semantics – Quantitative Time Abstraction

Here, we assume a quantitative time abstraction based on an internal clock. We consider an extended subset of statecharts containing also timeout events. The syntax of the statechart is captured in the same way as in Sect. 3.3, except that the set of events can contain timeout events. In Sect. 4.1 we formalize parts of the basic step algorithm related to timeout events and the internal clock. There are two time models in [7], Sect. 9, the synchronous and the asynchronous time model, which differ in the modeled relationship between processing steps and progress of time. In the synchronous time model system processing and internal clock are synchronized, while in the asynchronous model they are not. They are used in the algorithms Go-Step and Go-Repeat, respectively. In Sect. 4.2 we also formalize the timed part of the algorithms in terms of clocked transition systems. They are appropriate since explicit access to time is possible, i.e., there exists a variable T capturing the global time, and timers can be introduced [12].

4.1 Timeout Events

A timeout event '$tm(e, d)$' is generated iff the last occurrence of event e is $d \in \mathbf{N}$ time units ago. Part of the basic step algorithm is a list of timeout events and their time of occurrence.

Definition 7 Timeout Status, Initial Timeout Status. *The set of all time-out events included in the considered statechart is denoted by $Tmset$. A timeout status is a set of tuples $(tm(e, d), next) \in Tmset \times \mathbf{N}^{\infty}$ consisting of a time-out event $tm(e, d)$ and the time of its next occurrence. By Tmd_{all} we denote* the relation $Tmset \times \mathbf{N}^{\infty}$. A timeout status $\Theta_{Tm} \subseteq Tmd_{all}$ with $\Theta_{Tm}(Tm) \equiv$ $(\forall tm(e,d) \in Tmset : (tm(e,d), \infty) \in Tm) \wedge |Tm| = |Tmset|$ is called initial timeout status.

A part of the basic step algorithm changes the timeout status depending on the set of available events and the actual time, and generates the timeout events the time of which is due: For each pair $(E, next)$ in the timeout status with $E = tm(e,d)$ do the following: if e is generated, set $next := current\_time + d$, else if $next \leq current\_time$, then generate E and set $next := \infty$ ([7], Sect. 8). However, in the simulation algorithm Go-Step the condition $next \leq current\_time$ is replaced by the condition $next \in (current\_time, current\_time + 1]$. Therefore, we define a parameterized timeout evaluation step as a function over the set of all time intervals Int.

Definition 8 TmO. *The change of the timeout status and the generation of timeout events with respect to an interval $int \in Int$ is defined by the function* $TmO : Int \rightarrow ((2^{Tmd_{all}} \times 2^{Enames} \times \mathbf{N}) \rightarrow (2^{Tmd_{all}} \times 2^{Enames}))$*, such that* $TmO(int)((Tmd, E, T)) = (Tmd', E')$ *iff the following conditions are satisfied:*

1. $\forall(tm(e,d), next) \in Tmd :$
   $(e \in E \qquad\qquad\qquad \Rightarrow (tm(e,d), T+d) \in Tmd') \wedge$
   $(e \notin E \wedge next \in int \Rightarrow (tm(e,d), \infty) \quad \in Tmd' \wedge tm(e,d) \in E') \wedge$
   $(e \notin E \wedge next \notin int \Rightarrow (tm(e,d), next) \in Tmd')$, and
2. $\forall e_1 \in E' : (e_1 \in E \vee (\exists(tm(e_2, d), next) \in Tmd : e_2 \notin E \wedge next \in int))$.

4.2 The Timed Part of Go-Step and Go-Repeat

The timed parts of simulation algorithms Go-Step and Go-Repeat have explicit access to an internal clock T with discrete time domain. Therefore, we use for their formalization clocked transition systems [12] over $\mathbf{N}$ consisting of: 1.) a finite set of system variables $V = D \cup C$, where $D = \{u_1, \ldots, u_n\}$ is the set of discrete variables and $C = \{c_1, \ldots, c_k\}$ is the set of clocks. Clocks are of type $\mathbf{N}$. Discrete variables can be of any type. A special clock $T \in C$ represents a *master clock.* 2.) Θ : a satisfiable assertion with $\Theta \Rightarrow T = 0$, 3.) $\mathcal{T}$: a finite set of transitions, 4.) Π : a *time progress condition.* The set of transitions is extended by $\mathcal{T}_T = \mathcal{T} \cup \{tick\}$, where transition $tick$ is given by $\rho_{tick} \equiv \exists \Delta : (\Delta > 0 \wedge \forall t \in [0, \Delta) : \Pi(D, C+t) \wedge D' = D \wedge C' = C + \Delta)$, where $C' = C + \Delta$ abbreviates $c'_1 = c_1 + \Delta, \ldots, c_k + \Delta$ and $\Pi(D, C+t)$ abbreviates $\Pi(u_1, \ldots, u_n, c_1 + t, \ldots, c_k + t)$.

The algorithm Go-Step (cf. [7], Sect. 9) is : '1.) execute all external changes reported since the completion of the previous step, 2.) increment the clock by one, 3.) execute all timeout events whose due time falls inside $(T, T+1]$, 4.) execute one step.' Point 1 and 4 are formalized similarly to the untimed case and point 3 is formalized using Sect.4.1. The clocked transition system CTS_S is shown in Fig. 5. The clock T is allowed to progress simultaneously with timer t. Thus, time can not progress in location $1, 2, 4, 5$ and increments maximally by 1 time unit during the stay in location 3. Location 3 cannot be left before $t = 1$ holds, which is the guard of transition τ_{34}. Therefore, the clock increments by one time unit in location 3. By transition τ_{34} the timer is reset.

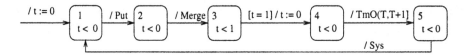

Fig. 5. Clocked Transition System CTS_S

The clocked transition system CTS_S consists of the following components:

1. A set of variables $V = V_{sys} \cup V_{env} \cup \{Tm\} \cup \{T, t\}$, where V_{sys} and V_{env} are defined in FTS_S, Tm captures a list of timeout events and their time of occurrence, T the current time of the internal clock, and t the timer. The domain of T and t is $\mathbf{N}$.
2. Initial states given by $\Theta(V) : \Theta_{sys}(V_{sys}) \wedge \Theta_{env}(V_{env}) \wedge \Theta_{Tm}(Tm) \wedge T = t = 0$.
3. A set of transitions $\mathcal{T} = \{\tau_{12}, \tau_{23}, \tau_{34}, \tau_{45}, \tau_{51}\}$, where time does not progress. These are defined by predicates, for which we give examples below:
$$\rho_{12}(V, V') : \pi = 1 \wedge Put(V_{Env}, V'_{Env}) \wedge V'_{sys} = V_{sys} \wedge \pi = 2 \wedge$$
$$Tm = Tm' \wedge (T', t') = (T, t)$$
$$\rho_{45}(V, V') : \pi = 4 \wedge TmO((T, T + 1))((Tm, V_{sys}, T), (Tm', V_{sys}')) \wedge$$
$$V'_{Env} = V_{env} \wedge \pi' = 5 \wedge (T', t') = (T, t)$$
4. A time progress condition Π specifying the global restrictions on the progress of time. $\Pi(t) : (\pi \in \{1, 2, 4, 5\} \to t < 0) \wedge (\pi = 3 \to t < 1)$. Therefore, progress of time is modeled by a transition τ_{tick} determined by
$$\rho_{tick} : \exists \Delta \in \mathbf{N}_{>0} \forall d \in [0 \ldots \Delta) : \Pi(t + d) \wedge$$
$$(T', t') = (T + \Delta, t + \Delta) \wedge (V'_{sys}, V'_{env}, Tm') = (V_{sys}, V_{env}, Tm) \ .$$
This is equivalent to
$$\pi = 3 \wedge t = 0 \wedge (T', t') = (T'+1, t'+1) \wedge (V'_{sys}, V'_{env}, Tm') = (V_{sys}, V_{env}, Tm) \ .$$

The algorithm Go-Repeat (cf. [7], Sect. 9) is: '1.) execute all external changes reported since the completion of the previous step, 2.) execute all timeout events whose time is due (up to and including the current time), and 3.) repeatedly execute one step till the system is in a stable state.' These steps do not increment the internal time clock. Nothing is said in [7] when and how time advances. The points 1.) and 3.) are formalized as in the untimed case and point 2.) using formalization of Sect. 4.1. The clocked transition system is shown in Fig. 6.

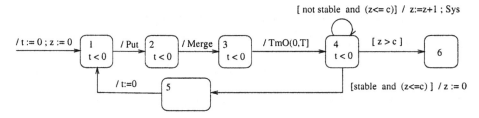

Fig. 6. Clocked Transition System CTS_R

Other simulation modes of [7] advance the clock to the time point when the next timeout event is due. This can be formalized using the condition $t <$ $Min\{ next \mid (tm, next) \in Tm\}$, for instance, in location 5 of Fig. 6.

Since time progresses in Go-Step by one, we can replace in TmO (cf. Def. 8) the condition $next \in (T, T+1]$ by $next = T+1$. As long as for Go-Repeat for the progress of the clock $\Delta \leq Min\{ next \mid (tm, next) \in Tm\}$ holds, the condition $next \in (O, T]$ in TmO can be replaced by $next = T$.

5 Concurrency and Concepts of Synchronous Languages

Reactive systems perform a permanent interaction with their environment [8]. They involve both concurrency between the system and its environment and between its system components. For the specification of such systems the following abstraction assumptions of synchronous languages have been made (cf. [2, 16, 17]): 1.) Processes work synchronously. 2.) Process combination does not introduce non–determinism. 3.) Emission of input and emission of output are synchronous. We divide the third assumption into the following two points. 3.1.) System Reactions take no observable time (perfect synchrony hypothesis). 3.2) The output of a step is also an input of the same step. Below, we discuss in which way concurrency and these concepts have been modeled by the formalized semantics.

Concurrency of Processes, (Internal). Concurrent execution of processes is modeled as follows: OR substates of the same AND state are viewed as concurrent processes. Then, a process is enabled if a transition within this OR state is enabled and no transition with higher a priority is enabled. A process makes a step if a transition within the OR state is taken. In a *Sys* step, for instance $Sys((S, E, C), \{t_1, \ldots, t_n\}, (S', E', C'))$, processes '$scope(t_i)$', $i \in \{1, \ldots, n\}$ can be viewed as working synchronously (cf. Theorem 6), where the output of a step is not an input of the same step.

The combination of processes introduces non–determinism. For instance, when two processes write to the same variable C by $fs!(C)$ and $tr!(C)$ the new value of C can be *true* or *false*. The evaluation function $EvalCo$ is not commutative. Given a set of true conditions C, then $EvalCo(C, fs!(C) * tr!(C)) \neq$ $EvalCo(C, tr!(C) * fs!(C))$. In such cases STATEMATE emits a warning signal. To avoid this phenomenon, restrictive read and write disciplines on shared variables, or commutative evaluation functions, as in Esterel [3], can be introduced.

The semantics models strong synchronization of processes, i.e., they are closely coupled. However, a shared variable concurrency semantics, which is an interleaving semantics, is appropriate for the view of loosely coupled processes.

Concurrency of System and Environment, (External). The basic step algorithm models the situation that the system takes its input from a list containing the external changes generated by the environment since the last step. When the system takes a new input it can just detect whether an input has been produced since the last *Merge* step. Note that the interface between the environment and the system and the interface between parts of the system are modeled differently. The algorithms Go-Step and Go-Repeat model the relation between internal system processing based on the step *Sys* and the communication with the environment based on step *Merge*. The transition system FTS_S shown in Fig. 3 models a continuous interaction with the environment because $\pi = 2 \Rightarrow \Diamond \pi = 1$ is valid. This is not the case for the FTS_R shown in Fig. 4 since only $\pi = 2 \Rightarrow \Diamond(\pi = 1 \lor \pi \in \{3, 4\})$ holds. The transition system CTS_R shown in Fig. 6 models that a reaction due to an input ends when the system reaches a stable state, i.e. involves in general a sequence of *Sys* steps, and that this reaction needs zero time. For the CTS_R it follows that if $\pi = 2$ and the local clock satisfies $T = a$, then the time does not change in locations $2, 3, 4$, i.e., $T = a$ unless locations 5 or 6 are reached, where variable a records the value of the clock at the observation point $\pi = 2$. This is given in temporal logic by $(\pi = 2 \land T = a) \Rightarrow ((T = a)\mathcal{W}(\pi \in \{5, 6\}))$. The transition system CTS_S shown in Fig. 5 models reactions consisting of a *Merge* and a *Sys* step and that this reaction needs one time unit. In fact, CTS_S satisfies $(\pi = 1 \land T = a) \Rightarrow ((T \leq a + 1)\mathcal{W}(\pi = 5 \land T = a + 1))$.

6 Conclusion

We have presented a formal semantics for the simulation algorithms Go-Step and Go-Repeat of STATEMATE as described in [7]. We have defined an abstract textual syntax for the complex graphical representation of Statecharts, where we considered full compound transitions. The description of [7] turned out to be very rigorous. For instance, several interpretations of conflicting transitions turned out to be equivalent. We have introduced several steps for the formalization of the basic step algorithm. Based on these steps we have formalized the untimed part of the simulation algorithms using fair transition systems and the timed part using clocked transition systems over **N**. This semantics models parallel processes and important concepts of synchronous languages.

There exist proof systems for fair and clocked transition systems [15, 12], such that STATEMATE specifications even with shared variables over infinite domains can be verified. Clocked transition systems are extensions of timed automata [1]. A consequence of this is that finite–state clocked transition systems can be verified by model checking algorithms developed for timed automata.

Our semantics can be used as a reference point: 1.) to identify underlying concepts appropriate for certain application areas, e.g., that an event can only take effect in the next step as assumed in VHDL, a standard description language for hardware ([7]), 2.) for the definition of more abstract semantics, compositional semantics, and appropriate semantics for efficient verification, and 3.) for extensions, especially real–time features, because the definitions are given in a modular way.

Acknowledgment

We thank Amir Pnueli for proposing the topic, especially for pointing out problems to consider and approaches to take. We thank David Harel, Amnon Naamad and members of the staff of i–Logix for explanations on Statecharts as implemented in STATEMATE. Carlos Puchol suggested to confine ourselves to the class of Statecharts for which the scheduling algorithm Go-Repeat terminates. Special thanks go to Yassine Lakhnech, Erich Mikk, Willem–Paul de Roever, and Michael Siegel.

A   Remarks and Proofs

We make remarks on and give the main ideas for the proofs of the theorems for states and transitions of Statecharts, and the system step of the basic step algorithm, respectively.

We assume that an AND state is only followed by OR states to avoid counter–intuitive specifications like the following one:

Let $S = \{r, s, s_1, s_2\}, down(r) = \{s\}, down(s) = \{s_1, s_2\}, type(s) = AND,$ $type(s_1) = type(s_2) = BASIC,$ and $t = (\{s_1\}, \{s_1\})$. When transition t_1 is taken, not only state s_1 is exited but also state s. Our assumptions ensure that only state s_1 is exited. The assumption is also needed to prove Theorem 2.

Lemma 1. Let $C \in C_{all}(s_r)$ and $B = \{s \in C \mid down(s) = \emptyset\}$, then $up^*(B) \cap down^*(s_r) = C$.

Proof. To prove this we use that there does not exist any infinite path in a state hierarchy and all states above a basic state of a basic configuration are included in the configurations related to the basic configuration.

Theorem 2. *A set of states is an allowed target set of a legal full compound transition $t \in T_w$ and $En = EnterMax(t)$ iff it is a basic configuration relative to a state $En \in States$.*

Proof. Let $En \in S$ be a state.

1. Let X be a basic configuration relative to En, and $C = up^*(X) \cap down^*(En)$. That $X \neq \emptyset$ follows directly from $C \in C_{all}(En)$ and $En \in up^*(X)$. That X is legal can be shown straightforward by contradiction. Below, we prove that the condition on the target set of states of a full compound transition holds for X.

   Assume $s \in down^*(En)$ and $type(s) = OR$.

   <u>Case 1</u> : $s \notin C$: Since $s < En$ and $En \in C$ there exists $s' \in up(s)$ with $s' \notin C$ and $up(s') \in C$. Because $C \in C_{all}(En)$ and $type(up(s)) = OR$ there exists $s'' \in down(up(s'))$ with $s'' \in C$ and therefore $s'' \in up^*(X)$.

   <u>Case 2</u> : $s \in C$: Since $type(s) = OR$ and $C \in C_{all}(En)$ there exists $s' \in down(s),\ s' \in C$. With $X \in B_{all}(En)$, then $s' \in up^*(X)$ and $down(s) \cap up(X) \neq \emptyset$.

2. Let $t = (X, l, Y) \in \mathcal{T}_w$ with $EnterMax(t) = En$. The proof idea for $down^*(En) \cap up^*(Y) \in \mathcal{C}_{all}(En)$ is that for each OR state exact one substate is element of $up^*(Y)$. This is ensured by the conditions for legality and full compoundness. If an AND state is included in $down^*(En) \cap up^*(Y)$, then its substates are also included in it because of the full compound condition and the fact that AND states are followed by OR states. $\forall s_1, s_2 \in Y : \neg(s_1 < s_2 \vee s_2 < s_1)$ implies that all states of Y are basic states.

That a new configuration is reached by a systems step follows directly by induction using Theorem 3.

Theorem 3. *Let $\mathcal{C} \in \mathcal{C}_{all}$, $t = (X, l, Y) \in \mathcal{T}_w$. Then*
$$X \subseteq \mathcal{C} \Rightarrow (\mathcal{C} \setminus Exit(t, \mathcal{C})) \cup Enter(t)) \in \mathcal{C}_{all} \ .$$

Proof. The proof idea is as follows. In configuration $\mathcal{C}$ the configuration related to $ExitMax(t)$ is replaced by a configuration related to $EnterMax(t)$. Since $ExitMax(t)$, $EnterMax(t) \in down(scope(t))$ and $type(scope(t)) = OR$ follows that a new configuration is reached.

Theorem 4. *Assume $\mathcal{C} \in \mathcal{C}_{all}$ with $X_1, X_2 \subseteq \mathcal{C}$. Then in the definition of conflict between transitions, page 6, conditions 1–5 are equivalent.*

Proof. Condition 2 $\Rightarrow$ Condition 3:
If $(down^*(ExitMax(t_1)) \cap \mathcal{C}) \cap (down^*(ExitMax(t_2)) \cap \mathcal{C}) \neq \emptyset$,
then $(down^*(ExitMax(t_1)) \cap down^*(ExitMax(t_2)) \neq \emptyset$
Since for every common state there exists only one path from root to it. Therefore, $ExitMax(t_2) \leq ExitMax(t_1) \vee ExitMax(t_1) \leq ExitMax(t_2)$.
  Condition 3 $\Rightarrow$ Condition 2: Assume w.l.o.g. $ExitMax(t_1) \leq ExitMax(t_2)$. As $X_1 \subseteq \mathcal{C}$ also $ExitMax(t_1) \in \mathcal{C}$ and $ExitMax(t_1) \in down^*(ExitMax(t_1)) \cap \mathcal{C}$. With $ExitMax(t_1) \leq ExitMax(t_2)$, then $ExitMax(t_1) \in down^*(ExitMax(t_2)) \cap \mathcal{C}$.
  Condition 1 $\Rightarrow$ Condition 3: Assume w.l.o.g. $Exit(t_1, \mathcal{C}) \cap X_2 \neq \emptyset$. Then, $down^*(ExitMax(t_1)) \cap X_2 \neq \emptyset$ and there exists $s \in X_2$ s.t. $s \leq ExitMax(t_1)$ and $s \leq ExitMax(t_2)$ hold.
Since there exists exactly one path from the root to each state. Therefore, $ExitMax(t_2) \leq ExitMax(t_1) \vee ExitMax(t_1) \leq ExitMax(t_2)$ holds.
  Condition 3 $\Rightarrow$ Condition 1: Assume w.l.o.g. $ExitMax(t_2) \leq ExitMax(t_1)$. Then, $down^*(ExitMax(t_2)) \subseteq down^*(ExitMax(t_1))$
and $(down^*(ExitMax(t_2)) \cap \mathcal{C}) \subseteq (down^*(ExitMax(t_1)) \cap \mathcal{C})$ hold.
Since $X_2 \neq \emptyset$ and $X_2 \subseteq (down^*(ExitMax(t_2)) \cap \mathcal{C})$ there exists a state $x \in X_2 \subseteq (down^*(ExitMax(t_1)) \cap \mathcal{C})$.
  The proof of Condition 2 $\Leftrightarrow$ 3 is similar as above but simpler.
  Condition 4 $\Rightarrow$ Condition 3: As $X_1, X_2 \subseteq \mathcal{C}$ also $scope(t_1), scope(t_2) \in \mathcal{C}$.
$type(LCA(scope(t_1), scope(t_2))) = OR$ implies that
$scope(t_1) \leq scope(t_2)$ or $scope(t_2) \leq scope(t_1)$.
Case 1: $scope(t_1) = scope(t_2)$
From $ExitMax(t_i) \in (down(scope(t_i)) \cap \mathcal{C})$ for $i \in \{1, 2\}$, and $type(scope(t_1)) =$

$type(scope(t_1)) = OR$ we obtain $ExitMax(t_1) = ExitMax(t_2)$.

Case 2: $scope(t_1) < scope(t_2)$.

From $ExitMax(t_2) \in (down(scope(t_2)) \cap C)$ and $type(scope(t_2)) = OR$ follows $scope(t_1) \leq ExitMax(t_2)$. From $ExitMax(t_1) < scope(t_1)$ follows $ExitMax(t_1) < ExitMax(t_2)$.

Case 3: $scope(t_1) > scope(t_2)$ analogously.

Condition 3 $\Rightarrow$ Condition 4:

Case 1: $ExitMax(t_1) = ExitMax(t_2)$.

From $ExitMax(t_i) \in (down(scope(t_i)))$ for $i \in \{1,2\}$ it follows that $scope(t_1) = scope(t_2)$, $LCA(\{scope(t_1), scope(t_2)\}) = scope(t_1)$, and $type(LCA(\{scope(t_1), scope(t_2)\})) = type(scope(t_1)) = OR$.

Case 2: $ExitMax(t_1) < ExitMax(t_2)$.

From $ExitMax(t_1) \in (down(scope(t_1)))$ it follows that $ExitMax(t_1) < scope(t_1) \leq ExitMax(t_2) < scope(t_2)$, $LCA(\{scope(t_1), scope(t_2)\}) = LCA(\{scope(t_1)\}) = scope(t_1)$ and $type(LCA(\{scope(t_1), scope(t_2)\})) = type(scope(t_1)) = OR$.

Case 3: $ExitMax(t_2) < ExitMax(t_1)$ analogously.

Condition 4 $\Leftrightarrow$ Condition 5 :

From $type(LCA(scope(t_1), scope(t_2))) \neq BASIC$ follows $type(LCA(scope(t_1), scope(t_2))) = OR \Leftrightarrow \neg type(LCA(scope(t_1), scope(t_2))) = AND$.

Lemma 5. *Let $S \in C_{all}, t_1, t_2 \in T_l$ with $type(LCA(scope(t_1), scope(t_2))) = AND$. Then, $Exit(t_1, S) \cap Exit(t_2, S) = \emptyset$ and $Exit(t_1, S) \cap Enter(t_2) = \emptyset$.*

Proof. From $type(LCA(scope(t_1), scope(t_2))) = AND$ follows $\neg(scope(t_1) \leq scope(t_2)) \vee (scope(t_2) \leq scope(t_1))$ and $down^*(scope(t_1)) \cap down^*(scope(t_2)) = \emptyset$.

Since $Exit(t_i, S), Enter(t_i) \subseteq down^*(scope(t_i))$, $i \in \{1,2\}$ the lemma holds.

Theorem 6. *Let $(S, E, C), (S', E', C') \in SysSt_{all}$, $n \in \mathbf{N}$, $\{t_1, \ldots, t_n\} \subseteq T$ with $Sys((S, E, C), \{t_1, \ldots, t_n\}, (S', E', C'))$. Then,*
$$S' = (S \setminus \bigcup_{\{i \in 1, \ldots, n\}} Exit(t_i, S)) \cup \bigcup_{\{i \in 1, \ldots, n\}} Enter(t_i).$$

Proof. Let $(S, E, C), (S', E', C') \in SysSt_{all}$,

$n \in \mathbf{N}$, $\{t_1, \ldots, t_n\} \subseteq T$ with $Sys((S, E, C), Tr, (S', E', C'))$ and $S = S_0$, $S_{i+1} = (S_i \setminus Exit(t_{i+1}, S_i)) \cup Enter(t_i)$ for $i \in \{0, \ldots n-1\}$.

Then, $S' = S_n$. Claim : $S' = (S \setminus \bigcup_{\{1, \ldots n\}} Exit(t_i)) \cup \bigcup Enter(t_i)$.

Base step: $n = 1$, then $S' = (S \setminus Exit(t_1, S)) \cup Enter(t_1)$.

Induction step: $n \to n+1$

$(S \setminus \bigcup_{\{1, \ldots n+1\}} Exit(t_i, S)) \cup \bigcup_{\{1, \ldots n+1\}} Enter(t_i)$

$= (S \setminus \bigcup_{\{1, \ldots n\}} Exit(t_i, S)) \setminus Exit(t_{n+1}, S) \cup \bigcup_{\{1, \ldots n\}} Enter(t_i) \cup Enter(t_{n+1})$

by Lemma 5

$= ((S \setminus \bigcup_{\{1, \ldots n\}} Exit(t_i, S)) \cup \bigcup_{\{1, \ldots n\}} Enter(t_i) \setminus Exit(t_{n+1}, S) \cup Enter(t_{n+1})$

by induction hypothesis

$= (S_n \setminus Exit(t_{n+1}, S)) \cup Enter(t_{n+1})$

572

by $S \cap down^*(ExitMax(t_n)) = S_n \cap down^*(ExitMax(t_n))$ (use Lemma 5)
$= (S_n \setminus Exit(t_{n+1}, S_n)) \cup Enter(t_{n+1}) = S'$.

References

1. R. Alur and D. L. Dill. A Theory of Timed Automata. *Theoretical Computer Science*, 126:183–235, 1994.
2. A. Benveniste and G. Berry. The Synchronous Approach to Reactive and Real-Time Systems. *Proceedings of IEEE*, 79(9):1270–1282, 1991.
3. G. Berry and G. Gonthier. The Esterel Synchronous Programming Language: Design, Semantics, Implementation. *Science of Computer Programming*, 19(2):87–152, 1992.
4. D. Harel. Statecharts: A Visual Formalism for Complex Systems. *Science of Computer Programming*, 8:231–274, 1987.
5. D. Harel and E. Gery. Executable Object Modeling with Statecharts. In *18th ICSE, Berlin*, 1996.
6. D. Harel, H. Lachover, A. Naamad, A. Pnueli, M. Politi, R. Sherman, A. Shtull-Trauring, and M. Trakhtenbrot. Statemate: A Working Environment for the Development of Complex Reactive Systems. *IEEE Transaction on Software Engineering*, 16(4):403–414, 1990.
7. D. Harel and A. Naamad. The STATEMATE Semantics of Statecharts. *ACM Transaction on Software Engineering and Methodology*, 5(4):292–333, 1996.
8. D. Harel and A. Pnueli. On the Development of Reactive Systems. In *Logics and Models of Concurrent Systems*, pages 477–498. Springer-Verlag, 1985.
9. D. Harel, A. Pnueli, J. Schmidt, and R. Sherman. On the Formal Semantics of Statecharts. In *LICS'87*, pages 54–64. Computer Society Press, 1987.
10. J. Helbig and P. Kelb. An OBDD-Representation of Statecharts. In *EDAC'94*, pages 142–149, 1994.
11. C. Huizing and R. T. Gerth. Semantics of Reactive Systems in Abstract Time. In *Real-Time: Theory in Practice*, LNCS 600, pages 291–314. Springer-Verlag, 1991.
12. Y. Kesten, Z. Manna, and A. Pnueli. Verifying Clocked Transition Systems. In *Hybrid Systems III*, LNCS 1066, pages 13–40. Springer-Verlag, 1996.
13. Y. Kesten and A. Pnueli. Timed and Hybrid Statecharts and their Textual Representation. In *FTRTFT'92*, LNCS 571, pages 591–619. Springer-Verlag, 1992.
14. A. Maggiolo-Schettini and A. Peron. Retiming Techniques for Statecharts. In *FTRTFT'96*, LNCS 1135, pages 55–71, 1996.
15. Z. Manna and A. Pnueli. *The Temporal Logic of Reactive and Concurrent Systems*, volume 1. Springer-Verlag, 1992.
16. F. Maraninchi and N. Halbwachs. Compositional Semantics of Non-deterministic Synchronous Languages. In *ESOP'96*, LNCS 1058. Springer-Verlag, 1996.
17. A. Pnueli and M. Shalev. What is in a Step: On Semantics of Statecharts. In *TACS'91*, LNCS 526, pages 244–264. Springer-Verlag, 1991.
18. A.C. Uselton and S.A. Smolka. A Process Algebraic Semantics for Statecharts via State Refinement. In *PROCOMET'94*, IFIP, pages 262–281, 1994.
19. M. von der Beeck. A Comparison of Statecharts Variants. In *FTRTFT'94*, LNCS 863, pages 128–148. Springer-Verlag, 1994.

Using PVS to Prove a Z Refinement: A Case Study

David W.J. Stringer-Calvert[1], Susan Stepney[2], Ian Wand[1] *

[1] Department of Computer Science, University of York, U.K.
[2] Logica UK Ltd., Cambridge, U.K.
{davesc,icw}@minster.york.ac.uk, stepneys@logica.com

Abstract. The development of critical systems often places undue trust in the software tools used. This is especially true of compilers, which are a weak link between the source code produced and the object code which is executed. Stepney [23] advocates a method for the production of *trusted* compilers (i.e. those which are guaranteed to produce object code that is a correct refinement of the source code) by developing a proof of a small, but non trivial compiler by hand in the Z specification language. This approach is quick, but the type system of Z is too weak to ensure that partial functions are correctly applied.

Here, we present a re-working of that development using the PVS specification and verification system. We describe the problems involved in translating from the partial set theory of Z to the total, higher order logic of the PVS system and the strengths and weaknesses of this approach.

1   Introduction

Computer systems are increasingly being used in applications where their failure could lead to financial or environmental disaster, or even to loss of life. Such systems are called *Critical* and as such must be engineered to the highest quality, to anticipate potential faults and to reduce the possibility of errors in the system.

The major enemy in seeking assurance in a computer system is complexity. Complex systems are difficult to specify and to reason about, hence mistakes and omissions *will* be made during the design and implementation process. One characteristic of a good design process is that it should provide for validation and verification of the 'product' at every stage, so as to catch introduced errors earlier (allowing solutions to be implemented more cheaply) and to provide a trace of the development, which may be used in a safety argument.

At the highest level of rigour, we would use a refinement process to provide a fully formal development route from the requirements specification (expressed

---

* Logica UK Ltd carried out the original work on the compiler method for RSRE (now DRA Malvern), and is continuing the development for AWE plc. D.W.J. Stringer-Calvert is funded by a CASE studentship from the Engineering and Physical Sciences Research Council and Siemens Plessey Systems.

in some suitable formal notation), via formal refinement rules (which have been proven to preserve meaning), to code in a high level language, say Ada.

Having now, at great expense, formally refined our requirements into a concrete implementation in Ada, we have a dilemma. As noted, Ada is a *high level* language, indicating that it contains constructs intended to make the programming task easier and less error prone. However, nothing comes for free and the payment for this is made by the need to use a compiler or interpreter (a large and complex piece of software) in order for the program we have written to be executed on a real computer. Thus, the compiler and associated tools (including an assembler, linker and libraries) are in a position of great trust in the building of our software system.

Formal methods are often seen as the solution to the problem of assurance in critical systems, but their application is usually limited to the most critical parts of a system, as they are mostly seen as costly and difficult to use. Thus a cost/rigour tradeoff has developed, with 'formalised' methods (such as Z [22] with hand proofs) which provide less than full verification, becoming the popular choice in industry.

Recent developments in full strength *mechanised* verification have lent more credibility to the possible use of full formal verification on larger numbers of critical systems developments. Systems such as the Prototype Verification System (PVS) [16,19] provide the necessary automation of much of the tedious detail of fully formal proofs, and also allow for the construction of proof strategies specific to the problem domain where necessary.

This paper presents the initial stages of our work on compiler correctness, moving from a specification in Z, with hand proofs, through to a rigorous treatment with PVS. This treatment has revealed several errors in the original hand development, and forms the basis for further investigation into the extent to which mechanisation can be applied to automate proofs in this problem domain.

2 The Starting Point

In this paper we build on the work of Stepney [23] who has developed a *demonstrably correct* compiler for a simple (but non-trivial) language Tosca, targeted at an imaginary assembler Aida (similar to that used on the Viper [5] processor). Tosca contains the usual features of a high level language — sequencing, assignment, choice, while loops, and a simple model of input/output based on streams of integers. The target language (Aida) is a simple assembly language with load/store, input/output, and arithmetic/logical operations.

Both languages are defined denotationally (using the Z specification language [22]), and the source language is given an operational semantics in terms of templates of target instructions, thereby defining a compiler. Correctness proofs are discharged by hand, using the principle of structural induction over source language constructs.

The work described here is a re-engineering of those hand proofs within the framework of the PVS specification and verification system. The specification language of PVS is based on classical, typed, higher order logic. It contains constructs intended to ease the natural development of specifications such as parameterised modules, records, subtypes, and abstract datatypes. Unlike Z, the PVS logic does not admit partial functions, although this can be modelled using subtypes and dependent types.

The PVS proof checker is interactive, using a sequent style presentation. It provides powerful basic commands, and a mechanism for building re-usable strategies based on these. The power of the system comes from the use of decision procedures to automate efficiently the decidable aspects of the logic, and their close integration with rewriting.

As the type system of the PVS logic is so rich and expressive, type checking is undecidable. To overcome this, the type checker emits type correctness conditions (TCCs) to which the full weight of the theorem prover can be applied. Most of these TCCs are discharged automatically by standard strategies. TCCs are also emitted during proof as extra subgoals where required to ensure type correctness, for example when instantiating a lemma.

PVS was chosen over, say, a Z-based prover such as Z/EVES [20] because we anticipated that the automation it provided would make the verification task easier. In addition, we expected that the PVS type system would make the development less error prone than a hand development in Z, as PVS has both domain checking (i.e. ensuring that functions are applied only to arguments within their domain) and conservative definitions.

The remainder of this paper provides a short outline of the original Z development, followed by a discussion of some of the problems encountered in translating this into the PVS system. A brief discussion of related work is included, together with our future plans for research in this area.

3   Z Development

In this section we give an overview of the original Z development of the compiler, with an explanation of why the various design decisions were made. More detail is given elsewhere [23].

The development of a compiler by this method has three components:

1. **Specification**: The denotational semantics of both the high level source language (Tosca), and the low level assembly language (Aida), are specified in Z, as is the operational semantics of the high level language in the form of a set of templates of low level language instructions.
2. **Implementation**: The Z specification of the Tosca semantics are translated into Prolog, where they are executable. Executing the denotational semantics gives an interpreter; executing the operational semantics gives a compiler.

3. **Proof:** The operational semantics are proved to be equivalent to the denotational semantics: the compiler transformation is *meaning preserving*, and hence the compiler is correct.

For example, the meaning of Tosca's assignment statement x := e is a state change: the state σ is updated so that x maps to the value of the expression e. In Z this can be written as[1]:

$$\mathcal{M}[\![assign(\mathbf{x}, \mathbf{e})]\!]\sigma = \sigma \oplus \{x \mapsto \mathcal{M}[\![\mathbf{e}]\!]\sigma\}$$

In Prolog this becomes

```
meaning(assign(Name,Expr),Pre,Post):-
    meaning(Expr,Pre,Value),
    update(Name,Value,Pre,Post).
```

Similarly, the meaning of Aida's store instruction (store the contents of the accumulator at the location l) updates its store[2]. In Z:

$$\mathcal{A}[\![store\ \mathbf{l}]\!]\rho_\iota\theta\sigma_\iota = \theta(\sigma_\iota \oplus \{l \mapsto \sigma_\iota A\})$$

Here, σ_ι represents the Aida store, ρ_ι the environment mapping from program labels to continuations, θ the current continuation, and the term $\sigma_\iota A$ the value contained in the accumulator.

The operational semantics define the sequence of Aida instructions corresponding to the translation of each Tosca instruction. The assignment statement is translated into a sequence of instructions to evaluate the expression, followed by an instruction to store that value at the appropriate location. In Z:

$$\mathcal{O}\langle\!| \ assign(\mathbf{x}, \mathbf{e}) \ |\!\rangle = \mathcal{O}\langle\!| \ \mathbf{e} \ |\!\rangle \ ^\frown \langle store\ x\rangle$$

In Prolog this becomes

```
compile(assign(Name,Expr),[InstrList,store(Name)]):-
    compile(Expr,InstrList).
```

To show that the compiler is correct, we need to show that the translation into Aida preserves the semantics of the Tosca instruction. We do so by structural induction over Tosca's abstract syntax, proving that for each construct, the Aida meaning of the translation template is the same as the Tosca meaning of the original instruction. For the assignment example we need to prove that:

$$\vdash \mathcal{M}[\![assign(\mathbf{x}, \mathbf{e})]\!] = \mathcal{A}[\![\mathcal{O}\langle\!| \ assign(\mathbf{x}, \mathbf{e}) \ |\!\rangle]\!]$$

As we can see from above, the specifications serve (at least) three conflicting purposes in this approach:

---

[1] The square brackets **[ ]** are the conventional denotational semantics brackets, *not* Z's bag brackets.

[2] The semantics of Aida is more complicated than Tosca's, and needs to use 'continuation' arguments, because the assembly language allows arbitrary jumps. See [23] for more explanation.

1. **Language definition**: the denotational semantics act as the language definition, and so the specification style should be as clear and abstract as possible, to make the definition comprehensible to human readers [1].
2. **Implementation**: the various semantics are translated into an executable language, and so should be written in a concrete, algorithmic, style that facilitates this translation. The declarative language Prolog, rather than some imperative language, is chosen as the target language in order to minimise this implementation step.
3. **Proof**: the various semantics need to be manipulated mathematically, in order to perform the correctness proofs, and so should be written as abstractly as possible.

In the original work the only tool available was ƒUZZ, a Z type checker [21]: no proof tools were used, and hence 'suitable for tools' was not a design criterion. In particular, Z's partial functions were exploited to structure the specifications, and to provide Tosca with various static checking semantics.

4 Translation to PVS

The first attempt to translate the Z specifications into PVS took a direct *naive* approach, where the specifications were relatively quickly translated into the logic of the PVS system with little modification. With this approach the main branch of the correctness theorems followed closely the original hand proofs, except for a few cases where unproven assumptions had been made, where the translation had been incorrect and also where the detail of a series of complex reasoning steps was omitted and presented as one step.

We therefore set about re-working the specification to allow the correctness theorems to be proved. This work involved the tightening of the specification, thereby making assumptions explicit, as will be shown in the following sections.

4.1 PVS Types

Whilst augmenting the functions in the specification, we found it very useful to also augment the types of those functions. As type information is available to the ground prover in PVS, this approach minimises the number of type correctness conditions generated as side effects of proof steps. For example, the following function shows the use of a dependently typed argument, and a predicate subtype for the range:

```
OE(epsilon : Expr)(rho_o : Inj_Env)
  (SP : {l : Locn | l >= top(rho_o)}) :
  RECURSIVE {l : list[Instr] | cons?(l) AND sequential?(l)} =

  . . .
```

Here, the function OE returns a list of Instr, which satisfies the predicates cons? (i.e. it is a non-empty list), and sequential?, a predicate which we have defined to mean the list contains no jump or goto instructions.

In the remainder of this section we discuss some of the more interesting aspects of this conversion from Z to PVS, highlighting some of the original assumptions and describing the approaches taken to overcome them. Fragments of PVS specifications appear as boxed figures.

4.2 Total functions

Partial functions are a natural method for modelling many situations, and heavy use is made of them in Z specifications. It is difficult however to provide support for mechanical reasoning using partial functions, and as such PVS does not support their use. Therefore, the most challenging part of translating a Z specification into the logic of the PVS system is removing the use of such functions.

There are three basic methods for making a partial function into a total one:

1. Cause the function to return a specific, fictitious value (a *bottom*) for undefined cases.
2. Cause the function to return an arbitrary value of the correct type for undefined cases.
3. Constrain the type of the function arguments so that it is a total function over a restricted domain.

The second option can be achieved by the use of Hilbert's epsilon operator [13], which, given a predicate, returns a value which satisfies that predicate (if possible) and if it is not satisfiable returns an arbitrary value of the appropriate type. Epsilon is a useful specification tool, as it allows for a clever abstraction from detail, but for our purposes here, options one and three seem more appropriate[3].

In our specification of the compiler problem in PVS, we have experimented with the use of methods one and three from the above list. We believe there is a tradeoff in their use between the readability of the specification, and ease of proof. Whereas both of these methods make explicit the inherent partial nature of a function, the use of a bottom element (method one) tends to clutter the body of the function, and the use of complex types (method three) tends to make the function 'head' quite opaque and results in extra type correctness conditions to ensure applications of the function are within its domain.

After experimenting with the use of both approaches (as will be seen later in this paper), we would now advocate the use of complex types to approach this problem. If we use a bottom element, the tool can give us no assistance in noting our mistakes and inconsistencies, but the correctness conditions generated by the use of complex types are extremely valuable for locating errors and omissions.

---

[3] See section 2.4.2 of [19] for more discussion on the use of the epsilon operator in PVS

Such support leads us to believe that PVS would be a useful tool for language designers starting from scratch, using the PVS type system to explore and define various static semantics for the language after noting where and which obligations were generated.

4.3 Store

The most significant change to the specification involved the memory maps at both the Tosca and Aida levels. Pictorially, they are as follows:

Tosca Memory Map

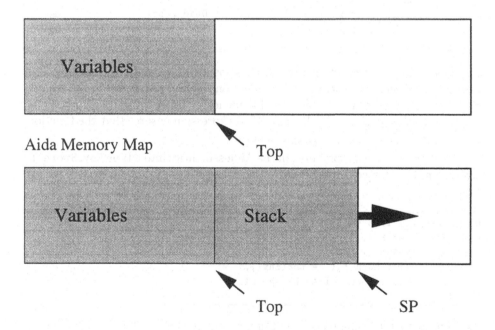

Fig. 1. Tosca and Aida Memory Maps

All variables in Tosca have global scope, so they are allocated storage statically, at compile time. Aida has static storage of the equivalent Tosca variables. It also has a stack, which grows from above the highest allocated memory location, to store temporary variables needed during expression evaluation.

The Z specification defines a function `restrict`, which performs a range restriction on the store, to yield the locations that are currently in use:

$$restrict : Env_O \times Locn \times State_I \to State_I$$

$$\forall \rho_o : Env_O; \ \lambda : Locn; \ \varsigma_\iota : Store_I; \ in : Input; \ out : Output \bullet$$
$$restrict(\rho_o, \lambda, (\varsigma_\iota, in, out)) =$$
$$((\{A\} \cup \operatorname{ran} \rho_o \cup (top .. \lambda - 1)) \lhd \varsigma_\iota, in, out)$$

Our new treatment introduces a stack pointer, which in conjunction with the use of a dependent type removes the need for the restrict function. The basic type is Inj_Env:

```
Dead_Locn : Locn = 0

Inj_Env    : TYPE =
  [# top : Locn,
     map : {f : [Name -> {1 : Locn | 1 < top}] |
       FORALL (xi1, xi2 : Name) :
         ((f(xi1) = f(xi2) AND NOT f(xi1) = Dead_Locn)
           IMPLIES xi1 = xi2)}
  #]
```

Inj_Env provides the function map, which maps variable names to locations. The range of this function is locations dependent on the first parameter in the record, top, but its domain includes *all* variable names — unused variables map to an unused location Dead_Locn. The quantified expression ensures that the function is injective (modulo the use of Dead_Locn).

The Inj_Env type is combined in the Aida semantics into a type Env_Store_I, which combines the concepts of environment and store into one dependent record type:

```
Env_Store_I : TYPE =
  [# Env : Inj_Env,
     A   : Value,
     SP  : {1 : Locn | 1 >= top(Env)},
     Mem : [{1 : Locn | 1 < SP} -> Value]
  #]
```

'A' represents the accumulator, containing a single value. 'SP' is a stack pointer, which is constrained to be a location greater than or equal to the highest location allocated to a Tosca variable. Thus, the memory (Mem) is a mapping from locations to values, where it is only defined for locations below the stack pointer.

Two extra instructions were added to the instruction set of the low level machine to increment (**spinc**) and decrement (**spdec**) the stack pointer, and these were inserted into the operational semantics at appropriate points in expression evaluation. The decrement operation makes use of the PVS function **restrict**[4], which takes a function defined over a type X and gives one which has a domain which is a subtype of X.

---

[4] This is not related to the Z function **restrict** defined earlier.

```
SP_INC(sigma_i : Env_Store_I) : Env_Store_I =
  (# Env := Env(sigma_i),
     A   := A(sigma_i),
     SP  := SP(sigma_i)+1,
     Mem := Mem(sigma_i) WITH [(SP(sigma_i)) := Unknown]
  #)

SP_DEC(sigma_i : {e : Env_Store_I |
                     SP(e) - 1 >= top(Env(e))}) : Env_Store_I =
  (# Env := Env(sigma_i),
     A   := A(sigma_i),
     SP  := SP(sigma_i) - 1,
     Mem := restrict(Mem(sigma_i))
  #)
```

This allows us to ensure that when the stack pointer is decremented, the domain of the function representing the memory shrinks appropriately.

Earlier we stated that all declarations in our high-level language are static. Now we have combined the environment and store in the same datatype, the state transition functions in the dynamic semantics could modify the environment, both by extension or by contraction. If a state transition removes mapping between a program variable and its location in memory, then subsequent transitions may fail.

Due to this, PVS emits TCCs during the proof, obliging us to prove that the environment remains static. For example, the last line of this TCC asks us to prove that the environment after executing $rho_i(phi)$ (a continuation) is the same as that in the initial state:

```
% Subtype TCC generated (line 109) for  rho_i(phi)(sigma_i)
  % Proved -- Complete
MI_TCC3: OBLIGATION
(FORALL (phi: Label, gamma: Instr,
         rho_i: Env_I, sigma_i: State_I, vartheta: Cont):
 NOT Halted?(sigma_i) AND NOT Step(sigma_i) = 0 AND gamma = goto(phi)
 IMPLIES Halted?(rho_i(phi)(sigma_i))
 OR Env(StoreOf_I(rho_i(phi)(sigma_i))) = Env(StoreOf_I(sigma_i)));
```

These TCCs are easily proved, but it is also straightforward to avoid their generation at proof time by constraining the type of state transition functions so that they cannot modify the environment. The following definition is the type of arbitrary state transitions (continuations) in the low level language:

```
Cont : TYPE = [s1 : State_I -> s2 : State_I |
                    (Halted?(s1) IMPLIES Halted?(s2)) AND
                    (Env(StoreOf_I(s1)) = Env(StoreOf_I(s2))) AND
                    (Step(s1) = 0 IMPLIES s1 = s2)]
```

4.4 Halting

The original Z specification made heavy use of partial functions to structure the specification. For example, the dynamic meaning of Tosca's assignment statement (x := e) is partial: it says nothing about what state change occurs if, say,

- the lhs-name (x) is undeclared
- there are some uninitialised values in the rhs-expression e
- the lhs and rhs have different types

Making the dynamic meaning function total to include these checks would clutter the specification, and compromise the understandability of the language definition. So instead, the complete Tosca specification includes several other, static, meaning functions, such as type checking, and declaration-before-use checking, defined in a manner very similar to the dynamic meaning. If an assignment statement passes these checks in the context of some program, then it is guaranteed to be in the domain of the dynamic meaning function.

We have already noted that PVS does not admit partial functions, and as such the direct implementation of the Aida semantics generated many type correctness conditions highlighting the partial areas of the specification. Many of these cases were dealt with by augmenting the original semantics with sensible extensions, but there were several areas which dealt with 'exceptional' behaviour, for example arithmetic overflow/underflow. To deal with these cases, we added a Halted? flag to the low level state, which is set True when an error occurs. A similar concept is introduced at the high level, where a flag Okay? is introduced into the state. A high level state which is NOT Okay? is equivalent to any low level state which is Halted?.

4.5 Termination

The largest assumption made in the hand proof is that loops and hence programs terminate, therefore it is a 'partial-correctness' proof. The following definition of the dynamic semantics of loops gives a potentially infinite recursion:

$$
\begin{aligned}
&\mathcal{M}_C[\![\text{loop } (\epsilon, \gamma)]\!]\rho\sigma = \\
&\quad \text{if } \mathcal{M}_E[\![\epsilon]\!]\rho\sigma = bool_v\,\mathrm{T} \\
&\quad \text{then } \mathcal{M}_C[\![\text{loop}(\epsilon, \gamma)]\!]\rho(\mathcal{M}_C[\![\gamma]\!]\rho\sigma) \\
&\quad \text{else } \sigma
\end{aligned}
$$

The termination assumption is necessary in order to use proof by induction, and if the loop is non-terminating then this induction is not well founded. In [23, Appendix B], a non-recursive definition of the dynamic semantics of loops is given, using an infinite family of functions:

$$W : \mathbb{N} \to (CMD \times EXPR) \to Env \nrightarrow State \nrightarrow State$$

$$\forall n : \mathbb{N};\ \gamma : CMD;\ \epsilon : EXPR;\ \rho : Env;\ \sigma : State \bullet$$
$$\mathcal{W}_0(\gamma, \epsilon)\rho = \varnothing[State \times State]$$
$$\wedge\ \mathcal{W}_{n+1}(\gamma, \epsilon)\rho\sigma =$$
$$\quad \text{if } \mathcal{M}_E[\![\epsilon]\!]\rho\sigma = bool_v\mathrm{T} \text{ then } \mathcal{W}_n(\gamma, \epsilon)\rho(\mathcal{M}_C[\![\gamma]\!]\rho\sigma) \text{ else } \sigma$$

$$\mathcal{M}_C[\![\mathrm{loop}(\epsilon, \gamma)]\!] = \bigcup\{n : \mathbb{N} \bullet \mathcal{W}_n(\gamma, \epsilon)\}$$

This definition does not easily translate into the logic of the PVS system, so we took a slightly different approach based on a loop counter.

The loop counter is made part of the state at the Tosca and Aida levels, and decrements by one every time a loop body is executed. Thus, we can use induction over the naturals to prove that $\forall n : n$ unfoldings of the loop are correctly translated. The dynamic semantics of loops at the Tosca level therefore becomes:

```
MC(gamma : Cmd)(sigma : State) : RECURSIVE State =
  CASES gamma OF
    ...
    loop(epsilon,gamma) :
      IF ME(epsilon)(sigma) = BoolV(TRUE) THEN
        MC(loop(epsilon,gamma))
          (MC(gamma)(sigma) WITH [(Step) := Step(MC(gamma)(sigma)) - 1])
      ELSIF ME(epsilon)(sigma) = BoolV(FALSE) THEN
        sigma
      ELSE
        sigma  WITH [(Okay?) := FALSE]
      ENDIF
    ...
  END CASES
```

This form of definition also allows the recursive function MC to be guaranteed to terminate. Non-terminating recursive functions are in essence partial functions, and as such are not permitted in PVS. A termination TCC is generated to ensure that, on each recursive call to a function that its *measure* decreases. A measure function is attached to every recursive function in PVS, and here we use:

```
MEASURE sizeof(gamma) + Step(sigma)
```

sizeof is a function we have defined which gives the 'size' of a Tosca command (which is represented as an abstract datatype). This decreases on the recursive call (for evaluating embedded commands) in every case except loop, where the 'embedded' command is not just the loop body, but the *loop itself*, which has the same 'size'. However, using the loop counter, the Step decreases on each execution of the loop, hence the overall measure also decreases.

4.6 Remaining Assumptions

There are several axioms in our specification, detailing things that cannot be directly derived from the functional description of the languages and compiler. Three of these relate to the partial nature of the Z specification:

1. Any two Tosca states that are NOT Okay? are equivalent.
2. Any two Aida states that are Halted? are equivalent.
3. Any Tosca state that is NOT Okay? is equivalent to any Aida state that is Halted?.

The other remaining assumptions concern the environment Env_I which maps from labels in an Aida program to the continuations which they represent. It is not possible to 'build' this environment as the compiler progresses through the source text, as many label references in goto and jump instructions are forward references. Also, to build the continuations to which they would refer would require knowledge of the entire target program text, which is not available until after compilation.

Hence, we have generated two axioms (for loop and choice instructions) which give a representation of how this environment maps into the final program text: This axiomatisation is sufficient for our purposes, but not ideal — it is far too easy to introduce inconsistencies into the specification with the use of axioms.

```
rho_i_loop : LEMMA
  FORALL (gamma : (loop?), rho_i : Env_I, phi : Label, n : nat,
          sigma_i : {s : State_I | NOT Halted?(s)}, sigma : State) :
    (FORALL (vartheta : Cont) :
       rho_i(1 + PROJ_1(OC(c(gamma : (loop?))))(Env(StoreOf_I(sigma_i)))
                        (SP(StoreOf_I(sigma_i)))(phi))) = vartheta
    AND rho_i(PROJ_1(OC(c(gamma : (loop?))))(Env(StoreOf_I(sigma_i)))
                      (SP(StoreOf_I(sigma_i)))(phi))) =
        MI_Star(PROJ_2(OC(gamma)(Env(StoreOf_I(sigma_i)))
                        (SP(StoreOf_I(sigma_i)))(phi)))
                (rho_i)(vartheta))
```

5 Correctness Theorems

The main branches of the correctness theorems follow the hand development quite closely. The exceptions are where our augmentations of the specification come into play, and where the hand proof makes light of some tricky details. The best examples of this are in the proof of the translation of block commands and entire programs, where Stepney assumes that these will follow directly (and simply) from earlier lemmas, which is not entirely true.

The effort required to perform the proof with PVS has been large (a person year, with the usual interruptions — considerably more that that to perform the proof by hand). It has been noted by the authors of PVS that this is one of the largest and more complex theorems passed through their system, and the theorems we are required to discharge here are of a very different nature from the theorems that have been specified in PVS previously. We have thus been stretching the limits of the type system, for example in the use of doubly-dependent types and abstract datatypes with subtypes.

We have succeeded in implementing strategies for discharging several of the correctness theorems in a near automatic manner. The next stage of this research is to see how robust these strategies are to changes in the specification, as a result of adding more high-level language statements.

6 Related Work

One of the earlier works in the area of compiler verification is that by Polak [18], who performed a partial correctness proof of a non-optimising compiler for a substantial subset of Pascal, using the Stanford Pascal Verifier [9]. However, it is reported by Young [25] that there are a large collection of unproven assumptions within his formal theory, and several inconsistencies in the axioms.

Computational Logic Inc. have performed verification of a compiler [14] for a simple language Micro-Gypsy using the Boyer-Moore (NQTHM) system [3] as part of their work on a trusted stack of system components [25]. The European ProCoS (Provably Correct Systems) project [2] also attempted use of NQTHM for their work on an Occam compiler, but with little success [24]. Recent work at Kiel [4] and Ulm [7] is using the PVS system with much greater success. A formalisation of denotational semantics is now available within the PVS framework [17].

Several works have been based on the HOL system [8] — verification of an assembler (Curzon) [6] and compilers for a small real-time language (Hale) [11] and a simple imperative language (Joyce) [12]. A notable rigorous by-hand work is that performed at Mitre and North Eastern University [10] for a compiler for Scheme.

7 Conclusions

We have seen how it is possible, with some work, to use PVS to prove a theorem cast in Z. This exercise highlighted some problems with the original proof, and also some problems with using a proof tool in a somewhat 'unnatural' manner.

Often, the *process* of performing a proof is more instructive than getting the yes/no answer out at the end. With a hand proof, that process can deepen the understanding of the original specification structure. It is important that this source of insight not be lost when using a tool. In this case other insights came from using PVS: the way of using it to explore the static semantics, for example.

PVS gives us greater confidence in the result of the compiler via several routes. With its expressive type system, and the requirement to discharge type correctness conditions, we have a method for noting incompleteness and weakness in the specification at a very early stage (which is therefore cheap to rectify). Discharging putative theorems about the specification gives us more confidence, noting hidden assumptions and blatant incorrectness in the specification, but we have noted this to be a very expensive activity, and will require more work on automation before this is a viable industrial proposition for proofs of compiler correctness.

We noted that the standard heuristics and built-in proof strategies of PVS were not well suited to this problem domain, largely due to the very specific ordering in which re-write rules must be fired. We are in the process of developing strategies which automate re-writing in this domain by specific ordering of applications, and controlled eagerness. Also, SRI are implementing more sensible methods for instantiation of universal strength quantifiers, possibly using unification or tableaux procedures, which should succeed in our proofs where the current heuristics fail.

However, it should be remembered that there is more to a specification than just its proof opportunity: the other purposes of the specification must not be compromised in the pursuit of ease-of-proof, lest assurance be lost in other areas such as clarity, or translation to executable form.

7.1 Future Work

The work detailed here is ongoing, both at York and Logica. Since the original small language was specified in [23], further development of this approach has continued at Logica, on a compiler for AWE's high assurance ASP processor. The method has been used on a high level language that extends Tosca by adding more data types (bytes, unsigneds, arrays), functions and procedures, and separate compilation of modules, with a high-integrity linker [15].

At York, we are intending to extend the PVS treatment of the compiler, by augmenting the source language (and possibly target language) with new features including local scope, procedures and functions, an array datatype and separate compilation. Our plan is to manufacture proof strategies such that the augmentation of the source language requires as little manual intervention to re-run the correctness proofs as is possible.

8 Acknowledgments

Our thanks to John Rushby, Jeremy Jacob and the anonymous referees for their useful comments on drafts of this paper. For help with PVS, our thanks to Natarajan Shankar and Sam Owre of SRI International.

References

1. Rosalind Barden, Susan Stepney, and David Cooper. *Z in Practice*. BCS Practitioners Series. Prentice Hall International, 1994.
2. Jonathan Bowen, C.A.R. Hoare, Michael R. Hansen, Anders R. Ravn, Hans Rischel, Ernst-Rüdiger Olderog, Michael Schenke, Martin Fränzle, Markus Müller-Olm, Jifeng He, and Zheng Jianping. Provably correct systems - FTRTFT'94 tutorial. In *Proceedings of FTRTFT'94*, number 863 in Lecture Notes in Computer Science. Springer-Verlag, September 1994.
3. Robert S. Boyer and J. Strother Moore. *A Computational Logic Handbook*. Academic Press, 1988.
4. Karl-Heinz Buth. Automated code generator verification based on algebraic laws. ProCoS Project Document Kiel KHB 5/1, September 1995.
5. W.J. Cullyer. Implementing safety critical systems: The VIPER microprocessor. In G. Birtwistle and P.A. Subrahmanyam, editors, *VLSI Specification, Verification and Synthesis*, pages 1–25. Kluwer Academic Publishers, 1988.
6. Paul Curzon. A verified vista implementation final report. Technical Report 311, University of Cambridge Computer Laboratory, September 1993.
7. Axel Dold, F.W. von Henke, H. Pfeifer, and H. Rueß. Formal verification of transformations for peephole optimizations. 1997. These proceedings.
8. Mike Gordon. A proof generating system for higher-order logic. Technical Report 103, University of Cambridge Computer Laboratory, January 1987.
9. Stanford Verification Group. Stanford Pascal verifier user manual. Technical Report 11, Stanford Verification Group, 1979.
10. Joshua D. Guttman, John D. Ramsdell, and Vipin Swarup. The VLISP verified scheme system. *LISP and Symbolic Computation*, 8:33–110, 1995.
11. R.W.S. Hale. Program compilation. In Jonathan Bowen, editor, *Towards Verified Systems*, chapter 6. Elsevier Science Publishers Series on Real-Time Safety Critical Systems, Amsterdam, 1993.
12. Jeffrey J. Joyce. A verified compiler for a verified microprocessor. Technical Report 167, University of Cambridge Computer Laboratory, March 1989.
13. A.C. Leisenring. *Mathematical Logic and Hilbert's ε-symbol*. Gordon and Breach Science Publishers, New York, 1969.
14. J. Strother Moore. A mechanically verified language implementation. Technical Report 30, Computational Logic Inc., September 1988.
15. I. T. Nabney and S. Stepney. *High integrity separate compilation*. In preparation.
16. Sam Owre, John Rushby, Natarajan Shankar, and Friedrich von Henke. Formal verification for fault-tolerant architectures: Prolegomena to the design of PVS. *IEEE Transactions on Software Engineering*, 21(2):107–125, February 1995.
17. H. Pfeifer, A. Dold, F. W. v. Henke, and H. Rueß. Mechanized Semantics of Simple Imperative Programming Constructs. Ulmer Informatik-Berichte 96-11, Universität Ulm, Fakultät für Informatik, 1996.
18. Wolfgang Polak. *Compiler Specification and Verification*. Number 124 in Lecture Notes in Computer Science. Springer-Verlag, 1981.
19. J.M. Rushby and D.W.J. Stringer-Calvert. A less elementary tutorial for the PVS specification and verification system. Technical Report CSL-95-10, Computer Science Laboratory, SRI International, August 1996.
20. Mark Saaltink. The Z/EVES system. In *ZUM '97: The Z Formal Specification Notation; 10th International Conference of Z Users*, number 1212 in Lecture Notes in Computer Science, pages 72–85, Reading, UK, April 1997. Springer-Verlag.

21. J. M. Spivey. *The fUZZ manual.* Computing Science Consultancy, 2 Willow Close, Oxford, UK, 1988.

22. J.M. Spivey. *The Z Notation: A Reference Manual.* Prentice Hall International, 1989.

23. Susan Stepney. *High Integrity Compilation: A Case Study.* Prentice Hall International, 1993.

24. Deborah Weber-Wulff. Proven correct scanning. Procos internal report, August 1992.

25. William D. Young. A verified code generator for a subset of Gypsy. Technical Report 33, Computational Logic Inc., October 1988.

Verification of Reactive Systems Using DisCo and PVS

Pertti Kellomäki

Tampere University of Technology
Software Systems Laboratory
Finland

Abstract. We have provided mechanical verification support for DisCo, an object oriented language and method for the specification of reactive systems. The paper has two main contributions. The first one is a mapping of object oriented specifications to the PVS theorem prover, where their invariant properties can be mechanically verified. The second one is the use of the theorem prover together with the animation facility of the DisCo environment when strengthening invariants.

1   Introduction

This work was done in the DisCo project, whose aim is to develop a methodology and associated tools for the specification of reactive systems. The work on the specification language and the tools has been described elsewhere [1, 15, 17], so we only introduce them briefly here. Since the DisCo language has a well defined semantics, it is possible to reason formally about DisCo specifications. This paper describes how invariant properties are verified using the PVS [20] theorem prover.

Figure 1 gives an overview of the system. The user first constructs a specification in the DisCo language. The specification can be examined using the animation tool, which can also be used to validate the specification against the informal requirements. Once the user is satisfied that the specification captures the requirements, formal verification can be used to increase confidence in the specification. During verification we sometimes need to find a stronger invariant that implies the invariant we want to verify. We use the theorem prover together with the animation tool for strengthening invariants.

The main contributions of this paper are the mapping of object oriented specifications to the PVS logic, and the use of the theorem prover and the animation tool together for strengthening invariants.

We use a familiar example, the alternating bit protocol [6], to give a flavor of what DisCo specifications look like and how they are mapped to the logic of the theorem prover. The rest of the paper is structured as follows. Section 2 reviews some related work. Section 3 introduces the DisCo specification language using the alternating bit protocol as an example. Section 4 gives our formalization of the Temporal Logic of Actions in PVS, and Section 5 describes the mapping of DisCo constructs to this logic. Section 6 illustrates how invariants are proved, and Section 7 draws some conclusions and outlines future work.

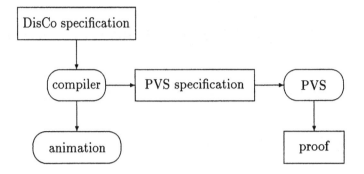

Fig. 1. The DisCo specification environment

2 Related Work

TLA reasoning has been mechanized by von Wright and Långbacka using the HOL prover [19, 22], by Kalvala using Isabelle [16], and by Engberg et al. using the Larch Prover [11]. These are more or less complete formalizations of TLA, which can be used for reasoning about arbitrary TLA specifications. This is not our goal, since we are only concerned with the subset of TLA used for DisCo specifications.

The execution model of Unity [7] is similar to that of DisCo. The Unity logic has been embedded in various theorem provers by several authors: in COQ by Heyd and Crégut [14], in HOL by Andersen et al. [3], and in the Larch Prover by Chetali [9]. Our work could be used as a starting point for a PVS embedding of Unity, if so desired. The main differences between the Unity embeddings and ours is that whereas in Unity the state consists of a fixed set of named variables, in our case the variables are embedded in an unknown number of anonymous objects.

The embedding of Duration Calculus [8] by Owre and Skakkebæk [21] lets a user write specifications in PVS so that they are a close transliteration of the Duration Calculus notation. Closer to our work is an experiment described by Agerholm [2], where existing specifications written in VDM-SL were translated by hand to the PVS logic. The main difference to our work is that we have a mechanical translation from the specification language to the target logic.

Havelund and Shankar [13] use PVS and the Murφ state exploration tool for specifying the bounded retransmission protocol, an extension of the alternating bit protocol. Our use of the animation tool is somewhat similar to their use of the state exploration tool.

Chou [10] describes a general framework for reasoning about distributed algorithms with the HOL theorem prover. Properties of programs are verified by verifying the properties of their more abstract counterparts, and using a mapping between concrete and abstract programs.

3   DisCo

The DisCo specification language is based on the *joint action* approach of Back and Kurki-Suonio [4, 5]. A joint action system consists of a set of objects, and a set of actions. Whenever the guard of an action is true for some combination of participating objects, the action can be executed for them. The execution of an action is atomic, and parallelism is modeled using nondeterministic choice. The meaning of a DisCo specification is the set of execution sequences it allows.

Rather than presenting all the details of the DisCo specification language, we show how a familiar example is specified using it. We do not use the language support for stepwise refinement in DisCo, but rather give the specification as a monolithic whole. In specifications of realistic size, stepwise refinement would be used, however.

For brevity, we do not give the full specification here, just some representative parts of it. Figure 2 illustrates the specification in the DisCo animation tool.

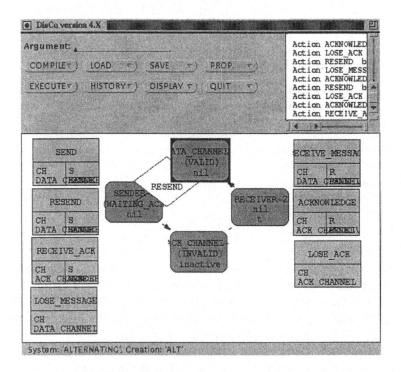

Fig. 2. Specification in the DisCo animation tool

3.1   The Alternating Bit Protocol

We now briefly outline the version of the alternating bit protocol we use as an example. The protocol ensures correct delivery of messages over an unreliable

592

channel, which may lose messages but not corrupt them. In our version, there are two channels. The sender places messages on a message channel which the receiver can read, and the receiver places acknowledgments on an acknowledgment channel which the sender can read.

Both the sender and the receiver maintain one bit of additional information, which is transmitted in the messages and acknowledgments to the other party. In the initial state, the values of the bits are the same in the receiver and in the sender, and there are no messages nor acknowledgments in transit. When the sender wants to send a message, it stores the message on the message channel along with its bit, and enters a state indicating that it is expecting an acknowledgment. In this state it can then repeatedly send the message, until an acknowledgment with the same bit is received. When the acknowledgment is received, the sender inverts its bit, and enters a state where no acknowledgments are pending.

The receiver repeatedly sends acknowledgments with the negation of its bit. When it reads a message with a bit equal to its own bit, it receives the message and negates its own bit. It then continues to send acknowledgments with the negation of the new value of the bit.

3.2 Specification of the Alternating Bit Protocol in DisCo

We first give a definition of the data channel. It has a single top level state indicating whether the channel contains a valid message. A message consists of the alternating bit and some data to be sent.

```
class data_channel is
  state *invalid, valid;
  extend valid by
    data : integer;
    bit : boolean;
  end;
end;
```

DisCo objects have a hierarchical state structure similar to Statecharts [12]. The **extend** clause declares the variables *data* and *bit* to reside within the state *valid*. When a data channel enters the state *invalid*, the variables become inactive. The asterisk in front of *invalid* indicates that it is the default state. The definition of *ack_channel* is similar, so it is omitted here.

A class definition describes the structure of the objects belonging to the class. There can be any number of objects, even infinitely many. An implementation of a specification fixes the number of objects of each class. Animation also requires a specific instance of the specification. Figure 2 shows an instance of the specification consisting of one object of each class.

The class *sender* is defined next. It has two constant attributes *in_ch* and *out_ch*, which are references to channels. The history variable *sent_messages* is used when formulating the main invariant about ordering of messages. The definition for class *receiver* is similar, so it is omitted here.

```
class sender(in_ch : ack_channel := null;
             out_ch : data_channel := null) is
  state *ready, waiting_ack;
  last_sent : integer;
  bit : boolean;
  sent_messages : sequence integer;
end;
```

A number of assertions about the structure of the system are needed. They give the necessary conditions an implementation needs to fulfill in order for the verified invariants to hold. These assertions are also initial conditions for the system. Some representative assertions are listed below.

assert data_receiver_exists **is**
  $\forall$ d : data_channel :: $\exists$ r : receiver :: r.in_ch = d;

assert well_connected **is**
  $\forall$ r : receiver :: $\forall$ s : sender ::
  (s.out_ch = r.in_ch) = (s.in_ch = r.out_ch);

assert unique_ack_sender **is**
  $\forall$ r, rr : receiver ::
  r.out_ch = rr.out_ch $\Rightarrow$ rr = r;

The assertions *sender_data_exists*, *receiver_data_exists*, *sender_ack_exists*, *receiver_ack_exists*, and *unique_data_sender* are omitted, as they are similar to those presented.

We also give here the assertion *delivered_messages* corresponding to the main invariant we want to verify, stating that the protocol preserves message ordering. We return to it in Section 6 when discussing verification.

assert delivered_messages **is**
  $\forall$ s : sender; r : receiver ::
  (s.out_ch = r.in_ch $\wedge$ s.in_ch = r.out_ch)
  $\Rightarrow$ (s.sent_messages = r.received_messages)
    $\vee$
  (<s.last_sent> & s.sent_messages = r.received_messages);

We next give the actions objects can participate in. The actions *send* and *resend* move a message from the sender to the data channel. The message to be sent in the *send* action is modeled as an action parameter, which receives an arbitrary integer value each time the action is executed. The message is stored in *last_sent* for subsequent use in the action *resend*. The action *resend* is similar to *send*, and is omitted here.

```
action send(m : integer)
by s : sender; ch : data_channel is
when s.out_ch = ch ∧ s.ready
do
  →s.waiting_ack;        -- state transition to state waiting_ack
  s.last_sent := m;
  →ch.valid;
  ch.valid.data := m;
  ch.valid.bit := s.bit;
end;
```

A message is received if its bit matches the bit of the receiver. Receiving a message removes it from the channel. The received message is appended to the sequence of received messages, and the alternating bit at the receiver is negated.

```
action receive_message
by r : receiver; ch : data_channel is
when r.in_ch = ch
∧ ch.valid ∧ ch.valid.bit = r.bit
do
  r.bit := ¬ r.bit;
  r.received_messages := <ch.data> & r.received_messages;
  →ch.invalid;
end;
```

The actions *acknowledge* and *receive_ack* are similar to the actions *send* and *receive_message*. The actions *lose_message* and *lose_ack* lose the contents of a channel by entering the state *invalid*. We omit these actions here for brevity.

4 Temporal Logic

In this section, we give a formalization of a temporal logic in the PVS logic. The logic is essentially Lamport's Temporal Logic of Actions, even though there are some differences to the description of TLA in [18]. This is the logic to which the syntactic forms of the DisCo language are mapped.

We start by formalizing state, which is simply an uninterpreted abstract data type in our formalization:

```
state : TYPE
```

Behaviors are sequences of states, so they are formalized as such:

```
behavior: TYPE = [nat -> state]
```

The types for temporal formulas, actions, and state predicates are the expected mappings

```
temporal_formula : TYPE = [behavior -> bool]
state_predicate  : TYPE = [state -> bool]
action           : TYPE = [state,state -> bool]
```

We represent terminating computations as nonterminating computations by repeating the last state. For this a *stuttering* step is needed.

```
stutter(A : action) : action =
  LAMBDA (unprimed, primed : state) :
    A(unprimed, primed) or primed = unprimed
```

In order to be able to use actions and state predicates as temporal formulas, we introduce lifting functions, which are declared as *conversions* to PVS. Whenever an action or a state predicate is encountered in a context requiring a temporal formula, it is automatically converted by PVS using these conversions.

```
statepred2temporal((P: state_predicate)):
  temporal_formula = LAMBDA (b: behavior): P(b(0))

action2temporal((A: action)): temporal_formula =
  LAMBDA (b: behavior): A(b(0), b(1))
```

We next define the temporal operator [] for a temporal formula F and behavior b:

```
[]((F: temporal_formula), (b: behavior)): bool =
  FORALL (n: nat): F(suffix(b, n))
```

We are now ready to define what an invariant is. A state predicate P is an invariant for a system with initial condition I and actions A under some assumptions iff [] (P,b) holds for all behaviors b satisfying the assumptions and the initial condition, and consisting only of A steps or stuttering steps.

```
invariant((P: state_predicate), (assumptions: bool),
          (I: state_predicate), (A: action)): bool =
  FORALL (b: behavior):
    assumptions AND I(b(0)) AND [](stutter(A),b) => [](P,b)
```

The **assumptions** argument collects the requirements an instance of the specification needs to fulfill. For example, in the protocol example we require that for each data channel there exists a receiver (assertion *data_receiver_exists*). We represent DisCo classes as uninterpreted subtypes of PVS record types, so **assumptions** essentially constrains the subtypes representing classes. The verified invariants do not hold if the assumptions are not satisfied.

We derive theorems corresponding to the inference rules of TLA. These theorems can then be used in invariant proofs. The theorem **invariant_rule** is the standard technique for establishing invariants: show that the predicate holds in the initial state, and that none of the actions can invalidate it. The second theorem, **invariant_intro_rule**, allows us to introduce previously established invariants as assumptions in a proof. Both of these are straightforward to prove.

```
invariant_rule: THEOREM
    FORALL (P: state_predicate, assumptions: bool,
            I: state_predicate, A: action):
      (FORALL (b: behavior):
        NOT (I(b(0)) AND [](stutter(A),b))
            OR
        ((assumptions AND I(b(0)) => P(b(0)))
            AND FORALL (n: nat):
            assumptions AND P(b(n)) AND A(b(n), b(n + 1))
                => P(b(n + 1))))
        => invariant(P, assumptions, I, A)


invariant_intro_rule: THEOREM
    FORALL (assumptions: bool, P: state_predicate,
            I: state_predicate, A: action):
      invariant(P, assumptions, I, A)
        => FORALL (b: behavior):
        assumptions
          AND I(b(0))
          AND [](stutter(A),b)
        => FORALL (n: nat): P(b(n))
```

It is often convenient to derive a stronger invariant implying the invariant we want to prove, and prove the stronger invariant. The invariant implication rule allows for this.

```
invariant_implication_rule: THEOREM
    FORALL (assumptions: bool, Pstrong: state_predicate,
            Pweak: state_predicate,
            I: state_predicate, A: action):
      invariant(Pstrong, assumptions, I, A)
          AND (FORALL (b: behavior, n: nat):
                assumptions and Pstrong(b(n))
                    => Pweak(b(n)))
          => invariant(Pweak, assumptions, I, A)
```

5 Mapping DisCo to PVS

In this section we describe the mapping of DisCo constructs to PVS using the specification in Section 3 as an example.

We have implemented a compiler which automates the mapping of DisCo to PVS. The formalization of temporal logic and the mappings of the individual DisCo constructs are a definitional extension of PVS logic, so they cannot give rise to inconsistencies. It is certainly possible to give contradictory initial conditions and assumptions in a DisCo specification, but these would be detected by the animation tool which detects assertion failures when a specification is animated.

The correctness of the compiler crucially affects the value of the results of any verification performed using the resulting PVS theories. We have not attempted to verify the correctness of the compiler formally, neither do we see much added value in such an exercise. Much more useful would be to use the pretty printing support in PVS to facilitate easier checking of PVS theories against their DisCo counterparts.

5.1 Classes

A DisCo class is represented as an uninterpreted subtype of a record type in the PVS logic. Each of the components of the DisCo class gives rise to one or more elements in the record type. For example, the class *sender* maps to the type

```
sender:
    TYPE FROM
        [# in_ch: objid,
           out_ch: objid,
           last_sent: [state -> int],
           bit: [state -> bool],
           sent_messages: [state -> list[int]],
           state3: [state -> state3_type],
           ref: objid #]
```

There are two kinds of components in a class: parameters and variables. Parameters are constant components which do not change their values in actions, so they are represented as elements of the corresponding type. The field *in_ch* is an example of a parameter. Variables change their values in actions, so they are represented as functions from state to the appropriate type. The field *bit* is an example of a variable.

A DisCo state is an anonymous finite state machine. We represent a DisCo state as an enumerated variable, and name the variables state0, state1, etc. For each enumerated variable, a corresponding enumeration type is declared. In the example, the type of state3 is declared as

```
state3_type: TYPE = {ready, waiting_ack} .
```

The hierarchical structure of DisCo states is not preserved in the PVS representation. Parameters and variables embedded within states are converted to top level components by prefixing them with the names of the enclosing state items. For example, the variable *valid.bit* is mapped to valid_bit in the PVS representation.

5.2 Expressions

Mapping DisCo expressions to PVS is straightforward. DisCo constants map to PVS constants, DisCo operators map to PVS operators, etc. References to parameters and variables within objects use the accessor functions PVS creates for a record type. Let *s* be an object of class *sender*. The reference *s.in_ch* maps to in_ch(s), since *in_ch* is a parameter. The reference *s.bit* maps to bit(s)(*state*), where *state* is the appropriate TLA state. References to DisCo states map to references to the corresponding enumerated variables.

5.3 Assertions

As was mentioned in Section 3, there are two kinds of assertions. The first is exemplified by *data_receiver_exists*:

> **assert** data_receiver_exists **is**
> ∀ d : data_channel :: ∃ r : receiver :: r.in_ch = d;

The assertion only refers to constant attributes of objects, so it cannot be invalidated by actions. There is thus no need to prove it as an invariant. We map these state-independent assertions to boolean formulas, which are taken as assumptions when doing verification. The assertion *data_receiver_exists* maps to

```
data_receiver_exists: bool =
  (FORALL (d: data_channel):
    (EXISTS (r: receiver): in_ch(r) = ref(d)))
```

Assertions that can be invalidated by actions are mapped to boolean functions of state. For example, the assertion *delivered_messages* maps to PVS as follows.

```
delivered_messages_body((r: receiver), (s: sender),
                        (other: state)): bool =
  ((out_ch(s) = in_ch(r)) AND (in_ch(s) = out_ch(r)))
      IMPLIES
    ((sent_messages(s)(other) = received_messages(r)(other))
        OR
      ((append((: last_sent(s)(other) :),
               sent_messages(s)(other)))
        = received_messages(r)(other)))

delivered_messages((other: state)): bool =
  (FORALL (s: sender):
    (FORALL (r: receiver): delivered_messages_body(r, s, other)))
```

State-dependent assertions give rise to proof obligations. For each assertion, the following theorem is generated.

```
assertion_is_invariant :
  THEOREM invariant( assertion, ASSUMPTIONS, INIT, ACTIONS)
```

The predicate ASSUMPTIONS is the conjunction of assumptions about the system, INIT is the conjunction of initial conditions and assertions, and ACTIONS is the disjunction of the actions.

The bulk of the work involved in verifying an invariant goes into establishing that none of the actions can invalidate the invariant. It is often the case that most of the actions preserve the invariant almost trivially, and that only a handful of actions need special consideration. We produce a lemma *action_preserves_assertion* for each action-assertion pair. These lemmas together imply *assertion_is_invariant*, and help to modularize the proof.

5.4 Actions

An action is a relation between two states, so we map it to a boolean function of pairs of states. A DisCo action only gives the changes that take place, leaving implicit what is left unchanged. The PVS counterpart needs to spell out the new values also for the unchanged parts of the state. Figure 3 gives the mapping of the action *send* to PVS. Parameters and participants map to existentially quantified variables. We give the guard as a separate function, since this is sometimes convenient when doing the verification.

The body of an action consists of a sequence of assignments and state transitions, which are individually mapped to the corresponding PVS formulas. Assignments in DisCo map to equalities in PVS, with the left hand side mapping to a reference in the primed state. State transitions map to assignments to the corresponding enumerated variables.

6 Verification of Invariants

We set out to verify the assertion *delivered_messages*, which captures the informal requirement that messages should not be lost and that their order should be preserved:

> **assert** delivered_messages **is**
> $\forall$ s : sender; r : receiver ::
> (s.out_ch = r.in_ch $\wedge$ s.in_ch = r.out_ch)
> $\Rightarrow$ (s.sent_messages = r.received_messages)
> $\vee$ (<s.last_sent> & s.sent_messages = r.received_messages);

The first proof attempt reveals that *delivered_messages* is not inductive, so we need to strengthen it. Somewhat arbitrarily, we separate some of the strengthening conjuncts to separate assertions. We illustrate the strengthening procedure with one subgoal. Applying the generated strategy to the lemma **receive_ack_preserves_delivered_messages** results in the subgoal presented in Figure 4.

In terms of the protocol, the subgoal depicts a state where the acknowledgment channel contains a valid bit equal to the bit of the sender (formulas -8 and -9), and the values of the history variables *sent_messages* and *received_messages* are equal (formula -1). Animating the specification in the animation tool suggests that when an acknowledge is received, the values of the history variables cannot be equal. Thus, we strengthen *delivered_messages* with the conjunct

not(s.bit = ack.valid.bit $\wedge$ s.sent_messages = r.received_messages) .

```
send_guard((ch: data_channel), (s: sender), (m: int), (other: state)):
   bool = (out_ch(s) = ref(ch)) AND (ready?(state3(s)(other)))

send((unprimed, primed: state)): bool =
  (EXISTS (ch: data_channel, s: sender, m: int):
   (send_guard(ch, s, m, unprimed))
   AND (((waiting_ack?(state3(s)(primed)))
   AND ((last_sent(s)(primed) = (m))
   AND ((valid?(state2(ch)(primed)))
   AND ((valid_data(ch)(primed) = (m))
   AND (valid_bit(ch)(primed) = (bit(s)(unprimed))))))))
   AND (((FORALL (other: data_channel):
             ((other) /= (ch)) IMPLIES
                 ((state2(other)(primed) = (state2(other)(unprimed)))
                 AND ((valid_data(other)(primed)
                              = (valid_data(other)(unprimed)))
                     AND (valid_bit(other)(primed)
                              = (valid_bit(other)(unprimed))))))))
   AND (((FORALL (other: sender):
           ((other) /= (s)) IMPLIES
              (last_sent(other)(primed) = (last_sent(other)(unprimed)))))
   AND ((FORALL (other: sender):
           ((other) /= (s)) IMPLIES
              (state3(other)(primed) = (state3(other)(unprimed))))))))))
   AND (⟨ state1 and valid_bit unchanged in ack_channel⟩
   AND (⟨ bit unchanged in receiver⟩
   AND (⟨ received_messages unchanged in receiver⟩
   AND (⟨ bit unchanged in sender⟩
   AND ⟨ sent_messages unchanged in sender⟩)))))
```

Fig. 3. Mapping of the action *send* to PVS.

The other unresolved subgoals yield strengthening conjuncts in a similar fashion, resulting in the strengthened version of *delivered_messages*:

assert delivered_messages_aux **is**
$\forall$ s : sender; r : receiver; ack : ack_channel ::
  (s.out_ch = r.in_ch $\wedge$ s.in_ch = ack $\wedge$ ack = r.out_ch)
  $\Rightarrow$ ((s.sent_messages = r.received_messages)
     $\vee$
     (<s.last_sent> & s.sent_messages = r.received_messages))
  $\wedge$ not(s.bit = ack.valid.bit
          $\wedge$ s.sent_messages = r.received_messages)
  $\wedge$ not(s.bit $\neq$ r.bit $\wedge$ s.sent_messages = r.received_messages)
  $\wedge$ not(s.bit = r.bit $\wedge$ s.sent_messages $\neq$ r.received_messages);

```
[-1]     (sent_messages(s!1)(now) = received_messages(r!1)(now))
[-2]     ss!1 = s!1
[-3]     ASSUMPTIONS
[-4]     b!1(n!1) = now
[-5]     INIT(b!1(0))
[-6]     [](action2temporal(stutter(ACTIONS)), b!1)
[-7]     (in_ch(s!1) = ref(ch!1))
[-8]     (valid?(state1(ch!1)(now)))
[-9]     (valid_bit(ch!1)(now) = bit(s!1)(now))
[-10]    (out_ch(s!1) = in_ch(r!1))
[-11]    (in_ch(s!1) = out_ch(r!1))
   |-------
[1]      (cons(last_sent(s!1)(now), sent_messages(s!1)(now))
             = (received_messages(r!1)(now)))
[2]      (cons((last_sent(s!1)(now)),
             cons(last_sent(s!1)(now), sent_messages(s!1)(now)))
             = (received_messages(r!1)(now)))
```

Fig. 4. An unresolved subgoal from the proof of *delivered_messages*

The auxiliary assertions needed for establishing that *delivered_messages* is an invariant are shown in Figure 5. The assertions were produced with the same strengthening process, except for the assertion *channel_bits*, which was produced by observing how the alternating bits relate to each other when the specification was simulated in the animation tool.

6.1 Experiences on Verification

The DisCo specification of the alternating bit protocol does not describe a single instance of a sender–receiver pair and the associated channels, but rather a world of senders, receivers, and channels. The class definitions for *sender* and *receiver* state that they can be connected to channels, but do not imply any particular structure. The structure needs to be given explicitly using assertions. Most of the subgoals not resolved by the PVS decision procedures have to do with this generality of the DisCo specification. For example, when the prover constructs a subgoal corresponding the situation where two senders are connected to the same data channel, we need to refer to the appropriate assumptions in order to resolve the subgoal. In practice this means expanding definitions and instantiating the resulting quantified formulas with appropriate values. Installing all the assumptions as automatic rewrites is not feasible, because that would make the search space for PVS decision procedures too large.

Verifying a typical DisCo specification involves mostly reasoning about state machines, for which the PVS decision procedures are quite effective. Once an inductive invariant has been found, it is thus usually not a problem to prove it. The main problem is finding the invariant.

assert channel_bits **is**
∀ s : sender; r : receiver;
  data : data_channel; ack : ack_channel ::
  (s.out_ch = data ∧ data = r.in_ch
  ∧ s.in_ch = ack ∧ ack = r.out_ch)
  ⇒ ((s.bit = r.bit
    ⇒ (ack.invalid ∨ (not s.bit) = ack.valid.bit))
   ∧
   (s.bit ≠ r.bit
    ⇒ (data.invalid ∨ data.valid.bit = s.bit)));

assert data_not_corrupted **is**
∀ s : sender; d : data_channel ::
  s.out_ch = d ∧ s.bit = d.valid.bit ⇒ s.last_sent = d.valid.data;

assert ready_bits_aux **is**
∀ s : sender; r : receiver; d : data_channel ::
  (s.out_ch = d ∧ d = r.in_ch)
  ⇒
  not(s.ready ∧ s.bit=d.valid.bit ∧ s.bit=r.bit)
  ∧ not(s.ready ∧ s.bit ≠ r.bit)
  ∧ not(s.bit ≠ r.bit ∧ d.valid.bit = r.bit);

assert ready_bits **is**
∀ s : sender; r : receiver; d : data_channel ::
  (s.out_ch = d ∧ d = r.in_ch)
  ⇒
  not(s.ready ∧ s.bit=d.valid.bit ∧ s.bit=r.bit)
  ∧ not(s.ready ∧ s.bit ≠ r.bit);

Fig. 5. Auxiliary assertions

7 Conclusions

We have implemented a mechanized chain from DisCo specifications to the logic of the PVS prover. This can be used for formal verification of invariant properties of DisCo specifications. We use the failed subgoals together with the DisCo animation tool for systematic strengthening of invariants. We analyze the subgoal to see if it represents an unreachable state, using simulation with the animation tool to augment informal reasoning. Once we are convinced that we have identified an unreachable state characterized by some assignment a of values to variables, we strengthen the invariant with the conjunct $\neg a$.

The examples we have tried so far suggest that verification can be done with a reasonable amount of effort. It is difficult to estimate how much work has gone into the verification of the alternating bit protocol, as the tools have been under constant development, but we estimate that specifying and verifying a similar case would be under one week.

7.1 Future Work

It is quite often the case that the original invariant describes some intuitively understandable property of the system, but the strengthening conjuncts are not immediately obvious. It is thus easy to make mistakes with the strengthening conjuncts, which leads to wasted verification efforts. We are planning to use finite state methods as a quick check for the strengthened invariants before attempting a proof with PVS, in a fashion similar to [13].

The PVS logic has proved to be flexible enough to express the semantics of DisCo in a natural way. It would be interesting to compare how some other theorem provers using higher order logic would fare in this respect.

So far we have concentrated on invariants, but we are planning eventually to extend this work to the verification of liveness properties. Invariant proofs have been attempted first, because automatic support can be provided for them. Also, liveness proofs often need supporting invariants.

7.2 Acknowledgments

Financial support from the Academy of Finland and Emil Aaltonen foundation is gratefully acknowledged. We would also like to thank the reviewers for suggestions on improving the paper. Members of the DisCo project, most notably Reino Kurki-Suonio, have influenced and inspired the work reported here.

References

1. The DisCo project home page. http://www.cs.tut.fi/laitos/DisCo/.
2. Sten Agerholm. Translating specifications in VDM-SL to PVS. In J. von Wright, T. Grundy, and J. Harrison, editors, *Proceedings of the 9th International Conference on Theorem Proving in Higher Order Logics*, volume 1125 of *Lecture Notes in Computer Science*, pages 1–16. Springer-Verlag, 1996.
3. F. Andersen, K. D. Petersen, and J. S. Petterson. Program verification using HOL-UNITY. In J. J. Joyce and C.-J.H Seger, editors, *International Workshop on Higher Order Logic and its Applications*, volume 780 of *Lecture Notes in Computer Science*, pages 1–16, 1994.
4. R. J. R. Back and R. Kurki-Suonio. Distributed cooperation with action systems. *ACM Transactions on Programming Languages and Systems*, 10(4):513–554, October 1988.
5. R. J. R. Back and R. Kurki-Suonio. Decentralization of process nets with a centralized control. *Distributed Computing*, (3):73–87, 1989.
6. K. A. Bartlett, R. A. Scantlebury, and P. T. Wilkinson. A note on reliable full-duplex transmission over half-duplex links. *Communications of the ACM*, 12(5):260–261, May 1969.
7. K. M. Chandy and J. Misra. *Parallel Program Design: A Foundation*. Addison-Wesley, 1988.
8. Zhou Chaochen, C. A. R. Hoare, and Anders P. Ravn. A calculus of durations. *Information Processing Letters*, 40(5):269–276, December 1991.

9. B. Chetali. Formal Verification of Concurrent Programs: How to specify UNITY using the Larch Prover. Technical Report RR 2475, INRIA-Lorraine, Nancy, France, January 1995.

10. Ching-Tsun Chou. Mechanical verification of distributed algorithms in higher-order logic. *The Computer Journal*, 38(1), 1995.

11. Urban Engberg, Peter Grønning, and Leslie Lamport. Mechanical verification of concurrent systems with TLA. In G. v. Bochmann and D. K. Probst, editors, *Computer Aided Verification – Fourth International Workshop. CAV'92. Montreal, Canada. June 29 - July 1*, volume 663 of *Lecture Notes in Computer Science*. Springer Verlag, 1992.

12. David Harel. Statecharts: A visual formalism for complex systems. *Science of Computer Programming*, 8(3):231–274, June 1987.

13. K. Havelund and N. Shankar. Experiments in theorem proving and model checking for protocol verification. *Lecture Notes in Computer Science*, 1051, 1996.

14. Barbara Heyd and Pierre Crégut. A modular coding of UNITY in COQ. In J. von Wright, T. Grundy, and J. Harrison, editors, *Proceedings of the 9th International Conference on Theorem Proving in Higher Order Logics*, volume 1125 of *Lecture Notes in Computer Science*, pages 251–266, 1996.

15. Hannu-Matti Järvinen. *The Design of a Specification Language for Reactive Systems*. PhD thesis, Tampere University of Technology, 1992.

16. S. Kalvala. A formulation of TLA in Isabelle. *Lecture Notes in Computer Science*, 971, 1995.

17. Reino Kurki-Suonio, Hannu-Matti Järvinen, Markku Sakkinen, and Kari Systä. Object-oriented specification of reactive systems. In *Proceedings of the 12th International Conference on Software Engineering*, pages 63–71. IEEE Computer Society Press, 1990.

18. Leslie Lamport. The temporal logic of actions. *ACM Transactions on Programming Languages and Systems*, 16(3):872–923, May 1994.

19. Thomas Långbacka. A HOL formalization of the temporal logic of actions. volume 859 of *Lecture Notes in Computer Science*. Springer Verlag, 1994.

20. S. Owre, J. M. Rushby, and N. Shankar. PVS: A prototype verification system. In Deepak Kapur, editor, *11th International Conference on Automated Deduction*, volume 607 of *Lecture Notes in Artificial Intelligence*, pages 748–752. Springer Verlag, 1992.

21. Jens U. Skakkebæk and N. Shankar. Towards a Duration Calculus proof assistant in PVS. In H. Langmaack, W.-P. de Roever, and J. Vytopil, editors, *Formal Techniques in Real-Time and Fault-Tolerant Systems*, volume 863 of *Lecture Notes in Computer Science*, pages 660–679, Lübeck, Germany, September 1994. Springer-Verlag.

22. J. von Wright and T. Långbacka. Using a theorem prover for reasoning about concurrent algorithms. In G. v. Bochmann and D. K. Probst, editors, *Computer Aided Verification – Fourth International Workshop. CAV'92. Montreal, Canada. June 29 - July 1*, volume 663 of *Lecture Notes in Computer Science*. Springer Verlag, 1992.

Term Rewrite Systems to Derive Set Boolean Operations on 2D Objects [*]

David Cazier and Jean-François Dufourd

Laboratoire des Sciences de l'Image, de l'Informatique
et de la Télédétection (LSIIT, URA CNRS 1871)
Université Louis Pasteur, Département d'Informatique
7, rue René Descartes, 67084 Strasbourg Cedex
E-mail: {cazier, dufourd}@dpt-info.u-strasbg.fr

Abstract Set boolean operations between 2-dimensional geometric objects are crucial in computational geometry and deserve rigorous treatments. We build up a simple and convergent system of rewrite rules modulo equations to cope with their design. This system is complete is the sense that it gives a detailed description for all particular cases. This specification leans on a new operation of labeling self-refinement of planar subdivisions. Starting from these abstract descriptions, we design concrete algorithms with a new method. The rewrite system is successively transformed in specialized ones from which we derive efficient treatments, like plane-sweep algorithms.

1 Introduction

Designing reliable (set) boolean operations involving any number of objects remains a crucial and difficult task in geometric modeling, even in 2D. In the case of closed 2D objects, these operations appear in areas like cartography [1], drawing software design [2], 3D objects projection [3]. Moreover, 2D points sets without boundary are needed for modelling valid domains for certain differential equations [4].

This problem has been solved many times with rough software engineering methods and in specific cases, mainly in constructive solid geometry [5]. We present a new rewrite-based way to cope with the specification and the derivation of boolean operations in boundary representation. This approach takes place in the framework of the formal methods studied in our laboratory for geometric modeling [6, 7] and computational geometry [8].

Although we have dealt with these problems for 3D objects [9, 10], for simplicity and deeper discussion about sofware engineering, the objects we consider in this paper are 2-dimensional. But they are general and non-regularized [5]. In fact, they are defined by planar subdivisions, i.e. partitions of the plane into vertices, edges and faces, described by embedded combinatorial maps [11, 12, 2].

[*] This research is supported by the *GDR-PRC de Programmation* and the *GDR-PRC Algorithmes, modèles et infographie* of the French CNRS and MENESR.

An object is then any set of vertices, edges and faces of a given subdivision. It may consist of disjoint pieces, have holes and contain dangling edges or isolated vertices.

Boolean operations amount to the refinement of overlapping subdivisions or line arrangements as defined by Bentley-Ottmann [13]. We generalize these techniques with the self-refinement of embedded combinatorial maps in which each vertex, edge and face is labeled with the set of objects it belongs to. The self-refinement has been approached incrementally [1] or more generally [13, 2, 14, 15]. The resulting algorithms are usually described by conventional methods, i.e. written in a pseudo-code or a programming language, most often on concrete data structures, and say nothing about borderline cases.

Our definition of self-refinement and boolean operations relies on the use of formal methods, especially algebraic specifications [16, 17] allied to rewriting [18]. Firstly, this approach allows us to focus on conceptual and logical aspects of the problems to solve. Formal objects are described with abstract data type generators and the behavior of operations on these objects is modeled by rewrite rules and equations. Secondly, a logical prototyping, followed by symbolic calculations, points out possible design errors. These techniques have been seldom but fruitfully used in computer graphics languages [19, 20], mechanical proof in geometry [21], and geometric modeling [22, 6, 7].

The method we propose allows us to define correctly and logically the self-refinement and leads to the construction of boolean operations as a label completion of maps based on their topology. By appropriate choices of data structures and strategies, it permits us to derive concrete algorithms, from the most naïve until the most efficient ones. One of the methodological novelties is the design of algorithms as specialized rewrite systems including and reflecting the choices of implementation.

Finally, we know that the question of numerical approximations is essential in this kind of problems. Our approach allows us to return a map that always satifies its integrity constraints and to locate the sensible points thanks to the separation maps provide between topology and embedding. But this paper is essentially turned into topological issues and eludes these difficulties that need specific studies [2, 23].

In section 2, we define the self-refinement of labeled subdivisions. In section 3, we specify maps in a formal and precise algebraic framework. In section 4, we describe the labeling self-refinement as a simple, convergent term rewrite system and the label completion used to complete boolean operations. In section 5, we present a new approach to derive concrete algorithms, and in section 6, we give some concluding remarks.

2 Self-Refinement of Subdivisions

To compute the union, intersection or difference between two 2D objects defined by given subdivisions of the plane, a convenient way is to construct a new subdivision, the *corefinement* of the initial ones, that contains all their elements, taking into account their intersections and overlappings. Precisely, superposed edges or vertices are merged, intersecting edges are cut at their intersection points and edges overlapping some vertices are cut at those incidence points.

Extending the work of [4], we generalize this idea to any number $p \geqslant 2$ of objects through the notion of *labeling self-refinement* of a set of vertices, edges and faces that are labeled with the set of objects they belong to. It consists in transforming it into another one that represents a correctly labeled subdivision of the plane. During this refinement all labels are completed to take into account the intersections that can be found thanks to topological properties.

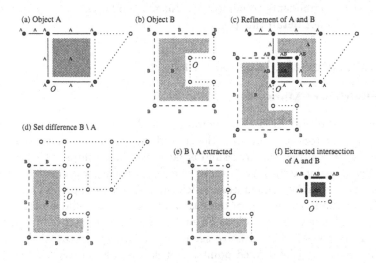

Figure1. *Example of labeling self-refinement*

To simplify the presentation, let us consider an example with $p = 2$ objects, but note that the results hold with any number $p \geqslant 2$. In figure 1 (a) and (b), we have two subdivisions with a common coordinate system of origin O. Two objects are thus defined.

Object A is formed by the square face, four edges and five vertices labeled by A of the left subdivision (a). Object B is formed by the face, three edges and four vertices labeled by B of the right one (b). The drawing conventions are the following: among the faces and vertices, those of A are grey, those of B are light-grey and the others are white. Among the edges, those of A are plain lines, those of B are dashed lines and the others are dotted lines.

Thanks to their common coordinate system, the two subdivisions are superposed to form a labeled set of vertices, edges and faces which is self-refined (c). In the result, vertices, edges and faces that belong to A and B are labeled with AB. The vertices and edges labeled AB are drawn in black and the faces are in dark-grey.

The result of a boolean operation is then an object modeled by a unique labeled subdivision after the self-refinement. This object is extracted by deleting the label of the non required parts. By example, the parts of the set difference $B \setminus A$ are those whose label contains B but not A, as shown in (d).

When the self-refinement contains only one connected component, as in the previous example, all parts of the result of the boolean operations we are not interested in, i.e. whose label is empty, can be deleted. For instance, (e) represents $B \setminus A$ and (f) represents $A \cap B$ whose vertices, edges and faces are those whose label contains A and B.

When the result of the self-refinement contains two or more connected components, each of them is completely included in a face (possibly the external unbounded one) of another component. To manage this case, *dummy* edges are added between components to correctly transmit the labels, then removed. For simplicity, we do not detail this point.

3 Combinatorial Maps and Labels

3.1 Definition of Maps

In a geometrical object, it is usual nowadays to distinguish topology from embedding [24]. The topology concerns the cells of the object, i.e. its vertices, edges and faces, as well as their incidence and adjacency relationships. The embedding concerns the position and shape of these cells. The two aspects coexist in the notion of combinatorial embedded map which supplies an easy, precise and concise description of subdivisions and of their traversal and manipulation [12].

Let us recall some basic notions on maps. A *combinatorial map* is a triplet $M = (B, \alpha_0, \alpha_1)$ where B is a finite set whose elements are called *darts*, α_0 is an involution on B without fixed points, that is to say a permutation such that $\alpha_0(\alpha_0(x)) = x$ and $\alpha_0(x) \neq x$, for all x, and α_1 is a permutation on B.

For a permutation σ in B, the *orbit* $\langle\sigma\rangle(x)$ of x with respect to σ is the set $\{x, \sigma(x), \ldots, \sigma^k(x)\}$, where k is the smaller non negative integer such that $\sigma^{k+1}(x) = x$. Clearly, all the elements of $\langle\sigma\rangle(x)$ have the same orbit $\langle\sigma\rangle(x)$.

In a map M, an orbit with respect to α_0 is called a *topological edge* and an orbit with respect to α_1 a *topological vertex*. Since α_0 is an involution without fixed point, for any x, $\langle\alpha_0\rangle(x) = \{x, \alpha_0(x)\}$. The darts of a same orbit with respect to α_i are said to be i-linked. Thus, a vertex is a sequence of 1-linked darts. In the plane, darts are usually interpreted as half-edges, as shown is figure 2.

A dart :   Two 0-linked darts :   Three 1-linked darts :

Figure 2. *Conventions and graphical representations*

Example 3.1 *Figure 3 shows a map with $B = \{1, \ldots, 7, -1, \ldots, -7\}$ and, in cyclic notation, $\alpha_0 = (-1, 1)\,(-2, 2)\,(-3, 3)\,(-4, 4)\,(-5, 5)\,(-6, 6)\,(-7, 7)$ and*

$\alpha_1 = $ *(1, 2) (-2, 3) (-3, -4, 7) (4, -6) (-7, 6, 5, -1) (-5). Thus, $\alpha_0(1) = -1$, $\alpha_0(-1) = 1$, and the orbit $\langle\alpha_0\rangle(1) = \{1, -1\}$ is the common edge of darts 1 and -1. Similarly, $\alpha_1(6) = 5$, $\alpha_1(5) = -1$, $\alpha_1(-1) = -7$, $\alpha_1(-7) = 6$ and so $\langle\alpha_1\rangle(6) = \{5, -1, -7, 6\}$ is the common vertex of darts 5, -1, -7 and 6.* ☐

Maps provide a simple way to traverse (oriented) faces. If we denote by $\varphi(x)$ the function $\alpha_1^{-1}(\alpha_0(x))$, where α_1^{-1} is the inverse of α_1, then an orbit with respect to φ forms a *topological face*. With this convention, the face $\langle\varphi\rangle(x)$ of x lies on the left of the edge oriented from x to $\alpha_0(x)$.

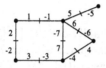

Figure3. *An example of combinatorial map*

Example 3.2 *In figure 3, $\varphi(7) = -1, \varphi(-1) = 2, \varphi(2) = 3, \varphi(3) = 7$, and thus $\langle\varphi\rangle(7) = \{-1, 2, 3, 7\}$ is the common (square) face of darts -1, 2, 3 and 7. The same way, $\{-4, -6, -7\}$ is the triangular face and $\{4, -3, -2, 1, 5, -5, 6\}$ is the unbounded external face. Thus, this map has three (oriented) faces.* ☐

The *geometry* of subdivisions is formally described by the *embedding* of combinatorial maps. Here, it simply consists in associating each topological vertex with a *point* in the plane. Then, each topological edge is implicitly embedded on the line segment defined by its extremities and each face is implicitly embedded on the polygon defined by the embedding of its darts.

As previously explained, the objects are defined through the notion of label. In a map, each vertex, edge and face is labeled with the set of (names of) objects it belongs to, possibly the empty set if it belongs to no objets.

To simplify the management of labels and to allow the labels completion, all the darts of a vertex, the two darts of an edge and all the darts of a face are labeled, of course in a similar way. Thus, each dart has three labels: a 0-label for its vertex, a 1-label for its edge and a 2-label for its face.

Note that the topological structure allows us to have only one embedded dart and one labeled dart by vertex, edge or face. But the efficiency of the self-refinement is improved when each dart is explicitly embedded and labeled.

Example 3.3 *In figure 4, the 2-labels are depicted as boxes linked by dashed lines to their darts. The 2-labels of darts 6 and -6 are $\{B\}$ and $\{A\}$. Thus the edge $\{6, -6\}$ is on the boundary between A and B.*

The same way, the 2-labels of 7 and -7 are $\{A, B\}$ and $\{A\}$, thus the edge $\{7, -7\}$ lies in the interior of A. The object A is the union of the square and triangular faces and the object B is the whole plane with a triangular hole. ☐

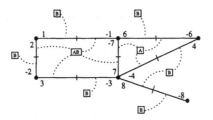

Figure4. *Example of labeled map*

3.2 Planarity

Although this notion can be formally defined [11], we simply say that a map is *planar* if it can be embedded in the plane without any intersection or overlapping of vertices, edges or faces. It must satisfy the following five conditions: (*i*) two distinct vertices have to be embedded on distinct points; (*ii*) all the darts of a vertex are embedded on the same point; (*iii*) the segments on which edges are embedded do not overlap any embedding of the vertices; (*iv*) the embedding of two distinct edges are not secant; (*v*) the vertices are *arranged*. The last condition means that when the edges of a given vertex are traversed following the α_1 permutation order, the associated segments turn counter-clockwise around the vertex (see figure 5). That is a need for a coherent orientation in boundary representation. To those necessary conditions, we add one more that leads to a better representation: (*vi*) the map must not contain any null edge.

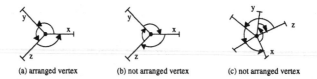

| (a) arranged vertex | (b) not arranged vertex | (c) not arranged vertex |

Figure5. *Arranged and non-arranged vertices: circle arcs represent 1-links*

These conditions imply that two distinct faces do not overlap. That way, the self-refinement of any embedded map with possible intersections or overlapping transforms it into a planar map that correctly models a subdivision of the plane. Finally, the result of the labeling refinement has to be correctly labeled. This implies that all the darts of any vertex (resp. edge, face) have the same 0-label (resp. 1-label, 2-label).

To manage the boolean operations, a single map is used to model any number p of objects. At the beginning each object is modeled by a connected component of the map. These p distinct components may intersect or overlap each other. After the refinement the map models a subdivision of the plane from which the result of any compound boolean expression with the p objects may be extracted (as in figure 1).

3.3 Basic Specification of Embedded Labeled Maps

The first stage of our formalization consists in giving an algebraic specification [16] of embedded maps and operations handling them in the MAP1 module shown in table 1. It extends a specification module called BASE that defines the basic sorts *Bool, Int, Point, Label* and their operations. The used language is ad hoc but rather close to OBJ3 [25].

Table1. *First level of map specification*

Spec MAP1 extends BASE by

   Sorts $Map, Dart = Int$

   Operators

     $v : \longrightarrow Map$

     $l0, l1 : Map\ Dart\ Dart \longrightarrow Map$

     $em0 : Map\ Dart\ Point \longrightarrow Map$

     $lb0, lb1, lb2 : Map\ Dart\ Label \longrightarrow Map$

     $\alpha_0, \alpha_1, \alpha_1^{-1} : Map\ Dart \longrightarrow Dart$

     $gem0 : Map\ Dart \longrightarrow Point$

     $label0, label1, label2 : Map\ Dart \longrightarrow Label$

   Axioms $(M : Map\ ;\ x, y, z, t : Dart\ ;\ ...)$

     $\alpha_0(v, z) \to z$

     $\alpha_0(l0(M, x, y), x) \to y$

     $\alpha_0(l0(M, x, y), y) \to x$

     $\alpha_0(l0(M, x, y), z) \to \alpha_0(M, z)$ **if** $(z =/= x) \wedge (z =/= y)$

     $\alpha_0(l1(M, x, y), z) \to \alpha_0(M, z)$

     ...

     $l0(l0(M, x, y), z, t) = l0(l0(M, z, t), x, y)$

     $l1(l1(M, x, y), z, t) = l1(l1(M, z, t), x, y)$

     $l0(l1(M, x, y), z, t) = l1(l0(M, z, t), x, y)$

     ...

   Preconditions $(M : Map\ ;\ x, y : Dart\ ;\ ...)$

     prec $l0(M, x, y) \equiv (x =/= y) \wedge \alpha_0(M, x) == x \wedge \alpha_0(M, y) == y$

     ...

End

Here, the darts are simply considered as integers by the $Dart = Int$ declaration. Maps are defined from seven basic functional *generators*: $v, l0, l1, em0, lb0, lb1, lb2$ [22, 7]. Generator v creates the empty map, $l0(M, x, y)$ links two darts x and y by α_0 in M, i.e. creates an edge $\{x, y\}$, and $l1(M, x, y)$ links x to y by α_1. Generator $em0(M, x, p)$ embeds dart x on point p and $lbi(M, x, S)$ i-labels x with the set S of object names, where $0 \leqslant i \leqslant 2$.

A set of *observers* of maps, $\alpha_0, \alpha_1, \alpha_1^{-1}, gem0, label0, label1$ and $label2$, get the direct or inverse topological links, the embedding and the i-labels of darts. For instance, $\alpha_0(M, z)$ gives the image of z by α_0 in map M and $gem0(M, z)$ its embedding.

The axioms are given as rewrite rules or equations that describe possibilities of permutation between generators. Here it is impossible to give all of them, so, only some rules for α_0 and some equations are written in table 1. The observers are used to define preconditions for the basic generators. Table 1 only contains the precondition of $l0$ using α_0. Note that because of the equations, the order the generators are applied is indifferent provided that the preconditions hold. So, a map is described by a class of first order congruent terms, by the congruence denoted by $\equiv_{E}$, where applications of $l0$, $l1$, $em0$, $lb0$, $lb1$, $lb2$ are the same but permutated.

Finally, this specification has the shape of an *algebraic conditional rewrite system modulo* the permutation equations [26]. Let us recall that for such a system R, the rules are applied modulo the set E of equations. In our case, a map M rewrites in a map M', what we denote $M \xrightarrow{R/E} M'$, if $M \equiv_{E} u[l\sigma]_p$ and $M' = u[r\sigma]_p$, for some context u, position p in u, substitution σ and conditional rule $l \longrightarrow r$ if $c_1 \wedge \ldots \wedge c_n$ in R, where $c_i \xrightarrow[R/E]{\cdot} true$ for $1 \leqslant i \leqslant n$, as written in [26]. Moreover a rule can apply if and only if the substitution of the rewritten subterm of M do not raise errors of precondition.

It can be proved as in [27] that this specification has the *no junk* and *no confusion* properties [16, 17, 25] with respect to the BASE specification and that the corresponding rewrite system modulo is *terminating* and *confluent* [18, 26].

3.4 Specification of Second Level Operators

The module MAP2 extending MAP1 in table 2 defines the higher level topological observers φ, eqv and eqe. In M, $\varphi(M, z)$ gives the successor of z in its oriented face, and $eqv(M, z, t)$ and $eqe(M, z, t)$ respectively compare in M the vertices and edges of z and t. Note that the rules for eqv, in fact, reproduce the well-known Warshall's algorithm. MAP2 also specifies topological map constructors. Thus, $edv(M, z)$ extracts z from its vertex and $cute(M, x, x', y')$ cuts the edge of x inserting the new vertex $\{x', y'\}$ between x and $\alpha_0(M, x)$.

Moreover, in MAP2, geometrical observers are defined: $eqev(M, z, t)$ and $eqee(M, z, t)$ respectively compare in M the embeddings of the vertices and edges of z and t. Constructors modify the topology and the embedding of a map. Thus, $dee(M, x)$ deletes in M the edge of x with its attributes and $cutee(M, x, p)$ cuts the edge of x inserting a new vertex at point p. The darts x' and y' are both created by the *newdarts* function during the cut. They are labeled at each level with the labels of x and $\alpha_0(x)$ (not shown in table 2). The operator $mee(M, x, y)$ merges the edges of x and y and realizes the union of their labels. The constructor $mev(M, x, y)$ merges the vertices of x and y, reordering the 1-links and 0-labeling all darts with the union of the starting labels.

In table 2, only some operators axioms and preconditions of MAP2 are written. Moreover, other easily understandable observers, that appear in the rules

Table2. *Second level of map specification*

Spec MAP2 **extends** MAP1 **by**

  Operators
    φ : *Map Dart* $\longrightarrow$ *Dart*
    eqv, eqe : *Map Dart Dart* $\longrightarrow$ *Bool*
    edv : *Map Dart* $\longrightarrow$ *Map*
    cute : *Map Dart Dart Dart* $\longrightarrow$ *Map*
    ...
    eqev, eqee : *Map Dart Dart* $\longrightarrow$ *Bool*
    dee : *Map Dart* $\longrightarrow$ *Map*
    cutee : *Map Dart Point* $\longrightarrow$ *Map*
    mee, mev : *Map Dart Dart* $\longrightarrow$ *Map*
    ...

  Axioms (M : *Map* ; x, x', y, y', z, t : *Dart* ; p : *Point* ; ...)
    $\varphi(M, z) \rightarrow \alpha_1^{-1}(M, \alpha_0(M, z))$

    $eqv(v, z, t) \rightarrow false$
    $eqv(l0(M, x, y), z, t) \rightarrow eqv(M, z, t) \lor (z == x \land t == x) \lor (z == y \land t == y)$
    $eqv(l1(M, x, y), z, t) \rightarrow eqv(M, z, t) \lor \Big(eqv(M, z, x) \land eqv(M, t, y)\Big)$
                            $\lor \Big(eqv(M, z, y) \land eqv(M, t, x)\Big)$
    ...

    $cute(l0(M, x, y), x, x', y') \rightarrow l0(l0(M, x, x'), y, y')$
    $cute(l0(M, x, y), y, x', y') \rightarrow l0(l0(M, x, x'), y, y')$
    $cute(l0(M, x, y), z, x', y') \rightarrow l0(cute(M, z, x', y'), x, y)$ **if** $(z =/= x) \land (z =/= y)$
    $cute(l1(M, x, y), z, x', y') \rightarrow l1(cute(M, z, x', y'), x, y)$
    $cutee(M, x, p) \rightarrow em0(em0(cute(M, x, x', y'), x', p), y', p)$
        with $(x', y') = newdarts(M)$
    ...

  Preconditions (M : *Map* ; x, y, z, t : *Dart* ; ...)
    prec $cute(M, z, x, y) \equiv \alpha_0(M, z) =/= z \land x =/= z \land y =/= z$
    ...

End

---

of section 4, are omitted. The specification MAP2 has the same good properties than those given for MAP1 in section 3.3.

4   Rewrite System for the Labeling Self-Refinement

The labeling self-refinement of a given map is performed through two stages. The first one is the self-refinement of this map that transforms it into a planar map. During this stage the labels are preserved and transmitted to the new created darts. The second stage is the label completion that transforms the map into a correctly labeled one.

4.1 Self-Refinement

We define the self-refinement of maps through a set of elementary and independent operations that are nicely described as 6 rules, R_1 to R_6, of a third conditional modulo rewrite system R. Because R is more complex than the previous rewrite systems, in table 3, the rules are depicted in a more visual *fractional* fashion, where the numerator is the starting map and the denominator the resulting map after the rewrite step. Moreover, the rules are graphically depicted in figure 6.

To condense the rule description, we take the following convention: the term $x \in M$ means that x is a parameter of sort Dart of some generator of the map M. For instance, as all darts have to be embedded, x exists in M if it has been embedded. Thus $x \in M$ may be seen as a shortcut for $M = em0(M', x, p)$ and $x \in M \wedge z \in M$ stands for $M = em0(em0(M', x, p), z, q)$ modulo the permutations. Note that we have a true rewrite system in the sense of [26] without variables introduction in the right-hand sides, as may appear at first sight.

Table3. *Rewrite system for embedded map self-refinement*

$$R_1 : \frac{M}{dee(M,x)} \text{ if } \begin{cases} x \in M \\ nullee(M,x) \end{cases} \qquad R_4 : \frac{M}{cutee(cutee(M,x,i),z,i)} \text{ if } \begin{cases} x \in M \wedge z \in M \\ secant(M,x,z) \end{cases}$$

$$\text{with } i = intersection(M,x,z)$$

$$R_2 : \frac{M}{mee(M,x,z)} \text{ if } \begin{cases} x \in M \wedge z \in M \\ \neg eqe(M,x,z) \\ eqee(M,x,z) \end{cases} \qquad R_5 : \frac{M}{mev(M,x,z)} \text{ if } \begin{cases} x \in M \wedge z \in M \\ \neg eqv(M,x,z) \\ eqev(M,x,z) \\ mergeable(M,x,z) \end{cases}$$

$$R_3 : \frac{M}{cutee(M,x,p)} \text{ if } \begin{cases} x \in M \wedge z \in M \\ \neg nullee(M,z) \\ incident(M,z,x) \\ p = gem0(M,z) \end{cases} \qquad R_6 : \frac{M}{edv(M,x)} \text{ if } \begin{cases} x \in M \\ \neg arranged(M,x) \end{cases}$$

Thus, R_1 deletes a null edge, represented in figure 6 as a loop. If there is a dart x in map M ($x \in M$) that belongs to a null embedded edge ($nullee(M,x)$), then this edge is deleted from M ($dee(M,x)$). R_2 merges superposed edges. So, if the darts x and z belong to distinct topological edges ($\neg eqe(M,x,z)$) embedded on equal segments ($eqee(M,x,z)$), then the edge of z is deleted from M and its labels are transmitted to the edge $\{x, y\}$ of x. Thus, at levels 0, 1 and 2, the labels of x and y are replaced by the unions, denoted $Lx + Lz$ and $Ly + Lt$ in figure 6, of the starting labels Lx, Ly, Lz and Lt ($mee(M, x, z)$).

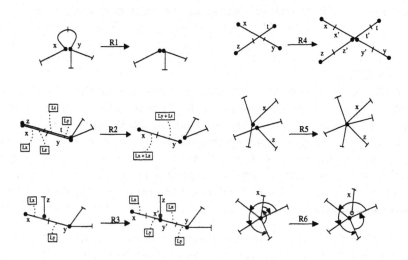

Figure6. *Graphical illustration of the rewrite rules*

R_3 performs the incidence cutting. It cuts in two parts an edge incident to a vertex. If the vertex of z is embedded on a point p incident to the edge of x ($incident(M, z, x)$) and if the edge of z is not null, then the edge of x is cut at point p. The point p is obtained by $gem0(M, z)$. Remember that the new darts x' and y' are labeled with the labels of x and y, by $cutee(M, x, p)$ (section 3.3).

R_4 realizes the intersection cutting. If the edges of two darts x and z are secant ($secant(M, x, z)$), then they are cut at their intersection point $i = inter$-$section(M, x, z)$. Here again, the new darts are labeled at each level with the labels of the cut edges as in R_3. For legibility reasons, the labels are not represented in figure 6 for R_4.

The two last rules handle vertices. R_5 merges two distinct vertices embedded on equal points, if possible. If the vertices of x and z are distinct in M ($\neg eqv(M, x, z)$) and are embedded on equal points ($eqev(M, x, z)$), then they are merged. This fusion can be done if the two vertices are mergeable ($mergeable(M, x, z)$), i.e. if they are arranged. The darts of the new vertex are 0-labeled with the union of the 0-labels of x and z, by $mev(M, x, z)$ (section 3.3). Finally, R_6 extracts a dart x whose 1-links prevent its vertex to be well arranged ($\neg arranged(M, x)$). This rule does not change any label.

Rewrite system R is *terminating*, what is proven with the techniques of [28] and the building of a measure m of maps reflecting the progress of the refinement. The measure counts the number of null edges, couples of equal or secant edges, overlapping and non arranged vertices. Note that m can also be algebraically specified. It is then easy to prove that each rule application decreases this measure with lower bound 0, what leads to the termination of the system.

Let us examine informally the proof, for instance for R_1. The conditions to start R_1 are $x \in M$ and $nullee(M, x)$. The preconditions of $nullee$ stipulate that x is 0-linked to another dart, denoted y, and that x and y are embedded on points, denoted p and q. After permutations, we can find a term of the class of M that has the shape $em0(em0(l0(M'', x, y), x, p), y, q)$, what is proven by structural induction on the shape of the terms that represent M. This step is an inductive proof of theorems, valid in the finitely generated algebras [17] corresponding to the specification.

We have $M \xrightarrow[R/\mathcal{B}]{} dee(M, x) = M''$ thanks to the specification of dee. Finally, the definition of m is used to prove that $m(M) > m(M'')$, the number of null edges being reduced. The other rules are handles, rather easily, the same way.

The *confluence* of the rewrite system can also be proven. But this is more difficult because the rewriting is conditional and is done modulo the permutations. Moreover, two different terms may represent two isomorphic maps, i.e. two maps where the links and the embedding are the same, but the dart names are permutated, and thus we have to consider them as equal. However, the initiating conditions of the rules are separated what simplifies the study.

The only way we found to prove the local confluence is the exhaustive analysis of *critical pairs*, i.e. cases where two rules may be initiated by two different darts or couples of darts. Here again, the preconditions are used to obtain the shape of the terms to be rewritten. Then we can check by hand that all critical pairs are joinable [10].

Our rewrite system is then *convergent*. Thus, for each map, the rewriting leads to a single normal form modulo map congruence. So, the term rewrite system can be seen as a function of map normalization which projects any map into its self-refinement. The convergence gives us the possibility to choose any convenient or efficient strategy for the rules application.

4.2   Label Completion

During the self-refinement stage, the topology of the refined map changes. New vertices, edges and faces are created. The 0 and 1-labels are locally updated. But 2-labels of the darts belonging to a same new face can now be different. The goal of the label completion is to update the labels of all darts of all faces of a map, until the map is correctly labeled.

Figure7. *Graphical illustration of the label completion rule*

The label completion is achieved by a single rewrite rule (figure 7, table 4). If the 2-labels of two consecutive darts of a face are distinct, they are completed.

Precisely, after refinement, if dart x and its successor $z = \varphi(M, x)$ have distinct 2-labels Lx and Lz, their edges were, before refinement, boundaries of faces of distinct objects. Their unique face belongs to the intersection of those objects. Thus, x and z have to be 2-labeled with the union $Lx + Lz$.

Table4. *Rewrite rule for label completion*

$$R_{label} : \frac{M}{transmit(M, x, z)} \quad \text{if} \quad \begin{cases} x \in M \\ z = \varphi(M, x) \\ \text{2-label}(M, x) =/= \text{2-label}(M, z) \end{cases}$$

Moreover, before the refinement, the face f_z of z was perhaps continuing on the right side of x (the grey zone in figure 7). The objects of f_z that lie after refinement on the right of x are those of $Lz \setminus Lx$, i.e. those whose boundaries do not contain the edge $\{x, y\}$. Thus these objects are added to the 2-label of y that becomes $Ly + (Lz \setminus Lx)$. It follows that the edge $\{x, y\}$ and the vertex of x lie in the interior of the objects of $Lz \setminus Lx$, thus these objects are also added to the 0-label of the darts of the vertex of x and to the 1-label of x and y (what is not represented in figure 7). Labels of t and z are updated the same way. These changes on the labels of x, y, z and t are done by the function $transmit(M, x, z)$.

When the rule is applied, objects are always added to the labels. As the labels are bounded by the set containing all objects, after a finite number of changes there cannot exist two darts of a same face that have distinct 2-labels. If not, those labels would be filled up and therefore become equal. Thus, the label completion is a terminating process, which can be formally proven by the technique of [28] sketched in section 4.1.

After the label completion, all darts of a given face have the same 2-label. Thus the result is a correctly labeled map. Moreover, as the labels of a given dart always contain the objects of its initial labels, the final map is definitely the expected result.

4.3 An Example of Rewriting

An example of labeling self-refinement is shown in figure 8 where only 2-labels are depicted as letters on the left side of edges. Subfigure (a) contains an embedded map defining three objects A, B and C. Subfigure (b) shows its self-refinement. Subfigure (c) contains the map after four executions of R_{label}. The circle arcs mark where R_{label} has been applied. Subfigure (d) gives the final result.

The use of rewriting techniques allows us to completely express a complex problem as a set of elementary and independent transformations in a formal way. Let us see now how this result can be used to derive concrete algorithms.

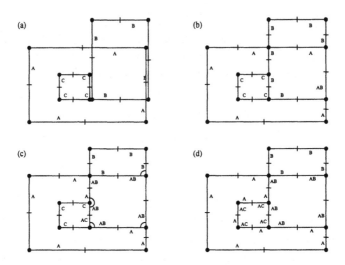

Figure8. *Example of labeling self-refinement*

5 Deriving Simple Concrete Algorithms for Self-Refinement

5.1 A Naïve Algorithm

A naïve use of the self-refinement rewrite system described above is to test for each dart, or couple of darts, if a rule can be executed. The corresponding algorithm has the following shape:

Repeat
 | Choose x in M
 | Try to apply R_1 and R_6 with x
 | Repeat
 | | Choose z in M
 | | Try to apply R_2 to R_5 with x and z
 | Until no rule can apply with x
Until no rule can apply

Such an abstract algorithm is not deterministic, because darts are randomly chosen. To describe a concrete, i.e. real and efficient, algorithm, we have to hold a strategy to choose darts. We achieve this goal adding to the term rewrite system a *control structure* that yields the dart, or couple of darts, that is going to be examined. A rewrite rule then describes the transformations of the map *and* those of the control structure.

5.2 A Simple List-Oriented Algorithm

The above-mentioned algorithm is not efficient because each dart can be chosen more than once. A first idea of improvement is to use *linear lists*. The algorithm begins with a list of all darts of M. Each step, a dart x is chosen for a rule application, and removed from the list when no rule can be executed on it. The algorithm ends when the list is empty. As we need to select couples of darts, for each dart taken in the first list, we handle a second list to choose another dart z. The selected darts x and z are always at the head of the two current lists.

Table5. *Lists structured rewrite system*

$$R_{L1} : \frac{L, L', M}{d(d(L, x), y), d(d(L', x), y), dee(M, x)} \quad \text{if} \quad \begin{cases} x = first(L) \wedge y = \alpha_0(M, x) \\ nullee(M, x) \end{cases}$$

$$R_{L2} : \frac{L, L, M}{d(d(L, z), t), d(d(L', z), t), dee(M, z)} \quad \text{if} \quad \begin{cases} x = first(L) \wedge z = first(L') \\ t = \alpha_0(M, z) \\ \neg eqe(M, x, z) \wedge eqee(M, x, z) \end{cases}$$

$$R_{L3} : \frac{L, L', M}{[x', y'|L], L', cutee(M, x, gem0(M, z))} \quad \text{if} \quad \begin{cases} x = first(L) \wedge z = first(L') \\ \neg nullee(M, z) \wedge incident(M, z, x) \end{cases}$$

$$R_{L3'} : \frac{L, L', M}{[z', t'|L], L', cutee(M, z, gem0(M, x))} \quad \text{if} \quad \begin{cases} x = first(L) \wedge z = first(L') \\ \neg nullee(M, x) \wedge incident(M, x, z) \end{cases}$$

$$R_{L4} : \frac{L, L', M}{[x', y', z', t'|L], L', cutee(cutee(M, x, i), z, i)} \quad \text{if} \quad \begin{cases} x = first(L) \wedge z = first(L') \\ secant(M, x, z) \end{cases}$$

$$R_{L5} : \frac{L, L', M}{L, L', mev(M, x, z)} \quad \text{if} \quad \begin{cases} x = first(L) \wedge z = first(L') \\ \neg eqv(M, x, z) \wedge eqev(M, x, z) \wedge mergeable(M, x, z) \end{cases}$$

$$R_{L6} : \frac{L, L', M}{L, L', edv(M, x)} \quad \text{if} \quad \begin{cases} x = first(L) \\ \neg arranged(M, x) \end{cases}$$

$$R_{L7} : \frac{L, L', M}{L, d(L', z), M} \quad \text{if} \quad \begin{cases} z = first(L') \\ \neg(R_{L_2} \vee \ldots \vee R_{L_6}) \end{cases}$$

$$R_{L8} : \frac{L, [ ], M}{d(L, x), d(L, x), M} \quad \text{if} \quad \begin{cases} x = first(L) \\ \neg(R_{L_1} \vee R_{L_6}) \end{cases}$$

Table 5 shows the term rewrite system R_L derived from R. It contains 8 rules R_{L_1} to R_{L_8} similar to those of R apart from the use of two lists as control structures. The lists are generated by the constructors [ ], that is the empty list, and $[x|L]$, that adds dart x at the head of list L. The destructor $d(L, x)$ deletes x from L, where x is not always in first position in L. As the rewrite rules are independent, the changes on the rewrite system can simply be made rule by rule.

So, in R_{L_1} and R_{L_2}, the darts of the deleted edges just have to be deleted from the two lists. The case of R_{L_3} is more subtle. Indeed, R_3 is not symmetric for darts x and z. Thus we divide it in R_{L_3}, where z is incident to x, and $R_{L'_3}$, where x is incident to z. In case of R_{L_3}, the edge of x is cut, what creates two new darts x' and y' that have to be inserted in L. As we are not concerned about the order of darts in L, L is simply replaced by $[x', y'|L]$. As obviously, x' and y' cannot interfere with x, they are not added to L'. In $R_{L_3'}$, the roles of x and z are just inverted. In the same way, in R_{L_4}, darts x', y', z' and t', that are created when edges are cut, are added in front of L. R_{L_5} and R_{L_6} are quite similar to R_5 and R_6, excepting the use of the lists to select darts.

R_{L_7} and R_{L_8} manage the cases where no previous rule can be fired. They only modify the control structures. When z cannot activate any rule for a given x, it is deleted from L', by R_{L_7}, so that its successor will be selected in further rules conditions. Thus, formally, when the rules that need a couple of darts, i.e. R_{L_2} to R_{L_6}, cannot be executed, which is denoted by $\neg(R_{L_2} \vee \ldots \vee R_{L_6})$, the first dart of L' is removed from L'. When L' is empty, i.e. when x has been checked against all other darts, and if R_{L_1} and R_{L_6} cannot apply, R_{L_8} removes dart x from L by $d(L, x)$. The second list is then also initialized with this list. All couples of darts are thus examined only once.

System R_L is a formal description of a strategy to compute a map self-refinement obtained from a pleasant study by cases. An algorithm can be easily derived from R_L. The rewrite rules share the common conditions $x = first(L)$ and $z = first(L')$. To construct our algorithm, we factorize them and handle directly the control rules R_{L_7} and R_{L_8} and the two lists:

```
L = list-of-darts(M)
While L ≠ []
  │ x = first(L)
  │ Try to apply R_L₁
  │ If R_L₁ fails Then
  │     │ Try to apply 6 with x
  │     │ L' = L
  │     │ While L' ≠ []
  │     │     │ z = first(L')
  │     │     │ Try to apply R_L₂ with x and z
  │     │     │ If R_L₂ fails Then
  │     │     │     │ Try to apply R_L₃ to R_L₅ with x and z
  │     │     │     │ L' = d(L', z)
  │     │ End {while L'}
  │     │ L = d(L, x)
End {while L}
```

If we count the number of rule fires attempts, this list algorithm has a complexity in $O((n+i)^2)$, where n is the number of darts and i the number of couples of darts that interact.

5.3 More Efficient Algorithms

More efficient algorithms can be derived, the same way. We shown in previous papers [29, 8] that the use of a *priority queue* and a *dictionary*, instead of lists, can produce a classical *plane-sweep* algorithm [13, 14], the complexity of which is in $O((n + i)\ln(n))$. More sophisticated algorithms, like the one of [15] that adds new edges to make convex the subdivision's faces, with a complexity in $O(n\ln(n) + i)$ thanks to this improvement, can be rigorously designed that way.

The label completion can also be described by an efficient algorithm using a FIFO queue. It starts with a queue containing all darts. The first dart x of the queue is checked by R_{label}. If changes arise on the labels of some darts, these darts are added to the end of the queue. This step is repeated until the queue becomes empty. The complexity of the label completion is then in $O(pn)$ where n is the number of darts and p the number of objects. Indeed, a dart is added to the queue only if its labels are changed. Since the changes on labels only add objects, a dart can be put in the queue no more than p times.

We have proposed a general mechanism to describe a concrete self-refinement algorithm. Different control structures lead to different algorithms. The interest of this approach is the clear separation between data structures used to handle maps and data structures used to improve the control and thus the complexity of the algorithms. A classification of refinement algorithms can thus be done. It is based upon the kind of structures and research functions that are used.

6 Conclusions

We have defined topological and geometrical operations for the construction and the handling of labeled planar subdivisions. To achieve this, we have based our approach on the combinatorial map mathematical model and on rewriting techniques, which led us to express a non trivial problem at different levels as a set of elementary and independent transformations. The result is a complete formal specification of general boolean operations on p 2-dimensional objects. We have shown that efficient algorithms, like the plane-sweep algorithm in $O((n+i)ln(n))$, may be derived from this formal definition. Thus, the method we propose provide good tools for algorithms design, even in computational geometry.

One may wonder why, despite a rather good experience about these questions, for instance through OBJ3 [22, 27, 6], we do not use existing specification languages or systems to support our approach. That is because our concerns are too specific. First, set theory-oriented frameworks, like VDM [30] or Z [31, 32], are not well adapted to our problems, where complex reccursive data structures play a predominant role. Second, algebraic specification systems, like Larch [33] or OBJ3 [25], where these data structures can be more easily modeled, can only help in a syntactical checking stage. In a semantical stage, i.e. during a running, they only propose data representations as formal big terms which are unworkable, while true drawings are expected. Third, no system can nowadays support our methodology of rewrite systems derivation by introduction of control data structures. A further challenge is to bring solutions to these questions.

Thus, in a first stage, operations on maps and rewrite rules were directly implemented in a graphical Prolog. Using this logical prototyping, we were able to check quickly, in a practical way, the validity of our specifications. In a second stage the different algorithms we defined were implemented in C with pointers and linked data structures, as described in [6, 22], and the graphical X11 library. These programs allowed us a practical study of the different strategies and control structures for rules application [10].

We have completed the rewrite systems to handle more complex structures, like 2- and 3-generalized maps which models topological 3D varieties [12]. In [9], we go about the problems of 3D boolean operations in boundary representation, that involve a lot of difficulties and in particular that need a correct and efficient definition of faces intersections.

A project is to deal with the numeric approximations. We feel that our approach, which separates on the one hand topology and embedding and on the other hand logic and control, can help to locate the sensible points were these questions have to be treated and to propose solutions. Moreover, this separation allow us to always return a correct topological result, i.e. that verifies the map integrity constraints, even if the best numerical result, in a certain sense, is not always obtained for the embedding.

Finally, specification formalism and rewriting expressiveness provide good tools for a safe and rigorous algorithm design, also in computational geometry. Moreover, these techniques can also be used to study complexity of algorithms.

References

1. J.F. Dufourd, C. Gross, and J.C. Spehner. A digitization algorithm for the entry of planar maps. In *Proc. Computer Graphics International Conf.*, pages 649–661, Leeds, U.K., 1989. Springer-Verlag.
2. M. Gangnet, J.C. Hervé, T. Pudet, and J.M. van Thong. Incremental computation of planar maps. In *Proc. of ACM Siggraph Conf., Boston, Computer Graphics*, volume 23, pages 345–354, July 1989.
3. Y. Gardan and E. Perrin. An algorithm reducing 3D boolean operations to a 2D problem: concepts and results. *Computer-Aided Design*, 28(4):277–287, 1996.
4. J.R. Rossignac and M.A O'Connor. SGC: A dimension-independent model for pointsets with internal structures and incomplete boundary. *CAD*, 1991.
5. A.A.G. Requicha and H.B. Voelcker. Boolean operations in solid modeling: Boundary evaluation and merging algorithms. In *Proc. of IEEE*, volume 73, january 1985.
6. Y. Bertrand, J.F. Dufourd, J.F. Françon, and P. Lienhardt. Algebraic specification and development in geometric modeling. In *LNCS*, volume 668 of *EATCS conf. TAPSOFT*, pages 75–89, Orsay, France, 1993. Springer-Verlag.
7. Y. Bertrand and J.F. Dufourd. Algebraic specification of a 3D-modeler based on hypermaps. *CVGIP : Graphical Models and Image Processing*, 56(1):29–60, 1994.
8. D. Cazier and J.F. Dufourd. Rewrite-based derivation of efficient algorithms to build planar subdivisions. In *Proc. Spring Conf. on Comp. Graphics*, pages 45–54, 1996.
9. D. Cazier and J.F. Dufourd. Reliable boolean operations on polyhedral solids defined as rewrite systems. In *Proc. WSCG'97*, pages 40–49, Plzen, 1997.
10. D. Cazier. *Construction de Système de réécriture pour les opérations booléennes en modélisation géométrique*. PhD thesis, Université L. Pasteur, Strasbourg, 1997.
11. W. Tutte. Graph theory. In *Encyclopedia of Mathematics and its Applications*, chapter 21. Cambridge University Press, 1984.

12. P. Lienhardt. Topological models for boundary representation : a comparison with n-dimensional generalized maps. *Computer-Aided Design*, 23(1):59–82, 1991.

13. J.L. Bentley and T. Ottmann. Algorithms for reporting and counting geometric intersections. *IEEE Trans. Comput.*, 28:643–647, 1979.

14. J. Nievergelt and F.P. Preparata. Plane-sweep algorithms for intersecting geometric figures. *Com. of ACM*, 25(10):739–747, 1982.

15. B. Chazelle and H. Edelsbrunner. An optimal algorithm for intersecting line segments in the plane. *Journal of ACM*, 39(1):1–54, 1992.

16. H. Ehrig and B. Mahr. *Fundamentals of algebraic specification 1. Equations and initial semantics*, volume 6 of *EATCS Monograph on Theoretical Computer Science*. Springer, 1985.

17. M. Wirsing. Algebraic specifications. In *Formal models and semantics*, Handbook of Theoretical Computer Science, chapter 13, pages 675–788. Elsevier, 1990.

18. N. Dershowitz and J.P. Jouannaud. Rewrite systems. In *Formal models and semantics*, Handbook of Theoretical Computer Science, chapter 6, pages 243–320. Elsevier, 1990.

19. W.R. Mallgren. *Formal specification of interactive graphic programming languages*. ACM Dist. Dissertation. MIT Press, USA, 1982.

20. D.A. Duce, E.V. Fielding, and L.S. Marshall. Formal specification of a small example based on GKS. *ACM Trans. on Graphics*, 7(3):180–197, 1988.

21. B. Brüderlin. Using geometric rewrite rules for solving geometric problems symbolically. *Theoretical Computer Science*, 116:291–303, 1993.

22. J.F. Dufourd. Algebraic map-based topological kernel for polyhedron modellers: algebraic specification and logic prototyping. In *Proc. Eurographics*, pages 649–662, 1989.

23. V.J. Milenkovic. Practical methods for set operations on polygons using exact arithmetic. In *Proc. Canadian Conf. on Computational Geometry*, Qubec, 1995.

24. A.A.G. Requicha. Representation for rigid solids: theory, methods and systems. *Computing Survey*, 12(4):437–463, 1980.

25. J. A. Goguen, T. Winkler, J. Meseguer, K. Futasugi, and J.P. Jouannaud. *Introducing OBJ*, Cambridge University Press edition, 1992.

26. N. Dershowitz and M. Okada. A rational for conditional equational programming. *Theoretical Computer Science*, 75:111–138, 1990.

27. J.F. Dufourd. An OBJ3 functional specification for the boundary representation. In ACM Press, editor, *First ACM-SIGGRAPH Symp. on Solid Modeling*, pages 61–72, Austin, Texas, 1991.

28. E. Bevers and J. Lewi. Proving termination of (conditional) rewrite systems. A semantic approach. *Acta Informatica*, 30:537–568, 1993.

29. D. Cazier and J.F. Dufourd. A rewrite system to build planar subdivisions. In *Proc. Canadian Conf. on Computational Geometry*, pages 235–240, Qubec, 1995.

30. C.B. Jones. Systematic software development using VDM. In *Texts and Monographs in Computer Science*. Prentice-Hall international, 2nd edition, 1990.

31. J.B. Wordsworth. *Software development with Z: a practical approach to formal methods in software engineering*. Addison-Wesley, Workingham, England, 1992.

32. J.M. Spivey. *The Z notation – A reference manual*. Prentice-Hall international, 2nd edition, 1992.

33. J.V. Guttag and J.J. Horning. Larch: language and tools for formal specification. In *Texts and Monographs in Computer Science*. Springer-Verlag, 1993.

A Normal Form Reduction Strategy for Hardware/Software Partitioning

Leila Silva, Augusto Sampaio and Edna Barros

Depto. de Informática - UFPE
Caixa Postal 7851 - Cidade Universitária
CEP 50740-540 Recife - PE - Brazil
{lmas,acas,ensb}@di.ufpe.br

Abstract

In this paper we present a characterisation of the hardware/software partitioning problem as a program transformation task. Both the input and the output of the partitioning are expressed as processes in occam, and the partitioning itself is conducted by the application of a set of rules derived from an algebraic semantics of occam. The partitioning is designed in such a way to allow the complete separation of the efficiency and the correctness aspects of the process. A complete set of rules to turn an arbitrary program into a normal form is presented; this form is the parallel composition of very simple subprocesses, allowing a very flexible analysis of how they can be combined (in clusters) to produce the final result of the partitioning.

1 Introduction

Hardware/Software codesign is the design of systems comprising two kinds of components: specific application components and general programmable ones. The latter kind is referred here as software component, whereas the former is also called hardware component.

An essential aid to hardware/software codesign is the availability of approaches to hardware/software partitioning. Gupta and De Micheli [10] carry out the hardware/software partitioning by moving operations from hardware to software to reduce system costs. Ernst and Henkel [7] moves operations from software to hardware to meet performance goals. Barros [2] and Vahid and Gajski [20] propose clustering heuristic algorithms to improve system performance and costs. Ismail *et al.* [12] proposes an interactive system level partitioning method and tool, using data flow graphs with extended finite state machine as nodes. Knudsen and Madsen [14] present a dynamic programming algorithm, using control data flow graphs and taking communication overheads into account.

All the approaches above emphasise the algorithmic aspects of hardware/software partitioning. More recently, some works have suggested the use of formal methods for the partitioning process. In [6] Cheung *et al.* use a functional notation called *form* which facilitates algorithm derivation, structural transformation and verification. Carreras *et al.* [5] use LOTOS in the specification phase and estimation methods at different levels of abstraction in the partitioning phase. Balsoni *at al.* [1] use occam as the internal model onto which the system exploration and partitioning strategy are based. Although these approaches use formal methods to hardware/software partitioning, neither of them includes a formal verification that the partitioning preserves the semantics of the original description.

In [3] Barros and Sampaio presented some initial ideas towards a partitioning approach whose emphasis is correctness. The proposed approach uses occam[16] as a description language and suggests that the partitioning of an occam program should be performed by applying a series of transformations to obtain a set of parallel processes, some of which to be implemented in software and the others in hardware.

This work is based on the ideas suggested in [3]. While [3] suggests that the partitioning can be characterised as a program transformation task, no formal strategy of how this can be obtained was presented. The ideas were illustrated through a small case study. The work presented here further develops the ideas described in [3] and gives two major contributions: the first is a more precise characterisation of the partitioning phases, where we clearly separate efficiency from correctness issues; the second is the complete formalisation of one of these phases, the *splitting*, which transforms the original description into a *normal form* suitable for partitioning.

As suggested in [3], we use occam as the source programming language. The main reason for choosing occam is that occam obeys a large set of algebraic laws [17] which can be used to carry out program transformation with the preservation of semantics. Furthermore, occam includes features to express parallelism and communication. Note that these are essential to express the result of the partitioning in the programming language itself: the hardware and software components generated by the partitioning are represented as communicating processes.

This work is part of the PISH project, a co-design environment that is being developed by four brazilian universities [4]. The project comprises all the steps from the partitioning of (an initial description of) the system into hardware and software components to the layout generation of the hardware. Here we are concerned only with the partitioning, but similar algebraic techniques are used both to compile the software components into machine code [18] and the hardware components into a hardware description language [13]. The final steps are concerned with hardware generation (high-level synthesis, logic synthesis and layout synthesis).

This paper is organised as follows: after an informal description of the partitioning process (Section 2), a short description of (a subset of) occam and some of its laws are presented (Section 3). Then we show how the partitioning can be entirely reduced to a program transformation task (Section 4). Section 5 describes a strategy for the splitting phase. Finally, Section 6 summarises the contribution of this paper and discusses topics for further research.

2 The Hardware/Software Partitioning Approach

This section describes the phases of the hardware/software partitioning process adopted in the PISH project. The partitioning is based on the approach proposed by Barros [2], which supports a detailed exploration of the design space, permitting the whole description be analysed at the level of primitive commands. Additionally, distinct implementation possibilities of hardware components are considered during the partitioning process. Originally, [2] has used UNITY as description language. In order to adapt it for occam, some modifications on the original approach were necessary: the major one was a consequence of the fact that communication in UNITY is based on shared variables, while in occam it is based on message passing. So, the modified partitioning algorithm has to consider different metrics to compute communication costs.

As the hardware/software partitioning of a system is strongly dependent on the underlying target architecture, a description of this architecture is presented, before describing the main phases of the partitioning process.

2.1 The underlying target architecture

The target architecture underlying our approach to partitioning is presented in Figure 1. It includes a single software component. The hardware components, on the other hand, can exhibit distinct degrees of parallelism. Due to the fact that parallelism in occam is based on message passing, the memory is distributed through the components, unlike the target architecture taken in the original partitioning approach proposed by Barros (based on UNITY) [2]. Therefore each set of processes kept in the same cluster has its local variables stored in the component where it is allocated into.

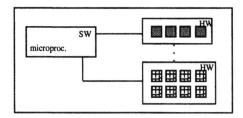

Fig. 1. The underlying target architecture.

2.2 The Partitioning Phases

The general structure of the partitioning process is depicted in Figure 2. The phases represented by normal boxes belong to the approach proposed by Barros [2]. The phases represented by dashed boxes have been originally proposed in [3] and are further investigated here with the aim to allow a characterisation of

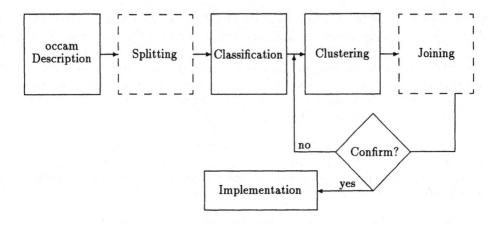

Fig. 2. The general structure of the partitioning process.

the partitioning as a program transformation task. In what follows we give an overview of each of these phases.

The partitioning accepts as input an occam description of a system. This description is **split** in such a way that the original program is transformed into a set of *simple*[1] processes, all of them in parallel. The **classification** phase takes place and the set of implementation alternatives, for each process, is established considering various features of the original description, such as concurrent behaviour, data dependence, multiplicity, non-determinism and mutual exclusion.

After that the **clustering** phase takes place. One of the alternatives is chosen as the current one. This choice can be made interactively (by the user) or automatically (by the system). When performed automatically, the alternative leading to a balanced degree of parallelism among the various statements and minimising an area-delay cost function will be taken as the current one.

The partitioning is achieved by a multistage hierarchical clustering algorithm. At the first stage, clusters are built according to the similarity of the functionality of the processes and the similarity of the degree of parallelism exhibited by their current implementation alternative. After that a cluster tree is built to permit the analysis of which clusters will be combined in the same hardware or software component. To build the cluster tree, some metrics were defined based on some guidelines, such as: processes exhibiting similar parallelism degree are kept closer to each other, and processes with data dependence are also kept close to minimise communication cost. Based on these metrics, a distance matrix D is built, where each D_{ij} represents the degree of similarity between the implementation of processes i and j. The algorithm for building the cluster tree from a distance matrix can be found in [2]. At the second stage, a new distance matrix for the clusters resulting from the first stage is established and from it

---

[1] A formal definition of a simple process is given in Section 4. For the moment it is sufficient to think of assignment statements as our level of granularity.

a new cluster tree is built. The goal of the clustering at the second stage is to share resources among processes that were kept separate in the first stage. The clustering phase is responsible only for determining which processes should be combined to form the clusters, but it does not actually carry out the necessary transformations to combine the processes. Notice that the classification and the clustering phases do not involve any kind of transformation. These phases only analise the description generated by the splitting phase.

At the **joining** phase each of the identified clusters is effectively formed by combining the relevant processes. Like the splitting, this involves program transformation. Finally, at the **implementation** phase the generated clusters are allocated into the underlying target architecture.

Observe that this strategy allows full flexibility to explore the design space. As a result of the splitting, we obtain a set of simple parallel processes. Since parallelism is a commutative operator (at least in occam), the clustering phase is able to analyse all possible permutations of this set. The hardware/software partitioning itself occurs in the joining phase; the result is a partition of the original set in the precise mathematical sense.

There are some important points to be emphasised about our approach to partitioning. Note that the whole process can be carried out on the same semantic model (as transformations of occam programs), allowing a simple characterisation of the correctness proof of the partitioning. Another advantage is that, as the result of the partitioning process is an occam program, it is possible to simulate the system before the implementation phase. But, most importantly, observe the orthogonality of our design regarding the two main features of the partitioning approach: correctness and efficiency. Correctness is related to the preservation of the semantics of the original description and (as proposed here) is based on a firm mathematical basis. On the other hand, efficiency is based on heuristics and is a measure of how fast the partitioned program will run, and what is the gain obtained when contrasting to the original program. It may be the case that, for a given input, the output produced by the partitioning is even less efficient than the original input (simply because the heuristics were not adequate for the problem addressed). However, this output (although useless for practical purposes) will still preserve the semantics of the original input, provided, of course, we prove the correctness of the splitting and the joining phases.

Figure 2 reflects the independence of concerns: the dashed boxes are relevant to guarantee the correctness of the partitioned process, whereas the normal boxes are related to efficiency. An immediate consequence of this separation of concerns is that we can reuse the same transformation phases (splitting and joining) as part of several different strategies for hardware/software partitioning. For example, if we decide to use a different cost-function or distinct metrics than those proposed by Barros [2], we need to change only the classification and clustering phases.

3   A Language of Communicating Processes

The goal of this section is to present the language which is used both to describe the applications and to reason about the partitioning process itself. This language is a representative subset of occam. For convenience, we sometimes linearise occam syntax in this paper. For example, we may write $\mathtt{SEQ}(P_1, P_2,..., P_n)$ instead of the standard vertical style. The subset of occam adopted here is defined by the following BNF-style syntax definition, where [clause] has the usual meaning that clause is an optional item.

```
P ::= SKIP | STOP | x := e
    | ch ? x | ch ! e
    | IF [ rep IF] (c1 P1, c2 P2,..., cn Pn)
    | ALT [ rep ALT] (c1&g1 P1, c2&g2 P2,..., cn&gn Pn)
    | SEQ [ rep SEQ] (P1, P2,..., Pn)
    | PAR [ rep PAR] (P1, P2..., Pn)
    | WHILE c P
    | VAR x: P
    | CHAN ch: P
```

Informally, these processes behave as explained below.

- SKIP has no effect and always terminates successfully.
- STOP is the canonical deadlock process which can make no further progress.
- x := e is executed by evaluating the expression e and then assigning its value to the variable x. Parallel assignments of the form $x_1, x_2,..., x_n := e_1, e_2,..., e_n$ are also allowed.
- ch ? x and ch ! e are the input and the output commands, respectively. They allow parallel processes communicate through channels. The communication occurs when a given process P is willing to receive a message and another process Q is ready to send a message through the same channel (*synchronous* communication). For convenience, we assume that x and e may be lists of variables and expressions, respectively. Consider an input process of the form ch ? ($x_1, x_2,..., x_n$) and an output process ch ! ($e_1, e_2,..., e_n$) running in parallel. When they synchronise, the effect is that of the parallel assignment $x_1, x_2,..., x_n := e_1, e_2,..., e_n$.
- IF is a conditional command which takes a list of arguments of the form c_i P_i, where c_i is a boolean expression and P_i is a program. It is the lowest index boolean guard to be true that activates the corresponding P_i.
- ALT is also a conditional command which takes a list of arguments of the form $c_i\&g_i$ P_i, where $c_i\&g_i$ is a guard (c_i is a boolean expression and g_i is either SKIP or an input command) and P_i is a program. The first guard $c_i\&g_i$ to be satisfied (this happens when c_i is true and g_i is either SKIP or an input command ready to engage in a communication) activates the corresponding P_i. If more than one guard is satisfied at the same time, ALT activates non-deterministically one of the corresponding P_i's. If none of the guards is satisfied, ALT behaves like STOP.

- SEQ($P_1, P_2,..., P_n$) denotes the sequential composition of processes $P_1, P_2,...,$ P_n. If the execution of P_1 terminates successfully then the execution of P_2 follows that of P_1, and so on, until P_n is executed.
- PAR($P_1, P_2,..., P_n$) stands for the parallel composition of processes $P_1, P_2,...,$ P_n. These processes run concurrently, with the possibility of communication between them. Communication is the only way two parallel processes can affect one another, so (when combined in parallel) one process cannot access a variable that another one can modify.
- WHILE c P denotes a loop which executes the process P until the condition c becomes false.
- VAR x: P declares the local variable x (which may be a list of the form x_1, $x_2,..., x_n$) for use in the process P. In occam, a type for the variables is used in place of the keyword VAR. Here we avoid mentioning a particular type for the declared variables; the rules (presented in Section 5) which use this form are valid for variables of any type.
- CHAN ch: P declares the local channel ch (which may be a list of the form $ch_1, ch_2,..., ch_n$) for use in the process P. Like variables, channels in occam are also typed, but here we abstract away from their types, for the same reason as explained above for variables.

The optional argument **rep** which appears in the IF, ALT, SEQ and PAR constructs stands for a replicator of the form i = m FOR n where m and n are integer expressions. Replicators allow the construction of an array of processes, and they are especially useful to deal with array variables. Only one process can be associated with replicated constructs. This is why we need to repeat IF, ALT, SEQ and PAR constructs when replicators are used.

For conciseness, we use the following abbreviations:

Notation	Meaning
$SEQ_{k=1}^n P_k$	SEQ($P_1, P_2,..., P_n$)
$PAR_{k=1}^n P_k$	PAR($P_1, P_2,..., P_k$)
$IF_{k=1}^n c_k P_k$	IF($c_1 P_1, c_2 P_2,..., c_n P_n$)
$ALT_{k=1}^n c_k \& g_k P_k$	ALT($c_1 \& g_1 P_1, c_2 \& g_2 P_2,..., c_n \& g_n P_n$)
$VAR_{k=1}^n c_k$	VAR $c_1, c_2,..., c_n$
$CHAN_{k=1}^n ch_k$	CHAN $ch_1, ch_2,..., ch_n$

We extend the subset of occam here adopted with four new constructors: BOX, HBOX, SBOX and CON. The syntax of these constructors is <constructor> P, where P is a process. The introduction of these constructors in occam has no semantic effect; they can be regarded just as annotations, useful for the classification and the clustering phases. A process included into a constructor BOX is not split and its cost is analised as a whole at the clustering phase. We can see BOX as a black box for the splitting. The constructors HBOX and SBOX are used to define a BOX that we know beforehand that it will be implemented in hardware or in software, respectively. In this paper we use BOX to refer to BOX, HBOX or SBOX. These constructors help to raise the granularity level of the splitting phase when this happens to be convenient for a given application. As a result, they allow flexibility concerning user interaction. The constructor CON is an annotation for a *controlling process*; this is defined in Section 5.

Algebraic Laws

In order to carry out program transformation we need a semantics in addition to the above syntax of the occam operators. A set of algebraic laws which completely characterises the semantics of WHILE-free occam programs is given in [17]. In this section we present only a small subset of these laws which will be used to illustrate the style for proving the rules of the splitting phase. Each law is given a number and a name suggestive of its use, and the operational justification for each law is taken from [17].

The SEQ operator runs a number of processes in sequence. If it has no arguments it simply terminates.

Law 3.1 (*SEQ-SKIP unit*) SEQ() = SKIP

Otherwise it runs the first argument until it terminates and then runs the rest in sequence. Therefore it obeys the following associative law.

Law 3.2 (*SEQ-assoc*)
$SEQ(P_1, P_2, \ldots, P_n) = SEQ(P_1, SEQ(P_2, P_3, \ldots, P_n))$

It is possible to use the above laws to transform all occurrences of SEQ within a program to binary form.

Evaluation of a condition is not affected by what happens afterwards, and therefore SEQ distributes leftward through a conditional.

Law 3.3 (*SEQ-IF distrib*) $SEQ(IF_{k=1}^{n} c_k P_k, Q) = IF_{k=1}^{n} c_k SEQ(P_k, Q)$

Assignment distributes rightward through a conditional, changing occurrences of the assigned variables in the condition. We use c[e/x] to stand for the substitution of e for every occurrence of x in c.

Law 3.4 (*assignment-IF distrib*)
$SEQ(x := e, IF_{k=1}^{n} c_k P_k) = IF_{k=1}^{n} c_k[e/x] SEQ(x := e, P_k)$

More generally, the operator IF can distribute rightward through SEQ, provided some conditions are satisfied.

Law 3.5 (*SEQ-IF right distrib*)
$SEQ(P, IF_{k=1}^{n} c_k Q_k) = IF_{k=1}^{n} c_k SEQ(P, Q_k)$,
if $c_1 \lor c_2 \lor \ldots \lor c_n \equiv TRUE$ and no variable in any c_k is altered by P.

The following two laws deal with nested conditionals. The first law permits us to unnest IFs and the second law states a property of nested conditionals.

Law 3.6 (*IF assoc*) $\text{IF}(C_1, \text{IF}(C_2), C_3) = \text{IF}(C_1, C_2, C_3)$

Law 3.7 ($\wedge$-*IF distrib*)
$\text{IF}(C, b \text{ IF}_{k=1}^n b_k P_k) = \text{IF}(C, \text{IF}_{k=1}^n b \wedge b_k P_k)$

To unnest ALTs, we use the following law.

Law 3.8 (*ALT assoc*) $\text{ALT}(\text{ALT}(G_1), G_2) = \text{ALT}(G_1, G_2)$.

A **PAR** command terminates as soon as all its components have; the empty **PAR** terminates immediately. Furthermore, **PAR** is an associative operator. As with **SEQ**, we can use the two laws below to reduce **PAR** to a binary operator.

Law 3.9 (*PAR-SKIP unit*) $\text{PAR}( ) = \text{SKIP}$

Law 3.10 (*PAR-assoc*)
$\text{PAR}(P_1, P_2, \ldots, P_n) = \text{PAR}(P_1, \text{PAR}(P_2, P_3, \ldots, P_n))$

If a declared variable is never used, its declaration has no effect.

Law 3.11 (*VAR elim*) $\text{VAR } x: P = P$,   if x is not free in P.

The scope of a *bound* variable[2] may be increased without effect, provided it does not interfere with another variable with that same name. The next law states that if each component process of a conditional declares the variable **x**, and this variable is not free in the boolean conditions, then the declaration may be moved outside the constructor.

Law 3.12 (*VAR-IF distrib*)
$\text{IF}_{k=1}^n c_k (\text{VAR } x: P_k) = \text{VAR } x: \text{IF}_{k=1}^n c_k P_k$

There is no point in assigning to a variable at the very end of its scope since the value given to it can have no effect.

Law 3.13 (*assignment elim*) $\text{VAR } x: (\langle x \rangle + y) := (\langle e \rangle + f) = \text{VAR } x: (y := f)$

If a conditional has a condition c that (logically) implies another preceding condition b, the branch with condition c will never be executed, and therefore can be eliminated. This law can actually be derived from more basic laws of occam, as shown in [19].

Law 3.14 (*IF branch elim*)
$\text{IF}(C, b P, c Q, D) = \text{IF}(C, b P, D)$,   provided $c \Rightarrow b$.

---

[2] If P is some occam term and x is a variable, we say that an occurrence of x in P is *free* if it is not in the scope of any declaration of x in P, and *bound* otherwise.

As discussed in the previous section, the new constructors **BOX, HBOX, SBOX** and **CON** are used only for the purpose of annotation; they have no semantic effect. This is formally captured by the following laws. They are not part of [17] and can be considered as definitions of the new operators.

Law 3.15 *(BOX unit)* <box> P = P, for box = BOX, HBOX and SBOX

Law 3.16 *(CON unit)* CON P = P

4   Partitioning by Transformation

The emphasis of this section is the characterisation of the partitioning as a program transformation task. Therefore we will restrict ourselves to the splitting and joining phases. Recall from Section 2 that these are totally independent of the efficiency aspects involved in the classification and clustering phases; for a detailed explanation of these phases we refer the reader to [2].

During the splitting phase, the original description is transformed into a set of **k** *simple* processes, all of them in parallel, resulting in a program of the form:

$$\text{CHAN } ch_1, ch_2, \ldots, ch_n: \text{PAR}(P_1, P_2, \ldots, P_k) \qquad (1)$$

where each P_i, $1 \leq i \leq k$ is a simple process, as defined below. This is the normal form of the splitting phase. In order to simplify the exposition, the definition of a simple process given below does not take replicators into account. In [19] a generalisation of this definition considering replicators is presented.

Definition 4.1 A process P is *simple* if it is *primitive* (SKIP, STOP, x := e, ch ? x, ch ! e), or has one of the following forms:
   (i) ALT(b_k&g_k c_k:=TRUE).
   (ii) IF(b_k c_k:=TRUE).
   (iii) BOX Q, HBOX Q and SBOX Q, where Q is an arbitrary process.
   (iv) IF(c Q, TRUE SKIP), where Q is primitive or a process as in (i),(ii) or (iii).
   (v) SEQ(C_i, Q, D_j), where Q is simple and C_i and D_j are communication commands, possibly combined in sequence or in parallel.
   (vi) WHILE c Q, where Q is simple.
   (vii) VAR x: Q, where Q is simple.
   (viii) CON Q, where Q is simple. □

Observe that the forms we need for IF and ALT in (i) and (ii) are very restricted. The reason is that the branches of these constructs will be transformed into parallel processes (with the form described in (iv)), and the role of (i) and (ii) is to keep track of which branch should actually be executed (by assigning TRUE to one of the c_k's).

If the BOX constructors are not considered, the normal form presented above guarantees that each simple process has at most one assignment in its most internal level. The only exceptions are IF's and ALT's in the forms (i) and (ii), respectively. This allows the analysis of every possibility of combining the commands of the original program, exploiting the different ways of sharing resources. However, this level of granularity can be too small in some situations. For example, if the designer knows previously that a process P will necessarily be implemented in hardware, say to make use of existing hardware components, it is not interesting splitting P. In that case, we can annotate P with the constructor HBOX, transforming P into an atomic process.

By analysing the description generated by the splitting phase, the classification and clustering phases define which processes will be grouped at the same cluster and to what extent they should be serialised. These phases will not be described here; see [2, 3].

It is important to observe that the form generated by the splitting phase can be used by another partitioning algorithm, provided, of course, the granularity of the normal form presented above is suitable for this algorithm.

Based on the information of the clustering phase and on the description resulting from the splitting phase, the joining phase generates a final description of the partitioned program in the form:

$$\texttt{CHAN } ch_1, ch_2, \ldots, ch_m \colon \texttt{PAR(SW}, H_1, H_2, \ldots, H_r) \qquad (2)$$

where SW and each H_s, $1 \leq s \leq r$, are the generated clusters. Each P_i generated by the splitting phase (1) is in exactly one of these clusters. Note that in this way we capture the precise mathematical notion of partition. The SW, by convention, stands for the software process and each H_i for one hardware process.

5 The Splitting Strategy

The goal of the splitting strategy is to transform the original program into a set of parallel processes, each one obeying the *simple* form described in Section 4. This is achieved in two main steps, described below.

Step 1: IF/ALT simplification.

The goal of this step is to transform the original program into one in which all IF's and ALT's are simple processes. To accomplish this we use some basic laws of occam [17] and the following transformation rules. Each of these rules can be easily derived from the more basic laws given in [17].

In this section we present the reduction rules without considering replicators, for legibility. The generalisation of these rules, taking replicators into account, can be found in [19].

The first rule deals with the conditional. It transforms an arbitrary IF into a sequence of conditionals, one for each branch of the original IF. The application of this rule permits a flexible analysis of each subprocess of a conditional by the clustering phase.

Rule 5.1

$$IF_{k=1}^{n} \; b_k \; P_k$$

$=$

$$VAR_{k=1}^{n} \; c_k$$
SEQ
$\quad$ $SEQ_{k=1}^{n} \; c_k := FALSE$
$\quad$ $IF_{k=1}^{n} \; b_k \; c_k := TRUE$
$\quad$ $SEQ_{k=1}^{n} \; IF(c_k \; P_k, \; TRUE \; SKIP)$

provided each c_k is a fresh variable (occurring only where explicitly shown).

Note that the role of the first **IF** operator on the right-hand side of the rule above is to make the choice and to allow the subsequent conditionals to be carried out in sequence. This is why we need the fresh variables $c_1, c_2, \ldots,$ c_n. Otherwise, execution of one conditional could interfere in the condition of a subsequent one in the sequence.

All the rules presented in this section have particular cases. For example, when the variables of b_k are not assigned by any P_k, in Rule 5.1, we could avoid introducing the corresponding variable declaration c_k and use b_k itself. In this paper such optimisations are not explored.

To be simple, the subprocess of a conditional are either primitive commands or can only include **ALT**, **IF** or **BOX** processes. The rules 5.2 and 5.3 distribute **IF** over **SEQ** and over **PAR**, respectively. Notice that by exhaustively applying these rules we can guarantee that no **IF** will include any of these operators in its internal process.

Rule 5.2

$$IF(b \; VAR \; x : \; SEQ_{k=1}^{n} \; P_k, \; TRUE \; SKIP)$$

$=$

$$VAR \; c : \; SEQ(c := b, \; VAR \; x : \; SEQ_{k=1}^{n} \; IF(c \; P_k, \; TRUE \; SKIP))$$

provided c is a fresh variable.

Rule 5.3

$$IF(b \; PAR_{k=1}^{n} \; P_k, \; TRUE \; SKIP)$$

$=$

$$VAR \; c : \; SEQ(c := b, \; PAR_{k=1}^{n} \; IF(c \; P_k, TRUE \; SKIP))$$

provided c is a fresh variable.

To illustrate how the hardware/software partitioning in the style suggested in this paper may be proved to be a semantic-preserving transformation process, we present the proof of Rule 5.2, considering the binary case. The complete proofs of all rules of the splitting phase can be found in [19]. We start with the right-hand side of the rule and show that, by simple equational reasoning, we obtain the corresponding left-hand side.

Proof of Rule 5.2:

> VAR c : SEQ(c := b,
>
> $\qquad$ VAR x : SEQ(IF(c P$_1$, TRUE SKIP), IF(c P$_2$, TRUE SKIP)))
>
> = {(3.3)$< SEQ - IF\ distrib >$}
>
> VAR c : SEQ(c := b,
>
> $\qquad$ VAR x : IF c SEQ(P$_1$, IF(c P$_2$, TRUE SKIP))
>
> $\qquad\qquad$ TRUE SEQ(SKIP, IF(c P$_2$, TRUE SKIP)))
>
> = {c **does not occur in** P$_1$, (3.5)$< SEQ - IF\ right\ distrib >$}
>
> VAR c : SEQ(c := b,
>
> $\qquad$ VAR x : IF (c (IF c SEQ(P$_1$, P$_2$), TRUE SEQ(P$_1$, SKIP)),
>
> $\qquad\qquad$ TRUE (IF c SEQ(SKIP, P$_2$), TRUE SEQ(SKIP, SKIP)))))
>
> = {(3.1)$< SEQ - SKIP\ unit >$, (3.7)$< \wedge -IF\ distrib >$,
>
> and Boolean algebra}
>
> VAR c : SEQ(c := b, VAR x : IF(c SEQ(P$_1$, P$_2$), c P$_1$, c P$_2$, TRUE SKIP))
>
> = {(3.14) $< IF\ branch\ elim >$, c **does not occur in x**,
>
> (3.12)$< VAR - IF\ distrib >$}
>
> VAR c : SEQ(c := b, IF(c VAR x : SEQ(P$_1$, P$_2$), TRUE VAR x : SKIP))
>
> = {(3.11) $< VAR\ elim >$, (3.4) $< assignement - IF\ distrib >$}
>
> VAR c : IF(b SEQ(c := b, VAR x : SEQ(P$_1$, P$_2$)), TRUE SEQ(c := b, SKIP))
>
> = {c **does not occur in** P$_1$ **and** P$_2$, (3.12)$< VAR - IF\ distrib >$,
>
> (3.13)$< assignment\ elim >$, and (3.11)$< VAR\ elim >$}
>
> IF(b VAR x : SEQ(P$_1$, P$_2$), TRUE SKIP) □

If a conditional has a WHILE as its internal command, we can unnest the WHILE using the following rule:

Rule 5.4

> IF(b WHILE d P, TRUE SKIP)
>
> =
>
> VAR c : SEQ(c := b, WHILE (d $\wedge$ c) P)

provided c is a fresh variable.

We can apply the distribution Rule 5.5 to unnest simple IF's. Observe that, as our strategy is bottom-up, we can assume that the most internal IF is already simple.

Rule 5.5

> IF(b_1 IF(b_2 P, TRUE SKIP), TRUE SKIP)
>
> =
>
> IF(($b_1 \wedge b_2$) P, TRUE SKIP)

To transform an arbitrary **ALT** to a simple form, we break the **ALT** into a sequence of assignments, a simple **ALT** and a sequence of **IF**'s. After the application of Rule 5.6, we have to deal only with the **IF** operator, using the rules previously described. Like the conditional, the simplification of alternation allows us to explore the possibility of combining its subprocesses in a very flexible way.

Rule 5.6

> $\text{ALT}_{k=1}^{n}(b_k \& g_k\ P_k)$
>
> =
>
> $\text{VAR}_{k=1}^{n}\ c_k$
> SEQ
> $\quad\text{SEQ}_{k=1}^{n}\ c_k := \text{FALSE}$
> $\quad\text{ALT}_{k=1}^{n}\ (b_k \& g_k\ c_k := \text{TRUE})$
> $\quad\text{SEQ}_{k=1}^{n}\ (\text{IF}(c_k\ P_k, \text{TRUE SKIP}))$

provided each c_k is a fresh variable.

Step 2: Parallelisation of the intermediate description generated by Step 1.

The goal of this step is to transform the intermediate description generated by Step 1 into the simple form stated by Definition 4.1. We assume that the **SEQ** and **PAR** operators are in binary form. This can be achieved using the laws of associativity of **SEQ** and **PAR**, as presented in Section 3. Another restriction is that each channel, not into a **BOX** constructor, can be used only once for input and only once for output. This restriction is because the original input and output commands (that is, those entered by the user in the source program) will be transformed into parallel processes at the end of the splitting, and occam does not permit that two or more parallel processes input or output through the same channel. The new channels that may be introduced in this step will also obey this restriction.

The rules to perform this step are presented below. The following auxiliary notation will be used. We denote by **ASS(P)** the list of free variables that are assigned in process **P** (either through an assignment or an input command), and by **USED(P)** the list of free variables used in expressions of **P** (either on the right-hand side of an assignment statement or in a boolean expression or in an output command).

Notice that after Step 1, only SEQ, PAR and WHILE operators are not (possibly) in the simple form, and we have basically to deal with these commands in this step.

Before presenting the rule that deals with SEQ, we will motivate the need for this rule by using an example.

Consider the program fragment below, as part of an arbitrary context, where P_1 and P_2 are labels for explanation purpose.

```
...
SEQ
  x := x + 2            P₁
  y := x + z            P₂
...
```

According to the normal form definition, we have to put P_1 and P_2 in parallel. However, we cannot do that by simply replacing SEQ by PAR, because the resulting process would not have a valid syntax in occam (as P_1 and P_2 share the variable x).

We investigate three alternative solutions to this problem. We can make x local to P_1 and then implement the sequential flow using synchronisation:

```
CHAN ch₁, ch₂:
PAR
  VAR x: SEQ(ch₁ ? x, x:= x + 2, ch₂ ! x)      P₁'
  SEQ(ch₁ ! x, ch₂ ? x, y := x + z)            P₂'
```

Observe that the first action to happen is the synchronisation between P_1' and P_2' on the channel ch_1. As a result, the value of x (which is still global to P_2') is sent to P_1' and assigned to the local variable x declared in P_1'. Then P_1' executes the assignment x := x + 2 and sends the updated value of x back to P_2'. In this way, the parallel composition of P_1' and P_2' behaves the same as the sequential composition of P_1 and P_2.

Another way of achieving the same result is by making x local to P_2, rather than to P_1. In this case, we need a single channel:

```
CHAN ch:
PAR
  SEQ(x := x + 2, ch ! x)              P₁''
  VAR x: SEQ(ch ? x, y := x + z)       P₂''
```

Yet another alternative is to make x local to both P_1 and P_2, and create a new process which controls the communication between them:

```
CHAN ch₁, ch₂, ch₃, ch₄:
PAR
  VAR x: SEQ(ch₁ ? x, x := x + 2, ch₂ ! x)        P₁'''
  VAR x,y: SEQ (ch₃ ? x, y := x + 2, ch₄ ! y)     P₂'''
  SEQ (ch₁ ! x, ch₂ ? x, ch₃ ! x, ch₄ ? y)        controller
```

This is certainly the most expensive of the three solutions, since the communication between P_1''' and P_2''' is indirect, through the **controller**. Nevertheless, this solution is more uniform because it avoids the assymetry of making global variables local to one process or another. Rather, we turn the original processes (P_1 and P_2) into *closed* processes in the sense that all their variables are local, and the only way each one interacts with the environment is through communication with the controlling process, except, of course, in the case that the original processes include input or output commands. The controlling process acts as an interface between P_1''' and P_2''', and between them and their environment. Due to its uniformity, we found this solution more suitable for generalisation, as captured by Rule 5.7 below.

Rule 5.7

```
VAR z : SEQ(P₁, P₂)

=

CHAN ch₁, ch₂, ch₃, ch₄:
PAR
    VAR x₁: SEQ(ch₁ ? x₁, P₁, ch₂ ! x₁')
    VAR x₂: SEQ(ch₃ ? x₂, P₂, ch₄ ! x₂')
    VAR z : CON (SEQ(ch₁ ! x₁, ch₂ ? x₁', ch₃ ! x₂, ch₄ ? x₂'))
```

provided ch_1, ch_2, ch_3 and ch_4 are not free in P_1 or P_2.

where z is a list of local variables of $SEQ(P_1, P_2)$, $x_i = USED(P_i) \cup ASS(P_i)$ and $x_i' = ASS(P_i)$, $i = 1, 2$. We need to pass assigned variables because P_1 or P_2 may be a conditional command including an assignment that can or cannot be executed.

Controlling processes are annotated with the operator **CON**; recall from Section 3 that this has no semantical effect. As mentioned above, the controlling process acts as an interface between the processes under its control and the rest of the program. This kind of annotation is useful during the clustering phase, allowing a distinction between the application process and those introduced during normal form reduction.

In principle, processes originally in parallel do not need to be further transformed. As part of our normal form reduction strategy, however, it is convenient that parallel processes have the form illustrated by the right-hand side of Rule 5.7. The next rule captures the desired transformation, where x_i and x_i' have the same meaning as in Rule 5.7.

Rule 5.8

```
PAR(P₁, P₂)

=

CHAN ch₁, ch₂, ch₃, ch₄:
```

```
PAR
    VAR x₁: SEQ(ch₁ ? x₁, P₁, ch₂ ! x₁′)
    VAR x₂: SEQ(ch₃ ? x₂, P₂, ch₄ ! x₂′)
    CON(PAR(SEQ(ch₁ ! x₁, ch₂ ? x₁′), SEQ(ch₃ ! x₂, ch₄ ? x₂′)))
```

provided ch_1, ch_2, ch_3 and ch_4 are not free in P_1 or P_2.

If P_1 and P_2 are simple processes in Rule 5.7 and in Rule 5.8, the splitting is done. Otherwise, as our strategy is bottom-up, both P_1 and P_2 must already be in the form $PAR(Q_1, Q_2,..., Q_n)$, where each Q_i is simple.

Rule 5.9

```
    VAR x :
    SEQ(ch₁ ? x, CHAN ch : PAR(PAR_{k=1}^{n-1} Q_k, VAR z : CON Q_n), ch₂! x′)
=
    CHAN ch :
    PAR
       PAR_{k=1}^{n-1} Q_k
       VAR x : CON(SEQ(ch₁ ? x, VAR z : Q_n, ch₂ ! x′))
```

provided x is not free in each Q_k, $k = 1, 2,..., (n-1)$, and ch_1 and ch_2 do not belong to ch (which may be a list of channels).

Note that x may be free in Q_n. This will be usually the case since Q_n is the controlling process in $PAR(Q_1, Q_2,..., Q_n)$. Also, because Q_n is the controlling process, the communication between the environment and each Q_k, $k = 1, 2,..., n-1$ is done through Q_n. In particular, as a result of the application of rules 5.7 and 5.8 we can be sure that the process $Q_1, Q_2,..., Q_{n-1}$ have no global variables.

The next rule deals with the WHILE operator, if it is not simple yet.

Rule 5.10

```
    VAR z : WHILE d (CHAN ch : PAR(PAR_{k=1}^{n-1} Q_k, CON Q_n )
=
    CHAN ch, CHAN_{k=1}^{n-1} ch_k:
    PAR
       PAR_{k=1}^{n-1} (VAR c : SEQ(ch_k ? c, WHILE c SEQ(Q_k, ch_k ? c))
       VAR z : CON(SEQ(WHILE d SEQ(PAR_{k=1}^{n-1} ch_k ! TRUE, Q_n),
                        PAR_{k=1}^{n-1} ch_k ! FALSE))
```

provided each ch_k and c are not free in each Q_k, $k=1, 2,..., n-1$.

where z is a list of local variables of the WHILE on the left-hand side of Rule 5.10.

After applying these rules exhaustively, the only remaining task is to eliminate nested occurrences of PAR; this is achieved using the basic associativity law of the parallel operator.

The normal form reduction process is summarised by the following theorem.

Theorem 5.1 *An arbitrary program* P *(according to the syntax defined in Section 3) can be reduced to the normal form*

$$\text{CHAN } ch_1, ch_2, \ldots, ch_n \colon \text{PAR}(P_1, P_2, \ldots, P_k)$$

where each P_i *is simple (see Definition 4.1).*

Proof: By applying exhaustively the laws 3.6 and 3.8 we transform P into a program such that all IF and ALT commands are unnested. Then we proceed with the application of rules 5.1, 5.2, 5.3, 5.4, 5.5 and 5.6, which transforms P into an intermediary description P', where all IF and ALT commands are simple. After that, we apply the laws 3.2 and 3.10 to turn P' into binary form. Next, the application of rules 5.7, 5.8, 5.9 and 5.10 reduces P' to a form composed by simple parallel processes. Finally, we apply Law 3.10 to unnest PAR constructs, achieving the normal form for the splitting phase. □

6 Conclusions

This paper has characterised the hardware/software partitioning problem as a program transformation task. The partitioning is divided into five distinct phases: splitting, classification, clustering, joining and implementation. The orthogonality between the efficiency and the correctness aspects of the partitioning is an important achievement. The main contribution of this paper is a formal strategy for carrying out the splitting phase automatically. One important advantage of this approach to partitioning is uniformity: the reasoning formalism is just occam and its algebraic laws. The fact that the output of the process is still an occam program may be very useful to carry out simulation in a very early stage of the development process.

We believe that this approach is very promising, and we are not aware of any other work which presents a complete formal characterisation of the partitioning problem as we have done here. Nevertheless, it is worth mentioning that the kind of algebraic framework used here to formalise the partitioning process has been used previously to characterise and reason about a number of other applications. For example, apart from the laws presented in [17], Roscoe and Hoare develop a strategy which allows WHILE-free occam programs to be reduced to a normal form suitable for comparison. In [18], Sampaio shows how to reduce the compiler design problem to one of program transformation; his reasoning framework is also a procedural language and its algebraic laws. In [13], He Jifeng, Page and Bowen show how the same framework can be used to design hardware compilers. All these works can be regarded as applications of refinement algebra.

The joining phase should also be designed as a set of transformation rules. Some of these rules are just the inverses of the ones discovered for the splitting. For example, instead of introducing channels to allow that sequential processes operate in parallel (as done in the splitting), in the joining we will need to eliminate local communication of processes in the same cluster. But the joining is inherently more difficult than the splitting. When we combine two simple processes, the result is a process which is not simple anymore. There seems to be no obvious normal form to characterise the result of the joining in general. Also, one must take care for not introducing deadlock when serialising processes in a given cluster. A complete characterisation of the joining phase is one of the immediate topics for further work. At the moment, the joining phase can be carried out using The occam Transformation System [9] which allows one to apply the basic laws of occam interactively.

Our ultimate goal is to code the transformations as rewrite rules using an algebraic system such as OBJ3 [8], or a functional language such as SML[15], enabling us to mechanically check the correctness of each transformation; but most importantly, the rewrite rules will serve to prototype the partitioning automatically. In our approach, therefore, the prototype of the partitioning algorithm is obtained as a by-product of its own proof of correctness.

As mentioned above, similar approaches have been defined to carry out compiler design [18] and hardware implementation [13]. These can be taken as complement of our work in the sense that the approach presented in [18] can be used to perform the compilation of software processes into the transputer, whereas the one presented in [13] can be used to synthesise the hardware components using FPGA's. Put together, this allows a complete formal characterisation of the partitioning, where the original description is mapped into a suitable target architecture. Some experiments are being carried out using the HARP2 Board developed jointly by Oxford University and Sundance Multiprocessor Technology Ltd [11].

Acknowledgments: The authors acknowledge the financial support given by the Brazilian Research Council, CNPq, and by the Keep-In-Touch exploratory activity, grants KIT-128 and KIT-142. Leila Silva also acknowledges the Federal University of Sergipe, for financial support.

References

1. A. Balsoni,W. Fornaccari, D. Sciuto. Partitioning and Exploration Strategies in the TOSCA Co-Design Flow. In *Proceedings of Fourth International Workshop on Hardware/Software Codesign*, (1996) 62–69, IEEE Press.
2. E. Barros. *Hardware/Software Partitioning using UNITY*. PhD thesis, Universität Tübingen, 1993.
3. E. Barros and A. Sampaio. Towards Probably Correct Hardware/Software Partitioning Using Occam. In *Proceedings of the Third International Workshop on Hardware/Software Codesign Codes/CASHE94*, (1994) 210-217, IEEE Press.

4. E. N. S. Barros, M. E. de Lima and A. Sampaio. From Hardware/Software Partitioning to Layout Synthesis: A Transformational Approach. In *Proceedings of VIII Brazilian Symposium on Integrated Circuits*, Gramado - RS, (1994) 89–100.

5. C.Carreras, J.C.López, M.L.López, C.Delgado-Kloos, N.Martinéz, L.Sánchez. A Co-Design Methodology Based on Formal Specification and High-level Estimation. In *Proceedings of Fourth International Workshop on HW/SW Codesign*, (1996) 28–35, IEEE Press.

6. T. Cheung, G. Hellestrand and P. Kanthamanon. A Multi-level Transformation Approach to HW/SW Co-Design: A Case Study. In *Proceedings of Fourth International Workshop on HW/SW Codesign*, (1996) 10–17, IEEE Press.

7. R. Ernst and J. Henkel. Hardware-Software Codesign of Embedded Controllers Based on Hardware Extraction. In *Handouts of the International Workshop on Hardware-Software Co-Design*, October 1992.

8. J. Goguen *et al*. *Introducing OBJ*. Technical report, SRI-CSL-92-03, SRI International, 1993.

9. M. Goldsmith. *The oxford occam transformation system*. Technical report, Oxford University Computing Laboratory, January 1988.

10. R. Gupta and G. De Micheli. System-level Synthesis Using Re-programmable Components. In *Proceedings of EDAC*, (1992) 2–7, IEEE Press.

11. C. A. R. Hoare and I. Page. Hardware and Software: The Closing Gap. In *Transputer Communications*, **02**, (1994) 69–90.

12. T. B. Ismail, K. O'Brien and A. Jerraya. Interactive System Level Partitioning with PARTIF. In *Proceedings of the European Conference on Design Automation*, February 1994, IEEE Press.

13. Jifeng He, I. Page, and J. Bowen. A Provable Hardware Implementation of occam. In *Correct Hardware Design and Verification Methods (Advanced Research Working Conference, CHARME' 93)*, *Lecture Notes in Computer Science*, Springer Verlag, **683**, (1993) 214–225.

14. P. V. Knudsen and J. Madsen. PACE: A Dynamic Progrmming Algorithm for Hardware/Software Partitioning. In *Proceedings of Fourth International Workshop on HW/SW Codesign*, (1996) 85–92.

15. L. Paulson. *ML for the working programmer*. Cambridge University Press, 1991.

16. D. Pountain and D. May. *A Tutorial Introduction to OCCAM Programming*. Inmos BSP Professional Books, (1987).

17. A. Roscoe and C. A. R. Hoare. The laws of **occam** programming. In *Theoretical Computer Science*, **60**, (1988) 177–229.

18. A. Sampaio. *An Algebraic Approach to Compiler Design*. Volume 4 of Algebraic Methodology and Software Technology (AMAST) Series in Computing, World Scientific, 1997.

19. L. Silva, A. Sampaio and E. Barros. *A Normal Form Approach to Hardware/Software Partitioning Using Occam*. Technical Report, RT-DI/UFPE 001/97, Federal University of Pernambuco, Recife, Brazil.

20. F. Vahid, J. Gong and D. D. Gajski. A Binary-constraint Search Algorithm for Minimizing Hardware During Hardware/Software Partitioning. In *Proceedings of European Design Automation Conference*, (1994) 214–219.

Viewpoint Consistency in Z and LOTOS: A Case Study

Eerke Boiten, Howard Bowman, John Derrick and Maarten Steen

Computing Laboratory, University of Kent, Canterbury, CT2 7NF, UK.
(Email: E.A.Boiten@ukc.ac.uk.)

Abstract. Specification by viewpoints is advocated as a suitable method of specifying complex systems. Each viewpoint describes the envisaged system from a particular perspective, using concepts and specification languages best suited for that perspective.

Inherent in any viewpoint approach is the need to check or manage the *consistency* of viewpoints and to show that the different viewpoints do not impose contradictory requirements. In previous work we have described a range of techniques for consistency checking, refinement, and translation between viewpoint specifications, in particular for the languages LOTOS and Z. These two languages are advocated in a particular viewpoint model, viz. that of the Open Distributed Processing (ODP) reference model. In this paper we present a case study which demonstrates how all these techniques can be combined in order to show consistency between a viewpoint specified in LOTOS and one specified in Z.

Keywords: Viewpoints; Consistency; Z; LOTOS; ODP.

1 Introduction

Specification by viewpoints is advocated as a structuring method for the description of large software systems [14]. One advantage of this method of specification is a true separation of concerns, due to each viewpoint representing only one perspective on the envisaged system. Additionally, each viewpoint can use a specification language which is dedicated to its particular perspective – acknowledging the generally held belief that no formal method applies well to all problem domains.

Our motivation for studying viewpoint specification derives from its use in distributed system design, in particular in the Open Distributed Processing (ODP) standard [19]. There are five viewpoints with fixed pre-determined roles in ODP: *enterprise, information, computational, engineering* and *technology*. The perspectives they represent are at potentially different levels of abstraction (this is in contrast to many other viewpoint models). For example, the *computational* viewpoint is concerned with the algorithms and data flow of the distributed system function. It represents the system and its environment in terms of objects which interact by transfer of information via interfaces. The *engineering* viewpoint, on the other hand, is more concerned with distribution mechanisms, and defines the building blocks which can be combined to provide the system's functionality.

Inherent in any viewpoint approach like ODP's is the need to check or manage the *consistency* of viewpoints and to show that the different viewpoints do not impose contradictory requirements. The mechanisms needed to do this depend on the viewpoint languages used. Consistency checking becomes particularly challenging when the viewpoints are described in different specification languages or even according to different paradigms. Of the available formal techniques we are interested in the use of Z and LOTOS, due to their potential use in specific ODP viewpoints and also because they are representative of different kinds of specification languages.

In previous papers we have described a number of individual techniques and aspects of consistency checking: a general framework for defining consistency [4], techniques for LOTOS [26], techniques for Z [3, 10], and techniques for relating LOTOS and Z [13, 11]. However, so far these have not been brought together in a single case study. In this paper we present such a case study: existing techniques will be combined in an example, demonstrating how consistency can be shown between one viewpoint specified in LOTOS, and another specified in Z.

This paper (sections 3-6) illustrates each of these techniques with reference to our running example of a protocol specification (introduced in section 2). By combining these techniques we check the consistency of an engineering viewpoint written in Z with a computational viewpoint written in LOTOS as follows. We first translate the LOTOS specification to an observationally equivalent one in Z, then we check the consistency of the two viewpoints now both expressed in Z. The constructive method used for this results in a common refinement of the two Z viewpoints, whose existence demonstrates consistency of the original viewpoints.

However, these mechanisms largely deal with viewpoints written at the same level of abstraction, and they need to be extended to deal with the differing levels of abstraction found in various viewpoints. The final section of the paper discusses what support might be made available by using appropriate specification styles or methods of refinement that are compatible with viewpoint modelling and consistency checking.

2   A Simple Example

We illustrate our work by reference to a simple example, which we outline in this section. The example we describe specifies a communications protocol from two ODP viewpoints - a computational viewpoint and an engineering viewpoint (although the fit is not perfect). The example is based on the specification of the Signalling System No. 7 protocol described in [30] (a more extensive description of it is given in [17]). Because the engineering viewpoint in this example is heavily state dependent we have specified it in Z. However, the choice of language in the viewpoints is immaterial to the essence of the work described here.

2.1 The Computational Viewpoint in LOTOS

Suppose the protocol handles messages of type *element*, which contains a distinguished value *null*. The protocol is described here in terms of two sequences *in* and *out* (which represent messages that have arrived in the protocol (*in*), and those that have been forwarded (*out*)). Incoming messages are added to the left of *in*, and the messages contained in *in* but not in *out* represent those currently inside the protocol. The specification ensures that the *out* sequence is a suffix of the *in* sequence, so that the protocol delivers without corrupting or re-ordering.

The data typing part of the LOTOS specification specifies an algebraic type seq of sequences which in practice would be drawn from a standard library. For this reason, also the equations defining the standard operations on sequences have been omitted. A less traditional one is suffix subtraction: $x - y = z$ iff x is the concatenation of z and y.

Two actions model the behaviour of the protocol, which describe the transmission and reception of messages. *transmit* accepts a new message and adds it to the *in* sequence. The *receive* action either delivers the latest value as an output (which is then also added to the output sequence), or a null value is output, modelling the environment's "busy waiting" (in which case *out* is unaltered). Initially, no messages have been sent. This viewpoint is specified as follows.[1]

specification
type seq **is** element, bool **with**
       sorts *seq*
       opns *empty_seq* :→ *seq*
            add : *element*, *seq* → *seq*
            $\neq$: *seq*, *seq* → *bool*
            first : *seq* → *element*
            last : *seq* → *element*
            front : *seq* → *seq*
            $-$: *seq*, *seq* → *seq*
            cat : *seq*, *seq* → *seq*
            # : *seq* → *nat*
       eqns
            (* definition of operations omitted *)
endtype
behaviour
       Protocol[*transmit*, *receive*](*empty_seq*, *empty_seq*)
where
       process *Protocol*[*transmit*, *receive*](*in*, *out* : *seq*) : **noexit** :=
       transmit?*x* : *element*; *Protocol*[*transmit*, *receive*](*add*(*x*, *in*), *out*)
       []
       receive!*null*; *Protocol*[*transmit*, *receive*](*in*, *out*)

---

[1] Note that this is not the simplest possible LOTOS specification of this protocol, in particular the use of two sequences *in* and *out* seems slightly artificial. However, this is also how the protocol is described in textbooks, e.g. [24].

$$[]$$
$$[in \neq out] \rightarrow receive!last(in - out);$$
$$Protocol[transmit, receive](in, add(last(in - out), out))$$
    endproc
endspec

An alternative, but equally acceptable, specification at this level of abstraction would be to require that *receive* has some (non-*null*) effect as long as there are still messages within the system. To model this we would add a guard $[in = out]$ to the second branch of the choice. This specification, in fact, is in itself composed of two LOTOS specifications of parts of its behaviour, cf. section 6. We will see the consequences for consistency checking of this seemingly small change later.

2.2 The Engineering Viewpoint in Z

This engineering viewpoint describes the route the messages take through the medium in terms of a number of sections represented by a non-empty sequence of signalling point codes (SPC). Each section may send and receive messages of type M, and those that have been received but not yet sent on are said to be in the section. The messages pass through the sections in order. In the state schema, *ins i* represents the messages currently inside section i, *rec i* the messages that have been received by section i, and *sent i* the messages that have been sent onwards from section i. The state and initialization schemas are then given by

$$[M, SPC]$$

```
┌─ Section ──────────────────         ┌─ InitSection ──────────────
│ route : iseq SPC                     │ Section'
│ rec, ins, sent : seq(seq M)          ├────────────────────────────
├─────────────────────────────         │ ∀ i : dom route •
│ route ≠ ⟨⟩                           │     rec i = ins i = sent i = ⟨⟩
│ #route = #rec = #ins = #sent         └────────────────────────────
│ rec = ins ⌢⌢ sent
│ front sent = tail rec
└─────────────────────────────
```

where $\frown\frown$ denotes pairwise concatenation of the two sequences (so for every i we have $rec\ i = ins\ i \frown sent\ i$). The predicate *front sent = tail rec* ensures that messages that are sent from one section are those that have been received by the next. This specification also has operations to transmit and receive messages, and they are specified as follows:

$\boxed{\begin{array}{l} \underline{\text{Transmit}}\\[2pt] \Delta Section\\ m?: M\\ \hline route' = route\\ head\ rec' = \langle m?\rangle \frown (head\ rec)\\ tail\ rec' = tail\ rec\\ sent' = sent \end{array}}$
$\boxed{\begin{array}{l} \underline{\text{Receive}}\\[2pt] \Delta Section\\ m!: M\\ \hline route' = route \wedge rec' = rec\\ front\ ins' = front\ ins\\ last\ ins' = front(last\ ins)\\ front\ sent' = front\ sent\\ m! = last(last\ ins)\\ last\ sent' = \langle m!\rangle \frown (last\ sent) \end{array}}$

In this viewpoint, the new message received is added to the first section in the route in *Transmit*, and *Receive* will deliver from the last section in the route. In the computational viewpoint, messages arrive non-deterministically, but in this viewpoint the progress of the messages through the sections is modelled explicitly. To do this we use an internal action *Daemon* which chooses which section will make progress in terms of message transmission. The oldest message is then transfered to the following section, and nothing else changes. The important part of this operation is:

$$\boxed{\begin{array}{l} \underline{\text{Daemon}}\\[2pt] \Delta Section\\ \hline \exists i: 1..\#route - 1 \mid ins\ i \neq \langle\rangle \bullet\\ \quad ins'i = front(ins\ i)\\ \quad ins'(i+1) = \langle last(ins\ i)\rangle \frown ins(i+1)\\ \quad \forall j: \mathrm{dom}\ route \mid j \neq i \wedge j \neq i+1 \bullet ins'j = ins\ j \end{array}}$$

3 Consistency and Correspondences

In order to be able to check the consistency of multiple viewpoint specifications (such as the two just presented) we first need to define what is meant by consistency - at one time the ODP reference model alluded to three different definitions. However, this can be resolved by adopting a formal framework as described in [4]. This provides a definition of consistency between viewpoints general enough to encompass all three ODP definitions.

Correspondences. Because viewpoints overlap in the parts of the envisaged system that they describe (e.g. the viewpoints above both specify the result of receiving a message) we need to describe the relationship between the viewpoints. In simple examples, these parts will be linked implicitly by having the same name and type in both viewpoints – in general however, we may need more complicated descriptions for relating common aspects of the viewpoints. Such descriptions are called *correspondences* in ODP.

What are the correspondences in the above example? Certainly the protocol transmits one type of message, so M and *element* should be identified. The operations and actions described in the two viewpoints are different·perspectives of the same function, so we should link *Transmit* to *transmit* and *Receive* to *receive* (and implicitly the inputs and outputs of the operations are identified). Finally, it is clear that *in* and *out* in the computational viewpoint in some way represent information that is also represented by *rec, ins* and *sent* in the engineering viewpoint. However, unlike the other correspondences this is not a matter of simply identifying these components. We note that they are related via the following predicate: *head rec* = *in* $\wedge$ *last sent* = *out*. These correspondences can then be documented succinctly as a relation

$$\{(M, element), (Transmit, transmit), (Receive, receive), (head\ rec, in),$$
$$(last\ sent, out)\}$$

Consistency. The concept of a *development relation* plays a key role in our definition of consistency. Such relations relate specifications during the development process. Many different development relations occur in practice, each with different fundamental properties, e.g. *conformance relations, refinement relations, equivalence relations* and *translations*. The latter of these enables different languages to be moved between, by translating from the syntax of one to the syntax of the other in such a way that the semantics are preserved.

Using the concept of a development relation, we can define consistency:

A set of viewpoint specifications are consistent if there exists a specification that is a development of each of the viewpoint specifications with respect to the identified development relations and the correspondences between viewpoints. This common development is called a unification.

Least Developed Unification. Besides a definition of consistency, we have also investigated methods for constructively establishing consistency [5]. This involves defining algorithms which build unifications from pairs of viewpoint specifications. An important notion in this context is that of a *least developed unification*. This is a unification that all other unifications are developments of. Thus, it is the *least developed* of the set of possible unifications according to the development relations of the different viewpoints.

Using least developed unifications as intermediate stages, global consistency of a set of viewpoints can be established by a series of binary consistency checks. Unfortunately, it is not the case that least developed unifications can always be derived. [5] considers the properties that development relations must possess for such unifications to exist. In most cases development relations possess the required properties (in particular, Z refinement produces a least developed unification) and as a reflection of this, we will use a least developed unification strategy below in order to check the consistency of the protocol viewpoints.

4 Relating LOTOS and Z

Comparing viewpoints written in LOTOS and Z requires that we bridge a gap between completely different specification paradigms. Although both languages can be viewed as dealing with states and behaviour, the emphasis differs between them. Our solution for consistency checking between these two languages so far is to adopt a more behavioural interpretation of Z. We do so by using an object-oriented variant of Z called ZEST [8], developed by British Telecom specifically to support distributed system specification. ZEST does not increase the expressive power of Z, and a flattening to Z is provided. This enables us to produce output in a standardised language, whilst supporting the need to provide object-based capabilities in formal techniques used within ODP.

Object-based languages have a natural behavioural interpretation, and we have exploited this by defining a common semantics for LOTOS and a subset of Z in an extended transition system, which is used to validate a *translation* from full LOTOS into Z [13]. The essential idea behind the translation is to turn LOTOS processes into ZEST objects, and hence if necessary into Z.

The definition of *element* (which was omitted in the LOTOS specification) would be translated to a definition of *element* in Z, for example:

$[element]$

$| \quad null : element$

For the data typing part, the ADT component of a LOTOS specification is translated directly into the Z type system. For example, the above LOTOS viewpoint's ADT can be translated directly to an axiomatic declaration in Z, viz:

$[seq]$

$empty\_seq : seq$
$add : element \times seq \to seq$
$last : seq \to element$

$\forall x, y : element, q : seq \bullet last(add(x, empty\_seq)) = x$
$\qquad \land last(add(x, add(y, q))) = last(add(y, q))$

Moreover, any realistic consistency checking toolbox will also contain direct translations from axiomatic descriptions of standard structured types (e.g. sets and sequences) into their Z mathematical toolbox (cf. [25]) equivalents. We will assume that this translation has indeed been made in this example (and hence identify $empty\_seq$ and $\langle\rangle$).

For the LOTOS behaviour expression, we first derive its representation in the common semantic model. The common semantic model is an extended labelled transition system, within which each transition represents a possible transition of the LOTOS behaviour. It is an *extended* transition system because transitions are annotated with guards and data-typing information derived from the LOTOS specification. Having derived such a representation for a LOTOS behaviour, we generate the Z specification from the transition system. This will involve translating each transition (which represents a LOTOS action) into a ZEST operation schema with explicit pre- and post-conditions to preserve the temporal ordering. The pre- and post-conditions are derived from the start and end state of each transition together with the guard of the transition. The data-typing content of a transition is incorporated into the operation schema's declaration. Note that we assume (as usual in ZEST) a firing condition interpretation [27] of operation pre-conditions to ensure the interpretation of LOTOS actions corresponds correctly to that of Z operations.

For example, the above LOTOS viewpoint will be translated into a Z specification which contains operation schemas with names *transmit* and *receive*. The operation schemas have appropriate inputs and outputs (controlled by channels *ch?* and *ch!*) to perform the value passing defined in the LOTOS process. Each operation schema includes a predicate (defined over the state variable s) to ensure that it is applicable in accordance with the temporal behaviour of the LOTOS specification. Thus the behaviour expression in the above viewpoint is translated to the following Z schemas.

$$
\begin{array}{|l}
\hline \textit{State} \underline{\hspace{4cm}} \\
\hline s : \{s_0, s_1, s_2, s_3\} \\
in, out : seq \\
x : element \\
\hline
\end{array}
\qquad
\begin{array}{|l}
\hline \textit{Init\_State} \underline{\hspace{3cm}} \\
\Delta State \\
\hline s' = s_0 \\
in' = empty\_seq \\
out' = empty\_seq \\
\hline
\end{array}
$$

$$
\begin{array}{|l}
\hline \textit{transmit} \underline{\hspace{3cm}} \\
\Delta State \\
ch? : element \\
\hline s = s_0 \land s' = s_1 \land x' = ch? \\
\hline
\end{array}
\qquad
\begin{array}{|l}
\hline \textit{receive} \underline{\hspace{3cm}} \\
\Delta State \\
ch! : element \\
\hline (s = s_0 \land s' = s_2 \land ch! = null) \lor \\
(in \neq out \land s = s_0 \land s' = s_3 \\
\land ch! = last(in - out)) \\
\hline
\end{array}
$$

$$
\begin{array}{|l}
\hline i \underline{\hspace{8cm}} \\
\Delta State \\
\hline (s = s_1 \land s' = s_0 \land in' = add(x, in) \land out' = out) \lor \\
(s = s_2 \land s' = s_0 \land in' = in \land out' = out) \lor \\
(s = s_3 \land s' = s_0 \land in' = in \land out' = add(last(in - out), out)) \\
\hline
\end{array}
$$

Because the translation was defined indirectly via the semantics, recursion is dealt with by using an internal action, which is translated as an internal Z operation with special name i. However, we can re-write it without the internal action by replacing the three operation schemas by the following two. In order to reason about Z specifications which contain internal actions we have defined a generalisation of refinement in Z called weak Z-refinement [10], and the specification without the above internal operation is weak Z-refinement equivalent to the original.

$$
\begin{array}{l}
\underline{\ transmit\ }\\
\Delta State\\
ch? : element\\
\hline
in' = add(ch?, in) \land out' = out
\end{array}
\qquad
\begin{array}{l}
\underline{\ receive\ }\\
\Delta State\\
ch! : element\\
\hline
in' = in\\
(out' = out \land ch! = null)\lor\\
(in \neq out \land ch! = last(in - out)\land\\
\quad out' = add(ch!, out))
\end{array}
$$

The two viewpoints are now both expressed in Z, and the following section shows how we can check them for consistency. However, knowing that both viewpoints are consistent (after translation) with respect to Z refinement may not always be enough. The LOTOS viewpoint had an associated development relation, which does not necessarily correspond to Z refinement under translation. Thus, we have begun to investigate how the development relations in Z and LOTOS relate, with interesting and promising results [11]. For example, a failure-traces reduction in a LOTOS viewpoint will imply a Z-refinement after translation into Z.

5 Consistency in Z

Now the two viewpoints are specified in Z, we can apply the consistency checking techniques for Z described in [3]. This involves constructing a least refined unification of the two viewpoints, in two phases. In the first phase ("state unification"), a unified state space (i.e., a state schema) for the two viewpoints has to be constructed. The essential components of this unified state space are the correspondences between the types in the viewpoint state spaces. The viewpoint operations are then adapted to operate on this unified state. At this stage we have to check that a condition called *state consistency* is satisfied. In the second phase, called *operation unification*, pairs of adapted operations from the viewpoints which are linked by a correspondence (e.g. *Transmit* and *transmit*) have to be combined into single operations on the unified state. This also involves a consistency condition (*operation consistency*) which ensures that the unified operation is a refinement of the viewpoint operations.

5.1 State Unification

To simplify the presentation, we replace the state space of the computational viewpoint by the following[2], which is a reversible data-refinement step that excludes some unreachable states (note that *out* being a suffix of *in* is indeed an invariant of the computational viewpoint). It also removes the component x which has become superfluous once the internal operation has been removed.

```
┌─ NState ────────────────────────────────────────────
│  in, out : seq M
├──────────────────────────────────────────────────────
│  out ∈ suffixes in
└──────────────────────────────────────────────────────
```

We describe the correspondences between the two viewpoints (see section 3) as a schema between the state spaces *Section* and *NState*, this is then used to build the unified state schema.

$$R \mathrel{\widehat{=}} [\, Section;\ NState \mid head\ rec = in \wedge last\ sent = out \,]$$

R is total in both directions, we prove this by showing that it includes a total function in both directions.

- From *Section* to *NState* : $R = \lambda\, rec,ins,sent,route \bullet (head\ rec, last\ sent)$. This is a total function since *Section* ensures that *rec* and *sent* are non-empty, and also that *last sent* is a suffix of *head rec*.
- From *NState* to *Section*: $R \supseteq \lambda\, in,out \bullet (rr,ii,ss,rt)$, for example choosing all sections empty except for the first one, i.e. *head ii = in−out*; *head rr = in*; $^\frown/(tail\ ii) = \langle\,\rangle$; ran $ss =$ ran(*tail rr*) $= \{out\}$.

[3] describes how a correspondence relation needs to be totalised in order to form a correct unified state space; however, as the correspondence relation here is total in both directions it can be used directly to form the unified state. The condition of state consistency, viz. that the viewpoint state predicates are equivalent for any pair of states in R, is guaranteed to hold in this example because R's predicate includes the viewpoint predicates. Thus, the unified state space of the protocol viewpoints is

---

[2] A formal definition in Z of suffixes would be

```
══[X]═══════════════════════════════════════════════
│  suffixes : seq X → ℙ seq X
├──────────────────────────────────────────────────────
│  ∀ x,y: seq X • y ∈ suffixes x ⟺ rev y ⊆ rev x
└──────────────────────────────────────────────────────
```

which makes use of sequences being particular sets, on which set inclusion turns out to be the prefix relation.

```
┌─Un──────────────────────────────────────────
│ Section
│ NState
├──────────────────
│ head  rec=in
│ last  sent=out
└───────────────────────────────────────────────
```

which is essentially *Section* extended with derived components *in* and *out*.

The totality of R also greatly simplifies operation adaptation. All the viewpoint operations are adapted simply by making them operate on the unified state. The engineering viewpoint operations will thus become

$$AdTransmit \mathrel{\widehat{=}} [\,\Delta Un \mid Transmit\,]$$
$$AdReceive \mathrel{\widehat{=}} [\,\Delta Un \mid Receive\,]$$
$$AdDaemon \mathrel{\widehat{=}} [\,\Delta Un \mid Daemon\,]$$

The *AdDaemon* operation plays no further role: it is not linked to any operation from the computational viewpoint by a correspondence, so its adaptation is already part of the unified specification and automatically consistent. The external operations will become, similarly

$$Adtransmit \mathrel{\widehat{=}} [\,\Delta Un \mid transmit\,]$$
$$Adreceive \mathrel{\widehat{=}} [\,\Delta Un \mid receive\,]$$

Now we have adapted the operations, we apply operation unification to the receive and transmit operations.

5.2   Operation Unification and Consistency

The general rule for operation unification is as follows [1, 3]. Two operations $Op1$ and $Op2$, both changing state S and with input $x?:T$, are unified to

```
┌─Op──────────────────────────────────────────
│ ΔS
│ x?:T
├──────────────────
│ pre Op1 ⇒ Op1
│ pre Op2 ⇒ Op2
└───────────────────────────────────────────────
```

For this unified operation to be a common refinement of the original operations, the condition of *operation consistency* needs to hold: whenever both preconditions hold, $Op1 \wedge Op2$ must be satisfiable. This clearly represents the informal notion that the two viewpoint operations should not impose contradictory requirements.

For the *transmit* operations, both adapted operations are total, i.e. their pre-conditions always hold. The unified transmit operation will thus be

$$unTransmit \mathrel{\widehat{=}} [\,\Delta Un \mid AdTransmit \wedge Adtransmit\,]$$

It remains to check that $unTransmit$ is satisfiable whenever both pre-conditions hold. For this, it is only necessary to check that the "derived" components in' and out' get consistent values: their new values can be computed from the old values of rec and $sent$ via Un' and $AdTransmit$, or via $Adtransmit$ and Un. These turn out to give the same values:

$$in'$$
$$= \{Un'\}$$
$$head\ rec'$$
$$= \{AdTransmit\}$$
$$m? \frown head\ rec$$
$$= \{Un\}$$
$$m? \frown in$$
$$= \{Adtransmit\}$$
$$in'$$

$$out'$$
$$= \{Un\}$$
$$last\ sent'$$
$$= \{AdTransmit\}$$
$$last\ sent$$
$$= \{Un\}$$
$$out$$
$$= \{Adtransmit\}$$
$$out'$$

Thus, the unified transmit operation refines both original operations, and therefore the original *transmit* operations were consistent.

For the *receive* operations, consistency checking is a little more complicated. The adapted *receive* operation is total, however, $AdReceive$ is only defined when there is a message in the last section. Thus, the unified receive operation is

---
unReceive

ΔUn
$m! : M$

$last\ ins \neq \langle\rangle \Rightarrow Receive$
$in' = in$
$(out' = out \wedge m! = null)\vee$
$(in \neq out \wedge m! = last(in - out) \wedge out' = \langle m!\rangle \frown out)$

Consistency is again determined by $Adreceive$ and $AdReceive$ both being satisfiable when both pre-conditions (so in this case, $last\ ins \neq \langle\rangle$) hold. What needs to be checked is the values of the derived components in' and out', like above for the transmit operations. The value for $m!$ in that case would also need to be checked, but since it is in both cases identical to the value which is added to out this causes no extra complications. For in', it is simply

$$in' = head\ rec' = head\ rec = in = in'$$

(according to Un', $AdReceive$, Un, and $Adreceive$), whereas for out' we have

$$out'$$
$$= \{Un\}$$
$$last\ sent'$$
$$= \{AdReceive\}$$
$$last(last\ ins) \frown last\ sent$$
$$= \{Un\}$$
$$last(last\ ins) \frown out$$
$$= \{Section, Un\}$$
$$last((last\ rec) - out) \frown out$$

$$out'$$
$$= \{Adreceive\}$$
$$last(in - out) \frown out$$

It can indeed be proved that, whenever both $(last\ rec)-out$ and $in-out$ are defined, their last elements are equal – this is essentially the proof that the sectional viewpoint does not distort the order in which elements travel through the protocol.

In this case, the specifications turn out to be consistent. However, with two minor but reasonable modifications they are not. Consider the alternative computational viewpoint mentioned in section 2.1; its *receive* operation would be translated from LOTOS to the following impatient receive in Z:

$$
\begin{array}{l}
\underline{impreceive} \\
\Delta NState \\
m! : element \\
\hline
in' = in \\
(in = out \land out' = out \land m! = null) \lor \\
(in \neq out \land m! = last(in - out) \land out' = \langle m! \rangle \frown out)
\end{array}
$$

If we also modify the engineering viewpoint's receive operation to be total, by making it have no effect outside its precondition except for returning a *null*, i.e.

$$TotReceive \hat{=} Receive \lor (\neg\ \mathrm{pre}\ Receive \land \Xi Section \land m! = null)$$

the resulting specifications become *inconsistent*. When the last section is empty, but there is a message in some other section, *TotReceive* will insist that the state remain unchanged. However, in that situation *impreceive* states that this message should be added to *out*. Unsurprisingly, the only way to prevent this situation and make these operations consistent is to ensure there is no more than one section... clearly not what was intended by the viewpoint specifiers.

6 Consistency in LOTOS

In addition to the techniques discussed so far, we have also developed mechanisms to check the consistency of two viewpoint specifications written in LOTOS. This section reviews our work in this area.

Instantiations of Consistency. A major influence on consistency in LOTOS is that the language supports a large spectrum of development relations. Elsewhere we have categorised consistency according to these different relations [6, 26, 4], which is summarised in figure 1. The development relations highlighted are the following:

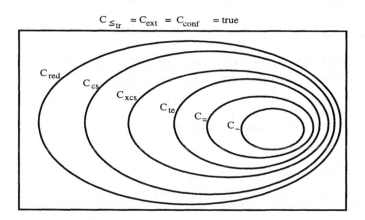

$$C_{\leq_{tr}} = C_{ext} = C_{conf} = true$$

Fig. 1. LOTOS Consistency Relations

$\leq_{tr}$ - *trace preorder (i.e. refinement as preservation of safety properties)*, *ext* - *extension (i.e. refinement as addition of functionality)*, *conf* - *conformance*, *red* - *reduction (i.e. refinement as reduction of non-determinism)*, $cs = conf \cap conf^{-1}$, $xcs = ext \cap conf^{-1}$, *te* - *testing equivalence*, $\approx$ - *weak bisimulation equivalence*, $\sim$ - *strong bisimulation equivalence*.

The figure considers instantiations of consistency with each of these development relations, e.g. C_{red} denotes consistency when the development relation is instantiated as *red*. The figure illustrates, as a Venn diagram, the relative strengths of the different instantiations of consistency. For example, it indicates that $C_{\sim}$, consistency according to strong bisimulation, is the most discriminating check. In other words, if two specifications are consistent by $C_{\sim}$ they will be consistent by all other instantiations of consistency, however, there is at least one pair of specifications that is consistent by all other instantiations, but not by $C_{\sim}$. At the other extreme, the instantiations $C_{\leq_{tr}}$, C_{ext} and C_{conf} are completely undiscriminating, in the sense that all pairs of LOTOS specifications are consistent according to these checks.

A full discussion of the different development relations we have considered and the resulting notions of consistency is beyond the scope of this paper. However, a general point should be clear, which is that there are many different notions of consistency all arising from different notions of development, and these can be related according to their relative strength. This enables appropriate consistency checks to be employed according to the class of viewpoint specification being considered.

Example. We illustrate the LOTOS consistency checking techniques using our running example. Due to space limitations the illustration is slightly artificial, but it will serve to highlight our approach.

The LOTOS process *Protocol* presented in section 2 can be viewed as a unification of two partial specifications. The first is a generic protocol, called *GenProt*:

process *GenProt*[*send*, *deliver*](*q* : *seq*) : **noexit** :=
  send?*x* : *element*; *GenProt*[*send*, *deliver*](*add*(*x*, *q*))
  []
  [*q* ≠ *empty_seq*] → *deliver*!*last*(*q*);
                          GenProt[*send*, *deliver*](*front*(*q*))
endproc

which has a very simple behaviour, that of a queue which can grow arbitrarily; it is well known that the observable behaviour of a protocol can be viewed as a queue. *GenProt* offers two actions *send* and *deliver*. The first allows a user to input an element into the protocol, while the second enables a user to output an element from the other end of the protocol. As expected, a *deliver* action can only occur if *q* is not empty.

We envisage that such a description might be made available in a library of generic specification components. In addition, the ADT definition presented in section 2 with *Protocol* is assumed to be generic and hence available to all the partial specifications we consider here.

We also assume the following partial specification:

process *BusWait*[*transmit*, *receive*] : **noexit** :=
  receive!*null*; *BusWait*[*transmit*, *receive*]
endproc

which models the busy waiting behaviour that we see in *Protocol*. Specifically, *BusWait* will continually offer the action *receive*!*null*, denoting the possibility that the user attempts to output an element from the protocol when it is not ready to do so.

Assuming the following correspondences between the partial specifications,

{(*send*, *transmit*), (*deliver*, *receive*)}

we can view the second specification, *BusWait*, as defining additional behaviour which can be used to specialize the generic protocol *GenProt*. Implicitly, in this example, the behaviour of each partial specification extends the behaviour of the other specification. For example, *BusWait* adds the ability to perform the action *deliver*!*null* to the behaviour of *GenProt*. Thus, the appropriate refinement relation to use when unifying these two partial specifications is extension, *ext*.

Research based on work performed by Leduc [22] can be used to characterise the least developed unification according to extension. Specifically, if we denote a least developed unification of two processes P and Q by U then the following trace/refusal property characterises U (the reader unfamiliar with trace/refusals is referred to [7]):

$$Tr(U) = Tr(P) \cup Tr(Q) \quad \wedge$$
$$\forall \sigma \in Tr(U),$$
$$\sigma \in Tr(P) \cap Tr(Q) \implies Ref(U,\sigma) = Ref(P,\sigma) \cap Ref(Q,\sigma) \quad \wedge$$
$$\sigma \in Tr(P) - Tr(Q) \implies Ref(U,\sigma) = Ref(P,\sigma) \quad \wedge$$
$$\sigma \in Tr(Q) - Tr(P) \implies Ref(U,\sigma) = Ref(Q,\sigma)$$

In fact, it can be shown that up to testing equivalence the following process:

process *Prot*[*transmit*, *receive*](q : *seq*) : **noexit** :=
  transmit?x : *element*; *Prot*[*transmit*, *receive*]($add(x, q)$)
  []
  [$q = empty\_seq$] $\rightarrow$ *receive*!*null*; *Prot*[*transmit*, *receive*](q)
  []
  [$q \neq empty\_seq$] $\rightarrow$ *receive*!*last*(q); *Prot*[*transmit*, *receive*]($front(q)$)
endproc

is the least developed unification of *GenProt* and *BusWait*. Notice that this unification has inherited the naming of *BusWait*, the "specializing" process. Thus, we have assumed that our correspondences define a renaming of *GenProt*.

Finally, we can observe that *Prot* has the same trace/refusal characterisation as the process:

process *Protocol*[*transmit*, *receive*](in, out : *seq*) : **noexit** :=
  transmit?x : *element*; *Protocol*[*transmit*, *receive*]($add(x, in)$, out)
  []
  [$in = out$] $\rightarrow$ *receive*!*null*; *Protocol*[*transmit*, *receive*](in, out)
  []
  [$in \neq out$] $\rightarrow$*receive*!*last*($in - out$);
          Protocol[*transmit*, *receive*](in, $add(last(in - out), out)$)
  endproc

which is the alternative LOTOS specification that we considered in section 2. The reason that *Protocol* and *Prot* are equivalent is that their externally visible behaviour is the same. This can be observed from the fact that at all corresponding points in the behaviour of the two processes, $in - out$ equals q.

7   Issues in Viewpoint Specification and Refinement

The key component of the consistency checking strategy presented here is to be able to identify common refinements of the multiple viewpoints. Such refinements can also be viewed as common *models* for the collection of viewpoints.

These common models will typically be expressed in terms of the most primitive entities in the viewpoints, for example in the protocol viewpoints typical entities included: actions or operations, e.g. *transmit* and *Receive*; data variables, e.g. the sequence *out* representing messages delivered by the protocol.

However, finding a suitable set of primitives is not always possible. In particular, different ODP viewpoints occur at different levels of abstraction, thus identifying one-to-one correspondences is almost certain to be impossible in general. In fact, these correspondences can be extremely complex with what are primitive entities in one viewpoint being related to whole portions of behaviour in another viewpoint. For example, the execution of a remote procedure call operation in the computational viewpoint would actually correspond to a body of primitive interactions in the engineering viewpoint, e.g. interactions between stub objects, binding objects and protocol objects in order to invoke an RPC transport protocol.

Such changes of abstraction level add extra complications to viewpoints modelling and consistency checking, since the models of the two viewpoints are expressed in terms of different (but non-independent) primitives, thus, hindering the search for a common model. Potential solutions include the use of appropriate styles of specification and suitable methods of refinement.

Action Refinement incorporates a change of action granularity into the refinement. It fits naturally into a process algebra setting where actions serve as the primitive unit of computation. For example, in the computational viewpoint written in LOTOS one branch dealt with reception of a message[3]:

$$receive;\ Protocol[transmit, receive](in, add(last(in - out), out))$$

and we may wish to refine this to show how the message is passed down the layers in the protocol stack:

$$reclyr_1;\ \ldots;\ reclyr_n;\ Protocol[transmit, receive](in, add(last(in - out), out))$$

where the action *receive* has been action refined into the "partial behaviour" $reclyr_1;\ \ldots;\ reclyr_n$.

The first behaviour could be viewed as more "abstract" in its modelling of the transmission process; the actual mechanism for communication is abstracted away from and represented by a single action. This method of action refinement enables us to relate viewpoints at different levels of abstraction to the same unification. For example, one viewpoint, expressed in terms of coarse grain primitives, could be action refined to a model that is expressed in terms of the finer grained primitives of another viewpoint.

Such action refinement has been quite extensively investigated within the process algebra field, although little work has to date been performed in the context of LOTOS. Action refinement has proved a hard problem to resolve. In particular, it has been realised that it is difficult to handle in the context

---

[3] For simplicity, we have removed *receive*'s output here.

of an interleaving semantics (which is the standard approach), because central to interleaving semantics is the assumption that actions are atomic. Clearly, if actions can be refined into arbitrarily complex behaviours, the assumption of atomic actions is lost.

Current research has suggested that true concurrency models are better behaved in the presence of action refinement [28], since true concurrency models do not rely on the assumption of atomic actions. We are currently investigating the feasibility of moving to a true concurrency setting in order to integrate action refinement into consistency checking.

Promotion is a specification style often used in Z specifications for combining specifications at different levels of abstraction. Promotion works when a global operation on a number of components is defined in terms of a local operation on a single component. Using a special promotion schema *Promote*, the global operation is then defined by (where *Local* is the local state etc): $\exists \Delta Local \bullet Promote \land LocalOperation$. Promotion can also be used to define global operations in terms of multiple (possibly different) local operations on different instances of the local state, i.e. they may change the state of several local components at once.

This technique can be profitably used for specifying *viewpoints* at different levels of abstraction, in a manner which automatically guarantees their consistency: one viewpoint defines the global operations, but also this viewpoint includes the local state and its operations – but only their signatures (in Z terms, by including them as empty schemas). The global viewpoint thus does not make any assumptions about the local state and operations apart from their existence. Another viewpoint will then actually *define* the local state and its operations, see [12, 20] for examples of this in practice.

For example, suppose an additional viewpoint is to be combined with the engineering viewpoint of the protocol. This viewpoint wishes to use a number of protocols on a collection of routes (identified by *Id*), with an operation, *GlobalTransmit*, to transmit a message down a chosen route. We can specify the viewpoint as follows:

```
┌─ Section ─────────────────        ┌─ Transmit ─────────────────
│                                    │
└────────────────────────────       └────────────────────────────


┌─ Global ──────────────────        ┌─ Promote ──────────────────
│ series : Id → Section             │ ΔGlobal
│                                    │ ΔSection
│ ∀ i, j : dom series •             │ id? : Id
│ (series i).route = (series j).route├─────────────────────────────
│ ⇒ i = j                           │ series id? = θSection
│                                    │ series' = series' ⊕ {id? ↦ θSection'}
└────────────────────────────       └─────────────────────────────
```

$$GlobalTransmit \;\widehat{=}\; \exists \,\Delta Section \bullet Promote \land Transmit$$

Then the unification techniques described above will deliver the correct combination of viewpoints if they are specified in this promotion style – namely, the syntactic inclusion of the local viewpoint – and the viewpoints are automatically consistent.

With this technique we are no longer restricted to modelling Z viewpoints at an equal level of abstraction, but we can also model the situation where one viewpoint provides the implementations of standard components to be used in another one. This is exactly the relationship that arises between a number of the ODP viewpoints. For example, the engineering viewpoint may provide standard communication components that are assumed when describing a computational viewpoint specification.

8 Related Work

Several other research groups have studied partial- or viewpoint specification, in particular in Z. Ainsworth, Wallis, et al [1, 2] studied unification ("amalgamation") of Z viewpoints, using an extended notion of refinement ("co-refinement"). Daniel Jackson's work on specification by views, also in Z, uses a syntactical notion of view composition, which does not always coincide with our, more semantical, one. The approach by Frappier et al. [15] is similar to ours in the more abstract setting of homogeneous binary relations. Most of the cited papers contain small to medium examples of consistency checks within one formal method.

There are also a large number of viewpoint specification research groups in the area of requirements engineering, most of which are represented in the recent ACM FSE workshop [14]. Consistency checking, though considered essential, is not studied extensively in that context, partly due to the notations used being less formal. However, for an interesting example of viewpoint unification and inconsistency handling between an OMT object diagram viewpoint and a dataflow diagram viewpoint, cf. [9].

Various authors have reported on specification styles which use subspecifications in different languages, often with different paradigms. Most of these, however, manage to avoid the consistency issue by using the various languages in different stages of development, or by the careful use of layering techniques. (The latter is actually an indication that consistency checking between specifications at different levels of abstraction need not be hard, provided the viewpoints are well separated.) Languages and methods that have been combined in such a way with Z include action systems [21], state charts [29], JSD and CSP [18] and SSADM [23]. However, we are not aware of any published case study of consistency checking and unification between two partial specifications in two different formal languages.

More information about our work (which is partially funded by BT Research Labs. and the EPSRC under grant number GR/K13035) can be found at:
http://alethea.ukc.ac.uk/Dept/Computing/Research/NDS/consistency

References

1. M. Ainsworth, A. H. Cruickshank, P. J. L. Wallis, and L. J. Groves. Viewpoint specification and Z. *Information and Software Technology*, 36(1):43–51, February 1994.

2. M. Ainsworth, S. Riddle, and P.J.L. Wallis. Formal validation of viewpoint specifications. *Software Engineering Journal*, 11(1):58–66, January 1996.

3. E. Boiten, J. Derrick, H. Bowman, and M. Steen. Consistency and refinement for partial specification in Z. In Gaudel and Woodcock [16], pages 287–306.

4. H. Bowman, E.A. Boiten, J. Derrick, and M. Steen. Viewpoint consistency in ODP, a general interpretation. In E. Najm and J.-B. Stefani, editors, *First IFIP International workshop on Formal Methods for Open Object-based Distributed Systems*, pages 189–204, Paris, March 1996. Chapman & Hall.

5. H. Bowman, E.A. Boiten, J. Derrick, and M. Steen. A formal theory of viewpoint consistency. Submitted for publication, 1997.

6. H. Bowman, J. Derrick, and M. Steen. Some results on cross viewpoint consistency checking. In K. Raymond and L. Armstrong, editors, *IFIP TC6 International Conference on Open Distributed Processing*, pages 399–412, Brisbane, Australia, February 1995. Chapman and Hall.

7. E. Brinksma, G. Scollo, and C. Steenbergen. Process specification, their implementation and their tests. In B. Sarikaya and G. v. Bochmann, editors, *Protocol Specification, Testing and Verification, VI*, pages 349–360, Montreal, Canada, June 1986. North-Holland.

8. E. Cusack and G. H. B. Rafsanjani. ZEST. In S. Stepney, R. Barden, and D. Cooper, editors, *Object Orientation in Z*, Workshops in Computing, pages 113–126. Springer-Verlag, 1992.

9. H.S. Delugach. An approach to conceptual feedback in multiple viewed software requirements modeling. In Finkelstein and Spanoudakis [14], pages 242–246.

10. J. Derrick, E.A. Boiten, H. Bowman, and M. Steen. Weak refinement in Z. In J.P. Bowen, M.G. Hinchey, and D.Till, editors, *ZUM '97: The Z Formal Specification Notation*, volume 1212 of *Lecture Notes in Computer Science*, pages 369–388. Springer-Verlag, 1997.

11. J. Derrick, H. Bowman, E. Boiten, and M. Steen. Comparing LOTOS and Z refinement relations. In *FORTE/PSTV'96*, pages 501–516, Kaiserslautern, Germany, October 1996. Chapman & Hall.

12. J. Derrick, H. Bowman, and M. Steen. Maintaining cross viewpoint consistency using Z. In K. Raymond and L. Armstrong, editors, *IFIP TC6 International Conference on Open Distributed Processing*, pages 413–424, Brisbane, Australia, February 1995. Chapman and Hall.

13. J. Derrick, E.A.Boiten, H. Bowman, and M. Steen. Supporting ODP - translating LOTOS to Z. In E. Najm and J.-B. Stefani, editors, *First IFIP International workshop on Formal Methods for Open Object-based Distributed Systems*, pages 399–406, Paris, March 1996. Chapman & Hall.

14. A. Finkelstein and G. Spanoudakis, editors. *SIGSOFT '96 International Workshop on Multiple Perspectives in Software Development (Viewpoints '96)*. ACM, 1996.

15. M. Frappier, A. Mili, and J. Desharnais. Program construction by parts. In B. Möller, editor, *Mathematics of Program Construction: Third International Conference*, volume 947 of *Lecture Notes in Computer Science*, pages 257–281. Springer-Verlag, 1995.

16. M.-C. Gaudel and J. Woodcock, editors. *FME'96: Industrial Benefit of Formal Methods, Third International Symposium of Formal Methods Europe*, volume 1051 of *Lecture Notes in Computer Science*. Springer-Verlag, March 1996.

17. I. Hayes, M. Mowbray, and G.A. Rose. Signalling system no. 7 – the network layer. In *PSTV IX*, pages 3–14, 1990.

18. M.G. Hinchey. JSD, CSP and TLZ. In *Methods Integration Workshop*, Leeds, 1996.

19. ITU Recommendation X.901-904 — ISO/IEC 10746 1-4. *Open Distributed Processing - Reference Model - Parts 1-4*, July 1995.

20. D. Jackson. Structuring Z specifications with views. *ACM Transactions on Software Engineering and Methodology*, 4(4), October 1995.

21. V. Kasurinen and K. Sere. Integrating action systems and Z in a medical system specification. In Gaudel and Woodcock [16], pages 105–119.

22. G. Leduc. *On the Role of Implementation Relations in the Design of Distributed Systems using LOTOS*. PhD thesis, University of Liège, Liège, Belgium, June 1991.

23. F. Polack and K. C. Mander. Software quality assurance using the SAZ method. In J. P. Bowen and J. A. Hall, editors, *Z User Workshop, Cambridge 1994*, Workshops in Computing, pages 230–249. Springer-Verlag, 1994.

24. J. Ronayne. *The Integrated Services Digital Network: from concept to application*. Pitman, London, 1987.

25. J. M. Spivey. *The Z notation: A reference manual*. Prentice Hall, 1989.

26. M. W. A. Steen, H. Bowman, and J. Derrick. Composition of LOTOS specifications. In P. Dembinski and M. Sredniawa, editors, *Protocol Specification, Testing and Verification, XV*, pages 73–88, Warsaw, Poland, 1995. Chapman & Hall.

27. B. Strulo. How firing conditions help inheritance. In J. P. Bowen and M. G. Hinchey, editors, *Ninth Annual Z User Workshop*, LNCS 967, pages 264–275, Limerick, September 1995. Springer-Verlag.

28. R.J. van Glabbeek. The refinement theorem for ST-bisimulation semantics. In *Programming Concepts and Methods*. Elsevier Science Publishers, 1990.

29. M. Weber. Combining statecharts and Z for the design of safety-critical control systems. In Gaudel and Woodcock [16], pages 307–326.

30. J. Woodcock and J. Davies. *Using Z: Specification, Refinement, and Proof*. Prentice Hall, 1996.

A UNITY Mapping Operator for Distributed Programs

Michel Charpentier

INPT-ENSEEIHT / IRIT
2, rue Charles Camichel
31071 Toulouse cedex, FRANCE
e-mail: charpov@enseeiht.fr

Abstract. When describing a distributed application within the UNITY framework, one usually uses the composition by union to express the interaction between processes. Unfortunately, the semantics of union is not well-suited to express the possible true parallelism between the different parts of a program. However, the different processes of a distributed application do not share any memory. Thanks to this particularity and the definition of an abstract communication model, the composition by union can be modified to fit the parallelism of distributed programs. This paper gives a set of theorems that characterize the UNITY properties of a union program that remain valid when the processes of the program are composed with the new operator. Therefore, this operator can be used to formalize the mapping of programs to distributed architectures.

1 Introduction

The work presented here is related to our current project called DADA for *Distributed Algorithms Design Assistant*. The DADA project aims to help the design and the proof of asynchronous distributed programs, that is to say programs sharing neither memory nor a common clock. This project involves a three way research:

- distribution formalization: we are working on a well-formalized definition of distribution to be incorporated into the UNITY framework. We have developed a new communication abstraction based on the *observation* relation [4, 6] described in Sect. 4. This observation relation extends the UNITY logic and appears to be helpful to describe and prove distributed algorithms [5];
- automatic proof of parallel programs: the kind of proofs we have to design are very difficult and tedious and need the help of automatic tools. For that purpose, we have developed a UNITY-based environment working on a subset of the language [7, 8]; the environment allows us to automatically check the consistency of a specification with its corresponding implementation.
- program refinement: automatic tools are not always able to prove the properties of a large or complex program. Our idea, in this case, is to refine a centralized (or not fully distributed) program description towards another

expression well-suited to distribution. We investigate such transformations, able to introduce distribution into a program without loosing its correctness [10].

In this context, the reminder of the paper deals with distributed programs which are described, together with their properties, within the UNITY formalism extended with observation. More precisely, we investigate the consequences of union semantics on the mapping of programs to distributed architectures. This leads to the definition of a new composition operation which appears well-suited to formalize the mapping step in the design of a distributed application.

First, we introduce the UNITY framework and some specific notations in Sect. 2. Section 3 gives an example showing the difficulties arising when mapping programs composed by union to distributed architectures. Then, we present our communication model and the logical relation it is based on in Sect. 4. A new composition operation, called product, is defined in Sect. 5. We investigate more precisely the relationship between union and product in Sect. 6. This is achieved by considering the transformation from union into product and the converse transformation. The theorems presented in this part are then proved in Sect. 7.

2 The UNITY Framework

2.1 Introduction

This section describes briefly the UNITY formalism. A more comprehensive presentation can be found in the given references, especially [3, 12].

The UNITY framework consists of two parts:

- a programming notation semantically based on fair transition systems;
- a specification language based on a linear temporal logic, able to express the safety properties and the progress properties of the former systems.

Different semantic models have been proposed [2, 3, 9, 15, 17] both for the language and for the logic. These models are related to each other but are not equivalent. We now make precise the choice used for this work.

2.2 The Language

A UNITY program comprises three main parts, namely the declaration of the state variables (`declare`), their initial values (`initially`) and the description of the system transitions (`assign`).

For a given program F, $F.declare$ contains the declaration of the state variables of the program along with their types. We are not interested in types in this paper and we consider, for the sake of simplicity, $F.declare$ simply as the *set* of state variables. In particular, we use set operations like $\in$, $\cup$ or $\cap$.

$F.init$ is used to constrain the initial values of the state variables. In [3, 12], $F.init$ assigns an initial value to some of the variables. Following [9, 15, 17], we prefer to see *F.init* as a *predicate* stating the acceptable initial states. This is useful to state initial conditions like $x \geqslant 0$ or $x < y$ without assigning explicit values to variables. We suppose that *F.init* is satisfiable.

The *F.assign* part is the set of the program statements. It describes all the valid transitions of the system with multiple guarded assignments, separated by the $\|$ mark. These assignments are of the following form:

$$\begin{aligned} \bar{v} := &\bar{e}_1 \quad \text{if} \quad g_1 \\ \sim &\bar{e}_2 \quad \text{if} \quad g_2 \\ &\cdots \\ \sim &\bar{e}_n \quad \text{if} \quad g_n \end{aligned}$$

where $\bar{v}$ is a list of references to be assigned, $\bar{e}_i$ is a list of values and $\sim$ acts as an *"else if"* operator. A UNITY statement must be deterministic: when several guards are simultaneously true, the right-hand side values must be the same. More precisely, the statement must satisfy $\langle \forall i, j :: g_i \wedge g_j \Rightarrow \bar{e}_i = \bar{e}_j \rangle$. Moreover, the assign section of a program is always supposed to contain, in addition to the statements explicitly described, the *skip* statement that has no effect on a state [12].

The $\|$ mark denotes the simultaneous assignment of several variables: $x := a \| y := b$ is the same as $x, y := a, b$. More generally, if $\bar{v}$ and $\bar{w}$ contain no common references, $\bar{v} := \bar{e}$ if $p \parallel \bar{w} := \bar{f}$ if q represents:

$$\begin{aligned} \bar{v}, \bar{w} := &\bar{e}, \bar{f} \quad \text{if} \quad p \wedge q \\ \sim &\bar{e}, \bar{w} \quad \text{if} \quad p \wedge \neg q \\ \sim &\bar{v}, \bar{f} \quad \text{if} \quad \neg p \wedge q \end{aligned}$$

Semantically, executing a UNITY program F consists in choosing non-deterministically one assignment in *F.assign* and then executing it atomically. This choice is repeated infinitely, assuming weak fairness: each statement is executed infinitely often.

Therefore, an operational semantic model for UNITY is a characterization of all the possible computations given the program text. For program F, we denote the set of possible computations by $\mathcal{O}.F$. A computation σ is a sequence of states σ_i. For an expression e, the notation $\sigma_i.e$ represents the value of the expression e in the state σ_i. Several models $\mathcal{O}$ were proposed [9, 17] and we define another in Sect. 4.3 in accordance with our communication model.

2.3   The Logic

The UNITY framework also provides a linear temporal logic to describe and prove some properties of programs. This logic is based on the operators *unless*, *stable, constant, invariant, leads-to* ($\mapsto$) and *until*[1]. Because they are fundamental properties of systems [16], we only consider *invariant* and *leads-to* relations.

---

[1] In a purely operational semantic model, where only computations are considered, the operator *ensures* is removed from the theory presented in [3].

However, we also give the operational definition of *stable* which is useful to state properties about *leads-to* in Sect. 6.

Given a program F, its operational semantics $\mathcal{O}.F$ and state predicates p and q, the *stable*, *invariant* and *leads-to* properties are defined as follows:

$$\text{invariant } p \text{ in } F \equiv \langle \forall \sigma : \sigma \in \mathcal{O}.F :: \langle \forall t :: \sigma_t.p \rangle \rangle$$
$$p \mapsto q \text{ in } F \quad \equiv \langle \forall \sigma : \sigma \in \mathcal{O}.F :: \langle \forall t :: \sigma_t.p \Rightarrow \langle \exists t' : t' \geq t :: \sigma_{t'}.q \rangle \rangle \rangle$$
$$\text{stable } p \text{ in } F \quad \equiv \langle \forall \sigma : \sigma \in \mathcal{O}.F :: \langle \forall t :: \sigma_t.p \Rightarrow \langle \forall t' : t' \geq t :: \sigma_{t'}.p \rangle \rangle \rangle$$

2.4 Program Composition by Union

The UNITY logic provides an operator, called *union* and denoted by $[\![$, to compose different programs. The state variables of programs F and G are gathered to become the variables of the program $F[\![G$. The statements of $F.assign$ and $G.assign$ are also collected into $(F[\![G).assign$ and any initial state of $F[\![G$ must be a valid initial state both for F and for G. Formally:

$$(F[\![G).declare = F.declare \cup G.declare$$
$$(F[\![G).init \quad = F.init \wedge G.init$$
$$(F[\![G).assign = F.assign \cup G.assign$$

This composition by union is used to:

- write programs in a modular way;
- represent the different parts of a distributed or concurrent application.

The distributed application built from the processes described by programs P_i is represented by the program $\langle [\![i :: P_i \rangle$. By analogy, each part P_i of the union is called in this case a UNITY *process*.

No memory is shared between the different processes of a distributed program. Therefore, different UNITY processes must not share any state variable. In this case, the composite program is said to be *well distributed*:

$$\langle [\![i :: P_i \rangle \text{ is well distributed } \equiv \langle \forall i, j :: P_i.declare \cap P_j.declare = \emptyset \rangle$$

This definition of *well distribution* may look too restrictive. It eliminates all kinds of shared variables instead of classifying them carefully by specifying how they can be accessed. For instance, this classification can rely on type extension [13] or on predicate transformers [17]. We must outline that the problem of interaction between programs is not the matter of this paper. Instead, we are interested in mapping, and from the mapping point of view, distributed programs have no shared variables.

However, well distributed programs need a communication mechanism to exchange information. We use a communication mechanism based on observation which is described in Sect. 4.

2.5 Mapping Programs to Architectures

The UNITY formalism was intended to abstract program design from architecture. Therefore, the formalism was not designed for one specific architecture. Instead, UNITY programs can be implemented on many architectures, but a mapping step is necessary.

This mapping step is an informal part of a program description. It says how the program can be executed on a specific architecture. Different mappings for different architectures are described in [3]. In particular, for distributed architectures, the mapping must partition the set of statements and the set of variables among processors, so that any statement is on the same processor as the variables it uses. The mapping must also choose a control flow for each processor with respect to the weak fairness constraint. Lastly, the mapping must define a communication mechanism, for instance by assigning variables of type sequence to communication channels.

3 Presentation of the Problem

Describing distributed programs with the composition by union of UNITY involves considering programs of the form:

$$P = \langle [\![i :: P_i \rangle$$

Remember that the composition by union only gather the statements from the processes P_i into the **assign** part of the program P. Therefore, due to the semantics of UNITY, these statements are mutually exclusive, even when they come from distinct processes P_i.

When mapping such a program on a distributed architecture, two statements from two different UNITY processes go on two different real processors. Therefore, no mutual exclusion is guaranteed between these two statements: different sites are always likely to execute one statement each, exactly at the same time. Moreover, there is no way to prevent processes not sharing any clock to do so.

By transgressing this mutual exclusion constraint, a distributed program may behave in a slightly different way from its UNITY model as shown in the following example. Consider two processes and their UNITY descriptions F and G:

Program F	Program G
Declare $x : int$	Declare $y : int$
Initially $x = 0$	Initially $y = 0$
Assign $x := 1$	Assign $y := 1$

The concurrent computation of these two processes is then described by the composition $F[\![G$, which is only a shorthand for:

Program $F[\![G$
Declare $x, y : int$
Initially $x, y = 0, 0$
Assign $x := 1$
$[\![\qquad y := 1$

If processes F and G are mapped on a distributed architecture, the computation

$$(x, y) : (0, 0) \rightarrow (1, 1) \rightarrow (1, 1) \rightarrow \ldots \tag{1}$$

should be valid, since it corresponds to the case of the two processes executing their statement at the same time. But this behaviour is not allowed for $F \| G$ because the two statements are mutually exclusive in this program.

This differences between the operational semantics of the distributed application and that of the UNITY program is a serious problem because one may prove within the UNITY framework properties that will be falsified on a distributed architecture. For example, the property $x + y = 0 \mapsto x + y = 1$ can be proved for the program $F \| G$, but is falsified by the computation (1) of the processes F and G in a distributed context.

Therefore, it appears that the traditional mapping of programs composed by union is not well-suited to distributed architectures. Such a mapping does not take into account all the concurrency between the different processes of a distributed application. In this paper, we define precisely another kind of mapping, able to represent simultaneous computation of statements from different processes. This mapping relies on the separation of variables (idea of well-distributed programs) and the choice of an abstract communication model (observation).

4   Observation-based Communication

4.1   Presentation

In the UNITY model, communication between processes relies on shared variables. Generally, variables of type sequence are used to describe distributed applications. These sequences correspond to a low-level model of communication based on message exchanges. However, this communication model makes difficult both the description and the proof of algorithms: readability is poor since message passing is not part of the syntax, and proofs are difficult since message semantics is not part of the logic.

We gave in Sect. 2.4 the definition of a well-distributed program. In such a program, processes share no variables. Therefore, we were led to define another communication abstraction more consonant with UNITY principles. This abstraction, called *observation*, weakens the shared variable model to adapt it to distribution. It is based on a kind of weak consistency between variables. It can be seen as a relation (extending the logic) or as a mechanism (extending the model) relying on the relation.

4.2   Observation Relation

The observation relation describes the relationship between a *source* variable and an *image* variable in a program. It takes the form of a temporal operator based on any operational semantic model of UNITY. This operator has its own properties (in particular, it is an order^2) and properties related to other UNITY logical operators.

Given two variables v and $'v$ of a program F and an operational semantics model $\mathcal{O}$, the relation $'v \prec v$ (read $'v$ *observes* v) is defined as follows:

$$'v \prec v \text{ in } F \equiv \langle \forall \sigma : \sigma \in \mathcal{O}.F :: \langle \exists C : Clock(C) :: \langle \forall t :: \sigma_t.'v = \sigma_{C.t}.v \rangle \rangle \rangle$$

$Clock(C)$ means that C is an abstract clock, that is a mapping from natural numbers to natural numbers such that:

1. $\langle \forall t :: C.t \leqslant t \rangle$: an abstract clock never outgrows the ideal time;
2. $\langle \forall t :: C.t \leqslant C.(t+1) \rangle$: an abstract clock is monotonously increasing;
3. $\langle \forall k :: \langle \exists t :: C.t > k \rangle \rangle$: an abstract clock eventually increases.

The relation $'v \prec v$ means that, at any time t, the image variable $'v$ has the value the source variable v had at time $C.t$. Therefore, the relation states that any value of $'v$ is a previous value of v (clock property 1), that $'v$ is assigned its values in a chronological order (clock property 2) and that $'v$ is eventually assigned more recent values of v (clock property 3), even though the delay between v changes and $'v$ updates is unbounded and some changes of v may be lost.

A more comprehensive presentation of the observation relation and its properties can be found in [6, 5].

4.3 Observation Mechanism

The observation *mechanism* is part of a program description. It is made of assumed observation *relations* between some variables of the program. In the next section, this mechanism will be used to represent communication between processes.

A new section, named **observe**, is introduced into UNITY programs. It consists of a set of observation relations, the truthfulness of which the program environment is responsible for. There are constraints on these observation relations so that the mechanism maps straightforwardly on distributed architectures: image variables are supposed to be assigned by the observation mechanism alone. In particular, they cannot appear on the assignments left-hand side. Moreover, no variable can be image in more than *one* observation relation, even though a variable can be both image and source in two different relations. For example, $x \prec y$, $y \prec z$ is a correct **observe** section, but $x \prec y$, $x \prec z$ is not.

When satisfying these hypotheses, a UNITY program with an **observe** section can be translated into a standard program without observations [6]. However, this effective fulfillment of the observation relations must not be given explicitly if we want the mechanism to remain abstract. Therefore, we have to consider the **observe** section of a program at the semantics level.

This can be achieved by considering the environment part in the operational semantics of a program. Such semantic models are used in [9, 17]. They are based

---

^{2} The relation $\prec$ is not strictly antisymmetric. We can only deduce an invariant of the program, that is to say: $x \prec y$ in $F \wedge y \prec x$ in $F \Rightarrow$ invariant $x = y$ in F.

on an interleaving between the program transitions and the environment transitions, the latter possibly being restricted with logical specifications. However, the observation mechanism cannot rely on such semantic models. Due to the observation relation definition, an image variable and its source must be able to change their value *at the same time*, that is to say on the same state transition. That means a program transition and an environment transition take place simultaneously. This is impossible in these interleaved semantic models[3].

Moreover, in these models, the environment is constrained at the *transition* level, not at the *computation* level, and only safety is considered. This is not enough to describe observation relations.

Therefore, a new operational semantic model is defined that allows image variables to change their value while a program assignment is executed and in accordance with the observation relations. The computation of the next state in a sequence of states must therefore take the observation relations into account.

This new semantic model, called Obs, is defined as follows:

- $F.Img$ is the set of the image variables of F, that is to say the variables in the left-hand side of (exactly) one observation relation:

$$F.Img \ = \ \{x \in F.declare \mid \langle \exists y : y \in F.declare :: x \prec y \in F.observe \rangle\}$$

- $F.NImg$ is the set of the variables of F *not* image in any **observe** relation, that is to say the variables assigned by the program statements. The variables of the program F are then partitioned:

$$F.Img \cup F.NImg = F.declare \quad \wedge \quad F.Img \cap F.NImg = \emptyset$$

- $\mathcal{O}_{assign}.F$ is the set of the computations σ such that:
  - $\sigma_0.F.init$,
  - $\langle \forall t :: \langle \exists s : s \in F.assign :: \sigma_t \xrightarrow{s} \sigma_{t+1} \rangle \rangle$ and
  - $\langle \forall s : s \in F.assign :: \langle \forall t :: \langle \exists t' : t' > t :: \sigma_{t'} \xrightarrow{s} \sigma_{t'+1} \rangle \rangle \rangle$.

  where $\sigma_t \xrightarrow{s} \sigma_{t+1} \equiv \langle \forall x : x \in F.NImg :: \sigma_{t+1}.x = (s.\sigma_t).x \rangle$[4];

- $\mathcal{O}_{observe}.F$ is the set of the computations σ such that:

$$\langle \forall \ x \in F.Img : x \prec y \in F.observe :: \langle \exists C : Clock(C) :: \langle \forall t :: \sigma_t.x = \sigma_{C.t}.y \rangle \rangle \rangle;$$

- $Obs.F = \mathcal{O}_{assign}.F \cap \mathcal{O}_{observe}.F$.

On the one hand, $\mathcal{O}_{assign}$ describes the states of the variables as determined by the program assignments with respect to the weak fairness. The statements are executed on a complete program state (with the image variables), but the images are free to be assigned with any value. On the other hand, $\mathcal{O}_{observe}$ describes the states of the images determined by the observation relations of the **observe**

---

[3] The ∥ operator would not even be able to later introduce this simultaneity because the state changes due to the observation mechanism would not be described with UNITY assignments (cf Sect. 5).

[4] $s.\sigma_t$ denotes the image of the state σ_t by the statement s seen as a mapping.

section. The operational model *Obs* is made of the computations satisfying both constraints.

Note that the definition of the observation relation as a logical operator, given in Sect. 4.2, is based on *any* operational semantic model of UNITY. In particular, the operator and its properties can be used on a UNITY program with an **observe** section within the semantic model *Obs*.

4.4 Communication Representation

Communication between processes can be described with the observation mechanism presented above in a more abstract way than with explicit messages sequences.

This is achieved by stating, in the **observe** section of a UNITY process, some observation relations with their sources located in other processes. The processes remain well-distributed if they were, but each process now has an approximated view of the other processes. We choose the observation relations between two UNITY processes (one that observes and one that is observed) to be located in the **observe** section of the process that observes. In other words, the images are local to processes and the sources are remote-located[5].

The composition by union is extended to handle UNITY programs with an **observe** section. The different **observe** sections are gathered to become the **observe** section of the composite program:

$$(F[\!]G).observe \;=\; F.observe \cup G.observe$$

A given variable is supposed not to be the image of different observation relations from different **observe** sections so that the new **observe** section remains consistent. Note that any well-distributed program automatically satisfies this assumption.

The variables of a well-distributed program using an observation-based communication model can be seen by all processes but can only be assigned by *one* process (including its observation mechanism). Such variables are sometimes called *distributed variables* [14], or *output variables* [17], or *private variables* [17], or *read variables* [13], or *owned variables* [11].

Finally, due to the definition of the observation relation, the internal computations of processes and the communication are strictly concurrent: the images are altered by the observation mechanism and may change their value at the same time (that is to say during the same transition) as any ordinary assigned variable.

---

[5] That means we have to state, in a program F, relations like $x \prec y$ with possibly $y \notin F.declare$. This is only a matter of syntax. In fact, we consider the relation $x \prec y$ to be part of the description of the program $F[\!]G$ and the relation is not handled outside this program.

4.5 Example

Let us consider the following two UNITY processes:

Program F	Program G
Declare $x : int$	Declare $y, z : int$
Initially $x = 0$	Initially $z = 0$
	Observe $y \prec x$
Assign $x := x + 1$ if $x < 10$	Assign $z := y$

The variable x from the program F is increased from 0 to 10 by increments of one. The program G communicates with F through observation and has an image y of x. With respect to the semantic model $\mathcal{O}bs$, the variable z is monotonously increasing and bounded with 10 in the program $F[\![G$. Properties such as $true \mapsto z = 10$ in $F[\![G$ and $z \prec x$ in $F[\![G$ can also be proved.

A more comprehensive example can be found in [5] where a mutual exclusion algorithm based on logical clocks is fully described with observation. The proofs of its fundamental safety and liveness properties are also given.

5 A New Program Composition Operation

The communication between UNITY processes composed by union can be represented with the observation mechanism. As we saw previously, the communication is then strictly concurrent with the internal computations and need no additional transitions. Therefore, this communication model is compatible with the concurrency due to the mapping to a distributed architecture. However, the problem introduced in Sect. 3 still remains: the mapping must still forbid assignments to be executed at the same time by different processes.

In this section, a new composition operation is defined. It stems from the composition by union but handles simultaneous execution of statements by different processes. Therefore, this composition operator maps correctly on distributed architectures.

5.1 Principles

Due to the atomicity of UNITY statements, perfect simultaneity is the only case of overlapping between statements[6]. Indeed, two atomic statements take place at two different moments or at the same time but there is no other possibility. The composition by union does not handle the later case.

The idea of the new composition is to represent this possible simultaneity with additional synchronous statements. Each additional statement takes place for two or more assignments executing at the same time.

---

[6] If a partial overlapping need to be considered, that means the granularity chosen for the UNITY model is not the right one.

For example, the **assign** section of the program of Sect. 3 could be:

$$\text{Assign } x := 1$$
$$\qquad \| \quad y := 1$$
$$\qquad \| \quad x, y := 1, 1$$

The computations of this program into the UNITY model and the computations of the two processes $F : x := 1$ and $G : y := 1$ concurrently are the same, even when F and G execute one statement each at the same time. Therefore, any distributed mapping of the two processes will satisfy all the properties proved on the program above.

5.2 Definition of the Product Operator

The ideas introduced above are now formalized. A new operator for program composition, called *product* and denoted by $\|$, is defined.

In addition to the *skip* statement introduced in Sect. 2.2, we now assume that every UNITY program has the statement $fair := \neg fair$. The boolean variable $fair$ is never declared and is not considered to be a variable of any process. It is only used for product composition. It cannot appear elsewhere in the program or in its properties. If such a variable already exists, it must be renamed. When reasoning on program computations, we always consider that the variable $fair$ is part of the program state: a state of a program F is a mapping from $F.declare \cup \{fair\}$.

We can now formally define the product composition. Given two UNITY programs F and G, possibly extended with an **observe** section, and such that $F\|G$ is well-distributed, the product $F\|G$ is defined as follows:

- $(F\|G).assign = (F\|G).assign$
  $\qquad \cup \{(s_F\|s_G) \text{ if } fair \mid s_F \in F.assign \wedge s_G \in G.assign\}$
- the other sections of $F\|G$ are the same as in $F\|G$.

Because $F\|G$ is well-distributed, the programs F and G share no variable outside the **observe** sections. Therefore, the synchronous statements $s_F\|s_G$ are correct UNITY statements (that is to say non conflicting).

The notation "$(s_F\|s_G)$ *if fair*" only means that the conjunction "$\wedge fair$" is added to the guards of s_F and s_G. The variable $fair$ is used to break the weak fairness of UNITY. Statements of the form $s_F\|s_G$ do not represent statements of the processes, but only the simultaneous execution of such statements. Therefore, they do not require any fairness. Maintaining fairness for such statements would correspond to consider that simultaneous execution *must* occur infinitely often, which is not consonant with the actual behaviour of an asynchronous distributed program. However, in UNITY, the weak fairness rule applies to *all* the statements of the **assign** section. This is the reason why we need to remove weak fairness for the statements introduced by product composition: due to the variable $fair$, no additional statement execution is forced.

Simultaneous execution of statements from different processes is now handled with the product operation by implicitly adding the corresponding assignments. The computations of the processes F and G in a distributed context and those of $F \| \| G$ in the UNITY model are the same.

As we will see, the additional statements need not be explicitly manipulated to reason about the program $F \| \| G$. As these additional statements are usually numerous, the theorems of Sect. 6 are very useful in hiding them from the user.

5.3 Simple Properties

In this section, simple properties of composition by product are stated. The reasoning in the next sections is made easier using these properties, in particular when generalizing theorems for any number of processes. The equalities are pure syntax: two programs are equal when they have the same set of statements.

$$F \| \| G \;=\; G \| \| F$$
$$F \| \| (G \| \| H) \;=\; (F \| \| G) \| \| H \;=\; F \| \| G \| \| H$$
$$F \| \| (G \| H) \;=\; (F \| \| G) \| (F \| \| H)$$

The first two properties state that the composition by product is commutative and associative as was the composition by union. They rely on the commutativity and the associativity of $\|$ when defined. The last property states that $\| \|$ distributes over $\|$.

6 Converting Union into Product

6.1 Introduction

The composition by product allows simultaneity of execution in the description of a distributed application. On the one hand, using this form of composition may facilitate the mapping step. But on the other hand, all the additional statements of the form $s_F \| s_G$ must a priori be considered to prove properties on the program $F \| \| G$. These statements become numerous when the number of UNITY processes increases. All the possibilities of parallelism between two statements, between three statements, and so on, must be considered. A program with ten processes of ten statements each leads to ten billions additional statements.

Moreover, using the product composition when designing a UNITY program freezes the future mapping of the program: it precisely expresses which abstract UNITY process goes on which node. Since UNITY principles are to postpone such a mapping step, product operations should not appear too soon in the design of a program.

For both these reasons, it seems interesting to have a way to introduce product operations at the end of the design and without making all the additional statements explicit. This can be achieved by characterizing, for a well-distributed program composed by union with an observation-based communication model, the UNITY properties that still hold when the composition by product is used.

Referring to the example program of Sect. 3, we already know that some properties of $F[\![G$ are not preserved in $F[\![\![G$, but if the class of preserved properties is large enough, one may keep doing proofs on $\langle[\![i :: P_i\rangle$ and then convert some unions into products depending on the desired mapping without loosing correctness.

6.2   Theorems

The theorems stated in this section show the preservation of some properties when converting from a composition by union into a composition by product. Only *invariant* and *leads-to* properties are considered, but similar results hold for *stable*, *constant* or *unless* and can be proved from the proof principles given in the next section.

In the following, F and G are two UNITY programs with observe sections such that $F[\![G$ is well-distributed (the product $F[\![\![G$ is defined). P and Q are state predicates over the variables of F and G. Then, the following theorems hold:

$$\frac{\text{invariant } P \text{ in } F[\![G}{\text{invariant } P \text{ in } F[\![\![G} \tag{2}$$

$$\frac{P \mapsto Q \text{ in } F[\![G \wedge Q \text{ local to } F}{P \mapsto Q \text{ in } F[\![\![G} \tag{3}$$

$$\frac{P \mapsto Q \text{ in } F[\![G \wedge \text{stable } Q \text{ in } F[\![G}{P \mapsto Q \text{ in } F[\![\![G} \tag{4}$$

Theorem (2) states that *all* the invariants are preserved when converting from composition by union into composition by product. Theorem (3) states that $P \mapsto Q$ is preserved as soon as the predicate Q is local to one process (that is to say all the free variables of the predicate Q are variables of a single process). Finally, Theorem (4) states that $P \mapsto Q$ is also preserved when the predicate Q is stable.

These theorems extend in case of a composition between N processes. For example, (3) becomes:

$$\frac{P \mapsto Q \text{ in } \langle[\![i : 1 \leqslant i \leqslant N :: F_i\rangle \wedge \langle \exists i : 1 \leqslant i \leqslant N :: Q \text{ local to } F_i\rangle}{P \mapsto Q \text{ in } \langle[\![\![i : 1 \leqslant i \leqslant N :: F_i\rangle}$$

The three theorems state that, when converting from union into product, all the safety *invariant* properties are preserved and that the liveness *leads-to* properties not preserved must involve a *global* and *transient* state, and therefore are not significant in distributed application descriptions (since processes cannot detect them).

Note that these theorems are theorems of the conversion from union into product and they are not composition theorems since properties of $F[\![\![G$ are deduced from properties of $F[\![G$ and not from properties of F and G separately.

One may wonder if new properties can be proved in a composition by product that were falsified in the corresponding composition by union. The answer is that the converse transformation (from product into union) is a program *refinement*. The following properties hold:

$$\frac{\text{invariant } P \text{ in } F \| G}{\text{invariant } P \text{ in } F \| G} \tag{5}$$

$$\frac{P \mapsto Q \text{ in } F \| G}{P \mapsto Q \text{ in } F \| G} \tag{6}$$

From (2) and (5), we deduce that the programs $F\|G$ and $F\|\|G$ have *exactly* the same set of invariants, that is to say the same set of reachable states.

6.3 Example of Composition by Product

Let us consider a mutual exclusion algorithm for N nodes. The nodes are set along a logical ring, each having a predecessor and a successor. They handle counters so that, at any time, only *one* node has a counter smaller in value than the counter of its predecessor. This node may then enter the critical section. It releases access right to its successor by increasing its counter.

This algorithm requires communication between nodes so that a node knows about its predecessor. More precisely, each node *observes* the counter of its predecessor. The following UNITY program describes the behaviour of a node:

```
Program  Node_i
Declare   c_i, t_i : int
          req_i, excl_i : bool
Initially c_i = i ∧ ¬req_i ∧ ¬excl_i
Observe   t_i ≺ c_{i⊖1}
Assign    req_i := true
      []      excl_i := true if req_i ∧ c_i ⩽ t_i
      []      excl_i, req_i, c_i := false, false, t_i + 1 if excl_i ∨ ¬req_i
```

The variables req_i and $excl_i$ represent respectively a request for the critical section and the actual access to this section. The variable c_i is the counter of the node i and t_i is the image the node i has of the counter of its predecessor, the node $i \ominus 1$. The observation mechanism is responsible for updating the variable t_i.

The application made of N such nodes ($N > 1$) is described by the UNITY program:

$$\langle [] i : 1 \leqslant i \leqslant N :: Node_i \rangle$$

This program satisfies usual properties of mutual exclusion algorithms:

invariant $\langle \forall i, j : 1 \leqslant i, j \leqslant N :: c_i \leqslant t_i \wedge c_j \leqslant t_j \Rightarrow i = j \rangle$: frontier uniqueness

invariant $\langle \forall i, j : 1 \leqslant i, j \leqslant N :: excl_i \wedge excl_j \Rightarrow i = j \rangle$: mutual exclusion

$\forall i : 1 \leqslant i \leqslant N :: c_i \leqslant t_i \mapsto c_{i\oplus1} \leqslant t_{i\oplus1}$: frontier movement

$\forall i : 1 \leqslant i \leqslant N :: req_i \mapsto excl_i$: algorithm fairness

The hypotheses of the theorems of Sect. 6.2 are satisfied by the program and its properties:

- each node only uses local variables outside its `observe` section and never assigns its image variable;
- the first two properties are *invariant* properties and are therefore automatically preserved;
- the last two properties are *leads-to* properties with a right-hand side local to a node ($i \oplus 1$ in the first case and i in the second case). Therefore, they are also preserved.

Since all the four properties are satisfied by the program composed by union, and since they are preserved, they still hold for the distributed program:

$$\langle [\![i : 1 \leqslant i \leqslant N :: Node_i \rangle$$

7 Proofs

7.1 Important Lemma

The proof of the theorems of the preceding section relies on the following important lemma that shows a close relation between each computation of $\mathcal{O}bs.(F[\![G)$ and a corresponding computation in $\mathcal{O}bs.(F[\![G)$.

Given two UNITY processes F and G such that $F[\![G$ is well-distributed and $s_F \| s_G$ if *fair* a statement of $(F[\![G).assign$ with $s_F \in F.assign$ and $s_G \in G.assign$. Then, with respect to the notations introduced in Sect. 4.3:

$$\langle \forall \sigma : \sigma \in \mathcal{O}bs.(F[\![G) :: \langle \forall i : \sigma_i \xrightarrow{s_F \| s_G} \sigma_{i+1} ::$$
$$\langle \exists \sigma' : \sigma' \in \mathcal{O}bs.(F[\![G) :: \langle \exists j :: \sigma'_j = \sigma_i \xrightarrow{s_F} \sigma'_{j+1} \xrightarrow{s_G} \sigma'_{j+2} = \sigma_{i+1} \rangle \rangle \rangle \rangle \tag{7}$$

This lemma can be read as follows: in any computation of $F[\![G$, the state transformation produced by executing an additional statement when *fair* is *true* is the same as the state transformation produced by executing, one after the other, the two parts of the statement in a particular computation of $F[\![G$ (Fig. 1). Of course, when *fair* is *false*, the additional statement has no effect.

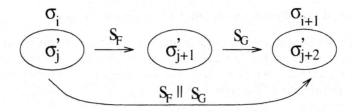

Fig. 1. Additional statements interpretation

To prove (7), one must show the existence of the sub-sequence $\sigma'_j \xrightarrow{s_F} \sigma'_{j+1} \xrightarrow{s_G} \sigma'_{j+2}$ in a computation of $\mathcal{O}bs.(F\|G)$. This is done in three steps:

- The separation of variables due to the well-distribution of F and G ensures:

$$\langle \forall \sigma_i :: (s_F\|s_G).\sigma_i = s_F.s_G.\sigma_i = s_G.s_F.\sigma_i \rangle$$

  The executions of s_F and s_G on a state σ_i are fully independent. The resulting state is the same, whether the statements are executed in any order or at the same time. This can be shown for instance by calculating the *weakest precondition* of $s_F\|s_G$, $s_F; s_G$ and $s_G; s_F$.

- Then, we assume $\langle \exists \sigma' : \sigma' \in \mathcal{O}bs.(F\|G) :: \langle \exists j :: \sigma'_j = \sigma_i \rangle \rangle$, that is to say σ_i is reachable in at least one computation σ' of $\mathcal{O}bs.(F\|G)$, and we show that the states with indexes greater than j can be chosen[7] for σ' so that $\sigma'_j \xrightarrow{s_F} \sigma'_{j+1} \xrightarrow{s_G} \sigma'_{j+2} = \sigma_{i+1}$. This is achieved by showing that the image variables can change their values concurrently with s_F and s_G in σ' in the same way they change concurrently with $s_F\|s_G$ in σ. If '$\bar{v}$ represents *all* the image variables in $F\|G$, then $\sigma'_j.'\bar{v} = \sigma_i.'\bar{v}$ (since $\sigma'_j = \sigma_i$). The computation σ' is then chosen so that $\sigma'_{j+1}.'\bar{v} = \sigma'_j.'\bar{v}$ (the image variables do not change while executing s_F) and $\sigma'_{j+2}.'\bar{v} = \sigma_{i+1}.'\bar{v}$ (the image variables change while executing s_G in the same way they change while executing $s_F\|s_G$ in σ). These changes of the image variables are in accordance with the observation definition. Therefore, the desired computation σ' is built.

- In fact, the argument above proves the lemma for the *first* occurrence of an additional statement in σ. We conclude that the state σ_{i+1} is then reachable in a computation σ' and the same argument can be used again. Therefore, the proof of the lemma is extended by induction for all the occurrences of additional statements.

From the construction above, we see that σ' can be chosen in $\mathcal{O}bs.(F\|G)$ with the image variables not changing while executing s_F. This proves the stronger lemma:

$$\langle \forall \sigma : \sigma \in \mathcal{O}bs.(F\|G) :: \langle \forall i : \sigma_i \xrightarrow{s_F\|s_G} \sigma_{i+1} :: \\ \langle \exists \sigma' : \sigma' \in \mathcal{O}bs.(F\|G) :: \langle \exists j :: \sigma'_j = \sigma_i \wedge s_F.\sigma'_j = \sigma'_{j+1} \xrightarrow{s_G} \sigma'_{j+2} = \sigma_{i+1} \rangle \rangle \rangle \rangle \tag{8}$$

which is used later in the proof.

7.2 Proof of the Theorems from Union into Product

Once the lemma is established, the theorems stated in Sect. 6.2 are easily proved. This lemma states that the additional statements have no effect but the bypass of exactly one state. Therefore, no new state becomes reachable and all *invariant* properties are preserved (Theorem (2)).

---

[7] Starting in a given state, the execution of a given statement can lead to different states depending on how images change.

Concerning *leads-to* properties, the hypothesis $P \mapsto Q$ in $F[\!]G$ states that, in any computation σ' in $Obs.(F[\!]G)$, a P-state will always be followed by a Q-state. The only way not to respect this constraint for a computation σ in $Obs.(F[\!|\!]G)$ is to bypass the last Q-state (if their number is finite) or all Q-states from a point (if their number is infinite). In both cases, executing $s_F \| s_G$ must bypass a Q-state between two $\neg Q$-states to falsify the property (Fig. 2). Moreover, we saw that

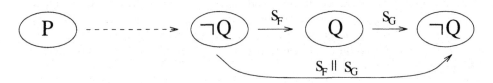

Fig. 2. Case of a *leads-to* property not being preserved.

σ' can be chosen so that images do not change while executing s_F (Lemma (8)). If the predicate Q is local to process G (Theorem (3)), the transition $\neg Q \xrightarrow{s_F} Q$ is impossible (the case of Q local to F is proved with a symmetrical argument), and if the predicate Q is *stable* in the program $F[\!]G$ (Theorem (4)), the transition $Q \xrightarrow{s_G} \neg Q$ is impossible. That proves both theorems about *leads-to*.

7.3 Proof of the Theorems from Product into Union

The refinement property of the converse transformation (from product into union) is easy to prove since we took care of breaking the weak fairness of UNITY for the additional statements. This allows to assert that, for two programs F and G:

$$\langle \forall \sigma' : \sigma' \in Obs.(F[\!]G) :: \langle \exists \sigma : \sigma \in Obs.(F[\!|\!]G) :: \natural\sigma = \natural\sigma' \rangle \rangle \qquad (9)$$

The operator $\natural$ is used to abstract from stuttering [1]. More precisely, $\natural\sigma$ is the same as σ except that all the maximal finite segments of identical states in σ are replaced by the single state in $\natural\sigma$. For a given computation σ', the corresponding computation σ is obtained by always executing the additional statements of the form "$s_F \| s_G$ *if fair*" when the variable *fair* is *false*.

We cannot assert that $Obs.(F[\!]G) \subset Obs.(F[\!|\!]G)$ since a computation of $Obs.(F[\!]G)$ only executing a finite number of times the *skip* statement when the variable *fair* is *false* is not in $Obs.(F[\!|\!]G)$: due to weak fairness, the computations of $Obs.(F[\!|\!]G)$ must have an infinite number of *skip* transitions starting from a $\neg fair$-state, corresponding to the execution of the additional statements.

Having proved (9), and since the computations σ and $\natural\sigma$ satisfy the same set of UNITY properties, it is obvious that the UNITY properties of $F[\!|\!]G$ are valid properties of $F[\!]G^8$.

---

[8] This is a strong form of refinement. Weaker forms are possible. For example, a transformation can preserve all the UNITY properties of a program without preserving

If the additional statements were obeying the weak fairness rule, (9) would not be true. Consider, for instance, the following programs F and G:

Program F	Program G
Declare $x : int$	Declare $y : int$
Assign $x := 1$	Assign $y := 1$
$[\![$ $x := 0$	$[\![$ $y := 0$

Without removing the weak fairness, their product would contain the statement $x, y := 1, 1$. Therefore, the property $true \mapsto x + y = 2$ would be true for $F [\![\!] G$ and not for $F [\![G$. This is another justification for having introduced the boolean variable $fair$, even if it could be shown that only transient global *leads-to* properties are involved.

8   Conclusions

Because it forces mutual exclusion between statements, the composition by union cannot express the possible simultaneity when executing statements in different processes. Therefore, programs composed by union do not map in a straightforward way to distributed architectures.

However, synchronous statements can be described within the UNITY language, and this kind of statements can represent simultaneity. Therefore, these synchronous statements are added to the composition by union to define a new form of composition called *product*.

Moreover, we have shown that composing processes by product preserves most of the properties proved in a composition by union: all invariants are preserved and only some liveness properties about global and transient states are falsified. Thus, as shown with the example of Sect. 6.3, one may keep making proofs on the simpler union program without explicitly considering the additional statements.

Within our context of a design by stepwise refinement, two transformations may be distinguished when converting a centralized program into a distributed program:

– the localization of abstract processes among nodes;
– the increase of parallelism inherent to distribution.

The first point involves a mapping step which is not formally described in the UNITY framework, and the composition by union does handle correctly the second point. The criterion of *well-distribution* and the composition by product answer both these problems by formalizing the mapping and by enabling some true parallelism between statements of different nodes.

---

a single computation. This is due to the fact that two programs may have exactly the same set of UNITY properties and different computations, even when abstracting from stuttering [18].

In this work, we only consider UNITY programs using an observation-based communication model. It would be interesting to extend it to a more standard communication model like message-passing. However, this less abstract model would probably make the proofs more difficult.

The UNITY language was very appreciated for its ability to express synchronous statements. However, the formalism forces weak fairness for all statements. Thus, the definition of the product composition is more awkward than if the kind of fairness (including the complete absence of fairness), could be chosen for each statement, as it is the case for example in [11, 16].

Acknowledgements

Special thanks to G. Padiou and P. Quéinnec for their valuable comments on earlier drafts and their help in preparing the final version of this paper. The author is also grateful to the anonymous referees for careful reading of the manuscript and helpful comments.

References

1. M. Abadi and L. Lamport. The existence of refinement mappings. In *3rd Annual IEEE Symposium on Logic in Computer Science*, pages 165–175, Washington D.C., July 1988. Computer Society Press.
2. N. Brown and A. Mokkedem. On mechanizing proofs within a complete proof system for Unity. In *Algebraic Methodology and Software Technology*, Concordia University of Montréal, 1995.
3. K.M. Chandy and J. Misra. *Parallel Program Design: A Foundation*. Addison-Wesley, 1988.
4. M. Charpentier, M. Filali, P. Mauran, G. Padiou, and P. Quéinnec. Observer pour Répartir. In *Journées du GDR programmation*, Grenoble, novembre 1995.
5. M. Charpentier, M. Filali, P. Mauran, G. Padiou, and P. Quéinnec. Abstracting communication to reason about distributed algorithms. In Özalp Babaoğlu and Keith Marzullo, editors, *10th Int'l Workshop on Distributed Algorithms (WDAG'96)*, volume 1151 of *Lecture Notes in Computer Science*, pages 89–104, October 1996.
6. M. Charpentier, M. Filali, P. Mauran, G. Padiou, and P. Quéinnec. Répartition par observation dans Unity. Technical Report 96-01-R, IRIT, 27 pages, janvier 1996.
7. M. Charpentier, A. El Hadri, and G. Padiou. A Unity-based Algorithm Design Assistant. In *Workshop on Tools and Algorithms for the Construction and Analysis of Systems*, pages 131–145, Aarhus, Denmark, May 1995. BRICS Notes Series NS-95-2.
8. M. Charpentier, A. El Hadri, and G. Padiou. Preuve Automatique dans un Environnement de Développement Unity. *T.S.I. Technique et Science Informatiques*, 15(1), janvier 1996.
9. P. Collette. *Design of Compositional Proof Systems Based on Assumption-Commitment Specifications. Application to UNITY*. Thèse de docteur en sciences appliquées, Faculté des Sciences Appliquées, Université Catholique de Louvain, June 1994.

10. M. Filali, Ph. Mauran, and G. Padiou. Raffiner pour répartir. In *Quatrièmes rencontres du parallélisme*, Villeneuve D'Ascq, 1992.

11. Z. Manna and A. Pnueli. *The Temporal Logic of Reactive and Concurrent Systems: Specification.* Springer-Verlag, 1992.

12. J. Misra. A Logic for Concurrent Programming. Technical report, The University of Texas at Austin, Austin, Texas 78712, April 1994.

13. J. Misra. A Logic for Concurrent Programming. Technical report, The University of Texas at Austin, Austin, Texas 78712, September 1994. Chapter 6: Closures Properties.

14. M. Raynal. *Algorithmique du parallélisme : le problème de l'exclusion mutuelle.* Dunod, 1984.

15. B.A. Sanders. Eliminating the Substitution Axiom from UNITY Logic. *Formal Aspects of Computing*, 3(2):189–205, April-June 1991.

16. A. U. Shankar. An Introduction to Assertional Reasoning for Concurrent Systems. *ACM Computing Surveys*, 25(3):225–262, September 1993.

17. R. T. Udink. *Program Refinement in Unity-like Environments.* PhD thesis, Utrecht University, September 1995.

18. R.T. Udink and J.N. Kok. On the relation between Unity properties and sequences of states. In J.W de Bakker, W.-P. de Roever, and G. Rozenberg, editors, *Semantics: Foundations and Applications,* volume 666 of *Lecture Notes in Computer Science*, pages 594–608, 1993.

Author Index

Springer
and the
environment

At Springer we firmly believe that an international science publisher has a special obligation to the environment, and our corporate policies consistently reflect this conviction.
We also expect our business partners – paper mills, printers, packaging manufacturers, etc. – to commit themselves to using materials and production processes that do not harm the environment. The paper in this book is made from low- or no-chlorine pulp and is acid free, in conformance with international standards for paper permanency.

Lecture Notes in Computer Science

For information about Vols. 1–1238

please contact your bookseller or Springer-Verlag

Vol. 1275: E.L. Gunter, A. Felty (Eds.), Theorem Proving in Higher Order Logics. Proceedings, 1997. VIII, 339 pages. 1997.

Vol. 1276: T. Jiang, D.T. Lee (Eds.), Computing and Combinatorics. Proceedings, 1997. XI, 522 pages. 1997.

Vol. 1277: V. Malyshkin (Ed.), Parallel Computing Technologies. Proceedings, 1997. XII, 455 pages. 1997.

Vol. 1278: R. Hofestädt, T. Lengauer, M. Löffler, D. Schomburg (Eds.), Bioinformatics. Proceedings, 1996. XI, 222 pages. 1997.

Vol. 1279: B. S. Chlebus, L. Czaja (Eds.), Fundamentals of Computation Theory. Proceedings, 1997. XI, 475 pages. 1997.

Vol. 1280: X. Liu, P. Cohen, M. Berthold (Eds.), Advances in Intelligent Data Analysis. Proceedings, 1997. XII, 621 pages. 1997.

Vol. 1281: M. Abadi, T. Ito (Eds.), Theoretical Aspects of Computer Software. Proceedings, 1997. XI, 639 pages. 1997.

Vol. 1282: D. Garlan, D. Le Métayer (Eds.), Coordination Languages and Models. Proceedings, 1997. X, 435 pages. 1997.

Vol. 1283: M. Müller-Olm, Modular Compiler Verification. XV, 250 pages. 1997.

Vol. 1284: R. Burkard, G. Woeginger (Eds.), Algorithms — ESA '97. Proceedings, 1997. XI, 515 pages. 1997.

Vol. 1285: X. Jao, J.-H. Kim, T. Furuhashi (Eds.), Simulated Evolution and Learning. Proceedings, 1996. VIII, 231 pages. 1997. (Subseries LNAI).

Vol. 1286: C. Zhang, D. Lukose (Eds.), Multi-Agent Systems. Proceedings, 1996. VII, 195 pages. 1997. (Subseries LNAI).

Vol. 1287: T. Kropf (Ed.), Formal Hardware Verification. XII, 367 pages. 1997.

Vol. 1288: M. Schneider, Spatial Data Types for Database Systems. XIII, 275 pages. 1997.

Vol. 1289: G. Gottlob, A. Leitsch, D. Mundici (Eds.), Computational Logic and Proof Theory. Proceedings, 1997. VIII, 348 pages. 1997.

Vol. 1290: E. Moggi, G. Rosolini (Eds.), Category Theory and Computer Science. Proceedings, 1997. VII, 313 pages. 1997.

Vol. 1291: D.G. Feitelson, L. Rudolph (Eds.), Job Scheduling Strategies for Parallel Processing. Proceedings, 1997. VII, 299 pages. 1997.

Vol. 1292: H. Glaser, P. Hartel, H. Kuchen (Eds.), Programming Languages: Implementations, Logigs, and Programs. Proceedings, 1997. XI, 425 pages. 1997.

Vol. 1294: B.S. Kaliski Jr. (Ed.), Advances in Cryptology — CRYPTO '97. Proceedings, 1997. XII, 539 pages. 1997.

Vol. 1295: I. Prívara, P. Ružička (Eds.), Mathematical Foundations of Computer Science 1997. Proceedings, 1997. X, 519 pages. 1997.

Vol. 1296: G. Sommer, K. Daniilidis, J. Pauli (Eds.), Computer Analysis of Images and Patterns. Proceedings, 1997. XIII, 737 pages. 1997.

Vol. 1297: N. Lavrač, S. Džeroski (Eds.), Inductive Logic Programming. Proceedings, 1997. VIII, 309 pages. 1997. (Subseries LNAI).

Vol. 1298: M. Hanus, J. Heering, K. Meinke (Eds.), Algebraic and Logic Programming. Proceedings, 1997. X, 286 pages. 1997.

Vol. 1299: M.T. Pazienza (Ed.), Information Extraction. Proceedings, 1997. IX, 213 pages. 1997. (Subseries LNAI).

Vol. 1300: C. Lengauer, M. Griebl, S. Gorlatch (Eds.), Euro-Par'97 Parallel Processing. Proceedings, 1997. XXX, 1379 pages. 1997.

Vol. 1301: M. Jazayeri (Ed.), Software Engineering - ESEC/FSE'97. Proceedings, 1997. XIII, 532 pages. 1997.

Vol. 1302: P. Van Hentenryck (Ed.), Static Analysis. Proceedings, 1997. X, 413 pages. 1997.

Vol. 1303: G. Brewka, C. Habel, B. Nebel (Eds.), KI-97: Advances in Artificial Intelligence. Proceedings, 1997. XI, 413 pages. 1997. (Subseries LNAI).

Vol. 1304: W. Luk, P.Y.K. Cheung, M. Glesner (Eds.), Field-Programmable Logic and Applications. Proceedings, 1997. XI, 503 pages. 1997.

Vol. 1305: D. Corne, J.L. Shapiro (Eds.), Evolutionary Computing. Proceedings, 1997. X, 313 pages. 1997.

Vol. 1307: R. Kompe, Prosody in Speech Understanding Systems. XIX, 357 pages. 1997. (Subseries LNAI).

Vol. 1308: A. Hameurlain, A M. Tjoa (Eds.), Database and Expert Systems Applications. Proceedings, 1997. XVII, 688 pages. 1997.

Vol. 1309: R. Steinmetz, L.C. Wolf (Eds.), Interactive Distributed Multimedia Systems and Telecommunication Services. Proceedings, 1997. XIII, 466 pages. 1997.

Vol. 1310: A. Del Bimbo (Ed.), Image Analysis and Processing. Proceedings, 1997. Volume I. XXI, 722 pages. 1997.

Vol. 1311: A. Del Bimbo (Ed.), Image Analysis and Processing. Proceedings, 1997. Volume II. XXII, 794 pages. 1997.

Vol. 1312: A. Geppert, M. Berndtsson (Eds.), Rules in Database Systems. Proceedings, 1997. VII, 214 pages. 1997.

Vol. 1313: J. Fitzgerald, C.B. Jones, P. Lucas (Eds.), FME '97: Industrial Applications and Strengthened Foundations of Formal Methods. Proceedings, 1997. XIII, 685 pages. 1997.

Vol. 1314: S. Muggleton (Ed.), Inductive Logic Programming. Proceedings, 1996. VIII, 397 pages. 1997. (Subseries LNAI).

Vol. 1315: G. Sommer, J.J. Koenderink (Eds.), Algebraic Frames for the Perception-Action Cycle. Proceedings, 1997. VIII, 395 pages. 1997.

Vol. 1317: M. Leman (Ed.), Music, Gestalt, and Computing. IX, 524 pages. 1997. (Subseries LNAI).

Vol. 1320: M. Mavronicolas, P. Tsigas (Eds.), Distributed Systems. Proceedings, 1997. X, 333 pages. 1997.

Vol. 1321: M. Lenzerini (Ed.), AI*IA 97: Advances in Artificial Intelligence. Proceedings, 1997. XII, 459 pages. 1997. (Subseries LNAI).

Vol. 1324: C. Peters, C. Thanos (Ed.), Research and Advanced Technology for Digital Libraries. Proceedings, 1997. X, 423 pages. 1997.